# COGNITIVE PSYCHOLOGY

## PHILIP QUINLAN & BEN DYSON

PEARSON
Prentice
Hall

Harlow, England • London • New York • Boston • San Francisco • Toronto • Sydney • Singapore • Hong Kong
Tokyo • Seoul • Taipei • New Delhi • Cape Town • Madrid • Mexico City • Amsterdam • Munich • Paris • Milan

**Pearson Education Limited**
Edinburgh Gate
Harlow
Essex CM20 2JE
England

and Associated Companies throughout the world

*Visit us on the World Wide Web at:*
www.pearsoned.co.uk

**First published 2008**

ISBN 978-0-13-129810-1

**British Library Cataloguing-in-Publication Data**
A catalogue record for this book is available from the British Library

**Library of Congress Cataloging-in-Publication Data**
A catalog record for this book is available from the Library of Congress

10 9 8 7 6 5 4 3 2 1
12 11 10 09 08

Typeset in 10.5/12pt Minion by 35
Printed and bound by Rotolito Lombarda, Italy

*The publisher's policy is to use paper manufactured from sustainable forests.*

# Dedication

PQ: To Amanda

BD: To Mum and Dad

# British Psychological Society Standards in Cognitive Psychology

The British Psychological Society (BPS) accredits psychology degree programmes across the UK. It has set guidelines as to which major topics should be covered within cognitive psychology. We have listed these topics below and indicated where in this textbook each is covered most fully.

| Topic | Chapter |
|---|---|
| Perception: visual information processing, auditory perception and speech recognition | Chapters 2–6 |
| Attention | Chapters 8, 9 |
| Visual and spatial imagery | Chapters 7, 15 |
| Comprehension | Chapters 14, 15 |
| Conceptual knowledge | Chapter 12 |
| Learning | Chapters 10, 12, 13 |
| Skill acquisition and expertise | Chapter 13 |
| Memory: encoding and retrievalprocesses, working, autobiographical, episodic and semantic memory, implicit and explicit memory, memory improvement | Chapters 10–13 |
| Thinking and reasoning, problem solving, decision making | Chapter 15 |
| Language: structure, comprehension, production, reading | Chapter 14 |
| Connectionist models | Chapters 12, 14 |
| Emotion and cognition | Chapter 16 |

# Brief contents

## Supporting resources

Visit **www.pearsoned.co.uk/quinlan** to find valuable online resources

**Companion Website for students**

For each chapter you will find the following resources

- **Remind yourself**
  - A quick test to get an idea of how well you understand the main topics covered in a chapter;
  - A names and dates quiz to help recall important figures and their time of writing;
  - A concentration game to test your understanding of key terms.
- **Test yourself** – For the main topics in each chapter, explore animations and diagrams from the text. Assessed multiple choice questions will help test your understanding of key concepts in Cognitive Psychology.
- **Going further** – Annotated weblinks to classic experiments and annotated weblinks to the latest research allow you to explore topics in more depth.

On entering the site for the first time select **Register**. You will then be asked to provide some personal details when you create your user account.

**Also:** the Companion Website provides the following features:
- Search tool to help locate specific items of content
- E-mail results and profile tools to send results of quizzes to instructors
- Online help and support to assist with website usage and troubleshooting

**For instructors**
- Online testbank of over 400 questions
- PowerPoint slides featuring figures and tables from the book
- PowerPoint set of lectures in *Cognitive Psychology*
- A set of teaching ideas for use with the book

For more information please contact your local Pearson Education sales representative or visit **www.pearsoned.co.uk/quinlan**

# Contents

## Chapter 3   Visual processes and visual sensory memory          64

## Chapter 4    Masking, thresholds and consciousness    105

## Chapter 6    Theories of perception                                                         **185**

## Chapter 7    Mental representation      228

## Chapter 11   Human memory: fallibilities and failures   387

# List of figures and tables

# Guided tour

**Learning objectives** outline what you should expect to learn from the chapter.

**Chapter opening examples** and **Reflective questions** encourage you to relate your own experiences to what you are about to read in the chapter.

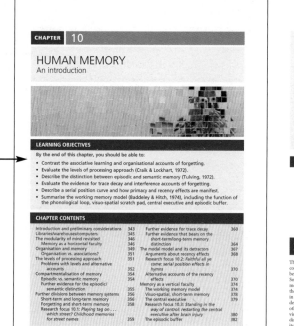

**Chapter contents** provide an overview of all topics that are covered in the chapter.

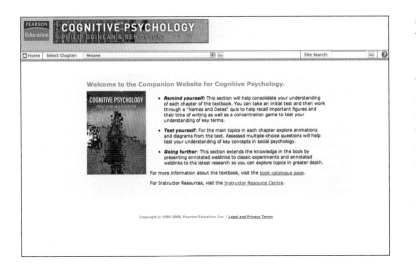

A Companion Website accompanies this book please go to:

## www.pearsoned.co.uk/quinlan

This website features a range of resources that will allow you to consolidate your understanding, test your knowledge and explore a particular area of interest in more depth.

On entering the site for the first time select Register. You will then be asked to provide some personal details when you create your user account.

# Develop your knowledge

**Pinpoint questions** provide a chance to check your knowledge and understanding of the chapter so far. Answers are provided at the end of the each chapter.

**For example . . .** boxes highlight the application of Cognitive Psychology in the real world.

---

**338** Chapter 9 Attentional constraints and performance limitations

a sense the previous task set must be released from inhibition. Following this argument, it can be seen that the task set inertia hypothesis predicts a very particular pattern of results – namely that performance on switch trials will be particularly impaired following an incongruent trial. This is a prediction about a specific between-trial congruency effect. Critically the data reported by Goschke (2000) were perfectly in line with this very particular prediction.

In thinking about such a pattern of performance it becomes almost immediately apparent that it fits reasonably uncomfortably with the task set reconfiguration hypothesis as originally stipulated. Why should it take longer to reconfigure the system after an incongruent trial than after a congruent trial? Indeed, Pashler (2000, p. 287) has stated, 'Perhaps the most intriguing aspect of task switching is the lingering effect of the irrelevant mapping – the "task congruity

effect".' Although Monsell (2003, p. 137) has offered some speculations as to why this might occur – 'The detection of cross-task interference during a trial might also prompt the ramping-up of endogenous control' – it remains anyone's guess as to what this actually means.

More generally, it should come as no surprise that the literature is now awash with findings that variously support either the notion of task set reconfiguration or the notion of task set inertia. Many other reasons for task-switching costs are also currently being explored. The field remains wide open and the killer experiments have yet to be carried out!

**Pinpoint question 9.10**

What evidence is there to suggest that task-switching costs are not simply the result of executive control?

**Research focus 9.3**

### Totally wired? The effect of caffeine on task switching

The evidence for switching costs is beyond doubt and it is interesting to consider other factors that may impinge. So we can ask, what are the cognitive effects of caffeine exactly? Tieges, Snel, Kok, Wijnen, Lorist and Ridderinkhof (2006) took it upon themselves to examine the effects of caffeine during task switching, predicting that a boost of caffeine should help in task set reconfiguration, especially if individuals are given sufficient time to prepare for the switch.

Eighteen participants were used in the study, with each individual taking part in three separate experimental sessions involving either the consumption of a placebo, a low dose of caffeine or a high dose of caffeine. To their credit, Tieges et al. (2006) examined many different types of measurement in their study, although here we'll just be focusing on the behavioural results. In an adaptation of the alternating-runs task (Rogers & Monsell, 1995), participants either judged the colour (task A) or the consonant/vowel nature (task B) of letters presented on a computer monitor. During single-task conditions, only the colour or the identity task was completed. During mixed-task conditions, the two tasks alternated in a predictable manner, with two trials of task A followed by two trials of task B and so on. The gap in between response at one trial and stimulus presentation at the next (RSI) varied over 150, 600 and 1500 ms.

In general, participants seemed pretty buzzed as a result of their caffeine shot since RTs were generally faster in the caffeine conditions relative to the placebo condition, although there were marginal differences between the effects of high and low doses of caffeine. More importantly, the behavioural data revealed that switch costs were substantially reduced following caffeine intake, although this was especially true for the condition in which participants had the greatest time to prepare for the task switch (RSI 1500 ms).

Tieges et al. (2006) discussed the reduction of switching costs in the presence of caffeine ingestion as a consequence of the relationship between caffeine and dopamine activity (see Garrett & Griffiths, 1997). Therefore, it seems that a cup of GMA (Good Morning America) really does help in the planning of anticipatory behaviour as demanded by a predictive task switch! Of course, we're not suggesting that you now run out and buy a sackful of coffee beans. You'll need to read a different textbook to ours to find out about dependency, habituation and withdrawal . . .

Source: Tieges, Z., Snel, J., Kok, A., Wijnen, J. G., Lorist, M. M., & Ridderinkhof, R. (2006). Caffeine improves anticipatory processes in task switching. Biological Psychology, 73, 101–116.

---

**122** Chapter 4 Masking, thresholds and consciousness

**For example . . .**

If all of this is starting to feel a little remote, then the work of Connolly, Wayne, Lymperis and Doherty (2000) should act as a sobering reminder of how important issues concerning masking and perceptual thresholds can be. In their review, Connolly et al. (2000) discussed the efforts of tobacco companies who are introducing additives to cigarettes. The intention is that additives should mask the sensations

associated with environment tobacco smoke. Clearly if we can't detect (either by smell or by sight) tobacco in the air because it is being masked by these additives, then we will be more likely to think we're in an environment free from the effects of second-hand smoke inhalation. So while we're discussing these apparently theoretical issues, they do have real-life and potentially life-threatening consequences.

which it decides when to come on! Given this, we need to consider how the psychological state of the participant may affect the setting of a threshold. How might the participant's motivations and expectations affect the difference between being aware of the stimulus and being unaware of it?

supra-threshold Above threshold.

sub-threshold Below threshold – subliminal.

subliminal perception Perception thought to occur below the threshold of consciousness.

stimulus factors Dimensions upon which a stimulus may vary.

subjective factors Factors that are inherent to participants – indicative of individual differences.

psychophysical function A graphical/mathematical means for relating a participant's responses to some variation in a stimulus factor.

### Thresholds and perceptual defence

There are no dirty words, only dirty minds

*(attributed to Lenny Bruce)*

The difference between the participant as passive sensor and the participant as decision-maker featured heavily in the early studies of perceptual defence. Perceptual defence refers to reports that participants 'exhibited higher perceptual thresholds for negatively valued or taboo materials than neutral or positively valued materials' (Postman et al., 1953, p. 215). For example, Postman et al. (1953) used a masking by light technique in which on a given trial a single word was presented very briefly. Initially the luminance of the word display was well below that of the pre- and post-fields.

After every stimulus presentation the participant was asked to report anything they thought they saw. The luminance of the target field was incremented slightly after every trial and the same target word was repeatedly presented over a sequence of 18 trials. Now a classic perceptual defence effect in these circumstances would be that participants would take longer to report taboo words correctly (such as 'raped' and 'filth') than neutral words (such as 'mixer' and 'clove'). That is, neutral words could be 'seen' at lower levels of luminance than could the taboo words – taboo words had higher perceptual thresholds than neutral words.

Taken at face value, such a result does have quite important consequences for understanding perception because perceptual defence can be construed as being an example of semantic activation without conscious identification. How could the perceptual threshold of the taboo and neutral masked words be differentially affected unless the meaning of the words had been accessed? In this regard perceptual defence poses difficulties for any simple sequential stage theory of perceptual processing in which stimulus encoding must run to completion before any processes concerning the interpretation/identification of the stimulus takes place. The existence of perceptual defence seems to suggest that the meaning of the stimulus is affecting sensory encoding!

Given these sorts of considerations, there ensued much discussion over the claim that perceptual defence reflects a tendency to resist recognising threatening stimuli (Postman et al., 1953). Without doubt, this is quite an alarming thing to claim: do we really want a perceptual system that insulates us from threatening stimuli? If you are about to be hit by a speeding car, you need to know about this pretty quickly in order to try to avoid it! Maybe a more sensible approach is to argue that perceptual defence effects show that anxiety-provoking stimuli are detected, but at an unconscious level. This act of recognition then pre-empts anxiety

---

**Research focus** boxes provide an insight into classic or more recent examples of research conducted in specific subject areas.

# Develop your knowledge (*continued*)

**Figures** illustrate key concepts, visually reinforcing your learning.

**Key terms** are highlighted in the text when they first appear, followed by a full definition at the end of a section. Key terms are also included in the Glossary at the end of the book.

---

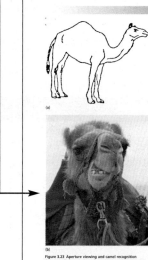

**Figure 3.23 Aperture viewing and camel recognition**
Cut out a slit from a piece of card large enough to cover the whole of figure (a). Then either move the slit over the figure or hold the card still and move the figure behind it. It remains to be seen whether the effects generalise to (b).
Sources: (a) Snodgrass, J. G., & Vanderwart, M. A. (1980). Standardized set of 260 pictures: Norms of name agreement, usage agreement, familiarity, and visual complexity. *Journal of Experimental Psychology: Learning, Memory, and Cognition, 6*, 174–215 (43, p. 198). Reproduced with permission from APA. (b) J. Marshall/Tribal Eye/Alamy.

is applied – the canvas retains stimulus information until the complete picture is built up. Indeed this particular metaphor has been used directly to explain aperture viewing in terms of something known as **retinal painting** (Morgan, Findlay, & Watt, 1982). According to the retinal painting hypothesis, in conditions of aperture viewing the eyes follow the direction of the shape as it moves behind the slit, even though the slit itself remains stationary. A consequence of these involuntary eye movements is that a different part of the retina is exposed to the shape as it moves. An ordered sequence of images falls on consecutive parts of the retina and in this way the complete shape is painted onto the retina.

However, if the retinal painting account of aperture viewing were found to be true, then there would be good grounds for arguing that it is irrelevant to discussion of iconic memory. The argument would be that aperture viewing is yet another demonstration of visible persistence and, as we have seen, there are good grounds for arguing that informational persistence (i.e., iconic storage) is different from visible persistence. This is where the distinction between the two sorts of aperture viewing comes to the fore. In the moving slit example it seems reasonable to argue that retinal painting may be the explanation because the slit moves and the figure remains stationary. Different aspects of the figure are successively falling on different parts of the retina. However, the retinal painting account falters in the stationary slit case since different parts of the figure are being successively exposed to the same part of the retina.

In addressing this point, Morgan et al. (1982) ran an experiment on aperture viewing in which they carefully controlled the display presentation so that retinal painting could be ruled out. They designed computer-controlled displays in which the participant was presented with a sequence of static snapshots of what would be visible through the aperture over time. Each snapshot provided a new static view and adjacent snapshots shared no overlapping elements. Figure 3.24 provides an illustration of one such sequence of snapshots. Importantly, even with these kinds of displays participants did report the impression of a real object moving behind the slit.

Critically, the position of the participants' eyes was monitored during the display sequence to ensure that the slit was stabilised on the back of the retina. This was vital so that each new snapshot stimulated the same part of the retina. So under these conditions both voluntary and involuntary eye movements have been eliminated from consideration. The results unequivocally

---

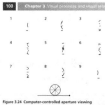

**Figure 3.24 Computer-controlled aperture viewing**
The sequence of stimulus fragments (top panel) presented by Morgan et al. (1982) in their simulation of viewing a moving wagon wheel (bottom panel) through an aperture.
Source: Morgan, M. J., Findlay, J. M., & Watt, R. J. (1982). Aperture viewing: A review and a synthesis. *The Quarterly Journal of Experimental Psychology, 34A*, 211–233. Reproduced with permission from Taylor & Francis.

demonstrated that, even though the complete figure was never exposed, participants reported perceiving a real object moving behind a slit. This shows that 'partial views of a shape presented in temporal succession can give rise to the perceptual impression of a whole shape in motion' (Morgan et al., 1982, p. 231 – a conclusion more recently endorsed by Fendrich et al., 2005). → See 'What have we learnt?', below.

**Pinpoint question 3.10**

What critical condition ruled out retinal painting as an account of aperture viewing?

**aperture viewing** Viewing a stimulus through a slit.
**anorthoscopic perception** Perception of a world through a slit or aperture.
**retinal painting** According to Morgan, Findlay and Watt (1982), the piecemeal exposure of a stimulus over adjacent parts of the retina as is assumed to take place in studies of aperture viewing.

**→ What have we learnt?**

This sort of data suggests that there is indeed a form of visual memory that operates so as to integrate information over brief intervals so as to provide a coherent picture of the constantly changing visual environment. Such a memory system is seen to take different time-stamped snapshots of the stimulus and organise these into a coherent impression of the visual input – a post-retinal storage buffer (Parks, 1965). The data from Morgan et al. (1982) reveal that participants can recover the impression of a complete object even though it is exposed in a piecemeal fashion to the same place on the retina. Here the contents of the aperture are completely over-written at each point in the sequence and yet a coherent impression of the shape is achieved. So although Adelson (1983) discussed iconic memory much like a light-sensitive 2D photographic plate, this simple analogy will not work for the case where the spatial structure of a shape can be recovered in the aperture viewing case. Indeed it seems much more likely that the sort of mechanisms being tapped in such aperture viewing experiments is different from iconic memory. By

this view the aperture viewing experiments are tapping into a form of visual short-term memory that may be useful in integrating information over very brief intervals and that operates subsequent to iconic storage.

Accordingly, the visual array is initially captured as a 2D retinal copy of the world (in the icon) but this is merely a precursor to other forms of short-term visual memory. By this view, the partial-report studies are seemingly tapping into iconic storage but the aperture viewing experiments reflect the operation of other forms of visual storage. We have essentially argued that performance in the various tasks so far described reflects the properties of either of two forms of visual memory, namely (i) an iconic fast-decaying memory, and (ii) a later, more durable form of storage. We may therefore cling on to the classic form of icon as a cyclopean retinocentric representation but leave open the possibility of a further short-term store that is also sensitive to the visual characteristics of visible stimuli. It is this later memory system that is responsible for integrating information over brief intervals.

---

**What have we learnt?** boxes summarise the material covered in the previous section and allow you to check your understanding.

## Check your understanding

**Chapter summaries** recap and reinforce the key points to take away from the chapter. They also provide a useful revision tool.

**Answers to pinpoint questions** present suggested answers to pinpoint questions in each chapter.

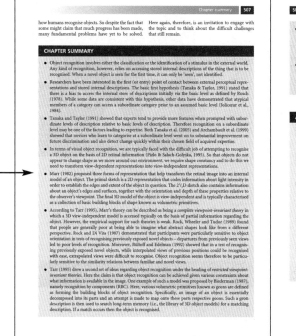

For each chapter, go to the website to explore a range of **interactive resources** that allow you to check your understanding of important terms, concepts and ideas.

Take a **quick test** to get an idea of how well you understand the main concepts covered in a chapter.

Try the **names and dates quiz** to help connect important cognitive concepts with who introduced them and when.

A **concentration game** tests your understanding of key terms.

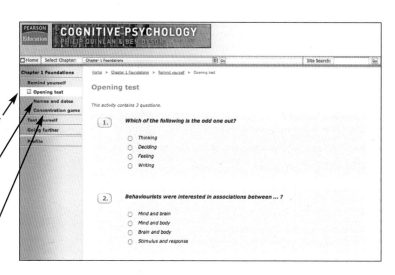

## Check your understanding (*continued*)

Within the **test yourself section**, you will find a series of questions based around the learning outcomes for each chapter. Explore the animations and diagrams and answer the questions to check your understanding.

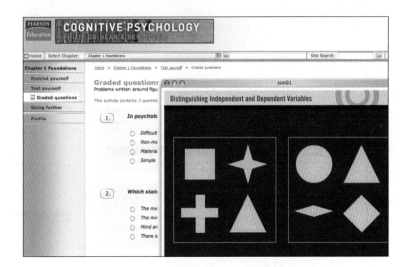

## Extend your study

Explore topics in more depth using the **weblinks** to classic experiments and the latest research. Use our guide to authoritative websites to help you in your independent and further research.

# Preface

Why deal with differences in reaction times when we can access people's opinions using questionnaires? Why worry about how quickly to present a visual mask when we can observe parents and children interacting with each other? There is little doubt that students often have an initial difficulty getting to grips with cognition relative to other aspects of Psychology. One of the reasons for this is that Cognitive Psychology can often appear rather abstract and, as a result, lack an obvious connection with the real world that makes other topics much more enticing. This book is an attempt to present Cognitive Psychology in a way that covers the detailed experiments that underlie the development of dominant theories about mental processes, while at the same time reminding the reader of the implications that these ideas have in the outside world. Why worry about reaction time: what would happen if you stopped too late at a red light in your car? Why worry about masking: what would happen if you couldn't smell or see cigarette smoke?

However, our aim has never been to produce a tabloid version of Cognitive Psychology; to do so would be a disservice to the legions of researchers gone before and the complexity of the arguments offered. Moreover, some sense of the chronological development of cognitive research is also necessary to appreciate how far we have come (or how far we still have to go) in understanding the relevant issues. Ultimately, we hope to show in this book that Cognitive Psychology is all around us, flourishing inside the laboratory and of pragmatic value outside the laboratory.

## Book structure

The book begins by setting the foundations for studying Cognitive Psychology in terms of outlining an abstracted, information processing account of the mind. Both relatively thorny philosophical problems are introduced in addition to pragmatic concerns involving hypothesis testing. The book begins its trawl through the empirical data in earnest in Chapter 3 by identifying visual sensory memory as one particular entry point into Cognitive Psychology. The reader will have covered all points in between including perception, memory, language, reasoning and skill acquisition, before reaching the final Chapter 16 and the discussion of emotion and cognition. Consequently, the book covers all the British Psychological Society (BPS) required topics as demonstrated in the table below.

| Topic | Chapter |
|---|---|
| Perception: visual information processing, auditory perception and speech recognition | Chapters 2–6 |
| Attention | Chapters 8, 9 |
| Visual and spatial imagery | Chapters 7, 15 |
| Comprehension | Chapters 14, 15 |
| Conceptual knowledge | Chapter 12 |
| Learning | Chapters 10, 12, 13 |
| Skill acquisition and expertise | Chapter 13 |
| Memory: encoding and retrieval processes, working, autobiographical, episodic and semantic memory, implicit and explicit memory, memory improvement | Chapters 10–13 |
| Thinking and reasoning, problem solving, decision-making | Chapter 15 |
| Language: structure, comprehension, production, reading | Chapter 14 |
| Connectionist models | Chapters 12, 14 |
| Emotion and cognition | Chapter 16 |

## Pedagogical features

A textbook need to do much more than to transmit information from the writer to the reader. The reader needs to be able to check their understanding of basic concepts, feel confident that they have grasped the details of specific experiments, and also appreciate the wider issues involved. With this in mind, each chapter has an equivalent structure incorporating a number of aids to understanding. At the start of each chapter, the reader will be presented with an **Opening example**. Rather than begin each chapter at the deep end, we set the themes of the chapter within some fairly autobiographical (and some not-so autobiographical) scenarios in which the reader is reminded how exactly the chapter topic might relate to everyday life. Following the opening example, the reader is presented with two **Reflective questions** that provide further links between the forthcoming ideas and real life in the form of open-ended questions that should be held in mind as the chapter progresses. A number of **Learning outcomes** are then provided, identifying the specific goals that each chapter aims to meet. Each topic ends with a **Chapter summary** in which the main points of the chapter are presented in brief form.

Within the text itself lie an additional layer of features designed to further assist the reader in their understanding of Cognitive Psychology. Each chapter contains 10 **Pinpoint questions,** which are aimed at testing the reader's understanding of core concepts and findings. A number of **Key terms** are identified throughout the chapter, the definitions for which are supplied in a **Glossary** at the back of the book. Every chapter also contains 3 **Research focus** boxes in which contemporary research is presented and evaluated with respect to the themes of the current chapter. To remind the reader of the real-life application of the current topic, we provide **For example . . .** boxes in which examples from popular culture are presented to further illustrate principles within the chapter. We also offer moments of reflection in the form of **What have we learnt?** boxes, in which we evaluate exactly how far we have come in the chapter and what remaining ground there is left to cover.

## Reviewers

We would like to thank the following reviewers:

Dr Thom Baguley, Nottingham Trent University, England

Professor Graham C. L. Davey, University of Sussex, England

Dr Graham Dean, University of Teesside, England

Dr Lisa Hinkley, Oxford Brookes University, England

Dr Magnus Lindgren, Lund University, Sweden

Dr Jean McConnell, Glasgow Caledonian University, Scotland

Stephen Nunn, Middlesex University, England

Dr Anna-Carin Olsson, Umea University, Sweden

Dr Sylvain Sirois, University of Manchester, England

Professor Eric Soetens, University of Brussels, Belgium

Dr Ian Walker, University of Bath, England

Dr Susanne Wiking, University of Tromsø, Norway.

# Acknowledgements

It is now several months since I 'finished' working on the book and I was hoping that this hiatus would have made reflection easier. If anything, the opposite has happened and now it is proving to be immensely difficult to make sense of it all. Nonetheless, what is very clear is that things would have turned out very differently if it had not been for Amanda Sowden and Ben Dyson. Amanda's unfathomable optimism provided a necessary stabiliser. Unfortunately, her tolerance was, at times, stretched to the limits: Mere 'thanks' is not enough. In turn, Ben came to the rescue, late in the project, when I was about to succumb to other pressures. So my real gratitude goes to them.

However, it would be remiss not to thank several others. In no necessary order: Max Coltheart, Robert Goldstone, Gillian Rhodes, Mike Miller, Ian Neath, Charles Hulme, Mark Hurlstone, Rebekah Dutton, Padraic Monaghan, Nikos Andreadis, Gareth Gaskell and Alan Baddeley helped set the record straight in various respects. I have also benefited a great deal from discussions with Richard Wilton and Alan Kingstone: their influence may only be clear to them but it would be disingenuous not to acknowledge it here.

This has been a rather demanding, and, in places, arduous endeavour. There is a view that the writing of textbooks is an indulgence that can only be pursued to the detriment of proper academic research. Unsurprisingly, this has proved to be not the most encouraging backdrop against which to work. Even though I do not subscribe to such a view, I do promise that I won't attempt it again.

As is the way with this sort of thing, it took a little longer than anyone predicted. Although the project started in the very capable hands of Morten Fulgevand and David Cox at Pearson, the majority of the work, at that end, has been carried out both assiduously and cheerfully by Janey Webb, Steven Jackson and Joe Vella. Their contributions have been significant. We will just have to agree to differ about the appropriateness of the terms 'interim' and 'mooted'.

Finally, it is only proper to attribute some of the blame to Diana Kornbrot, Neville Austin and Leslie Henderson. They taught me the basics of experimental cognitive psychology and are primarily responsible for my engagement with this most fascinating and important science.

*Philip Quinlan*
*York, April 2008*

I would like to thank the numerous individuals who had the misfortune to be around while the book was being written. Special apologies must go to Andrew Dunn, Claude Alain, Mark Bewley and Gordon Baxter, all of whom had to wait just that little bit longer for their respective e-mails, manuscripts, text messages and music. Special mention also to Phil Kerfoot for allowing evidence of the Ibiza bike incident to receive a wider audience, to Mark Blythe who helped track down some of the more cultural references as the deadline approached and to Jim Parkinson for 'the noise'. Finally, thanks to Andy Field who provided his own unique input during the more trying periods of writing and also to Peggy St. Jacques who continues to provide the support that makes everything possible.

*Ben Dyson*
*Sussex, April 2008*

# About the authors

**Philip Quinlan's** first lecturing appointment was in 1988, in Cognitive Science at the Department of Psychology, Birkbeck College, The University of London. As both luck and youth were on his side, he was then able to move, in 1989, to a lecturing position in the Department of Psychology at (the now) Royal Holloway, University of London. He stayed and terrorised the students for about a year before heading north to The University of York, in 1991. Despite the almost overwhelming opposition, he retains his commitment to Cognitive Psychology, thinks much of connectionism is just plain daft, and feels that the immense financial costs far outweigh the gains of a lot of the current work in Cognitive Neuroscience.

**Ben Dyson** was awarded his PhD at the University of York, UK, carried out a post-doctoral research fellowship at The Rotman Research Institute, Canada, and is currently a lecturer in the Department of Psychology at the University of Sussex, UK. Ben's core research interests focus on the passive and active cognitive representations of sound using behavioural and event-related potential (ERP) methodologies. More recently, he has become interested in auditory memory and the psychological mechanisms involved in the production and perception of art.

## CHAPTER 1

# FOUNDATIONS

## LEARNING OBJECTIVES

**By the end of this chapter, you should be able to:**

- Recognise the distinction between physical and abstract properties.
- Describe the assumptions of behaviourism, the laws of behaviour and the principles of associationism.
- Explain how empirical research allows for experimental investigations of the mind.
- Identify two desirable properties of scientific theory: falsification (Popper) and simplicity (Occam).
- Identify the difference between the type and token versions of central state identity theory.
- Describe what it means to provide a functional account of any aspect of human cognition.
- Explain the analogies that exist between the mind/brain distinction and the computer software/hardware distinction.
- List the three different levels of description according to Marr (1982).
- Understand the threat posed to cognitive psychology by reductionism.

## CHAPTER CONTENTS

▶

# 'If you don't believe, she won't come' Playground hypothesising about the tooth fairy

The playground is like a young person's internet – rife with information, some of it important, some of it completely spurious, with no real way of separating one kind from the other. One compelling topic tends to be how best to make additional pocket money, and consequently break-time discussions can turn to that magical source of income, the tooth fairy. 'But it's true!' blurts the girl, 'when your tooth falls out, you put it under the pillow, and then the fairy comes, and then she takes the tooth and gives you some money.' The boy looks on sceptically. 'It's true!' the girl insists, 'it happened four times already! Every night for a week my tooth fell out, and every night I'd put my tooth under my pillow, there was a shiny coin the morning after. Straight away – not three days later, not a month – straight away!' Again, the boy remains unconvinced: 'I heard that your mum comes in the middle of the night and does it, it's not the tooth fairy at all.' To emphasise his point, he wipes his nose on his sleeve. The girl thinks for a moment and then replies, 'Well, yes, your mum puts the money underneath your pillow, but it's the tooth fairy that gives her the money in the first place.' 'But how does the tooth fairy carry all that money around?' 'She has a magic pocket!' The boy rolls his eyes to the sky, notices a football flying overhead and runs off to meet it land. The girl, meanwhile, begins to wiggle a fifth tooth in preparation for tonight's payout.

How do we know what is real? Does the tooth fairy really exist? If the tooth fairy doesn't exist, why are some explanations of important events more convincing than others? During the course of this first chapter, we'll discuss a problem more worrying than any mythical cash-distributing sprite, namely, do our minds really exist? We'll tackle various approaches that attempt to account for human behaviour, and argue why it might be necessary to invoke mental processes when describing the causes of human behaviour. Specifically, we'll make a broad distinction between cognitivism and behaviourism in a bid to make some general points about what it means to be human. Moreover, we'll present several different philosophical perspectives on the relation between mind and body so as to prepare you for the remainder of the book (and of course to really get you wondering whether you exist at all).

## REFLECTIVE QUESTIONS

1. Think about your childhood in terms of reward and punishment (we hope more of the former and less of the latter). How did you learn not to touch an electrical socket? How did you learn to be polite to your grandparents? Did the feedback happen straight away after the event or some time afterwards? Did the feedback happen often or only once?

2. Take an average day and consider what is causing you to do the things you do. Why did you decide to go to college this morning? Why did you take the scenic route instead of the normal one? How did you figure out what you were going to have for dinner? Did you do these things today because you did them yesterday? Did you do them because someone told you to? Or do you act in a purposeful way and decide to do them?

## PART 1

# An historical perspective and why there is more to cognitive psychology than meets the eye

## Introduction and preliminary considerations

One of the challenges in writing this book is trying to imagine what the material means to someone who is studying human cognition for the first time. Over the course of the history of cognitive psychology particular ways of thinking and talking about the human mind have evolved, and these are now firmly ingrained in present-day attitudes. To those in the know, all of it is just so obvious and reasonable. Yet in being placed in the position of trying to explain this material to a novice cognitive psychologist, much of what is taken for granted – as being self-evident – quite clearly is not. Indeed, it is only when we reflect upon the terms that are used, and the concepts that are accepted, does it become clear that rather a lot needs explaining. Of course you will be getting your fill of the core topics of cognition (e.g., attention, object recognition, thinking, perception, memory, etc.) as the book unfolds, but without a serious consideration of the foundational issues and assumptions, much of that material will make little sense. At the outset therefore, we have decided to try to get you to think about the basics of cognitive psychology before we launch into the particularities of the different mental faculties.

Put simply, it seems to us vital that we address some rather basic issues in order to explain the 'cognitivist' point of view. Indeed, in attempting to do this, it has become very quickly apparent that even the simplest

cognitive account is based on a rather complicated network of presuppositions and assumptions that do need to be carefully examined and explained. For instance, the typical cognitive psychologist assumes that it is perfectly sensible to argue that your thoughts reside in your inner world – an internal space in which the external 'real' world is in some sense 'represented in your mind'. Indeed, it is because this notion of an inner world is so central to the study of cognition that it is easy to forget that this is merely an assumption and (as we will see) not one that is accepted throughout the scientific community.

In adopting a cognitivist point of view, it can be slightly irritating to realise that not everyone believes that the study of human cognition is a worthwhile enterprise at all – the very idea! Indeed there are even some who have argued that the discipline is inherently incoherent (see e.g., Skinner, 1985). As we will see, cognitive psychologists are quite happy to discuss mental representations and processes, but not everyone is comfortable with such talk. Detractors such as Skinner believed that a scientific psychology should not concern itself with unobservable entities such as the mind (the 'inner world' mentioned above). In contrast, psychologists should only concern themselves with things and events that occur in the real world. As Flanagan (1984, p. 94) noted, according to Skinner, 'if we are merely interested in explaining the occurrence of the overt behavioral responses we can do so without any mention of mental events'.

Clearly there are many vexed and important issues here, and because of this we need to proceed with extreme caution before getting further into the complexities. For now, though, it is enough just to state that the study of human cognition is based on some reasonably contentious assumptions, and it is only fair to you, as the reader, to be open about this at the outset. Therefore it is important to us to try to paint a clear picture of what it is that cognitive psychologists are attempting to achieve and how it is that they go about their business. You may, of course, end up expressing doubts about the sensibleness of the discipline, but at least you should be able to see what cognitive psychology is and what it entails. Having been exposed to the basic assumptions, you should then be in a position to judge whether cognitive psychology is in any sense a worthwhile enterprise.

Structurally this first chapter is divided into two parts. In Part 1, some historical material is covered in an attempt to set the context for the study of human cognition. In doing this, alternative ways of thinking about human psychology are set out, and you will be able to see that these deny most (if not all) of what cognitive psychologists assume. By seeing what cognitive psychology is not, this may help clarify what cognitive psychology is. Such a manoeuvre is useful in much the same way that an understanding of right-wing politics may help shed light on the nature of left-wing politics.

Various philosophical approaches to understanding the mind are also explored. The invitation to consider philosophical viewpoints may seem a little out of place because this book is primarily about psychology, not philosophy. Nonetheless, consideration of some philosophy provides an interesting slant on the foundational assumptions of the cognitivist approach to the study of the mind. Without some understanding of the philosophical issues that underpin the discipline, cognitive psychology may, indeed, come across as incoherent. This initial material provides a necessary backdrop to the eventual framework for thinking about the mind: a framework that underpins the vast majority of theories of cognition.

So, in summary, the early material in the book provides an introduction to, and discussion of, the very foundations of cognitive psychology. Definitions of some basic and key terms are included and clarification of the foundational assumptions that underpin the cognitive approach to understanding human intellectual abilities is also provided. Contrasting (indeed diametrically opposed) views are also covered in a bid to clarify what cognitive psychology is all about.

Part 2 builds on the material covered in Part 1, and explores more closely the possible relations between the mind and brain. Part 2 also develops the basic concepts that define what a cognitive account of some aspect of human performance actually looks like. Concepts such as **function** and **functional role** are described and the distinction between structure and function is spelt out. The notion of an **information processing system** is introduced and consideration is

given to how best describe the operation of information processing devices. A description of what it means to provide an explanation at the cognitive level is given, and some contrasting ideas about **reductionism** and **eliminative materialism** are also included. Some effort is also expended on explaining why mind science does not reduce to brain science, and why it is that brain science can never replace mind science.

---

**function** A term used to refer to what a thing does.

**functional role** A phrase used to refer to what the purpose of a component of an information processing system is.

**information processing system** A descriptive phrase that is used to refer to any kind of device whose operations are causally defined in terms of the information presented to it.

**reductionism** The notion that we can reduce ideas relating to mental events to a basic physical level. At a fundamental level, mental events can be understood in terms of the operations of physical mechanisms.

**eliminative materialism** The viewpoint that once we understand the precise electro-chemical workings of the brain, we will understand the mind. When we reach this point, we can eliminate any talk of the cognitive level.

---

## The abstract nature of cognitive psychology

A key term that is used repeatedly in cognitive psychology is **abstract**, and it is unfortunately the case that this term has unwanted connotations like 'difficult' and 'complex'. For example, it is sometimes claimed that understanding quantum physics depends on understanding *abstract* mathematics. In psychological terms, however, all we need accept is that the term 'abstract' is used to designate something that is defined without reference to the material (physical) world – that is, without reference to the world of chairs and tables, rivers and trees, bangs and crashes. By this definition, things like thoughts, ideas, beliefs, desires, feelings and attitudes are all abstract because, although these may be about the physical world, they are not, in themselves, physical entities. The important implication is that we can discuss the abstract nature of the mind, and in the context of this book, this is hardly a contentious statement to make. For some, though, such a discussion is very problematic. They see such a discussion to be based upon a rather shaky distinction between the mental and the physical, and they have profound problems in making sense of this distinction. To appreciate this more fully, it is important to consider the physical/mental distinction in the context of the extremely influential philosophy of mind known as Cartesian dualism (or more simply, **dualism**).

---

## Pinpoint question 1.1

**Is guilt over breaking your little brother's model aeroplane physical or abstract? Why?**

---

**abstract** A term that is used to refer to anything that is defined without reference to the material world.

**dualism** The philosophical position that the mind is a mental entity distinct from the physical world.

---

## Dualism and one of the many mind/body problems

According to dualism – a philosophy generally attributed to René Descartes (1591–1650) – the world is made up of two incompatible substances, namely, the mental and the physical, respectively. There is a mental world and there is a material world. Cartesian dualism posits that the mind is a non-physical (i.e., abstract) entity that is different from any form of physical entity. Within this framework it is perfectly acceptable to discuss the mental causation of behaviour, e.g., 'William decided to make a sandwich because he felt hungry'. What we have here is a statement that William's *feeling* gave rise to a *decision* ('feeling' and 'deciding' are the mental events) that caused him to make (the physical act) the sandwich. Such ideas are so intuitively plausible that it is difficult to see how they could be problematic, or even wrong!

So what could possibly be objectionable in what we have been discussing? Well, as Flew (1979, p. 86) noted, 'A great deal of work . . . has been devoted to trying to avoid Descartes' absolute division between the mental and the physical.' This is primarily because the framework provides no indication of the means by which the mental and the physical are supposed to interact (Fodor, 1981a). How could it be that a mental

event causes a physical event if the mental and the physical are fundamentally different sorts of things? Clearly, therefore, this is a very serious mind/body problem to which no one has ever managed to provide an adequate solution. This is not to argue that dualism is hopelessly misguided, but merely that it gives rise to some very difficult issues. It is therefore important to show how it is possible to be a cognitive psychologist without being wedded to dualist assumptions.

The central point is that it is quite possible to discuss mental states and processes in the absence of any discussion of physical states and processes. In this sense, it is possible to state that the mind is an abstract entity, with the only implication being that it can be discussed and defined without reference to physical states and processes. In this regard, cognitive psychologists are not so much concerned about the physical states and processes that take place between your ears; they are much more concerned with what mental states and processes might be like in their own right. Do not get too hung up about this for the moment because a much more thorough discussion of this point can be found later in the chapter. However, if the basic point is accepted, then it is also quite reasonable to question whether the study of the mind falls within the realm of science. That is, can science, which is concerned with the study of the physical nature world, help us understand the nature of the mind that is defined as an abstract entity? Is there any way in which we can use scientific methods, which have been developed to explain the physical world, to study the mind?

All of this may be very difficult to come to terms with because it is easy to free associate and begin to equate the mind with the soul, to locate the soul in the spirit world, and then think that the study of human cognition is no different from the study of the paranormal because both involve the study of abstract entities. This is indeed a possible train of thought, but just because we are concerned with mental states and processes this does not mean that we will end up ghost hunting. Rather, what psychologists try to do is understand human behaviour, and what they assume is that a large component of this understanding requires the detailing of how the mind works (see e.g., Pinker, 1997, for a thorough exposition). As with many complex arguments, things tend to become clearer when we think in terms of particular examples. A useful example in this context involves a contrasting approach to the study of human nature to that accepted by cognitive psychologists, and this is known as *behaviourism*.

## Behaviourism

Textbook treatments of the history of psychology tend to convey that, prior to the emergence of the cognitive revolution (in the first half of the twentieth century), all of academic psychology took place within a behaviourist framework. This may well be a reasonably accurate description of how the discipline developed in North America (however, see Lovie, 1983), but other quite different schools of thought were influential during this period, especially in Europe. For instance, the early development of psychoanalysis (Freudian theory – see Freud, 1952) took place in Europe during the 1920s and 1930s. Nevertheless, it is the case that the most challenging alternative to cognitive psychology is **behaviourism**, and behaviourism was the major movement in academic psychology in the first half of the last century.

### The laws of behaviour

Behaviourism is the view that a true science of psychology strives to achieve a description of human nature in terms of **laws of behaviour**. We must strive to generate such laws of behaviour couched in terms of physical events and physical processes. In other words, the laws will contain statements only about observable things that can be measured. If we wish to understand behaviour then we must aim to set out basic laws, and it will be via such laws of behaviour that we will then be able to control behaviour and predict it correctly. In this regard, the aspiration is to generate a theoretical account of behaviour that operates much like Newton's laws of motion. For example, we can calculate force by finding the product of mass and acceleration. Newton's laws help us to understand the physical world because they successfully predict and, generally, allow us to control events in the physical world. Of course, we can question the validity of such laws (as did Einstein), but science advances by attempting to understand the laws of nature.

Behaviourists aspire to a theory of human behaviour that is successful in the same way that Newton's laws are successful. By this view the eventual theory of behaviour will contain certain universally established principles (or laws), and the theory will hold true if these laws correctly predict behaviour. For instance, our theory might say that any given human will seek out pleasurable things over unpleasant things and, because of this, and given two different outcomes, the human will choose the pleasurable option over the unpleasant. Indeed, a very similar principle was con-

sidered to be one law of behaviour known as the **law of effect**. Although the term 'behaviour' has featured heavily in the foregoing, the behaviourist tradition was (essentially) concerned with attempting to provide theoretical accounts of learning. In this regard, a fundamental aim was to identify the necessary and sufficient conditions for learning to occur. Given this, the law of effect is actually a statement about learning.

The law was put forward by an American psychologist working at the very beginning of the twentieth century named E. L. Thorndike. Thorndike had undertaken a thesis on animal intelligence with an aim to explore how certain basic **associative processes** might account for learning. These will be explored in more detail shortly, but through his work with non-human animals, Thorndike put forward the idea that animals learn responses that result in rewarding consequences, and they drop responses that result in punishing consequences. This was known as the law of effect because the effect (or consequence) of making a particular response was hypothesised to govern learning. Responses that result in positive outcomes are likely to be repeated whereas responses that result in negative outcomes are not. Figure 1.1 provides an illustration of the sort of experiment that was used in the past to demonstrate such points.

Using this framework for thinking, it is easy now to posit *bonds* or, alternatively, *associations* between stimuli and their contingent responses, and discuss how such *bonds* can either be strengthened or weakened. Strengthening a so-called stimulus–response (S–R) bond implies that the tendency to make a response (R) to stimulus (S) is increased so that next time the S is presented, R becomes a more likely consequence. Similarly, weakening an S–R bond implies that next time the S is presented, the probability of producing R is decreased. Figure 1.1 provides an example where the stimulus (S) is the sound of the tuning fork and response (R) is the raising of the leg. In this case the S–R bond will be strengthened because in making the response the dog avoids an unpleasant electric shock. By the law of effect, Thorndike had provided an account of learning that proceeds on the basis of the consequences of the animals' behaviour: appropriate responses will be increased and inappropriate responses will be dropped because of the respective consequences of making these responses.

### Pinpoint question 1.2

**How would the law of effect account for the behaviour of someone who was hopelessly addicted to biscuits?**

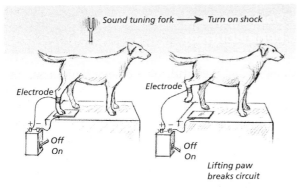

Sound tuning fork ⟶ Turn on shock

Electrode

Electrode

Off
On

Off
On

Lifting paw
breaks circuit

**Figure 1.1 The law of effect in practice**
This figure provides an example of something known as *instrumental conditioning*. In this case, the experimental subject's behaviour serves to determine the presence or absence of the reward. In traditional terminology, the sound of the tuning fork acts as the stimulus, the response is the raising of the leg, and the shock is known as the reward (albeit a rather unpleasant one). Within this particular experiment, the contingencies are set up between responses and rewards (raising leg terminates the shock) but of course interest also lies with the associations that are formed between the sound of the tuning fork and the raising of the leg.

*Source*: Rachlin, H. (1976). *Introduction to modern behaviorism* (2nd ed., fig. 2.13, p. 81). San Francisco: W. H. Freeman.

## The principles of associationism

The law of effect provides one account of learning and how this proceeds when responses are rewarded or reinforced. Other laws of learning were captured by various other **principles of associationism** in which reinforcement was not a necessary component. Such was the psychology of John Watson (1878–1958) and Clark Hull (1884–1952) (see Macphail, 1998, for a more thorough discussion). In such accounts two factors were seen to be important, namely the frequency and the recency of the co-occurrence of the S(timulus) and the R(esponse).

With respect to the first factor, the strength of the associative link between S and R is directly related to the frequency with which S and R co-occur. In this way, the likelihood that S will elicit R in the future reflects the frequency that S has elicited R in the past. This is something we saw in the introduction. The girl appears to be more convinced about the existence of the tooth fairy because the stimulus (tooth under pillow)/response (shiny coin) association had occurred four times in a row. Indeed this claim was

also encapsulated in the second law of behaviour discussed by Thorndike known as the **law of exercise**. This stated that 'The more often a given situation is followed by a particular response, the stronger will be the associative bond between them' (Miller, 1962, p. 227).

The second factor – recency – emphasises the proximity of S and R in time. That is, the association between S and R will also reflect how closely S and R have co-occurred in the past. The implication here is that an association between an S and an R will most likely be established, and then strengthened, the more closely the R has followed the S in the past (Blumberg & Wasserman, 1995, p. 139).

Such ideas as these form the basis of the principles of associationism. By this view, useful learning takes place from being able to register the contiguity (i.e., the closeness in time and space) and the frequency of co-occurrence of stimuli and responses (i.e., how often such things co-occur). Learning depends on the ability to register the covariation, or correlation, of particular stimuli and their corresponding responses. Things that co-occur more frequently together (i.e., highly correlate) in close spatial and/or temporal proximity will be strongly associated. So the basic idea is that it will be easier to learn about how your actions and their consequences are related if the consequences follow in quick succession to the actions. Think of it this way – learning how best to use the console with a new game will be easier if a certain key press has immediate consequences than if there is a delay between the key press and how the game responds.

So far discussion of both the law of effect and the other principles of associationism has been limited to how S–R bonds are established. The ideas that stimulus–stimulus (S–S) bonds or response–stimulus (R–S) bonds might also be possible were ruled out by the early behaviourists (Macphail, 1998, p. 84). This was presumably on the grounds that these implicate unseen forces at work, such as expectations and anticipations: behaviourists only discuss directly observable events, and so avoid any mention of mental entities. It is worth noting, however, that these very constructs (i.e., S–S and R–S bonds) were discussed in theoretical terms by William James in his foundational textbook entitled *Principles of Psychology*, a work that pre-dated experimental behaviourism by around 50 years. However, it is not difficult to see how the principles of associationism can be extended so as to allow learning in the absence of any reinforcement, or, indeed, any form of response. Indeed, modern associative theory embraces such possibilities.

## Associative processes and learning about causation

In thinking about the various sorts of putative associative processes, **association formation** provides an apparently straightforward account of learning about causation. For example, given that event *B* always follows event *A* in close temporal proximity, it is reasonable to predict that next time *A* occurs, *B* will be along shortly. The believer in the introduction was at pains to point out that the reward of money came straight after putting a tooth underneath your pillow, not a month, not even three days later. Noting this association between *A* and *B* can then be seen to lead to the conclusion that there is a causal link between *A* and *B*: *A* causes *B*. Of course, whether this sort of account strikes you as being at all reasonable is another matter, but it cannot be denied that this is a particularly important point. As Macphail (1998, p. 135) stated, 'the only way to predict the future is to uncover causal relationships'. Anything that provides a plausible account of learning about causality is therefore worthy of our consideration. So if we are inclined to dismiss the philosophical underpinnings of behaviourism, we need to be very careful in dismissing the principles of associationism in a similar fashion. How else are we to account for the understanding of causality?

> **behaviourism** A research programme that attempts to describe human nature but only in terms of observable events and entities.
>
> **laws of behaviour** Statements that specify the conditions under which certain types of behaviour will come about.
>
> **law of effect** A behaviourist law proposing that responses are strengthened when associated with positive outcomes and weakened when associated with negative outcomes.
>
> **associative processes** Psychological processes by which two entities are related. The registration of the co-occurrence of two entities.
>
> **principles of associationism** Statements that collectively specify how association formation takes place.
>
> **law of exercise** A behaviourist law proposing that associative bonds are strengthened the more often a particular stimulus is followed by a particular response.
>
> **association formation** The laying down of associative bonds between two otherwise separate entities. Responses can be associated with stimuli, hence on associative bond is formed between the stimulus and response.

## Some general points about behaviourism

In applying the principles of associationism, the behaviourists hoped to show how behaviour could be predicted and controlled. Such ideas were tested out in terms of rearing non-human animals in well-controlled environments and by constraining their experiences with particular schedules of reinforcement (regimens governing the provision of rewards and/or punishments). The psychology of the rat and pigeon came to the fore. The hope was that by controlling the animal's environment, the future behaviour of the animal could be predicted on the basis of knowing its previous history of reinforcement and by applying the laws of behaviour. The ultimate goal was to extrapolate the results from these animal experiments to the whole of human society and hence provide a theoretical (and perhaps chilling) framework for explaining and understanding human behaviour (Skinner, 1948/1976). Such behavioural accounts are striking because they deliberately avoid using the mind as an explanatory concept (Skinner, 1985).

All of this leads to one possibly unpalatable implication of the behaviourist research programme, namely that humans and other animals are considered to be nothing other than machines. Even the human bits of *RoboCop* are mechanical! That is, given the laws of behaviour, we can predict behaviour by identifying antecedents (stimuli) that have previously been linked with behavioural outcomes (responses). Consider the following example. If, in the past, dinner has always been signalled by the ringing of the dinner bell and the ringing of the dinner bell results in Harry turning up at the dining room, then we should predict that Harry will turn up at the dining room next time the dinner bell sounds. In this regard the stimulus (the antecedent) is the ringing of the dinner bell and the resulting response (the consequent) is Harry's arriving at the dining room. By the behavioural view, the ringing dinner bell causes Harry to behave in certain ways and the laws of the behaviour specify the causal link between the stimulus and the response. We can control behaviour to the degree that if we want Harry to come to the dining room, we need only ring the dinner bell. Nowhere in this kind of account are any kinds of mental entities (such as thoughts, wants or needs) mentioned.

The general point being conveyed is that, according to behaviourism, human behaviour is seen to be described in terms of a **deterministic system** whereby

## For example . . .

In order to evaluate the ambivalent feelings most individuals have towards such ideas, the interested reader would do well to compare two works of fiction, both pursuing ideas of behaviourism within a societal context. The first is *Walden Two* written by B. F. Skinner (1976; one of the founding fathers of modern behaviourism), who portrays a utopian society built around behaviourist principles (see Figure 1.2a), and *A Clockwork Orange* by Anthony Burgess (1962), who's main protagonist Alex, undergoes the Ludovico Technique – a form of behavioural aversion therapy designed to eliminate the anti-social and violent urges he experiences (see Figure 1.2b).

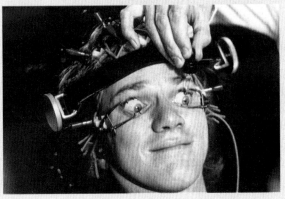

(a)                                                          (b)

**Figure 1.2 The consequences of behaviourism?**
Will the principles of behaviourism lead us to a utopian society of joy and harmony (a), or a dystopian society of manipulation and control (b)?
*Sources*: (a) Janine Wiedel Photolibrary/Alamy; (b) Kobal Collection Ltd/Warner Bros.

## Research focus 1.1

### Are you looking at me? The role of race when fear stares you in the face

While behaviourism can lead to the creation of all sorts of contingencies such as a dolphin who will swim through a hoop so as to receive a fish reward, or the employee who jumps through different kinds of hoops at the threat of unemployment, the kinds of stimulus–response associations that we've been talking about might also be applied to critical social issues, including the origins of racism. Olsson, Ebert, Banaji and Phelps (2005) took this highly contentious issue into the laboratory.

In the critical experiment, black and white American participants were presented with two unfamiliar black and two unfamiliar white faces. During the fear acquisition stage, and for each race, one of the faces was paired with a mild electric shock while the other face was not. Therefore, using such behavioural techniques, Olsson et al. (2005) were teaching participants to be fearful of one white face and one black face. During a subsequent extinction stage, all four faces were presented in the absence of shock. Skin conductance responses (SCRs) were collected for both stages of the experiment as a measure of reaction to the faces.

During the extinction phase, in which no shocks were given, individuals presented with racial outgroup faces (black participants' responses to white faces and, respectively, white participants' responses to black faces) that had previously been paired with a shock, showed a higher SCR relative to when individuals where presented with racial in-group faces (black participants' responses to black faces and, respectively, white participants' responses to white faces) that had previously been paired with a shock.

Olsson et al. (2005) argued that this shows that there is a bias to associate 'racial outgroup members more easily with an aversive stimulus' (p. 786). They went on to speculate that while natural selection is perhaps not the root of why blacks might inherently fear whites and vice versa, more generally, individuals who are not part of one's own social group may be perceived as more threatening than those that are. Happily though, Olsson et al. (2005) concluded on a positive note, stating that since socio-cultural learning is likely to have at least partly caused the effect, increased inter-group contact might help to unravel this rather unpleasant disposition.

*Source*: Olsson, A., Ebert, J. P., Banaji, M. R., & Phelps, E. A. (2005). The role of social groups in the persistence of learned fear. *Science*, *309*, 785–787.

certain stimuli cause (determine) certain responses. So, as with any other machine, as long as we can identify the physical antecedents to some form of behaviour, we can then claim to understand the causes of that behaviour. In other words, the behaviour is fully determined by physical antecedents. Furthermore, if we accept this, then there are grounds for believing that a scientific account of behaviour is tractable.

Couched in this way, the account is very much in the spirit of other scientific theories of the world. Objects and events are linked by certain causal relations, and future actions can be predicted perfectly by the occurrence of their causal antecedents. In this way the behaviourists quite rightly claimed that the theories they were pursuing were identical in nature to those pursued by any other scientist who is trying to explain the physical world. In this way the behaviourist research programme treats humans and other animals as the same sort of devices – albeit biological devices – as any other kind of machine. It is perhaps useful to explore this a little further.

## Methodological behaviourism

Physical machines, like wind-up clocks, behave in lawful ways that can be understood in terms of causal deterministic principles. This means that nothing is left to chance – particular consequents are caused by certain antecedents. In winding a clock, the rotational energy applied to the key is stored in the internal spring and the release of this energy results in the hands of the clock rotating. In adopting a behavioural framework for thinking about humans, behaviourists aim to provide deterministic accounts similar in nature to that provided for the behaviour of the clock. They aim to identify the effective stimulus (the winding of the clock) and the resulting response (the movement of the hands of the clock) and, as long as they can specify which stimuli go with which responses, they have a lawful account (or theory) of behaviour. This sort of approach to understanding behaviour, Searle (1994, p. 33) labelled **methodological behaviourism** because it is an endeavour that consists merely of 'discovering the correlations between stimulus inputs and behavioural outputs'. If we can identify the effective stimuli and their contingent responses, then job done.

## Behaviourism and free will

Having reduced us to nothing other than machines, the behaviourists make another (perhaps) unpalatable claim and state that, if we know the laws of behaviour, then we can control behaviour. Collectively what this leads to is a very clear statement about the status of **free will** – the notion that human beings are free to choose how to behave and the belief that their behaviour is not solely governed by deterministic principles of cause and effect. Simply put, behaviourists have outlawed any further discussion of free will because their aim is to provide an account of human behaviour that avoids any mention of decision-making or choice. As machines, humans are simply at the mercy of whichever effective stimuli have featured in their previous reinforcement history: remember, an effective stimulus causes its response. This is why, in *A Clockwork Orange* (Burgess, 1962), Alex cannot help but feel nausea when he hears 'Symphony Number Three of the Danish Veck Otto Skadelig' after exposure to the Ludovico Technique.

Behaviourists limit themselves to describing behaviour solely in terms of deterministic principles. Nearly everyone has problems with the notion of free will – behaviourists deal with the problem by denying it – but such a concept proves equally uncomfortable for some cognitive psychologists. Nevertheless, by failing to acknowledge free will, the behaviourist analogy – of humans as nothing more than machines – is exact.

## Behaviourism and the science of psychology

Before leaving this discussion of behaviourism it is useful to explore some issues further. Initially, there are two main points:

1. From the behaviourist perspective, the theory of behaviour is defined with respect to a set of laws of behaviour. In this regard the theory is very much like any other scientific theory such as that which predicts that when water is heated to 100°C, it boils. The aim behind behaviourism is to uncover the laws of behaviour, such that we can predict and control it.

2. A somewhat special feature of some behaviourist theories, though, is that they are constrained in rather peculiar ways. That is, any such theory must only contain statements about observable objects and events. Nowhere in the theory must there be any mention of anything that is not part of the known physical world. Cast in this way, Searle (1994, p. 33) refers to this sort of behaviourism as logical behaviourism (see below).

Point (1) is clearly a laudable aim but may actually fall short of what it is that we as psychologists are trying to do. We are not only trying to predict and possibly control behaviour, but we are also trying to understand it in ways other than by prediction and control (this is set out in detail below). In addition, in thinking about point (2) – the 'special feature' of behavioural accounts – the constraint seems too restricting. It seems to fail to recognise that, as in any other branch of science, as long as we can generate testable predictions that involve measurement, then we can study any sort of abstract entity we want. For instance, scientists theorised about possible mechanisms for genetic inheritance in abstract terms long before DNA was discovered.

The critical thing is that the validity of our predictions must be open to empirical test, where **empirical** means relating to a scientific experiment or observation in which measurement plays a critical role. We can discuss and study all things abstract (including the fairies at the bottom of the garden) in a scientific way, as long as we also have a means to test such statements. In terms of science, this means that it is perfectly valid to theorise about an abstract entity as long as the theory supports a testable prediction that can be examined by experiment or observation. So although the behaviourists did have laudable aims, they perhaps failed to appreciate that anything can be studied scientifically as long as appropriate testable statements can be made (Wilton, personal communication). So as long as we can generate testable predictions about the mind (about mental states and processes) then we can adopt a scientific approach and study the mind.

### Pinpoint question 1.3

How does the empirical approach allow for the study of mind rather than just behaviour?

## Logical behaviourism

At one level methodological behaviourism reduces to nothing more than a rather sophisticated version of train spotting, that is, it entails the simple recording of various contingencies that occur in the real world: B follows A, D follows C, etc. A more sophisticated form of behaviourism, known as **logical behaviourism**, presents itself as a much more challenging enterprise altogether. Indeed it is this form of behaviourism that threatens the very foundations upon which cognitive psychology is based.

Logical behaviourism is a rather extreme position to take because it categorically rules out discussion of anything but observable events and entities in our accounts of behaviour. It aims to rid our explanations of any mention of mental states or processes in a bid to focus only on observable events and entities. Central to this way of thinking is the basic assumption that all mental terms can be defined in relation to behaviour. So to say that 'William is thirsty' is the same as saying 'William is disposed to behave in a particular way'. The aim is to replace the phrase (i) 'William is thirsty' by stating (ii) 'If there were water available then William would drink', together with a whole host of other statements about what William could do to quench his thirst. According to logical behaviourism, everything that you might wish to predict about William's behaviour by stating 'William is thirsty' is adequately accounted for by stating things like (ii). Statements such as (ii) are more commonly referred to as **behavioural dispositions**.

Logical behaviourists prefer statements like (ii) because they make no mention of anything other than observable behaviour. So by replacing mental terms like 'is thirsty' by phrases like 'is disposed to drink', we rid our explanations of any mention of the mental. To take another example, to say (i) 'Harry believes it will rain' is equivalent to saying (ii) 'Harry will be disposed to wear a raincoat and carry an umbrella when he goes outside'. However, nothing in (ii) makes reference to anything mental. As Churchland (1984, p. 23) notes, by such a behavioural perspective, mentioning mental entities is nothing more than a 'shorthand way of talking about actual and potential patterns of behaviour'. Given that logical behaviourism is treated as being a serious philosophical approach as to how best to explain human nature, it poses as a considerable challenge to the cognitivist position. It is therefore incumbent on us to try to show how it can be resisted.

## Criticisms of logical behaviourism

Encouragingly, there are several very good reasons to resist this line of argument. For instance, the framework begins to creak when you attempt to analyse carefully any particular behavioural disposition. As Harman (1989) noted, 'Whether you are disposed to take an umbrella with you depends on not just your belief that it will rain but also your desire not to get wet, your perception of the umbrella in the corner, your further belief that umbrellas are good for keeping rain off, and so on' (p. 833). In this regard, a difficulty in attempting to analyse any one behavioural disposition is that it seems to lead inevitably to some form of reference to mental states and/or processes such as further beliefs, perception, feelings, thoughts, etc.

Aside from this technical point, there is also a common-sense objection to logical behaviourism that Searle discussed (1994, p. 35). He reflected about what it means to be human and asks whether you can honestly say that the logical behaviourist view corresponds with the 'ordinary experiences of what it is like to be a human being'. For instance, can we really explain your behaviour without mentioning your thoughts and feelings? Is 'to be religious' really only a collection of dispositions such as attending a place of worship on holy days? Despite this being merely a common-sense objection, rather than a logical argument, philosophers have taken it seriously because logical behaviourism can be construed as almost a denial that humans are sentient beings – 'almost' because even if it is conceded that we are sentient beings then the denial is that we need not discuss things like sensations, thoughts and emotions in order to explain our behaviour.

This is best conveyed in the following example. Logical behaviourists would have us believe that to have a pain is nothing more than to be 'inclined to moan, wince, to take an aspirin and so on' (Churchland, 1984, p. 24). That is, according to the logical behavi-

ourists, to be in pain merely means that we are disposed to behave in particular ways. This is a quite astonishing claim to make. Remember what it feels like when you trapped your fingers in a car door. To deny that the experience of pain causes people to behave in particular ways seems to run counter to our basic notions about what it is to be a sentient being. So despite what the logical behaviourists claim, their line of argument fails to address quite fundamental aspects of the causes of human behaviour.

In summary, logical behaviourists substitute statements about mental states and processes with statements about dispositions to behave in certain ways. Yet in attempting to explain all of human behaviour in terms of behavioural dispositions, the approach fails to acknowledge that we (as humans) are sentient beings and that we typically act in ways that are determined by our thoughts and feelings and beliefs. Of course, nothing in what has been written here fundamentally undermines the logical behaviourist position. Instead, an appeal has been made to your intuitions and impressions of what it is like to be human. Based on these intuitions and impressions, the sorts of accounts of human behaviour that logical behaviourists offer are going to be, at the very best, incomplete. Indeed, upon reflection it seems that the failures of the behaviourist tradition to provide answers to very straightforward questions about human nature were instrumental in the development of cognitive psychology – a discipline whose primary objective is to understand the mind.

---

**deterministic system** Consequents are causally determined by their antecedents. For instance, each response is causally linked to a stimulus.

**methodological behaviourism** A kind of behaviourism which aims to detail the correlations between stimuli and responses.

**free will** The idea that an entity is free to choose how to behave and is capable of deciding how to behave. Linked to the idea that although I did do x I could have done y if I had so wished.

**empirical** A scientific experiment or observation involving measurement.

**logical behaviourism** The doctrine that all talk about mental states and processes can be replaced by talk of behavioural dispositions. For example, to say that Andrew is clever is to say nothing other than that Andrew behaves in an intelligent way.

**behavioural dispositions** Statements about common ways of behaving.

## 'Testability is falsifiability': cognitive psychology and theory testing

The preceding sections contain a general introduction to what it means to develop a behavioural account of some aspect of the human condition on the understanding that this provides a useful context for thinking about what a cognitive account might look like. Broadly speaking, from the cognitivist point of view (and in stark contrast to the behavioural view) the study of human cognition is based on the assumption that there is an abstract entity called the mind and that this is composed of mental states and mental processes; it is concerned with exploring the nature of mental states and mental processes. From a cognitive point of view, it is perfectly reasonable to discuss and study things like thoughts, beliefs, ideas and attitudes. Cognitive psychology may be described as the scientific study of the mind, on the understanding that we can generate testable statements about these abstract entities.

So as with any other science, in cognitive psychology we operate within a framework whereby we make certain assumptions about the subject of enquiry, and on the basis of these assumptions we generate certain hypotheses that result in testable predictions. Importantly though, for our science to work properly we must attempt to generate theories that are falsifiable. What this means is that we should strive to generate predictions that, if shown to be false, would show that the theory upon which they are based is false. This is perhaps a difficult point to appreciate fully but it might help to think in the following terms.

In designing a new aircraft, concerns about safety dictate that we test the prototype version to destruction. It would be foolish to only test the prototype when it is a nice sunny day with no wind (conditions we know that the airframe will withstand) because we are ultimately not concerned with how it will behave in good flying conditions. We are primarily concerned with whether the aircraft is safe to fly when it is −30° F, when there are severe hailstones and it is blowing a gale, etc. In this regard it is best to test the prototype (i.e., the theory) to its limits in order to find out the conditions under which it will fail. Theories of human cognition will only be of any use to us if we can generate a test that will show the theory to be false if it fails the test.

This sort of argument is most readily associated with an extremely influential philosopher of science known as Karl Popper. Popper (1963/2000), in writing about the usefulness of putting forward a theory of anything, concluded the following (among other things):

- It is easy to obtain confirmations, or verifications, for nearly every theory – if we look for confirmations.
- A theory which is not refutable by any conceivable event is non-scientific.
- Every genuine test of a theory is any attempt to falsify it, or refute it. Testability is falsifiability.
- Confirming evidence should not count except when it is the result of a genuine test of the theory; and this means that it can be presented as a serious but unsuccessful attempt to falsify the theory.

According to Popper, a scientific theory is one that is incompatible with certain possible observations – the theory needs to be clear about what possible outcomes of an experiment would result in the theory being falsified. My theory predicts $x$ and if $x$ does not occur then my theory is false. In contrast, a theory that is compatible with all possible observations, or one that has been modified solely to accommodate such observations, is unscientific and therefore of little worth.

These are very general statements about scientific theories, but they have considerable impact in discussing cognitive psychology. Cognitive psychologists are allowed to posit abstract entities on the assumption that these can be tested in a scientific way. Part of this process is to generate a theory that may be falsified by empirical evidence. As a cognitive psychologist you need to be clear about whether the critical experiments have been carried out. Is there a possible result from the experiment that would refute the theory? You also need to satisfy yourself that any modifications to the theory, in light of the evidence, are reasonable – perhaps the data demand a different theory? If some version of the theory can be developed so that it can account for any possible observation then it probably is not that useful after all.

These problems are particularly acute for cognitive psychologists because the discipline is primarily concerned with abstract entities, and there is a danger of getting carried away and deriving very complex accounts of even the simplest behaviours. Indeed, we must guard against developing accounts in which various abstract entities are generated almost indefinitely, in an unconstrained and arbitrary fashion. Such has been the criticism of cognitive psychology in the past (see Skinner, 1985), and although it is sensible to dismiss much of the behaviourist rhetoric, these are very real concerns.

Cognitive psychology therefore only makes sense on the assumption that cognitive theories give rise to testable predictions. However, some caution is warranted before we get too carried away and begin thinking how best to study the fairies at the bottom of the garden. First we need to consider whether: (i) the complexity of the account is warranted by the evidence – could we get by with a simpler behavioural account? – and (ii) would we want to use the same sort of account when explaining quite different things that exhibit similar behaviours?

## Occam's Razor: the beauty of simplicity

There is an old story about how space agencies were concerned for some time with the problem of astronauts having to write in weightless conditions. Ordinary pens taken into space would burst, leak and just fail to write in zero gravity. US research and development went into overdrive at some expense to produce the space pen – the first pen capable of writing upside down. Russian astronauts used a pencil.

Let us first consider the notion of complexity and here concern is with a principle that is used in other sciences called **Occam's Razor**. This principle is attributed to the fourteenth-century logician and Franciscan friar known as William of Occam (having been born in the Sussex village of Ockam). The principle states that 'Entities must not be multiplied unnecessarily.' In other words, things should be kept as simple as possible. Unnecessary complexity in our explanations should be avoided. In its original conception William of Occam used the principle to justify many conclusions, including 'God's existence cannot be deduced by reason alone.' However, a modified principle is applied when attempting to draw much more modest conclusions in science, namely 'When you have two competing theories, which make exactly the same predictions, the one that is simpler is the better.' The simpler account should be favoured over the more complicated account.

Occam's principle is particularly pertinent when trying to explain human behaviour. It is sobering to think that, despite elegant theories about mental events causing us to behave in one way or another – for instance, I feel thirsty so I go and make a cup of tea – we need to consider carefully whether a simpler account will do – for instance, one that makes no mention of mental entities whatsoever. It just is far simpler to accept that your mum is the tooth fairy,

after all. In this respect, we need to be clear about when a complicated cognitive account is to be preferred over a much simpler behavioural account. Under what conditions is a cognitive account warranted by the evidence?

## Simplicity and the thermostat

An alternative way of thinking about these issues is with respect to entities other than humans. One famous example that has been discussed in the literature is the humble central heating thermostat. The question here has been, 'Is it at all reasonable to ascribe mental qualities to a central heating thermostat in order to explain its behaviour?' This may come across as being quite an astonishing question, but it has, nevertheless, exercised some very serious scientists. Why? Well, at first glance, the overt behaviour of the thermostat may be explained if we assume that the thermostat has certain beliefs about room temperature and the conditions under which the heating should come on and go off. This example was originally set out by McCarthy (1979) and, according to him, typically a thermostat has three beliefs: 'the room is too hot', 'the room is too cold' and 'the room is okay'. Moreover, the thermostat's behaviour can be fully understood and predicted on the assumption that it operates according to these beliefs. So if the thermostat believes that the room is too hot it switches the central heating off. He goes on to bolster this argument by saying that ascribing such beliefs to this particular thermostat helps us to understand the operation of thermostats, in general. Such an argument is reasonably unconvincing though.

For instance, insofar as electricians are able to service thermostats, without ever assuming that the thermostats believe anything, this seems to undermine the position. With due respect to electricians, the example illustrates that it is quite possible to understand how thermostats generally function, without having to ascribe a system of beliefs to these devices. This is a clear example of how Occam's Razor can play a useful role. We can fully account for the operation of the thermostat from understanding the physical operation of its internal components. There is no need to posit any additional form of internal belief system. Therefore, at the risk of hurting the feelings of thermostats, we can avoid any further discussion of thermostats having beliefs because this is both unwarranted and it is not parsimonious.

This is just one example of where Occam's Razor can be applied with some force, but more generally, the principle underpins much of behaviourist theorising.

For instance, from the behaviourist position the issue is 'If we are wary of ascribing beliefs to thermostats, what are the grounds for ascribing beliefs to humans?' We readily ascribe beliefs and goals to humans, but we are less ready to make such ascriptions to simple mechanical devices. The behaviourist challenge to cognitive theorising is that we ought to be striving for the simplest accounts of human behaviour. By the behaviourist view the simplest accounts make no reference to the mind. Do we really need to assume that humans hold beliefs in order to explain their behaviour?

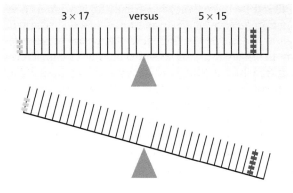

Figure 1.3 **Balance beams 'do' mental arithmetic?** Schematic representations of a balance beam and its ability to 'figure out' which of two products (i.e., weights × distance on the left vs. weights × distance on the right) is the greater.

## Simplicity and cognitive theory

The foregoing discussion of the thermostat provided a useful case of where Occam's Razor can be applied successfully. There simply is no need to appeal to a thermostat's belief system in order to understand what it is doing. Let us now take a quite different example and consider why we might wish to offer a complex account of some aspect of human behaviour even though a much simpler device seems to mimic this behaviour. Here the example concerns mental arithmetic. Although we differ in our abilities to carry out mental arithmetic, from a cognitive perspective it seems fairly reasonable to assume that this ability depends on mental representations and mental processes. Mental arithmetic (and the name really does wear its assumptions on its sleeve in this respect) is defined as being a set of numerical operations that are carried out in the mind. For example, your task is to multiply 17 by 3, to multiply 14 by 5 and then to respond with which product is the greater.

From a cognitive perspective, it is assumed that such mental arithmetic problems engage psychological processes such as holding in memory representations of the numbers and operating upon these in order to carry out the computation. The critical question, however, is whether such a form of explanation is really necessary. One reason for some caution is that there exists a rather simple device that can 'solve' these sorts of problem. However, in considering what this sort of device is, we think that you would be reluctant to suggest that there are any sorts of cognitive operations going on.

The device in question is a few pieces of wood knocked together to form a balance beam (see Figure 1.3). Let us assume that we have a balance beam such that on each side of the supporting mid-point (the fulcrum), the beam is divided into 34 peg locations. Each peg can take a weight and to simplify the problem all the weights are the same. If we place 3 such weights at position 17 on the left arm and 5 such weights at position 13 on the right arm, the balance will fall to the right. What the balance beam is doing is to signal that the product of 17 and 3 is greater than the product of 13 and 5.

The dilemma here is the following. Whereas cognitive psychologists would wish to offer a cognitive account of the behaviour of the human in solving the problem, they would not wish to provide such an account for the operation of the balance beam. Balance beams do not think, yet they can 'do' multiplication. In the same way that we were averse to suggesting that thermostats believe anything, we are also reluctant to claim that the balance beam is doing anything like mental arithmetic. This is despite the fact that the balance beam is responding as though it were doing mental arithmetic. Okay, it won't actually say the answer, but it will indicate which product is the larger.

One way out of this dilemma is to consider other differences between humans and balance beams. One critical difference lies in humans' ability to do all sorts of other mental arithmetic such as the dreaded long division. The balance beam is stuck at the level of simple multiplication and, consequently, the special-purpose mechanistic approach to mental multiplication offered by the balance beam fails to provide a more comprehensive explanation of how mental arithmetic is carried out in general. Nevertheless, such examples as these do force us to consider the circumstances under which a cognitive account – an account based on abstract mental entities – is appropriate and when it is not. A critical point is that, regardless of the complexity of the cognitive account put forward, the actual behaviour under consideration may actually arise because of the operation of some very simple principles: we may wish to wield Occam's Razor.

As with the thermostat example, the example of the balance beam has, we hope, forced you to consider the problems and difficulties present when trying to offer a cognitive account of some behaviour. These examples show that caution must be exercised in attributing mental states and processes to these kinds of physical devices. The concern is that if we are not going to attribute mental states and processes to these devices, then why are we so ready to attribute these to humans? This is a fundamental issue and can only be addressed by a careful consideration of how the mind has been defined in cognitive psychology and what it means to offer some form of cognitive account of behaviour. A more detailed discussion of these concerns is contained as the material unfolds over the ensuing chapters. We hope, however, that the foregoing has exposed to you the difficulties that the cognitive psychologist faces in attempting to explain behaviour by appealing to abstract entities. → See 'What have we learnt?', below.

| Pinpoint question 1.5 |
| --- |

Why would a cognitive psychologist attribute a mental state to an articulate adult but not to a talking parrot?

| Pinpoint question 1.6 |
| --- |

Why would a behaviourist have concerns about you undertaking a careful consideration of how the mind has been defined in cognitive psychology?

## → What have we learnt?

So far several rudimentary and key points have been made about the scientific nature of cognitive psychology, and a very general description of the 'cognitivist' view has been provided. Most of the discussion has focused on behaviourism on the grounds that the cognitive perspective can best be appreciated by comparing it against its most radical theoretical alternative. What behaviourism forces us to do is to consider simple explanations of what may otherwise appear to be very complex processes. However, as the discussion has shown, there are both advantages and disadvantages to such an approach. The principle of Occam's Razor holds that we should aspire to generate simple over complex theories – if two theories can explain the same set of phenomena equally well then we should choose the simplest. However, in thinking about the complex nature of the human mind it may be very misleading to think in terms of very simple devices. Balance beams 'do' multiplication but only up to a point! Fundamentally, cognitive psychology is a discipline that is primarily concerned with the mind as an abstract entity, and, as a consequence, cognitive psychologists should not be constrained by a misconception of what is and what is not a scientific endeavour. The basic point is that our theories should provide testable predictions. If we can generate appropriate testable predictions then we can study abstract entities.

In considering how cognitive psychology developed over the twentieth century, it seems that the emergence and current dominance of cognitivism can be traced, in part, to a dissatisfaction with the sorts of constrained accounts that behaviourists put forward. It would be a grave mistake, however, to discard the whole of behaviourism on the grounds that it is the antithesis to cognitivism. Many of the principles of association and association formation remain foundational. Think of this next time you hear someone attempting to convince you of their regime for weight loss, giving up smoking or of ridding you of your phobias. Typically, the most effective (non-invasive, i.e., no drugs, surgery or electric shocks) forms of treatment can be found in behavioural psychology. As cognitive psychologists, though, we are much more interested in the events that intervene between stimuli and their contingent responses than we are in the stimuli and responses themselves.

## Research focus 1.2

### Reefer madness: behavioural solutions to marijuana problems

Amazing. It's the first chapter in an undergraduate textbook and already we're talking about recreational drug use. Nevertheless, marijuana is the most common illegal drug and its use is both an important individual and social issue. Kadden, Litt, Kabela-Cormier and Petry (2007) were interested in the extent to which marijuana dependence could be treated by principles derived from behaviourism.

Two hundred and forty participants were selected to take part in this study, all of whom were heavy smokers who self-reported as being unable to stop using marijuana. Individuals were encouraged to abstain from smoking according to one of four conditions. The first condition acted as a control, while the second condition carried out contingency management (i.e., ContM) establishing a reinforcement programme in which participants who provided drug-free urine samples were given vouchers that could be exchanged for goods and services. A third condition examined a combination of motivational enhancement therapy (i.e., MET) and cognitive behavioural therapy (i.e., CBT) which we won't go into in too much detail here, and a fourth condition combined the interventions of ContM and MET+CBT.

The data revealed that at the end of treatment, those individuals in the contingency management intervention in which they were positively reinforced for non-drug use produced the highest rates of abstinence. Three months after the treatment, those individuals who had received the combination of ContM and MET+CBT showed greater avoidance of the herb. Approximately one year after treatment, 27 per cent in the ContM and MET+CBT condition continued to show abstinence.

Kadden et al. (2007) speculated about why it was that the treatment that only involved behavioural intervention (ContM) initially produced the highest rates of abstinence, rather than the condition that combined treatments (ContM and MET+CBT). Although procedural differences existed between the two conditions, ContM actually took 15 minutes per session while the ContM and MET+CBT session lasted one hour per session, so duration cannot explain superiority in the former case directly after treatment, as it is in the opposite direction to that which we would expect. So, we've done our conscientious citizen bit by demonstrating that the same behavioural principles that probably get you smoking marijuana in the first place can also get you off it.

*Source*: Kadden, R. M., Litt, M. D., Kabela-Cormier, E., & Petry, N. M. (2007). Abstinence rates following behavioral treatments for marijuana dependence. *Addictive Behaviors, 32*, 1220–1236.

---

**Occam's Razor** The principle that, given two competing theories that make the same predictions, the preferred theory is the one that is simpler.

## PART 2

### An introduction to the nature of explanation in cognitive psychology

Having established a very general framework for thinking about what cognitive psychology is and what its concerns are, it is important to now consider a more detailed appraisal of different perspectives on the mind. It is hoped that we can draw a veil over simplistic behavioural accounts of human nature and be more confident that there is something more to the human condition than meets the eye. Just look at the man in Figure 1.4 and try to convince yourself that there is nothing of interest that can be said about what he might be thinking! Nevertheless, having already covered much ground there is still a little further to go before we can fully appreciate what a cognitive account of some aspect of behaviour actually looks like. To carry the discussion forward we must now consider a particular mind/body problem: how are the mind and brain related?

**Figure 1.4 Are humans really only biological machines?**
Put yourself in his place and try and convince yourself that we can avoid the assumption that humans are anything other than sentient beings.

## How the mind and the brain are related

### Central state identity theory

Aside from the various flavours of behaviourism that we have considered so far, how else might we address the problem of explaining human behaviour? Well, the most obvious possibility is that our mental lives are intimately connected with the things that go on in our brains – 'obvious' in the sense that it is patent to everyone that damage to the brain can have profoundly deleterious effects on an individual's cognitive abilities. The paradigm examples here are the language

problems that typically arise following a stroke that affects the left cerebral hemisphere (i.e., damage to the left side of the brain). In accepting this, various attempts have been made to explore the mapping between mental states (e.g., having the thought that it might rain) and neurological events (such as brain cells firing in a particular part of the brain). Clearly therefore the brain and the mind are related, but we need to try to clarify exactly what the link might be.

The first such theory for thinking about this mapping is known as **central state identity theory**. The basic assumptions of central state identity theory form the bedrock of all current work in human neuroscience (the study of how the human brain works). So, at one level, it would be quite bizarre to try to argue that central state identity theory is misconceived. It just is the case that the theory encapsulates the widely accepted view that to understand the mind we must understand the brain. In fact, this claim is becoming so ingrained in thinking in cognitive psychology that many now tend not to pause to consider what the consequences of accepting it are. However, given that being a cognitive psychologist is all about thinking through the consequences of various assumptions, we will take time to explore just what consequences follow from accepting these ideas. Central state identity theories come in two versions, namely *type identity theory* and *token identity*. We will consider each version in turn.

### Type identity theory

A basic tenet of central state identity theory is that mental events are identical with neurophysiological events in the brain. For example, remembering that you promised to feed next door's budgie corresponds to a particular pattern of nerve cells (neurons) firing in the brain. In one version of central state identity theory, known as **type identity theory**, each type of mental event maps onto a different type of neurological event; for example, remembering to feed the budgie maps onto pattern *A* of nerve cells firing, and choosing not to feed the budgie maps onto pattern *B* of nerve cells firing.

Some caution is warranted here, as is revealed by the use of phrases such as 'maps onto' and 'corresponds to' since the argument from type identity theory really is that 'deciding to feed budgie' is nothing more than (or is the very same thing as) a certain pattern of nerve cells firing. Such a view captures the materialist framework for discussing the mind (Fodor, 1981a). In contrast with dualist theorists who posit physical and mental entities, materialist theorists assume only physical entities. According to materalists, everything exists in the material (physical) world. There is no non-material world and because of this materialists equate mental states and processes with brain states and processes.

Stated this way, it is clear that problems emerge almost immediately. Take, for example, the extremely painful case of trapping fingers in a car door. The defining element of being in pain is the sensation of hurting (e.g., the throbbing fingers). So having a pain is having a particular **sensory experience**. Pain has a particular sensory quality associated with it and it is this that differentiates it from any other sensation. Experiencing pain is a subjective experience in that it is your pain and no one else's.

A problem with identity theory is that it seems to force different things to be the same, so there is the feeling of pain (which is a mental event) and there is this pattern of nerve cells firing (which is a physical event), but identity theory wants to claim that these two different things are actually one and the same thing. However, as with Searle's (1994) common-sense objection to logical behaviourism, this is all very odd. To state that being in pain is nothing more than having a particular pattern of nerve cells firing seems to negate any serious discussion of what it feels like to be in pain. As a consequence it omits essential aspects of the experience that aid our understanding of the behaviour of those who are in pain. Knowing that someone is in pain means that we can predict with reasonable certainty how they are going to behave and makes us treat them differently to when they are not in pain. This is clearly a problem for type identity theory, but a more serious difficulty has been raised by Searle (1994). This is that the theory falls foul of the fact that every brain is different from every other brain: this can be referred to as the **different brains problem**.

## The different brains problem

Consider the following example. Let us assume that when Jones thinks it might rain, nerve cells *A*, *B*, *C* and *D* fire. Smith's brain is different from Jones' brain and when Smith thinks it might rain, nerve cells *E*, *F*, *G* and *H* fire. Both men are entertaining the same thought, but different nerve cells are firing in the different brains. This is the fundamental problem that *type* identity theory faces – different types of neural events are underlying the same thoughts in the two different brains. What this means is that we might well be able to map out the complete repertoire of neural events of Jones' thoughts (cells *A* + *B* + *C* + *D* firing = looks like rain, cells *E* + *F* + *G* + *H* firing = desire to go trampolining), but there is no guarantee that this will be of any help in understanding what Smith is thinking because his brain is very different.

## Token identity theory

Given these sorts of problems a second version of central state identity theory has been discussed and this is known as **token identity theory**. This asserts that mental events correspond with neurological events, but there is an acceptance that there may well be a variety of neurological events that underlie each mental event. In this way we can allow different patterns of firing nerve cells to underlie the thought that it may rain. It is quite acceptable that the firing of nerve cells *A*, *B*, *C* and *D* and, separately, the firing of nerve cells *E*, *F*, *G* and *H* correspond to the same thought in different brains. As it stands, it is token identity theory's brand of **materialism** that provides the foundations for all current work in human neuroscience.

So far so good, but upon reflection we see that this version of central state identity theory again fails to provide any insights into understanding subjective experience. If we really are trying to understand the psyche then it seems that materialism may not provide all of the answers that we are looking for. However, we are just going to have to accept the fact that all materialist theories fail in this regard (see Searle, 1994, ch. 2).

On a less daunting level, the theory faces other difficulties. In overcoming the 'different brains problem', token identity theory has opened itself up to another criticism. How can we ever decide what it is about different patterns of nerve cells firing that makes them correspond with the same mental event? If we accept that different patterns of nerve cells firing may give rise to the same thought, we need to be clear about what it is about these patterns of firing that give rise to this particular thought. To address this we need to consider the notions of *function* and *functional role* in more detail. In discussing these topics you can be assured that we have nearly reached our final destination and can begin to explore what a cognitive account of some behaviour really looks like.

---

### Pinpoint question 1.7

**What is the critical distinction between type and token identity theory?**

## Function and functional role

To understand these issues we need to consider how the term *function* is going to be used. One way of thinking about the function of a thing is to ask about what its intended purpose is. So we can think of the purpose of a petrol pump in a car as being transferring petrol from the tank into the carburettor, while the purpose of the carburettor is to ensure that there is a correct mix of petrol and air prior to combustion. So we can distinguish between the structure or form of the pump (what its physical make-up is) and its function (what it does).

By this means we can provide a complete structural account of the whole of the car's engine by simply describing the physical make-up of each component, carburettor, pump alternator, starter motor, ignition, etc., and showing how these parts are interconnected, without any reference to function whatsoever. This would constitute one description of the car's engine. However, in order to understand the workings of the engine and its constituent parts we need also to describe what function each component serves. We need to provide a description of the functional role of each component. In this regard we are no longer concerned with the physical make-up of the pump – whether it has parts of carbon steel or graphite – we are purely concerned with what it does. So in offering a **functional description** of the engine we specify what the purpose of each component is. The assumption is that to attain a full understanding of the workings of a car's engine we need to have:

1. A description of the structure of the components.
2. A specification of how these are interconnected.
3. A complete description of the functional role of each of the components.

In this regard, Figure 1.5 is of some help, but it is lacking in some critical aspects. Figure 1.5 shows a basic circuit diagram of just a fraction of a car's engine components. It is helpful at one level because it provides a listing of the various components, together with some indication of how these parts are connected together. Nevertheless, it would be far more helpful if it also contained a description of what the various bits do. What we need is a functional description of the components. For instance, clearly the distributor is important (because if it played no useful role it could be left out), but what does it do?

In designing a new car engine we could reasonably begin by stating, at a very general level, what we want the engine to do. We need to state its intended purpose, namely that the engine needs to power the car's transmission. We might then begin to divide this overarching aim into smaller problems and so compartmentalise the large problem into constituent sub-problems. All along we are asking questions about function and so, incrementally, we will arrive at a design in which particular components serve particular functions. For example, if we need to deliver petrol into the carburettor then, we will need a pump to force the petrol from the tank into the carburettor.

Traditionally this form of design eventuates in a blueprint or **schematic diagram** that specifies each component and shows how each component is connected with other components (see Figure 1.5). Such a diagram may also reveal the flow of control between various components (hence the associated name flow chart). For instance, the diagram reveals the direction that petrol flows from the tank via the pump to the carburettor. (There is some indication of flow of control in Figure 1.5 but, without further specification of what the arrows stand for, the diagram is not that helpful.) So although the diagram is ultimately

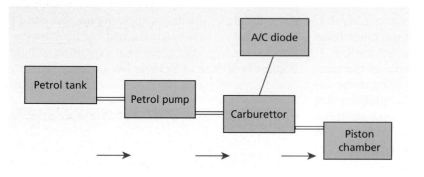

**Figure 1.5 The usefulness of a blueprint**
A schematic representation of some of the components of a car's engine.

concerned with specifying the critical components and how these are interconnected, it may also provide some indication of the sequencing of events as mapped onto the individual components.

An important point is that at the level of the diagram we are not so bothered about how close the different components are to one another – whether the pump is next to the tank or the carburettor – we are primarily concerned with how the components are interconnected with one another. For such a diagram to be complete, though, we need to embellish the structural information with a description of the functions of the individual components. (What does the A/C diode do, again?) At a very general level such a blueprint would be incredibly useful.

Of course in many cases it is important to know where the different components of some multi-component system are. To take a familiar example, clearly it is critical to know where the network printer is when you print a private e-mail out. In terms of the operation of the system, however, it really does not matter if the departmental printer is next door or downstairs. Indeed, in providing a flow chart of the department's intranet the physical location of the different components is irrelevant.

One critical aspect of such an approach to design is that the individual components can be discussed in the abstract, that is, without commitment to any particular physical entity. So we can discuss the functional role of a petrol pump without committing ourselves to a carbon steel or graphite model, and without having to make a difficult colour scheme decision between blue and grey. This is also the case for Figure 1.5 in that there is no indication of what any single component looks like; nevertheless, the diagram does contain very useful information. To take another example, we can discuss the necessity of having a brake to engage whenever the car is stationary – the function of this brake is to fix the car in its current position. Typically, this is instantiated as a handbrake, but such a brake might otherwise be a foot brake. As long as we have something that functions as a brake we need not care too much about what it looks like.

The foregoing examples clearly show that functional role can be discussed without any commitment to any particular instantiation of a physical component. Expressed thus, any component will do, as long as it fulfils its designated functional role. What is going on here is a manoeuvre whereby the explanation of any device is shifted from concerns about structure to concerns about function. We are interested in what the device does, not in how it is made.

## Functionalism

By analogy, therefore, it is possible to see now how two different neurophysiological (brain) states may underlie the same mental state – as long as the two neurophysiological states serve the same functional role then they capture the same mental state. That is, mental state $x$ is defined purely in terms of its function. Such a claim as this is central to the philosophical take on the mind known as **functionalism**. More particularly, the term *function* is now defined in terms of causation – mental state $x$ has a particular function insofar as it leads to the same consequences, be these new mental states or some form of overt behaviour. For instance, Anne thought it was going to rain and remembered she had left her kitchen window open. The thought caused her to remember the open window. Mental event $x$ caused mental event $y$. Moreover, because Anne remembered that she had left the kitchen window open she returned home earlier than usual. That is, the remembering caused her to leave work early. Mental event $y$ caused behaviour $z$.

Importantly, in shifting the level of analysis from the physical level to the functional level, functionalism allows for the possibility that the same mental processes may exist in different brains – it gives licence to token identity theory and also provides an answer to the different brains problem. As long as the functional description of the mental states and processes is the same for different individuals then our understanding of their behaviour does not depend on understanding the particularities of the underlying neural apparatus. In this way the different brains problem can be avoided.

## Flow charts of the mind: distinctions between mind, brain, software and hardware

The standard way of thinking about how the same mental processes exist in different brains is in terms of the hardware/software distinction that lies at the heart of all computer technology. Hardware refers to any physical device that is either a computer itself or is some peripheral that may be linked up to a computer such as a webcam or printer. Software refers to the programs that run on the computer. The hardware/ software distinction is particularly pertinent here because it maps onto the physical/abstract distinction that has been mentioned before. The computer is a physical device but its programs are abstract. Again the term 'abstract' means 'defined without reference to a physical object'. In arguing this, it is quite appropriate to discuss software without having any real understanding or concern for the sort of hardware (the computer) that it runs on.

Consider the following: if money were no object it is feasible that you would have the most up-to-date computer systems at work and at home. What this allows for, for example, is that the very same latest update for your favourite word processor can be used on two different computers. For the sake of argument, let us agree that the two computers share no common components – they have different keyboards, screens and chips but nevertheless both computers run the very same program. It is therefore true that the same program runs on two very different computers. This is where functionalism plays a critical role because it shows us that we can discuss the operation of the computer without having any clear understanding of its physical make-up. The operation of the computer is governed by the programs that run on it, and if we want to understand its behaviour we need to understand the programs.

By adopting such a functional approach we can argue that, by analogy, 'The mind is to the brain as the program is to the hardware' (Searle, 1994, p. 200). Put briefly, what cognitive psychologists are attempting to do is specify mental software. Cognitive psychologists endeavour to understand the programs that collectively make up mental activity: they essentially deal with the *flow charts of the mind*.

Having stated this, however, a common misconception is that the argument is that the brain is a computer and mental states and processes are identical in all respects to a computer program. Although some cognitive psychologists may be wedded to such ideas, this is not a necessary implication. All that is being stated is that we can discuss the mind and its states and processes in much the same way that we discuss computer software, that is, without reference to its physical instantiation. This view is central to functionalism. More particularly, when cognitive psychologists make reference to functional descriptions, the reference is with respect to something very much like the blueprints or schematic diagrams that were used in the example of designing a car engine. What cognitive psychologists are trying to do is to specify component

internal states and processes but only with reference to their functional roles.

## Functional description and a return to the thermostat

Although previously we were rather dismissive of thermostats, Figure 1.6 provides a blueprint or schematic diagram of the workings of the thermostat in the abstract! As can be seen, the diagram consists of a series of boxes that are interconnected with arrows and because of this the flow chart is also referred to as (somewhat unimaginatively) an **arrows-and-boxes diagram**. The boxes designate component processes such as the first – 'Read temperature setting "T" on thermostat box', whereas the interconnecting arrows merely indicate which is the next step in the whole procedure. In more advanced systems the arrows may have other connotations, such as some form of communication channel, but we will discuss these in more detail later. So for the time being, having read the setting on the thermostat box the next process is to 'Read actual room temperature "R" from thermometer or other sensor'.

This diagram provides a useful functional account of the operation of the thermostat. In other words, it

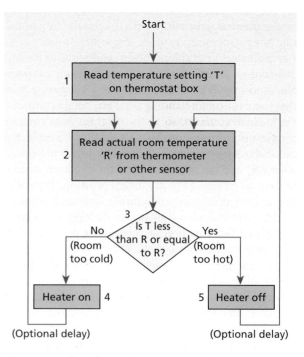

**Figure 1.6 A flow chart of the operation of a thermostat**
*Source*: Zaks, R. (1980). *Programming the 6502* (fig. 1.1, p. 9). Berkeley, California: Sybex.

provides a description of the component processes and the sequencing of these processes, together with a description of what functions these processes serve. Critically it does so in the absence of any mention of physical components whatsoever. Indeed the flow chart is hardly likely to be of much help if we wish to build a thermostat. To build a thermostat we have to take the functional account shown in Figure 1.6 and instantiate this in some kind of physical device. As a consequence, we now have to think in terms of physical components, and we will need to understand the physical nature of these components in order to build our thermostat. So in this case, a full understanding of the nature of the thermostat rests upon understanding (i) its physical make-up and the physical nature of its components, and (ii) what it is that these components actually do.

Problems abound, though, when we begin to apply these ideas to human cognition. Unlike trying to build a thermostat, we already have our device (the brain) fully formed and we are trying to figure out just what is going on. We cannot dismantle it and try to put it back together and because of this we actually undertake something known as **reverse engineering**. We are not, in the case of forward engineering, trying to build something we have already designed. More particularly, we are trying to understand how the workings of the brain underpin the mind. Perhaps now you can begin to appreciate the enormity of the problem. We have a physical device (the brain) that we do not fully understand, and we are convinced that the workings of this device are critically related to mental states and processes that constitute the mind, but we have no real understanding of these either. This is a fairly bleak scenario, so what we need therefore is a framework for thinking that might make the problems tractable.

## Functionalism and information processing systems

For a start we must begin by accepting that the brain is complicated in ways that thermostats and balance beams are not. As we have seen, there are good grounds for arguing that the brain is much more like a programmed computer than are these simple devices. If we accept this, then concerns relating to mental states, representations and processes (i.e., mental entities) come to the fore because by analogy these are akin to computer states, representations and processes, respectively. This is what the mental software analogy is all about.

Such ideas as these will be developed much further in the next chapter, but if we are to accept the mental software idea, then certain other things follow. For instance, like the computer, the brain can be characterised as being an *information processing system*. It takes in information from the world (the input), it converts this into codes that represent the input, and it then (one hopes) produces sensible responses to the input. Similarly, the computer takes in information from the keyboard (which keys have been pressed), it then represents this in its own internal codes, and (if working properly) it will produce sensible outputs. Such ideas about information processing simply do not apply to things like thermostats and balance beams because these (as characterised above) are not programmable devices.

**central state identity theory** The idea that to understand the mind we must understand the brain. Mental states and processes are identical with neurological states and processes.

**type identity theory** A version of central state identity theory which asserts that there is a one-to-one mapping between each mental event and its corresponding neurological event.

**sensory experience** The subjective sensations associated with stimulation of the senses.

**different brains problem** An issue for type identity theory in that no two brains are the same, hence the same mental event cannot be associated with a particular neurological event because different neurological events take place in different brains.

**token identity theory** A version of central state identity theory which argues that any one of several different sorts of neurological events gives rise to a particular sort of mental event.

**materialism** The philosophical position that mental events equate with/reduce to physical events.

**functional description** A description of some form of device that sets out what function each component has.

**schematic diagram** A visual representation specifying each component of a system and how the components link together.

**functionalism** The endeavour to attempt to define the properties of any device in terms of the functions that it and its components serve.

**arrows-and-boxes diagram** Similar to a schematic blueprint; a visual representation specifying the components of a system and how the components are interconnected.

▶

**reverse engineering** Attempting to understand how a pre-existing device works on the basis of how it behaves.

## Marr's levels of explanation and cognitive psychology

How, therefore, can such information processing devices be best understood? To answer this, we must now turn to a framework for thinking that was provided by Marr (1982). According to him it is possible to discuss three levels of description of any kind of information processing device, namely:

1. The level of the computational theory.
2. The level of the representation and the algorithm.
3. The level of the hardware implementation.

### The level of the computational theory

At the **computational theory level**, concern is with what the device does and why it does it. It is at this level that the 'logic of the strategy' (Marr, 1982, p. 28) is spelt out. Consider the following example of an electronic calculator and the question of how it carries out arithmetic. Analysis at the level of the computational theory would address the fact that the calculator carries out various arithmetic operations (the 'what it does') and the fact that it uses a particular method for carrying these out (the 'why it does what it does'). For instance, an early Hewlett Packard calculator (the HP35) used a method based upon something known as Reverse Polish. So expressions such as:

$(1 + 2) \times 3$

were entered as

$1\ 2\ 3 \times +$

which accords with something known as postfix notation (or Reverse Polish – and because of this, and perhaps the price, it is no wonder this model quickly died out). The computational theory would be therefore be concerned with issues like why Reverse Polish was used and what the principles of Reverse Polish are.

### The level of the representation and the algorithm

At the **representation and the algorithm level** much more detailed questions are asked about the nature of the calculator's operating system and the manner in which numbers and arithmetic processes are embodied in the device. In this respect, we are interested in how information is stored (i.e., represented) within the device and also how various arithmetic operations are instantiated. We will discuss in much more detail the notion of representation as we proceed through this book (see Chapter 7, for instance). For now, though, we will stick with a simple definition and assert that for any information processing device, information from the outside world is represented internally within the device. So when the number 2 is entered into the calculator this is represented via some form of electronic code. This form of **internal representation** stands for the number 2. By analogy, where the mind is concerned such internal (mental) states stand for (i.e., represent) actual states in the real world.

What then happens to such representations is a matter for the **algorithm**, or more particularly, the set of operations that are carried out on these representations. In computer science the term 'algorithm' is mainly used interchangeably with the phrase 'computer program', but we may take a more general reading and define it as a procedure that, when correctly applied, ensures the correct outcome. If you entered a '+' sign into the calculator and it is working properly then it should invoke its addition algorithm. The addition algorithm comprises the sequence of operations that determine that two numbers are added together. So understanding the nature of the calculator depends on trying to specify the nature of internal representations and the associated internal algorithm. In terms of understanding human cognition, and by analogy, we need to consider both mental representations and mental processes. In this respect our functional account should not only provide a flow chart that maps out the relations between component processes, but also some description of the sorts of internal representations that are also implicated. A much more thorough exploration of these ideas is contained in the next chapter, but in summary, at the level of the representation and the algorithm we are committed to being precise about (i) how states of the world are represented by the device, and (ii) what the contingent internal processes are.

### The level of the hardware

Finally there is the **hardware implementation level** and, as we have already noted, flow charts such as that shown in Figure 1.6 are of little use. Concerns at this level are with how the designated representations and processes are implemented physically. What physical components do we need to build the device? As has been discussed, the one purpose of a functional description is to avoid any commitment to physical instantiation, but of course to attain a full understanding of any physical device details at all three levels of explanation will need to be addressed.

## Pinpoint question 1.9

**According to Marr (1982), what are the three levels of description for any device?**

## Levels of explanation and information processing systems

Let us examine the notion of levels of explanation in more detail and apply this in an attempt to understand the operation of a programmed computer: the paradigm case of an information processing system. One way of conceptualising how a computer operates is in terms of the following levels:

1. The intended program.
2. The actual computer program.
3. Translation.
4. Machine instructions.
5. Transistors.

The level of the intended program – Level 1 – is where discussion of what it is that the program is designed to do takes place. Using Marr's framework, this is couched at the computational level and may be fleshed out by stating what we want the program to do – we need to specify the goals and objectives behind the program. For instance, we want the program to produce a bank statement that itemises all in-goings and out-goings on an account in a month. At this point there is no need to make any reference to any specific kind of computer or hardware of any kind. At the next level (i.e., at Level 2) the necessary step is to commit ideas to 'paper' by writing a computer program in a particular language, e.g., BASIC, PASCAL, FORTRAN, etc. In completing these two stages both the level of the computational theory and the level of the representation and algorithm have been captured. Importantly, both of these levels have been addressed without any concern whatsoever about the nature of the computer that the program will run on.

For computer languages to be at all useful, however, there needs to be a means of converting (i.e., translating) an actual program into a form that can be run on a particular computer. Stated thus, concerns about hardware are paramount. In some programming languages the translation stage may involve two steps: (i) converting the computer program into an intermediate code known as assembly language, and then (ii) converting assembly language into machine instructions. It will be something of a relief to learn that we need not concern ourselves with the detailed nature of assembly language.

The critical point is that the stage of translation takes a representation of the program and converts it into something known as binary code – a series of 0s and 1s where each 0 and 1 is known as a bit. For instance, the command PRINT might be translated into 0101000010101010. The 0s and 1s are vital because they correspond to the respective OFF/ON states of the critical electronic components of your computer – here referred to as transistors. Think of these as being akin to simple switches in an electric circuit: if the switch is ON, electricity flows this way round the circuit; if the switch is OFF, the circuit is closed. So there is a fundamental level at which properties of the program correspond exactly with physical states of the machine. The machine code corresponds to the physical state of the computer's 'switches' and these cause the computer to behave in particular ways. Any change in state of the switches results in the computer doing something else.

This example provides a concrete illustration of how Marr's levels of analysis may be useful in attempting to explain the operation of a computer. The central idea is that the computer can be described at a number of different levels, and that there is no sense in which a description at any particular level is more correct or valid than a description at any other level. The different descriptions serve different purposes. If the questions are about what the program is supposed to do, then these concern the level of the computational theory. If the questions concern the design of the program, then these will be answered most appropriately at the level of the representation and the algorithm. If the questions concern whether the program uses an 8-bit or 16-bit representation of numbers (don't worry, your computer science friends will be only too delighted to tell you what these are), then the answers will be at the level of the machine code and therefore at the level of hardware implementation.

## What's a computer? Half a century playing the imitation game

You are sitting in front of a computer, idly instant messaging. But how do you know the person on the other end is really another human being? What if the human responses were occasionally replaced by computer-generated responses? Do you think you would be able to tell? This proposal is a variation of the famous imitation game, now commonly referred to as the Turing Test first proposed by Alan Turing in 1950, and as summarised by French (2000). In it, Turing was attempting to define the sufficient conditions under which a computer could be attributed with thinking and intelligence – two of the most human of all cognitive faculties.

While the relevance of the Turing Test is doubted by some, French (2000) stated that the imitation game will continue to raise important questions as the bridge between human and machine becomes closer, such as: 'To what extent do machines have to act like humans before it becomes immoral to damage or destroy them?' (pp. 116–17). Anyone who cradles their MP3 player in a rather loving way might appreciate the sentiment here.

The Turing Test has been criticised as being a rather behaviourist approach to the definition of intelligence, in that all the machine needs do is succeed in the game, and this does not really constitute an adequate conceptualisation of what it is to think (see Gunderson 1964, cited by French, 2000; and, Searle, 1980), while others have argued that to 'play the game' is not a single ability but one that requires numerous cognitive faculties.

Despite the Turing Test being proposed over 50 years ago, it still provokes intense debate. This is perhaps most represented by the Loebner Prize, which offers a $100,000 reward for the first person who can design a computer that passes the Turing Test. French (2000) stated, however, that few computer programs have even come close and that the prize might actually impede serious discussion of the philosophical issues arising from the test itself. So the next time you're instant messaging, it might be worth thinking about who might be on the other end.

*Source*: French, R. M. (2000). The Turing test: The first 50 years. *Trends in Cognitive Science, 4*, 115–122.

## Levels of explanation and reductionism

Having considered how it is that computers operate, it seems odd to try to argue that one level of explanation is better or more valid than any other since different questions demand answers at different levels. Nevertheless, in questioning the utility of having more than one level of explanation we are beginning to consider what is known as *reductionism* – the doctrine that we can reduce all accounts of behaviour to a very basic physical level (perhaps even to the atomic or even subatomic level – see Penrose, 1989). If we accept some version of central state identity theory, then we are accepting that mental states and processes are nothing other than neural states and processes. According to reductionists, understanding the mind reduces to understanding the basic electro-chemical states and processes that characterise the behaviour of neurons (brain cells). If we understand these physical states and processes, we understand the mind.

A more virulent version of reductionism is known as *eliminative materialism*. Churchland (1984) states, essentially, that once we have a full understanding of the behaviour of neurons in terms of basic electrochemical principles, we can then eliminate any mention of any other level of description from our science. Mental states and processes reduce to neural states and processes, and if we understand neurons then we understand the mind. Churchland (1984, p. 44) is particularly taken with eliminative materialism because, on his reading of history, this sort of theorising has been successfully applied in ridding science of unnecessary concepts such as 'phlogiston' (i.e., a spirit-like substance that had been assumed to be given off when materials burn or metal rusts). The argument is that, given that eliminative materialism worked for physics, why can't it work for cognitive psychology? Maybe we can get rid of the mind after all?

This line of argument is very threatening to those of us who study cognitive psychology because it seems to suggest that as soon as we have a complete understanding of the brain, there will be nothing left for cognitive psychologists to do. More importantly, it seems to lead to the conclusion that mind science should be completely replaced by brain science! However, this conclusion can be resisted and a reasonable rebuttal is that even if you did have a complete account of the nature and operation of neurons, this is couched at a completely different level to the one that we as cognitive psychologists are concerned with. Indeed, such an understanding would have little utility if we want to make predictions about the everyday life of human beings. For instance, we may conjecture that the primary reason that Harry went to the florist's and bought his girlfriend a bunch of flowers was because he thought she was still angry at him after she caught him gazing longingly at her best friend. This is not to argue that such a physical (neuronal) account is not possible, in principle, but just that it would be of little use in trying to understand Harry's concerns about trying to figure out his girlfriend. These sorts of considerations lead to the conclusion that both reductionism and eliminativism are misguided (for a much more technical exploration of these ideas see the introduction of Fodor, 1975). On the contrary, what we have argued is that mental states and processes can only be understood if we have some understanding of their functional roles. As cognitive psychologists we are interested in uncovering the functional nature of the mental components that constitute the mind – the flow charts of the mind – and in this regard the properties of neurons will be of little help.

In this respect Marr's (1982) framework for thinking is so important. In using his kind of analysis the characteristics of any information processing device can be laid bare. It is also assumed that in using his analysis the relation between the mind and the brain becomes tractable. For cognitive psychologists the levels of the computational theory and the level of the representation and the algorithm come to the fore. This is not to dispute the fact that considerable progress continues to be made in human neuroscience. The main point is that we, as cognitive psychologists, focus on the two levels – which are essentially the cognitive levels – that do not concern anything that might be going on at the level of neurons. In the same way that the very same program can run on two different computers, we assume that the same kinds of mental representations and processes are embodied within different brains. In this way cognitive psychologists can (and do) operate without any regard for the brain.

## Pinpoint question 1.10

**How does reductionism threaten cognitive psychology?**

**computational theory level** Marr's (1982) first level of description is concerned with what the device does and why it does it.

**representation and the algorithm level** Marr's (1982) second level of description concerned with how a device represents information and how such representations are operated upon.

**internal representation** Some property of the inner workings of a device that stands for some property of the outside world. For instance, in a computer 01 represents '1'.

**algorithm** A well-specified procedure (such as a computer program) that ensures the correct outcome when correctly applied.

**hardware implementation level** Marr's (1982) third level of description concerned with the physical nature of an information processing device.

## Concluding comments

There is no doubt that we have covered quite a bit of territory in moving from behaviourist beginnings to contemporary theorising in cognitive psychology. Along the way we have established that there is a basic method to the madness of trying to understand the abstract entity that is the human mind. If we can make testable predictions about mental events in terms of some form of measurable behaviour, then it is quite legitimate for us to study mental events. Such a claim, however, must be approached with some caution and we have been mindful of the problems in attempting to accept a complex cognitive account when competing simple behavioural accounts exist. When should we appeal to Occam's Razor and when should we not?

We have also noted with some concern a desire to reduce our cognitive theories to the level of neural processes on the assumption that once we understand the brain we will understand the mind. Again we have expressed caution here. It seems that where complex information processing systems are involved, it is probably better to adopt a more circumspect approach and accept that such devices can be understood at various levels. Neither level is more valid or correct than any other level.

## CHAPTER SUMMARY

- Cognitive psychology concerns itself with the abstract nature of the mind – abstract in the sense that it is primarily concerned with non-physical, that is, mental, entities such as thoughts, beliefs and desires. This distinction, between abstract and physical properties, fits most comfortably with Cartesian dualism (after Descartes), in which there is a division between the mental and the material world. A critical problem for dualism though is, 'How can there ever be mental causation of physical behaviour?' As the mental and physical are so different, then it is unclear how they interact (Fodor, 1981a). This is a very serious unanswered problem, so how is it possible to be a cognitive psychologist and avoid the charge of being a dualist? The answer to this problem is discussed from an historical perspective and forms the basis of the chapter. Initially the focus is with behaviourism as a stark contrast to cognitivism. Contrasting behaviourist views are described and dissected.

- In contrast to the discussion of an internal mental world, behaviourism seeks to explain human nature solely in terms of observable things. According to the behaviourist manifesto, laws of behaviour should be developed on and be defined purely in terms of observable (i.e., measurable) events and states. Such laws can then be used to control and predict behaviour. The law of effect is one such law, and this proposes that associations between a stimulus (S) and a response (R) can be strengthened or weakened according to the positive or negative consequences of a person's actions.

- Further principles of associationism were put forward. According to the law of exercise, association formation most likely comes about when an S and an R co-occur frequently and in close proximity with one another. The behaviourist approach aims to do away with discussion of mental states and processes, choosing only to view humans and other animals as S–R machines. Human behaviour is treated as being the observable characteristics of a deterministic system.

- One school of behaviourism, known as methodological behaviourism, seeks to lay bare exactly which sensory inputs are associated with which behavioural outputs, therefore detailing the correlations between Ss and corresponding Rs. One consequence of the behavioural framework is that free will is stripped out, eliminated in lieu of the causal nature of S–R bonds. However, behaviourism stands on somewhat shaky grounds and may suffer from the misconception that only theories about physical entities can be tested. On the contrary, abstract theoretical constructs can be studied as long as these generate testable predictions.

- A different and more extreme form of behaviourism, known as logical behaviourism, stipulates that talk about mental events must be replaced by talk of behavioural dispositions. All explanations of the mental are redundant in respect of corresponding statements that stipulate behavioural consequences. To state that 'Harry is hungry' conveys nothing more than 'if food were available Harry would eat it'. Terms that previously referred to mental entities are replaced with terms that refer to observable entities without loss of meaning. Against such a view, an appeal was made to your introspections and intuitions. The philosophical perspective that is logical behaviourism does not gel with the ordinary experience of what it is like to be human (Searle, 1994) and the idea that our own behaviour is typically caused by thoughts, desires and feelings.

- Cognitive psychology works on the basis that, as long as testable predictions involving measurement can be generated, we can test any kind of entity we like – physical or abstract. However, in stating this, an important stricture is that any cognitive theory should be falsifiable (Popper, 1963/2000). The conditions under which the theory can be shown to be false should be made transparent. An additional guiding principle is that our explanations of human cognition should honour the principle of Occam's Razor, which states that when presented with two theories, each making similar predictions, the best theory is the simplest: it is the one that makes the fewest assumptions.

- Occam's Razor can be used to argue against the idea that thermostats have beliefs about room temperature. Although it is possible to describe the behaviour of the thermostat as though it does have such a belief system (McCarthy, 1979), such a conclusion can be resisted. Rather, electricians can build and repair thermostats without any reference to any putative thermostat belief system. Such devices can be understood both in terms of the structure of their physical components and what functions the components serve. But why can't similar arguments be applied to the understanding of human nature? Why is it that we might hesitate in applying Occam's Razor when attempting to explain human cognition? Caution is warranted because the human mind exhibits complexities that analogies with simpler devices cannot support. For example, both humans and the humble balance beam can be said to perform multiplication, but humans can go on to perform a variety of other mental arithmetic calculations that balance beams cannot. To therefore argue that balance beams carry out some form of mental arithmetic cannot be justified.

- In the second half of the chapter attention became focused on the particular nature of cognitive accounts. Again appreciation of these rested upon appreciating various philosophical perspectives on the relation between mind and brain. Central state theory is based on a fundamental assumption that the mind is embodied in the brain and two different flavours of the theory have emerged. Type identity theory claims that each mental event maps onto its own particular neurological event. Token identity theory makes a lesser claim, namely that underlying each mental event is a neurological event and different neurological events can give rise to the same mental event. Both sorts of identity theory are problematic and the dilemmas that arise can be addressed when the notion of functional role is introduced.

- Discussion of the notion of functional role laid the basis of discussion of functionalism. Functionalism fundamentally underpins cognitive psychology. In order to understand any sort of device it is important to understand the functions it performs and the functions that its components perform. In particular, it is accepted that our understanding of mental states and processes can only proceed if we address issues of what functions such states and processes fulfil.

- Functionalism therefore provides a means by which token identity theory can be extended. Different patterns of neurological activity can produce the same sort of mental event, but mental events are defined in terms of their functional roles. Of most help here is the software/hardware distinction as used in computer science. By analogy the mind is the mental software that runs on the brain's hardware (Searle, 1994).

- Such ideas can be more fully understood in terms of Marr's (1982) framework of thinking about information processing systems. The brain is like a computer insofar as information about the external world is represented internally. Such information processing devices can be best understood at each of three levels. At the computational level, what the device does and why, are the foci of interest. At the representation and algorithm level, the particularities of the internal representations and processes are spelt out. At the hardware implementation level, concern is with how the device is physically instantiated. While neuroscientists concern themselves with the hardware implementation level, cognitive psychologists concern themselves with the computational and representation and algorithm levels of explanation.

- Despite all that has been argued, a final threat to cognitive psychology comes in the form of reductionism – the idea that a true understanding of any device can only be achieved by essentially understanding physical structure and physical processes. An extreme version of reductionism known as eliminative materialism states that once a complete description of neural behaviour is provided, then any talk about the mental can be eliminated from our concerns. Mind science reduces to brain science and when we understand the brain then we also understand the mind. This conclusion, however, can be resisted.

## ANSWERS TO PINPOINT QUESTIONS

1.1 Guilt over a snapped Lancaster Bomber is abstract because it is a mental state. Of course, this guilt might manifest itself physically if you eventually purchase a new model kit for your weeping sibling.

1.2 A biscuit addict would continue eating according to the law of effect since the positive outcome of the taste and texture of the biscuit would be likely to lead to repeated snacking.

1.3 As long as an empirical approach involves the derivation and testing of predictions, it does not constrain what kind of entity may be studied. Both physical and abstract properties can be examined in this way.

1.4 According to Popper, scientific theories should be falsifiable, and according to the principle of Occam's Razor, scientific theories should be simple.

1.5 All the parrot can do is imitate talking; there is no sense in which it has any understanding of what it is saying. In this respect, it is simply a biological form of tape recorder.

1.6 Considering how the mind has been defined is an abstract mental process and not one that behaviourists would acknowledge.

1.7 Type identity theorists claim that a specific type of mental event maps onto a distinct neurological pattern of activity, while token identity theorists claim that a specific type of mental event can map onto one of a number of different tokens of neurological patterns of activity.

1.8 The common function of all these different structures is to store musical information.

1.9 The three levels of description are: (i) computational theory, (ii) representation and algorithm, and (iii) hardware implementation.

1.10 Reductionism threatens cognitive psychology with the assertion that once a physiological understanding of the brain is complete, there will be nothing left for the cognitive psychologist to do.

## CHAPTER 2

# INFORMATION PROCESSING AND NATURE OF THE MIND

## LEARNING OBJECTIVES

**By the end of this chapter, you should be able to:**

- Distinguish between different methodological approaches used to study human cognition; namely, the cognitive psychology approach, the artificial intelligence approach, the neuroscience approach and, finally, the cognitive neuropsychological approach.
- Describe in broad terms the information theory (Shannon & Weaver, 1949) as applied to human cognition.
- Summarise the basic concepts of human information processing.
- Discuss the computational metaphor of the mind with reference to physical symbol systems.
- Recognise the difference between rule-governed and rule-following systems.
- Define the principles of modular design (Marr, 1982).
- Distinguish between horizontal and vertical faculties.
- Summarise the modularity of mind hypothesis (Fodor, 1983).
- Realise the link between the modularity hypothesis and cognitive neuropsychology.
- Understand the logic of association, dissociation and double dissociation deficits.

## CHAPTER CONTENTS

▶

Cars cruising up and down the front, bright lights, fortunes won and lost, a constant stream of hedonism – it could only be one place: Blackpool. So there you are, sitting in a corner in one of the amusement arcades along the Golden Mile, ploughing next week's shopping budget into a fruit machine. Like an automaton, you continue dropping coins into the slot, as the machine registers how much money you put in and how many chances you have left of moving beyond bread and water next week. The 'spin' button begins to flash, waiting for your hot sweaty hand. It's clearly been a while since the machine got a service, what with the years of sand blowing in from the front, so you've taken to thumping the button down so as to take no chances in activating the spinning wheels. Wait a minute – three plums! Jackpot! A rather conspicuous yellow light on top of the fruit machine starts flashing and the machine begins to vibrate in a very pleasing fashion. However, the display of plums is not followed by the satisfying chink-chink-chink of cash. Nothing! 'But surely the machine knows it's a jackpot – look, the flashy lights, the noises!' you explain feverishly to a passing mechanic. 'Looks like the money dispensers got clogged again,' he sighs, as a spanner is jammed unceremoniously into the innards of the machine. Time passes. The faint smell of fish and chips enters the room. 'Ahh,' the mechanic says, appearing from round the back of the thieving box of metal, 'it wasn't the dispenser at all, it's the spinning mechanism that got jammed. What you actually got was two plums and a cherry. Sorry mate. Here, have the next game on me.' And with that, he flips you a coin and walks away.

# Hold the bells! The unfortunate case of the modular fruit machine

## REFLECTIVE QUESTIONS

1. How logical do you think you are? How much do you think you are defined by rules? Will you always go to the pub after work on a Friday night? If people ask 'How are you?' do you always have the same answer? Do you always cook chicken in the same way? How flexible are you in deviating from set patterns? Under what circumstance does this happen?

2. In what ways are you different to a computer (hopefully in addition to physical appearances)? Do you save information? Are there any techniques you have when storing data so that you can easily retrieve it again? What do you do when you know a piece of information but you can't quite get at it? How do you know when you've forgotten something?

## PART 1

## An introduction to computation and cognitive psychology

## Introduction and preliminary considerations

Feeding slot machines provides an example of humans interacting with machines, but one question we will be grappling with here is how much like machines humans are. Indeed, playing the slots can be so addictive that it seems that the machines can take control of your behaviour. What we intend to do here is discuss some of the assumptions behind adopting an information processing approach to behaviour, explaining that many things – even your interactions in the arcades at Blackpool – can be described using some sort of communication theory in which information is transmitted from a sender to a receiver. In this way we will touch on how you might be similar to and different from machines. Although it is stretching our fruit machine analogy a little far, you will discover that some cognitive psychologists have drawn very close parallels between minds and computers. We will examine such claims rather closely in this chapter. Finally we'll introduce the concept of modularity and show how this has been used to try to account for the mind.

So in this chapter, we range from discussing how a fruit machine has functionally separate components that each perform a specific job such as dispensing cash or spinning the wheels, to introducing you to the idea that mental processes may be thought of in a very similar way. The basic idea is that different parts of the mind are dedicated to different tasks, such as appreciating music, doing maths, understanding language, recognising objects, etc. Having introduced such notions of modularity we conclude by explaining how it is that evidence from brain-damaged individuals may inform our theories about the modular mind.

So far we have decided that behaviourism, despite its lofty ambitions of predicting and controlling human actions, falls short in not providing a very useful framework for thinking about human cognition. As cognitive psychologists we are primarily interested in developing flow charts of the mind, and consequently, we focus our attention and efforts on attempting to understand mental states and mental processes. Given this, we are happy to admit the importance of the brain, but are

nevertheless clear that mind science and brain science are different disciplines: we can study cognition and leave the neurons (brain cells) to the neuroscientists.

In pursuing these goals, we have also been introduced to the notion of information processing systems, but so far have given little away about what such systems are actually like. A very brief introduction to the operation of a digital computer was included in Chapter 1 because this provided one example of an information processing system that we fully understand. However, the current chapter contains quite a lot more detail about the operation of computers, and it is therefore completely reasonable to ask what exactly these digital boxes have to do with the nature of the human mind. The main reason for this is that many commentators have drawn rather strict analogies between the operation of a programmable computer and that of the human mind (see for instance Johnson-Laird, 1989, and Pinker, 1997). In drawing such comparisons the commentators have introduced the notion of so-called *computational processes*, and arguments have been made that mental processes are, essentially, **computational processes** (see Fodor, 1981b). Given that we fully understand how computers operate, then maybe we will be able to understand the mind, after all? Such sentiments as these are fully explained as the discussion proceeds.

Much of this material has a philosophical flavour to it and most experimental cognitive psychologists never let these basic issues get in the way of running experiments. It is therefore possible to argue that these issues are simply irrelevant – so why bother with them? In contrast to such a negative view, we feel that it is important to get acquainted with the sorts of assumptions that underpin the experimental work, even though these may not have been discussed or even stated. The issues are fundamental, and it is without doubt that such ideas are particularly important when we discuss (later in the book, see Chapter 12) a very particular type of research known as **connectionism** (see Quinlan, 1991, for a review). Connectionism is a discipline in which computer programs (or computer models) are developed in order to try to simulate various kinds of cognitive processes using networks of simple processing units interconnected with many adaptable links or connections. Here it suffices to note that connectionism depends on a quite different set of assumptions to those that have so far been discussed (see Chapter 1). Therefore connectionist and information processing models of the mind are typically cast as being contrary accounts of the same mental phenomena.

Initially, therefore, the basics of the information processing approach are explored and the so-called **computational metaphor** of mind will be discussed. Much of the material concerns work carried out decades ago, but the issues are foundational and these do provide the backdrop for much of what is to be discussed in the ensuing chapters. As with Chapter 1, this chapter is divided into two main parts. In the first we thoroughly explore the computational metaphor of mind and how this forms the basis of the computational theory of mind. It is accepted that this basic framework provides the theoretical basis for much of present-day cognitive psychology, but it is also acknowledged that there are critical differences between minds and computers. Grounds for resisting the conclusion that the human mind is exactly the same sort of machine as a digital computer (or indeed a fruit machine) are also therefore considered.

In the second part of the chapter, we will explore different ideas about how the mind may be constituted. Such considerations are sometimes referred to as **architectural characteristics**. Is it best to think of general characteristics that cut across all cognitive domains? Is it best to think in terms of special-purpose, domain-specific processes? Or is there a completely different way to carve up our mental faculties? In addressing these sorts of questions, one approach that is particularly relevant is known as **cognitive neuropsychology**. Cognitive neuropsychology focuses on the operation of damaged brains and how associated cognitive deficits may inform theories about cognition couched at the functional level. The chapter therefore closes with a discussion of this approach to the study of cognition. Its methods and its logic are scrutinised and the sort of evidence that it uncovers is also briefly summarised. Before we can begin to tackle issues concerning mental dysfunction, however, it is best to begin by examining different methodologies that are applied to trying to understand the mind as it functions normally.

**computational processes** Individual operators that can be specified in terms of a physical symbol system.

**connectionism** A discipline that attempts to generate computer models of the mind based on brain-like architectures – simple processing units (based on brain cells) are interconnected with adaptable connections or links. Very much a telephone exchange approach to modelling the mind.

**computational metaphor** The position that the mind/brain relation is the same as the computer software/hardware relation. Mental processes are computational processes.

**architectural characteristics** When used in the context of the mind, this phrase refers to how the mind may be composed and organised into its constituent components.

**cognitive neuropsychology** A cognitive approach that concentrates on comparisons between performance of individuals suffering from some form of brain damage with individuals with intact brains.

## Different methodological approaches to the study of the mind

Let us begin by reconsidering the task that cognitive psychologists face. We have in front of us one of the most complicated things in the known universe and we are trying to figure out how best to understand it: we are faced with the black box that is the human mind (see Figure 2.1). The rules of engagement are quite clear. We cannot physically attempt to open the black box: the ethical reasons are clear – who wants to be the first volunteer? Instead we have to try to figure out the inner workings of the box merely by observing what it does. The task is daunting, and in order to try to make some headway, we simply accept the foundational assumption that the black box contains an information processing system. We therefore set ourselves the goal of trying to understand the nature of its putative internal states and processes.

So where are we to begin? Perhaps it is best to start with a simple example and work by analogy. Consider the question: 'How are we going to understand what a computer is doing when it is running a particular

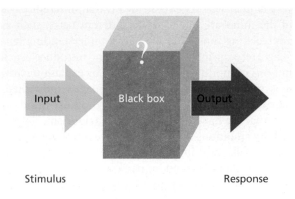

**Figure 2.1 The black box that is the human mind**
As cognitive psychologists, we are trying to figure out the internal workings of this black box merely from observing its behaviour.

program?' In this hypothetical case we have already written a computer program and the aim is to try to get someone else (a naïve observer) to uncover what is going on when the computer runs the program. In this contrived example, if we run the program it will simply type out 'Are we having fun yet?' and wait for a typed response. When a typed response is made the program will decide if the answer is 'Yes', and if it is then the program will quit; otherwise the program will ask the question again. The program will iterate until the response 'Yes' is typed. A skeleton of the program for doing this looks like this:

```
Line1.  Program FunYet
Line2.  Begin
Line3.  Print "Are we having fun yet?"
Line4.  Get (response)
Line5.  IF response ="Yes" GOTO Line6
        OTHERWISE GOTO Line3
Line6.  End.
```

The bits in bold are commands and operations that are defined for the particular language. 'response' is a contrived variable that can be assigned a value taken from a keyboard input. 'Get' is a command that accepts keystrokes until the <Return> key is pressed. Somewhat reminiscent of the Turing Test described in Research focus 1.3, the program might have to be running for quite some time before it can quit:

```
> Are we having fun yet?
> What do you think?
> Are we having fun yet?
> Absolutely not.
> Are we having fun yet?
> If I say 'yes' will you leave me alone?
> Are we having fun yet?
> Yes
>
```

## The cognitive approach

Initially, the naïve observer is simply allowed to interact with the program by typing in certain responses and observing and measuring the outcomes. In adopting a strictly cognitive approach the observer adopts a strictly non-invasive approach to the study of the device. The observer attempts to vary the input to the program (i.e., types in different responses) and notes down any systematic changes that relate to this variation. Which behaviours are reproducible and why? The hope is that by noting any such systematic variation in what is typed in and what occurs as a consequence,

this will allow the observer to generate a flow diagram of hypothesised component processes. For instance, certain input processes will be proposed (how does the program accept input?), certain decisional processes will be proposed (how does the program decide to repeat or quit?) and, finally, certain output processes will be proposed (how does the program produce its outputs?). The details of this approach are fleshed out in the forthcoming chapters.

## The artificial intelligence approach

An alternative (perhaps even a complementary) approach might be termed the **artificial intelligence (AI) approach**. Now the aim is to try to generate a new computer program that mimics the behaviour of the observed program. Here success would be gauged by providing a new program that mimics the behaviour of our observed program in all critical respects. This sort of solution has gone further than that of simply providing a flow chart because we have operationalised our ideas in the new computer program. We have gone further because, apart from mapping out assumed representations and processes in a flow chart, we have provided what is known as a **demonstration proof** that the particular representations and processes embodied in the new program are sufficient to solve the task. Our ideas actually work because our program mimics the behaviour of the program we are trying to understand.

A claimed benefit of adopting this approach is that it forces the theorist to formulate, very precisely, the assumptions that underlie the theory. The ideas must be precise because they are to be operationalised in a computer program (as anyone who has tried their hand at programming will know). Computers are extremely exacting mechanisms and because of this every command in the program must be correctly specified – down to the last comma and full stop. (Indeed, quite a lively debate sprang up over claims that the Mariner 1 space probe failed because of a missing hyphen in its controlling software.) As a consequence the theorist must be precise in fleshing out the theoretical ideas because such ideas will have to be converted into programming code.

We might worry that the particular programming language places some unnecessary constraints on the theory – such that everything is converted to **binary coding** – but this need not detract from the advantages of having to specify our theoretical assumptions in detail. If this exercise is successful and the program runs successfully then we have a demonstration proof that the operations specified in the program are sufficient to explain the behaviour. The theory has been shown to work. When described in these terms, it is clear that this kind of AI provides a very useful approach to understanding cognitive processes. It provides a means to address detailed issues at the level of the representation and the algorithm (Marr, 1982).

Indeed we might get quite carried away and try to argue that the observed program and new program are actually the same. Patently though, this is not a necessary conclusion to draw, but we have shown, quite categorically, that our particular theory of the operation of the target program has been shown to be plausible. Our theory (as embodied in our new program) has passed a test of sufficiency.

Perhaps counter-intuitively, one of the biggest benefits of adopting an AI approach is in cases where, despite how hard we try, we cannot get our programmed theory to work. In this respect we have good grounds for ruling out the theory. Although the failure to pass a test of sufficiency need not be completely fatal for the theory, such failures cannot help but cast a shadow: we have tried to demonstrate the utility of our theory in terms of a computer program, but no matter how hard we have tried it does not work!

## The neuroscience approach

Alternatively, if we are really desperate, we might decide to try to observe and, possibly, measure the inner workings of the particular computer that the program runs on. However, given that we are not allowed to break open the computer's casing, nor tamper with any of the internal components in any way, this drastically limits our options – maybe we should measure changes in the magnetic fields that are generated by the computer's components as the program runs? The ultimate hope, in adopting such a stance, is that if we observe the changes in the states of its physical components (i.e., of the transistors) as we run the program, then this will tell us something fundamental about the nature of the program itself.

Although this might sound a quite bizarre way to try to discover how a computer operates, very similar techniques are currently being developed in a bid to understand how the mind works. This neuroscience approach is very much in its infancy, and although some claim that it holds much promise, it is difficult to be clear what its ultimate contribution will be (for an entertaining and thought-provoking piece, see Fodor, 1999). We are beginning to map out which areas of the brain become particularly exercised when a person is engaged in certain cognitive tasks. However, so far little has been learnt about cognitive processes that are assumed to be associated with such changes in brain activation. Much is being learnt about the structural organisation of the brain (where stuff happens) but, as of this time of writing, little has been learnt about cognitive functioning (what stuff is happening and how). As this book is primarily concerned with the nature of cognition, little further attention will be devoted to this particular kind of neuroscience approach. Of course we will occasionally make reference to work in cognitive neuroscience, but a primary aim of this book is to examine evidence that speaks directly to the cognitive level. → See 'What have we learnt?', below.

### → What have we learnt?

What the foregoing passages have done is perhaps caricature three approaches to attempting to understand the mind. (We will focus on a final approach – the cognitive neuropsychological approach – as we draw the chapter to a close.) The cognitive approach is primarily concerned with generating flow charts on the basis of measuring observable behaviour; the AI approach is primarily concerned with developing computer simulations, typically on the basis of certain intuitions about what may be going on; and the neuroscience approach is primarily concerned with how brains work. In practice, you will discover that aspects of all three approaches creep under the umbrella of cognitive psychology. Quite unashamedly, though, this book focuses primarily on cognitive and AI accounts of human cognition. This is not to argue that knowledge of the brain is completely irrelevant to understanding the mind. On the contrary, what has been argued is that cognitive psychology is primarily concerned with functional accounts and neuroscience has contributed little in informing theories couched in functional terms: remember, as cognitive psychologists we are primarily concerned with the mental software, not the neural hardware. This book therefore attempts to lay bare what has been discovered about the mind from those researchers who have adopted a functional point of view.

**artificial intelligence (AI) approach** Attempts to mimic intelligent behaviour via computer simulation.

**demonstration proof** Taking any hypothesis and demonstrating that it can work in practice. Demonstrating that something works.

**binary coding** Representations that can contain only 0s and 1s.

## Information theory and information processing

For cognitive psychologists the primary aim is to put forward a **functional account** of some aspect of human cognition. For proponents of the AI approach, the ultimate aim is to provide such an account in terms of the operation of a computer simulation (or alternatively a computer model). This might seem clear enough, but there are many subtleties here and we need to tread carefully so as to understand the implications more fully. Much hinges on the notion of information processing and information processing systems, and although the basic ideas have already been introduced (in Chapter 1), we need to explore these more thoroughly in order to proceed. A starting point is to consider, in broad strokes, **information theory**.

## A brief introduction to information theory

Information theory was introduced by Shannon and Weaver (1949) as a mathematical account of the operation of any type of communication system. As such it provides basic assumptions that underpin our ideas about information processing systems. Consider the example of two people (Speaker Andy and Listener Lou) conversing over the telephone where both participants are talking via a landline. (Remember, the ideas were

developed in the 1940s – a very long time before the advent of mobile phones or internet messaging!) As with any communication system, it is possible to define:

1. An information source (i.e., Speaker Andy – the person speaking).
2. A transmitter (i.e., Speaker Andy's telephone).
3. A channel (i.e., the cable interconnecting the two handsets).
4. A receiver (Listener Lou's telephone).
5. The destination (Listener Lou).

Shannon and Weaver were also concerned with the idea that noise might occur on the line during the conversation, for example, a crossed line with a pizza delivery firm, Speaker Andy's flatmate hoovering in the background, or static produced by a dodgy connection at the wall. Figure 2.2 provides a schematic representation of the general set-up as captured in a so-called communication system.

In this communication system, the auditory input (Speaker Andy's speech) is converted (or encoded) by the transmitter into an electrical signal which then travels down the line. This signal is then re-converted into auditory output at the receiver. For Shannon and Weaver (1949), the important issues concerned how efficiently such a system might operate. In this regard, they attempted to quantify the system's efficiency in terms of a number of variables, namely:

1. The channel capacity (how many signals the system could deal with at any one time).
2. The rate of transmission (how quickly the system could transfer the signal).
3. Redundancy of encoding (how much of the original input needed to be sent).
4. Noise (essentially interference within the system).

The major contribution that Shannon and Weaver (1949) made was that they developed a general statistical formulation for describing the inter-relationships between these variables. Importantly their account was

**Figure 2.2 The basics of a communication system**
A schematic representation of a communication system as described by Shannon and Weaver (1949) in their discussion of information theory.

*Source*: Haber, R. N. (1974). Information processing. In E. C. Carterette, & M. P. Friedman (Eds.), *Handbook of perception* (Vol. 1, fig. 1, p. 315). London: Academic. Reproduced with permission from Elsevier.

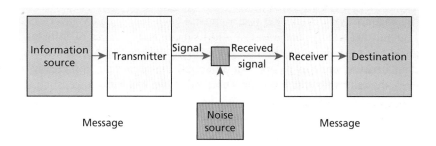

couched at an abstract level because their ideas were developed independently of how the communication system might actually be physical instantiated (e.g., via a telephone network). As Haber (1974) wrote, their objective was to describe a communication system with general statistical concepts 'independent of the specific types of channels, the types of senders and receivers, and most critically, the nature or content of the information flowing through the channels' (p. 315). In this regard their account is a functional account as discussed in Chapter 1.

At the time, what psychologists were particularly taken with was the notion of **redundancy** or amount of information present in a given signal (and here 'signal' refers to a given stimulus). The important point was that, in being able to define and quantify information, it is also possible to measure it. This was vital because it provided psychologists with an insight about how to define an abstract entity in such a way that it could be measured. Psychologists could now conceive of ways of measuring something couched at the psychological level; that is, independently from stimuli and responses.

### Pinpoint question 2.1

**Why is the Shannon and Weaver (1949) model a functional account of communication?**

## Information and the notion of redundancy

One way of thinking about redundancy is in terms of how much of the signal can be correctly predicted from other parts of the signal. A highly redundant message is highly predictive. A critical issue now was how to go about measuring the redundancy or, conversely, the amount of information present in the signal. In addressing this, the aim was to try to quantify how predictive signals are. For example, if a message is highly predictive we could get away with deleting the irrelevant bits and just leaving the relevant. In the case of our telephone conversation between Andy and Lou, the vacuum noise might get pretty intense such that Lou only hears 'Mary had a ++++ ++++ its fleece ++++ ++++ as ++++'. However, this message is highly redundant because you can recover the intended message even though most of it has been obscured. If we can delete a lot of the message and still understand it, then the message is said to have low information content. However, with the message, 'We should meet tonight because that's a good time to elope', there is very little

redundancy. Lou would be unable to reconstruct the intended meaning if all that he heard was 'We should meet ++++ because that's a good ++++ to ++++.'

Shannon and Weaver took it upon themselves to try to quantify information purely in terms of statistical means by using things like the frequency of co-occurrence of parts of the message. For instance, they realised that the amount of information increases with the number of possible things that might have occurred at a given point in the signal. In our second example, Andy could have asked Lou to meet 'at the corner', 'at 9pm', 'in Glasgow', 'at Barry's place' or 'at once'. In this respect the message has low redundancy. In contrast, take another example: if $y$ invariably follows $x$, and hearing $x$ implies hearing $y$ next, then $y$ is fully redundant with respect to $x$. The receiver can, in a sense, write down $y$ as soon as $x$ is heard irrespective of whether $y$ reaches the receiving end of the communication system ('Will you please shut up and sit dow . . .'). More generally, the amount of information conveyed increases as the number of potential events that may follow $x$ increases ('Will you please shut up and . . .'). Information theory provides the statistical methods for quantifying the information that is present in a given signal.

> **functional account** A description of a system primarily in terms of what purpose(s) it serves.
>
> **information theory** A mathematical account of how a communication system works (Shannon & Weaver, 1949).
>
> **redundancy** The extent to which a message can be predicted or recovered from other parts of the message.

## Information theory and human information processing

The fact that the modern world depends on telecommunication systems that are fundamentally based on the properties and principles identified by Shannon and Weaver (1949) is a clear testament to the usefulness of information theory. Indeed these early ideas about communication systems and information transmission greatly influenced cognitive psychologists. For instance, such ideas provided them with a functional framework for thinking about how the human mind might operate in the abstract. It provided the foundations for the assumption that the mind may be characterised as an information processing system whereby stimulation at the senses enters into a complex communication system. Indeed the theoretical framework dovetailed nicely with other sentiments in the literature about analogies between the operation of the human central nervous system and a 'complicated telephone switchboard' (Tolman, 1948, p. 190).

Models of cognitive processing soon began to appear that were based on the central tenets of the so-called *information processing framework*. Nonetheless, psychologists were quick to realise that for humans, at least, the notion of the amount of information was more difficult to define than by the simple sorts of statistical measures used in information theory. It is not so much which words are spoken but what meanings are trying to be conveyed (MacKay, 1961): 'dog bites man' is much less informative than 'man bites dog'! However, information theory forced psychologists to consider a whole new approach to thinking about human cognition. Now the view was that the human mind could be treated as being an information processing system: there is some input to an internal communication system that is transformed or encoded in particular ways. This encoded information is then transmitted through the system. Eventually, further operations may lead to an output from the system in the form of some sort of observable behaviour.

By way of example, such a system may be posited to explain how it is that you can see the sentence 'Mary had a little lamb, its fleece was white as snow . . .' (the written sentence is the input) and go on to read it aloud (the spoken sentence is the output). The information contained in the written form of the sentence is encoded, transmitted and eventually transformed into a spoken output. The underlying operations of encoding and transforming the information in the input to produce the output are to be explained in terms of the operations of an information processing system.

The now classical information processing view is that the human organism consists of certain sensory systems (eyes, ears, etc.) which operate as receivers of external inputs; these receivers operate to encode these inputs via sensory encoding or sensory transduction. This encoded information is then passed on, via abstract information processing channels, to more central systems. The central systems operate on the information in such a way that an appropriate response can be made. At a distance, this description is very much like a behaviourist S–R theory: an external stimulus elicits a response from an organism. However, in attempting to develop functional accounts of behaviour, cognitive psychologists are mainly concerned with the putative internal (abstract) events that intervene between the stimuli and responses. They treat these as being of more importance than the correlative nature of the stimuli and contingent responses. → See 'What have we learnt?', below.

### → What have we learnt?

Following on from the birth of information theory, psychologists were quick to realise that in trying to explain human nature, something other than stimuli and responses could be quantified and measured. The concept of information came to the fore, and, in turn, information processing accounts of human cognition soon began to emerge. Such accounts hold that a sensory input gives rise to an internal signal that represents the stimulus. That is, the internal signal stands for or designates the stimulus. Hence a phrase that we will repeatedly come across is **stimulus representation**. This stimulus representation is then operated upon in such a way that it can be converted into a behavioural response. The important distinction here is between mental representations and mental processes. The stimulus representation is an internal, mental representation and there are internal processes that operate on such a representation. Mental processes are internal operations that are invoked once the senses receive stimulation. As we go on to discuss, sensory stimulation invokes processes whereby the signal is encoded and transmitted through the human information processing system.

As cognitive psychologists recognised that the goal was to generate functional information processing accounts of cognition, it was accepted that such *internal representations* and processes can be discussed without reference to neurophysiology. Indeed, in laying the foundations for the AI approach to cognitive psychology, Newell, Shaw and Simon (1958) were convinced that the most appropriate way to proceed was to generate working computer programs that mimicked or simulated the particular cognitive ability under consideration. Such ideas as these will be discussed in more detail shortly, but they are very closely linked with something that is known as the *computational metaphor of mind*.

**Pinpoint question 2.2**

If both behavioural S–R theories and information processing theories use ideas regarding stimulus and response, how do they differ?

**stimulus representation** The phrase used to refer to how a stimulus is encoded following the operation of the perceptual mechanisms.

## The computational metaphor of mind and human cognition

Since the inception of information processing accounts of human cognition, and the growth in AI, a widely influential view is that mental states and processes can be best understood by analogy with those that characterise the operation of a digital computer. In this way information processing accounts of human cognition invoke something known as the *computational metaphor of mind*. Essentially, by this view, the brain, in operationalising the mind, behaves in much the same way as does a digital computer when it runs a program. To understand this assertion, we need to consider the sorts of things that computers do.

### The naked desktop: the internal workings of a digital computer laid bare

I think you all ought to know that I'm feeling very depressed.

*(Adams, 1979)*

Presuming that machines such as Marvin the Paranoid Android in *The Hitchhiker's Guide to the Galaxy* can only get depressed in works of fiction, we have no qualms in stripping our computer bare on the assumption that embarrassment is also out of the question (see Figure 2.3). In very simple terms, there is a central processing unit (the CPU that contains an arithmetical unit and a control unit), a program memory, a data memory and a data bus. Operations that are carried out within this system are defined in terms of the sorts of binary coding we have already discussed (see Chapter 1). The computer operates according to the ON/OFF states of its transistors and this is captured by a coding scheme in which a 0 signifies OFF and a 1 signifies ON. This binary code is fundamental and the power and usefulness of the computer rests upon the fact that, to a very large extent, any form of stimulus information can be captured by a signal composed of 0s and 1s. If you remain unconvinced by the awesome power of these two numbers, then it is worth remembering that all your prized DVD of *The Matrix* contains is a very well-organised set of 0s and 1s (see Figure 2.4).

The computer shown in Figure 2.3 operates by (i) dividing up these binary signals into workable chunks of, say, 8 characters (or bits) in length such as 00100110, where each 1 and 0 represents a bit in the code; and (ii) shifting these chunks about via the data bus (the main communication channel between the components). Even the computer program itself is rendered into constituent binary chunks, and these, like the other forms of data, are stored in a particular place in memory (i.e., in the program memory in Figure 2.3).

In running the program, the first chunk of the program code is taken from the program memory and moved via the data bus into the CPU. This CPU is the heart of the computer and is composed of a variety of dedicated temporary stores (or registers) and other components that interpret the current states of the registers. One such register will contain the chunk of program just read from the memory. Let us assume

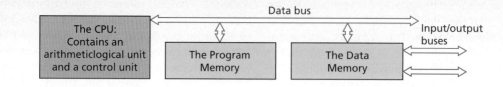

**Figure 2.3 A schematic representation of the internal components of a very simple digital computer**
The main components shown are the central processing unit (the CPU), which comprises the arithmetic–logical unit and the control unit, the program memory, the data memory, the data bus and the input/output buses. The term 'bus' is used in the same way as is 'channel' in information theory. The data bus acts as the communication channel between the memory and the CPU. The input/output buses allow for communication to and from the outside world.

undertaken by a computer. So, for instance, Palmer and Kimchi (1986) have stated that 'mental operations are ones that select, transform, store, and match information arising from the present situation, from memories of past situations, from plans for future situations, or (usually) some combination of these' (p. 39).

## Physical symbol systems

In taking these kinds of ideas about computation much further, Newell (1980) discussed something he termed a **physical symbol system**. He defined a physical symbol system as consisting of:

1. A memory.
2. A set of operators.
3. A control.
4. An input and an output (see Figure 2.5).

Before continuing with describing these components, it is important to consider what **symbolic representation** means in this context.

### Symbolic representation

Any symbol is something that stands for, designates or represents something else. (Remember the time that TAFKAP – The Artist Formerly Known As Prince – 'became' a symbol?) The symbols used in a digital computer are binary numbers. A given binary number can stand for a piece of information that represents a person's name, their bank account number, the colour of a pixel on a computer screen, the first note of the theme tune to *Neighbours*, etc. Formally, the number one can be represented, in binary notation, by 0001, the number two by 0010, the number three by 0011, the number four by 0100 and so on. The way it works is that in binary notation, the only allowable characters are 0 and 1 so if we wish to represent something in binary we must have a means of transforming it into 0s and 1s. Of course, what the binary numbers themselves represent is given by the person who wrote the program (e.g., either names, bank account numbers, colours of pixels, notes in a tune). We have much more to say about symbolic representation as the discussion proceeds. For now, though, let us keep it simple and merely accept the definition of symbolic representation as given and agree that it is a very useful way of thinking about how digital computers operate. Closely aligned to this idea of symbolic representation is the idea that such representations are stored in memory.

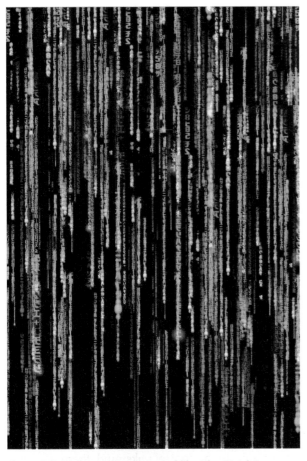

**Figure 2.4 How much is your mind like *The Matrix*?**
*Source*: Kobal Collection Ltd/Warner Bros.

that this chunk carries an instruction that now determines the next step. For instance, the instruction might specify the operation to access a chunk of data from a particular place in the data memory. The control unit, in contrast, is responsible for ensuring that the sequencing of these kinds of operations is kept in check. It determines that when the current instruction has completed, the next chunk of program is copied into the CPU via the data bus from the data memory. Such operations continue until the program has completed (or, possibly, it crashes).

So what we have here is the notion of programmed control together with ideas about storing and retrieving data that are represented in memory. Such concepts, when used in the context of human cognition, are central to the computational metaphor of mind. The claim is not so much that the brain is nothing more than a digital computer, but rather that mental operations are directly analogous with the operations

SS: Example symbol system

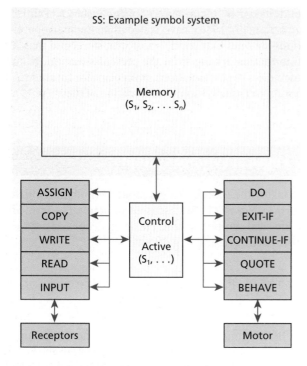

**Figure 2.5 A physical symbol system**
Newell's (1980) schematic representation of the critical components of a physical symbol system.

*Source*: Newell, A. (1980). Physical symbol systems. *Cognitive Science, 4*, 135–183 (fig. 2, p. 145). Reproduced with permission.

## Symbolic representation and memory

One way of thinking about memory is to conceive of it being akin to a series of pigeonholes such that each can hold a particular chunk of data. Each of these pigeonholes has a unique address and so in order to retrieve or store a given data chunk, a necessary first step is to recover the correct address of the relevant pigeonhole. In this respect, in order to retrieve or store a particular memory it is necessary to access the particular address of that memory. This is essentially how a computer's memory is organised. By analogy, the postal service receives millions and millions of data chunks (i.e., letters and parcels – let us call these packets), and in order for this system to work, each packet must be delivered to the correct address.

By way of example, it is possible for a computer to store the numbers 1–4 in its memory by assigning the binary patterns 0001, 0010, 0011, 0100 to, say, addresses #1345, #1346, #1347, #1348, respectively. The critical point is that the patterns 0001, 0010, 0011, 0100 are taken as being symbols for the numbers 1, 2, 3 and 4, respectively. It is these symbols that are stored in the computer's memory. In this way the numbers 1–4 are represented internally – in memory.

So a basic idea is that memory can be compartmentalised in such a way that different sorts of information are stored in different places – in much the same way that books are stored in a library. Using memory correctly means being able to store information in and retrieve information from the relevant places. To make Figure 2.5 more concrete, let the $S_1$ stand for the symbol 0001 which represents the number '1', $S_2$ for the symbol 0010 representing number '2', and so on. These are the sorts of internal, symbolic representations that the system deals in. Such symbolic representations are stored in memory and may act as inputs to the control system.

Where the human mind is concerned, and according to the computational metaphor, it is assumed that knowledge of the world is stored as memories: such memories represent aspects of the world. For instance, recalling the recipe for white sauce is understood to be a process of retrieving this information from memory in much the same way that data chunks are retrieved from a computer's memory when it runs a program. Committing something to memory – such as the

---

**For example . . .**

This is the beginning of one of Shakespeare's famous speeches from *Hamlet*, 'To be or not to be, that is the question', converted into binary code:

0101010001101111001000000110001001100101 0010000000110111101110010001000000110111011 0111101110100000100000011101000110111100 1000 0001100010011001010010000001110100011010000

1100001011101000010000001101001011100110010 0000011101000110100001100101001000000111000 1011101010110010101110011011011101000110100 10 110111101101110

Ah, the beauty of language.

――――――
Note: Conversion by http://www.roubaixinteractive.com/ PlayGround/Binary_Conversion/Binary_To_Text.asp

phone number of a rather fabulous-looking individual – is the same sort of process as assigning a data chunk to some particular place in the computer's data memory. Being able to recall the phone number is taken as evidence that the number must have been represented and stored internally in memory. We have much more to say about human memory later in the book (see Chapters 10 and 11), but for now what we have done is summarise, briefly, the view of human memory as characterised by the computational metaphor. As we will see, such a view has been incredibly influential and forms the bedrock of much research on human memory.

## Information processing and the internal set of operations

In addition to internal representations, there are also internal processes. Within the physical symbol system these processes are captured by the so-called operators. These specify particular operations that can be carried out by the system. For instance, a symbol can be retrieved from the memory and copied into the control unit (designated Control in Figure 2.5) and therefore this symbol acts as the input to the control unit. *Retrieving* and *copying* are examples of basic operations. Other operations may then take place in the Control unit with the result that a different symbol is produced as output, and then stored in memory. Imagine a pile of dirty plates in the kitchen. The idea here is that the dirty plates are stored temporarily on the kitchen work surface, but in order for them to become clean, they must be operated upon. They must enter the sink (the Control unit), be washed and dried and returned to the cupboard.

Figure 2.5 provides examples of ten operators (i.e., the internal processes of ASSIGN, COPY . . . QUOTE, BEHAVE). These define possible processes that take place in the control unit, for instance, retrieving (i.e., reading) a symbol from memory, and storing (i.e., writing) a symbol to memory. In our kitchen example, the sink only allows for the WASH operation (SMASH, STACK or IGNORE are other operations, which may have some attractions, and probably feature in more real-world 'systems').

In setting out this particular framework for thinking, Newell (1980) drew the analogy that, there is a general level at which mental representations and mental processes map onto the sorts of representations and processes defined, respectively, in this kind of physical symbol system. In particular, it was assumed that, in discussing the mind, there is a well-defined set of

symbols and a well-defined set of operations that manipulate these symbols. In our computer example, however, the binary symbols are well defined – they must be of a certain length and can contain only 1s and 0s. By 'manipulate', reference is to the primitive sets operations as defined in Newell's symbol system (1980, fig. 4, i.e., READ, WRITE, etc.). Such operations as these are central to the idea that the mental processes are akin to the sets of instructions in computer software. Indeed such ideas as these are central to Newell's notion of control.

## Control

In general terms the understanding is that there is an overall program that specifies, for each current state of the Control unit, what the next state should be – this is essentially what a digital computer's operating system does. In pursuing this line of reasoning, Newell was wedded to the idea that the behaviour of any information processing system as defined as a physical symbol system is governed by a set of basic **rules of operation**. For him each of these rules specified an antecedent state (the before state) and consequent state (the after state), otherwise known as a **condition/action pair**. For instance, 'If the WRITE operator is active then STORE the currently active symbol in memory.' In other words, the rule may be interpreted as stating 'If condition $x$ (is satisfied) then take action $y$.' ('If the WASH operation is called for then scrub with hot, soapy water.'). This sort of rule is much like a primitive test such that if the condition of the rule matches the current state of the control unit then the action defined by the rule is invoked. It is useful to also remember that such rules of operation are stored in memory alongside all other forms of data.

We hinted at some of the rules of operation in our end-of-the-pier fruit machine introduction. For example, one of the first functions it must perform is to figure out how much money has been entered and whether it is enough to start playing. Therefore we can think of this as a SUM operation within the fruit machine, and when the total cash equals the required amount, then the PLAY routine is invoked. → See 'What have we learnt?', page 44.

→ See 'What have we learnt?', page 44.

### Pinpoint question 2.3

**What is the role of a control unit in a physical symbol system?**

## → What have we learnt?

In summary, in a physical symbol system (i) there is a set of well-defined symbols and operations, and (ii) the overall behaviour of the device is governed by a controlling program that specifies the rules of operation. That is, the control of the device is governed by a set of rules of operation that are specified in terms of condition/action pairs – if the condition is satisfied then invoke the action. Such rules of operation govern the order and timing of when the basic operators come into play (Newell, 1973, p. 297). The rules are represented in memory alongside the other forms of data. Such is the framework for thinking about human cognition that is provided by the computational metaphor of mind.

What has happened, though, is that over the years the computational metaphor has evolved into something much more like a theory – a computational theory of mind (Fodor, 1975, 1981b; Pinker, 1997). The theory has certain foundational assumptions, namely:

1. The mind contains internal representations (such as the data in the memory in Figure 2.5) that stand for (designate) aspects of the external world. Such representations comprise one or more symbols from a well-defined set: well-defined in the sense that for our 8-bit digital computer the symbol set contains all possible 8-bit patterns. It simply cannot deal with anything other than patterns in this well-defined set.

2. In addition to the internal representations referred to in point 1, internal processes are posited. Such processes are construed as being akin to the sorts of information processing operations that are carried out by a digital computer – such as reading and writing to memory. (Other examples such as COPY and ASSIGN have been provided by the sorts of operators defined by Newell in his description of a physical symbol system.)

3. Finally, in addition to the storage of data in memory, rules of operation are also stored (such as condition/action pairs discussed above). That is, there is some form of rule-specified control system that governs how the basic operators are deployed. These determine what should happen next given the present state of the system.

physical symbol system  A kind of symbol system, defined by Newell (1980), as comprising mental representations and mental processes as defined in computational terms.

symbolic representation  Some form of notational system used to denote, depict or represent an entity or set of entities.

rules of operation  Statements specifying condition/action pairs that determine and control computational processes.

condition/action pair  Conditional statement specifying that if a condition is met then the action will be taken. Discussed here in terms of the computational processes of control.

So far the discussion has explored how it is that minds and computers may be construed as being very similar devices. Clearly though, if we do not stop ourselves heading down this road, then we may end up concluding that we are all Mensch-Maschines (man-machines), as envisioned by those electronic music pioneers Kraftwerk (see Figure 2.6). Soon we will discuss the primary reasons that minds and computers are different, but for now we need to pursue the computational theory of mind a little further. This is because it sets out a rather provocative claim as to why it is that minds and computers are special. This relates to the notion of control mentioned in the third characteristic of the computational theory of mind set out above.

## The special nature of minds and computers

| Wir sind auf Alles programmiert | We are programmed just to do |
|---|---|
| Und was du willst wird ausgeführt | Anything you want us to |
| Wir sind die Roboter | We are the robots |

*Kraftwerk (1978). 'The Robots' on* The Man-Machine *(LP recording). Hollywood, CA: Capitol.*

## Rule-following vs. rule-governed systems

Theorists, such as Newell (1980), have taken the notion of control (in point 3 above) to mean 'defined by a rule-based system'. By this view, cognition is characterised, in part, by a system of rules that describes the set of mental operations that underlie all forms of intellectual ability. In this regard, the mind is seen to be a rule-following device. **Rule-following device**s may be distinguished relative to rule-governed devices.

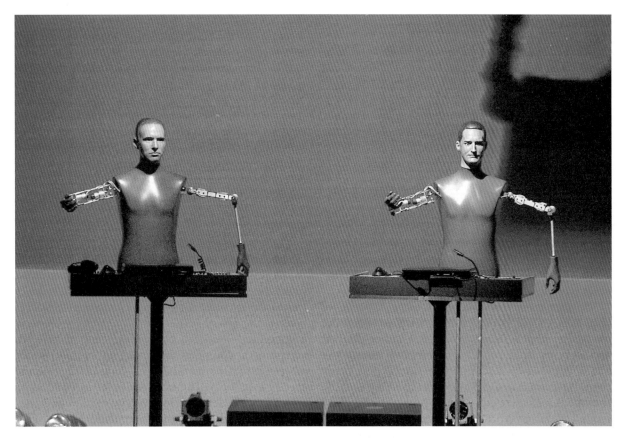

**Figure 2.6 How far should we take the computational metaphor of the mind?**
*Source*: John Alex Maguire/Rex Features.

**Rule-governed device**s are said to act in accordance with a set of rules. The critical difference between rule-following and rule-governed devices regards whether or not the rules are assumed to be embodied in the device. In our discussion of physical symbol systems (the paradigm rule-following device) we tried to emphasise the claim that the rules of operation of the device are stored alongside all other kinds of data. However, a critical concern is that even though we may be able to specify precisely the set of rules that perfectly predicts the behaviour of the device, this does not mean that such rules are represented within the device.

Reconsider our thermostat example in Chapter 1. The thermostat is a case of a rule-governed, not a rule-following device. Although it is possible to provide a rule-based account of the behaviour of the thermostat – we can explain how room temperature affects the internal workings of the thermostat – we do not need to assume that any form of rule that defines these relations is represented within its internal workings. By contrast, the notion of rule following applies only to cases where 'a representation of the rules they follow constitutes one of the causal determinants of their behavior' (Fodor, 1975, p. 74). So the critical difference is between cases where the rules of operation are represented and determine the behaviour of the device (rule following) and cases where the behaviour of the device can be merely explained by a set of rules (rule governed).

To be blunt, this is the distinction that sets apart computers (and any other form of programmable device) and minds from all other forms of devices. The claim is that both computers and minds contain rules of operation that govern their behaviour. Given this, the computational metaphor is limited to only these kinds of devices. There is computer software and there is mental software.

## Pinpoint question 2.4

**Why is a radiator not a rule-following device?**

## Mental computation

So what is really meant by the phrase 'mental software'? Central is the idea of 'computation', and this has been taken to refer to the operations defined in a physical symbol system. It is important to distinguish this interpretation of the term 'computation' from an unnecessary connotation relating to arithmetic or, more generally, mathematical operations. In more common usage there is the notion of computing defined relative to some form of number puzzle. In the present context, though, the terms 'computation' and 'computational' are used in reference to the basic operations defined in the physical symbol system just described, for example, shifting, transforming, storing, copying, reading and writing information. In this regard we need to keep our ideas about mathematics and computation quite separate.

Why are these concerns of importance? Well, we need to take stock of what has been argued. What the physical symbol system provides is a rather detailed and specific framework for thinking about the functional level of description that underpins many cognitive accounts of behaviour. In fleshing out the computational metaphor of the mind, the physical symbol system lays bare what the intended meaning of *information processing* is and it sets out, in fairly basic terms, what memory may be like. That is, memory is an internal store of information wherein the stored information represents aspects of the external world. Remembering, in this scheme, is recovering information from the internal store, and learning, in part, means storing new information in the internal store.

In addition, this computational metaphor also implies some overall 'program' of control. By this view there is a general sense in which the mind is governed by a set of basic rules of operation that specify causal relations between mental states. These rules of operation define the mental software. If the current state matches the condition for Rule *x* then the action of Rule *x* will be brought about. In this way we have been able to specify the operation of an automatic machine such that it 'works away by itself, reading and writing moving to and fro . . . At every step its behaviour would be completely determined by the configuration it was in and the symbol it had read' (Hodges, 1983, p. 98).

In adopting the computational metaphor, we have characterised the mind as an abstract machine independently of its physical instantiation. Our actual machine could be made of hydraulic components, ropes and pulleys, transistors, water pumps, etc., but in accepting the computational theory of mind we are accepting an account couched in mechanistic terms. At a very basic level, the physical symbol system provides a framework for thinking in which the mind is viewed as being very much the same sort of complex machine as a digital computer. So in accepting the computational theory of mind, the theorist may be described as providing a **mechanistic account** of some form of cognition. As with every other sort of machine, the operations of the mind are seen to obey deterministic principles of cause and effect. Thereby we are able to avoid any discussion of free will at all.

## The formality condition

We have come a long way from our simple behaviourist beginnings and, to be fair, much of what is assumed in the computational theory of mind gives rise to quite heated debate even among cognitive psychologists. Is it really the case that the mind is nothing more than a computer? We need exert some caution here. In accepting the computational metaphor of mind we are accepting that both minds and computers are quite special sorts of machines and similar in both being rule-following devices. However, we need to be somewhat cautious because the computational theory of mind may only take us so far in understanding human nature. It seems that even if we are able to provide adequate functional accounts of some aspects of cognition, we may still be left with the nagging doubt that we have left something out (see Wilton, 2000, for a much more thorough exposition of these ideas).

In this regard, we need to consider in a little more detail how is it that computers compute. In this context a critical term is formal because we can say that our physical symbol system (our abstract machine) is a **formal system**. Again there may be unnecessary connotations, such as getting dressed up to go to a job interview, or using 'vous' instead of 'tu' in French, but a quite different sense is implied in the current context. In using the term 'formal' the connotation is with respect to form or structure. For instance, the fact that the symbols '0010' and '0010' are the same is because they have the same form.

This may seem blindingly obvious, but stick with it. If we ask our computer to compare two symbols (two binary patterns), what it will do is check off each bit in one with the corresponding bit in the other – it will see if the form of the symbols is identical with respect to one another. Therefore it is quite correct to state that the computer is a formal system because its operations are governed only by the form of the symbols, and not by what they stand for, designate or represent. Fodor (1980) has referred to this as the *formality condition*. The computer will do one thing when 00001010 is copied to the CPU and another thing when 00001011 is copied into it. Therefore it really is true that the computer is nothing other than a dumb deterministic machine. This is despite the fact that computers are incredibly useful to have around. Just think – without them, no eBay, YouTube or even MySpace.

Another way of thinking about this is that the computer has no conception of whether you are registering online for a dating service or playing an online game of Texas Hold-'Em. The computer distinguishes one symbol from another because the different symbols cause the computer to do uniquely different things. Critically, though, the computer has no conception of what, if anything, the symbols refer to. It neither knows nor cares whether the symbol such as 01010010 signifies the colour of a pixel on the computer screen, the intensity of a sound it is emitting from its speakers, or indeed a word in a Shakespearian sonnet.

By contrast, humans (typically) do know that their thoughts and feelings are about particular things (see Churchland, 1984, p. 63). For instance, when someone says, 'Please pass the salt,' they are referring to the particular salt cellar just outside their grasp. Thoughts and feelings are with reference to (are about) particular things and typically with reference to things in the external world. This sort of so-called 'aboutness' is known as **intentionality**, and, according to Searle (1980), no amount of computer programming or computational theory is going to help us understand intentionality. In this respect our computational theory may not be much help in understanding intentionality at all (see for instance Fodor, 2000).

## The formality condition and strong AI

In the foregoing we have accepted that AI refers to research concerned with attempting to write computer programs that behave in ways that mimic human cognitive abilities. However, Searle (1994) discussed a more specific distinction between different flavours of AI, namely that between **weak AI** and **strong AI**.

In undertaking weak AI, the aim is to write a computer program in such a way that the process of writing and refining the program aids our understanding of some aspect of human cognition. For instance, we may have certain ideas about how people recognise faces and we feel that we can gain a better under-standing of this if we attempt to program a computer to recognise faces. A useful description of weak AI was provided, incidentally, by Newell, Shaw and Simon back in the 1950s (1958). According to them, an ultimate aim is to develop an explanation of an observed behaviour by providing 'a program of primitive information processes that generates this behaviour' (p. 151).

Strong AI is based on quite different assumptions, and a central claim now is that a properly programmed computer 'is not merely a tool in the study of the mind: rather (it) is a mind in the sense that computers given the right programs can be literally said to understand and have other cognitive states' (Searle, 1980, p. 417). That is, as long as you can derive a computer program that mimics perfectly some aspect of human intellectual behaviour then both the human and the computer possess the same mental states and processes. Indeed, a critical implication of adopting functionalism is the possibility that devices other than humans can have 'mental' states (Fodor, 1981a) – yes, your very own laptop might actually be capable of thought after all!

If the computer simulation of mental addition is indistinguishable in terms of its behaviour from a human doing mental addition then functionalism attributes the same mental states to the computer and the mind. The operations contained in the computer's program are assumed to correspond with mental operations in virtue of their corresponding functional roles. Both the human and the computer are claimed to be doing mental arithmetic, so we really do have an argument here for the thinking computer.

However, a moment's thought about the formality condition should allow us to resist this conclusion. In considering the formality condition, it has been argued that functionalism may not provide answers to some of the fundamental questions about what it is to be a sentient being. For instance, although we are very likely to make some progress in understanding the sorts of cognitive operations that humans engage in, by adopting the functionalist theoretical framework, we are very unlikely to make any progress in understanding the nature of subjective feelings, affect and emotions by adopting such a framework. Despite the claims of strong AI, a working computer simulation may not provide the final answers to the questions about what it is to be human: for whereas the human knows and thinks about the external world, the computer does not. The computer only has access to its internal representations that consist merely of 1s and 0s. It has no conception of what these representations stand for, designate or mean. On these grounds it seems that there is little sense in asserting that your PC thinks, has emotions or is conscious of anything whosoever.

Much has been written on these types of issues over the years (see Fodor, 1975, 1980, 2000; Searle, 1980, 1994, 2001; Wilton, 2000) and to pursue them further would take us into the provenance of the philosophy of mind rather than empirical cognitive psychology. As Morris and Hampson (1983, pp. 53–4) wrote, 'Consciousness is not something we know how to incorporate into our theorising. It may be necessary to give consciousness a central place, but as yet no one has suggested either how consciousness makes possible any sort of cognitive functioning which could not be carried out by an unconscious system, nor, indeed, any way in which consciousness per se could contribute at all' (see Wilton, 2000, ch. 1, for further discussion). So we will need to tread very carefully whenever we are tempted to appeal to the notion of consciousness as an explanatory construct.

So where does this lead us to? On the one hand, much of the content of this book rests on adopting the functionalist framework. The belief is that we can make significant progress in understanding human cognition by adopting a functionalist approach. This allows us to study mental states and processes and try to map out those particular mental states and processes that intervene between specific stimuli and their responses. However, on the other hand, we accept that this approach may not provide answers to all the questions we might like to ask about human nature. → See 'What have we learnt?', below.

## Pinpoint question 2.5

**Why does strong AI bridge the gap between computers and humans?**

## → What have we learnt?

We have examined the fact that cognitive psychologists have embraced the computational metaphor in putting forward their accounts of human cognition. This metaphor has been described and foundational ideas to information processing accounts of cognition have been explored. Further discussion has been directed at issues concerning the nature of computation. Particular attention has been paid to the operations undertaken by a digital computer as these provide a useful basis for understanding mental computation as defined in a physical symbol system.

Functionalism has been discussed at some length and some implications of adopting this doctrine have been spelt out. Despite the tremendous success that has followed from adopting functional accounts of the mind, some caution has also been expressed over the degree to which this approach can help answer some of the bigger questions we may ask about what it is to be a human being. So although we may gather together minds and computers under the category of rule-following devices, accounting for one may only provide limited insights into accounting for the other.

**rule-following device** A device acting according to a set of rules which are represented within the device itself (i.e., minds and computers).

**rule-governed device** A device acting according to a set of rules which are not represented within the device itself.

**mechanistic account** One which details operations that could be undertaken by some form of machine or device.

**formal system** A notational system governed by the form of symbols (their structure) with no reference to what those symbols represent or mean.

**intentionality** When thoughts and feelings refer to particular things in the world.

**weak AI** One version of artificial intelligence in which computer modelling is taken to be a methodological tool that aids our understanding of human cognition.

**strong AI** One version of artificial intelligence in which an appropriately programmed computer is assumed to have the same sorts of mental states as humans.

## PART 2
## So what is the mind really like?

In Part 1 of this chapter, we have spent quite a lot of time exploring the computational theory of mind, and we are now in a position to appreciate the limitations of this approach. It provides very useful guidelines defining a particular methodological approach to the study of human cognition, but it may be ill equipped to provide answers to all the questions we may wish to ask (see Fodor, 2000, for more on this). Nevertheless, the basic theoretical landscape inhabited by cognitive psychology has now been mapped out, and we can begin to address more detailed questions about what the mind is really like.

We are now in a position to focus on how the mind might be constituted, and here our concerns turn to what are known as structural or architectural considerations. Indeed there are those who are quite happy to discuss these issues in terms of the so-called **functional architecture** of the mind (Fodor, 1983). To appreciate this, however, we will need to examine different notions of *modularity*, and eventually we will consider a particular version of modularity known as the **modularity hypothesis** (Fodor, 1983, 1985). It is only fair, at the outset, to be open and admit that not all cognitive psychologists are entirely happy with the details of the modularity hypothesis (see for example Marshall, 1984; Putnam, 1984; Shallice, 1984), but this should not detain us unnecessarily. The main point behind discussing the hypothesis here is that it provides a useful context for considering competing ideas about how the mind is constituted. First, we will consider how Marr (1982) approached the issue of modularity and then discussion focuses on the writings of Fodor (1983).

> **functional architecture** A specification of the components of an information processing system, how they are interconnected and what functions the components serve.
>
> **modularity hypothesis** The idea that the mind may be decomposed into smaller and discrete sub-processes (or modules) (after Fodor, 1983).

## Marr's principle of modular design

The first use of the term 'modularity' is not associated with Fodor, but with Marr (1982). Marr (1982) was particularly interested in something he termed the *principle of modular design* (p. 102) and he advanced the argument in terms of the example of a computer programmer who is designing a large and complex computer program. One approach to this problem has already been sketched out in terms of the example of designing and building a car engine (see Chapter 1). The central idea is to break down the overall endeavour into manageable sub-projects where each sub-project maps onto a particular component (or module). In terms of designing a computer program, though, the analogy is with respect of parts of the program known as **sub-routines** that we may otherwise call modules. Here the idea is that the program can be divided into separate modules that can be developed independently of any other part of the program. Indeed with very large software packages, each sub-routine will have its own dedicated set of programmers who collectively work to develop it: the final package is then pieced together from all these different sub-routines.

Take for example your 'favourite' graph drawing package. Within the program, there may be a whole set of sub-routines that are concerned with getting input from the keyboard and checking that the input corresponds to what is expected – for example, checking the input contains numbers rather than letters. Other parts of the program will then be concerned with carrying out different operations, such as drawing a graph of the inputted numbers. The point is that, at the design-and-build stages, the sub-routines for checking the input and those for drawing the graph can be developed independently of one another.

Although Marr (1982) wrote with respect to implementing large and complex computer programs, his points should be taken as applying, by analogy, to the evolution of intellectual capabilities. According to him, there are clear advantages in having a complex system evolve along the lines of being composed of many 'small, nearly independent specialised sub-processes' (or modules, p. 325). One particular claimed advantage of having a system evolve like this is that it becomes resistant to damage – it exhibits **resistance to damage**. That is, if the system is composed of independent (although) interconnected components, then damage to one component need not have catastrophic consequences for the operation of the other components.

To invoke the programming example again, if the computer program comprised just one monolithic set of instructions then a change in any one instruction would have consequences for all ensuing instructions. In this respect, any changes in the program would have implications for the whole system. In contrast, if the program is composed of independent routines, then it is possible to see how damage to one routine could have hardly any negative consequences for other routines in the program.

Finally, Marr (1982) was also particularly taken with this principle of modular design because it allowed for a degree of operational independence across the different core components. So with our graph drawing package, although the input checking routines do not depend on whether the graph drawing routines are working correctly, the converse is not true: unless the graph drawing routines get the right sort of numbers then the graph will not be drawn. More generally, the idea is that within a complex information processing system, the different modules can be getting on with their own tasks quite independently of what is going on in other parts of the system. → See 'What have we learnt?', page 51.

## Pinpoint question 2.6

**Would you prefer to fly in a modular or non-modular airplane and why?**

## Research focus 2.1

### We are not amusia-ed: is music modularised?

While we can discuss the modularity of video game design of fruit machine operation, a far more intriguing prospect (and, we hope, one of the reasons that you're reading this book) is the idea that certain mental faculties such as musical comprehension could be modularised too. Anyone who has listened to somebody tone-deaf singing in the shower will probably not have stopped to contemplate whether it is merely this individual's pitch system, rather than their rhythmic system, that has gone awry. However, Piccirilli, Sciarma and Luzzi (2000) did address these concerns in a **single-case study**.

In December 1997, a 20-year-old male was referred to Piccirilli et al. (2000) complaining of violent headaches, which were also accompanied by the onset of a language disorder. After a brain scan, the patient was shown to have a haematoma (a blood clot) in the left temporal region of the brain (just above the ear). After treatment, damage to the brain was found at the site of the haematoma. While substantial improvement was observed for the language disorder that initially indicated the presence of the haematoma, the patient began to complain: 'Sounds are empty and cold. Singing sounds like shouting to me. When I hear a song, it sounds familiar at first but then I can't recognise it' (p. 542). The authors then sought to investigate whether the patient was suffering from something called amusia – basically a loss in the comprehension or production of tonal music.

In completing a **battery of tests**, the patient performed within the normal range on over 30 procedures that sought to tackle a variety of verbal and non-verbal cognitive abilities. Moreover, the patient could recognise environmental sounds such as typewriters and trains, and could distinguish between male and female voices as well as foreign languages. While the male patient was able to recognise different types of musical instrument as a result of their different timbral properties, and also distinguish between different kinds of rhythm, severe difficulty was expressed in the recognition of familiar melodies and also for memories of tones.

Piccirilli et al. (2000) concluded that damage in the left temporal area of the brain (the left superior temporal gyrus, if you want to get technical) was related to the specific deficit in pitch perception experienced by the patient. Moreover, the data were interesting in the respect that other domains related to music perception were not damaged, such as the ability to distinguish a rhumba from a cha-cha-cha, or a French horn from a clarinet. Therefore the processing of music appears to be modular, with individual modules being responsible for pitch, timbre and rhythm. That's still cold comfort when you have to listen to those in-the-shower superstars, but at least if they can't sing, then their capacity for rhythm might be intact such that they might still be able to make a good drummer.

*Source*: Piccirilli, M., Sciarma, T., & Luzzi, S. (2000). Modularity of music: Evidence from a case of pure amusia. *Journal of Neurology, Neurosurgery and Psychiatry, 69*, 541–545.

## → What have we learnt?

What Marr (1982) has provided here are a set of a priori reasons as to why cognitive psychologists may be right to pursue theories based on the sorts of arrows-and-boxes diagrams discussed in Chapter 1 (see Figure 1.6). Here, in brief, is the argument. Cognitive psychologists believe that one useful way to proceed is to provide functional accounts of the mind based on the notion of **modular decomposition**. That is, they believe that it is right to attempt to set out a description of putative internal component processes that intervene between stimuli and their associated responses. By this view, stimulation of the sense organs eventuates in an internal signal that represents properties of the external world, and different component processes (modules) may be invoked as the signal is propagated through the information processing system. We therefore decompose the information processing system into its constituent modules such that each of these corresponds to a different box in our arrows-and-boxes diagram. Such is the first notion of modularity that has been discussed in the literature.

**sub-routines** Smaller sections of a larger program which can run independently of one another.

**resistance to damage** The way in which a larger system can still retain its functions even though some components of the system fail. The lights on the car have gone out but the engine keeps on turning.

**single-case study** Research that involves the examination of only a single participant's performance. Most typically used in cognitive neuropsychological research.

**battery of tests** A series of psychological tests carried out in order to assess an individual's ability across a number of domains.

**modular decomposition** Specifying the intervening component processes involved in some functional account of the mind.

## Other conceptions of modularity

The second notion of modularity that has been discussed in the literature is contained in Fodor's (1983) modularity hypothesis, but to understand this it is important to adopt something of an historical context. In introducing these ideas Fodor began by discussing what he called 'Faculty Psychology' – a loosely held set of beliefs that maintains that the mind is composed of very many different sort of special-purpose components. According to Marshall (1984), the bases of these ideas may be traced back to the Ancient Greek philosopher Aristotle. Aristotle's framework for thinking starts with consideration of the five sense modalities (sight, sound, touch, smell and taste), which map onto the respective sense organs (eyes, ears, viscera, nose and tongue). It is the sense organs that are ultimately responsible for sensory encoding or, alternatively, **sensory transduction**.

Sensory transduction is the process by which stimulation of the sense organs is transformed into an internal signal that is subject to further processing. (Recall our earlier discussion of information processing defined in the context of a communication system.) According to this view, sensory transduction associated with each of the sense organs eventuates in information being transformed into a common perceptual code – information presented in any modality is rendered into the same code. Light entering the eyes and sound entering the ears are transformed into signals in the same code. This code is then operated on 'in sequence, by the faculties of perception, imagination, reason and memory' and each of these faculties 'effected its own intrinsic operations upon input representations irrespective of the nature or type of those representations' (Marshall, 1984, p. 213).

## The nature of horizontal faculties

Defined in this way, the faculties of perception, imagination, reason and memory are what Fodor (1983) labelled **horizontal faculties**. In simple terms, horizontal faculties reflect general competencies that cut across different domains. For instance, many cognitive abilities may be conceived as containing a memory component and, therefore, memory can be construed as a horizontal faculty. To clarify this, let us reconsider the mental arithmetic example discussed in Chapter 1.

Here the task was to work out two different products (e.g., $17 \times 3$ and $14 \times 5$) and compare these to see which was greater. By a very simplistic account, the assumption is that performance in the task depends, to some extent, on memory: the answer to the first question must be retained until the answer to the second product is derived. It is only then that the two quantities may be compared. In this regard, it is legitimate to argue that the task depends on memory. So one limitation, in being able to complete the task, can be attributed to memory. If this is not so obvious, imagine what it would be like to report the largest of five or six such products without the aid of pencil and paper. Memory can therefore be construed as a horizontal faculty insofar as similar memory constraints underlie other quite unrelated competencies, such as trying to learn a poem off by heart. According to Fodor (1983), horizontal faculties are defined with respect to what they do and are not defined in terms of what they operate on. For instance, the same memory limit applies to numbers as it does to poems.

## The nature of vertical faculties: a different kind of pot head

In contrast to carving up the mind in terms of horizontal faculties or horizontal strips, the alternative is to consider vertical strips. That is, we may also conceive of **vertical faculties**. So what are vertical faculties? Fodor (1983) cited the work of Francis Joseph Gall (1758–1828). Gall's idea was that the mind is composed of distinct mental organs, with each mental organ defined with respect to a specific content domain (Marshall, 1984, p. 215). For instance, there is a mental organ that underlies musical ability and a different mental organ that underlies the domain of mathematics, and so on and so forth. So whereas horizontal faculties are defined with respect to what they do, vertical faculties are defined with reference to their subject matter; for example, music, mathematics, language, etc. We might describe the amusia patient in Research focus 2.1 as losing a vertical faculty.

Having made such a strong assertion, Gall went further and argued that each of these different mental organs could be identified with a unique region of the brain. That is, he firmly believed that individual intellectual abilities, such as being musically adept, were directly linked with particular brain regions – that there really was a distinct area of the brain that embodies a special-purpose mechanism for music and a different brain region that embodies a special-purpose mechanism for mathematics. This view formed the basis of Gall's **phrenology** where particular bumps on the head could be interpreted as being associated with particular regions of the brain. Each of these regions embodied a particular intellectual ability and

the prominence of the bump was indicative to the size of the underlying brain region, the simple notion being that increased size was indicative of how well developed the corresponding cognitive function was. (See, in some contexts, size does matter!) Clearly such ideas were taken very seriously because pot heads based on the scheme shown in Figure 2.7 were produced. Having one of these meant it was now very easy to pinpoint where inside the human head each intellectual faculty was supposed to reside.

To return to our mental arithmetic example, by the vertical faculty characterisation, all of the aspects of the task reflect the operation of the mathematical mental organ. Even though there may well be memory constraints associated with the task, these constraints should not be taken as being indicative of cognitive limitations in general. In contrast, they should be construed as being specific to the mathematical mental organ. Knowledge about numbers and knowledge of particular arithmetic operations are also assumed to be contained within the mathematical mental organ.

Gall, in positing vertical faculties (mental organs), also provided a critique of the traditional view of horizontal faculties (Fodor, 1983, p. 16). The notion of general-purpose faculties for memory, perception, etc.,

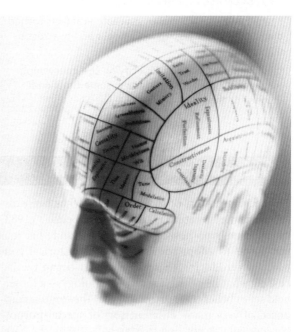

**Figure 2.7 There are pot heads and pot heads**
Phrenology – the attempt to associate particular mental faculties with specific regions of the brain as indicated by bumps on the head.
*Source*: Wolfgang Flamisch/Zeta/Corbis.

was dismissed in favour of a framework for thinking in which a whole battery of distinct mental organs are posited, each one of which has particular characteristics with respect to memory, perception and the like. Gall's vertical faculties 'do not share – and hence do not compete for – such horizontal resources as memory, attention, intelligence, judgment or whatever' (Fodor, 1983, p. 21).

Overall therefore it is possible to set aside the classical view of the mind from Gall's modular view because the two imply different functional architectures. The classic view posits general-purpose mechanisms that operate globally across all domains, whereas Gall posited distinct special-purpose mental organs, each with its own unique characteristics. Fodor (1983) proposed an alternative view and it is to this that we now turn.

## Pinpoint question 2.7

**What is the difference between vertical and horizontal faculties?**

sensory transduction Transforming stimulation of the sense organs into some form of internal signal.

horizontal faculties General competencies such as memory or attention that cut across all cognitive domains.

vertical faculties Specific competencies that reflect independent intellectual capacities, such as being a competent musician, language user, mathematician, etc. Such capacities are assumed to have domain-specific characteristics.

phrenology After Francis Joseph Gall (1758–1828), the idea that vertical faculties could be measured relative to the sizes of bumps on the head. Each bump was related to an underlying brain region.

## Fodor's modules

With the publication of Fodor's seminal book, *The Modularity of Mind* (1983), a quite different meaning of the term 'module' was introduced, and this can best be appreciated in terms of the functional architecture of the human mind that Fodor put forward. Fodor (1983) distinguished between sensory transducers, input systems and central processors. In thinking about what these are, a distinction that you may find

helpful is that between the proximal and the distal stimulus. The **proximal stimulus** is the stimulation of the sense organs, whereas the **distal stimulus** is the actual external object responsible for the sensory stimulation. For example, the distal stimulus could be a stereo system and therefore the associated proximal stimulus would be the sound vibrations you receive in the ear when you play some music.

The sensory transducers are the sense organs, and are responsible for taking the proximal stimulus and converting this into a basic sensory code. This coding then acts as the input to the corresponding input system. For Fodor (1983), input systems are the modules referred to in the modularity hypothesis. In simple terms, modules operate as the interface between the sensory transducers and the central processors. They deliver to the central processors (what amounts to) the best first guess of what the distal stimulus is that gave rise to the sensory stimulation. We can call this representation of the sensory stimulation the stimulus representation. The final decision, about what the distal stimulus may actually be, is made by the central processors. As Marshall (1984, p. 216) stated, 'Central processors are concerned with the fixation of belief (including perceptual belief) and the planning of intelligent action.' The fixation of a perceptual belief is the act of making a final decision about what the distal stimulus is. Figure 2.8 provides a schematic representation of the basic ideas.

All the really interesting things about thinking, believing and feeling are undertaken by the central processors. Although Fodor (2000) was happy to admit that cognitive psychologists have made much progress in understanding the operation of the input systems (the modules), he also claimed that the operation of the central processors remains essentially unknown. So at the heart of Fodor's functional architecture of the mind lies a very black box indeed! The black box contains the central processors and, according to Fodor, we know hardly anything about their operation at all (Fodor, 2000). Nevertheless, the general distinction between input mechanisms and central mechanism recurs time and time again in the literature, and we will constantly be considering the nature of this distinction as we proceed.

Many vexed questions remain and it is premature to discuss these issues in detail in advance of considering the nature of perception. However, in broad strokes, what we have here is a view of the mind in which the sense organs are fundamental. Stimulation of the sense organs is converted into some form of internal codes that are fed into the corresponding

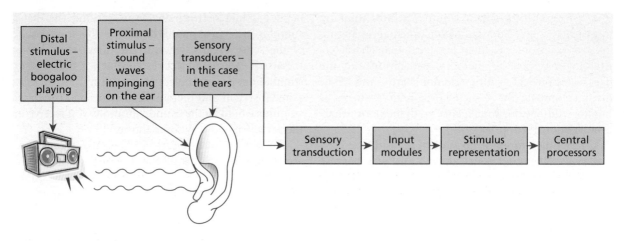

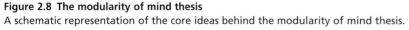

**Figure 2.8 The modularity of mind thesis**
A schematic representation of the core ideas behind the modularity of mind thesis.

input modules. The modules take the sensory codes and convert these into internal representations that code rough guesses as to what the distal stimuli are. However, it is the central processors that arrive at a decision about what it is that is out there. The central processors assign meaning to the proximal stimulus on the basis of the information delivered by the input modules together with relevant world knowledge.

## How is it best to characterise modules?

In setting out the nature of the modules, Fodor (1983) provided a description of a number of their characteristics. Not all of these are relevant in the present discussion, but one that is, is the claim that modules are **domain-specific**. At first glance, it might appear that this is referring to the possibility that there is a different module for each of the separate sense modalities. However, Fodor made a different suggestion; namely, that there are many more modules than sense organs. For example, he argued that the visual system comprises many different modules, each of which takes on a different job: separate modules exist for 'color perception, for the analysis of shape and for the analysis of three-dimensional spatial relations' (Fodor, 1983, p. 47).

Within the domain of language processing, Fodor (1983) discussed, at some length, the possibility that different modules exist for encoding different sorts of linguistic input. More particularly, he alluded to special-purpose modules for the analysis of visual and spoken language, respectively. In this context the concerns are with the processes responsible for the analysis of written language and separately for speech, and, that these, respectively, map onto different types of language modules. In this way a particular input module is posited for a specific domain of processing.

A more recent proposal has been ventured by Coltheart (1999) who stated that 'a cognitive system (*i.e., a module*) is domain-specific if it only responds to stimuli of a particular class' (such as the class of colours; p. 118, text in italics added). By way of example, Coltheart speculated that there might exist a module responsible purely for face recognition: such a module only comes into play with faces and for no other sort of visual object.

What is going on here is that assumptions are being made about how the mind might be composed of different sorts of processing modules, and how such modules can be defined with reference to a particular subject matter (or domain), for example, text recognition, speech recognition, face recognition, etc. The problems associated with trying to establish the number and type of modules, though, are set aside for experimental cognitive psychologists to answer. The overriding theoretical claim is that different modules operate in different domains, and they are defined in terms of these domains. → See 'What have we learnt?', page 55.

**Pinpoint question 2.8**

**What does it mean for a module to be domain-specific?**

## → What have we learnt?

According to Fodor (1983), cognitive psychologists can make the most progress by thinking about the operation of the mind in terms of information processing modules. In contrast to the classical idea of the mind comprising horizontal faculties, and Gall's notion that the mind comprises vertical faculties, Fodor described a different position. He advocated a framework for thinking in which various input systems (modules) correspond to vertical faculties and these operate as input systems to central systems (that are themselves contained in an innermost black box). Each input module is viewed as a special-purpose (domain-specific) computational device that transforms sensory information into a form that is then subject to further analyses. It is the job of the central systems to make sense of (that is, assign meaning to) the outputs from the input modules.

---

**proximal stimulus** Stimulation of the sense organs that is caused by a particular distal stimulus.

**distal stimulus** The external entity in the outside world from which stimulation of the sense organs arises.

**domain-specific** The notion that individual processing modules are responsible for a discrete aspect of processing. For example, there is a particular module responsible for colour perception and a different module for pitch perception, etc.

## Modularity and cognitive neuropsychology

Apart from the domain-specific nature of modules, Fodor examined other assumed characteristics of the processing modules, two of which deserve further attention now. These are that:

1. Modules are associated with fixed neural architecture (where fixed neural architecture refers to the adult human brain in which the structure does not change).
2. Modules exhibit characteristic and specific breakdown patterns.

Both of these characteristics are very much in line with Gall's ideas concerning independent mental organs and both concern mind/brain relations. In this regard, it is undeniably true that if we accept points (1) and (2) as being defining characteristics of information processing modules, then we are conceding that a critical dependency relation holds between the mind and brain. If the brain is damaged then it is very likely that there will be negative consequences at the cognit-ive level. More particularly, the claim is that direct evidence of these claims can be forthcoming from the study of the cognitive performance of individuals with particular forms of brain damage. Such research is known collectively as *cognitive neuropsychology* and this clearly is implicated when we consider points (1) and (2) as set out above. Indeed cognitive neuropsychologists accept that much can be learnt about the cognitive level when brains do not function normally. In particular, they accept that evidence from brain-damaged individuals can provide converging evidence for particular functional accounts and may also provide critical constraints for such accounts.

## Cognitive neuropsychology

Both points (1) and (2) above are fundamental assumptions that underpin cognitive neuropsychology (see Coltheart, 2001). In turn, much of the evidence from cognitive neuropsychological studies has traditionally been used to bolster claims about the modular nature of mind (see for instance the collected papers in Rapp, 2001). So what does neuropsychological evidence look like and how is it best interpreted?

Cognitive neuropsychology is an umbrella phrase for research concerning the operation of disordered brains. *Developmental cognitive neuropsychology* is the branch of the discipline concerned with brain disorders that develop as a person ages and that lead to some form of cognitive impairment. Such problems may arise because of certain adverse genetic factors or problems during pregnancy or birth. In contrast to such **developmental disorders**, there are also **acquired disorders**. Acquired disorders occur during the normal course of development and arise when the brain is damaged through injury or illness. Given that this book is primarily concerned with adult human cognition, we will focus on acquired rather than developmental disorders.

In adopting the cognitive neuropsychological approach, the theorist attempts to understand the cognitive deficits following brain damage, by accepting certain key assumptions. Some of these are shared with cognitive psychology in general. For instance, Coltheart (2001) discussed the foundational assumption that the same functional architecture is assumed to operate in all normal individuals. According to Coltheart (2001), cognitive psychology would simply fail in its endeavours if 'different individuals had different functional architectures for the same cognitive domain' (p. 10). If it were accepted that different individuals carry with them radically different functional architectures then attempting to generalise from one individual to another is essentially pointless. Remember, if we are trying to pursue a science of cognitive psychology then we are attempting to establish general principles that apply across individuals. Such generalisations can only hold if the underlying functional architecture is the same across different individuals. Critically though, in accepting the basic point about 'the same functional architecture', we are actually accepting point (1); namely, that information processing modules are associated with fixed neural architectures. → See 'What have we learnt?', page 57.

## Research focus 2.2

## Life after trauma: the astonishing case of Phineas Gage and the iron rod

A rather spectacular case of an acquired brain disorder is that provided by the example of Phineas Gage. Gage, an American railway construction worker, living in the middle of the nineteenth century, survived an horrific work-related accident in which a 3'8" long 13.5-pound iron rod exploded through his forehead and removed large portions of his left frontal lobes (i.e., brain structures just behind the left side of the forehead). Figure 2.9 reveals a present-day reconstruction of the path of the rod through Gage's frontal lobes, and although it has been generally accepted that damage was specific to his ventromedial prefrontal cortex, we will never actually know what specific structures were actually damaged (see Wagar & Thagard, 2004).

The first surprise was that Gage actually survived the passing of the iron rod through his head. The second, perhaps more theoretically interesting finding, was that, although Gage underwent a major personality change after the accident, the majority of his cognitive faculties remained largely intact (see Selnes, 2001). Initially this was taken as evidence against a strictly modular view of the brain – the fact that so much of the frontal lobes were damaged and yet there was very little cognitive impairment was taken as evidence against strict localisation of function. Apparently no particular cognitive ability was impaired (i.e., from being localised in the frontal lobes). However, in a later reinterpretation it was claimed that the changes in personality were consistent with damage to something known as supervisory or executive functions. Gage now exhibited

lack of self-control. He was now 'fitful, irreverent, and grossly profane', and according to Wagar and Thagard (2004), 'He was . . . unable to settle on any plans he devised for future actions.' Consequently 'he lost all his friends and was unable to hold down a job' (Wagar & Thagard, 2004, p. 68).

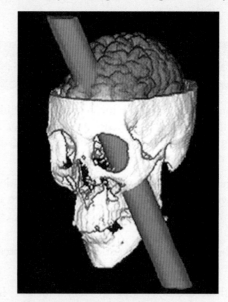

**Figure 2.9 Phineas Gage and his iron rod**
A reconstruction of the path that an iron rod took through Phineas Gage's frontal lobes. Ouch!

*Source*: Damasio, H., Grabowski, T., Frank, R., Galaburda, A. M., & Damasio, A. R. (1994). The return of Phineas Gage: clues about the brain from the skull of a famous patient, *Science, 264(5162)*, 1102–1105. Reproduced with permission from AAAS.

The Phineas Gage case is particularly striking for a number of reasons. First, the fact that Phineas was able to live through this quite horrific injury meant that his behaviour could be observed after this traumatic event. Such observations have since been used to infer what cognitive functions the missing parts of his brain were responsible for at a cognitive level. Second, the case was important as it is a relatively rare example of *clean damage*: while the damage was extensive, it was also localised. The case stands in contrast to the many other cases of acquired disorders that arise following stroke, asphyxiation, viral infection, etc. in which the damage is diffuse and affects many brain regions. With diffuse damage many different areas are affected and so the mapping between brain and cognitive functioning becomes impossible to grasp.

*Source*: Wagar, B. M., & Thagard, P. (2004). Spiking Phineas Gage: A neurocomputational theory of cognitive–affective integration in decision making. *Psychological Review, 111*, 67–79.

## → What have we learnt?

Cognitive neuropsychology is wedded to the idea that functional architecture may be characterised as an information processing system composed of independent, special-purpose processing modules where each module corresponds with a particular box in an arrows-and-boxes flow diagram. The traditional cognitive neuropsychological approach to thinking about how brain damage affects the mind is in terms of sketching out an information processing arrows-and-boxes diagram and by assuming that there is a relatively straightforward mapping between parts shown in the diagram and parts of the brain. Accounting for decrements in performance now reduces to lesioning (cutting out) or damaging certain routes and/or components within the diagram on the understanding that these correspond to damaged parts of the brain.

In this respect, the evidence from cognitive neuropsychological studies is taken to inform functional accounts of human cognition that have been developed from observing the performance of normal functioning participants. It is in this way that cognitive neuropsychology and cognitive psychology can be seen as being complementary disciplines.

## Pinpoint question 2.9

**How does the case study of Phineas Gage support a modular view of the mind?**

## The logic of the cognitive neuropsychological approach

In practice, cognitive neuropsychology is primarily concerned with the patterns of similarities and differences between normal cognitive abilities and the abilities of those who possess a disordered/damaged brain. Typically, interest is with the performance across a whole battery of tests. Within the battery, each test is designed to examine a particular cognitive operation. Cognitive neuropsychology is distinctive in that it is the intensive study of single cases that is central. In any given study, the single case is a person or 'patient' who presents with some form of brain damage. Performance of the patient on the battery of tests is then compared with individuals with intact brains (also known as **control participants**). Comparisons across the whole profile of test scores are then carried out.

It is assumed that the modular decomposition of the mind can be worked out by examining how performance across a number of tasks is affected by brain damage. Various possible outcomes are possible and these are discussed in detail next.

## Association deficits

Relative to the profile of control participants, one sort of patient deficit that might arise is known as an **association deficit**. This is where the patient performs poorly on, say, two different tests. For example, the patient is impaired in understanding both written and spoken words (Coltheart, 2001). This pair of impairments is said to be associated because they arise in the same person. It might be tempting to conclude that performance in both tests (i.e., comprehending text and speech) depends on the operation of a single underlying module that has been damaged in the particular patient. You should be clear that even though this is a possible conclusion, it is *not* a *necessary* conclusion. To see this, think of a different functional architecture in which each test depends on the normal operation of its own underlying module. Damage may have occurred to both of these modules.

## Dissociation deficits

Funnell (1983) reported one patient who was able to read aloud more than 90 per cent of words but was unable to read even the simplest non-word correctly ('dreed' was read as 'deared' and 'ploon' as 'spoon'). With such characteristic cases, the abilities (in this example, reading words and reading non-words, respectively) are said to dissociate because, within the same person, one is impaired but the other remains intact. Therefore, a **single dissociation** or, more simply, a **dissociation deficit** occurs when the patient performs well on task A (i.e., performs within the normal range on task A) but poorly on task B. A dissociation deficit may also arise when the patient performs poorly on both tasks but is particularly impaired on one relative to the other.

It is easy to see, therefore, how finding a single dissociation might lead you immediately to claim evidence for the operation of cognitive modules – with module *a* being responsible for performance in task A and a different module *b* being responsible for performance in task B. Maybe there are different modules that underlie the reading of words and the reading of non-words respectively? Unfortunately, though, this line of reasoning is not completely watertight because of the following.

## Cognitive deficits and cognitive resources

It is often assumed that performance in a given cognitive task – such as solving anagrams – depends on some form of mental effort or mental work. As with any notion of work, mental work uses up energy. So in carrying forward the notion of mental work there is the notion of mental energy or **mental resources**. In this way any cognitive task may be assumed to consume mental resources. These ideas will be more thoroughly fleshed out when we consider attention (see Chapter 8), but for now it suffices to consider basic issues. Perhaps an alternative concrete example will help.

Let us assume initially that the cognitive system is akin to an electrical circuit linked up to a 12 volt battery. We can build the circuit by adding components to it – for instance, making up a string of lights to be

hung from trees in a garden. Here the resources are fixed – there is only one 12 volt battery and the electrical current is fixed. A consequence of this is that there will come a point at which the more lights you add to the circuit, the less bright each light will shine. Each light brings with it certain resource demands.

It may help to think of mental resources to be akin to the 12 volts provided by the battery in our simple circuit. Each task we ask of the cognitive system places associated demands on mental resources. In terms of our single dissociation we have a case of two tasks that may either arise because of the operation of two different modules, each of which possesses its own pool of resources (there is more than one battery), or we can think of a non-modular system that contains a single pool of resources (there is only one battery). In explaining the single dissociation we were immediately inclined to accept our modular account (the one with more than one battery). But could such a dissociation arise from the operation of the alternative non-modular system? Well, the short answer is 'Yes, in principle it can', and this all relates to something known as the problem of **resource artefacts** (Dunn & Kirsner, 1988; Shallice, 1988). It may be that the two tasks are not equated in their inherent difficulty so that the single dissociation may merely reflect the different demands that the two tasks place on a single (non-modular) pool of mental resources. We will return to the notions of mental effort and mental resources when we discuss attention later in the book (see Chapter 8).

Assume that the dissociation shows that task A performance is unimpaired or relatively unimpaired whereas task B performance shows a substantial deficit. By the resource argument, this can arise if task A is an easier task than task B. Task A makes fewer demands on resources than does task B so any damage that results in a depletion of mental resources will have more catastrophic consequences for task B performance than task A performance. In this way the presence of the dissociation is perfectly in line with predictions drawn from damage to a non-modular system.

### Pinpoint question 2.10

What are two interpretations for the observation of a single dissociation?

## Double dissociations

Neither the demonstration of an association deficit nor a single dissociation provides watertight evidence in favour of the operation of an underlying modular cognitive architecture. On these grounds, it is sometimes argued that firmer evidence for mental modules arises when we consider the notion of a **double dissociation**. The critical conditions for demonstrating a double dissociation are two tasks (*A* and *B* as above) and two different patients (patients I and II). A double dissociation arises when patient I performs well on task *A* but poorly on task *B*, and, in contrast, patient II performs well on task *B* but poorly on task *A*.

Coltheart (2001) provided the following plausible example: 'Patient A is impaired on comprehending printed words, but normal at comprehending spoken words; patient B is normal at comprehending printed words but impaired at comprehending spoken words' (p. 14). From the example, there are seemingly good grounds for concluding that different modules underpin text and speech comprehension, respectively. More particularly the double dissociation is most consistent with the idea that there is at least one module that is unique to comprehending printed words (and that this is damaged in patient A) and that there is at least one distinct module unique to comprehending spoken words (and that this is damaged in patient B).

Moreover, such a double dissociation cannot be explained away in terms of resource allocation within a single non-modular system (Shallice, 1988, pp. 232–7). In simple terms, if task *A* demands fewer resources than task *B* (task *A* is easier than task *B*) then, as we saw above, task *A* performance can remain intact even if task *B* performance is impaired. The reverse pattern cannot occur if the problem is assumed to lie in the allocation of resources in a single non-modular system. Any problem in resource allocation will hurt the difficult tasks first, so any decrement in performance on an easier task will only come about after a decrement in the more difficult task has been observed. So this seems to suggest that we are on much firmer ground in arguing for modular decomposition of the mind in the presence of a double dissociation. Damage in patient I selectively affects the operation of module *a* whereas damage in patient II selectively affects the operation of module *b*.

At first glance, therefore, the demonstration of a double dissociation across different types of patient is entirely consistent with an underlying modular architecture. Different and selective modules are damaged across the different patients. Indeed a double dissociation may constitute very strong evidence for some form of modular architecture. However, as Coltheart (2001) was at pains to point out, this should not be confused with definitive proof for an underlying modular architecture. Indeed, it has been repeatedly argued (and demonstrated) that double dissociations can arise in models of processing that do not fractionate according to modules. There is some evidence to suggest that double dissociations can arise in cases where different impairments to the same unified information processing system arise (for a recent illustration see Plaut, 2003). However, the evidence is contentious and, as Coltheart and Davies (2003) have argued, any such demonstration 'certainly does not show that a theory of that (non-modular) kind provides the best explanation of the double dissociation' (p. 190).

**Research focus 2.3**

## It's rude to point: double dissociations and manual behaviour

As a child, you have probably been told, on numerous occasions, that it is rude to point, and it therefore may come as something of a surprise to learn that one recently documented double dissociation relates to pointing. Back in 1922 the term 'autotopagnosia' was coined to refer to the condition in which a person is unable to point to their own body parts when given a verbal command. This has got nothing to do with shyness or anything of that sort, but seems to have a lot more to do with impairments regarding how information regarding body parts is represented internally. In exploring this and related disorders, Felician, Ceccaldi, Didic, Thinus-Blanc and Poncet (2003) tested a variety of elderly people on their ability to carry out several simple tasks. The results are shown in Table 2.1.

JR are the initials of a 73-year-old right-handed male who presented with a recent history of being unable to perform accurate motor movements (such as writing and dialling telephone numbers) with his right hand. AP are the initials of a 68-year-old right-handed woman. Until the age of 55 she had worked as a cashier, but she presented with a recent history of making spelling and calculation errors. She also presented with difficulties regarding knowledge of the spatial disposition of body parts (*Question*: 'Is the shoulder above or below the knee?' *Answer*: '?').

Both patients and a group of age-matched control participants were tested across the battery of simple tasks shown in Table 2.1. The notation *x/y* refers to the numbers correct (i.e., *x*) out of a possible total (i.e., *y*). Clearly the age-matched controls performed generally at ceiling in all cases. However, an interesting double dissociation can be seen across certain of the tasks for JR and AP (see the cells in Table 2.1 in bold).

Whereas JR was (essentially) unimpaired in his ability to point to the body parts of someone else, he was (essentially) unable to point to his own when asked to. In contrast, AP was impaired in being able to point to the body parts of someone else, but she was quite able to point to her own.

The deficits of neither patient could be traced to problems in pointing *per se*, to follow verbal commands or, indeed, name body parts. For JR his problem was diagnosed as being a classic case of autotopagnosia. His problems concerned either some form of corruption in the manner in which he represented his own body parts, or some form of difficulties in accessing this information (or indeed both).

In contrast, AP was diagnosed as having 'heterotopagnosis' – an inability to point to the parts of other people's bodies. In turning to her case, Felician et al. discussed the possibility of a specific module dedicated to processing information about other people's bodies (p. 1313). In AP but not JR this module was damaged. By extension, a separate module that codes information about one's own body parts is needed to explain the double dissociation. This module was impaired in JR but not AP.

**Table 2.1** Summary data of performance of the patients and control participants across a range of simple pointing tasks

|  | JR | AP | Controls |
| --- | --- | --- | --- |
| Naming body parts |  |  |  |
| Own (visual input)[a] | 20/20 | 20/20 | 20/20 |
| Own (tactile input)[b] | 20/20 | 20/20 | 20/20 |
| Others (visual input)[c] | 20/20 | 20/20 | 20/20 |
| Pointing to body parts |  |  |  |
| Own (verbal command) | **4/20** | **20/20** | 20/20 |
| Others (verbal command) | **18/20** | **3/20** | 20/20 |
| Pointing to objects |  |  |  |
| Objects within reach | 20/20 | 20/20 | 20/20 |
| Object in the room | 20/20 | 20/20 | 20/20 |
| Pointing to parts of pictures |  |  |  |
| Parts of an animal | 12/12 | 12/12 | 12/12 |
| Parts of a bike | 20/20 | 16/20 | 20/20 |
| Parts of a human body | 20/20 | 20/20 | 20/20 |

Notes: [a] Refers to a task in which the examiner pointed to the participant's own body parts to name.
[b] Refers to a task in which the examiner touched the participant's own body parts to name.
[c] Refers to a task in which the examiner pointed to his own body parts for the participant to name.

*Source*: Felician, O., Ceccaldi, M., Didic, M., Thinus-Blanc, C., & Poncet, M. (2003). Pointing to body parts: A double dissociation study. *Neuropsychologia, 41*, 1307–1316.

**developmental disorders** Neurological problems that develop as a person ages. Typically such problems are noted in childhood and may arise as a result of genetic factors, during pregnancy or birth.

**acquired disorders** Neurological problems that arise during the normal course of development through injury or illness.

**control participants** A group of individuals with intact brains who provide a profile of normal performance on some test or battery of tests in a cognitive neuropsychological study.

**association deficit** A neuropsychological case in which an individual with brain damage presents with deficits in two different domains such as an inability to understand (i) written and (ii) spoken forms of language.

**single dissociation** See dissociation deficit.

**dissociation deficit** A neuropsychological case in which an individual with brain damage presents with a marked deficit in one domain but has preserved, or relatively preserved, function in a related domain. For instance, a person is able to read words but not non-words.

**mental resources** The mental equivalent of energy or power that supports cognitive performance in some task. Difficult tasks are assumed to demand more mental resources than simple tasks.

**resource artefacts** This refers to accounting for a single dissociation by claiming that task difficulty is not equated across the various tasks that show the dissociation.

**double dissociation** Where individual 1 performs well on task A but poorly on task B, but individual 2 performs poorly on task A but well on task B.

## Concluding comments

In the second half of the chapter we have gone some way to introduce you to the basic modularity of mind hypothesis. This is because it provides the foundations for much of what is to follow in the rest of the book. In large part we will accept the view of the mind set out by Fodor (1983) and, as we proceed, we will attempt to see how well this view is supported by the evidence.

The final sections of the chapter have been concerned with the cognitive neuropsychological approach. Like much of present-day cognitive psychology, much of cognitive neuropsychology is wedded to the notion of a modular functional architecture as discussed by Fodor (1983). Although the details of any particular theoretical framework can be debated at length, the notion of semi-independent processing modules crops up time and time again in the cognitive psychology literature and, over recent history, this view of the mind has been bolstered by cognitive neuropsycho-

logical evidence. Nevertheless, it seems that each kind of deficit that we have described – association deficit, single dissociation and double dissociation – poses problems for interpretation. Caution therefore must be exercised.

Others have been even more sceptical. For instance, Gregory in 1961 voiced some concerns over just how much a broken brain can possibly tell us about a normal brain. Think about it. Remove the fuse box from your car and none of the electrics will work. So not only do the lights, heater and CD player no longer work but neither will the engine. In this rather extreme example, therefore, observing the behaviour of this broken car will tell us almost nothing about the normally functioning car.

Gregory (1961), though, was much more concerned with the brain on the understanding that this is a very complicated 'machine'. As he stated, if a single component is removed from a complex, multi-component machine, 'anything may happen' (p. 320). He continued by saying that a typical finding with electronic equipment (remember, this was written in the early 1960s) was that 'several different faults may produce the same "symptom" . . . anything affecting the (power) supply will tend to produce the same fault' (p. 322). Here the example was of removing some resistors from the radio set with the consequence that the radio begins to emit howls. So what should we conclude from such a demonstration? Gregory was at pains to point out that it should not lead to the conclusion that the function of the resistors is to suppress howls. Yet similar claims about inhibitory mechanisms are occasionally made by neurophysiologists when discussing damaged brains!

In developing his argument, and in providing such examples, Gregory was actually building a case for *functionalism*. As he stated, understanding the properties of a damaged machine is made considerably easier if a functional account of the intact system is available. In this regard, cognitive neuropsychology will be made much easier if functional accounts of the normal intact system are available.

So where does all of this leave us? Well, perhaps the most obvious conclusion to be drawn is that it would be folly to try to defend a whole theory of the architecture of the mind on the basis of just one result – be it an association deficit, a single dissociation or even a double dissociation. Statements about functional architecture are generally on a much firmer footing if backed up by a whole range of (what is known as) **converging evidence**. Our theory of mind ought to be consistent with a range of phenomena and be testable to the point of being falsified (see discussion of Popper in Chapter 1). Most importantly, the theory must make testable predictions concerning the outcomes of experiments that have yet to be carried out, and observations that have yet to be made. It is by this means that we hope to be able to decide about the appropri- ateness of our claims about modular decomposition and the modularity of mind.

> **converging evidence** A variety of different forms of evidence that all lead to the same sort of conclusion. The evidence converges on the one conclusion.

## CHAPTER SUMMARY

- Three approaches to the study of the mind are the cognitive, artificial intelligence and cognitive neuroscience approaches. Each has its different methods but the first two are of prime concern here. We are interested in attempting to provide functional accounts of the mind and these can be derived without any discussion of the underlying neurology.

- Information theory (Shannon & Weaver, 1949) provided a means to quantify the amount of information in terms of redundancy. The theory provided the basis of understanding communication systems in terms of information processing. Within a communication system, information is sent by a source (the sender) via a channel of transmission. Outputs from the channel arrive at a receiver. The efficiency of the communication system can be quantified according to criteria such as channel capacity, rate of transmission, redundancy of encoding and noise. Such proposals formed the basis of characterising human cognition in terms of information processing theory. A central idea is that external stimuli give rise to sensory signals that encoded them. Such signals can be defined as being internal representations, which stand for or designate external things.

- The computational metaphor highlights similarities between minds and computers. A digital computer is designed to store, operate on and retrieve large amounts of information characterised as strings of 0s and 1s in something known as binary code. The basic ideas that draw the analogy between computers and minds are set out in the physical symbol system as defined by Newell (1980). Here there is a well-defined set of symbols and a well-defined set of operations, with the overall behaviour of the system governed by a control program specifying the rules of operation. When considering the computational metaphor of the mind, therefore, we must also consider the use of internal representations or symbols that stand for aspects of the external world, internal processes that define operations upon these symbols, and an internal control system (Pinker, 1997). Cast in this way the metaphor becomes the computational theory of mind.

- What the computational theory of mind leads to is the understanding that minds and computers (programmable devices) are a very special kind of machine. A critical distinction here is between rule-following and rule-governed systems. A rule-governed system is one that acts according to a set of rules that are not represented within the device itself, whereas for rule-following systems, the rules of operation are represented internally in some form. Both minds and computer are taken to be rule-following devices. However, where minds and computers differ is with respect to the formality condition. A computer has no understanding of what the symbols it is using actually represent whereas minds do comprehend the link between thoughts and the things to which these thoughts refer.

- The formality condition reveals that computational theory can only provide, at best, an incomplete view of the mind. In offering the physical symbol system as a characterisation of the mind, it is clear that the claim is that mental operations have access only to the form of the internal codes and not their content. The computer has only access to the binary codes and has no conception of what such codes stand for or refer to. Humans, in contrast, typically have immediate access to what they are thinking about and how they are feeling. In this respect the computational theory of mind may be profoundly limited in its scope. Nevertheless, the computational theory of mind provides the most currently useful framework for thinking about human cognition and within this framework it is possible to consider how the mind may be constituted.

- Marr (1982) introduced the principle of modular design in which large-scale problems should be decomposed into many small problems, each being dealt with by an independent module. In this way, a big system could be resistant to damage in that if one module stopped working, this would not necessarily entail the whole of the system coming to a standstill. This kind of modular decomposition could be represented by the use of an arrows-and-boxes diagram.

- Alternative ideas about modular decomposition have recurred throughout the history of cognitive psychology. Horizontal faculties specify generic capabilities that cut across all domains, whereas vertical faculties specify particular domain-specific processes. The most thoroughly developed view of mental modularity is contained in the modularity of mind hypothesis (Fodor, 1983). By this view critical distinctions are drawn between the sensory transducers, input modules and central processors. The input modules can be best understood in terms of special-purpose computational devices: vertical faculties can be seen to fractionate into multi-modular systems. The input modules take stimulus information from the sensory transducers and transform it in such a way that a best first guess as to what is out there can be provided for further analysis. The central processes are responsible for assigning meaning and interpreting the proximal stimulus.

- The assumption of modularity fits comfortably with ideas relating to the breakdown of cognitive processing. For example, one of the general assumptions of cognitive neuropsychology is that if individuals experience focal brain damage or lesioning, then this is likely to impact on specific cognitive functions. This can lead to a number of empirical findings such as association deficits in which patients perform poorly on related tests, dissociation deficits in which a patient performs well on one task but less well on another, and double dissociation deficits in which one patient performs well on task A but not on task B whereas another patient performs well on task B but not on task A. Such cognitive neuropsychological data must be treated with care but when it is considered alongside other forms of converging evidence a case can be built for claims about putative modular architectures.

## ANSWERS TO PINPOINT QUESTIONS

2.1 The Shannon and Weaver (1949) model is a functional account of communication because the formulation of communication is independent of any form of physical instantiation.

2.2 Information processing theorists are concerned with abstract events that intervene between the stimulus and responses, whereas discussion of stimulus–response bonds is sufficient for behaviourists.

2.3 The control unit serves to operate upon symbols retrieved from memory.

2.4 A radiator is not a rule-following device because, although it acts according to rules set out by the central heating designer, those rules are not instantiated within the radiator itself.

2.5 Strong AI states that the mimicry of human behaviour is a sufficient condition for having mental processes.

2.6 A modular airplane would be preferable since it might be able to continue flying even if certain parts of the aircraft were not working properly.

2.7 Vertical faculties are domain-specific competencies. Horizontal faculties are general competencies.

2.8 A module is domain-specific when it only responds to a certain type of stimulus.

2.9 The case of Phineas Gage supports a modular view of the mind because the removal of his left frontal lobe seemed to be primarily associated with self-control and while this was compromised after the injury, his remaining cognitive system appeared to function normally.

2.10 A single dissociation (i) may reflect the operations of a modular mind, or (ii) it may simply arise as a result of a resource artefact. Either the brain damage has selectively impaired the operations of one particular module, as evidenced by poor performance on one particular task, or it might be that the particular task examined demands more mental effort to complete than others in the test battery.

## CHAPTER 3

# VISUAL PROCESSES AND VISUAL SENSORY MEMORY

## LEARNING OBJECTIVES

**By the end of this chapter, you should be able to:**

- Understand what is meant by naïve realism and define the three principles related to naïve realism (Neisser, 1967).
- Distinguish between full-report and partial-report conditions (Sperling, 1960).
- Identify the conditions under which partial-report superiority can arise.
- Distinguish between forward and backward masking.
- Distinguish between masking by integration and masking by interruption (replacement and curtailment).
- Contrast the dual-coding account of iconic memory (Coltheart, 1972) with the later three-component model (Coltheart, 1984).
- Contrast the discrete moment hypothesis with the travelling moment hypothesis.
- Define the various visual frames of reference discussed by Wade and Swanston (1991).
- Describe what aperture viewing is and what the basic findings are.

## CHAPTER CONTENTS

# Catching the last bus home?

Okay, so maybe the last Malibu and Coke wasn't such a good idea, especially after an evening of Bacardi Breezers, Black Russians and, of course, the Hell Shots. It also probably wasn't such a good idea to fall out with your best friend over . . . what was it now? Anyway, you stormed off, left the club, looked for a taxi, searched for your mobile phone, and are now walking down a road in the middle of nowhere, hoping it is in the right direction for town. Good, a bus stop. Not so good is that, although there is a timetable, there are no lights and it is getting very dark. Also not good is the fact that it is beginning to rain and it is beginning to rain quite hard.

Some parts of the timetable you can make out and it seems that the 49A is the one for you, even though you have no idea what time the next one is or indeed whether you are on the right side of the road. Anyway, what time is it now? (No phone, remember?) Not only is it raining but it now starts to thunder and with thunder there is lightning. You're leaning against the timetable, and the next lightning flash allows you to pick out the details. Okay, concentrate. It is turning out to be relatively easy to see what is written as long as it keeps lightning – why is that? If it keeps up, though, you should be able to figure out exactly when the next bus is. See, the last bus was 20.30 and the first bus is 7.13. It was 23.30 when you left the club . . .

## REFLECTIVE QUESTIONS

1. How do you see the world around you? How do you integrate visual information from one moment to the next? Do you record each moment onto individual film cells in your head or do you overlay each moment on top of each other? Why is it so easy to read in a lightning storm?

2. Think about a continuously noisy environment like a train station. Why is the act of listening difficult in these cases? What are the physical differences between that critical tannoy announcement and everything else you're trying to ignore? What would happen if a firework went off before or after the announcement? Would it make it easier or harder to hear? What might you do to make listening more successful in these cases?

## Introduction and preliminary considerations

Having considered in some detail the very basic theoretical foundations upon which cognitive psychology is built, we are now in a position to roll up our sleeves and get our hands dirty with the actual business of doing experimental research. We have considered foundational assumptions and general frameworks for thinking about human cognition, and now we need to focus on how cognitive psychologists go about studying the mind. To begin we are going to consider the very front-end of the visual system and discuss what the early stages of visual information processing might be like. You arrive at the airport, so what are the sorts of things that go on before you board the plane? In analogous fashion, information arrives at the senses, so what are the sorts of things that go on before it is fully identified and perhaps acted upon? In considering this particular aspect of human cognition, we are following an historical precedent set by Neisser in his seminal textbook (Neisser, 1967), and in following the threads of this particular line of research we can begin to appreciate how knowledge about the earliest stages of visual information processing unfolded over the years. In focusing upon just one aspect of visual processing, we can begin to understand some intricacies of experimental design and methodology, and appreciate how data and theory can be inextricably interlinked. We focus on the notion of **visual sensory memory**.

So to begin to get to grips with the experimental side of the discipline we are going to consider visual sensory memory as very much a case study. We will show how, from rather meagre beginnings, an immense amount of research has been generated. Not only do we cover specific issues concerning this kind of short-term memory system but, in order to understand what might be going on, we need to consider some general properties of the visual system. Moreover, some rather basic methodologies will also be introduced and dissected in a bid to set some firm foundations for the later materials. We will primarily be concerned with a technique known as **visual masking** because this has played such a central role in attempting to understand the nature of the short-term visual memory system. As with any unsolved mystery we need to think about the possibilities given the evidence, and to try to come up with plausible hypotheses about why the evidence is as it is. We can then set up experiments to test these ideas and as a consequence collect more evidence that bears on our thoughts. In reading the chapter you will see such a research strategy has been applied to the problems of trying to solve the mysteries of very short-term visual memory.

> **visual sensory memory** An assumed temporary memory system that fleetingly records the physical characteristics of sensory stimulation.
>
> **visual masking** A situation under which one visual event is obscured either by an immediately preceding event or an immediately following event.

## An introduction to sensory memory

We begin with consideration of a form of visual sensory memory that is assumed to come into play once the very earliest sensory encoding operations have run their course. The details will be fleshed out as we proceed. Traditionally, it has been accepted that **sensory encoding** operates so that a stimulus – for instance, light impinging on the back of the eyes (the retinae) – is transformed into some sort of coding that is propagated through the peripheral nervous system to the brain. Remember, we are treating the mind as an information processing system akin to an abstract communication system (see Chapter 2). Initially, light energy is transformed into some form of sensory code that is captured by the pattern of retinal nerve cells firing. However, the notion of a **coding transformation** is perhaps difficult to grasp when it is encountered for the first time. In this simple case, though, all that is being suggested is that one form of energy (e.g., light) is being changed into another form of energy (e.g., neural energy – the firing of nerve cells), just as the chemical energy within a battery turns into electrical

energy. The light-sensitive retinal cells (**photoreceptor cells**) begin to fire if the appropriate form of light energy falls within their receptive fields.

You might like to think of each cell as being akin to a hand-held torch and the receptive field of the cell is like the beam of light that illuminates the ground ahead of you. Anything that falls within the beam of light falls within the cell's receptive field, with the cell responding to critical stimuli within this receptive field. So the cell could be tuned to switch ON when a spot of light falls within its receptive field (see Hubel, 1963/1972). More generally, the term 'transformation' implies that a change takes place, and here the implication is that that stimulus information – such as light, heat or sound – is changed into some form of internal code via processes of sensory encoding. In terms of a more concrete example, every time you speak into your mobile phone the speech sounds are converted into a digital signal comprising 0s and 1s and it is this (binary) signal that is then transmitted to the phone network.

In discussing sensory encoding the implication is that each sense (hearing, vision, touch, olfaction, taste) generates its own sort of code – that is, the codes generated for a given stimulus are modality-specific (Cowan, 1988, p. 166; 1995, p. 53). What this means is that the sensory encoding of a visual stimulus will capture its visual (visible) characteristics such as its colour and luminance; the sensory encoding of an auditory stimulus will capture its frequency and intensity, and so on and so forth. A further implication is that such stimulus properties apply only in their particular modalities – the visual system does not encode sound intensity and the auditory system does not encode luminance. There are basic sensory encoding operations that are unique to each of the five senses (they are modality-specific).

So far and for simplicity, sensory encoding has been discussed in terms of patterns of nerve cells firing. However, in this book, we are primarily concerned with functional accounts of processing and this means that it is quite legitimate to discuss sensory codes at an abstract level (see Chapter 1). Indeed we are treating the human visual system as being akin to an information processing system as defined in Chapter 2. As a consequence, we need not commit ourselves further on the nature of possible neurophysiological processes that underpin sensory encoding. We are primarily concerned with human information processing accounts, and given this, our focus is attempting to specify, at an abstract level, the sort of sensory information that is coded at the early stages of processing.

Now it is quite easy to conceive of an information processing system in which sensory codes are immediately and seamlessly passed on to the higher cognitive centres which are assumed to undertake the difficult task of interpreting the sensory information (i.e., make sense of the sense data). This general account may, however, come across as being highly unrealistic. You only have to compare it with the experience flying back from your holiday in Florida. By the ideal view, when we arrive back from Florida we all simply get off the plane, pick up our bags and leave the airport. No one queues to pass through customs, or queues to get a taxi, or waits for a train, or gets stuck trying to leave the car park. There simply are no constraints on anyone leaving the airport. Back in the real world, though, such constraints do actually exist, and it seems that similar analogous **processing constraint**s can also be found in the nervous system. Clearly our sensory organs are constantly being bombarded by sensory stimulation, and on the assumption that not all of this information can be dealt with at once, it seems that the human information processing system has evolved to operate within certain processing constraints.

One such set of constraints reflects characteristics of sensory memory. By this view stimulus information must pass through a sensory memory system before it can be processed further. By our airport analogy, having got off the plane we all have to wait in the arrivals area before we pass through the passport check. So the arrivals area can be conceived as being a holding area or perhaps a buffer zone between the arrivals/departure lounge and the rest of the airport. All arriving passengers enter the arrivals area before passing through into the baggage reclaim. Given that there are typically only a very few customs officers to deal with the arriving passengers, then some if not all of the passengers must wait in the arrivals area before passing through into the baggage reclaim. In a similar fashion, sensory memory can be conceived as a holding area in which different aspects of the encoded stimulus are forced to wait until being passed on to the higher stages of processing.

Such higher stages of processing are typically discussed in terms of processes of stimulus identification (e.g., the customs officer must check your passport to see who you are) and it is assumed these are relatively complex and time-consuming. So whereas we all arrive at the same time when the plane lands, the passports must be checked one person at a time. An important additional assumption in this sort of account is that unless all sensory information is passed forward from this temporary buffer, it will be lost forever, and clearly this is where our simple airport analogy breaks down.

In summary, a basic assumption is that because of the wealth and amount of sensory stimulation that takes place constantly throughout our waking lives, not all of this information can be properly dealt with at the same time. In attempting to impose some order on this potential chaos, sensory memory acts as a buffer between the early sensory pick-up of stimulus information and the later processes. These later processes operate so that we can begin to try to make sense of the environment. In the present discussion, we are primarily concerned with the constraints on processing that operate very early on in the visual system and discuss these in terms of a very particular kind of sensory memory.

## Pinpoint question 3.1

**What is the main processing constraint that you might experience at a supermarket checkout?**

**sensory encoding** The manner in which stimulus information that impinges on the senses is transformed into some form of internal code.

**coding transformation** Used in reference to stimulus processing – taking one internal code and translating this into another. For instance, the earliest representation of the stimulus is converted into a code that specifies its name, its physical appearance, its identity, etc.

**photoreceptor cells** Cells that make up the retina and that are sensitive to light.

**processing constraint** A non-architectural limitation within a system that places an upper bound on the amount of information that can be processed at any one time.

## Visual sensory memory: iconic memory

Let us now move from this very general discussion of the nature of sensory memory to a much more detailed discussion of a particular body of research concerning visual sensory memory. As noted above, a seminal reference here is to the textbook treatment provided by Neisser (1967). He set the context for the topic in terms of three naïve beliefs about the nature of visual perception – so-called **naïve realism**, namely that:

1. Visual experience directly mirrors the stimulus.
2. The visual experience starts and ends with the corresponding onset and offset of the stimulus itself.
3. The visual experience reflects a passive copy of the stimulus that may be fully understood by noting down the participant's verbal reports.

Neisser referred to these assumptions as adding up to a *naïve realist view of perception*: the view that our perceptions of the world are direct and truthful copies of it – exactly the kind of thing a judge would want to believe when relying on your eye-witness testimony.

Prior to learning about the experimental study of perception, most of us would probably be happy to accept all three of these statements as amounting to a reasonable description of a given visual experience – we are all naïve realists. When you introspect about what goes on when you look at the world around you, the idea of watching an internal three-dimensional (3D) movie in your theatre of consciousness seems to be a pretty reasonable account of what is going on. Your internal movie is, apparently, a perfect holographic copy of the external world. Yet, despite how compelling this impression may be, it seems that such a simplistic view cannot be correct. Given the detailed evidence that has been amassed from experimental studies on human perception over the years, quite a different view emerges. Indeed, Neisser (1967) considered such evidence and came up with a view of processing that implicates a kind of visual sensory memory that he called **iconic memory**. The overall view of processing contrasts markedly with the naïve realist account of perception.

## Early experimental investigations of iconic memory

One way of beginning is to set up an experimental situation in which we measure a participant's verbal reports of some briefly flashed visual stimulus. We flash the stimulus and get the participant to say what they saw. In this context it is normal to refer to the stimulus as being contained in a **stimulus display**. To make the task simple, each stimulus display comprises an array of printable characters such as individual letters or individual digits (sometimes these are also known as **display elements** or items) and in some cases the stimulus display may also be referred to as the **target display**. The critical point is that the characters should be highly familiar and easily nameable – if the display were presented for an unlimited amount of time then participants should have no trouble in naming all of the characters present. Should participants show difficulties in reporting the display elements in our proposed experiment, then we need to be sure that this cannot be due to the fact that the characters are unfamiliar or are hard to name such as '¥'. Poor performance in that task might be taken as indicative of a memory limitation when in fact the problem reflects the participants' inability to name the stimuli – how could they possibly report a stimulus that they cannot name?

In the experiments to be described, the critical unit of design is the experimental trial wherein at least one stimulus is presented and the participant makes at least one response. An experiment typically comprises one or more blocks of trials such that a block is simply a sequential series of trials (hence a block of trials). Two experiments immediately suggest themselves. For instance, we can control the length of time that the display is presented for – this is known as the **stimulus duration** – and vary the number of to-be-reported characters – known as the **display set size** – across the trials. (Here the display set size refers to the number of characters presented in a given display.) Alternatively, we can hold the display set size constant and vary the stimulus duration across the trials. Of course we can vary both the stimulus duration and the display set size across trials, but let's keep it simple and consider the case where display size is held constant and the stimulus duration is varied across trials.

In perhaps the simplest experimental set-up, we present a briefly flashed stimulus display to a participant and get them to either write down what they saw or simply tell us what they saw. Such techniques were used for around 80 years prior to the time Neisser (1967) was writing (von Helmotz, 1894, cited by van der Heijden, 2003). On the basis of this sort of research it had been concluded, and generally accepted, that if a display was presented for up to about half a second, then participants could report up to about five items (Coltheart, 1972). So a display might look something like this:

A G J K
F D E L
V O P Z

and the participant might be able to report D, E, G, V, or A, G, L, or indeed just D. Such a result was initially interpreted as showing that the participant could only perceive these letters in the display (Coltheart, 1972). Despite this conclusion, though, it became apparent (Sperling, 1960) that participants were aware that the displays contained far more items than they could report. This was a reasonable hint that verbal reports may only be a rather imperfect tool for studying perception! Participants reported *seeing* more than they could actually report.

So how might we provide evidence in support of this claim independently of the anecdotal reports from participants? Can we provide quantitative measures that might help illuminate what is going on? Well, pursuit of such questions sparked the interest in studying iconic memory. One seminal reference here is to the work of Sperling (1960). He presented participants with displays of the type shown above and tested performance in, essentially, two conditions. In both conditions a trial began with the presentation of a central fixation point. The participant pressed a key and then 500 milliseconds (ms) later the fixation point was replaced by a stimulus display for only 50 ms which itself was then replaced by the original fixation field. (To be clear, there are 1000 milliseconds in 1 second – so 50 ms is 0.05 of a second, 500 ms is half a second.)

In the **full-report condition** participants simply had to report all of the letters that they were able to from the stimulus display. Under full-report conditions the average correct report was of the order of 4.5 items for displays containing 5–12 characters. This is roughly what would have been predicted on the basis of the previous work, and Sperling (1960) referred to this as the *span of immediate memory*. However, a quite surprising result obtained in the other condition. In this condition – the **partial-report condition** – participants were *cued* to report the letters from only one particular row. Now what happened was that, at the offset of the stimulus display, a tone (*the cue*) was played. The tone varied in pitch such that a high-pitched tone signalled that the participant should report the top row of letters, a medium-pitched tone signalled that the participant report the middle row and a low-pitched tone signalled that the participant report the bottom row of letters.

Under these conditions participants were now able to report correctly about three of the four possible letters in the cued row. As Coltheart (1980a) argued, this result shows that – despite what might have been concluded on the basis of the full-report data – on average, the same number of items must have been stored in some form of memory from the other two uncued rows. The participants did not know which row to report from in advance of the cue so, unless they retained nearly all of the information in the display, their partial reports of the items could not have been this good. So whereas the full-report data suggest a very limited store of information from the display, the partial-report data suggest a memory store in which quite a lot of (perhaps all) the original stimulus information is retained.

## Pinpoint question 3.2

**How do you turn a full-report condition into a partial-report condition?**

### *Partial-report superiority*

What we have here are two different estimates of memory capacity: one from the full-report condition, and a dramatically larger one from the partial-report condition. The implication is that the estimate based on full report significantly falls short of what the true storage capacity is. It is not that verbal reports are inaccurate reflections of perception so much, but it does seem that the way in which such verbal reports are solicited is crucial. This conclusion must make us think hard about how best to get participants to report on their perceptions of the world. Nevertheless, the most important finding is that the capacity estimates of the memory store from the partial-report conditions are greater than those from full-report conditions. This is known as a partial-report advantage or partial-report superiority. The **partial-report superiority** (or partial-report advantage) was taken to show the large capacity of iconic memory – perhaps all of the display items are captured in the icon.

### *What kind of information is stored in the icon?*

To understand the nature of the memory system that we have identified, we can begin to ask just what sort of information is stored in the system. Is it simply a copy or mental photograph of the display? This is where the ingenuity of researchers really does begin to show. The basic idea now is to consider other characteristics of the stimulus elements that might be stored alongside their location in the display. In fact, we often take for granted that we recover location information as well as item information, otherwise the act of reading a textbook would beocme evry dffiultc edined. Given that the tone cues were effective, this revealed that the relative position of the characters had been retained in memory. If the cues had not worked then participants would not have been able to use the tone to recall items from the cued row.

So what other sorts of information are captured by the icon? To address this we need to begin to explore different sorts of manipulations of the display items. For instance, we could vary the colour of the items, their brightness, their shape, their size, and we could even go completely crazy and mix in letters and numbers together and hence vary the **categorical identity** of the items in the display. All of the above manipulations were dutifully carried out (Banks & Barber, 1977; Clark, 1969; Turvey & Kravetz, 1970; Sperling, 1960; von Wright, 1968, 1970) and the findings revealed that whereas a partial-report advantage was shown for all of the physical characteristics of the items, this was not so when categorical identity differentiated the cued items from the uncued items. Whereas participants could selectively report items of a particular colour, brightness, size or shape, they were unable to report selectively items from different categories when asked. Participants were unable to, for example, just report the letters and ignore the digits (Sperling, 1960). What this was taken to show was that the particular memory system being tapped contained something very much like a copy (i.e., a mental photograph) of the relevant characteristics of the stimulus display. Think of it this way: a colour photograph of next door's cat contains patches of colour and nothing else. You have to work on this information to decide that, 'Yes, indeed, the photograph contains an image of the cat.' To underline the *visual* nature of this sort of mental representation Neisser (1967) coined the phrase 'iconic memory'.

Indeed Coltheart, Lea and Thompson (1974) went on to show that participants were unable to use the sounds of the display items as an effective selection criterion because they failed to show a partial-report advantage when asked to report those letters with an *ee* sound in. Participants were unable to select out *D*, *B*, *C*, etc. from *F*, *L*, *M*, etc. The claim was that, whereas iconic memory contained an explicit representation of the *visual* properties of the items, further mental work was needed to extract their corresponding sounds. Neither categorical information (e.g., this item is a number) nor phonological information (e.g., this item contains an *ee* sound) appeared to be represented in the icon. So iconic memory was said to have a large capacity because the partial reports indicated that nearly all of the items in the display were retained. In addition, it was also claimed that the information contained in it was said to be *visual* and **pre-categorical** – the category identity of the characters (i.e., whether a given display element was a letter or number) was not made explicit.

## The time span of the icon

As a present I brought one of those Fred Flintstone cameras, the kind where the film canister is also the body of the camera, and I presented it to the chief. He seemed delighted and began to click off pictures. He wasn't advancing the film between shots, but since we were told we shouldn't speak unless spoken to, I wasn't able to inform him that he wasn't going to get twelve pictures, but only one, very, very complicated one.

*(Anderson, 1995)*

A third characteristic of iconic memory – that it has a very brief time span – was shown via the introduction of another experimental manipulation. Now a delay was introduced between the offset of the stimulus display and the presentation of the tone cue. By varying the delay to the cue over trials it was then possible to measure partial reports over increasingly longer periods. Figure 3.1 shows a schematic representation of the sort of data that was obtained when a delay was

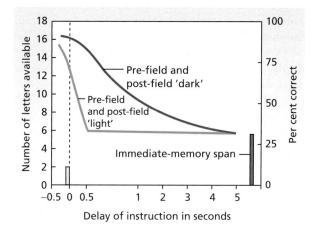

**Figure 3.1 The decay of iconic memory**
A schematic representation of data taken from Sperling's (1963) early experiments on iconic memory. Two curves are shown and these relate (i) the delay between the onset of a target display and the cue to respond (on the *x* axis) with (ii) the amount of information reported from the target display (on the *y* axis). The different curves show performance according to whether the pre- and post-fields were light or dark, respectively. The life of the icon is clearly extended when dark fields are used. The small vertical pale blue bar that defines the 0 time-point signifies the timing of the stimulus display. The taller vertical dark blue bar indicates immediate-memory span under no mask conditions.

*Source*: Coltheart, M. (1972). Visual information processing. In P. C. Dodwell (Ed.), *New horizons in psychology 2* (fig. 1, p. 64). Harmondsworth, England: Penguin Books. Reproduced with permission.

introduced between the offset of the display and the presentation of the cue. Full-report performance was unaffected when participants were similarly asked to delay their responses for up to 1 second on each trial – the span of immediate memory was said to be invariant over these delays. Using this technique, estimates of the lifetime of the icon were gauged relative to the point at which the partial-report advantage was abolished. The duration of this very short-term memory system was taken to be the point at which estimates of the number of items available were the same for partial and full report.

To understand Figure 3.1 completely, some further technical language needs to be introduced. The sequence of events on a trial is taken to comprise a sequence of display fields – for instance, an initial display containing a fixation mark (the fixation field), followed by a stimulus display (the stimulus field or target field) followed by a blank screen (a blank field). Using this terminology, any field presented immediately before the stimulus field is known as a **pre-field** and any field presented immediately after the stimulus field is known as a **post-field**. As can be seen from Figure 3.1, when the pre- and post-fields were dark rather than bright (a black screen rather than a white screen) the life of the icon was of an order of seconds. However, when the pre- and post-fields were bright, the life of the icon was shortened to around half a second.

This particular pattern of results was taken to underline the visual nature of the memory representation. As Sperling (1963) noted, 'the accuracy of partial reports strongly suggests their dependence on a persisting visual image' (p. 21). Remember, the stimulus display was only presented for 50 ms yet the lifetime of the icon extended well beyond this. So to answer the question 'How long does the icon last?' the data so far discussed suggest that it can range from less than a second to several seconds depending on the visual context of the displays. Performance was critically dependent on whether the stimulus display was more or less intense than its surrounding context.

One interpretation of the effect of presenting a bright post-field was that it reflected a limitation of sensory encoding – somehow the encoding of the stimulus field was being influenced by the luminance of the post-field. If one brief visual event is immediately followed by another, then they may become fused together in the same psychological moment. By this **integration hypothesis** (Kahneman, 1968) it is as if the perceptual system is unable to differentiate between where one briefly flashed event stops and another starts – the two are encoded as one. In this way it is as

**Figure 3.2  Okay, okay, it's my turn to do the washing next week**
The spooky result of coding two events as one. Old spiritualist photography was created by overlaying one 'real' world photograph on one of the 'spirit' world. In this case, the image of the apparition is integrated with its background. The mental equivalent is implicated in the integration hypothesis of masking (Kahneman, 1968).
*Source*: Bettmann/Corbis.

if the two events add (or sum) together as one – think of a double exposure on a photograph (see Figure 3.2) where successive images are superimposed on one another as described in the quotation from Anderson (1995). In following this logic, the relative legibility of either event will be tied to the relative amounts of stimulus energy in the two events. So, in simple terms, if the stimulus field is brighter than the surrounding pre- and post-fields then it will be more legible than if it is darker than the surrounding fields. This is exactly what the data show.

A further implication of the results shown in Figure 3.1 is that the representation of the items in iconic memory (a shorthand way of stating this is to say 'the items that are stored in iconic memory') will decay and be lost if they are not processed further – for instance, unless they are transformed or recoded into a more durable form then participants will fail to report them (Coltheart, 1972). → See 'What have we learnt?', page 72.

## Blinking heck! What happens to iconic memory when you blink?

One hypothesis that the research on iconic memory seems to suggest is that our visual perception of the world is derived from individual snapshots. One observation that should make this seem more reasonable is the simple act of blinking. As Thomas and Irwin (2006) pointed out, we blink once every four seconds for about a quarter of a second. Although our pupils are covered for about 100 ms every time this happens, amazingly our visual perception does not seem to be bothered by this almost constant interruption to the visual world. While this might be true in the grand scheme of things, it's quite possible that these regular disruptions to our visual system might cause problems for less durable types of visual information such as iconic memory.

In the primary experiment, 12 individuals were shown brief 3 × 3 target display of letters for 106 ms and then a tone cue followed 50, 150 or 750 ms later, with the pitch of the tone cueing which row they should report. This kind of paradigm should be pretty familiar to you now as it is exactly the kind of thing Sperling (1960) was doing in his partial-report task. The novel aspect of this experiment, however, was that participants completed both 'blink' and 'no-blink' conditions. While the no-blink condition should be self-explanatory, in the blink condition, participants were instructed to blink as soon as they saw the letter array. This resulted in an average blink occurring 225 ms after the presentation of the stimulus array and lasting for 265 ms.

Thomas and Irwin (2006) found that at cue delays of 50 ms, participants reported significantly fewer items from the appropriate row of the array when they were blinking relative to absence of a bit of shut-eye. Moreover, participants were also more likely to report letters from other rows in the array (something called mislocation errors) under blinking condition at 50 ms cue delay. Over subsequent experiments, Thomas and Irwin (2006) set out to show that cause of disruption was not due to other phenomena related to eye blinks. For example, they ruled out the possibility that changes in light intensity when the eye reopened acted as a visual mask (Experiment 2), and also that the cognitive consequences of motor responding (Experiment 3) and the closing of the eyes more generally (Experiment 4) were different to the act of blinking itself.

The authors concluded that the fact that there were problems in partial report when participants blinked only at very short delays between stimulus display and cue implies a disruption in iconic memory and the confusion of stimulus identity with stimulus location, hence the increase in mislocation errors. Thomas and Irwin (2006) suggested that this cognitive blink suppression effect might be due to our eye blinks acting as our very own personal visual masks! So the old saying does appear to have some truth – blink and you may, indeed, miss it.

*Source*: Thomas, L. E., & Irwin, D. E. (2006). Voluntary eyeblinks disrupt iconic memory. *Perception & Psychophysics, 68*, 475–488.

## → What have we learnt?

## The traditional view of iconic memory

The traditional view of iconic storage therefore is that within the first few tens of milliseconds of the first fixation on the stimulus (Coltheart, 1983a), information is transferred into a short-term visual store that holds, essentially, a mental photograph of the stimulus. Although the physical characteristics of the display characters are represented, further interpretative work is needed to recover the categorical nature of the items. Are they letters or numbers? Which letters or numbers were actually flashed? Information about the items in the display rapidly decays – the mental photograph fades – and will be lost unless there is further read-out from this store into a more durable form of storage. Much of what follows builds on these basic ideas about the nature of iconic memory; however, there have been challenges and disagreements and some of these we will consider as the discussion proceeds.

**For example . . .**

A fairly graphic example may help you think about iconic memory. The next time you can bring yourself to watch the original Tobe Hooper 1974 film *The Texas Chainsaw Massacre* (don't worry, you don't need to watch the whole thing), the first couple of minutes actually give a pretty good approximation of what the content of your iconic memory might look like. For those who haven't seen the film, you see a bunch of briefly flashed images that very quickly fade from view, some of which are over far too quickly to grasp exactly how gory they are. Although this is a fairly good visualisation of the rapid decay in iconic memory, we hope that the actual *content* of your iconic memory is very different.

## Iconic memory and visual masking

Other important evidence regarding iconic storage arose from different experimental manipulations in which the nature of the pre- and post-fields was varied. Indeed, quite intriguing patterns of performance emerged when different sorts of pre- and post-fields were used instead of blank fields. So far we have discussed bright and dark pre- and post-fields with the implication that the whole of these fields contain an homogenous colour – respectively, white and black. However, it is possible to design a **visual noise mask** defined as a field containing densely scattered letter fragments or randomly positioned black and white squares. Let us consider one condition in which Sperling (1963) presented an homogenous black pre-field and a post-field that contained a visual noise mask (see Figure 3.3). Here the mask followed the presentation of the stimulus display and this experimental set-up has come to be known as visual **backward masking** (Turvey, 1973). (You will therefore be completely unsurprised to learn that visual **forward masking** occurs when the mask is presented immedi-ately prior to the target.) The implication of backward masking is that the ensuing post-field mask somehow conceals the nature of the stimulus presented before the mask. How might this be?

**Pinpoint question 3.3**

In another in a long line of holiday moments captured on film, you're finding it hard to focus back on your margarita after looking at the camera flash. Is this an example of forward masking or backward masking?

### Masking by integration and masking by interruption

We have already discussed the integration hypothesis, namely, that the mask and the stimulus are combined into a single montage (as when a television picture is obscured by the snow-like appearance of interference). By this view such masking is known as **integration masking**. Alternatively, the mask could interrupt the processing of the stimulus and as a consequence whatever processes are operating on the stimulus cease when the mask is presented. This is known as **interruption masking**. Two possible means of interruption have been discussed: one form – known as **replacement** (after Turvey, 1978) – describes the interruption of processing in terms of the current stimulus information being completely over-written by the delivery of the next. In this way any trace of the first stimulus is lost. This is the same sort of masking demonstrated earlier by Averbach and Coriell (1961) that they called **erasure**. In the second – known as **curtailment** – the processing of the first stimulus simply stops when the next arrives. Curtailment allows for the possibility that some record of the first stimulus may still be available even though processing has moved on.

As you can possibly imagine, there has been some controversy over whether an integration account (Holender, 1986) or interruption account (Allport,

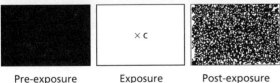

| Pre-exposure | Exposure | Post-exposure |

**Figure 3.3 Individual frames used in a typical backward masking experiment**
An example of the sorts of displays used by Sperling (1963). In this case the pre-exposure field is completely dark and the post-exposure field contains a visual noise mask. Over time, the three fields (left to right) are presented and the exposure field holds the target display.

*Source*: Sperling, G. (1963). A model for visual memory tasks. *Human Factors*, 5, 19–31 (fig. 3, p. 24). Reproduced with permission from Human Factors. Copyright © 1963 by The Human Factors and Ergonomics Society. All rights reserved.

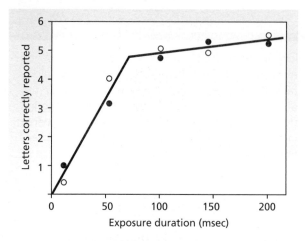

**Figure 3.4 Effect of exposure duration on amount reported in a typical iconic memory backward masking paradigm**
A schematic representation of data from Sperling's (1963) masking experiments. This shows the function relating amount of items correctly reported (on the y axis) plotted relative to the exposure duration of the letter stimulus display (on the x axis). The exposure duration was controlled by varying the onset of a visual-noise mask after the target display was presented. The data are taken from two different participants, shown respectively by the open and filled circles.

*Source*: Coltheart, M. (1972). Visual information processing. In P. C. Dodwell (Ed.), *New horizons in psychology 2* (fig. 2, p. 67). Harmondsworth, England: Penguin Books. Reproduced with permission.

1977; Coltheart, 1972, 1980a; Scharf & Lefton, 1970), or, indeed, a dual account (Turvey, 1978) best explains the backward masking of iconic memory but we shall return to this issue when we take a closer look at visual masking later. For now consider Figure 3.4 because this provides a schematic representation of data relevant to this issue.

The data shown in Figure 3.4 are taken from an experiment reported by Sperling (1963). He systematically examined the effect that backward masking had on full-report performance (where participants have to report all the display) by varying the stimulus duration and by presenting a visual noise mask at the offset of the stimulus display. The time between the stimulus onset and the mask onset is known as the **stimulus onset asynchrony** (or SOA) and, as Figure 3.4 shows, the number of items correctly reported is now critically dependent on the SOA between the onset of the stimulus and the onset of the visual noise mask.

Remember that in cases where the stimulus display is briefly flashed and there is no ensuing mask, participants can report between 4 and 5 items in full-report conditions (check out Figure 3.1 again if you're a little

hazy). In that experiment Sperling (1963) used a very brief stimulus duration (i.e., of only 5 ms!) and light pre- and post-fields, and still participants were able to report between 4 and 5 items. So the first thing to note about Figure 3.4 is that, if the mask is presented within 70 ms of the onset of the stimulus, that is the SOA is 70 ms or less, there is a dramatic reduction in a participant's ability to report the display items. This has been taken to show that iconic memory is abolished by visual backward masking (Coltheart, 1972; Gegenfurtner & Sperling, 1993; although this particular conclusion has been questioned, Smith & Fabri, 1975; and see later discussion of Smithson & Mollon, 2006). In and of itself this result was taken to further reveal the visual nature of iconic memory, such that if a visual masker is presented rapidly after the stimulus display, then the item report may be compromised.

What is particularly striking about the function shown in Figure 3.4 is that it seems to reveal the operation of two quite different mechanisms. Let's look at this in more detail. The first thing to note is that there is a steep rise in the number of items correctly reported within the first 70 or so milliseconds; there is then a more gradual rise for longer durations. Coltheart (1972) interpreted these particular data in terms of the operation of two sorts of processes – one process is reflected in the first component of the function (the early steep rise) and a different process is reflected in the second component (the later, less steep rise). It was argued that at the onset of the display there is rapid encoding of the visual characteristics of some of the items in the display – by around 80 ms around 4 items have been so encoded and so by a quick division it was assumed that it must take around 20 ms to generate a **visual code** for a particular item. At the same time, however, a less rapid form of encoding is initiated and this involves the recovery of the sounds of the names of the items – as specified in the **name code**. This process is considerably slower than visual encoding and generating the name code for any given item takes about 100 ms.

What we have here is an elaboration of the view that items are initially deposited in a very brief visual store. Unless information about these items is extracted or read out from this store, it will likely be lost. In other words, items must be selected for further processing if they are to be reported. In this regard, two notions of selection have been discussed, namely (i) *non-selective read-out* in which the participant essentially reports those items that are available at random, and (ii) *selective read-out* in which the participant attempts to report items of a particular sort. A simple starting point is to assume that participants use non-selective read-out when they are instructed in whole-report conditions

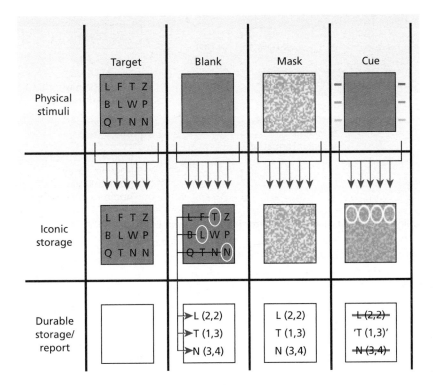

**Figure 3.5  A traditional account of iconic memory**
Schematic representation of the backward masking paradigm and the standard account of iconic memory and read-out from iconic memory. The first row shows the physical events that unfold over time on a given trial. The second row shows the internal visual representations and processes that operate over time. Column 2 shows non-selective read-out of the display elements into the more durable store prior to the cue. The third column shows the presentation of a random noise mask. Here items in the icon may be obscured, but items in the durable store are retained. The fourth column shows the presentation of a final visual cue, but in this case any record of the cued elements has been lost. Only the *T* can be reported because this has already been deposited in the durable store and was presented in the cued row.

*Source*: Smithson, H., & Mollon, J. (2006). Do masks terminate the icon? *The Quarterly Journal of Experimental Psychology, 59*, 150–160 (fig. 1, p. 152). Reproduced with permission of Taylor & Francis Ltd.

and selective read-out in partial-report conditions. However, more recently Gegenfurtner and Sperling (1993) have shown that, even in partial-report conditions, both non-selective and selective read-out does occur. Prior to the cue, items are read out in a non-selective fashion (although there is bias to select items from the middle row of the character array) and when the cue occurs participants switch to read out items selectively from the cued row. The critical point remains that, unless items are read out or transferred from iconic memory into a more durable form, they will be lost. Figure 3.5 provides a useful schematic representation of some of these ideas.

## The dual-coding account of iconic memory

In the dual-coding account of read-out from iconic memory, Coltheart (1972) argued that the visual code contains information about the physical characteristics of the items whereas the name code contains information about the sound of the name of the items. One set of coding operations captures the visual nature of the stimulus (its colour and shape) and a different set of operations is set in motion to recover its more abstract characteristics such as its name. This is by no means the only account of iconic storage that is conceivable but it does allow us to discuss what amounts to our first example of an arrows-and-boxes flow chart of some aspect of human information processing and this is provided in Figure 3.6. Here information is passed from iconic memory to a visual encoding box. The visual encoding box takes input from iconic memory and transforms it into a code that specifies the visual characteristics of the presented items. Similarly the name encoding box takes input from iconic memory and transforms it into a code that specifies the sounds

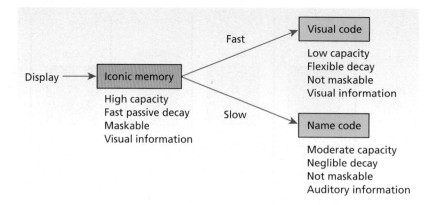

**Figure 3.6 The dual-coding account of read-out from iconic storage (from Coltheart, 1972)**

*Source*: Coltheart, M. (1972). Visual information processing. In P. C. Dodwell (Ed.), *New horizons in psychology 2* (fig. 7, p. 75). Harmondsworth, England: Penguin Books. Reproduced with permission.

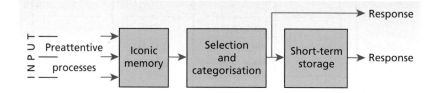

**Figure 3.7 From input to output via the visual system**
A very general information processing account of the stages of processing that characterise vision; from stimulus input to response.

*Source*: Turvey, M. T. (1973). On peripheral and central processes in vision: Inferences from an information-processing analysis of masking with patterned stimuli. *Psychological Review, 80*, 1–52 (fig. 1, p. 2). Reproduced with permission from APA.

that are associated with the displayed items. Indeed a basic claim was that iconic memory is located at the entrance to visual information processing in general.

As is shown in Figure 3.7, iconic storage is seen as a precursor to further processing: stimulus information must pass through the iconic memory system before further processing is possible. By this account, if an item never enters iconic memory or decays from it, it will never be perceived. In this regard this sensory memory system is seen as the very beginnings of visual perception. → See 'What have we learnt?', page 77.

→ See 'What have we learnt?', page 77.

### Pinpoint question 3.4

**According to the dual-coding account (Coltheart, 1972), after iconic storage, what two kinds of coding are there?**

## Iconic memory and visible persistence

Having set out the abstract nature of iconic memory as specified in the information processing accounts

shown above (Figures 3.6 and 3.7), one particular question has plagued the concept since it was first described: is iconic memory anything other than visible persistence? Since Sperling's (1960) earliest studies of iconic memory, there has been an uneasy tension over the degree to which iconic memory reflects anything other than **visible persistence** (see for example Sackitt, 1976). Although a more sensible definition of visible persistence is given below, a readily understood example of visible persistence relates to the sort of after-image that you experience after someone takes a flash photograph and you happen to be looking at the camera when the photograph is taken. The image of the flash bulb remains with you for some time after the flash has taken place. This example sets out an extreme form of visible persistence, but other more subtle forms have been documented (see Coltheart, 1980a, for a comprehensive review). So the central issue is: given that iconic memory has been defined as a persisting visual trace of the stimulus, is it really anything other than visible persistence? Indeed, here is a very good example of where Occam's Razor may

So in the face of the research on iconic memory, where does this leave the naïve realist view of perception? Well, the evidence clearly goes against the idea that our visual experience starts and ends with the corresponding onset and offset of the stimulus itself. Moreover, although the data apparently show that there is a stage at which visual experience reflects a passive copy of the stimulus, there are problems in trying to uncover the nature of this representation merely by getting participants to report everything they think they saw. The difference between full and partial reports reveals this. What remains is the issue of whether visual experience directly mirrors the stimulus.

Although the data discussed so far in no way settles this issue, the spirit of the model set out by Coltheart (1972; and see Figure 3.6) is that visual information presented to the eyes undergoes a series of transformation/re-coding operations that gives rise to an output that is 'something other than a mere relaying of the input' (Turvey, 1973, p. 17). Such codings preserve certain characteristics of the stimulus, but this is quite different to the naïve realist idea of mirroring the stimulus (Neisser, 1967). The full force of this possibility will be covered in much more detail later when we discuss theories of perception. More pressing here, though, are other concerns about the nature of the memory system that we have been considering. In a nutshell, the basic concern is with whether iconic memory reveals anything other than something known as *visible persistence*.

be of help. Why posit a complicated set of abstract mechanisms when the behaviour to be explained can be understood in terms of the basic physiology of the visual system? Why shouldn't iconic memory be anything more than a camera flash in the eye?

## Visible vs. informational persistence

In the most thorough defence of the idea that iconic memory and visible persistence are quite different, Coltheart (1980a) drew a very clear distinction between visible persistence as defined by the fact that 'some or all of the neural components of the visual system which respond when a visual stimulus is present continue their activity for some time after the offset of the stimulus' (p. 184) and **informational persistence** indexed by the partial-report advantage as studied in experiments on iconic memory. This is a good place to again refer to the notion of an abstract code. Here, Coltheart is arguing that information from the stimulus is being preserved in an abstract form but that this form of storage should not be equated with an extended pattern of visual nerve cell firing. In attempting to establish the difference between these two alternatives, Coltheart (1980a) reviewed a large body of work showing that properties that can rightly be attributed to visible persistence are different from those that can be attributed to the icon as gauged by the partial-report advantage.

### Getting a grip on visible persistence

One way in which visible persistence has been examined is by presenting participants with a visual stimulus for a given duration and by getting them to estimate how long this duration actually was. In a study by Efron (1970), the participants' task was to estimate the duration of an illuminated orange disk of light. He did this by having participants estimate when the offset of a target orange disk of light occurred simultaneously with the onset of a probe green disk of light. First the orange disk was illuminated for 500 ms, and some time after the onset of the orange disk, the green disk was illuminated for 500 ms. In other words, the SOA between the two disks was varied in a systematic fashion. In fact the SOA initially was set at over 500 ms so that there was an obvious gap between the offset of the orange disk and the onset of the green disk. The SOA was then decreased in 10 ms steps until the participant reported no gap between the two illuminated disks.

Clearly if the participant overestimated the duration of the first orange disk then the interval between the two disks would be greater than the actual duration of 500 ms and this was indeed what was found. Typically, participants overestimated the duration of the orange disk and this was put down to visible persistence of the sort described by Coltheart (1980a). Participants failed to detect a physical (albeit small) gap that existed between the offset of the orange disk and the onset of the green disk. Hence we have a means for measuring the duration of visible persistence. The judged delay between the offset and onset is taken as the measure of visible persistence.

### Direct and indirect measures of persisting traces

The technique described by Efron (1970) has been discussed as a direct method because participants' responses are taken as direct measures of the duration of visible persistence. Studies of the partial-report advantage, however, are assumed to employ an *indirect method* because these involve comparisons between two different performance indicators. Comparisons of partial and whole report are needed in order to make the necessary inferences. Coltheart's (1980a) main point is that direct and indirect methods are measuring and reflecting very different things and therefore it is sensible to claim that visible persistence and iconic memory can and should be distinguished.

For instance, it had been well established that (counter to intuitions!)(Coltheart, 1980b) (i) visible persistence decreased as display duration increased (i.e., shorter amounts of persistence for longer display durations; think of it this way – as the orange disk stayed on for longer, the estimates of its duration became less); and (ii) that visible persistence also decreased as the luminance of the display increased (where luminance refers to how bright the stimulus display is). Again, as the orange disk got brighter, the estimates of its duration became less. Coltheart (1980a, b) reviewed evidence showing that the same sorts of systematic variation in the duration of iconic memory did not occur. This was good news for those who wanted to claim that iconic memory and visual persistence are not the same.

If only life (and science) were that simple, because just a few years later, Coltheart (1984) cited newer evidence showing that, under certain circumstances, both visible persistence and iconic memory show similar variation when manipulated by changes in stimulus duration and stimulus luminance (Long & McCarthy, 1982; see also Long & Beaton, 1982). Here the evidence was that both sorts of traces were positively related to display duration and display luminance. Consequently, the previously clear distinction between iconic memory and visible persistence, as defended by Coltheart (1980a, b), was no longer sustainable. Here the argument is quite subtle, though, and is worth a little consideration before we move on. Previously the evidence was that visible persistence and iconic memory behaved differently according to manipulations of stimulus duration and luminance, hence visible persistence and iconic memory were seen to be different. However, cases were uncovered that showed that there is a type of visible persistence that behaves in a similar fashion to iconic memory when stimulus duration/luminance are varied.

One conclusion you might draw, therefore, is that iconic memory is nothing other than visible persistence because they exhibit the same behaviour under particular circumstances. But this is quite a dangerous conclusion to draw because it does not necessarily follow from the evidence. Merely because two things behave in the same way does not mean that they are the same. When released from the eighth floor of a hotel window, both chalk and cheese are travelling at the same speed just before they hit ground. In 1984 Coltheart was of the view that iconic memory and visible persistence are different and should be treated as such (despite some evidence to the contrary).

### Iconic storage is different from visible persistence

More recently this particular issue has been very carefully re-examined by Loftus and Irwin (1998). To cut a very long story short, they showed that Coltheart's conjecture – that iconic memory and visible persistence are different – is seemingly correct. In their critical experiment participants were presented with brief target displays each containing a 2 × 5 matrix of letters in a variant of an earlier paradigm described by Averbach and Coriell (1961). In this so-called bar-probe task, participants were cued to report just a single (target) letter indicated by a small bar marker (probe) adjacent to the to-be-reported (target) item (see Figure 3.8 for an illustration of the basic task). Both the target duration and the time between the offset of the target and the onset of the probe – the **inter-stimulus interval** (the ISI) – were varied.

---

### Pinpoint question 3.5

**What's the difference between SOA and ISI?**

---

In the study by Loftus and Irwin (1998), two different measures of performance were taken. On some trials participants were instructed to undertake the bar-probe task and report the probed letter, while on others they were asked to rate 'the subjective completeness of the

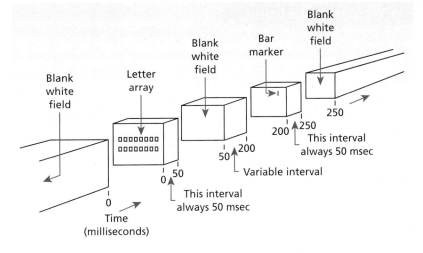

**Figure 3.8 Schematic representation of the Averbach and Coriell (1961) bar-probe task**

Loftus and Irwin (1998) used slightly different target displays and timings.

*Source*: Averbach, E., & Coriell, A. S. (1961). Short term memory in vision. *Bell Systems Technical Journal, 40,* 309–328 (fig. 2, p. 313). Reproduced with permission of John Wiley & Sons.

ensemble formed by the stimulus array and the probe' (pp. 168–9). In other words, participants were asked to rate the degree to which the initial stimulus array and following bar probe were seen to be part of the same visual event. How clear is the impression that the stimulus array and bar probe appear to be parts of the same visual scene? If visible persistence was operating in this case, then the impression would be one in which the letter array and bar probe were treated as a single perceptual event. In other words, the impression of the letter array would be that it persisted after the display was terminated and until the bar probe was physically present. What is particularly appealing about this experimental set-up is that comparisons between visible persistence (impressions of the cohesiveness of the array and bar probe) and the duration of iconic memory (letter reports) were made under identical display conditions.

Letter report accuracy was measured as in the standard sort of iconic memory experiment and this was discussed as being an objective measure. Letter accuracy could be validated objectively because on each trial the participant was either right or wrong. However, the subjective-completeness ratings were classified as being a subjective measure. 'Subjective' here refers to the fact that we have to take the ratings in good faith because there is no objective way of validating these reports – a participant could be guessing (or even lying!) on a given trial and we could never know. A rating of 1 meant the letters and bar probe appeared to be concurrent, whereas a rating of 4 meant the letters and bar probe appeared to be temporally separate events. The degree to which the letters and bar probe were rated as cohering when a delay was introduced between them was taken to reflect the operation of visible persistence.

In summary, the data revealed that item report decreased in a linear fashion as the delay between the letters and the bar probe increased. There was, however, no effect of display duration on letter report accuracy. A quite different pattern arose for the subjective ratings. Now the impression of perceptual cohesion decreased as a linear function of the time gap between the array offset and the probe onset. This is exactly what we'd expect – as the delay between the two events increases, the less likely they are to merge into one another. Importantly, though, there was a notable effect of display duration. Generally speaking, the longer the display was presented, the less the letters and the bar probe were seen as being concurrently present. In other words, there was a robust inverse relation between display duration and impressions of perceptual cohesion. As the display duration increased, impressions of perceptual cohesion decreased.

What all this means is that the effects of display duration were different across the measures of visible persistence and iconic memory. The data therefore provide good grounds for arguing that visible persistence and iconic memory are different things. Indeed, having run many experiments of this sort, Loftus and Irwin (1998) concluded by confirming Coltheart's (1984) conjecture that 'visible persistence (the lingering visible trace of a stimulus after its offset) differs from informational persistence (knowledge about the properties of a recently extinguished stimulus)' (p. 189). The importance of this conclusion cannot be overstated because it means that the study of iconic memory falls rightly within the realm of cognitive psychology and not visual neurophysiology. In this regard it is important to re-focus our efforts and concentrate on the functional properties of this sensory memory system.

→ See 'What have we learnt?', page 80.

The experiments of Sperling (1960, 1963) were originally taken as providing evidence for a transient form of storage that is present at a very early stage of visual information processing. It is as if there is some form of pictorial snapshot of the current scene that, under normal daylight conditions, dissipates over a relatively brief but measurable amount of time. It contains a record of the visual properties of the scene just glanced upon. From a physiological point of view, the most parsimonious account of the findings is that they arise because of visible persistence. Visible persistence is a well-known physiological process that is well understood and has certain well-established characteristics. For instance, brief flashes appear to persist longer than less brief flashes.

Quite clearly, therefore, if iconic memory is nothing other than visible persistence then performance in iconic memory tasks should reveal similar characteristics to those observed when visible persistence is measured. When Loftus and Irwin (1998) carried out such comparative experiments, however, they found that iconic storage (informational persistence) exhibits different characteristics to visible persistence. Hence informational and visible persistence are different. Icon memory is not simply visible persistence measured in a novel way. Consequently, the icon survives and continues to inhabit our thoughts about how best to construe visual information processing in functional terms.

## Puzzling findings and the traditional icon

What emerged from the early experiments on iconic memory was essentially a two-component account of processing. At a first stage 'very early in the lifetime of the visual display' (Coltheart, 1983b, p. 286) a visual representation of the stimulus is built up in iconic memory. This representation is short-lasting and can be severely disrupted by masking. So unless the information is recoded into a more durable form it will be lost and cannot be recovered. That is, iconic memory is a precursor to a more durable, longer-lasting form of storage.

In addition, the early research had apparently established the pre-categorical nature of iconic representation. For instance, whereas a partial-report advantage obtained when participants were cued to report items on the basis of their spatial position (for instance), such an advantage was not found when items had to be reported on the basis of their categorical identity (Sperling, 1960; von Wright, 1968). It was apparently impossible to report selectively by item category; for instance, participants were unable to report only the letters and not the digits in a mixed array of letters and digits. This contrasting pattern of performance had been taken to support the idea that, whereas iconic memory captured the physical characteristics of the display items, categorical information (i.e., item identity letter or digit) was not represented.

The traditional view of iconic memory is that, although the physical characteristics of the display characters are represented, further interpretative work is needed to recover the categorical nature of the items. The icon codes physical but not categorical information about the display items. By this view iconic representation was *pre-categorical* in nature and not *post-categorical*. Post-categorical information is recovered at a later (post-iconic) stage of processing. However, as the years and subsequent research unfolded, this traditional view became strained to breaking point.

For instance, Merikle (1980) revisited the situation in which participants are presented with briefly flashed displays containing both letters and numbers. This study therefore revisited the seminal finding reported by Sperling (1960), that there was no partial-report advantage when participants were cued to report either the letters or the numbers. Merikle tested performance across a range of conditions by varying the onset of the cue relative to the onset of the target display (so this is a manipulation of SOA rather than ISI; see Pinpoint question 3.5). Four such conditions were tested. In the −900 condition the cue preceded the target by 900 ms, in the −300 condition the cue preceded the target by 300 ms, in the +300 condition the cue followed the target by 300 ms and in the +900 condition the cue followed the target by 900 ms. Across these conditions, Merikle (1980) found evidence for a partial-report advantage of alpha-numeric class. So despite Sperling's (1960) failure to find a partial-report advantage for items defined by alpha-numeric class, Merikle (1980) reported a completely contrasting effect. Critically this arose when the cue preceded the target and was also statistically reliable when the cue followed the display by up to 300 ms.

So why did Sperling and Merikle find these contrasting patterns of results? The answer to this lies with the different task demands in the whole- and partial-report conditions. Typically, under whole-report conditions participants know that, on every trial, they must attempt to report all of the items. In contrast, in partial-report conditions participants are uncertain as to which items they must report. Therefore, whereas there is no uncertainty in whole-report conditions, there is high uncertainty in the partial-report conditions. Participants are particularly disadvantaged in the partial-report conditions and therefore it is probably not so surprising if we fail to find a partial-report advantage for any particular selection criterion (such as alpha-numeric class).

Merikle (1980) tried to equate uncertainty across the two conditions by mixing whole-report and partial-report trials in the same block. Now the cue on each trial told participants to either make a whole-report or a partial-report response, so the level of uncertainty was the same for both conditions. Participants never knew which sort of trial would come next. With this control designed into the experiment, Merikle (1980) showed that participants were, in fact, able selectively to read out display items on the basis of their alpha-numeric class. This indicated that, with the very brief intervals, typically used in iconic memory experiments, the categorical nature of the items had been determined (see Bundesen, Pedersen & Larsen, 1984, for further supporting evidence). Even with brief intervals, participants could select only the letters or only the numbers. So whatever memory system was being tapped, it was *post-* and not *pre-*categorical in nature.

## Puzzling findings and the three-component model

In considering this sort of finding, Coltheart (1983b, 1984) began to develop a three-component view of what is going on (see Figure 3.9). Now we have:

1. A pre-categorical iconic memory system.
2. A post-categorical durable store.
3. An output component or a response buffer.

The pre-categorical store is essentially where the traditional notion of iconic representation is located. The post-categorical store is the durable memory system in

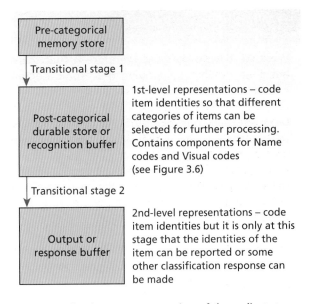

**Figure 3.9 The three-component view of the earliest stages of visual processing (based on the writings of Coltheart, 1983b, 1984)**

which item identities are made explicit (alternatively, this component was known as a recognition buffer; Coltheart, 1983b, p. 287). We might also consider how this store may be structured because with nameable characters (such as letters and digits) a visual code and a name code can be derived (see previous discussion of the two-stage account). In this regard, the recognition buffer may fractionate into two sub-components in the way shown in Figure 3.6 – there are processes concerned with name retrieval and processes concerned with visual encoding. Finally, the output component (response buffer) is essentially where a response is organised such that the participant can now report what has been presented.

So there is a distinction between **first-level representations** (Duncan, 1980) couched at the level of the post-categorical store and **second-level representations** couched at the level of the output stage. In order for an item to be reported it must be recoded into a second-level representation. So even though first-level representations code item identities, this form of representation does not support item report or any other form of categorical response. It is only at the output stage where second-level representations are coded that a categorical response can be organised. Being at the post-categorical stage would be like knowing the answer to a phone-in radio quiz but being unable to get through to the studio – the information is present but the response cannot be completed.

## → What have we learnt?

What we have established therefore is that there are good grounds for arguing that iconic storage can be distinguished from visible persistence, but in order to explain fully performance in partial-report tasks we need to invoke other forms of storage – performance in the partial-report paradigm map reflects other more durable forms of memory. For the time being, we may also hang on to the notion that iconic representation provides a momentary retinal snapshot of the visible world (the pre-categorical memory store, see Figure 3.9). Although this rapidly decays, its purpose is to prolong 'the availability of unprocessed visual information so as to give relatively slow-acting identification mechanisms more time to do their job' (Coltheart, 1980a, p. 222).

Such conclusions may seem straightforward but they do, however, lie at the heart of a particular controversy regarding the nature of visual perception. The basic claim is that if we accept this account of the early stages of visual processing, then this leads to a particular view of visual perception that seems to be untenable (see Haber, 1983, and the various commentaries on his paper for a thorough discussion of this point). Such a view of perception is now considered.

In this three-component model, there are two clear limitations or processing constraints. The first constraint concerns recoding information from an iconic form of representation into a first-level representation – let us call this transitional stage 1. The second constraint concerns recoding information from the durable store into the output stage (i.e., recoding first-level representations into second-level representations) – let us call this transitional stage 2.

One important feature of this three-component account is that it allows for selection to take place at either of the two transitional stages. Moreover, what the data from the Merikle (1980) study show is that the cues for item selection can operate at the post-categorical stage of processing located at transitional stage 2. Previously, the fact that participants could not select items on the basis of their categorical identity was taken to show that iconic memory is a purely visual store. Such a view, though, was apparently undermined by the evidence that participants can select items for report on the basis of their categorical identity from very brief displays. Given the three-component account, however, it is possible to retain the iconic store, but now argue that partial-report cues operate upon first-level post-categorical representations. Indeed it is tempting to contemplate the idea that, whereas non-selective read-out reflects the nature of transitional stage 1, transitional stage 2 is best characterised by selective read-out (e.g., transfer all digits but not letters). → See 'What have we learnt?', above.

**naïve realism** The idea that the perception directly and passively mirrors the stimulus as it is presented at the senses.

**iconic memory** Traditionally, taken to be a very short-term visual memory system which briefly preserves the physical characteristics of the stimulus.

**stimulus display** The presentation of visual information that the participant must operate upon so as to respond accordingly.

**display elements** Individual components of a stimulus display. For instance, the individual letters in a matrix of letters.

**target display** Alternative phrase for the imperative stimulus (i.e., the stimulus that the participant must act upon). See stimulus display.

**stimulus duration** The length of time that a stimulus is presented.

**display set size** The number of individual display elements in a stimulus display.

**full-report condition** In the Sperling (1960) paradigm, reporting all the display items from some form of briefly presented and masked display.

**partial-report condition** In the Sperling (1960) paradigm, reporting only the cued items from a briefly presented and masked display.

**partial-report superiority** The finding that estimates of iconic memory derived from partial report are larger than those derived from full report.

**categorical identity** A specification of the category to which a stimulus belongs.

**pre-categorical** When a representation of a stimulus does not contain the category identity of the stimulus.

**pre-field** Some form of visual event immediately before the stimulus field on a given trial.

**post-field** Some form of visual event immediately after the stimulus field has been presented on a given trial.

**integration hypothesis** According to Kahneman (1968), cases where two visual events are coded as one.

**visual noise mask** A display field containing densely scattered letter fragments or randomly positioned black and white squares. A mask that contains no pattern information.

**backward masking** A situation under which one visual event is obscured by an immediately following event (known as the mask).

**forward masking** A situation under which one visual event is obscured by an immediately preceding event (known as the mask).

**integration masking** When mask and stimulus are combined (psychologically) into a single montage.

**interruption masking** When processing of a stimulus is stopped by the presentation of an ensuing stimulus or masker.

**replacement** A form of masking by interruption where the processing of one stimulus is over-written when a second stimulus is presented.

**erasure** A form of interruption masking in which the current stimulus is completely over-written by the delivery of the mask.

**curtailment** A form of masking by interruption where the processing of one stimulus stops when a second stimulus is presented.

**stimulus onset asynchrony (SOA)** The time between the onset of one stimulus and the onset of a subsequent stimulus.

**visual code** Encoding that captures the visual characteristics of a stimulus.

**name code** A mental encoding that captures information about the name of a stimulus.

**visible persistence** Neural activity following the offset of a visually presented stimulus. Think of the impression created when you look at the camera and the flash accompanies the photograph.

**informational persistence** The retention of information following the offset of a stimulus, as revealed by the partial-report advantage. A technical phrase for iconic memory in its traditional guise.

**inter-stimulus interval (ISI)** The time between the offset of one stimulus and the onset of a subsequent stimulus.

**first-level representations** A representation of the stimulus that contains a record of its identity.

However, further operations are needed before a response can be generated.

**second-level representations** A representation of the stimulus that contains a record of its identity. Sufficient information is coded such that a response can be organised.

## The 'eye-as-a-camera' view of visual perception

We shall begin to address these concerns by concentrating on the 'eye-as-a-camera' view of perception (see Figure 3.10). This is a view of perception that fits most comfortably with the traditional view of iconic storage. Before continuing, though, it is important to realise that the discussion is now shifting between memory and perception and this shows just how blurred some of our 'dichotomies' actually are (cf. Newell, 1973). Implicit here is the assumption that in order to understand perception we cannot disregard the operation of certain memory systems!

Traditional accounts of visual processing may be characterised by the 'eye-as-a-camera' view of perception that asserts that light enters the eye, is projected onto the retina by the lens, and a 2D retinal image is

**Figure 3.10 Where does the camera end and the eye begin?**
*Source*: Peggy St Jacques.

**Figure 3.11 Static views of a changing world**
A collection of static, non-overlapping 2D images can be used to convey a changing 3D world.

created. It is this retinal image (or icon) that constitutes the first stage in visual perception (see Wade & Swanston, 1991, for a thorough historical account of this view), and it is asserted that our perception of the ever-changing world is built up from a sequence of such 2D static views (Turvey, 1977) (see Figure 3.11). For instance, just think of how we might use a flick book to convey the impression of a seal juggling a beach ball or a man on a unicycle. Indeed Coltheart (1983a) apparently endorsed this view when he stated that 'perception depends upon further analysis of the icon not the stimulus itself' (p. 18). Nevertheless, such a view is not without its critics (Haber, 1983; Neisser, 1976), and it is important to appreciate what their concerns are.

What is at stake is the validity of the claim that our seamless perception of a continuously changing world is constructed from a sequence of static retinal snapshots (i.e., icons). How might we best go about understanding this claim? Perhaps the simplest analogy here is with regard to how a traditional reel-to-reel movie camera operates. A reel of film comprises a sequence of fixed frames and during the filming stage this is passed behind an aperture at a speed of 24 frames a second. In order words, a different photographic frame is exposed to light roughly every 40 ms. So the visual scene is recorded on a sequence of fixed frames at 24 frames a second. This film is then played back in the

movie projector such that the cinema viewer watches a sequence of static images presented at 24 frames a second.

Two points are relevant here. First this analogy gives a reasonably clear impression of how iconic memory might be operating – this is examined more carefully below. Second, insofar as watching films is very much like watching the world go by, then maybe the iconic approach to understanding human visual perception is not so far fetched as Haber and Neisser would have us believe (Loftus, 1983). Nevertheless, a more careful analysis of these issues has been provided by Turvey (1977), who discussed a distinction, originally made explicit by Allport (1968), that sets out two different ways of thinking about visual perception over time. Interestingly, though, both of these assume that the current psychological moment is captured by the contents of a fixed memory buffer. These are framed, respectively, in terms of the *discrete moment* and the *travelling moment hypotheses*.

## The discrete moment and the travelling moment hypotheses

The **discrete moment hypothesis** is akin to the sequence-of-snapshots idea where it is assumed that, over time, the perceptual system takes one look at the world followed by another look and so on and so

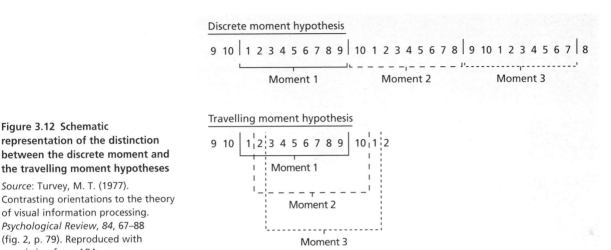

**Figure 3.12 Schematic representation of the distinction between the discrete moment and the travelling moment hypotheses**

*Source*: Turvey, M. T. (1977). Contrasting orientations to the theory of visual information processing. *Psychological Review, 84,* 67–88 (fig. 2, p. 79). Reproduced with permission from APA.

forth (the eye-as-a-movie-camera metaphor). This fits with one view of iconic memory whereby perception is built up from a series of discrete static snapshots of the world over time – the stroboscopic account of perception. The way the hypothesis is set out, however, critically depends on there being no overlap in the snapshots over time. It is as if the contents of the memory buffer are completely over-written at each moment in time – there is only one movie still that can be projected at any one time. In contrast, there is the **travelling moment hypothesis** which asserts that the perception of the world is built up from an overlapping sequence of 'looks' at the world. In contrast to the discrete moment hypothesis, the contents of the buffer are not completely over-written at each moment but are continuously updated. Figure 3.12 provides, in schematic form, these different hypotheses.

Perhaps the easiest way of thinking about this difference is in terms of a day in the life of a trainspotter. When the trainspotter watches a train pass by, his impression of the inside of a carriage is built up from a series of glimpses through the individual carriage windows (this would be the perceptual theory provided by the discrete moment hypothesis). Alternatively, the passenger, in watching the world pass by, sees the world framed by the carriage window but this view is continuously updated as the train moves on. New stuff appears on the leading edge of the frame and old stuff disappears from the trailing edge (this would be the perceptual theory provided by the travelling moment hypothesis). For Turvey (1977, and Allport, 1968), it is the travelling moment hypothesis that provides a much more sensible framework for thinking about visual perception than does the discrete moment

hypothesis – at least, the continuous nature of information uptake is mirrored in our impressions of a seamlessly changing external world.

Upon reflection, it is not impossible to see how a mechanism that operates according to the travelling moment hypothesis could function under stroboscopic lighting in the disco. Indeed, even though we might accept the travelling moment hypothesis as being entirely plausible, the fact that we do go to the cinema suggests that we can build up an impression of a seamlessly changing world on the basis of a sequence of static snapshots. Being forced to operate according to the discrete moment hypothesis does not seriously undermine our ability to perceive. However, we do not need to base an argument on intuitions and impressions because more recent evidence suggests that something very much like discrete moment processing is exactly what is going on (cf. VanRullen & Koch, 2003).

## Pinpoint question 3.6

**What is the main difference between the travelling moment and discrete moment hypotheses?**

### *Recent support for the discrete moment hypothesis*

A familiar complaint about research on iconic memory is that it was discovered in the lab, it lives in the lab, and consequently, it does not survive outside the tightly controlled conditions that exist in the lab. It will therefore come as something of a relief to realise that the data to be discussed were not gathered in the lab, but in the kitchen. As strange as it may seem, evidence

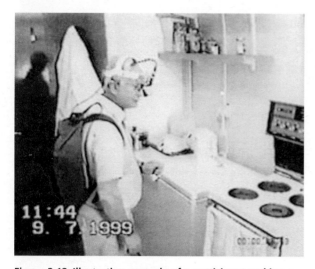

**Figure 3.13 Illustrative example of a participant making a cup of tea in Tatler's (2001) experiment**

*Source*: Tatler, B. W. (2001). Characterising the visual buffer: Real world evidence for overwriting early in each fixation. *Perception*, *30*, 993–1006 (fig. 1(a), p. 994). Reproduced with permission from Pion Limited, London.

for the discrete moment hypothesis comes from studies concerned with how it is that you go about making a cup of tea.

Tatler (2001) had volunteers make a cup of tea while wearing a rather unattractive piece of equipment that measured eye-position and eye-movements (see Figure 3.13). The equipment comprised optical devices that collected measures of eye-position data on a moment-to-moment basis together with a video record of the scene that the person was viewing. In combining both records, it was possible to recover where and to what the person was looking throughout the tea-making exercise. Volunteers were warned that at some point the lights in the kitchen would be extinguished. When this happened the participant was asked to report details of where and to what they had just been looking at.

Certain key findings emerged from this experiment but to understand these it is important to realise what is actually going on as we move our eyes around, looking at the world. In very broad strokes, eye movements are characterised by fixations (periods where the eyes are focused at one point in space) interspersed with so-called saccades. The eyes focus on one point in the scene, namely, the point of fixation, and then they jump to another. Jumps between fixations are known as **saccades**.

What emerged from the data was very intriguing. First, participants all reported the impression of a vivid image of the scene immediately prior to the blackout. They were able to report the details of the scene to which they were looking immediately prior to the blackout – evidence for a visual snapshot of the scene. Second, participants experienced extreme difficulties in being able to describe details of the penultimate fixation prior to the blackout. Collectively, these findings showed that participants could readily access the visual 'snapshot' for the current fixation, but could not access snapshots of previous fixations (paraphrasing, Tatler, 2001, p. 999).

Figure 3.14 provides a schematic representation of how processing unfolds over a pair of successive fixations – look at the mug, then look at the teapot. As can be seen from Figure 3.14, the basic ideas accord well with both the discrete moment hypothesis and the notion of iconic storage (see also Becker, Pashler & Anstis, 2000). In this account, immediately after a new fixation is made, a retinal snapshot/iconic representation is derived. This representation will be retained until it is over-written by the information taken up from the next fixation. At each fixation, information from the previous fixation is over-written.

So although Turvey (1977) contrasted the discrete moment and travelling moment hypotheses (in a bid to undermine the idea that our impression of the world can be built up from a sequence of static snapshots), the more recent data are far more supportive. Iconic memory and the discrete moment hypothesis are alive and well and exist outside the laboratory!

## Icons as retinal snapshots

Overall therefore the cited evidence has been taken to support the notion of the icon as a retinal snapshot. Qualifications have also been added about the existence of other more durable forms of visual memory that also seem to play a role in a variety of so-called iconic memory tasks. In this way the experiments have provided examples as to why the visual system comprises a number of different sub-systems or processing modules. Iconic memory apparently maps onto one such module. This is located at the very earliest stages of processing and is separate from the later, more durable forms of memory.

It is important therefore to try to understand the particularities of the iconic memory system if we are to be able to distinguish it from other forms of visual memory. In this regard, one issue that has exercised researchers over the years is with trying to establish the locus of iconic storage – whereabouts in the stream of internal visual processes does iconic representation

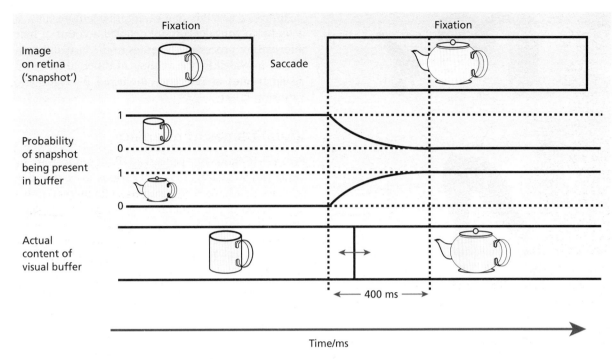

**Figure 3.14 The ever-changing nature of the icon**
Schematic representation of the events that unfold over time as first a mug is fixated and then a teapot (from Tatler, 2001).

*Source*: Tatler, B. W. (2001). Characterising the visual buffer: Real world evidence for overwriting early in each fixation. *Perception*, *30*, 993–1006 (fig. 7, p. 1004). Reproduced with permission from Pion Limited, London.

reside? In order to do this they have asked questions about the nature of the coding system that is used in iconic representation. To what degree is iconic storage really akin to a retinal image?

> **discrete moment hypothesis** Where visual perception over time is derived from individual non-overlapping snapshots of the world.
>
> **travelling moment hypothesis** Where perception is built up from an overlapping sequence of snapshots.
>
> **saccades** Generally used as short-hand of eye movements, but a saccade is the jump between one fixation and the next.

## Coding in the visual system

From neurophysiology we know that the retina is made up of a mosaic of photoreceptors, and as a first approximation, it is possible to consider the retina as being composed of a 2D array of light-sensitive points, and once again we can return to a computer analogy. Although a computer monitor projects light and the retinae receive light, it might help to think in terms of the pixels on your computer screen and the retinal image being composed of pixels. The photoreceptive cells on the retinae can be taken to be like the pixels on a computer screen – pixels that receive rather than project light. To speak of a **retinal co-ordinate system** therefore would be to define a position in terms of the points on this 2D retinal surface. In simple terms, we could give $x$ (left/right) and $y$ (up/down) values as we would on a traditional graph. This form of coding can be maintained throughout the visual system so we can talk of a retinal co-ordinate system – alternatively a **retinotopic map** – without necessarily implying that such a map can only reside in the retinae. However, on the most literal reading, a retina image would be taken to be the distribution of light over a simple 2D array of light-sensitive points defined over the retina. Each point represents the amount of light present at that retinal position. Again tradition dictates that a different retinal image is produced by each eye and it is the combination of these two images that gives rise to a single so-called cyclopean view of the world (see Figure 3.15).

**Figure 3.15 The eye has it**
How to achieve cyclopean perception without having to integrate information from two eyes. The purple hair is optional though.

*Source*: 20th Century Fox/Everett/Rex Features.

To appreciate this line of argument more fully, it is useful to consider a more detailed account of how information processing operates in the visual system. This is provided by the analysis of different so-called **visual frames of reference** discussed by Wade and Swanston (1991).

## Visual frames of reference

Figure 3.16 shows one general account, put forward by Wade and Swanston (1991), of various sorts of coding schemes that have been assumed to be present at different levels of the visual perceptual system. We have already discussed the notion of retinal coding whereby the position of the proximal stimulus is defined in terms of a retinal co-ordinate system. It has been suggested that one way to think about this is in terms of the space mapped out by a simple 2D graph in terms of $x$ and $y$ axes. What is critical in this scheme is where these two axes intersect – the point of origin – and the points in the 2D space defined by the axes are specified in terms of $x/y$ co-ordinates that are fixed relative to this point. In this general scheme the axes are sometimes referred to as frames of reference and

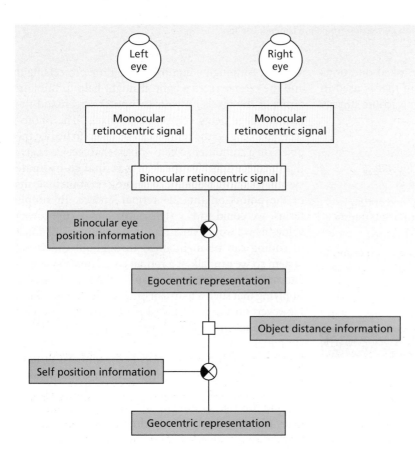

**Figure 3.16 Visual frames of reference**
Schematic representation of the different frames of reference used to code information in the human visual system (from Wade and Swanston, 1991).

*Source*: Wade, N. J. (1996). Frames of reference in vision. *Minimally Invasive Therapy and Allied Technologies*, 5, 435–439 (fig. 1, p. 436). Reproduced with permission from Taylor & Francis Ltd.

here the axes provide the frames of reference for every point in the space.

## Monocular retinocentric frames of reference

If we take this graph analogy and apply it directly to the idea of retinal coding, the centre of the eye – the fovea – offers itself as a natural point of origin. Furthermore we can also define an *x* axis as passing through the fovea (the horizontal midline) and a *y* axis intersecting the *x* at the fovea (the vertical midline) so that such midlines provide the retinal frames of reference for each point on the retina as defined by the individual photoreceptors. Wade and Swanston (1991) referred to this form of coding as monocular retinocentric. The implication is that such a **monocular retinocentric frame of reference** provides the initial co-ordinate system for coding the stimulus information. Importantly, each eye contains its own retinotopic co-ordinate system (see Figure 3.17).

## Cyclopean (binocular) retinocentric frames of reference

Given that we do not normally see the world through a single eye, there must be a stage at which information across the two eyes is combined to form a so-called *cyclopean view of the world* – we see one world, not two. Wade and Swanston (1991) referred to such a combined representation as being coded in terms of a **cyclopean retinocentric frame of reference**. At this level, information from the two eyes is combined to form a **binocular retinocentric representation**. Here we can think of taking the left and right retinal graphs and super-imposing them over one another such that they share a common origin (see Figure 3.18). Psychologically the origin occupies a point located between the two eyes known as the cyclopean eye or the egocentre. Such a point will be located in the centre of the head if information from both eyes is weighted equally. The egocentre may, however, be offset slightly in the direction of the dominant eye. At this level, information from the two eyes is combined to form a binocular retinocentric representation. Wondering which one is your dominant eye? Very easy. With both eyes open, create a circle with both your hands and capture a small object in its bull's eye. Now close your left and right eye in turn. Whichever eye is open when the object moves less is your dominant eye.

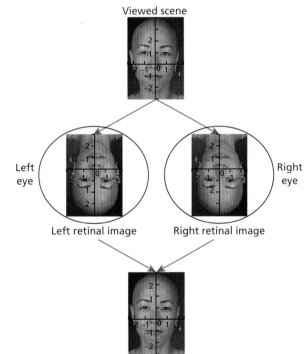

Figure 3.18 **Achieving a cyclopean view of the world**
Information is combined from the two eyes so that information contained in two separate monocular retinocentric frames of reference are then registered in a single binocular co-ordinate frame (see text for further details). The origin of this co-ordinate system is now in terms of some form of cyclopean frame of reference.

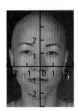 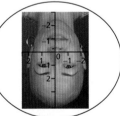

Figure 3.17 **A monocular retinocentric frame of reference**
The image on the left is the environmental scene. Superimposed over this is a co-ordinate system projected onto the image that specifies *x* and *y* axes whose origin is fixed at the nose. The image on the right is supposed to convey the retinal image – the image is inverted because the lens of the eye projects an inverted image. In this case, the frame of reference preserves the spatial nature of the dimensions in the scene but the *x* and *y* co-ordinates are defined relative to an origin specified on the viewer's retina. Therefore co-ordinates in the right image provide a monocular retinocentric frame of reference. Each eye of the viewer possesses its own monocular retinocentric frame of reference. The scene-based co-ordinates are fixed on an origin (the nose in this case) in the scene but the retinal co-ordinates are fixed on an origin in the retina, for instance on the fovea.

## Egocentric (head-based) frames of reference

If the eyes remain still, then any movement in the visual field will be coded relative to the egocentre. However, whenever the eyes move this must be taken into account. It would be catastrophic if every time we moved our eyes the world were seen to move in the opposite direction. In fact, if you keep your head still for a minute and look around, it's pretty amazing exactly how stable things appear despite the eye movements. Wade and Swanston (1991) therefore discussed the egocentric frame of reference. At this level, the binocular retinocentric representation is combined with information about eye movements so that the movement of the eye in the head can be discounted. In this regard, the **egocentric frame of reference** is also known as a *head-based frame of reference*. At this level it is as if there is a single eye in the centre of the head that moves with every head movement, so although we may not much look like a Cyclops, the visual system is certainly cyclopean in nature. This sort of co-ordinate system codes the relative distance of objects in the environment relative to the observer's head independently of where the eyes are pointing.

## Geocentric (scene-based) frames of reference

The final frame of reference Wade and Swanston (1991) discussed is the **geocentric frame of reference**.

So far we have discussed (i) the retinocentric frame that codes information in term of retinal co-ordinates but this will change every time the eyes move, and (ii) the egocentric frame that codes information in terms of a head-based co-ordinate system but this will need to be updated every time the head moves. The geocentric frame codes information about the disposition of objects in the environment independently of movement of the observer – this has been alternatively termed a scene-based frame of reference (Hinton & Parsons, 1988). This level of representation is the most stable of the three because it remains fixed when the observer moves, the objects in the visible environment move or both move. → See 'What have we learnt?', below.

### Pinpoint question 3.7

According to Wade and Swanston (1991), what are the four visual frames of reference?

---

**retinal co-ordinate system** Defining retinal positions in terms of a 2D co-ordinate system. For example, using *x* (left/right) and *y* (up/down) values with the origin fixed at the fovea. Such codings are preserved at some of the higher levels of the visual system. It is possible to find retinotopic maps in the cortex.

**retinotopic map** See retinal co-ordinate system.

---

## → What have we learnt?

The main reason in discussing the various putative frames of reference in vision at this juncture is that this framework is useful for thinking about the nature of iconic storage – just what sort of co-ordinate system captures the icon? Aside from this, the framework comes in useful when we discuss visual object recognition (see Chapter 13). So when we get round to discussing visual object recognition you will already be in a position to appreciate some of the issues. For example, what sorts of co-ordinate systems are used when internal representations of objects are derived? Nonetheless, it should now be clear that it is quite reasonable to discuss the icon as preserving information in terms of a retinal co-ordinate system – this codes the position of the stimulus elements in the target display – without also committing ourselves to the idea that iconic memory necessarily resides in the retinae (Wade & Swanston, 1991, p. 91).

In this regard therefore the abstract framework for thinking put forward by Wade and Swanston (1991) provides a very useful means to try to understand the detailed nature of iconic representation. We have accepted that the icon preserves the visual characteristic of the stimulus (e.g., red items, large items, items in a particular position in the display, etc.), but we have yet to understand fully what sort of co-ordinate system this information is captured in. For instance, one plausible suggestion is that iconic storage resides at a level at which information is integrated across the two eyes and is therefore a form of binocular retinocentric representation as described by Wade and Swanston (1991). Further evidence that bolsters this claim resides in the literature on visual masking, and it is to this that discussion now returns.

**visual frames of reference** After Wade and Swanston (1991), a collection of coding schemes that exist at different levels of the visual system. Each codes the spatial disposition of the parts of a stimulus in its own co-ordinates such as positions relative to the fovea – as in a retinal frame of reference.

**monocular retinocentric frame of reference** Spatial co-ordinates derived within an eye and defined in terms of some form of retinal co-ordinate system.

**cyclopean retinocentric frame of reference** Spatial co-ordinates derived from combined information from both eyes.

**binocular retinocentric representation** A representation of the visual world derived from both eyes but which preserves locational information in terms of retinal co-ordinates.

**egocentric frame of reference** A head-based frame of reference used by the visual system to specify object positions relative to the viewer's head.

**geocentric frame of reference** A scene-based frame of reference in vision which takes into account both body-centred and scene-based attributes.

---

**Research focus 3.2**

## Honk if you can hear me: listening to trains inside cars

Although this chapter is primarily concerned with vision, it's important to remember that masking can occur in other modalities – not just vision. So, it should be quite easy to think of cases of integration masking in audition, where loud and soft sounds presented at the same time compete for entry into our processing system. Dolan and Rainey (2005) provided the example of detecting approaching trains at a rail crossing while you wait inside your car. Although this is less of an issue in Europe since we tend to have those nice barriers that go up and down, it is more problematic in the US. There are often no such safeguards and drivers often have to rely on the sound of the train's horn as the primary cue for the imminent Amtrak. They also noted that this problem was compounded by the fact that certain states sought to ban train whistles due to noise pollution. So, exactly how does being inside a car mask the sound of the train?

Dolan and Rainey (2005) first began by creating a variety of sounds of approaching trains within various cars under various conditions. To begin, the same train was recorded passing a rail crossing (with horn blazing) within three different stationary cars. These cars were then taken to a quiet residential area and interior noise within the automobile was recorded with (a) engine idling with ventilation off, (b) engine idling with ventilation on, (c) car moving at 30 miles an hour with fan off, and (d) car moving at 30 miles an hour with fan on. The sound of the train and the internal noise were then played together and 20 participants with normal hearing were asked to indicate when they could hear the train approaching. The sound of the train horn was then increased if the participant couldn't hear it and decreased if the participant could hear it, until a threshold for the train horn within the various conditions was established.

The thresholds for hearing that long train a-comin' varied widely across the various conditions, with participants requiring louder train horn sounds when the vehicle was in motion at 30 miles an hour, and also when the ventilation fan was on. It was also found to be the case that the type of vehicle also influenced the threshold of the horn, with thresholds 'being highest for the older model pickup truck and lowest for the luxury sedan' (Dolan & Rainey, 2005, p. 623).

As the authors stressed, there are an incredible number of factors to consider in determining how well drivers, when tucked away snug in their cars, can hear external sound sources such as an approaching train. The vehicle's internal noise is generated by the engine, exhaust, radio, windshield wipers, tyres, air turbulence (the list goes on) and that's also assuming that the drivers have normal hearing in the first place. All these factors contribute to the masking in which we have to hear out the signals of interest while driving, be it train horns, other drivers honking at us or the attendant at the other end of the speaker box at the drive-through. So next time you're cursing your luck by getting stuck behind a rail crossing barrier for 10 minutes, just be thankful that someone else is looking out for your safety, rather than you having to rely on your ears.

*Source*: Dolan, T. G., & Rainey, J. E. (2005). Audibility of train horns in passenger vehicles. *Human Factors, 47*, 613–629.

## Turvey's (1973) experiments on masking

Figure 3.5 (top row – see page 75) illustrates a typ-ical sequence of events on a given trial in a backward masking paradigm. Remember here that the presenta-tion of the mask is said to disrupt the processing of the earlier stimulus target, and as we have already noted, such disruption may be due to the mask being integrated with the target or the mask may be said to interrupt the processing of the target. We therefore have two different means by which a mask may have its effects, respectively, via a process of integration with the target stimulus or via the presentation of the mask interrupting the processing of the stimulus. What Turvey (1973) did was to examine very carefully the conditions under which integration and interruption masking may take place.

Figure 3.19 provides examples of two different sorts of masks that Turvey used in his experiments. The

| Random noise (RN) | Pattern mask (PM) | Example of target |

**Figure 3.19 Examples of different sorts of visual masks and a target letter used in masking experiments (after Turvey, 1973)**

*Source*: Turvey, M. T. (1973). On peripheral and central processes in vision: Inferences from an information-processing analysis of masking with patterned stimuli. *Psychological Review*, 80, 1–52 (fig. 2, p. 4). Reproduced with permission from APA.

random visual noise mask (see also Figure 3.3, page 73) was essentially a random texture of small black and white squares: black snow against a white sky. The critical aspect of a mask such as this is that it contains no pattern information – that is, across the texture there are no discernible lines, edges, contours, angles, etc. In contrast to the random noise mask, there is the pattern mask that, unsurprisingly, does contain pat-tern information.

Now in Turvey's experiments the standard task was to present a target stimulus – a single capital letter – for a brief amount of time and to mask this. Given this letter character set, the pattern mask contained a random juxtaposition of line segments that were similar to those used to define the letters. The pattern mask contained pattern information as defined by visual features of the target letters. So at a very intuitive level, any visual encoding processes that are peculiar to let-ters may also be engaged by the pattern mask because both contain letter features. In contrast, given that tar-get letter and the random noise mask share no pattern information then there is no reason to assume that letter encoding operations will be engaged by the mask. At the outset therefore it is assumed that random noise masks and pattern masks should give rise to different forms of masking.

## Visual masking and the organisation of the visual system

Importantly the logic of Turvey's early experiments depends on accepting certain assumptions about how the human visual system operates, given its struc-ture. Figure 3.20 provides the necessary details, and here it suffices to say that it assumed that each retina is divided into a right and left **hemi-retina** about a

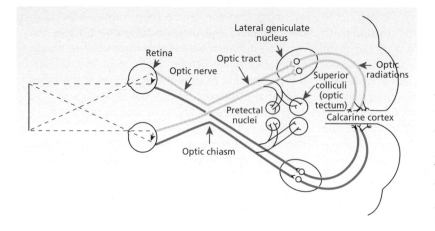

**Figure 3.20 Schematic representation of the structure of the visual pathways in the human brain**

*Source*: Posner, M. I., & Rogers, M. G. K. (1978). Chronometric analysis of abstraction and recognition. In W. K. Estes (Ed.), *Handbook of learning and cognitive processes*. *Vol. 5. Human information processing* (pp. 143–188, fig. 2, p. 149). Hillsdale, New Jersey: Erlbaum.

vertical midline. Turvey referred to the hemi-retina nearest the nose as the **nasal hemi-retina** and the hemi-retina furthest from the nose as the **temporal hemi-retina**. Basic physiology (see Figure 3.20) tells us that the physical projections from each temporal hemi-retina remain on the same side of the head (they are **ipsi-lateral** projections) whereas projections from each nasal hemi-retina cross over the midline of the head (they are **contra-lateral** projections). This means that information from the rightmost hemi-retina in each eye ends up in the occipital lobe of the right hemisphere of the cerebral cortex, whereas information from the leftmost hemi-retina in each eye ends up in the occipital lobe of the left hemisphere of the cerebral cortex. Figure 3.20 provides a schematic representation of these different so-called visual pathways.

Based on this understanding of how the visual system is structured, Turvey (1973) systematically varied whether the mask and the target letter were presented to the same hemi-retina of one eye (under so-called **monoptic** conditions) or whether the target was presented to one hemi-retina of one eye, and the mask was presented to the associated hemi-retina in the other eye. Put more simply, under monoptic conditions the target and mask travelled the same route from peripheral eye to the same (central) cortical hemisphere, whereas under **dichoptic** conditions, the target and the mask travelled via different peripheral routes to the same (central) cortical hemisphere. Figure 3.21 provides illustrative examples.

## Pinpoint question 3.8

**What is the difference between monoptic and dichoptic presentation conditions?**

We will constrain the discussion to that of backward masking in which the target display is followed by a mask. However, as we have already noted, Turvey examined performance separately, with random noise and with pattern masks. So we have type of mask (random noise vs. pattern) and type of presentation (monoptic vs. dichoptic) and when these are combined we have the four possibilities outlined in Table 3.1.

To cut a very long story short, Table 3.1 provides a summary of the evidence regarding whether backward masking effectively masked the perception of the target letter.

Case 1 is distinctive because participants' reports of the target letter depended on both the energy of the target and the amount of time that transpired before the mask was presented (i.e., the target/mask ISI). To make the target legible, increase either the energy of the target relative to the mask (make the target brighter), or increase the length of the pause between the offset of the target and the mask, or do both. All of this seemed to point to the idea that this kind of masking was, essentially, masking by integration primarily because the relative amounts of energy in the target and the mask were so critical. A dim target was obscured by a brighter mask.

Case 2 is also distinctive because, under these conditions, when the random noise mask was presented to one eye and the target display to the other eye, no masking effect was found. Participants were able to see and report the target letter despite the presentation of the backward random noise mask. In other words, a random noise mask was ineffective when it was not delivered to the same eye as the target.

In contrast in Cases 3 and 4, when pattern masks were used, masking occurred whether or not the target letter and mask were presented to the same eye. With

**Table 3.1** Different combinations of mask types and presentation conditions together with evidence for effective backward masking.

| | Random noise mask | | Pattern mask | |
|---|---|---|---|---|
| | **Monoptic presentation** | **Dichoptic presentation** | **Monoptic presentation** | **Dichoptic presentation** |
| Case | 1[ab] | 2[ab] | 3[c] | 4[bc] |
| Effective masking? | ✓ | ✗ | ✓ | ✓ |

[a] Findings reported by Turvey (1973, Exp. III, IV)
[b] Findings reported by Turvey (1973, Exp. IV)
[c] Findings reported by Turvey (1973, Exp. VI)

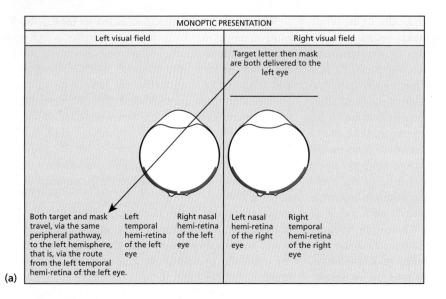

(a)

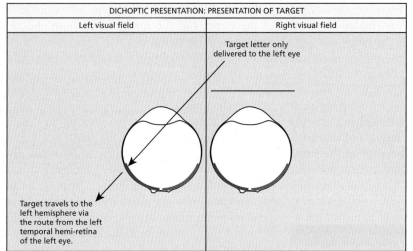

(b)

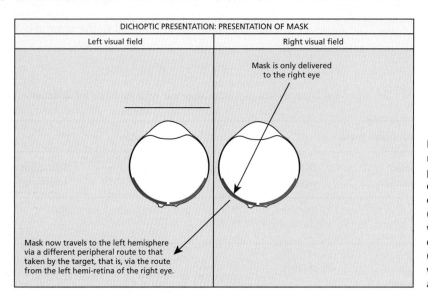

**Figure 3.21 Schematic representation of the monoptic presentation conditions and dichoptic presentation conditions used by Turvey (1973)** (a) Monoptic presentation in which target and mask are delivered to the same eye. (b) Dichoptic presentation in which the target and the mask are delivered to different eyes.

## → What have we learnt?

Clearly the experimental terrain has become a little overgrown. What has emerged, though, is that when discussing the very early stages of visual processing and the nature of iconic representation we must be very careful in taking into account the manner in which masking is undertaken. Very different patterns of performance emerge when either visual noise masks or pattern masks are used. If we were just to consider the results with masking by noise then we might be seduced into thinking that iconic representation was captured at a purely retinal level simply because such masking does not occur with dichoptic presentation. However, this is completely the wrong conclusion to draw because dichoptic masking does arise when pattern masks are used.

This result is important because it rules out the idea that the icon is merely a retinal image of the stimulus. Information across the two retinae is being integrated and the pattern masker is disrupting some form of binocular representation. Iconic storage is not therefore akin to a single retinal image of the input, because the visual input is captured in terms of a binocular retinal frame of reference (see Wade & Swanston, 1991). In accepting this we are in a sense shifting the icon from the back of the retina to the binocular retinocentric level.

dichoptic presentation, though, the relative amounts of energy in the target and mask were not influential.

### Peripheral and central masking

What is emerging here are patterns of masking that seem to reflect the operations of two different sorts of mechanisms, namely, peripheral encoding mechanisms and, respectively, central decision mechanisms. In using different sorts of masks (i.e., random noise vs. pattern), Turvey was attempting to tap selectively into these different mechanisms. So in certain cases the data were taken to reveal more about one of the mechanisms than the other. On this assumption therefore it is possible to refer to **peripheral masking** and **central masking**. It is tempting simply to equate peripheral masking with cases where the target and the mask are present monotopically and central masking with cases where dichoptic presentation is used, but the argument was more subtle than this. Other important differences were uncovered concerning the two different sorts of masking.

For instance, one such critical difference between central and peripheral masking was that central masking was shown to depend on the SOA between target and mask and not on the relative amounts of energy in the target and the mask. Indeed, Turvey was clear that in cases where masking occurs and the mask contains less energy than the target, this is the signature of central and not peripheral processes. A preliminary conclusion therefore was that central masking reflected 'interruption in the normal functioning of central mechanisms' (Turvey, 1973, p. 18).

What we have here therefore is an understanding that masking may reflect the characteristics of either or both of two underlying visual processes, respectively, peripheral and central processes. In simplifying Turvey's analysis substantially it is tempting to claim that the work shows that peripheral masking reflects purely processes of stimulus integration whereas central masking reflects processes of interruption. The eventual account was much more involved than this and we will briefly return to this at the beginning of the next chapter. → See 'What have we learnt?', above.

### Pinpoint question 3.9

**According to Turvey (1973), which form of masking turns out to be ineffective?**

hemi-retina Either the left half or the right half of the retina.

nasal hemi-retina The half of the retina closest to the nose.

temporal hemi-retina The retinal half furthest from the nose.

ipsi-lateral Same side to that being discussed.

contra-lateral Opposite side to that being discussed.

monoptic Cases where the stimulus is delivered to only one eye.

dichoptic Cases where one stimulus is delivered to one eye and a different stimulus is delivered to the other eye.

**peripheral masking** According to Turvey (1973), masking occurring at the level of peripheral encoding mechanisms.

**central masking** Masking occurring at the level of central decision mechanisms. Introduced in terms of the concurrent and contingent model of Turvey (1973).

## Further evidence on where the icon is

In following the elusive trail in trying to track down where the icon is, a very ingenious set of experiments were reported by Davidson, Fox and Dick (1973). Here the target display comprised a row of five letters. This was presented briefly (for 10 ms) and, in the conditions of interest, one of the letter positions was followed by a mask. The task was to try to report the letters and their positions together with the position of the mask. Matters were further complicated because participants were also instructed to alternate eye gaze between letter position 2 and letter position 4 starting prior to the onset of the display but continuing once the display was presented (see Figure 3.22). To facilitate this sequence of eye movements, two fixation lights were physically present at these locations and flashed alternately. Participants were instructed to fixate each of the currently illuminated lights in turn. The remaining details of the design can be conveyed with reference to a particular example. Assume the letter display contained S H V R Y. Take the case where the eye is fixed at letter position 2 (i.e., on the H). Now the letter display was presented but as soon as the eye moved to position 4 the letter display was replaced by the mask. The position of the mask varied over trials, but let us assume it was presented at letter position 5 (in the same physical location as the Y). In this example, the eye initially fixated on H, it then moved to the R (see Figure 3.22 for more details).

The critical question now was, at which position would the mask have its effect? If the icon is essentially a retinal image (or even located in binocular retinocentric co-ordinates) then the mask ought to erase the letter that falls at the same retinal location as the mask – in this case the V. If, however, the icon is coded in an egocentric reference frame (Wade & Swanston, 1991) or spatial co-ordinate system (Davidson et al., 1973), then the mask should erase the letter Y because the mask and the letter Y were presented at the same spatial location.

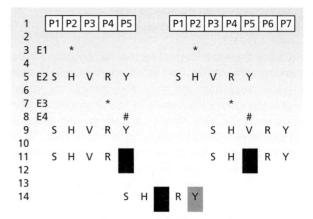

**Figure 3.22 Schematic representation of two alternative accounts of performance in the backward masking task devised by Davidson et al. (1973)**
The left-most column of numbers indicates how time (in steps) unfolds from the beginning of a trial. The left half of the figure provides a schematic of what is expected to transpire if the iconic representation of the five-letter display is defined in external, spatial co-ordinates. The right half of the figure provides a schematic of what is expected to transpire if the iconic representation of the five-letter display is defined in retinal co-ordinates.

- Line 1. P1 . . . P5 define the character positions in the letter display. P6 and P7 are included for completeness to mark letter positions if these move with the eye.
- E1 indexes the first event on a trial in which the light indicator illuminates letter position 2.
- E2 indexes the presentation of the letter display.
- E3 indexes the illumination of the light at letter position 4. This signals to the subject to initiate an eye movement to that position.
- E4 indexes the presentation of the masker.
- Line 9 provides the alternative representations that are assumed to be operating if, on the left, the icon retains its external co-ordinates, or whether, on the right, the icon moves with the eyes.
- Line 11 provides the respective percepts under these two different hypotheses.
- Line 14 provides a schematic representation of participants' perceptual reports. Namely, the letter V is rendered illegible by the mask but participants report seeing the masking character superimposed over the letter Y.

What Davidson et al. (1973) reported, however, was a very puzzling state of affairs. Take the particular case under discussion. Participants reported seeing the mask superimpose the letter Y but they were unable to report the letter V. So the mask was located (perceptually) in spatial co-ordinates but it was having its effects in retinal co-ordinates. One way to think about this is that whereas iconic representation is coded in terms of retinal co-ordinates, the percept of the current psychological moment is couched in terms of spatial co-ordinates. So there seem to be two levels of visual representation that are being revealed here: (i) a retinal iconic form of representation where the masking takes place (presumably couched in terms of the binocular retinocentric co-ordinates), and (ii) a higher-level of representation that supports our perceptual impressions of the world (presumably at the geocentric level).

Following up on this work, Irwin, Brown and Sun (1988) distinguished between *retinotopic visible persistence* that is susceptible to masking and *spatiotopic visible persistence* that is not. Spatiotopic visible persistence provides a means by which information is integrated over brief intervals. Irwin et al. found that both the appearance of the mask and its effects were at the same retinal location. There was no evidence of spatial fusion of the letters and the masker discussed by Davidson et al. (1973). Irwin et al. (1988) concluded that post-retinal integration probably does take place, but that it is most likely at a much more abstract level than iconic representation. The ability to integrate successive glances at the world underlies our ability to derive a stable representation of the visible environment and our place in it. It is therefore tempting to argue that this sort of operation takes place at the level of the geocentric frame of reference (Wade & Swanston, 1991, see further discussion of *Aperture Viewing*).

---

## Research focus 3.3

## Going, going, gone: iconic memory in dementia patients

So far we have been considering iconic memory with respect to normal and healthy individuals, which more often than not involve undergraduate samples (yes, we do consider you normal and healthy!). However, in addition to trying to understand typical cognitive functioning, the examination of atypical cognitive functioning is also of import (see Research focus 2.2 and the example of Phineas Gage in Chapter 2). So Lu, Neuse, Madigan and Dosher (2005) looked at iconic memory in individuals with mild cognitive impairment (MCI) to further appreciate the mechanisms involved in visual processing.

Three groups of participants were selected. The first was a group of 11 volunteers (average age 84.8 years) who were diagnosed with a suggestive impairment with respect to clinical dementia. These individuals were characterised by forgetfulness, having difficulty in time relationships and problem-solving impairment, but were also capable of self-care and had interests in the community and home life. A second group of 16 individuals had a ballpark equivalent age (average age 81.9 years) but did not show any of the negative characteristics listed above. A third and final group consisted of 23 examples of the good old undergraduate student (average age 20.4 years). All groups were required to complete a partial-report task in which the cue could either come before or after the critical display which was,

in this case, a series of eight letters making up a circle round a central fixation cross. Lu et al. (2005) were particularly interested in performance across the three groups as a function of time, and whether the cue was pre- or post-display.

Of particular interest was that, for both pre-display cueing and cases where the cue was presented at the same time as the display (i.e., simultaneous presentation), while the youngsters outperformed the oldies, there were no significant differences between the elderly group with suggestive dementia and the elderly group without suggestive dementia. Moreover, Lu et al. (2005) found that dementia participants also performed as well as the control elderly group under conditions where the longest post-cue SOA (stimulus onset asynchrony) was used. The important implication here was that individuals with dementia might be as good as normal elderly individuals both in terms of transferring information from iconic memory to short-term memory, and simply 'seeing' the stimulus. Where the dementia group performed less well was with shorter post-display cues ranging from around 100 to 300 ms.

Lu et al. (2005) took this data to imply that it was iconic memory *per se* (rather than memory in general) that decayed more rapidly in individuals with dementia than individuals of the same ballpark age

▶

who did not show signs of dementia. Moreover, this difference was still apparent when these slight differences in age between the two groups were controlled for. Therefore, such data point the way towards the possibility of using traditional cognitive paradigms such as partial report to help detect early-on the early onset of diseases such as dementia. So

next time you go to the doctor, it might not be just your blood pressure and reflexes they measure – they might ask you to respond to letter arrays too!

*Source*: Lu, Z., Neuse, J., Madigan, S., & Dosher, B. A. (2005). Fast decay of iconic memory in observers with mild cognitive impairments. *Proceedings of the National Academy of Sciences of the USA, 102*, 1797–1802.

## Iconic memory and the more durable store

In discussing iconic memory we need to keep in mind that such a short-term store has been discussed as being a precursor to a secondary, more durable form of storage (e.g., see Coltheart, 1972, 1984; Navon, 1983a). What we have therefore is the idea that visual sensory memory comprises two components – the iconic level and the more durable short-term store. Indeed Navon (1983a) discussed the latter post-iconic form of short-term store as being immune to masking (as shown in the Davidson et al., 1973 experiment – Figure 3.22). Although it is easy to make the distinction between the two components on paper, in reality there has been some confusion and the distinction has been blurred. In particular, some controversy has arisen over what exactly is going on in cases of what is known as **aperture viewing** or **anorthoscopic perception**.

### Aperture viewing

In aperture viewing the participant fixates on an aperture that can be as simple as a slit cut in a piece of card. Two cases can be distinguished – in the first the slit is moved over a line drawing of a familiar figure that remains stationary behind the slit. In the second the slit remains stationary and the figure is moved behind it (Haber & Nathanson, 1968). In the former case, and given an appropriate speed of movement of the slit, participants report seeing 'a full and undistorted shape' but when the figure is moved behind the slit participants can identify the figure but describe it as being compressed in the direction of movement (paraphrasing Fendrich, Rieger & Heinze, 2005, p. 568). In other words, move the slit left to right and the figure looks as though it is being compressed from the left to the right. (Typically, the figure is a line drawing of

a camel because then the camel can be seen to pass through the eye of a needle – see Figure 3.23.)

We will consider both cases (i.e., moving vs. stationary slit) as we proceed, but the latter case is particularly interesting. If you think a little more about what actually transpires, it is quite remarkable. The whole of the figure is never exposed yet the participant is able to build an impression of a coherent object from a very limited set of glimpses. Coltheart (1980b) discussed a slightly different example. Consider the case of walking past a slatted fence on the outside of a cricket ground, in which the pitch is easily visible between the slats. If you time your walk correctly it is possible to gain an uninterrupted impression of the whole ground as you walk past.

So what has this all got to do with iconic memory? Well, Parks (1965) was the first to point out that the phenomenon of integrating the different glimpses of the object over time implicates some form of short-term visual memory. He went on to make that connection with iconic memory: perhaps aperture viewing reflects the operation of the very same sort of visual storage as is being tapped in Sperling's tasks (1963)? Indeed, such a view was expanded upon by Adelson (1983) who went further to suggest that the brief storage duration afforded by iconic memory allows for visual information to be co-ordinated over time, especially in cases where there is little light. Adelson used the example of a photographer who lengthens the exposure duration when taking a picture in poor lighting conditions. In extending the exposure duration the photographer ensures a longer period for photons to build up on the film so that a more complete image is captured. The underlying idea is that the icon provides a brief but necessary visual buffer or short-term store which provides additional time for processing an immense amount of stimulus information that makes up the current visual world.

More particularly, in this context, the idea is that iconic memory is akin to a canvas upon which paint

(a)

(b)

**Figure 3.23 Aperture viewing and camel recognition**
Cut out a slit from a piece of card large enough to cover the whole of figure (a). Then either move the slit over the figure or hold the card still and move the figure behind it. It remains to be seen whether the effects generalise to (b).

*Sources*: (a) Snodgrass, J. G., & Vanderwart, M. A. (1980). Standardized set of 260 pictures: Norms of name agreement, usage agreement, familiarity, and visual complexity. *Journal of Experimental Psychology: Learning, Memory, and Cognition, 6*, 174–215 (43, p. 198). Reproduced with permission from APA. (b) J. Marshall/Tribal Eye/Alamy.

is applied – the canvas retains stimulus information until the complete picture is built up. Indeed this particular metaphor has been used directly to explain aperture viewing in terms of something known as **retinal painting** (Morgan, Findlay, & Watt, 1982). According to the retinal painting hypothesis, in conditions of aperture viewing the eyes follow the direction of the shape as it moves behind the slit, even though the slit itself remains stationary. A consequence of these involuntary eye movements is that a different part of the retina is exposed to the shape as it moves. An ordered sequence of images falls on consecutive parts of the retina and in this way the complete shape is painted onto the retina.

However, if the retinal painting account of aperture viewing were found to be true, then there would be good grounds for arguing that it is irrelevant to discussion of iconic memory. The argument would be that aperture viewing is yet another demonstration of visible persistence and, as we have seen, there are good grounds for arguing that informational persistence (i.e., iconic storage) is different from visible persistence. This is where the distinction between the two sorts of aperture viewing comes to the fore. In the moving slit example it seems reasonable to argue that retinal painting may be the explanation because the slit moves and the figure remains stationary. Different aspects of the figure are successively falling on different parts of the retina. However, the retinal painting account falters in the stationary slit case since different parts of the figure are being successively exposed to the same part of the retina.

In addressing this point, Morgan et al. (1982) ran an experiment on aperture viewing in which they carefully controlled the display presentation so that retinal painting could be ruled out. They designed computer-controlled displays in which the participant was presented with a sequence of static snapshots of what would be visible through the aperture over time. Each snapshot provided a new static view and adjacent snapshots shared no overlapping elements. Figure 3.24 provides an illustration of one such sequence of snapshots. Importantly, even with these kinds of displays participants did report the impression of a real object moving behind the slit.

Critically, the position of the participants' eyes was monitored during the display sequence to ensure that the slit was stabilised on the back of the retina. This was vital so that each new snapshot stimulated the same part of the retina. So under these conditions both voluntary and involuntary eye movements have been eliminated from consideration. The results unequivocally

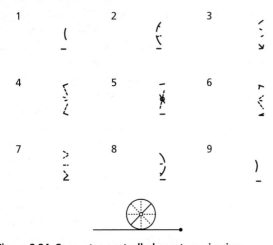

**Figure 3.24 Computer-controlled aperture viewing**
The sequence of stimulus fragments (top panel) presented by Morgan et al. (1982) in their simulation of viewing a moving wagon wheel (bottom panel) through an aperture.

*Source*: Morgan, M. J., Findlay, J. M., & Watt, R. J. (1982). Aperture viewing: A review and a synthesis. *The Quarterly Journal of Experimental Psychology*, 34A, 211–233. Reproduced with permission from Taylor & Francis.

demonstrated that, even though the complete figure was never exposed, participants reported perceiving a real object moving behind a slit. This shows that 'partial views of a shape presented in temporal succession can give rise to the perceptual impression of a whole shape in motion' (Morgan et al., 1982, p. 231 – a conclusion more recently endorsed by Fendrich et al., 2005). → See 'What have we learnt?', below.

## Pinpoint question 3.10

**What critical condition ruled out retinal painting as an account of aperture viewing?**

**aperture viewing** Viewing a stimulus through a slit.

**anorthoscopic perception** Perception of a world through a slit or aperture.

**retinal painting** According to Morgan, Findlay and Watt (1982), the piecemeal exposure of a stimulus over adjacent parts of the retina as is assumed to take place in studies of aperture viewing.

## → What have we learnt?

This sort of data suggests that there is indeed a form of visual memory that operates so as to integrate information over brief intervals so as to provide a coherent picture of the constantly changing visual environment. Such a memory system is seen to take different time-stamped snapshots of the stimulus and organise these into a coherent impression of the visual input – a post-retinal storage buffer (Parks, 1965). The data from Morgan et al. (1982) reveal that participants can recover the impression of a complete object even though it is exposed in a piecemeal fashion to the same place on the retina. Here the contents of the aperture are completely over-written at each point in the sequence and yet a coherent impression of the shape is achieved. So although Adelson (1983) discussed iconic memory much like a light-sensitive 2D photographic plate, this simple analogy will not work for the case where the spatial structure of a shape can be recovered in the aperture viewing case. Indeed it seems much more likely that the sort of mechanisms being tapped in such aperture viewing experiments is different from iconic memory. By

this view the aperture viewing experiments are tapping into a form of visual short-term memory that may be useful in integrating information over very brief intervals and that operates subsequent to iconic storage.

Accordingly, the visual array is initially captured as a 2D retinal copy of the world (in the icon) but this is merely a precursor to other forms of short-term visual memory. By this view, the partial-report studies are seemingly tapping into iconic storage but the aperture viewing experiments reflect the operation of other forms of visual storage. We have essentially argued that performance in the various tasks so far described reflects the properties of either of two forms of visual memory, namely (i) an iconic fast-decaying memory, and (ii) a later, more durable form of storage. We may therefore cling on to the classic form of icon as a cyclopean retinocentric representation but leave open the possibility of a further short-term store that is also sensitive to the visual characteristics of visible stimuli. It is this later memory system that is responsible for integrating information over brief intervals.

## Concluding comments

Since the 'discovery' of iconic memory in the 1960s there has been an immense amount of effort expended trying to nail down the properties and characteristics of this very short-term form of visual memory. Much has been learnt and it has become clear that this type of memory is most easily understood in terms of where it stands in relation to a whole raft of subsequent processes that underpin the ability to make sense of the visual world. Nearly all of this work has been concerned with visual masking and that is why our understanding of iconic memory has so closely been related with our understanding of how visual masking operates.

In this regard even though masking started out as being the tool used to understand iconic representation, almost by necessity, researchers have been rightly concerned with attempting to understand how masking itself operates. Clearly there are very different mechanisms involved when masking by visual noise and masking by pattern, and it is only by understanding the details of these processes of masking that advances have been made in understanding iconic storage. Indeed by covering these basic points about masking, we have laid the groundwork for the next chapter where we will discuss how masking has played a central role in attempts to understand things like visual awareness.

In closing it is useful to consider the following. In very general terms, Loftus and Irwin (1998) pointed out that the visual system is faced with two competing goals. On the one hand it has to be able to distinguish successive events that should be kept apart – for instance, being able to discriminate glances at the book from glances at the television. On the other hand, it has to be able to integrate temporally separate events that belong together. Think of the trainspotter and think of the train passenger. This distinction between segregating and integrating the continuous stream of input may provide some basic insight into what is going on (see Figure 3.25). Iconic representation and storage may provide a first approximation for segregating the input into distinct perceptual moments. Everything captured in the icon provides a first guess as to what goes with what at each particular moment in time. The fact that certain temporally successive events may also have to be integrated implies a function for a later visual short-term store (the more durable form of memory) which operates over successive glimpses of the world.

What we have learnt about iconic memory primarily concerns how the notion of a 2D retinal snapshot has been elaborated upon. We have concluded that the icon represents information combined from the two eyes but preserves the information in terms of a retinal coding system. Such a form of representation might be useful in providing a first guess as to what goes with what at each particular perceptual moment. Indeed, this particular conclusion is, according to O'Regan (1994, p. 270), what most authors agree on and it has been taken to undermine any attempt to try to argue that iconic memory provides a mechanism for integrating information across eye movements. As Pashler (1998) has also noted, 'there is no reliable evidence that iconic memory lets us hold onto the contents of one fixation and compare them with the contents of the next' (p. 108). Of course this is not to say that such comparative processes do not take place, but merely that they do not take place on the basis of some form of iconic representation (for a more detailed examination of these ideas see Hayhoe, Lachter, & Feldman, 1991).

**Figure 3.25  Can you lend me 10p?**
Not only do we have to segregate input into discrete moments, but we also have to integrate successive events across time. How else would we know how to operate a fruit machine?

## CHAPTER SUMMARY

- Cognitive psychologists have been fascinated by the possibility that there exists a very early and transient form of visual memory that is created as the result of sensory encoding operations. Light energy from the external world is transformed into sensory codes that are propagated from the eye to the brain. However, since we are constantly bombarded with sensory information, not all the energy from our environment can make it through to our higher-level cognitive centres. Therefore certain processing constraints exist, limiting the amount of information that we eventually experience.

- Neisser (1967) defined three beliefs about visual perception under the heading of naïve realism. Specifically, visual experiences were thought to mirror the external stimulus, the visual experience started and ended with the onset and offset of the external stimulus, and visual experiences were based on passive copies of the outside world which could be described using verbal reports. However, many of these assumptions have been questioned by the data accumulated in studies concerning visual iconic memory.

- In studies of visual iconic memory, participants are traditionally presented with an array of items (such as random letters) that appears only briefly. Their task is to report what they saw. One critical distinction is between full-report conditions and partial-report conditions (Sperling, 1960). In full-report conditions, participants are asked to report all items from the display. In partial-report conditions, participants are asked to report a sub-set of items. The sub-set of to-be-reported items is signalled by some form of signal that acts as a cue, such as tone of a certain pitch.

- Partial-report superiority is revealed when the capacity estimates of the memory store from the partial-report conditions are greater than those from full-report conditions. On the basis of estimates garnered from full report, it seems that only a handful of items from the array are captured. However, from estimates garnered from partial-report conditions, it seems that most (indeed perhaps all) of the items are registered.

- It was originally concluded that the partial-report superiority effect only occurs when the sub-set of items is defined relative to physical characteristics (such as colour or location) of the items rather than their categorical identity (such as whether they were letters or numbers). This led researchers to conclude that information in iconic memory was pre-categorical in nature. The identities of the items in the icon are not specified.

- In addition, estimates of the duration of iconic storage critically depend on presentation conditions. Specifically, performance in the tasks can be seriously disrupted if to-be-recalled displays are masked. Two views on the nature of visual masking emerged. Masking by integration is where the target stimulus is combined with the masking display to give rise to composite or visual montage in which information about the stimulus items become less legible. Masking by interruption is where the processing of the items in the target display is either replaced or curtailed by the presentation of the mask. In backward masking, the masker is presented after the target display. In forward masking, the masker is presented prior to the target display.

- Coltheart (1972) suggested that information can be read out from iconic memory with respect to two sorts of coding operations. In the first, visual characteristics of the items are recovered and this read-out takes place very rapidly. In the second, the names of the items are recovered and this name coding takes more time to complete. This dual-component view accords well with the observation that item report accuracy operates as a function of delay between the onset of the target display and the onset of the masker in backward masking paradigms. The first component (associated with the visual code) is revealed by a relatively steep increase in the number of items recalled when the stimulus array is backward masked at very short stimulus onset asynchronies (SOAs). The second component (associated with the name code) is revealed by a relatively shallow increase in the number of items recalled when the stimulus array is backward masked at longer SOAs.

- Some debate has opened up regarding whether iconic memory should be perceived as anything other than visual persistence, which is simply the result of physiology and an extended pattern of visual nerve cell firing. Although claims were made that iconic memory is nothing more than visual persistence (see evidence reviewed by Coltheart, 1984), the general conclusion now is that iconic memory and visual persistence are distinct (Long & McCarthy, 1982). Iconic memory relates to informational persistence (the retention of abstract information following the offset of a stimulus) and is therefore a topic that cognitive psychologists can claim an interest in.

- On the basis of the dual-coding account (Coltheart, 1972), iconic memory captures the physical characteristics of display items but further work is needed if the categorical identity of the item is required. Therefore iconic memory is thought to be a precursor to a more durable long-term store. However, Merikle (1980) provided evidence to suggest that when using briefly presented stimulus arrays under certain conditions, partial-report selection could be based on the categorical nature of the target items. In considering these data, Coltheart (1984) developed a three-component model in which there is a pre-categorical iconic memory system, a post-categorical durable store and a final output component or response buffer.

- Ideas about the nature of iconic memory and the early stage of information processing are intimately connected with some fairly fundamental ideas about the nature of visual perception. Two ways of thinking about visual perception were considered by Allport (1968). In the discrete moment hypothesis, the way you see the world is determined by a series of discrete snapshots that occur one after another and do not overlap. In the travelling moment hypothesis, visual perception is thought to be built up from an overlapping sequence of snapshots of the world in which regularities begin to form. Evidence for the discrete moment hypothesis came from Tatler (2001) who showed that while visual snapshots based on current eye fixations could be used to describe the environment, snapshots of the penultimate fixation appeared to be lost.

- Further detailed evidence about the locus of iconic memory was considered in terms of the sorts of frames of reference that operate in vision. In particular discussion focused on the description of visual frames of reference provided by Wade and Swanston (1991). Specifically, a monocular retinocentric frame of reference specifies the retinal coding of information presented to each eye. A binocular retinocentric frame of reference provides a cyclopean co-ordinate system that combines information from the two eyes. An egocentric frame of reference is couched at a higher level in which a head-based co-ordinate system is adopted; and finally there is a geocentric frame of reference in which information about both body-centred and scene-based attributes are combined.

- One proposal is that iconic memory coding operates using a binocular retinocentric frame of reference, therefore the icon cannot be simply a retinal image of the stimulus. Turvey (1973) conducted a number of experiments in which the presentation of stimulus and mask were varied across the same or different halves of the retina, in addition to using both random noise and pattern masking. Turvey (1973) found that random noise masking only had an effect when both stimulus and noise mask were presented under monoptic conditions. In contrast, pattern masking had an effect even when stimulus and noise were presented under dichoptic conditions. Ideas related to peripheral and central masking were summarised and it was concluded that different mechanisms reflect masking by interference and masking by interruption, respectively.

- Further evidence that bears on the nature of iconic memory seems in fact to reflect the operation of the secondary, more durable form of memory and not iconic memory itself. Here the evidence is taken from studies of aperture viewing. Participants can perceive a complete object even when the object is presented in a piecemeal fashion over a period of time to the same place on the retina (Morgan et al., 1982). Therefore there must exist another form of short-term visual memory store in which information is integrated over time.

## ANSWERS TO PINPOINT QUESTIONS

3.1 At a supermarket checkout, the main processing constraint is that only one shopper can be dealt with at any one time at the till.

3.2 Rather than get participants to report everything they saw in the target display as in a full-report condition, in a partial-report condition participants are cued as to which sub-set of items they should report.

3.3 Being temporarily blinded by a camera flash is an example of forward masking.

3.4 Visual codes and name codes are generated as information is read out from iconic memory according to the dual-coding account of Coltheart (1972).

3.5 SOA refers to the time in-between the onset of one stimulus and the onset of the next. ISI refers to the time in-between the offset of the first stimulus and the onset of the second.

3.6 The discrete moment hypothesis asserts that perception is based on a sequential series of non-overlapping snapshots of the world. In contrast, the travelling moment hypothesis asserts that perceptual experience is based on a continuous smooth updating of overlaying snapshots of the world.

3.7 There are monocular retinocentric, cyclopean retinocentric, egocentric and geocentric frames of references.

3.8 With monoptic presentation more than one stimulus is presented to the same eye. With dichoptic presentation different stimuli are presented to the two eyes.

3.9 Turvey (1973) was unable to show effective masking when dichoptic presentation of a target and a random noise mask were used.

3.10 A retinal painting account of aperture viewing was ruled out by stimulating the same part of the retina during the presentation of snapshots.

# MASKING, THRESHOLDS AND CONSCIOUSNESS

## CHAPTER CONTENTS

Stumbling into the kitchen, you decide to forget about your hangover and engage the mind in the most important task of the morning – brewing up. It is not an easy task and your bleary sleep-filled eyes are making it hard to see where those little bags of goodness might be. Finally, you locate the relevant items and now face that difficult choice of what's going to constitute your first meal of the day. Without really thinking, you make a couple of

# While you were sleeping The continuing joys of communal living

cups of Lapsang Souchong and throw two *pains au chocolat* in the oven to warm gently. Your flatmate comes into the room as you begin wearily to munch and slurp. 'Sorry about last night, I hope I didn't wake you when I got in?' they inquire. 'I listened to the radio for a bit – the World Service said there was a really bad earthquake in China last night – then I watched a documentary on the Louvre in Paris on the TV, and then I nodded off. Looked like you were out like a light the whole time.' You stare down at your cup of Lapsang Souchong and warm *pain au chocolat* and wonder whether you really had made independent choices about your breakfast selection . . .

## REFLECTIVE QUESTIONS

1. Play around with the volume control on your TV and radio. What happens as you increase the volume on your radio from silence? Does the sound gradually fade in or does the radio suddenly burst into life? If it's a song you know, does this make it easier or harder to detect? Why might this be? Now put the TV on in the background. How has this changed your ability to hear the radio? What kind of things are influencing your decision as to whether you can hear the radio signal or not?

2. Do you ever get a craving for a particular drink or brand of chocolate while out shopping? Why do you think this might be? To what extent do you see the advertising that is around you and to what extent do you process this information? Do you think you might not be able to see something physically but it still has an effect on you? Under what conditions might this happen?

# Introduction and preliminary considerations

In this chapter we are concerned with a variety of issues, all of which relate to the distinction between conscious and unconscious perceptual processes. As was probably clear, from the sentiments expressed in Chapter 2, attempting to explain consciousness is quite tricky, and some even have expressed doubts that we will ever be able to explain it satisfactorily (see for example McGinn, 1994). So we do need to be on guard as soon as consciousness is mentioned – especially if it is being used as an explanatory construct. How can anything be used to explain something when it needs to be explained itself? Nevertheless, we hope we can agree that it is not a completely meaningless construct. We all have some grasp of what it is to be conscious even if none of us can explain it that well. Now you are awake, but last night you were (probably) asleep. We all readily distinguish states of consciousness from states of unconsciousness, despite also being aware of the difficult cases – dozing in lectures, falling asleep in front of the TV, zoning in and zoning out of incredibly boring conversation, passing out in the back of a taxi on the way home from a party, and so on and so forth. Despite the misgivings, however, an incredible amount of research has been based on the understanding that the distinction between conscious and unconscious perceptual processes can be drawn and that it can be studied.

Such issues do bear on how best to think about the nature of the mind in functional terms. The view of the mind discussed so far might be described as being a linear, sequential account (see Chapter 2, Figure 2.8). First the senses are stimulated; next, processes of sensory transduction are engaged; and, eventually, a representation of the stimulus is derived in which only the physical characteristics of the stimulus are coded (e.g., it's red, it's big and it's on the left). In broad strokes, such operations characterise the perceptual mechanisms. The argument runs that once a stimulus representation has been derived, central processes now come into play so that the stimulus can be identified and some form of action can be taken. It follows that the meaning of the stimulus is accessed after the perceptual mechanisms have run their course. Conscious identification is achieved eventually, but only after a considerable amount of work has been carried out on the stimulus. In this chapter we will begin by examining a particular version of this sort of account in a little more detail: later we will contrast it with quite different ideas.

**Figure 4.1 The magic of visual masking?**
*Source:* Blend Images LLC/Photolibrary.com.

You may be surprised to learn that in most of the studies that have attempted to understand the boundary between consciousness and unconsciousness, visual masking has played a pivotal role. Indeed, as Figure 4.1 shows, some form of visual masking is clearly going on when the magician reveals only part of his assistant. The trick is to try to figure out what sort of masking it is. We will begin by following up on some of the ideas about visual masking that we introduced in Chapter 3. A basic assumption has been that visual masking is an effective methodological tool because it limits the amount of stimulus information that enters consciousness. Given that this is such a fundamental assumption, we will need to consider the supporting evidence quite closely.

Initially we will discuss two particular accounts of visual processing derived from experiments on visual masking. These illustrate some very general ideas about how internal mental processes may be arranged. We then move on to consider a slightly different literature that reveals how various masking techniques have been used to study a related issue. The issue is whether it is possible to access the meaning of a stimulus, but have no conscious experience of having been presented with the stimulus. In more lurid terms we may ask, 'Can our behaviour be influenced by unconscious messages?'.

In order to appreciate these issues more fully, the middle sections of the chapter contain an introduction to something known as **signal detection theory** (SDT for short). It is the case that many of the arguments made about the unconscious control of behaviour depend on understanding SDT. More generally, SDT crops up all over the place in the cognitive psychology literature (and if you look at the index you will find that SDT crops up all over the place in this book). SDT has such generality that it has been repeatedly used by cognitive psychologists as a means to address a very broad range of issues in perception, memory, attention and language use. It is therefore important to examine the reasoning behind the theory in some detail.

> **signal detection theory** A theoretical framework that provides a rationale for separating the effects of perceptual sensitivity from those of response bias.

## The sequential account of processing and Turvey's work on visual masking

One thing to emerge from our discussion of visual sensory memory and iconic storage was that advances in understanding these psychological constructs were intimately linked with understanding visual masking. From the outset, it has turned out that the problems in trying to understand iconic storage were compounded by the other difficulties in trying to understand visual masking. It became easier to address issues about iconic memory once progress was made in understanding masking. As we have seen, there is a whole raft of issues that concern experimental parameters such as stimulus timings and the type of masks used: Turvey (1973) concentrated on two forms of masking – random noise masking and pattern masking; Sperling (1960) examined masking by light. There is a quite different raft of issues with attempting to tie down, in functional terms, how these different types of masks operate. In this regard, and at a very general level, two alternatives were considered: masking by integration vs. masking by interruption. More particularly, a finer distinction was drawn between interruption by replacement (the processing of the mask takes priority over that of the target) and interruption by curtailment (the processing of the target stops immediately when the mask is presented – after Turvey, 1978).

We concluded that masking may reflect the characteristics of either or both of two underlying visual processes, respectively, peripheral and central processes.

Additionally, there was the conjecture that peripheral masking reflects purely processes of stimulus integration whereas central masking reflects processes of interruption. However, Turvey (1973) provided a much more elaborate view of masking in his concurrent and contingent model. The conjecture was not adequate, given the variety of masking effects then present in the literature. Discussion of the model allows us to demonstrate how intricate a functional account of some behaviour can be, and it also provides a very clear example of a sequential account of processing.

## The concurrent and contingent model of masking

In this account Turvey concentrated on the distinction between peripheral and central processing in terms of a sequential stage account – following the registration of the stimulus, first peripheral encoding operations are set in motion, then the **central processes** are engaged (in very broad strokes, similar ideas are encapsulated in the modularity of mind hypothesis – see Chapter 2). Initially the stimulus is registered via **peripheral coding mechanisms** that Turvey called *peripheral nets*. The idea is that there is a set of feature-specific peripheral detectors (or **feature detectors**, known as peripheral nets) which are individually sensitive to the visual characteristics of the stimulus such as its size, shape, orientation, position, etc. Information is initially picked up at this level and is then passed on to the central mechanisms (known as *central nets*).

The central nets function to (i) assemble an iconic representation of the stimulus from the outputs of the peripheral nets (see Michaels & Turvey, 1979), and (ii) identify what the stimulus might be. The central nets ultimately have to arrive at a decision as to the nature of the input stimulus (e.g., to assign it to the category 'letter A'). By the most simple view, peripheral masking reflects interference with read-into iconic storage whereas central masking reflects problems in read-out from the icon (Turvey, 1973, p. 46).

### Feedforward systems

In this scheme, information from the peripheral nets feeds forward to the central nets. So the stimulus activates its relevant feature detectors which, in turn, activate particular central processes concerning stimulus identification. One way to think about this is in terms of the following contrived scenario. Let's think of a native English speaker who knows nothing about Chinese orthography (i.e., the Chinese writing system). This English observer is placed in isolation in a quiet room with a television screen and telephone link to another testing room. Inside the other testing room is a Chinese/English bi-lingual receiver who can only hear what the English observer has to say through the telephone link. The observer is now presented with a Chinese character on the screen of the television and has to try to describe the character to the receiver over the telephone link. The receiver has to try to identify which character is being currently shown. So the analogy here is between the English person as a peripheral net and the Chinese person as the central net. The Chinese person is constantly monitoring what the English person is saying but cannot influence in any way what the English person is reporting. This example conveys in simple terms the basis of a purely **feedforward system**.

### The concurrent and contingent account of processing

In this account of processing, the different peripheral nets are seen to vary in their processing speeds – for example, colour analysis might take less time than shape analysis. Moreover the central nets are constantly being updated by information from the peripheral nets and the speed with which the peripheral nets produce output reflects the amount of the energy present in the stimulus. Peripheral processing will complete sooner for intense stimuli than for weaker stimuli. Different peripheral nets are seen to operate concurrently (at the same time) and outputs from the peripheral nets feed forward to the central decision processes. The decisions made at the central level are, in this sense, contingent on (or dependent on) the outputs provided by the peripheral nets. As a consequence, the account is known as a *concurrent and contingent account of processing*.

Masking may take place at the level of the peripheral mechanisms if the target and mask engage the same peripheral nets – for instance if the target and mask are presented to the same eye. At this peripheral level, integrative masking may take place if the target and mask contain similar levels of energy. The information contained in the target and the information contained in the mask will be indistinguishable because both stimuli engaged the same peripheral nets. Such is the explanation of integrative peripheral masking.

Masking may also arise at the level of the peripheral nets for another reason, however. Turvey concluded that if two successive stimuli occupy the same peripheral nets, then the stimulus with the greater energy will be prioritised. When the mask is more intense

than the target, this means that the peripheral encoding of the mask completes prior to that of the target even when the mask is presented after the target. The encoding of the mask in a sense overtakes the encoding of the target and it is the representation of the mask that is fed forward to the central mechanisms. The information for the target and the mask is kept separate; it is just that the mask wins the race to the central nets and it is this that is perceived and not the target. In this regard this form of masking does not reflect integrative processes.

In addition, it was also asserted that if successive stimuli compete for the same central nets, that is, if the target and the mask demand a similar interpretation such as when both target and mask are both words, for instance, then the stimulus that arrives second will be prioritised. By the replacement view of interruption, the representation of the target in the central nets is replaced by the representation of the mask. This form of interruption masking is akin to the *erasure* view of masking advanced by Averbach and Coriell (1961) in which the iconic representation of the target is simply over-written by the iconic representation of the mask. A less severe form of interruption would be where the target identification processes are curtailed by the later arrival of information concerning the mask (i.e., masking by curtailment). In this way the target is only partially processed before the mask arrives. → See 'What have we learnt?', page 110.

→ See 'What have we learnt?', page 110.

### Pinpoint question 4.1

**Why is the concurrent and contingent model referred to as a sequential account?**

**central processes** Internal operations that eventuate in the assignment of a stimulus representation to a mental category. Processes that are concerned with stimulus identification; interpretative mechanisms.

**peripheral coding mechanisms** Internal operations that are responsible for generating sensory codes for a given stimulus.

**feature detectors** A putative neural mechanism such as a brain cell that is dedicated to collect evidence in favour of one particular kind of perceptual feature such as line orientation, size, position, colour, etc. A feature detector is switched ON (alternatively, it fires) when evidence consistent with the target feature is present in the input.

**feedforward system** Information processing system in which only feedforward operations are carried out.

## → What have we learnt?

We have introduced ideas about sequential processing and have explained what feedforward processes are. We have also sketched the concurrent and contingent model as put forward by Turvey (1973) and have shown how varieties of masking were accounted for in the model. Fundamentally, the model is a sequential account of processing – first the peripheral nets come into play and then the central nets do. In addition, the operation of the central nets is contingent on the outputs of the peripheral nets. The peripheral nets feed information forward to the central nets. The central nets, essentially, do nothing until called upon by the peripheral nets. Integrative masking and the various forms of interruption masking were well accommodated by the model.

However, two further developments have transpired since the model was put forward, and we will discuss each of these in turn. First, a brand new variety of masking effects have recently been documented. Second, different kinds of processing assumptions have had to be made, because of these effects. The newer ideas provide alternative ways of thinking about how internal operations may be ordered. The simple sequential view of processing has been re-thought and processes of feedback have been discussed.

## Masking by object substitution

Ever since I put your picture in a frame

> *Waits, T. (1995). Picture in a frame.* On Mule Variations
> *(CD Recording). Los Angeles, CA: Anti.*

So far we have been gathering up evidence of an impressive variety of different kinds of masking paradigms: forward masking, backward masking, masking by light, masking by noise, and masking by pattern; but our collection would not be complete without consideration of the work of Di Lollo, Enns and Rensink (2000). They have documented a different variant of masking which they called **masking by object substitution**.

In the original demonstrations of masking by object substitution, the masked display item fell within the confines of an encompassing masking boundary (a mask is to a target as a frame is to a picture). Figure 4.2 provides examples of the sorts of display items and masks used. However, the effect arises even in cases when the mask comprises four dots placed at the individual corners of an invisible square within which the target item is located. In other words, masking by object substitution may occur when the masker has no contours at all!

A critical aspect of object substitution is that it occurs only under very particular conditions; specifically:

1. The target display and masker are initially presented simultaneously.

2. Then the target display is removed (but the masker remains present).

3. Finally the masker is removed.

Under these conditions the masker renders the target item invisible. Critically, no masking occurs when only a single target item is presented and no masking

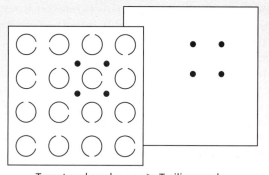

Target and mask ———→ Trailing mask

**Figure 4.2 Schematic representation of the sorts of target and masking displays used in studies of masking by object substitution**

Time, from the onset of the mask, moves from left to right across the page. Under these conditions the direction of the gap within the target circle would be difficult, if not impossible, to report. At the time of writing interesting demonstrations of the basic effects could be found at http://www.sfu.ca/~enzo/.

*Source*: Enns, J. T., & Di Lollo, V. (2000). What's new in visual masking? *Trends in Cognitive Science, 4*, 345–352 (fig. 4, p. 348). Reproduced with permission from Elsevier.

occurs if the target and mask are removed at the same time.

We can discount masking by integration as a potential explanation for object substitution because if the target item and mask were to be physically superimposed then the target item would be perfectly visible because there is no overlap between any aspects of the target and the mask. Integration masking only works if the superposition of the target and the mask renders the target illegible. Interruption accounts seem to fare equally badly. In the case of object substitution, the target and mask are presented concurrently, but interruption theories account for masking via the argument that it is the later onset of the mask that disrupts the ongoing processing of the target. Consequently, it seems that neither integration nor interruption masking can account for object substitution masking. Therefore Di Lollo et al. developed an alternative theory based on the notion of **re-entrant processing**.

## Feedforward and feedback processes

A useful distinction here is to consider the difference between **feedforward** and **feedback** processes. Previously the current and contingent account of masking was discussed in terms of purely feedforward processes. According to this sort of account, processing is known also as **stimulus-driven** – the stimulus drives the processing in a slavish linear (one step follows the other) fashion. A stimulus enters the system and consequently the train of processes is set in motion in a strictly linear sequence: first there is process 1, then process 2, then process 3 and so on until some end point is reached. Most importantly, there is no way in which a later stage of processing can influence an earlier stage.

However, it is exactly this possibility that is allowed in systems with feedback. For instance, stage 1 is initiated and the products of this stage are fed forward to stage 2, which, in turn, feeds back information to stage 1 – in such a system a so-called feedback loop is instantiated. Indeed such a feedback loop is central to the re-entrant account because this posits both feedforward and feedback processes. In considering how feedback may be instantiated in the visual system, Di Lollo et al. (2000) invoked the notion of re-entrant processing in attempting to explain masking by object substitution. The eventual re-entrant account is very much couched at the level of the neurophysiological structure of the visual system, but it is possible to discuss the model's abstract properties and Figure 4.3 provides a schematic outline of the basic ideas.

## Feedback as re-entrant visual processes

In many respects the model developed by Di Lollo et al. (2000) is similar to Turvey's in that it is assumed that the input stimulus activates many different sorts of processing modules akin to those shown in Figure 4.3. These in turn feed forward information to more central mechanisms. Although many different processing modules are posited across the whole of the retinal mosaic, let us consider the most simple case and focus on just one item location in the stimulus display – on just the operation of one processing module. The *input layer* is defined in terms of a retinal (point-for-point) representation of the display item (it is a retinotopic map – see Chapter 3). Information from the input layer feeds directly into the *working space layer* that codes information in a similar point-for-point manner. However, at each stage in processing, comparisons are made between the input layer and working space layer representations (in the same way that an artist

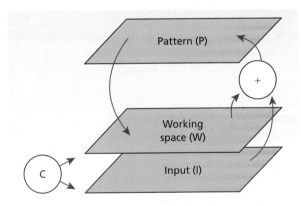

**Figure 4.3 Schematic representation of the re-entrant model of processing set out by Di Lollo et al. (2000)**
The input layer contains a record of the input stimulus and this is fed forward to the working space immediately following the onset of the stimulus. The working space representation, in turn, feeds forward to the pattern space. The pattern space contains stored pattern knowledge such as what an 'A' looks like. If the working space representation is consistent with a stored pattern then information from the pattern layer is fed back onto the working layer. Such feedback (i.e., re-entrant processes) means that the working layer representation is over-written by the pattern information. Comparisons between the working space representation and the input (the © in the illustration) are continuously being undertaken and the whole set of processes iterates until a pattern detector in the pattern space reaches some criterion level of activation.

*Source*: Enns, J. T., & Di Lollo, V. (2000). What's new in visual masking? *Trends in Cognitive Science*, 4, 345–352 (fig. 5, p. 348). Reproduced with permission from Elsevier.

continues to compare their drawing with real life while making a sketch), such that the eventual working space layer representation captures the combination of these two. At the start of processing the working space will be empty (an artist's blank page) and when a stimulus is presented its input representation is merely copied into the working space. There is nothing to combine with the input representation.

Pattern information is represented at the final *pattern layer* where shape characteristics are made explicit. The pattern layer is activated by the working space representation. So in simple terms, if the working space representation is consistent with the presence of the letter 'A' then this pattern information will be activated at the level of the pattern layer. Following this, pattern information is fed back onto the working space. What this actually means is that the activated pattern information over-writes the contents of the working space buffer. This sort of feedback defines the re-entrant aspect of the model. Processing then proceeds whereby the input layer and working space layer representations are again compared and a new working space representation is constructed. The time to identify the stimulus is gauged by the time it takes a given pattern detector (such as the letter detector for the letter 'A') to reach a pre-defined level of activation.

It is the over-writing processes that are used to explain masking by object substitution. In very simple terms, initially the input layer will contain a composite representation of the target item and the surrounding masker and this is immediately propagated onto the working space layer. This in turn produces activation at the level of the pattern layer which may be ambiguous to the nature of what is present – the retinal input contains information about both target and mask so any feedback from the pattern layer will also be ambiguous. Next the target is removed but the mask remains and so now all that will be consequently active at the pattern layer is the detector for the mask. This activation will over-write any residual representation of the target in the working space layer. Hence the target will be rendered invisible.

In the re-entrant account we have a rather extreme form of feedback being discussed. The present best guess as to the nature of the stimulus is being used to over-write (erase) the current output from stimulus encoding mechanisms. So although Enns and Di Lollo (2000) are keen to distance themselves from simple interruption accounts of masking, the re-entrant account does assume that, at a very basic level, the input representation is erased by the currently present stimulus. This does seem therefore to be fundamentally an account of masking based on the notion of replacement. → See 'What have we learnt?', below.

## → What have we learnt?

The present discussion of feedback processes has provided one specific example but, as you will discover, many different sorts of feedback processes have been discussed in the literature. In one respect, the re-entrant processes seem extremely constraining. Consider working in market research. You make an initial appraisal of the evidence in favour of a certain product and send this forward to head office, who then simply over-write your appraisal and state that 'This is what the evidence is actually telling us.' Of course, this may actually be a fair appraisal of the processes underlying object substitution. However, other less severe accounts of feedback have been discussed and we will consider these as the material unfolds.

Further discussion of the re-entrant model, however, would be premature in advance of considering of the nature of visual attention. At the level of detail, the account is one based on assumptions about directed visual attention. We will consider the nature of attention later in the book. However, discussion of the re-entrant model has provided us with our first example of how knowledge of the world may affect our perception of it. The re-entrant processes in the model play an important role in deriving a perceptual representation of the input. In this regard, we are now beginning to question the whole notion of a strictly sequential stage account of processing because this is contradicted by the model. Following the first initial feedforward of information in which the three layers are activated in series, the re-entrant processes allow the flow of control to operate in both directions. More particularly information from a later level of analysis can influence processing at an early stage. Such ideas as these are central to debates about how it is that knowledge may affect perception and ultimately how these may inform questions about the nature of conscious perception.

**How does masking by object substitution work on the Enns and Di Lollo (2000) model?**

**masking by object substitution** Specifically, this occurs when the target display and masker are initially presented simultaneously, then the target display is removed (but the masker remains present), and finally the masker is removed. The effect can even occur when the masker has no contours (e.g., it is composed of a small number of dots).

**re-entrant processing** Operations that feed back information from higher stages of processing to lower levels. A particular form of feedback in which previously derived stimulus representations are over-written by higher levels (see Enns & Di Lollo, 2000).

**feedforward** Where earlier processes provide information to (or influence, in some other way) later processes.

**feedback** Where later processes provide information to (or influence, in some other way) earlier processes.

**stimulus-driven** Operations that are invoked by the stimulus – see bottom-up processing.

## Masking and consciousness

Much has been written on how best to shore up the distinction between conscious and unconscious processes, and because of the surrounding philosophical quagmire, cognitive psychologists have tried to simplify matters and have merely offered operational definitions. For instance, all of this exciting talk about 'the nature of consciousness' becomes terribly mundane when the discussion is confined to talk about performance in visual masking experiments. A basic assumption is that one critical aspect of being conscious is being able to report on your thoughts and experiences. So if participants can report items correctly from a briefly presented and backwardly masked letter array, then we claim that such items have been consciously perceived.

Okay, this is not completely watertight because (of course) participants may simply guess and get lucky – they didn't actually perceive an E but there was something E-like in the array and so they guessed and got it right. However, there are ways round this problem – for instance, we could get participants to report what they saw but also ask them to rate how confident they were in making these item reports. Okay, you say you

saw an E but how confident are you that you actually saw an E (1 – a pure guess, . . . 10 – absolutely certain). Using such confidence ratings, in tandem with the perceptual report data, we can be more certain about what information has truly been perceived. The central problem is that because consciousness is by definition subjective, we have no objective criteria against which to judge it. We can only go on what the participants (in a sense) tell us. Indeed, we will see just how important concerns about guessing are as we proceed.

The nature of consciousness may seem a very long way from any possible differences between random noise and pattern masking, etc., but it simply is the case that the consideration of the nature of various masking effects has been used to adjudicate between so-called conscious and non-conscious (un-conscious) processing. As a starting point we will consider the work of Allport (1977). Although this study used visual masking and examined the nature of iconic memory, it also provides an example of how visual masking techniques have been used to address some fairly fundamental issues about human cognition.

## Semantic activation without conscious identification?

Our discussion of the study of iconic memory and visual masking has converged on some rather general statements about the nature of perception. We have also considered various examples of the manner in which information about the stimulus is recovered once it has been presented to the senses. The standard view has been that initially only the physical characteristics of the stimulus are made available (and are captured in the icon), and that the higher-order characteristics such as identity information and meaning only become available via the operation of the later central mechanisms. According to a strictly serial sequential view of processing, first the physical characteristics are recovered and then meanings are accessed. Alongside this view is the acceptance that the stimulus is only consciously perceived once its meaning or identity has been recovered.

As we have seen, such a strictly sequential view of processing is questioned if it is accepted that feedback processes can come into play (as is the case in the re-entrant model). If such feedback is allowed then it is possible to argue that the meaning of a stimulus (typically located in terms of the central mechanisms) may influence how that stimulus is itself encoded. Moreover, if such a possibility is entertained, then it is not beyond the bounds of plausibility to see how the meaning of a stimulus can be recovered but that no record of the actual stimulus enters into consciousness. We can demonstrate some knowledge of what was presented but we cannot report exactly what it was. So in the terminology used in the literature, **semantic activation without conscious identification** refers to the possibility that the meaning of a stimulus can be accessed (can be activated) without the person being aware of what exactly the stimulus was or indeed whether a stimulus was actually present (see Holender, 1986, and commentaries).

We need to tread carefully here before switching completely into ghost-busting mode. The issues should not be mixed up with the notion of a premonition. With a premonition it is claimed that a person experiences a feeling that something calamitous is about to happen before it does. Semantic activation without conscious identification is something quite different, but it may, nevertheless, come across as being a bit spooky. Semantic activation without conscious identification is taken to occur under the following conditions. A stimulus is presented but the person is not consciously aware that anything has happened. Nevertheless, other aspects of the person's behaviour indicate that they must have accessed the meaning of the stimulus. So the corresponding empirical question is, 'Is it possible to recover the meaning of an event without also having any clear impression of what stimuli gave rise to this event?' Allport (1977) reported a study that addressed exactly this question.

## Allport (1977)

In a critical experiment participants were presented with a target display containing four words, each situated at a different corner of an imaginary square. This target display was briefly presented and pattern masked. The SOA between target and mask was set individually for each participant such that, on average, a given participant was able to report correctly one of the four words. Two conditions were designed such that (i) in the *non-selective condition* participants were told simply to report anything that they thought they saw, and (ii) in the *selective condition* they were told that one of the words was an animal name and they had to try their best to report this as well as anything else they thought they saw. In the non-selective condition none of the words in the display was an animal name.

The first important finding was that data from the selective condition revealed that accurate reports of animal names outweighed accurate reports of other words in the display. That is, the results showed a significant tendency to report animal names selectively. Interesting comparisons were then drawn with data from a *control condition* in which participants were presented with the displays from the selective condition and were asked to report anything they thought they saw. Under these conditions there was no similar bias to report the animal name.

Overall this pattern of findings suggests that, for these very brief and pattern-masked displays, participants were able to retrieve something about the content or meaning of the target items when instructed to do so. In this regard, the data may be taken as another example of **post-categorical selection** (remember the discussion of Merikle's 1980 experiment in which participants were able to select items from masked displays on the basis of alpha-numeric class, in Chapter 3?). The argument is that participants could only selectively report the animal names if the corresponding words had made contact with stored semantic knowledge. A critical item must (in some sense) have been identified as an animal in order for it to be selected. In other words, the data seemed to indicate that selection from iconic memory could be based on the meaning of the words – something completely at odds with the traditional pre-categorical nature of iconic representation.

Of subsidiary interest Allport (1977) also reported an analysis of the errors that participants made. Across all of the displays used he found that approximately 6 per cent of the errors could be classified as being **semantically related** to one of the words in the display. For example, the target word 'blues' was reported as 'jazz', 'deal' as 'ace' and 'drink' as 'wine', etc. Allport took this as converging evidence for the idea that the backward mask was operating at a stage after which the displayed words had accessed their meanings. Such a view is entirely consistent with the three-component account of processing (Coltheart, 1984), in which selection is seen to be operating on the more durable post-categorical store (see Chapter 3). Even though participants were unable to report accurately a particular target item, the evidence from their inaccurate reports suggested that the target item had made contact with its meaning. If this had not occurred, how could it have been that participants incorrectly reported that a semantically related item had been presented?

Now the account was not so much that the pattern mask interfered with read-out from the icon, but that it interfered with higher-level processes of establishing a match between the visual code generated for the target word and its stored **orthographic description**. Briefly, what is being argued is that part of stored knowledge about a given word is its so-called orthographic description. This sort of description specifies the sequence of letters that make up the word. In this regard the masker interfered with visual and not semantic processes. Information from the masked stimulus word did, however, make contact with the appropriate stored meaning. In other words, Allport claimed that his data, taken as a whole, supported the notion of semantic activation without conscious identification (Holender, 1986). To reiterate: *even though participants were unable to report accurately a particular target item, the evidence from their inaccurate reports suggested that the target item had made contact with its meaning.*

Such a view poses some difficulties for the strictly sequential view of processing discussed previously. It seems not to be the case that semantic activation only takes place for items that are consciously identified! Indeed, given the importance of such a possibility – it has profound consequences for information processing accounts of perception – then we need to be confident that Allport's conclusions are warranted by the data.

### Pinpoint question 4.3

How do the errors generated in the Allport study provide evidence for semantic awareness without conscious identification?

## Problems for Allport (1977) and a re-interpretation of his data

Of the two central findings that Allport reported (1977), it is that regarding the **semantic errors**, or so-called **paralexic errors**, that generated the most interest. Indeed it was this finding that was subsequently undermined by later research. In two follow-up studies (Ellis & Marshall, 1978, and, separately, Williams & Parkin, 1980), it was quite convincingly shown that such errors do occur solely by chance and may therefore be accounted for by participants' guessing. In other words, the paralexic errors arose merely as a consequence of participants' guessing. On these grounds, the paralexic errors provide no convincing evidence for semantic activation without conscious identification – all they reflect is a strategy based on guessing.

However, as Ellis and Marshall (1978) admitted, the subsequent analyses do not completely undermine Allport's other finding regarding post-categorical

selection, namely that participants were reasonably accurate in reporting the actual animal name that was present in the selective displays. Even though this is true, we would be on much firmer ground had these data also been corrected for any reasonable guessing strategies that participants may have used. Indeed later commentators (see Cheesman & Merikle, 1985) have been far less forgiving and have argued that semantic errors made to masked words provide no convincing evidence for semantic activation without conscious identification at all!

Nevertheless, despite these particular criticisms of Allport's study and other concerns about semantic activation without conscious identification, the basic ideas have been examined repeatedly throughout the history of cognitive psychology. The central issue remains, 'Can meanings be recovered from stimuli that are not consciously perceived?' Indeed this is such an important psychological question that it is necessary to consider such a possibility in much more detail.

**semantic activation without conscious identification** The claim that the meaning of a stimulus can be accessed even though the person has no conscious awareness that any stimulus has been presented.

**post-categorical selection** Selection on the basis of semantic information.

**semantically related** Items that share commonalities in meaning (e.g., doctor–nurse).

**orthographic description** A mental coding that specifies a sequence of letters. It is assumed that something like an orthographic description must be stored internally for us to read and spell words.

**semantic errors** Errors in report that are semantically related to the desired target response.

**paralexic errors** A fancy phrase for semantic errors.

## Drawing the line between conscious and non-conscious processing

The very idea that a person might be affected by a stimulus in the absence of any awareness of the stimulus can be traced back, in the experimental literature, to early in the first half of the twentieth century. Then this topic was examined in terms of something known as **perceptual defence** (Postman, Bronson & Gropper, 1953). In order to understand what perceptual defence is, we need to understand the concept of a **perceptual**

**threshold**. We need to try to draw a line (i.e., establish a threshold) between pre-conscious and conscious processing. In order to make claims about semantic activation without awareness, it is critical that we can clearly distinguish between cases where a stimulus is consciously perceived and where it is not. In experimental terms, being able to make this distinction depends on being able to derive a threshold that sets the boundary at which consciousness is achieved.

## Perceptual thresholds

In the foregoing, the discussion unwittingly strayed into a form of language use and theorising that, although commonplace in present-day cognitive psychology, needs some further consideration. We have already come across the notion of a *feature detector* in the discussion of the concurrent and contingent model, but this has not been fully explained and this needs rectifying.

We might think of a complex object – let's take a plastic pig sitting on top of a filing cabinet (see Figure 4.4) – as being composed of a number of basic attributes that can be described in terms of perceptual features: the colour is predominantly pink, the shape of the tail is curly and so on. The idea is that there are specific brain cells (known as feature detectors) that are each dedicated to register one particular kind of perceptual feature. One very simple feature detector that has been frequently discussed is the **line detector**

(see for example Lindsay & Norman, 1972). Although it is usually assumed that the neurophysiological evidence for the existence of such detectors in the striate visual cortex is well established (Hubel & Wiesel, 1977), the interpretation of this evidence is contentious (see Purves & Lotto, 2003). We will side-step these issues momentarily while we consider the operation of such a detector at an abstract level.

The basic understanding is that a given line detector has a receptive field defined at a particular region of the retina, such that if a line of a particular orientation and size falls within this area on the retina (i.e., within the so-called **retinal receptive field**) then the detector will 'fire'. The firing of the detector signifies, at some very basic level, that a line of a particular size, orientation and position has been identified (see Figure 4.5 for an illustrative example). Clearly many different sorts of such detectors are needed if we are to account for detection of the indefinite number of other line segments that occur in the real world, but let us pretend such difficulties do not exist. Nevertheless, there are some other hidden assumptions that do need further elaboration.

### *All-or-nothing systems*

It may help to think in terms of the central nervous system as being akin to a simple electricity circuit containing various components together with the wiring between them. By this analogy, we can think of each

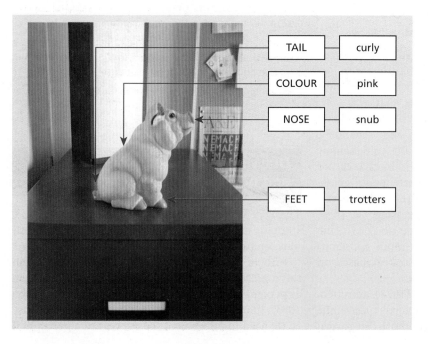

**Figure 4.4 What are the basic perceptual features of the plastic pig?**

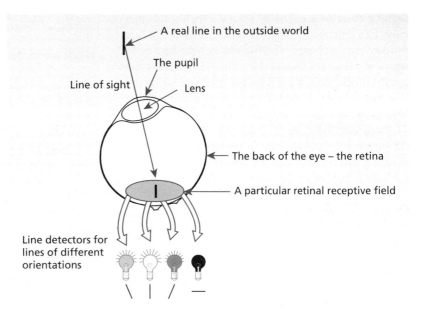

**Figure 4.5 A schematic representation of a collection of abstract line detectors**
A real vertical line is viewed and this falls in a particular retinal receptive field (the small circular region on the retina), which the various line detectors share, in this example. The level of activation of the detectors is shown, with bright meaning highly activated and dark meaning not active at all. The actual target lines associated with the various line detectors are shown so as to indicate the respective target line for each detector.

line detector in the cortex as being akin to a light bulb, wired up to a set of photoreceptors (light detectors) located at the back of the retinae. When light falls on these photoreceptors they transmit 'electricity' or energy down the wiring to the line detector. At the level of cognitive theory, the term for this electricity/energy is activation. In an **all-or-nothing system**, the light bulb remains off until it receives a critical amount of energy – the threshold amount – at which point any further energy will turn the light bulb on. In this system the light bulb obeys what is known as a step function – the light bulb stays off until the energy it receives surpasses a threshold level. When this happens the light bulb/feature detector is said to become activated. So with our example of a line detector, if enough 'line information' of the right sort impinges on the photoreceptors associated with our line detector then the detector fires and the associated line is registered.

### Continuous systems without thresholds

We can contrast this sort of **thresholded system** with another in which the intensity of the light bulb varies continuously as a function of the input – there is no threshold applied to the level of activation that the detector receives. The intensity of the light varies from a completely off state to a state of maximum brightness in a continuous way. Think of how room lights behave when a dimmer switch is turned up. So, for the all-or-nothing system we had an on/off switch, and for the continuous system we had a dimmer switch. In this system there is no notion of a threshold because

there is no clear distinction between the light being on and it being off.

### Continuous systems with thresholds

Indeed, more complicated scenarios can also be contemplated. For instance we can think of a continuous system that also has a threshold (i.e., the detector accumulates energy in a continuous fashion but only comes on if this exceeds a threshold value). You might have an old radio that has this feature on the volume control dial. That is, you need to turn the dial a little bit before the reception is audible but then, after that, the dial operates as a normal volume control: the volume increases as the dial is turned. So the dial has a threshold in terms of the radio being on or off, and then acts as a continuous system with respect to the loudness of 'Gardeners' Question Time' after that.

### The notion of partial activation and priming

Aligned to these notions of activation is a related idea that the detector may be described in terms of it being partially activated. The implication here is that the detector has received some activation but not enough for the detector to become fully activated, fire, or switch on. For instance, if our critical line does not fall exactly within the receptive field of the line detector then the line detector is partially but not fully activated. So the line detector for 45° lines will be partially activated by a line of 46° and less so by a line of 47°, and so on. One further consequence of allowing partial activation is that if a detector is partially activated then it takes less energy to activate it fully subsequently than if it were not partially activated. Having presented a line of 46° we now present a line of 45°. The 45° detector fires more quickly than if a 5° line precedes the 45° degree line. In the latter case the 5° line fails to activate the 45° detector at all (see Figure 4.5).

More generally, such assumptions about partial activation play a basic role in understanding various **priming effects** that can be found in the literature (although this is by no means the only sort of account of priming that there is!). With any priming experiment it is possible to distinguish between one stimulus known as the **prime** and a second stimulus known as the **target**. It is typically the case that the prime stimulus is presented before the target and it is its responses to the target stimuli that are of main importance. In any priming experiment the relationship between the prime and the target is varied across trials. If responses to the target following a prime are different from responses to the target following some sort of control stimulus, this would be known as a priming effect.

In the language of the priming literature various sorts of control stimuli are possible, for instance, some form of neutral stimulus or indeed no stimulus at all (in a so-called no-prime case). Performance with control stimuli is classified as being baseline performance, hence baseline trials or conditions are defined. Priming effects are typically gauged relative to performance in some form of baseline condition. However, what sort of baseline condition is the most appropriate for any given priming effect has been the topic of some controversy (see Jonides & Mack, 1984).

Various sorts of priming effects can be found in the literature. A typical **repetition priming** effect is where responses to a target are facilitated if the target is a repetition of the prime. A typical **semantic priming** effect is where responses to a target are facilitated if the target is semantically related to the target. In such cases **facilitation** is where the primed responses are faster or more accurate than those on baseline trials. The reasons that such facilitation takes place are many and varied. If responses on prime trials are slower or more inaccurate than they are on baseline trials, then this is taken as evidence of **inhibition**. Again explanations for inhibition also abound. We will have much more to say about priming as the discussion proceeds.

**perceptual defence** A form of semantic activation without conscious identification in which taboo words are harder to detect than neutral words.

**perceptual threshold** The point at which a stimulus of a certain kind is said to be perceptible. Usually defined in terms of some stimulus factor such as stimulus intensity that can be varied experimentally.

**line detector** An abstract feature detector that is dedicated to registering information in the proximal stimulus that corresponds to a line of a particular length, orientation, position, etc. in the external world.

**retinal receptive field** The region of the retina that can be linked directly to feature detectors of a particular sort – such as a line detector.

**all-or-nothing system** A thresholded system that is either in an ON state or an OFF state. There is no state in-between ON and OFF.

**thresholded system** A system whose outputs are not a continuous function of their inputs.

**priming effects** Changes in behaviour that are due to relations that hold between a prime stimulus and target stimulus. Priming effects are observed on responses to targets.

**prime** In a priming experiment, a stimulus that occurs before a target stimulus.

**target** A generic term for a stimulus that demands some form of response. Within a priming experiment it is preceded by a prime stimulus.

**repetition priming** When a stimulus is repeated, responses to the second presentation are changed relative to when the stimulus is not repeated. A priming effect is typically revealed as facilitation whereby responses are quicker and/or more accurate on a repeated presentation than on a non-repeated presentation.

**semantic priming** Where responses to a target stimulus are influenced by the semantic nature of the prime.

**facilitation** When performance is faster (and/or more accurate) on a given type of trial relative to performance on some form of comparison, baseline, control or neutral trial.

**inhibition** When responding is slower (and/or less accurate) on a given type of trial relative to performance on some form of comparison, baseline, control or neutral trial.

## Pinpoint question 4.4

**What kind of system is the browning wheel on a toaster?**

## Thresholds and conscious perception

Although this brief digression has taken us some way from the nature of consciousness, we hope that the notion of a threshold is becoming clearer by consideration of these simple examples. In the same way that a threshold may apply in determining when a simple line detector fires or a light bulb turns on, we may discuss a *perceptual threshold* as determining when a stimulus is perceived. Following this line of reasoning, this invites us to consider the claim that if an event occurs above a perceptual threshold, then it will be perceived (it is **supra-threshold**). In contrast, if it occurs below this threshold, then the event will not be perceived (it is **sub-threshold** or *subliminal* – as will become clear, the notion of partial activation is typically invoked in discussions of semantic activation without conscious identification). Understanding all of this now depends on having a clear idea about what constitutes a perceptual threshold.

In trying not to get too bogged down in attempting to explain consciousness, research psychologists have merely offered operational definitions of what it means to be conscious of something. According to Holender (1986), one such definition 'equates conscious identification with the ability to respond discriminatively to a stimulus at the time of presentation' (p. 3). In simple terms this means that we have to take participants at their word – if they say they saw the word *camel* with conviction, then we must assume they are reporting truthfully on their conscious experience of the visual presentation of the word *camel*.

It is very difficult not to think that such issues about consciousness are problems for philosophy and not cognitive psychology, but given that psychologists have shown an interest in **subliminal perception** (in this context 'subliminal' means literally 'below threshold'), it is important that we get a good handle on the concept of a perceptual threshold (see Macmillan, 1986). Indeed, what became the focus of much effort was attempting to understand situations in which a stimulus may exert an influence on behaviour even though the participant reports no conscious experience of it (remember Allport, 1977?). Clearly semantic activation without conscious identification is a relevant example, but many other examples have been discussed in the literature on subliminal perception and perceptual defence (see Dixon, 1971, for a review).

## Research focus 4.1

## Did you say something? Subliminal priming in audition

Essentially our current discussion of semantic processing without conscious awareness relates to the more popular notion of subliminal perception and whether we can really get messages into people's brains without them realising it. That said, one might be forgiven for thinking that humans are just a big pair of eyes, given how so much of the literature we've been discussing is devoted to vision. So it's important to recognise that many of the principles in this chapter also apply to other senses. In terms of subliminal perception, we might as equally be exposed to an inaudible voice telling us that 'the trolls are coming to get you' as we would fail to see a picture of the troll leader taunting us from the TV screen. However, for those of you who like your subliminal messages sprinkled with a dash more reality, Kouider and Dupoux (2005) discussed the case of subliminally priming speech in the laboratory.

Kouider and Dupoux (2005) found that the key to subliminal speech priming, which had so far eluded researchers, was first to hide the subliminal speech within speech-like noise that was spectrally equivalent to the subliminal speech itself. The resultant sound was reported as an 'unintelligible babble' (p. 617) similar to background noise at a party. The second trick was to time-compress the speech such that it was played much faster than it was originally spoken. In the first experiment, 88 French students were exposed to such babble, with some additional target speech being played at normal volume and speed. Participants had to decide as quickly and as accurately as possible whether the target speech was a word or a non-word. However, unbeknown to the participants, these target words had been immediately preceded by some prime speech contained in the babble. The priming speech contained material which was morphologically related, phonologically related or semantically related to the target word. In addition the target speech could be a simple repetition of the prime. Non-words trials were also varied with respect to their prime-target relationship. In English, assuming the target word is *tune*, then a morphologically related prime would be *tuned* – both *tune* and *tuned* share the same unit of meaning (i.e., in this case, *tune*). A phonologically related prime would be *chew* (*tune* and *chew* sound similar) and a semantically related prime would be *song* (as *tune* and *song* have very similar meanings).

In order to provide evidence for the success of the subliminal speech, participants should have been quicker to respond to the target when the prime and target were related than when there was no relation between the prime and target words. The data showed that when the participants failed to identify the prime (providing at least some evidence for the subliminal nature of the effect), subliminal speech priming was restricted to words rather than non-words, and was apparent only for cases where the prime was a complete repetition of the target. In contrast, when the participants reported hearing the prime (providing evidence for the nature of effects when the prime is supraliminal), then participants were faster to respond to target words with semantic and morphological primes. With clearly heard primes, non-word complete repetition priming was also in effect.

Despite some differences between sound and vision, Kouider and Dupoux (2005) concluded by drawing parallels in subliminal priming between the auditory and visual modalities. For instance, both modalities show subliminal priming effects more for words rather than non-words, and both also show little evidence of semantic priming. They also discuss how real-world examples of subliminal sound, such as those 'so-called subliminal audiotapes, which supposedly convey relaxing subliminal audio messages' (p. 617) have tended to fail as a result of unsatisfactory masking. The benefits accrued from these methods of delivery are more likely to be the result of supraliminal priming rather than subliminal priming. Therefore Kouider and Dupoux (2005) have provided an outline for future, albeit limited, adventures into subliminal audio presentation. Watch out, the trolls might be coming after all . . .

*Source*: Kouider, S., & Dupoux, E. (2005). Subliminal speech priming. *Psychological Science, 16*, 617–625.

## The traditional view of an absolute threshold

One traditional view of a perceptual threshold mirrors the notion of an absolute threshold as measured in physics. The freezing point of water is 0°C and the boiling point is 100°C. By such an analogy the idea of an absolute perceptual threshold is that it reflects a fixed constraint on sensory encoding. The reason that we cannot see in the dark is because our photoreceptors cannot operate if the amount of light entering the eye is below a certain minimum. Therefore it ought to be possible to measure the absolute minimum of detectable light – the absolute threshold of luminance detection. Now you see it, now you don't (see Figure 4.6a). In this regard, much effort was expended in trying to arrive at the best (psychophysical) method for ascertaining various sorts of perceptual thresholds (see Haber & Hershenson, 1979, for a very accessible introduction, ch. 5). However, it soon became apparent that the idea of an absolute perceptual threshold is not without its problems.

## Variable thresholds and subjective factors

As is perhaps obvious, people really are very different from pieces of coal and blocks of ice – if we try to measure their luminance threshold on Tuesday we will most likely get a different result to the measurements we take on Thursday. More pressing, however, is that if we estimate threshold at 11.00 on Tuesday, this value is likely to change if we re-test at 11.05. As Haber and Hershenson (1979) argued, this may be because we may have poor control over **stimulus factors** – our light source may vary in an erratic fashion. More importantly, though, we may have very little control over **subjective factors**. The participant might be bored/excited, tired/alert, happy/sad, drunk/sober and so on. The participant's psychological state can vary and, as experimenters, we probably will have little (possibly no) control over this. It is therefore highly unlikely that we will ever record a step function with a fixed threshold for some perceptual decision task. It is far more likely that the so-called **psychophysical function** relating accurate reports to a given stimulus variable (such as luminance) will be best approximated by a continuously smooth curve (see Figure 4.6b). If we admit this, however, we then have to decide where to place the threshold.

So one way to proceed is to design an experiment whereby on each trial we present the participant with a spot of light and simply get them to report what they see. Over trials we vary the intensity of the light (how dim or bright the light is) and note the participants' responses. (Did they see that very dim light just presented or did they not?) Assuming that a value of 0 signifies the light is off and 7 signifies the light is fully

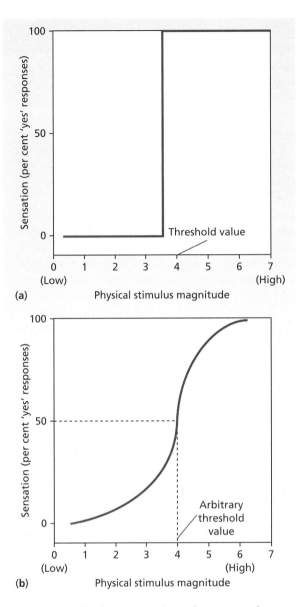

**Figure 4.6 Graphical representations of two sorts of thresholds**
(a) An example of step function associated with an absolute threshold. The perception of the stimulus only takes place once the stimulus strength has exceeded a certain threshold value. The stimulus is either present or it is absent and there is no in-between. (b) A continuous monotonically increasing function with an arbitrary threshold applied. Evidence in favour of a stimulus increases in a smooth fashion but the person is only prepared to respond that the stimulus is present once the stimulus strength exceeds the threshold value.

*Source*: Haber, R. N., & Hershenson, M. (1979). *The psychology of visual perception* (fig. 5.1, p. 89). London: Holt, Rinehart and Winston. Reproduced with permission from Ralph Haber.

on (i.e., very bright), then the light intensity values range from 0 to 7. For every light intensity value we presented we have data showing whether the participant saw the light being on or off. On the basis of these data (i.e., these perceptual reports) we can plot a psycho-physical function of the sort shown in Figure 4.6b).

So for every value of the stimulus intensity tested, we plot the probability that the participant actually reported seeing the stimulus. The problem now is to estimate the perceptual threshold, and this is where we have essentially a free hand. On the understanding that there is no useful sense in which an absolute threshold can be derived, we often end up choosing an arbitrary point as the threshold. Figure 4.6b shows a 50 per cent threshold. What this means is that, for the given level of stimulus energy, the participants will report seeing it on half the times it is presented. More typically though, a 75 per cent correct threshold is chosen. This is the point at which the participant is correct on 3/4 of the trials. Such a threshold can then be converted into a value on the actual light intensity dimension, for example, candelas/metre$^2$ (cd/m$^2$). In our light detection experiment what this means is that over the complete set of trials when the light was presented, the participant detected the light correctly on 75 per cent of occasions when the intensity was of a particular value estimated from our psychometric function. The particular intensity value signifies the 75 per cent correct threshold.

By now it should be clear that this rather detailed discussion of thresholds is leading towards consideration of how best to draw the line between non-conscious (or perhaps more fittingly *pre-conscious*) and conscious, between being unaware of the stimulus and being aware of the stimulus? More worrying, though, is that the 75 per cent correct threshold may be of little use in helping us draw a distinction between pre-conscious and conscious processing because on some trials the participant will be aware of the stimulus that falls below this threshold.

Clearly there are many methodological issues being side-stepped – such as how best to present the lights and what judgement we might ask of the participant – but most importantly we have failed to consider in any detail the psychological state of the participant. We have taken the participant to be essentially a passive sensor of stimulus information (the feature detector either comes on or it stays off and this is fully determined by the amount of energy present) and what we have failed to recognise is that the participant is a decision-maker and now there is a clear difference with the simple feature detector. There is no sense in

## For example . . .

If all of this is starting to feel a little remote, then the work of Connolly, Wayne, Lymperis and Doherty (2000) should act as a sobering reminder of how important issues concerning masking and perceptual thresholds can be. In their review, Connolly et al. (2000) discussed the efforts of tobacco companies who are introducing additives to cigarettes. The intention is that additives should mask the sensations associated with environment tobacco smoke. Clearly if we can't detect (either by smell or by sight) tobacco in the air because it is being masked by these additives, then we will be more likely to think we're in an environment free from the effects of second-hand smoke inhalation. So while we're discussing these apparently theoretical issues, they do have real-life and potentially life-threatening consequences.

which it decides when to come on! Given this, we need to consider how the psychological state of the participant may affect the setting of a threshold. How might the participant's motivations and expectations affect the difference between being aware of the stimulus and being unaware of it?

**supra-threshold** Above threshold.

**sub-threshold** Below threshold – subliminal.

**subliminal perception** Perception thought to occur below the threshold of consciousness.

**stimulus factors** Dimensions upon which a stimulus may vary.

**subjective factors** Factors that are inherent to participants – indicative of individual differences.

**psychophysical function** A graphical/mathematical means for relating a participant's responses to some variation in a stimulus factor.

## Thresholds and perceptual defence

There are no dirty words, only dirty minds.

*(attributed to Lenny Bruce)*

The difference between the participant as passive sensor and the participant as decision-maker featured heavily in the early studies of perceptual defence. Perceptual defence refers to reports that participants 'exhibited higher perceptual thresholds for negatively valued or taboo materials than neutral or positively valued materials' (Postman et al., 1953, p. 215). For example, Postman et al. (1953) used a masking by light technique in which on a given trial a single word was presented very briefly. Initially the luminance of the word display was well below that of the pre- and post-fields.

After every stimulus presentation the participant was asked to report anything they thought they saw. The luminance of the target field was incremented slightly after every trial and the same target word was repeatedly presented over a sequence of 18 trials. Now a classic perceptual defence effect in these circumstances would be that participants would take longer to report taboo words correctly (such as 'raped' and 'filth') than neutral words (such as 'mixer' and 'clove'). That is, neutral words could be 'seen' at lower levels of luminance than could the taboo words – taboo words had higher perceptual thresholds than neutral words.

Taken at face value, such a result does have quite important consequences for understanding perception because perceptual defence can be construed as being an example of semantic activation without conscious identification. How could the perceptual threshold of the taboo and neutral masked words be differentially affected unless the meaning of the words had been accessed? In this regard perceptual defence poses difficulties for any simple sequential stage theory of perceptual processing in which stimulus encoding must run to completion before any processes concerning the interpretation/identification of the stimulus takes place. The existence of perceptual defence seems to suggest that the meaning of the stimulus is affecting sensory encoding!

Given these sorts of considerations, there ensued much discussion over the claim that perceptual defence reflects a tendency to resist recognising threatening stimuli (Postman et al., 1953). Without doubt, this is quite an alarming thing to claim: do we really want a perceptual system that insulates us from threatening stimuli? If you are about to be hit by a speeding car, you need to know about this pretty quickly in order to try to avoid it! Maybe a more sensible approach is to argue that perceptual defence effects show that anxiety-provoking stimuli are detected, but at an unconscious level. This act of recognition then pre-empts anxiety

## For example . . .

At the time, the mere experimental demonstration of subliminal perception in studies of perceptual defence gave rise to worries that took hold about the possible misuse of subliminal messages in advertising and film-making (see Hochberg, 1978, p. 216). For instance, there were reports that unsuspecting filmgoers were presented with subliminal messages such as 'Eat popcorn' and 'Drink Coke' interspersed as a few frames of film so that they were essentially invisible with the consequence that sales of these items rose appreciably (Loftus & Klinger, 1992). Whether or not such events ever happened, the mere thought that it could led to a certain amount of concern in the media (subliminal mind control – shock, horror, probe, etc.). However, psychologists have become more concerned in trying to understand the basic effects rather than in generating possible underhand applications in the film industry.

spreading to consciousness (Dixon, 1971, p. 181). In this way the system is not placed in a situation of denial, but has instead been issued with a kind of benign warning – there is something scary out there but don't panic.

Unfortunately the literature is now littered with many contradictory findings (e.g., Worthington, 1964, vs. Barber & de la Mahotiere, 1982). Indeed, Postman et al. (1953) were unable to replicate the basic perceptual defence effect and found instead the reverse – taboo words had somewhat lower thresholds than neutral words. Indeed, this particular effect has more recently given rise to some further controversy (Dijksterhuis & Aarts, 2003; Labiouse, 2004; Dijksterhuis, Corneille, Aarts, Vermeulen, & Luminet, 2004). It is the case that now there are a variety of different subliminal effects in the literature. In acknowledging such controversial issues, and following an in-depth review of the work on perceptual defence, Dixon (1971) concluded with a rather vague statement that, 'thresholds for the correct report of emotional, threatening or anxiety-provoking, words or pictures significantly differ from those for more neutrally toned stimuli' (p. 179): a conclusion that fails to specify the direction of the difference in perceptibility across taboo and neutral words. Indeed, as Erdelyi (1974) stated, **perceptual vigilance** in which thresholds are lowered for emotional words actually pre-dates the idea of perceptual defence. Nevertheless, the mere possibility of subliminal perception was taken at face value by Broadbent and Gregory (1967a) and they went on to try to make sense of how perceptual defence might come about. What sort of cognitive mechanisms could possibly account for such findings?

## Research focus 4.2

### Slap or tickle: do we have a preference for the detection of negative or positive words?

As we mentioned in the text, there is some controversy over the perceptual defence hypothesis and the idea that we shield ourselves from negative words and instead prefer the company of bench, pencil and egg. Dijksterhuis and Aarts reopened this can of worms in 2003, which will serve as a way into understanding contemporary ideas regarding this topic. Dijksterhuis and Aarts (2003) began by discussing an evolutionary perspective and considering the humble case of the wildebeest. In providing justification for the need to recognise negative stimuli before neutral or positive stimuli, they stated that 'being a few hundred milliseconds late in detecting a lion is extremely dangerous, whereas being a little late in detecting edible vegetation is not so problematic' (p. 14). So far, so good for the wildebeest, but what we really need to do here is look at the data.

Three experiments were carried out in which participants were presented with subliminal stimuli. In experiment 1, participants were presented with a negative word, a positive word, or no word, and asked to report whether they thought they had seen a word. In experiment 2, participants were presented with either positive or negative words and asked to categorise them as either positive or negative. In experiment 3, participants were shown positive and negative words and again had to categorise them as positive or negative, but this time they also had to say which of two words was the synonym of the presented word. So, in the case of 'great super smashing', all these three words essentially mean the same thing and so are synonyms of one another.

The data showed that negative words were reported more often than positive words (experiment 1), that negative words were more accurately categorised as negative words relative to positive words (experiments 2 and 3), but that there were no differences in selecting synonyms for negative and positive words (experiment 3).

Dijksterhuis and Aarts (2003) concluded that the data do support a general evolutionary argument in that negative words are processed faster than positive words, in the same way that we need to process

negative stimuli (oncoming bus) faster than positive stimuli (oncoming strawberries and cream) if we are to stay alive. Dijksterhuis and Aarts (2003) stressed that some words, like *boredom*, are negative but not necessarily threatening (although it depends how much you value your creativity and free time) and so future distinctions need to be made as to whether it is the negative or threatening quality of the stimulus that is important. Such a contentious issue, however, did not go unchallenged as a counter-argument was made by Labiouse (2004), which was followed by a counter-counter-argument by Dijksterhuis et al. (2004). So, depending on who you read, it seems some of us prefer a slap rather than a tickle, while some prefer a tickle over a slap. Vive la différence!

*Source*: Dijksterhuis, A., & Aarts, H. (2003). On wildebeests and humans: The preferential detection of negative stimuli. *Psychological Science, 14*, 14–18.

## Pinpoint question 4.5

**How does perceptual defence manifest itself in masking studies?**

## Perceptual defence: a perceptual effect?

Again taken at face value, perceptual defence seems to suggest the operation of two sorts of recognition devices sitting side by side. Figure 4.7 provides a general schematic framework for thinking about this possibility. According to Dixon (1971, p. 371), one of these mediates overt behaviour in connecting stimuli to responses (the unconscious agency) and the second serves conscious perceptual experience (the conscious agency – see Figure 4.7). One way of thinking about perceptual defence effects is that the mechanisms responsible for transforming stimulus information into responses can affect whether the stimulus is consciously registered. This system operates a veto over whether information about the stimulus enters consciousness or not.

Broadbent and Gregory (1967a) were particularly concerned about how sensible such a dual mechanism theory is and they focused on one particular issue to try to examine the account further. Fundamentally, they were not convinced that the basic perceptual

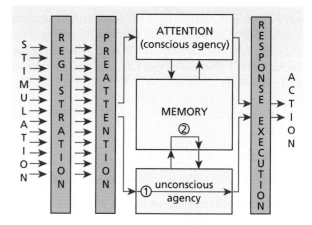

**Figure 4.7 Arrows-and-boxes and the unconscious**
Schematic representation of an information processing account showing various internal components implicated in the debate about unconscious processing (adapted from Greenwald, 1992). In some accounts of perceptual defence, the unconscious agency operates as a gatekeeper to consciousness. Route 1 indicates the flow of information in cases where there is no conscious processing going on whatsoever. Think of the case of walking up a flight of stairs – the control of balance and the act of climbing the stairs (typically) take place outside conscious awareness. Route 2 provides a means for understanding semantic activation without conscious identification.

*Source*: Adapted from Greenwald, A. G. (1992). New look 3: Unconscious cognition reclaimed. *American Psychologist, 47*, 766–779 (fig. 1, p. 767). Reproduced with permission from APA.

defence effect was anything other than a reflection of decision/response mechanisms. Maybe participants were perfectly aware of the unpleasant nature of the stimulus being presented, but they were simply reluctant to report such material for fear of embarrassing themselves in front of the experimenter? Such a possibility is perhaps hard to grasp in the present day, but social constraints were quite different in the middle of the twentieth century. Yes, 'belly' really was once a taboo word.

Where this is leading is a situation in which we need to be able to distinguish effects that may be reasonably attributed to early sensory encoding mechanisms from those that may be similarly attributed to later decision/response processes. In this regard, Dixon (1971) considered three possibilities. The first relates to sensory encoding mechanisms whereas the second and third concern factors located at a more central origin. The possibilities are as follows:

1. Perceptual defence reflects the fact that the immediate detection of a negative stimulus alters the sensitivity of the sensory encoding mechanisms in such a way that it becomes more difficult to encode the stimulus further. In this way the induced emotional state of the observer is affecting perceptual mechanisms – it is inhibiting the encoding of threatening stimuli. For instance, we can in a sense mis-tune the radio or de-focus the binoculars and hence lower the sensitivity with which the sensory apparatus can pick up stimulus information. In this way the first possibility concerns sensing – it is simply harder actually to detect threatening materials.

2. The immediate detection of the threat could simply block out the stimulus from further processing so that it does not enter consciousness.

3. The observer becomes less willing to identify the threat. In this way the third possibility locates perceptual defence at the level of deciding about what has been presented. The stimulus is fully encoded but the observer is more cautious in admitting the threat.

So whereas the first possibility is that perceptual defence reflects properties of perceptual mechanisms being altered so as to insulate the central mechanisms from the threat, the latter two possibilities posit that it reveals something more about higher-level cognitive processes. In attempting to unravel these different possibilities, experimenters turned to techniques developed in the field of signal detection theory.

**perceptual vigilance** A form of semantic activation without conscious identification in which emotional words are easier to detect than neutral words.

## Thresholds and signal detection theory

Realisation of the problems of attempting to determine a perceptual threshold gave rise to an extremely elegant theory concerning stimulus registration and recognition. Central to the theory is the idea that there is a fundamental difference between (i) the processes concerned with sensory encoding of the stimulus, and (ii) processes concerned with assigning this information to a pre-defined mental category. Given this, an overriding ambition was to try to discriminate sensory processes from decisional processes using empirical evidence.

To reiterate: sensory processes concern sensory encoding mechanisms as discussed previously (think of Turvey's 1973 peripheral processes), and as a starting point we will assume that these are in large measure beyond the control of the participant. In contrast, central or decisional processes are, by definition, post-perceptual, and are, by large measure, under the participants' volitional control. Until quite recently, it was generally accepted that methodologies derived from something called *signal detection theory* (SDT) could help discriminate between effects arising from sensory processes and those arising because of decisional processes.

From a traditional point of view, one framework for thinking about this is in terms of Figure 4.8. In very broad strokes, the model provides a means for thinking about how best to assign a signal to a particular category when the situation is one of uncertainty. Given the context of a very busy restaurant, was that your mobile phone ringing just then or was it someone else's? By this view, evidence in favour of a given signal (the sound of your mobile phone) is provided by a single number that falls somewhere on the abstract evidence continuum shown as the *x* axis in Figure 4.8 (see Wickens, 2002, for a relatively straightforward introduction to SDT). The problem is that the ringing of other mobile phones and other similar sounds also produce evidence that falls on the same signal continuum as your phone. The problem therefore is to try to discriminate when your phone rings in the presence of other phones ringing and other forms of noise.

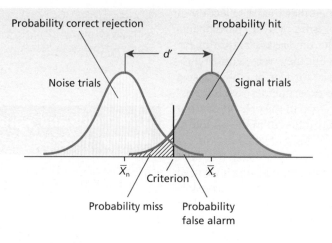

**Figure 4.8 Signal detection theory**

Schematic representation of the statistical model that underlies signal detection theory. A key concept is the continuum of evidence shown in the figure as the horizontal axis. The leftmost distribution provides a representation of the amount of noise that is present across all of the trials of the experiment. Most of the time the noise averages out at the $\bar{X}_n$ value. The height of the curve indicates how often a given amount of evidence on the continuum occurs across trials. Sometimes, but not often, very much lower levels of noise occur (signified by the leftmost tail of the distribution). Similarly sometimes, but not often, very much higher levels of noise occur (signified by the rightmost tail of the distribution).

When a signal is presented on a trial it is superimposed on the background noise – so there will generally be more evidence in favour of a signal on the signal trials than on noise-alone trials. The rightmost distribution signifies the amount of evidence that occurs across the signal trials. It is known as the signal + noise distribution. Remember noise is present on every trial.

In the simplest case, on each trial the participant simply indicates whether a signal was presented or not. The fact that the two distributions overlap indicates that the decision is difficult and there will be many trials that are ambiguous. Given this, the participant must set a criterion – a threshold on the continuum of evidence – such that any amount of evidence that exceeds this criterion will be classified as a 'signal present' trial. However, because the distributions overlap, such decisions are error-prone. Two sorts of errors are possible: (i) *misses* – the signal is missed and the trial is classified as a noise trial, and (ii) *false alarms* – the signal was not present but the participant believes that it was. In addition, two sorts of correct responses are possible: (i) *hits* – the signal was present and was detected, and (ii) the signal was not present and an absent response was made.

Over trials the incidence of the various response types is noted. It is possible, by examining the frequency of the different response types, to compute a measure of the distance between the noise and the signal + noise distributions. This is known as $d'$ or *sensitivity*. The location of the criterion β can also be computed. β reflects the level of evidence that the participant is prepared to accept as being indicative of the signal – it is also referred to as *response bias*. Anything that falls below (to the left of) the criterion is taken to be noise; anything above (to the right of the criterion) is taken to be signal. See text for further details.

*Source*: Willingham, D. (2004). *Cognition: The thinking animal* (2nd ed., p. 511). Upper Saddle River, New Jersey: Prentice Hall. Reproduced with permission of Pearson Education, Inc.

In SDT, it is assumed that there are essentially two basic states of affairs – one in which there is no signal actually present and one in which the signal is present. In the simple case, the participant must try to discriminate between when the signal is present (when my phone is ringing) and when it is not. Uncertainty in the model is provided because such judgements are always made in the presence of random noise (see Figure 4.8). Think of it this way: the claim is that, even when very little else is going on in the immediate environment, the basic sensory hubbub (i.e., activity in the central nervous system) is enough to introduce uncertainty into any signal processing situation.

In the left of Figure 4.8 there is a normal distribution which represents the random fluctuation of noise (both environmental and that from nerve activity) over time with the height of the distribution corresponding to the probability of a given value of noise being present. The normal distribution shows that on a small number of occasions there is low level of noise (the left tail of the distribution) and on a corresponding small number of occasions there are very high levels of noise (the right tail of the distribution). Most of the time, though, the level of noise is intermediate between these two values (the peak of the distribution is centred with respect to the tails) and it varies randomly over time.

So to be clear: uncertainty in the model is provided by random variability of noise in the system and the participants' task is made difficult because of this uncertainty. In the presence of all this noise, how is it possible to decide when a signal is actually present? In the abstract (and shown in Figure 4.8), the state of affairs of when the signal is present is given by the distribution to the right of the evidence continuum. Remember, judgements about the presence of a signal are always made in the presence of noise, hence the distribution to the right of the noise distribution is called the signal + noise distribution. Think of this in terms of the signal being always added to the noise distribution. So whenever a signal is present this will be superimposed on the noise provided by the environment and activity in the nervous system.

Nonetheless, on average the amount of evidence in favour of the signal when it is present will be greater than in cases when it is not present. The critical thing to remember is that, in this framework, evidence for the presence of a signal is represented by a single number that falls somewhere on the $x$ axis. In some cases classifying this number will be easy. For instance, when the number is very, very low then the participant can be reasonably confident that no signal was present; in addition, when the number is very, very high then the participant can be reasonably confident that the signal was present. Between these extremes, however, the situation is ambiguous. This is because, in the intermediate cases, the two distributions overlap to a considerable extent. So in many situations the participant must essentially try to make a best guess as to whether or not the signal was present.

Consider another example. You are sitting at home listening to the radio but the batteries are almost flat and the signal from the radio is coming and going and it is also very fuzzy. You (the listener) are trying to make out a radio programme that you know is being broadcast, and you (the listener) stand for the central decision processes in SDT. The problem is to try to discriminate the actual radio programme from the other sounds (the noise) coming from the radio. Sometimes you will mistake some of the random sounds as speech because you know that the actual radio programme is being superimposed over the random noise coming from the radio.

## SDT and sensitivity

One way to improve your chances of hearing the radio programme would be to change the batteries – this would improve the signal-to-noise ratio because the random noises would diminish, and the signal would be dramatically improved. This change would essentially reflect what is known as a change in the sensitivity of the radio to receive and transmit the signal. Graphically any improvement in sensitivity will force the signal + noise and the noise distributions apart. The whole of the signal plus noise is shifted rightwards away from the noise-only distribution. In this way, increasing the sensitivity of the system means that, on average, it will be easier to detect the signal when it is present because the two distributions will overlap less. The signal-to-noise ratio is increased. In signal detection theory the distance between the two distributions is known as the **sensitivity**. So a bigger distance between the two distributions signifies a larger sensitivity value. Bigger distances are better in terms of being able to discriminate the signal from the noise when the signal is actually presented.

## The notion of a criterion in SDT

Within this scenario, decisions have to be made, at each point in time, over whether the current event contains a signal or not. Given the random fluctuations in activation, and the fact that the two distributions overlap to some extent, it is unlikely that you will always be sure when a signal is actually present – especially if the signal is weak and the noise is strong. Nevertheless, decisions have to be made. How such decisions are made is defined in SDT in terms of the placement of a **criterion** (akin to a threshold) on the continuum upon which the noise and signal + noise distributions are defined. This is what the vertical line in Figure 4.8 represents. If the evidence in favour of the signal being present is sufficiently large, then the $x$ value will fall above or to the right of the criterion. In contrast, if the evidence is sufficiently low, then the $x$ value will fall to the left or below the criterion. According to the theory the placement of the criterion is under the control of the participant. You decide how much evidence needs to accumulate before you decide the signal is present. How far the two distributions are apart, however, is outside the control of the participant.

If the criterion is placed well to the right of the continuum this signifies that the participant is being very cautious in accepting any event as containing a signal. In contrast, if the criterion is placed well to the left of the continuum, this signifies that the participant is being very liberal in accepting any amount of evidence as being indicative of a signal. Remember, according to the theory the placement of the criterion is assumed to be under the volitional control of the participant. So any changes in the placement of the criterion are assumed to reflect decisional processes. Placing the criterion anywhere between the two extremes means that the participant is bound to make some mistakes, and such mistakes come in two forms: (i) **misses** – a stimulus is presented but the participant fails to notice it; and (ii) **false alarms** – a stimulus is not presented but the participant mistakenly believes that one was present. How best to balance the incidence of making these errors relative to making correct responses is central to understanding the application of SDT to cognition.

Previously a different analogy to our radio example was in terms of radar operators trying to detect enemy missiles approaching sovereign territory. Given that the cold war is thankfully far behind us, we will stick with our radio example and extend it a bit. The added twist now is that there is a competition running such that the winner will be the first person to ring up the radio station once they hear 'Money' by Pink Floyd. The first correct respondent wins £1,000,000. You decide to take part. Under these circumstances, as soon as you think you hear the slightest thing that resembles the opening sounds of the cash registers, you should phone the radio station. You must realise, however, that you are likely to make many mistakes – you will commit false alarms – because you have set your criterion for detecting the target song very low. Anything that sounds slightly like a cash register gets you reaching for the phone.

Let's change the scenario slightly so that the prize is still £1,000,000 but now you have only one chance at winning. If you ring up and get it wrong then you are eliminated from the competition. Now you are more likely to shift your criterion for detecting the song to be much higher because the consequences of making a mistake are now catastrophic. In this way you can see how the placement of the criterion is under the participant's control. Don't ring the station until you are much more confident about the cash registers.

Correct responses also come in two forms: (i) **hits** – a signal is presented and the participant notices it; and (ii) **correct rejections** – a stimulus is not presented and the participant realises this. In analysing the probability of making these types of responses (especially of making hits and false alarms) it is possible to derive separate estimates of (i) sensitivity – the distance between the noise and signal + noise distributions (known

as **d prime** or **$d'$**), and (ii) bias – the placement of the criterion on the activation continuum (measures concerning the placement of the criterion are sometimes referred to as **beta** or **β**). Using these estimates the assumption has been that it is possible to isolate factors that affect sensitivity (i.e., alterations to the perceptual coding mechanisms) and factors that affect bias (i.e., the central decisions or post-perceptual mechanisms).

## Pinpoint question 4.6

What are the two parameters of signal detection theory and what do they measure?

**sensitivity** In signal detection theory, the distance between the noise and the signal + noise distributions. An index of the efficacy of perceptual encodings mechanisms (i.e., $d'$).

**criterion** In signal detection theory, a movable threshold that determines the decision as to whether or not the signal or target stimulus was present on a given trial.

**misses** Cases where a signal is present and an incorrect absent response is made.

**false alarms** Cases where a signal is not present and an incorrect present response is made.

**hits** Cases where a signal is present and a correct present response is made.

**correct rejections** Cases where a signal is not present and a correct absent response is made.

**d prime ($d'$)** In signal detection theory, perceptual sensitivity or the distance between the noise and the signal + noise distributions. According to Estes (1994, p. 232), a $d'$ of 0 indicates a complete inability to distinguish a signal from noise (the distributions overlap completely); a $d'$ of 2 or 3 reflects a high degree of discrimination between signal + noise and noise (the distributions are spaced far apart).

**beta** In signal detection theory, the symbol for the location of the criterion. Changes in beta are typically taken to reflect changes in response bias.

## The traditional interpretation of SDT in information processing terms

As we have discussed, sensitivity is defined as the distance between the noise and the signal + noise distributions. If this distance is large, the value of sensitivity (i.e., $d'$) is large, and this means that the signal ought to be relatively easy to detect. In contrast, if the noise and the signal + noise distributions overlap to a considerable extent, then the distance between them will be small ($d'$ will be small), and this means that the signal will, most likely, be difficult to detect. Changes in signal strength are mirrored by changes in the distance between the noise and the signal + noise distributions. Although sensitivity can be manipulated externally – for instance we can simply increase the energy of the stimulus by making it louder, brighter, etc. – we are much more interested in whether we can get changes in sensitivity for reasons other than changes in signal strength. Of course, having introduced this possibility, we will discuss particular examples in more detail shortly. More specifically, traditionally, any such effects on $d'$ have been taken to reflect changes in the sensitivity of the perceptual encoding mechanisms (all other things being equal).

Tradition also dictates that we need to assume that the human information processing system is plagued with noise. Remember that we have defined human information processing as being akin to a communication system in which a communication channel connects a sender with a receiver. Noise on the channel can severely interfere with signals that are being transmitted. In the current context, though, noise is taken to be the random fluctuations in the neural mechanisms responsible for sensory encoding.

It is also accepted that the evidence continuum defines sensory properties of the stimulus event (see Pastore, Crawley, Berens & Skelly, 2003, p. 559; and Pastore, Crawley, Skelly & Berens, 2003, for further discussion). Information about both the signal and the background noise are represented by values on the evidence continuum. Nevertheless, by the traditional view, an increase in $d'$ signifies that it has become easier to encode the signal, and hence easier to discriminate the signal from the noise. A decrease in $d'$ signifies that it has become more difficult to discriminate the signal from the noise.

So whereas traditionally it was accepted that any changes in $d'$ reflect changes in the efficacy of the encoding mechanisms, in contrast, changes in β (i.e., changes in the position of the criterion) reflect later stages concerning subjective decision. As we saw in our radio example, the placement of the criterion is, essentially, under the participant's control. Your decision about when a signal is present is to some degree dependent on what the payoffs are for getting this judgement right. Hence changes in β have been taken to reflect later decisional processes. The beauty of signal detection theory (as originally developed) was that psychologists now had different measures that were taken to reflect early sensory encoding mechanisms ($d'$) and later decisional processes (β), respectively. In summary, changes in $d'$ are taken to reflect changes in sensory encoding or, more generally, perceptual mechanisms, whereas changes in β are taken to reflect changes in the decisional criterion regarding whether a signal was present or not. So changes in β are taken to reflect post-perceptual mechanisms. Given this framework, we now have a means to try to adjudicate between the three alternative interpretations of perceptual defence set out by Dixon (1971) and discussed above.

## Perceptual defence a perceptual effect? Broadbent and Gregory (1967a) revisited

Although Broadbent and Gregory (1967a) did not use the exact version of SDT outlined above to examine perceptual defence, they did use a very similar line of reasoning. They were attempting to ascertain whether perceptual defence reflects something fundamental about perception or whether the effects are post-perceptual in nature. In their experiment they examined auditory instead of visual perception, but this change in modality need not concern us greatly because what is at stake is the nature of perceptual defence in general.

Broadbent and Gregory recorded single words onto audiotape and then mixed these recordings with random noise (an auditory masker). The words, embedded in the auditory noise, were then presented to participants one at time. After each stimulus presentation participants had simply to write down what they thought they had heard. Two stimulus variables were manipulated: (i) the emotionality of the words classified as good (e.g., *nice*), neutral (e.g., *plain*) or bad (e.g., *fear*), and (ii) their frequency of occurrence in the language – there were common/high frequency words (such as *deep*) and there were rare/low frequency words (such as *chant*).

Broadbent and Gregory reported a mixed pattern of findings with the strongest evidence for perceptual defence being found with the rare words. Participants were less accurate in their reports of low frequency bad words than they were in reporting either low frequency neutral or good words. For high frequency words, however, reports of both good and bad words were worse than reports for neutral words. So performance with the common words revealed an effect of emotionality, but the classic perceptual defence effect only occurred with the rare words. Rare bad words were detected less well than either rare good or neutral words.

Having considered the overall pattern of correct responses, Broadbent and Gregory then went on to examine the types of errors participants made. Here interest was with the type of misperceptions that the participants reported. These data revealed that on both high and low frequency word trials, participants erred in reporting having heard a neutral word. That is, there was an overall bias to report neutral words. This bias was seen as being understandable on the grounds that there are far more neutral words in the language than there are good or bad words. So if you are going to guess, then guess a neutral word because this enhances your chances of being correct.

Although Broadbent and Gregory did not carry out a full SDT analysis of their data, they concluded that the effect of the emotionality of the words shown in the different proportions of correct responses reflected a change in sensitivity and not bias: bad rare words really were difficult to perceive! In contrast, the effect of word frequency in different types of errors made, reflected a change in bias and not sensitivity. If you are not sure what you heard then guess a neutral word because there are lots more of these in the language than either good or bad words. Given these contrasting effects, Broadbent and Gregory concluded (p. 583) that 'emotional words do not behave like words of low probability'. There is generally a bias against reporting low frequency words but there is no corresponding bias in reporting negatively charged emotional words. → See 'What have we learnt?', below.

## Pinpoint question 4.7

Why is guessing a neutral word rather than a good or bad word a reasonably sensible strategy to adopt when listening to speech in noise?

## → What have we learnt?

Broadbent and Gregory were very resistant to the idea that the effect for emotional words truly reflected the operation of an unconscious agency that protects the conscious agency from threatening or anxiety-provoking stimuli. They were loath to locate the perceptual defence effect at the level of the sensory encoding mechanisms, preferring to think in terms of how the effects may have arisen at the level of central mechanisms. Nevertheless, on the face of it, the effect of sensitivity in their data, namely, that reports of bad rare words were relatively poor, could be taken to reflect some form of interference from higher mechanisms on the operations of the sensory encoding mechanisms. For instance, it could be that the negative content of the words was registered immediately, and then operations came into play that somehow impeded a full analysis of the stimulus. In this way the full impact of the threatening material was blocked out from consciousness.

Indeed, for Dixon (1971), the sensitivity effect reported by Broadbent and Gregory (1967a) is evidence of some form of perceptual discrimination without subjective awareness – in more recent terminology, evidence for some form of semantic activation without conscious identification. However, Broadbent and Gregory downplayed such an interpretation of their results, preferring instead to argue that the effects may have arisen because of factors located more centrally. The argument is subtle and need not detain us here.

What the work of Broadbent and Gregory has provided is an example of how methods, such as SDT, have been used to try to tease apart effects that may be indicative of perceptual mechanisms from effects that may be indicative of central/decisional mechanisms. We will return to such issues as the material unfolds. For now though, it is important to consider more recent evidence that bears on the notion of semantic activation without conscious identification.

## For example . . .

Although there has been a recent resurgence in interest in perceptual defence (see Research focus 4.2), there has been continued interest in semantic activation without conscious identification. Indeed, there is still something of a debate, in the scientific literature, over the evidence regarding whether such a thing actually exists (see Draine & Greenwald, 1998). More troubling, though, is what has happened when the topic of subliminal mind control has been entertained in a court of law. There has been serious concern over whether subliminal messages can drive someone to commit suicide. A case in point relates to an example, discussed by Loftus and Klinger (1992) and documented in the film 'Dream Deceivers: The Story Behind James Vance vs. Judas Priest' (van Taylor, 1992). In this case, the families of two men who had entered into a gun-shot suicide pact took the rock band Judas Priest to court. The claim was that Judas Priest had included 'subliminal' (although they could be more accurately described as supraliminal backwards) messages about Satanism and committing suicide (such as 'do it') on their album *Stained Class*.

One of the individuals was successful in the suicide attempt, while the other survived but had to undergo extensive facial reconstructive surgery. This survivor went on to develop depression and eventually took his own life by taking a medication overdose three years later.

Lawyers for the families of the two men claimed that inclusion of the subversive messages was in part responsible for causing them to take their own lives. However, the eventual ruling was that there was no scientific evidence to suggest that subliminal messages can control behaviour to this degree. The ruling took account of the fact that Judas Priest identified additional subliminal messages on their record such as 'I asked for a peppermint, I asked for her to get one'.

Despite such lurid possibilities about subliminal messages exerting such a profound control over people's behaviour, psychologists are stuck with the more mundane possibility as to whether subliminal stimuli can affect behaviour at all!

## More recent accounts of semantic activation without conscious identification

SDT shifts the emphasis away from the concept of an absolute threshold of consciousness to one in which any effects of stimulus discrimination may be associated with a change in perceptual sensitivity, a change in subjective bias or both of these. Nevertheless, the preoccupation with perceptual thresholds will not go away, and much of the debate about semantic activation without conscious identification rests upon being able to state categorically when a stimulus fails to enter consciousness. Arguments rest on being able to distinguish the conscious from the unconscious/pre-conscious, and again visual masking comes to the fore. In this regard, the work of Marcel (1983a) took on much significance.

## Marcel's work on semantic activation without conscious identification

In a critical experiment, Marcel (1983a) presented participants with a display sequence comprising an initial fixation cross for 500 ms followed by a stimulus field for a variable interval, then a final pattern mask. The stimulus field either contained a printed word or the field was blank. On each trial the participant was presented with such a sequence and then asked to make one of three judgements:

1. In making a presence/absence judgement, the participant was asked whether a word was actually presented or whether the stimulus field was blank.

2. In making a graphic judgement, the participant was presented with two alternative (probe) words and had to judge which of these was more graphically similar to the stimulus word.

3. Finally, in making a semantic judgement, the participant had to choose which of two alternatives was most semantically similar to the stimulus word.

Few details are given but initially Marcel undertook to ascertain a threshold stimulus duration (or target–mask SOA – the time between the onset of the target and the onset of the mask) at which each individual participant began to experience difficulties in reporting whether a word had been presented or not. The method was roughly to reduce the SOA until the participants began to experience real difficulties in reporting what they saw. Having homed in on this so-called *detection threshold*, Marcel then systematically increased the target–mask SOA in a series of experimental trials and measured the accuracy of participants' judgements separately for the three judgement types. What he found, essentially, was that, as the target–mask SOA was increased from the detection threshold, accuracy increased in a monotonic fashion (participants became increasingly more accurate as the SOA increased). However, accuracy increased at different rates for the three judgement types.

Contrary to what might have been expected, as the SOA was increased slightly, participants began to improve in their semantic judgements. With further increases in the target duration their accuracy at the graphic task improved. Strikingly, however, even though accuracy improved on these judgements as SOA increased, participants' presence/absence judgements remained at chance as the SOA increased. In other words, there was apparently clear evidence of semantic activation without conscious identification. At certain exposure durations participants were unable to report accurately whether a word had actually been presented, yet when a word was presented for that duration, they were able to make reasonably accurate reports about its semantics. Although participants were unable to say whether a word had been presented or not, when a word was presented they were able to make a reasonable stab at its meaning.

Under these experimental conditions, it was argued that the backward pattern mask did not so much impede or interfere with the perceptual encoding of the word but that it essentially blocked out the stimulus information from entering consciousness. By this view the pattern masking was operating centrally, once the perceptual encoding had completed. Irrespective of any detailed consideration of the theoretical interpretations of the work (see Marcel, 1983b), Marcel's experimental findings provoked much interest and many replications were attempted and these met with

mixed success. However, serious doubts were cast on the original findings by Cheesman and Merikle (1984, 1985, 1986).

## Pinpoint question 4.8

What finding from Marcel's (1983a) study provided evidence for semantic awareness without conscious identification?

## Perception without awareness? A re-appraisal of Marcel's findings

The general methodological framework for thinking about Marcel's results has been nicely summarised by Merikle (1992). First, identify a measure of conscious perceptual experience (call it C: in Marcel's study, C is the presence/absence judgement). Next, identify a measure that reflects unconscious perceptual processes (call this U, e.g., the semantic judgement in Marcel's study). We now need to set up an experiment in which the stimulus fails to produce any effect on C but at the same time does produce an effect on U. Under these conditions we can conclude that perception without awareness has been demonstrated. Taken at face value, therefore, Marcel's results show that at certain critical target–mask SOAs there was no effect on his C (presence/absence) measure, but there was an effect on his U (semantic judgement) measure: hence the claim of perception without awareness!

What Cheesman and Merikle were particularly concerned with, however, was whether Marcel had truly established the correct conditions for showing perception without awareness. They felt there were serious problems with Marcel's measure of conscious perceptual experience (C) and whether participants in the experiment were truly unaware of the stimuli. In order to address this Cheesman and Merikle adapted another of Marcel's experiments to examine something known as the Stroop effect (Stroop, 1935).

### The Stroop effect

In a standard Stroop task, on each trial, the participant is presented with a printed word. The colour of the typeface varies over trials and the participant has to name the colour of the ink on each trial. In the standard effect there is a difference in performance between cases where the word is a colour name and it is printed in its own colour (e.g., BLACK – these are known as congruent cases) and cases where the word is a colour name but printed in a different colour (e.g., RED – these are known as incongruent cases). Performance is much better with the congruent than the incongruent cases. Typically no such effects arise when participants are asked simply to read the words (see MacLeod, 1991, for an extensive review, and Durgin, 2000, for a discussion of the reverse Stroop effect, i.e., interference effects on word naming trials). Figure 4.9 provides more extensive examples.

So the standard Stroop effect occurs when colour names are used, the colour of the ink of the text is varied across trials and participants have to name the colour of the ink. Sometimes these naming speeds can be compared to performance in control cases in which

a colour patch is presented instead of a coloured word and participants simply have to name the colour. Here again incongruent stimuli take considerably longer to name than colour patches. Cheesman and Merikle (1984), however, examined a slightly more complicated variant on this sort of Stroop interference.

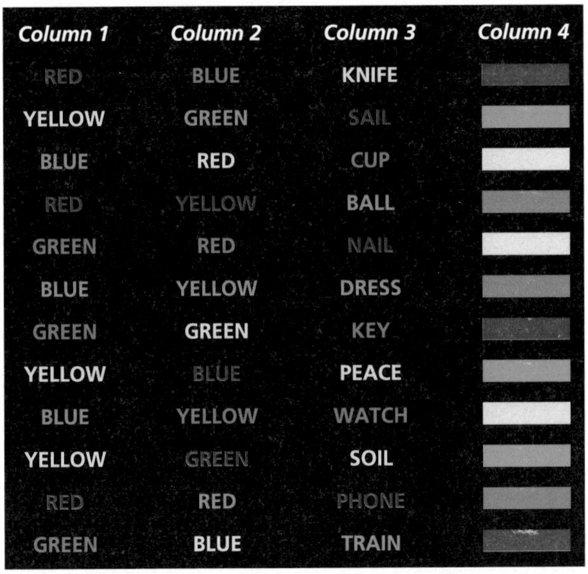

## Cheesman and Merikle (1984)

Initially, Cheesman and Merikle (1984) ran a simple detection task. On each trial one of four colour words (i.e., BLUE, GREEN, ORANGE or YELLOW), printed in black, was presented. This was presented to the non-dominant eye and then was followed immediately by a pattern mask to the dominant eye. (We have another case here of dichoptic pattern masking as discussed in Chapter 3.) At the start of each trial participants fixated on a centrally positioned unfilled rectangle and the word and its ensuing mask fell either slightly above or slightly below this. Participants simply had to respond by stating which of the four colour words they thought they saw. Figure 4.10a provides a schematic of the sequence of the events on a trial in the detection task. Naming speeds were not taken because it was accuracy of report that was the measure of interest.

The SOA between the word and mask were varied until it was so brief that participants were performing at chance, i.e., the point at which participants were correct 25 per cent of the time. (Okay, this is the first trial of the experiment, now guess which of the four colour words will be presented. You will be correct on 25 per cent of occasions.) This SOA was known as the *detection threshold* and played a very important role in a subsequent task. The aim of the detection task was simply to arrive at the detection threshold – the duration at which participants were no longer able to report accurately the name of the colour word that had been presented.

Cheesman and Merikle then went on to examine performance under various masked priming conditions. On trials in the 25 per cent detection condition participants were initially presented with one of the previous four colour words or the neutral letter string XXXXX as the prime for the duration given by the detection threshold. Following this, the central rectangle was filled with colour and next a mask was presented. Performance was also examined in a no-mask condition. Here the prime stayed on for the detection threshold SOA; this was followed by the coloured rectangle but the colour word was not masked. On all trials participants had to name the colour of the (target) rectangle as quickly and as accurately as they could.

| Column 1 | Column 2 | Column 3 | Column 4 |
|----------|----------|----------|----------|
| RED | BLUE | KNIFE | |
| YELLOW | GREEN | SAIL | |
| BLUE | RED | CUP | |
| RED | YELLOW | BALL | |
| GREEN | RED | NAIL | |
| BLUE | YELLOW | DRESS | |
| GREEN | GREEN | KEY | |
| YELLOW | BLUE | PEACE | |
| BLUE | YELLOW | WATCH | |
| YELLOW | GREEN | SOIL | |
| RED | RED | PHONE | |
| GREEN | BLUE | TRAIN | |

**Figure 4.9 Examples of various sorts of Stroop materials**
In the first column are *congruent stimuli* – the ink colour and named colour match. In the second column are *incongruent stimuli* – each colour name is printed in a colour different to that named. In the third column there are *control* or *neutral stimuli*, in this case, coloured words that are not colour names. A different sort of control stimulus is a coloured patch (see column 4).

The standard Stroop effect occurs when you attempt to name the colour of the ink of the colour names – you should be slower to progress down column 2 than column 1. There should be little difference in naming speeds if you now try to read out loud the names that are printed (compare the ease or difficulty of attempting columns 1 and 2). If you do find that there is a difference, with performance being slower in column 2 than column 1, when you read out the colour names, then this would be evidence of something called a *reverse Stroop effect*. Reverse Stroop effects do sometimes occur and the interested reader is referred to Durgin (2000) for further details.

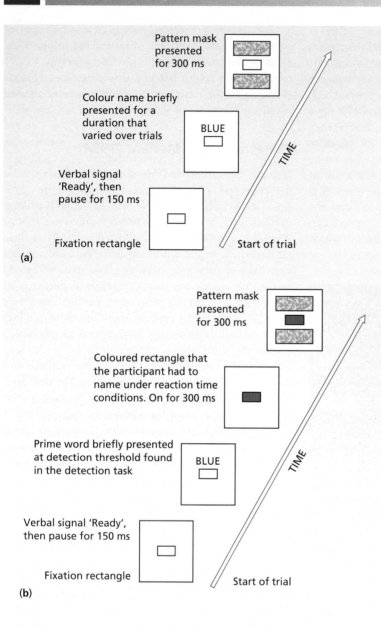

(a)

(b)

**Figure 4.10 Schematic representation of trial events in the tasks reported by Cheesman and Merikle (1984)**
(a) A sequence of events on a trial in the detection task reported by Cheesman and Merikle (1984). Time moves across the page, left to right, from the start of the trial. (b) Sequence of events on a trial in the colour naming task. Here a congruent trial is illustrated – the prime names the colour of the target patch. More specifically, the figure illustrates the 25 per cent detection condition in which the prime was presented briefly and followed by a colour patch. The sequence ends with the presentation of a pattern mask to obscure the prime word.

Figure 4.10b provides a corresponding schematic representation of the events on a trial in the colour naming task.

What is critical here therefore is the relation between the nature of the prime and the colour of the target rectangle. Congruent trials were where the colour word and the colour of the rectangle matched and incongruent trials were where the colour word and the colour of the rectangle mismatched.

The results were relatively clear cut. In the no-mask condition, participants were much slower on incongruent than congruent cases. More particularly, participants were much quicker in naming the colour patch when the prime was congruent than when the prime was the neutral XXXXX. This is evidence of facilitation due to the prime. In contrast, participants were much slower in naming the colour patch when the prime was incongruent than when the prime was neutral. This is evidence of inhibition due to the prime. Therefore overall pattern of facilitation and inhibition in the no-mask condition fits comfortably with standard Stroop effects even though the colour word and the to-be-named colour were separated in time.

Of critical importance, however, was performance in the 25 per cent detection condition in which pattern masks were used. Now there was no facilitation and there was no inhibition. If we take facilitation and inhibition to reflect semantic activation of the meaning of the prime words, Cheesman and Merikle concluded that there was none when participants were unable to identify the colour words at a level greater than chance. When participants were unable to detect accurately the target colour word, the Stroop effect was abolished: there was no evidence of semantic activation without conscious identification.

This finding was further substantiated by the data from two further conditions. Further detection trials were run in which a blank interval was inserted between the offset of the prime and the onset of the mask. Estimates of SOAs were established for a 55 per cent and a 90 per cent correct detection rate (of correct report of the prime words) prior to running the masked priming trials by increasing the duration of the blank frame. For both of these priming conditions,

facilitation and inhibition occurred and the size of these increased as accuracy improved. So even under masking conditions and as long as the participant was able to report correctly the identity of the target at levels above chance, the Stroop effects were observed. What was particularly interesting, however, was that despite participants being above chance in their reports of the prime identities in these conditions (remember, chance reporting was 25 per cent correct), they informally reported only very rarely *seeing* the primes.

## Pinpoint question 4.9

What do the stimuli have to look like and what must the participant do in order for a standard Stroop effect to manifest itself?

## Research focus 4.3

## Paying your way into consciousness: can post-decision wagers measure awareness?

On the basis of the work by Cheesman and Merikle (1984), it can be seen that measures of conscious awareness are fraught with difficulty. This frustration is also echoed in a recent paper by Persaud, McLeod and Cowey (2007) who stated that getting people to report their conscious experience is much more difficult than it first seems. For example, we could use numerical scales to gauge the confidence with which certain decisions are thought to be conscious, but people might underestimate their confidence or simply have no impetus to show it. So Persaud et al. (2007) hit upon the idea of motivating individuals to reveal the contents of their consciousness, and what better incentive than a bit of the old dirty cash. The idea here is that individuals bet on the contents on their consciousness, and if they fail to finish the experiment in profit, then it is likely that the information on which they are basing their decisions is outside the realm of consciousness.

To take one example, Persaud et al. (2007) examined an individual (GY) with blindsight, which is a remarkable condition that they define as the 'ability to make visual discriminations in the absence of visual awareness' (p. 257). Specifically, the participant was a 52-year-old man who, at the age of 8, had the left side of his striate cortex (primary visual cortex) destroyed. While essentially blind in his right

hemifield, GY was still able to report and discriminate certain stimuli presented there, despite the fact that he was not consciously aware of any visual event. Therefore GY was told that on half of the trials a stimulus would be presented in his right hemifield and on half the trials it would not. His task at each trial was to 'guess' whether a stimulus had been presented, then bet either 50p (low wager) or £1 (high wager) on his choice.

The first startling result was that out of 200 trials, GY correctly reported the presence or absence of stimuli in his 'blind' right hemifield 141 times, which was a result significantly better than chance. The second startling result was that only 48 per cent of correct responses were followed up with a high wager, which was a result no better than chance. Persaud et al. (2007) summarised thus: 'That GY was capable of using visual information in his scotoma (basically an area of visual impairment) to perform the discrimination, yet did not maximise his winnings by consistently wagering high after correct classifications, indicates that he was not always aware that he was making correct decisions' (p. 258; comments in parentheses added). In contrast, and under alternative conditions of presentation, when stimuli were present in his left hemifield that GY could consciously see, then correct responses were nearly always followed by a high wager.

▶

Although Persaud et al. (2007) reported other examples, the case of GY is interesting because it introduces us to an additional situation in which conscious identification is not a necessary step in making above chance responses to stimuli. Moreover, it provides an additional metric for measuring consciousness, with participants essentially being asked to put their money where their (conscious) mouth is. This could turn out to be a costly enterprise for psychologists as we become more like book makers, but if that's the price we pay (ahem) for novel insights into consciousness, then so be it.

*Source*: Persaud, N., McLeod, P., & Cowey, A. (2007). Post-decision wagering objectively measures awareness. *Nature Neuroscience*, *10*, 257–261.

## *Objective vs. subjective thresholds*

From this overall pattern of performance, Cheesman and Merikle drew a distinction between the **objective threshold** and the **subjective threshold**. An objective threshold is one that specifies chance level of performance: it is the level at which perceptual discrimination is at chance. In contrast, the subjective threshold is the point at which the participant reports an inability to perform than at a better than chance level. The distinction is crucial because although participants may be convinced that they are guessing – for instance, they are unable to report seeing a stimulus – objectively their responses show better than chance performance. They may feel as though they are guessing but objectively they are performing at levels better than chance. Cheesman and Merikle (1985) went further and provided an operational definition of conscious perception in stating that 'perceptual information presented below subjective threshold but above objective threshold is unconsciously perceived and that perceptual information presented above the subjective threshold is consciously perceived' (p. 339; see Figure 4.11 for an illustrative diagram).

They were also very critical that previous claims concerning apparent demonstrations of semantic activation without conscious identification (e.g., Marcel's) were based on unsound evidence, the point being that the relevant data had been collected under conditions where differences between subjective and objective thresholds had not been distinguished successfully. They were concerned that Marcel had inadvertently established subjective rather than objective thresholds in running his experiment, hence his claims about semantic activation without conscious identification were not well founded.

Following this line of reasoning, the most stringent test of semantic activation without conscious identification would be where semantic effects could be shown at the level of the objective threshold. For instance, in

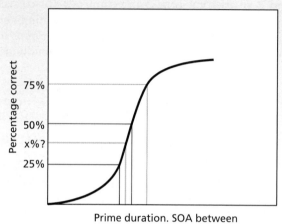

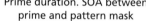

**Figure 4.11 The distinction between an objective and a subjective threshold**
After Cheesman and Merikle (1984, detection task). On each trial one of four colour words is presented briefly and pattern masked. The duration of the prime is varied over trials so that the SOA increases on the *x* axis from left to right. Plotted is a hypothetical psychophysical function that relates percentage correct responses to SOA. Four thresholds are presented. The 75 per cent correct threshold indicates the SOA at which the participant is correct on ³/₄ of the trials. Similarly, the 50 per cent correct threshold indicates the SOA at which the participant is correct on ¹/₂ of the trials. The green threshold (i.e., x per cent) is where the participant reports that they are guessing and are no longer confident in their responses. This is known as the *subjective threshold*. The final red line is where the participant is actually performing at chance – it is the *objective threshold*. The key point is that this shows that there can be situations in which a participant is convinced that they are guessing but their responses still remain above chance.

the task reported by Cheesman and Merikle (1984), such an effect would be where participants in the 25 per cent detection condition still showed facilitation and inhibition in their naming speeds.

## Perception without awareness? More provocative evidence

Cheesman and Merikle (1984, 1985) have offered us a very negative appraisal of the work that had attempted to show evidence for semantic activation without conscious identification. We need to be mindful of their very clear guidance over how best to set a perceptual threshold and we need to remember such notes of caution when masking is being used to make claims about unconscious perception or the like. However, it would be misleading not to note that there are now some reasonably compelling examples that do show various forms of semantic activation without conscious identification. One example will suffice at this juncture.

Hirshman and Durante (1992) ran two priming experiments on word recognition. Each prime was a word but on half the trials the target was either a word or a non-word. On a trial-by-trial basis participants were cued at the start of the trial to report the identity of the prime word or they were cued to make a speeded response to the target. That is, they had to press one key if the target was a word and a different key if the target was a non-word. This is known as a **lexical decision task**. Response times were measured to the nearest ms and accuracy measures were also taken. Figure 4.12 shows a schematic of the events on a trial in the experimental paradigm that they used.

The final variable of interest was known as **semantic relatedness**. On half of the word trials the prime and target were unrelated (e.g., table – lawn) and on the remaining trials the prime and the target were semantically related (e.g., doctor – nurse). As semantic relatedness only applies to words, it could not be manipulated on non-word trials. For example, the prime 'horse' is as unrelated to 'fong' as it is to any other non-word target. In this case, a semantic priming effect would be where responses to a related target are facilitated relative to responses to an unrelated target. For example, lexical decisions to the target (responses to the target 'cart') will be made more quickly and more accurately following a related prime (e.g., horse) than will lexical decisions to a target that follows an unrelated prime (e.g., fruit).

To repeat Merikle's (1992) terminology, we have a C measure, namely the prime identity reports, and we also have a U measure, namely the semantic priming effect. To show some form of semantic activation without awareness, we need to be able to show no effect on C but some effect of U.

On masked trials the prime was followed by a backward mask comprising a row of Xs and the duration of the prime (the prime-mask SOA) varied from 33 ms to 116 ms and data from this masked priming condition were very instructive. First, at the very short SOAs participants were generally unable to report the identity

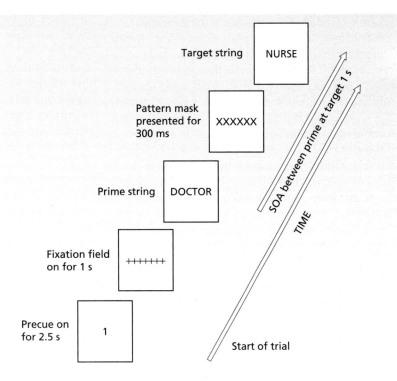

**Figure 4.12 A sequence of events on a trial in Hirshman and Durante (1992)**
The precue signalled the type of response required. A *1* meant 'report the prime', and a *2* meant 'make a lexical decision to the target'. A prime report trial is shown. The prime string was presented very briefly and then pattern masked. Time moves across the page left to right from the start of the trial.

## → What have we learnt?

Clearly the evidence so far reviewed for semantic activation without conscious identification is rather slight and the cautious approach to the problem advocated by Cheesman and Merikle carries some considerable force. Nevertheless, the data by Hirshman and Durante are provocative. The evidence is that there are very tightly controlled cases in which the meaning of a stimulus exerts an influence in the absence of the participant being able to report exactly what the stimulus actually was. This is a very far cry from the rather lurid claims we have considered about the potency of subliminal signals. Nevertheless, the mere possibility that semantic

activation can take place in the absence of conscious identification does have rather serious implications. For instance, it does imply that the perceptual mechanisms are such that the meaning of a stimulus can be accessed in the absence of having any record of what the physical characteristics of the actual stimulus was. A more challenging possibility is that the meaning of the stimulus can determine just how it is perceived. We will consider this sort of possibility in much more detail in the next chapter. Before we get too carried away, however, it is fitting to end on a further cautionary note regarding visual backward masking.

of the prime – this was especially true at the shortest SOA. At longer SOAs prime reports improved and at an SOA of 50 ms an additional effect of semantic relatedness was found. Participants were significantly better in reporting semantic related than unrelated primes. (Such retrospective priming may seem to be quite odd but it is reasonably well established in the literature: see Hirshman & Durante, 1992, p. 258, and Draine & Greenwald, 1998, for a slightly sceptical view.) The data for the lexical decisions were not as clear cut as they might be, but generally speaking, a typical semantic priming effect was found for these data.

Nevertheless, in a second experiment robust semantic priming was found when the masked primes were presented for only 33 ms. Although prime identification was very low (less than 8 per cent) semantically related primes were reported more accurately than semantically unrelated primes; a typical semantic priming effect did obtain in the lexical decision data to the targets. Hirshman and Durante therefore concluded that semantic priming does occur in such a way that it is not completely dependent on being able to identify the prime. Even though participants were unable to identify the primes correctly there was semantic activation that influenced the subsequent processing of the target: 'semantic activation can occur before word identification' (p. 264). → See 'What have we learnt?', above.

## Pinpoint question 4.10

How did Hirshman and Durante (1992) provide evidence from semantic awareness without conscious identification?

## Just how effective is visual masking in halting stimulus processing?

Given that backward masking techniques play such a prominent role in our discussions of the difference between conscious and unconscious processing, then it is important that we are clear that we fully understand just what is going on. So far we have been reasonably rigorous in setting out the conditions under which masking will and will not be effective. For instance, traditionally it was accepted that iconic memory is abolished by backward pattern masking (Coltheart, 1972; Gegenfurtner & Sperling, 1993). This fits with the view that, unless items from the target display are read out from iconic memory before the masker arrives, they will be lost. That is, the items will not be perceived – they will not enter consciousness. Given that such important claims have been made, then it is fairly critical that the supporting evidence is unequivocal.

For instance, the traditional view of the effectiveness of backward masking led to the assumption that the experimenter had a rather strict control of the contents of consciousness – roughly, only four items will be read out from the icon and it is only these that are consciously perceived. However, we can contrast the idea of masking by replacement with that of the notion of interruption by curtailment. To reiterate: by the replacement view, information about the current target is completely over-written by information about the next stimulus (i.e., the mask). According to the curtailment view, however, it is assumed that the processing of the first stimulus simply stops when the next arrives, and it is not necessary to suppose that masking eradicates all trace of the target. Curtailment allows for the possibility that some record of the target may still be available even though processing has moved on. Accordingly, the idea is that iconic representation may survive following the presentation of a backward visual-noise mask. Given this possibility it then becomes no easy matter to try to control the duration of iconic storage or indeed be confident that masking blocks or erases events from consciousness. Indeed recently, evidence that the icon may survive backward visual-noise masking has been provided by Smithson and Mollon (2006).

What they did was run a variant of the standard Sperling paradigm (see Figure 3.5), but importantly, they did not present the cue until after the presentation of the mask (see Figure 4.13, and Smith & Fabri, 1975, for similar manipulation). Clearly if the mask eradicates iconic representation, then participants should be unable to report cued items correctly, because the cue follows the mask and the mask erases the icon. However, what Smithson and Mollon (2006) showed was the following:

- There was no partial report advantage when the mask was presented at the offset of the target display, so an immediately following mask did eradicate the representation of the target display.

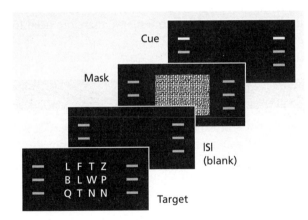

**Figure 4.13 Examples of displays used by Smithson and Mollon (2006)**
The target display was presented for <10 ms and followed either immediately or after 100 ms by a 'checkerboard pattern mask'. The mask was presented for <20 ms and then after a variable delay the cue (the bar markers) were presented. Time moves across the page left to right from the start of the trial.
*Source*: Smithson, H., & Mollon, J. (2006). Do masks terminate the icon? *The Quarterly Journal of Experimental Psychology, 59,* 150–160 (fig. 2, p. 153). Reproduced with permission from Taylor & Francis Ltd.

- There was, however, a robust partial-report advantage when the mask followed the offset of the target display by 100 ms, thereby replicating the basic Sperling (1960) effects.

- Most critically, the partial-report advantage occurred even when a delay was introduced between the offset of the mask and the onset of the cue. The effect was large when the cue immediately followed the mask but this declined gradually as the delay between the mask and the cue increased to 700 ms. Indeed the data indicated that the partial-report advantage survived for up to 400 ms after the onset of the mask.

Such a pattern of results clearly stands in contrast to the claim that the mask eradicates the icon in all cases. If the cue follows the mask to up to about 400 ms then the partial-report superiority survives.

Smithson and Mollon (2006) went further and argued that the data bolstered the discrete moment hypothesis (see Chapter 3). What their data suggest is that as visual events unfold over time, there is an internal sequence of snapshots that is generated in much the same way that movies are made up from a sequence of frames. Each visual event is captured in a frame on this kind of internal roll of film. So the sequence of visual events is represented in the visual system in some form of memory trace that preserves the sequential order of the input. By this view the icon survives the mask because it is coded as one discrete perceptual event and because this event is different from the other discrete perceptual event that captures the mask.

In conclusion, what we have here is further evidence in favour of the discrete moment hypothesis together with some rather alarming evidence that shows how backward masking may not act to erase or block items from entering consciousness in the way that has been traditionally accepted. Backward masking may not act according to interruption by replacement in all cases. Clearly such evidence is important to bear in mind if we are attempting to achieve experimental control on the contents of consciousness. We will return to such issues when we address effects of so-called *subliminal* face processing (see Chapter 16).

**objective threshold** The point at which perceptual discrimination is at chance.

**subjective threshold** The point at which a person feels as though they are performing at chance even though, in actual fact, they are performing better than chance.

lexical decision task  An experimental paradigm in which participants must judge whether, on a given trial, a letter string is a word or a non-word. Typically performance is carried out under reaction time conditions.

semantic relatedness  Typically, the degree to which items are related by virtue of the fact that they share the same category.

## Concluding comments

Although many of the basic ideas about establishing a boundary between conscious and non-conscious processing have been traced back to the first half of the twentieth century, it is clear that much remains unresolved and there is still much work to do. We can, perhaps, be confident in asserting that, at the very least, we have a much firmer understanding of the nature of perceptual thresholds than was the case 100 years ago. In addition, much progress has been made methodologically. We are now much clearer empirically about how best to establish a perceptual threshold and what establishing such thresholds means in terms of information processing. Nevertheless, the degree to which subliminal stimuli control our behaviour remains moot.

Evidence has emerged that subliminal stimuli may indeed be processed to a semantic level in the absence of explicit awareness. However, this evidence is only present in very transitory effects in tightly controlled experiments on word recognition. The effects, such as they are, seem only to reveal something about the very earliest stages of word recognition. This is a far cry from the more grandiose claims about how semantic information more generally affects the processes of sensory encoding. So although some aspects of advertising, and other attempts at mind control, are based on assumptions about the power of subliminal processing, the actual empirical data are far from compelling.

Despite the rather mixed evidence that has been reviewed in terms of semantic activation without conscious identification, the discussion has allowed us to introduce many basic concepts and methodological tools that have much more general application. Signal detection theory crops up time and again in the literature. The distinction between effects of perceptual sensitivity and bias will be revisited as we examine more thoroughly claims that have been made in the literature about the nature of human perception. What should be appreciated, however, is that in many, many cases when cognitive psychologists discuss the difference between conscious and unconscious processing, somewhere lurking in the background is an experiment involving masking. From what we now know about the limitations of this technique we therefore need to be very, very cautious.

## CHAPTER SUMMARY

- The chapter begins by drawing out what a sequential account of processing looks like – namely, the stages of processing are set out in a chain such that this stage can only begin once information from the immediately preceding stage arrives. Turvey's concurrent and contingent model of processing is described and an important distinction between early peripheral mechanisms responsible for stimulus encoding and later central interpretative mechanisms is set out. The model is based on arguments concerning feedforward processes in which information flows from the stimulus to the central mechanisms in a bottom-up, stimulus-driven way. In contrast there are feedback processes in which information may flow in the opposite direction.

- An explanation of masking by object substitution was provided by Di Lollo et al. (2000) in terms of re-entrant processes. In their model of visual processing, a distinction is made between an input layer, a working space layer and a pattern layer. The input layer represents retinal information, which is then passed to the working space layer. The pattern layer makes shape explicit and then passes this information back to the working space layer. Masking by object substitution occurs as a result of over-writing any representation of the target + mask in the working space layer with a representation of the mask alone.

- These principles of masking can be used to address some fairly fundamental questions in cognitive psychology, including the nature of consciousness. On the basis of the re-entrant model, stimulus identity at the pattern layer might influence the working space layer, and as a result of this feedback, it is possible that semantic activation could occur without the stimulus actually being consciously identified at all. Allport

(1977) presented data to suggest that while participants could not accurately report a target item (a word) that had been masked, the errors that participants made suggested that the semantic meaning of the target had been activated. For example, participants might not have reported seeing the word 'beach' but instead responded 'pebble'. However, it is important in such studies to control for the likelihood that these semantically related errors occurred by chance (Williams & Parkin, 1980).

- Perceptual thresholds are critical to the understanding of conscious awareness. The issues were discussed in the following example. The assumption is that a number of internal feature detectors become active when certain properties are present in the environment. The feature detector might operate according to a simple all-or-nothing rule, in which the detector is on once evidence has accrued past a particular threshold, and is off when evidence is below that threshold. Alternatively, the feature detector might operate with respect to a continuous system, in which the amount of detector firing is directly related to the amount of evidence for that feature. A hybrid model can also be thought of in which both threshold and continuous systems are combined. If stimulus presentation is above perceptual threshold it is said to be supraliminal, and if it is below perceptual threshold it is said to be subliminal. For cognitive psychology, absolute thresholds might be difficult to obtain as a result of stimulus and participant factors. Therefore, experimenters aim to create psychophysical functions that map out the likelihood of stimulus detection over a range of different factors.

- One piece of evidence for semantic activation without conscious awareness is perceptual defence (Postman et al., 1953). Here, different perceptual thresholds were found for neutral and taboo words, with taboo words requiring greater levels of luminance relative to neutral words. The conclusion was that the meaning of the word was affecting its sensory encoding. While the direction of this effect suggested that threatening stimuli tend to be resisted, contradictory evidence has since been found (Barber & de la Mahotiere, 1982). In addition, it wasn't clear whether perceptual defence was indeed a perceptual effect or whether it existed at the level of more central decision-making processes (Dixon, 1971).

- Signal detection theory (SDT; see for example Wickens, 2002) has been used to try to adjudicate between the perceptual and response-based accounts of the effects. Two parameters known as $d'$ (d prime) and $\beta$ (beta) can be derived and respectively these have been taken to reflect the operation of the perceptual analysers and mechanisms responsible for making a decision and making a response. In an early study by Broadbent and Gregory (1967a), the evidence was mixed. Low frequency bad words were hard to detect – with the implication that the perceptual analysis for these stimuli is affected by their meaning – whereas participants tended to guess neutral words over good and taboo words.

- Marcel (1983a) compared presence/absence, graphic and semantic judgements for words over a range of detection thresholds. As the SOA between target and mask increased, the accuracy of judgements also increased, but at different rates. Interestingly, there were SOAs in which participants could perform relatively well on the semantic judgements but not very well on the presence/absence judgements. Therefore, under certain conditions of stimulus presentation, semantic activation seemed to be occurring in the absence of conscious identification.

- However, Cheesman and Merikle (1984) pointed out that what is critical in these kinds of studies is the whether the measure of conscious perceptual experience is valid. Using a Stroop paradigm in which colour words are presented in different kinds of ink colour, they showed that when participants were performing at chance accuracy, neither facilitation with congruent stimuli nor inhibition with incongruent stimuli was observed. In this respect, the distinction between objective and subjective threshold is paramount and the task for future research is to show semantic activation in the absence of conscious awareness at the level of objective threshold.

- One critical assumption of the iconic memory literature is that backward masking erases the icon. That is, when the stimulus of interest is immediately followed by the presentation of a masker, the target stimulus fails to enter a more durable form of memory and is lost forever. Smithson and Mollon (2006) provided evidence to suggest that this may not be the case. In a variant of the Sperling paradigm in which the cue for partial report was presented after the mask, a partial-report advantage was shown when a delay was introduced between mask offset and cue onset. The data provide evidence for the discrete moment hypothesis as well as suggesting that backward masking does not necessarily erase the icon.

## ANSWERS TO PINPOINT QUESTIONS

4.1 The concurrent and contingent model is referred to as a sequential account because the model operates according to strictly feedforward principles. Information produced by the peripheral nets is fed forward to the central nets. First the peripheral nets are engaged by the stimulus, then the central nets are.

4.2 Masking by object substitution works by overwriting any representation of the target in the working space layer with a representation of the mask.

4.3 The errors in the Allport study provided evidence for semantic awareness in the absence of conscious identification since, although participants could not report a particular target, their errors tended to be semantically related to the target.

4.4 The browning wheel on a toaster is a continuous system.

4.5 Perceptual defence is revealed by taboo words requiring a higher perceptual threshold than neutral words.

4.6 $d'$ is a measure of sensitivity and $\beta$ is a measure of response bias.

4.7 Good and bad words are relatively rare. Neutral words are much more common so if you have to guess you are more likely to guess right if you guess with a neutral word.

4.8 Marcel (1983a) found that at certain SOAs, participants could not accurately report the presence or absence of a target, but could report which of two words was more like the (unseen) target in meaning. Therefore semantic information was independent of conscious identification.

4.9 A traditional Stroop stimulus must be a colour word printed in a certain colour, with ink colour and the colour name being different from one another. Participants are particularly impaired in naming the ink colour when this differs from the colour name.

4.10 The data from Hirshman and Durante (1992) suggest that even though participants were unable to identify the primes correctly, there was semantic activation that influenced the subsequent processing of the target.

# AN INTRODUCTION TO PERCEPTION

**By the end of this chapter, you should be able to:**

- Distinguish between perceptual and cognitive processes.
- Discuss how the familiarity effect relates to both late and early processes.
- Identify how the principles of familiarity, recency and expectancy operate in perception.
- Distinguish between the Old Look and New Look schools in perception.
- Detail the principles of Bruner's perceptual readiness theory (1957).
- Understand the significance of illusions for theories of perception.

## CHAPTER CONTENTS

Camping out in the woods with school friends was a rite of passage during the summer holidays. Stocked to the brim with incredibly unhealthy sweets and fizzy pop with neither a piece of fruit nor a decent toothbrush in sight, you set about bedding down for the night after a full day's open air fun. Some time after the obligatory exchange of ghost stories, and just before the last comforting square of chocolate has been consumed, an eerie

# 'It only attacks when the moon is aglow' The Beast of Burnley

sound fills the tent. For once, this isn't one of your companions letting off 'steam' but something rather more sinister. 'What the hell was that?' 'Oh, it'll be a cow – I saw a whole bunch of them in the next field this afternoon.' 'It's a rabid sheep! I knew one was going to attack me one day after eating all that lamb.' 'I heard that there's a beast that roams these parts, my dad told me the story of the Beast of Burnley just before I left. He especially told me to look out for strange shadows moving in front of the tent.' At that point, the torch batteries fail and more than one scream can be heard over the Burnley moorland . . .

When we don't know what a stimulus is, how do we estimate it? How does what we've experienced before colour our judgement? What happens when a stimulus is completely ambiguous, even after staring at it for what seems like hours? Answers to these and other related questions will be addressed in this chapter, although we may never know the true identity of the Beast of Burnley . . .

## REFLECTIVE QUESTIONS

1. How much of what you see and hear is caused by your environment and how much is caused by you? Do you tend to interpret the world in terms of what is most familiar, what has been seen most recently or what is more expected? How might these different influences interact with one another?

2. Have you ever looked at something and done a double take? What happens when you see something you don't understand? How do you know when something doesn't look right and how do you try to resolve these ambiguities in our environment? When we experience multiple interpretations of the same thing, what does this tell us about how we perceive the world?

## Introduction and preliminary considerations

Having considered the particularities of visual encoding, visual sensory memory and visual masking, the intention now is to examine broader questions about the nature of human perception. We will be concerned with the degree to which perception is governed, not so much by what is out there, but by what the person brings to the task. Basic questions exist over the extent to which our perceptions of the world are governed by our experience of the world and as we will see, according to one fairly radical perspective, it is claimed that our perceptions of the world are built up from knowledge of previous experience of it.

Clearly such a presupposition stands in stark contrast with the naïve realist view of perception as set out by Neisser (1967; and described previously, see Chapter 3). By the naïve realist view, our perceptions of the world are taken to mirror the world, but if we admit that our perceptions of the world are affected by our past experience of it, then something has to give – something more than mirroring is going on. An entailment of this is that everyone's experience of the world is unique, but if this is true, then how can it be that we all perceive the same world? On the one hand, we all happily admit that our experiences of the world are different – two people cannot be at exactly the same point in space at the same time. On the other hand, we must also admit that there is some common ground for how else could we successfully communicate among ourselves? We need to consider these issues very carefully.

Initially we will survey some basic points about human perception that have emerged in the literature, and then move on to examine some basic effects that have been taken to reflect general characteristics of the human perceptual system. Some of the evidence comes from the literature on word recognition, but the aim is to take from these studies evidence for general principles of perception. We will consider, in turn, **familiarity effects, recency effects** and **expectancy** or **set effects**.

> **familiarity effects** Empirical findings that reveal how familiarity influences our perceptions of the world.
>
> **recency effects** In perception research, experimental findings that reveal how the recency with which a stimulus has been encountered influences the perception of the stimulus. In memory research, how items towards the end of a list of to-be-remembered items are well recalled.
>
> **expectancy (set) effects** Empirical findings that reveal how expectancy can influence our perceptions of the world.

## Distinguishing perception from cognition

Before getting too engrossed in the details, it is important to set the work within a general framework for thinking. To provide a context for appreciating the relevant data, it is useful to consider some general theoretical issues first. One very useful framework for thinking was provided by Fodor (1983) and is captured by his modularity of mind hypothesis (see Chapter 2). A schematic representation of Fodor's architecture of the mind is provided in Figure 5.1, and this clearly shows that each of the five senses is decomposed into its own sub-set of input modules. Following sensory encoding, the input modules act as the interface between the world and the mind of the observer.

Here the distinction between the proximal and distal stimulus will, again, turn out to be useful. To reiterate: the proximal stimulus is the stimulation of the sense organs, while the distal stimulus is the actual physical thing that gave rise to proximal stimulus. So the brown leather chair is the distal stimulus and the corresponding pattern of light that impinges on the retinae is the proximal stimulus.

Initially, the stimulus energy (i.e., the proximal stimulus) that arrives at the epithelium (i.e., the surface of the body) is encoded by the sensory transducers. The eventual stimulus information is then passed on to the input modules, which in turn generate outputs that feed into the central processors. The central processors then function to try to make sense of the sense data. The central processors attempt to identify the distal stimulus that gave rise to the proximal stimulus. In very broad strokes, this is the general view of processing set out by Fodor in his modularity of mind hypothesis (1983; see Chapter 2).

Figure 5.1 also maps the distinction between **perception** and **cognition** onto the functional distinction between, respectively, the operation of the input modules on the one hand, and the operation of the central processes on the other. At a stretch, we could also cite Turvey's concurrent and contingent model here (see Chapter 4), since the peripheral and central nets in his model bear a certain resemblance to the input and central mechanisms, respectively. There is a division between relatively dumb peripheral mechanisms and the relatively clever central mechanisms.

Couched in this way the framework for thinking rests upon a seemingly simple distinction between perception and cognition. As an act of simplification, in the figure a line has been drawn between the perceptual mechanisms (the input modules) and cognitive processes (the central processors). Of course, whether it is at all sensible to accept such a clean division between perception and cognition is something that will preoccupy us throughout this chapter. It should come as no surprise to learn that many have taken issue with this distinction: it is controversial and it continues to be hotly debated (see Pylyshyn, 1999, and commentaries). Controversy surrounds such questions as: Can we sensibly distinguish properties of the perceptual system from properties of the cognitive system? Is there a useful distinction to be drawn between perceiving and conceiving? Is the 'seeing' vs. 'deciding' distinction valid? These questions will be addressed as discussion proceeds.

Despite such concerns, we will adopt Fodor's theory (see Chapter 2) as a useful starting point because it provides such a very clear framework for thinking about many fundamental issues in cognitive psychology. Ultimately, though, the psychological validity of the model stands or falls by whether it can adequately account for the data. We will therefore need to examine the sorts of empirical claims that the model makes about human information processing and see whether these stand up to scrutiny.

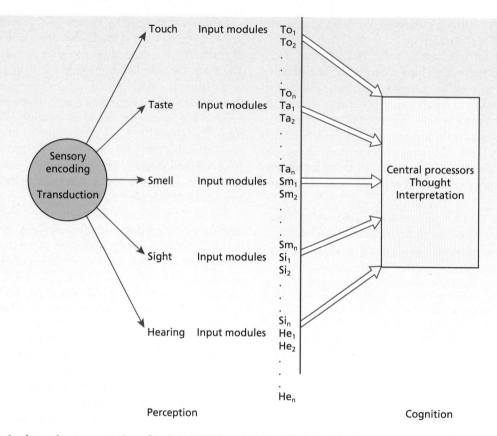

Figure 5.1 A schematic representation of Fodor's (1983) modularity of mind hypothesis and the architecture of the mind

Among the many characteristics of input modules that Fodor (1983) outlined, he asserted that input modules are **informationally encapsulated** (p. 64). By this he means that once a module receives input, it produces a corresponding output that 'is largely insensitive to what the perceiver presumes or desires' (p. 68). So regardless of what the perceiver hopes to see or hear or feel, etc., the input modules operate according to certain principles that are insensitive to these higher-order considerations. The assumption is that a perceiver is built so as generally to 'see what's there, not what it wants or expects to be there' (p. 68).

A complementary way of thinking about this is that the **processing** that goes on in the input modules is **bottom-up** or *stimulus driven*. Higher-order knowledge does not influence processing at this stage – the input modules operate in a purely feedforward manner and there is no feedback from central processes to the input modules (see Chapter 4). Input modules merely slavishly operate on the proximal stimulus and produce an output that approximates to the best first guess as to what is out there. They produce a first stab as to what the corresponding distal stimulus might be.

The input modules operate in a purely feedforward manner and there is no feedback from the central processors. Think of it this way: you (an input module) are working in a parcel sorting office and have been asked to separate out very large parcels from those that could possibly fit through a standard letter box. In making such a distinction you are merely operating on one set of criteria (such as size and volume) and your decisions are not based on what is contained in the parcels. Identifying what is in the parcels is up to someone else – someone who cannot alter your decisions in any way whatsoever.

So according to this view the input modules (the perceptual mechanisms) produce the best first guess as to what sort of object may have given rise to this pattern of input. In contrast, it is the job of the central processors (the cognitive mechanisms) to assign meaning to this input and so make sense of the sense data. The central mechanisms make a more informed judgement as to what the distal stimulus actually is by taking into account what the input modules are signalling and what the person knows about the world. By this view, the perceptual mechanisms operate quite independently of any cognitive influence. It therefore follows that perception and cognition are different and can be studied – to a certain extent – independently of one another. What we have here is a very clear statement of the distinction between perception and cognition.

Although there is something of a philosophical flavour to what is being discussed, as we shall see, there are empirical consequences that follow from holding such views. In this regard, initially we will continue to adhere to the tradition that has concentrated on trying to ascertain the degree to which a particular experimental effect reflects characteristics of encoding mechanisms (the perceptual system) as opposed to characteristics of more central decision mechanisms (the cognitive system). In pre-empting a very involved discussion of the evidence, though, we begin by considering the general modularity framework for thinking in some more detail. Moreover, before any congratulations are offered over novelty and originality, it should be stated at the outset that similar ideas have been around since the turn of the last century enshrined in the 'classic sensation-interpretation doctrine' associated with Wundt and Titchener (see Rock, 1983, p. 299).

## Pinpoint question 5.1

**According to Fodor (1983), which mechanisms are responsible for (a) your reading the sentence 'your in-laws are coming to visit' and (b) either jumping for joy or weeping openly?**

perception According to Fodor (1983), operations associated with the input modules.

cognition According to Fodor (1983), operations associated with the central processes.

informationally encapsulated A property of a processing module (Fodor, 1983) in which its operations are determined locally by information contained within the module.

bottom-up processing Processes driven by the stimulus in a feed-forward fashion.

## Drawing a distinction between the perceptual system and the cognitive system

To frame the present discussion we will freely use the phrase the **perceptual system** as being shorthand for the underlying mechanisms that produce an internal representation of the input stimulus (this will be known as the **perceptual representation**). In the preceding material, the perceptual system has been variously discussed in terms of encoding/peripheral/early mechanisms. In contrast, the **cognitive system** will be used as shorthand for the underlying mechanisms that operate on the perceptual representation to provide an interpretation of the input stimulus (the higher-order/later/central mechanisms). By this view the perceptual system operates so as to take the proximal stimulus and generate an internal representation of this. This perceptual representation is then amenable to further interpretative analysis that is undertaken by the cognitive system. (The nature of the perceptual representation will be discussed in more detail as we proceed.)

The purpose of the cognitive system is to take the perceptual representation and to assign an interpretation to it: the cognitive system generates a specification of the distal stimulus given the proximal stimulus as contained in the perceptual representation. Continuing in this vein, the eventual percept contains a specification of both the physical characteristics of the input together with a decision about what the distal stimulus actually is. There is a perceptual record of the stimulus which has been produced by the perceptual system and there is an interpretation of what this record specifies as supplied by the cognitive system.

For perception to work properly we want the perceptual system to deliver a representation that is a truthful record of the environment – something that is also known as a **veridical representation**. In other words, ideally the mapping between the proximal stimulus (the input) and the distal stimulus (an entity in the real world) should be correct. For example, if a tiger is currently present in the immediate environment then the perceptual system should deliver a

## For example . . .

You might be surprised to read about fictional superheroes in these pages, but it turns out that the cry, 'Is it a bird? Is it a plane? No, it's Superman!' could be interpreted as multiple decisions (of varying success) of the cognitive system as to what could possibly be that flying distal stimulus in the sky creating the related retinal proximal stimulation.

representation that leads the cognitive system to decide that there is a tiger present in the immediate environment. It should do this as quickly and effectively as possible. Clearly the perceptual system must be pretty good at this because we humans have survived despite not being the strongest or fastest predators on the planet.

Within the present framework for thinking, the observer's perceptual representation is assumed to contain a specification of patches of brown and black colours that, in combination, add up to a coherent tiger-like shape – it contains a record of the physical attributes of the proximal stimulus. Importantly, though, such a representation must allow the cognitive system to decide quickly that this representation signifies the presence of the tiger. Optimally, the perceptual system should be providing the cognitive system with a veridical (i.e., truthful) record of the environment that provides a very good basis upon which the cognitive system can decide what is out there.

These ideas will be fleshed out in more detail as we proceed, but for now we need to consider whether the evidence collected from experiments that we will review reflect the operation of perceptual mechanisms (as just described) or whether they are more indicative of the operation of interpretative (cognitive) mechanisms. We have drawn upon a rather simple distinction between (i) the perceptual system that encodes the proximal stimulus in such a way that a perceptual representation is generated and (ii) the cognitive system that provides an interpretation of the perceptual representation. The fundamental question now is whether we can marshal evidence that supports this distinction in such a way that the characteristics of these two systems are made clear.

When cast in these terms, there is a clear link with the material in the previous chapter. A similar aim was behind the experiments of Broadbent and Gregory (1967a) in their attempt to establish whether perceptual defence – the apparent failure to perceive threatening words – was due to a change in perceptual sensitivity or a change in response bias. Indeed the signal detection theory parameters of sensitivity ($d'$) and bias ($\beta$) came to prominence on the understanding that effects on measures of sensitivity reflected some aspect of the perceptual system and that effects on measures of bias reflected some aspect of the cognitive system. To be clear, the simple logic is that any $d'$ effect is associated with perceptual mechanisms whereas any $\beta$ effect is associated with interpretative/decisional mechanisms that constitute the cognitive system.

Much of the early work that we will review here was concerned with trying to tie down whether effects could be used to adjudicate between perceptual and cognitive mechanisms. More generally, this kind of issue is critical because if we take some observation (or more generally an experimental effect such as perceptual defence) to be indicative of an interpretation placed on some stimulus, then what we are admitting is that the observation reveals very little (even possibly nothing) about perception. The effect is more likely telling us something about how we interpret the world and we should set this aside from issues regarding the operation of the perceptual system.

> **perceptual system** Mechanisms responsible for the generation of an initial internal representation of a stimulus.
>
> **perceptual representation** Stimulus representation derived through the operation of the perceptual mechanisms.
>
> **cognitive system** Interpretative mechanisms.
>
> **veridical representation** An internal record of an external stimulus that is a truthful specification of it.

## Familiarity and perception

Let us return to our tiger example to carry the discussion forward. In recognising the patches of brown and black as signifying the presence of a 'tiger', the visual input has been assigned to a particular mental category. In this way stored knowledge of the world allows us to make sense of the data from the senses. The phrase **mental category** will be discussed in much more detail later (see Chapter 12), but, for now, it can be used as shorthand for stored knowledge about the nature of a class of things. Recognising a given stimulus means assigning the perceptual representation of the proximal stimulus to a mental category. Of course, you will be unable to do this if the stimulus is unfamiliar because, by definition, you have no mental categories for unfamiliar things. Critically, though, this does not mean that you will be unable to perceive an unfamiliar stimulus.

For instance, you have probably never come across the letter string NEBRUE before but this does not mean that you cannot perceive it. Patently, therefore, there is an important sense in which perception and interpretation are different. The perceptual system generates a perceptual representation of NEBRUE, but the cognitive system fails to generate a very meaningful interpretation of the input. Here the interpretation

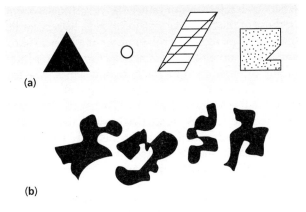

(a)

(b)

**Figure 5.2 Seeing vs. recognising**
Examples of (a) easy to describe, and (b) difficult to
describe figures.

*Source*: Kanizsa, G. (1985). Seeing and thinking. *Acta
Psychologica, 59*, 23–33 (fig. 1, p. 24). Reproduced with
permission from Elsevier.

assigned to the marks on the page may be nothing
other than an attempted pronunciation of the letters.
Hence, NEBRUE is seen but it is not recognised.

To cement this particular point, consider Figure 5.2
(taken from Kanizsa, 1985). In the upper half of the
figure are various geometric shapes. In a hypothetical
case one participant (the sender) is presented with
these and must get a second participant (the receiver)
to reproduce these but the sender may only describe
the figures to the receiver. The claim is that this task is
relatively straightforward because both participants
can easily relate these to familiar mental categories
such as a black equilateral triangle, a small ring on a
blue background, and so on. However, if the sender is
now presented with the blob-like configurations in the
lower half of the figure, the task becomes incredibly
difficult.

The more cynical among you might be thinking
that all of this is simply common sense so what is the
point in discussing it? Well, what the example should
make clear is that, as Kanizsa (1985) stated, 'there is no
difference between the two situations with regard to
the visual aspect as such' (p. 25). Both sets of marks on
the page are clearly visible and can therefore be easily
seen. However, in the former case the marks on the
piece of paper constitute familiar shapes and in the
latter they do not. Here, therefore, there is apparently
a very clear-cut distinction between perceiving and
conceiving. The process of seeing is the same for both
familiar and unfamiliar cases, yet something else
appears to be going on when we are confronted by
familiar entities as compared with unfamiliar entities.

Consideration of this kind of point leads us seamlessly
on to a discussion of familiarity effects in perception.

## Familiarity and word recognition

Intuitively it may seem that familiar things are easier
to perceive than unfamiliar things, and this is indeed
what is implied on a superficial understanding of what
familiarity effects in perception reveal. However, as
our discussion of perceptual defence showed, we need
to tread carefully and be much more analytic in our
approach. Does familiarity really affect perception?
Are familiarity effects indicative of the operation of
the perceptual system? or do they tell us more about
the operation of the cognitive system?

To address these questions, psychologists have been
preoccupied with experiments on word recognition.
As Michaels and Turvey (1979) noted, since the time
of Cattell (1886), it has been known that words are
more accurately identified from a briefly presented
display than are random letter strings. One obvious
reason for this is that words are simply more familiar
than a random string of letters. Upon reflection,
however, words and random letter strings differ on
several other things as well – such as meaningfulness
and, possibly, pronounceability (see Pollatsek, Well, &
Schindler, 1975, for a brief review). So the above so-
called **word recognition advantage** may not be solely
due to words being simply more familiar than random
letter strings; other factors may be at play and may be
confounded with our familiarity variable.

Given such difficulties in comparing the perception
of words with the perception of random letter strings,
an alternative has been to just consider the perception of different types of words, where the different
word types are defined according to their *frequency of
occurrence in the language*. We can therefore control
items by matching them on meaningfulness and pronounceability, but can also allow them to differ on their
frequency (e.g., 'fable' vs. 'table'). It will generally be
the case that a given word will be more meaningful
and pronounceable than a random string of letters
so to overcome such confounds it is better to examine
the perceptibility of words that differ in familiarity.
In the simplest case we can compare the perceptibility
of common vs. rare words (cf. Broadbent & Gregory,
1967a).

As Broadbent and Gregory (1971) stated, one
advantage of doing this sort of experiment with words
is that we have an objective measure of how familiar
the items are because there exist norms that contain
actual frequency counts of words taken from large

samples of written and transcribed spoken language. For instance, a very famous word count is the Kučera and Francis (1967) word count, and if you look at this particular set of word norms you will discover that THE is the most common word and ZOOMING and ZOOMS languish towards the bottom of the table. Indeed, the existence of such word norms and the ability to control systematically for stimulus frequency is one very good reason that words have been so intensively studied in experiments on perception.

This is not to argue that such experiments cannot be carried out with other forms of stimulus materials, but merely that it has proved easiest to carry them out with words. Indeed, a possible confusion – that must be avoided – is that the results of the experiments recounted here *only* reflect properties of the human word recognition system. Well, some of the effects are peculiar to the perception of words, but originally the experiments were motivated by a desire to understand more general properties of the perceptual system.

The **word frequency effect** is our first indication of a familiarity effect in perception. Broadbent and Gregory (1967a) began their paper with the statement that, 'It is, of course, normal to find that words common in the language are more easily perceived than are words which are uncommon' (p. 579), but two different sorts of accounts of this frequency effect have been contrasted. According to the first, the understanding is that the effect reflects sensory mechanisms – for instance, that 'sensory mechanisms are selectively adjusted so as to collect more evidence about the occurrence of probable events (than rare events)' (Broadbent & Gregory, 1971, p. 1: material in parentheses added). In contrast, and according to the second class of theories, the frequency effect reflects a decision or response bias located at a later, more central stage of processing. The basic question is therefore: is the word frequency effect telling us something about the perceptual system or is it telling us something about the cognitive system? Is the word frequency effect a so-called perceptual effect?

## Pinpoint question 5.2

**Why are rare words a better control than non-words when examining the processing of familiar words?**

## Sensory/perceptual accounts of the effects of familiarity

So the central issue is whether the word frequency effect (in particular) and familiarity effects (in general) reflect characteristics of either the perceptual system or those of the cognitive system. To get a better handle on this, let us reconsider the notion of a line detector and also assume that different detectors exist for lines of any orientation (one for horizontal lines, one for vertical lines, one for a rightward diagonal, one for a leftward diagonal, and so on). Therefore we might describe the letter V as one rightward diagonal and one leftward diagonal joined at the base. Let us also assume that in the corresponding hypothetical world, horizontal and vertical lines are more plentiful than diagonal lines. Consequently, horizontal and vertical lines will be more familiar than diagonal lines. How might an organism evolve to take advantage of this? Well, on a sensory account the organism may well have acquired more receptive fields for horizontal and vertical lines than for diagonal lines. In this regard the sensory mechanisms have been selectively adjusted throughout the evolutionary history of the organism to take advantage of the basic statistical nature of the world.

Alternatively, or indeed in addition to this, the perceptual mechanisms could be tuned throughout the course of the developmental history of the individual. Evidence for this idea comes from the work of Blakemore and Cooper (1970). In brief, they reared two kittens in highly constrained visual environments such that one kitten was only exposed to vertical lines and edges and the other kitten was only exposed to horizontal lines and edges. Later, recordings were taken of single neurons inside the brains of these kittens. Generally speaking, when orientation-selective cells were found (neural line detectors of the type already discussed), all were found to have preferred orientations of within 45° of the orientation to which the kitten had been first exposed. No cells were found that were linked to directions orthogonal (at right angles) to the original exposed orientation. Indeed simple behavioural tests revealed that the kittens were essentially blind to lines and edges in the non-preferred direction. So Kitty H reared in a horizontal world could see horizontal but not vertical lines. Kitty V reared in a vertical world could see vertical but not horizontal lines.

More provocative are the claims that such perceptual tuning can take place over much shorter time spans. Here it is not so much that an individual possesses disproportionately more feature analysers of a particular type than another (i.e., vertical line detectors over horizontal line detectors), but that particular feature analysers become more highly tuned than do others. To take an example from the concurrent and contingent account of processing (Turvey, 1973; see Chapter 4), the peripheral nets for familiar stimuli operate much more quickly than do those for unfamiliar stimuli. Hence they deliver their outputs to the central nets much sooner than do those for unfamiliar stimuli. Over time, therefore, the peripheral nets for familiar stimuli are 'tuned up' in the sense that they become 'well oiled' in delivering fast outputs. Such tuning does not take place for unfamiliar stimuli because they are encountered much less often.

As we will see shortly, there are also other accounts of perceptual tuning in which such processes arise under the control of the participant. It is not so much that the perceptual system passively changes as a consequence of being exposed to environmental influences but that the participant actively takes control over the operation of perceptual analysis. Such accounts as these are particularly controversial because they stand in complete contrast to the stimulus-driven, modular account of processing described in Figure 5.1. So, in contrast to such sensory accounts of familiarity effects (i.e., the perceptual mechanisms for familiar instances perform better than those for rare instances), the alternative is to consider decision or response bias accounts.

## Decisional/post-perceptual accounts of familiarity

Let us assume that each line detector has a threshold such that when the relevant line falls within the detector's receptive field, activation accrues at the detector (in the manner described in Chapter 4). When this activation exceeds the threshold, the detector fires and the line is identified. In this sort of system it is possible to think that each line detector has its threshold set at a particular level which is given by the probability of how often its corresponding line is encountered. So lines that are highly probable (say, horizontal and vertical lines) give rise to lower thresholds than lines that are rare (say, the diagonal lines).

What this means is that a detector with a lower threshold will fire more easily (or more quickly) than one with a higher threshold because the detector with a lower threshold needs less activation to fire (see Figure 5.3). Lowering the threshold implies that a much more liberal criterion is applied to detecting when the critical stimulus is present. So more probable lines will be detected more easily than will less probable lines. Less evidence needs to be present for detection of a probable line than an improbable line because of the difference in the respective threshold levels of activation on the corresponding line detectors.

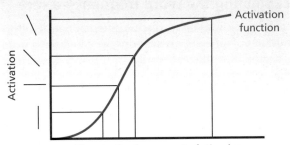

**Figure 5.3 Schematic representation of various line detectors and their different thresholds**
The *y* axis reflects the amount of activation provided by an input stimulus. The different line detectors are ordered according to the amount of activation that is needed for them to 'fire'. The understanding is that the thresholds, in this example, reflect how frequently the actual lines have been encountered. So the vertical line detector has a lower threshold than the others because vertical lines have been encountered the most often.

At one level the argument is quite subtle because there is a distinction being drawn between encoding and deciding/responding. By the sensory account, familiar items are encoded more quickly and/or more accurately than are unfamiliar items. By the later decision/response account, all items are encoded in the same fashion, it is just that familiar items are categorised more quickly than unfamiliar items. A decision about a familiar item is reached more quickly than a decision about an unfamiliar item because the observer is using a less stringent criterion for category membership for familiar than unfamiliar items. So, to use the language of signal detection theory, a purely sensory account predicts an effect on $d'$. $d'$ values for familiar items should be greater than unfamiliar items by the sensory account. The noise and the signal + noise distributions are far apart for familiar items and close together for unfamiliar items. In contrast, the decision/response bias account predicts an effect on $\beta$ and now the difference between familiar vs. unfamiliar items should be reflected in $\beta$. Participants should miss more unfamiliar than familiar items.

**Pinpoint question 5.3**

In a city, which do you think would have the lower threshold – the smell of car fumes or alpine air – and why?

## Explaining the word frequency effect

In the same way that we discuss different line detectors for lines of different orientations, we can discuss word detectors for different words. In this way we assume that each familiar word has its own word detector and each has a threshold set by the frequency of occurrence of the word in the language. In discussing such a framework for thinking about word recognition, Broadbent and Gregory (1971) located the word frequency effect at the level of central and not sensory mechanisms; that is, they located the familiarity effect in word recognition at the level of the word detectors. They argued that the word frequency effect reflects the fact that word detectors for common words have lower thresholds and hence need less evidence to fire, than do the detectors for rare words. By extension, they argued that familiarity effects, in general, reflect the operation of central decision mechanisms rather than perceptual encoding operations.

## Active vs. passive theories of perception

On the basis of this kind of word frequency effect, Broadbent (1977) introduced a more general framework for thinking about perception by contrasting **active theories** of perception with **passive theories**. For him the word frequency effect is indicative of a passive mechanism in which judgements are made about evidence for relevant stimuli that accrues at the level of corresponding stimulus detectors (i.e., word detectors). Word detectors with lower thresholds fire more quickly than do detectors with higher thresholds. The contrasting view is that active mechanisms are responsible for the effect. For instance, it could be that the participant has, in a sense, the ability to alter the perceptual system in line with knowledge and expectations about the world. By this view, the person is able to take control over the perceptual system to such an extent that they can selectively tune the perceptual encoding of common over rare stimuli. We will return to the distinction between active and passive views of perception later and we will explore more thoroughly active accounts of perception. For now, though, we need only note the distinction. Bearing this in mind, we can reconsider familiarity effects that have been documented in the literature.

## Familiarity effects reflect late processes

In using the term 'late' in the present context, the intended reference is with respect to accounts in which

there are stages of information processing that are arranged in a sequence such that certain processes come into play later than do others. We can then discriminate early from later stages of processing in much the same way that Turvey (1973) distinguished peripheral from central nets. According to the general framework sketched in Figure 5.1, sensory encoding operates (early) prior to any (later) decisional or response processes. The relevant distinction here is between perceptual and post-perceptual processes. By this view, a 'late' process refers to a post-perceptual process and an 'early' process refers to some form of perceptual/encoding process. As we have seen, Broadbent and Gregory (1967a) favoured a post-perceptual account of the word frequency effect which has its locus at a relatively late stage of processing.

Evidence that familiarity effects in perception do not reflect properties of sensory encoding was discussed by Hochberg (1968). In a critical experiment, on each trial he presented a pair of letter strings printed either side of a central fixation point for a very brief interval. Each letter string was presented vertically, not horizontally (see Figure 5.4). On each trial the participant simply had to say whether the letter strings were identical or not. This is known as a simultaneous **same/different judgement task** or more simply a *same/different task*. Each pair of letters was repeatedly presented over trials and the display duration was incremented slightly over trials. This was continued until the participant made a correct judgement. So as the exposure duration increased, the perceptibility of the letter strings also increased.

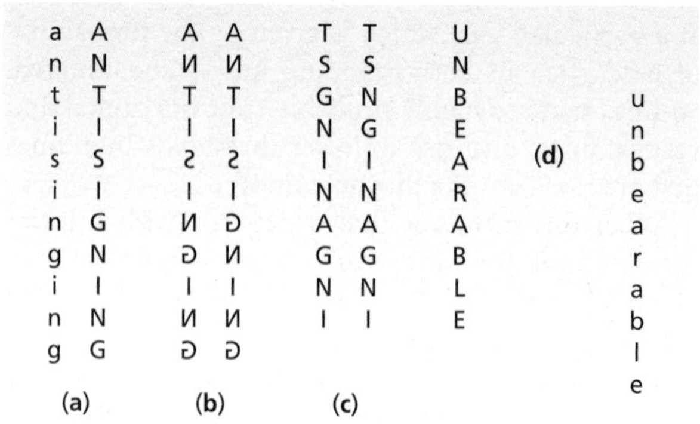

**Figure 5.4 Examples of the letter string stimuli that Hochberg (1968) used in his same/different matching experiments**

*Source*: Hochberg, J. E. (1968). In the mind's eye. In R. N. Haber (Ed.), *Contemporary theory and research in visual perception* (fig. 16, p. 327). New York: Holt Rinehart & Winston.

What Hochberg found was that there was no difference in performance across different types of letter strings when the strings of letters were spaced closely together (i.e., positioned closely side by side). That is, participants were unaffected by whether the strings were meaningful or pronounceable as compared to when the strings were meaningless and unpronounceable. Judgements were also unaffected by whether the individual letters were printed in normal or reversed print (see Figure 5.4). If the letter strings were spaced far apart (or the strings were presented sequentially with one string being presented and then removed before the other), matching was better for words than illegible or unpronounceable letter strings. According to Hochberg, under these conditions the task demanded temporary storage of the letters for comparison purposes. Now the results showed that familiarity aided the formation of memory traces for the words but not non-words.

What these data suggest therefore is that when the task judgement could be carried out at the level of sensory analysis (i.e., when the strings were spaced close together), the familiarity of the materials was of no consequence. It was therefore concluded that the effect of familiarity in perception is located at the level of central and not sensory mechanisms. Indeed such a conclusion gained further support in the more recent replication and extension carried out by Pollatsek et al. (1975) (see Figure 5.5). → See 'What have we learnt?', below.

## Familiarity effects reflect early processes

Having considered the evidence that suggests a late locus of the effects of familiarity, we now turn to the contrasting evidence that suggests an earlier locus. Two examples will be considered in this regard. The first

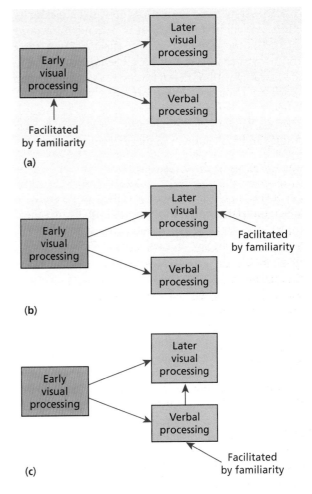

**Figure 5.5 Familiarity effects in word perception**
Various ideas concerning where, in the processing system, familiarity exerts its influence (taken from Pollatsek *et al.*, 1975).

*Source*: Pollatsek, A., Well, A. D., & Schindler, R. M. (1975). Familiarity affects visual processing of words. *Journal of Experimental Psychology: Human Perception and Performance, 1,* 328–338 (fig. 1, p. 337). Reproduced with permission from APA.

### → What have we learnt?

The view that emerges from consideration of this body of work on familiarity effects in processing of letter strings is that any such effects reflect the operation, not of sensory encoding mechanisms, but of more central processes concerning storage, comparison and decision. More recently, though, other data have been collected and these suggest that not all effects of familiarity in word recognition are the same. Therefore there may indeed be grounds for arguing that sensory analysis can be influenced by the familiarity of the stimulus.

Remember, what we are trying to do here is ascertain what processing mechanisms are responsible for particular behavioural effects – are familiarity effects (like the word frequency effect) indicative of perceptual or cognitive mechanisms?

concerns something known as the **word superiority effect**. As will become clear, it is perhaps misleading to discuss *the* word superiority effect because there are many such effects that have been documented in the literature. All of these, however, share a common property, namely that performance with words is shown to be superior to performance with non-words across a range of different tasks. Here we take two studies and look at them in more detail.

### Doyle and Leach (1988)

For instance, Doyle and Leach (1988) ran a study in which on trial a central fixation was initially presented prior to a rapid serial visual presentation (RSVP) sequence of display frames. Figure 5.6 provides a schematic of the various frames and timings used in the sequence. The two special frames were labelled as interval X and interval Y, respectively. X and Y were very brief, being in the order of 25 ms, and the target string of letters could appear in either interval on a given trial. As Figure 5.6 shows, immediately following each of these intervals was a rapid sequence of four masking displays. Collectively this sequence was known as a **dynamic mask**. In each frame of the dynamic mask, and at each target letter position, a different nonsense character was presented. Across the different frames of the masks different nonsense characters were presented and this created an impression of random characters rapidly changing in shape as the sequence unfolded.

All the participant had to do was to indicate whether the target letter string was presented in interval X or interval Y. Such a paradigm is known as a **two-alternative forced choice** (a 2AFC) task. The participant is forced (okay, 'encouraged') to make a decision about one of two alternatives. In this case, what partici-

pants actually did was to rate their confidence on a four-point scale as to how sure they were that the target occurred in interval X or that it occurred in interval Y.

Part of the reason that this is such a clever experiment is that the participants were not being tested on their ability to identify the target letter strings; they were being tested on their ability to perceive where in the sequence the target appeared. In this regard, an important manipulation was that on half the trials the target letter string was a word and on half the trials the target string was a non-word. If participants had been tested on their ability to identify the letter strings then any difference in performance across familiar words and unfamiliar non-words may have been due to good guessing on the word trials. If the target is HOME and all you saw was HOM*, then why not guess HOME. In contrast, in their actual task Doyle and Leach (1988) measured perception of the letter strings in such a way that any influence of familiarity could only show up indirectly.

Indeed, the central result was that, generally speaking, judgements for words were more accurate than were judgements for non-words. Participants were more accurate in locating which interval a word occurred in than they were in locating the interval in which a non-word occurred in. There was a word superiority effect because participants were more accurate on word than non-word trials. More critical, though, was that the effect was revealed in measures relating to $d'$ and, as was explained above, this effect was therefore taken to reflect perceptual sensitivity and not response bias. → See 'What have we learnt?', page 155.

### Merikle and Reingold (1990)

The second example of a 'perceptual' familiarity effect in word recognition is taken from a paper by Merikle

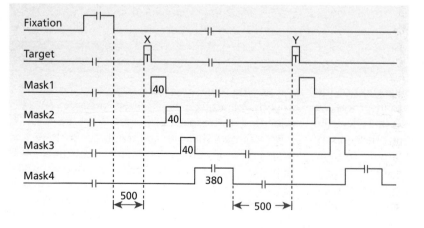

**Figure 5.6 Schematic representation of the RSVP displays that Doyle and Leach (1988) used in their experiments**

The target occurred either before the pattern mask located at X or before the pattern mask located at Y. A target never appeared at both positions within a trial.

*Source*: Doyle, J. R., & Leach, C. (1988). Word superiority in signal detection: Barely a glimpse, yet reading nonetheless. *Cognitive Psychology, 20,* 283–318 (fig. 1, p. 301). Reproduced with permission from Elsevier.

## → What have we learnt?

In summary, what we have here is an effect of familiarity that shows that familiar items (words) are more easily detected than are unfamiliar items (non-words). This effect cannot be attributed to participants lowering some response criterion for words relative to non-words (better guessing on word trials) because the effects were revealed in $d'$ rather than $\beta$. The effect of word familiarity seems to be operating at the level of an early perceptual encoding stage of processing. We may conclude that at some perceptual level the processing of familiar items is facilitated relative to unfamiliar items.

In terms of real life, the suggestion is the following: assume you are standing on a railway platform and aimlessly watching the trains go by. What the experimental evidence suggests is that you are more likely to detect the presence of a friend or relative on a train that moves past than someone you barely know. This is even though the presence of your friend is completely unexpected! The implication of the work of Doyle and Leach (1988) is that such an effect actually does reflect something about perceptual encoding. Familiar items are more easily encoded than are unfamiliar items.

and Reingold (1990). They ran a series of experiments, only one of which will be mentioned here. On a given trial and following the offset of fixation display presented to both eyes, a forward mask of a random string of letters was presented to the right eye for 50 ms. There was then a short pause followed by presentation of the target field to the left eye, which itself was followed by the mask being re-presented to the right eye. In the experiment under consideration the target frame duration was set at 50 ms. On half the trials, the target field contained a target letter string and on the remaining half trials the target field was blank.

For their first response on each trial participants merely had to report whether or not a target string was presented. This requirement was taken to define the **detection task**. In addition, in a second *lexical decision task*, participants then had to respond whether the target string was a word or a non-word. The experiment extends the basic methodology that Cheesman and Merikle (1984) developed, as we discussed in Chapter 4. Critically on the trials in which a target string was presented, a word appeared on a random half of the trials. On the remaining trials the target was a non-word. From the participant's viewpoint, the experiment may have seemed a little odd because even on trials when they thought no target had been present they still were expected to make a lexical decision response!

The data from the detection responses showed that detection performance was better for words than non-words; that is, there was again a robust word superiority effect. Participants were more accurate in deciding that a target string rather than a blank frame had been presented when the target string was a word than when it was a non-word. Again this result was

found when comparing scores computed as a variant of $d'$. Hence the conclusion was that stimulus familiarity did affect stimulus detection at the level of perceptual mechanisms. The findings could not be explained adequately in terms of a difference in bias in responding to words relative to non-words because of the effect being manifest through differences in $d'$ and not $\beta$. Word familiarity seems to exert an influence at a relatively early perceptual encoding stage of processing. Such evidence converges on the same conclusion as that put forward by Doyle and Leach (1988).

The findings on the lexical decision responses were equally provocative. Again measures of sensitivity were computed as a function of whether participants were correct in their detection decisions. The data were broken down as to whether participants scored a hit or a miss on the detection task. Now it was found that participants generally performed well when they detected the target string (on hit trials). If they detected the target then they could judge reasonably well if it was a word or a non-word. A different pattern arose on trials where the participants missed the target. Now they were reasonably accurate in making a word response, but they were essentially guessing when the target was a non-word. If participants failed to detect the target, they were still reasonably good at responding that it might have been a word. Critically therefore, as Merikle and Reingold (1990) stated, 'only familiar stimuli were perceived when participants failed to detect a stimulus but that both familiar and unfamiliar stimuli were perceived following stimulus detection' (p. 582). The fact that participants could perform above chance with words that they were unable to detect was taken to show that some form of knowledge about words had been accessed without participants being consciously aware of this. Such an effect therefore is another indication of semantic activation without conscious awareness – see Chapter 4.

Collectively, the data from the detection and lexical decision tasks reported by Merikle and Reingold (1990), has shown that stimulus familiarity affects both perceptual and interpretative stages of processing. Familiar stimuli were detected better than unfamiliar stimuli. In addition, familiar stimuli, but not unfamiliar stimuli, were seen to engage with cognitive mechanisms concerned with stored knowledge. In this regard, there is a rather clear indication of how *word* familiarity operates: perceptual mechanisms are apparently tuned to the detection of familiar over unfamiliar stimuli. Furthermore, familiar stimuli apparently engage interpretive process in a way that unfamiliar stimuli do not. → See 'What have we learnt?', below.

### Pinpoint question 5.4

If a word superiority effect shows up for the measure of $d'$ rather than $\beta$, does this mean perceptual or response mechanisms are responsible?

**mental category** Stored knowledge regarding the nature of a class of objects or entities.

**word recognition advantage** For example, the finding that words are more accurately recognised from a briefly presented display than strings of random letters. More generally, where performance with words is better than with any other form of strings of letters.

**word frequency effect** Differences observed in word processing as a result of the frequency of occurrence in natural language. Common words are typically dealt with more effectively than rare words.

**active theories** A phrase used to refer to theories of perception in which the person can exert some control over how they perceive the world.

**passive theories** A phrase used to refer to theories of perception in which the person has no control over their perceptions of the world.

**same/different judgement task** Experimental paradigm where, on each trial, participants are required to compare two stimuli and respond as to whether they are the same or whether they differ from one another.

**word superiority effect** Generally speaking, when performance with words is superior relative to performance with non-words.

**dynamic mask** A mask that changes over time.

**two-alternative forced choice** Paradigm in which participants are required to choose between one of two possible alternatives on every trial.

**detection task** An experimental task in which the participant simply has to respond on every trial as to whether a stimulus is present or not.

### → What have we learnt?

Initially the early work on familiarity effects was taken to show that familiarity operates at a level after sensory analysis is complete. In this regard the familiarity effects were interpreted as showing decision/response biases. Given this, it was concluded that familiarity exerts its influence at a post-perceptual stage of processing and therefore such effects tell us relatively little (perhaps nothing) about the nature of the perceptual system. The more recent studies, in contrast, have demonstrated quite convincingly that (at least where words are concerned) familiarity can exert an influence at an earlier perceptual stage of processing. Word familiarity conveys a benefit at the level of sensory analysis.

This is not to argue that the earlier and more recent data sets contradict one another. On the contrary, what seems to have emerged is that certain tasks have revealed familiarity effects that do not reflect the operation of perceptual mechanisms, and as such they suggest that the corresponding familiarity effects arise through the operation of post-perceptual mechanisms. Other tasks have quite clearly revealed how familiarity influences sensory analysis. On these grounds, it is most sensible to conclude that familiarity effects can arise at various stages throughout the processing system. Importantly, there is evidence to suggest that sensory mechanisms may become particularly attuned to familiar stimuli.

# Recency and expectancy

From a common-sense point of view it seems reasonable to claim that what observers actually perceive is, to large measure, determined by what they expect to perceive. You get on a bus and you expect to see an adult bus driver sat behind the wheel. Such a claim is enshrined in studies of expectancy on perception. In contrast, effects of recency on perception are studied on the assumption that a stimulus is more readily perceived if it has recently been encountered than if it has not. This probably has nothing to do with common sense, but the idea is that if you have just seen next door's dog rummaging in the hedge, then you will most probably see next door's dog next time you glance up and look at the bundle of fur in the garden. In examining effects of recency and expectancy on perception we will begin by considering experimental evidence that has been used to back up such intuitive, common-sense claims about the nature of human perception. However, we need to assess carefully whether there is any empirical evidence for such claims.

Other studies are then considered that have attempted to establish the locus of such effects in the human information processing system. So in the same way that research was directed to trying to find out where in the processing system familiarity was exerting its influence, we now must consider where recency and expectancy exert theirs. We can ask whether effects of recency and expectancy are located at perceptual or post-perceptual stages of processing. To address these issues much of the evidence comes from studies of the perception of so-called **ambiguous figures** and it is to these that the discussion now turns.

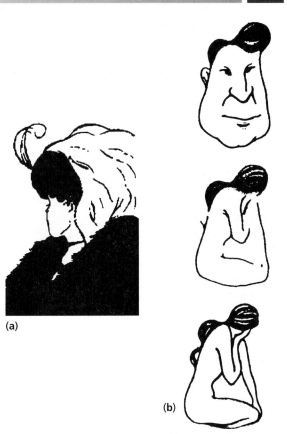

(a)

(b)

**Figure 5.7 Perceptually ambiguous figures**
(a) The now classic, ambiguous figure: Boring's old/young woman. (b) Examples of the nude/face figure. Ambiguity, varying from male to female, changes down the page, with the middle figure being the most ambiguous.

*Source*: (a) Fisher, G. H. (1966). Materials for experimental studies of ambiguous and embedded figures. *Research Bulletin*, No. 4. Department of Psychology, University of Newcastle upon Tyne. Reproduced with permission.

## The perception of ambiguous figures

Let us begin this discussion with a consideration of a classic stimulus in perceptual psychology known as an ambiguous figure. One of the most famous of these is that shown in Figure 5.7a and this has come to be known as Boring's (1930) figure of a young/old woman. If you're having trouble seeing either, the choker on the neck of the young woman is the mouth of the older woman. As Figure 5.7b also shows, it is quite possible to generate a set of figures that vary along an ambiguity continuum. At one end of the continuum is a figure that unambiguously depicts a face of a man and at the opposite end is a figure that unambiguously depicts a young woman. The central figure is ambiguous. Being able to vary figural ambiguity in this way has proved

to be a critical factor in studies of expectancy and recency in perception.

In an early study Leeper (1935) initially presented participants with an unambiguous version of Boring's figure and then went on to examine how the participants would interpret a subsequent presentation of the corresponding ambiguous figure. A central result was that participants tended to report resolving the ambiguity in terms of the interpretation of the unambiguous figure they had previously been given. So if they had been presented with the young woman version of the figure, they then interpreted the ambiguous figure as depicting a young woman. This was taken as evidence of how previous experience can affect present perceptions – participants tended to report the most recently accounted interpretation of the stimulus.

In a much later study Rock and Mitchener (1992) provided other evidence relevant to the general idea that expectancy affects perception. Now participants were chosen so that they were completely naïve with respect to ambiguous figures. That is, the participants had no previous knowledge of ambiguous figures and were therefore unaware that such figures could have more than one interpretation. Rock and Mitchener ran two conditions: in the *uninformed condition* participants were just asked to report what they saw when presented with an ambiguous figure. It is well established that in free viewing conditions informed participants first report one interpretation of the stimulus and then, at some time later, this flips or reverses and they then report the other interpretation of the stimulus. This is known as **ambiguous figure reversal**. Indeed with prolonged viewing the different interpretations alternate repeatedly (and why this happens has been the topic of some concern: see Horlitz & O'Leary, 1993). Nevertheless, in the uninformed condition, only one-third of the participants reported seeing the figures reverse. That is, they typi-cally reported one, but not both interpretations of the figures.

In a second, *informed condition* participants were now presented with the ambiguous figures and were told that the figures could be seen in either of two different ways. In this way participants were instilled with an expectancy over the nature of the stimuli – each participant had been told that the figures could be seen in more than one way. Now all of the partici-pants reported both interpretations and all reported that the figures reversed with prolonged viewing. Rock and Mitchener were very keen to underline how the contrast between performance across the two condi-tions provided further evidence of how knowledge affects perception – if participants did not know that the figures could be given either of two different inter-pretations, then they generally perceived the figure in a particular way and maintained that reading of the stimulus. In contrast, when the participants were informed about the nature of the ambiguity they were able to assign both interpretations and generate two quite different percepts.

## Research focus 5.1

### Flip-flopping: children's responses to ambiguous figures

Being students of psychology, we are all probably very suspicious of whatever kind of stimulus some-body shows us in a lab. We might get people to look at faces in the hope that this will reveal something about race bias or we might show individuals arti-ficial creatures to see whether it can tell us something about face processing. Therefore, when we present our participants with ambiguous figures, it's likely that they already have some prior experience with such figures and know all about the different inter-pretations of the images. In addition, some of the participants will be eager to please as well! To avoid such confounds, Mitroff, Sobel and Gopnik (2006) were interested in children's responses to ambigu-ous figures since it's likely that children will approach them in a naïve (in the nicest sense of the word) fashion.

Data from 34 children aged 5–9 were analysed in the experiment. Mitroff et al. (2006) used a classic ambiguous figure known as the duck/rabbit, in addi-tion to more unambiguous versions of the same pic-ture (see Figure 5.8). Children were asked to report

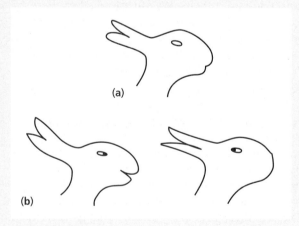

**Figure 5.8 Fair game**
The consequences of a duck and rabbit mating – the infamous ambiguous dabbit (or ruck) shown in (a). Unambiguous versions are shown in (b).

*Source*: Mitroff, S. R., Sobel, D. M., & Gopnik, A. (2006). Reversing how to think about ambiguous figure reversals: Spontaneous alternating by uninformed observers. *Perception, 35*, 709–715 (fig. 1, p. 711). Reproduced with permission from Pion Limited, London.

what they saw when presented with the ambiguous figure. If children reported both interpretations during the initial phase of the experiment, then this was considered a *spontaneous reversal*. Following the first presentation, participants were shown the unambiguous version to spoil the fun, and then were presented with the ambiguous figure again. If participants reported both interpretations in this second phase, this was labelled an *informed reversal*.

Only 12 of the initial 34 children were reported as experiencing spontaneous reversal, and of the remaining 22 children, 20 reported seeing multiple interpretations following instructions, thereby giving rise to a larger percentage of informed reversals. Importantly, Mitroff et al. (2006) also conducted further tests with the children to assess their theory of mind, that is, the extent to which they were aware of other people's feelings and perspectives. Specifically, children who reported spontaneous reversals performed particularly well on one particular test, in which the child had to report where in a fictitious village one member thought another person was situated: 'John thinks that Mary is at the park' (Mitroff et al., 2006, p. 712).

Mitroff et al. (2006) concluded that the data do not sit well with a purely bottom-up account of ambiguous figure reversal, in which the observer experiences neural saturation in relation to one interpretation so as switches over to the other interpretation. This is because bottom-up effects do not account for failures to reverse spontaneously. Neither does the data fit with a purely top-down account, in which the person has to know about the ambiguous nature of the figure prior to exposure. This is because top-down effects do not account for spontaneous reversals. A link between theory of mind and spontaneous reversals is suggested, although some children achieved one without the other. Perhaps the interpretation of ambiguous figures just got a little bit more ambiguous!

*Source*: Mitroff, S. R., Sobel, D. M., & Gopnik, A. (2006). Reversing how to think about ambiguous figure reversals: Spontaneous alternating by uninformed observers. *Perception, 35,* 709–715.

## Attempting to disentangle effects of recency from those of expectancy

Taken together these experiments provide evidence in support of the common-sense ideas that recency and expectancy affect perception. Of course the data are silent on where such recency and expectancy effects may be located, but we will return to this issue shortly. In simple terms, the original Leeper study concerned how recency may affect perception, and the later Rock and Mitchener study examined how expectancy affects perception. In a further important study, Epstein and Rock (1960) examined the perception of ambiguous figures in a bid to see whether recency or expectancy was the overriding factor in determining the current perception.

On a typical trial, the participant was presented with a sequence of stimuli where each stimulus apart from the last was an unambiguous version of Boring's figure. The different versions of the figure were presented in an alternating sequence (i.e., old, young, old, young, . . . ). Let us assume the last unambiguous figure to be presented in the sequence was of the old woman. However, the actual sequence ended when the ambiguous version was now presented. As a consequence, participants could not predict when the sequence would end but when the last figure was presented they had to report whether they saw the old or young woman. If they reported 'old' it was assumed that their report had been influenced by recency – the most recently presented version of the figure influenced their report of the ambiguous figure. However, if they reported 'young' then it was assumed that expectancy and not recency had influenced their report. The young version is the one that was predicted (i.e., expected) on the basis of the alternating sequence. Epstein and Rock found that current interpretations of the ambiguous figure tended to reflect an effect of recency. Participants reported the interpretation consistent with the figure most recently presented (in our case, old) and not the one that was expected on the basis of the alternation (in our case, young).

Unfortunately, as is the tendency with these kinds of things, ensuing research has tended to cloud the picture. For instance, in a later paper, Girgus, Rock and Egatz (1977) reported a failure to find any effect of recency on the perception of ambiguous figures. In an initial exposure phase participants were presented with a series of pictures and they had to rate each of them for attractiveness. In the experimental condition two unambiguous versions of a standard ambiguous figure were included in this exposure sequence of pictures. In the control condition these two pictures were replaced by neutral pictures. The whole series of pictures were repeatedly shown to the participants five times.

## → What have we learnt?

The evidence for effects of recency on the perception taken from the work on ambiguous figures is slight. Indeed, the fragility of such effects has been emphasised most clearly by Wilton (1985). In a series of experiments he was able to demonstrate that recency can be shown to influence the interpretation of ambiguous figures but in ways that remain unclear. Indeed the manner in which this factor operates in concert with others is still quite mysterious. So whereas the effects of familiarity in perception have been relatively straightforward to deal with, the picture is far from clear regarding the evidence for recency effects in perception.

What we are trying to do here is focus on what might be termed the common-sense view of perception that associates all so-called perceptual effects with the operations of the perceptual system. The claims are as follows:

1. Familiar things are easier to perceive than are unfamiliar things.
2. More recently encountered things are easier to perceive than are things encountered less recently.
3. You perceive what you want to; what you expect to perceive.

We need to assess the evidence both in terms of trying to elevate such common-sense notions to the level of scientific fact and also in terms of trying to locate where in the processing system the factors are having their influence. We have addressed point 1 and concluded that the evidence for point 2 is, so far, equivocal. We will turn to point 3 in a moment. Before that, though, we need to acknowledge that a much stronger case can be built for effects of recency in perception from studies with other kinds of materials. It is to these that we now turn.

---

The main measure of interest was the number of experimental and control participants that spontaneously reported seeing the ambiguous figure reverse when this was presented in a 60 second test phase subsequent to the exposure phase. The results revealed that there was no difference across the two conditions because, respectively, 7 out of 12 and 8 out of 12 participants reported reversals in the experimental and control groups. So it was concluded that the recent exposure of the two different interpretations of the ambiguous figures did not materially affect the tendency to report these interpretations at test. → See 'What have we learnt?', above.

## Recency and repetition priming

The mixed results in trying to establish an effect of recency on the interpretations of ambiguous figures should not distract us from the very robust effects of recency found in studies of repetition priming. Although there are many different kinds of repetition effects to be found in the literature, let us define the standard repetition effect as showing that the identification of a given stimulus is improved if it is repeated. Stated thus, it is easy to see how familiarity can be construed in terms of repetition over the long term: more familiar items have been encountered more often. So again there is a possible problem in trying to disentangle repetition from familiarity. A considerable amount of literature on repetition priming concerns single word recognition. However, comparable experiments using a variety of other materials do exist, and, in the current context, the study by Benton and Moscovitch (1988) is of some importance.

### Benton and Moscovitch (1988)

Consider their Experiment 1. In their lexical decision task on each trial participants were presented visually with a single string of letters and they had to respond as quickly and as accurately as they could to whether the string corresponded to a word or not. Here reaction times (RTs), recorded in ms, and accuracy were the main measures of interest. (There are 1,000 milliseconds in a second, so 500 ms is half a second.) On a random half of trials a word was presented and on the remaining trials a non-word was presented. Participants pressed one response key to signal 'word' and a different key to signal 'non-word'. Within the experimental blocks of trials, however, some of the stimuli were repeated.

Three different sorts of repetitions were examined. On Lag 0 trials the stimulus on trial $n$ was immediately repeated on trial $n + 1$ (the same target string was repeated on the next trial), and as such there was no lag between the repeated item. On Lag 4 trials the stimulus on trial $n$ was repeated on trial $n + 5$ (there were 4 intervening trials between the first and second presentations of the target string); on Lag 15 trials the stimulus on trial $n$ was repeated on trial $n + 16$ (there were 15 intervening trials between the first and second presentations of the target string). Table 5.1 provides examples.

**Table 5.1** Schematic representation of various trial dependencies in the lexical decision task carried out by Benton and Moscovitch (1988).

| Trial | Lag 0 – Word repetition | Lag 0 – Non-word repetition | Lag 4 – Word repetition | Lag 4 – Non-word repetition | Lag 15 – Word repetition | Lag 15 – Non-word repetition |
|---|---|---|---|---|---|---|
| 1 | **HOUSE** | VOWEL | **HOUSE** | HOLLY | **HOUSE** | **CRIPE** |
| 2 | **HOUSE** | DRIFT | SWAER | BERRY | AREA | CASTLE |
| 3 | LAND | SMALE | FICK | **CRIPE** | KILM | CANNON |
| 4 | FORM | ASILE | GRIGH | RADIO | YEAR | GINO |
| 5 | TILT | QUIET | LAWN | WENT | ULIM | HIDDEN |
| 6 | FROST | **CRIPE** | **HOUSE** | NIGBIPS | BIONE | ITEM |
| 7 | SORG | **CRIPE** | BIRDS | TOAST | WIBE | GRID |
| 8 | NOUR | GHOST | GOUR | **CRIPE** | YOST | SOCKS |
| 9 | GLUM | MOUSE | ROUGH | SWIND | HOST | WENT |
| 10 | FIRE | FRIN | HIFT | TABLE | FLOOR | MONTH |
| 11 | DORL | SWIRL | MASK | VIXE | BAND | YOUR |
| 12 | SIPH | GRAFT | AMOCK | FINT | MUG | LOOR |
| 13 | NOUGHT | KRINE | DEOY | LIPE | UNTIL | MIST |
| 14 | ABLE | DOWN | FRION | CHRIM | WERN | MINT |
| 15 | DREN | SPRITE | BORT | SLAPE | RENT | OVEN |
| 16 | GLOT | MOVE | RIFLE | CLOSE | BELT | CAVO |
| 17 | ZERO | NICE | STRIPE | VIOL | **HOUSE** | **CRIPE** |

Each column contains a possible sequence of trials. The actual types of repetitions co-occurred in a block of trials. Here they are separated out for illustrative purposes only. On each trial a letter string was presented and the participant simply had to press one key as a word response and a different key for a non-word response. The first and second stimulus presentations are shown in **bold**.

In an additional face/non-face discrimination task participants again made a binary decision on each trial, but now the stimulus was either a proper photograph of a face or a doctored photograph of a face. With these latter stimuli – known as non-faces – the internal features of a face had been rearranged by switching the position of the eyes, nose and mouth. The structure of the face/non-face task was the same as the lexical decision task with the same sorts of repetition trials being included. See Figure 5.9 for a particularly gruesome example of this sort of non-face.

With this design it is possible to see how familiarity and repetition can be examined separately. The nonwords and non-faces were completely unfamiliar to the participants. In addition, although each face was easily classified as a being a face, the actual faces were unfamiliar to the participants. Finally, each word was familiar in its own right. So across these different types of stimuli familiarity varied, but each stimulus type was examined in the various repetition conditions.

The results of the experiment were striking. First there was a large repetition effect for stimulus type on Lag 0 trials. Participants were facilitated in responding on these trials relative to when the stimulus was not repeated. In addition, repetition effects were found for words at all three lags. To be clear, in this experiment a repetition effect was observed if the average RT on repeated trials was shorter than the average RT on trials where the stimulus was presented for the first time. So for words there was a very large repetition effect on immediate repetition trials – of the order of 100 ms – this reduced on Lag 4 trials (to about 60 ms) and reduced again on Lag 15 trials (to about 40 ms). In this way the data revealed an effect of recency that dissipated with time. The repetition effect decreased as a function of recency – the more recently the stimulus word had been presented, the quicker participants were to make the classification response.

For all of the other unfamiliar stimuli the repetition effect was only statistically significant on Lag 0 trials. Here there was a strong recency effect but this was very short-lived. If any other stimulus intervened between the two presentations of the item the repetition effect was abolished. So the overall contrast between performance with words and the other items shows that the repetition effects for words reflects things other than perceptual processes – things relating to knowing the particular items used. Participants were generally

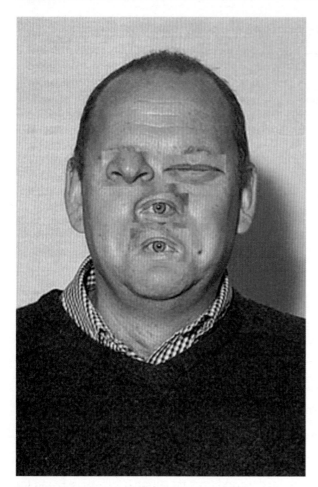

**Figure 5.9 Beauty is in the eye of the beholder**
A non-face stimulus akin to those used by Benton and Moscovitch (1988).

Although analogous face detectors may exist, only unfamiliar faces were used in the experiment. Therefore such putative mechanisms could play no role – there are no face-specific face detectors for unfamiliar faces. Consistent with this idea is that the long-lasting repetition effects were only found with words and not the face stimuli. This gives further credence to the idea that the longer-term repetition effects reflect some property of some form of long-term memory representations (i.e., word-specific detector). Such longer-term repetition effects only occur with familiar stimuli. Nevertheless all stimulus types produced an immediate repetition effect. This immediate repetition effect was taken to reflect the facilitation of perceptual encoding processes. → See 'What have we learnt?', page 163.

> ### Pinpoint question 5.5
> **What's the definition of a repetition effect?**

## Expectancy and set

In many respects the notions of familiarity and recency relate, essentially, to stimulus factors on the grounds that both can be objectively quantified. The experimenter can either choose materials that vary in frequency of occurrence in everyday life, or can carefully control the recency of exposure of a given stimulus. This is not to argue that there can be no control over a participant's expectancies, but that it is a much more difficult subjective factor to gain control over. For instance, it is possible simply to tell a participant to expect certain stimuli during an experiment, but it is something of an act of faith to assume that the participant then sets up the desired expectancy during the task.

Such concerns are critical because now we are turning to a particularly radical version of the claim that past experience together with current stimulation determines our perceptions of the world. In this regard psychologists have considered how it might be that observers' mental states can affect their perceptions (we approach this important topic in a different way in Chapter 16). The naïve default position is that if an observer is *set to* or *expects to* perceive a stimulus of a particular type then this will materially affect how the observer perceives the world. For instance, even the slightest evidence consistent with the stimulus will be taken as evidence of the stimulus (Cherry, 1978, p. 276). Indeed Rock, Hall and Davis (1994) discussed this sort of issue in describing some general principles regarding the perception of ambiguous figures.

facilitated on repeated word trials because they possessed stored knowledge about these particular stimuli prior to the experiment. This suggests that the word repetition effects reflected, in part, a memory component – performance was facilitated because of some form of memory representation of the actual items used.

How might this be? Well, on the understanding that there exist word detectors, of the sort described by Broadbent and Gregory (1971), then the presentation of a particular word results in the lowering of the threshold on its own particular detector. A consequence of this lowering of the threshold is that less evidence is required for the detector to fire next time the word is presented. The fact that the repetition effect dissipated with lag can be interpreted as showing that the detection threshold returns relatively to its original baseline level gradually over time.

Benton and Moscovitch (1988) described evidence for repetition effects that were taken to reflect facilitation of perceptual encoding processes and other repetition effects that were taken to reflect an additional benefit due to stored knowledge. Most important are the data that suggest that recency does influence perceptual encoding mechanisms. If either a letter string or an unfamiliar face were immediately repeated then its recognition was facilitated relative to cases where different stimuli occurred on successive trials. On these grounds, there is evidence to suggest that the perceptual system is sensitised to detect items that have recently been encountered.

However, it should be borne in mind that the effects are not as profound as might have been assumed on the basis of certain traditional ideas found in the literature. The perceptual effects are very short-lived indeed and only survive for a matter of seconds (as gauged by the time between successive trials). The more pronounced repetition effects with words than faces, reported by Benton and Moscovitch (1988), seem to reflect the operation of later interpretative mechanisms linked to stored knowledge. When these are stimulated, any contingent facilitation is much longer lasting than when unfamiliar stimuli are repeated. Yet again therefore the evidence suggests that some of the effects being reported reflect particular properties of the human word recognition system and we need to be mindful about this when attempting to draw conclusions about the perceptual system in general.

According to them, for reversals to occur the participant must know that the figure is ambiguous, and they must also be aware of exactly what the alternative interpretations of the figure actually are. These claims are about **mental set** but theorists have also discussed the notion of **instructional set** and it is to this that we turn first.

## Instructional set

According to Hochberg (1978), 'if the viewer is *set* to expect a particular *kind* of material, he will see it better at a shorter exposure' (p. 165). The basic idea that instructional set can be an important determiner of perception is perhaps best conveyed by the following simple example. In Figure 5.10 two patterns are provided and both contain well-known symbols – one a letter and the other a number. One implication of this is that, prior to knowing about the constitution of the patterns, you may well have been unable to see the E and the 3. However, as soon as you were informed about the inclusion of the symbols you were *set* to find them. How instructional set affects perception has been the topic of much debate. Rather critically, though, we need to be clear about whether such effects reflect perceptual or later decision mechanisms. We cannot dispute the fact that such factors produce effects, but we do need to be clear exactly what it is in functional terms that the effects are telling us.

**What sort of instructional set would help to see the number in this sentence?**

## Mental set

With instructional set, participants are specifically told to focus on some particular stimulus characteristic and to report on this. However, of some additional interest are cases where the effects of set are shown unintentionally. Several examples are worthy of comment. The first such example is a study by Bruner and Postman (1949). This has been discussed as providing evidence for a set effect in perception (Steinfeld, 1967), but it is instructive to think about whether the evidence is

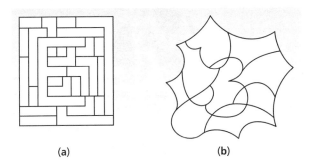

**Figure 5.10 Embedded figures**
Examples of hidden figures. As a hint, a letter is embedded in (a) and a digit in (b).
*Source*: Cherry, C. (1978). *On human communication* (fig. 7.8, p. 278). Cambridge, Massachusetts: The MIT Press. Reproduced with permission.

so clear-cut. The data clearly show an effect of past experience on perception but we will need to consider carefully whether this evidence really is indicative of an effect of mental set.

Bruner and Postman (1949) presented participants with brief visual displays, each of which contained a depiction of a playing card. An ascending **staircase method** of presentation was used in which each display was presented three times at 10, 30, 50, 70, 100, 150, 200, 250, 300, 400, 500, 600, 700, 800, 900 and 1,000 ms. (The staircase refers to the increments in display duration over trials and, given that the display duration increased monotonically over trials, the staircase is ascending.) At each exposure participants had to report what they had seen. What the participants did not know was that some of the stimuli contained what were known as incongruous cards, that is, cards in which the suit was presented in the wrong colour (e.g., the six of spades in red, see Figure 5.11). The basic results were straightforward and showed that for each display duration normal cards were recognised more accurately than were the incongruous cards.

This general pattern of results was taken to reflect an influence of set, that is, participants had difficulties in perceiving the incongruous cards because these stimuli violated their expectations about how playing cards should be. Indeed on some trials participants reported seeing compromise stimuli. For instance, the red six of spades was reported to have been presented in 'brown', or in 'purple', 'lighter than black', 'blacker than red', etc. Again these sorts of errors have been discussed as being a compromise between the actual stimulus and the expected stimulus (Gordon, 1989). However, it is difficult to see why these particular effects reflect something particular about expectancy rather than familiarity. Normal cards are more familiar than incongruous cards, hence the effects might be just as easily explained via familiarity as expectancy. So how might we distinguish between these two factors?

Well, ideally we need to use unfamiliar stimuli, but induce a particular mental set in the participants. Exactly this sort of manipulation was carried out by Steinfeld (1967). Here three independent groups of participants were tested. In Group A participants were read a short story about a sinking ocean liner. Group B participants were read a story completely unrelated to the ocean liner story and Group C participants were read no story. In the test phase all participants were shown a fragmented figure that was difficult to see as a ship (see Figure 5.12). The measure of interest was how long participants needed to view the figure before seeing it as a ship. The central result was that Group A participants took considerably less time to report seeing the ship than did the other two groups.

**Figure 5.11 Okay, who dealt this hand?**
Examples of the sorts of playing card stimuli used by Bruner and Postman (1949) in their experiments on the perception of incongruity.

**Figure 5.12 Life is full of possibilities**
The sort of fragmentary figures used in the experiments by Steinfeld (1967).

*Source*: Leeper, R. (1935). A study of a neglected portion of the field of learning: The development of sensory organization. *Journal of Genetic Psychology, 46*, 41–75 (fig. 1, p. 49). Reproduced with permission of the Helen Dwight Reid Educational Foundation.

In his recent review of set effects in perception, Pashler (1998) was very circumspect in his conclusions. From his review of the literature he concluded that the effects, such as they are, are very limited. At the most, the effects are generally consistent with the following idea. What expectancy does do is allow for the selective exclusion of noisy and irrelevant information when making judgements about stimuli that are difficult to otherwise perceive, such as in cases where the important stimuli are briefly presented and masked or they are presented in other forms of irrelevant noise.

More generally the claim is not that 'the perception of an object is changed or that an object is perceived . . . as something other than itself' but that expectancy can improve the efficiency with which a more precise description of the actual stimulus will be derived (Huang & Pashler, 2005, p. 156). So whereas an unexpected stimulus might be coded as being a short line oriented at *approximately* 45° to the right, the corresponding expected stimulus would be coded as being a short line oriented at exactly 45° to the right. What expectancy can do, therefore, is improve the precision with which a veridical – a truthful and more exact – description of a stimulus can be derived.

These data are important because the test stimulus was completely unfamiliar to the participants yet prior exposure to a relevant story induced a particular perceptual organisation of the stimulus. The data are clear in and of themselves, but it is not so transparent as to where to locate this set effect. That is, Steinfeld's result might reflect some form of perceptual 'tuning' of encoding processes (Steinfeld, 1967, p. 520), or the effect might reflect later decision or response processes. The point is that, unless we can locate where particular effects of associated variables may be operating, it is impossible to claim with any certainty that they inform about perception. → See 'What have we learnt?', above.

## More general conclusions

More generally, the foregoing discussion has been based on adopting the distinction between the perceptual system and the cognitive system. It has been assumed that the perceptual system is responsible for generating a perceptual representation of the proximal stimulus. The perceptual system comprises mechanisms concerned with encoding the proximal stimulus into a form that allows the cognitive system to arrive at a sensible interpretation of what is actually out there. The discussion has focused on some general principles that are assumed to underpin the operation of the perceptual system. Implicit in the discussion has been a certain presupposition about how human perception operates with regard to how it might be that past experience critically affects our perceptions of the world. This discussion has been set against the generally accepted ideas that (i) familiar items are easier to perceive than unfamiliar items, (ii) more recently experienced items are easier to perceive than not-so-recent items, and (iii) expected items are easier to perceive than unexpected items.

In each case, though, more detailed questions have been asked about whether the related effects reflect the operation of perceptual rather than cognitive/interpretative mechanisms. Most of the evidence has favoured accounts that locate the effects at later rather than earlier stages of processing. It has been accepted that in many respects the effects reflect decisional processes in which certain interpretations of the stimulus are favoured over others. In the absence of any further context '?able' is taken to signal the presence of 'table' rather than 'fable' merely because 'table' is more likely. The perceptual representation is ambiguous with respect to whether 'fable' or 'table' is really out there. The interpretation of this representation is biased towards 'table' because of its familiarity. In contrast, expectancy would favour 'fable' given the context. 'A short story leading to a moral conclusion is usually known as a ?able'.

In such passive accounts of processing the perceptual system merely runs off a perceptual representation of the stimulus and the rest is left to interpretative mechanisms that are located at later processing stages. Accordingly, it is at these post-perceptual stages of processing that the effects of familiarity, recency, expectancy and set are located. All of the effects are therefore post-perceptual in nature and all of this fits very well with the strictly modular account of processing discussed by Fodor (1983) and set out in Figure 5.1. By that account the input modules are 'largely insensitive to what the perceiver presumes or desires', and as was noted above, the perceiver is built so as generally to 'see what's there, not what it wants or expects to be there' (p. 68). Perceptual analysis is insulated from higher-order factors and cannot be altered by how the participant construes the world. So much for only seeing what you want to see.

In contrast, and perhaps more provocative, are the claims that even perceptual encoding can be altered by the participant's knowledge of the world. Several such effects have been described here and the data do indicate that perceptual mechanisms are differentially sensitive to the familiarity, recency and expectancy of the stimuli. How might this be? Well, it has been suggested that such effects reflect the fact that the perceptual system can be selectively tuned to collect evidence of a particular type. In addition, or indeed alternatively, there is the idea that such factors influence the selective uptake of information such that irrelevant sources of stimulation can be filtered out or excluded from further analysis (see Pashler, 1998).

These points are subtle but can be clarified by considering these sentiments expressed by Huang and Pashler (2005, p. 156) regarding the role that attention plays in perceptual processing: 'paying attention to a red object will not make it redder or brighter, but will only make the redness more precise and the related judgment more accurate'. An implication is that a similar conclusion applies in thinking about how familiarity, recency and expectancy operate in perception. It is not that they fundamentally alter the manner in which perceptual analysis takes place, rather they can improve the precision with which a stimulus is analysed.

This is indeed a very far cry from the rather strong statements about how perceptual analyses can be controlled or changed by the participant on a whim. To appreciate this fully, though, it is important to see how ideas about subjective factors in perception have sparked much controversy throughout the history of experimental cognitive psychology.

### Pinpoint question 5.7

**How do the effects of recency, familiarity and expectancy manifest themselves in perception?**

**ambiguous figures** A stimulus that has more than one interpretation and there is no obvious reason as to which is the 'correct' one.

**ambiguous figure reversal** The point at which an ambiguous figure switches between two different interpretations.

**mental set** A person's frame of mind or expectancies about an up-and-coming stimulus.

**instructional set** An expectation towards a certain kind of stimulus, usually as a result of explicit guidance by the experimenter.

**staircase method** A psychological procedure whereby the limits of performance are assessed by an experimenter systematically increasing or decreasing a parameter over trials.

## The Old Look/New Look schools in perception

So far it has been suggested, according to the modular view sketched in Figure 5.1, that the perceptual system operates in very much a feedforward manner: the input modules passively produce outputs that are then operated upon by the central (cognitive) mechanisms. However, such a passive view of perception stands in stark contrast to one traditional and important alternative.

In the late 1940s several perceptual theorists began to emphasise how inner states such as needs, emotions and values might contribute to a participant's perceptions. This particular school of thought became known as the **New Look** approach to perception and a basic premise here was that the affective (emotional) state of the observer plays a fundamental role in determining that observer's perceptions of the world. This is a very broad acceptance of the view that knowledge of the world fundamentally determines perception. To arrive at a reasonable appreciation of this so-called *New Look approach* it is useful to know what the **Old Look** looked like (so to speak). In this regard, and according to Swets (1973), the Old Look comprised, primarily, the Gestaltists who concentrated on the stimulus determinants of perception (the physical nature of the stimulus) and not subjective factors. So to best understand the New Look we need to first consider the Old.

### The Old Look: Gestalt theory

A central feature of Gestalt theory is its emphasis on trying to establish what is the correct unit of perceptual analysis. Whereas we might focus on the nature of primitive (i.e., elemental) perceptual features (such as short lines and edges) and their corresponding feature detectors (such as our now good friend the line detector), Gestalt theorists focused on the distinction

**Figure 5.13 The whole is different from the sum of its parts**
Examples of how the global aspects of different figures
may be the same but that their local aspects differ.

*Source*: Haber, R. N., & Hershenson, M. (1979). *The psychology
of visual perception* (fig. 8.10, p. 191). London: Holt, Rinehart
and Winston. Reproduced with permission from Ralph Haber.

**Figure 5.14 Do not attempt this at home**
One of the authors providing an example of the difference
between figure and ground. In this case, though, the figure
is on the ground.

between the perceptual whole and its parts. They
stressed that it is the relations between the parts and
their overall arrangement that is most important: our
perceptual impressions are governed by interpreting
wholes and not parts. Although the classic phrase here
is that 'the whole is more than the sum of its parts',
Gestalt theorists emphasised a slightly different take,
namely that the whole is *different from* the sum of its
parts. Less catchy perhaps, but just as theoretically
important, is, as Haber and Hershenson (1979) stated,
the whole has unique attributes that are independent
from the nature of its parts.

Figure 5.13 provides a schematic example of this.
The four elements in each figure are arranged in
such a way that the impression is of a global square.
Moreover the impression of the square is maintained
even though the nature of the elements can change.
The same impression of a square is conveyed when
triangles or unfilled circles are substituted as parts. If
such a transposition of parts does not alter the impression of the whole, then it is clear that the whole is
independent of the nature of its parts. The perception
of the whole is not fundamentally dependent on the
nature of its parts. In this way the notion of primitive perceptual features and their assumed detectors
plays no critical role in the theory. The theory is more
concerned with global aspects of perception than
elemental details.

## The Gestalt laws of perceptual organisation

In addition to this emphasis on the correct level of
perceptual analysis, Gestalt theory also set out principles concerning perceptual organisation. These are
typically referred to as the **Gestalt laws** of perceptual
organisation and they define how it is that unrelated
parts are assembled into perceptible wholes. In this
regard, the notion of figure/ground segregation is

central. The account focuses on perceptual principles
that give rise to assumed plausible segregations of the
stimulus array that at first blush distinguish objects
from their backgrounds. The Gestalt laws of grouping
provide useful rules of thumb as to how best to divide
the array into discrete objects. So the distinction is
between objects (figures) segregated from the background (ground). (Figure 5.14 provides an example of
where one figure, falling off a bike, was photographed
against a background, which in this case was thankfully sand.)

At a more general level, the account is that there are
certain principles of perceptual encoding that operate
to provide a 'best first guess' as to which aspects of
the stimulus information correspond to meaningful
chunks (perhaps even objects) in the input. These
principles can be applied to any form of input without
regard to whether the environment is familiar or not.
The laws of grouping merely offer suggestions as to
how best to divide up the input into separate chunks:
the decision as to what sort of objects are present is left
to the more central (interpretive) processes to work
out. Several laws of grouping were put forward during
the first half of the twentieth century and these relate
to how stimuli give rise to certain sorts of interpretations
and not others. It seems that the perceptual system
exhibits certain preferences in choosing certain forms
of organisation over others. Such sentiments as these
are best conveyed by concrete examples.

Figure 5.15 illustrates the points for us. In (a) the
dots in the matrix are spaced evenly from one another,
hence there is no clear organised percept that emerges.

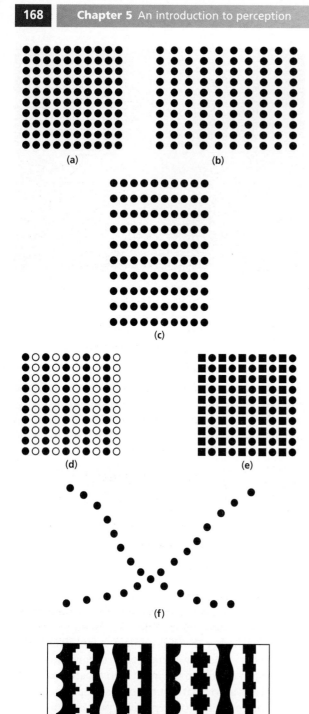

**Figure 5.15 Examples of the Gestalt laws of perceptual organisation**
See text for further details.

*Source*: (g) Gordon, I. E. (1989). *Theories of visual perception* (1st ed., fig 3.3, p. 54). Chichester, England: John Wiley & Sons.

However, when the factor of **proximity** is acting, elements are organised in groups by the closeness of the elements – so in Figure 5.15(b) the dots are grouped into columns and not rows, whereas the opposite is true in Figure 5.15(c). Grouping may also be determined by the **similarity** of the elements such as in Figure 5.15(d) and (e) where the elements group respectively by common colour and common form respectively. In both cases the elements organise themselves into columns.

Various other factors relate to something known as good continuations: common fate, direction, good curve. These are conveyed with respect of Figure 5.15(f). Closure and symmetry are related factors and these are illustrated in Figure 5.15(g). In summarising the factors, Robertson (1986, p. 164; see Figure 5.16, taken from Palmer, 1992) also discussed the idea of objective set by which certain organisations can be induced by prior experience (but here we are beginning to blur the distinction between stimulus determinants and subjective factors). However, she related that Gestalt theorists did discuss the subjective factors of experience or habit as defining predispositions to organise stimuli in particular ways. At the time, however, this was of marginal interest given the emphasis on stimulus and not participant variables.

## The Principle of Prägnanz

The main point of the Gestalt approach was to describe principles of organisation that gave rise to certain predepositions about how best to organise the proximal stimulus into meaningful wholes. To this end the Gestaltists also derived the **Principle of Prägnanz**. In its original form the principle was that 'perceptual organization will always be as "good" as the prevailing conditions allow' (Koffka, 1935/1963) and here the term 'good', although undefined, related to the application of stimulus factors such as regularity, similarity, symmetry, simplicity and so on. More generally, this principle of Prägnanz has been interpreted as a statement of the **minimum principle** (Hochberg & McAllister, 1953), namely, that of all the possible organisations consistent with a proximal stimulus the preferred one will be the one that is the simplest. We shall discuss the minimum principle in much greater depth later. For now it is most sensible to just describe the material rather than analyse it in depth.

## Gestalt theory and the brain

A different aspect of Gestalt theory also warrants a mention. This is that the theory presupposed that

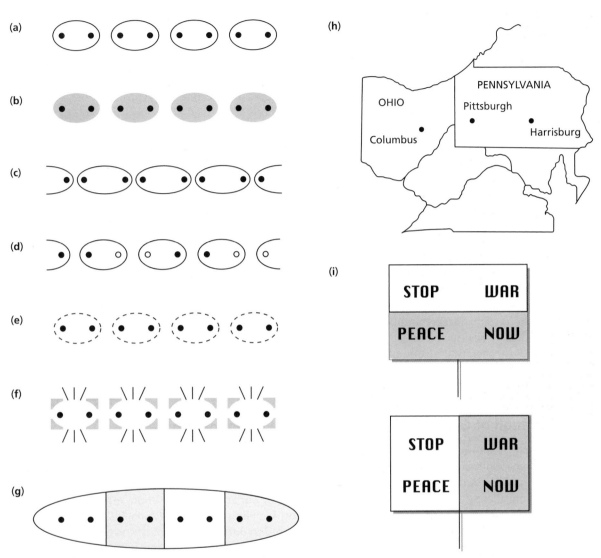

**Figure 5.16 Examples of grouping by common region (as documented by Palmer, 1992)**
Elements that fall within the same common region group together. Grouping by common region also seems to override grouping by proximity (c) and grouping by similarity (d). In (f) the notion of a region can be defined by illusory contours is shown. In (h) and (i), real-world examples are provided. In (i) different meanings are induced according to how the words are grouped together.

*Source*: Palmer, S. E. (1992). Common region: A new principle of perceptual grouping. *Cognitive Psychology, 24*, 436–447 (fig. 2, p. 439). Reproduced with permission from Elsevier.

perceptual organisation came about because the brain is structured to pick up the holistic properties of the stimulus as given by configural cues such as symmetry and closure. In this regard, the theory was fleshed out at the level of assumed electrical field properties of the brain. When a given stimulus acted as an input to sensory analysis the brain in turn resonated to the structural aspects of the stimulus and eventually settled on a pattern of activity that reflected 'an equilibrium involving minimum energy load' (van der Helm, 2000, p. 774). Given that almost no one now takes this theoretical excursion seriously, there is little point in dwelling too long on the details (for a very readable account, though, see Gordon, 1989). Despite the fact that there is little interest in the neural aspect of the theory, the Gestalt laws have had a profound and enduring impact on thinking about human perception. They remain the topic of much contemporary research and, in this regard, Figure 5.16 provides examples of a more recently described principle of perceptual organisation (taken from Palmer, 1992). Before we move on, it is important to appreciate one last aspect of Gestalt theory.

## Mental copies and perceptual organisation

This is that if we accept that the Gestalt principles of organisation do play a central role in perception, then we have further grounds for arguing against the idea that, fundamentally, the internal representation of the proximal stimulus is something other than a mere copy of sensory stimulation. To reiterate, whereas in vision it is tempting to discuss the notion of a retinal copy of a visible stimulus, this fails to capture, in an important sense, the nature of perceptual representation. If we accept that the Gestalt laws provide something of an account of why certain interpretations are preferred over others, then it is difficult to see how this can be merely due to generating a copy of the stimulus.

Perceptual organisation implies that the input is structured in such a way that certain relations between the parts are specified and others are not. Figure 5.15(c) is structured according to rows and not columns so there is a fundamental sense in which the rows are captured by the internal representation whereas the columns are not.

This sort of idea will be returned to shortly but in the current context it is possible to classify the Old (Gestaltist) Look as being essentially a passive view of perception in which encoding principles are applied to any stimulus independently of its nature and of the mental state of the participant. By this view the operation of the perceptual system cannot be altered or influenced by prior knowledge. To understand this, however, we need to contrast the Old Look with the New.

### Pinpoint question 5.8

What is a defining principle of the 'Old Look' Gestalt accounts of perception?

### Research focus 5.2

#### The gestation of Gestalt: how infants learn to group perceptually

Babies are pretty interesting things. To see directly into their perceptions and cognitions would be truly a phenomenal step in uncovering how mental faculties develop. Clearly, given the concerns in this chapter, it is interesting to ask how it is that babies develop a sense of Prägnanz. The problem is, of course, getting some sort of meaningful response from infants, apart from the occasional giggle and stream of milky sick.

Quinn and Bhatt (2006) argued that one way to examine perceptual grouping in babies is to adopt a familiarisation–novelty preference paradigm (after Fantz, 1964). Here, ickle participants are presented with an initial stimulus until they become familiar with it. Then two new stimuli are presented, one that is similar to the familiar stimulus and a novel stimulus. By measuring looking time, if the infant looks longer at the novel stimulus, then the idea is that the baby has a representation of the familiar object such that the novel stimulus can be distinguished from it.

Over a series of experiments, Quinn and Bhatt (2006) tested both 3–4- and 7–8-month-old children. In the first experiment, infants were presented with

solid bars organised in vertical columns or horizontal rows, and also with a 4×4 grid of squares which could either be filled in to represent the same vertical or horizontal organisation. Infants could either be familiarised with the bars first and then compared to different versions of the grid, or presented with the grid first and then compared to different versions of the bars – see Figure 5.17(a). According to looking times, infants preferred the novel stimulus in both cases, indicating grouping by lightness since the filled-in squares formed one (perceptual) group and the unfilled squares formed another. Quinn and Bhatt (2006) then ruled out the idea that the use of identical shapes facilitated perceptual organisation in the first experiment by defining rows and columns according to random squares and diamonds – see Figure 5.17(b). Again, on the basis of looking times, infants preferred the novel stimulus, again indicating grouping by lightness. However, in a third experiment – Figure 5.17(c) – when form became the grouping attribute that distinguished familiar from novel test stimuli, infants did not as readily show a preference for the novel stimulus.

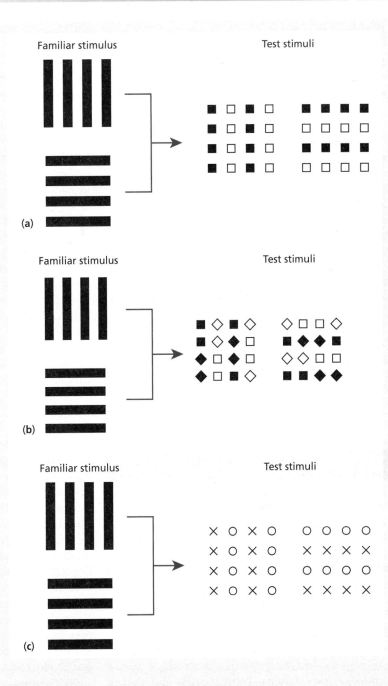

**Figure 5.17 Examples of the sorts of displays used by Quinn and Bhatt (2006)**

*Source*: Quinn, P. C., & Bhatt, R. S. (2006). Are some Gestalt principles deployed more readily than others during early development? The case of lightness versus form similarity. *Journal of Experimental Psychology: Human Perception and Performance*, *32*, 1221–1230 (fig. 1, p. 1223, fig. 2, p. 1225, fig. 3, p. 1226). Reproduced with permission from APA.

Quinn and Bhatt (2006) concluded that grouping according to lightness is a much stronger cue for perceptual organisation in infants than form, which raises the question why? Well, the authors go on to suggest that form grouping is slowly learnt while lightness grouping might be acquired much earlier for the infant. So you need to give those gurgling and smelly humans a little more credit, as at 8 months old they are well on their way to developing some incredibly complex perceptual grouping mechanisms. Sounds exhausting – no wonder they sleep all the time.

*Source*: Quinn, P. C., & Bhatt, R. S. (2006). Are some Gestalt principles deployed more readily than others during early development? The case of lightness versus form similarity. *Journal of Experimental Psychology: Human Perception and Performance, 32*, 1221–1230.

New Look The idea that our perceptions of
the world are influenced by our knowledge,
expectations, beliefs, needs and desires about the
world.

Old Look A passive view of perception in which
encoding principles are applied to any stimulus
independently of its nature and irrespective of the
mental state of the participant.

Gestalt laws A set of statements backed up by
demonstrations of how it is that the perceptual
system groups elements (the parts) into coherent
wholes. Collectively the laws specify principles of
perceptual organisation.

proximity As pointed out by Gestaltists, elements
that are close together tend to group together.

similarity As pointed out by Gestaltists, elements
that are similar tend to group together.

principle of Prägnanz As pointed out by Gestaltists,
perceptual elements tend to cohere into 'good'
groupings.

minimum principle The idea that of all possible
perceptual organisations, the one that will be
selected will be the simplest.

## The New Look

A pivotal figure in the New Look theoretical movement
was Jerome Bruner (see collected papers in Anglin,
1974) and of particular interest is his seminal paper
written in 1957. His theoretical approach is worthy of
some detailed consideration because it provides a very
good summary of some key ideas that are implicated
in many attempts to understand human perception. It
also allows us to reconsider the difference between
passive and active views of perception.

The general New Look approach is that our perceptions of the world are very much determined by our
knowledge, expectations, beliefs, needs and desires
about the world. Perceptual defence (see discussion in
Chapter 4) is one example taken to justify this claim,
but many other examples exist. An important and early
study was carried out by Bruner and Goodman (1947).
They tested participants individually and the task was
to alter the size of a spot of light so that it matched a
comparison disc. The discs varied in size and varied in
nature. Generally participants were reasonably good in
their estimates of size when the discs were neutral but

this changed dramatically when the discs were replaced
with coins. Now participants generally overestimated
the size of the coins and these estimates tended to
increase with the value of the coins.

More unfortunate, though, is the realisation that the
findings were further complicated by socio-economic
factors. The participants in the experiment were 10-
year-old children and half were classified as rich and
half were classified as poor. When the size ratings were
broken down according to the socio-economic class
of the children, a rather upsetting result emerged.
Although both sets of children overestimated the size
of the coins, the poor children's estimates were more
extreme than those of the rich children. Moreover the
poor children's overestimates increased quite dramatically with the value of the coins: this was not true of
the rich children's estimates.

Regardless of what the correct interpretation of these
data is, the impact of the study was profound and the
findings formed the foundations for the idea that *need*
and *value* fundamentally determine our perceptions of
the world. Such a view was clarified further in Bruner's
later *perceptual readiness* theory.

## Bruner's perceptual readiness theory

Central is the idea of a **perceptual cue** as defined as a
property of the proximal stimulus. For Bruner the act
of perception is taking the information provided by
proximal cues and assigning this to a mental category.
Fundamentally this means that perception implies the
existence of certain mental categories. For instance,
this might mean taking this particular spot of light
on the retina and assigning it to the category 'a visual
impression'. More generally it would mean being able
to interpret the spot of light as (say) arising from the
usherette's torch in a cinema. What we have here is a
claim that perception means going from perceptual
cues to mental categories. As Bruner (1957, p. 125)
asserted, 'all perceptual experience is necessarily the
end product of a categorization process'.

By assigning a given input to a mental category the
implication is that the act of perception is said to 'go
beyond' the information given. So as soon as you draw
the perceptual inference that the spot of light indicates
the presence of the usherette's torch, you can begin to
draw certain other inferences about properties of the
distal object that are plausible – in this sense, you have
gone beyond the information that is the spot of light
that was given. For instance, you can make predictions
about the size of the torch in relation to the usherette's

body and the fact that it will contain a switch for operating it and so on. As Bruner stated, such inferences imply **predictive veridicality**. The act of perception implies that the observer can go on to make predictions about the unseen environment on the basis of what has already been seen. The usefulness of such predictions depends on how elaborate the corresponding mental categories are. So a torch expert will begin to make far more sophisticated predictions about the 'spot of light' than the novice.

These are very important points because they begin to show how it is that perception is intimately tied up with prediction. By this view the perceptual system is taken to provide the observer with a representation of the world that is useful for prediction. So the perceptual representation of the brown and black striped 'tiger-like' shape will also provide some indication of the position of this object relative to the observer. This can then be used as a basis to decide to run or stay very still indeed! (See Allport, Tipper, & Chmiel, 1985, p. 109.) Predictions about what to do next are based on the information transmitted by the perceptual system. As a consequence it is important that whatever information is conveyed, is done so in a manner that makes it easy for the cognitive system to work on. The cognitive system must arrive at a reasonable interpretation of the outside world quickly and effectively (especially where perceiving tigers is concerned!).

In addition, Bruner discussed the notion of the accessibility of mental categories. That is, classifying 'the spot of light' as 'the usherette's torch' depends to some degree on the accessibility of the latter category. By the perceptual readiness account, the accessibility of a given category depends on essentially two factors, namely (i) the expectancies that the observer has of the likelihood of certain events, and (ii) the observer's needs. So the usherette's torch category will be highly accessible within the cinema rather than outside the cinema and it will be more easily accessed if you arrive late for the film and the cinema appears full than if you arrive in plenty of time and the cinema is not full. These notions of accessibility refer to the 'readiness' in 'perceptual readiness'.

---

**perceptual cue** An aspect of the proximal stimulus that is used to infer what the distal stimulus is.

**predictive veridicality** Going beyond the information provided by the current stimulus representation so as to predict future events.

---

# Perception as a process of unconscious inference

Aside from the notion of category accessibility, central to the account is the notion of a **perceptual inference**. Much like Sherlock Holmes goes about solving a case, the perceptual system is seen to engage in taking a series of cues (clues) provided by the sensory stimulation and figuring out how best to interpret these cues. Perceptual inferences are made in assigning these cues to these categories. From registering this particular spot of light you draw the inference that it arises from the usherette's torch. Given that such inference making is not a conscious activity, we have the notion of perception being based on making **unconscious inferences**. This is very much in line with the traditional view of perception which is typically traced back to Helmholtz (1867/1962) – that perceptual processes act as though solving a problem by taking various cues and forming the best hypothesis as to the most likely distal stimulus that gave rise to the proximal stimulus.

## The likelihood principle

In this regard, we have a different principle of perception from the minimum principle given to us by the Gestalt theorists. This alternative is known as the **likelihood principle** – 'sensory elements will be organized into the most probable object or event (distal stimulus) in the environment consistent with the sensory data (the proximal stimulus)' (Pomerantz & Kubovy, 1986, pp. 36–9). As Gregory (1970) stated, 'We are forced . . . to suppose that perception involves betting on the most probable interpretation of sensory data, in terms of the world of objects' (p. 29). Pylyshyn (1999) went even further and stated that, according to the New Look, perception involves a cycle of hypothesis and test whereby an initial best guess is made on the basis of some set of cues together with the current subjective state of the observer, this is checked against the stimulus information and, if needs be, the hypothesis is refined, reformulated and re-checked.

There are many fundamental issues here. For instance, ensuing arguments focused on various distinctions such as that between perception and cognition, between observation and inference (Fodor, 1984), between stimulus-driven and knowledge-based processes, between peripheral and central processes, etc. We will consider some of these as the discussion proceeds. However, the New Look approach only really makes sense in the view that, in general, the proximal stimulus is fundamentally ambiguous. The New Look approach is based on what has come to be known as a **poverty of the stimulus** argument (Fodor, 1985).

## The poverty of the stimulus argument

By the poverty of the stimulus argument, the claim is that each proximal stimulus is an impoverished version of what is actually out there. In vision the perceptual system operates upon 2D impressions of a 3D world, and this may lead to problems and difficulties. For instance, given the right lighting conditions and angle of regard, a square patch of light may appear to signify the presence of a tilted oblong (Broadbent, 1971, p. 12). In the above example, featuring 'The Two Ronnies', 'four candles' and 'fork handles' may be indistinguishable in the absence of further disambiguating information, such as being in a home furnishing store as opposed to a garden centre. These sorts of examples are taken to show that any given proximal stimulus may be consistent with a number of different states of the environment (Broadbent, 1971, p. 12). Such a claim does not have universal support and it has been categorically denied by Gibson (1986) and the many followers of the direct perception school of thought. Consideration of the ensuing, rather heated debate would lead us in a direction away from cognitive accounts of perception. Interested readers may be entertained by the fray by consulting Fodor and Pylyshyn (1981) and Turvey, Shaw, Reed and Mace (1981).

Perhaps consideration of a classic example – known as the Necker cube (see Figure 5.18) – will help cement these ideas. This figure is inherently ambiguous because various actual objects could produce such a 2D projection – you are either looking down on a wire cube or looking up at one. More generally, though, it is claimed that every proximal stimulus is inherently ambiguous because it could have arisen from any one of an indefinite number of distal causes. The basic claim is that, in general, the proximal stimulus is

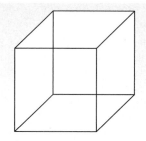

**Figure 5.18 The classic Necker cube figure**

an impoverished specification of the distal stimulus, and because of this the perceptual system necessarily engages in some form of inference-making. On the basis of this evidence (this sensory stimulation, i.e., a spot of light) your best guess is that this particular object (the distal stimulus, i.e., the usherette's torch) is actually out there in the real world. You make an inference about the nature of the distal object on the basis of the perceptual cues provided in the proximal stimulus. The argument is that if the information available at the senses uniquely specified the distal stimulus, then there would be no need for perceptual inference-making, as Gigerenzer and Murray (1987) rightly point out (p. 69).

### Pinpoint question 5.9

'Let him have it, Chris', was the (alleged) sentence uttered by Derek Bentley as he and an armed Chris Craig were cornered on the roof top of a building in Croydon by police after they were disturbed while planning to rob a warehouse. Why was this spoken utterance ambiguous?

## Perceptual inference-making

It is very easy to get confused here and, as Pinpoint question 5.9 demonstrates, perceptual ambiguity in some extreme cases can mean the difference between

## Research focus 5.3

# You saw the whole of the cube: spatial neglect and Necker drawings

When a brain-damaged individual falls into the hands of a psychologist, they are often asked to perform a number of weird and wonderful tasks in order to assess their mental capacities. One such type of brain damage is spatial neglect and one such type of task is to draw a Necker cube. Typically, individuals with spatial neglect will fail to draw one half of the visual scene, typically the half of the scene opposite (or **contralateral**, as we like to say in the trade) to the side of the brain that has received the damage. Seki, Ishiai, Koyama, Sato, Hirabayashi and Inaki (2000) were particularly interested in why certain individuals with spatial neglect could successfully complete a drawing of the Necker cube while others couldn't.

An impressive sample of 100 right-handed patients with right hemisphere stroke was used in the study. This meant that these individuals would show neglect in the left side of space. Participants were split into two groups according to the severity of their neglect (mild and severe) and were also administered a test of verbal intelligence. Individuals were then asked to go ahead and draw a Necker cube with no time restrictions.

Upon a close examination of exactly how each individual drew the Necker cube, Seki et al. (2000) found that verbal IQ was positively correlated to the number of correct vertices the patient drew. Importantly, while verbal IQ did not appear to be a factor in determining the number of correct vertices for patients with mild neglect, a fair verbal IQ for those individuals with severe neglect helped to maintain performance at mild neglect levels. That is, it was only the combination of poor verbal IQ and severe neglect that caused the problem in drawing the Necker cube. This is clearly represented in Figure 5.19(b), in which the left halves of the cube and flower are missing.

Seki et al. (2000) concluded that both the severity of the spatial neglect and the verbal intelligence of the patient play critical roles in determining performance in post-trauma tasks such as those reported

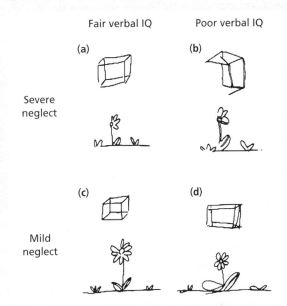

**Figure 5.19 Drawings of various figures by individuals suffering from spatial neglect**
Verbal intelligence can overcome drawing problems in patients with spatial neglect. The left-side neglect of a Necker cube in severe neglect patients appears to be more apparent for individuals with poor verbal IQ (b) relative to fair verbal IQ (a). Those with mild neglect and fair verbal IQ (c) perform relatively well at these tasks.

*Source*: Seki, K., Ishiai, S., Koyama, Y., Sato, S., Hirabayashi, H., & Inaki, K. (2000). Why are some patients with severe neglect able to copy a cube? The significance of verbal intelligence. *Neuropsychologia*, *38*, 1466–1472 (fig. 5, p. 1470). Reproduced with permission from Elsevier.

here. Therefore, not only is the Necker cube an interesting stimulus from a standard cognitive point of view, but it can also tell us something about the abilities of individuals who have suffered brain trauma. Not bad for a collection of 12 lines, really.

*Source*: Seki, K., Ishiai, S., Koyama, Y., Sato, S., Hirabayashi, H., & Inaki, K. (2000). Why are some patients with severe neglect able to copy a cube? The significance of verbal intelligence. *Neuropsychologia*, *38*, 1466–1472.

life and death – Derek Bentley was eventually convicted and sent to the gallows. Typically, when inference-making is discussed, the implication is that someone is engaged in some form of difficult problem-solving

activity such as completing a crossword puzzle. The aim here is to go from a set of clues to filling in the letters in the crossword. For example, given the clue 'Coin used as an image of worship (4)', one way to proceed is simply to think of different coins whose names are four letters long. So the (bottom-up) inference is that the solution is a name of a coin that is four letters in length. The word length ('4') initiates the hypothesis-and-test cycle. So 'dime' might be the first hypothesis but then 'cent' fits this description as well and the current input is ambiguous with respect to both of these (top-down) predictions. However, an alternative hypothesis can be considered and this comes from knowledge about how crosswords work. Here the idea is to rearrange the particular letters of COIN and test out these possibilities. In doing this, a much more plausible solution is discovered.

This example stresses how problem solving can involve inference-making, generating hypotheses and testing these against the evidence. However, the example also emphasises conscious processes in which participants would be able to provide a running commentary of how they were proceeding while engaged in the task. This is quite unlike the sort of problem solving that is taken to characterise perception. The idea that perception is like problem solving must not be taken to imply that perceptual analysis is dependent on being aware of the underlying processes. As Gregory (1980) stated, 'Much of human behaviour controlled by perception can occur without awareness: consciousness is seldom, if ever, necessary' (p. 196). So the problem-solving terminology applied to perceptual analysis describes the way in which the underlying processes are assumed to operate, by analogy.

The overarching point is that the perceptual system is faced with the problem of deciding which distal stimulus gave rise to this particular proximal stimulus. The argument goes that it achieves a solution by a process of unconscious inference-making. Certain plausible hypotheses are made about the possible link between the proximal and distal stimuli and these are then tested out against the available sensory evidence.

This will become much clearer if we consider what a perceptual inference might look like and here we can turn to an abridged example taken from Gigerenzer and Murray (1987, p. 63). They defined a perceptual inference in terms of something they call a **probabilistic syllogism**. Any syllogism contains a series of statements that are divided into initial premises and a final conclusion. So an example of a perceptual inference is taken to include:

- *a major premise*: concurrent stimulation of the same right-hand position on both retinae is *normally* associated with a luminous object being present in the left visual field

- *a minor premise*: there is currently stimulation of these right-handed retinal locations

- *a conclusion*: a luminous object is currently present in the left side of space.

Gigerenzer and Murray (1987) stated that, according to the traditional Hemholtzian view of inference-making in perception, the major premise is a generalisation learned by experience, but it seems also quite possible that the premise could specify some constraint that has evolved over the emergence of the human visual system – for example, shadows cast on the ground tend to provide information about the actual position of the light source. Now of course these sorts of constraints could be learnt but they could also reflect evolutionary adaptations.

The major premise also contains the important hedge 'normally', and this gives licence to the term 'probabilistic' in 'probabilistic syllogism'. The assumption is that perceptual inferences are not water-tight and can only provide best first guesses as to the nature of the environment. Indeed the fact that the visual system can be fooled by visual illusions shows that the perceptual system is fallible: the initial inferences made about the sensory data are often incorrect.

## Lessons from perceptual illusions

Optimally, the perceptual system should be providing the cognitive system with an accurate (veridical) record of the environment that unambiguously specifies what is out there. However, outside this 'best of all possible worlds' scenario, the truth is that the perceptual system is fallible and mistakes do arise. Indeed there is a vast literature on how the perceptual system may be fooled by various kinds of perceptual illusions (see Wade, 1982) and some of these (see Figure 5.20) are extraordinarily compelling. The existence of such illusions provides clear examples of mismatches between our perceptions of the external world and the actual nature of the external world. Indeed examples such as these again stand in contrast to the naïve realist view of perception in which our internal world simply mirrors the external world. Our perceptions of the world cannot be mere copies because if they were then there would be no such things as perceptual illusions. There really is no need to conclude that the stick bends merely because it is half submerged in water. Even though the perceptual representation specifies a bent stick, the real world contains a straight stick. The stick appears to be bent even though we know that the stick is straight. In this case, and despite knowledge to

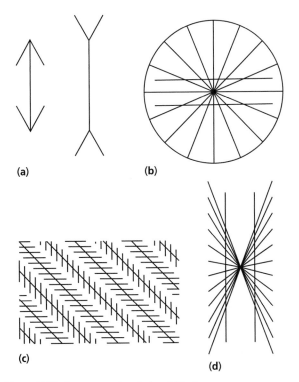

**Figure 5.20 A cornucopia of visual illusions**
(a) The Muller–Lyer illusion: the right vertical line appears longer than the left. (b) The two parallel, horizontal lines appear to bow. (c) The long diagonal lines appear not to be parallel. (d) The two parallel, vertical lines appear to bow.

*Sources*: (a) Robinson, J. O. (1972). *The psychology of visual illusion* (fig. 2.1, p. 21, fig. 3.3, p. 67, fig. 3.19, p. 73 and fig. 3.33, p. 7). London: Hutchinson. Reproduced with permission. (b–d) Palmer, S. E. (1992). Common region: A new principle of perceptual grouping. *Cognitive Psychology, 24*, 436–447 (fig. 7, p. 445). Reproduced with permission from Elsevier.

the contrary, the world appears differently from what it actually is. So what are such apparent anomalies telling us?

The understanding here is that the perceptual system has evolved in such a way that it delivers as truthful a representation of the environment as possible given certain facts about the nature of the world together with physical constraints embodied in the central nervous system. For instance, our ability to perceive the depth of surfaces relative to our angle of regard is in part driven by the fact that we have two eyes that are symmetrically positioned relative to the midline of our bodies. This is a rather obvious physiological constraint. In addition, we can only detect certain wavelengths of light (contained in the visible spectrum) and we cannot hear dog whistles, even if we'd want to. The perceptual system operates within such physical constraints that, according to evolutionary theory, reflect a sensitivity to those properties of the world that have adaptive significance to us as biological organisms.

More interesting, perhaps, is the possibility that the perceptual system has evolved in such a way that it reflects particular properties about real-world structure (i.e., objects). In this regard, Marr (1982) considered a number of processing constraints that likely reflect properties of the nature of objects such that they are cohesive and may be rigid. Points on the surface of an object that are adjacent will likely stimulate adjacent retinal cells. Hence the firing of two adjacent retinal cells implies two sources of light that arise from a single object. In this way the sorts of perceptual inferences that characterise the perceptual analysis stage (about contour extraction and figure/ground segregation) can

## For example . . .

Physiological constraints do not just restrict laboratory experiments – they also have been used and abused in the outside world too. For example, **presbycusis** is the common complaint suffered by many older individuals who lose sensitivity in higher frequency regions (low frequency sounds are rumbles and booms, high frequency sounds are shrills and whistles). According to one article from *The New York Times* (Vitello, Hammer & Schweber 2006), presbycusis was manipulated in two different social contexts. In the first devious manoeuvre, annoying high frequency sounds, which younger people could

hear but older people could not, were installed around bus stops and other favourite haunts of the adolescent to disperse large groups in public settings. In a second, equally devious manoeuvre, the kids decided to use similar high frequency sounds as ring tones, such that they could remain in the loop regarding phone calls and text messages in class without that ancient, grey-haired teacher at the front being able to hear what was happening. Touché!

*Source*: Vitello, P., Hammer, K., & Schweber, N. (2006, June 12). A ring tone meant to fall on deaf ears. *The New York Times*.

make clever suggestions about the sorts of structures out there that correspond to objects. Gregory (1970) provides some further examples. The critical point, though, is that, in some cases, such knowledge (as embodied in the processing constraints) may not apply equally well in all cases.

Consider the classic Muller–Lyer figure shown in Figure 5.20(a). The figure on the right is typically interpreted as a receding corner of a room whereas the figure on the left is interpreted as a protruding corner of a room. The so-called fins attached to the line ends are taken by the visual system to correspond to cues to distance as to how far the edge is from the viewer. In the real world the cues indicate that the respective edges are at different distances from the viewer. So if a metre-tall fencing post is situated one metre from the viewer and there is another situated 10 metres away, the latter gives rise to a smaller retinal image than the former – the more distant post 'looks smaller' than the nearer one. More formally, Emmert's rule states that 'the image of an object is inversely proportional to distance' (Rock, 1983, p. 302). So as Rock stated, in

applying the rule, 'the greater the perceived distance of the image, the larger the object must be' (p. 302). To compensate for this the visual system is said to invoke **size constancy/invariance**. Merely because objects recede into the distance does not mean that they decrease in size, so to preserve the idea that objects retain their size this perceptual inference is built into the system. However, the violation of size constancy can also lead to some interesting holiday photos (see Figure 5.21).

According to Gregory (1970), it is the misapplication of size constancy that gives rise to the Muller–Lyer illusion. In the right-hand version of Figure 5.20(a) the edge appears further away than it does in the left-hand version, hence the system tries to compensate for this by producing an impression of a line that is longer than it actually is (on the right) and a line that is shorter than it actually is (on the left). It would be disingenuous to convey that this is the only account of the illusion – it is not (see Robinson, 1972) – but the example is nevertheless intriguing. It shows how arguments have been made to try to substantiate the claim

**Figure 5.21 Violations of size constancy make for great holiday photos**
*Source*: Alamy Images/Peter Jordan.

**Figure 5.22 A visually confusing scene (from Kanizsa, 1969)**

*Source*: Kanizsa, G. (1969). Perception, past experience and the 'impossible experiment'. *Acta Psychologica, 31*, 66–96 (fig. 18, p. 85). Reproduced with permission from Elsevier.

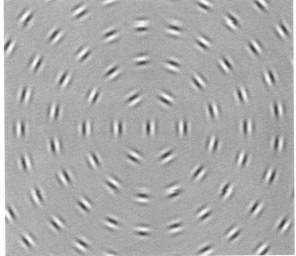

**Figure 5.23 An example of how isolated elements cohere to form the impression of surfaces and contours**

*Source*: Achtman, R. L., Hess, R. F., & Wang, Y.-Z. (2003). Sensitivity for global shape detection. *Journal of Vision, 3*, 616–624 (fig. 2j, p. 619). Copyright © The Association for Research in Vision and Ophthalmology (AVRO). Reproduced with permission.

that knowledge about the physical world may form the basis of perceptual analysis, and, moreover, that there are clear cases where such knowledge is misapplied.

Indeed, this sort of consideration has been brought to the fore on several occasions by Kanizsa (1969, 1985). For instance, in Figure 5.22 the impression is that the sails of the boats are nearer than the fishing rod despite everything we know about fishing rods and their size in relation to the size of a sail. In this way it is seen that certain perceptual inferences are drawn that starkly contradict common sense – in this case it seems that the visual system prefers to interpret larger objects as nearer (Kanizsa, 1969).

### Pinpoint question 5.10

Why don't perceptual illusions support a naïve view of perception?

## Modularity revisited

If this inference-making view of perception is accepted, then one sensible way to proceed is to try to figure out what sorts of perceptual inferences there are. One first approximation to an answer is provided by the Gestalt laws. For instance, the fact that these elements line up in a systematic way suggests that they form part of a single edge or contour (see Figure 5.23, taken from Achtman, Hess & Wang, 2003). A more detailed account, though, has been put forward by Fodor (1983, 1985).

We have already discussed the notion of a perceptual module in the Fodorian sense and how this may be characterised by *information encapsulation*. That is, each module has access only to a limited module-specific store of knowledge. So for instance, the speech processing module would most likely have access to information regarding word boundaries and properties of the sound signal specific to speech, the visual module concerning figure/ground segregation would have access to information regarding the nature of contours and edges, and so on. The critical thing, however, is that both modules are limited in only having access to information within their respective domains. The speech module has no access to information about edges and the figure/ground module has no access to information about spoken words.

In addition, neither module has access to semantic/conceptual knowledge about what a cat is or what /cat/ (the spoken form of 'cat') means. Although these ideas are contentious, one simple way of thinking about perceptual modules, and the perceptual system in general, is that it takes sensory data and generates some form of representation of this in terms of a specification of a segregation between objects and background without any commitment to what the objects are. For ease of exposition this has been referred to here as a perceptual representation. The perceptual representation therefore is a structured representation

**Figure 5.24 Yet another example of a fragmentary figure**

*Source*: Leeper, R. (1935). A study of a neglected portion of the field of learning: The development of sensory organization. *Journal of Genetic Psychology*, *46*, 41–75 (fig. 1, p. 49). Reproduced with permission of the Helen Dwight Reid Educational Foundation.

in which the stimulus information has been divided up into plausible figures and plausible ground – it specifies 'the arrangement of things in the world' (Fodor, 1983, p. 42). It is the work of the central systems to now generate a plausible interpretation of this perceptual representation.

### 'Seeing' vs. 'Seeing as'

A very useful distinction in this context is between 'seeing' and 'seeing as'. This can be most easily grasped by considering Figure 5.24. Initially you probably see just a jumble of black blobs on a white background – we see the blobs and we see them *as* blobs. However, it is also possible to see the blobs as a man riding a horse. In both cases it is appropriate to discuss the perceptual representation as merely specifying individual red blobs. In the first case our interpretation of the figure is essentially black blobs on a white background. In the second case our interpretation is that the figure depicts, albeit in a very impoverished way, a man riding a horse. The claim is that the perceptual representation underlying these different interpretations is the same – the seeing is the same in both cases. What changes is the interpretation – the seeing as.

## Bottom-up vs. top-down modes of processing

In contrast to this analysis, in the New Look approach even perceptual processes (i.e., the seeing) are influenced by general knowledge. Here the basic idea is that knowledge of the world in large part determines our perceptions of it to the extent that it will fundamentally alter the perceptual representation. So if we need to eat we will actually begin to see food. The differences between the two theoretical approaches can be better understood in terms of the difference between stimulus-driven and knowledge-driven processes or alternatively between bottom-up and top-down processes. To reiterate: stimulus-driven/bottom-up processes are those that are essentially put in motion by the stimulus – it is difficult not to state that such processes are automatically invoked by the physical nature of the stimulus. The ace of hearts automatically produces activation in the red detectors (see Figure 5.11). In contrast, knowledge-driven or top-down processes 'control and structure information delivered by input processes' (Gordon, 1989, p. 137).

So whereas in the modular account inferences work from the bottom up, inferences in the New Look operate from the top down. To invoke top-down processes in perception seems to allow for the possibility that the act of seeing can be fundamentally altered by our desires, needs, wants, expectations, etc. So the New Look account of perception is active, not passive, and as Broadbent (1977) stated, the implication is that the central mechanisms essentially interrogate the input, 'testing hypothetical models of the world against the sensory evidence' (p. 113). Perhaps the most extreme form of top-down processing is that implemented in the re-entrant model of Di Lollo and colleagues in which the pattern information represented at the level of the pattern layer over-writes the current representation of the input in the working space (see Chapter 4). However, less extreme forms of top-down processing are possible (see Figure 5.25). Figure 5.25 is taken from Gregory (1998) and sets out a framework for thinking about perception that encompasses the New Look. By this view, top-down processes may be invoked when an error in interpreting the proximal stimulus occurs.

**perceptual inference** Certain plausible hypotheses are made about the possible link between the proximal and distal stimuli and these are then tested out against the available sensory evidence.

**unconscious inference** A perceptual inference that operates unconsciously.

**likelihood principle** The idea that 'sensory elements will be organized into the most probable object or event (distal stimulus) in the environment consistent with the sensory data (the proximal stimulus)' (Pomerantz & Kubovy, 1986, pp. 36–9).

**poverty of the stimulus** The assumption that the proximal stimulus is a very poor under-specification of what the distal stimulus is.

**contralateral** Opposite side to the side being considered.

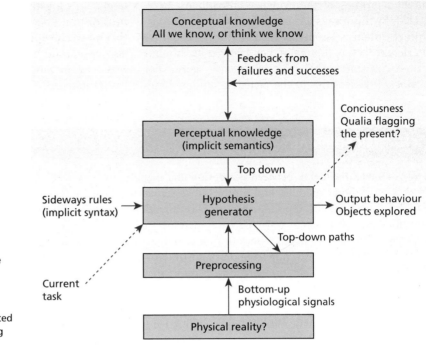

**Figure 5.25 Gregory's (1998) schematic representation of the organisation and operation of the human perceptual system**

Source: Gregory, R. L. (1998). Brainy minds. *British Medical Journal, 317,* 1693–1695 (fig. 3, p. 1694). Reproduced with permission from BMJ Publishing Group.

**probabilistic syllogism** A collection of statements in which the major premise and minor premise lead to a likely conclusion.

**presbycusis** Loss of high frequency sensitivity in hearing traditionally associated with aging.

**size constancy/invariance** The perceptual inference that an object retains its size regardless of the size of its image on the retina. The ability to discount absolute size in identifying shape.

## Concluding comments

So where does this leave us? Well, it appears that we have two alternative accounts of inference-making in perception. By the modularity of mind view (Fodor, 1983) each perceptual module contains certain principles of operation (these define the corresponding perceptual inferences) that are applied to any stimulus in a bid to parse the input into plausible objects, from the bottom up. The input modules feed forward the first best guess as to the nature of the stimulus. The eventual perceptual representation is then operated upon by the central mechanisms that offer an interpretation of the input (e.g., a few random black blobs on the page, a huntsman on a horse). In contrast to

this, and according to the New Look, the actual perceptual analysis is driven by the mental categories that the participant possesses in a top-down fashion. If I am hungry enough, any large yellow 'M' in the high street will do.

The central dilemma remains. This revolves around whether or not our knowledge of the world can influence stimulus coding in such a way that our perceptions primarily reflect our wants, needs and desires instead of what is really out there. In considering this dilemma we have attempted to base the discussion on an apparently clear distinction between a passive (Old Look) account of perception and an active (New Look) account. However, a more complicated view has emerged from consideration of the issues. Indeed, as Broadbent (1977) stated, there is possibly a better framework for thinking about perception.

By this view there is an initial perceptual analysis stage that is passive and which takes evidence that arrives at the senses and then goes on to *suggest* possible interpretations of the environment. This is then followed by a stage in which the most promising interpretation is followed by active interrogation of sensory stimulation to check for the presence of features that have yet to be detected. According to Navon (1981) it is useful therefore to distinguish between *suggestion* as the label for the 'flow of information from the environment into the perceptual system' and *inquiry* as the label for the later probing of the evidence (Broadbent, 1977, p. 115). By this means it is possible to see how the perceptual system is essentially insulated from cognitive interference even though it has evolved to honour certain constraints that exist in the real world. For instance, it is sensitive to the fact that similar things tend to go together and that similar things that are near one another go together, and that similar things that move coherently together go together, etc. We can also appreciate how the interpretation of a stimulus may be guided by the selective uptake of information from the senses.

## CHAPTER SUMMARY

- A simple distinction between perception and cognition is provided and this mapped onto the difference between input modules and central processes as discussed by Fodor (1983) in his modularity of mind hypothesis. In this respect, perception is informationally encapsulated such that the outputs from the input modules do not in any way reflect an individual's expectations, wants, desires or needs. In contrast, higher-order influences such as wishes or desires only come into play during the operation of central processes, when the system is trying to understand (interpret) the sense data. The perceptual system (and the concomitant perceptual representation) therefore may be said to be veridical (truthful), although the interpretations of this representation may not be.

- Even though it is possible to perceive a stimulus without necessarily being able to recognise it, familiarity clearly plays an important role in perception. However, in order to assess whether familiarity impacts upon perception or cognition, word recognition experiments have been particularly useful (Broadbent & Gregory, 1967a). The word frequency effect is perhaps the most obvious manifestation of how familiarity impacts on perception: common words are more easily perceived than are rare words.

- Nevertheless, it is not clear whether frequency effects come about through an enhancement of sensory mechanisms (i.e., perception) or whether central and more response-based mechanisms (i.e., cognition) are responsible. Blakemore and Cooper (1970) found that kittens raised in environments in which only vertical or horizontal lines were present were essentially blind to orientations to which they had not been exposed. Such data support a perceptual account of familiarity. Alternatively, familiar stimuli might be thought of as having a lower threshold than unfamiliar stimuli, thereby supporting a decisional account of familiarity. Perceptual and decisional accounts may be distinguished using signal detection theory and the observation of an effect of familiarity on $d'$ or $\beta$, respectively.

- In accounting specifically for the word frequency effect, empirical support has been garnered for accounts that argue for the locus of this effect at a perceptual (early) level and those that argue for a post-perceptual (late) level. For example, using a same/different paradigm, Hochberg (1968) showed that the ability to respond same/different was equivalent for meaningful and meaningless letter strings when they were placed close together. The idea here was that when such judgements could be made at the level of sensory analysis, then familiarity was not important. Consequently, such effects had to exist at the level of post-perceptual processes.

- However, additional evidence supporting the perceptual nature of familiarity effects is provided by research into word superiority. Doyle and Leach (1988) asked participants on which of two intervals either a word or non-word appeared given very fast rates of presentation. A word superiority effect was found – i.e., perceptual report of words was better than for non-words – and the effect was manifest in $d'$ (a measure of sensitivity), thereby supporting a perceptual account of familiarity. Merikle and Reingold (1990) also found a word superiority effect in visual masking studies on $d'$ providing further support for this claim.

- Our sensory world is also influenced by what we expect to experience and how recently we have encountered certain events. The study of ambiguous figures (such as the classic old/young woman) helps to compare the relative contribution of these two factors. Epstein and Rock (1960) presented participants with an alternating sequence of unambiguous old or young woman pictures followed by a target ambiguous figure. If recency was the most important factor influencing judgement, then participants should interpret the ambiguous figure according to the last picture. If expectancy was more important, then participants should interpret the ambiguous figure according to the expected pattern of the previous stimuli. While support for recency over expectation was provided, more recent evidence (Girgus, Rock, & Egatz, 1977; Wilton, 1985) has called this conclusion into question.

- Ideas related to the effects of recency are also represented by the literature on repetition priming, in which stimulus identification is improved if a stimulus is repeated (Humphreys, Besner, & Quinlan, 1998). Benton and Moscovitch (1988) examined the interaction between familiarity and repetition. For unfamiliar stimuli such as non-words, repetition only had a very short-lived effect. For familiar stimuli such as words, repetition had a longer-lasting effect. Therefore, although perception is sensitive to recently encountered stimuli, the role of long-term representations such as those associated with familiar stimuli also seems to influence judgement.

- Expectancy can influence perception in many different forms. Instructional set refers to explicit commands influencing a participant's perception (Hochberg, 1970). In contrast, mental set is where a participant is implicitly put in mind of a certain perception (Steinfeld, 1967). In sum then, familiarity, recency and expectancy are all thought to influence perception, although it is hard to disentangle these influences and also hard to locate the actual site of these effects (Huang & Pashler, 2005).

- Notions of participant factors influencing current perception stand in contrast to the 'Old Look' Gestalt school. The Gestalt laws or principles of perceptual organisation such as proximity and similarity were used to explain how individuals derive perceptual representations without reference to beliefs, desires, expectations, etc. A more overriding principle is that of the principle of Prägnanz – 'perceptual organization will always be as "good" as the prevailing conditions allow' (Koffka, 1935/1963).

- In contrast, the New Look school of perception (Bruner, 1957) did, however, acknowledge that our prior knowledge, needs and experience of the world heavily influence what we currently perceive. Perceptual readiness was put forward as a concept by which the individual was able to assign perception to mental categories and consequently go beyond the sense data to make inferences about what else might be out there (predictive veridicality).

- In the (Old Look) minimum principle, of all possible organisations the one that will be selected will be the simplest. In contrast, in the (New Look) likelihood principle it is the organisation that is most likely that will be selected. Also associated with the New Look school is that idea that individuals engage in a form of perceptual hypothesis testing regarding their environment. These kinds of perceptual inferences can be important when our sensory input is impoverished.

- Such a binary Old Look vs. New Look distinction may not be that helpful after all and if we are to make significant progress in understanding perception then aspects of both active and passive modes of operation will need to be considered (cf. Broadbent, 1977).

## ANSWERS TO PINPOINT QUESTIONS

5.1  Perception and input modules are responsible for (a) the first initial reading of the sentence. Cognition and central mechanisms are responsible for (b) its interpretation.

5.2  It is better to compare rare words with familiar words rather than random letter strings, since potential confounds such as meaningfulness and pronounceability are controlled for.

5.3  The smell of car fumes should have a lower threshold in the city because of its increased familiarity.

5.4  Traditionally, it has been accepted that an effect of $d'$ implies operations at the level of perceptual mechanisms.

5.5  A repetition effect is where responses to the repeated presentation of a stimulus is facilitated relative to a case where the stimulus is not repeated.

5.6    Look between words rather than within the words themselves ( . . . instructional se**t wo**uld help . . . ).

5.7    More recent, more familiar and more expected stimuli will be identified more effectively than distant, rare and unexpected stimuli.

5.8    The Old Look Gestalts posit a passive view of perception in which encoding is driven by basic grouping mechanisms rather than the mental state of the person.

5.9    'Let him have it, Chris' could have been referring to Chris handing over the gun, or it could have been an encouragement to shoot at the police.

5.10    Perceptual illusions have multiple interpretations and as such perception cannot simply be based on simple copying operations.

# THEORIES OF PERCEPTION

**By the end of this chapter, you should be able to:**

- Review and distinguish between the minimum principle and the likelihood principle.
- Evaluate the evidence for a crude-to-fine account of perceptual processing using both global-to-local (Navon, 1977) and change blindness (Rensink, 2002) studies.
- Summarise the analysis-by-synthesis account of speech processing.
- Discuss the notion of a frame (Minsky, 1975).
- Evaluate the data relating to phonemic restoration.
- Describe an alternative account of the effects of $d'$ and $\beta$.

## CHAPTER CONTENTS

# But is it art? Aesthetic observations and Twiglets

Another Friday night, another private art gallery opening in the funky end of town. This time, you've actually got an invite thanks to your flatmate, who knows the waiter who used to work with the brother of the guy who sold the artist their pencils. Or something. The room is filled with angular hair-cuts, olives on cocktail sticks and some decidedly funny-tasting punch. 'An interesting piece, would-n't you say?' 'Not really,' you reply, noticing that the room is swaying more than it did at the start of the evening. You stare at the title in order to confirm your rather brash statement: 'pass in tow'. Hmm. The shapes in the painting come into focus and then the textures and details slowly follow. Try as you might, there really is nothing in the picture that gets you the sense of a slow-moving vehicle pulling another one along by a piece of rope. You alter your view-point, as far as your balance will allow, to attempt to reconstruct what really should be two vehicles in tandem. Nothing. 'Quite brilliant how the artist has adopted a pseudo-mathematical approach to each sketch,' your companion insists: '"Exponential", "Ogive" and this one, "Asymptote".' As the word slowly erases any image of a broken-down car behind a van and is instead replaced by a really quite pleasing array of wavy lines, you realise that maybe the punch was pretty strong after all.

## REFLECTIVE QUESTIONS

1. Have you ever misread a newspaper headline or misheard a song lyric? Did this initially mistaken perception seem as valid as any of your other perceptions? How do you know what you're seeing and hearing is actually out there in the environment and not simply a product of your own cognition? How might we be able to tell the two apart?

2. Take a look at your current environment. What kind of things do you notice straight away? When do you notice the details, the objects and the relationship between objects? Is there any pattern to the way in which you take in a visual scene?

## Introduction and preliminary considerations

In the previous chapter we discussed some general factors – familiarity, recency and expectancy – that have been studied in the context of attempting to understand human perception. All three factors have been shown to influence our impressions of the world, but as cognitive psychologists we need to try to understand where such factors exert their influence in the chain of processes leading from sensory reception to conscious awareness. More particularly, the research questions have been framed in terms of whether factor $x$ operates at a perceptual or a post-perceptual stage of processing. Does factor $x$ reflect fundamental properties of the perceptual system or simply biases in the way that we interpret the world?

An additional, much more basic question now deserves our attention. This question is fundamental, but rather surprisingly, it does tend to get ignored in discussions of human perception. We have concluded that, following sensory encoding, some form of perceptual representation is derived, and that consequently this representation is assigned some form of interpretation. However, we have yet to consider what sorts of overarching principle, or principles, may be at play in determining the nature of the eventual percept. The basic question is: 'What sort of percept is actually generated?' Here an attempt at an answer is framed in terms of the distinction between the minimum principle and the likelihood principle.

## Simplicity and likelihood

As noted in Chapter 5, according to the (Old Look) Gestalt principle of Prägnanz, or alternatively, the *minimum principle*, 'We perceive whatever object or scene would most simply or economically fit the sensory pattern' (Hochberg, 1981, p. 263). In contrast, according to New Look theorists, there is the *likelihood principle* by which 'We perceive whatever object or scene would, under normal circumstances, most likely fit the sensory pattern' (Hochberg, 1981, p. 263). Although these contrasting views do not square up as polar opposites, they certainly are very different: on the one hand, it is claimed that perceptual analysis suggests *simple solutions* to establishing the cause of the proximal stimulus (it's a bird, it's a plane), and on the other, the claim is that perceptual analysis suggests *likely solutions* to establishing the cause of the proximal stimulus (given the presence of Lex Luther, it probably is Superman). More detailed analyses have been carried out in the literature, and it is to these that we now turn as we attempt to answer questions about the fundamental nature of human perception. First we will consider the evidence relevant to the minimum principle and then we turn to the likelihood principle.

## The minimum principle

### Structural information theory

Let us begin by considering how the notion of simplicity has been used in one theory of visual information processing and we will see that things are perhaps not

so simple after all! The most detailed account of the minimum principle is contained in **structural information theory** (SIT) as developed, over the past 40 years or so, by Leeuwenberg and colleagues (Boselie & Leeuwenberg, 1986; Leeuwenberg, 1969; Leeuwenberg & Boselie, 1988; Leeuwenberg & van der Helm, 1991; van der Helm & Leeuwenberg, 1996). The basic aim of the theory is to explain why particular interpretations of visual stimuli are preferred over others. It has also been applied to other aspects of perception, but, for present purposes, we shall concentrate on only this. The theory provides a detailed specification of how the minimum principle, in which the most simple representation is derived, underlies perceptual encoding. The theory is primarily concerned with the principles that govern the coding of the contours of shapes on the understanding that these principles describe how abstract sensory coding operations function.

It is easiest to explain the theory with recourse to a simple example. Figure 6.1a provides an illustration of the sort of line drawing that has featured heavily in the development of the theory (after Pomerantz & Kubovy, 1986, fig. 36.43). Although there is an indefinite number of distal stimuli that could correspond to the picture, two primary possibilities are given, respectively, by (i) two overlapping squares (Figure 6.1c), and (ii) a square abutting a chair shape (see Figure 6.1b). The problem posed for the theory is to explain why it is that the overlapping square interpretation is preferred.

To keep matters as simple as possible, we will initially consider how the theory first accounts for the generation of an internal representation of a line drawing of a square. The theory is concerned with the internal

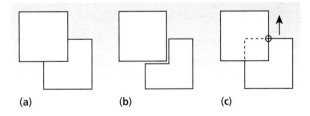

(a)　　　　　(b)　　　　　(c)

**Figure 6.1 Further examples of ambiguity in visual perception**
In (a) the figure is ambiguous. Either there are two squares with one overlapping the other or there is one square abutting a chair shape. The two alternative readings are provided in (b) and (c), respectively.

*Source*: Pomerantz, J. R., & Kubovy, M. (1986). Theoretical approaches to perceptual organization. In K. R. Boff, J. P. Kaufman, & J. P. Thomas (Eds.), *Handbook of perception and human performance* (fig. 36.43, pp. 36–42). New York: Wiley. Reproduced with permission of John Wiley & Sons.

**Figure 6.2 How would you go about describing the relationship between the lines in this picture?**

*Source*: Rex Features/Buenavista/Everett.

coding principles that underpin the derivation of a stimulus representation. The theory focuses on perceptual coding mechanisms that are assumed to play a very basic role in the visual encoding of shape information. Central here is the idea that the contour of the square is coded in terms of a symbolic representation that specifies elemental line segments and angles that define the bounded contour – these primitive elements are specified in the perceptual representation via **primitive symbol**s. Elementary coding operations are invoked that trace around the contour. Once such an operation is applied, it generates a **primitive code** that specifies for a given point on the figure, the nature of the contour.

In simple terms, this is exactly like making a copy of a drawing of a shape using paper and pencil. However, the copy operations are governed by a description of the strokes of the pen for each position on the shape's contour. To begin with, we need a starting point (an origin) for the pencil and its direction of travel. As the pen traces round the contour we note the orientation of every elemental line segment. Each primitive line is noted together with each change in

direction (i.e., each angle and its magnitude are noted). So for instance, one primitive code of the square could be '$a\ \alpha\ a\ \alpha\ a\ \alpha\ a\ \alpha$' in which '$a$' signifies a line of unit length and where $\alpha$ signifies a 90° clockwise rotation (in this example the '$a$' and '$\alpha$' are the primitive symbols). Alternative codes are generated for different points of origin and directions of travel for the same figure. For example, '$a\ \delta\ a\ \delta\ a\ \delta\ a\ \delta$' could be another way of representing a square, with '$\delta$' signifying a 90° counter-clockwise rotation. By thinking beyond the simple case of a square (see, for example, Figure 6.2), you can begin to appreciate how the number of possible codings can be immense, and because of this a basic problem is to decide which of the many possible codings is to be preferred (see Figure 6.3).

The SIT account proceeds by stipulating that, as an intermediate step, each generated code is itself subject to further coding operations by which any inherent redundancies are removed. So in our current example, '$a\ \alpha\ a\ \alpha\ a\ \alpha\ a\ \alpha$' can be recoded into a form with fewer symbols such as '$4 * (a\ \alpha)$' and this is now known as the **end-code**. Three such redundancy reducing operations have been discussed repeatedly:

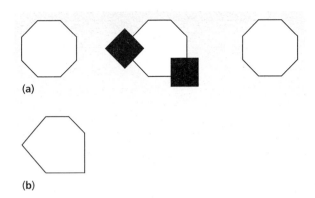

**Figure 6.3 The minimum principle in action?**
The minimum principle predicts that the central figure in
(a) will be seen as in (b). This is because the end-code is
shorter for two straight lines intersecting at a right angle
than is the end-code for three lines and two angles.
Alternatively you may gain the impression of a regular
octagon. (This demonstration might work best when (b) is
covered up and you ask a naïve friend to report what they
see in (a).)
*Source*: Kanizsa, G. (1985). Seeing and thinking. *Acta
Psychologica*, *59*, 23–33 (fig. 3, p. 30). Reproduced with
permission from Elsevier.

1. *Iteration* – the code '*aa*' can be replaced with the
   end-code '*2 \* (a)*'. In other words, $2 \times a$ (2 times *a*).
2. *Symmetry* – the code '*abcba*' can be replaced with
   '*S[(a)(b),(c)]*'. In other words, *c* is centred relative
   to *ab* and *ba*.
3. *Alternation* – the code '*abac*' can be replaced with
   '*<(a)>/<(b)(c)>*'.

For our purposes we do not have to be too concerned with these details because the general point
is that we are trying to minimise the primitive code
that is being used to describe the shape. We do this by
removing any redundancy in the generated codes. For
instance, the text 'I LUV U' (i.e., seven characters) is a
compressed form of 'I LOVE YOU' (i.e., ten characters).
We have transcribed the message of ten characters into
a shorter form (of seven characters) which retains all
of the information contained in the original.

## Pinpoint question 6.1

**How might an equilateral triangle be represented by
a primitive code?**

However, we do have a problem here since, given
that there may be more than one end-code for a given
figure, a decision has to be made about which is the
preferred code. The basic idea now is that the preferred

code corresponds to the shortest code and the shortest
code is the one that contains the smallest number of
primitive symbols. In an early version of the theory each
end-code was assigned a number known as the **structural information load** (SIL) (Buffart, Leeuwenberg,
& Restle, 1983) which corresponds to the number
of primitive symbols in the end-code. The preferred
interpretation of the figure was therefore given by the
shortest code.

In the above three cases given, only the primitive
symbols are counted (i.e., the italicised lower-case letters); consequently, the SIL for the iteration example
is 1, for the symmetry example it is 3 and for the
alternation example it is also 3. In each case there is
a saving in the end-code over the number of initial
letters derived from the input patterns. In this way
and because we have generated a shorter code than the
original, we have demonstrated how the minimum
principle could be working. We choose the shortest
code – the code with no redundancies – and it is this
that indicates the assumed nature of the perceptual
coding operations. The theory therefore provides an
example of how perceptual coding is governed by the
minimum principle.

One way of thinking about this is to realise that
the sorts of codings that the theory is concerned with
are analogous to the sorts of commands that could be
given to a computer controlled graph plotter to trace
out the contour of a shape. Each symbol defines a
particular plotting operation and the complete code
specifies the entire program to draw the figure. An
important point about such codings is that whatever
reads the code must be able to retrieve a veridical
(truthful) specification of the input from the code.
The plotter must be able to reproduce the figure given
the code. What this means is that, regardless of how
compact the code is, it must preserve enough information so that the original figure can be reproduced
from it. There would be little point in generating a
short code for some stimulus if critical aspects of the
stimulus were lost in the process.

So, according to SIT, the reason that the overlapping squares interpretation of Figure 6.1a is preferred
is that this interpretation yields the shortest code.
Indeed, empirical support for the theory was provided
by Buffart et al. (1983). Various sorts of overlapping
figures, of the sort shown in Figure 6.1a, were constructed and hard copies of the figures were individually presented to participants. The participants were
then asked how they interpreted the figures by providing figural completions – for instance, is the impression of overlapping figures or is the impression of a

chair shape abutting a square? Each completion was then assessed against two plausible solutions for the given item: one with a low SIL (overlapping squares) and one with a higher SIL (abutting shapes). Support for SIT, and its formalism of the minimum principle, was provided by the fact that approximately 96 per cent of the participants generated responses in line with the lower SIL interpretation.

## Critical appraisal of SIT

Despite such positive beginnings, confidence in the particular coding scheme set out in SIT has been somewhat undermined since the publication of this early empirical study. First Pomerantz and Kubovy (1986) were able to suggest the same preferred interpretation of Figure 6.1a as SIT, but on the basis of a different set of coding principles. On these grounds, the choices participants make about interpreting line drawings do not provide unequivocal support for SIT.

Second, Peterson and Hochberg (1983) showed that interpretations of line figures could be critically affected by whereabouts participants were told to fixate (see Figure 6.4). If you recall the duck/rabbit illusion from Chapter 5 (see Figure 5.8), you get a stronger sense of a duck if you focus on the left-hand side of the picture and a stronger sense of a rabbit if you focus on the right-hand side. Critically SIT, as originally conceived, provides no insights as to how or why this happens. So this point is not so much about the theory being wrong but it being incapable of explaining related phenomena. What is the point of a theory of gravity that applies only to pancakes and house bricks but not to articles of discarded clothing? Indeed, Peterson and Hochberg (1983) found that participants were most likely to report an overlapping squares impression of Figure 6.1a when they fixated the uppermost intersection. However, if they were instructed to fixate the lower intersection, the impression was of a chair shape in front of a square. So depending on where you fixate, you can gain either the impression of overlapping squares, or the impression of a chair being in front of a square.

This particular finding was taken to be at odds with SIT as originally conceived: regardless of where the participant fixates, the minimum code is the minimum code, and point of fixation should not matter. In contrast, Peterson and Hochberg (1983) took their findings to undermine any notion of the application of a *global* minimum principle that determines a coding of the entire stimulus pattern. Participants' impressions of the figures seemed to depend critically

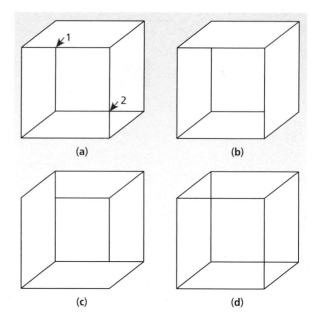

**Figure 6.4 The multi-stability of perception**
In (d) the figure is the classic Necker cube – interpretation of the cube reverses over time (see previous discussion in Chapter 5). The drawing is rendered unambiguous in (b) and (c). (a) is more intriguing. If intersection 1 is fixated a stable percept is achieved however if intersection 2 is fixated then the interpretation of the figure is less stable. The depth information at this junction is ambiguous and the figure begins to flip. (Some people sometimes report figure (a) 'flipping' into an impossible case.)

*Source*: Peterson, M. A., & Hochberg, J. (1983). Opposed-set measurement procedure: A quantitative analysis of the role of local cues and intention in form perception. *Journal of Experimental Psychology: Human Perception and Performance*, 9, 183–193 (fig. 1, p. 184). Reproduced with permission from APA.

on the current analysis of some sub-part of the figures. This was taken to bolster the view that the overall impression of a figure is essentially built up from a kind of piecemeal analysis of its local parts. As Hochberg (2003) has noted, such demonstrations rule out 'any exclusive whole-based simplicity or minimum principle' (p. 220). Such issues also impinge on the perception of impossible figures (see Figure 6.5).

What impossible figures demonstrate is that when the individual parts are scrutinised nothing seems awry; it is only when attempting to derive a coherent interpretation of the whole figure that problems occur. This is consistent with the piecemeal approach to vision that Hochberg (1981, 2003) discussed. It is assumed that the interpretation of any one part is generated independently of others. As a result there is no guarantee that the set of local interpretations

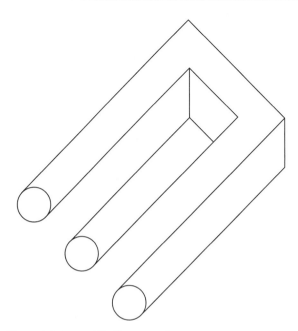

**Figure 6.5 Impossible figures and scenes**
A classic impossible figure sometimes known as the 'Devil's pitchfork'. Each local aspect of the figure makes perfect visual sense on its own – it is only when attempts are made to assemble the local parts into a coherent whole that problems abound.

would correspond to the parts of any naturally occurring object. Each local interpretation is plausible, but collectively these just do not fit together! → See 'What have we learnt?', below.

## The likelihood principle

As we have just noted, a particular strength of the minimum principle is that it can be specified with precision. This means that very clear predictions can be made. The very particular coding principles embodied in SIT stand as a testament to this. Such principles have given rise to detailed empirical predictions, and although such predictions have not received unanimous support, the minimum principle, as embodied in SIT, is clearly testable. It is pertinent to ask, therefore, if there is any way that we might be able to get a similarly tight grip on the likelihood principle. Unsurprisingly, the answer to this is 'Yes'. To appreciate this, though, we need to consider a different example of a perceptual inference provided by Gigerenzer and Murray (1987, p. 88). According to them, one characterisation of the likelihood principle is provided in the following so-called 'probabilistic syllogism' (we will learn much more about syllogisms in Chapter 15 but, for now, let us just remind ourselves from Chapter 5 that it is a well-formed statement comprising two premises and a conclusion):

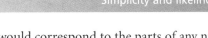

### → What have we learnt?

On the basis of the more recent data, concerns have been raised over any simple application of the minimum principle, and more particularly, serious concerns have also been aroused over the details of SIT. This does not mean that we ought to abandon the whole SIT framework, for, as we shall see (when we discuss mental representation in the next chapter), the basic notions about the nature of perceptual encoding of shape remain of interest. All that has been concluded is that the particular instantiation of the minimum principle as couched in terms of SIT appears wanting. Indeed, the details of the SIT formalism need not detain us too long because the theory appears to be in a constant state of flux (see, for example, the most recent incarnation of the theory – the 'holographic theory' – by van der Helm & Leeuwenberg, 1996). It seems that, in order to accommodate freshly acquired data, the theory merely expands to incorporate more and more coding principles. However, even with these more recent embellishments, the general framework for thinking has been undermined by subsequent empirical tests (Olivers, Chater & Watson, 2004; Pothos & Ward, 2000; Wagemans, 1999). In such cases there does come a point at which a basic rethink is required and perhaps this time has now come.

In conclusion, the general SIT framework for thinking about perceptual analysis has had very mixed success and it is no longer tenable as originally conceived. This is not to argue that the minimum principle is, *in general*, of little worth, but merely that the specific instantiation of the minimum principle in SIT has repeatedly been shown to be inadequate. The strength of the theory is that it has been specified in sufficient detail that it has generated fairly precise and testable predictions. Unfortunately this strength has turned out to be a fatal weakness because these predictions have failed to be confirmed. The theory does a relatively poor job in accounting for the relevant data.

*Major premise:* The retinal input D (the sensory data) normally occurs when the external object H (the hypothesis – the external object) is present.
*Minor premise:* D is present.
*Conclusion:* Therefore the external object H is present.

This kind of syllogism sets out quite precisely the sort of perceptual inference that is assumed to underpin the attempt to link a representation of the proximal stimulus with the actual distal stimulus. In the last chapter, we were introduced to the notion of perceptual inference on the understanding that this provides one characterisation of how it is that the perceptual system takes a stimulus representation and interprets it. The term 'probabilistic' is used here because of the term 'normally' in the major premise. The reasoning can be summarised along the following lines:

*Major premise:* That kind of spot of light normally occurs when the usherette is waving her torch around.
*Minor premise:* You can see the spot of light.
*Conclusion:* Therefore the usherette is waving her torch around.

Remember (from Chapter 5), this form of 'reasoning' is known as unconscious inference. There is no implication that you are actually consciously aware that any form of *perceptual* problem solving is going on as you perceive the world. Nor is the assumption that there is any way in which you might be able to control such perceptual operations. All that is being asserted is that it is one way to characterise the operations undertaken by the perceptual system. Importantly, such a view only makes any sense if a basic poverty of the stimulus argument is also accepted (see Chapter 5).

On the understanding that the proximal stimulus is an under-specification of the distal stimulus, it is taken to be a matter of fact that there is a **many-to-one mapping** between the possible distal causes and the proximal stimulus. More than one distal stimulus is taken to be consistent with this particular proximal stimulation (the poverty of the stimulus reappears and we're back to our fork handles). This means that for any given input there will be more than one plausible hypothesis as to its distal cause (does the picture contain two overlapping squares or a chair shape and a square abutting one another?).

The poverty of the stimulus is crucial here because if it were the case that every proximal stimulus un-ambiguously signalled its own unique distal stimulus,

then there would be no need to make an inference – D always occurs when object H is present so D means that H is present. The likelihood principle is not a certainty principle – H is the most likely cause of D. On these grounds the perceptual system must choose between these different interpretations of the input and decide what is actually out there. What is the most likely distal stimulus (the most likely hypothesis) given the proximal stimulus (the data)? According to the likelihood principle, the system chooses the hypothesis that is most likely given the data.

### Pinpoint question 6.2

**As you scan through a letter from the gas board, on the basis of the likelihood principle, are you more likely to read that you owe the gas board money, or that they owe you money?**

Put bluntly, if the human perceptual system has evolved according to the likelihood principle then its default position is to conclude that any given proximal stimulus is caused by the most likely distal stimulus given the current sensory stimulation. By this view the aim is to establish the most likely distal stimulus for every proximal stimulus. There is no acknowledgement in this account of simplicity of coding, and because of this it is typically taken to stand in contrast with the minimum principle. However, more recently the idea that the two principles are fundamentally different from one another has been challenged by Chater (1996).

**structural information theory** A model originated by Boselie and Leeuwenberg (1986) which attempts to operationalise how the minimum principle might work in vision.

**primitive symbol** The atomic symbolic unit contained in a primitive code.

**primitive code** According to the structural information theory (Boselie and Leeuwenberg, 1986), a collection of primitive symbols that are used in generating the internal code for a shape.

**end-code** According to SIT, the end-code is the ultimate version of an internal description of a shape when all of the redundancy reducing operations have been carried out.

**structural information load** The number of primitive symbols contained within an end-code.

**many-to-one mapping** When a single proximal stimulus may have been produced by several distal causes. The many distal causes map onto the one proximal stimulus.

## Simplicity and likelihood reconsidered

So we may ask, to what degree is this form of characterisation of perception different from that of the minimum principle? Are the minimum principle and the likelihood principle really that fundamentally different from one another? A thorough treatment of these issues is outside the scope of this book, but what Chater (1996) has claimed to have demonstrated is that, given basic tenets of information theory (see Chapter 2), the minimum principle and the likelihood principle can be shown to be mathematically equivalent. Essentially, both principles are about minimising the uncertainty over what actual state of the world (the distal stimulus) caused this particular sensory data (the proximal stimulus). When examined at a mathematical level, Chater (1996) has shown that both principles reduce to the same sort of equation. Clearly, if this conclusion is revealing a fundamental truth, then it casts the long-running debate over the relative importance of the two principles in rather poor light. There is little point in trying to devise experiments that attempt to favour one principle of perceptual organisation selectively over the other because at a deep level the principles are the same.

A very detailed critique of these ideas has been provided by van der Helm (2000), but a full consideration of these would take us far from present concerns. However, following on from van der Helm's exploration of the ideas, it seems that all Chater has done is show how the minimum principle and the likelihood principle can be conceived as being equivalent when a very particular mathematical argument is made. Unless this argument can be shown to be water-tight, which van der Helm (2000) has disputed, then there are grounds for continuing to try to collect selective evidence favouring one or other of the principles. The two principles may not reduce to a single mathematical form after all.

More critically, though, and despite these concerns over mathematical equivalence, we may still ask questions about how sensible the principles are at a higher level. The invitation now is to ask deeper questions about the nature of perception and one way forward is to consider the issues from an evolutionary perspective. Why has the perceptual system evolved in the way that it has done? What is the ultimate purpose of the perceptual system? In refocusing attention in this way it is useful to reintroduce Marr's (1982) framework for thinking (see Chapter 1). At the level of the representation and the algorithm we are interested in questions concerned with how particular functions are implemented – secure the most simple interpretation vs. secure the most likely interpretation. At the level of the computational theory, though, we may ask why a given function might be implemented after all. In the present case, it may turn out that decisions about the level of the representation and the algorithm may be solved by taking a hard look at the computational level. Has the human perceptual system evolved so that it is governed by principles of simplicity or by principles of likelihood? Are we better able to survive because we perceive the most simple of things or because we perceive the most likely of things?

## Simplicity, likelihood and the nature of perception

In exploring Chater's arguments, van der Helm (2000) introduced the notion of evolutionary usefulness, and used this to appraise the minimum and likelihood principles. He concluded that, on evolutionary grounds, the minimum principle ought to be favoured over the likelihood principle. In summary, he asserted that whereas the likelihood principle operates best within the constraints of this particular world, the minimum principle can operate in any particular world. Therefore the minimum principle is more useful because it is not constrained by the environment. Caution is perhaps warranted, however, in accepting this conclusion too readily. We need to be clear. What sort of perceptual system has actually evolved? Has the system evolved to generate short codes? Or has the system evolved to convey the most likely codes? Obviously there are benefits to both sorts of system, but which of these best characterises the human perceptual system?

### Are short codes all they are cracked up to be?

First consider the short codes system: one advantage of generating short codes is that savings are made in transmission times. Think in terms of a standard PC Zip file. If you save a large document on your computer you can use an encryption program such as Zip to remove redundancies in the file and hence save a much smaller compressed file. The Zip program has generated a file containing shorter codes than is contained in the original document. As anyone who still accesses the internet over a modem line knows, transmission times can be painfully slow, so the benefits of accessing compressed documents becomes immediately apparent. It is quicker to download a small than a large file, hence the usefulness of generating short codes – it is quicker to download the Zip file than the original document. Using this analogy it can be seen that the perceptual system might also benefit from short codes in terms of transmission times. It is much better (more adaptively useful) to have a quicker perceptual system than a slower one.

Given these sentiments, there are apparent benefits in using short codes. However, a down side of using short codes – one that is hardly ever mentioned – is that at some point they need to be *decompressed* and this takes time. So although short codes may facilitate transmission times, they do carry a processing overhead. Generally speaking, the more compressed a message is, the longer it will take to decompress it. So although generating short codes can confer some processing advantages, these may also carry a significant cost.

More pointed, perhaps, is the fact that this desire to generate short codes may be at odds with the way the nervous system actually operates. In modern-day digital computers, and other forms of telecommunication devices (such as mobile phones), it is vital to compress the last drop of redundancy out of the signals that are transmitted (small is indeed beautiful). As our discussion of SIT has shown, it is easier to transmit '*1000000 x a*' than one million *a*s. However, such forms of optimisation may not provide the most adequate model for the sort of coding undertaken in the nervous system (for more on this see Barlow, 2001). Perceptual codes may be highly redundant for good reasons. Nerve cells may operate unreliably or they may become damaged. If the message is to have any success in getting through then the system may have to operate in a highly redundant fashion. Think about it: if you really want to ensure that your document gets through, then fax it, send it as an e-mail attachment and send a hard copy. Each of these forms of transmissions is redundant with respect to the others because they are all dealing with the same message. However, an advantage of this sort of redundancy is that the chances of the message getting through are increased.

**Pinpoint question 6.3**

Why are redundancies in any information processing system useful?

## The advantages of the likelihood principle

In contrast, what of a system that has evolved to convey the most likely codes? Clearly such a system will face problems in cases where the most likely object is not actually present. The spot of light in the cinema is not given off by the usherette's torch but by someone's mobile phone. However, if the system has evolved to prioritise the most likely hypothesis about the distal stimulus (the torch) given this particular proximal stimulus (the spot of light), then this may be seen to be very advantageous. By definition it will work effectively most of the time. This leads to a rather striking conclusion that it is likelihood rather than simplicity that is the fundamental factor: a conclusion that is diametrically opposed to that put forward by van der Helm (2000). How might we might provide further weight to this conclusion?

Well, as Sutherland (1988) stated, in relation to visual perception, 'we must as far as possible see what is really there and that to be effective vision must follow the likelihood principle'. Moreover, 'In so far as the minimum principle operates, it surely does so only because it usually gives rise to the perceptual representation that is most likely to correspond with the real world' (p. 384). Although these comments are limited to vision, they of course apply to perception in general. The claim is that if the perceptual system is seen to operate with short codes this will be because these are in the service of providing a perceptual representation that specifies the most likely distal cause. By this view it is the likelihood principle that is paramount. If the minimum principle is seen to operate then it does so in helping achieve a perceptual representation that codes the most likely cause.

One concrete example helps here. Consider the shape Y; if you sketch this out on a piece of paper you will see that there are two plausible interpretations of the shape: a protruding corner of, say, a table, or a receding corner of, say, a room. Let us now assume (for the sake of argument) that that corner of the room results in a shorter code than the corner of the table. According to the minimum principle, Y will always be interpreted as signalling a room corner. However, on the assumption that there are a lot more tables than rooms, it seems plausible that the most likely interpretation of Y is as a corner of a table. Nevertheless, if a room corner results in a shorter code then this will be the favoured interpretation. Such a contrived example shows that when the minimum principle and the likelihood principle are placed in opposition to one another it is difficult to conceive of why the perceptual system would have evolved to operationalise the minimum principle.

To hammer this point home Sutherland (1988) set out various examples that prove difficult to reconcile with the minimum principle and two are repeated here:

1. A general assumption is that light tends to come from above and this determines which aspects of the stimulus are seen as hollows and which are seen as protuberances. The minimum principle fails to account for this because light coming from above is no simpler than light from below, yet the perceptual bias of light shining down on us determines the interpretation that is made.

2. Smaller areas tend to be classified as figure and larger areas tend to be classified as background. In addition, areas containing concavities tend to be seen as figure and areas containing convex regions tend to be seen as ground. The minimum principle provides no account of either of these facts yet they are perfectly in line with the notion that these interpretations are most likely given the world we inhabit.

For some, therefore, the importance of the likelihood principle is overwhelming. ➜ See 'What have we learnt?', below.

## ➜ What have we learnt?

The debate continues over which of the minimum and likelihood principles best characterises perception and, historically, the practice has been to provide examples that can be readily accounted for by one principle but prove problematic for the other. However, Chater's (1996) proof of equivalence casts some considerable doubt on the usefulness of continuing in that vein. How can you possibly refute one principle without refuting both? What we have done, however, is extend the argument a little and have asked more far-reaching questions about evolutionary usefulness. When framed in these terms, it seems that there are good grounds for arguing for the primacy of the likelihood principle. If the minimum principle does actually operate in perception, it does so because this aids in the derivation of the most likely environmental cause of the current sensory stimulation. There seems little point to a system that is primarily driven by a desire to derive short codes.

A rather definite position has been taken on the debate over the minimum principle vs. the likelihood principle with a rather strong case being built for favouring the likelihood principle. The arguments for this conclusion seem compelling, but there are, of course, some grounds for caution. Alongside the various examples that have been taken to support one principle over the other selectively, examples have been discussed that prove difficult for both principles. Figure 6.4a provides a case in point. Although the figure is perfectly consistent with a view of a real object, it is also possible to get into a bit of fix and see it as an impossible object. According to Pomerantz and Kubovy (1986, pp. 36–27), 'many observers report spontaneous and in fact indifferent perceptual alternations between the possible and impossible interpretations'. Both the minimum principle and likelihood principle favour the plausible readings of the figure and neither predicts the impossible impressions.

Kanizsa (1985) has also argued that demonstrations, such as those contained in Figure 6.4a and Figure 6.6, indicate that the situation is perhaps much more complex than proponents of the minimum principle and proponents of the likelihood principle would have us believe. He used such demonstrations to argue that the visual system works according to 'autonomous principles of organization' (p. 33) that are independent of logic, expectations and knowledge. By this view, perception is a much more complex process than any single-principle doctrine would have us believe.

**Figure 6.6 Not well parked**
Kanizsa's car in the woods (from Kanizsa, 1985).

*Source*: Kanizsa, G. (1985). Seeing and thinking. *Acta Psychologica*, *59*, 23–33 (fig. 8, p. 32). Reproduced with permission from Elsevier.

## Global-to-local processing

At a very basic level the minimum principle vs. likelihood principle debate is about what, fundamentally, the perceptual system is trying to achieve – short codes or codes that specify the most likely distal stimulus given the current proximal stimulus. In considering the issues, simple 2D shape perception has been the main battleground – two overlapping squares, or a chair and a square? Given this rather narrow context, it is easy to come away with a rather narrow view of how perception operates. The different adversarial camps seem to propagate a rather rigid view in which invariably the system generates either the shortest or the likeliest reading of the input in a completely slavish fashion. Such a perspective, though, avoids any serious discussion of active processes in vision, and as we saw towards the end of Chapter 5, this is probably an oversight.

It seems that, to achieve a better understanding of what is going on, we would be well advised to think in terms of both active and passive perceptual processes. Such advice stems from consideration of the suggest/inquire account of perception (Broadbent, 1977; Navon, 1977, 1981). To reiterate, according to this view there is an initial passive perceptual analysis stage. This processes information that arrives at the senses and goes on to *suggest* possible interpretations of the environment. This passive stage is then followed by an active stage in which the most promising interpretation is followed by interrogation of the proximal stimulus to check whether the initial suggestion is sensible. In this respect, we might wish to adopt a middle ground and assume that the minimum principle vs. likelihood principle debate only addresses issues concerning the initial passive stage.

In fleshing out the suggest/inquire account of perception, it has been asserted that perceptual processing proceeds in a so-called global-to-local manner (Broadbent, 1977; Navon, 2003). So to get a better handle on the suggest/inquire account it is important to understand what is meant by **global-to-local processing**. This sort of idea has been originally attributed

**Figure 6.7 Stood up again?**
What do you notice about this scene? Which aspects do you note first and which aspects become apparent later?

to the followers of the Gestalt movement (Kohler, 1930/1971; Wertheimer, 1925/1967). According to them, any given stimulus can be conceived as comprising a whole (the Gestalt) together with constituent parts. So for instance, the human body (the whole) possesses an overall shape but this is made up of a head, various limbs and a torso (the parts); a whistled tune contains an overall melody (the whole) but this can be decomposed into individual notes (the parts).

According to Palmer and Kimchi (1986), not only did the Gestalt theorists claim that the perceived object (the whole) is different from the sum of the parts, but also that the whole is perceived prior to its parts. We see the wood before the individual trees. At a functional level, the claim is that there is a strict ordering to perceptual processes – the overall nature of the stimulus is recovered prior to its constituent parts. We may refer to this assertion as a statement about **global precedence**: the global nature of the stimulus becomes apparent prior to the nature of its local constituents. (A small point perhaps, but as Navon (1981) has stated, the term 'global' should not be confused with the term 'whole' because a whole comprises both global and local aspects; p. 2.) The whole emerges from consideration of both the global and local characteristics.

## For example . . .

Take a quick look at Figure 6.7. How would you immediately describe the scene? It's a dinner table, right? Exactly – no trickery this time! What about if you take another look at the scene – what do you see now? It looks like there's bread in one of the bowls, and some salt and pepper shakers behind the bottle of wine too. What's that blue object in the left-hand corner – is it a yoga ball? If you thought like this, it seems you were just carrying out some global-to-local processing of your own.

```
S S S S        H H H H H        O O O O O
S              H                O
S              H                O
S S S S        H H H H H        O O O O O
      S                H                O
      S                H                O
S S S S        H H H H H        O O O O O


H       H      S       S        O       O
H       H      S       S        O       O
H       H      S       S        O       O
H H H H H      S S S S S        O O O O O
H       H      S       S        O       O
H       H      S       S        O       O
H       H      S       S        O       O

Consistent     Inconsistent         Neutral
```

**Figure 6.8 Examples of composite letters as used in a typical global-to-local processing experiment**

## Experiments with compound letters

In pursing this line of inquiry, Navon (1977) devised a novel stimulus known as a **compound letter** (i.e., large letter made of small letters) and used this sort of stimulus in various identification tasks (see Figure 6.8). With compound letters the identities of the large, global letter (the whole) and the small, local letters (the parts) can be varied independently of one another. Navon's (1977) third experiment is of main interest here.

There were two main conditions in this experiment: in the global condition, on each trial a compound letter was presented and participants had to respond (under RT instructions) to the identity of the large letter; in the local condition, participants had to respond to the identity of the small letters. Although the large and small letters could be the same as one another, or different from one another, all of the small letters shared the same identity. Participants had to make one key press to the letter S and another to the letter H. In the global condition, the large letters (*H* or *S*) were composed of Hs, Ss, or Os, whereas in the local condition, Hs, Ss, and Os were composed of Hs, or Ss. Performance was compared across these two conditions and across three general sorts of trials.

On consistent trials the identity of the global and local letters were the same (e.g., an S made up of Ss). Neutral trials were those when an O occurred at the global level in the local condition and at the local level in the global condition. Os were designated neutral because the participant never had to base a response on detecting this letter. Inconsistent trials were those where an H was made of Ss or where an S was made of Hs. Consistency was therefore defined according to

whether the local and global letters shared the same identity. On each trial, the global letter appeared randomly for a very brief period of time (i.e., for only 40 ms) in one of the quadrants of the visual display (in the *periphery*). It was then masked with a large square filled with dots – yes, this is another case of backward masking (see Chapter 3).

The results of the experiments can be summarised thus. First, responses to the global letters were faster overall than responses to local letters. This effect is typically referred to as the **global advantage**. Second, within the local condition, responses to inconsistent trials were slower than either responses to neutral or consistent trials. This effect is typically referred to as **global-to-local interference** and is generally interpreted as showing that the identity of the global letter somehow interferes with the processing of the local letters. Finally there was no effect of inconsistency on RTs to the global letters; there was no **local-to-global interference**. When participants were responding to the identity of the global letter they were not slowed in cases where the local letter and the global letter signalled different responses.

### Evidence for global-to-local processing?

Taken together, these results support the idea that the whole is perceived both prior to, and independently of, the parts. The overall global advantage shows that participants were faster in making decisions to the global letter than the local letter. This is consistent with the notion of global precedence. In addition the pattern of interference effects converges on the same conclusion. Perhaps the simplest way to understand this is again in terms of the operation of some form of internal letter detectors. Take for example a large S composed of Hs. On presentation of the compound letter both the S and H detectors will become activated. However, according to the global precedence, the global S detector will become activated prior to the local H detector. In the global condition this means that global RTs will be shorter than local RTs because of the relative speed of activation of the respective letter detectors. Moreover, on this simple speed-of-processing account there is no reason to assume that the identity of the local letter should in any way interfere with responses to the local letter. The global letter detector always becomes activated first, hence a decision and response about the global letter can be elicited quickly.

Using a similar logic there is also every reason to assume that there will be global-to-local interference in the local condition. By the simple speed-of-processing

**For example . . .**

Similar forms of conflicting information can be created at tea time using a tasty combination of spaghetti loops and ravioli (see Figure 6.9). Under which conditions would global-to-local interference occur here?

**Figure 6.9 Navon (1977) in the kitchen: global-to-local processing with spaghetti loops**

account the idea is that the identity of the global letter becomes available prior to that of the local letters so the decision stage of processing is having to ignore or discount this information because in the local condition the task is to respond to the identity of the local letters. Therefore the system is, in a sense, having to wait around until the local letter detector fires and provides the correct information upon which to base a response. At this point in time the decision stage really has to put some work in. It now has conflicting information to resolve in order to make the correct response, since the global processor is screaming S while the local processor is shouting H. The global-to-local interference arises because of having to resolve this conflict.

## Accounting for global-to-local processing

As you can probably imagine, there are many and various sorts of accounts of processing that can be contemplated, but Navon (1981) focused on just two. For instance, in the strictly serial account, all of the tests for the global letter run to completion before any mental work can be expended on the local letter (see

Figure 6.10a). Alternatively, processing may proceed in a parallel fashion such that both the global and local letter detectors operate at the same time but that the so-called rise time for the activation of the global letter detector is shorter than the rise time for the activation of the local letter detector (see Figure 6.10b). Indeed this parallel processing account is sometimes referred to as a **simple horse-race account** of processing. By this view there is a global letter horse and a local letter horse. Stimulus onset signals the start of the race and both horses set off: the one that reaches the finishing line first wins the race.

It should come as no surprise that subsequent research with compound letters has variously supported,

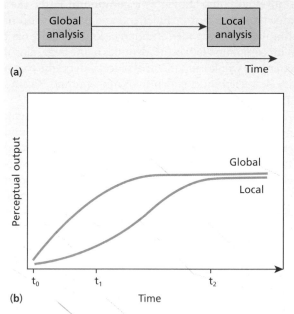

(a)

(b)

**Figure 6.10 Contrasting views of global and local processing**
(a) provides a simple sequential stage account of global-to-local processing. (b) provides a perhaps more plausible parallel account in which the global precedence arises because of the relative speeds with which global and local characteristics of a stimulus are recovered. Local aspects are recovered more slowly than global aspects.

*Source*: Navon, D. (1981). The forest revisited: More on global processing. *Psychological Research*, *43*, 1–32 (fig. 3a and b, p. 6). Reproduced with kind permission from Springer Science and Business Media.

rejected or modified the original account. For instance, the ensuing research has shown that the pattern of effects can change as a function of a variety of task demands and display factors. These include the following:

- Sparsity of the local elements (e.g., Martin, 1979; Navon, 1983b). This factor refers to how many local elements are used to define the global letters.
- The visual angle sub-tended by the stimulus (Amirkhiabani & Lovegrove, 1996; Kinchla & Wolfe, 1979; Lamb & Robertson, 1988). This is a technical way of referring to how big the stimuli are.
- The retinal position of the letters (Amirkhiabani & Lovegrove, 1996; Grice, Canham & Burroughs, 1983; Hoffman, 1980; Lamb & Robertson, 1988; Navon & Norman, 1983; Pomerantz, 1983). This refers to where the letters were positioned relative to the fixation.

- The exposure duration/degree of masking used (e.g., Paquet & Merikle, 1984). How long were the letters presented for? Was the letter presentation curtailed by a mask? (See Table 6.1 for a summary of the relevant findings and Kimchi (1992) for a much more extensive review.)

The aims of this large body of research were to try to establish (i) if the basic Navon effects with composite letters are replicable and (ii) the conditions under which the effects occur/break down. The ultimate goal is to use such empirical techniques to bolster the theoretical conjecture that perception in the real world proceeds in an essentially crude-to-fine fashion. First you get the overall gist of the thing out there and then you get the details. As you can see from Table 6.1, this conclusion provides a very reasonable account of the basic effects – generally speaking, the global advantage

**Table 6.1** A brief sample of studies that have examined performance in classifying composite letters.

| Study | Display positional characteristics | Display duration (in ms) | Local element density | Overall speed of response | Interference |
|---|---|---|---|---|---|
| Navon (1977) | P | 40+ | D | G < L | GI only |
| Navon and Norman (1983) | 1. Large (P) | 150 | D | G < L | GI = LI |
| | 2. Small (C) | 150 | D | G < L | GI only |
| Paquet and Merikle (1984) | C | 10 | D | G < L | GI only |
| | C | 40+ | D | G < L | GI = LI |
| Martin (1979) | P | 100 | D | G < L | GI > LI |
| | P | 100 | S | G = L | GI = LI |
| Grice et al. (1983) | P | Unlimited | D | G < L | GI > LI |
| | C | Unlimited | D | G = L | GI = LI |
| Kinchla and Wolfe (1979) | 1. Large | 100 | D | L < G | |
| | 2. Small | 100 | D | G < L | |
| Pomerantz (1983) | P | Unlimited | D | G < L | GI > LI |
| | C | Unlimited | D | G <= L | LI = GI |
| Hughes, Layton, Baird and Lester (1984) | P | Unlimited | D | G < L | GI only |
| Boles (1984) | P | 150 | D | G < L | GI > LI |
| Lamb and Robertson (1988) | 1. P | 100 | D | G < L | GI > LI |
| | C | 100 | D | G <= L | GI = L |
| | 2. C | 100 | D | L < G | LI > GI |

Display positional characteristics – this refers to the overall size of the compound letter and whereabouts it was presented in the display, that is, either centrally (C) at fixation or somewhere unpredictably in the periphery (P).
Local element density – this refers to the spacing and number of local letters contained in the compound letter – either sparse (S) or dense (D).
Overall speed of response – this refers to the overall speed of response in the global and local conditions (G < L – indicates the presence of a global advantage; L < G – indicates the presence of a local advantage).
Interference – GI refers to global-to-local interference; LI refers to local-to-global interference.

is robust and generally speaking global-to-local interference is typically stronger or as strong as local-to-global interference.

## Pinpoint question 6.4

**When would a local advantage occur?**

## Navon's (2003) account of global-to-local processing

However, Navon (2003) quite openly discussed the fact that it is probably a misconception to think in terms of some invariant form of global precedence. It is only to be expected that performance can be modulated by other task demands and display characteristics. It is

more appropriate to view global precedence as being indicative of a general disposition of the perceptual system to favour wholes over parts. According to Navon (2003, p. 282), it is only plausible to assume that the perceptual system embodies 'a built-in formation preference . . . to select cluster properties rather than element properties provided that the cluster makes up a good form or a familiar pattern'. How might such a preference operate?

In order to address this question the discussion shifts from modes of perceptual processing to a consideration of how knowledge about objects is stored in memory. By this view, knowledge of a particular object is captured in something known as an **object schema**. An object schema is taken to be the long-term memory representation of a familiar object (see Figure 6.11). Aligned to this is the idea that this form

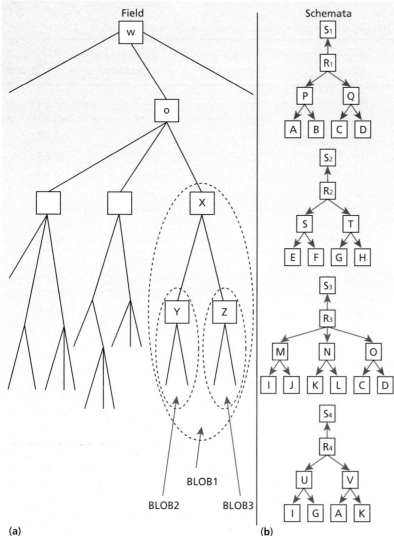

(a)

(b)

**Figure 6.11 Hierarchical representations of composite objects in a cluttered scene**
(a) provides a schematic representation of the hierarchical nature of a cluttered scene. (b) provides an illustration of schemata as held in long-term memory. The whole field *w* is composed of a series of objects (*o*), each of which is composed of a set of componential parts (*X*, *Y*, *Z*). The problem is to try to secure a match between the structures (blobs) in the field and the appropriate object schemata as stored in long-term memory. In the right of the diagram are four object schemata (i.e., $S_1$, $S_2$, $S_3$ and $S_4$). The issue is whether $S_1$ is activated by matching *X* with $R_1$ or because of matching *Y* with *P*. According to global addressability it is the latter that prevails – 'global constituents serve as entry points to their schemata' (Navon, 2003, p. 284).

*Source*: Navon, D. (2003). What does a compound letter tell the psychologist's mind? *Acta Psychologica*, *114*, 273–309 (fig. 2, p. 283). Reproduced with permission from Elsevier.

of knowledge is captured via hierarchical structures or **tree structure**s (as shown in Figure 6.11). This sort of representation comprises nodes (the bottom-most nodes are known as leaves) and connections between nodes (branches). Each node corresponds to a particular aspect of the object whereby the highest node in the tree specifies the identity of the object and the nodes further down the tree specify parts of the object. The constituent nature of this representation corresponds to the structure of the object being described. So the relation between a superordinate and its subordinate nodes would correspond to the constituency relations that hold between the global and local aspects. To contrive an example: the human body schemata would contain one node specifying 'face' which in turn would connect with various subordinate nodes for 'eyes', 'nose', 'mouth', 'ears', etc.

The more general claim therefore is that knowledge of familiar objects is captured in some form of knowledge store that comprises object schemata. For Navon (2003), a central idea is known as **global addressability** (p. 284). Global addressability is a statement about how contact is made between incoming stimulus information and the knowledge store. Initial entry to the store progresses such that the current input is presumed to be the global constituent of some object schema rather than the local constituent. That is, the system is set up to treat each stimulus as being an object in and of its own right. For example, consider Figure 6.12. At a literal level this is simply a montage comprising various fruit and vegetables; however, it is the global impression of a face that is most apparent. As Navon (2003) argued, it seems unlikely that this face impression is driven by analysis of the 'facial' features because these are most appropriately matched with the corresponding schemata for fruit and vegetables. Using the principle of global addressability it is claimed that 'the global constituents of the face schema are invoked by the overall pattern' (p. 284). The face is seen, not the fruit.

In more familiar terms the general view being discussed here is that the typical mode of processing is from crude to fine. Following sensory analysis a crude first guess is suggested; this is then followed up by more fine-grained analyses (see Figure 6.13 for an example taken from the visual processing literature – Watt, 1988). In line with this crude-to-fine idea, Navon and Norman (1983) draw a distinction between a **suggested identity** and a **confirmed identity**: initially the identity of the stimulus is merely suggested and, if the conditions demand it, then further confirmation may be achieved through a process of actively seeking supporting

**Figure 6.12 Ripe old age**
An example of global precedence in which the initial impression is of a face and not of a random collection of fruit.
*Source*: Giuseppe Arcimboldo. *Vertumnus*. 1590–1591. Oil on wood. Skoklosters Castle, Balsta, Sweden/Samuel Uhrdin.

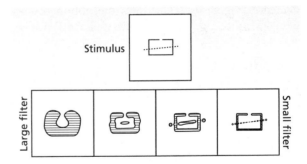

**Figure 6.13 Shape analysis in the visual system**
An example of how global precedence may actually be operating at the level of shape coding in the visual system (taken from Watt, 1988). Here it is assumed that different neurophysical analysers (or *filters*) are differentially sensitive to the various levels of a shape's description. The basic idea is that there are specialised filters, each of which is sensitive to a particular grain of analysis. From left to right the filters are arranged in a crude to fine manner in which the leftmost filter outputs a crude description of the overall disposition of the complete figure. In contrast, the rightmost filter outputs a description that codes the fine details.
*Source*: Watt, R. J. (1988). *Visual processing: Computational, psychophysical, and cognitive research* (fig. 5.9, p. 134). Hove, England: Erlbaum. Reproduced with permission.

**Figure 6.14 The difference between a suggested and confirmed identity**
'Is it Sarge? – 'No.'
'Is it Rosemary the telephone operator? – 'No.'
'Is it Henry, the mild-mannered janitor?' – 'Could be!'
*Source*: Rex Features/Hanna-Barbera.

evidence (Figure 6.14 illustrates the notion of suggested identity). → See 'What have we learnt?', below.

## Change blindness

Further evidence for this general view of perception comes from a relatively recently discovered phenom-enon known as **change blindness** (Rensink, O'Regan, & Clark, 1997; Simons & Ambinder, 2005). A detailed discussion of this would take us too far away from current concerns but it is appropriate to discuss the basic effects because, at a very general level, they are entirely consistent with the notion of crude-to-fine processing.

Figure 6.16 provides a diagrammatic illustration of the sorts of displays used on a given trial (Rensink et al., 1997). As is shown, the displays were dynamic in the sense that they comprised a repeating sequence of display frames. Of primary importance are the alternating photographs, known (for ease of exposition) as P1 and P2. The critical aspect of this design is that although P1 and P2 were pictures of the same scene, they differed by one critical aspect: an object or feature present in P1 was deleted in P2; its colour changed across P1 and P2; or its position changed. The participants' task was to press a key as soon as they detected this change. In addition they had to report the nature of the change to the experimenter – they had to report the nature of the so-called change signal (Simons & Ambinder, 2005). In one experiment (Rensink et al., 1997, Experiment 1) the change signal was defined as either being of central interest or of marginal interest. Independently a group of partici-pants had been asked to describe the scenes and from these descriptions if a majority of participants men-tioned the critical aspect then it was designated of cen-tral interest, otherwise it was designated of marginal interest. The first striking result was the amount of time that participants took to register some of the changes – on average around 11 s and for some of the displays in the order of 50 s. Also, perhaps unsur-prisingly, marginal interest changes took less time to detect than central interest changes.

## → What have we learnt?

Navon's account provides a very useful framework for thinking about the nature of perception in gen-eral. For most of the time, and in moving through the world, the observer need only operate at a level at which general labels for things are available, e.g., there is a dog running loose in the park. The natural mode of operation progresses from a crude to fine level. Within Navon's account the addi-tional claim is that crude analysis is mandatory with the proviso that more detailed analyses may be undertaken if needed. The degree to which the stimulus is interrogated further is under a certain amount of volitional control. That is, having realised that there is a dog running loose in the park it may well be in your best interests to begin to track its movement and to try to figure out what sort of dog it is – Rottweiler or not? Following the initial first pass at the world, further analyses may be under-taken – the stimulus is actively interrogated (Broadbent, 1977, p. 113) – and such analyses can be directed under subjective control (see Figure 6.15 for an example of where our current interpretation of the world is constantly being updated – Power, 1978).

(a)

(b)

(c)

(d)

(e)

(f)

(g)

**Figure 6.15  Sheds, I told you so**

Here, in a sequence of photographs, are various
snapshots taken in approaching a row of agricultural
sheds from a distance along a road. Power (1978)
presented versions of these photographs in sequence
to participants and asked them to generate their
impressions of what they saw. Typically participants
began by reporting a very clear unambiguous
impression of a bridge, but their impressions changed
as the sequence progressed. Indeed typically three
different hypotheses were considered before the scene
was correctly identified.

*Source*: Power, R. P. (1978). Hypotheses in perception:
their development about unambiguous stimuli in the
environment. *Perception*, *7*, 105–111 (fig. 1, p. 106).

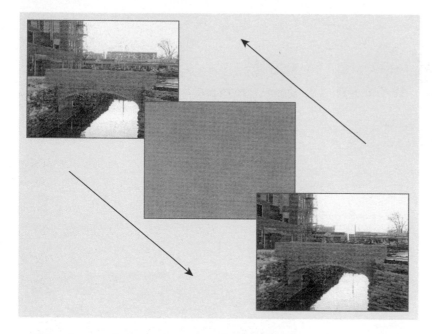

**Figure 6.16 Spot the difference**
An example of a stimulus sequence taken from a change blindness experiment. The first frame is shown and replaced by an intervening lightness mask, which is itself replaced by the third frame. This sequence is iterated many times and the participant is asked to report any change across the two images. In this case the change is obvious, right?

*Source*: Simons, D. J., & Ambinder, M. S. (2005). Change blindness: Theory and consequences. *Current Directions in Psychological Science, 14*, 44–48 (fig. 1, p. 45). Reproduced with permission from Blackwell Publishers, Ltd.

Since these early data were reported there has been much further work carried out on the effect and there remains much to understand. However, the generality of the effect has been amply demonstrated by the work of Simons and Levin (1998) who contrived real-world examples (see Figure 6.17 for a more thorough illustration). From this work they concluded that, 'Provided the meaning of the scene is unchanged, changes to attended objects can escape detection even when they occur during a natural, real-world interaction' (p. 644). This fits well with the data above showing that changes to objects of central interest were detected earlier than those of marginal interest. → See 'What have we learnt?', page 206.

---

**Research focus 6.1**

## Touchy touchy: the inability to detect changes in the tactile modality

Where would we be without the sense of touch? Your romantic dates would be a lot less exciting, your pet rabbit would suddenly stop being all fluffy and soft, and the poisonous tarantula crawling up your arm would go undetected. Clearly, then, we need touch to operate successfully in the world just as we need vision and audition. Although the complete loss of touch would be quite a dramatic event, Gallace, Tan and Spence (2006) were interested in the extent to which the tactile sense was susceptible to change blindness.

Ten participants were fitted with a number of vibrotactile inducers. These were, essentially, sensors that would vibrate according to when the experimenter wanted them to. Seven sensors were fitted in total at various points on the participant's body including wrist, elbow, waistline, ankle and knee. At each trial, multiple sensors were activated; however, which of the sensors were activated varied across

three conditions. In the first *sequential no-gap condition*, two sensor patterns were activated sequentially for 200 ms. In the second *sequential gap condition*, one sensor pattern was activated for 200 ms, there was then no stimulation for 110 ms, and then a second sensor pattern was activated for again 200 ms. In the third *masked interval condition*, two sensors patterns were activated, but the 110 ms interval between activations consisted of 50 ms of no simulation, a tactile mask if you will of 10 ms in which all sensors were activated, followed by another period of 50 ms of no simulation. Participants were asked to respond whether the pattern of stimulation changed position across presentations. In half of the trials position stayed constant and in the other half of the trials, position moved.

Gallace et al. (2006) found an effect on *d'*, indicating that participants were best at detecting change in the first no-gap condition, worst at detecting change during the masked interval condition, and intermediate when there was an interval with no mask (i.e., in the gap condition). Estimates of β were generally low and equivalent across the three conditions, indicating no evidence of concomitant changes in response bias.

The data were taken as providing evidence for change blindness in touch. That is, under conditions where the tactile patterns were interrupted by a mask, participants were less able to tell that stimulation had changed position. Of particular interest to Gallace et al. (2006) is the idea that change blindness might occur in all of the modalities. The current evidence is that it does occur in all of the modalities that have been currently tested. However, the data are clear. If you want to make sure you don't miss out on any changes in tactile sensation during your hot date, make sure there are no interruptions (or masks!).

*Source*: Gallace, A., Tan, H. Z., & Spence, C. (2006). The failure to detect tactile change: A tactile analogue of visual change blindness. *Psychonomic Bulletin & Review, 13*, 300–303.

(a)  (b)  (c)  (d)

**Figure 6.17 One enchanted meeting**
An example of change blindness in the real world. A bearded gentleman is stopped in the park by a perfectly innocuous young man 'for directions'. Mid-conversation two other men intervene carrying a large board – this is where the switch takes place and a different young man now takes up the conversation. The data reveal that not many people notice the change in identity of the person asking directions. Easy enough to try but probably not something to attempt after dark and after last orders.

*Source*: Simons, D. J., & Ambinder, M. S. (2005). Change blindness: Theory and consequences. *Current Directions in Psychological Science, 14*, 44–48 (fig. 2, p. 46). Reproduced with permission from Blackwell Publishers, Ltd.

## → **What have we learnt?**

Importantly the data converge on the framework for thinking about perception as set out by Navon (2003). Not all aspects of a scene are analysed immediately and completely: there seems to be a general crude-to-fine progression such that initially the gist of the scene is encoded and this may become elaborated upon over time if circumstances permit and the situation demands it. Moreover, the degree to which further analyses are undertaken is, in some critical respects, under attentional control. As Simons and Ambinder (2005) noted, unless participants direct attention to the change signal it may go undetected.

## Pinpoint question 6.5

How do the data from change blindness relate to the idea of crude-to-fine processing?

**global-to-local processing** The idea that the general nature of a stimulus is derived prior to its local aspects.

**global precedence** The idea that the global aspects of a shape are recovered prior to its local aspects.

**compound letter** A stimulus in which a larger letter is composed of smaller letters (after Navon, 1977).

**global advantage** When responses to the general nature of a stimulus are better than responses to its local aspects.

**global-to-local interference** Cases where responses to local aspects of a stimulus are impeded by conflicting global information.

**local-to-global interference** Cases where responses to global aspects of a stimulus are impeded by conflicting local information.

**simple horse-race account** Where the processes associated with different aspects of a stimulus race to completion.

**object schema** Similar to Minsky's (1975) frame, a memory representation that codes the perceptual nature of a familiar object.

**tree structure** A form of representation which is composed of nodes and connections between nodes. From a topmost node the structure branches out until at the very bottom are the leaves.

**global addressability** The assumption that any input segment corresponds to a global constituent of some object and not to some local constituent.

**suggested identity** First guess of an object's identity.

**confirmed identity** Final judgement of an object's identity based on available perceptual evidence.

**change blindness** The inability to detect a critical change in alternating images of the same scene.

## Context effects in perception

So far we have discussed the operation of passive perceptual mechanisms in terms of how the early stages of processing may proceed – are short codes delivered or do the codes specify the most likely distal stimulus given the evidence at the senses (i.e., the proximal stimulus)? A case has been built for the latter – it has been accepted that, on balance, the likelihood principle is of primary import. If the minimum principle does operate, it does so because it is in the service of the likelihood principle. It may be that short codes facilitate the derivation of the most likely representation. In addition, we have also explored the suggest/inquire account of perception in terms of the literature on global-to-local processing. First a relatively crude description is derived, and active processes may be invoked in a bid to be clearer about the details.

A limitation of all of this is that discussion seems to have taken place in something of a vacuum and little attention has been paid to what are known as *context effects in perception*. Figure 6.18 provides an illustration of a case in point. The central quadrilateral in both cases is identical and in the absence of the bounding contour would be seen as a trapezium. However, the tendency is to report seeing a rectangle in (a) and a

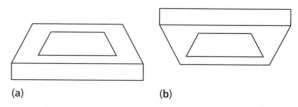

(a)                    (b)

**Figure 6.18 Context and shape perception**
Despite first impressions the central region is identical in both (a) and (b).

*Source*: Leeuwenberg, E. L. J., & van der Helm, P. A. (1991). Unity and variety in visual form. *Perception, 20*, 595–622 (fig. 19, p. 617). Reproduced with permission from Pion Limited, London.

trapezium in (b) (Leeuwenberg & van der Helm, 1991). Context is clearly being taken into account here. So although there is evidence for the independent derivation of interpretations for the different parts of a figure (as Hochberg, 2003, has amply demonstrated), this process can crucially depend on the context within which the stimulus occurs. As a consequence, the eventual interpretation of a given stimulus may reflect both the nature of its inherent properties and the scene within which it is present. In this regard, Figure 6.6 shows how trying to understand the interplay of figural and contextual factors remains astonishingly challenging. In this regard it is perhaps a shortcoming in the debate over simplicity vs. likelihood that not enough attention has been paid to the complexities of perception in the real world. When these are acknowledged, concerns rapidly turn to how perception is influenced by context and it is to exactly these sorts of concerns that discussion now turns.

## Context in the perception of speech

One relatively early attempt to explain how context may be taken account of in perception was provided by a very influential theory of speech perception known as **analysis by synthesis**. In broad strokes, in this theory a distinction is drawn between an initial stage of analysis followed by a subsequent stage of synthesis, yet, as we shall see, the actual model is more complicated than this simple distinction allows for. In very general terms, whenever there is sensory stimulation, basic perceptual features are registered at an initial analysis stage of processing. This is the stage in which the stimulus is decomposed into its constituent elements – in other words it is analysed. To reinvoke our tiger example, the tiger's black and brown stripes are registered. Functionally, this stage contains preliminary encoding operations in which salient and elemental characteristics of the proximal stimulus are registered.

To refer back to the suggest/inquire account, this analysis of the stimulus provides a *suggestion* as to the nature of the distal stimulus. The first stage gives rise to a rough indication of what it is in the environment that gave rise to the proximal stimulation. For instance, this stage might suggest that the stripes cohere in a rather ominous, tiger-like way. The crude-to-fine assumption is accepted.

On the basis of this preliminary analysis a secondary stage is invoked in which an hypothesis about the actual distal stimulus is made. Now knowledge about plausible causes of the proximal stimulus are integrated – that is, synthesised – with the outputs of the initial analysis stage. Operations at the synthesis stage give rise to a composite representation that specifies the first best guess as to the nature of the distal stimulus. This form of integration of combining information from the senses with stored knowledge is known as a **constructive process** and this is why analysis by synthesis is taken to be a **constructivist theory** of perception (Norman, 2002). The percept is built up from both bottom-up (or stimulus-driven) and top-down (or knowledge-driven) sources. The eventual perceptual representation is not just a specification of the sensory stimulation; it is this together with a contribution from stored knowledge.

By this account the eventual perceptual representation is the sum of sensory stimulation plus stored knowledge. Indeed, Neisser (1967) used this assumption of the theory to account for why it is that errors in perception may actually occur. Such errors are explained by assuming that the participants are making hypotheses about the nature of the input that are incorrect. The active, constructivist aspects of the theory are captured via the processes of projecting onto the world expectations and predictions about its nature. It is in this way that perception is in part determined by stored knowledge. Critically in this theory perception is an active, not passive process, and fundamentally, our perceptions of the world are governed by how we construe the world.

## For example . . .

Participants sometimes hear words that were not present in spoken input or they see letters of words that were not actually displayed. For example, Queen's magnum opus *Bohemian Rhapsody* does not contain the lyrics 'the algebra has a devil for a sidekick' or 'spare him his life and his lone slice of cheese', as good as these actually sound (see www.kissthisguy.com for more examples). What is interesting, however, is that while these mis-heard song lyrics have gone awry in terms of semantic content, they appear to have retained the original syllabic and phonological structure.

In the original analysis-by-synthesis account, following the initial perceptual analysis and generation of the first hypothesis there then follows a comparison stage in which the outputs of the perceptual analysis are compared with the current hypothesis. If there is a match then the current hypothesis is taken as being confirmed and the distal stimulus is perceived. In case of a mismatch, though, a new hypothesis is generated and this is now tested; that is, an **hypothesis-and-test cycle** is initiated.

In this account we have the distinction between bottom-up processes – outputs from the perceptual analysis stage – and top-down processes – the hypotheses that are generated and are then compared with these outputs. In addition we have several clear statements about the constructive nature of perception; that is, the eventual perceptual representation is constructed out of contributions from sensory analysis and from stored knowledge. Both the generation of perceptual hypotheses and the construction of the perceptual representation are taken to be active processes. However, the model is not simply a two-stage account in which the first analysis stage is followed by the second synthesis stage, because the hypothesis-and-test cycle operates in an iterative fashion. In other words, perceptual analysis continues as different interpretations of the input are tried out and tested in a sequential manner one after the other until a match is secured.

Is this a real Leonardo da Vinci sketch or not? Well, the figures do resemble Leonardo's artwork so is there a signature? Look for a signature? If there is a signature it will be at the bottom right of the sketch so look there? Yes, there is some writing, but does it say da Vinci?

**Pinpoint question 6.6**

Which part of analysis by synthesis is bottom-up and which is top-down?

## Analysis by synthesis and speech perception

Despite a certain degree of abstraction, the analysis-by-synthesis account has been applied to everyday problems such as how we understand what someone is saying. Indeed, a complete account of analysis by synthesis was developed by Stevens and Halle (1967) in their model of speech perception. So although we have been predominantly fixated on the visual modality, attention now turns to audition. Figure 6.19 provides the arrows-and-boxes diagram associated with their model.

Input to the model S′ undergoes some form of auditory analysis by which certain salient auditory features are extracted from the speech signal and the outputs from this stage are then entered into the store. The store is essentially a short-term memory buffer.

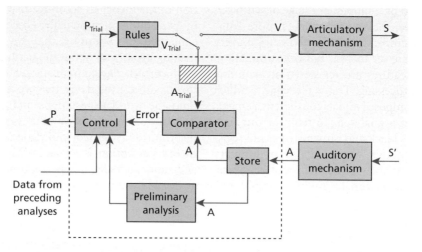

**Figure 6.19 The arrows-and-boxes of analysis by synthesis**
Schematic representation of the original analysis-by-synthesis model of speech perception. S = sound output; S′ = sound input; A = auditory patterns; P = abstract representation of phonology; V = instructions to articulatory mechanism; 'Trial' subscript denotes internally-generated hypotheses.

*Source*: Stevens, K. N., & Halle, M. (1967). Remarks on analysis by synthesis and distinctive features. In W. Wathen-Dunn (Ed.), *Models for perception of speech and visual form*. Proceedings of a Symposium sponsored by the Data Sciences Laboratory Air Force Cambridge Research Laboratories, Boston, Massachusetts, November 11–14, 1964 (pp. 88–102, fig. 3). Cambridge, Massachusetts: The MIT Press. Reproduced with permission.

Read-out from the store is fed into two places, namely preliminary analysis and the comparator. Initially the comparator plays no role (we don't have anything to compare yet!) so the main focus is with preliminary analysis, and as its name implies the output from the store undergoes further analysis in which possible speech features are extracted.

At the level of the control the first hypothesis is made about what may have been spoken. The control outputs a sequence of codes that specifies the first best guess of the actual speech signal. In the context of previous speech, then, a record of the previous utterance can now be used to help generate this first best guess as to what is now being spoken. This in turn is now combined with knowledge about the nature of the spoken form of the language captured by the rules box in the model. The idea is that rules that specify the spoken form of the language now come into play. Such rules are known as **phonological rules** because these specify legal (pronounceable) strings of sounds that occur in the particular spoken language under consideration. The idea is that the input codes that carry information about speech are now converted into some form of representation that actually specifies a possible spoken form – the noise from the ears is converted into a representation of the sounds *kuh a tuh*, that is, /cat/. It is a sound-based representation – it specifies a possible spoken form of an utterance. This code specifies the speech signal in terms of the basic building blocks of sound – the code does not, however, convey anything about meaning. (In a rather loose way, anything bounded by backslashes is taken to signify spoken sounds.)

This sound code is then operated upon to produce something called the V specification and this contains actual motor commands that govern the control of the speech articulators, namely the various parts of the vocal tract – the lips, the tongue, the voice box, etc. – that come into play during speech production. What has happened here is that a code that specifies the phonological nature of speech has been transformed into a different one that specifies something known as a motor command. The *kuh a tuh* is converted into a set of commands that specify how to move your mouth so as to produce these very same sounds. In this account being able to understand the speech signal depends upon being able to recover the motor commands that could be used to produce the speech.

More particularly, the motor command is an abstract representation that includes instructions about how to initiate and control an actual utterance. These commands govern the control of the articulatory system.

For instance, these specify the sequence and timing of movements of tongue and lips during speaking. It is this set of articulatory instructions that is compared with the acoustic pattern stored in the comparator. If the predicted utterance and the sound pattern stored in the comparator match, then the predicted speech is heard. If any discrepancy occurs between the predicted and the actual, then an error signal is passed on to the control and the next hypothesised speech string is generated for test. This is where the hypothesis-and-test cycle is instantiated.

In summary, the analysis-by-synthesis view of speech perception (after Broadbent, 1971, p. 270) is that, on the basis of a preliminary analysis of the speech signal, the listener generates an hypothesis about what has been heard to have been spoken in terms of a code that specifies movements of the articulatory system. The listener compares this code with a stored representation of the sensory input. Modification of the code is undertaken in the face of any mismatch that arises. The eventual percept specifies the speech elements that match with the internally generated code.

To get a better handle on this let us assume that, up to the critical time point, the speech has so far contained /The cat sat on the m/. Analysis by synthesis now provides a straightforward account as to why /at/ will be so readily heard. First, /a/ is a highly plausible next sound, given the phonological constraints of English. A sound such as /g/ is most unlikely given the low probability of ever having heard /mg/ before. In addition, the completion /at/ is most likely given knowledge about actual real-world scenarios and certain children's books. Hence the model acknowledges two top influences in speech perception, namely (i) knowledge of the phonological constraints of the language and (ii) general world knowledge.

## Initial appraisal of analysis by synthesis

As Broadbent (1971) summarised, the theory was based on three lines of evidence:

1. The sort of effects we have already discussed as showing how experience affects perception (i.e., effects of familiarity, recency and set).
2. Differences between acoustic aspects of the speech signal and articulation.
3. How speech sound discrimination is affected by the ability to articulate those same sounds.

We have already spent some time discussing the first of these so it is only right to now concentrate on the last two.

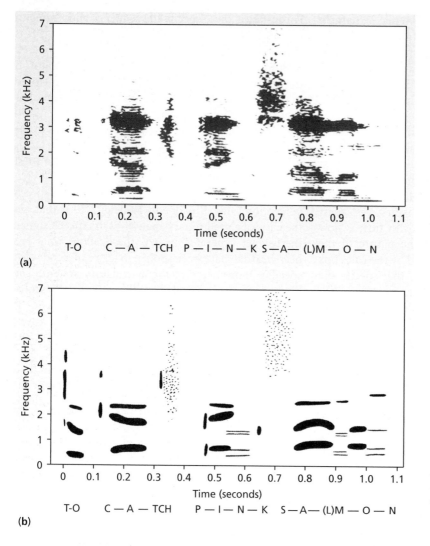

**(a)**

**(b)**

**Figure 6.20 Visible speech**
A schematic representation of a speech spectrograph of the spoken utterance 'TO CATCH PINK SALMON'. The graphs are defined relative to an *x* and a *y* axis. The *x* axis specifies elapsed time from the start of the utterance. The *y* axis specifies the component frequencies of the speech signal. The intensity (or amplitude) present at a given frequency is given by the depth of shading. So very dark patches signify large amounts of energy in the signal at the particular frequency (see Figure 6.21). (a) actual sound spectrogram and (b) simplified version painted by hand.

*Source*: Warren, R. M. (1999). *Auditory Perception. A new analysis and synthesis* (fig. 7.5, p. 165). Cambridge, England: Cambridge University Press. Reproduced with permission.

## The physical nature of speech and an introduction to phonemes

If speech is recorded and rendered into something known as a **speech spectrograph**, what is produced is a visual representation of the sound energy contained in the sound signal. This makes explicit the sound intensity values for different speech frequencies at each time point in the signal. Figure 6.20 provides such an example of a speech spectrograph. One traditional linguistic description of speech defines the **phoneme** as the elemental unit of speech – the atom or minimum unit of sound that forms the basis of all speech of a given language (Stork & Widdowson, 1974). Each natural language can be defined relative to its set of phonemes and clearly not all phonemes are present in all languages. For example, Khowar (a language spoken predominantly in northwest Pakistan) has over ten unique phonemes including /tsh/ and /zh/. By this view,

any spoken utterance can be rendered into a sequence of phonemes (e.g., 'cat' can be rendered into the following phonetic transcription, /K/ /a/ /t/). At a higher level of analysis the speech stream can be divided into constituent syllables: whereas 'cat' contains a single syllable (it is a monosyllable word), 'cattle' contains two syllables (it is a bi-syllabic word). So, in speech, syllables may be described as being composed of phonemes, and words may be decomposed into syllables.

Acoustic analysis of speech gives rise to the following surprising fact: even though a given phoneme may be contained in different syllables (the /g/ in /game/; the /g/ in /girl/), the spectrographs of these different syllables show that the physical nature of the phoneme is not the same in the two cases. Nevertheless, different acoustic patterns give rise to perception of the same phoneme. How can this be? Well, according to Stevens and Halle (1967), this is because the perception of the phoneme is based on a recovery of the motor commands that specify the articulation of the phoneme. When an analysis of the speech articulators is undertaken, the articulation of /g/ is essentially the same in these different contexts. This sort of consideration led to the claim that to perceive an utterance is to recover a specific pattern of intended (phonetic) gestures (or motor commands) of the articulators (see Liberman & Mattingly, 1985). The same motor commands are used in producing a target phoneme in different contexts. Hence the claim is that hearing /g/ in all its contexts implies recovering the same set of motor commands in all these contexts.

## Phoneme recognition and categorical perception

The final thread of evidence, which Broadbent (1971) quoted as being generally supportive of analysis by synthesis, is the following. If asked to discriminate between different speech sounds, then discrimination performance is better for different variations of two different phonemes than for speech sounds that map onto the same phonetic category. The basis of this claim arose originally from a study by Liberman, Harris, Hoffman and Griffith (1957).

As we have seen, each part of speech is defined by an energy profile as shown in the speech spectrograph. Synthetic speech can be created (using some sort of sound editing package) by manipulating the timing and energy content of this signal. In this way Liberman

et al. created a range of 14 vowel–consonant syllables that varied from /be/ to /de/ to /ge/ (see Figure 6.21). If the /be/ to /ge/ continuum were to be mapped out, then the 14 syllables fell at equal intervals along this continuum and the continuum itself could be defined into three regions that mapped onto the three phonetic categories given by /b/, /d/ and /g/ (see Figure 6.21b).

On each trial a participant was presented with three sounds in something known as an ABX paradigm. The first sound (A) was followed by the second sound (B) and the participant had to respond with whether the third sound (X) was a repetition of A or B. The central result was that participants' classifications were better if A and B were taken from different phonetic categories than if A and B fell within the same phonetic category (see Figure 6.21b). This was even when the physical difference between A and B in two cases was equated – take any adjacent phonemes on the continuum. This basic finding was taken to demonstrate something known as **categorical perception** – in this example speech sound perception fundamentally depends on the nature of the phonetic categories that the participant brings to bear. In other words, two things that sound like the same phoneme (e.g., /b/) are more difficult to tell apart than when the two things sound like two different phonemes (e.g., /b/ and /g/). This occurs even when the physical separation of the members of the respective pairs of stimuli is the same. Given that different phonemes are defined relative to different motor commands, then here there is

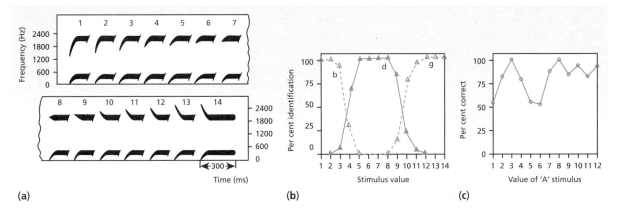

**Figure 6.21 The categorical perception of phonemes**
Examples in (a) of speech sounds ordered on a syllabic continuum. The sounds map from 1 – /b/, through 7 – /d/, to 14 – /g/. In (b) the identification responses are plotted out for the 14 different sounds. Versions 1–3 were clearly identified as belonging to /b/; versions 5–8 were clearly identified as belonging to /d/; versions 11–14 were clearly identified as belonging to /g/. In (c) the per cent correct scores from the ABX task are shown. Each point reflects performance when adjacent stimuli were presented. So the first point on the curve represents when *1* and *2* were the *A* and the *B*. As can be seen, performance varies according to whether the stimuli are both taken from the same phonetic category. Discrimination performance is best when the stimuli are taken from different categories (see text for further details).

*Source*: Fry, D. B. (Ed.), (1976). *Acoustic phonetics* (fig. 1, p. 335, fig. 2, p. 338). Cambridge, Massachusetts: Cambridge University Press. Reproduced with permission.

evidence that knowledge of how sounds are articulated influences perception of these sounds.

### Further evidence from the perception of visible speech

In addition to the three lines of evidence cited by Broadbent (1971) in support of the general analysis-by-synthesis view of speech perception, other data also speak to the theory. Indeed the basic idea that knowledge of how speech sounds are articulated plays some role in the perception of speech is revealed by a fascinating effect discovered in studies of so-called visible speech. The effect is known as the McGurk

effect (McGurk & MacDonald, 1976) and is a rather compelling illusion that can arise when participants watch and listen to a film of someone apparently talking. In one such example the participant is presented with a sound track that accompanies a movie of a face articulating a sequence of syllables. The sound track contains the sequence /bah/ /bah/ /bah/; however, the moving face depicts the spoken sequence /beh/ /veh/ /deh/. The perceptual impression is of hearing the sequence /bah/ /vah/ /dah/. That is, the percept is a strange blend of the sights and sounds with the auditory impression being one that is mainly consistent with the visual articulatory gestures. Of course this evidence does not show that the particular analysis-

## Research focus 6.2

### Hear my lips: visual and auditory dominance in the McGurk effect

Anyone who has sat through a ventriloquist's act (gottles of geer, etc.) will know all about the combination of separate auditory and visual events. Although the dummy is only moving their wooden lips (and in fact, they aren't even doing that autonomously), the voice is being thrown from the ventriloquist to the stooge, with the final percept being a lip-moving, vocal-producing dummy. The McGurk effect (as described) also points to some interesting forms of integration between sound and vision, although the interest here is more with how incongruent auditory and visual information become fused to create illusory perceptions. Van Wassenhove, Grant and Poeppel (2006) sought to investigate exactly when the visual and auditory portions of the McGurk effect have to be presented in order for the effect to occur.

Groups of around 20 participants took part in the study. In one condition, participants were presented in auditory form with /b/ (or 'ba') and in visual form with /g/ ('ga'), which at some point in the great scheme of things should recombine to form the illusory percept of /d/ (or 'da'). Van Wassenhove et al. (2006) manipulated the extent to which both auditory and visual information appeared together. Audio-visual pairs were presented simultaneously, but the audio information could also lag behind the visual information (/g/ then /b/), or lead in front of the visual information (/b/ then /g/). Lagging and leading times increased by 67 ms multiples until there was a temporal distance of 467 ms between

the two pieces of speech information. Participants were instructed to indicate whether the percept was more like 'ba', 'ga' or 'da'.

The data revealed that there was a very clear illusory perception of /d/ at 0 ms (something to be expected, since this would be the ventriloquist working at their best), but also when auditory information lagged behind visual information up until around 200 ms. It was also interesting to note that participants very rarely reported hearing the visually driven percept of 'ga' something not revealed so strongly in the original McGurk and MacDonald paper (1976).

Van Wassenhove et al. (2006) concluded that auditory and visual information have, quite literally, a small window of opportunity to integrate together to form a fused multi-model (that is, audio-visual) percept. Specifically, the auditory portion of the signal has about 200 ms to arrive after the visual portion of the stimulus to stand a chance to be integrated with it. One reason for this asymmetry is thought to be due to the amount of time it takes for auditory and visual information to reach their respective cortical areas. Van Wassenhove et al. (2006, p. 605) discussed this effect in terms of analysis by synthesis, since 'the dynamics of auditory and visual speech inputs constrain the integration process'. Try telling that to the dummy next time you see him.

*Source*: van Wassenhove, V., Grant, K. W., & Poeppel, D. (2006). Temporal window of integration in auditory-visual speech perception. *Neuropsychologia, 45*, 588–607.

by-synthesis account of speech perception has been validated, but nevertheless, the McGurk effect fits comfortably with the idea that speech perception and speech production share some rather intimate connections.

**analysis by synthesis** Perception viewed as a process of integration of sensory information and shared knowledge on the basis of generating and testing hypotheses about the input.

**constructive process** Perception construed as a process in which the percept is built up from sensory information and stored knowledge.

**constructivist theory** A theory of perception that assumes constructive processes; that is, the percept is built up from the evidence at the senses together with knowledge about the world.

**hypothesis-and-test cycle** First a hypothesis is generated and then analyses are carried out to test the validity of the hypothesis. If the test fails, the cycle begins again with another hypothesis, and so on.

**phonological rules** The specification of the rules of pronunciation.

**speech spectrograph** A visual representation of sound energy in speech.

**phoneme** The minimum unit of speech in a natural language.

**categorical perception** Where the detection of the difference between an A and a B stimulus is better if A and B are taken from different psychological categories than when A and B are taken from the same psychological category.

## Perception as a process of embellishment

A basic implication of analysis by synthesis is that perception is, in part, defined as an act of embellishment: the eventual percept includes a combination of information from the senses and information contributed by the central mechanisms. The term 'embellishment' is being used because it is assumed that the central mechanisms add or contribute to the

construction of the eventual percept (as discussed above). The apparent necessity for this has been taken by some to follow from a rather strict reading of the classic 'poverty of the stimulus' approach to perception. On the understanding that the proximal stimulus is only a very imperfect and inadequate counterpart to the distal stimulus, the perceptual system must embellish or add information during the processes of constructing the percept (Michaels & Carello, 1981). Such a process is inherent in analysis by synthesis because the perception of speech is determined by reference to the proximal stimulus and articulatory movements that probably caused the utterance. Other examples of this kind of theory of perceptual embellishment have been discussed in the literature on visual information processing and it is to one of these that discussion now turns.

## Minsky's (1975) frame theory

Central to Minsky's (1975) account of perception are various assumptions about how knowledge of the world is stored (in memory) and subsequently used during the course of perception. The basic assumption is that perception critically depends on making the connection between the proximal stimulus and knowledge stored in memory (as in the tradition of the New Look – see Chapter 5). Accessing appropriate stored knowledge allows sensible predictions to be made about the nature of the external world given the current sensory stimulation (after Bruner, 1957). To understand the nature of perception therefore means understanding something about how knowledge about the world is specified in the head. In examining the possible manner in which knowledge is stored, Minsky (1975) generated a general framework for thinking in terms of his frame theory. Unsurprisingly the notion of a **frame** is central.

For him a frame is an internal specification of a stereotypical thing (where 'thing' can be any familiar real-world entity, object or event). Figure 6.22 illustrates what the frame for a room might contain – namely a specification of a bounded rectangular area comprising four walls, a ceiling and a floor. Chances are, you're in a bounded rectangle area right now. More particularly, what this specification contains is not only a list of plausible properties of the thing being considered, but default assumptions about the nature of those properties. For instance, the frame for a living room probably has a default that specifies that the ceiling will contain a light, and it might even include a default assumption about porcelain ducks

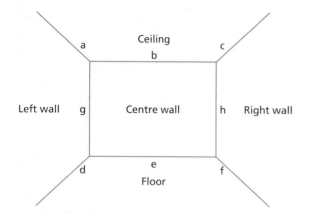

**Figure 6.22 A frame for a room**
An illustration of what the frame for a room might contain
– namely a specification of a bounded rectangular area
comprising four walls, a ceiling and a floor.

*Source*: Minsky, M. (1974). A framework for representing
knowledge. MIT-AI Laboratory Memo 306, June 1974 (fig. 1.5).
Reproduced with permission from Prof. Marvin Minsky.

**Figure 6.23 Is a living room still a living room if it doesn't
have flying ducks?**
*Source*: Photolibrary.com.

on the wall (see Figure 6.23). The central point is that
the living-room frame will contain a fairly complete
specification of the typical living room. In this way,
before being told that you are now about to enter a
living room you will be able to bring to mind a set of
expectations about a typical living room.

By this view perception is merely an act of updating
the current frame by over-writing the defaults that do
not match with the current situation. Someone might
have opted for a cuckoo clock instead of the ducks.
The current percept therefore is the current frame. An
alternative way of thinking about a frame is that it is
composed of various slots where each slot contains a
certain default. Hence the so-called **slot-and-filler**
framework for thinking. So the number-of-walls 'slot'
will be filled with the number four on the understanding that the typical room contains four walls.

Frame theory is far more detailed than might
be supposed on the basis of the current account, but
only the general characteristics are of interest here. For
instance, although the theory provides an interesting
framework for thinking about how stored knowledge
may be characterised, it also provides something of an
insight into how expectancy may operate in perception and why perception is so quick and efficient. The
basic idea is that perception is primarily **knowledge
driven**. You start with what you expect (as given by your
prior knowledge) and over-write only those things that
do not fit with your expectations. As Minsky stated, the
frame directs the whole hypothesis-and-test cycle that
is central to all top-down theories of perception.

## Problems for knowledge-driven accounts of perception

Despite supporting evidence for something like analysis by synthesis going on behind speech perception
and the intuitive plausibility of frame theory, there has
been much controversy over these kinds of knowledge-
driven accounts of perception (Fant, 1967; Morton &
Broadbent, 1967; Neisser, 1976). In particular, a recurrent concern has been expressed over how best to
control the hypothesis-and-test cycle in cases when
errors (mismatches) occur. If the current hypothesis
is wrong, how does the system generate the next best
guess and the next after that and the next and so on?
As Neisser (1976) pointed out, the hypothesis-and-test
cycle seems to imply that an implausibly large number
of incorrect guesses are generated all of the time. Moreover, the sequential nature of testing one hypothesis at

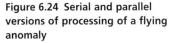

**Figure 6.24 Serial and parallel versions of processing of a flying anomaly**

*Source:* Image from Kobal Collection Ltd/Warner Bros./DC Comics.

a time seems to render the mechanisms implausible (Broadbent, 1971, p. 273). A very bad first guess may result in the mechanisms taking an inordinate amount of time to home in on the correct percept.

### Serial and parallel matching

To try to shore up the general analysis-by-synthesis framework for thinking about perception, Broadbent (1971) suggested some particular modifications. Remember, Broadbent (1977) himself was generally sympathetic to the view of an initial passive stage of processing followed by an active stage – suggestion followed by inquiry. To this end Broadbent (1971) suggested that the process of securing a match between the input and stored knowledge does not operate serially (one hypothesis at a time) but that many different categories are considered in parallel at the same time (see Figure 6.24). In simple terms, the difference is between a mechanism that can consider one thing at a time (i.e., a **serial processor**) and a mechanism that can consider more than one thing at once (i.e., a **parallel processor**).

By way of example, assume the spoken stimulus /coil/ has unfolded to the point of /coi/. By the standard serial analysis-by-synthesis account, first /n/ will be tested, then /l/ will be. This is because /coin/ has a higher frequency of occurrence in the language than does /coil/. The predictability of the final phoneme will be based on how frequently it has occurred in the past. In contrast, in a parallel system both /n/ and /l/ can be considered at the same time. So whereas the first serial system takes the sum of two tests to arrive at a decision, the second parallel system just has to wait for the quicker of the two tests to finish. In these simple terms the parallel system seems to offer a more plausible account of how speech perception operates in the real world in real time.

### Perception in unfamiliar contexts

Although there is much to take from these ideas about how it is that people may make sensible predictions about the nature of the external world on the basis of sensory evidence, caution is still warranted in being too accepting of the general knowledge-driven framework. For instance, although frame theory manages well in dealing with the perception of familiar entities, it throws little light on how the perceptual system operates in unfamiliar situations. How does perception operate in the absence of a frame? The theory provides no answer to this.

### Discriminating the real from the possible

In addition, concerns have been aired over the idea that the eventual percept includes a combination of information from the senses and information contributed by the central mechanisms. If the eventual percept is nothing other than the sum of the combination of sensory information and stored knowledge, then this leads us to consider the frightening question of how can a person discriminate between what is out there and what is not? How could a person ever discriminate between the real and the imagined? According to the theory, everything is captured by the current frame, and there is no distinction drawn between what has been contributed by the external stimulus and what has been contributed by stored knowledge.

Such concerns as these have led some (see Gibson, 1986; Michaels & Carello, 1981) to dismiss the whole constructivist approach to perception as completely wrong-headed. It is far beyond the scope of the present book to examine thoroughly the alternative views. It is, however, much more appropriate to take a careful look at the relevant data and try to decide how such data inform our theories. It is most pertinent to ask about what sorts of data constrain ideas about possible processes of embellishment in perception.

---

**frame** After Minsky (1975), a mental representation of a stereotyped or typical real-world event or object. Slots in the frame are associated with attributes and the slots are filled with default or prototypical values.

▶

> **slot-and-filler** In thinking about a stereotypical object or event, there are a number of characteristics (or slots) that the entity has (e.g., legs) and these must be assigned (or filled) with a certain value (e.g., four).
>
> **knowledge driven** A claim about perception being governed by stored knowledge.
>
> **serial processor** A mechanism that can only operate on one thing at once.
>
> **parallel processor** A mechanism that can operate on more than one thing at once.

## Phonemic restoration as an act of perceptual embellishment

Although frame theory has been discussed in terms of it providing a useful approach to thinking about vision, perhaps the strongest evidence for the basic embellishment view of perception comes again from studies of speech perception. It is for this reason that we now turn to the phenomenon of **phonemic restoration**. According to Samuel (1996a) the original experiments on phonemic restoration were carried out by Warren (1970). In these experiments participants were presented with a recording of the spoken sentence 'The state governors met with their respective legislatures convening in the capital city.' However, the recording had been doctored such that the word 'legislatures' had been changed in a particular way. The spoken segment starting from the first /s/ and lasting for 120 ms had been removed and replaced with a cough of the same duration. We can indicate this by using the notation 'legi**atures'. Participants were played this recording and were asked to indicate, on a written form of the sentence, when the cough started, how long it lasted, and most importantly, whether it replaced the spoken sounds. Participants were essentially being asked whether the cough replaced the phoneme /s/ or whether it was presented in addition to the phoneme.

The central finding was that the overwhelming majority of the participants reported that all the speech sounds had been presented. In terms of the current example the results showed that, even though the /s/ had been removed, participants reported hearing it. In other words, at the level of perceptual awareness, the phoneme /s/ had been restored – hence the phrase *phonemic restoration*. The imperfect, impoverished stimulus had been perceived as being intact. Such

evidence is consistent with the idea of perception as a process of embellishment.

From the original experiments several of the other subsidiary findings are also of interest. For instance, similar results obtained when a tone replaced the cough. However, when the target segment was removed and replaced with silence, then there was no illusory recovery of the missing phoneme. Performance in the task was qualitatively different when extraneous noise replaced the phoneme as compared with when the phoneme was simply missing from the speech. Whereas participants were relatively poor in locating the position of the added noises, they were extremely accurate in locating the position of the gap. We will return to consider such details in a moment.

As you can possibly imagine, since the publication of the paper there has been an explosion in the number of studies published on phonemic restoration (see Samuel, 1996a, for a review), and several quite different avenues of research have been pursued on the back of the basic phenomenon. However, most pressing here is the issue of the degree to which the data truly reflect processes of embellishment in perception. Traditionally phonemic restoration has been treated as providing a paradigm case for examining whether there are top-down influences in perception as set out in analysis by synthesis and frame theory.

### Establishing the true nature of phonemic restoration

Given our previous concerns about the distinction between perceptual versus cognitive effects (see Chapter 5), it is pertinent to ask about the degree to which phonemic restoration is truly a perceptual phenomenon or whether it is merely another indication of response bias. When couched thus, it immediately conjures up the possibility of examining the effect in the context of signal detection theory (see Chapter 4). Can we link the effect to changes in $d'$ (changes in the sensitivity of the phonetic analysers) or is the effect carried by changes in $\beta$ (changes in response bias)? Remember, any changes in $d'$ have been taken to reflect something about changes in perceptual encoding mechanisms, whereas changes in $\beta$ are taken to reflect changes in a post-perceptual stage of processing. The aspiration here therefore is to be able to adjudicate between the possibility that participants are actually 'hearing' the missing speech (as would be shown by changes in $d'$) or that they are simply convincing themselves that the speech was present because in natural discourse it typically is (an effect that would show up in a change in $\beta$).

Such experiments have indeed been carried out. For instance Samuel (1981a, 1981b) generated two sorts of stimuli – known, respectively, as **added stimuli** and **replaced stimuli**. Both sorts of stimuli were spoken items in isolation. The recordings were doctored so that the stimuli in the added cases were where an extraneous noise (a tone or noise burst) was superimposed on the speech, and in the replaced versions, the extraneous noise replaced speech sounds erased from the recordings. On a given trial a single stimulus was presented over headphones to the participants and they simply had to categorise the stimulus as 'added' or 'replaced'. In this way participants were being forced to discriminate between added and replaced cases and, as a consequence, measures of $d'$ and $\beta$ could be derived (see Chapter 4). In such cases a low value of $d'$ would indicate that a participant was unable to tell apart when the speech signal was intact from when it was not. A low value of $d'$ would indicate high levels of phonemic restoration. In turn large values of $\beta$ would indicate a bias towards responding 'noise replaced', whereas small values would indicate the opposite bias towards responding 'noise added'.

Critically performance was assessed when participants were presented with real word stimuli and when they were presented with non-words. In one important experiment Samuel (1981b, Experiment 2) used a task in which the complete spoken item was presented first on a given trial and then this was followed by the doctored version of the item (either added or replaced). Participants then had to make their decisions about the second item. In comparing performance across words and non-words, Samuel was able to address the issue of the degree to which stored knowledge influenced phonemic restoration. With familiar words participants have stored knowledge about these items (because that is what being familiar means). With the non-words, however, because these had been made up for the experiment, none of the participants would have knowledge of these items. By comparing performance across words and non-words the reasoning was that this would reflect the influence of stored knowledge in phonemic restoration.

### Pinpoint question 6.8

**Why was the distinction between words and non-words important in assessing the phonemic restoration effects by Samuels?**

## Detailed theoretical accounts of performance

Before discussing the actual findings, it is important to consider the sorts of theoretical ideas that are at stake. The traditional approach to theorising provides the following rationale. An effect on $d'$ would reflect how word knowledge influenced the operation of perceptual mechanisms. If $d'$ was smaller on word than non-word trials then this could be taken to show that the perceptual mechanisms can be altered by higher-level expectations about the nature of the speech signal. In the limit a $d'$ of 0 would show that participants were unable to discriminate when the phoneme was actually presented from when it was replaced. Such a situation is perfectly consistent with the notion of phonemic restoration. In contrast, an effect on $\beta$ would be taken as reflecting systematic changes in post-perceptual mechanisms concerning decision and response. That is, if there was a difference in $\beta$ across word and non-word trials then this would indicate that participants were merely guessing in a rather sophisticated way in line with their expectations given by their knowledge of the spoken form of their language.

However, Samuel made a slightly different claim and argued that phonemic restoration is perhaps better explained in terms of what he called 'bottom-up confirmation of expectations' (1981a, p. 1124). By this view the basic phonemic restoration effect is taken as evidence of a mixture of both top-down and bottom-up influences – 'the listener uses the linguistic context to restore the appropriate (expected) phoneme. However, the illusion also depends on bottom-up factors' (1981b, p. 476). This latter point is most clearly supported by the fact that phonemic restoration does not take place when silence replaced a phoneme (as documented by Warren, 1970). For Samuel this is in line with the hypothesis because silence does not provide any confirmation for expected phonemes. In the absence of any bottom-up activation (i.e., acoustic stimulation at the appropriate point), then phonemic restoration does not occur. In addition, phonemic restoration was more likely to occur when the acoustic nature of the noise matched the characteristics of the critical speech sound than when it did not (see Samuel, 1981a). Such findings fit well with the general idea that phonemic restoration ought to vary as a function of both top-down expectations and the acoustic nature of the speech signal.

## Sorry, I'll read that again: phonemic restoration with the initial phoneme

Thanks to mobile phone drop-out, sneezes, noisy eaters on the next dinner table, Walkmans, car horns and the occasional fire alarm, we increasingly find it difficult to make ourselves understood. However, as we have already seen, thanks to the wonders of phonemic restoration, we are often able to 'fill in the blanks' under the most cacophonous environments imaginable. In the original studies that we discussed above, Warren (1970) looked at phonemic restoration in the middle of a word (i.e., 'legi**atures'). Sivonen, Maess and Friederici (2006), however, were interested in phonemic restoration at the beginning of words and also what electrical brain activity might be able to tell us about the perceptual and cognitive processes involved.

Thirty-seven German speakers were exposed to a variety of sentences in which the final word was highly predictable (Der Hund jagte die Katze auf den Baum) or not so predictable (In seinen Kaffee tat er Zucker und Sahne). And if you don't speak German: 'The dog chased the cat up the tree' and 'In his coffee he took sugar and cream'. In addition, the last word in the sentence was complete or the first phoneme was replaced with a silent interval. As Sivonen et al. (2006) pointed out, a cough (as used in the original studies) is a high frequency noise which probably stimulated the same regions of the auditory system as the speech would have done, if it was present. In contrast, and as also found in the original studies, a silent interval did not help to restore the phoneme.

Sivonen et al. (2006) examined certain components of the electrical signals recorded from the scalp known as the N1 and the N400. The nice thing about recording electrical brain activity is that there is a strong assumption that certain components

such as the N1 relate to automatic and stimulus-driven processes, whereas other components such as the N400 relate to more cognitive effects, such as whether the final word in a sentence is highly predictable or not. The data revealed greater N1 amplitude (the size of the N1) for silent final words than complete final words. With respect to the N400, responses were larger when the final word was unexpected relative to expected. Importantly, there was no effect of silence/presence for the N400. In a separate behavioural study involving 17 additional participants, Sivonen et al. (2006) also confirmed that reaction times were longer for unexpected words than expected words, and also longer for when the first phoneme was silent as opposed to present.

In sum, the data revealed that the brain, incredibly early on in processing, can detect the presence of gaps in phonemes. This occurs around about 100 ms after stimulus onset, as hinted at by the label 'N1' with the '1' standing for 100 ms. Despite this, later processes associated with retrieving the semantic nature of the word (the N400) were not sensitive to the presence or absence of the first phoneme of the final word in a sentence, but the N400 was sensitive to whether it was a highly predictable word or not. Therefore the phonemic restoration effect really does seem to provide our brain with a reconstruction of sensory input, which at later stages of processing is indistinguishable from actually having heard the word in the first place! Therefore, it **comes ***prisingly *asy to **derstand text when the ***mary ***neme is ****ing.

*Source*: Sivonen, P., Maess, B., & Friederici, A. (2006). Semantic retrieval of spoken words with an obliterated initial phoneme in a sentence context. *Neuroscience Letters, 408*, 220–225.

## Top-down processing and interactive activation models

Although this account fits reasonably comfortably with an analysis by synthesis view of processing, it is best understood in terms of the sort of architecture sketched in Figure 6.25. This is not supposed to be a detailed example of an actual model of speech perception, but the figure does provide an illustration of the sorts of

processes and representations that are germane to so-called **interactive activation models** (McClelland & Rumelhart, 1981; Rumelhart, 1977).

Structurally we may distinguish several stages of processing. Initially there are the low-level acoustic analyses that give rise to some basic representation of the speech signal and for ease of exposition we are simply going to discuss an early level of representation that is captured by abstract phoneme detectors. Each

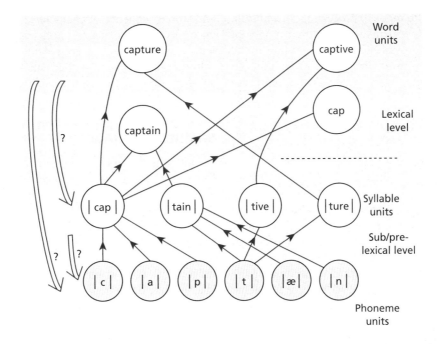

**Figure 6.25 A schematic representation of a hypothetical interactive activation model of speech perception**
Three levels of processing units are posited: (i) *phoneme units* (i.e., phoneme detectors) – each unit responds to a particular phoneme in the language; (ii) *syllable units*/detectors – each unit responds to a particular syllable in the language; and (iii) lexical or *word units*/detectors – each unit responds to a particular word in the language.

The phoneme and syllable units are known as *pre-lexical* or *sub-lexical* units whereas the word units are known as *lexical units*. Collectively the word units constitute something known as the *mental lexicon* – the internal store of knowledge about words in the language. In this case, each word unit contains a specification of how a particular word sounds. The solid arrows stand for connections between units in which information is fed forwards. The back arrows signify feedback connections from the higher-level units to the lower-level units. In interactive activation models, information can flow in both directions and the feedback connections convey how stored knowledge may affect the perceptual analysers.

phoneme in the language has its associated phoneme detector; for instance, the /t/ light will switch on whenever /t/ occurs in the speech signal. At the next level we have set out syllable detectors. Following on from the logic just set out, there now is a syllable detector for each syllable in the language – the 'tain' light will switch on whenever /tain/ is present in the speech signal. Finally in our caricature of the spoken word recognition system, there are word detectors.

Now the understanding is that knowledge of words of the language is stored in something akin to a mental dictionary (or alternatively a **mental lexicon**) – among other things, knowledge of a given word's spelling (its so-called *orthographic description*) and how a given word sounds when pronounced (its **phonological description**) are assumed. In this way it is argued that each word has its own so-called lexical entry (its place in the dictionary). There is an abstract word detector for each familiar word in the language and made-up pseudo-words or non-words have no such lexical entries.

To adopt more common language, we can refer to the phoneme, syllable and word detectors as being akin to simple processing units and, having introduced this terminology, phoneme and syllable units are known as 'sub-lexical' units (Samuel, 1996b) and the word units are known as lexical units. One way of thinking is that the sub-lexical units are beneath the lexical units and this fits with our simple diagram because the architecture sketched out is hierarchical in nature. As we progress through the diagram from the bottom to the top, the higher units are built on the lower units such that the lower units are in a sense constituents of the higher units.

Having sketched out the architecture of the model it is now important to discuss processing. In a standard feed-forward account, processing starts at the bottom of the model and activation percolates all the way to the top. First the phoneme units become activated; they then pass activation forward to the syllable units; and finally the word units become activated. This is the classic bottom-up mode of processing. In addition, we may also ask as to whether top-down modes of processing are also possible. Can activation flow in the opposite direction – from the higher-order units to the lower-order units? In the same way that phoneme detectors are activated from incoming stimulus information, is it also possible that they can become activated from the higher-level units? The idea that feedback can operate in this manner lies at the heart of interactive activation accounts of processing.

Within this kind of interactive activation framework it is possible to conceive of a speech processing system that operates in the following manner. As soon as speech enters the system, activation begins to flow towards the lexicon, and as soon as any lexical unit becomes activated, activation then begins to flow in the opposite (top-down) direction. So on hearing the /ca/ in /captain/ the constituent /c/ and /a/ phoneme units become activated and these in turn activate all lexical units beginning in /ca/. These lexical units now begin to propagate activation back down towards the sub-lexical units and their constituent phoneme units become activated from the top down. In this way expectations about the world are driven by knowledge of the world. On hearing /ca/ an expectation is generated about the possibly up-and-coming /ptain/.

## Interactive activation and phonemic restoration

So how does all this relate to phonemic restoration? Well, these basic ideas allow quite a number of predictions to be made about the nature of the effect. For instance, if the effect reflects top-down influences, we can predict that there ought to be larger phonemic restoration effects for words than for non-words, the reason being that whereas words possess lexical entries, and these can generate top-down activation of the phoneme detectors, non-words possess no lexical units hence there can be no top-down activation. However, we need to relax this assumption a little because there is no reason to suppose that non-words will never activate word detectors. It is hard to see why 'desparate' should not activate the word detector for 'desperate', especially if you're bad at spelling. So although 'desparate' has no lexical entry of its own, it seems highly likely that it will partially activate at least one word detector. By this view, any string of letters or phonemes is capable of activating word detectors such that the level of activation of a given word detector will reflect the degree of overlap between the input

and stored sequence of characters. The critical difference between a word and a non-word stimulus is that with a word there is a consistent pattern of activation that obtains across a particular set of lexical and sub-lexical units. Non-words will typically give rise to inconsistent patterns of activation.

## Samuel's findings

In line with this kind of argument Samuel (1981b) found that more restoration (lower $d'$ values) occurred for words (such as prOgress) than for phonologically legal pseudo-words (such as crOgress – in these examples the capital O is the critical phoneme). This shows that participants were essentially worse in their judgements concerning words than they were in their judgements concerning non-words. They were less able to make the added/replaced judgements for words than non-words. Their impression of the words was, in a sense, clearer than that for the non-words – they were less able to hear what was wrong with the words than they were the non-words. Moreover, and taken at face value, the results indicate how subjective factors can alter the sensitivity of the perceptual analysis. Within the traditional SDT framework for thinking, such a change in $d'$ is related to the stored knowledge that the participant brings to the task. Stored knowledge about the acoustic nature of words was taken to influence the acoustic analysis for those words. In this respect the data have been taken to show how top-down influences can operate at a perceptual stage: a conclusion that fits comfortably with interactive activation accounts of speech perception.

More particularly, according to Samuel's 'partially interactive' account (Samuel, 1981b), lexical units activated corresponding phoneme detectors and this was taken as evidence of a top-down influence in perception. Information from the speech signal made contact with stored knowledge about particular words and because of this appropriate phoneme detectors became activated. In other words, the top-down activation of word knowledge brought about tuning of particular perceptual mechanisms as evidenced by the effect on $d'$.

Although later work has replicated this so-called lexical effect, Samuel (1996b) did offer a cautious appraisal, in arguing that these effects are real, but fragile. However, in addition to the lexical effect on $d'$, Samuel (1981b) also reported an additional effect of response bias. Now when listeners were provided with a leading sentential context (Mary had a little l*mb) they were more likely to say that a word was intact when it was expected than when it was not (Peter saw a little l*mb).

As an overall pattern of findings, therefore, the data suggest that phonemic restoration can arise for a variety of reasons. It is far too much of an over-simplification to think the data reflect only changes in sensitivity or only changes in bias. Depending on the testing conditions, the effect can arise for a number of different reasons and these have to be taken into account in trying to explain the various patterns of performance. The most provocative findings relate to the effects on $d'$. → See 'What have we learnt?', below.

## Pinpoint question 6.9

**What critical data point reveals a top-down effect on phonemic restoration in Samuel (1981a)?**

# Perception as constrained hallucination?

By extension a more far-reaching conclusion, and one that is resisted by some (see Fodor, 1985; Norris, McQueen & Cutler, 2002), is that constrained hallucination provides a useful framework for thinking about perception in general. This conclusion, though, has been, and continues to be, hotly contested. Indeed there is a fiercely defended alternative view that all of the evidence that is garnered in support of top-down (feed-back) influences in perception can also be accom-modated by feed-forward systems (see Norris et al., 2002; and for commentaries for a lively discussion, and for the alternative view, see McClelland, Mirman, & Holt, 2006). Accordingly, neither embellishment nor tuning of perceptual mechanisms is necessarily warranted by the data. The counter-view is essentially that the perceptual representation of the stimulus remains a raw record of bottom-up processing, and that it in no way contains any added components from the top down!

The debate is both involved and long-standing and there is simply no way in which justice can be done to the subtleties of the many points made. However, just one issue will be discussed and this relates to the view that changes in $d'$ arise purely as a function of percep-tual analyses and that response bias effects (as revealed by changes in β) arise purely as a function of post-perceptual mechanisms. The contrasting claim is that if we assume a number of distinct stages of process-ing, then each of these may have their own sensitivity and bias characteristics and that there is no necessity in assuming that a change in $d'$ reflects a particular property of perceptual mechanisms and β reflects response bias.

## What is the correct interpretation of changes in d′ and changes in β?

From our previous discussion of SDT (see Chapter 4), $d'$ reflects the distance between the signal + noise distribution and the noise alone distribution. The

## → What have we learnt?

In summary, the evidence of phonemic restoration can be taken to show how embellishment might take place in perception. By this view it is perfectly acceptable to argue that the eventual perceptual representation is a blend of bottom-up stimulus information and information contributed on the basis of expectations and knowledge. As Samuel (1981b) concluded, this is not to imply that listeners 'hallucinate' everything they hear: 'the percep-tual system does not indiscriminately synthesize phonemes: rather speech is generated only when there is confirmation in the acoustic signal that the expected sound really is present' (p. 1131). In this regard the notion is of perception as a very con-strained form of hallucination.

The intuitive appeal of this line of argument is that such a form of hallucination may confer an advantage because of the nature of the problem facing the auditory system. The speech signal unfolds over time so in the absence of a very good acoustical memory, and in cases where it is impos-sible to ask the speaker to repeat themselves, there literally is no going back. In this regard, it is in the listener's best interests to extract as much useful information as possible on the first pass and to work on this as best they can. It is also typically the case that speech is present in a background filled with extraneous noise. Given such profound constraints – speech is transient and it is sometimes obscured by noise – it is argued that the perception of speech has evolved to tolerate such imperfection. Maybe constrained hallucination is the best solution to this very difficult problem? (See Warren, 1999, ch. 6, for a much more thorough discussion of these ideas.)

underlying continuum was traditionally discussed as capturing variation in the outputs of the sensory encoding mechanisms. Although this is a very common characterisation, Pastore, Crawley, Berens and Skelly (2003) have asserted that this view is simply wrong. All that needs to be assumed is that the continuum provides 'some measure of evidence for (or against) a particular alternative' (Wickens, 2002, p. 150). Even though it is possible to argue that measures of sensitivity may reflect the operation of encoding or sensory mechanisms they need not do so. In accepting this argument, it weakens any claimed link between $d'$ and the operation of purely perceptual mechanisms. This is especially so in multi-stage models – each stage may be characterised as having sensitivity and bias parameters defined relative to its own evidence continuum.

To provide a particular example, Masson and Borowsky (1998) considered performance in a lexical decision experiment and discussed what may happen on a given trial when a word is presented. In making a word response the decision can be influenced by the familiarity of the word's orthographic pattern and by semantic information. In other words, how it is spelt and what it means separately contribute to the lexical decision. So we have processes associated with orthographic familiarity and separate processes concerning the derivation of meaning. The point is that

any effect of sensitivity may be due to either or both of these processes. As Masson and Borowsky (1998) concluded, 'unless we can be certain that task performance is determined exclusively by perceptual processes, sensitivity effects cannot unambiguously be attributed to changes in perceptual processing'.

Indeed further problems have been identified by Norris (1986, 1995). He claimed to have shown how changes in $d'$ may actually arise from changes in criteria. Therefore, in contrast to the assumptions we have made previously, changes in $d'$ may therefore reflect changes in some form of post-perceptual mechanism (though for a careful and contrary appraisal of these ideas see Pastore, Crawley, Skelly, & Berens, 2003). So together the claims (a) that $d'$ does not necessarily reflect the operation of sensory mechanisms, and (b) that changes in $d'$ may reflect changes in some form of post-perceptual mechanisms, seriously undermine the argument that SDT can be used to adjudicate between perceptual and post-perceptual mechanisms. The whole edifice begins to crumble. → See 'What have we learnt?', below.

## Pinpoint question 6.10

Why might changes in $d'$ not be related to perceptual processes after all?

## → What have we learnt?

So where does this leave us? Well, recently a rather dark shadow has been cast over the traditional application of SDT and the contingent interpretation of $d'$ and β in terms of perceptual and post-perceptual mechanisms, respectively. Perhaps with the benefit of hindsight, this is not surprising, for as Pastore, Crawley, Skelly et al. (2003) argued, 'any dependent measure ([such as] $d'$ . . . reaction time etc.) . . . must reflect the combined action of all of the processes between stimulus and response'. Furthermore, 'SDT models decision making based on the distributions of available, evaluated information but does not model the processes intervening between the presentation of the information and the decision' (p. 1264). A stark conclusion can be drawn. This is that the traditional application of SDT, to the issue of perceptual vs. conceptual processes, cannot be sustained in the absence of a detailed specification of the nature of the intervening processes between stimulus and response. We

cannot take changes in $d'$ to be an unequivocal index of changes in some form of perceptual analysis in the absence of a very precise account of processing.

Debate continues over the particularities of auditory word perception and the specific issue of how best to interpret lexical influences on phoneme detection (see Magnuson, McMurray, Tanenhaus & Aslin, 2003; McClelland et al., 2006; Samuel, 2001). There is no doubt that a much clearer understanding of SDT has emerged (Pastore, Crawley, Berens et al., 2003; Pastore, Crawley, Skelly et al., 2003), but a consequence of this is that the interpretation of effects showing a change in sensitivity must be now treated with some caution. The central issue, of whether feedback from the higher conceptual levels to lower perceptual levels does actually take place, remains hotly contested and has yet to be resolved to anyone's satisfaction (see Pylyshyn, 1999, and commentaries, and McClelland et al., 2006).

phonemic restoration The perception of an intact phoneme when it is in fact not present in a spoken utterance.

added stimuli In the phonemic restoration paradigm, where noise is added to the critical phoneme.

replaced stimuli In the phonemic restoration paradigm, where the critical phoneme is replaced by noise.

interactive activation models Processing systems in which information can both feed forward information from lower levels to higher levels and be fed back from higher levels to lower levels.

mental lexicon The 'mental' dictionary in which knowledge about words in a given natural language is represented.

phonological description The internal specification of how a word is pronounced. A pronounceable non-word also has a phonological description.

## Pulling it all together

We've come quite a long way in this chapter, from the consideration of how we may perceive the outline of a square to how individuals detect changes in complex real-world scenes. In standing back from this material, certain themes have emerged and certain conclusions suggest themselves. Perhaps the easiest way to begin to sum up is to consider what the ultimate purpose of the perceptual system actually is.

Arguably a critical consequence of reaching a decision over what caused the proximal stimulus is that we can begin to make predictions about our immediate environment. We can begin to make predictions about the next perceptual moment, both in terms of (i) how entities in the world will interact with one another and (ii) how we should interact with them. The central claim therefore is that the perceptual system has evolved to provide a representation of the world that supports useful predictions to be made about the world. To discuss knowledge-driven processes in perception is an implicit endorsement of this view – predictions are constantly being made about the next state of the world on the basis of the current perceptual moment and what has gone before. An inability to make predictions such as these would most likely result in sudden death – think about not having the ability to predict the direction of oncoming traffic while crossing the road. Indeed this notion of generating and testing predictions lies at the very heart of the

analysis-by-synthesis view of perception. Having stated this, however, we need to tread carefully before we embrace analysis by synthesis fully. There are concerns about (i) embellishment in perception, and (ii) top-down influences in perception.

## Embellishment in perception revisited

The first cause for concern is with the notion of embellishment in perception. Whether or not there truly is embellishment in perception remains, essentially, unresolved. By the modularity view (Fodor, 1983) the perceptual system is by necessity insulated from any form of cognitive intervention – the perceptual system should merely deliver a veridical (truthful) representation of the environment so that the cognitive system can then go to work and make necessary inferences. More particularly, the cognitive system should not alter the perceptual representation in any way because the consequences of making a wrong guess could prove to be fatal. This view stands in contrast to that provided by embellishment theories such as analysis by synthesis. By these accounts the perceptual representation contains a combination of both aspects of the stimulus and aspects of stored knowledge.

Such problems may be sidestepped on the understanding that it is sensible to distinguish a perceptual representation from any interpretation that is placed on the proximal stimulus (Wilton, personal communication). Consider Figure 6.26. According to the present view, the perceptual representation provides a specification of a series of unconnected black segments on a white background. Two plausible interpretations of this representation are black blobs on a white background (Rock, 1986, called this the *literal solution*) or 'lady and lapdog'. It is for this reason that

**Figure 6.26** Obvious, right?

*Source*: Leeper, R. (1935). A study of a neglected portion of the field of learning – The development of sensory organization. *Journal of Genetic Psychology, 46*, 41–75 (fig. 1, p. 49). Reproduced with permission of the Helen Dwight Reid Educational Foundation.

it is best to separate out a perceptual representation from an interpretation that is placed on it. The perceptual representation supports 'seeing', whereas the interpretation provides the 'seeing as'.

By the modularity of mind view (see Fodor, 1985, for example), the perceptual representation is the product of purely bottom-up figure–ground segmentation processes and this should be treated as being separate from any interpretation of the stimulus. Moreover, in keeping the perceptual representation separate from some form of interpretation there is no need to assume that the eventual percept is simply the sum of contributions from input and stored knowledge – the marks on the piece of paper are represented veridically in the perceptual representation and any knowledge about ladies and lapdogs is quite separate from this. How such knowledge is brought to bear to form an impression of the stimulus falls within the realm of cognition, not perception. By this view embellishment plays no role in how we perceive the world.

## Top-down influences in perception revisited

Closely aligned to these concerns about perceptual embellishment are the many vexed and unsettled issues over the involvement of top-down factors in perception. A recurrent cause for concern has been the degree to which (indeed if at all) the perceptual analysis stage is affected by knowledge – to what degree is perceptual analysis knowledge driven? Purely bottom-up (modularity) theorists argue that perceptual processes are essentially insulated from any form of cognitive intervention (Fodor, 1983; Pylyshyn, 1999; Rock, 1986). For example, as has been repeatedly argued (Fodor, 1983; Rock, 1983, ch. 11; Rock 1986), the Muller–Lyer illusion simply will not go away if the participant is informed that the two lines are of equal length. No matter how hard you try, the two lines do look different in length. Despite what you know, the percept refuses to change in line with this knowledge. This sort of evidence has been taken to show that the input modules are autonomous – that they operate independently of one another and of the central mechanisms.

This notion of autonomy has been justified on the grounds that the eventual perceptual representation must be largely insensitive to what the perceiver presumes, needs or desires as a matter of reliability. For the system to function reliably it should provide a veridical (truthful) representation of what is actually out there, rather than one that specifies what is expected or desired. Now, of course, given that perceptual illusions

do exist, then this shows that the perceptual system does not function optimally in all cases – in the Muller–Lyer illusion the lines are not different lengths, they are the same length. To reiterate, however, Kanizsa (1985) has taken such evidence to argue that the visual system works according to 'autonomous principles of organization' (p. 33) that are independent of logic, expectations and knowledge. We need therefore to go some way before we fully understand the principles of stimulus encoding. The perceptual system offers a best first guess as to what is out there; it is then up to the interpretative mechanisms to arrive at a decision.

Nevertheless, the arguments go to and fro. One point of agreement is that everyone accepts that the human information processing system capitalises on the predictable nature of the structure of the world. The disagreements are with how this comes about. According to interactive activation accounts, predictability is used to tune the perceptual analysers such that expected information is in some sense prioritised over the unexpected. For instance, top-down activation of perceptual analysers results in particular analysers being facilitated relative to others. For instance, the T detector reaches threshold before the F detector because in the context of '?able', 'table' is the more likely candidate than 'fable.' By this view, top-down factors are instrumental in showing how evidence consistent with one interpretation of the world is processed faster than a different interpretation. In this way the expected is prioritised over the unexpected (see McClelland et al. 2006, for a more thorough exposition of this point).

In contrast to this, it is argued that the unexpected ought not to be disadvantaged in any way because it is the unexpected that can prove fatal for the organism (Gregory, 1980). Consistent with this view is the idea that top-down effects actually reflect post-perceptual stages of processing. According to the modular view of processing, top-down effects reflect interpretations placed on a perceptual representation and that the corresponding effects are located at a post-perceptual level (after Fodor, 1983, and Pylyshyn, 1999). However, this general view has struggled to accommodate any related effects attributed to changes in sensitivity (i.e., $d'$) where the effects have been interpreted either as the tuning of particular perceptual analyses or the moderation of these analyses by so-called knowledge-driven processes. Such possibilities are ruled out by the strictly modular view.

Proponents of the modular account have argued that, in the absence of any other compelling evidence, changes in $d'$ cannot be equivocally attributed to changes taking place during perceptual encoding. We have seen that, in the context of a multi-stage processing system, such a simple explanation is problematic. As Rhodes and Kalish (1999) stated, 'sensitivity and bias can be measured for discriminations mediated by any level of the system and changes in sensitivity will be evidence for perceptual change only if the discrimination is based on perceptual, rather than post-perceptual or semantic cues' (p. 391).

In conclusion, arguments about the nature of top-down effects in perception continue and remain, essentially, unresolved. Controversy remains and there simply are at present no easy answers. We will, however, continually return to this issue as we proceed to consider (i) the nature of attention and its relation to perception, and (ii) the nature of language and its relation to perception. In the meantime it is best to draw the chapter to a close by simply summarising the general framework for thinking that has emerged from our discussion.

## Concluding comments

We have accepted the idea that the human perceptual system operates so as to generate a perceptual representation of the external world that specifies objects within the current environment. It has been accepted that there is an initial stage of perceptual analysis that produces a suggestion as to what is present in the immediate environment. By the present view the Gestalt laws are central at this initial stage because they provide useful ways of carving up the sensory stimulation into plausible figures and plausible ground from the bottom up. These sorts of segregation processes oper-

ate in the same way for both familiar and unfamiliar stimuli alike (Marr, 1982). The default position in this account is to assume that the generation of this perceptual representation operates initially in a bottom-up fashion according to certain hard-wired operations that have evolved over the course of human evolution. In this sense, the human perceptual system implements the likelihood principle – the hard-wired constraints in the human perceptual system reflect properties of the world.

This initial stage produces a suggestion about the possible cause of the proximal stimulus. Such a suggestion is primarily derived from the bottom up and in order for this suggestion to be confirmed, it is necessary to invoke further active processes of inquiry. Such further analyses of the input can now be undertaken under volitional control. More particularly the initial perceptual suggestion is typically couched at a crude level such that an object type is suggested – this is Navon's principle of global addressability (2003) and this forms the initial interpretation of the stimulus. The subsequent analyses constitute a much more fine-grained examination of the stimulus. In keeping the perceptual representation separate from its interpretation, it becomes clearer how the suggest/inquire framework may operate. From the perceptual representation certain interpretations are suggested and it is these that are followed by the selective probing of this representation (cf. Navon, 2003, pp. 287–8).

Clearly this general account can be challenged by any argument for or demonstration of top-down influences at the level of perceptual encoding. In this regard the assumption for bottom-up only processing at the perceptual level is both controversial and vulnerable. We will return to this assumption as discussion proceeds and we will need to reconsider it carefully as the material unfolds.

## CHAPTER SUMMARY

- Both the minimum principle and the likelihood principle have been put forward as explanation as to how we might build an impression of the world. For the minimum principle, we choose the most economic fit. For the likelihood principle, we choose the most likely fit.

- The structural information theory (SIT; Boselie & Leeuwenberg, 1986) suggests one way in which simple interpretations of visual scenes are preferred over complicated interpretations. Here, primitive codes are developed which attempt to encapsulate a visual scene in various ways and the preferred interpretation is the one that eventuates in the shortest internal code. While the SIT is an extremely well-specified theory, the empirical support is somewhat lacking.

- In terms of comparing the minimum and likelihood principles, it has been shown that these approaches are mathematically equivalent (Chater, 1996) and that in both cases, the general aim is to minimise uncertainty within a visual scene. Although van der Helm (2000) has offered a critique of Chater's approach to the issues, he asserted that the minimum principle is better from an evolutionary perspective since it can be applied within any common or uncommon environment. Despite this (claimed) evolutionary advantage, the case for the minimum principle is not convincing. As Sutherland (1988) pointed out, when the minimum and likelihood principles are put in opposition to one another, it is not clear that the minimum principle would provide the preferred solution.

- A limitation of the minimum principle vs. likelihood principle debate is that it seems not to consider, in any serious way, active processes in vision. In fact it is possible that the issues relate more to the initial derivation of a stimulus representation than to the final means by which a decision is made about the possible distal stimulus. The suggest-then-inquire framework for thinking was reintroduced and fleshed out in terms of the evidence for global-to-local processing. In a typical experiment, compound letters (e.g., Navon, 1977) – in which larger letters were built up of smaller letters – were presented and participants were required to categorise either the global or local identity of the letter. Two robust effects have been observed: (i) a global advantage such that responses are generally better when judgements are made about the global letters than when they are made about the local letters; and (ii) global-to-local interference in the absence of local-to-global interference. Generally speaking, participants' responses to local letters are impeded in the presence of conflicting global information. This overall pattern of effects reflects the notion of global addressability and a crude-to-fine scheme of perceptual analysis.

- Another paradigm that supports the notion of crude-to-fine processing is change blindness (Rensink, 2002). Here, subjects are presented with two alternating pictures that differ according to a single aspect. Subjects are faster at detecting change when this is of central interest as opposed to marginal interest (Rensink, O'Regan, & Clark, 1997), suggesting that the gist of a scene is encoded before specific details of that scene.

- Another major theme in perception research concerns how to resolve the issue of how it is that context may affect perception. The analysis-by-synthesis approach to speech perception attempts to consolidate ideas about how the eventual percept may be a blend of information derived from the stimulus and information provided by stored knowledge. Specifically, an initial estimate of the distal stimulus is generated by perceptual analysis and then this estimate is synthesised with previously stored knowledge, giving rise to a percept. This percept is compared with the input and if a mismatch is found, then the analysis by synthesis undergoes another cycle of hypothesis testing. Evidence for analysis by synthesis has been provided by demonstrations of speech perception (Stevens & Halle, 1967) and categorical perception (Liberman et al., 1957).

- One aspect of analysis by synthesis suggests that perception is in part an act of embellishment. That is, prior knowledge helps to flesh out an otherwise impoverished proximal representation of the distal stimulus. Another theoretical approach that addresses the notion of prior knowledge is Minsky's (1975) frame theory. This is essentially a slot-and-filler framework of thinking in which knowledge of stereotypical objects and scenes are stored in memory and these guide our perceptions of the world. Each frame has a number of slots and these must be filled with certain values. However, such knowledge-driven accounts of perception cannot explain how perception operates in completely unfamiliar or unexpected environments.

- Despite this, embellishment accounts of perception such as the frame theory have found support in the data derived from experiments on phonemic restoration. Here, subjects were played speech with certain phonemes being replaced with noise or simply having noise added to them (Samuel, 1981a). Interest was in the extent to which subjects heard the speech as complete, and under which conditions the phonemes were restored. By comparing between words and non-words, it was possible to assess the contribution of prior knowledge on perception. In short, phonemes in words were restored more often than in non-words, demonstrating the interaction between bottom-up (stimulus-driven) and top-down (prior knowledge) effects on perception. This led some researchers to wonder whether perception wasn't more generally a constrained hallucination, given that what individuals experienced was a mixture of both external and internal information.

- Issues remain over whether the evidence points to the conclusion that perceptual analysis is an autonomous stage of processing or whether, in contrast, it can be influenced by stored knowledge.

## ANSWERS TO PINPOINT QUESTIONS

6.1  An equilateral triangle might be represented by the primitive code '$a\,\delta\,a\,\delta\,a$' where $a$ represents a line of fixed length and $\delta$ represents a clockwise or counter-clockwise rotation of 120°.

6.2  Since you are more likely to owe them money, then you are more likely to read that you owe them money.

6.3  Redundancies in any information processing are useful because in the case of some form of system failure, although some copies of a message may be lost, some information may reach its destination.

6.4  A local advantage would occur when responses to some local aspect of a stimulus were in some sense more efficient than responses to a global aspect.

6.5  Change blindness supports notions of crude-to-fine processing since participants do not recover scene details immediately. First they acquire the gist and it is only after repeated viewings that they may be able to recover a specific change across the two images.

6.6  In analysis by synthesis, the perceptual analyses are bottom up whereas the hypotheses are top down.

6.7  Categorical perception would state that the distinction between the 8 oz baby and the 9 oz bag of flour would be easier to detect since these objects belong to different categories.

6.8  Both words and non-words were used in order to assess the influence of prior knowledge on the phonemic restoration effect. Prior knowledge should only be available for words.

6.9  A top-down effect on phonemic restoration was revealed in that participants were relatively unable to discriminate added vs. replaced phonemes in words. They had much less difficulty in making similar judgements with non-words. In this regard, it was concluded that stored knowledge about words (rather than non-words) was influencing the acoustic analysis of the stimuli.

6.10  $d'$ does not necessarily relate to perceptual processes if we assume that there are many intervening stages between receiving sensory stimulation and making a response for the effect and operations at any one of the stages may be responsible (Masson & Borowsky, 1998).

## CHAPTER 7

# MENTAL REPRESENTATION

## LEARNING OBJECTIVES

**By the end of this chapter, you should be able to:**

- Describe different views on analogical representation.
- Understand what is meant by a cognitive map and explain the virtues of holding one in mind.
- Detail features of the dual-format theory (Kosslyn, 1980) and the difference between depictive and descriptive mental representations.
- Understand what is meant by mental scanning (Kosslyn & Pomerantz, 1977; Pylyshyn, 1981) and describe related experiments.
- Discuss the debate on the ambiguous nature of visual images.
- Understand what is meant by mental rotation (Shepard & Cooper, 1982) and describe related experiments.
- Explain key features of mentalese and propositional representation.

## CHAPTER CONTENTS

# You are nothing!

Sorry to have to break this to you, but really, you are nothing. You have no inner life. There might as well just be a big empty space where your brain should be because all you do, all day every day, is just make these mindless responses to your environment. Don't believe us? Well, imagine that you're walking down your local high street at the weekend. In the window of a large department store, you see the advert that you saw on TV last night for the Flashy3000, the all-in-one digital music player, pet locater and espresso machine. Because the TV advert was so funny and the colours and patterns of the advert were so appealing, you enter the shop to make an impulse buy because you know how good that will make you feel. Arriving at the Flashy3000 stand, you notice that you can buy it in all different colours. Since it's a nice sunny day, you decide to buy the yellow one and try not to think about how that will look when it's raining. You wonder exactly how much smaller it is compared to your old Flashy2000 and you imagine them both side by side. It's tiny and will fit in your jeans pockets. Great! Looking for a cash desk, you notice that the one at the front is crammed with a large number of equally eager Flashy3000 consumers. Since you used to work at this particular store, you know that there's a cash desk on the second floor that's always much quieter. You decide to take the lift up to the second floor, but it's broken. No matter, you remember where the stairs are and take the alternative route. Approaching the desk, you feel the surge of adrenalin. The exchange of money. That kick as the goods get handed over. This joy is slowly replaced by anxiety as you realise you now have no money left to buy groceries. However, since you used to work here, you also know where the returns counter is . . .

## REFLECTIVE QUESTIONS

1. Think about a large place that you know very well. This might be a city you once lived in. Have a start and end point and think about travelling between them. What sorts of information are stored in your cognitive map of this mental environment? Do you know whether you need to turn left or right at the end of the street? Do you know where the nearest dustbins or telephone boxes are? Would you know an alternative route if your imagined path was blocked?

2. Think about an object of sentimental value that you own. What kind of view do you have of the object – are you looking at it straight on or from the side? Are you able to look at the underside of the object? How are you able to do this? Is this a fine-grained representation you have with lots of detail? What kinds of information are you unable to retrieve simply by examining your mental representation of this object?

## Introduction and preliminary considerations

This chapter is about knowledge. This may all sound terribly philosophical; however, it is not so much concerned with the content of knowledge – what such knowledge is about – but much more to do with the format of knowledge. How is knowledge specified? How is knowledge represented in the mind? From Chapter 2 we have seen how the computational theory of mind is based on assumptions about internal representations and processes, yet very little has so far been given away about what **mental representation** may actually be like. To rectify this, the present chapter provides a general survey of various accounts of mental representation and considers how such ideas have been motivated by experimental data. Rather surprisingly, perhaps, the basic issues will be initially discussed in terms of behaviourist theorising.

As was spelt out in the earlier chapters, a central difference between cognitive and behavioural psychology is the degree to which assumptions are made about mental entities – few, if any, are made in behavioural accounts, and many and various assumptions are made in cognitive accounts. Behavioural psychologists have either completely avoided any talk about mental entities, or have theorised in language that disguises the fact that mental entities are being talked about. So in discussing the approach adopted by Clark L. Hull (a particularly influential behaviourist), Miller (1962) stated that, 'His ambition was to specify rigorously a small number of mathematical variables inside the organism that would account for all of the observed correlations between stimulation and response' (p. 215). Cognitive psychologists, in contrast, have embraced the concept of mental representation. Indeed, we are almost at a point where it seems no longer possible to offer an account of some aspect of behaviour if it fails to acknowledge the necessity of internal mental processes and mental representations. This chapter, therefore, is focused on the basic notion of mental representation and how different accounts of mental representation have been put forward in the literature. How is knowledge represented in the mind?

It would be easy to state that the best way to proceed falls somewhere between the polar caricatures of the behaviourist and cognitivist approaches. A much more interesting discussion, though, can be offered if some of the basic assumptions about knowledge are laid bare and are examined carefully. Behaviourists have a very dim view of any talk about mental representation

(see, for example, Skinner, 1985) so maybe we can explain behaviour without any consideration of how knowledge is represented in the mind? Given that this book is about cognitive psychology, it is quite important to be able to counter such views and examine the evidence that has been used to argue for mental representation. It is for this reason that we begin by considering how and why the concept of mental representation has its roots in behavioural psychology. It could be argued that cognitive psychology as a discipline grew out of a deep-seated dissatisfaction with psychological theories that denied any talk of mental representation; however, a much more subtle story can be told and it is to this that we now turn.

> **mental representation** Stored knowledge as captured by internal forms of presentation in the mind.

## How rats running mazes led to some insights about mental representation

If you were a rat looking for employment in the early twentieth century, then the chances are that you could have ended up being involved in some form of behavioural research. In a bid to examine various aspects of learning, researchers took it upon themselves to observe the behaviour of rats in mazes. A typical maze would contain a start box in which the rat was placed at the beginning of the trial, a goal box in which some form of reward (typically food or water) was placed, and a connecting set of passage ways between the start and end boxes. Tolman (1948) described such a typical experiment.

On day 1 a hungry rat is placed in the start box and left to its own devices. Being a reasonably inquisitive animal, the rat will typically begin to explore the maze and, given enough time, may well chance upon the goal box and therefore eat (or drink). If this procedure is repeated (one trial a day for several days) then the typical, and perhaps not surprising, result is that the rat will tend to speed up in the amount of time it takes to travel between the start and goal boxes. This speeding up is taken to be an index of learning and is assumed to reflect the fact that the rat eventually learns the quickest route through the maze from start box to goal box.

So far none of the foregoing should be contentious. What is contentious, though, is the issue of what exactly underlies such learning. To answer this question, Tolman discussed the so-called *stimulus–response (S–R) school of behaviourism*. This form of behaviourism explained the learning in terms of the strengthening of a whole chain of stimulus–response bonds (see Chapter 1). Here the idea is that the rat, in traversing the maze from start to goal box, is learning to strengthen a particular intervening chain of S–R pairings. By this kind of account, and from the animal's point of view, the initial impression of the start box is associated with placing this paw down in order to move out of the start box, the next impression of the maze is associated with placing this next paw down in order to move further along the maze, and so on. Each impression of the maze acts as a stimulus for a particular bodily movement or response. Ultimately, the animal would be rewarded by arriving at the goal box and by gaining access to the food or water. In repeating the previous sequence of movements on the ensuing days the whole chain of S–R associations would be strengthened by successfully finding the reward: it is this that is reflected in the rat quickening over subsequent testing sessions.

## Pinpoint question 7.1

**According to a strictly behaviourist account, why does a rat get quicker at finding food in a maze when it is placed at the same location day after day?**

The preceding description has been couched at a level that only makes mention of external events, but Tolman (1932/1967) conceded that the S–R school did also allow for the fact that the S–R bonds could reflect structural changes at the level of the central nervous system (CNS). The assumption was that the CNS could be construed as being akin 'to a complicated telephone switchboard', the analogy here being that 'There are incoming calls from the sense organs and there are outgoing messages to the muscles' (p. 243). Learning is therefore equated with the strengthening of appropriate connections between input and output mechanisms together with the weakening of inappropriate connections. It is assumed that the S–R chains can reside internally in the animal, hence this form of behavioural theorising acknowledges the importance of internal representations and processes (it just fails to discuss them in terms of mental entities – see Chapter 1).

On the face of it, the earliest S–R accounts of learning are attractive because they are simple (remember

Occam's Razor?) and make no reference to unobservable events (see Chapter 1). Nevertheless, we need to ask the more penetrating question about whether such accounts provide adequate explanations of the rats' learning. Is this an adequate description of what is going on when the rat learns to find the reward? In adopting a critical tone, Tolman offered a contrasting account in terms of something he called **field theory**. Now the telephone exchange analogy (set out above) was replaced with a 'map control room' analogy (p. 244). According to Tolman, 'incoming impulses are usually worked over and elaborated in the central control room into a tentative cognitive-like map of the environment' (p. 245). What Tolman is arguing here is that the rats' behaviour in learning the routes through the maze reflects the acquisition of a *cognitive representation* that is like a *map*.

> **field theory** Tolman's account of the learning behaviour of rats in mazes explained in terms of means–end expectation.

## Maps and cognitive maps

Much of the ensuing material has been distilled through notes provided by, and discussion with, Richard Wilton of Dundee University. Some of the issues to be addressed are covered in Wilton (2000). In order to understand what is being claimed here, it is important to understand what sort of representation a map is. Let us take the case of a standard street map of London as a simple example. A useful distinction here is that between the **represented world** and the **representing world** (Rumelhart & Norman, 1985). In the present example, the represented world is the set of streets (the external world) that make up London: the representing world is the actual map of the streets of London. In contrasting the information in the represented world with that in the representing world, it is important to realise that only some of the information in the represented world is present in the representing world. An obvious example is that the 3D external world is reduced into the 2D bird's eye of view that is captured by a street map. Not all information present in the represented world is included in the representing world. For instance, information about the height of the buildings has been discarded.

Something else that makes a map a special form of representation is its spatial nature. According to

Gallistel (1990), a map represents **geometric relations** that are present in the represented world (p. 9). Having stated this, though, we have to tread carefully because the map may capture only some of the spatial relationships in the represented world. With the street map example we have already seen how things like the height of buildings or indeed the height of the actual terrain is not represented. The street map does not capture spatial relations in the vertical direction (you would need an Ordnance Survey map for this). However, in other respects what the street map does capture is a reasonably complete record of the planar (horizontal) spatial relationships that are present in the represented world.

## Analogical representation

If the map is very detailed then it is possible to imagine that this would correspond perfectly with a line drawing made from a satellite photograph of the mapped area. (One way to grasp the point is by going to Google Maps and typing in your favourite location and then toggle back and forth between the Satellite and the Maps option; see Figure 7.1.) In this regard, the spatial relationships present in the map are *analogous* with those presented in the represented world. The length of Oxford Street corresponds directly with the length of the line on the map that denotes Oxford Street. In this respect, the street map is a form of **analogical representation**. There is a correspondence between the length of the represented streets and the length of the marks on the piece of paper that signify the streets themselves. That is, long lines signify long streets, and short lines signify short streets. In this way the lengths of the lines on the map share an analogical relation with actual distances in the real (represented) world.

Indeed, with the street map example, the spatial correspondences go further because locations that are near one another in the real world are near one another on the map. So the street map of London represents in an analogical way because of the correspondence between (i) the marks on the piece of paper and (ii) entities, such as buildings and streets, in the real world. There is a related general point here that should also be introduced before we proceed. A useful distinction can be drawn between (i) things in the world (e.g., the buildings) and (ii) relations between those things (e.g., 'to the west of'). Given this distinction, the representing world will need to capture both (i) the things in the represented world and (ii) the relations between those things.

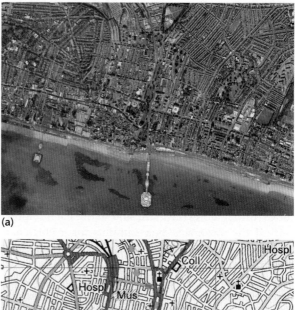

(a)

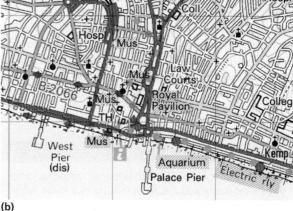

(b)

**Figure 7.1 Two representations of the same spatial layout** (a) shows an aerial photograph of a rather tawdry seaside resort in the south of England. (b) shows a corresponding map of the same area. The map shares strict analogical relations with the photograph in so far as parts of the drawing coincide exactly with features in the photograph.

*Sources*: (a) Skyscan; (b) Ordnance Survey.

### Analogical representations in the strict sense

Our street map is a form of analogical representation in a rather strict sense – dimensions in the represented world have analogous dimensions in the representing world (see Gregory, 1961). Palmer (1978) offered the following characteristics of **strict analogical representation**: 'Spatial information is not only preserved but it is preserved in (1) a spatial medium, and (2) in such a way that the image resembles that which it represents' (p. 295). So the map itself provides information about the real world in 2D and the information is conveyed in a way that it resembles what is being represented: long lines, long streets.

## Analogical representation in the lenient sense

All of this may come across as being quite obvious but such correspondences do not exist for all maps and not all forms of representations are analogical in this strict sense. Other forms of maps constitute what may be called **lenient analogical representation**. For instance, things are slightly more complicated for a map of the London Underground.

This map is an impoverished form of representation because only very few spatial relations in the represented world are captured in the representing world. All this map consists of (in essence) is a set of small circles and tick marks that are interconnected with lines of various colours. The map does, though, preserve some spatial information in a very approximate way, for instance, 'to the west of' in the world is conveyed by 'to the left of' in the map. Stations that are next to one another in the Underground network are next to one another in the map. Given this, it is useful to think of analogical representation in a less strict sense. Again Palmer (1978) provides a very use-

ful definition. In this case, the basic assumption is that such representations merely preserve spatial information in some way or other, 'if object A is above object B in the represented world, then the representing world – whatever that is – will have objects A and B in some relationship that functionally corresponds to "aboveness" in the real world' (Palmer, 1978, p. 295). To take the Underground map example, the fact that Piccadilly Circus is to the left of Leicester Square on the map is because Piccadilly Circus is to the west of Leicester Square in the real world.

In summary, a defining aspect of analogical representation is that 'an analogical representation has a structure which gives information about the structure, of the thing denoted, depicted or represented' (Sloman, 1978, p. 165). We should also be mindful, though, that, as Sloman (1978) has asserted, 'not ALL the properties and relations in analogical representation need be significant' (p. 165). For example, it is probably of no concern whether the map is drawn in pencil or black ink on pink or green paper, etc. Nonetheless, for the representation to be at all useful, the person must know what is important and what is not (see Figure 7.2).

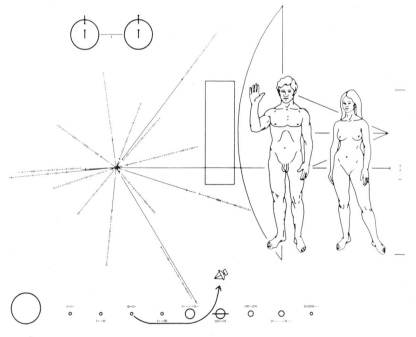

**Figure 7.2 The Pioneer plaque**
This image was created and attached to the Pioneer 10 space probe in case the spacecraft was intercepted by extraterrestrial beings. As can be seen, it contains a mixture of analogical representations and other more abstract symbols. The man and woman are shown as standing in front of an outline of the spacecraft in such a manner so as to convey the absolute size of humans. For those of you still in the dark, the dumb bell (upper left corner) represents the hyperfine transition of neutral hydrogen. (Obvious, right?) If you are still confused then take pity on the poor aliens because they have just come to the conclusion that there is a species out there whose members look like two circles connected by a line.
*Source*: Courtesy of National Aeronautics and Space Administration (NASA) (www.nasa.gov).

Having introduced the concept of analogical representation, we have gone one step further and distinguished a strict form of analogical representation from a lenient form of analogical representation:

- In the strict form of analogical representation (e.g., the street map), dimensions in the represented world have analogous dimensions in the representing world.

- In the lenient form of analogical representation (e.g., the Underground map), it is only the case that some spatial and some structural information is preserved in some fashion or other.

## Symbols and symbolic representation

Although we have classified our Underground map as being a lenient form of analogical representation, there are other aspects of this kind of representation that allow us to discuss some more general characteristics of **symbol system**s. For instance, it is possible to think of the map as being based on a *symbol system*. Both the stations and the spatial relations between the stations are captured in an abstract system of representation (known as a **representational system**). This system comprises symbols for the stations (the circles and tick marks) and symbols that signify the actual tracks (the lines) that connect the stations. To be exact, a representational system comprises both symbols and rules for combining and using the symbols. Such a system applies to our map of the Underground. For instance, a station can either be represented by a tick mark or by a circle, but not by both. A circle signifies an interchange station. Different stations are connected to one another via one or more lines, each of a particular colour, with the different colours reflecting different Underground lines.

To reiterate, although it is true that this particular map provides a 2D representation of particular places and routes in London, only certain spatial relations that exist in the represented world are present in this representing world. In this regard the map only captures 'next-to' or 'connected-with' relations that exist in the real world, together with some other relations concerning spatial layout. If the top of the map is taken as corresponding to north, then above–below

relations in the map signify north–south and left–right relations in the map signify west–east. In these respects the map is a lenient form of analogical representation. However, caution is warranted here because it can be particularly confusing to attempt to use this Underground map to explore London above ground. Places that seem close to one another in the map may be far apart in the world and also places far apart on the map may be very close above ground. The distances on the map between the stations do not correspond with the distances of the stations in the real world. Indeed, anybody who has taken the tube from Embankment to Charing Cross rather than walk it, will have got close to the definition of a futile exercise.

In conclusion, our map of the Underground provides an example of a lenient form of analogical representation because only some spatial relations are preserved. It is also an example of a symbolic representational system. The map comprises basic symbols (the station markers and the connections between these) that are governed by certain rules of combination (e.g., two markers for different stations that are connected together in the Underground network must be joined together by a line). For these reasons it may not be too helpful to try to draw a strict distinction between symbolic vs. analogical representations. Any given example may contain aspects of both (see Figure 7.2). Some further useful distinctions are drawn out in Figure 7.3.

Although such a digression into the nature of maps may seem to have taken us far from the topic of rats running mazes, Figure 7.4 shows a striking correspondence between the sort of Underground map we have been discussing and the sort of **cognitive map** that Tolman (1948) assumed the rats acquired as they became familiar with the structure of a given maze. In fact, anybody who has attempted to change from the Northern line to the District line at Embankment may actually begin to feel like a rat in a maze, so perhaps the analogy is not so far fetched. → See 'What have we learnt?', page 236.

→ See 'What have we learnt?', page 236.

### Pinpoint question 7.2

In what sense is a street map an analogical representation?

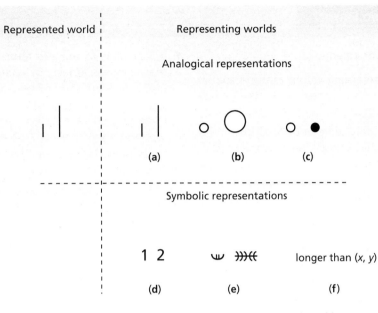

**Figure 7.3 Examples of different representational systems for the same represented world**
On the left of the figure is the external world (the represented world) comprising two vertical lines of different lengths. Various representing worlds (representational systems) are shown on the right of the figure. In the upper panels are various forms of analogical systems. (a) contains a literal representational system in which the representation contains a copy of the lines. (b) and (c) contain examples of different forms of non-literal systems. (b) is where the dimension of size of circle mirrors the length dimension, and (c) is where the dimension of brightness of circle mirrors the length dimension (i.e., the darker the circle, the longer the line).

In the lower panel are various forms of symbolic systems. In (d) line length is conveyed via Arabic numerals (i.e., a bigger number signifies a longer length). In (e) a completely arbitrary symbol system is used. In (f) a propositional form of representation is used (see later in the chapter). Although some of these systems are intuitively obvious, the central point is that they can only work when appropriate interpretative mechanisms are brought to bear. The mind of a Martian may be as in (e) but this can only be if the Martian has access to the meanings of the symbols. The Martian must be in possession of a representational system together with an understanding of how this links with the represented world.

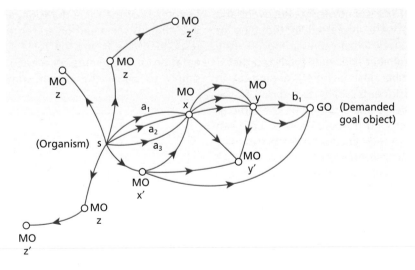

**Figure 7.4 Schematic representation of a cognitive map as discussed by Tolman (1948)**
*Source*: Tolman, E. C. (1967). *Purposive behavior in animals and man* (fig. 61, p. 177). New York: Appleton-Century-Croft.

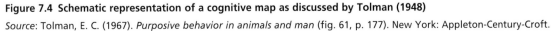

## → What have we learnt?

Several critical points emerge:

1. A map (the representing world) captures spatial relations that exist in the real world (the represented world).

2. Maps represent only some but not all such relations – they are, by necessity, an incomplete form of representation.

3. Maps can either represent the world in a strict analogical fashion in which there is a one-to-one correspondence between the nature of the map and the nature of the world (e.g., long lines stand for long streets) – dimensions in the represented world have analogous dimensions in the representing world. Other forms of maps are not strictly analogical, in this sense. With more lenient forms of analogical representation all that is assumed is that spatial relations are preserved in some fashion or other.

4. It is possible to think in terms of hybrid systems that combine aspects of analogical representation with some form of symbol system. We have provided the example of the map of the London Underground as a case in point. This form of representation is exactly of the form discussed by Tolman (1948) in his discussion of cognitive maps.

In discussing the abstract nature of maps we have also introduced the notion of a symbol system. A symbol system is a form of representational system that comprises both symbols and rules for combining the symbols. In the current context, we are attempting to understand the sort of representational system that underpins the mind. As discussion proceeds, you will discover that a central concern is with trying to tie down whether the mind uses analogical representations.

## Research focus 7.1

## Is 8 to 9 further than 10 to 9? Representing the mental number line

We hope that this far you will have learnt that, at the very least, you should not attempt to use the London Underground map to estimate the time it takes to walk from Embankment to Charing Cross: use an A-to-Z instead. In exploring the nature of a different form of stored knowledge, Reynvoet and Brysbaert (1999) were interested in the type of organisation involved when representing quantity along a mental number line. They predicted that if the mental number line is purely analogical in nature, then participants' ability to respond to the difference between 8 and 9 should be the same as their ability to respond to the difference between 10 and 9 due to the equivalent distance of 1 between both pairs of numbers. The point is that by the strictly analogical view, the mental distance between 8 and 9 should be exactly the same as the mental distance between 9 and 10. Check it out, look at a ruler. This is despite the alternative suggestion that the processing of single- and double-digit numbers invoke different mental representations.

In one experiment, ten participants, over a series of trials, were presented with prime–target combi-

nations, in which both prime and target were numbers ranging from 5 to 15. Basically, a forward mask (remember these? see Chapter 3) was presented for 66 ms, followed by the prime stimulus for 66 ms, followed by a backward mask (and these? see Chapter 3) of the same duration, and then the target stimulus remained on screen until participants responded (see Figure 7.5 for a schematic representation of the events on a trial). Their task was simply to name the target stimulus as fast as

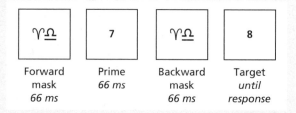

**Figure 7.5 A schematic representation of the sequence of events on a trial in the experiment reported by Reynvoet and Brysbaert (1999)**
Time from the onset of the trial travels from left to right across the page.

possible, with reaction times being measured with a microphone.

The idea here was that if the mental number line was not analogical then there might be something special about the jump from single- to double-digit numbers (or indeed double- to single-digit numbers) across primes and targets. If this is the case then different reaction times (RTs) should be observed for responding to the prime-target pairing of, say, 7 and 9 relative to 11 and 9. Reynvoet and Brysbaert (1999) found the fastest RTs were when prime and target were identical, although response speeding was still in evidence when the prime was about 2 or 3 away from the target. Despite the priming effect being slightly stronger when the prime target stayed within the same decade (e.g., 7 and 9; 9 ms per distance unit) relative to moving between decades (i.e., 11 and 9; 5 ms per distance unit), the difference was not statistically significant. In order to check that these results were not due to making a vocal response, in a second experiment they asked participants to respond manually to the even or odd status of the target via key presses, and similar findings obtained.

Although their conclusion rests upon finding no difference between the conditions, the authors found that single- and double-digit numbers appear to exist along the same mental number line, given as how effects of priming were equivalent across within-decade and between-decade conditions. Reynvoet and Brysbaert (1999, p. 200) concluded that their data are consistent with 'models that see the core of the numerical system as an analogue magnitude system'. However, other evidence suggests that the mental number line is not as simple as all that since participants are also quicker to indicate that 2 is smaller than 3, relative to indicating 8 smaller than 9 (cf. Brysbaert, 1995)! Therefore even our understanding of processing the simplest of numbers appears to be quite complicated.

Source: Reynvoet, B., & Brysbaert, M. (1999). Single-digit and two-digit Arabic numerals address the same semantic number line. Cognition, 72, 191–201.

**represented world** The set of things being represented in a representing world (e.g., the London Underground system in a map of the Underground).

**representing world** A means by which information in a represented world is captured. For instance, a map of the London Underground system is a representing world of the actual represented Underground system.

**geometric relations** Spatial relationships as defined within a geometric system.

**analogical representation** A form of representation in which there is a correspondence between parts and relations in the representing world and parts and relations in the represented world.

**strict analogical representation** According to Palmer (1978), in this form of representation 'Spatial information is not only preserved but it is preserved in (1) a spatial medium and (2) in such a way that the image resembles that which it represents' (p. 295).

**lenient analogical representation** Such representations merely preserve spatial information in some way or other.

**symbol system** A representational system comprising a set of well-defined symbols, each of which stands for a particular entity, and a set of rules by which such symbols can be manipulated.

**representational system** A set of symbols and their rules of combination that form the basis of capturing information about a particular set of entities in some represented world.

**cognitive map** An internal representation of an external environment that captures salient landmarks and salient spatial relations between those landmarks.

## Tolman's alternative theoretical perspective to behaviourism

Tolman was particularly concerned with a distinction he drew between **molecular descriptions** and **molar descriptions of behaviour**. A molecular description of a rat running a maze has been discussed in terms of the S–R account. Here the description is completed by specifying, essentially, the smallest building blocks of behaviour (the component reflexes) and describing how these behavioural 'molecules' are combined into a single chain that runs from start to finish. In contrast, a molar description begins by posing questions about what the ultimate goal of the behaviour is. In the case of the rat in the maze it is to gain access to sustenance (e.g., food or water) – the goal is to feed or drink.

By this molar account, having established the ultimate goal, it is only then appropriate to consider the means by which the goal is to be achieved. To understand a rat's behaviour, we must consider the sort of means–end analysis that the rat engages in: in this case, the means to achieve the goal is to traverse the maze from start to goal box. Once the ultimate or superordinate goal has been identified it is now possible to subdivide the problem into subordinate goals. For instance, the first subordinate goal could be to arrive at the first choice point in the maze such as that provided by a T-junction. The rat now has to decide whether to turn left or right. Having achieved this subordinate goal, the next subordinate goal should be considered, and so on.

Although this sort of approach may seem tortuous, a very similar task analysis can be offered for simple everyday tasks such as making a cup of tea. We can describe the behaviour by breaking it down into a sequence of sub-goals, such as first fill the kettle, then switch it on, etc. The overall goal, however, is to quench your thirst with a cup of tea. The basic point is that behaviour may only become understandable if it is assumed that the animal/person is striving to achieve certain goals.

In couching the description of behaviour at this molar level, discussion of exactly which sequence of movements the animal makes in traversing the route is irrelevant (in the same way that it does not ultimately matter whether you hop, skip or jump while making the tea). Tolman was clear in suggesting that there is an indefinite number of ways in which the animal moves from one choice point in the maze to the next, but discussion of these is essentially irrelevant in understanding what the animal is doing and why it is doing it. The particular bodily movements that allow the animal to move from one choice point to the next are of only secondary interest in terms of what the animal is actually learning about traversing the maze. In this regard he discussed the idea that the animal exhibits **means–end expectations**. For instance, the rat will exhibit a 'selectively greater readiness for short (i.e., easy) means activities as against long ones' (1932/1967, p. 11). Why prolong the time until the next meal if you do not have to? So if the rat is given a choice between a short route to the goal box and a long route, it will tend to choose the short one.

At this point it could be claimed that the rat engages in **rational decision-making**, for as Searle (2001) stated, rational decision-making is a matter of selecting certain means that will bring about certain ends. For example, if you have to get up tomorrow to get to

that 9 o'clock lecture, then the rational decision is to get an early night and put the alarm clock on. The more enjoyable (irrational?) option is to go to the pub and stay out drinking. In discussing human decision-making, Searle stated that 'We come to the decision making situation with a prior inventory of desired ends, and rationality is entirely a matter of figuring out the means to our ends' (2001, p. 1). This provides a clear description of the kind of framework for thinking that Tolman adopted to explain the rats' maze-learning behaviour. Clearly this is a fundamentally different perspective to the S–R (chains-of-associations) approach.

## Some examples of Tolman's experiments on cognitive maps

Unsurprisingly, experimental data can be brought to bear on these issues. In one experiment discussed by Tolman (1948), a given rat was placed in the start box of a Y maze located at the base of the vertical line and released. During a pre-exposure phase the rat was simply returned to its home cage whenever it reached either the left or the right goal box. Water was available in the right goal box and food was available in the left goal box. Now half the rats were deprived of food and half were deprived of water. Following this deprivation phase, and when each rat was returned to the maze for the first time, the tendency was for the hungry rats to choose left and the thirsty rats to choose right. This pattern of results shows that during the pre-exposure phase the rats were learning something about the location of the food and that of the water even though they had not exhibited any particular preference for taking one limb or the other during the pre-exposure phase. Indeed performance on the first test trial is commensurate with the idea that the rats possessed a means–end expectation, namely that in following a particular route they would find a particular goal object – either food or water.

### Pinpoint question 7.3

How does a rat turning left towards food when it was deprived of food, and turning right towards water when it was deprived of water, support the idea of rational decision-making?

One other example is also worthy of note. In this experiment three groups of hungry rats were allowed to explore the maze shown in Figure 7.6a. In the case of the control group of rats, food was provided in the goal box so whenever an individual entered the goal box that animal could eat. Performance was gauged in terms of the number of dead ends the rats entered between release from the start box and entry into the goal box. As can be seen from Figure 7.6b, as the days transpired the control rats made fewer navigational errors.

In a first experimental group of rats (Group III) no food was provided in the goal box for the first two days but food was provided on subsequent days. In a

second experimental group of rats (Group II) no food was provided in the goal box on the first six days but was provided thereafter. The data from these two groups show the same striking pattern. As soon as food had been provided in the goal box the animals made dramatically fewer navigational errors on subsequent days. So what are we to take away from such a demonstration?

Well, according to Tolman, the dramatic improvement in performance is indicative of the fact that, despite the fact that the experimental animals had received no rewards early on in training, they had learnt something about the spatial layout of the maze. In just being allowed to wander around the maze these rats had acquired some knowledge about the spatial structure of the maze. Such a process Tolman (1948) referred to as **latent learning**. This is quite a clear demonstration that learning can occur in the absence of any reward or contingent feedback – quite a significant conclusion in and of itself. However, more contentiously perhaps, Tolman argued that, in merely exploring the maze, the rats had acquired a cognitive map of the structure of the maze.

As is shown in Figure 7.4 the sort of representation that Tolman described was exactly the same as our example of the map of the London Underground. Both are symbolic representational systems that capture critical spatial relations in a represented world. Given such a hypothesis, we can begin to ask more penetrating questions about how such a kind of internal representation might be at all useful. How might an animal benefit from having a mental faculty (akin to a map control room) in which a cognitive map is consulted rather than just having a simple switching mechanism (akin to a telephone exchange) from stimulus to response?

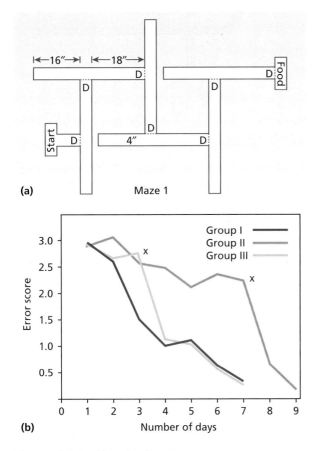

**(a)**      Maze 1

**(b)**      Number of days

**Figure 7.6 Latent learning in mazes**
(a) provides a bird's-eye view of the structure of the maze used. (b) provides a graph of the data collected. The graph maps out the relation between number of days in the maze and the number of errors committed (i.e., wrong turns that the rats made) in reaching the goal box for each group of rats. Group 1: the food in the goal box was available from day 1. For the other two groups the X marks the day on which food in the goal box was made available.

*Source*: Tolman, E. C. (1967). *Purposive behavior in animals and man* (fig. 7, p. 48; fig. 8, p. 49). New York: Appleton-Century-Croft.

**molecular descriptions of behaviour** Behaviour described in terms of atomic units. For example, behaviour broken down into sequences of S–R bonds.

**molar descriptions of behaviour** Behaviour described in terms of the ultimate goals that the organism is attempting to achieve.

**means–end expectations** Knowledge that carrying out a certain set of behaviours will result in a specific goal.

**rational decision-making** The selection of appropriate means to produce the desired result.

**latent learning** The acquisition of knowledge in the absence of reward or feedback.

# Mental operations carried out on mental maps

The evidence so far considered above merely confirms that the animals acquired some form of memory from their experiences in the maze, but Tolman's field theory goes further than this. It posits that only particular spatial relations are committed to memory, and that it is only by consulting such memory representations that the rat can behave adaptively in the future. The animal should be able to consult the cognitive map and work out novel routes despite never having taken these routes in reality. The rat should be able to (in a sense) figure out how best to arrive at the goal box even when the shortest route is blocked or unavailable for some other reason. This is despite the fact that not all possible spatial relations that could possibly be used to describe the world are contained in the cognitive map.

With such difficult circumstances (as when the quickest route is blocked), the brute force approach would be to engage in a simple trial and error exploration of the maze so as to chance upon an unblocked route. Try all other routes until by chance you hit on one that leads to the goal box. The animals are cleverer than this, though, and it is clear that they can work out alternative routes in ways other than by trial and error. A critical experiment in this regard was carried out by Tolman and Honzik (reported by Tolman, 1932/1967). Figure 7.7 shows a schematic representation of the maze used in this experiment. During preliminary training rats were forced to take certain routes through the maze. For instance, in blocking path 1 at X, the animals soon begin to take path 2. In blocking both paths 1 and 2 respectively at X and Y, the animals began to take path 3. In this way the rats were forced to acquire knowledge of each of the three routes through the maze.

The critical stage of the experiment was when a barrier was placed at N. This barrier compromised both paths 1 and 2 and now when the animals were replaced in the start box they overwhelmingly chose to take path 3. The rats' behaviour is readily explained in terms of being able to draw an inference on the basis of knowledge of the spatial layout of the maze. In other words, in solving this navigational problem the understanding was that the rats consulted a cognitive map of the maze that they had acquired over the preliminary training sessions. Clearly this is not the only possible account of these data. Nonetheless, the mere thought

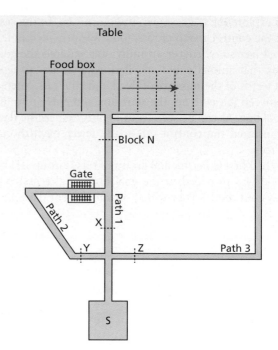

**Figure 7.7 Aerial view of the maze apparatus used by Tolman (1932/1967)**

*Source*: Tolman, E. C. (1958). *Purposive behavior in animals and man* (fig. 7, p. 48; fig. 8, p. 49). Berkeley, CA: University of California Press. Reproduced with permission.

that it could be plausible, opened up the serious possibility of generating cognitive (instead of purely behavioural) accounts of learning.

Indeed, this experiment reveals one clear advantage that a cognitive representation can confer on an animal, namely that in being able to consult such a representation, the animal need not engage in energy-consuming, trial-and-error behaviours. On finding the barrier at block N, the animals did not slavishly traverse the next shortest route to the goal box, but inferred that the most reasonable alternative was to take the longest route. More interesting, though, is the possibility that such a cognitive representation provides a means by which the animal can engage in novel and appropriate behaviours that are not simply repetitions of previous behavioural repertoires (such as re-running a previously taken path 3). It seems that the cognitive map allows the animal to combine previously learnt behaviours in novel ways.

The simple idea is that in consulting a cognitive map the animal can arrive at completely new routes that it has never before taken. For instance, let's assume that you have committed to memory the map of the London Underground. While waiting for a train to Oxford Circus at Holborn there is an announcement that the Central line is closed between Tottenham Court Road and Oxford Circus. On hearing this and on consulting your cognitive map of the Underground, you decide to take the Piccadilly line to Piccadilly Circus and change onto the Bakerloo line. This is despite the fact that you have never taken this rather circuitous route before.

Although all of this may strike you as nothing other than a statement of common sense, the actual account assumes the following:

1. that you possess a mental representation that specifies structural relationships of the London underground system;

2. that you consult such a representation; and

3. that you draw particular inferences on the basis of the information captured by such a representation.

The conclusion is that, by bringing to bear mental operations on a particular mental representation, you can generate novel behaviours in solving navigational problems. Experimental evidence reveals that rats are also apparently capable of similar mental dexterity, and once again the work of Tolman (1932/1967) is important here.

During an initial exploration phase, rats on an individual basis were allowed to roam freely about a table strewn with various objects and obstacles, like a sort of assault course for rodents. No rewards were provided during this preliminary phase. Next the rats learnt to traverse an elevated maze that led from one closed-off corner of the table (the start box) to another closed-off corner at which food was provided (the goal box). Finally each rat was placed on the table top just outside a wire enclosure that barred access to the food corner of the table. After some futile attempts at forcing the wire enclosure, a typically observed behaviour was that the rat spontaneously moved to the start box of the elevated maze and onwards to retrieve the food. This was despite the fact that entry to the start box was obscured by various obstacles on the table.

The most relevant point is that the rats moved directly from the wire enclosure to the start box in the final phase even though 'they had probably never once taken the direct course' during their initial random explorations of the table top. Importantly, this particular observation was taken to support the following conclusion: the rats were able to construct new routes across the table top on the basis of the map-like representation that they had acquired through mere exploration of this world. → See 'What have we learnt?', below.

## Pinpoint question 7.4

**What benefits does a cognitive map confer?**

## → What have we learnt?

The basic idea therefore is that a cognitive map contains a specification of the key parts of the represented world and a specification of some of the spatial relations among those parts. Importantly, and as Gallistel (1990) has argued, the strict correspondence between the representing and the represented worlds (i.e., between the map and the world) is that it is possible to 'use operations in one system to draw conclusions about the other' (p. 1). In other words, it is possible to work mentally on the map so as to draw conclusions about the spatial relations that hold in the world. Importantly, the outcomes of such mental operations can be used to predict or anticipate external events and relations (Gallistel, 1990, p. 2).

As we proceed, the case for making assumptions about the usefulness of mental representation is being steadily built up. Indeed, it should be becoming apparent just how critical mental representation is in understanding human nature. It lies at the very heart of our ability to solve problems and make predictions about the world. If we are prepared to accept this, and so reject behaviourism, then we can begin to ask more detailed questions about just what mental representation is really like and why it is like it is. More generally we can ask, 'What is the format of mental representation?'

## You can't get there from here: the cognitive map of a brain-damaged London taxi driver

While the rats in the above discussion had to cope with developing a cognitive map of an experimenter's table top, clearly there are many more complex cases to be considered. One such example is that bewildering mess of lines and intersections known as the London road system. Therefore we might expect London cab drivers to have an excellent cognitive map of London (involving the acquisition of the layout of over 25,000 streets, informally known as 'The Knowledge'), but what happens when that map gets damaged? Maguire, Nannery and Spiers (2006) examined the case of a brain-damaged London cab driver and how this damage impacted on his very own 'knowledge' of the highways and byways of old London town.

This particular individual, known as TT, was a 65-year-old man who had been working as a London cab driver for 37 years. After being taken ill, TT was found to have limbic encephalitis and a structural examination of his brain, using MRI technology, revealed damaged hippocampi – areas of the brain thought to be intimately linked to navigation and the acquisition of cognitive maps. In order to test TT's navigation abilities, ten additional control participants were recruited who had also worked on the London roads for an average of 41 years. One particularly novel aspect of this study was that all individuals were asked to navigate a driver (one of the authors) round a virtual representation of London, complete with one-way systems and traffic restrictions, although presumably with fewer pigeons and tourists.

Both TT and control participants 'picked up' passengers at one location and then navigated through the virtual streets of London to the passengers' required destination. The success of the journey was calculated on the basis of the optimal distance in terms of the shortest possible route versus the actual distance travelled. TT was found to operate as well as control participants for certain journeys (Piccadilly Circus to Big Ben). However, for other journeys TT took a much more circuitous route (Berkeley Square to Berwick Street) while other trips simply could not be completed at all (British Museum to St Paul's Cathedral).

Maguire et al. (2006) sought to find the cause of these round-the-houses routes such as the Berkeley Square to Berwick Street example which involved TT taking a much more indirect route. It was revealed that when TT's routes required him to deviate from the main roads of London (known as A roads), then navigation was impaired. Therefore it seems as though the hippocampi are indeed important in terms of detailed spatial representation, although, as Maguire et al. (2006) state, this is not to rule out the possibility of damage elsewhere in TT's brain. So the next time a cabbie takes you the long way round, it might not be because they're trying to squeeze a bit more money out of you, but because they're having trouble with the fine-grained details of their cognitive map.

*Source*: Maguire, E. A., Nannery, R., & Spiers, H. J. (2006). Navigation around London by a taxi driver with bilateral hippocampal lesions. *Brain, 129*, 2894–2907.

## Maps and pictures-in-the-head

Previously we have explored the possibility that a cognitive map contains a record of some but not all spatial relations that hold in the represented world. This view contrasts most markedly with the idea that this form of internal representation is like a picture (Levine, Jankovic & Palij, 1982). The alternative view is that a cognitive map is akin to a picture-in-the-head. In raising this issue, it should be clear that the discussion is moving on from an acceptance that internal representations are justified to a more detailed examination of what the nature of such representations might be. The discussion now turns to the problem of trying to work out the format of internal representations. We begin by posing the question: are mental representations analogical in nature?

### Mental pictures

It is very important to consider carefully what is at issue here because some of the conclusions to be drawn may prove to be very difficult to accept. For instance, despite the conclusions about what constitutes a cognitive map on the basis of the data reported by Tolman, a radically different alternative is that it could also be construed as being a mental picture akin to some form of photographic copy of an aerial view of a given landscape. Indeed something that is so seductive about the idea of mental pictures is that, as Pylyshyn (2002) has noted, 'it seems intuitively obvious that what we have in our mind when we look out onto the world, as well as when we imagine a scene, is something that *looks like* the scene' (p. 157). There is, however, exceptionally good evidence that the mental picture view of internal representation is problematic and therefore our intuitions may be quite misleading.

As the notion of a picture is going to feature heavily in this discussion, it is perhaps useful to remind ourselves just what sort of representation a picture is. Let us first define a **literal picture** as being a 2D representation of something but critically what is shown *resembles* the thing that it is representing (it is an analogical representation). So if you were to draw next door's cat, then the drawn cat ought to *resemble* the actual cat. The drawing should contain a facsimile (or approximate facsimile) of the cat. To take an example from Dennett (1981), in his discussion of images, he states that literal pictures 'must resemble what they represent and not just represent it' (p. 129). So a picture showing something hard, square and black cannot be a literal picture of something soft, round and white.

It is quite another matter to discuss **symbolic pictures** for now the notion of resemblance is set aside and, given the nature of contemporary art, notions of symbolic representation stretch far and wide. Now it is quite possible to consider a picture showing something hard, square and black on the understanding that this is intended to represent next door's cat. Figure 7.8 provides a different illustration of the same point:

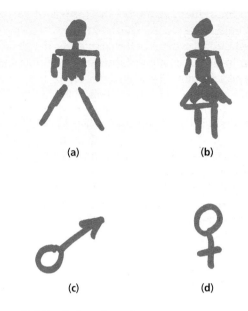

(a)    (b)

(c)    (d)

**Figure 7.8  Symbols and gender**
The upper two symbols represent by resemblance, whereas the lower two symbols represent by convention.

(a) and (b) are taken as being literal pictures (albeit at a very crude level of approximation) because the shape of the figures resembles the things they represent, namely male and female, respectively; (c) and (d) can be taken as symbolic pictures because now there is no resemblance between the individual symbols and the things that they represent (again male and female, respectively). Both (a/b) and (c/d) convey the same meanings but (c) and (d) do not represent by resemblance. There is an arbitrary relation between each symbol and its real-world referent. The fact they are symbols for the things that they represent is decided upon by convention or cultural acceptance.

## For example . . .

In discussing the difference between literal and symbolic pictures, we would be just as at home in the art gallery as we would in the psychology lab. As already noted, in modern art it is quite possible to make a picture showing something hard, square and black on the understanding that this is intended to represent next door's cat. In this vein, if you track down a picture of Picasso's Cat Sculpture, you'll notice that while it does represent a cat, the actual feline in question was probably not blue, yellow and red as the literal interpretation of the art work would suggest. Things get a little more confusing when considering the work of René Magritte and his famous image *La trahison des images* (The Treachery of Images; 1928–29). Here, there is a picture of a pipe with the caption 'Ceci n'est pas une pipe' (This is not a pipe). Magritte is quite right – it is not a pipe, it is a *picture* of a pipe – and in this way he makes an important point about the sign (picture of a pipe) and the signified (an actual pipe). Although we should probably save those kinds of philosophical musing for the gallery itself . . .

In posing questions about the format of mental representation we can ask which of these two forms of representational systems best characterise what resides in the mind. Do mental representations resemble what they represent (are they depictive?) or are they more symbolic in nature (are they symbolic)? It will therefore come as no surprise to learn that there are those who defend each format (i.e., the depictive and the symbolic, respectively) and there are those who defend hybrid systems. Let us consider the position of those who defend the notion of mental pictures first.

> **literal picture**  A representation of an object or scene that strictly resembles the subject of the picture, in the same way that an undoctored photograph depicts a scene.
>
> **symbolic pictures**  A symbolic picture is a representation of an object or scene that does not necessarily resemble the subject of the picture.

## Kosslyn's view of mental pictures

One implication of positing mental pictures is that these preserve some of the geometrical properties of the thing being represented. The implication is that these are more like literal than symbolic pictures. As Kosslyn (1994) has noted, 'each part of an object is represented by a pattern of points, and the spatial relations among these patterns . . . correspond to the spatial relations among the parts themselves' (p. 3; see also Pylyshyn, 2003). Kosslyn has repeatedly argued that there is an important sense in which at least some forms of mental representation – so-called **mental images** – are couched in a depictive format. As Kirby and Kosslyn (1990) noted, **depictive representation**s (such as literal pictures) convey meaning by visual resemblance. So far all of this seems relatively straightforward, but there are thorny issues. There does seem to be something of a philosophical quandary over whether it makes any sense to claim that there are 'elements in perception that represent in virtue of resembling what they represent' (Dennett, 1981). If there are no pictures in the brain, what sense can we make out of the resemblance claim?

Try to dispel such concerns for the time being, because, despite such philosophical musings, the notion of mental depictive representations is alive and well in some quarters of the psychological literature. For instance, Kosslyn, Ganis and Thompson (2003) have stated that in a depictive representation '(i) each

portion of the representation corresponds to a representation of a portion of the object, such that (ii) the distances (defined within the metric of the representational space) among the representations preserve the corresponding distances among the represented portions of the object' (p. 110). A depictive representation is clearly a particular form of analogical representation, as we described previously. Nonetheless, a concrete example may help. Take the real-world object to be an adult human male (this is 'the object' in the above). Take the representational space to be a piece of paper and the depictive representation to be a drawing of a stick-figure of the man. Now the structure of the stick-figure mirrors that of the man's body, and the lengths of the lines correspond with the lengths of the parts of the male body.

According to Kosslyn and colleagues, there are good grounds for asserting that mental images are analogical in nature. Although this may seem a perfectly reasonable claim to make, it has caused an astonishing amount of dispute in the literature. To appreciate the causes for concern, it is useful to consider Kosslyn's ideas in a little more detail.

## Mental images and the mental cathode-ray screen

We can be assured that no one believes that there are literally pictures-in-the-head (Kosslyn & Pomerantz, 1977, p. 57), but there are those who argue it is *as if* there are mental pictures or mental images. For instance, there are those who have discussed a **cathode-ray tube metaphor** (Kosslyn, Pinker, Smith & Shwartz, 1979; Kosslyn & Pomerantz, 1977) in which it is assumed that a stored image is projected onto a mental display which is then read off by the perceptual system. These are very contentious ideas, and we need to examine the arguments very carefully.

Perhaps the easiest way to proceed is to think in terms of something like a pixelated image on a real computer screen. Such an image can be saved as a bit map where, for each bit in the stored image, a number is stored that represents the light intensity value for a particular pixel on the screen. Now this bit map can be stored in a variety of ways in the computer's memory, but to make the picture metaphor exact it would have to be that the information in the bit map is stored as a 2D *x/y* array. In this way the representation would not only preserve the point-for-point characteristics of the input stimulus (the individual light intensity values), it would also retain the 2D spatial nature of the stimulus (see Figure 7.9).

**Figure 7.9 Pixelated imagery**
An 8 × 8 pixel grid of part of an image to be found
elsewhere within this book (and a bottle of champagne for
the first person to tell us where this image has come from!).
The representation codes the individual light intensity
values in a point-for-point fashion. This form of
representation preserves the 2D nature of the input image.

**mental images** A mental image is taken to be a
visual recreation in the mind of some concrete object
or event. A picture in the mind.

**depictive representation** A form of representation
that denotes by resemblance.

**cathode-ray tube metaphor** The proposal that the
internal medium of representation used in various
mental imagery tasks corresponds to a 2D array of
light intensity values.

## Dual-format systems

Overall therefore there is very little going for this form
of point-for-point representation in the absence of
some additional means of indexing what is represented.
We may have the files, but they are little use to us in
the absence of meaningful filenames. In accepting this,
Kosslyn (1980) discussed two forms of representation,
namely (i) a depictive representation that is akin to
the sort of bit-map representation discussed above,
together with (ii) a separate **descriptive representation** that contains an hierarchically structured list
of facts about the contents of the stored image. Each
depictive representation has a corresponding descriptive representation. So if the stored image is of a record
player, then the corresponding descriptive representation will include a generic label together with the
names of the various components arranged in a hierarchical fashion – it's a record player that contains a lid,
turntable, switches, sliders, a stylus arm and so on (see
Figure 7.10). So alongside the depictive representation
there is a corresponding descriptive representation
that specifies the content of identifiable chunks in the
image (Kosslyn, 1980, p. 143).

In this respect the eventual theory developed by
Kosslyn is a dual-format theory in that it posits both
depictive and descriptive forms of representation (see
also Anderson, 1978, and Paivio, 1990, 1991). However,
in focusing on the depictive format we are dealing with
mental images, and as Kosslyn et al. (1979) remarked,
not only do 'images . . . represent geometrical distance'
but 'images have spatial extent' (p. 537). For Kosslyn,
at least, it is the nature of the depictive representation
that fundamentally determines behaviour across a
range of cognitive tasks. We will return to descriptive
representations in a moment but, for now, it is important to consider some of the empirical evidence that
has been cited as converging on the idea of depictive
representations. → See 'What have we learnt?', page 246.

Given that this bit-map form of representation captures the point-for-point characteristics of the input
image, we might want to state that it is a *complete*
form of representation. Yet in adopting a 2D picture
metaphor we are leaving out the third (depth) dimension and therefore it cannot be a complete form of
representation. We should also note that this form of
storage is also known as 'uninterpreted' (Pylyshyn,
1973; Kosslyn & Pomerantz, 1977). What this means is
that all the bit-map captures are points of light, and
there is no other form of information encoded in the
representation. The stored image is neither parsed nor
segmented into meaningful chunks, and, given this,
there are no explicit labels attached to the significant
entities contained in the input image. It seems therefore that, without additional assumptions, there is
no obvious way that mental pictures could be easily
organised and accessed – the technical-speak for this is
that such representations are not *content addressable*.
Just think of searching through the contents of your
PC when the files have random strings of characters
as names!

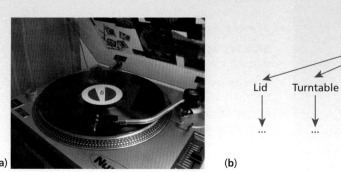
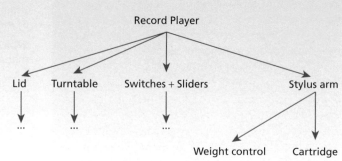

(a)　　(b)

**Figure 7.10 Depictive vs. descriptive representation**
(a) Depictive representation of a record player comprising individual point-for-point light intensity values for one particular 2D view. (b) A corresponding descriptive representation providing a hierarchically structured list of labels about the components of the record player as represented in the image in the upper panel.

## → What have we learnt?

So far we have introduced a number of different issues relating to mental representation. Most of the discussion has concerned the notion of analogical representation. We have distinguished between two general forms of analogical representation: (i) analogical representation in a strict sense and (ii) analogical representation in a lenient sense. We have discovered that Kosslyn is a keen supporter of the notion of strictly analogical representation in the conservative sense: when he has discussed *mental images* the implication is that this form of representation is strictly analogical in nature. To re-quote Palmer (1978), 'Spatial information is not only preserved but it is preserved in (1) a spatial medium and (2) in such a way that the image resembles that which it represents' (p. 295).

The situation is a little more complex because Kosslyn has also conceded that such representations are of little use without some form of additional indexing. Given this, the ultimate framework he adopted is one in which both depictive and descriptive forms of representation are needed. Presently we are concentrating on the nature of depictive representations and the evidence that has been garnered to support such notions. Later we will discuss descriptive forms of representation in much more detail. Now it is important to consider further the arguments and the critical data that have been used in the debates about the true nature of the format of internal representation.

## Pinpoint question 7.5

What are the two different types of representation generated for an object according to dual-format theorists (e.g., Kosslyn, 1980)?

**descriptive representation** A form of representation that denotes by description.

## Mental scanning

Some of the most relevant data relating to depictive representations are those taken from experiments on mental scanning. In a typical experiment participants were given a schematic map of the sort shown in Figure 7.11 to commit to memory. The map is distinctive in having seven clearly identifiable landmarks and it is the position and nature of these landmarks that have to be remembered. Participants were tested in being able to draw the map accurately from memory and when they could reproduce the map, to within certain objective levels of tolerance, the final phase of the experiment was begun. Now participants were tested under timed conditions. On each trial they were told to form a mental image of the map and focus attention on a named location (such as the sandy cove). When they indicated a state of readiness they were then given another named location and they had to make one key response if the named location was contained on the map and they had to make another key response if the location were not so contained. Importantly, participants were instructed to scan their image mentally, starting at the first named location. The critical data are shown in Figure 7.12. Now the duration of the timed response shows a linear relationship with actual physical distance. When RT is plotted as a function of the distance between the named locations on the original map, there is a linear relation between the two. Scanning time is directly proportional to the distances between landmarks on the actual map.

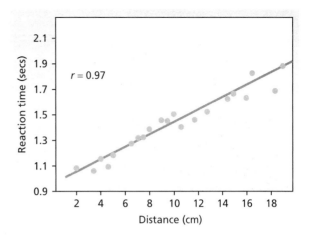

**Figure 7.12 A graphical function relating time to respond to the actual physical distance between two target places on a learnt map in a mental scanning experiment**
The *r* value provides the correlation coefficient showing the linear fit between the function and the data points.

*Source*: Kosslyn, S. M. (1980). *Image and mind* (fig. 3.7, p. 44). Cambridge, Massachusetts: Harvard University Press. Copyright © 1980 by the President and Fellows of Harvard College. Reproduced by permission.

**Figure 7.11 Example of a schematic map used by Kosslyn, Ball and Reiser (1978)**

*Source*: Kosslyn, S. M. (1980). *Image and mind* (fig. 3.6, p. 43). Cambridge, Massachusetts: Harvard University Press. Copyright © 1980 by the President and Fellows of Harvard College. Reproduced by permission.

Such data as these have been repeatedly cited as showing that mental images are spatial in that they preserve the actual geometrical properties of the thing being imaged. More particularly these data and many more like them motivated the cathode-ray model of Kosslyn and colleagues (Kosslyn et al., 1979; Kosslyn & Pomerantz, 1977; Kosslyn & Shwartz, 1977). By this view the stored image of the map is projected on the internal cathode-ray screen and information about the image is then read off from this screen, for instance, by scanning. The notion of a cathode-ray screen is much more than a simple metaphor because such a 2D array representation formed a central component of the computer model developed by Kosslyn and Shwartz (1977). It provided the so-called *representational space* or *internal spatial medium* within which mental images were projected. Via this construct the mental picture idea is fleshed out. The mental image preserves spatial information in this spatial medium in such a way that the image resembles that which it represents. So if object A is above object B in the represented world then the representation of A is above the representation of B in the representing world (cf. Palmer, 1978). In other words, if the sandy cove is below and to the right of the well on the actual island itself, then in my mental representation of the island projected by my own internal cathode-ray tube, the sandy cover would also have to be below and to the right of the well.

## For example . . .

JERRY: Anywhere in the city?
GEORGE: Anywhere in the city – I'll tell you the best public toilet.
JERRY: Okay . . . Fifty-fourth and Sixth?
GEORGE: Sperry Rand Building. 14th floor, Morgan Apparel. Mention my name – she'll give you the key.
JERRY: Alright . . . Sixty-fifth and Tenth.
GEORGE: (Scoffs) Are you kidding? Lincoln Center. Alice Tully Hall, the Met. Magnificent facilities.

*Seinfeld and David (1998)*

Now for those of us geeky enough to know where Jerry Seinfeld's fictional apartment is (129 West 81st Street, fact fans) one might wonder about George Castanza's mental scanning abilities in his search for the perfect toilet. Although not conducted in very controlled circumstances, if George's mental representation of Manhattan was analogical in nature, we might expect the time taken for him to arrive at the facilities located at 54th and 6th mentally to be longer than the time he took to reach in his mind 65th and 10th. This is because he is further away from the former restroom than the latter.

The associated claim is that operations on mental images are fundamentally constrained by how such images can be manipulated within the representational space. According to Kosslyn, such a medium provides a spatial analogue for reasoning about real-world scenes. Aligned to this is the idea that to move around in this space from, say, point A to point B, implies traversing intervening points (Wilton, 1978). So moving from the well to the sandy cove means passing by the lake (see Figure 7.11) as defined within the representational space. Such an idea is completely consistent with the data from the experiments on mental scanning outlined above. Indeed it is seen as a critical lynchpin in the argument that images have spatial extent. In the same way that a real map takes up (2D) space, then the same claim is made about mental images!

### Further provocative data

Some caution is warranted here because quite different conclusions have been reached by Pylyshyn (1981) on the basis of data from his mental scanning experiments. In these experiments participants were familiarised with a fictitious map of the sort described previously and were tested in being able to reproduce the map accurately as before. At test they were expected to form an image of the map. In one condition participants were instructed to imagine a speck of light traversing from a first named landmark to a second and to press a key when the speck arrived at the second. In replicating the original results (see Figure 7.12), the data revealed a linear relation between RT and actual distance. So far so good. However, a quite different pattern emerged in a second condition.

Now participants were given a first named landmark and were then asked to respond with the compass bearing of a second landmark relative to the first (N, NE, E, SE, etc.). Under these conditions RTs no longer increased linearly with map distances. A similar pattern was also observed when participants were asked to respond with the compass bearing from the second location to that of the first. This task was deemed necessary to try to ensure that participants were forming and consulting an image while engaged in the task. These latter results showed that relative positional judgements about a learned map could be made in a manner independent of distance. So whether or not the RTs depend on map distances seems to be critically dependent on task constraints. Given this, performance in mental scanning tasks is not fundamentally constrained by the spatial nature of an image defined within some form of assumed internal representational space. If it were, then the same patterns of performance ought to emerge across all 'scanning' tasks.

The more general implication is that the original image scanning data are, perhaps, not as revealing as might have been first thought. If participants are asked to scan images, then the data reveal that they can follow instructions and behave in a manner consistent with them scanning images. However, if the task constraints are changed, then participants perform in ways that are more in line with these task demands. If the task does not ask for scanning then participants do not scan. In this respect, the results of the mental scanning experiments may reveal more about what participants believe the experiment is actually about and behave in ways that accord with these assumptions:

the data do not reflect fundamental characteristics of image processing. As a brief aside, Finke and Pinker (1982) have shown cases of mental scanning even when participants have been provided with no instructions to scan. What we can take away from this, though, is open to argument because, as we will see, such examples fall in line with a more general tendency to mimic internally how the task might be solved in actuality. This point will be discussed more fully below when we discuss mental rotation.

### Pinpoint question 7.6

What did Pylyshyn (1981) find that fits uncomfortably with the notion of an analogical medium?

## Real space in the head: what is mental space really like?

Figure 7.13 provides a reasonable framework for thinking about the issues. As was noted above, no one seriously accepts the view that there is a literal copy of the external world residing in the mind, so all serious discussion about internal representation is about the nature of the mental **functional space**. According to Kosslyn, the functional space is fundamentally constrained to be like real space, in that both are assumed to have spatial extent. Mental images projected onto the mental cathode-ray screen serve as analogical representations of the things imagined and for Kosslyn the mental scanning data reflect fundamental properties of this functional space. They provide clear indications about the format of the internal

representations that underpin imaginal inference. Let us first consider some more evidence for this claim and then go on to consider the counter-arguments.

## Further evidence for analogical representation

For instance, Kosslyn (1976) ran an imagery experiment consisting of three conditions in which a designated group of participants was assigned to each condition. For all groups there were two phases of the experiment: in phase one (known as the *no-imagery condition*), and on a given trial, the participant was presented with a spoken animal name (e.g., Mouse) and then following either no delay or a 5 s pause a property name was presented (e.g., Whiskers). (Given that the presence of the pause had no material affect on the results then no further mention will be made of this manipulation.) Participants were expected to make a forced choice decision as to whether the property was a constituent feature of the animal. Two types of name/property pairs were tested. For high association/low area pairs (e.g., Mouse – Whiskers) the property referred to a small feature of the animal that was highly associated with the animal. For low association/high area pairs (e.g., Mouse – Back) the property referred to a large feature of the animal that was not highly associated with the animal.

In the second phase of the experiment, known as the *imagery condition*, the same property verification task was repeated but now different instructions were used with the different groups. Participants in the Whole groups were told to form an image of the entire animal while performing the property verification task, whereas participants in the Part group were told to only image the relevant part of the animal.

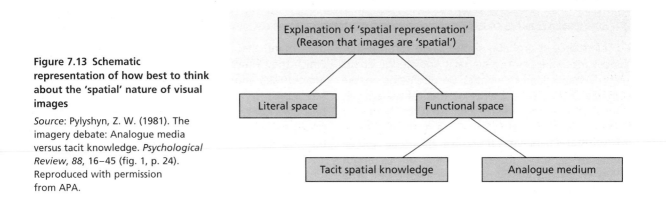

**Figure 7.13 Schematic representation of how best to think about the 'spatial' nature of visual images**

*Source*: Pylyshyn, Z. W. (1981). The imagery debate: Analogue media versus tacit knowledge. *Psychological Review*, 88, 16–45 (fig. 1, p. 24). Reproduced with permission from APA.

In the no-imagery conditions the general finding was that there was an effect of association such that responses were faster to high association pairs than to low association pairs: participants responded quicker to the Mouse/Whisker pairs than the Mouse/Back pairs. However, in the imagery conditions exactly the reverse effect obtained. Now generally speaking, participants took longer to respond to small features than to large features (although this effect of size did not reach statistical significance for the Part group). In other words, in the imagery conditions the size of the property only affected performance when participants formed an image of the entire animal. In none of the groups, however, was there an effect of animal name/part name association.

From this pattern of effects, Kosslyn (1976) concluded that, in cases when participants form images of whole objects, smaller properties are less easy to 'see' than larger properties. One implication, therefore, is that there is a rather strict correspondence between viewing an actual object and imaging that same object. In the same way that it is less easy to discern small features than large features of actual seen objects, this is taken to hold true for viewing parts of imaged objects. According to Kosslyn, therefore, these findings endorse his views about the analogical nature of mental representation.

## The dissenting view: descriptive, not depictive representations

At first blush this data set seems quite compelling in revealing fundamental characteristics of images and imagery. However, Pylyshyn (2002) has repeatedly taken a contrary position. He has set out an alternative view in terms of the so-called **tacit knowledge** that participants bring to bear in these tasks. Tacit knowledge refers to knowledge that participants have about some aspect of the world that they are unable to articulate with any degree of authority; sometimes this is referred to as *implicit knowledge*.

How does this relate to the imagery experiments discussed above? Well, according to Pylyshyn (2002), when participants are asked to imagine some object or event, they use their tacit knowledge of what seeing that object or event would be like and use this in carrying out the task. Therefore their behaviour is entirely consistent with what they believe to be true of the corresponding object or event. Consequently, the data that have been taken to reflect fundamental aspects of the format of the representational space may be nothing more than an indication of the tacit knowledge that the participant brings to bear on the task. More particularly, take the case of the mental scanning tasks. Participants are bound to know that for any given speed of travel, longer distances will take more time to traverse than shorter distances. Therefore performance in the tasks may simply reflect this. Scanning times should take more time for longer than shorter distances. In this regard, the data need not necessarily reflect fundamental characteristics of some internal representational space. On the contrary, it may merely reflect the tacit knowledge about travelling between real places that the participants bring to bear on the task.

---

**functional space** The idea that there is some form of psychological workspace that allows a person to reason about spatial relations in the real world.

**tacit knowledge** The knowledge that a person has but which they are unable to express in language.

---

## For example . . .

For instance, it probably comes as no surprise that most footballers only have tacit knowledge about aerodynamics and kinematics. Despite being unable to dissect the finer points of theoretical physics, they all know how to kick a ball so it lifts high over the heads of the defenders. For a start, they know they should lean back. If pressed, they may well be able to generate some reasonable advice about how to do this when coaching someone else. The basic point, though, is that tacit knowledge is that which they know but are unable to express in language. Take another example: if you know how to ride a bike, try explaining how to do this to someone who does not know how to ride a bike. You clearly have the knowledge of how to ride a bike but you cannot express this knowledge in words. Your bike riding knowledge is tacit.

## Depictive representations and a pause for thought

One final point to be considered about depictive representations relates to the claim that in such representations all spatial relations are 'immediately accessible' (Kosslyn et al., 2003, p. 200). For instance, look at the character 'A' and it is immediately apparent that the shape contains an enclosed triangle, that the apex of the A is above the centre of the horizontal bar, that the apex is above the feet, etc. Now imagine an 'A' and, according to Kosslyn, the same visual characteristics that are immediately apparent in looking, are immediately accessible in imagining. Such a claim has an intuitive ring to it – just imagine any other capital letter and see for yourself. However, despite this cosy intuitive feeling, you might be slightly unnerved to learn that the empirical evidence is strictly against this claim. For example, findings that fit rather uncomfortably with this view come from a study by Palmer (1977). He developed something termed a *mental synthesis task* and this is best explained with regard to Figure 7.14.

At the top of the figure are two examples of random line figures composed by interconnecting adjacent dots in a regular 3 × 3 matrix of dots. Having generated such line figures, each was subdivided into two

sub-patterns or fragments where each fragment contained three lines. Now the division into the fragments was designated according to the degree to which they were considered to be good components of the original figures. As can be seen, three general categories of fragments were generated and designated as either of high, medium or low goodness. If we look on the very right-hand side of Figure 7.14, we'll see that a triangle stands for high goodness in view of the shape being both interconnected and having a closed contour. The second shape (the larger, open triangle) has slightly less goodness since, while it has interconnected, it no longer has a closed contour. The final shape (the 'nose' and the horizontal line) has neither interconnectedness nor closed contours and as such stands for low goodness components.

Now on each trial in the experiment participants were presented with a pair of fragments on either side of a central fixation. Participants were told that they had to synthesise the two fragments mentally into a globally connected figure and make a response when they felt that they had completed fusing the two together. Times to make these responses were recorded. Following a 500 ms pause a complete figure was presented and the participants had to respond as to whether the figure corresponded to what the composite of the two fragments looked like.

The results of the study are shown in Figure 7.15. The first thing to notice is that the time to synthesise the sub-patterns mentally varied according to their designated goodness. Responses were faster when presented with high rather than low goodness sub-patterns. These data are problematic for any simple-minded imagery account. If what the participants are doing is manipulating depictive representations of the sub-patterns, then there is no reason to assume that the mental synthesis should depend on component goodness. Think about it this way. Draw one figure fragment on one overhead transparency and draw a different figure fragment on another transparency. To enact mental synthesis, simply move the transparencies together until they superimpose one another. This lateral movement in no way depends on the structural nature of what appears on the two transparencies. So if these sorts of operations were being carried out, mentally, on depictive representations, then why should the goodness effects reported by Palmer (1977) have occurred?

Moreover, the decision response times in the figural matching task also showed an effect of component goodness. Responses for the high goodness cases were enacted faster than those for the low goodness cases. This is also contrary to the idea that all spatial relations

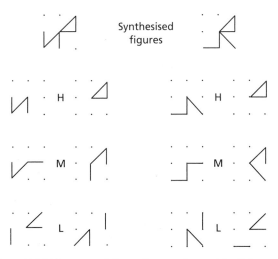

**Figure 7.14 Figures and figure fragments used by Palmer (1977) in his mental synthesis experiments**
'H' picks out fragments of high goodness; 'M' picks out fragments of medium goodness; 'L' picks out fragments of low goodness.

*Source*: Palmer, S. E. (1977). Hierarchical structure in perceptual organisation. *Cognitive Psychology*, *9*, 441–474 (fig. 7, p. 463). Reproduced with permission from Elsevier.

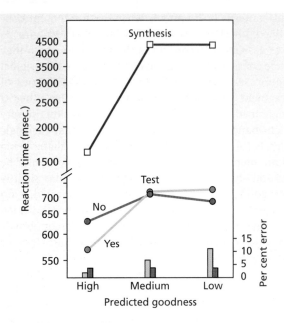

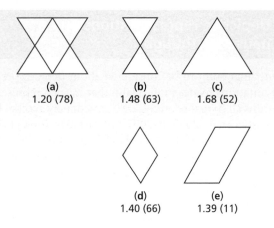

**Figure 7.15 Data showing performance in the mental synthesis and comparison tasks used by Palmer (1977)**
The upper part of the graph shows the average response times to synthesise the different fragment sorts. The lower panel provides latency and accuracy data for the figural matching task. In both sets of data, effects of figural fragments are present.

*Source*: Palmer, S. E. (1977). Hierarchical structure in perceptual organisation. *Cognitive Psychology*, *9*, 441–474 (fig. 8, p. 465). Reproduced with permission from Elsevier.

**Figure 7.16 Figures and data for the experiment reported by Reed (1974)**
Mean reaction times are presented in seconds. These times indicate how long participants took to respond that there was a correspondence between an initial figure and a second figure. In case (a) the whole figure was repeated. Numbers in brackets show the total number of participants (out of 80) who correctly detected the correspondence between the two figures.

*Source*: Reed, S. K. (1974). Structural descriptions and the limitations of visual images. *Memory & Cognition*, *2*, 329–336 (fig. 2, p. 330). Copyright © 1974 by Psychonomic Society, Inc. Reproduced with permission.

are equally available in the image. These data are much more consistent with the idea that, whatever the nature of the internal representation of the figures is, it seems to be quite unlike a mental picture. Rather, it appears that some form of structural organisation is being derived, and, in this regard, only some but not all spatial relations are being coded.

Indeed, it is exactly this conclusion that is bolstered by the findings reported by Reed across a range of experiments (1974; see also Reed & Johnsen, 1975). In one, now classic, experiment, participants were initially presented with a line drawing of a geometric figure (S1) for 1 s. This was removed and after a delay of either 1 s or 5.5 s a second figure (S2) was presented. Participants had to make a speeded choice response as to whether the two figures corresponded or not. To be precise, two positive cases were tested, namely (i) when S1 and S2 were identical, and (ii) when S2 was a sub-part of S1. On complete repetition trials S1 and S2 were the same figure and responses were very fast and accurate. However, more interest is with

the data from trials in which S2 was a sub-part of S1 (see Figures 7.16b–e). As can be seen from Figure 7.16, quite a few participants failed to make the correct connection between S1 and S2 when the sub-parts were presented and particularly noticeable is that the fact that only 11 out of the 80 participants correctly identified the parallelogram as being a constituent of the overall figure. Such data as these underline the fact that only some of the possible structural properties of a shape are derived and are represented internally. Whatever is being tapped here is quite unlike a photocopy or literal picture of the figures.

**Pinpoint question 7.7**

What does the role of 'goodness' in shape perception tell us about mental representation?

# The ambiguity of mental images

We have been considering evidence that bears on claims about the nature of depictive representation. Despite the claims about the availability of a 'near-infinite

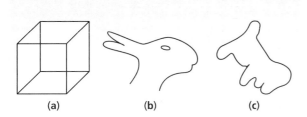

**Figure 7.17 Classic examples of ambiguous figures**
(a) shows a Necker cube, and (b) the duck/rabbit ambiguous figure. (c) is known as the chef/dog figure. Can you see why?

*Source*: Chambers, D., & Reisberg, D. (1985). Can mental images be ambiguous? *Journal of Experimental Psychology: Human Perception and Performance*, 11, 317–328 (fig. 1, p. 320). Reproduced with permission.

number of spatial relations' (Kosslyn et al., 2003) in mental images, the evidence points in a rather different direction. It seems, on the contrary, that only key parts and important relations between those parts are stored, and it is these that are readily accessible. Pursuing this line of argument brings us to a slightly different strand in the literature which has emerged relatively recently. This strand can be traced to an original paper published by Chambers and Reisberg (1985; although some of the basic ideas were carefully explored in an earlier paper by Hinton, 1979).

In the Chambers and Reisberg (1985) study, initially participants were acquainted with various ambiguous figures such as the Necker cube (Figure 7.17a) and were instructed as to how such figures can be given more than one interpretation. They were encouraged to discover the alternative interpretations of various ambiguous figures for themselves. Next they were shown the duck/rabbit figure (Figure 7.17b) and were instructed to form a mental image of the figure so that they would be able to draw it later. Then they were presented with the chef/dog figure (Figure 7.16c) and told how the different interpretations of this figure in part depend on the focus of attention. They were encouraged again to discover the different interpretations of the figure for themselves.

Next, participants were asked to reconstruct a mental image of the duck/rabbit figure and report their impressions of this. Originally all participants had reported the impression of either a duck or a rabbit and they were now asked to consult their image and report an alternative interpretation to the one they originally experienced. Finally they were asked to draw their image, inspect this drawing and report their impressions.

The data from this experiment are quite straightforward. Whereas all of the participants were able to report both readings of the duck/rabbit when asked to inspect their drawings of the figure, none of the participants were able to do this when they consulted their mental image of the figure. As we have already discussed, a typical finding is that when a person views such ambiguous figures, the different alternative interpretations fluctuate such that interpretation A is achieved for a certain amount of time (yes, it's a duck) and then is replaced by interpretation B (now it's a rabbit). This continues so that B remains stable for a certain period and then the interpretation reverts to A. This alternating between the different readings of the figure is known as ambiguous figure reversal. So the issue behind the Chambers and Reisberg (1985) experiment was whether participants experienced figure reversals when consulting a mental image. The fact that no participants did, was taken to reflect that mental images are quite unlike pictures. Figure 7.18 forcefully reinforces this point.

Generally, the claim is that whichever interpretation is placed on the figure initially, determines the nature of the representation of the figure that is stored. So if the participants perceived a rabbit when initially presented with the figure, then they stored a structurally organised representation of the figure that is consistent with this particular interpretation (e.g., ears to the left, eye centre, mouth towards the right). In contrast, if they perceived a duck, then their representation of the figure will be of a duck (e.g., bill towards the left, eye centre, ridge on the back of the head towards the right). The critical point is that there is no obvious way in which operations on the one form of representation will effortlessly give rise to the other

**Figure 7.18 The birds**
Look at these pictures carefully, choose one to concentrate on and then close your eyes and imagine that the figure is rotated by 90°. What do you now see?

*Source*: Pylyshyn, Z. W. (2002). Mental imagery: In search of a theory. *The Behavioral and Brain Sciences*, 25, 157–238 (fig. 6, p. 173). Cambridge, England: Cambridge University Press. Reproduced with permission.

form of representation. The data suggest, therefore, that only one reading of the figure is stored, and although a mental image of the figure can be achieved, this is a very different form of representation to that of a picture. As noted by Chambers and Reisberg (1992), what an image depicts depends on what an image means – it is nothing like a mental photocopy.

Such a conclusion is commensurate with other concerns that have been voiced in the literature about depictive representation. As Fodor (1975, pp. 179–80) discussed, if we replace the thought 'John is fat' by a mental picture revealing John with a large stomach, what mental picture is going to replace the thought 'John is tall'? The same picture or a different picture? If a different picture is to be used, then this picture will also depict John as a certain shape, but given that both pictures show John of a certain size and a certain shape, which picture stands for which thought?

These are serious concerns and have engendered a quite different theoretical approach to that adopted by Kosslyn. The alternative view is that mental images are generated from some form of stored description of the thing that is being imaged (Fodor, 1975, p. 193). Mental images are *images under a certain description*. If this is accepted, then it seems that the experiments on mental imagery are telling us something basic about fundamental cognitive representations and processes that are quite different from images and imaging.

Since the original Chambers and Reisberg (1985) paper, the original findings have been replicated and extended (Chambers & Reisberg, 1992; Reisberg & Chambers, 1991) and, perhaps unsurprisingly, evidence has been uncovered that some reversals of ambiguous mental images can occur for some people in some circumstances (Brandimonte & Gerbino, 1993; Peterson, Kihlstrom, Rose & Glisky, 1992; see Pylyshyn, 2002, for a brief review). Most recently, Mast and Kosslyn (2002) have reported that certain image reversals do occur for some people in very particular circumstances. Take a look at Figure 7.19 and you'll see that, viewed in one orientation, it looks like a young woman, but if you rotate the book through 180° within the plane then the same figure now looks like an old woman. Participants were presented with the figure in one orientation and then asked to form an image of the figure and rotate it accordingly. Interest was with whether or not participants could now report seeing the alternative

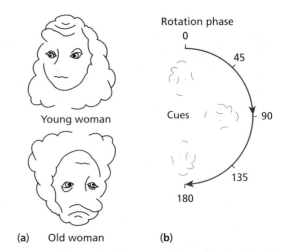

**Figure 7.19 Illustrating the Mast and Kosslyn (2002) task**
(a) Schematic representation of the figures used by Mast and Kosslyn (2002) together with (b) the 'hints' provided during the mental rotation phase of the experiment.

*Source*: Mast, F. W., & Kosslyn, S. M. (2002). Visual mental images can be ambiguous: Insights from individual differences in spatial transform abilities. *Cognition*, *86*, 57–70 (fig. 2, p. 61). Reproduced with permission from Elsevier.

interpretation of the figure when the image had been rotated.

Of a total 36 participants, 16 were able to report the alternative interpretation with 5 spontaneously reporting this and the remaining 11 after further hints were provided. So any claims that mental images cannot be reversed are simply wrong. Some caution is warranted here, though, because while engaged in the rotation phase of the experiment participants were presented with partial cues of the sort shown in Figure 7.19. They were instructed to imagine what the complete figure looked like in the context of these cues. We are therefore left with the following, more circumspect conclusion, namely that mental images may be reversible but only for some people and only in the presence of certain visual cues.  → See 'What have we learnt?', page 255.

→ See 'What have we learnt?', page 255.

## Pinpoint question 7.8

**What does it mean for a picture to be ambiguous?**

## → What have we learnt?

Clearly much more work is needed but, neverthe- less, there are some interim conclusions that can be drawn. It seems undeniable that *some* people experi- ence mental images, some of the time. This has led to the conclusion that some mental representations are therefore depictive in nature. Indeed some aspects of problem solving seem inextricably linked to the sorts of images that people form. As Kubovy (1983) has commented, 'before we carry out a phys- ical operation on an object, we often first imagine how we would perform it' (p. 662). Think in terms of going about putting together flat-pack furni- ture. It is generally far simpler to try to figure out how the pieces should go together before actually attempting to put them together. We might legiti- mately ask therefore whether the images merely accompany the real thinking or whether the ima- ging *is* the real thinking. The position adopted here is that the images, when they occur, are essentially a by-product of the thinking. The data overwhelm- ingly suggest that mental images are fundamentally constrained by an underlying interpretation that is applied. In line with this is the idea that images are in some sense generated from a stored description of the imagined scene or object (Fodor, 1975). The counter-argument (to the idea of mental pictures) is that, fundamentally, mental representation is descriptive, not depictive, in nature. This is not to deny that people experience mental images (just imagine your favourite painting). What is at stake is the critical issue of what such evidence is actually telling us about the nature of mental representation.

## Mental rotation

It would be completely remiss in discussing mental images not to consider mental rotation. Indeed, in reviewing the now classic book on this topic (Shepard & Cooper, 1982), Kubovy (1983) concluded by stating that this described 'some of the best research ever done in cognitive psychology' (p. 663). Figure 7.20 provides details of the most important experiments and results (see Shepard & Metzler, 1971). Basically on every trial in the experiment participants were presented with perspective views of two 3D figures. Participants were timed to decide whether the two figures were different views of the same object or whether they were mirror- reversed views of the same object. The main independ- ent variable of interest was the angular separation in 3D space between the two views. Take one pen in your left hand and one in your right and hold them so that they are in the same orientation to your line of sight. Now hold one steady and rotate the other. As you rotate the pen the angular separation between the two changes. The critical finding was that RTs increased linearly with the degree of angular separation between the two views.

Despite the simplicity of these data, it is very easy to confuse what they reveal. For instance, it is very easy to accept incorrectly that the data reveal evidence for the rotation of mental images (Shepard, 1990; Shepard & Cooper, 1982). Given that there are no pictures-in- the-head, then it makes little sense to talk in terms of rotating images and, consequently, we have to tread very carefully here. The most sensible way to proceed is to discuss participants as 'imagining the rotation of an object' (Kubovy, 1983) and therefore there is no commitment to any particular form of internal repres- entations or processes. Further empirical evidence is needed to narrow down the options. Of more import is what these data do *actually* show. This is that 'parti- cipants were mentally representing an object in succes- sively more and more rotated orientations' (Shepard, 1990, p. 369) until one of the figures was imagined to be aligned with the other. In imaging the two objects to be in the same orientation, a decision could then be made about whether they were structurally ident- ical or not. You'll notice that these kinds of arguments are very similar to the ones we have already discussed regarding mental scanning (see Figure 7.12) and the distinction between tacit spatial knowledge and ana- logue medium.

When thought about in these terms, the data are both interesting and unintuitive. For instance, it seems to be a rather cumbersome way of going about the task. Why can't participants focus on a critical feature and simply check this across the two figures? If they could do this, then the angular separation between the two figures ought not to have such a dramatic effect as it does. Indeed, if you were going to develop a fast and efficient problem-solving device, then it seems par- ticularly inefficient to have it behave in the way that

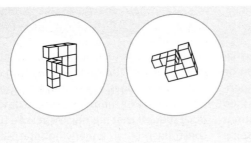

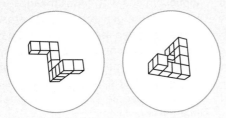

**(a)**

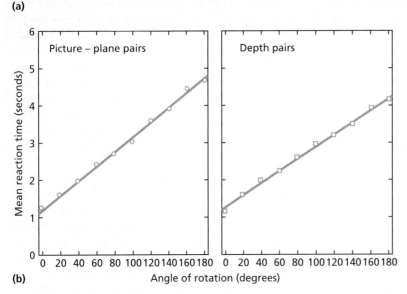

**(b)**

**Figure 7.20 The classic mental rotation experiments**
(a) Examples of the sorts of illustrations used to convey 3D block figures in the original mental rotation experiments reported by Shepard and Metzler (1971). (b) shows the RT data plotted as a function of angular separation between the figures. The left panel shows the data when the rotation was around the clock-face (within-the-plane/picture plane). The right panel shows the data when the rotation was through-the-plane (depth rotated).

*Source*: Shepard, R. N., & Cooper, L. A. (1982). *Mental images and their transformations* (fig. 3.1, p. 35; fig. 3.2, p. 36). Cambridge, Massachusetts: The MIT Press. Copyright © 1982 by the Massachusetts Institute of Technology. Reproduced with permission of The MIT Press.

participants do. It should be able to ignore the angular separation of the two figures, recover the structural nature of each, and then simply decide same or different. In contrast, the data show a very particular constraint of human processing.

It seems that people have to go through the steps of imagining what would physically take place if pre-sented with real objects and the task was to see whether they were the same or not. Quite simply the easiest thing to do would be to pick them up and rotate them until they aligned. In this regard it seems that what is going on here is that participants are mentally simu-lating real-world scenarios – remember the flat-pack furniture? It is far easier to imagine how the parts may go together than physically attempt to put them together in particular ways, which is again also true of flat-pack furniture. However, what the 'mental rotation' data reveal is that participants actually simulate physical processes in order to solve the problem. In this case, they solve the problem by imaging how they would go about physically manipulating the actual objects. In this respect the mental rotation experiments may be telling us more about mental problem solving (i.e., internal processes) than they are about mental representation.

Since the earliest reports of mental rotation, there has been a mountain of papers published on the effects. Indeed, if you think of a possible experiment that you would like to do on this area, then it is best to check the literature first because it is highly likely that some-

one somewhere will already have done it. Moreover, despite the very particular nature of the mental rotation findings reported by Shepard and Metzler (1971), the general area of research leads to a very clear conclusion and this is the very close link between problem solving and perception. Indeed, Wilton (1978) has gone so far as to argue that 'the processes of thought are limited in their operations by having evolved from processes that make predictions in perception' (p. 564; see also similar ideas discussed by Goldstone & Barsalou, 1998). What the rotation effects reveal is an ability to predict what an object probably looks like when viewed from a different angle of regard. One way in which this is achieved is by mentally simulating the actions that would bring this about in the real world.

## Research focus 7.3

## Monkey see, monkey do, monkey rotate? The mental life of a macaque

If someone accused you of being a 'product of your environment', it would be an unlikely compliment. However, Burmann, Dehnhardt and Mauck (2005) discussed being a product of one's environment in more positive terms and how different kinds of environment may lead to the evolutionary development of different kinds of mental activity. Specifically, Burmann et al. (2005) summarised evidence to suggest that mental rotation is actually a loss of flexibility in perceiving orientation-independent views, as a result of humans abandoning the arboreal (tree-dwelling) environment in favour of walking upright. Because we aren't swinging around any more, we have a pretty boring upright view of the world which inhibits our ability to recognise objects any which way. Therefore, it would be an interesting question as to whether a species such as the lion-tailed macaque, which still lives in an arboreal environment, reveals mental rotation effects.

A 5-year-old female lion-tailed macaque was eventually tested, after a period of training, under a two-alternative matching-to-sample procedure. This means that, at each trial, the monkey was initially presented with the image of a 'sample' stimulus consisting of an asymmetrical shape. The monkey was required to touch the sample within 5 seconds in order to display two comparison stimuli. The monkey was then required to touch the image that matched the sample image. The target stimulus could either be clockwise or counter-clockwise

rotated by 0°, 40°, 80° or 120°. Upon responding correctly, the macaque received as a reward either cereal or meal worm. Tasty.

Generally speaking, the macaque produced both slower reaction times and more errors as the angle of rotation between sample and comparison stimuli increased. However, in terms of statistical significance, the authors found that only reaction times at 0° rotation were faster than 40°, 80° and 120° rotation. In other words, there was no evidence of a linear increase in reaction time as angle of rotation increased, which would be generally supportive of the macaque imagining the rotation of the object.

Burmann et al. (2005) discussed that their data do not conclusively point either to full mental rotation (in which a linear increase in reaction time with angle of rotation should have been observed), nor to rotational invariance (in which reaction time should have been constant with respect to angle of rotation). Rather, the data point to a state somewhere in between mental rotation and rotational invariance, as a result of the macaque representing an intermediate step in the evolution of cognition. It seems that in evolving an upright gait, we really do see the world in a different way.

*Source*: Burmann, B., Dehnhardt, G., & Mauck, B. (2005). Visual information processing in the lion-tailed macaque (Macaca silenus): Mental rotation or rotational invariance? *Brain, Behavior & Evolution, 65*, 168–176.

## Descriptive representations

So far we have introduced and discussed analogical representation and we have devoted quite a lot of attention to various ideas about depictive forms of mental representation. Issues and problems have been discussed and it has been concluded that alternative ideas are perhaps needed. To this end, let us briefly remind ourselves about the nature of cognitive maps as described by Tolman, and the conclusion that these are quite unlike pictures. Using the example of the map of the London Underground, we noted that this sort of map is not a simple 2D copy of the target landscape because only some of the spatial relations present in the landscape are preserved. We have built a case that this provides a very good example of how best to think about the nature of mental representation. Whatever form of representation is being derived and stored, it is not a copy or facsimile. We have concluded that the internal representation of some input is a specification in which significant parts and significant relations between those parts are captured. Some but not all parts of a stimulus are captured and some but not all relations between those parts are captured.

If this is accepted then it can be concluded that an internal representation of a stimulus is a description of the stimulus couched in some form of internal language. Such ideas have been fleshed out in terms of a mental language variously referred to as **mentalese** (Fodor, 1975), the **lingua mentis** (Jusczyk & Earhard, 1980; Pylyshyn, 1978), or more simply, the **language of thought** (Fodor, 1975). Evidence for this line of reasoning has already been discussed, in passing, with respect to perceiving shapes (see the previous references to the work of Palmer and Reed). Indeed, to appreciate what is being asserted, it is important to reconsider claims about the nature of perceptual encoding operations that are assumed to underlie shape processing. We need to revisit the notion of a **structural description** that was introduced in our discussion of SIT (see Chapter 6).

### Mentalese – the language of thought

A critical aspect of this mental language (as with natural language) is that it has a componential structure (see Chapter 14 for much more on this point). The analogy here with natural language is that, in natural language, sentences are composed of phrases and phrases are composed of words. Fundamentally the idea is that internal language contains a vocabulary. In natural language the vocabulary comprises the words of the language. In mentalese (i.e., mental language, or the language of thought) the vocabulary is taken to comprise unanalysed semantic elements (Fodor, 1975) – the atoms of thought. There have been quite controversial debates about how best to pursue this line of argument (Fodor, Fodor & Garrett, 1975; Jackendoff, 1977; Katz & Fodor, 1963), but on one reading, such unanalysable units of meaning are sometimes referred to as **semantic primitives** (Katz & Fodor, 1963; Winograd, 1978) or alternatively **cogits**, where a cogit is 'the smallest information structure perceptually or cognitively delineated' (Hayes-Roth, 1977, p. 261). In addition to such meaning primitives, language has something that is known as a **combinatorial syntax** (i.e., grammar – a formal system for generating sentences). The rules of grammar specify how the different components can be combined – they specify combinatorial processes (Gallistel, 1990; Jusczyk & Earhard, 1980). Given such combinatorial rules, just think of the number of sentences you can generate from 'we', 'go', 'can', 'now', 'home'.

It is easy to make the mistake and conclude that this internal language is simply an internalisation of external language – a Welsh person's mentalese is not simply internalised Welsh, nor is a Scottish person's mentalese simply internalised Gaelic. Indeed, to provide a completely different non-verbal example, consider a photofit kit in which there is a whole range of different facial features (the primitive elements) and a basic set of rules for combining these features (e.g., the nose must be located above the mouth). The possibilities are endless. Quite clearly, therefore, there are combinatorial systems other than natural language. To avoid any confusion, it is best to think that mentalese is an abstract system (such as algebra and its formulae of $x$s and $y$s) and it should not be confused with the notion of some form of 'inner voice'. Indeed there is a very important point to make here about the nature of human thought: namely that it is the ability to take elemental units (whatever they stand for) and to combine them in novel ways that appears to be a defining characteristic of intelligent behaviour.

Insofar as the notion of a cognitive map can be fleshed out as being more like a description than a picture, the basic idea can be extended and be applied more generally. It is possible to envisage that any stimulus in any modality is transformed into a description in an abstract mental language. This is exactly how a computer works – all forms of input are translated into digital (i.e., binary) signals. In this way, this framework can be applied more widely to thinking about perception in general (Fodor, 1975; Sutherland, 1968).

So although the preceding discussion focused on the concept of a cognitive map, the basic characteristics of these internal representations are taken to be the very same as those that underpin more elementary pattern recognition (Sutherland, 1968, 1974). It is assumed that, in general, stimuli are recoded into a form in which their elemental features are specified, together with certain salient structural relations that hold between those features. The claim is that the internal representation of a shape, which is produced via perceptual encoding operations, is in the form of a *structural description*. The description codes significant parts and significant relations between those parts. In this respect, this general theoretical approach to how the language of thought works in perception, bears a certain analogy with SIT (as described in Chapter 6).

Okay, that's quite a lot to take in at once, so just stop for a minute and consider your own mental language. Introspection tells us that our perceptions of the world seem quite different from what might be expected on the basis of trying to decipher abstract codes. Perceiving seems quite unlike attempting to understand a description of the world such as when reading a descriptive passage in a novel. Intuition suggests that what is transpiring is a never-ending visit to the cinema in which the mind's eye is watching some form of internal movie. The impression is that this is something quite different to that of reading a screenplay. The problem is the following. Our impressions of the world give rise to a seamless chain of smoothly changing events. However, what the psychological evidence suggests is that these impressions are misleading, if we are trying to figure out what is really going on. It seems as though the internal representations and processes operate according to strict rules in the generation of language-like descriptions. Our seamless view of the world – our perception of the world – is based on operations in an internal language of thought.

It is important, therefore, to examine the data that lead to these conclusions. When we trace the evidence back through time, it again turns out (cf. our previous discussion of Tolman's research) that the foundational ideas were worked out in studies with non-human species (henceforth, animals).

## Structural descriptions of shapes

A typical experiment (e.g., Bowman & Sutherland, 1969) was one in which, during an initial training phase, the participants (in this case, goldfish) were trained to take food from a particular place holder and then they were trained to discriminate between a positive reinforced option (e.g., a W shape) and a negative non-reinforced option (e.g., a V shape). That is, the goldfish were trained to associate one shape (positive) with food and a second shape (negative) with no reward. The fish were therefore motivated to select the shape with the positive outcome and learning was assumed to have taken place after the fish exhibited 18 correct out of 20 trials. Following this training period a transfer phase was initiated. Now the training shapes were changed and performance was now reassessed. A new pair of shapes was tested and the idea was to see which of the two would be treated as being most like the previous positively reinforced shape. The basic rationale here is as follows.

The most basic assumption is that animals exhibit various forms of generalisations in their pattern classifications. When asked to pass the salt we will effortlessly pick up the nearest salt cellar even though we may never have seen that particular salt cellar before. In the context of these transfer test experiments, the degree to which a response associated with one pattern transfers to a different pattern can be used to address questions about the sorts of internal codes that are being used to represent the patterns. For example, assume that an animal, having learnt something about E, categorises F in the same way, but discriminates E from L. On the basis of this pattern of performance, it can be concluded that the code being used for the category E must contain some specification of the presence of the top horizontal bar. The internal representation of the E is in terms of a structural description that codes the various parts of the letter and the relations between those parts. It is quite unlike a mental picture or a mental photocopy.

Figure 7.21 shows the sorts of transfer responses that the goldfish trained on discriminating W from V showed. As you can see, the goldfish performed very well on cases of 90° and 180° rotation of both shapes, and also when the same number of points were used at the top or left of the shapes. So much for their three-second memory! The general conclusion to emerge from the empirical work with animals was that they make use of very abstract descriptions in classifying shapes (Sutherland, 1974; see Figure 7.18). Indeed, Sutherland (1968) discussed various empirical findings across a range of studies on animals that pose challenges for any theory of pattern recognition.

### Shape recognition and various constancies

Among these findings is the ability to discount absolute size in making shape discriminations. Animals exhibit

| | Group I | Group II | Group III |
|---|---|---|---|
| | Training shapes | | |
| | M A (shapes) | W ⋁ (shapes) | 𝟛 ❭ (shapes) |
| | Transfer series I | | |
| 1 180° rotation of 'W' | W A  92** | M ⋁  65 | ⧣ ❭  85** |
| 2 180° rotation of 'V' | M ⋁  78** | W A  60 | 𝟛 ◀  78** |
| 3 180° rotation of both shapes | W ⋁  88** | M A  82** | ⧣ ◀  78** |
| 4 90° rotation of both shapes | 𝟛 ❭  73** | ⧣ ◀  77** | W ⋁  80** |
| 5 Same number of points at top or left of shapes | (shapes)  87** | (shapes)  85** | (shapes)  83** |
| 6 Same number of points at base or right of shapes | (shapes)  57 | (shapes)  55 | (shapes)  77* |
| 7 Same number of knobs at top or left of shapes | (shapes)  78** | (shapes)  80** | (shapes)  83** |
| 8 Same number of knobs at base or right of shapes | (shapes)  55 | (shapes)  55 | (shapes)  77** |
| 9 | (shapes)  47 | (shapes)  67 | (shapes)  68* |
| 10 | (shapes)  63 | (shapes)  72* | (shapes)  60* |
| 11 | (shapes)  62 | (shapes)  65 | (shapes)  55 |
| 12 | (shapes)  55 | (shapes)  62 | (shapes)  50 |

**Figure 7.21 Actual figures used by Bowman and Sutherland (1969) in their fish training experiments**
The numbers show the percentage of trials on which the left-hand member of each pair was treated as being equivalent to the W-shape used during training and the right-hand member of each pair as equivalent to the V-shape used during training. Asterisks show cases where the outcomes differ significantly from chance.

*Source*: Bowman, R., & Sutherland, N. S. (1969). Discrimination of 'W' and 'V' shapes by goldfish. *The Quarterly Journal of Experimental Psychology, 21*, 69–76 (fig. 1, p. 72). Reproduced with permission from Taylor & Francis Ltd.

something known as *size constancy* or size invariance. When animals were trained to discriminate between a pair of shapes they continued to discriminate the shapes successfully even when the size of the shapes was altered (Sutherland, 1968). This shows that the animals had cottoned on to the fact that shape identity, but not size, was the critical factor. The animals learnt something about shape as abstracted away from shapes of particular sizes. To account for this, it is assumed that the structural description codes the relative size of the parts of the shape and not the absolute size.

Rather unsurprisingly the animals also exhibited **retinal position constancy (invariance)**: shape discrimination generalised from one part of the retina to another and, moreover, discriminations learnt with one eye transferred to the other (Myers & McCleary, 1964). The structural description is abstracted away from a retinal co-ordinate system – the information is coded in some other form of co-ordinate system that is not tied to a retinal frame of reference (see Chapter 3).

It was also established that the animals overcame some changes in brightness to maintain shape discriminations across different lighting conditions; that is,

More striking perhaps are the generalisations that animals make when confronted by more complex patterns. Figure 7.23 provides various examples. What seems to be going on is that the animals (the rat, octopus and goldfish) are sensitive to so-called higher-order or more abstract properties of the patterns. They treat a whole variety of checkerboards as being equivalent regardless of the absolute number of squares that they contain (Sutherland & Williams, 1969). In this regard,

**Figure 7.22 A contrast inversion effect**
By inverting the grey level of a colour picture, even very famous individuals can be rendered unidentifiable (?).
*Source*: Olivier Douliery/ABACA/PA Photos.

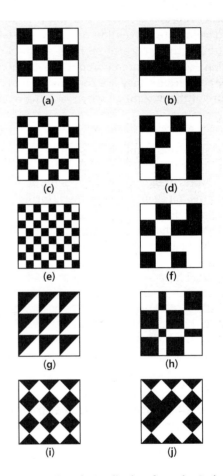

**Figure 7.23 Examples of stimuli taken from the Sutherland and Williams study (1969)**
The animals (rats) were trained to discriminate regular (a) from irregular (b). The remaining pairs of the shapes in the different rows were used in transfer tests. The figures in the left column (starting with (c)) were treated by the animals as being equivalent to (a) at test and the figures in the right column were treated as being equivalent to (b) at test. In all cases the rats were responding according to pattern regularity, showing that they had abstracted something other than simple templates during training.

*Source*: Sutherland, N. S. (1974). Object recognition. In E. C. Carterette, & M. P. Friedman (Eds.), *Handbook of perception III* (pp. 157–185; fig. 3, p. 165). Reproduced with permission from Elsevier.

they show limited **brightness constancy (invariance)**. From the human point of view, it is intuitively obvious that shapes can be easily recognised despite changes in the ambient light; however, the fact that brightness invariance does break down is shown by the fact that face recognition can be particularly impaired if the grey levels in the images are inverted (see Figure 7.22). A related finding (described by Sutherland, 1968) was that shape discrimination survived when an outline figure was substituted for a filled-in shape. Evidence taken to show that the structural description does not code the surface brightness of a given figure. Collectively all of this evidence reveals that the animals were recovering something about shape that is not linked inextricably to particular instances. The animals were abstracting general properties of the shapes independently of the particularities of any individual shape.

## → What have we learnt?

We have reached a point where we are beginning to make links between issues about the format of mental representation, on the one hand, and the nature of perception, on the other. The basic point is that there must be some reason as to why mental representations are the way that they are. The data suggest that the derivation of some form of internal representation of the world is intimately connected with perception of the world, which is, in turn, in the service of problem solving and prediction. Mental representations are the way that they are because they are constrained both by the nature of the perceptual system and the operations that are fundamental to problem solving. There is simply no point in having some form of representation (such as a raw bit-map) if this form of representation serves no useful purpose. In the current context, we can get a much better grip on the problems concerning mental representation if we examine the data from experiments on pattern perception and stimulus generalisation. Such points as these are further reinforced if we begin to consider how ideas about the perceptual coding of shape have been incorporated in models of shape recognition and the processes of recognising shapes.

---

it is the structural regularities (such as symmetry and repetition) that are being coded rather than a list of visual features or indeed templates of the original training patterns. Yet again therefore this is further evidence of structural descriptions – it is the general structure of the shapes that is driving behaviour rather than templates of particular shapes. The structural description is coding something about figural regularity.
→ See 'What have we learnt?', above.

### Pinpoint question 7.9

What kinds of visual properties can vary, without shape discrimination being disrupted in animals?

## Shape discriminations and template matching

Apart from using the data from the animal experiments to build arguments about the nature of internal representation, they have also been used to inform debates about the process of shape recognition. Central to all accounts of shape recognition is the idea that the derived perceptual representation is compared against corresponding representations of shapes that are stored in memory. A shape is recognised when its input representation is matched with a stored counterpart. A basic assumption therefore is that the format of the derived representation must be the same as the format of the stored representation, otherwise how could any useful comparisons take place? The basic question is: what is the purpose of mental representation? In the present context, the answer is that it underpins object recognition. We will discuss object recognition in much more detail in Chapter 13, but it is useful here to introduce a handful of relevant concepts.

A rather important conclusion is that what is stored is intimately connected to what is perceived. According to Neisser (1967) this sort of consideration led Gestalt theorists to the conclusion that the stored (so-called *central*) representation was 'an exact copy of the perceptual event that had occurred previously' (p. 30). In other words, what was being stored was a **template** of the input stimulus. So when stimulus *x* is presented it is recognised by a process of **template matching**. It is identified by noting how similar the encoding of stimulus *x* is with a corresponding stored template. By way of a concrete example, Neisser (1967) cited the case of matching a fingerprint against stored images of fingerprints in a database. The unknown fingerprint is compared against each stored image in turn by simply overlaying the input image over each in turn. A match is secured when the overlap between two images is perfect or almost so.

The reason that template matching is no longer taken as seriously as it once was, is that it seems implausibly rigid. Unless the input representation matches perfectly with a stored counterpart then the input shape will never be recognised. Against this, though, is the evidence cited in Figure 7.23. This sort of evidence undermines any simple template-matching account of shape recognition: the animals are particularly adept at picking up on the higher-order characteristics of shapes and template matching provides no explanation of how this can be.

These data show that the animals do not behave as though they are simply comparing picture-like templates with one another and using simple point-for-point comparisons to generate some overall metric of pattern similarity. Within the experimental context, a failure to discriminate between two patterns is taken as being evidence that the animal is treating the two target patterns as being similar. So if we assume that the internal representation of the patterns is couched in some form of picture or template, we must then ask how the similarity of the two 'pictures' is derived. The answer is in terms of a point-for-point comparison. A problem now is that the data do not fit within this framework at all. It is the regularity of the pattern that the animals are sensitive to. An implication of the findings with the checkerboard stimuli is that the animals would transfer learning of one checkerboard to another in which the black and white squares had been swapped. Such a result would, however, not be predicted on the basis of template matching. If these two checkerboards were to be superimposed then there would be no overlap at all and not one of the point-for-point comparisons would result in a match.

There seem, therefore, good grounds for dismissing template matching as being a ridiculous account of shape recognition. However, we must tread carefully here because, when pared back to its basics, the account shares some fundamental assumptions with other more grandiose theories. The notion that an input representation is derived and is compared with some stored counterpart is a central and ubiquitous assumption (as we discuss in Chapter 13). Moreover, as Sutherland (1974) has argued, any account that posits feature detectors, such as the line detectors discussed previously, is based on assumptions about template matching albeit at a very elemental level. Each feature detector acts as an elemental template.

To overcome the obvious problems with the template-matching accounts of shape recognition, Sutherland developed the notion of a *structural description*. Figure 7.24 provides examples of the sorts of codings that Sutherland (1968) thought underlined the process of generating an abstract, structural description of a shape. As can be seen, such a scheme bears close resemblance to the sorts of codings discussed in the context of SIT (see Chapter 6; although no claims are being made about the description comprising minimal codes!). The basic claim is that the perceptual encoding of shape eventuates in a mental representation of shape that is rendered into a language-like code. In order to understand this language-like code, however, we must explore certain other ideas about propositional representation. → See 'What have we learnt?', page 264.

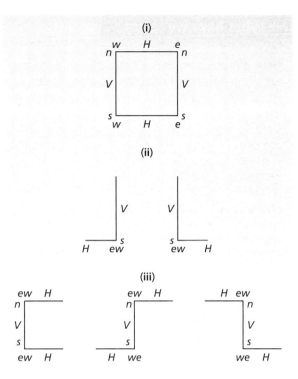

**Figure 7.24 The sorts of codings that Sutherland (1968) used to illustrate the notion of a structural description**
'H' and 'V' stand for horizontal and vertical, respectively. The other letters are abbreviations of compass directions (**n**orth, **s**outh, **e**ast and **w**est). Using such a coding system both the orientation and directions of the contours of a shape are captured.

*Source*: Sutherland, N. S. (1968). Outlines of a theory of visual pattern recognition in animals and man. *Proceedings of the Royal Society of London, Series B, 171*, 297–317 (fig. 16, p. 306). London: The Royal Society. Reproduced with permission.

## The lingua mentis and propositional representation

Much of what is known about mental representation can be accommodated within a framework for thinking in which propositions play a central role. At the heart of this framework is something known as a **predicate** defined as a generic function that specifies the relation that holds between entities known as **arguments** (after Norman & Rumelhart, 1975). Formally a predicate can be written:

$$P[\text{range}_1, \text{range}_2, \ldots \text{range}_n]$$

where P is the predicate and the *range* notation specifies the sets of allowable arguments. So in analysing the term 'give' the corresponding predicate would be:

give[agent, object, recipient, time]

Here it is accepted that a basic level of perceptual encoding is a process of assigning a description to a stimulus in some form of internal language. In discussing this possibility, the relevant data have been used to argue against simple template-matching accounts of shape recognition. Template matching was seen to be a fairly rudimentary idea that could be traced to the Gestalt movement, but the more recent data stand in contrast to this idea. On a more positive note, though, the data do accord with other aspects of Gestalt theorising. For instance, it is clear that the claims about an internal representation containing a description of a stimulus fit comfortably with the notions of perceptual organisation set out by the Gestalt theorists (see Sutherland, 1974). If we accept that the perceptual representation is, in part, derived through the application of the Gestalt laws of perceptual organisation, then, whatever is going on during the perceptual encoding, it is not a mere process of copying (see Wilton, 2000, for a more thorough exposition of this). The implication here is that the perceptual representation is a structured representation that contains a record of only the salient parts of the stimulus and the relations that hold between those parts – in other words, the perceptual representation may be thought of as providing a structural description (Sutherland, 1968). The Gestalt laws provide some insights into how the salient parts of a stimulus may be derived in the first instance.

This general conclusion is exactly in line with the previously discussed evidence described by Palmer and Reed. If this is accepted, then we should be able to dispel any notion of pictures-in-the-head. Indeed, as Johnson-Laird (1980, 1983) has repeatedly argued, any theory that posits pictures-in-the-head is in dan-

ger of an infinite regress because 'a picture requires an homunculus (a little man) to perceive it . . . and big homunculi need little homunculi to perceive their pictures' (1983, p. 147) (as Figure 7.25 illustrates).

**Figure 7.25 Unravelling the perception of ambiguous figures**
Why pictures-in-the-head theories don't work.

*Source*: Henderson, L. (1982). *Orthography and word recognition in reading* (fig. 11, p. 228). London: Academic. Reproduced with permission from Elsevier.

In the simple case, the *agent* is an animate (possibly sentient) being, as is the *recipient*, whereas *object* is a physical object and *time* is the when of the state of affairs. The natural language sentence '*Mary gave John the ticket yesterday*' would be captured in the corresponding proposition:

give[Mary, the ticket, John, yesterday]

In this form a proposition is a predicate with all its variable values filled in. (Clearly our simple example is stretched with sentences of the type '*The mirror gave Mary a nasty fright the other day*' but we hope the basic points are clear.) As we will see, on the assumption that propositions can be assigned a truth value (the proposition is either true or false), then we can also begin to see how propositions could play a useful role in inference making.

Indeed we can also see how such a representational system can underpin the derivation of structural descriptions. For instance, consider the following predicate:

Intersection[line1, line2, angle]

This can be used to code the corners of a square:

Intersection[horizontal, vertical, 90°]

Such ideas will be expanded upon shortly.

It is not difficult to see how a set of propositions can be treated as giving rise to a full-blown representational system as set out above. To reiterate, a representational system comprises a set of symbols or primitives and rules of combination that define how such symbols can be manipulated. With propositions, the primitives are the predicates and the arguments, and the arguments are constrained to take on allowable values. Indeed Jusczyk and Earhard (1980) have expressly stated that the lingua mentis is essentially a **propositional system** in which each individual proposition is a well-formed string of elements wherein each element (each primitive) is taken from the set of human concepts.

Indeed, given the abstract nature of propositions, it is also possible to see how both verbal and visual information could be captured in the same underlying propositional representational format. Although it may not be immediately obvious, the schematic representation shown in Figure 7.26 provides a propositional breakdown of the compositional nature of a face (Palmer, 1978).

### Propositions and network diagrams

More generally such a schematic illustration is known as a **network diagram** (or in this case a **propositional network**) comprising nodes and interconnections between nodes. This form of tree structure occurs time and again in the cognitive psychology literature and we will consider them again when we address other issues concerning mental representation in the chapter on long-term/semantic memory (see Chapter 12). In this particular example, the nodes (the ovals) represent particular predicates and the connections are labelled

arguments. In this particular model there are four predicate types coding, respectively: (i) relative location (the arrow symbols), 'location[*object, referent*]'; (ii) relative orientation (the degree values), 'orientation[*object, referent*]'; (iii) relative size (the ratios), 'size[*object, referent*]'; and (iv) shape (labelled shape), 'shape[*object, value*]'. There is no intention here to defend this particular representational system, but merely to use it to illustrate the flexible nature of propositions. They can be used as a generic form of coding system. Indeed, as is clear from Figure 7.26, propositions can be used to encode quantitative information (think of the ratios, for instance) as well as qualitative information (as is the case with the attributes – nose, eyes, mouth).

Indeed, it is because of this that claims have been made that a propositional system can be used to simulate the data from the mental rotation experiments. Here data have been taken to reveal a continuous analogical process. As noted by Kubovy (1983), introspection suggests that we perform such tasks 'in a continuous and unbroken run through all the stages of the action we are contemplating' (p. 662). Such mental transformations appear to simulate the continuous nature of the physical operations that would be brought to bear on the task. Therefore how could such a propositional representational system simulate such continuous analogical operations? Well, in answer to this question it has been argued (Hinton & Parsons, 1981; Palmer, 1975) that small discrete changes in the value of variables cast in a propositional description could simulate these data.

As is shown in Figure 7.27, the wire configuration (Figure 7.27a) can be represented by the network diagrams shown in Figure 7.27b. In this case, the nodes (the ovals) represent the parts of the configuration. Each link captures an angular relationship (e.g., $R_{wx}$) between a subordinate component and its superordinate whole. Simulating moving a given flap ($x$, $y$ or $z$) in and out corresponds to updating the corresponding $R$ values. The 'in and out' rotation of a part is therefore mimicked by changing a quantity as specified within a structural description of the 3D shape. Of course, as Wilton (1978) stated, such a theoretical manoeuvre does not in any way explain why people exhibit such a distinctive way of solving 'rotation' tasks; all it shows is how analogical processes can be mimicked by a propositional representational system. This point is relatively important because it illustrates how a discrete form of representation comprising propositions can simulate thinking about continuous changes that can take place in the real world.

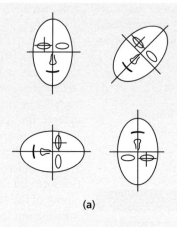

(a)

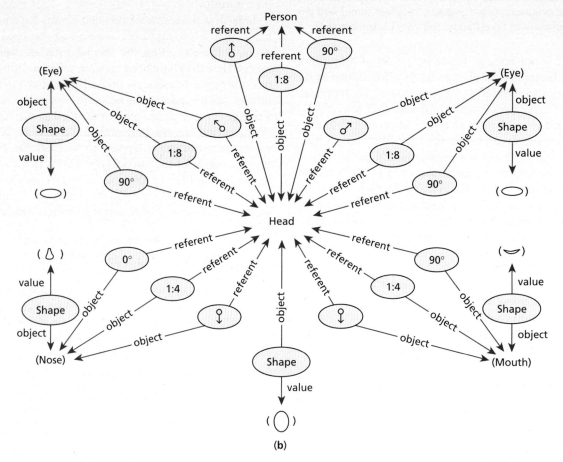

(b)

**Figure 7.26 A propositional representation of a face**
A propositional form of representation, discussed by Palmer (1975), that provides a structural description of a face (see text for further details).

*Source*: Palmer, S. E. (1975). Visual perception and world knowledge: Notes on a model of sensory-cognitive interaction. In D. A. Norman, & D. E. Rumelhart (Eds.), *Explorations in cognition* (pp. 279–307; fig. 11.4, p. 290). San Francisco: W. H. Freeman.

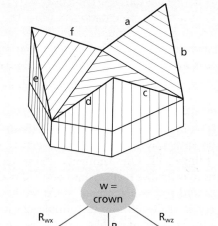

**(a)**

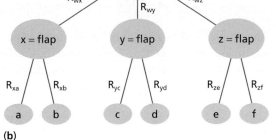

**(b)**

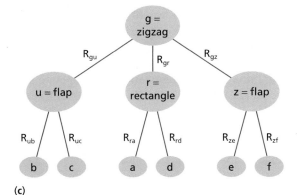

**(c)**

**Figure 7.27 Different structural descriptions of the same shape**
(a) Depicts a figure comprising six solid bars joined end to end to make a solid object. The object is perceptually ambiguous because it can be seen either (i) as a crown shape or (ii) as a zigzag shape. These different readings of the shape are supported by different structural descriptions (shown respectively as 'w' and 'g' in the lower panels (b) and (c)). These tree diagrams provide the structural descriptions in terms of different propositional networks (from Hinton & Parsons, 1981).

*Source*: Hinton, G. E., & Parsons, L. M. (1981). Frames of reference and mental imagery. In J. Long, & A. D. Baddeley (Eds.), *Attention and performance, IX* (pp. 261–277; fig. 15.1, p. 262; fig. 15.2, p. 263). Hillsdale, New Jersey: Erlbaum. Reproduced with permission.

**mentalese** A term to describe mental language as discussed by Fodor (1975), for instance.

**lingua mentis** A phrase synonymous with the language of thought.

**language of thought** A phrase used to refer to the internal system of representation and the operations that take place within this system in order to explain thought and thinking (after Fodor, 1975).

**structural description** A form of internal representation that codes key parts of a shape and some of the salient relations between those parts.

**semantic primitives** Atomic units of meaning within mental language.

**cogit** The smallest unit of information within mental language. Cogits are the atoms of thought.

**combinatorial syntax** A system of rules for combining units of some form of language or form of representational system.

**retinal position constancy (invariance)** The ability to discount retinal position in identifying shape.

**brightness constancy (invariance)** The ability to discount absolute brightness in identifying shape.

**template** According to Gestalt theories, an exact perceptual copy of an input stimulus.

**template matching** Taking a representation of an input stimulus and attempting to match this against stored templates of known stimuli.

**predicate** Within propositional representation, a generic function which applies to one or more arguments.

**arguments** One or more variables that apply to a predicate. A predicate structure is of the sort – Predicate [Argument1, Argument2, . . . Argumentn].

**propositional system** A formal system of representation based upon propositions.

**network diagram** See tree structure.

**propositional network** A representational system in which propositions are coded in terms of nodes and links.

# Concluding comments

The present chapter has provided an introduction to the notion of mental representation and has set out some of the more basic reasons as to why cognitive psychologists have felt that such a notion is necessary to their theories. Fundamentally, it is difficult to see how thinking and problem solving could take place without some form of internal representational system. Primarily the work covered here has been directed towards the question of what the *format* of internal representation is. Various alternative suggestions and relevant data have been examined. Despite the richness of this evidence, a rather important nagging doubt hangs over the field and this concerns the degree to which behavioural evidence can be used to adjudicate between ideas about mental representations and ideas about mental processes.

The foregoing has attempted to concentrate on issues concerning the format of mental representation. For example, how like a picture is a cognitive map? However, issues have also been raised about the nature of mental operations (processes) such as scanning images and mental rotation. There are many issues and some of the problems in interpreting the empirical results may reflect difficulties in trying to discriminate constraints due to representational format and those concerning mental processes (see the protracted debate involving Anderson, 1978, 1979; Hayes-Roth, 1979; and Pylyshyn, 1979).

What we have tried to do here is develop a particular line of argument in favour of descriptive, not depictive, forms of mental representation. It has been claimed that mental representation is the way that it is because it fundamentally underpins our ability to make sense of the world. This is why we have focused quite a lot of attention on perception. The understanding is that the perceptual mechanisms deliver representations of the world that readily support problem solving and the ability to make predictions about the world. So if we understand perceptual coding then we may understand mental representation more generally. A basic claim is that, fundamentally, mental representations are coded in a language-like format – a language of thought.

So although we have discussed analogical and more particularly depictive representations, the evidence seems to point in a different direction: a direction in which descriptive representation resides. This is not to argue that people cannot reason in an analogical fashion because a central point has been that our ability to solve problems is constrained by what we know about the world. So our understanding of gravity is in large measure based on our experience of seeing things fall over. In this regard, it makes perfect sense to assume that when we think about gravity we do so in a way that mimics our experiences of having things fall. Our thoughts about particular problems may involve mental simulation of real-world scenarios and real-world events. What we have done here is try to spell out how such thinking can be accounted for by a language-like system that comprises descriptions.

The problems, though, cannot be overstated. A computer analogy may help here. Fundamentally, the only form of internal representation in a computer are binary signals (the 0s and 1s discussed in Chapter 2). By analogy, in some quarters, it is accepted that the fundamental codes in the brain are the firing patterns of neurons (neurological 0s and 1s). In this sense, therefore, we know what the format of the internal representations are. Leaving the explanation there is deeply unsatisfying. What we would really like to know are answers to questions couched at what Marr (1982) termed *the level of the representation and algorithm* (see Chapter 1). Can we get a handle on the sorts of programmes and representations that operate at the psychological level? From this perspective it is quite sensible to ask whether mental representations are more like bit-maps or propositions. When cast in such terms it seems that the task in front of us is similar to that of trying to figure out whether a computer is running a program written in PROLOG or C by merely observing its behaviour. In these terms, it is a testament to the creativity and ingenuity of experimental cognitive psychologists that any pro-gress in understanding has been made at all.

## CHAPTER SUMMARY

- Behaviourist accounts of learning differ from cognitive accounts in that behaviourists fail to recognise the importance of mental representation. For example, according to S–R theory, a rat finds its food in a maze on the basis of strengthening appropriate stimulus–response bonds. Evidence has been described that questions this view and provides support for the idea that the rat, in learning about the spatial layout of a maze, acquires a cognitive map.

- A map is an example of a representing world depicting a represented world. Typically maps do not contain a complete specification of everything in the represented world. Maps show the represented world by preserving certain geometrical relations between elements within the represented world. Two forms of analogical representation were discussed. With strict analogical representation, and according to Palmer (1978), 'Spatial information is not only preserved but it is preserved in (1) a spatial medium and (2) in such a way that the image resembles that which it represents' (p. 295). Importantly, dimensions in the represented world are captured by analogous dimensions in the representing world. With lenient analogical representation, spatial information is merely preserved in some way or other.

- It is also possible to consider cases where hybrid systems are conceived in which a representation system has both analogical and symbolic characteristics. Various sorts of symbolic systems are discussed.

- In contrast to molecular descriptions of behaviour as put forward by S–R theorists, a molar description of behaviour introduces the idea of goal-directed action (Tolman, 1948). Animals can demonstrate rational decision-making and reveal behaviour consistent with the idea of operating according to certain means–end expectations. Different sets of actions lead to different outcomes and one selects the actions that will lead to a desired goal.

- A cognitive map can be developed simply on the basis of latent learning or simple interaction within a represented world. Not only does this allow for efficient navigation, but also adaptive behaviours such that novel routes from A to B may be generated if usual pathways are obstructed. The critical point is that a mental representational system underpins the ability to apply learnt behaviours to novel situations. Previously learnt behaviours can be combined to bring about novel actions that have never been tried out.

- In pursuing ideas about analogical representation, the notion of picture-like, depictive representations were considered. Evidence regarding mental images and their picture-like qualities were addressed. Questions about whether they correspond to literal pictures were examined. With literal pictures, the representation resembles the object of interest whereas in other forms of non-literal representation there is no necessary resemblance between the representing and represented object. In this regard a distinction was drawn between depictive and descriptive representations. Simply put, depictive representations are picture-like and descriptive representations are language-like.

- Theorists like Kosslyn (1994) hold that mental images are analogical in nature. Using the cathode-ray tube framework for thinking (Kosslyn & Pomerantz, 1977), it is assumed that an image of an object is akin to a 2D display on a mental movie screen. It is tempting to claim that these sorts of representation are assumed to be complete but this is mistaken as they lack information about depth. Such representations merely capture point-for-point aspects of surface detail and they do not contain any information about what is being represented.

- A revision to literal representation theories (Kosslyn, 1980) acknowledged the absence of object description and proposed that depictive representations of objects are stored in addition to descriptive representations, thereby leading a hybrid model of mental representation. It is simply hopeless to think that mental files are stored without mental filenames.

- Mental scanning experiments have been used to support ideas relating to the analogical nature of the mental representation of spatial layout in maps. If subjects are asked to focus on one landmark and to respond whether a second landmark is present within the representation (Kosslyn & Pomerantz, 1977), time to respond is linearly related to the distance between landmarks.

- However, the depictive nature of mental representation has been questioned by evidence arising from further mental scanning experiments (Pylyshyn, 1981). A case was built for the notion of descriptive representation by an appeal to ideas concerning tacit knowledge (Pylyshyn, 2002). Subjects in mental scanning experiments can behave in various ways depending on the task constraints and subjects' interpretations of what is expected of them. Converging evidence for descriptive forms of representation came from studies of mental synthesis (Palmer, 1977), figural decomposition (Reed & Johnsen, 1975) and whether mental images are ambiguous (Chambers & Reisberg, 1985).

- Mental rotation experiments (Shepard & Cooper, 1982) also shed light on the way in which internal representations may be manipulated, although similar difficulties in separating out the use of functional, analogue space or tacit knowledge still apply. Evidence from these studies provides very strong evidence for the close-knit relation between how the world is perceived and how it is construed. The evidence suggests that mental problem solving is very much mental simulation in which physical actions (actions that could take place in the real world) are simulated in the head.

- Fundamental to the notion of descriptive representations is the notion of some form of language of thought (mentalese – Fodor, 1975; or lingua mentis – Pylyshyn, 1978). The language of thought should not be confused with any given natural language such as English or French, but is explained in terms of a representational system in which the basic building blocks of thought are combined in ways determined by rules.

- Not only are attributes of the world captured by such a representational system but of equal import are the relations between such attributes. Support for these ideas is provided by animal research (Sutherland, 1974). Here animals were initially trained to discriminate between a pair of shapes, for example, and then they were tested in making similar discriminations with different shapes. Of particular interest were the patterns of generalisation that the animals made. Collectively, these data support the idea that in representing shapes the animals were generating a structural description that codes both salient parts and relations between these parts. Such a descriptive representation is not like an image nor a picture.

- The chapter concluded with an examination of the claim that fundamentally the language of thought is composed of propositions. Evidence showing how propositional representation can underpin aspects of perception and mental problem solving (i.e., mental rotation) was discussed.

## ANSWERS TO PINPOINT QUESTIONS

7.1 A chain of stimulus–response bonds are set up during maze exploration and these bonds are strengthened when the food reward is discovered.

7.2 With analogical representations there is a correspondence between aspects of the representing world and aspects of the represented world. So with the street map the length of the lines depicting the streets are analogical with the actual length of the streets in the real world.

7.3 The rat has acquired knowledge that one set of actions will lead to one goal and a second set of actions will lead to another, and that it is able to select which set of actions will produce the goal of fulfilling its current need.

7.4 A cognitive map allows for efficient navigation around an external environment as well as the ability to generate novel routes.

7.5 First, each object will have a depictive or literal representation in which information regarding the spatial nature of an object is captured in 2D planar projection. Second, descriptive labels

that specify the content of the stored image are also needed.

7.6 When participants were asked to respond to the relative position of a second landmark, relative to another, according to compass bearings, then no linear relation between speed of response and distance between landmarks was shown.

7.7 Evidence from studies of fragment 'goodness' (e.g., Reed & Johnsen, 1975; Palmer, 1977) contrast with depictive accounts of mental representation as it appears only some of the possible structural properties of a shape are represented internally.

7.8 A picture can be ambiguous in the sense that what it shows is open to question – is there a young woman or an old woman shown? The critical research question is whether mental images can be ambiguous in the same way.

7.9 Size, retinal position and brightness can all change without substantial loss in shape discrimination.

7.10 Daddy is taking us to the zoo tomorrow.

## CHAPTER 8

# ATTENTION
## General introduction, basic models and data

## LEARNING OBJECTIVES

**By the end of this chapter, you should be able to:**

- Summarise the early selection structural constraint models of attention by Broadbent (1953) and Treisman (1964).
- Summarise the late selection structural constraint models of attention by Deutsch and Deutsch (1963).
- Summarise the ideas of resource allocation set out by Kahneman (1973).
- Appreciate how both structural and processing constraints are incorporated in Pashler's (1998) framework for thinking.
- Discuss load theory (Lavie, 2000).

## CHAPTER CONTENTS

Anybody who has tried to DJ (and some of us are still trying) will appreciate how difficult it can be to listen to two things at once. Imagine the scene – you've just played a few great tunes to build up the crowd and now are getting ready to drop that track that will seal your reputation as a true master mixer (see Figure 8.1). The problem is that you've

# A cognitive psychologist in the DJ booth

got to make sure that the two records are playing at the same speed and that those rhythms fit nicely. So, using a single left-ear headphone, you listen to the record already playing and cue up the vinyl you want to play before unleashing it onto the unsuspecting crowd. So now you're listening to both the playing and the to-be-played record through the same 'input channel'. But are we really able to listen to two things at once? Would it be more reasonable to assume we switch between sources of information? What

**Figure 8.1 Attentional control and the modern world**
Being a successful DJ requires phenomenal attentional capabilities (as well as being able to put your hand in the air).
*Source*: Katy Beswetherick/Rex Features.

would happen if one song were fed through the left headphone and the other through the right headphone? Would this make mixing easier or harder? And how about doing all of these things while ignoring those flashing lights and dry ice? Is someone calling your name from behind the DJ booth? Quick, your dance floor is waiting . . .

## REFLECTIVE QUESTIONS

1. Think about an airline pilot and the various kinds of information that they have to deal with (the view out of the cockpit window, visual computer displays, auditory warning signals, communication with ground control, co-pilot and passengers). How can you apply the concepts from this chapter such that you might improve the way in which the pilot deals with these inputs?

2. Think about your immediate context right now as you read this book. Try to make a list of all the potential inputs in your environment (remember to think about all the senses). Are you being successful in attending? Is there an input that you would like to ignore that you can't? Why do you think this is? On the basis of what you've learnt in the chapter, how can you make your environment an easier one to work in?

## Introduction and preliminary considerations

Psychologists use the concept of attention to explain how it is that we are able to select aspects of our environment that we are interested in while ignoring others. If we are being eyed up from across a busy wine bar, we might focus on picking up non-verbal cues from our potential suitor, while disregarding our friend's (currently irrelevant) demonstration of their new golf swing. How we might effectively juggle such concurrent and competing activities has become a question of central importance and serves as the focus of this chapter. We will look at a number of theories of attention and attentional control and discuss a number of experiments that have been put forward to help explain how we achieve attentional selection, that is, the ability to focus on the important stuff and ignore everything else. Generally speaking, attentional selection is apparently so effortless that you are probably taking it for granted right now.

In more formal terms, we will discuss contrasting views about whereabouts in the human information processing system exactly such selection takes places. Does selection occur very early on in processing or does it occur much later? Accordingly, we will discuss the division between so-called 'early selection' and 'late selection' theories. We will also discuss how selection has been thought of either in terms of *structural constraints* or in terms of *processing constraints*. Such

mysterious possibilities will be thoroughly explored as we proceed.

But just for the moment, think about where you are right now. Perhaps you're reading this on the bus. How are you blocking out the noise of the other passengers? Can you be sure your attention will switch if your mobile suddenly starts ringing? How do you know when to get off if you're engrossed in this book – wait, you haven't gone past your stop, have you?

## Out with the new and in with the old

Quite a lot of advertising capitalises on the naïvely held belief that this year's model is much better than last year's; modern living encourages the view that it is only right to discard the old version in favour of the new. Despite this, the disappointment can be palpable when it suddenly dawns that there really is very little to tell the new and old apart. As in life, this happens quite a lot in cognitive psychology. In many cases, it turns out that the only difference between this year's model and last year's is the packaging – old wine/new bottles. Indeed one of the mildly depressing characteristics of the history of cognitive psychology is how often old ideas are discarded, or otherwise forgotten, only to be rediscovered and repackaged at a later date.

So what are we to make of all this? Well, it does suggest that progress can only be made if the old ideas are properly evaluated. We need to be able to discriminate the useful from the useless so that we can set firm foundations for theorising. It is for this reason that the current discussion of attention starts with a consideration of Broadbent's filter theory of attention which dates back to 1958. Most of the ideas present in that model feature, in some form or other, in most models of attention ever since. So clearly these 'old' ideas have turned out to be incredibly useful. In general terms, the theory was based on a particular view about why attention is necessary. The basic idea is that attention is necessary because the central mechanisms cannot cope with the amount of sensory stimulation present at any given time. As Allport (1989) noted, by this view, the fundamental 'purpose of attentional mechanisms is to protect the brain's limited capacity system (or systems) from informational overload' (p. 633).

At the risk of revealing too much personal information, at the time of writing one of the authors is at home, there is a chirpy sparrow in a tree in the garden which is interfering with the CD currently playing, he has a slight headache from talking on the phone until 4am this morning, he is resting his foot on the corner of the dining table (not as comfortable as it sounds) and he is also digesting a sausage sandwich and a cup of tea. There are some thoughts about brewing up again, maybe taking the day off and reading the Saturday paper on the beach, and then there are decisions to be made about what to take to the barbeque he's been invited to tomorrow. Now the sparrow is back and chirping louder than usual, the phone has started to ring and the kettle has boiled and the CD needs changing and . . . Even in this state of relative inactivity, there is a lot going on in terms of sensory stimulation and clearly there are important decisions to be made about what ought to be attended to.

## Early filtering accounts of selection

Broadbent's (1958) filter theory of attention is notable as being one of the most famous arrows-and-boxes accounts within the human information processing framework for thinking about cognition. It is an abstract, functional account (as described in Chapters 1 and 2) and describes putative component stages of processing that are assumed to intervene between a given stimulus and the corresponding response. There

is, essentially, no discussion of physiology or neurophysiology. Even though there are clear physical constraints that set the boundaries on human information processing – for instance, we only have two eyes and two ears, that brain cells can only fire a certain number of times a second, etc. – the limitations of the human processing system were discussed in the model in abstract terms. More particularly, the idea is that the brain ought to be conceived as being akin to a communication system along the lines that we discussed in Chapter 2.

As with any communication system, there is the notion of a limited capacity channel that connects the sender with the receiver. In terms of human information processing, the sender is, essentially, the outside world (the bird song, whistling kettle, ringing telephone, etc., are being sent by the outside world) and the receiver is the participant as defined by the central interpretive mechanisms (i.e., the conscious perceiver). Limited capacity, in this context, refers to an upper bound placed on the amount of information that can be transmitted down the channel at any given time: as in a meat packing factory, there are only so many frozen chickens that can go down the conveyor belt at once. Intervening between the outside and the inside worlds are various other processes concerning sensory encoding/perceptual analysis and so on. What the filter theory does is flesh these intervening processes out in some detail. Central, though, is the idea that, at an abstract level, the human central nervous system could be conceived as comprising a limited capacity information transmission channel.

At this juncture, it is worth recalling Turvey's (1973) concurrent and contingent model (see Chapter 4). In that model, whereas the peripheral mechanisms can handle much information quickly and in parallel (concurrently), the central mechanisms operate more slowly and can only sensibly deal with one item at once (the central mechanisms are contingent on the peripheral mechanisms). Sensory information is initially registered in parallel, but further processing operates in a serial (one-at-a-time) mode. Moreover, because of the constraint of the **limited capacity channel**, only some of the information presented to the senses can be dealt with at once. Some of this information needs to be selected as being currently relevant – the rest is, essentially, ignored. It is this notion of selection that underpins the notion of attention in the theory.

To get a better handle on all this, it is simplest to consider the actual information processing account set out by Broadbent (1958). As can be seen from Figure 8.2, input to the senses is registered initially and

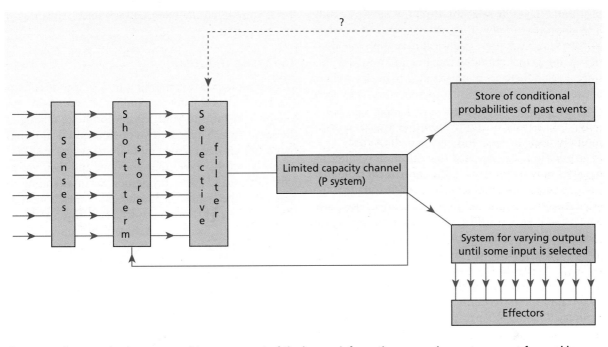

**Figure 8.2 The now classic arrows-and-boxes account of the human information processing system as put forward by Broadbent (1958)**

*Source*: Broadbent, D. E. (1958). *Perception and communication* (fig. 7, p. 299). Oxford, England: Pergamon Press.

is then passed forward to a short-term store or sensory memory system (the **S system**) in parallel (at the same time). One way to think of the S system is in terms of the body's total sensory apparatus – that is, the body's sensory receptors. As our previous example showed, there is an immense amount of sensory stimulation all of the time (the sight of the sausage sandwich, the whistling kettle, ringing telephone, etc.), and it is assumed that, because of this, the S system handles the various different kinds of information in parallel.

Rather unfortunately, the S system has also been discussed in terms of comprising parallel **input channels** which map onto the different senses such as vision, hearing and touch (Moray, 1969). A further complication, though, is that sometimes the auditory system is discussed as being composed of left and right ear channels (Broadbent, 1958, p. 58). So the mapping of input channels onto the different senses is not exactly correct, since we can also think of individual eyes and ears as input channels. So we must be careful of the distinction between input channels (so defined) and the central limited capacity processing channel. The basis idea is that the S system comprises many input channels that deliver information continuously (and in parallel) as stimulation from the outside world

impinges on the body. These many input channels act as the front end to the human information processing system. The problem now is to decide which aspects of this stimulation are worthy of attention. Only a subset is selected for further processing and so enters the next stage which is characterised by the operations of the limited capacity processing channel. The basic issue is to decide which of the many input channels should be the focus of attention.

## Selection by filtering

The basic idea here is that a selective filter affects the read-out or output of items from the short-term store so as to pass them on for further processing (for similar ideas see Chapter 3 and the discussion of information transfer from iconic memory). In this model, the operation of the filter acts as the first form of selection discussed by Broadbent (1958) and, unsurprisingly, this form of selection was known as *filtering*. A defining aspect of this **selection by filtering** is that it operates on the information stored in sensory memory, and as we have already discussed, such information specifies only the physical characteristics of stimuli. Sensory memory is said to represent the physical characteristics of stimuli, therefore selection from this store can only operate relative to physical features. In this way, selection by filtering is pre-categorical in nature; the identity of the actual stimulus remains unknown at this stage. (Again there are many parallels to be drawn here between this sort of sensory memory and the early discussions of iconic memory – see Chapter 3.) Select only those aspects of stimulation that possess a common physical attribute and filter out all the rest.

In addition, it is assumed that selection by filtering operates only upon items in the short-term store that share the currently pertinent common feature that the filter is set to. So read-out from your short-term store while standing in a field might deliver all the brown items (if the filter is set for brown items) *or* all the items on the right-hand side of space (if the filter is set for all the items to the right), but not all the brown items *and* all the items on the right-hand side of space. To use appropriate terminology, read-out from sensory memory operates at a **pre-categorical level**. Selection operates at a level prior to the stage at which the stimulus is identified, or, alternatively, assigned to some form of mental category. Having been confronted with a big brown shape while walking through the Rocky Mountains you now need to decide whether this actually warrants further action. Clearly the assignment of the big brown shape to the mental category of 'bear' would have significantly different consequences than assigning it to 'large rustling shrub', but at the earliest stages of processing such assignments cannot be made – only physical characteristics of the stimuli are registered.

Another important point about the short-term store is that, despite the fact that it has a very large capacity, items will decay from the store within a matter of seconds if they are not read out by the filter. For example, if two items arrive simultaneously in the S system, one will be passed on immediately, but the other will have to wait until the limited capacity channel frees up. It is also assumed that an item's probability of being selected increases directly as a function of its physical intensity. Just think about how hard it is to eavesdrop on a whispered conversation, in contrast to responding to someone shouting 'Fire!' in a doctor's waiting room. In terms of sound, a shout is more intense than a whisper, and so it is more likely that a shouted message will be passed on for further processing than a whispered message. In addition, it is also assumed the filter can switch between different selection criteria but that such switches take time. So you may feel that you can listen to one conversation while attending to another, but according to the theory, you can only do

this if you switch the filter between them. How might this happen?

### Switching the filter

Well, assume you are standing in a group of friends and high-pitched Janet is standing to your right and low-pitched John to your left and both are talking at the same time. There are two obvious physical things that differ between Janet and John; namely, the speakers are standing in different positions and their voices have different acoustic properties. So in attending to Janet, the filter could latch onto either a location cue (listen to the right) or an acoustic cue (listen to high-pitched voice). Switching between the conversations means **switching the filter** from either right to left or from high pitch to low pitch. The point is that you will not be able to process the two conversations at once because the filter can only follow one physical cue at once.

So although you may feel that you can process Janet and John at the same time, according to filter theory, the only way this is possible is to switch rapidly between the two conversations. However, according to the theory this switching takes time and so some information from the conversations will likely be lost during the time it takes to switch the filter. In this regard filtering is seen to be an all-or-nothing operation. Items are either selected for further processing or they are left in the S system to decay. In general, selection by filtering is assumed to be useful in cases when the participant is presented with a number of concurrent and complex events. In choosing to attend to (i.e., to select) one class of events it will be most likely that other events are less well processed and indeed may never be.

### Rehearsal

All of these ideas are summarised in Figure 8.3. Items that are selected for read-out by the filter are passed on to the limited capacity channel, shown as the P (or perceptual) system in the figure. This **P system** is assumed to operate serially such that selected items are processed one at a time. A further important component of the model now may come into play and this is known as **rehearsal**. We have already seen that unless an item is selected for read-out from the short-term store it will be lost within a matter of seconds. If the system is in danger of information overload then any item selected for read-out can be passed back from the P system and rehearsed, such that it is recirculated into the short-term store. In this way the limitations

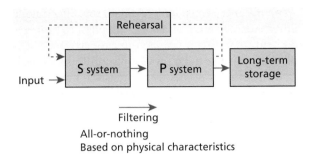

**Figure 8.3  A skeletal account of Broadbent's (1958) model of processing**

of the central channel can be overcome, to a certain extent. Of course, rehearsing items in this way carries an overhead that may, in turn, deflect other items from being selected from the short-term store. Critically, though, only items that have been selected and have exited from the P system stand any chance of entering the long-term memory system. In this way it is only items that are selected from the S system and are processed by the P system that can enter long-term storage.

In the original discussion of the model (Broadbent, 1958), not very much was given away about the long-term memory system. As can be seen in Figure 8.2 this system in part contains some form of record of the conditional probabilities of past events – in other words it is conceived as being an **associative memory**. In simple terms the idea is that this system keeps track of associations between items. So long as A and B co-occur then a record is kept of the strength of this co-occurrence in long-term memory. For example, the strength of association between salt and vinegar will be greater than that between salt and pepper if you live next to a chip shop rather than a fancy restaurant. The second component of long-term memory is contained on the route to the effectors and, by this, Broadbent meant the bodily mechanisms necessary for making a response. However, it is difficult to be more specific about this particular component because, again, very little else was given away about its properties (see Broadbent, 1971, p. 16).

### The P system

In the original discussion of the model, the operation of the P (perceptual) system was also under-specified. Initially, some doubts were expressed about whether what came out of the limited capacity channel was the same as what went into it (Broadbent, 1958, p. 227). Was the same sort of information circulated around the system? Or was it the case that the P system actu-

ally transformed inputted information into a different sort of code? A more definite proposal was, eventually, put forward by Broadbent (1971, p. 178). Now he suggested that the P system affects perceptual–semantic categorisation, in that items in the P system are assigned to their corresponding mental categories. In other words, the outputs from this system coded **postcategorical information**: the previous brown shape is assigned to the rather alarming mental category of 'human predators' and not the friendly flora category!

Based on this discussion, it can be seen that the items that are not selected, and therefore do not enter the P system, are 'excluded from semantic categorisation or identification' (Allport, 1989, p. 633). On the understanding that the items exiting from the P system are represented in a code that specifies the post-categorical nature of the item, this was later interpreted as indicating that the P system used a different form of memory system to that of the original sensory buffer. Sensory information is initially registered in the S system in some raw form that codes the physical nature of the stimulus (e.g., large brown shape), while outputs from the P system code the categorical nature of the stimulus (e.g., bear) – semantic information is now made explicit. The representation of the stimulus entering the P system from the S system simply codes physical characteristics of the stimulus (i.e., its size, shape, position, colour, etc. (e.g., large brown shape) but it does not code its identity. At this stage the commitment to 'bear' has not been made. On leaving the P system the stimulus has been identified, hence 'bear' is now coded. The concern was with whether the so-called sensory codes and semantic codes demanded different forms of storage. Such concerns about different sorts of stimulus coding and different sorts of memory systems are covered in much more detail later (see Chapter 10). Here we merely introduce you to the sort of issue that the model throws up and we will be much more careful in our appraisal later.

## Information processing constraints in the model

In Broadbent's (1958) original filter theory we can identify various sorts of processing constraints. The limited capacity channel, or P system in Figure 8.3, provides what is known as a **structural bottleneck** – the body of the bottle holds a lot of wine but only a small amount escapes through the neck of the bottle when the bottle is inverted. Whereas sensory stimulation is captured in parallel by the S system, the processing on the limited capacity channel is sequential in that only one item can be processed centrally at a time. You'll be aware of both the CD playing and the sparrow in the garden, but only actively able to listen to one at once. Similarly the limited capacity channel has a strict upper bound on how quickly any item can be cleared from the S system. It is quite possible for a logjam to occur in the S system if information is arriving too quickly for it all to enter the P system. This form of bottleneck is known as a **structural constraint** because it is part of the architecture of the model. Think in terms of a departmental store containing a lift (see Figure 8.4). The lift operates as a structural bottleneck because only a small number of people enter the lift at a given time. The speed with which the lift operates, though, would be akin to a *processing constraint* and the filter theory also contains various sorts of processing constraints.

For instance, consider the filter: the filter selects items that are defined by a common physical property and items that do not possess this property are essentially ignored. The main processing constraint in dealing with complex events therefore is the time it takes the filter to switch from one pertinent feature to the next. Again information may be lost from the S system because this decays before the filter is switched to the appropriate stimulus characteristic.

So given this theory, what is the evidence? What are the relevant data? Despite the cursory treatment of the model here, the whole of Broadbent's 1958 book provided the empirical justification for the model, but in a kind of brave and foolish way we will only consider two sorts of experiment that set the foundations for the theory.

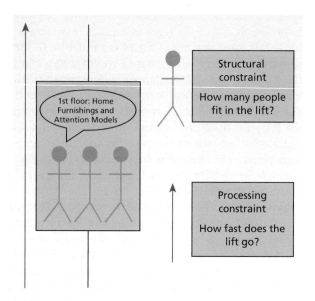

**Figure 8.4 Structural vs. processing constraints**
An illustrative example of the difference between structural constraints and processing constraints.

### Pinpoint question 8.1

**How might we avoid item decay if information is left in the sensory system in the Broadbent (1958) model?**

## Split-span experiments

The first kind of experiment that provides support for the filter theory are known as split-span experiments, initially reported by Broadbent (1954) and demonstrated in schematic form in Figure 8.5. On each trial participants were presented with a recording of a spoken list of digits over headphones, either under presentation conditions known as (i) a *conventional list* or under presentation conditions known as (ii) a *binaural list*. In a conventional list, the same series of digits were spoken in unison down the left and right headphone channels. So say the list was 734215, then both left and right input channels would carry 'seven', 'three', 'four', 'two', 'one' and 'five' in synchrony. All the participant

### For example . . .

Structural constraints don't just occur in models of attention – you only need to think about a tennis ball serving machine for a real-world example. The top basket holds many balls waiting to be launched, but only one can be fired at once. The actual serving mechanism and its one-ball-at-once operations constitutes a structural bottleneck. Which in this case is pretty useful otherwise you'd never be able to practice your half volley. This is very much like the neck of a bottle of wine, and the limited capacity channel that Broadbent talked about in his model. You could also think of a processing constraint using the same example, the processing constraint being how fast the machine can reload and fire balls at you.

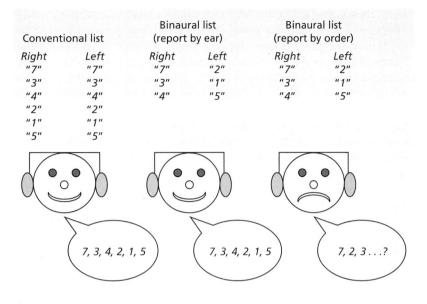

**Figure 8.5 Split-span experiments**
Illustrative examples of different conditions in the split-span experiments reported by Broadbent (1954).

had to do was to listen to the list and then write down the actual sequence of digits heard. With conventional list presentation over 90 per cent of the lists were reported correctly.

In the case of binaural presentation simultaneous pairs of digits were presented to the left and right channels but different items were presented to the two ears. So the sequence of items now for the left and right ears would be the pairs 'seven'/'two', 'three'/'one' and 'four'/'five' spoken in unison. For one group of participants they were told simply to report as many items as they could. The most striking observation was that they overwhelmingly chose to attempt to report all the items from one ear before they reported any of the items from the other. So, in our example, a typical response for the order of report would be 734215. Participants were able to report approximately 60 per cent of the lists correctly if they adopted this recall strategy. In contrast, performance dropped dramatically when participants were instructed to report the digits in an alternating report condition. Now they had to alternate between the ears of delivery. From our example, the participant was expected to report the digits in the order 723145. Under these conditions, performance was compromised.

Critically, performance also depended on the rate of presentation of the pairs. In the conditions we have been discussing, the rate of presentation of the pairs was one pair every 1/2 s. With this rate of presentation, in the alternating report condition, participants were only able to report approximately 20 per cent of the lists correctly. However, if the rate of presentation

of the lists was slowed down to one pair every 2 s then report approximated the 50 per cent correct level.

To begin to explain these data we have to accept the notion that the ear of delivery is conceived as an input channel and that the filter selects items only from one of these channels. We choose to attend to either the left or right ear in a similar way to which we choose to attend to Janet or John. Furthermore it was also asserted that switching between these channels takes time. So when participants were presented with binaural lists and were free to use whichever strategy they wished in terms of reporting, they chose to report the content delivered to one ear and then report the content delivered to the other ear. Such a strategy led to the least amount of filter switching. Performance was relatively good because during list presentation the filter is set to one channel (the left ear) and forwards the items from this channel. The items from the other channel (the right ear) are registered and remain in the sensory buffer (the S system) until the filter is switched so that these items can be read out for further processing. Moreover, when the rate of presentation of the list was short enough, none of the items from the later selected channel decayed and were lost.

In contrast, in the alternating report condition, when participants were required to report alternating digits from both ears, performance was poor and this was taken to reflect limitations in having to switch the filter. Now during list presentation the participant attempted to switch the filter between the left and right ears rapidly so that alternate items from the different ears could be passed to the limited capacity channel. At high presentation rates (1/2 s) the filter was simply unable to fluctuate fast enough and items were therefore lost. However, if the presentation rate was slow enough (2 s) then it is possible to switch between the input channels and recover the items in the correct way.

Similar data were also collected in a later variant of the split-span procedure (Broadbent, 1956) in which the presentation of the items was divided across sight and sound (the visual and auditory modalities) in a cross-modal condition. This time, digit sequences were divided up so that pairs were presented simultaneously with one member being presented visually and the other being presented aurally. A within-modality condition was also run in which the digits were presented either in the visual or auditory modality. The central finding was that memory in the cross-modal task was equivalent to that in the within-modality task, but only if the participants adopted the correct strategy. To do well in the cross-modal task, participants had to attempt to report all the items from one modality before switching to the other. Attempting to alternate between the modalities resulted in inferior performance. In this regard, the eyes and, separately, the ears could be taken to correspond to different input channels, with switching between the two input channels taking time.

**Pinpoint question 8.2**

What are the two ways in which digit recall can be improved for the binaural condition in split-span experiments?

## Shadowing experiments

The second type of experiment that provided data that motivated Broadbent's (1958) filter theory of attention can be traced to the shadowing studies of Cherry (1953). These experiments were similar to split-span studies in terms of bombarding participants with lots of acoustic information, but, as we will see, the tasks were quite different. Here we can again adopt the notion of the two ears (i.e., the left ear and the right ear) being defined as separate input channels, and distinguish between an **attended channel** and an **unattended channel** with this distinction becoming apparent in a moment. In a basic shadowing experiment, separate messages are played concurrently down the left and right speakers of headphones. Such an experiment is also known as a **dichotic listening** experiment because messages are being played down the two channels at the same time. The aim of the experiment is to

force the participant to attend to one channel but the objective is to try to assess what information is being recovered from the unattended channel. How much of John can you perceive when paying attention to Janet? The ingenious aspect of these experiments is the manner in which participants were forced to repeat out loud the attended message as it was being played. They were asked to **shadow** (immediately repeat aloud) the attended message. As Moray (1969) noted, the messages were presented at a rate of about 150 words per minute and after some practice most participants were able to report the attended message correctly.

The beginning and end portions of the unattended message always comprised a male voice speaking English, but the middle portion of the message changed in different ways across different conditions such as changing the sex or nationality of the speaker. Using this shadowing technique, Cherry quizzed his participants afterwards on what they noticed about the message on the *unattended* channel. Cherry found that participants did notice a gross change in pitch (low male voice to high female voice, and whether a pure tone was played) but they did not notice the introduction of a foreign language or reversed speech. In short, participants could say whether the unattended message contained speech and whether it was spoken in a male or female voice, but they were unable to report anything about the content of the message.

A general conclusion therefore was that all that can be recovered from the unattended message is some specification of its physical characteristics and it seemed as if there was no semantic analysis (analysis of the meaning or content) of the unattended message at all. Such a conclusion is generally in line with the predictions of the original filter theory: unless items are selected for further processing they remain coded in terms of their pre-categorical characteristics. The content of the unattended message cannot be recovered because, according to filter theory, the filter prohibits the unattended message from entering the limited capacity channel where semantic analysis takes place. It is only the attended message that undergoes a full analysis.

## Provocative data – challenges to the early filter account

Having concluded that participants in his study were unable to report a change to the unattended channel involving reversed speech, Cherry (1953) also noted that some participants did detect that something odd had occurred when the unattended message changed in this way. A possible conclusion therefore is that these participants may have picked up a distinction between a meaningful and meaningless message even though, according to the original filter theory, the unattended message never gains access to any kind of semantic analysis. However, according to Broadbent's (1958) filter theory, such a state of affairs might occur if participants either intentionally, or unintentionally, switched the filter to the unattended channel when the reversed speech was presented.

A more recent and careful appraisal of this particular experimental manipulation has been provided by Wood and Cowan (1995a). They were able to confirm that the detection of the reversed speech did depend on shifts of attention to the unattended channel, but the central issue was: why did such shifts occur? Were such switches random or did they reflect a more interesting possibility? Did the unattended message actually undergo some form of semantic analysis? We might assume that, in the normal course of events, the unattended message does undergo some form of semantic analysis and when this is disrupted – such as when it changes to reversed speech – attention is summoned over to the unattended channel by switching the filter. Clearly such a possibility fits rather uncomfortably with the original all-or-nothing conception of the filter in Broadbent's theory (see Figure 8.3).

However, other evidence began to emerge which suggested that this rather uncomfortable possibility might have some truth behind it. For instance, Moray (1959) contrived a rather devious shadowing experiment in which he embedded instructions to change ears or stop shadowing in the messages. Such commands were easily detected if presented on the attended channel but went undetected on the unattended channel. However, if the command was prefixed by the participant's own name, on the unattended channel, then it was heard on about 30 per cent of occasions. Yet, as Wood and Cowan (1995b) noted, participants hardly ever followed the commands. The only evidence that the commands were detected came from subjective recollections immediately after the shadowing trial.

Wood and Cowan (1995b) were able to replicate Moray's findings in much more tightly controlled conditions. They concluded that participants who were able to detect their own name on the unattended channel also showed evidence of shifting their attention to the unattended channel following registration of their own name. In this regard, presentation of the name did summon attention to the unattended channel. Importantly, this reveals that there was some semantic analysis of the unattended message even though this was not entirely consistent with the conception of attentional constraints described in the original filter theory.

**Research focus 8.1**

## I think my ears are burning: why do I hear my name across a crowded room?

While our own conversation is clearly going to be the most riveting in any party setting, it seems as though we are also hopelessly drawn to the sound of our own name across a crowded room. Researchers have been particularly interested in the attentional demands of cocktail parties for about half a century now, which presumably has nothing do to with the alcohol involved. Conway, Cowan and Bunting (2001) wondered about individual variation in the ability to divide auditory attention across two channels and whether this would be related to something known as working memory (i.e., a short-term memory system – see Chapter 10 for a more thorough description). Working memory is thought to be involved in maintaining attentional focus upon task-relevant information (Baddeley & Hitch, 1974). This is why Conway et al. (2001) thought that it might be related to performance in studies where attention has the potential to be divided across

multiple input channels. Therefore individuals with poor working memory might be able to hear their name across a crowded room better because they find it difficult to maintain attention on their own conversation in a distracting environment.

Forty participants were used, half of whom were identified as having low working memory span, while the other half had high working memory span. All participants were then presented over headphones with two different messages, one to each ear as in the original Cherry (1953) study. Participants were required to shadow one message in the right ear while ignoring a simultaneously presented message in the left ear. Unbeknown to the participants, their name had been inserted into the unattended message, in addition to a control name that was not their own. After shadowing, participants were asked whether they found anything unusual about the unattended message and if so, what it was.

▶

Sixty-five per cent of individuals characterised with poor working memory heard their own name on the unattended channel in contrast to only 20 per cent of those with good working memory capacity. The distracting effect of hearing one's own name in an unattended channel also persisted for one or two words after the event, as revealed by a larger number of shadowing errors committed by individuals who had been drawn to their own name.

At a basic level, Conway et al. (2001) support the idea that sometimes information on unattended channels can be semantically analysed just as Moray (1959) showed. However, this study also emphasises the importance of individual differences in performing these kinds of dichotic listening tasks, suggesting that any structural limited attentional capacity must be considered on a person-to-person basis. A final conclusion could be that your performance at a cocktail party might not have anything to do with drinking Long Island Iced Teas after all.

_Source_: Conway, A. R. A., Cowan, N., & Bunting, M. F. (2001). The cocktail party phenomenon revisited: The importance of working memory capacity. _Psychonomic Bulletin & Review, 8_, 331–335.

**limited capacity channel** A notion that is based on the view that information must be transmitted in human information processing between different processing modules – for instance, between the peripheral and the central mechanisms. The understanding is that processing modules are connected by processing channels, any one of which can only cope with a certain amount of information at any given time.

**S system** The early sensory storage and coding mechanisms in Broadbent's 1958 model of human information processing.

**input channels** The idea that the sensory apparatus can be divided into independent streams of processing. Descriptions of an input channel can include whole senses (e.g., touch) or specific sensory transducers (e.g., the left ear).

**selection by filtering** A specific kind of selection taken from Broadbent's (1958) filter theory in which information is chosen from sensory memory on the basis of physical characteristics of the input.

**pre-categorical level** A stage in processing at which the categorical identity of the stimulus is not known. For example, it's red and it's small but what is it?

**switching the filter** In Broadbent's (1958) account, whereby the focus of attention is changed from one input channel to another.

**P system** Strictly, the perceptual system in Broadbent's (1958) filter theory of attention. In this scheme the P system assigns meanings to signals propagated down the limited-capacity channel.

**rehearsal** Allowing information to be recirculated in a processing system. In Broadbent's (1958) account, information from the P system is returned to the S system.

**associative memory** Information storage that keeps track of the associative relations between two events. Typically the strength of an associative link is indexed by the co-occurrence between the two associates.

**post-categorical information** A specification of the categorical nature of a stimulus.

**structural bottleneck** A claim that not all information arriving at a particular stage of processing can be dealt with concurrently; only information associated with one task can pass through to the next stage at once.

**structural constraint** A limitation within the architecture of the system that limits the amount of information that can pass through at any one time. Also known as a structural bottleneck.

**attended channel** An input channel that participants concentrate on.

**unattended channel** An input channel that participants are asked to ignore.

**dichotic listening** Situations that involve different acoustic material being presented to left and right ears at the same time.

**shadow** To report back verbally the contents of an attended channel in real time.

## Pinpoint question 8.3

How does the work of Wood and Cowan (1995b) challenge the filter theory of Broadbent (1958)?

## The attenuated filter model of attention

In addition to the provocative data reported by Cherry (1953), other evidence also began to emerge that indicated that unattended messages may be analysed at the semantic level. Indeed, a now classic piece of evidence was reported by Treisman (1964) and this resulted in a modification to the original filter theory. Again participants were tested in shadowing tasks and again a rather devious manipulation was employed. Each message was 50 words long and each individual message was either comprehensible text or a stream of spoken words that came across as some kind of garbled English. As in standard shadowing experiments, different messages were simultaneously delivered to the left and right headphone speakers. On each trial though, the messages could switch channels. Schematically this is conveyed thus:

Attended channel        . . . I SAW THE GIRL/song was WISHING . . .
Unattended channel    . . . me that bird/JUMPING in the street . . .

Text on a given line corresponds to what was actually presented on the designated channel. The '/' indicates that point at which the messages were switched and the capitalised text indicates what the participant actually vocalised during the shadowing trial. What this indicates is that occasionally participants followed the content of the message across the channels for one or two words after the messages switched but they then immediately reverted back to the attended channel.

This particular pattern of performance was peculiar to cases where the messages comprised comprehensible text and significantly fewer shadowing switches occurred when the messages contained only approximations to English. This finding reinforced the conclusion that some form of semantic analysis of the unattended message must have been taking place, otherwise how could it be that the participants mistakenly followed the content of the messages across the channels when the switch occurred? If the messages were not semantically coherent then such channel switches tended not to occur. We shall cover Treisman's detailed account of her data later, but for now all we need note is the following. This sort of finding led Treisman (1964) to suggest that, in contrast to the original all-or-nothing filter in the original filter theory, unattended messages were attenuated (dampened down) and were not completely blocked out from further analysis. This suggestion forms the basis of the **attenuated filter account** of processing and in its general form this was accepted as a sensible modification to the original filter theory (Broadbent, 1971, 1982).

One way to think about the attenuated filter theory is to conceive of the unattended message as having a lower signal-to-noise ratio (see Chapter 4) than that of the attended message. The filter operates to dampen down the unattended message but it does not block it out completely. The reason that participants sometimes followed the content across onto the unattended channel is that the unattended message was, in some sense, being analysed at a semantic level. Semantically relevant items on the unattended channel were therefore easily recognised – they were in a sense primed by the context provided by the leading attended message.

## Further revisions to the original filter theory

So far we have examined the original filter theory (Broadbent, 1958) and the attenuated filter theory (Treisman, 1964). Both of these were attempts to explain how it is we can selectively attend to some of the vast amount of sensory stimulation and discard the rest. However, we have only focused on one form of selection – selection by filtering – but two other forms of selection were introduced and discussed later by Broadbent (1971). These were **selection by categorisation** and **selection by pigeonholing** and it seems that discussion of these other forms of selection were an attempt to extend the theory so as to encompass the more challenging data.

### Selection by categorisation

The first (new) form of selection, known as *categorising*, featured little in the extended theory (Broadbent, 1971). Nevertheless, from what is given away, it clearly is central to ideas about object recognition and identification in general. We shall return to these points when we discuss these topics in more detail later (see Chapter 13). Categorising was said to involve both input and output selection and refers to assigning stimuli to mental categories. The outputs from the limited capacity channel were termed *category states* because the purpose of the limited capacity channel was to take an item and assign it to an appropriate mental category. In this regard, the outputs from the limited capacity channel code post-categorical information.

At a further level of detail it was noted that many different stimuli may be assigned to the same category state; for example, pug, labrador, and poodle are all members of the category DOG. In addition, it was also recognised that each stimuli may evoke a variety of similar responses (e.g., saying 'Look at the dog', 'Fetch', etc.). This is why categorisation is said to involve both stimulus (input) selection and response (output) selection. The participant must (on the input side) discriminate dogs from all other stimuli and produce the most appropriate of a variety of different possible responses (on the output side).

In discussing input selection, the idea is that the perceptual system must be able to discriminate relevant from irrelevant stimuli. With filtering, such selection is relatively straightforward because it refers to cases where relevant stimuli share a common feature so any stimuli missing this feature can be ignored as irrelevant – when shopping for an engagement ring, for example, it might be the case that anything other than gold would be ignored by your potential spouse. Categorising, however, involves cases where there is no single discriminating feature; for instance, there is no such perceptual feature common to all dogs. Certainly all dogs are supposed to bark but their actual barks are quite different from one another. On these grounds, categorising applies when category assignment depends on analysis of more than one feature (barks, four legs, tail, etc.). However, this does not necessarily mean that the stimulus must undergo a complete analysis as long as discriminating features can be recovered.

A concrete example is provided by the work of Rabbitt (1964, 1967). Here participants were asked to base a response on whether a C or O was present among other non-target letters. Participants needed time to practise the task, and early on in practice the time to find the target letter lengthened as the display set size increased (i.e., as the number of items in the display increased). However, later on in practice the irrelevant letters had less of an effect on target detection times. Initially participants searched for C or O among non-targets taken from the set AEFHIKL. Participants improved over time because they learnt the C/O category. They 'learnt' that this category contains only curves and no straight-line features. Having acquired this category, non-target items could be eliminated from further processing on the basis of detecting a straight line.

Supporting evidence for this view was found by switching the non-target items to either a new set containing other angular letters (e.g., TZXY) or one containing curved letters (e.g., BDGQ). Performance dropped considerably when curved non-targets were introduced. In contrast, performance did not suffer so much when the other angular non-target set was introduced. What this indicates is that selection by categorisation can be more much more complex than simple filtering. Moreover, changing the setting of the filter can be very quickly accomplished as we have seen in the split-span experiments of Broadbent (1954). In contrast, changing the setting of the category rule can take an immense amount of time.

### Selection by pigeonholing

The other (new) form of selection discussed by Broadbent (1971) is known as *pigeonholing* and this can only come about once mental categories, in the form described above, have been acquired. The general idea here is that the participant can bias certain category assignments over others. Instead of selecting items on the basis of a unique and common feature, as is the case with filtering, pigeonholing operates by changing the probabilities of the outputs (the category states) from the limited capacity channel. It is very much in the vein of a criterion shift as discussed in the context of signal detection theory (see Chapter 4). Think in terms of moving a threshold downwards such that only a minimal amount of information consistent with a favoured category will trigger the corresponding response.

For example, let's assume that you are waiting for a friend from a train at a busy station and she has told you that she will be carrying a red bag and a black umbrella. In the first instance you bias the category of red things so that you attempt to recognise your friend from her bag. If this is not working, now bias the black things category and attempt to recognise her on the basis of her umbrella. Switching the selection rule here can be carried out fairly quickly because it implies biasing a different but already established mental category. The general idea is that you will more readily recognise your friend because of these kinds of expectations than if you have no expectations at all.

## The differences between stimulus set and response set

Despite the discussion of categorisation, much more interest was placed on the differences between selection by filtering and pigeonholing, and indeed these notions have endured and have been incorporated into a much more recent account of attentional processing (see Bundesen, 1990). Specifically Broadbent discussed filtering in terms of something he called **stimulus set**, and pigeonholing in terms of something else he called **response set**. Stimulus set refers to the common physical characteristic unique to the relevant items – e.g., all the red items, all the low-pitch items, all the squares, etc. In contrast, response set refers to cases where the assignment of stimuli to responses is necessarily defined with respect to some form of mental category: for example, classifying $x$ as an arithmetic symbol rather than as being composed of two crossed diagonal lines.

In simple terms, whereas this stimulus set can be defined relative to the physical characteristic of the stimulus, this response set cannot. For instance, a stimulus set in a shadowing experiment might instruct the participant to report back everything spoken in a male voice and ignore anything spoken in a female voice, whereas a response set would instruct the participant to report back only the names of animals that are spoken in any voice. Similarly, in a display of red and black digits and letters, stimulus set might define the targets as all the black items or all the red items whereas response set might define the targets as all the digits or all the letters (Broadbent, 1970).

Filter theory predicts that selection by filtering should be easier than pigeonholing because of the manner and timing in which different aspects of the stimulus become available during processing. The attentional filter is said to operate early on in processing and latches onto a distinctive physical characteristic as registered in the sensory store (it can latch onto 'red things'). In contrast, selection by pigeonholing can only take effect once an item has entered and exited the limited capacity channel and has been assigned to a mental category (such as 'my friend'). Hence selection by stimulus set should be easier than selection by response set since, in order to decide whether an item is a target in a response set, the item must be assigned to an appropriate mental category. Broadly speaking, the data have confirmed this prediction (Broadbent, 1970). Indeed, the findings from the iconic memory literature, showing that selection by colour is far easier than selection by alpha-numeric class (see Chapter 3), provide converging support (Bundesen et al., 1984).

According to Broadbent (1971), by embellishing the original filter theory with the more detailed discussion of selection by filtering, categorisation and pigeonholing, this allowed him to provide a much more elaborate framework for thinking about the nature of attention and attentional constraints. For instance, by incorporating the notion of pigeonholing into the theory, a mechanism is provided for explaining how aspects of the unattended message might break through in shadowing experiments. For example, the biasing context used by Treisman (1964) on the attended channel lowered the thresholds for detecting relevant words. Hence recognition of contextually appropriate material was facilitated and participants unintentionally switched to the unattended message.

**Why is it harder to find the letters C and O among BDGQ rather than TZXY?**

**attenuated filter account** Treisman's (1964) revision of Broadbent's (1958) filter theory in which relevant portions of an unattended signal may be semantically processed. In this account filtering is partial and not all-or-nothing as in Broadbent's earlier theory.

**selection by categorisation** The ability to select items for further processing on the basis of the category membership.

**selection by pigeonholing** The ability to select items because of lowering of a category threshold – if it looks like a duck and walks like a duck, it must be a duck.

**stimulus set** The common physical characteristics shared by items that are designated targets.

**response set** Stimuli defined as targets because they share the same mental category. No one physical characteristic defines the targets.

## Late filtering accounts of selection

Although it became increasingly apparent that the all-or-nothing account of filtering in the original theory was untenable, Broadbent retained the notion of an early filter that picked out material for further processing purely on the basis of their physical characteristics. Select the red items, select the loudest items, select the item moving very quickly towards your head! A concession had been made, however, in that the filter merely attenuated irrelevant (unattended) stimuli and did not block them out completely. In contrast to this notion of early selection, a radical alternative was put forward in terms of a late operating filter, in which selection takes place at a much later stage of processing and involves much more complex categories than physical stimulus properties. This view is generally associated with Deutsch and Deutsch (1963), and is typically described relative to the schematic presented in Figure 8.6.

Deutsch and Deutsch discussed data, such as Moray's (1959), that were taken to reveal semantic analysis of

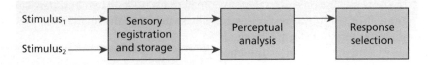

**Figure 8.6 An arrows-and-boxes account of late attentional selection**
Selection does not operate until all inputs have undergone perceptual analysis and category assignment. Selection for action does not operate until everything has been identified.

*Source*: Kahneman, D. (1973). *Attention and effort* (fig. 1.1b, p. 6). Englewood Cliffs, New Jersey: Prentice Hall. Reproduced with permission.

unattended material. By considering this sort of data, they dismissed the notion of an early filter situated at a stage where only the physical characteristics of stimuli were available. In contrast, they took the evidence to show that 'all sensory messages which impinge on the organism are perceptually analyzed at the highest level' (p. 85).

More recently such a view has been developed by Duncan (1980). According to him, prior to any selection taking place, each stimulus is fully identified and this means that a representation of the stimulus is derived that codes its physical characteristics, its name if this is applicable, and (critically) its category assignment (p. 284). A further elaboration on the Deutsch and Deutsch account was also provided by Kahneman (1973). According to him the late filtering model implies that 'the meanings of all concurrent stimuli are extracted in parallel and without interference' (pp. 6–7). Any form of selection therefore only takes place at a post-categorical stage of processing prior to response execution. It is as if everything is identified but that the critical constraints relate to responding.

If you have four pans of water all boiling at one time, then the one that is about to boil over will be the stimulus that is currently most important and the one that will require a response. You only have one pair of hands so only one of the pans can be dealt with at once. In this account the stimulus that will be responded to is the one that is momentarily designated the most important. It is the assignment of importance to the various stimuli that is what is implied by 'semantic analysis' in the Deutsch and Deutsch (1963) account. Moreover, as Kahneman (1973) notes, the weighting of importance can reflect momentary intentions (you reach for the mango chutney, not the raita) or enduring dispositions (you prefer beer to white wine).

There is a huge literature on the merits and shortcomings of early and late filter theories; however, one study is particularly relevant and will be discussed briefly here. Treisman and Geffen (1967) designed a dichotic listening task in which participants were given

two tasks to complete. The primary task was simply to report back (i.e., shadow) the designated attended message. The secondary task was physically to tap when a designated target word occurred on either the attended or unattended channel. The argument went like this. If selection was located at an early perceptual stage then targets on the unattended channel should be missed and therefore participants should be less accurate in tapping to unattended than attended targets. However, if the problem lay at a response selection stage – as argued by Deutsch and Deutsch (1963) – then taps to both sorts of targets should be equally as bad, regardless of whether the target occurs on the attended or the unattended channel.

In greatly summarising the results, what Treisman and Geffen (1967) found was that participants tapped to 87 per cent of the attended targets but to only 8 per cent of the unattended targets. Hence the data fit more comfortably with the early (attenuating) filter view than the late response selection view (see Deutsch & Deutsch, 1967; Lindsay, 1967; Treisman, 1967; for an interesting interchange on these findings). However, to be fair, the experiment addressed a very particular aspect of one late selection theory and the findings therefore do not undermine late selection theories *in general*.

## Evidence in support of late selection

So is there any convincing evidence in favour of late selection theories? Well, in fact there is, and some of the more intriguing evidence has been reported by Duncan (1980). Here performance was examined in some disarmingly simple, but subtle, visual search experiments (see Figure 8.7). Participants were presented with a series of four items on each trial (let's say the letters X, T, E and the number 3), and performance was compared across two main conditions. In the SIM (simultaneous) condition all four items were presented at once, whereas in the SUCC (successive) condition one pair of items was presented initially and then another pair followed this pair.

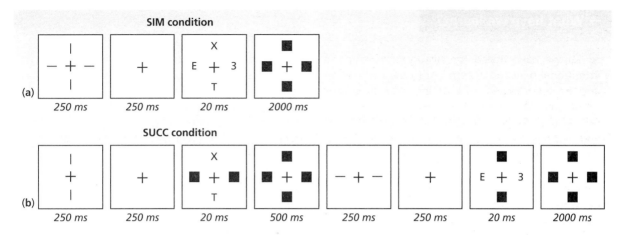

**Figure 8.7 Schematic representation of the sorts of displays and conditions used by Duncan (1980)**
(a) In the SIM(ultaneous) condition, participants were presented with stimuli on a vertical and horizontal limb at the same time. (b) In the SUCC(essive) condition, participants were presented with stimuli from one limb at a time. The task was to spot target digits presented among non-target letters. The start of a trial is at the leftmost side of the figure and the time line showing how events unfolded within a trial travels from left to right. In the SUCC condition the rows of events unfolded consecutively.

Any given item could appear at one of four positions that were located at the ends of an imaginary '+' centred on a display screen. The '+' was said to be composed of a horizontal and a vertical limb. Two items were presented top and bottom relative to centre, while two items were presented left and right relative to centre. In the SIM condition the four items were presented very briefly (e.g., for 20 ms) and were then immediately masked by individual rectangular light patches (this provides another example of backward masking; see Chapter 3). In the SUCC condition the items on the first limb were presented briefly and then masked; approximately a second later the items on the second limb were presented and then masked.

The participants' task was to look out for target digits presented among non-target letters (a 3, say, among the X, T and E in Figure 8.7). On a given trial the displays could contain either a single target (on one limb), one target on each limb (i.e., two targets in total), or no targets on either limb. Performance was also assessed in a so-called *combined task* and, separately, in a *separated task*. In the combined task, participants simply had to press a key if they detected the presence of a target anywhere. So even though, on some trials two targets were present, they could simply respond as soon as they detected either target. Participants merely had to respond if they saw a target – they did not have to report which target they saw. In contrast, in the separated task, participants had to make target present/absent judgements for each limb separately. Measures of accuracy were of central import

for (i) comparisons between the SUCC and SIM conditions and (ii) comparisons across cases where either one target or two targets were presented.

In considering the combined task data (in which the participant could respond to any target), there was little difference in performance across the SIM and SUCC conditions when only a single target was present. Participants were marginally more accurate in detecting the single target when each limb was presented in turn (in the SUCC condition) than when the whole display was presented (in the SIM condition). So there was a small cost in having to divide attention across the whole display relative to the cases where they could focus attention on each pair of items in sequence. Remember, in the SIM condition, participants were trying to concentrate on both limbs of the display at once and hence divide their attention across the whole display. In contrast, in the SUCC condition, they were trying to focus their attention on each limb at a time as each limb was presented in sequence.

Of more interest, though, are the data in the separated task, in which participants had to make judgements whether a target was present on each limb. Now there was a large effect of having to divide attention, with performance being worse in the SIM than the SUCC case. Not surprisingly perhaps, participants performed worse when having to process four simultaneous items than they were when faced with a sequence of two pairs of items. The most intriguing effects, however, occurred in the separated task when two targets were present – one on each limb. The critical finding

## → What have we learnt?

So far we have traced the history of research in attentional selection in terms of (i) the early all-or-nothing filter account of Broadbent (1958), (ii) the attenuated filter account of Treisman (1964), and, finally, (iii) the late selection account of Deutsch and Deutsch (1963). Broadbent extended his framework for thinking by discussing various ideas about how selection might operate. He discussed (i) selection by filtering, (ii) selection by categorising, and (iii) selection by pigeonholing. Each form of selection was discussed in terms of a general framework for thinking. Nevertheless, the data reported by Duncan (1980) are challenging and seemingly cannot be easily accommodated by the theory. In reply Broadbent (1982) insisted that until latency measures were taken as well as accuracy measures, then the costs in performance due to the presence of multiple targets should be interpreted with caution. Since then the arguments about where best to try to locate selection in the human information processing system have oscillated back and forth. More recently, various compromise positions have been put forward, as we will consider later in the chapter. For now, though, it is appropriate to discuss a quite different take on the issues. From this perspective, performance limitations should not be taken to reflect structural constraints present in the processing system, but the consequences of *resource constraints*.

was that participants were particularly impaired when two targets were concurrently present (in the SIM condition) and where they were expected to register and respond to both targets. In a later similar experiment, Duncan found that whereas the presence of more than one target disrupted performance, the number of concurrent non-targets was relatively unimportant.

So what does all this tell us about early vs. late theories of attentional selection? Well, the first point is that the limitations in processing that these experiments reveal seems to reflect problems the system has in processing concurrent targets – as Duncan stated, the data suggest that non-target elements 'do not compete for limited capacity processes' (p. 284). So how can this be? Well, as we have already noted, according to Duncan all items are fully analysed at an initial unlimited stage of processing. The critical constraint occurs at a subsequent stage in which items are selected for further processing. The identity of an item is recovered at the first stage and this means that each item will be identified as either a target (digit) or a non-target (letter). Non-targets can therefore be sensibly ignored but the targets must now compete for entry into a limited capacity system. Output from this limited capacity system eventuates in a perceptual record of the item in question, although problems arise if more than one target is present concurrently. Target items compete for entry into the limited capacity system and hence performance suffers accordingly. So the problems do not arise in identifying what is and what is not a target, they arise after the identity of the items has been recovered, and only when multiple targets compete for attention. → See 'What have we learnt?', above.

## Pinpoint question 8.5

What evidence is there in the Duncan (1980) experiment to suggest the existence of an information filter that occurs late on in processing, as Deutsch and Deutsch (1963) suggest?

## No 'structural bottleneck' accounts of attention

All of the theories we have so far discussed in this chapter have assumed some kind of structural bottleneck in the processing architecture that constricts the amount of material that can be dealt with at once. If you remember our lift example earlier on in this chapter, this is analogous to how big the lift is and therefore how many passengers can fit in the lift at any one time (are we dealing with a dumb waiter here or an industrial shaft?). However, performance also critically depends on how fast the lift moves from floor to floor. We can therefore distinguish between models of attention that focus on structural constraints (akin to the number of passengers that the lift can take at any one time) and those that concentrate upon processing constraints (akin to the maximum speed at which the lift can travel). It is to these latter models that we now turn.

As Figure 8.3 reveals, a filter provides a so-called *structural constraint* and the difference between so-called early and late filter theories concerns where the central bottleneck is assumed to be located in the sequence of internal processes. Despite that for most of the latter half of the twentieth century, attentional researchers were preoccupied in trying to establish which of these two general theories is correct, many also commented that such a simple binary opposition failed to do justice to the complex nature of human information processing (see Allport, 1989, for review). For instance, if we accept the modularity view of mind (Fodor, 1983; see Chapter 2), in which the mind is composed of discrete compartments dealing with specific cognitive functions, then it is most appropriate to think in terms of multiple constraints distributed across the different modules. Indeed many possibilities suggest themselves, and we will consider some of the more plausible alternatives as the discussion proceeds.

For instance, some theorists have discussed accounts in which the notion of a filter is simply avoided altogether. One such example was discussed briefly by Hochberg (1970). The basic idea rests on assuming some form of analysis-by-synthesis account of processing (see Chapter 6). Put simply, any material that confirms an expectation of what the stimulus is, will be held in memory and will be recalled if necessary. Anything that does not confirm expectations is not encoded and will be lost. Unfortunately, this account was not very thoroughly spelt out, and given that it has provoked very little interest in the literature (but see Kahneman, 1973), we can move on to perhaps more useful ways of thinking.

One such way of thinking has been provided by Norman (1969), and a schematic representation of his ideas is provided in Figure 8.8. In this scheme every stimulus undergoes sensory encoding, and if the stimulus is familiar, then stored knowledge about the

stimulus will be activated. For example, if we mention *American Psycho* then you might activate the fact that it was a book by Bret Easton Ellis, that the main character's name is Patrick Bateman, and when the original paperback was released it contained a Francis Bacon painting on the front cover which was replaced by a picture of Christian Bale when it got turned into a movie, etc. None of this will happen if you are unfamiliar with *American Psycho*.

However, to give proper justice to Norman's model, it is perhaps more appropriate to reconsider the notion of word detectors as discussed in the context of Broadbent and Gregory (1971; see Chapter 5). For simplicity's sake we have only discussed a word detector in abstract terms: it is a mechanism responsible for collecting evidence in favour of a particular familiar word – the word detector for NURSE will fire if 'NURSE', 'nUrSe', 'nurse', '*nurse*', etc. are encountered. In Norman's account, a more sophisticated notion of such a detector was implied. This mechanism is more than something like a mental light bulb that is switched on when a particular word is presented. On the contrary, in this scheme a given detector provides the entry point to all stored knowledge about the word. The implication is that when a detector becomes activated, then access to stored knowledge about the semantics of the stimulus is granted: for instance, access to the information that a nurse is a paramedic, typically encountered in a hospital setting, etc.

By this view the detector provides access to all knowledge about the stimulus that the participant possesses that is represented in long-term memory. In this way, and following sensory analysis, the long-term

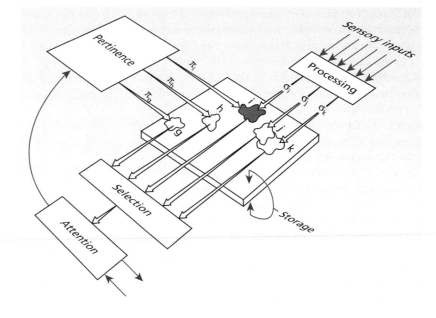

**Figure 8.8 A simple arrows-and-boxes account of Norman's (1969) theory of attention**
How attentional selection may operate in the absence of any structural constraints. 'Storage' refers to long-term memory (see text for further details).

*Source*: Norman, D. A. (1969). Towards a theory of memory and attention. *Psychological Review*, 75, 522–536 (fig. 1, p. 526). Reproduced with permission from APA.

memory representation of a given stimulus is activated to a certain degree depending on what was actually presented and what was delivered by the sensory analysis. So whereas NURSE is the ideal stimulus for the NURSE detector, the detector could become partially activated by 'N*RSE', 'NARSE', 'NURS', and so on. To return to the railway station, the detector for 'your friend' would become partially activated by seeing someone wearing 'her' coat.

Moreover, the activation of such long-term representations was also assumed to reflect top-down influences. So for instance, activation could spread on the basis of contextual information: the LAMB detector becomes partially active by reading 'Mary had a little . . .' (or indeed 'The Silence of the . . .' if we are to continue our macabre literature theme). Back on the railway platform, you have a sensible expectation that your friend will be arriving off the next train, hence 'your friend's' detector will be primed or partially activated by this kind of top-down influence. In terms of the model, Norman discussed such activation in terms of what he called **pertinence**. This refers to the level of activation of any given stored stimulus representation (the 'my friend' detector will be partially activated – it will have a high pertinence value). Moreover, the pertinence of any given stimulus can change over time if the current state of affairs demands this. Swerve to avoid the pedestrian that steps off the kerb and then brake to avoid the on-coming traffic. The critical aspect, though, is that the current pertinence value reflects both the products of sensory analysis together with any top-down influences. In this way, the distinction between attention and memory is blurred because the processing constraints that exist in the model refer to operations concerning memory access and retrieval. Indeed, Norman (1969) happily drew comparisons between his account and analysis by synthesis (see Chapter 6).

In the current context, the critical point is that there is no structural bottleneck in this account. At any given moment items are selected for further processing on the basis of their being the most currently pertinent. In this way attention can be focused on certain items but it can also be shifted around, depending on how the pertinence values change. In discussing this account, Hirst (1986) cautioned against confusing it with the late selection account put forward by Deutsch and Deutsch (1963). Remember that according to that account all items are fully analysed; in contrast, according to Norman, how thoroughly an item is processed is determined by its current level of pertinence. All items do make contact with their long-term memory representations, but the level of analysis of any particular item is determined by its current pertinence value.

> **pertinence** According to Norman (1969), the level of activation of any given stored stimulus representation calculated as a combination of sensory analysis and top-down influence.

# The notion of attentional resources

Consideration of the models of Deutsch and Deutsch and of Norman forces us to think of alternatives of how best to construe attentional constraints outside the confines of the early filter theory. Perhaps the most radically different sorts of ideas can be found in the context of discussions of **attentional resources**. Here, we are moving away from issues about structural constraints – where to place a filter – towards a consideration of processing constraints. For instance, quite different views of performance limitations are now forthcoming and these are not best conveyed in terms of attempting to squeeze too much information down a processing bottleneck. Whereas bottleneck accounts of processing constraints assume that the central limitation is structural in nature – only so much information from the input can be forced through the bottleneck at any one time – resource theories take a quite different view. It is to these that we now turn.

## A single pool of resources?

Perhaps the simplest analogy here is with the idea of a basic electric circuit connected up to a 12-volt battery (see Figure 8.9). The circuit has a finite electrical resource fixed at the upper bound of the current dissipated by the battery. If the circuit has one light bulb attached it will shine brightly because all of the resources in the circuit are devoted to powering this one bulb. If other light bulbs are all connected up to the same circuit, and they demand less than the upper bound of the available current, then they will all shine brightly.

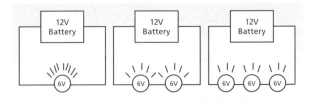

**Figure 8.9 Mental resources by analogy with a simple electric circuit**
A simple electric circuit illustrating how a fixed resource (the current provided by a battery) can be depleted as more components are added to the system – as more lights are added to the circuit each shines a little less brightly.

However, if more and more light bulbs are added then they all shine, but dimly. The light bulbs are demanding more from the battery than it can push out. The current provided by the battery is a fixed resource and adding components to the circuit can result in overload. At the limit none of the components in the circuit will operate properly.

### A brief introduction to dual-task methodology

Here part of the analogy can be fleshed out in terms of cognitive psychology and the common-sense belief that it can be quite demanding to try to do more than one thing at once. More formally this sort of issue has been examined in terms of dual-task experiments. A dual-task experiment takes the following form:

- Stage 1 – have participants carry out one task (task A) and measure how well they do at this task in isolation.
- Stage 2 – do the same for a second task (task B) in isolation.
- Stage 3 – now have participants complete both tasks A and B at the same time.

The typical expectation is that participants will perform less well at either or both tasks when they are combined than when they are completed in isolation. Such a result is known as a **dual-task decrement**. It is not a caricature of single resource theory to state that it assumes that the whole of cognition places demands on a single pool of resources, in that the completion of any two concurrent tasks may cause problems – yes, walking and chewing gum at the same time may interfere with one another! However, stated in such a way, it is perhaps not surprising that some have found this to be a genuinely implausible description of the limits placed on human cognitive performance. Given this, we will consider the alternatives in more detail shortly.

## Single resource accounts and the dual-task decrement

By a single resource account, the dual-task decrement arises because task A and task B compete for the same 'pool of resources' – there is only one 'battery' in the system. Of course the absence of a dual-task decrement can also be explained by single resource theory on the assumption that the combination of tasks does not exceed the upper bound on the available resources so both tasks can be completed without interference – there's plenty of juice in the battery to go round. So evidence for a single resource model can be derived from dual-task experiments. To flesh these ideas out, it is useful to concentrate on the most famous single resource model as described by Kahneman (1973).

Kahneman's model is shown in schematic form in Figure 8.10. The central premise in the account is that

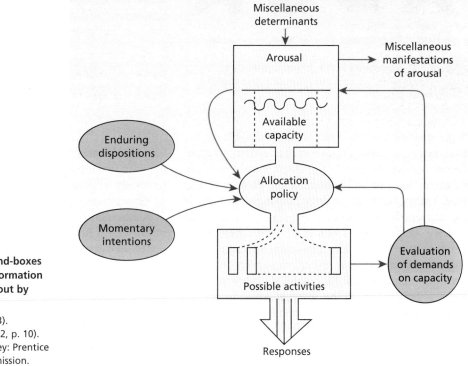

**Figure 8.10 The arrows-and-boxes account of the human information processing system as set out by Kahneman (1973)**

*Source*: Kahneman, D. (1973). *Attention and effort* (fig. 1.2, p. 10). Englewood Cliffs, New Jersey: Prentice Hall. Reproduced with permission.

## Patting my head and rubbing my belly: can I really do two things at once?

Patting the head while concurrently rubbing the stomach are two tasks whose joint mastery seems to be reserved only for those people with far too much time on their hands. Franz, Zelaznik, Swinnen and Walter (2001) referred to this special kind of dual-task interference as 'spatial coupling' which is observed when we try to get our hands to do two different things at once: typically, what we find is our head patting becomes a little more like rubbing and our stomach rubbing becomes a little more like patting. Franz et al. (2001) wondered whether dual-task interference could be reduced if these two tasks were somehow reconfigured into a single task.

Eight participants were asked to draw either the top or bottom half of a circle with their left or right hand. In uni-manual conditions, participants only used one hand to draw one half of the circle. In bi-manual conditions, participants drew with both hands, either two top halves, two bottom halves, or one top and one bottom half. Critically, these bi-manual conditions were categorised into cases where the two parts of the drawing completed a circle (top–bottom) and cases where the position of the two parts were reversed (bottom–top condition; like a letter u sitting on a letter n – see Figure 8.11).

Franz et al. (2001) reported that most participants found the bi-manual bottom–top condition to be the most difficult, with the top–bottom condition being easier because participants were able to bear in mind a circle. These qualitative comments were supported by quantitative analyses, in which a measurement of the spatial disruption of the bottom–top condition was larger than the top–bottom condition.

This study shows that there are both motor and cognitive constraints that influence dual-task performance. In the above example, the motor difficulty in performing bi-manual conditions may be alleviated by recasting the components of the task into a single image. The dual task essentially becomes a single task. The authors speculated about how this finding might extend to other examples of multi-tasking. For example, they stated that holding in mind two supposedly unrelated ideas is difficult but made easier if you are able to bridge the two ideas with a single concept. Therefore, perhaps patting your head and rubbing your belly might be difficult, but prubbing your helly could be less so.

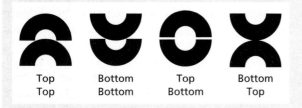

| Top | Bottom | Top | Bottom |
| Top | Bottom | Bottom | Top |

**Figure 8.11 Schematics of the target figures that participants were expected to produce in the study by Franz et al. (2001)**

*Source*: Franz, E. A., Zelaznik, H. N., Swinnen, S., & Walter, C. (2001). Spatial conceptual influences on the coordination of bimanual actions: When a dual task becomes a single task. *Journal of Motor Behavior, 33,* 103–112.

there exists an upper bound on the capacity to complete so-called mental work – there is only so much attention that can be devoted to any given task at a time. Using the work analogy, 'paying attention' in this account is akin to 'exerting effort' or 'investing capacity' (Kahneman, 1973, p. 8). The schematic in Figure 8.10 resembles the familiar arrows-and-boxes diagram, but as you can see, there appears to be no way in to the model. In this regard, it is very much an abstract description of the internal workings of the mind. Central to the model is the notion of arousal. At the limit, you are more likely to devote attention to the televised football game if your team is playing in the Cup Final than if you are drowsing in front of a match between two teams you have never heard of. In general terms, the allocation of attention will depend partially on your current state of arousal.

Kahneman (1973) reviewed much of the evidence in support of such a suggestion and noted that it is well established that both too little and too much arousal can have detrimental impacts on performance. Under-arousal is generally explained in terms of lack of motivation at a task, whereas over-arousal will result in the participant being unable to discriminate between relevant and irrelevant aspects of the task. Over-arousal can be compared to that initial rush you might get when they open the doors to the January sales: 'A teapot descaler! A tweed jacket! A nose hair remover! Wait, I only came in for an egg timer.' However, Kahneman went on to make a more general point, namely that, as a task becomes more difficult, it may be possible to increase the supply of resources because of the operation of physiological arousal mechanisms. In this way arousal may be able to compensate for the increased task difficulty. However, when task difficulty becomes immense, any compensation due to arousal may not be sufficient to meet the task demands.

Independently of arousal, two other components are also assumed to influence the deployment of attentional resources – an *allocation policy* and a further *control mechanism* that evaluates the current demands on capacity. Failures to evaluate the current demands properly are typically associated with under-arousal and we will have more to say about the allocation policy in discussing dual-task decrements later.

## Appraisal of single resource theories

Although the presence of a dual-task decrement fits comfortably with the idea of a fixed pool of common processing resources, Navon and colleagues in a series of papers (Navon, 1984, 1985, 1990; Gopher & Navon, 1980; Navon & Gopher, 1979, 1980) have thoroughly picked away at this idea and have arrived at a quite different view of processing constraints. First, though, let us be clear about what it is that single resource models actually predict. Single resource models assume that concurrent tasks compete for the same fixed pool of resources and therefore there should exist a trade-off in performing the tasks when they are combined (Navon, 1990). If both tasks draw on the same pool of resources there should be a dual-task decrement when the tasks are combined. Essentially, if task A demands more resources to complete than task B, then whereas performance on task A may improve or remain steady, performance on task B should decline.

Okay, you are sitting writing a course essay (task B – let's face it, it's always task B) and are also listening to the radio (task A) at the same time. Now by all accounts writing the essay is the more demanding exercise. However, let's assume your favourite programme is now aired and they begin to play an interview with your favourite celebrity/footballer/fashion icon (or indeed 'your favourite celebrity, footballer, fashion icon'). To attend fully to the interview has the consequence of demanding more resources, hence your ability to write the essay dries up.

In mapping out such possibilities, Norman and Bobrow (1975) introduced the notion of a **performance operating characteristic** (**POC**; examples are shown in Figure 8.12). Although the functions shown in the figure are idealised, it is possible to trace out a POC in a number of ways. For example, participants could be required to perform task A or task B to a particular level of competence. This could be achieved by instructing participants to make responses within a certain response deadline or make sure that they make few mistakes on the task. Alternatively, they could be instructed to prioritise task A over task B: concentrate primarily on task A but ensure not to ignore task B completely. Another possibility is to see what effect an increase in the difficulty of task A has on the ability to perform task B concurrently. In such cases, the assumption is that, as more resources are devoted to task A, performance on task A will improve, but performance on task B should reveal a concomitant decrease. More generally, it is assumed that the more of a drag task A places on the resource pool, the less resources can be devoted to task B.

Norman and Bobrow (1976) encapsulated these ideas in something they defined as the principle of **complementarity**. As before, it is assumed that there will be a dual-task decrement when two single tasks are combined – performance will be worse in this case than when either task is carried out in isolation. However, more generally there will be a trade-off between the two tasks. In other words, the more you try to listen to the radio, the worse the essay writing will get, and alternatively the more you try to write the essay, the less you will take in from the radio. In more formal terms, according to the principle of complementarity there is a more challenging prediction of single resource models. This is that there will be a reciprocal interaction between the resource demands of task A and of task B. The nature of this reciprocal relationship can best be tackled by examining performance across a range of combinations of different variations in the relative difficulties of task A and task B, and this means tracing out a corresponding POC. Compare writing down 'the the the . . .' with attempting to write an essay. Compare listening to ambient music with listening to a conversation on the radio. Now think of all the possible combinations, derive some measures of performance and then compute a POC.

Evidence in support of the single resource account of performance has indeed been forthcoming in the literature. For instance, Gopher and Navon (1980) examined performance in something called a manual tracking experiment, in which participants had control

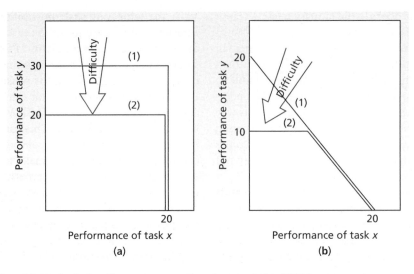

**Figure 8.12 Examples of hypothetical performance operating characteristics (POCs)**
The way to read these graphs is that large *y* values imply good performance on task *y* (i.e., task *y* is relatively easy). Likewise, large *x* values imply good performance on task *x* (i.e., task *x* is relatively easy). (a) shows the consequences of combining a more difficult task *y* with task *x*. As the difficulty of the task *y* increases, performance on *y* falls from a level of 30 (curve 1) to a level of 20 (curve 2) but there is no concomitant change in performance on task *x*. In other words, there are no common resources that task *y* and *x* draw upon. In (b) the situation is more complex. Curve 1 illustrates the principle of complementarity – there is a uniform trade-off in performance across the two tasks. A more difficult task *y* can only be dealt with in combination with a less difficult task *x*. Curve 2 shows the case where increases in task *y* difficulty can be tolerated up to a point (i.e., a value of 10 on the *y* axis) but after that there has to be compensation: task *x* must get easier. An implication is that there are sufficient resources to perform a relatively difficult task *y* up to a point, but further increases in difficulty do have implications for carrying out task *x*. In this case there is a mixture of resources that are shared by both tasks and resources that are unique to each task. These examples are taken from Navon and Gopher (1980), who consider even more complex cases of resource allocation.

*Source*: Navon, D., & Gopher, D. (1980). Task difficulty, resources, and dual-task performance. In R. S. Nickerson (Ed.), *Attention and performance VIII* (pp. 297–315, fig. 15.3 A and B, p. 309). Hillsdale, New Jersey: Erlbaum. Reproduced with permission.

over the movement of a visually presented $X$ on a computer screen via the left/right and up/down movements of a games controller. The computer controlled the up/down and left/right movement of a target square boundary on the computer's screen and the aim was to try to ensure that the $X$ remained within the square as the square moved about the screen. Here task A was defined as controlling the horizontal movements of the $X$ and task B was defined as controlling the vertical movements of the $X$.

In one experiment Gopher and Navon systematically investigated what happened when the difficulty of control over the horizontal, and separately, the vertical movements of $X$ were manipulated. Increasing task difficulty meant that slight movements of the controller greatly accelerated the moving $X$. What they found was that there was a trade-off between performing these tasks as control difficulty was systematically varied.

Moreover this trade-off was clearly in line with the idea that both tasks placed demands on the same pool of resources. Given that both tasks involved trying to control the movement of a single object with the same hand, it is perhaps not so surprising that a single resource model provided an adequate fit to the data.

Despite the evidence consistent with single resource assumptions, Gopher and Navon reported other similar tracking experiments in which the results were not so supportive. In discussing their data, Gopher and Navon introduced a contrast between (i) single resource models, and (ii) models that assume task-specific or multiple resources. We shall turn to multiple resource models shortly, but more pressing is consideration of data that urge caution in trying to interpret POCs in general. The conclusion will be that we need to be very careful in making claims about attentional resources on the basis of POCs alone.

If participants have to complete two tasks which both make demands from the same pool of resources, what *two* predictions can we make about dual-task performance?

## Resources and resource allocation in more detail

Navon (1990) ran a dual-task experiment in which task A involved the classification of a visually presented digit – participants had to respond as to whether the digit was odd or even. In task B participants had to respond to a concurrently visually presented Hebrew letter. They had to decide whether the letter came from the first or second half of the alphabet. Both tasks were carried out under reaction time (RT) conditions. The typical instructions to participants in such tasks are that they should try to respond as quickly as they can without making too many errors. Performance on the two tasks was also manipulated across two conditions.

In the *minimal requirements conditions*, participants were given continuous within-trial feedback on how well they were expected to perform on both tasks. Performance requirements were systematically varied within a range that the participants could easily achieve. Moreover, for each level assessed, slightly more weighting was to be attributed to one of the tasks over the other by setting the RT deadline at a slightly lower level for one of the tasks. What this means is that participants were pushed to respond within a certain time limit for one of the tasks. This was accomplished by shortening the RT deadline – either press the key within this deadline or the response will be treated as an error. In this way the hope was to achieve a performance trade-off for the two tasks. For example, as the RT deadline was lowered for task A, RTs on task B should lengthen.

In contrast, in the *optimum–maximum conditions*, participants were told to try to maximise their response speed on one task even though the difficulty of the other task was altered. Again, according to a single resource model, any variation in the difficulty of one task ought to produce a concomitant variation in performance in the other task – a more difficult task requires more resources. (Remember the *principle of complementarity*?) So even under the optimum–maximum requirements there ought to have been a trade-off in task performance.

A schematic representation of the data from the experiment is presented in Figure 8.13. Consider performance in the minimum requirements condition first. Here there is a clear performance trade-off between the two tasks such that improvement on one is associated with a decrement on the other. RTs on task A shorten as RTs on task B lengthen. Such a pattern is generally in line with single resource models. However, quite a different pattern emerged in the data for the optimum–maximum conditions: here there simply is no evidence of a similar performance trade-off. Now when participants attempted to maximise the speed of response on one task, performance was essentially unaffected by variation in the speed of response on the other task. So when maximising speed on task A, varying the speed of response on task B failed to produce any change in task A responses.

According to Navon (1990), this suggests that the trade-off seen in the minimum requirements condition apparently does not necessarily reflect any limit on being able to perform both tasks concurrently as described by single resource models. Rather, it seems that the pattern of performance reflects participants' compliance with what they consider to be the objectives of the experiment. The more general and important conclusion is that participants appear to have more control over dual-task performance than is implied by the single constraint defined by a finite pool of attentional resources. A performance trade-off may reflect nothing more than participants being able to perform in a manner that is asked of them. It therefore does not necessarily imply anything of significance about the nature and availability of attentional resources.

Indeed, Navon (1990) went further and argued that such demonstrations as these can undermine the faith that may be put in single resource models: merely demonstrating a performance trade-off in a dual-task experiment does not, in and of itself, indicate the constraints that apply when only a single pool of attentional resources is available. He went further, though, and in a detailed review began to question the general usefulness of thinking solely in terms of attentional resources. In some cases it might be better to think not in terms of scarcity of some form of limited resource but in terms of other forms of task interference: attentional resources provide just one way for thinking about how two concurrent tasks may interfere with one another. Evidence in support of this idea comes from a dual-task experiment reported by Navon and Miller (1987) (see Figure 8.14 for more details).

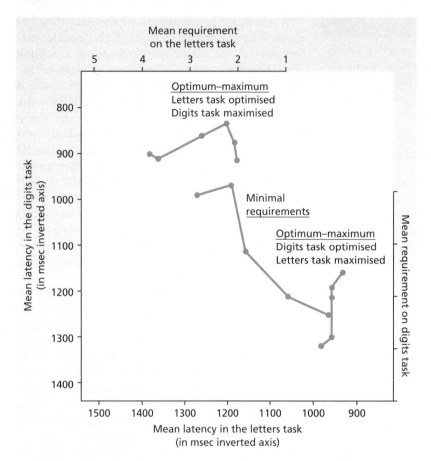

**Figure 8.13 Data from Navon (1990)**
In the minimum requirement task, that is, in the absence of any requirements to weight either task differentially, there is a clear performance trade-off. To meet a response deadline on one of the tasks, RTs on the other task suffered. In the optimum–maximum conditions, participants were instructed to maximise the speed of response on one task. Even though task difficulty was varied on the other task, there was no evidence of any forms of performance trade-offs (see text for further details).

*Source*: Navon, D. (1990). Do people allocate limited processing resources among concurrent activities? In L. Green, & J. H. Kagel (Eds.), *Advances in behavioral economics. Volume 2* (pp. 209–225, fig. 3, p. 219). Norwood, New Jersey: Ablex. Reproduced with permission of the Greenwood Publishing Group. Inc.

## Attentional resources or something else?

Let us take a simplified case and consider just those trials in which four words are presented concurrently on the screen of a computer. One pair was vertically aligned and one pair was horizontally aligned at the end points of an invisible '+'. Task A was to judge whether a boy's name was presented in the vertical limb. Task B was to judge whether a city name was presented on the horizontal limb. Performance was assessed in each task separately (task A *or* task B), and in a dual-task situation in which judgements about both limbs had to be made (task A *and* task B). Five types of word stimuli were defined:

1. An *on-channel target* – a city name (e.g., 'London') on the horizontal city limb or a boy's name (e.g., 'George') on the vertical boy's limb.

2. An *on-channel associate* – a city-related word (e.g., 'England') on the city limb or a boy's name related word (e.g., 'Jane') on the boy's limb.

3. An *off-channel target* – a city name on the boy's limb or a boy's name on the city limb.

4. An *off-channel associate* – a city-related word on the boy's limb or a boy's name related word on the city limb.

5. A *neutral word* unrelated to both city names and boys' names.

For ease of exposition the words defined in 1–4 are known here as *response-related words*. Each limb could contain either no response-related words or only one response-related word.

Various predictions were set out. First, consider those concerning performance in the single-task case. On the assumption that participants could selectively attend to the designated pair of items (on a given attended limb), then it was assumed that there should be no effect of the type of item included on the other limb. This prediction was borne out by the data. So if you are only doing the boy's name task, in isolation, then you are unaffected by anything that occurs on the

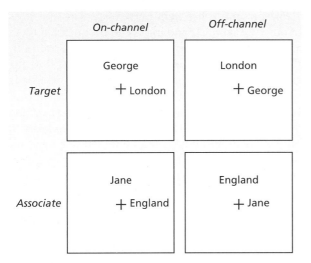

**Figure 8.14 Examples of some of the stimuli in Navon and Miller's (1987) dual-task experiment**
One task was to judge whether a boy's name was presented in the vertical limb and another task was to judge whether a city name was presented on the horizontal limb. As a result, on-channel targets were city names on the horizontal limb or boys' names on the vertical limb. On-channel associates were city-related names on the horizontal limb or boy-related names on the vertical limb. Off-channel targets were city names on the vertical limb or boys' names on the horizontal limb. Off-channel associates were city-related names on the vertical limb or boy-related names on the horizontal limb. Neutral words were also used, but are not shown here. In these cases displays of display size 2 are shown; discussion in the text focuses on cases where displays of display size 4 were used.

other horizontal limb. More involved, though, are the predictions concerning cases when a response-related word was included in the attended limb. Part of the rationale was based on the assumption that task difficulty relative to a neutral word would be increased in the presence of an on-channel associate. For example, the mere presence of 'Jane' on the vertical boy's limb should slow down the boy's name judgement. Again the data supported this prediction: participants were impaired in responding when an on-channel associate was present on the attended limb. Finally, items relevant to the other task should behave exactly as other neutral words even when included on the attended limb. Again the data were generally in line with this prediction.

More critical, though, is what happened in the dual-task situation. First it was predicted that there would be a dual-task decrement, and indeed overall it was found that average RTs were twice as slow in the

dual- than the single-task cases. Moreover, responses on both tasks were affected by the presence of any response-relevant item. Indeed the most interesting effects concerned cases where items relevant to one task occurred on the wrong limb. Performance was particularly slow if, say, 'George' appeared on the city limb or 'London' appeared on the boy's limb. Performance was also affected when an associate relevant to the other task was presented on the wrong channel. In contrast to single-task performance, the presence of, say, 'Jane' on the city limb dramatically slowed performance.

### Outcome conflict, not competition for a common resource

The conclusions that Navon and Miller drew from these results do not fit particularly comfortably with the notion of attentional resources. Something else must be going on in the experiments than mere competition for some form of common resource. What the data suggest is something quite different. In having to analyse the semantic content of both channels and make responses accordingly, performance reflected a particular type of task interference known as **outcome conflict**. As Navon and Miller (1987) stated, outcome conflict arises in dual-task situations when 'the outcome of the processing required for one task conflicts with the processing required for the other task' (p. 435).

In the context of their experiment, and from the participant's point of view, knowledge about boys' names and knowledge about city names is most pertinent to the tasks. The aims are (i) to try to avoid responding to any item that is associated with either of the target categories, so don't be fooled into responding to channel associates, and (ii) certainly to not respond to a target present on the wrong limb. Point (i) is made difficult by the fact that both targets ('George') and their associates ('Jane') will activate the corresponding mental category (boys' names). Point (ii) is made difficult by the fact that either target can appear on any limb but a target is only valid when it occurs on its particular limb. Any such disruptive effects can be gauged relative to neutral trials because neutral words will not activate either of the target categories.

It is as if the participant has to untangle and keep track of appropriate from inappropriate meanings invoked by the displayed words. The problem arises in trying to monitor semantic activation produced by the different response-related words in their conflicting categories. The data cannot be explained just in terms of scarcity of some fixed resource because the neutral words will also activate their relevant categories, yet these do not produce the interference found with the response-relevant items. For example, 'horse', on either the city or the boy's name limb would activate the ANIMAL category, but this category is completely irrelevant to either task. By this view the same amount of semantic activation is produced on all trials when the display contains the same number of words – every word produces semantic activation and as a consequence the same amount of this kind of word-processing resource is being used up on every trial. However, the response-relevant words produce an additional outcome conflict that is not produced when a neutral word is presented. Something other than competition for a common pool of resources is clearly going on.

Navon and Miller went on to discuss several sorts of outcome conflicts and in general they defined them as arising when a particular task produces 'outputs, throughputs, or side effects' that are harmful to the execution of another concurrent task (p. 435). The basic idea is that despite the fact that claims about attentional resources abound, there are other ways of construing processing limitations. Indeed, given the complexity of human cognition, it is perhaps only sensible to admit that there may be many different sorts of processing constraints that are quite different in nature to competition for a single scarce mental resource.

## Pinpoint question 8.7

**Why did the presentation of neutral words fail to impact upon resource allocation in the Navon and Miller (1987) study?**

## For example . . .

Despite the somewhat constrictive nature of the tasks that cognitive psychologists ask participants to perform in examining dual-task performance, real-life examples are all around us. Take the highly enjoyable case of taking notes in a lecture as an example of a real-life dual task. As Piolat, Olive and Kellogg (2005) pointed out, there are lots of problems faced by our intrepid note-taker. For example, there is a discrepancy between the average speed of writing and the average speed of talking which means you're always lagging behind the lecturer. More than that, you're having to monitor the speech continuously while writing so that you don't miss the thread of the argument. And then, of course, you've got to decide what's worth writing down and what isn't. It's a tricky business.

In detailing exactly how tricky note-taking is, Piolat et al. (2005) summarised a number of studies in which note-taking was compared with a number of other procedures such as playing chess and text copying, in a dual-task paradigm. As we have mentioned before, a dual-task decrement would be observed if participants were less able to complete both tasks at the same time, relative to only one task at a time. Under these conditions, it was shown

that the dual-task decrement for note-taking was larger than the simple copying of text and equivalent to playing chess. And we all know how taxing checkmating can be. In the cases of both note-taking and chess, Piolat et al. (2005, p. 299) stated that such activities demand the 'retrieval of large amounts of knowledge, conceptual planning, and the development of solutions to the problems posed in each situation'.

While it may seem like an incredible feat that we can note-take at all, there are always ways to improve this rather handy skill. For example, Piolat et al. (2005) stated that students learn more when they do not try to record everything in a linear fashion. Rather, identifying the connections between concepts and producing mental maps facilitates learning. At a very basic level, note-taking acts essentially as a memory dump, allowing you to save and retrieve information at a later date. If you're passionate about the subject matter, then it is going to be a lot easier for you to learn – which is something you should bear in mind as you're reading this book!

*Source*: Piolat, A., Olive, T., & Kellogg, R. T. (2005). Cognitive effort during note taking. *Applied Cognitive Psychology, 19*, 291–312.

**attentional resources** The equivalent of mental electricity. A finite amount of mental energy that must be distributed among competing stimuli and tasks.

**dual-task decrement** A reduction in performance when performing two tasks together, relative to performing the same two tasks separately.

**performance operating characteristic (POC)** A function relating performance on two tasks when the two tasks are combined. The POC functions can be traced out as the difficulty of the tasks is varied or as participants vary their commitment to either or both tasks.

**complementarity** The reciprocal interaction between the resource demands of two tasks. If the demands of one task increase, performance on a competing task suffers.

**outcome conflict** Conflicts that arise in cases where competing stimuli are present in a display and it is difficult to resolve which to respond to.

## Multiple resources?

Although it is possible to come away from reading Navon's papers with the conclusion that the concept of an attentional resource is both poorly specified and of little use, he is generally sympathetic to the idea that different tasks may place demands on different pools of resources (see Navon & Gopher, 1979). By this view, different processing mechanisms have their own processing characteristics and capacity limitations. An early example of such a view was put forward by Treisman (1969), by which sensory analysis is seen to proceed in terms of the operation of *independent input analysers*. (The analogy is not exact, but in simple terms it is possible to think of the analysers in much the same way as Fodor (1983) discussed *input modules* – see Chapter 2. Indeed, the notion is also reminiscent of the *perceptual nets* taken from Turvey's concurrent and contingent model of processing – see Chapter 4).

In this scheme, different analysers (different input channels) operate in parallel with one another but processing within an analyser is serial in nature. If we take these different analysers to represent the different senses, then an experiment reported by Treisman and Davies (1973) is highly relevant. They ran an experiment in which participants were asked to monitor information streams presented to the auditory and the visual modalities. Two visual streams were defined relative to two separate visual screen locations and two auditory streams were defined relative to the left and right speakers, respectively, of a pair of headphones. On each trial, participants were required to monitor for the presence of a given target. In a so-called *surface condition*, the target was the syllable 'end' embedded in a word (e.g., 'BrENDa'). So in the surface condition, target detection depended on an analysis of the physical or surface characteristics of the target (its written or spoken form). In contrast, in a so-called *semantic condition*, animal names acted as targets (e.g., 'baboon'). Target detection in this condition now depended on accessing word meanings. Overall, the patterns of performance were the same across these two conditions as gauged by measures of target detection accuracy.

Generally there was a dual-task decrement: participants performed worse when monitoring two streams than just a single stream. More importantly, though, participants were particularly poor when monitoring two streams within a given modality than when they were monitoring one stream in each modality. They were more likely to make errors when concentrating on both visual streams, or both auditory streams, than when they divided attention across one visual and one auditory stream.

Clearly such a pattern of results fits comfortably with the idea that two tasks within the same modality may compete for the same resources but concurrent tasks in different modalities do not. However, Kahneman (1973) urged some caution here. Even though participants performed better in the cross-modality than the within-modality condition, there still was a dual-task decrement relative to when participants were able to concentrate on a single task. So while there are resource implications for carrying out two tasks within the same modality, there is also a dual-task decrement when two tasks are carried out across different modalities relative to the completion of a single task.

## 'Sorry, I can't speak now, I'm in the hospital': mobile phone use and driving as dual task

While, for some of us, walking and chewing gum may seem like a daunting dual task, others are under the illusion that their multi-tasking abilities know no bounds. Unfortunately, such multi-tasking can take place in environments that pose serious risks, not only for that individual but also for those around them. One fairly contentious example is attempting to hold a conversation via a non-hands-free mobile phone while driving (something that is now illegal – at least in the UK). Support for this legislation comes from Strayer, Drews and Johnston (2003) who investigated how driving performance changes as a result of attempting to hold a conversation over a mobile phone. Here is a case where we have a very real example of a dual task that demands the division of attentional resources between vision (driving) and audition (talking).

Clearly as a result of the ethical issues involved in trying to run an experiment of this nature in a real-world setting, Strayer et al. (2003) utilised a high-fidelity driving simulator in order to test participants' driving performance under single-task (i.e., just driving) and dual-task (i.e., driving and talking) conditions. Importantly, the researchers also used a hands-free mobile phone, thereby ensuring that any dual-task interference was due to the act of communication rather than the motor behaviour associated with the use of a mobile phone.

Strayer et al. (2003) found that the dual-task decrement associated with mobile phone use while driving was most prominent during high-density traffic. Participants were involved in more accidents, slower in terms of braking onset and braking offset and they also took longer to reach a required minimum speed in the dual-task condition relative to the single-task condition. Nattering participants also took less notice of billboards while driving, correctly recognising fewer billboards as 'old' after completing the dual task relative to the single task.

Under safe and controlled conditions, these researchers have demonstrated that this kind of dual-task interference has important – potentially life-threatening – consequences. Moreover, the study does not provide support for the argument that using a hands-free mobile phone eliminates dual-task interference and is somehow a safe option. Maybe some of us should just stick to walking and chewing gum after all.

*Source*: Strayer, D. L., Drews, F. A., & Johnston, W. A. (2003). Cell phone-induced failures of visual attention during simulated driving. *Journal of Experimental Psychology: Applied, 9*, 23–32.

## When doing two things at once is as easy as doing either alone

We have already seen (in Research focus 8.2) how doing two things at once might become easier if they are seen as one task. Perhaps more impressive, though, are the dual-task studies that reveal how proficient participants can become after intensive practice. To take just three examples: (i) Hirst, Spelke, Reaves, Chaharack and Neisser (1980) taught participants to read prose while simultaneously writing single words and short sentences from dictation; (ii) Allport, Antonis and Reynolds (1972) practised participants at piano playing from a score while shadowing an auditory message; and (iii) Shaffer (1975) combined copy typing and shadowing. In all cases and after extensive practice (e.g.,

after six weeks in the Hirst et al. study) participants were shown to have improved dramatically and became competent in the dual-task situation. The impression is that participants became as efficient at doing both tasks at once as they were at doing either task alone.

In reviewing these particular studies, though, Broadbent (1982) was particularly sceptical that the data were as convincing as they might appear on a superficial reading. He pointed out that even though performance did improve dramatically over the course of the training sessions, there still remained some evidence of dual-task interference even after extended practice. The issue boils down to whether the data provide cast-iron evidence for time-sharing, that is, the ability to complete two tasks at the same time by being able to divide attention between two concurrently demanding tasks. In line with the notion of filter switching,

## For example . . .

If you've ever trained to become a majorette (if not, what are you waiting for?), you'll notice that your baton twirling becomes more and more fluid until you hardly notice that you're doing it at all. Therefore, it's not as though the finger movements demand the same amount of cognitive effort as you practise; rather, it seems that the skill becomes easier and actually demands less and less resources the better you get. So if anything, the suggestion is that one characteristic of skilled performance is that it depends on little or no attentional resources.

Broadbent was convinced that the data instead reflect strategies in task switching and scheduling that previously had not been thought possible. According to him, the data do not provide compelling evidence for time-sharing and for the claims about being able to divide attention in dual-task situations.

Regardless of what the 'right' conclusion is to draw from these studies (see Hirst, 1986, for a riposte) the dramatic improvements in performance are difficult to square with the notion of a single and fixed pool of attentional resources. This whole idea becomes untenable if the suggestion is that practice increases the pool of resources. As Hirst (1986) argued, the studies that do show effects of practice, are probably better interpreted in terms of skill acquisition than anything about the allocation of attentional resources.

In the absence of extensive practice (and indeed in some situations, despite extensive practice), it just is the case that some pairs of tasks will interfere more with one another than other pairs of tasks (cf. Treisman & Davies, 1973). In addressing the possible reasons for this, Wickens (1984) set out a three-dimensional space of possibilities within which multiple resources may be defined. The dimensions reflect (i) early vs. late processes, (ii) separate modalities and finally (iii) 'processing codes' (p. 302) (see Figure 8.15).

In (i) the division is between perceptual encoding/categorisation and response selection and execution. The implication here is that any two tasks that place demands on the same stage of processing are likely to interfere with one another. For example, attempting to turn down the volume on the TV via the remote control and pick up the ringing phone places demands on the same response components. In (ii) the implication is that tasks performed in different modalities are less likely to interfere than are tasks performed within the same modality (cf. Treisman & Davis, 1973). This may go some way to explain how people can continue to shop in a supermarket while continuing a conversation over a mobile phone. Finally the implication in (iii) is that tasks that give rise to different internal codes are less likely to interfere than tasks that generate the same sorts of codes. You might like to test this idea out by trying to complete a Sudoku puzzle at the same time as some long multiplication problems, and then doing Sudoku and a crossword. All other things being equal,

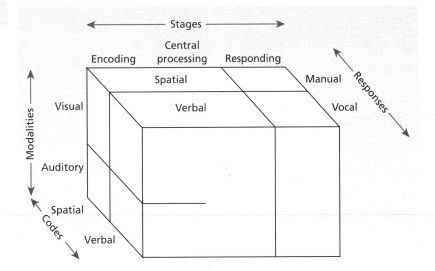

**Figure 8.15 Wickens' (1984) framework for thinking about cases under which competing tasks may interfere with one another**
The 3D space is given by dimensions defined relative to (i) the stage in the human information processing system where conflicts may arise, (ii) the modalities in which the tasks are presented and (iii) the mental codes that are called upon by the tasks.

*Source*: Wickens, C. D. (1984). *Engineering psychology and human performance* (fig. 8.7, p. 302). Columbus, Ohio: Charles E. Merrill.

the Sudoku plus crossword condition should be easier because you're dealing with numbers and letters, relative to dealing with only numbers when trying to complete the first pair of puzzles.

We have discussed some of the evidence that strengthens the plausibility of this framework and Wickens (1984) discussed more. It is without doubt, though, that Wickens has provided an entirely sensible framework for thinking about when and how concurrent tasks may interfere. However, it does not settle the deeper issue about whether there is a central processing constraint on attempting to do more than one thing at once. This is a very important question that has given rise to a rather extensive literature and we shall discuss this possibility in more detail in the next chapter.

### Pinpoint question 8.8

**According to Wickens (1984), what are the three ways in which the interference between two tasks can be reduced?**

### Pulling it all together

In attempting to provide an integrative overview of the various kinds of theories of attention that have been considered in the literature, Pashler (1998) put forward the scheme shown in Figure 8.16. Here, the space of possible theories is defined by a 2 × 2 matrix whose

dimensions define, respectively, (i) whether the theory allows for the possibility that unattended stimuli are identified and (ii) whether the theory allows for the possibility that multiple attended stimuli can be processed simultaneously. We have already considered: (i) early selection accounts in which multiple attended stimuli are not processed simultaneously and unattended stimuli are not identified, such as Broadbent's (1958) filter theory; and (ii) late selection accounts in which multiple attended stimuli are processed simultaneously and unattended stimuli are identified, such as Deutsch and Deutsch (1963). However, two cells of the matrix have yet to be discussed.

The '???' in the figure is taken to signify accounts in which all items are slavishly identified but in a sequential (one-at-a-time) manner. This would be like standing by a conveyor belt as freshly picked tomatoes are funnelled past one at a time: your job is to try to grade each for size and quality. Pashler termed this sort of account an **uncontrolled serial model** in which perceptual analysis is said to proceed serially but exhaustively – you can't leave the conveyor belt until all the tomatoes have gone past. In this sort of functional account there is no notion of selection, but processing is constrained to operate in a serial fashion. Where does such a strange notion come from?

The idea of **serial exhaustive processing** is most readily associated with the work of Sternberg (1967). In the now classic **Sternberg memory scanning task** participants are provided at the beginning of a trial with a **memory set** of characters, for instance the digits 3 and 7 presented on a visual display. The memory

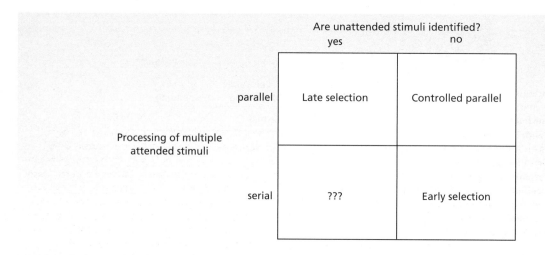

**Figure 8.16 The 2 × 2 space of possible theories of attention (taken from Pashler, 1998)**

*Source*: Pashler, H. E. (1998). *The psychology of attention* (fig. 1.6, p. 22). Cambridge, Massachusetts: The MIT Press. Copyright © 1998 Massachusetts Institute of Technology. Reproduced with permission of the MIT Press.

set is removed and replaced with a single **probe item** (a digit) and the participant has to press one response key if the probe is a member of the memory set (the participant must make a positive response) and another key if the digit is not (the participant must make a negative response). The experiments are run under RT conditions so response speed is the main measure of interest but accuracy is also recorded. Performance is measured for differing memory set sizes and the resulting averaged RT data are then plotted as a func-

tion of memory set size (see Figure 8.17 for an idealised example). As the figure shows, a central result is that RT increases linearly as memory set size increases but more particularly the rate of increase is the same for positive and negative responses. The standard theoretical analysis of the task is the following.

When the participants are provided with the memory set, they encode and store these in some form of temporary memory system. These items must be stored until the probe item is presented. The probe is then

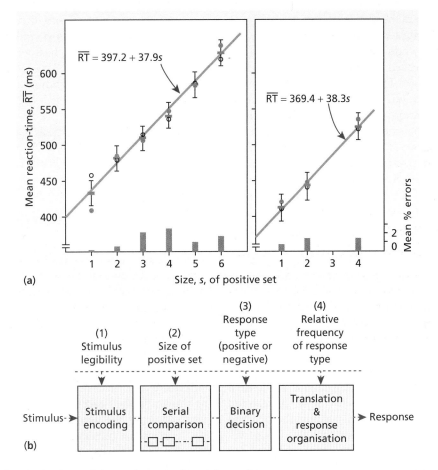

**Figure 8.17 Sternberg's classic mental scanning experimental paradigm**
(a) Shows typical data taken from a Sternberg memory scanning experiment. On the left, performance with memory sets that varied from 1 to 6 items – a different memory set was used prior to each trial. On the right, performance with a memory set (consisting of 1, 2, 3 or 4 items) that was kept constant over many trials. A critical finding is that response time increases linearly with memory set size – every added item to the memory set size incurs a constant increment in response time. Furthermore, identical functions are shown for present and absent responses. That is, on average a present response takes the same amount of time to make as an absent response (i.e., the data points overlap). Taken together, these two findings support the notion of serial exhaustive processing – don't make a response until you have considered every item in the memory set. (b) is a schematic arrows-and-boxes representation of the component stages of processing that Sternberg put forward for the memory scanning task. Of some additional interest is the fact that, over a series of experiments, he was able to infer whereabouts particular experimental variables were having their influence in this stages-of-processing account. For instance, stimulus legibility affects the earliest encoding stage of processing.

*Source*: Sternberg, S. (1975). Memory scanning: New findings and current controversies. *The Quarterly Journal of Experimental Psychology, 27*, 1–32 (fig, 2., p. 5, fig. 4, p. 6). Reproduced with permission from Taylor & Francis Ltd.

encoded and the participant must compare this input representation against the stored representations of the memory set digits. If a match is found, a positive response can be made; if no match is found, then a negative response can be made.

It was the nature of the memory search and comparison process that gave rise to the notion of *serial exhaustive processing*. This is most easily understood in relation to Figure 8.17. As with any straight line graph the function can be decomposed into a slope (the steepness of the line) and an intercept (the point at which the line crosses the vertical axis). Sternberg took the intercept to reflect the sum of (i) the amount of time needed to encode the probe item, and (ii) the amount of time needed to convert the eventual decision into a response. The slope of the function was taken to reflect the rate of the memory comparison process, simply how quickly individual items could be processed. Two properties of these lines are important for our discussion here.

First, the linear nature of the function was taken to indicate the operation of a serial mechanism: each character added to the memory set carried an overhead of an additional unit of processing time. Second, the fact that the slope of the negative response function was the same as for that for the positive response function was taken to show that exactly the same sort of comparison process was going on in both positive and negative trials.

What the data therefore seemed to rule out is something known as **serial self-terminating processing**. In this context a serial self-terminating process would mean that the slope on the positive trials would be half that on the negative trials. Why? Well, on target present trials sometimes the target will be the first item in the memory set, sometimes it will be the last and sometimes it will be somewhere between the first and the last. On average this means that the target will be found after half the memory set items have been checked. Remember, the process is self-terminating – so as you find the target, stop checking and respond 'present'. In contrast, on absent trials you can only press the 'absent' key once you have checked off all the items. In extending this analysis over the increasing memory set sizes tested, the conclusion is that the difference in slope between the positive and negative memory search functions should be 1:2. It should on average take twice as long to decide 'absent' as it does to decide 'present' for a given memory set size.

The problem with the memory scanning data, however, is that the memory search does not appear to reflect serial self-terminating processing because the slopes of the positive and negative functions are the same. As we have just argued, serial self-terminating processing would be most consistent with the negative slope being twice as steep as the positive slope, and it's nowhere near. On these grounds, Sternberg argued that the data were most consistent with the notion of a serial exhaustive process in which all items in the memory set were checked on every trial regardless of whether the probe was part of the memory set or not. So even in the case when '3' is the probe, and the memory includes both 3 and 7, the implication is that the stored 3 is checked and then the stored 7 is checked prior to a response being made. Although the adequacy of the reasoning has been challenged (see commentary by Sutherland, 1967), the notion of serial exhaustive processing has endured: hence the '???' in Figure 8.16.

### Pinpoint question 8.9

**What support is there for serial exhaustive processing?**

## Controlled parallel processing

The final alternative in Figure 8.16 that remains unexamined is that termed controlled parallel. **Controlled parallel processing** allows some flexibility which is ruled out by the simple caricatures of early and late selection theories. By this view, parallel processing of several stimuli is possible but a possible downside is that unattended stimuli may go unprocessed. The eventual model that Pashler (1998) provided is set out in schematic form in Figure 8.18. The model incorporates both a filtering mechanism and resource limitations (as shown by the beaker of 'capacity' in the bottom-right corner of the figure). The filtering mechanism selects items for further processing and the selected stimuli may then compete for the limited capacity that underpins semantic analysis. If the demands placed on this pool of resources are within the capacity limitations of the system, then parallel processing of several stimuli is possible. However, if the system is overloaded then processing efficiency is compromised. That is, if too many stimuli are competing for resources, then processing will falter.

As with Broadbent's (1958) early filter model, the controlled parallel processing model follows from a very careful review of the attentional literature – some of which we have examined here. According to Pashler (1998), overwhelmingly the evidence leads to such an account in which both structural (filtering

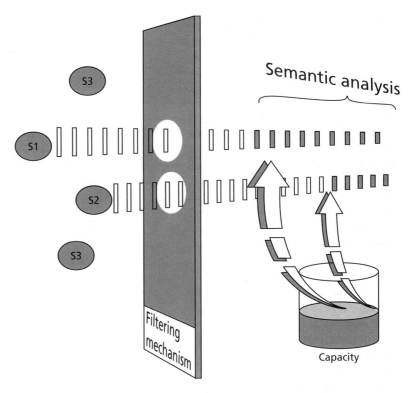

**Figure 8.18 A schematic representation of the human information processing system as described by Pashler (1998)** See text for further details.

*Source*: Pashler, H. E. (1998). *The psychology of attention* (fig. 5.1, p. 227). Cambridge, Massachusetts: The MIT Press. Copyright © 1998 Massachusetts Institute of Technology. Reproduced with permission. The MIT Press.

mechanisms) and processing (capacity/resource) constraints are needed.

**uncontrolled serial model** A framework of processing in which all items must be processed but in a sequential fashion.

**serial exhaustive processing** The sequential examination of a list of items, with testing continuing until all items have been considered.

**Sternberg memory scanning task** A task in which participants are initially given a set of possible target items to hold in mind; they are then presented with a single item and are asked to decide if it is a target.

**memory set** List of to-be-remembered items.

**probe item** In the Sternberg memory scanning task, an item to be compared with a memory set.

**serial self-terminating processing** The sequential examination of a list of items, with examination stopping after the item of interest has been found.

**controlled parallel processing** The general view, espoused by Pashler (1998), that parallel processing of stimuli is possible but this is not without restraint and is under executive control.

## Perceptual load theory

Before moving on from this discussion of general theories of attention, it is useful to consider a more recent account that bears some resemblance to Pashler's, although neither is discussed in relation to the other. This is the perceptual load theory put forward by Lavie (2000). Lavie distinguished between two types of control mechanisms, namely passive and active mechanisms. While it may be a step too far, there does appear to be rather close similarities between Lavie's (2000) 'passive' mechanism and Pashler's filter, and her 'active' mechanism and Pashler's semantic analysis/central mechanisms. Both also agree on the distinction between early (perceptual) vs. later (executive) stages of processing. The main point of contention, though, is whether some form of capacity limitation governs the early perceptual stage of processing: according to Lavie, it does. She has claimed to have shown how it is possible to overload an early perceptual analysis stage of processing. Accordingly, selection by filtering can be compromised if the task places heavy demands on the initial perceptual analysis stage of processing.

## Load theory and effects of varying perceptual load

Figure 8.19 provides examples of the sorts of visual displays used by Lavie (1995) to test her perceptual load theory. The task was to press one key if a target *z* was present and a different key if a target *x* was present. Response-relevant items were presented randomly at one of six pre-defined positions in a central row of the computer display. In the S1 condition there was only ever a single target present. In the S6 condition the target was embedded in a row of six characters. Also on every trial a non-target character was randomly positioned in the periphery of the display. As can be seen from Figure 8.19, the non-target could either be compatible with the central target (i.e., the central target was an *x* and the peripheral non-target was also an *X*), the non-target could be incompatible with the target (i.e., a *z*), or it could be neutral with respect to either response (i.e., a *P*).

In general terms two effects were of initial interest: first, whether the compatibility of the non-target would influence responses to the target; and second, whether there would also be an effect of display size (i.e., the number of items in the display) on responses. More interesting, though, was what the combined effect of these two factors would be – would the compatibility effect interact with the effect of display size?

The results of the experiment were relatively clear-cut. Responses were shorter on trials containing a small number of items than large. Although this factor has been referred to display size, Lavie termed the factor **perceptual load**. The understanding was that, by increasing the number of non-target items in the display, this would increase the load placed on perceptual encoding mechanisms. So a large display size was taken to reflect a high perceptual load being imposed, whereas a small display was taken to reflect a low perceptual load being imposed. The most interesting result, however, was that the effect of non-target compatibility varied across these two levels of perceptual load.

Let us stand back for a second so as to appreciate what the basic compatibility effect should look like. Here previous experiments had been able to establish firmly that responses in these sorts of task were heavily influenced by the nature of irrelevant non-target items concurrently present. The standard effect is that RTs are shortest on trials containing compatible items (both target and non-target are *x*), longer on neutral trials (target as *x* and non-target as *P*) and longest on incompatible trials (target as *x* and non-target as *z*).

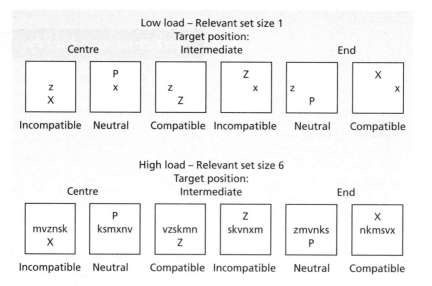

**Figure 8.19 Examples of displays used by Lavie (1995)**
The target letters are *z* (press one key) and *x* (press another key). Participants were told to focus attention on the central letters and decide which target was present there. The central letters were accompanied by the presence of a peripheral, non-target letter. As can be seen, the peripheral non-target could either be congruent with the central target, incongruent with the central target or response-irrelevant (i.e., neutral). Across the low and high perceptual load conditions the number of central letters varied. Perceptual load increased as the number of central letters increased.

*Source*: Lavie, N. (1995). Perceptual load as a necessary condition for selective attention. *Journal of Experimental Psychology: Human Perception and Performance*, *21*, 451–468 (fig. 1, p. 455). Reproduced with permission from APA.

Indeed, the lengthening of responses on incompatible trials is taken to reflect something known as **response competition**. Without going into too many details, the basic idea is that both the target and non-target are identified and as a consequence a conflict occurs at the level of response selection and execution. The target $x$ primes the $x$ response and the non-target $z$ primes the $z$ response. So which response is appropriate?

Now in Lavie's experiment the critical finding was that the standard compatibility effect only arose for the low perceptual load condition, when there was a small number of non-targets in the display. There was no corresponding effect for the high perceptual load condition, when there were several non-targets in the displays. Lavie explained this particular pattern of effects by reference to her perceptual load hypothesis. If the load on perceptual analysis is slight, then filtering is unnecessary and both targets and non-targets are processed. However, when perceptual analysis is made more demanding, then full (perceptual) capacity will be devoted to detecting targets. Given that all resources are dedicated towards target detection, none of the non-targets will be processed further. The perceptual analysis of the target is so demanding that the perception of the non-targets is said to be excluded.

Think of it this way. You are waiting to hear the football results on a pub's television set and the pub is crowded and very noisy. So the main perceptual task (hearing the telly) is very demanding. Under these conditions you are likely not to notice that your mate is asking whether you want another drink (he is the distracting non-target). Compare this with the situation in which the pub is empty, the telly is clearly audible and your mate asks whether you want another drink.

## Load theory and effects of varying memory load

More intriguing still was a further extension to the theory tested in more recent experiments. On the assumption that sometimes both relevant and irrelevant items exit from the perceptual analysis stage, then the active mechanisms now come into play in an attempt to discriminate the relevant from the irrelevant. On these grounds, if the active mechanisms are overloaded then any detrimental effect of irrelevant items might then be exacerbated. So whereas overloading the passive (perceptual) mechanism results in a lessening of interference from non-targets, completely the opposite is predicted if the active (central) mechanisms are overloaded. If the central mechanisms are overloaded, then, even in cases where the perceptual load is slight, the prediction is that interference from non-targets should be substantial.

This second strand to the theory has been tested on a number of occasions but one example will suffice here. De Fockert, Rees, Frith and Lavie (2001) ran the following dual-task experiment using stimuli similar to those depicted in Figure 8.20. In the attentional task the stimulus was a photograph of a famous face superimposed by a typed name. Participants were required to make a response to the face, classifying it as belonging to a politician or a pop star. A congruent stimulus contained the name and face of the same person (e.g.,

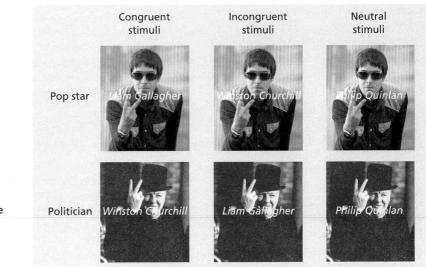

**Figure 8.20 Variations on a theme by de Fockert et al. (2001)**

*Sources*: (top row): Getty Images; (bottom row): Hulton-Deutsch Collection/Corbis.

Mick Jagger's face with Mick Jagger's name); an incongruent stimulus contained the face of a politician and the name of a pop star (e.g., Bill Clinton's face with David Bowie's name) or the face of a pop star and the name of a politician). Finally a neutral stimulus contained the face of a politician or a pop star superimposed by an anonymous name (e.g., Jim Smith). On the basis of previous experiments it was predicted that RTs to congruent stimuli should be shorter than RTs to incongruent stimuli. However, the main interest was with how this effect might be influenced by the nature of a secondary memory task.

Following the initial presentation of a central fixation cross, a memory set of five digits was presented. Participants were instructed to retain this ordered sequence until the end of the trial. Okay, so retain this set of numbers and keep reading: 0 3 1 2 4. Next there followed a varied number of display frames containing the face stimuli defined before. When the face frames had completed, a probe digit was presented and participants had to respond with the digit that *followed* it in the original sequence. So what was the number after the probe digit 2? Imagine having to do that as well as the face judgement task and you will get a fair idea of what it was like to be in the experiment (see Figure 8.21 for a schematic representation of the events at each trial).

In order to manipulate the active central mechanisms posited by Lavie (2000), memory load was varied by either having participants retain a fixed digit sequence over a complete block of trials (0 1 2 3 4 in the *low memory load condition*) or by having them retain a different sequence on every trial (the *high memory load condition*). If the perceptual load theory was correct, then the effect of an incongruent stimulus should be greater in the high memory load condition.

Overall, the concurrent memory load affected responses on the attentional task with RTs being shorter in the low memory condition than the high memory condition. Critically, though, the congruency effect was considerably larger in the high memory load condition than the low memory load condition. The implication was that when memory was overloaded, participants experienced substantial difficulties in suppressing the irrelevant typed name information.

One central assumption here is that the memory task tapped into the same active central mechanisms responsible for suppressing irrelevant semantic information activated by the presentation of the face. By this view, the degree to which a given non-target will interfere with some other task is critically dependent on the availability of capacity in the temporary mem-

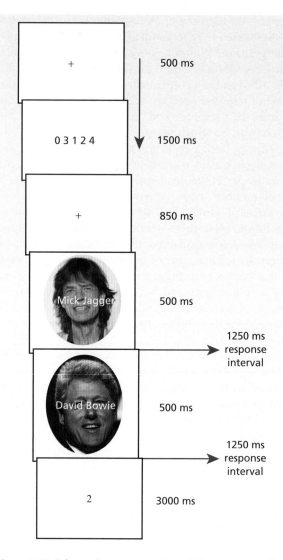

**Figure 8.21 Schematic representation of the sequence of events in the experiment reported by de Fockert et al. (2001)**
See text for further details.

*Sources*: de Fockert, J. W., Rees, G., Frith, C. D., & Lavie, N. (2001). The role of working memory in visual selective attention. *Science*, *291*, 1803–1806 (fig. 1, p. 1804). Reproduced with permission from AAAS.
Images: (top): Getty Images; (bottom): Corbis.

ory system. This hypothesis was supported because, as de Fockert et al. (2001) showed, the ability to ignore irrelevant information was *diminished* when memory load was increased. The conflict between responding to the face and the name was increased when the concurrent memory load was high.

The contrast between the earlier study by Lavie (1995) and the later work by de Fockert et al. (2001) is particularly interesting. In summary, overloading the passive (perceptual) mechanism results in a lessening of interference from non-targets (as shown by Lavie, 1995), but overloading the active (central) mechanisms leads to an increase in interference from irrelevant information.

### Pinpoint question 8.10

**How do high demands placed on passive perceptual analyses contrast with high demands placed on active central analyses?**

**perceptual load** The amount of perceptual analysis demanded by a given task.

**response competition** Conflict that occurs when more than one response is invoked by a stimulus.

## Concluding comments

You may well now be feeling that the number of different theories of attention that are out there is the same as the number of people who consider themselves to be researchers in attention. To allay these fears it is important to bear in mind that certain themes recur in the literature. Some examples are the differences between structural (bottleneck) constraints and processing (resource) constraints (see Figure 8.4); differences between the various ways in which information is selected or discarded, and the problems that exist in trying to do more than one thing at once. From Pashler's (1998) work it seems that both assumptions about structural and processing constraints are necessary. However, it may well turn out that even such hybrid theories are still too simplistic and that much more imaginative thought is needed on the ways in which the human information processing system may be constrained. Our theories need to take account of both structural and processing constraints but are we really thinking about these in the most appropriate fashion?

It may well be that our conceptions of the human information processing system are misguided and that the mind is much more complex than the parallel-then-serial framework as suggest by Pashler and others. Indeed, some very interesting and quite different speculations about human information processing have been put forward by Navon (1989a, 1989b). He speculated that the mind may actually comprise many different processing modules, each specialised for some particular purpose: sometimes the modules co-operate, sometimes they compete. By this view the mind is understood as an *anarchic intelligence system*. The modules are said to operate autonomously in attempting to fulfil their own purposes such as 'collecting information . . . , making interpretations, attempting prognoses, and initiating operations pertinent to the system's subsistence' (p. 195). Attention within this framework is 'assumed to regulate only the communication among modules' (p. 191). Within this framework the idea that the filter operates early or late is seen to be far too simplistic – each module has its own constraints and these may come into play at different stages throughout the system.

These ideas have yet to be fleshed out fully and the critical experiments have yet to be carried out. Nevertheless, such an alternative framework reveals that, despite what might seem to be an emerging consensus on how best to construe constraints in the human information processing system, interesting avenues remain to be explored.

## CHAPTER SUMMARY

- The world can be an overwhelming place in terms of the sensory information it provides. The aim of attention therefore is to allow us to focus on those things that are critical in our environment and filter out those aspects that are less relevant.

- Broadbent's (1958) filter theory proposed an early structural bottleneck, which acts as a gateway between early sensory analysis and later processes of stimulus identification. Although early processes handle vast amounts of information concurrently – in parallel – the more central processes operate less slowly in a serial one-at-a-time mode. Items that are deemed relevant are selected for further processing but such selection can only operate on the physical characteristics of the stimulus as represented in the early sensory store.

  Support for Broadbent's theory was provided by split-span experiments in which participants reported information split across two channels, and shadowing experiments in which participants were asked to report information from a single channel while ignoring a second channel.

▶

- Treisman's (1964) attenuated filter theory model revised Broadbent's (1958) idea and argued that sometimes information on unattended channels could be processed to a semantic level, such that meaning was derived. The evidence seemed to suggest that occasionally the meanings of items were recovered despite attention being directed elsewhere. One implication was that the division of attention between attended and unattended channels was not all-or-nothing.

- The late selection theory of Deutsch and Deutsch (1963) argued for a late structural bottleneck in that attentional selection takes place at a post-categorical stage, wherein all items are identified and selection is now carried out on the basis of meaning. This has the implication that attended and unattended information are processed to a semantic level. Further evidence for late selection comes from the experiments of Duncan (1980) who showed that limitations in processing only occurred when more than one target item competed for attention.

- Alternative accounts argued for processing rather than structural constraints. This is the difference between the speed of a lift (processing constraint) and the size of the lift (structural constraint). Theorists have debated the relative merits of single resource models in which all concurrent tasks draw on a single limited pool of attentional resources (Kahneman, 1973), and, alternatively, models in which multiple resources each relate to different input channels (Treisman & Davies, 1973).

- Pashler's (1998) controlled parallel model argued for the combined existence of structural and processing constraints in attention, with an initial filtering mechanism selecting items, and such items going on to compete for resources involved in semantic processing.

    Lavie (2000) used the concept of different sorts of mental load to argue for different kinds of processing limitations. From her experiments, the ability to ignore irrelevant information was *enhanced* when the perceptual load of the task was increased. In contrast, the ability to ignore irrelevant information was *diminished* when memory load was increased.

## ANSWERS TO PINPOINT QUESTIONS

8.1 Item decay can be avoided by rehearsal. This allows information that has already exited the S system to be recirculated via the P system back into the S system.

8.2 Participants performed better at the binaural condition when reporting the content of one ear followed by the content of the other ear, and when the rate of presentation was slowed.

8.3 Wood and Cowan (1995b) challenged Broadbent's (1958) model by arguing that unattended information (such as your own name) can be semantically processed.

8.4 B D G Q share curved properties with C and O whereas T Z X Y do not (Rabbitt, 1964). This is an example of categorising (Broadbent, 1958) in which learned categories can determine which items are selected and which are essentially filtered out or ignored.

8.5 Duncan (1980) provided evidence in support of the Deutsch and Deutsch (1963) model in that non-targets failed to impact upon responding while multiple targets did. This seems to indicate that that the nature of the item (target or non-target) is made explicit prior to selection. Selection seems therefore to take place at a post-categorical level.

8.6 A dual-task decrement should occur in that performance in the two tasks should not be as good as either task performed in isolation. According to Norman and Bobrow (1976), complementarity should also obtain in that the more resources allocated to task A, the worse participants should be at task B (or vice versa).

8.7 Neutral words did not impact upon responding in the Navon and Miller (1987) study because they were not relevant to either task.

8.8 Two tasks are less likely to interfere with one another if they (a) place demands on different stages of processing, (b) involve different modalities, and (c) do not share internal forms of coding.

8.9   The idea of serial exhaustive processing (Sternberg, 1967) is supported by the facts that (i) the increase in reaction time was linear with increases in memory set size, and (ii) identical functions obtained for both present and absent responses.

8.10   The ability to ignore irrelevant information was *enhanced* when the perceptual load of the task was increased. In contrast, the ability to ignore irrelevant information was *diminished* when memory load was increased.

## CHAPTER 9

# ATTENTIONAL CONSTRAINTS AND PERFORMANCE LIMITATIONS

## LEARNING OBJECTIVES

**By the end of this chapter, you should be able to:**

• Contrast between sequential and concurrent models of processing.

• Describe the principles associated with the psychological refractory period (PRP) paradigm.

• Produce empirical evidence in support of a central bottleneck (Pashler, 1994).

• Contrast between PRP models and central capacity sharing (CCS; Tombu & Jolicœur, 2003) models.

• Describe the principles associated with task switching.

• Contrast between the executive control account (Rogers & Monsell, 1995) and the task carryover account (Allport et al., 1994) of task switching.

## CHAPTER CONTENTS

So things have gone pretty well since our last visit to the DJ booth. Now world renowned for taking your audience on musical journeys of the highest

# Back in the booth

order, you're in great demand everywhere. Unfortunately, things have taken off a little too well. You're currently negotiating a new signing to your record label, designing the artwork for your new album, desperately trying to avoid your obligatory stalker who has appeared on the scene, trying to get a warm-up spot at the Miami Music Conference, chasing up the record-pressing factory after they sent you a warped pressing of your latest release, and to top it all off, the press have you involved in a seedy tryst with some D-list celebrity or other. Really, just how many things do you think you can do at once?

## REFLECTIVE QUESTIONS

1. Think about a really busy day you've had where it felt like there just weren't enough hours in the day to complete all the jobs you had to do. Did you end up trying to do two things at once? Did this really feel like doing two things at once or were you switching quickly between two jobs? Were certain combinations of job easier to perform together than others? Why do you think this might have been?

2. Think about a job that you or a friend may have had that demanded a lot of repetitive action (perhaps on a production line). What were you able to do at the same time as performing this job? What happened when your environment changed and you had to do something else? How easy was it for you to step out of one task and into another?

## Introduction and preliminary considerations

In the previous chapter we considered a range of theoretical ideas about how a person copes with the overwhelming bombardment of the senses by information from the external world. Selective attention was deemed necessary because of an inherent limitation in being able to deal with everything all of the time. Only a sub-set of the vast wealth of stimulation is taken to be pertinent at any given time and it is this that plays a primary role in determining our immediate course of action. Accordingly, attention is seen to be the gatekeeper to the more central processes of interpreting data from the senses and deciding about how best to operate on the basis of the selected stimulus information.

In this chapter we will explore attempts to define the conditions under which performance breaks down in the face of multiple and concurrent processing demands. This topic has largely been investigated by designing dual-task experiments in which participants are asked to attempt to carry out two independent tasks at the same time (see Chapter 8). Performance in such

dual-task situations is then compared with performance when participants complete either task alone. The aim here is to try to ascertain just how much we can do at a given point in time. An inability to perform as well in the dual-task as the single-task conditions is taken to reflect problems in attempting to do more than one thing at once. Clearly, if there is only a certain amount we can do at a given time, then it is in our best interests to be able to prioritise so that the important stuff gets our full concentration. Being able to attend selectively therefore makes perfect sense, and understanding performance in dual-task situations helps us to clarify the nature of attention and attentional control.

A fairly basic issue here is the degree to which such limitations in our ability to do two things at once reflect a so-called *structural constraint* of the processing system – like a processing bottleneck (see previous discussion of Broadbent's 1958 filter account of attention in Chapter 8) – or whether they reflect some form of default setting of the system that can be finely tuned with practice. Initially, your inability to juggle might seem like a structural constraint – you only have two hands and you can't seem to move and co-ordinate these fast enough, but then, given enough practice and determination, you should eventually learn to juggle.

It also might help to remember our lift analogy in Chapter 8 – if some aspect of performance is taken to reflect a structural bottleneck then this cannot be changed with practice, since structural constraints are assumed to be fixed. This is basically saying that the size of the lift does not change regardless of the amount of times it is used. However, if such initial difficulties can be overcome or modified by practice then this clearly does not reflect a structural limitation of the system. To re-use our juggling example: the fact that you can learn to juggle shows that your original inability was not due to any structural limitations because these have not changed over the course of practice – you still have two hands.

## Stages of information processing

In order to understand what is fundamentally at stake, it is important first to understand the sort of ideas that underpin the whole enterprise. Consider the very simple stages-of-processing account shown in Figure 9.1.

In very general terms, the figure shows, in schematic form, four sequential stages of processing, namely stimulus encoding, stimulus identification, decision and response organisation/execution. Stimulus encoding covers everything from registration at the senses of stimulus information, to the delivery of a representation that codes the physical characteristics of the stimulus, namely its size, shape, intensity, position and so on: yes, it's fat, furry and digging. Operations at this stage of processing are sometimes known as

input processes (also known as early or peripheral processes). Stimulus identification implies categorisation whereby the description of the stimulus information is assigned to a mental category: yes, it really is the neighbour's cat at the bottom of the garden. Operations at this level are sometime known as *central processes*. Finally, decision and response organisation/execution processes are sometimes known as **late processes**. The decision stage is where a conclusion is drawn about what to do now the stimulus has been identified: yes, it probably is a good idea to chase it off the tomato patch. At the response execution stage the actual plan of action is initiated: get out of the chair and run out of the back door with a large broom. Response execution processes are also sometimes known as **output processes**.

For simplicity it is assumed that the four stages are arranged sequentially such that each stage, in turn, is initiated. The first stage (let's call this stage $n$) sends its outputs to the second stage (stage $n + 1$) but stage $n + 1$ can only begin once stage $n$ has produced a final output, and so on. Described thus, the argument provides a serial or **sequential stage model of processing** – very much in the spirit of the sort of Sternberg account of memory search described in the previous chapter. You'll remember that participants on a given trial were asked to check whether a probe number was present in a remembered set of items. Performance in this relatively simple task was explained in terms of four sequential stages of processing – stimulus encoding, serial (memory) comparison, binary decision and finally translation and response organisation.

As you can possibly imagine, there has been some debate over whether such hypothesised stages operate in a truly sequential manner. The question has been posed as to whether stage $n + 1$ really has to wait until stage $n$ has run to completion (see the comprehensive and, in places, contrary reviews by Meyer, Yantis, Osman & Smith, 1985; and Miller, 1988). Is it absolutely critical that the stimulus is fully encoded before the serial comparison stage is set in motion? It will come as little surprise to discover that, depending on what you read, you are likely to arrive at different conclusions on this point. For example, the *concurrent and contingent model* of Turvey (1973; see Chapter 4) provides a quite different account of processing to the simple sequential stage model discussed here. In Turvey's model there was continuous information transmission from the peripheral to the central processes. The idea is that the central processes can begin at any point after the peripheral processes have been activated – they do not have to wait until the peripheral

Stimulus encoding
(Fat, Furry, Digging)

↓

Stimulus identification
(Neighbour's cat)

↓

Decision
(Tomato patch must
be protected)

↓

Response execution
(Get the broom)

**Figure 9.1 A simple sequential, stages-of-processing account going from stimulus to response**

processes provide a final and complete description of the input. In other words, you could at least start to get the broom out even though you are not 100 per cent confident that it is next door's cat. Clearly, therefore, there are very different and contradictory views on how best to think about the basic processing architecture.

**What is the difference between strictly sequential and concurrent models?**

In exploring these ideas, Miller (1982, 1983) asked whether response preparation can really begin before stimulus recognition is completed. In brief, his experimental paradigm was as follows. In the simple case and on each trial, participants had to make a speeded letter classification response to a single visually presented letter. Four response keys were used, two each for left and right hands and one member of each of these pairs for the index and middle finger, respectively. For simplicity, number the keys *1*, *2*, *3* and *4* from left to right and assign *1* and *2* to the left middle and index finger. Now assign keys *3* and *4* to the index and middle finger of the right hand (see Figure 9.2).

In the same-hand condition the letters *s* and *S* were assigned to keys *1* and *2*, respectively, and the letters *t* and *T* were assigned to keys *3* and *4*, respectively. From the participants' view, if you see some kind of '*s/S*' press a key with the left hand and if you see some kind of '*t/T*' press a key with the right hand. Of course this simple rule does not clarify exactly which key to press, but it does allow the participant to prepare to respond with a given hand. Indeed Miller (1982) was able to show that being able to prepare such a response conferred an RT (i.e., reaction time) advantage – that is, knowing which hand to use facilitated the speed of making a particular finger key press. Comparisons here

were with a different-hand condition such as where the key assignment was *s*/key *1*, *t*/key *2*, *S*/key *3* and *T*/key *4*. Responses were generally slower in the different-hand condition than in the same-hand condition.

The experiment was run under conditions in which participants were quicker to make the letter classification (letter *S* vs. *T*) than they were able to make the size judgement (i.e., the distinction between the upper- and lower-case letters). So the letter identity was resolved quicker than the size information and the assumption was that the preliminary perceptual analysis therefore delivered information about letter identity prior to letter size. Taken on its own, this result therefore suggested that, yes, a response could be prepared prior to the completion of stimulus recognition just like the concurrent and contingent model suggests. Participants were faster in making the letter judgement when a particular letter was associated with a given hand than when it was not.

However, there was a final twist to this story. Miller (1982) also examined cases where four separate letters were used (*M/N* vs. *U/V*). Now there was no difference in response speed across the same- and different-hand conditions. Participants were unable to prepare a response on the basis of '*M* or *N*' vs. '*U* or *V*'. So whereas response preparation effects were found when different letters were mapped onto different hands (*s/S* vs. *t/T*), and when letters were assigned to one hand (*U/V*) and numbers to the other (*4/9*), no such effects were found when four different letters were used (*M/N* vs. *U/V*) or when the characters (*U/4*) were mapped onto one hand and (*V/9*) were mapped onto the other. Collectively, therefore, the data qualify the claim that response preparation invariably begins before stimulus recognition is completed. More precisely, such response preparation is only possible under conditions where the route from stimulus to response involves the activation of a mental category that itself maps onto the response – for example, *S* vs. *T*, *letter* vs. *number*.

So as long as the preliminary perceptual analysis activates a unique code (it's a letter) that is mapped directly onto a response (press a left key), then response preparation can begin before stimulus recognition is complete. Clearly this state of affairs cannot take place if response preparation can only begin once the stimulus has been fully analysed and as such the data stand in contrast to the simple sequential model as specified in Figure 9.1. It is as if the stage of response output can be initiated even though prior stages have yet to run to completion. This is not to argue that the ordering of the stages is at fault, but merely that the stages do not

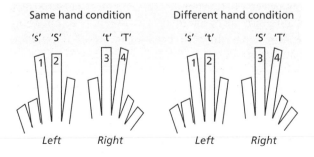

**Figure 9.2 Schematic representation of the response mappings used by Miller (1982)**

have to run to completion before the next can begin. Bad news for the neighbour's cat, then.

So even though the very strict notion of a completely sequential stages-of-processing account such as that shown in Figure 9.1 appears not to be fully supported, it nevertheless does provide a useful framework for thinking about other general issues in attention and performance. What the data show is that there are some clear examples where response preparation can usefully begin before a complete analysis of the stimulus has been completed, but this ought not to be taken to undermine the general framework completely. It is still useful to accept that certain processes operate prior to others, and that the manner in which such processes are organised temporally is fundamental. For instance, some form of stimulus analysis must take place prior to stimulus identification, and in the absence of wild guessing, identification must operate prior to decision and response. This is not to argue that each stage must run to completion prior to the next but merely that accepting some form of temporal ordering is a useful starting point for theorising.

### Pinpoint question 9.2

What enables response preparation under conditions where responses to *X* and *Y* are mapped onto the left hand and *1* and *2* are mapped onto the right hand, but not where *X* and *1*, and *Y* and *2* are mapped onto different hands?

## Further analyses of dual-task performance

Thinking about stages of processing and how such stages are sequenced leads naturally on to the question of whether fundamentally we can act on more than one thing at once. Now the critical question that has been addressed is, 'Is it possible to prepare and execute more than one decision/response at once?' and it is to this that discussion now turns. Is it possible to answer the phone, open the front door and get the broom out all at the same time?

Striking examples have been discussed, in the previous chapter, of how performance on two concurrently demanding tasks can be accomplished apparently without interference (e.g., reading a music score while verbal shadowing as documented by Allport et al., 1972). At a superficial level, such demonstrations may be taken as evidence that humans are quite capable of doing several things at once: the evidence can be interpreted as showing evidence of **multi-tasking**, or more particularly, of **time-sharing**. Multi-tasking/time-sharing here can be understood as being able to do more than one thing at once. However, we need to be much more specific and address the issue more carefully. For example, and in terms of the stages-of-processing account in Figure 9.1, we can pose the question, 'Can the processes associated with a given stage be devoted to more than one stimulus at once?' Answering 'Yes' to this question implies that some form of time-sharing is taking place such that more than one stimulus is being dealt with at the same time and by the same stage of processing.

The examples of proficient dual-task performance noted above (such as reading a music score while verbal shadowing) seem to suggest quite strongly that there is much flexibility in each of the stages of processing outlined in Figure 9.1, and indeed in this simple account, the idea of **parallel processing** is allowed because two different stages can be activated at once. For example, the work of Miller (1982) suggests that operations at both the stimulus encoding stage and the response organisation/execution stage can run concurrently. As we will see, though, the bigger issue is whether processing of different things can proceed at the same time at the same stage: is it possible to organise two different responses at the same time?

Some caution is warranted because it is very difficult to be clear about whether examples of proficient dual-task performance do actually provide cast-iron evidence of time-sharing or whether the data are more readily interpreted in terms of rapid **task-switching** (Broadbent, 1982; Pashler & Johnston, 1989). For example, given the luxurious situation of having two TVs in the same room tuned to different stations, would we really be able to watch two programmes at the same time (time-sharing) or would we instead quickly switch between watching one and then the other (task-switching), creating the illusion of watching both 'at once'. Indeed, Pashler (1998), in attempting to get a better handle on the issues, has discussed a different form of dual-task situation to those to which we have hitherto been introduced. In this alternative paradigm, it is not continuous performance at concurrent tasks that has been examined, but performance on discrete trials using two separate tasks. By this view, it is only by examining performance on the two tasks, at a very fine-grained level, that a much better understanding will be achieved. The evidence has been used to try to decide between the time-sharing and task-switching views of processing. We'll take a look at this now.

## Counting the cost: Alzheimer's disease and dual-task performance

In addition to examining dual-task performance in sprightly undergraduates, it is also interesting to examine how the elderly perform under such circumstances, which in turn helps us to understand how the cognitive system changes as a result of age. According to a report published in 2007 by the US Alzheimer's Association (www.alz.org), approximately one in eight people over the age of 65 show signs of Alzheimer's disease, which is a neurodegenerative disease characterised by a slow decline of cognitive functioning. Crossley, Hiscock and Foreman (2004) suggest that tasks susceptible to the early stages of Alzheimer's should be those that are highly demanding on the cognitive system, whereas more automatic tasks should show greater resilience to the disease.

Fourteen individuals with Alzheimer's disease were compared with 14 age- and gender-matched participants. Under single-task conditions, participants were asked to complete a 'tapping task' in which key presses were required as fast as possible using alternating fingers on one hand, and one of two 'speaking tasks'. One of the tasks (speech repetition) required participants to repeat the months of the year and was thought to involve low levels of cognitive effort. The second speaking task (speech fluency) required participants to name as many words beginning with a particular letter and as such was thought to involve greater cognitive effort.

Alzheimer and control individuals also completed concurrent task conditions in which either the tapping task or one of the speaking tasks was emphasised as being more important. Performance in the concurrent condition was examined relative to single-task performance.

Tapping rate decreased in the concurrent condition relative to the single-task condition, although interesting differences between the groups were also observed. During speech repetition, both Alzheimer and control participants showed a reduction in tapping rate of the same magnitude. However, when the speech fluency task was carried out, the Alzheimer group showed a significantly greater decrement in tapping rate relative to controls.

The data support the idea that dividing attention across two concurrent tasks is exacerbated in individuals with Alzheimer's disease only when the tasks place a large demand on the cognitive system. Crossley et al. (2004) argued that dual-task performance could contribute to the early diagnosis of Alzheimer's. The work also points to ways in which an individual's environment can be tailored to the needs of the patient so that they will be able to function effectively.

*Source*: Crossley, M., Hiscock, M., & Foreman, J. B. (2004). Dual-task performance in early stage dementia: Differential effects for automatized and effortful processing. *Journal of Clinical and Experimental Neuropsychology, 26*, 332–346.

input processes Early stage of processing associated with the initial physical registration and encoding of the stimulus. It is also referred to as early or peripheral processes or pre-bottleneck processes.

late processes Processes associated with decision/response stages of processing.

output processes Processes associated with physically making a response.

sequential stage model of processing A view of stimulus processing in which intervening stages of processing are ordered. In strictly serial accounts each stage must run to completion before the next stage can begin.

multi-tasking Being able to do more than one thing, at a cognitive level, at the same time.

time-sharing Where one stage of processing is dealing with more than one stimulus at the same time.

parallel processing Within some form of information processing system, allowing the system to process more than one stimulus at once.

task-switching Changing from doing one task to doing another.

## Studies of the psychological refractory period

The study of the **psychological refractory period (PRP)** has a long history – Kahneman (1973) traced the introduction of the phrase to a paper by Telford (1931)

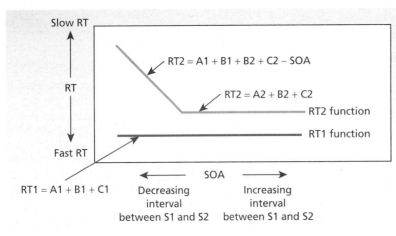

**Figure 9.3 Schematic representation of idealised data from a PRP experiment**
RT1 is unaffected by the interval between task 1 and task 2 (i.e., the SOA). RT2, however, shows a classic PRP effect. At the shorter SOAs RT2 falls linearly as the interval increases. After a critical time point, RT2 falls no more and ends up being equivalent to the case when task 2 is carried out in isolation from task 1.

– and it is clear that there is currently a resurgence of interest in the topic, triggered primarily by the work of Pashler (as reviewed in 1998). Initially, it is important therefore to establish exactly what the PRP refers to. We will start with a basic observation and arrive at an operational definition.

The basic phenomenon arises when participants are asked to make two sequential responses to two different tasks – a task 1 and a task 2 – in quick succession. Task 1 might be to press one key when a tone is heard and task 2 to press another key when a flashed light is seen. If the delay between the tasks is long enough, then there is no reason to assume that performance in either task will be impaired relative to when each task is performed in isolation. However, evidence for the PRP arises when delay between the tasks is reduced. As Kahneman (1973, p. 162) noted, when the delay between the critical stimuli on task 1 and task 2 is reduced to about 0.5 s then responses to task 2 can be dramatically slowed. Bringing the two tasks closer together results in slowing to task 2. Figure 9.3 provides an illustration of this general case and allows us to introduce some general PRP notation.

S1 refers to the imperative stimulus on task 1 – the stimulus that is associated with task 1 and demands a response. Similarly, S2 refers to the imperative stimulus for task 2. Although it is possible to define the temporal spacing between the tasks in various ways, it is now commonplace to use the *stimulus onset asynchrony* (SOA) or the time from the onset of the first stimulus (S1) to the onset of the second stimulus (S2) as the critical variable. The typical PRP experiment is run under RT conditions so although accuracy measures are taken, prime interest is with speed of response. RT1 refers to the average RT for task 1 as measured from the onset of S1, and RT2 refers to the average RT for task 2 as measured from the onset of S2.

Although Figure 9.3 provides idealised data in schematic form, Figure 9.4 provides a real example of performance in a PRP experiment. The actual data are taken from the first experiment reported by Broadbent and Gregory (1967b). Participants were sitting centrally facing an array containing a distant red warning light and a nearer row of four white lights. The four lights were divided into a left-hand side pair and right-hand side pair, so in this respect the experiment is reminiscent of the Miller (1982) studies. Each light had an associated response key so numbering the lights left to right *1–4*, respectively, gave rise to a corresponding pair of response keys on the left (key *1* and *2*) and a pair of response keys on the right (key *3* and *4*). In one condition task 1 was simply to press key *1* when light *1* was switched on and key *2* when light *2* was switched on. Task 2 was to press the alternative appropriate key when light *3* or *4* was switched on. Given that the lateral order of position of the lights mapped onto the same lateral order of the response keys, this situation was referred to as having **compatible S–R relations**.

As Figure 9.4 shows, SOA varied from the simultaneous presentation of S1 and S2 (that is, an SOA of 0 s) to a delay of just over 0.5 s (i.e., 550 ms) between S1 and S2. Within a block of trials the SOA was held constant and participants were told to respond as quickly as possible to S1 and to try their best and then respond to S2. The first general result, which is typical of many such experiments, was that RT1 was essentially unaffected by the delay between S1 and S2. This shows that participants were able to follow the experimental instructions and prioritise task 1 responding. Even when two lights were presented concurrently (i.e., the SOA was equal to 0), the participants were able to make first the task 1 response and then the task 2 response. In contrast, there was a very marked effect of SOA on the responses to task 2. The more conventional

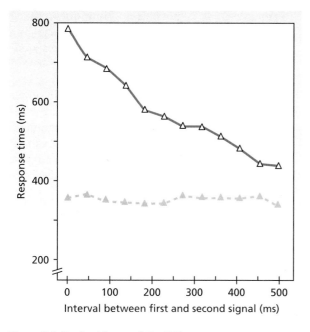

**Figure 9.4  Real evidence of the PRP**
Data from Broadbent and Gregory (1967b). RT1 (solid triangles) is unaffected by the time between task 1 and task 2. RT2 (unfilled triangles) declines in a linear fashion as the SOA between the tasks is increased. Eventually RT2 levels out as the delay between the tasks is increased dramatically.

*Source*: Broadbent, D. E., & Gregory, M. H. P. (1967b). Psychological refractory period and the length of time required to make a decision. *Proceedings of the Royal Society of London, Series B, 168*, 181–193 (fig. 3, p. 189). London: The Royal Society. Reproduced with permission.

way to discuss this is that as the SOA between the tasks is shortened, RT2 is lengthened: as the delay between the tasks is reduced responses to S2 slow down. This is one critical signature of the PRP effect.

Much has been taken away from this marked task 2 slowing. It is almost as if the second response must wait until the system clears itself of critical processes concerning task 1. At the very least the second response is postponed until the system can begin to cope with the response organisation for task 2. It is this notion of response postponement (the task 2 slowing) that lies at the heart of central bottleneck accounts of the PRP. There appears to be a 'lock-out' period that arises when the system is dealing with one stimulus (the task 1 stimulus), and during this time it simply cannot deal with any other stimulus (the task 2 stimulus). The duration of this lock-out is known as the *psychological refractory period* (PRP). The presence of the PRP has been taken to provide evidence for the idea that, fundamentally, the processing system operates in a serial manner: there is a basic constraint

in not being able to organise more than one response at once. So while a response is being organised for S1, response organisation for S2 cannot proceed, hence the slowing witnessed in RT2.

## Understanding the PRP

In order to understand the psychological refractory period, we'll have to introduce some relatively simple formulae – but don't worry, we'll work through these pretty slowly. Central to theoretical accounts of the PRP is the assumption that any task can be decomposed into three components that reflect separate and sequential stages of processing. These are (i) pre-bottleneck processing (indexed by A), (ii) central or bottleneck processing (indexed by B) and (iii) post-bottleneck processing (indexed by C).

As Figure 9.3 shows, the RT on a given trial is assumed to reflect, primarily, the sum of A, B and C. More formally, RT1, the RT for task 1, is given by:

$$RT1 = A1 + B1 + C1 \tag{9.1}$$

The A duration reflects the time taken by the perceptual analysis stage, the B duration reflects the time taken by the limited capacity channel (i.e., central processing), and the C duration reflects the time taken by the later response-related stages. What is being assumed here is that on every trial the total RT reflects the sum of the durations of three sequential stages. Although the account makes no claims about each stage running to completion prior to the next, it does assume that the stages are sequential and that the bottleneck stage cannot be bypassed.

The RT function for task 2 comprises two parts – an early sloping part and a later flat part (see Figure 9.3). Explaining this function is more complicated than for the RT1 functions because it seems to reflect two components rather than one. Before we progress much further it is probably best to frame the discussion in terms of a simple analogy. In this regard the overall processing system can be seen to be akin to the operations involved in visiting the bank. The presence of the PRP (the task 2 slowing) suggests that there is a sense in which the tasks have to form a sort of queue and, by analogy, the different tasks may be taken to correspond with customers in a bank. Here the assumption is that the central processes operate as a single bank teller and, because this bank teller is extremely conscientious, only one customer (task) can be dealt with at once – other customers have to form an orderly queue and wait until the bank teller is free. Each customer (or task) is dealt with sequentially, one at a time.

Using this analogy, each task contains three components: (A) the pre-bottleneck stage – entering the bank and waiting in the queue; (B) the bottleneck stage – time spent with the bank teller; and (C) the post-bottleneck stage – the time between finishing with the bank teller and leaving the bank. So in the same way that the reaction time for task 1 (RT1) reflects the times to complete A1, B1 and C1, so too we can think of RT2 as being associated with times to complete A2, B2 and C2. However, given that task 1 can add delays to task 2 responding – particularly when the onset of task 1 and task 2 are close together (i.e., at short SOAs) – RT2 is typically more than just the sum of A2, B2 and C2. To see why this might be so, we need to consider four principles that describe the central bottleneck account of processing as put forward by Pashler (1994).

**Pinpoint question 9.3**

**What are the three stages associated with the completion of a task according to a central bottleneck account of processing (Pashler, 1994)?**

## Pashler's (1994) four principles of the central bottleneck theory

**Principle 1.** Any delay incurred in the A and B components of task 1 will slow down RT1 and RT2 to the same degree.

In terms of the bank analogy, if customer 1 dawdles before moving forward to the counter, then this time penalty applies equally to customer 1 and customer 2. The time that the first customer spends with the teller corresponds to the duration of the lock-out (the PRP). However, this only holds for short SOAs between the tasks, as Figure 9.3 shows. At long SOAs both tasks can be completed, as if in isolation, as long as the delay between S1 and S2 allows S1 to clear the bottleneck before S2 is ready to proceed.

**Principle 2.** Any delay incurred in the C (post-bottleneck) component for task 1 has no consequences for task 2.

If customer 1 takes a long time to leave the bank after having moved away from the bank teller's window, then there is no effect on the total time spent by customer 2 in the bank.

**Principle 3.** It is possible to slow down the A component of task 2 (the pre-bottleneck stage) by a certain amount without introducing a corresponding slowing in the task 2 response.

This principle is considered thoroughly below. In simple terms, if customer 1 is engaged with the bank teller and customer 2 has to wait, then the time customer 2 has to wait is known as **slack time**. Customer 2 can get up to anything during this slack time and it may be that they are able to fill out one cheque or indeed five during this slack time (cheque filling-in is a pre-bottleneck – pre-bank teller operation). Given that customer 1 is taking so much time, it doesn't matter whether you have one cheque or five to fill in, you still have to wait and so the difference in time to do the cheque filling-in is not reflected in the total time you spend in the bank. Of course this is only true if you can fill in the five cheques before customer 1 moves off.

**Principle 4.** Adding any delay to the B or C component of task 2 will have no consequences for task 1 performance and will reveal a constant slowing of RT2 for all SOAs.

If customer 2 takes some time with the teller and/or delays in leaving the counter having been dealt with by the teller, then this will have no consequences for how long the first customer spends in the bank.

What these four principles do is set the foundational predictions for the central bottleneck account of processing.

### Predictions concerning RT2

In formalising the queuing idea Pashler and Johnston (1989) defined RT2 thus (deep breath now):

$$RT2 = \max(A1 + B1 + SW, SOA + A2) + B2 + C2 - SOA \qquad (9.2)$$

Here the 'max( . . . )' notation with all that stuff in the brackets simply means: take whichever is longer, either 'A1 + B1 + SW' or 'SOA + A2'. As an aside, SW is defined as the time to switch between task 1 and task 2 and although this may be considerable we can, for simplicity, assume that it is a constant, take it out of the equation and discuss it no further. Happily, we can think more clearly about the time to respond in task 2 in terms of two simpler equations. One version of equation (9.2) applies at short SOAs and a different one applies at long SOAs. One version of the equation describes the sloping part of the task 2 function (at shorter SOAs) in Figure 9.3 whereas the other version of the equation describes the flat part of the function (at longer SOAs).

At short SOAs (the sloping part of the function) RT2 is given by:

$$RT2 = A1 + B1 + B2 + C2 - SOA \qquad (9.3)$$

In this case (A1 + B1) is a longer duration than (SOA + A2) and as a consequence RT2, in part, reflects the pre-bottleneck (A1) and bottleneck (B1) components of task 1. Why? Well, customer 2 has to wait for customer 1 to leave the queue (A1) and finish with the teller (B1). Customer 2 then has to deal with the teller (B2) and then leave the bank (C2). The '− SOA' term refers to the fact that we need to measure RT2 from the onset of the second task when S2 is presented and not from when S1 is presented.

In terms of our banking analogy, this corresponds to the time at which the second customer enters the bank – not the time from which our first customer (S1) came in. So we need to subtract the time between the onset of the tasks (SOA) or the time between when the first customer joined the queue and when the second customer joined the queue. Indeed, as the SOA increases we have to take more and more away from the sum of the other components (A1 + B1 + B2 + C2). The time associated with pre-bottleneck, bottleneck and post-bottleneck processes remains the same, but the SOA is increasing, and since this value is subtracted from the sum, RT2 will decrease in a linear fashion as the SOA increases. For every 1 ms that the SOA increases, RT2 decreases by 1 ms. This is reflected in the sharp gradient for the RT2 function at the short SOAs.

At long SOAs, that is, when (SOA + A2) is a longer duration than (A1 + B1) (the flat part of the task 2 function – see Figure 9.3):

$$RT2 = SOA + A2 + B2 + C2 - SOA \qquad (9.4)$$

You can see that now the SOA cancels itself out and so we can write:

$$RT2 = A2 + B2 + C2 \qquad (9.5)$$

This reveals that, according to central bottleneck theory, at long SOAs task 2 responding is unaffected by the presence of task 1 (the line is flat – Figure 9.3). Since there are no components associated with task 1

in equation (9.5) (i.e., no A1, B1 or C1), it's all about task 2 now, hence the time to respond to task 2 should be the same as when it is carried out in isolation from task 1.

## Pinpoint question 9.4

According to central bottleneck theory (Pashler, 1994), what three components influence the reaction time of task 2 during short SOAs that do not play a role at longer SOAs?

The critical point in all of this is that only one task at a time can engage central processing, so if task 1 has access to the central processing component (the B component; the bank teller), task 2 has to wait until the B component is free. By instructing the participants to make sure that they respond to S1 before they respond to S2, the understanding is that S1 will engage central processing prior to S2: task 2 will therefore have to wait. B2 cannot begin until B1 is finished. If you are customer 2, then you are going to have to wait until customer 1 has moved away from the counter before you can engage with the teller. The B1 duration of task 1 (time with teller for task 1) cannot overlap with the B2 duration of task 2 (time with teller for task 2), because only one task can engage central (B) processes at once. As a consequence, the B1 and the B2 durations add together at the short SOAs and are reflected in RT2 – customer 2 has to hang around for customer 1 to move away from the counter. The time that customer 1 spends with the teller adds to the total time that customer 2 spends in the bank.

This waiting period (the slack time) can be estimated roughly from the negative gradient of the early portion of the RT2 function – how long is it before the RT2 line becomes flat? According to the bottleneck account, while (SOA + A2) is longer than (A1 + B1) the gradient of the RT2 function ought to be −1. In other words, every millisecond that task 2 is delayed relative to the bottleneck results in a millisecond saving in RT2. Ideally, do not enter the bank until the teller is free, otherwise you will have to wait and the wait will be determined by how long customer 1 takes with the teller.

Data most consistent with the central bottleneck theory would be where the RT2 function is as in Figure 9.3, comprising an initial linear function with a −1 slope (equation (9.3) applies) followed by a flat line (equation (9.5) applies). A different way to think about the −1 slope is that for the short SOAs, for every millisecond that task 1 engages the bottleneck,

1 millisecond is added to RT2. However, we must remember that humans are not automata, hence there will be variability in RTs and we should not be surprised if the data only approximate this state of affairs. For instance, the real data shown in Figure 9.4 provide only an approximate fit with the central bottleneck account. The initial slope is roughly −0.7 and this is followed by a gradual decline into an apparent plateau. We shall return to this point (and Figure 9.4) shortly because significant deviations from the −1 slope do not accord at all well with the central bottleneck theory (see Kahneman, 1973).

## Testing the principles of the central bottleneck account

As can perhaps now be appreciated, the central bottleneck account sets some fairly fundamental constraints on the ability to be able to do two things at once. Fundamentally, the idea is that the cognitive system, as defined by the central processes, can only service one task at once – only one individual may engage the bank teller at once. Hence mentally we really cannot do more than one 'thing' at once. However, as with any theory, the central bottleneck account stands or falls by how well the data fit with its predictions. Indeed, the worth of the theory must be gauged relative to the specificity of its predictions. Vague predictions are not much use because typically such predictions cannot be used to adjudicate between alternative accounts. In this regard one of the strengths of the central bottleneck account is that it provides very specific predictions about dual-task performance. The basic principles of central bottleneck theory give rise to the following predictions.

> **Prediction 1.** Any delay incurred in the A and B components of task 1 will slow down RT1 and RT2 to the same degree.

If the first bank customer engages in small talk before leaving the bank teller, then both customers (1 and 2) will be delayed in leaving the bank to the same extent. If we take Prediction 1, there is some supporting evidence, but it is also the case that this principle has not been rigorously tested. Some evidence is, incidentally, present in the experiment we have already introduced by Broadbent and Gregory (1967b). Participants had to make finger press responses to an array of flashing lights. Using the same basic experimental set-up and procedures they tested a second group of participants but now the participants were instructed to use

**incompatible S–R relations**. This means that now the light-to-key mappings were switched within the left and right pairs – light 1 pulses so press key 2; light 2 pulses so press key 1, and so forth. In using *incompatible S–R relations* the idea was to slow down the response selection stage of processing (so as to test other aspects of bottleneck accounts that we need not concern ourselves with here).

In addition, the probabilities of the two task 1 lights were changed so that one of the lights was switched on more often than the other. The idea was that responses to the frequent light ought to be executed faster than responses to the rare light. According to Pashler (1994, p. 224), stimulus probability is assumed to affect stimulus identification and response selection, and both are assumed to take place at or prior to bottleneck processes. The relevant data are shown in Figure 9.5. As can be seen from the figure, the difference in task 1 responding across the frequent and rare light conditions influenced task 2 responding. So a fast RT1

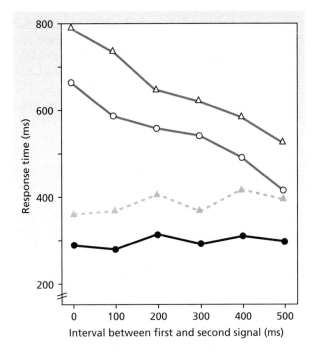

**Figure 9.5 Example of additive responding on task 2**
Data from Broadbent and Gregory (1967b). Filled circles: RTs to the faster alternative on task 1; filled triangles: RTs to slower alternative on task 1; unfilled circles: RTs to S2 after faster S1; unfilled triangles: RTs to S2 after slower S1.

*Source*: Broadbent, D. E., & Gregory, M. H. P. (1967b). Psychological refractory period and the length of time required to make a decision. *Proceedings of the Royal Society of London, Series B, 168*, 181–193 (fig. 4, p. 190). London: The Royal Society. Reproduced with permission.

was accompanied by a fast RT2 and a slow RT1 was accompanied by a slow RT2. Prediction 1 therefore has some empirical support.

**Prediction 2.** Any delay incurred in the C (post-bottleneck) component for task 1 has no consequences for task 2.

Prediction 2 has generated little interest in the literature, and although Pashler (1994, 1998) does cite some unpublished and supportive evidence, much more has been made of Prediction 3.

**Prediction 3.** It is possible to slow down the A component of task 2 (the pre-bottleneck stage) by a certain amount without introducing a corresponding slowing in the task 2 response.

Critical here are cases where the difficulty of task 2 is manipulated because the aim is to see how the effect of task 2 difficulty changes as a function of SOA. Common sense dictates that the more difficult version of task 2 should generally take more time to complete than the less difficult version of task 2. Recite the months of the year in chronological order, and now do it alphabetically! However, if we are to test Prediction 3, the effect of task 2 difficulty must be mapped out over SOAs. A primary aim is to see what the effect of changes in the duration of the pre-bottleneck (A2) stage has on RT2. In terms of our bank analogy: while the first customer is engaged with the bank teller, customer 2 can be filling out cheques. The question now is, 'What are the conditions under which customer 2 spends the same amount of time in the bank regardless of whether they fill out one cheque or several cheques?' (paraphrasing Pashler, 1994, p. 224). Understanding these states of affairs lies at the heart of PRP logic.

## Additivity and under-additivity on RT2

The basic idea is that we now need to examine various variables that will affect task 2 responding, and in particular we need to try to find a variable that will alter the pre-bottleneck (A2) stages of processing for task 2. The central bottleneck theory of processing makes very particular predictions about how RT2 will vary as SOA increases when the difficulty of the pre-bottleneck stages are also varied. To understand these predictions we need to introduce some more technicalities regarding additive and under-additive patterns of responding. Figure 9.6 illustrates the difference between an **additive pattern** of responding and an **under-additive pattern** of responding on task 2 performance. Figure 9.7 provides more details about the difference between an additive and an under-additive pattern of performance.

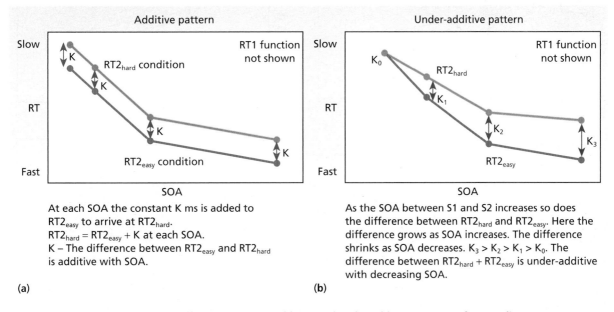

At each SOA the constant K ms is added to RT2$_{easy}$ to arrive at RT2$_{hard}$.
RT2$_{hard}$ = RT2$_{easy}$ + K at each SOA.
K – The difference between RT2$_{easy}$ and RT2$_{hard}$ is additive with SOA.

(a)

As the SOA between S1 and S2 increases so does the difference between RT2$_{hard}$ and RT2$_{easy}$. Here the difference grows as SOA increases. The difference shrinks as SOA decreases. $K_3 > K_2 > K_1 > K_0$. The difference between RT2$_{hard}$ + RT2$_{easy}$ is under-additive with decreasing SOA.

(b)

**Figure 9.6 An introduction to the difference between additive and under-additive patterns of responding on RT2**
In (a) an additive pattern on responding to task 2 is shown. At each SOA the constant K (ms) is added to RT2$_{easy}$ to arrive at RT2$_{hard}$. In this sense, the difference between RT2$_{easy}$ and RT2$_{hard}$ is additive with SOA for task 2.
In (b) an under-additive pattern on responding to task 2 is shown. As the SOA between S1 and S2 increases, so does the difference ($K_0$, $K_1$, $K_2$, $K_3$, respectively) between RT2$_{easy}$ and RT2$_{hard}$. The difference between RT2$_{easy}$ and RT2$_{hard}$ is under-additive with decreases in SOA.

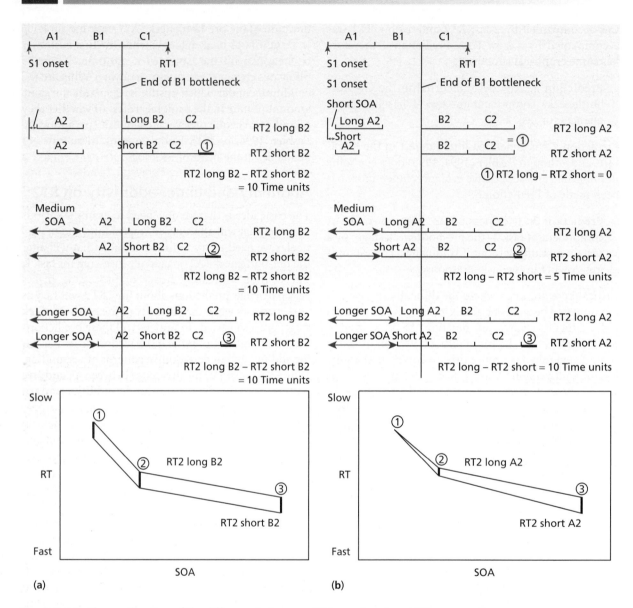

**Figure 9.7 Further explanation of the difference between additive and under-additive responding**
(a) Explanation of an additive pattern of responding on RT2.
(b) Explanation of an under-additive pattern of responding on RT2.

## Additivity

Here, an additive pattern (Figure 9.7a) reflects a constant time penalty that applies across all SOAs. In other words an additive pattern reveals that the effect of task 2 difficulty is the same right across the whole range of SOAs tested. The difference in RT between the difficult and easy task 2s is the same for all SOAs: this constant is *added to* the RT for the easy condition. According to central bottleneck theory, such an additive pattern is most likely to occur if a variable affects

the post-bottleneck stage of task 2 (i.e., the C2 stage). In our banking analogy, such a stage occurs after you (task 2) have finished with the bank teller and are about to leave the bank. So anything that slows you down in leaving the bank – such as bumping into someone for a chat – will alter the time of the C stage. Further relevant evidence for these claims is provided below. More formally Figure 9.7a shows the pattern of RT2s we would expect if we do find a variable that alters the duration of the post-bottleneck stage of processing for task 2.

## Under-additivity

More critically, and according to Prediction 3 of the central bottleneck account, there ought to be cases where an under-additive pattern of responding should also emerge when task 2 difficulty is varied (see Figure 9.7b). Here, an under-additive pattern is where the time penalty associated with the difficulty of task 2 gets smaller as the SOA between task 1 and task 2 decreases. Alternatively, the effect of task 2 difficulty increases as the SOA between task 1 and 2 increases. As Figure 9.7b shows, at the shortest SOA there is essentially no difference in RT for the easy and difficult task 2 conditions. However, as the SOA between task 1 and task 2 increases, so does the effect of task 2 difficulty. Indeed, at very long SOAs the effect of task 2 difficulty ought to be the same as when task 2 is tested on its own.

The basic scenario to consider is this: you (customer 2) move to the head of the queue but customer 1 is already with the bank teller. Now start the clock and begin timing, and stop the clock when customer 1 finishes at the counter – this is the slack period. Now let's think in terms of an easy task 2 and a difficult task 2. An easy task 2 is where you have one cheque to fill in and a difficult task 2 is where you have to fill in several cheques and one deposit slip. Both of these occur pre-bottleneck because you have to complete this paperwork prior to moving forward to the teller.

If in both the easy and difficult conditions you can complete all of the paperwork prior to customer 1 leaving the bank teller, then there will be no difference in your time spent in the bank across these two cases. You are still going to have to kill time (during the slack period) because customer 1 is engaged with the bank teller. This will most likely happen if there is only a short delay (a short SOA) between customer 1 moving towards the bank teller and you moving to the head of the queue.

A quite different pattern will emerge if you move to the head of the queue as customer 1 is about to leave the bank teller (at a long SOA). Now customer 1 is not holding you up to the same extent – there is either no slack time or very little slack time – and the difference between the easy condition and difficult condition will be reflected in your total time in the bank. It takes longer to do more paperwork in the difficult condition than the easy condition and this will now be reflected in the different amounts of time you spend in the bank across the two conditions. Even though the teller is now free, you still haven't filled in all five cheques and there is no point in moving forward until you have completed this paperwork. More formally, these predictions are spelt out in Figure 9.7b.

Let us concentrate on performance across two conditions: (i) an easy task 2 in which the corresponding A2 component is relatively short, and (ii) a difficult task 2 in which the corresponding A2 component is relatively long.

As long as both short and long A2 components complete before task 1 bottleneck processes are complete, then there should be no difference in RT2 across the easy and difficult conditions – the difference between these conditions is located at the pre-bottleneck stage to task 2 processing and this is absorbed into the slack time. As Figure 9.7b shows, this will typically take place at the shortest SOAs – there is no effect of task 2 difficulty at the short SOAs. Critically, though, if the impact of task 2 difficulty is located at the pre-bottleneck stage of processing, then as the SOA is increased, the difference across the easy and difficult conditions should begin to emerge.

This notion of an under-additive pattern fits most comfortably with having uncovered a variable that selectively operates at a pre-bottleneck stage of processing. Indeed, as McCann and Johnston (1992) pointed out, if a variable gives rise to an under-additive pattern of task 2 responding, then it must be having its effect at a pre-bottleneck stage of processing. In contrast, if the effect is additive then this suggests that the variable operates at or beyond the bottleneck. Data shown in

### For example . . .

You're making dinner for yourself and a loved one, and you're weighing up the virtue of either a couple of TV dinners or a freshly prepared romantic meal for two. Your flat-mate already has something in the oven (the central bottleneck stage, B, the oven, is engaged), so the pre-bottleneck stage (A) here refers to the extent to which you can prepare your meal before the oven becomes available. An easy A2 component would simply be a case of piercing the plastic film, whereas a hard A2 component would require (although certainly not be limited to) peeling the carrots, washing the potatoes, wrapping the fish in tin-foil, lighting the candles, opening the white wine . . .

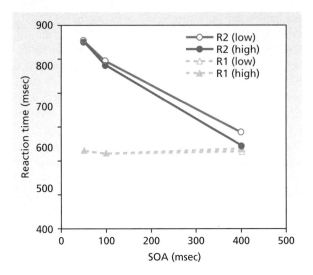

**Figure 9.8 An actual example of an under-additive pattern of responding on RT2 (taken from Pashler & Johnston, 1989)**
Various RT1s are shown in dashed and dotted lines. RT2s are shown in solid lines picked out by circles. Task 2 difficulty was manipulated by altering the contrast of S2 with a high contrast S2 being easier to respond to than a low contrast S2. At short SOAs there is no effect of this task 2 difficulty variable but at longer SOAs the effect is pronounced. This is consistent with the idea that the effect of the contrast manipulation was located at an early pre-bottleneck stage of processing.

*Source*: Pashler, H. E., & Johnston, J. C. (1989). Chronometric evidence for central postponement in temporally overlapping tasks. *The Quarterly Journal of Experimental Psychology, 41A*, 19–45 (fig. 3, p. 31). Reproduced with permission of Taylor & Francis.

Figure 9.8 reveal an under-additive relation and are taken from the first experiment reported by Pashler and Johnston (1989).

In task 1 participants made key press responses to the pitch of a tone (key 1 high pitch/key 2 low pitch). In task 2 participants identified a single letter (A, B or C) when each letter was mapped onto its own response key. Participants made task 1 responses with one hand and task 2 responses with the other hand. In the present context the main task 2 variable of interest was the visual intensity of the displayed letter. To make the letter harder or easier to see, it was presented against a black background and presented in grey (creating something called low contrast) or white (creating something called high contrast). Think of the high contrast conditions as the easy task 2 and the low contrast conditions as the difficult task 2.

The effect of stimulus contrast was taken to reflect something about the early stimulus encoding (pre-

bottleneck) stage of processing (see Figure 9.1). On this understanding that differences in letter contrast would reflect relatively early stimulus encoding operations, the idea was that this factor ought to reveal an under-additive pattern with SOA. As Figure 9.8 shows, the data fit perfectly with this general idea and it can be concluded that stimulus contrast has its effects prior to any processing bottleneck.

**Prediction 4.** Adding any delay to the B or C component of task 2 will have no consequences for task 1 performance and will reveal a constant slowing of RT2 for all SOAs.

Any delay that occurs at a post-bottleneck stage of task 2 processing will slow down RT2 but have no effect on RT1. You (task 2) leave the bank teller, notice a friend, and go over to talk to them before you leave the bank. Here a study by McCann and Johnston (1992) is particularly relevant. In the critical experiment for task 1 participants had to make a speeded verbal response to the presentation of a tone – they were to respond 'high' if the tone was of higher pitch than a reference tone and 'low' if it was lower. The reference tone was presented first for 500 ms, there was a 300 ms pause and then the target tone was presented for 500 ms. Task 2 was more complex. Participants had now to respond to the size of a presented rectangle or triangle. Each shape demanded a single key press from one of three designated keys on the computer keyboard. For instance the keys 'Z', 'X' and 'C' were assigned to the rectangle and the ';', '.' and '/' keys were assigned to the triangle. In addition there could be an ordered mapping of the keys onto the sizes in that increasingly larger sizes of shape were associated with increasingly rightward keys (for the rectangle, Z for small, X for middle and C for large) or there could be an arbitrary mapping of the keys onto the sizes (for the rectangle again, Z for large, X for small and C for middle).

Critically the understanding was that the difference between the ordered and arbitrary conditions would reflect on a difference in the difficulty of the response organisation stage of task 2. The B2 duration in the arbitrary condition ought to take longer than that in the ordered condition. Following Prediction 4, any additional time penalty ought to be the same across all SOAs and any such RT2 slowing should have no concomitant effect on RT1. There should be an additive effect of task 2 difficulty with SOA. As Figure 9.9 shows, the data from the McCann and Johnston experiment confirmed both aspects of Prediction 4. → See 'What have we learnt?', page 327.

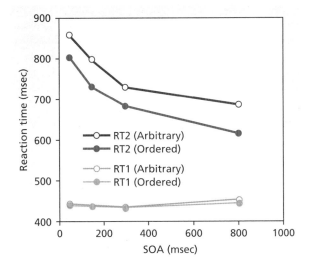

**Figure 9.9 An actual example of data showing an additive pattern on task 2 responding (taken from McCann & Johnston, 1992)**

In this case the task 2 difficulty was manipulated by varying the response mapping used. This variable was assumed to operate at or after the bottleneck stage. As can be seen, the more difficult task 2 takes a constant additional amount of time to complete than the easy task 2, at all SOAs.

*Source*: Pashler, H. E. (1998). *The psychology of attention* (fig. 6.7, p. 285). Cambridge, Massachusetts: The MIT Press. Reproduced with permission.

## Pinpoint question 9.5

**According to central bottleneck theory (Pashler, 1994), if you increase the post-bottleneck processing of task 1, what happens to the reaction time for task 2?**

**psychological refractory period (PRP)** The amount of temporal lock-out that occurs while one stimulus engages central (so-called bottleneck) processes.

**compatible S–R relations** Cases where the meaning or physical position of a stimulus maps directly onto the physical position of a response. A stimulus on the left of the display is assigned to the compatible left response.

**slack time** In PRP studies, the time the second task has to wait before the first task has cleared the central bottleneck.

**incompatible S–R relations** Cases where the meaning or physical position of a stimulus does not directly map onto the physical position of a response. For example, stimuli on the right of a display are mapped to a left response key.

**additive pattern** In the context of the PRP, the case where the same effect of task a difficulty is constant for all SOAs tested.

**under-additive pattern** In the context of the PRP the case where the effect of task a difficulty increases as SOA increases.

**response organisation** Stages of processing that concern the planning of the appropriate actions for a response.

## → What have we learnt?

From the review of the literature contained here, an impression might be that the evidence is unequivocally supportive of the central bottleneck theory. In describing the logic of the central bottleneck theory, however, we have simply amassed and described data that help make the points for us. As we shall see, there are some difficult and challenging data, and controversies abound. We will address some of the points of contention as discussion proceeds, but it is nevertheless true that there is an impressive and growing body of evidence that does converge on the central bottleneck theory. This is not to say that the theory applies to all cases, but merely that there is much evidence to suggest that certain tasks have picked on a processing constraint that currently is best interpreted as being a structural bottleneck. Such a profound processing constraint severely limits our ability to act on more than one stimulus at once.

Nevertheless, we need to be clearer about what the central bottleneck might actually be. Different theorists have used the notion of a central bottleneck to refer to a possible constraint at different processing stages. In the early literature analogies were drawn with Broadbent's original 1958 filter theory: The PRP reflects the operation of the serial P system (see Chapter 8). However, as Pashler and Johnston (1989) pointed out, in the 1958 theory the central bottleneck was taken to be a limitation in the number of stimuli that can be *identified* at any one moment. In contrast, in the PRP literature the critical bottleneck was taken to reflect a limitation in the later stages of decision and response selection (Welford, 1952). So within this context, the understanding is that the central bottleneck reflects a constraint concerning decision/response selection (Pashler, 1998) and the post-bottleneck processes concern response execution/production (Navon &

▶

Miller, 2002). By this view, it is as though problems exist in attempting to respond to more than one stimulus at once, and according to this form of bottleneck theory, it is impossible to organise more than one response at once. Stimulus identification occurs pre-bottleneck and, according to central bottleneck theory, the fundamental constraint is in **response organisation** (i.e., decision/response selection; alternatively, linking the stimulus with its correct response). There is sound evidence that the central bottleneck resides at some form of decision/response selection stage of processing. An interesting question remains over whether there is also a bottleneck in not being able to identify more than one stimulus at once.

At the time of writing, there is a large and growing literature that is based on PRP logic. Indeed, as discussed above, the PRP paradigm is an apparently powerful empirical tool because it provides a means for determining the locus of where, in the chain of internal processes, a variable is having its effects. In much of the relevant work in the twentieth century a considerable amount of time and effort was spent in trying to link changes in $d'$ or sensitivity with perceptual (pre-bottleneck) mechanisms and changes in $\beta$ or response bias with post-perceptual (post-bottleneck) mechanisms (see Chapters 5 and 6). In a complementary fashion the PRP paradigm promises to provide converging evidence on these issues. Additive patterns of a variable with SOA suggest a post-bottleneck (late) locus, whereas under-additive patterns suggest a pre-bottleneck (early) locus. Maybe some further progress could be made by systematically linking measures of these signal detection theory parameters with performance in PRP tasks?

## Standing back from the central bottlenecks

### Capacity sharing?

Despite the emphasis that has been placed on the central bottleneck account of processing, it would be remiss not to also discuss evidence of **capacity sharing** (indeed Kahneman, 1973, provided a rather scathing attack on the early evidence for central bottleneck accounts) which does not sit so comfortably with the central bottleneck account. Not all of the experimental data accord well with the strict ideas about lock-out and queuing as described in the theory (see Navon & Miller, 2002). As a consequence the idea of capacity sharing has been raised (a multi-tasking bank teller? Can it be true?). For instance, in embracing the standard PRP logic as set out above, Tombu and Jolicœur (2003, 2005) provided a well-defined, capacity sharing theory known as the central capacity sharing (CCS) model which assumes that processing is limited by the capacity of some central stages.

Unlike bottleneck accounts, however, in the CCS model different concurrent tasks are able to engage central processes at the same time. As discussed previously (see last chapter), this competition for resources may result in a slowing of both tasks (a dual-task decrement is found). As processing capacity is limited, shared processing eventuates in a lengthening of both RT1 and RT2. Importantly, though, the degree to which central resources are allocated to task 1 can be varied; so under some circumstances the system may allocate all processing resources to task 1 before continuing with task 2 (in other words, the standard bottleneck model is a special case of the more general capacity sharing model). In other circumstances, the system may allocate some central resources to task 2 while it is still engaged with task 1, slowing down processing of both tasks. Think of it this way: both customers 1 and 2 are standing at the counter and the bank teller is trying to deal with both at once.

More particularly, in the typical PRP paradigm, participants are specifically told to prioritise task 1 and to make sure to respond to S1 prior to making a response to S2. Under such conditions, and given that participants can follow these instructions, then there may well be no evidence of capacity sharing. RT1s therefore will show little effect of SOA and little effect of any manipulation of the difficulty of task 2. Evidence for capacity sharing therefore arises when RT1 does slow with decreases in SOA. As Tombu and Jolicœur (2003, p. 9) have stated, the CCS model predicts that 'RT1 at short SOAs will be larger than RT1 at long SOAs . . . The larger the proportion of central processing allocated to Task 1 . . . the smaller the SOA effect.' In addition capacity sharing may also be taking place when the increase in RT2 with decreases in SOA is considerably less than −1. Under these circumstances the trade-off in responding to the two tasks is not entirely consistent with the strict queuing idea advanced in the central bottleneck theory. In this respect, the data from the Broadbent and Gregory (1967b) experiment are tantalising – remember their slope of −0.7 instead of the ideal −1.

More particularly, Tombu and Jolicœur (2003) did provide some evidence for capacity sharing when conditions were relaxed such that participants were free to respond either to S1 or S2 first. So clearly evidence for capacity sharing may arise when capacity sharing is encouraged, in the same way that the sequential responding was encouraged in PRP paradigms. Clearly much more work needs to be done because, at present, there is little understanding of the general conditions under which capacity sharing can take place – as Tombu and Jolicœur (2005) readily admitted! Nevertheless the importance of the PRP cannot be underestimated. To consolidate all of this, let's look at a concrete demonstration described by Levy, Pashler and Boer (2006).

## Pinpoint question 9.6

**The evidence for capacity sharing seems critically dependent on the task instructions used. What are these?**

capacity sharing The idea that multiple tasks may be able to share central processes at the same time.

## PRP and driving

Levy et al. (2006) were keen to find out whether evidence for the PRP could be found in a more realistic setting and therefore contrived a PRP experiment in which performance was assessed in a driving simulator. The simulator comprised a large visual display of the optic flow as viewed from the driving seat of an automatic transmission car. The optic flow was controlled by movements of a standard steering wheel, and operation of brake and accelerator pedals. Participants were literally asked to 'follow that car!' by tracking a lead car down a winding road (not exactly like *The French Connection*, but as close as any psychology experiment is ever going to come). The speed of the so-called lead car varied and illumination of its brake lights indicated that the (virtual) driver was applying the brakes.

Participants were instructed to follow the lead car and to apply their brakes whenever the lead car indicated braking. In PRP notation, the braking task was task 2. Task 1 was to indicate whether a brief auditory or visual signal (S1) was presented once or twice. Given the tight software control afforded by the simulator, the SOA between S1 (the brief stimulus) and S2 (the brake lights) was systematically varied. In addition performance was examined according to whether S1 was an auditory tone or a visual stimulus (a change in the colour of the rear windscreen of the lead car) and according to whether a verbal or manual task 1 response was needed.

The results clearly showed that time-to-brake data were influenced by the proximity of the two tasks. As the time between S1 and S2 shortened, the time to brake lengthened in a linear fashion as predicted by the central bottleneck theory (see Figure 9.3 and the sloping part of the RT2 function). More interesting, perhaps, is that when the data were subdivided into (i) the time to apply the brake, and (ii) the time to let the foot off the accelerator, the same slowing was evident in both data sets. In other words, the slowing arose at a stage prior to response initiation. Indeed further support for the central bottleneck theory came from the breakdown of the data according to the stimulus and response modality of task 1. Neither of these factors dramatically affected braking performance. Response slowing was the same regardless of whether S1 was presented as a sight or sound, and regardless of whether the participant made a manual or vocal response. In simple terms, and as Levy et al. (2006) concluded, 'performing a concurrent task can seriously impair driving even when the two tasks do not overlap in their sensory or response modalities' (p. 233).

The implications are clear: it is simply inadvisable to try to attempt to engage in anything other than driving when controlling a car in traffic. This means that trying to engage in any form of concurrent conversation ought not to be attempted when driving through traffic. The case against using a mobile phone while driving ought to be clear enough, but these additional data reveal how dangerous it can be to engage in any form of concurrent conversation. To try to make a case that a hands-free phone is a much safer option appears completely unfounded (see Research focus 8.3). The size of the PRP effect reported by Levy et al. (2006) revealed a delay in responding of around 174 ms as gauged by the difference in the braking RT at 350 ms SOA and 0 SOA between S1 and S2. This translates into slightly more than 16 ft when travelling at 65 mph. So if anyone needs to be reminded about

## → What have we learnt?

So far the discussion about performance limitations reflects profound constraints that exist when a person attempts to respond to two conflicting stimuli that occur within very close temporal proximity to one another. Indeed, of several studies that have examined this, when a PRP effect does occur, it remains robust even in the face of very extensive practice (see Ruthruff, Johnston & van Selst, 2001; van Selst, Ruthruff & Johnston, 1999). Therefore the claim that the PRP can be abolished with practice (see Schumacher et al., 2001; and Research focus 9.2) has not withstood more careful analysis (Tombu & Jolicœur, 2004; see also Ruthruff, Johnston, van Selst, Whitsell & Remington, 2003). Indeed the data from the Levy et al. (2006) study are very revealing in this regard. They tested only participants who had at least two years' driving experience yet evidence of a PRP effect still obtained. Participants

were therefore highly practised at the task and yet still the PRP constraint was revealed. The evidence therefore does seem to suggest that there is a very general constraint in not being able to respond effectively to more than one stimulus at once.

Now discussion turns to a quite different set of constraints that also exist but now such constraints are revealed when a person switches between competing task demands. Stated thus, the experiments do not sound that different from PRP experiments. One clear difference, though, is that, whereas the second stimulus can be presented before a response to the first has actually been made in PRP experiments, in task-switching experiments there never is any occasion in which this happens: the second stimulus is presented only once the opportunity to respond to the first has expired.

the practical applications of cognitive psychology to the real world, the existence of the PRP shows that disengaging from a concurrent conversation so as to brake may in fact mean the difference between life and death! → See 'What have we learnt?', above.

### Pinpoint question 9.7

Why is the use of a hands-free mobile phone just as bad as any other mobile phone while driving?

## Research focus 9.2

### Because practice makes . . . : PRP, practice and the elderly

It may come as little surprise to learn that as one gets older, certain things become more difficult: remembering telephone numbers, skydiving, understanding the difference between dub step and grime, that kind of thing. It also shouldn't be a shock to anybody on the basis of the literature we've been talking about in this chapter to guess that elderly people perform worse than younger individuals on PRP tasks. However, one of the reasons for becoming worse at anything may just be related to lack of practice – the chances are you'll do the majority of your skydiving while you're still young. Maquestiaux, Hartley and Bertsch (2004) wondered whether a similar explanation might be applied to PRP performance in older individuals and set out to test this.

Six younger (mean age = 24 years) and six older (mean age = 65 years) individuals were given two tasks to complete. Task 1 was verbal categorisation of high and low pitch tones. Since this study was conducted in France, the responses were 'haut' and 'bas', respectively. Task 2 was manual categorisation of an alphanumeric character from a target set of eight letters and numbers. Over several blocks, the interference of task 1 on task 2 decreased, and older adults during their last blocks of trials were generally shown to be as good as the younger adults were during their first block of trials. However, it was also noted that practice helped to reduce PRP inference more in the young than the old.

Maquestiaux et al. (2004) then considered what would happen to the degree of PRP interference in the same older adults if task 1 became simpler. To make the verbal categorisation of tones easier, participants were simply required to say whether a pair of tones was the same or different in pitch. Interestingly, a simpler task 1 led to a reduction in PRP interference but only for the older adults. The authors argued that this was due to elderly individuals requiring 'an extra task-switching stage before Task 2 response selection regardless of whether the Task 1 response mapping was more . . . or less . . . complex' (p. 661). In a final experiment, again using the same individuals, task 2 was made easier with respect to response demands in that participants now only had to categorise an alphanumeric character manually from a target set of two letters and numbers. Interestingly, making task 2 easier also reduced PRP interference in the older but not the younger individuals.

The data led to some interesting conclusions. It seems that ideas relating to performance during dual-task processing might be critically different between younger and older adults. That is, while both young and old are sensitive to a central bottleneck, as demonstrated by PRP interference, there are other stages related to response mapping that take longer for the older sample tested here. However, perhaps the most optimistic point to take from this paper is that, with enough practice, older people can perform as well as younger (albeit unpractised) individuals. So the upshot of all of this seems to be: keep on skydiving!

*Source*: Maquestiaux, F., Hartley, A. A., & Bertsch, J. (2004). Can practice overcome age-related differences in the psychological refractory period? *Psychology and Aging, 19*, 649–667.

## Task switching

Central to the discussion of the PRP effect is the idea that participants must complete two concurrent tasks and switch between them. In the context of a typical PRP experiment, the effort expended on the act of switching is of little interest because it is assumed to be, on average, the same on all trial types. More generally, a **task-switching cost** refers to the degree to which changing between different tasks impairs performance on either or both of the tasks relative to when no such switch occurs. There are some points of contact with a previous discussion here because, in a more primitive form, switching costs have been raised in relation to Broadbent's filter theory (see Chapter 8): in that context, performance costs were associated with having to switch the filter from one selection criterion to another. For instance, costs in switching the filter, say, from the red items to the items on the left, could result in a failure to recover information from the short-term store because enacting a switch was assumed to be a time-consuming operation. Remember, items in the short-term store decay away so anything that consumes vital processing time will increase the likelihood of information being lost from the store.

More generally, though, the task-switching literature is concerned with more complex cases in which quite different tasks are combined across different trials in an experiment. Each trial is associated with a different task and the different tasks are interleaved in a block of trials. Participants must therefore hold in mind two quite different sets of task instructions and must be able to switch between these as the experiment progresses. For example, you might be a booking agent at a holiday call centre. Unfortunately, the person who usually deals with complaints is away today (the rumour across the office is that it's stress related) and you've been asked to take bookings (task A) as well as complaints (task B), depending on the nature of the call. Task switching aims to detail exactly what the cognitive consequences are of handling a booking and then having to switch immediately to the gripe of an irate customer.

## Basic concepts and findings from the task-switching literature

Let us again take the simple case in which two tasks (A and B) are presented and on different trials participants must undertake either task A or task B. A **switch trial** pair occurs when task A is immediately replaced by task B (or vice versa). A **non-switch trial** pair occurs when task A is presented twice or task B is presented twice. In both cases, it is the second task in each pair that dictates whether or not the pair involves switch or non-switch. Typically, a task-switching cost is revealed by relatively poor performance on a switch trial relative to a non-switch trial. In addition, switch trials can either be predictable, such as when the sequence A B A B A B is repeated, or they can be unpredictable, when the A and B trials are randomly determined. In the latter case, and in advance of the trial, the participant is unable to predict which task will be presented next. As you can probably see, the number of manipulations that could be carried out to examine task switching is legion. However, we will limit this discussion to the major studies and the central results that have been found. What is clear, though, is that task-switching costs occur all over the place, and despite their seemingly clear-cut nature, there has been a quite remarkable amount of controversy over what is actually going on (see Monsell, 2003, for a review).

An often cited and important early study was carried out by Jersild (1927). On a given trial the participant was presented with a printed list of two-digit numbers. Task A was to subtract three from each number and task B was to add six to each number. Participants worked their way down the list by saying aloud the result of the computation. Performance was assessed in pure and alternating blocks of trials. In **pure blocks** either task A or task B was performed throughout (for example, either add, add, add, add, or subtract, subtract, subtract, subtract), whereas in **alternating blocks** they switched between tasks A and B across adjacent trials (for example, add, subtract, add, subtract). So in the latter case the participants had to keep track of what the tasks were and also when they were supposed to carry out each task. In comparing performance across the pure and alternating lists, Jersild (1927) found a notable task-switching cost (or alternatively an **alternation cost**) – participants were slower in responding in the alternating than the pure condition. According to Allport et al. (1994), the alternation cost amounted to several hundreds of milliseconds per list item (p. 422) when computed from the time to complete a given block of trials. As we will see, the techniques have moved on considerably since Jersild's report because now reaction times can be collected on a trial-by-trial basis.

In beginning to get a handle on what is going on here, we need to consider the concept of a **task set**. Each task has its own instructions and requirements and the participant must bear these in mind in order to carry out the appropriate task at the appropriate time. In the present context, though, the phrase *task set* refers to 'the set of cognitive operations required to effectively perform the task' (Gilbert and Shallice, 2002, p. 298). In the Jersild experiment, the task set for the addition task includes the set of cognitive operations that underlie mental addition, and for the subtraction task the task set includes the set of cognitive operations that underlie mental subtraction.

Given this characterisation, a reasonable first step is to assume that detailed aspects of performance in task-switching paradigms provide fairly direct indications of executive control (Monsell, 1996). Indeed in undertaking their research Allport et al. (1994) noted their preliminary understanding was that voluntary shifting of task was a 'prototypical function of intentional control' (p. 431). The assumption here is that the task-switching paradigm provides a window on the operations of cognitive control, insofar as different sets of mental processes are being (in a sense) 'turned on' and 'turned off' at will by the participants (just like an internal light switch). Task-switching costs therefore provide an index of the amount of mental effort that is needed in mentally moving between one task set and another – switching off one task set and switching on a different task set; we might call this the *executive control account* (Gilbert & Shallice, 2002). Although this all seems indisputable, we need to examine this basic assumption fairly carefully.

Here you'll notice that we are beginning to stray into the territory of how it is that we organise our thoughts and actions on a moment-to-moment basis. How do I bring to bear the appropriate set of mental operations at any given moment in time? While engaged in a game of cards, should I stop thinking about what's for tea or play my trump card after all? However, in terms of the first Jersild experiment just described, the participant not only had to add or subtract numbers when prompted by the occurrence of the next, they also had to remember which operation was appropriate on a given trial. There was nothing about the stimulus that cued which operation was appropriate, so clearly the participant had to maintain some form of running order so that they could follow the instructions accordingly.

Pashler (2000, after Fagot, 1994) has referred to this case as one in which **bivalent lists** are used. For bivalent lists the same items are associated with two different task sets – depending on whether it occurs on an odd or an even trial, *43* indicates either 'do addition' or 'do subtraction'. This is in just the same way that when the telephone rings in the call centre, there is nothing about the ring, in itself, that can tell us whether it is a potential booking or a grievance. In contrast, **univalent lists** are those in which each type of item is only associated with one sort of operation. For instance, Jersild carried out another experiment in which the same subtraction task was retained but task B was now to provide the antonym (semantic opposite) of a printed word ('BLACK' for 'WHITE', for example). So numbers defined the stimulus set for task A and words defined the stimulus set for task B. In an alternating list the items might be '43', 'LOVE', '15', 'BLACK', '35', 'HOT', and so on. Such is the nature of a univalent list of items.

According to the task-switching hypothesis, why should alternating blocks be harder than pure blocks?

One possible conclusion from Jersild's first experiment was that the alternation cost arose primarily because participants were confronted with bivalent lists and as such had to remember which task to enact on each trial. If this were true, then by getting rid of this additional burden (by using univalent lists) the cost should disappear. Hence in Jersild's subsequent experiment the participant was alleviated of having to remember which task to carry on each trial – see a number, subtract three; see a word, say the opposite. In line with this basic idea, Jersild found that the cost was actually abolished when univalent lists were used (in fact performance was actually better now with the univalent than the bivalent lists – something that is still not fully understood). Indeed this contrast between the significant alternation cost with bivalent lists and the lack of such a cost with univalent lists rules out any simple memory account of the basic alternation effect (i.e., the time penalty in alternating between different tasks (ABAB) vs. not (AAAA or BBBB)). Simply put, switching from task A to task B does not necessarily lead to a task-switching cost. For both bivalent and univalent lists, participants must retain two different task sets, yet the switch cost arose only with the bivalent lists. Clearly, therefore, something else must be going on, and this is where the notion of **task set reconfiguration** comes in. Maybe switch costs only arise when a task set reconfiguration is called for?

## Task set reconfiguration

According to Pashler (1998), a preliminary explanation of task switching concerns the notion of task set reconfiguration. It is accepted that for both bivalent and univalent lists there are two competing task sets. For every item (after the first) in a bivalent list, the participant must (in a sense) turn off the task set associated with the last item and turn on the task set associated with the next. In a nutshell, this is what is implied by the notion of task set reconfiguration.

Having run off one set of mental operations for task A, the system must now be reconfigured so that the task B mental operations can take place. As participants are forced to alternate between different tasks, they have to switch between different task sets. By one view, when the mental light switch is set in one position, this makes the subtract task set active, and when it is set in the other position, this makes the language task set active. In fact Rogers and Monsell (1995) introduced a different analogy – that of a railway network in which some control process switches the connections (the railway points) so that a particular route from stimulus to response is configured properly. The points outside Micklefield are switched so that a train travels appropriately from Leeds to York. To take a different route – Leeds to Selby – the points outside Micklefield now need to be switched and this will take some noticeable time.

Although a similar account might be given for performance with the univalent lists, it seems that more than task set reconfiguration is going on. With univalent lists, the responses associated with the two tasks are very different. For instance, each number demands a 'number' response and each word demands a 'word' response. As Pashler, Johnston and Ruthruff (2001) pointed out, with univalent lists there is little tendency now to produce the wrong response. With bivalent lists conflicting rules concerning response selection are involved, and it is therefore not possible to maintain a constant S–R mapping throughout a block of trials. By this view, particular difficulties arise when the different tasks can produce conflicts in mapping stimuli onto responses. Spector and Biederman (1976) put this a slightly different way, saying that switch costs are likely to be minimal if the stimulus acts as an unambiguous retrieval cue for the appropriate task set. The costs are minimal when the stimulus provides a very clear steer as to what the appropriate response should be (see Figure 9.10). So even though every switch trial calls for a task set reconfiguration such reconfiguration is minimal if the stimulus-to-response mapping does not change on every trial, for instance, when numbers retain their mappings throughout and words retain theirs.

Clearly, therefore, we need further clarity on the nature of the switching costs. For instance, given that task set reconfiguration is a time-consuming operation or set of operations, then we could predict that performance on switch trials should show a significant improvement as the time between the trials increases. Indeed, arguably, given sufficient time between trials, there should be no cost at all – as long as the task set

Eat

Stand on

Eat
Stand on

**Figure 9.10 Examples of stimuli that vary in their ambiguity regarding response**
In contrast to the first two stimuli, the ambiguity for response for the third depends on whether you are hungry or thirsty.

can be reconfigured prior to the onset of the next trial. To examine this possibility, the simple idea was to examine switch costs as a function of the delay between one item and the next. How well do the Micklefield points deal with switching Leeds to York and Leeds to Selby when trains arrive in quick succession? More particularly, the idea was to run the experiment such that we present an item, wait for a response, pause, and only then present the next item. (The 'pause', just mentioned, is known as the **response-to-stimulus interval** or **RSI**). Using this design we can begin to examine how task set reconfiguration might operate.

**Pinpoint question 9.9**

Do univalent lists or bivalent lists produce larger task-switching effects?

On the 'flicking of the mental switch' characterisation of performance, enacting a so-called 'shift of set' takes a certain amount of time to complete but, once completed, the participant is perfectly prepared to respond to the next item. By this account, as long as the RSI (pause) is long enough, then performance on a switch trial should be comparable to that on a non-switch trial. A problem for this account, though, is that it is simply not supported by the data (Allport

et al., 1994). Although the size of the switch cost may reduce as the RSI increases (Rogers & Monsell, 1995), the cost seems not to dissipate completely. Indeed Allport et al. (1994) reported a case where there the switch cost reduced only marginally when the RSI was increased from 20 ms to 1100 ms.

A different example from Rogers and Monsell (1995) helps illustrate this point. The basic display contained an encompassing outline square divided into four quadrants and on each trial a pair of characters was positioned in the centre of one of these quadrants. For ease of exposition, task A will be designated the *letters task* and here participants had to classify the letter as either a consonant or a vowel. With task B (the *numbers task*) participants had to classify the number as either odd or even. On most trials, the pair of characters contained one letter and one number. On neutral trials, though, either a letter or a digit was presented together with a symbol not assigned to a response (for instance, '#'). Depending on which quadrant the characters fell in, participants enacted either task A or B. So for example, if you were a participant in the experiment you might be told that if the characters fell in the upper two quadrants then you must make the letter judgement, and if the characters fell in the lower two quadrants then you must make the number judgement. The critical thing was that the stimulus position was perfectly predictable following the first trial because the location of the stimulus pair was determined sequentially in a clockwise fashion. This gave rise to what has become known as an *alternating runs paradigm* – the sequence was AABBAABB etc.

With the alternating runs design, both non-switch A → A/B → B and switch A → B/B → A trials were tested within the same block of trials. The difference between switch and non-switch trials allows us to assess the size of the task switch cost. What Rogers and Monsell (1995, Experiment 3) showed was that, although the size of the switch cost decreased dramatically as the RSI increased, a significant cost still emerged at the point when the delay was over 1 second (see Figure 9.11). So when participants were given enough time to prepare for the ensuing switch, they were unable to overcome all of the cost – they were never able to perform as though there had been no switch at all. In other words, there was still a **residual switch cost** even when a relatively lengthy interval was introduced between the trials.

It is this sort of finding that stands in contrast to any simple account of task switching. Simply put, if switch costs merely reflect aspects of volitional control (i.e., the participants' ability to choose to decide to do

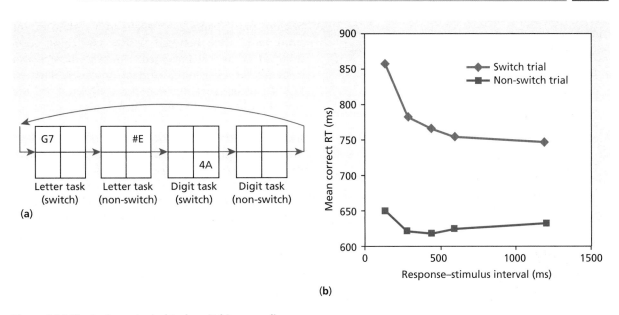

**Figure 9.11 Illustrating a typical task-switching paradigm**
(a) Schematic representation of a sequence of four trials in the paradigm developed by Rogers and Monsell (1995). The trial sequence moves in time from left to right. On every trial a pair of characters was presented in one quadrant of the screen. If the pair fell in the upper of the two quadrants, then the participants were expected to make a response to the letter. If the pair fell in the lower of the two quadrants, then the participants were expected to make a response to the number. The second trial shows a neutral trial where the imperative stimulus (i.e., the letter) is paired with a character not linked with a response. As can be seen, the order of trials was predictable because the characters moved round the screen, across trials, in an orderly clockwise fashion. In a sequence of four trials (discarding the first trial in a block), every first and third trial was a switch trial and every second and fourth trial was a non-switch trial. (b) shows the data broken down according to trial type and RSI. As can be seen, RTs on switch trials are slower than they are on non-switch trials. Moreover, the switching cost (the difference in RT between switch and non-switch trials) remains even at very lengthy intervals – there is evidence of a residual switch cost (see text for further details).

*Source*: Monsell, S. (2003). Task switching. *Trends in Cognitive Science*, *7*, 134–140 (fig. 2, p. 136). Reproduced with permission from Elsevier.

one sort of thing rather than another), then they should be abolished if participants are given plenty of time to prepare for the next stimulus event. The fact that participants cannot so prepare implies that there is something else going on – something else is responsible for the residual costs. So even though participants do benefit from being given some extra time to prepare for the next stimulus, they still show evidence of impairment from having to switch to a different task. Indeed, even when highly capable, highly motivated participants were tested under near optimal conditions, residual switching costs were still present in the data (Nieuwenhuis & Monsell, 2002).

**task-switching cost** The impairment in performance associated with changing between one set of operations and another. There are many reasons as to why such costs may occur.

**switch trial** A trial that implicates a task different from the immediately preceding trial.

**non-switch trial** A trial that implicates the same task as the immediately preceding trial.

**pure blocks** A set of trials in which only one task is demanded throughout.

**alternating blocks** A sequence of trials in which, respectively, odd and even trials are predictably related to two different tasks.

**alternation cost** Impaired performance observed during alternating blocks relative to pure blocks.

**task set** The collection of processes associated with the completion of a particular task.

**bivalent lists** Experimental stimuli in which each stimulus is associated with two tasks. In the absence of other information, such as a cue or its order in the list, the response is ambiguous.

univalent lists Experimental stimuli in which each stimulus is only associated with its own particular task. For instance, a vowel/consonant judgement can only be made of a letter, whereas an odd/even judgement can only be made of a number

task set reconfiguration The need to discard one set of processes and engage another set of processes when faced with a change in task.

response-to-stimulus interval (RSI) The time between the response made on the current trial and the presentation of the next stimulus.

residual switch cost In the task-switching literature, a performance decrement associated with changing tasks even in the presence of a substantial interval between the two tasks.

## Some additional theoretical ideas

How might we begin to explain such findings? In order to do this we must consider the sorts of psychological processes that are being tapped in these tasks. In terms of psychological theory, a relevant distinction is between some form of a controller (executive/central) system and the controlled (slave/input) systems. The basic central vs. input distinction reappears (remember the modularity of mind hypothesis? see Chapter 2) because now we have the idea that, whereas the slave systems are primarily stimulus driven (alternatively, exogenously triggered, i.e., from the bottom up), the executive system (the supervisory attentional system) is not primarily stimulus driven but initiates control from within (endogenously and in a top-down fashion) (after Allport et al., 1994, p. 450). Accordingly, it is assumed there is a unitary limited capacity central executive that is in overall charge of interpreting all of the current input and deciding what to do next – yes, there really is a mental equivalent of the Fat Controller!

By the most simple view, the central executive is in control of task switching – is in total charge of task set reconfiguration – and given this, the alternation costs in RT ought to reflect fairly directly the amount of time it takes to shift mentally between the competing task sets. However, given the evidence for the residual switching costs after quite long delays between trials, it seems that something else must be going on. The data from the Rogers and Monsell (1995) study reveal evidence for some form of **endogenous control** processes

because participants can benefit to a certain extent from more time between trials – switching costs declined as the RSI increased. However, there is also evidence for **exogenous control** processes. That is, task set reconfiguration may not complete until the arrival of the next stimulus – there is also evidence of residual switching costs even with long delays between trials. It seems that the (exogenous) stimulus triggers further reconfiguration processes once it is presented. So in advance of a given trial, participants can be partially prepared to make, for example, a number judgement, but they are unable to prepare completely for the particular number judgement that is demanded by the trial. It is only when the actual number occurs that they can then begin to execute the appropriate response.

Despite this general framework for thinking, Gilbert and Shallice (2002) noted that there are now essentially two competing accounts of task-switching costs. The first is associated with Monsell and co-workers as described above, that is the *executive control account*; the second is associated with Allport and co-workers (Allport et al., 1994; Allport & Wylie, 1999; Waszak, Hommel & Allport, 2003) and might be referred to as the **task carryover account** (after Gilbert and Shallice, 2002). Having considered the executive control account, it is only fitting to turn to the task carryover account.

## The task carryover account

According to Allport (and the task carryover account), switching costs are more readily understood in terms of carryover effects from the preceding task. By this view, the processing system remains (in a sense) primed to do what it has just done and any change is likely to result in performance costs. Back to the daily grind in our call centre example: you might find yourself 'on a roll' after taking a number of holiday bookings on the trot, only for your flow to be interrupted by some idiot complaining about the quality of in-flight peanuts. This account emphasises factors concerning interference, competition and conflict that can occur when the task changes. Collectively such factors are brought under the umbrella of so-called **task set inertia** and are taken to reflect 'persisting facilitation or suppression of competing processing pathways' (Allport & Wylie, 2000, p. 49). The system is set to do what it has just done, and trying to undo these operations (on a switch trial) is likely to result in a performance impairment. Problems on switch trials primarily reflect an inability to shake off what has gone on in the immediately previous trial.

It is always useful to try to set theories, such as the executive control theory and the task carryover theory, in opposition to one another, but in some ways this can be misleading. In this case, both the executive control theory and the task carryover theory accept that task switching may well reflect characteristics of attentional control together with the recent history of the processing system. For example, the task carryover account accepts a role for volitional control because participants clearly can follow the experimental instructions. The sticking point between the two accounts, though, is over the degree to which the switching costs provide a transparent window on operations associated with 'the time taken to reconfigure the processing system in readiness for the upcoming task' (Allport & Wylie, 1999, p. 278). According to Allport, there is evidence to suggest that the costs may more critically reflect factors associated with task set inertia. As Gilbert and Shallice (2002) noted, 'This (task carryover) account does not deny the involvement of control processes in task switching . . . What *is* denied by this account is that these control processes are measured in any direct way by the switch cost' (p. 299). One simple example suffices.

Goschke (2000) reported an experiment in which, on each trial, participants were presented with a single coloured letter. Task A was to classify the letter as either an *A* or a *B*. Task B was to classify the colour of the letter as either red or green. Critically the letter *A* and the colour red were assigned to one key press and the letter *B* and the colour green were assigned to a different key press. This allows us to discuss cases where the stimuli are congruent (*red A, green B*) and where they are incongruent (*green A, red B*). Neutral stimuli were also defined. When making colour decisions, the letters *C* and *D* (i.e., not response relevant) were presented; when making the letter decisions, the neutral stimuli were coloured blue and yellow. Given this design, it would be reasonable to expect effects of congruency such that congruent stimuli would be responded to fastest; followed by responses to neutral stimuli; followed by the slowest responses to the incongruent stimuli.

Both pure and mixed blocks were tested. In pure blocks, participants only responded to colour or they only responded to letter identity. In contrast, in mixed blocks participants alternated across trials – first enact task A (respond to letter identity), then B (respond to the colour), and so on. Performance was examined at both a short RSI (i.e., 14 ms) and a long RSI (i.e., 1500 ms). One preliminary result was that there were significant task-switching costs at the short RSI that

diminished but did not disappear at the long RSI. This is consistent with the idea of some benefit of preparation time together with robust residual switching costs at long intervals. The effects of congruency were also of interest.

## Switching costs and proactive interference

In this experiment we can discuss both within-trial and between-trial effects of congruency. We have already discussed within-trial congruency and this refers to whether or not the different stimulus attributes signal the same response or different responses. Effects of between-trial congruency are a little more involved.

One aspect of the task set inertia hypothesis is that variously the nature of the stimulus, judgement and response on trial *n* can influence performance on trial *n* + 1 irrespective of the delay between the two trials. To understand this, the concept of **proactive interference** is introduced. Proactive interference refers to how event attributes *now* can go on to influence performance at a later time. For example, the all-night party you're having now might severely 'influence' your performance at a family Sunday lunch tomorrow. In the task carryover account, the residual task-switching cost is assumed to arise because of proactive interference from, in this case, the immediately previous trial. From this point of view, Goschke (2000) reasoned that if the participant were forced to inhibit a response to an irrelevant stimulus characteristic on trial *n*, then this should produce slowing on the next trial if this irrelevant characteristic now becomes response relevant (see the alarmingly large literature on **negative priming** for further instances of this – see Fox, 1995, for a review).

Consider the case of being engaged in a mixed block of trials in which the participant is having to alternate between the letter and colour tasks. So let us assume that the participant on trial *n* is having to respond to the letter component of a *green A*. *A* is the relevant component and *green* is the irrelevant component – remember *green A* is an incongruent stimulus because *A* is signalling 'press one key' and *green* is signalling 'press the other key'. In this respect, participants have to inhibit the colour response when responding to the letter. The task set for letter identity is primed and the task set for colour identity is to be inhibited. Now assume on the next trial a *red B* is presented. This is a switch trial because now participants have to make a colour response and now the task set that was previously inhibited must be activated – in a sense the previous task set must be released from inhibition. Following this argument, it can be seen that the task set inertia hypothesis predicts a very particular pattern of results – namely that performance on switch trials will be particularly impaired following an incongruent trial. This is a prediction about a specific between-trial congruency effect. Critically the data reported by Goschke (2000) were perfectly in line with this very particular prediction.

In thinking about such a pattern of performance it becomes almost immediately apparent that it fits reasonably uncomfortably with the task set reconfiguration hypothesis as originally stipulated. Why should it take longer to reconfigure the system after an incongruent trial than after a congruent trial? Indeed, Pashler (2000, p. 287) has stated, 'Perhaps the most intriguing aspect of task switching is the lingering effect of the irrelevant mapping – the "task congruity effect".' Although Monsell (2003, p. 137) has offered some speculations as to why this might occur – 'The detection of cross-task interference during a trial might also prompt the ramping-up of endogenous control' – it remains anyone's guess as to what this actually means.

More generally, it should come as no surprise that the literature is now awash with findings that variously support either the notion of task set reconfiguration or the notion of task set inertia. Many other reasons for task-switching costs are also currently being explored. The field remains wide open and the killer experiments have yet to be carried out!

## Pinpoint question 9.10

What evidence is there to suggest that task-switching costs are not simply the result of executive control?

## Research focus 9.3

### Totally wired? The effect of caffeine on task switching

The evidence for switching costs is beyond doubt and it is interesting to consider other factors that may impinge. So we can ask, what are the cognitive effects of caffeine exactly? Tieges, Snel, Kok, Wijnen, Lorist and Ridderinkhof (2006) took it upon themselves to examine the effects of caffeine during task switching, predicting that a boost of caffeine should help in task set reconfiguration, especially if individuals are given sufficient time to prepare for the switch.

Eighteen participants were used in the study, with each individual taking part in three separate experimental sessions involving either the consumption of a placebo, a low dose of caffeine or a high dose of caffeine. To their credit, Tieges et al. (2006) examined many different types of measurement in their study, although here we'll just be focusing on the behavioural results. In an adaptation of the alternating-runs task (Rogers & Monsell, 1995), participants either judged the colour (task A) or the consonant/vowel nature (task B) of letters presented on a computer monitor. During single-task conditions, only the colour or the identity task was completed. During mixed-task conditions, the two tasks alternated in a predictable manner, with two trials of task A followed by two trials of task B and so on. The gap in between response at one trial and stimulus presentation at the next (RSI) varied over 150, 600 and 1500 ms.

In general, participants seemed pretty buzzed as a result of their caffeine shot since RTs were generally faster in the caffeine conditions relative to the placebo condition, although there were marginal differences between the effects of high and low doses of caffeine. More importantly, the behavioural data revealed that switch costs were substantially reduced following caffeine intake, although this was especially true for the condition in which participants had the greatest time to prepare for the task switch (RSI 1500 ms).

Tieges et al. (2006) discussed the reduction of switching costs in the presence of caffeine ingestion as a consequence of the relationship between caffeine and dopamine activity (see Garrett & Griffiths, 1997). Therefore, it seems that a cup of GMA (Good Morning America) really does help in the planning of anticipatory behaviour as demanded by a predictive task switch. Of course, we're not suggesting that you now run out and buy a sackful of coffee beans. You'll need to read a different textbook to ours to find out about dependency, habituation and withdrawal . . .

*Source*: Tieges, Z., Snel, J., Kok, A., Wijnen, J. G., Lorist, M. M., & Ridderinkhof, R. (2006). Caffeine improves anticipatory processes in task switching. *Biological Psychology, 73*, 101–116.

**endogenous control** The ability to change cognitive processing at will. In spatial cueing experiments, the idea that the movement of attention is under the control of the participant.

**exogenous control** Cognitive processes that are driven by events external to the person. A bright flash will grab your visual attention and there is nothing that you can do to avoid this from happening. In spatial cueing experiments, the idea that the movement of attention is governed by salient stimulus characteristics such as a sudden onset of a visual event.

**task carryover account** Task switching explained according to the presence or absence of priming from the previous trial.

**task set inertia** The claim that the processing system has a default of maintaining operations with an immediately preceding task even if the task demands change.

**proactive interference** The negative influence of present events on future performance. Interference of new material by old material.

**negative priming** Typically discussed in terms of performance on trial *n* + 1 of an adjacent pair of trials (trial *n* and trial *n* + 1). Negative priming is characterised by poor performance on trial *n* + 1 when an ignored stimulus characteristic on trial *n* becomes the imperative signal on trial *n* + 1.

## Concluding comments

In his recent review, Monsell (2003) has readily admitted that any account that posits just one mechanism as the sole cause of task switching is bound to be unsuccessful, given the variety of the task-switching costs that exist. There is good evidence that several endogenous and exogenous factors may be at play. Being fully able to understand how such factors interact in any given case poses the greatest challenge for future research. Nevertheless he also concluded that 'something of a consensus' has emerged over the presence of an effortful (time-consuming) 'endogenous, task-set-reconfiguration process, which, if not carried out before the stimulus onset, must be done after it' (p. 137). According to him, task carryover effects may well exist but the case for task-set reconfiguration is apparently incontrovertible.

Ultimately the real constraints in processing that both the PRP and task-switching costs reveal are of profound importance and have real-world significance. As Monsell (2003) noted, such facts need to be taken into account by designers of 'human–machine interfaces that require operators to monitor multiple information sources and switch between different activities under time pressure' (p. 138). He cites in this regard air-traffic control as being an obvious example, but as we have already seen, we need only consider the more mundane example of driving in to work to get the point.

## CHAPTER SUMMARY

- As a general framework for thinking, it has been considered that all processing might be thought of as being understood in terms of a sequential set of stages, comprising, roughly, stimulus encoding, stimulus identification, decision and response organisation/execution.

- Two competing ideas regarding the organisation of these stages have been put forward. A serial or sequential stage model argues that each stage must be complete before the next can start. In contrast, something like the concurrent and contingent stage model relaxes this assumption and states that subsequent stages of processing do not have to wait until the previous stage has run to completion. Evidence is presented that, under certain circumstances, response preparation can begin before stimulus identification is completed.

- The psychological refractory period (PRP; Kahneman, 1973) paradigm attempts to address whether each individual stage allows for time-sharing by which more than one stimulus can engage the associated processes at once. To test this in the PRP paradigm, participants have to respond to two stimuli, one presented after the other, and the interval between stimulus presentations (the SOA) is varied. PRP logic rests on assumptions regarding pre-bottleneck, bottleneck and post-bottleneck processing, with bottleneck processing indicating a structural constraint in which only one stimulus can be dealt with at a time.

- This central bottleneck processing account (Pashler, 1994) has four basic predictions: (i) slowing pre-bottleneck and central processing for the first task will slow reaction times for both the first and second task equally; (ii) variation in post-bottleneck processing for the first task will have no consequences for the second task; (iii) pre-bottleneck processing for the first task can be slowed without slowing the response to the second task; and (iv) slowing central and post-bottleneck processing for the second task will have no effect on the first task.

- While the idea of a central processing bottleneck in terms of response organisation has received various empirical support (Broadbent & Gregory, 1967b; McCann & Johnston, 1992; Pashler & Johnston, 1989), there are alternative accounts arguing that processing is limited as a result of the amount of capacity allocated between tasks.

- The central capacity sharing (CCS; Tombu & Jolicœur, 2003) model suggests that two tasks may be able to share central processes at any one time. At one extreme, the CCS model may mimic the central bottleneck account by allocating all central processing to only one of the tasks. At the other extreme, capacity may be shared between the two tasks, leading to response slowing for both tasks.

- In contrast to PRP research, in which the processing of two stimuli can simultaneously compete for the same processes, interest has also been raised for cases where two tasks might demand similar or different types of processes across trials. A basic task-switching effect is demonstrated in worse performance during cases where the task changes (switch trials) relative to when the same task is maintained (non-switch trials) across consecutive trials (e.g., Jersild, 1927).

- Two competing accounts of task switching have been put forward. In the executive control account (Rogers & Monsell, 1995), task switching is thought to be the cost incurred in activating and deactivating certain cognitive operations at will. In the task carryover account (Allport et al., 1994), task-switching costs are thought to be the result of violating task set inertia in which the cognitive system settles into a processing pattern. Both accounts, however, share ideas about attentional control and the history of processing,

## ANSWERS TO PINPOINT QUESTIONS

9.1 Strictly sequential models require the completion of one stage before the next can be carried out, whereas concurrent models allow for multiple stages to be carried out at any one time.

9.2 Response preparation is possible in cases where letters and numbers are assigned to different hands, since there is a direct relation between the mental category and the specific response hand (e.g., letters are assigned to the left hand and numbers to the right). There is no unique assignment between mental category and response hand in the X/1 and Y/2 case.

9.3 The three stages associated with the completion of a task according to Pashler (1994) are pre-bottleneck, bottleneck and post-bottleneck.

9.4 The time task 1 spends in the pre-bottleneck stage (A1), the time task 1 spends in bottleneck

processing (B1), and the SOA between the presentation of task 1 and task 2 all influence the overall response time of task 2 at short SOAs.

9.5 Increasing post-bottleneck processing for task 1 should have no effect on the reaction time for task 2.

9.6 When participants are instructed to respond to S1 and then S2 the evidence is, typically, in keeping with queuing. In contrast, when participants are allowed to respond to stimuli in any order, then the evidence may be more in keeping with capacity sharing.

9.7 It is the very presence of concurrent conversation that appears to be detrimental to driving performance and not the type of phone used.

9.8 Alternating blocks are harder than pure blocks because participants have to switch between the different cognitive operations to perform two tasks in the alternating block case.

9.9 Bivalent lists produce larger task-switching effects since there are conflicting rules regarding response selection for every stimulus presented.

9.10 Even if participants are given ample time to prepare for the next event, a residual task-switching cost is still obtained (Rogers & Monsell, 1995). Also, highly motivated individuals seem unable to avoid task-switching costs completely (Nieuwenhuis & Monsell, 2002).

## CHAPTER 10

# HUMAN MEMORY
## An introduction

**By the end of this chapter, you should be able to:**

- Contrast the associative learning and organisational accounts of forgetting.
- Evaluate the levels of processing approach (Craik & Lockhart, 1972).
- Describe the distinction between episodic and semantic memory (Tulving, 1972).
- Evaluate the evidence for trace decay and interference accounts of forgetting.
- Describe a serial position curve and how primacy and recency effects are manifest.
- Summarise the working memory model (Baddeley & Hitch, 1974), including the function of the phonological loop, visuo-spatial scratch pad, central executive and episodic buffer.

## CHAPTER CONTENTS

So you've left it a little late (again) and you're about to sit an exam with the barest amount of preparation. Cursing your decision to go camping at the weekend, you frantically skim-read the textbook that should've been more than skimmed a long time ago. There are three chapters you need to look over and you decide that the best approach is to search for key words. For the first chapter, you're operating fairly reasonably and spot key words and begin to make associations with other knowledge nuggets of information coming to mind. Stifling a mental groan, signal detection theory, you think, sounds familiar – that's where you judge whether behaviour is due to a response bias or a change in perceptual sensitivity – isn't that right? Didn't we do that when we looked at visual masking and conscious perception? Hmm . . . things seem to be going well. As you begin the second chapter, you're acutely aware of the clock ticking and decide just to try to remember the key words by getting them to rhyme with other words. Working memory? Flirting Henry. Episodic buffer? Melodic duffer. For the third chapter, blind panic sets in and you only really recognise the presence of lots of rather long and complicated-looking words before you pass out five minutes before the exam is due to begin.

# You must remember this?
## A levels of processing approach to exam cramming

## REFLECTIVE QUESTIONS

1. What kind of a situation helps you to improve your memory and what kind of situations make it easier to forget? How deeply are you thinking about the to-be-remembered material? Are there other competing sources of information? What kinds of relations are you drawing upon with the to-be-remembered material and information that already exists in your memory?

2. Think about the back catalogue of your favourite band. Which albums are easiest to remember? Is there anything about the position of these albums, within their grand canon of work, that makes these easier to retrieve? Is there anything other than when the album was released, that might influence the likelihood of retrieval?

## Introduction and preliminary considerations

The study of human memory is a major theme in cognitive psychology and it has a history that can be traced back alongside that of the discipline itself. So far we have discussed various sorts of short-term memory systems (see Chapter 3), but discussion of these acted primarily as a vehicle by which other topics in cognitive psychology could be introduced and described. For instance, our discussion of sensory and other short-term memory systems concentrated on visual information processing. Now it is important to discuss the nature of memory more generally, and in its own right.

Over years, many different metaphors have been used to aid understanding, and, although we will concentrate on a very particular framework for thinking, Table 10.1 (abridged from Roediger, 1980) provides a list of some of the many competing ideas that have been entertained. Rather than attempt to discuss each of these in turn, a more sensible strategy is to consider a general framework for thinking, and here we return to the computational metaphor of the mind (as we discussed in Chapter 2). We will, of course mention some of the other alternatives as discussion proceeds, but in order to provide a general framework for thinking we will focus on the computational metaphor. This has held a prominent position in the way that researchers have thought about the nature of memory and the nature of memory processes.

So we begin by sketching out some very basic ideas about how human memory has been thought about in general. We then move on to reconsider a more specific distinction that Fodor (1983) introduced in his discussion of the modularity of mind hypothesis. The distinction is between horizontal and vertical faculties (see Chapter 2) and we will see how this applies to memory. The discussion proceeds with a focus on different conceptions of how memory may be organised, how memory may be structured and how memory processes operate. The chapter draws to a close with a description and an appraisal of the extremely influential modern-day account of memory embodied in the *working memory account* (Baddeley & Hitch, 1974).

**Table 10.1** Various memory metaphors that have been discussed in the literature (taken from Roediger, 1980).

**A. Spatial analogies with search**

| | |
|---|---|
| wax tablet (Plato, Aristotle) | mystic writing pad (Freud, 1950) |
| gramophone (Pear, 1922) | workbench (Klatzky, 1975) |
| aviary (Plato) | cow's stomach (Hintzman, 1974) |
| house (James, 1890) | pushdown stack (Bernbach, 1969) |
| rooms in a house (Freud, 1924/1952) | acid bath (Posner & Konick, 1966) |
| switchboard (see John, 1972) | library (Broadbent, 1971) |
| purse (Miller, 1956a) | dictionary (Loftus, 1977) |
| leaky bucket or sieve (Miller, 1956a) | keysort cards (Brown & McNeill, 1966) |
| junk box (Miller, 1956a) | conveyor belt (Murdock, 1974) |
| bottle (Miller, Galanter, & Pribram, 1960) | tape recorder (see Posner & Warren, 1972) |
| computer program (Simon & Feigenbaum, 1964) | subway map (Collins & Quillian, 1970) |
| stores (Atkinson & Shiffrin, 1968) | garbage can (Landauer, 1975) |

**B. Other spatial theories**

organisation theory (Tulving, 1962)

hierarchical networks (Mandler, 1967)

associative networks (Anderson & Bower, 1973)

**C. Other analogies**

muscle ('strength') (Woodworth, 1929)

construction (Bartlett, 1932)

reconstruction of a dinosaur (Neisser, 1967)

levels of processing (Craik & Lockhart, 1972)

signal detection (Bernbach, 1967)

melodies on a piano (Weschler, 1963)

tuning fork (Lockhart, Craik & Jacoby, 1976)

hologram (Pribram, 1971)

lock and key (Kolers & Palef, 1976)

A – lists cases where it has been asserted that memory is like 'a receptacle containing objects'.

B – other cases that have a spatial character but no obvious real-world object for comparison.

C – other cases that do not fall readily into categories A and B.

## Libraries/warehouses/computers

One basic idea is that memory can be conceived of as being akin to a set of pigeonholes, or places in a mental store, each of which is associated with a particular address – each pigeonhole has a unique identifier, just as the mail for Professor Cromwell goes in a different place to the mail for Professor Cramwell. So if we wish to store something in memory or retrieve something from memory, we need to have access to an address, and then use this as a means to access the appropriate pigeonhole. By analogy, think of a library for books: each book in the library has a unique tag or catalogue number associated with it. This tag can be used to locate whereabouts the book is stored in the library. So if you want to retrieve a book from the library (e.g., *Ulysses* by James Joyce), first go to the catalogue and retrieve its address (e.g., *PF 88202 Uly* if you're after passing the University of Sussex Library), and then use this to go to a particular place in the library (e.g., turn right once you get in, go through the double doors, take the right side of the seventh row of books, find the fourth stack and it *should* be on the bottom shelf) and retrieve the book. Such a conception of memory is pervasive, and one reason that it seems so sensible is that it provides a very useful means to understand how information is actually stored in a computer. In this way we have a demonstration proof that this account of memory actually works. Of course, given the context of the present book, the ultimate question now is, 'How good an account of human memory is it?'

To address this, we will have to think about how it is that many different sorts of knowledge are memorised. Although the library analogy is useful, it is also limited. It only deals with how one type of thing can be stored and retrieved. It only deals with the storage and retrieval of books. Such a limitation is too constraining, and we need to consider how it is that a whole host of other things could be stored and retrieved. Maybe a warehouse analogy rather than a library analogy will work better for us? Again with the warehouse analogy we can distinguish between the thing that is to be stored (e.g., a green plastic garden chair) and its address or identifying tag (e.g., Aisle 3, Bay 7, Shelf 3). These aspects are shared with the library analogy, and again we can use the same principles of storage and retrieval as in the library analogy. First retrieve an address and then use this to place or retrieve an item in storage.

Both the library and the warehouse analogies are useful in setting out some, perhaps common-sense, ideas about memory, but there is a critical difference between these cases and memory. Whereas with the library and the warehouse actual physical items are being stored and retrieved, this is not the case with a computer, or indeed, human memory. With these latter forms of memory what are being dealt with are representations – binary in the case of the computer, mental in the case of human memory – and it is these that are being stored and retrieved. As soon as we invoke the notion of mental representation (see Chapter 7) then we must immediately address notions of how such representations are coded and in this respect the notion of mental coding comes to the fore. It is not the thing itself that is being stored and retrieved, but some form of mental record. For ease of exposition, this general view of memory will be referred to as the **computer metaphor of memory**, or, more simply, *the computer metaphor*.

In using such a computer metaphor when we discuss human memory it is usually very helpful to distinguish between *encoding*, *storage* and *retrieval*. When these distinctions are made it is possible to see how problems in remembering may arise. The to-be-remembered event may not have been encoded or it may not have been encoded properly. The event may not have been stored or it may have been stored in the wrong place. The event may not be retrievable. The event may have been encoded and stored properly but no record has been kept of where in memory it has been stored. The possibilities are legion, and some of these will be examined in the following.

However, some caution is warranted before we dive in at the deep end. We need to ask just how useful are the library/warehouse/computer analogies for thinking about the nature of human memory. No matter how easy it is to bandy about terms like *storage* and *retrieval*, for some (such as the behaviourists, e.g., Skinner, 1985) these ideas are merely fanciful. For them, even fence posts can be said to remember. The imprints of the sledgehammer blows on the top of the posts serve as a record (a memory) of the events that took place as the post was hammered into the ground. They therefore have posed the question, 'Does human memory operate in ways that are fundamentally different from the fence post?' If considered carefully enough, such concerns are extremely challenging for those who are more firmly rooted in the human information processing tradition (see Hintzman, 1993, for a very thought-provoking discussion of related issues). In this regard, we are again faced with the problem of having to decide just how simple accounts of human cognition ought to be.

For those keen to pursue the fence-post line of argument, then alternative sources will need to be consulted. It is the case that the present focus is with traditional cognitive accounts of memory that, to varying degrees, cling on to the human information processing framework for thinking. In such accounts, remembering is seen as something more than passive registration and then the ultimate recovery of information from some kind of mental store. We will see that many of the most famous human information processing accounts of human memory rest on several assumptions about a variety of different sorts of memory stores and memory codes. The behaviourist challenge to such accounts is to try to justify these assumptions in the face of much simpler mechanisms. Although the fence-post analogy is probably pushing the point a little too far, there is no harm in constantly asking whether the very complicated accounts that exist in the human memory literature are entirely justified – can simpler mechanisms suffice? Indeed, as we will see, there is currently something of an emerging counter-movement developing in memory research in which the aim is to push a few simple assumptions a very long distance indeed!

> **computer metaphor of memory** A view of the mind in which each memory trace or mental record is stored at its own place (address) in the mental store.

## The modularity of mind revisited

Having provided a very basic framework for thinking, it is important to move the discussion on by considering more particular ideas. As was pointed out in Chapter 2, Fodor drew a distinction between vertical and horizontal faculties. Put briefly, we can divide up the functional architecture of the mind either horizontally, across all cognitive domains, or vertically according to the different cognitive domains. So we can either assume that the same memory constraints operate in all domains or we can argue that each cognitive domain has its own unique memory constraints. We will begin by considering the idea that memory is constituted as a horizontal faculty, but we will soon move on to consider alternative views about how memory may, in fact, fractionate. Specifically, we go on to consider the alternative general view (of vertical faculties) that different kinds of memory systems exist across different cognitive domains.

## Memory as a horizontal faculty

The idea that the same memory constraints apply everywhere is firmly rooted in the history of the study of human memory, and forms the bedrock of much recent and, indeed, current thinking. According to the modularity of mind hypothesis (Fodor, 1983), a horizontal faculty may be defined relative to a set of processing constraints that apply across all modalities. Similar ideas relating to memory have been discussed, in some detail, by Crowder (1989) in terms of what he called **processing modularity**. By this view it is appropriate to think in terms of very general principles of memorising that apply throughout cognition. In this regard, it is fitting to begin by discussing, in very general terms, how we retain and forget information. What are the most effective ways of committing information to memory? What are the most effective ways of retaining the information in memory?

### Paired associate learning

In turning to this, we are yet again confronted with further evidence of how cognitive psychology has its roots firmly in the behaviourist tradition. For instance, in his review of the history of memory research, Bower (2000) began by tracing out studies on what is known as **paired associate learning**. Many of the basic ideas about forgetting can be traced to early experiments on paired associate learning. A typical paired associate learning experiment is divided into two phases: a *study (or exposure) phase* in which the to-be-remembered material is presented for learning, and a *test phase* in which memory for the material is tested. During the initial study phase, participants are presented with pairs of items to remember (the paired associates) where the items are things such as nonsense syllables, words, pictures, word/picture combinations, etc. One member of each pair is designated the **stimulus item** and the other is designated the **response item**. For simplicity, we will focus on cases where the to-be-remembered items are pairs of words. For instance, the list comprises *horse cart, cat broom, grape foot*, etc. We can think of each pair as comprising a stimulus word (e.g., *horse*) and a response word (i.e., *cart*). In the later test phase, participants are presented on each trial with a stimulus word (e.g., *cat*) and they have to try to reinstate the response word (i.e., *broom*) that was originally paired with the stimulus word during the study phase.

Within this framework all that is posited is some form of representation of the stimulus word (a memory trace for the stimulus word), some form of representation of the response word (a memory trace for the response word) and some form of associative bond between these two representations. During the study phase the assumption is that traces are laid down in memory for the stimulus and response words and critical associative bonds are also established between these two traces. The ability to recover a response word given a stimulus word (or a cue) depends essentially on the durability of the different traces and the strength of the associative bond between them.

A classic example of a paired associate experiment was reported by Bower in 1970. We will discover that the results have been taken to be problematic for the associative account of memory, but it is nevertheless useful to consider this study in some detail. Three separate groups of participants were recruited and each group engaged in a study phase of paired associates. For all groups the presentation of the paired associates was the same. Each pair of words was exposed for 10 s and three lists of 30 pairs of words were presented in total. After each list, the stimulus words were scrambled and intermixed with 30 new items. Each of these words was then presented to the participants. The task was to consider each of these words and to rate their confidence over whether each had just been presented in the immediately previous list – this was known as the **recognition test**. No response words were presented during this recognition test.

By way of explanation, in a recognition test a mixture of previously exposed and novel items are presented to participants and they have to decide, for each item, whether it is old or new. In contrast, in a recall test participants are asked to reinstate just those items that have been previously exposed. Two forms of recall test have been discussed in the literature: (i) in a **free recall test** participants have (essentially) no constraints and are asked to reinstate, by whatever means possible, just those items to which they have been previously exposed; (ii) in a **cued recall test** certain items are provided as cues to help recollection of other to-be-remembered materials. In addition to the recognition test, Bower (1970) also assessed participants in a variation of a cued recall task. In a final recall phase of the experiment, each of the original stimulus words were re-presented and participants were tasked with having to recall the response word that the stimulus word had been paired with.

It is the results of the recall test that are of most interest here, and these results were broken down according to study group. As noted above, three such study groups were tested, and across the groups different instructions were given as to how to commit the material to memory during the study phase. In the rote repetition group, participants were asked to overtly rehearse the pairs of items during the 10 s period each pair was exposed, e.g., start clock, present pair 'MONKEY–PIANO', participant repeats back, 'Monkey Piano, Monkey Piano, Monkey Piano, Monkey Piano, …' until 10 s elapses, then present next pair 'PENCIL–BENCH', and so on. In the interactive imagery group, participants were told that for each pair they had to form a mental image in which the named items were interacting in an imagined scene. Finally, in the separation imagery group, participants were instructed to form a mental image of the two items essentially side by side with one another. The implication was that these participants would therefore imagine the items but not in such a way that they were interacting.

The results of the experiment were clear-cut: recall performance was poor in both the rote repetition group and the separation group (i.e., correct recall was around 30 per cent correct in these groups). Recall performance was correspondingly much better in the interactive imagery group (i.e., 53 per cent). Although the reasons for these differences continue to be discussed (Hintzman, 1993; Wilton, 1990; Wilton & Mathieson, 1996), it is the poor performance of the rote repetition group that is particularly instructive. One reason that performance with this group was so surprising was that it contrasted sharply with basic tenets of associative learning. As Bower (2000) described, in repeating a particular S–R association the strength of the bond or the association is assumed to increase. Moreover, the strength of the association is taken to reflect the degree of learning, or how well the association will be retained in memory. The greater the strength of the association, the more resistant the association will be to forgetting.

On the basis of this kind of account of the associative principles of learning, the rote repetition group ought to have performed exceptionally well because in this group the particular S–R bonds were being strengthened because of the overt act of repetition during the study phase. Unfortunately for this account, however, the results revealed only meagre levels of retention in the rote repetition group. What the results instead revealed is that a much more useful **mnemonic strategy** (a mnemonic strategy is essentially a means to aid memory) is to form a mental image of the referents of the items interacting. Although the reasons as to why interactive imagery is such a useful mnemonic have been debated ever since (see Hintzman, 1993, and Wilton & Mathieson, 1996), at the time when they were originally reported the results were exceptionally challenging to standard behavioural accounts of learning and memory. Apparently, something other than learning as a consequence of the strengthening of particular S–R bonds appeared to have been revealed by the experiment.

### Pinpoint question 10.1

If you wanted to remember the pairing of ELEPHANT–RIBBON, what would be one successful way of doing this?

### Forgetting and S–R associationism

Despite the fact that Bower's results sit very uncomfortably with associative accounts of learning and memory, it would be far too bold to argue that they fatally undermined the framework. As Bower (2000) has more recently pointed out, such accounts do provide some fairly basic insights into why forgetting may take place. First, in much the same way that an associative bond can be strengthened, such bonds can also weaken. More particularly, associative bonds may weaken naturally because of something known as **decay**. The mental chain between MONKEY and PIANO simply rusts away because of lack of use. As we will see below, decay is typically assumed to be a passive process by which forgetting takes place, and one active mechanism that can be brought to bear to overcome decay is to reuse the associative bond through active rehearsal. Associative bonds can be strengthened through the act of rehearsal.

Although other evidence may be marshalled in favour of such a view, Bower's (1970) results are difficult to square with these particular ideas. The apparent strengthening of the associative bonds through overt rehearsal was not particularly effective in engendering good memory for the materials in his experiment. From an intuitive point of view, this is somewhat surprising because rehearsal lies at the heart of rote learning and rote learning is what cramming for an exam is all about, and cramming is the best way to learn (right?).

A second (associative) reason that Bower (2000) gave for forgetting is that the representation of the learnt material is liable to change over time. A consequence of this is that only some of material can be recoverable at test. For example, if a set of features or cues – let's call these *prime minister, Conservative, female, 1980s* – are associated with a response item 'Margaret Thatcher', and if *prime minister, Conservative, 1980s*

are lost over time, then it is unlikely that 'Margaret Thatcher' will be recalled on the basis of *female* alone. The thrust of this kind of account is that, even though material has been stored, unless a comprehensive set of original contextual cues (i.e., cues present during the study phase) are available at test then the material may not be recoverable. Although this account is seemingly sensible and can explain why 'Margaret Thatcher' may or may not be recalled, it does not explain how it is that the cues themselves are lost or forgotten.

The final factor discussed by Bower as responsible for forgetting is known as *interference*. In this regard, the memory for one paired associate is compromised by the learning of others. For instance, you may experience real difficulties in remembering your friend's new boyfriend simply because you cannot help but think of their previous boyfriend. In memory research two forms of interference are typically distinguished: (i) **proactive inhibition** – old material interferes with the learning of new; and (ii) **retroactive inhibition** – new material interferes with the memory of old material. Learning a new chord on the guitar may be compromised because of chords that you already know. You already know how to play *G* and *D* and *E* but all of this makes it difficult to hang on to how to play *C* – the chord you have just been taught today. This is an example of proactive inhibition – prior knowledge hurts memory for new material. In contrast, if after learning *C* you forget how to play *G*, then this is an instance of retroactive inhibition – newly acquired knowledge comprises what you already know. We will return to discuss proactive and retroactive inhibition in more detail shortly, but fundamentally they are central to associative accounts of forgetting.

Indeed, in thinking about interference as a cause of forgetting, theorists have attempted to explain Bower's (1970) findings concerning interactive imagery without any appeals to the special nature of imagery at all. As Hintzman (1993) discussed (see also Wilton & Mathieson, 1996), there is one important factor that is confounded in Bower's original study. Whereas in the separation group the same relation was used for every pair of associates (i.e., a monkey is *beside* a piano, a clown is *beside* some wine, etc.), in the interactive imagery group participants were free to generate their own relations for each different pair of associates (a monkey *playing* a piano, a clown *drinking* some wine, etc.). In this respect it is the number of different relations that are used with the materials rather than the type of relation per se that is important. In effect when different relations are used with the different paired associates in a list, interference between the different

## → What have we learnt?

In summary, and according to Bower (2000), the evidence surrounding the three (associative) causes of forgetting (decay, modification of traces over time, and interference) 'is simply overwhelming' (p. 13). Therefore it will come as no surprise that, as discussion proceeds, we will repeatedly consider how forgetting might best be explained – which of the three factors provides the best account? We will also see how attempts have been made to eliminate

some of the potential causes of forgetting from further consideration. For instance, is decay or interference the primary factor? Is either sufficient alone? However, initially it is useful to consider other factors that have been identified as being critical to the effective retention of material and in this regard we may ask whether we need anything other than associative accounts of memory at all.

---

paired associates is likely to be minimal. A standard assumption here is that interference in memory will most likely occur between similar materials, hence the difference between the interactive imagery group and the other groups is readily explained by (essentially) associative principles. → See 'What have we learnt?', above.

**processing modularity** Crowder's (1989) view that the same memory processes apply throughout cognition. For example, remembering and forgetting are the same regardless of which cognitive domain is being discussed.

**paired associate learning** An experimental paradigm in which participants are presented with pairs of items during a study phase, which must be committed to memory. In some cases, during a later test phase, participants are presented with one member of each pair (i.e., the stimulus item) and are asked to produce the other member (i.e., the response item).

**stimulus item** In paired associate learning, the item in the pair that is presented during the test phase.

**response item** In paired associate learning, the item in the pair that must be reinstated during the test phase.

**recognition test** Where previously seen items are mixed with previously unseen items, and participants are required to categorise each item as either being old or new.

**free recall test** Where participants are asked to reinstate previously exposed items in any order without the aid of cues.

**cued recall test** Where participants are asked, to reinstate a previously experienced item with the aid of a cue or cues.

**mnemonic strategy** An aid to memory.

**decay** Forgetting that occurs naturally as a function of time. Memory traces are said to fade away over time.

**proactive inhibition** The negative influence of present events on future performance. Interference of new material by old material.

**retroactive inhibition** Interference of old material by new material.

## Organisation and memory

As is probably clear, from a traditional behaviourist standpoint, standard associative principles were accepted as providing a sufficient theoretical framework within which to think about the problems of human memory. The same associative principles of learning and memory were assumed to apply in all areas of cognition, hence the idea of memory as a horizontal faculty. However, with the rise in popularity of the cognitivist approach, alternative and contrasting perspectives began to emerge. One of the most prominent among these was provided by Mandler (1967) in the so-called 'Mandler Manifesto' (Bower & Bryant, 1991). Put briefly, according to traditional associative theory, any item can operate as an effective memory cue for any other item as long as a strong enough associative bond exists between the memory traces for the two items. In other words, all other things being equal, it should be as easy to remember the paired associates 'horse–onion' as 'horse–cart'.

In complete contrast to this view, Mandler (1967) argued that there is much more to effective memorising than merely mentally linking items together. For him, memory is primarily determined by how learners organise the to-be-remembered materials during initial exposure. A seminal study was reported by Mandler and Pearlstone (1966). On a given trial, participants were presented with a list of words such that each word was printed on its own index card. Participants were encouraged to sort the words/cards into different piles according to whatever grouping principles that they thought were most natural for capturing relations between the words. For instance, the words might be grouped according to general conceptual categories such as 'food', 'mode of transport', 'man-made', 'naturally occurring', etc. The cards were then collected and participants were asked to sort them again. This procedure was repeated until the participants were consistent in their groupings across two consecutive attempts. It was found that for lists of 52 words, participants used between two and seven groupings. More critically, though, are the findings that relate to performance in an unannounced free recall test for the words which was carried out once the first phase of the experiment was complete.

The results showed a very clear pattern: memory for the words increased linearly as a function of the number of categories that participants had used during the exposure phase of the experiment. That is, the more finely the participants divided the words into groups (i.e., the more they organised the material), the better their memory for the material was. In this respect organisational factors were brought to the fore. 'Horse–cart' ought to be better remembered than 'horse–onion' on the grounds that horse and cart fall naturally into a familiar grouping. Indeed, something else to emerge, from the follow-up research, was that a primary determinant of memory was how well the participants were able to organise the material rather than how long they spent on the task or how many attempts at sorting the materials they undertook – factors that should be important according to associative theory.

For Mandler (1967, p. 328) such results as these show that 'organization is a necessary condition for memory',

and, by way of definition, organisation implicates 'the formation, availability, and use of consistent relations among the members of a set or subsets such as groups, concepts, categories and chunks' (Mandler, 2002, p. 334). In addition, it was also claimed that an important characteristic of such organisation is that the material be grouped in an hierarchical fashion. Evidence consistent with this was later provided by Bower, Clark, Lesgold and Winzenz (1969). Although the experiment was very involved, for our purposes, the most important difference was with the manner in which the to-be-remembered materials were presented in different conditions. In all conditions lists of words were used, but in blocked conditions the materials were presented in an organised fashion (see Figure 10.1). Here the words were grouped into conceptual hierarchies along with an explicit representation of what those hierarchies were. As the figure shows, the items were grouped according to certain category labels in an hierarchical fashion. In contrast, in random conditions the items were similarly grouped but the hierarchies were nonsensical and the words were (essentially) randomly assigned to the tree structures.

A central result was that the material presented in organised hierarchies was much better recalled (under free recall conditions) than was the corresponding material organised into meaningless tree structures. Indeed Bower et al. reported cases where memory for lists of 112 words was perfect when organised hierarchies were used. Clearly this is an extremely powerful demonstration of how organisational factors really can aid memory, but we need to be careful in not over-interpreting the effects. For instance, Watkins (1989) was keen to point out that the data reflect more about factors relating to stimulus organisation than any wilful attempts by the participants to organise the

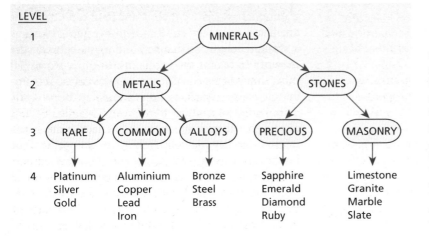

**Figure 10.1 Schematic representation of the structured lists that Bower, Clark, Lesgold and Winzenz (1969) used in their experiments on organisational principles of memory**

*Source*: Bower, G. H., Clark, M. C., Lesgold, A. M., & Winzenz, D. (1969). Hierarchical retrieval schemes in recall of categorized word lists. *Journal of Verbal Learning and Verbal Behavior*, *8*, 323–343 (fig. 1, p. 324). Reproduced with permission from Elsevier.

materials themselves. (If participants could wilfully organise the materials, then why was performance with the random group so poor?)

## Organisation vs. associations?

In addition, Bower and Bryant (1991) have also tempered the interpretation by suggesting that (maybe) the effects can be explained within a strictly associative framework after all. They accepted that the data clearly demonstrate the effectiveness of organisational principles in committing material to memory, but their primary concerns were with trying to explain why such effects may occur. Very briefly, they suggested that such effects might reflect the operation of 'a network of reactivated semantic associations which are used in encoding list items and in cuing their retrieval in inter-related clusters' (p. 166). In other words, the effects reflect (fundamentally) the operations of long-term, semantic memory as conceived as being an associative network comprising (essentially) nodes for items and links or connections that exist between such nodes.

This is not to argue that human memory ought to be conceived of as being an undifferentiated mass of nodes and connections. As Anderson (1976, p. 40) has stated, 'Nothing like direct stimulus-response pairs reside in memory.' In contrast, both Bower and Anderson (Anderson, 1976; Anderson & Bower, 1973, 1974; see also Kintsch, 1974) have expended an awful amount of time and effort in exploring ideas about how long-term semantic memory may be organised along propositional lines (see Chapters 7 and 12). By this view, facts, as represented in the knowledge store, are structured according to elementary propositions. The fact that roses are red would be stored propositionally as '*red(roses)*'; in other words, the node for *red* is linked to the node for *rose* via a relation link (as we will see when we discuss semantic memory in more detail, such a link is known as an *ISA link*). Understanding organisational factors in memory boils down to understanding the operations and nature of the putative long-term store. A basic assumption is that long-term or more specifically, 'long-term semantic' memory is a depository of abstract propositions that capture a person's knowledge about the world. We will discuss various kinds of models of long-term semantic memory in greater detail in Chapter 12. Briefly, one popular idea is that each concept (e.g., ONION, VEGETABLE) can be conceived as a node in a network and nodes are interconnected by various sorts of connections that signify relations between concepts (e.g., ONION *IS A* VEGETABLE).

What is at issue, though, is whether ideas about organisation add anything of substance that is not already covered by principles of associationism. Insofar as propositions are more than simple associations – for instance, a proposition can represent a relation between two items (such as a horse *pulls* a cart) that is something other than a simple association (such as horses and carts commonly co-occur) – then the implication is 'Yes'. However, we need to consider more empirical evidence before we can be comforted by this conclusion. Something else that is of some concern is the fact that, despite the early success and popularity of the organisational approach, it simply 'ran out of steam' towards the late 1970s (Bower & Bryant, 1991; Mandler, 2002). This might suggest that such an approach has only limited utility, but it also seems that other alternatives appeared to offer more attractive avenues for research. One of the most famous and alternative themes to emerge from this time has come to be known as the **levels of processing** approach.

### Pinpoint question 10.2

**Have you forgotten what the three associative causes of forgetting are yet?**

levels of processing  A theory of memory in which the strength of trace is related to the level of analysis, with shallower processing associated with the retrieval of physical characteristics and deeper processing associated with retrieval of semantic information. Deeper levels of processing produce better memory performance than does shallower processing.

## The levels of processing approach

The basic idea here is that memory is intimately tied up with perception insofar as 'the memory trace can be understood as a by-product of perceptual analysis' (Craik & Lockhart, 1972, p. 671). Remembering, by this view, reflects, to large measure, the sorts of perceptual analyses that were brought to bear on the material during initial exposure to it. The main thrust of the argument is based on the assumption that stimulus analysis can be rightly considered to contain various stages or levels of processing. As with other sequential stage models of processing (see Chapter 9), the idea is that a stimulus undergoes various sorts of coding operations such that different coding operations are undertaken at the different stages. At the early (or shallow) stages the physical characteristics of the stimulus are recovered. The later (or deeper) stages involve stimulus recognition and other forms of semantic interpretation. By this view, the durability of a trace for a given stimulus will depend critically on the depth of processing of the stimulus – 'trace persistence is a positive function of the depth to which the stimulus has been analyzed' (p. 671). In other words, the more deeply an item is processed, the better it will be remembered.

Although Craik and Lockhart (1972) outlined the basic levels of processing framework, the now famous empirical supporting evidence was published in detail by Craik and Tulving (1975). Here the basic paradigm involved something known as **incidental learning**. During an initial exposure phase participants were presented with items in the context of various orienting tasks. In a structural orienting task a participant might be asked something about the superficial physical characteristics of a given stimulus word: 'Is the word printed in capital letters?' In a phonemic task a participant might be asked, 'Does the word rhyme with train?' Finally, in a semantic task a participant might be asked, 'Is the word an animal name?' The 'incidental' part of the learning comes about by pretending that the experiment is really about performance in these orienting tasks, rather than about the later memory test of which the participants are currently unaware. The understanding was that, respectively, the different orienting tasks forced the participant to process the stimulus to a particular level such that the tasks, as described, line up in a shallow to deep order. The structural task was the most shallow task and the semantic task was the deepest task. Participants were then tested for memory of the original stimulus words in an unannounced memory test.

Simply put, support for the levels of processing account came from the fact that memory performance was systematically related to the depth of processing associated with the original orienting task – deeper processing gave rise to better levels of performance. Let us call this the **depth of processing effect**. The second clear, and unexpected, result (Craik, 2002) was that items that had been responded to positively during the exposure phase were better remembered than were items that had been responded to negatively and this result occurred for all types of orienting tasks used. So memory for the word 'DOG' was better having answered, 'Yes, it is an animal' than 'No, it is not a plant'. Let us call this the **congruity effect** – congruent (yes) encodings lead to better performance than incongruent (no) encodings.

Collectively, the depth of processing effect and the congruity effect led to the conclusion that two factors were needed in order to explain performance, namely depth and elaboration, respectively (Craik, 2002, p. 309). We have seen how deep processing supports good retention. Regarding the notion of elaboration, the idea was that congruent encodings reflected the fact that a greater number of informative links are established between the item ('DOG') and category (ANIMAL) of the orienting question than when incongruent encodings are available (DOG – PLANT?). With congruent encodings many such links are stored and are then used at the time of retrieval (paraphrasing Bower & Bryant, 1991, p. 157).

> ## Pinpoint question 10.3
>
> **What two effects were revealed in Craik and Tulving (1975)?**

## Problems with levels and alternative accounts

Although the validity and robustness of the effects are not at issue, the notion of depth of processing has never shaken off concerns about its definition. For instance, Eysenck (1978, p. 159) was soon to point out that 'there is danger of using retention-test performance to provide information about the depth of processing, and then using the putative depth of processing to "explain" the retention-test performance: a self-defeating exercise in circularity'. Indeed, as Craik (2002) has recently admitted, this remains something of a problem because the only independent measures of depth, that are seemingly reliable, are participants' own judgements of relative depth of processing (Seamon & Virostek, 1978).

More challenging perhaps are the claims that the phenomena described within the levels of processing framework can also be accounted for in terms of simple associative mechanisms. One alternative way of thinking about the data has been discussed by Bower and Bryant (1991), and this borrows heavily from the earlier accounts of human memory discussed by Anderson and Bower (1973; in their HAM model) and Anderson (1976; in his ACT model). Such models were network models of the kind described above with nodes standing for concepts and links between nodes standing for relations between concepts. In Anderson's model (1976), temporary (short-term or working) memory can be thought of as being a small sub-set of nodes in long-term memory that can be activated at any given time.

In a typical list-learning experiment, a temporary structure is set up that captures the items to be remembered, their serial order, and the fact that they belong to a particular list used in the experiment. Such a temporary structure is set up for every trial and a different temporary structure is constructed for each trial. Critically, if the items are also represented in long-term memory (for instance, if the items are words), then when such representations are activated during the exposure phase, activation will also spread down connections that exist in long-term memory for those items. Two factors now come into play. If an item in long-term memory shares many connections with others then many such connections will be strengthened. In addition, the more often such connections are activated, the more they will become strengthened. Such ideas are firmly rooted in the associative tradition. An item will be more easily remembered if it can be recalled from any of several retrieval cues. So if many connections in memory are strengthened, then this implies that there could exist many effective retrieval cues. An item will be more easily remembered if connections between it and the retrieval cue have been strengthened during initial exposure.

Think of it this way. If asked whether 'poodle', rhymes with 'doodle', then links between the representations that code how 'poodle' and 'doodle' sound are activated in long-term memory and such links will be strengthened. However, when asked whether 'poodle' is an animal, activation will now spread more widely throughout conceptual memory. For instance, you may even activate the memory that next door's dog is a poodle. In other words, the claim is that the sorts of tasks that are used in levels of processing experiments reveal the sort of activation that spreads through the knowledge store. If the task activates many connections between items, as is the case with semantic tasks, then memory is boosted. However, if the task activates few such connections, as in the structural task, then memory is poor. By this view, the levels of processing effect reflects differences in the sorts of existing memory structures that are activated by the different tasks. As Bower and Bryant (1991) have argued, 'The greater number of properties or relations noticed for a given list-word, the more property-to-word associations are strengthened, so that the list-word's recall is boosted' (p. 160).

Bryant and Bower (1991) used a similar argument to account for the congruity effect – the fact that items responded to with a 'Yes' during exposure are recalled better than items that were responded to with 'no'. 'Yes' items will activate connections that already exist in memory (for instance, the 'IS AN' connection between DOG and ANIMAL) and when connections are activated they are strengthened. Although it is possible to trace a pathway within conceptual memory between, say, DOG and ENGINE (so as to, for example, answer the question, 'Is a DOG an ENGINE?'), the basic idea is that activation decreases in strength as it passes through conceptual memory, so in these cases each connection is strengthened but only very weakly. Indeed, Bower and Bryant (1991) discussed further evidence that accords with Mandler's Manifesto: what seems to be critical is that participants actively attend to the categorical associations of the list-words as they are studied and, moreover, that participants use these noticed categories as retrieval cues to aid later recall (paraphrasing, pp. 160–1). ➔ See 'What have we learnt?', below.

## ➔ What have we learnt?

What is being argued here is that both organisational principles and associative principles are at work. Memory is critically dependent on how the participant may organise the material during exposure. Remembering, in this regard, reflects how well the to-be-remembered materials map onto extant knowledge structures in long-term semantic memory. However, what the later work has indicated is that other processes also have a role to play. According to Bower and Bryant (1991), a more complete understanding of remembering can only come about through considering principles of storage and retrieval that are fundamentally *associative* in nature.

To attempt to delve much deeper into these issues is beyond the scope of the present book. It suffices to note, though, that important issues do remain over whether human memory is fundamentally determined by propositional constraints or whether simple associations suffice (see Wilton, 1992, and the later detailed discussion included in Chapter 12). At a fairly basic level, therefore, interesting questions can still be asked about S–R accounts of learning and memory (see Bower, 2000, and also Hintzman, 1993, for more on this).

**incidental learning** A situation in which participants are oriented to materials without being aware that they will have to remember them and be tested on them later.

**depth of processing effect** Deeper (e.g., semantic) processing leads to better memory than does less deep processing. It is easier to remember material when semantic judgements are made than when judgements are made about the surface characteristics of the material. Is it the antonym of 'ambitious'?

**congruity effect** Responding with affirmation leads to better memory than does responding with negation.

## Compartmentalisation of memory

In moving the discussion forward, we turn away from very general claims about processes, to more particular concerns about architectural considerations. Figure 10.2 (abridged from Gregg, 1975) is useful in setting the scene for discussion. As can be seen, there is no mention in the figure of particular sensory modalities or cognitive domains and this is because the distinctions made between different types of memory systems are assumed to cut across these divisions and apply in all cases: hence the notion that memory can be conceived as being a horizontal faculty. The same remembering is going on when you whistle a familiar tune as when you recite your favourite poem.

Figure 10.2a provides a time line, and as Gregg (1975) noted, this ought not to be taken as being a characteristic of the different kinds of memory systems referred to in other parts of the figure. On the con-trary, it refers to the retention intervals that have been used to study the different memory systems.

## Episodic vs. semantic memory

Figure 10.2b draws out a distinction between so-called **episodic memory** and **semantic memory**. We have briefly introduced the notion of semantic memory and we will discuss it at greater length in Chapter 12. Here we need to consider in more detail episodic memory. The notion of episodic memory is gener-ally attributed to Tulving (1972, 1983) but in review, Tulving (2002) cited previous work by Nielsen (1958) that aptly summarises the difference between episodic and semantic memory. Episodic memory, in its most general form, is essentially a phrase used to describe 'memories of life experiences centering around the person . . . and basically involving the element of time' (p. 11). In contrast, semantic memory refers to 'intellectually acquired knowledge not experienced but learned by study and not personal' (p. 11).

So in distinguishing between semantic and episodic memory, whereas semantic memory codes the fact that Paris is the capital city of France, episodic memory codes the contextual features of where and when you learnt this particular fact. In many regards, episodic memory may be taken as being your own record of events that happened to you – it is the personal record of your experiences. The critical point is that such episodic information is coded in terms of spatial and temporal relationships with other salient life events. As Tulving has noted (2002, p. 3), 'Episodic memory is about happenings in particular places at particular times or about "what", "where" and "when".'

Facts stored in semantic memory are simply known. In contrast, a critical signature of episodic memory is the phenomenological experience of remembering.

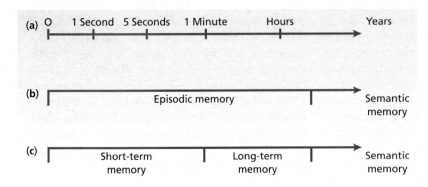

**Figure 10.2 Simple schema for thinking about different memory systems**
(a) provides a time line along which retention intervals have been defined so as to study the different memory systems. (b) draws out the division between episodic and semantic memory. (c) draws out the distinction between short-term, long-term and semantic memory.

*Source*: Gregg, V. (1975). *Human memory* (fig. 5.1, p. 60). London: Methuen. Reproduced with permission from Thomson.

Tulving (1985) has referred to this as the **autonoetic aspect of memory**. It is the claim that, during recollection of a particular event, the event is, in some sense, experienced again: the person becomes aware of having actually experienced the original event.

On the assumption that episodic memory underlies the reconstruction of some earlier experienced event, then other claims have been made about how this sort of episodic memory is responsible for so-called mental time travel (see Tulving, 2002; Suddendorf & Corballis, in press). According to Tulving (2002, p. 2), 'When one thinks today about what one did yesterday, time's arrow is bent in a loop. The rememberer has mentally travelled back into her past and thus violated the law of the irreversibility of the flow of time.' By extension, Suddendorf and Corballis (in press) have argued that the same mechanism surely underlies the ability to project oneself into the future in a bid to predict and plan future events and actions. It can be seen therefore that both forward and backward mental time travel convey adaptive benefits to those organisms that possess such capabilities, particularly as these are fundamental to successful decision-making (see Klein, Cosmides, Tooby & Chance, 2002, for a detailed exposition of this point). For instance, given that yesterday you put your hand in the fire and got burnt, then the very same thing is likely to happen if you do it again today or at any time in the future. On the basis of this form of memory system, you can decide to keep your hand well away from fires in the future. Clearly, therefore, episodic memory is a very useful form of memory to possess.

## Further evidence for the episodic/semantic distinction

Perhaps the most important evidence that has been used to support the division between episodic and semantic memory comes, not from experimental studies with normal healthy adults, but instead from cases in the cognitive neuropsychology literature. Tulving (2002) has provided a detailed description of an adult male known by his initials KC. During a motorcycle accident KC suffered a serious closed-head injury that left him with a very particular sort of amnesia (memory loss). Two sorts of amnesia can be distinguished: (i) **retrograde amnesia** which is an inability to recall memories prior to some particular time (such as the time when the damage to the brain occurred), and (ii) **anterograde amnesia** which is an inability to form

## For example . . .

A cinematic demonstration of backward and forward episodic memory time travel can be found in the Marx Brothers' film *Duck Soup*. As president of Freedonia, Groucho (playing Rufus T. Firefly) is escorted around his state by Harpo in a sidecar (see Figure 10.3). Or at least that's the idea. Revving the vehicle outside his palace, Groucho climbs into the sidecar only for Harpo to detach the motorbike from the sidecar and drive off without him. After a number of similar incidents, Groucho realises his error (travelling backwards in time; remembering numerous stationary outcomes) and figures it would be better if *he* were to drive (travelling forwards in time; predicting successful travel). At which point, Harpo detaches the sidecar and drives off with Groucho once again, going nowhere.

**Figure 10.3 Mental time travel**
Groucho attempting to undertake forward and backward mental time travel in the film *Duck Soup*.
*Source*: Rex Features.

new memories (subsequent to the time when the brain damage occurred). Now there are many and varied flavours of these two types of amnesia (see Baddeley, 1990 and Shallice, 1988, for reviews), but KC is particularly distinctive in the type of amnesia with which he presents.

KC was described as having both anterograde amnesia in being unable to generate new memories of ongoing experiences, in addition to a very particular kind of retrograde amnesia: his semantic memory for knowledge acquired prior to the accident was described as being reasonably intact but he was also described as being unable to remember 'any events, circumstances, or situations from his own life' (Tulving, 2002, p. 14), both prior to and subsequent to the accident. Such an example is a paradigm case of a single dissociation as defined in Chapter 2. The patient KC has an unimpaired semantic memory (strikingly, KC retained the ability to play chess!) but seriously impaired episodic memory. Such a single dissociation is at least consistent with the idea that there are separable (isolable) semantic and episodic memory systems. However, whether this distinction is as clear-cut as some might wish is another matter. Conway (1990, 2005), for instance, has repeatedly considered how memory of personal (autobiographical) details may be inextricably interwoven with other forms of non-personal conceptual/factual knowledge. On these grounds alone, therefore, much more careful analyses of the relations between episodic and semantic memory systems are apparently called for.

---

### Pinpoint question 10.4

**What is the distinction between episodic and semantic memory and how does patient KC support their dissociation?**

---

**episodic memory** Memories of life experiences (after Tulving, 2002).

**semantic memory** Memories of learnt rather than experienced knowledge (after Tulving, 2002).

**autonoetic aspect of memory** According to Tulving (1985), a phenomenological aspect of remembering in which previous events are re-experienced.

**retrograde amnesia** Inability to retrieve memories before a certain time point.

**anterograde amnesia** Inability to retrieve memories after a certain time point.

## Further divisions between memory systems

Figure 10.2c draws out divisions among short-term memory, long-term memory and semantic memory. The distinction between semantic memory and long-term memory seems to be merely a manoeuvre to clarify the difference between factual/conceptual knowledge and knowledge of everything else. Semantic memory is taken to be memory of objective facts about the world that remain true or false regardless of a person's relation to the world (see Chapter 12). More broadly, long-term memory is taken to constitute a person's knowledge of the world and this encompasses everything that they know. An alternative view merely collapses the semantic/long-term distinction and simply acknowledges that one component of long-term memory is semantic memory. In this respect, the critical issues lie with the short-term vs. long-tem memory distinction rather than the rather subtle difference between putative long-term and semantic memory systems.

### Short-term and long-term memory

As Tulving (1993) noted, 'Everybody knows about Donald Broadbent's *Perception and Communication*, a book that changed the history of experimental psychology' (p. 284). Not only did Broadbent summarise most of what was known about attention and attentional control at the time, but at the very heart of his boxes-and-arrows model of attention are distinctions between different types of memory systems and memory processes (see Chapter 8). Fundamentally the distinction between a short-term store and long-term memory is laid bare in the model. This is an architectural distinction based on the assumption that short-term and long-term memory are best conceived as being horizontal faculties as they cut across all cognitive domains. As noted previously (Chapter 8), Broadbent gave away scant details of the nature of long-term memory, although some comments were made about the nature of an associative memory. Much more was given away about the nature of remembering over the short-term. Indeed, in the model we have very clear statements about memory processes and, in discussing forgetting, both the notions of trace decay and item rehearsal were introduced.

In brief, in Broadbent's (1958) account, stimuli impinge on the senses and enter sensory memory (the S system) which has unlimited capacity. Unless items within the sensory memory are passed on for further

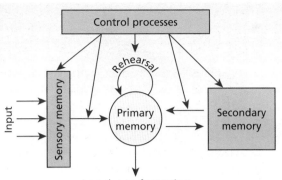

**Figure 10.4 Arrows-and-boxes account of the major memory components and processes as discussed by Kintsch (1970a)**

*Source*: Kintsch, W. (1970a). *Learning memory and conceptual processes* (fig. 4.5, p. 143). New York: Wiley. Reproduced with permission from John Wiley & Sons.

processing then they will decay within a matter of seconds and will be lost. The subsequent stage of processing (the P system) has only very limited capacity. Items are processed serially and there are other strict time constraints that operate now. Only short sequences can be successfully processed and items that are output from the P system may be fed back into the S system – we have the notion of a rehearsal loop (see Chapter 8 for the details).

Figure 10.4 provides a slightly different take on the general framework for thinking. The diagram honours all of the distinctions used in Broadbent (1958); however, in this case short-term memory is labelled primary memory and long-term memory is labelled secondary memory (taken from Kintsch, 1970a).

The now classic example of the existence of some form of short-term memory and the distinction between this and long-term storage is with respect to the ability to recall telephone numbers. (Unfortunately, the force of this example is perhaps now lost because of the advent and ascendancy of mobile telephones – why bother to remember any telephone number when you can get your mobile to do it for you?) In this example, the distinction is between being asked to provide your own telephone number as compared with the case of having to retain a number just read out from the phone book by someone else. Whereas some telephone numbers (such as your own and your best mate's) have been committed to long-term memory and can be easily retrieved from that, memory for novel numbers is both transient and frail. Indeed, thinking about this example allows us to refer to the

notion of rehearsal. Given that memory for the new phone number is so fragile – it will be lost after several seconds – the common strategy is to either physically repeat the number aloud over and over, or covertly repeat the number to oneself. Here the notion of rehearsal is being referred to and, as has been made clear, it can be either overt (out loud) or covert (silent). Covert rehearsal or sub-vocal rehearsal implies the operation of inner speech. Rehearsal is assumed to kick in when the pen and pad normally left beside the phone have gone missing (again!).

Indeed one main plank in the argument for the short-term/long-term distinction is that different forms of forgetting are associated with the two stores and this assumption was central to Broadbent's (1958) account of processing (see Chapter 8). Whereas forgetting associated with information committed to long-term memory was assumed to be at the mercy of the principles of interference, forgetting associated with information committed to the short-term store was assumed to be associated with decay (see Melton, 1963; and Underwood, 1976, p. 54). As we have seen, one strategy to overcome forgetting over the short term (i.e., decay) is to invoke rehearsal. (As Figure 10.5

**Figure 10.5 Short-term memory loss and the big screen**
In the film *Memento*, the character Leonard suffers from a very extreme form of short-term memory loss. To compensate for this he writes (tattoos) critical information on his body. Maybe he should've tried rehearsal! Now where did he put that shopping list?
*Source*: Rex Features/New Market/Everett.

shows, though, there are more drastic measures you can take to prevent forgetting!)

## Forgetting and short-term memory

Of course, having made this claim about different forms of forgetting, it is important to try to get a handle on how forgetting and particularly forgetting over short intervals actually takes place. The most famous examples of how forgetting in the short term may be at the mercy of processes of decay were provided by Brown (1958). The simple case is where a participant is presented with a list of items to remember, and then, following some delay, is asked to recall the list of items. In one example lists comprised one to four serially presented pairs of consonants (e.g., *K P, T S, G J, L Q*) and the delay to recall (i.e., the so-called **retention interval**) was set at around 5 s. Performance across two conditions was measured. Either the retention interval was filled with a digit-reading task (pairs of numbers were presented after the consonants) or it was simply unfilled. In the case of the unfilled retention period there was hardly any forgetting except when longer lists were tested. In contrast, when the delay was filled, much less was recalled and memory declined monotonically as a function of list length (the longer the list length, the more forgetting took place). So when item rehearsal is prohibited, by having participants engage in the distracting digit-reading task, items decay from memory and are lost.

One way to think of decay is in the following terms. There is some form of mental storage system in which so-called traces are deposited. A trace is a short-hand term for some form of mental representation of the to-be-remembered material such as a consonant triple *GHD*. Now think that each trace is like a photograph or painted sign left out in the sun (see Figure 10.6). The critical point is that, just as the photographic image/sign fades with the passage of time, the memory trace also decays. Typically it is assumed that all traces decay passively away – so as soon as a trace is deposited in the store it begins to fade and the only way to halt the decay is by, in a sense, refreshing the traces by rehearsal. In other cases the language of mental activation is discussed (see Nairne, 2002) so traces enter the store and are attributed with a high activation level. With the passage of time this activation dissipates unless the trace is re-activated through the operation of rehearsal.

Such are the explanations of forgetting based on the notion of trace decay. However, as we have seen, an alternative to this account of forgetting is the notion of

**Figure 10.6 An illustration of trace decay**
Decay over time is a fact of life. In the same way that this advertisement has faded through the years, decay theorists argue that so too will our memories.

interference, and although the study by Brown (1958) is toted as being the classic study on trace decay, in a second experiment he did examine whether the forgetting seen in his task might also be due to interference.

In a second experiment Brown (1958) compared performance across a variety of other conditions. For instance, in addition to the previous control condition in which the to-be-remembered materials were followed by an unfilled retention interval, performance was compared in two conditions in which irrelevant material was presented prior to the to-be-remembered consonants. In both these conditions an unfilled retention interval followed the presentation of the to-be-remembered material. Either pairs of digits were presented prior to the to-be-remembered items or pairs of irrelevant consonants were. Here the aim was to see whether prior presentation of irrelevant material would impede (i.e., interfere with) memory for the relevant items and, moreover, whether such an effect depended on the similarity of the relevant and irrelevant material, the underlying assumption being that the more similar the items are to one another, the more they will interfere with one another. In this respect, we would expect irrelevant consonants to have a much more damaging effect than irrelevant digits.

What Brown (1958) was attempting to do here was to contrast forgetting on the basis of decay with forgetting on the basis of interference. On the assumption that the memory traces of the to-be-remembered items decay away in the absence of rehearsal, then Brown made the following argument. Essentially, trace decay ought not to be affected by the nature of the similarity of relations between the presented items. A trace will simply decay, regardless of what is currently in the memory store. However, such ideas contrast with the notion of interference because now relations between presented items are of paramount importance. The more similar the items are, the more likely it is that their corresponding memory traces will interfere with one another. By this view, more interference ought to arise when the relevant and irrelevant material are similar to one another (e.g., *FG, EQ*) than when they are not (e.g., *13, EQ*).

**In order to stop a shopping list falling out of your short-term memory, what could you do and what should you avoid hearing?**

### Proactive and retroactive inhibition

The basic point here is trying to draw out the contrast between decay accounts of forgetting and interference accounts of forgetting, but as Brown (1958) discussed, interference in this context comes in two forms. To reiterate: there is so-called *proactive inhibition* in which material presented now interferes with material presented in the future, and in contrast, there is *retroactive inhibition* in which material presented in the future interferes with material presented now. (Remember learning to play the guitar?) What Brown (1958) was most interested in was proactive inhibition: (i) does irrelevant material presented prior to the relevant material impede memory for the relevant material, and if so, (ii) is interference greater when the relevant and irrelevant material are similar than when they are not?

What he found was that there was little evidence of any proactive inhibition – it did not seem to matter if any irrelevant material was presented or not. Hence the evidence was taken to be consistent with the decay account rather than the interference account. However, as Postman and Keppel (1969) pointed out, there was some slight evidence of forgetting when the relevant consonants were preceded by irrelevant consonants. In other words, there was also some slight evidence to suggest that interference could not be ruled out completely.

## Research focus 10.1

## Playing tag on . . . which street? Childhood memories for street names

With all this talk of decay and interference, you might be wondering how we remember anything at all. Yet it is testament to the wonder of our mental faculties that not only do we remember, but the extent of our memories can often be rather spectacular. Any discussion of childhood memories, for example, requires a consideration of storage and retrieval systems that often span certainly years, decades and even half-centuries. Schmidt, Peeck, Paas and van Breukelen (2000) were interested in these ideas in relation to very long-term retention, and sought to investigate how accurately individuals could remember the street names from their childhood neighbourhood.

Two hundred and eleven former pupils of a school in the Netherlands took part in the study, with ages ranging from 11 to 79. It should be noted, however, that this was the outcome of sending questionnaires to 700 individuals (yielding a response rate of about 30 per cent), so let that be a warning for those of you interested in questionnaire studies!

Participants were provided with a map of their old school neighbourhood (Molenberg) with the street names omitted. Each street had a number and participants were encouraged to write down street names that corresponded to the numbers of the map. In addition, each participant provided information regarding whether they ever lived in the Molenberg neighbourhood, how they got to school, where they used to play and whether they took different routes to school.

First, Schmidt et al. (2000) found that memory for street names differed according to retention interval (in other words, your age) – the older you are, the longer your retention interval to your childhood. While recall of street names was initially high, forgetting was pronounced over the first five years of retention but then stabilised for at least another 30 years or so after that. More street names were recalled as a result of individuals actually living in the Molenberg area, and who played out in the streets. Memories were also much better for individuals

▶

who had walked to school rather than having been driven to school.

Schmidt et al. (2000) were keen to point out that their study demonstrates that many of the phenomena discussed within the laboratory also apply to ecologically valid memories. Ideas related to increasing exposure to items and having a richness of encoding to improve the memory trace also apply to the current example, in that the longer an individual stayed within the Molenberg area and the more that individual interacted within its streets,

the better the retention of the street names. Moreover, the principle of retroactive interference appears to be in effect here since recall of childhood street names was negatively related to the act of moving home. Consequently, it's likely that the new street names would interfere with the memory of those well-loved streets of old. Whatever they were called.

*Source*: Schmidt, H. G., Peeck, V. H., Paas, F., & van Breukelen, G. J. P. (2000). Remembering the street names of one's childhood neighbourhood: A study of very long-term retention. *Memory, 8*, 37–49.

## Further evidence for trace decay

Further (and now classic) evidence for trace decay is shown in Figure 10.7. These decay functions show memory performance as a function of retention interval and of the to-be-remembered material. With these cases, a slightly different procedure to that of Brown's was instigated by Peterson and Peterson (1959). On each trial in the experiment, some to-be-remembered material was presented (e.g., a single **trigram** such as CHJ – see Figure 10.8), and then this was immediately followed by a three-digit number (e.g., *506*). Participants were instructed to count backwards in threes from this number and after some delay they were expected

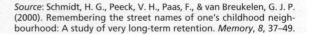
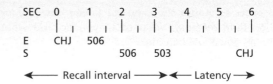

**Figure 10.8 Schematic representation of the events on a trial employing the Brown–Peterson technique**
First, a consonant triple is presented to the participant. Next, a random three-digit number is presented and the participant must begin to count backwards in threes from this number. When the retention interval expires (in this case after 3 s) the participant must attempt to recall the original consonant triple. E = experimenter's instructions; S = subject's utterances.

*Source*: Postman, L., & Keppel, G. (Eds.) (1969). *Verbal learning and memory. Selected readings* (fig. 1, p. 355). Harmondsworth, England: Penguin Books.

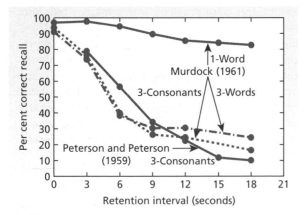

**Figure 10.7 Typical data from experiments that have employed the Brown–Peterson technique**
Various memory functions sketched out in terms of to-be-remembered materials and retention interval from experiments employing the Brown–Peterson technique (see text for further details).

*Source*: Kintsch, W. (1970a). *Learning memory and conceptual processes* (fig. 4.7, p. 148). New York: Wiley. Reproduced with permission from John Wiley & Sons.

to recall the to-be-remembered material. Given the similarity of the two kinds of tests used, across the Brown and the Peterson and Peterson experiments, the general paradigm is now referred to as the Brown–Peterson task. The general point, though, is that this procedure was being used as a tool to examine forgetting when rehearsal is prohibited by an essentially irrelevant task (such as counting backwards).

As can be seen from Figure 10.7, different types of consonant clusters and words have been used in the various cases. Murdock (1961), for instance, showed that performance was pretty good when only a single word was used (although performance did decline a little as the retention interval was increased). However, dramatic falls in performance, as a function of delay, were witnessed when more items for recall were used (such as three unrelated consonants or three unrelated words). From these sorts of results Kintsch (1970a)

## → What have we learnt?

So what are we to take away from this early work? Well, according to Nairne (2002), the results from the Brown–Peterson task are striking for two reasons. First, forgetting is demonstrated when the to-be-remembered materials were very simple (e.g., three consonants) and well below **immediate memory span**. Immediate memory span is determined in the following way. Grab the nearest person and read a random list of, say, three letters at them and then get them to report the letters back to you in exactly the same order as initially presented. If they are exactly correct (i.e., they provide the correct letters in the correct order), then increase the list by one item and repeat the procedure. Keep doing this until your participant makes an error. Using such techniques, it is possible to estimate a person's immediate memory span – the sequence length for which they can correctly recall all the items in the correct order. From the classic paper on memory span by Miller (1956b), the average span is approximately seven items (i.e., the magical number 7 +/– 2 items). More importantly, immediate memory span has been taken as a direct index of the capacity of the short-term store. On the face of it, therefore, performance in the Brown–Peterson task reflects the fact that when rehearsal is prohibited, forgetting (i.e., trace decay) takes place even when the capacity of the short-term store has not been exceeded. Three (consonants) is quite a long way from seven! On these grounds alone, therefore, it is not obvious why trace interference should have any role to play in forgetting in the Brown–Peterson task.

Nairne's (2002) second reason as to why the results are important relates to the previous points about similarity. Given that forgetting in the Brown–Peterson task takes place even when the retention interval is filled with material quite different to the to-be-remembered material (count backwards in

threes while remembering a consonant triple), then it seems that interference (i.e., retroactive inhibition) cannot be operating here. Underpinning this claim is the basic assumption that 'Similarity was the main determinant of interference' (p. 64). The earliest interpretations of the data from the Brown–Peterson task were couched in terms of item decay. In contrast, the later work of Keppel and Underwood (1962) suggested that the main source of forgetting in the Brown–Peterson task was due to proactive inhibition (see also Crowder, 1982): earlier items interfere with memory for the later ones. Given such opposed views, it is important to say a little more, and Figure 10.9 provides the critical data.

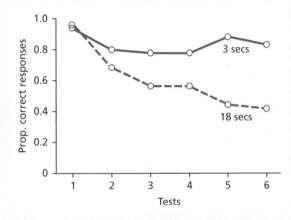

**Figure 10.9 Data taken from Keppel and Underwood (1962)**
The figure shows how performance in the Brown–Peterson task depends critically on (i) how many previous trials have been undertaken by a given participant, and (ii) the retention interval.
*Source*: Postman, L., & Keppel, G. (Eds.) (1969). *Verbal learning and memory. Selected readings* (fig. 2, p. 387). Harmondsworth, England: Penguin Books.

concluded that 'it is the number of units or "chunks" (Miller, 1956a), which determines the rate of forgetting rather than the number of physical elements within an item, such as letters or information units' (Kintsch, 1970a; p. 149). → See 'What have we learnt?', above.

### Release from proactive inhibition

Keppel and Underwood (1962) examined memory performance in the Brown–Peterson task in the fol-

lowing way. At the start of testing, a single trigram of consonants (e.g., *CHJ*) was presented as the to-be-remembered material. Next a number was presented and participants counted backwards in threes from this number for either 3 s or 18 s and then they attempted to recall the trigram. This whole procedure was repeated six times. Figure 10.9 shows the proportion of correct responses as a function of the number of prior trials broken down according to retention delay. The $x = 1$

points show performance on the first trial and, as can be seen, there is no difference in performance on the first trial across the two retention intervals.

Straight away, you'll notice that this basic effect runs completely contrary to the decay account of forgetting, on the assumption that the longer you have to keep the material in mind, the more forgetting ought to take place. Yet what the data show is not this pattern at all. On the first trial there is almost no forgetting, regardless of the delay to recall, in that similarly high levels of performance were observed for both 3 s and 18 s retention intervals. Instead performance in the task decreases as a function of the amount of prior material to which you were exposed. So by trial 6 you will have already been tested with five items, by trial 5 you will have seen four items and so on. Memory performance critically depends on the amount of prior material to which you have been exposed. Hence the data suggest that the primary determiner of forgetting in the Brown–Peterson task is proactive inhibition (current information interfering with later information) and not decay. The importance of these data cannot be underestimated. Indeed Crowder (1989) went to some lengths to substantiate the fact that there is almost no forgetting on the first trial in the Brown–Peterson task in a bid to undermine the notion of forgetting as a function of trace decay.

It would be unfair not to mention, at this juncture, the study by Baddeley and Scott (1971). They carried out a study in which 424 participants were tested in a single-trial Brown–Peterson task (in groups of three to eight at a time in 'a caravan parked in the middle of the University of Sussex Campus', p. 277). Each participant was given a sequence of three, five or seven digits. Either immediate serial recall was tested or a retention interval of up to 36 s was introduced. During the interval the participants were engaged in a letter-copying task. The data were instructive in revealing that forgetting did take place both as the retention interval increased and as the size of the letter sequence did. The critical aspect of the design was that participants were only tested with one sequence so, according to Baddeley and Scott (1971), proactive interference could play no role. Moreover, given the differences between digits (in the to-be-remembered material) and the letters (in the distractor task), retroactive inference was also ruled out. Therefore the most probable reason for the decline in performance was item decay. Against this though, Neath and Surprenant (2003) have recently demonstrated that the data reported by Baddeley and Scott (1971) can be accommodated by an account that the forgetting effect arises because of interference effects

between the items in the sequences. Interference increases with delay and it increases with the amount of information that has to be retained.

Additional evidence for the proactive inhibition account of performance comes from a rather ingenious twist to the Brown–Peterson task introduced by Wickens, Born and Allen (1963). Essentially by switching the category of the to-be-remembered materials (say, from letters to digits) on the very last trial in the task, they showed memory performance improved dramatically – an effect that is known as **release from proactive inhibition**. Again, this effect is most easily understood in terms of interference, with the proviso that interference most likely occurs between similar sorts of items. So if dissimilar items are introduced on the final trial then the prior items that have already been presented will tend not to interfere with them (see Figure 10.10). Memory for these final new category items can reach levels of the first items presented on the trial. This may also go some way to explaining how you're able to learn anything about attachment theory in a developmental psychology seminar after a three-hour workshop on research methods in the same day: the change in subject matter

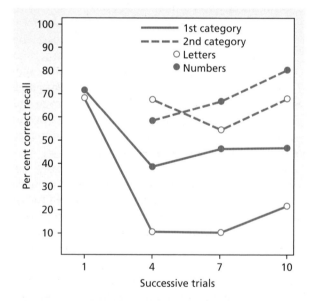

**Figure 10.10 Data discussed by Wickens et al. (1963) showing the now classic release from the proactive inhibition effect**

If the category of the to-be-remembered items is changed (as on the fourth trial here, see dotted lines), then performance improves dramatically relative to cases where the same category is retained over trials (solid lines).

*Source:* Underwood, G. (1976). *Attention and memory* (fig. 2.9, p. 93). Oxford, England: Pergamon Press.

frees you up from proactive inhibition, although whether you're good for anything after three hours' research methods is another issue in itself.

### Short-term forgetting and retroactive inhibition

On the basis of the data so far discussed there is now apparently little support for the notion of forgetting over the short term purely as a consequence of trace decay. The evidence, in contrast, seems to favour that the primary determiner of forgetting over the short term is trace interference. Further support for this conclusion comes from a study by Waugh and Norman (1965). They carried out seminal experiments with something they called the *probe-digit procedure*. On each trial in the experiment, participants were presented with an auditory list of spoken digits. The final digit in the list was a repeat of an item that had already occurred and this so-called probe digit was accompanied by a high-pitch tone. The tone signalled the presence of the probe and the fact that the participant had to try to report back which digit had immediately followed the probe in the list.

By way of example, assume the list was as follows:

4 8 0 9 2 3 4 5 6 8 TONE

Here 8 is the probe digit (because it ends the list and is signalled by the tone) and the correct response would be 0 as 0 immediately follows 8 in the list. Performance in the task is shown by the data in Figure 10.11 and, as you can see, the data are a little complicated. On the *y* axis is the probability of correct recall so large values indicate good memory performance and small values indicate poor levels of performance. On the *x* axis are the number of items that intervene between the two presentations of the probe digit. In our example, the *x* value would be 7 as there are seven intervening items between the first presentation and the second presentation of the digit 8.

As is clearly shown in the figure, performance decreases in a steadily decreasing fashion (monotonically) as the number of intervening items increases. In addition, the figure also shows the data for two rates of presentation. List items were presented either at a slow rate of one item per second or at a faster rate of four items per second. What is going on here is an attempt to adjudicate between forgetting as a process of decay and forgetting as a consequence of retroactive interference (where new information interferes with old information).

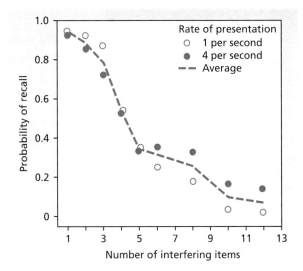

**Figure 10.11 Data described by Waugh and Norman (1965)**
Probability of recall is mapped out as a function of number of interfering items and rate of presentation (see text for further details). The major determiner of performance is the number of interfering items. In other words, interference is a much more potent determiner of memory than is decay in these cases.

*Source*: Waugh, N. C., & Norman, D. A. (1965). Primary memory. *Psychological Review*, *72*, 89–104 (fig. 3, p. 95). Reproduced with permission from APA.

Both accounts of forgetting can explain why the memory for items at the start of the list suffers the most. By the decay account, recall of these items is delayed the longest, that is, right until the presentation of the list is complete. By the interference account, the traces for the early items suffer the most because many items intervene between when the early items were presented and when they are to be recalled. Also, according to both accounts of forgetting, memory for the items at the end of the list suffer the least because the delay to recall is short and few items intervene between the end of the list and recall. To try to disentangle these two accounts, Waugh and Norman (1965) compared performance across two rates of presentation. In doing this, performance for an item at each list position could be compared with cases where the number of intervening items was being held constant but the time that the items were having to be held in memory was varied.

If some sort of time–decay process were important then the rate of forgetting ought to be greater for the slow as compared with the fast rate of presentation. With slow presentation rates the items had to be retained for longer than when a fast presentation rate was used. In contrast to this account, the data revealed

## → What have we learnt?

We have arrived at the following position. The primary basis for forgetting over the short term is apparently interference rather than trace decay as a function of the passage of time. Although there are those who still cling on to the notion of trace decay (Cowan, 1995, p. 105; Baddeley, 1986; Burgess & Hitch, 1999; Page & Norris, 1998; Repovš & Baddeley, 2006), not everyone is convinced by the claim that forgetting over the short term is best described as a process whereby memory traces simply fade away in the absence of some form of reactivation or rehearsal (see Nairne, 2002, for a review; Neath & Surprenant, 2003). This is not to argue that the idea of some form of forgetting due to time-based decay has no supporting evidence (see, for example, the recent carefully controlled studies of Mueller, Seymour, Kieras & Meyer, 2003), but merely that more powerful factors have been identified. In particular, and as Nairne (2002) has commented, 'the rate and extent of forgetting often depend on the specific activities that occur during the retention interval' (p. 63). To avoid any unnecessary controversy, though, it is perhaps best to concur with Baddeley (2000a) who has concluded, 'The issue of whether short-term forgetting reflects decay or interference remains unresolved.'

that the major determiner of performance was the number of intervening items. So yet again there is clear evidence for some form of item interference going on here – in this case the evidence is for retroactive inhibition. Having stated this, however, the data also hint at an effect of presentation rate because recall was slightly worse for the slow presentation rates. The actual statistical test of this effect was not reliable but then again we have to remember that only four participants were actually tested. → See 'What have we learnt?', above.

### Pinpoint question 10.6

Which is the biggest cause of forgetting: decay or interference?

## Further evidence that bears on the short-term/long-term memory distinction

> Homer Simpson: 'How is education supposed to make me feel smarter? Besides, every time I learn something new, it pushes some old stuff out of my brain.'
>
> *Daniels (1994)*

Clearly there is little consensus over the nature of forgetting over the short term (Baddeley, 2000a; Nairne, 2002; Neath & Surprenant, 2003, ch. 6). Even though these arguments are not settled, other concerns also exist over the traditional distinctions between short-term and long-term memory systems. At the very least, we have come to the conclusion that it has proved to be very difficult to base the distinction for different sorts of memory systems on different forms of forgetting. To reiterate: an early idea was that forgetting from short-term memory was assumed to be at the mercy of trace decay whereas forgetting from long-term memory was assumed to be as a consequence of interference (see Melton, 1963, for a very readable account). However, the actual evidence seemed to point to the fact that forgetting over the short term is well explained by processes of interference. It is therefore important to consider what other sort of evidence has been used to bolster the distinction between different short-term and long-term memory systems.

The model shown in Figure 10.4 (page 357), although abridged from Kintsch (1970a), was actually first discussed in detail by Waugh and Norman (1965). At the heart of the model is the distinction between primary (short-term) and secondary (long-term) memory. The critical points are that primary memory is strictly limited in capacity (7 +/− 2 items) and, as Waugh and Norman (1965) stated, 'every item that is attended to enters primary memory' (p. 93). If the capacity of the store is exceeded by the arrival of new items, then old items are displaced from the store (exactly as Homer Simpson described in the above quotation). You can also think of it in terms of packing a suitcase – if you can't get that vital third pair of designer jeans in, then maybe one pair of trainers will have to be ejected. The simple idea is that the short-term store contains a fixed number of slots, or pigeonholes, and if these fill up, the only way to retain a new item is to displace an old item in a first-in/first-out fashion.

If items are displaced from the store there are essentially three options:

1. The item can be read into secondary memory.
2. It can enter the rehearsal loop.
3. It will be lost (i.e., forgotten).

Important corollaries are that items can only enter secondary memory once having passed through primary memory, and also that the chances that an item will enter secondary memory are enhanced the more it is rehearsed. On the basis of all of this it is now possible to argue that memory over the short term can now reflect either or both of two memory systems – it is quite possible that an item can be recovered from either primary or secondary memory depending on where it currently resides. One important implication of this is that performance in a so-called short-term memory task can actually reflect properties of the long-term memory system (see, for example, Hulme, Roodenrys, Schweickert, Brown, Martin & Stuart, 1997; Roodenrys & Quinlan, 2000).

It is ideas such as these that have been exploited mostly in terms of graphical representations of data known as **serial position curves**. Serial position curves are typically generated for data either from a **serial order task** or from a *free recall task*. With a serial order task, items are presented to a participant and the participant then has to report back the items in the sequence that they were originally presented (see previous discussion of immediate memory span). In free recall, participants are presented with a list of items and are simply asked to report back anything that they can remember. The data shown in Figure 10.12 are

taken from a study by Murdock (1962). Here participants were presented with lists of common nouns and then were asked to report back any words that they could remember (under free recall conditions). List length varied from between 10 and 40 items and the nouns were presented either at a fast (1 item every s) or slow (1 item every 2 s) rate.

Such serial position curves (or bow-shaped functions) have a characteristic U-shape and are typically discussed in terms of the early part of the curve, the middle part and the end part, respectively. (The fact that, generally speaking, performance is better for shorter than longer lists is quite intuitive and is known as the **list length effect**.) The early part of the curve reveals a rapid decrease in performance for the first four to five items. The relatively good performance for the first one or two items is known as the **primacy effect**. Performance shown by the middle part of the curve is relatively poor and relatively stable. The dramatic improvement in performance for the last few items is known as the **recency effect** (cf. Craik & Birtwistle, 1971; Tulving & Colotla, 1970).

In simple terms, the basic ideas now are that the recency part of the curve is taken to reflect both the operation of read-out from primary memory and its capacity. An indication of the capacity of primary memory is assumed to be reflected by the asymptote of the recency part of the curve (where the curve reading from right to left, starts to go flat). As can be seen Figure 10.12, the recency effect is relatively stable across the different list lengths. In contrast, the primacy part of the curve is taken to reflect the operation of read-out from secondary memory. The earliest items in the list have been rehearsed the most, hence they have entered and can be recovered from secondary memory.

**Figure 10.12 Classic serial position curves (after Murdock, 1962)**
The notation 10–2 refers to list length (i.e., 10 items) and rate of presentation (i.e., 2 items per s). The curves conform to typical U-shaped functions. Good performance with the items early in the list illustrates the primacy portions of the curves. Good performance with the items later in the list illustrates the recency portions of the curves.

*Source*: Kintsch, W. (1970a). *Learning memory and conceptual processes* (fig. 4.13, p. 161). New York: Wiley. Reproduced with permission from John Wiley & Sons.

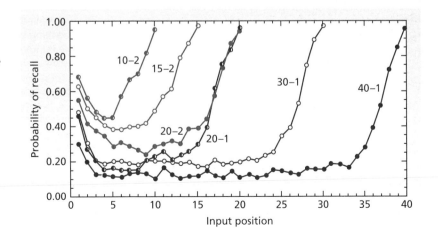

Evidence that converges on these basic ideas was provided by a study by Glanzer and Cunitz (1966). Their second experiment addressed the nature of the recency effect. Participants were presented with a list of words – ten words appeared in each list and after each list participants under free recall instructions were asked to report back the list items. The critical twist here, though, was that across the lists three different conditions were tested. In immediate recall, as soon as the list was completed the participants began to recall the words. In contrast, two further conditions introduced a delay between the end of the list and recall. Under these conditions a number was presented at the end of the list and the participant was instructed to count out loud backwards from the number until told to stop. Two retention intervals of 15 s and 30 s were tested. As can be seen from Figure 10.13a, the recency effect is robust for the immediate delay condition, it dissipates noticeably when a filled delay of 10 s was used and it was essentially abolished when a 30 s delay was introduced.

Such data as these are particularly noteworthy because the manipulation of retention interval selectively affected the recency parts of the curves – the early and middle parts of the curves were essentially unaffected by the factor. What this reveals is a selective dissociation – a factor selectively affects one aspect of performance but leaves others untouched. Such evidence is entirely consistent with the idea of an isolable sub-system – in this case a short-term memory store whose operation and capacity are reflected in the recency effect shown in the last part of the curve.

What is perhaps more impressive, though, is that Glanzer and Cunitz (1966) went on to demonstrate a kind of double dissociation (see Chapter 2). Now in their first experiment two other factors were examined: item repetition and item spacing (i.e., time delay between the presentation of one item and the next in the list). We will concentrate on the spacing variable as this gave rise to the most impressive effects. Now free recall performance was tested with delays of either 3 s, 6 s or 9 s between the words and lists of 20 items were used. The data (shown in Figure 10.13b) essentially replicate that reported by Murdock (1962) in showing that the earlier but not the later part of the curves were affected by the spacing manipulation. In other words, if you increase the pause between each pair of adjacent items in a to-be-remembered list, then memory for the earlier items will benefit. In contrast, the recency parts of the curves were essentially the same regardless of item spacing.

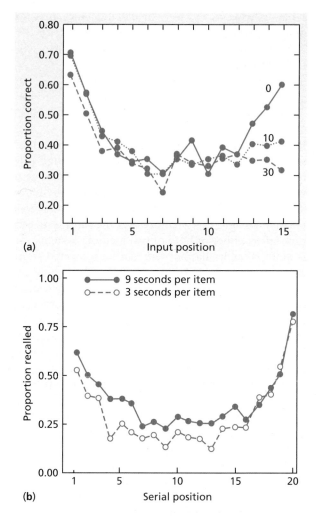

**Figure 10.13 Seminal data from Glanzer and Cunitz (1966)**
(a) Shows serial position curves for three critical cases. Here we have a variable that affects only the recency part of the curves. Performance is examined as a consequence of the delay to the recall cue (the retention interval). When a delay was introduced, participants were given a number to count backwards from at the end of the list. The retention interval was a filled interval. (b) Shows a variable that affects everything but the recency part of the curves. Here the variable is inter-item delay during list presentation. The fact that two variables have independent effects in this way is reminiscent of a double dissociation (see Chapter 2) and has been taken by some to indicate that the primacy and recency effects arise through the operation of quite different mechanisms.

*Sources*: (a) Kintsch, W. (1970a). *Learning memory and conceptual processes* (fig. 4.10, p. 156). New York: Wiley. Reproduced with permission from John Wiley & Sons.
(b) Gregg, V. H. (1986). *Introduction to human memory* (fig. 4.3, p. 98). London: Routledge & Kegan Paul. Reproduced with permission from Taylor & Francis Ltd.

So across these two experiments there is a kind of double dissociation – we have one variable, namely retention interval that affects the later but not the earlier parts of the curve, and there is a different variable, namely item spacing (i.e., presentation rate) that affects the earlier parts of the curve but not the later. Hence we can begin to build a case for two different memory systems – a short-term store evidenced by the recency effect and a long-term store evidenced by the primacy effect.

**list length effect** Memory performance for short lists is typically better than for longer lists.

**primacy effect** In a serial position curve, memory is good for the first few items in a list.

**recency effect (in serial memory)** In a serial position curve, where memory is good for the last few items in a list.

## Pinpoint question 10.7

**What two common effects may be observed in serial position curve data?**

**retention interval** The length of time that individuals are required to hold items in memory before memory is tested.

**trigram** A collection of three letters.

**immediate memory span** The length of sequence of items for which an individual can recall all the items in their correct order.

**release from proactive inhibition** Where memory performance improves as a result of switching the category of to-be-remembered items in a run of trials.

**serial position curves** The pattern of memory performance plotted as a function of whereabouts each item was presented within a list.

**serial order task** Where participants are asked to reinstate previously exposed items in the order in which they were presented.

## The modal model and its detractors

Data such as has just been discussed fit particularly comfortably with the model described by Waugh and Norman (1965) and similar sorts of theoretical ideas were historically discussed in terms of what has come to be known as the modal model. Figure 10.14 shows the account of memory put forward by Atkinson and Shiffrin (1968), and as can be seen, it shares many components with the Waugh and Norman (1965) account. This kind of multi-store, multi-component model came to be known as the **modal model** (because the core components began to occur in the most frequently discussed theories of memory in the literature). At the heart of the modal model is the distinction between short-term and long-term memory and the conception that these components are essentially horizontal faculties – the same memory constraints apply across the board in all domains.

Detractors have taken issue with the model on a number of fronts. One set of commentators have chosen to take a contrary position on the grounds that the distinction between the short-term and long-term systems is not sustainable, hence what we are really

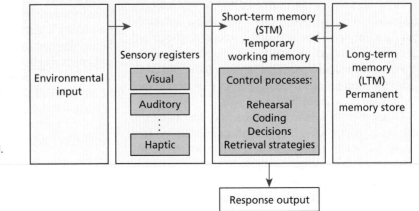

**Figure 10.14 The modal model**
The arrows-and-boxes diagram that summarises the so-called modal model as developed by Atkinson and Shiffrin (1968).

*Source*: Atkinson, R. C. & Shiffrin, R. M. (1976). The control of short-term memory. *Scientific American, 225*, 82–90. Copyright © 1976 Scientific American, Inc. Reproduced with permission.

observing in our experiments is the operation of a single unified memory system (see, for example, Melton, 1963; and also Crowder, 1989, 1993). The other set of detractors have gone in completely the opposite direction and have argued that the short-term/long-term memory distinction is not subdivided enough! A much more psychologically plausible account is one in which temporary memory itself fractionates into several interdependent processing systems (see, for example, Baddeley, 1986; Hitch, 1980; Monsell, 1984). Some of this in-fighting has taken place over how best to understand recency effects.

## Arguments about recency effects

Previously we concluded that the recency effects so far discussed arose because participants were simply reading out the last few items in a list from the short-term store. Such a conclusion was bolstered by the fact that if a filled retention interval of around half a minute transpired after the end of the list, then the recency effect was abolished. In other words, if there was a sufficient opportunity to forget items from the short-term store, then forgetting did indeed take place. In addition, the size of the recency effect was essentially unaffected by list length – again an indication that maybe the last few items were held in some form of short-term store.

However, several other effects were uncovered that seemed to clash with this sort of account. First are the results reported by Bjork and Whitten (1974). The procedure was a little convoluted but the data are striking nonetheless. On each trial the participant was given a list of word pairs to remember. Memory was tested after the end of the list under free recall conditions. In simple terms, each word pair was presented for 2 s and this was followed by a 22 s filled interval in which a distractor task (for instance, solving simple maths problems) was administered. So in-between each presentation of each word pair there was a distractor task to complete. Twelve word pairs were contained in each list and occasionally the distractor activity was interrupted and participants were either asked to recall the immediately preceding word pair or rehearse the immediately preceding word pair.

Three such lists were presented and, following the last list, participants were given an unannounced free recall task in which they had to report all of the members of the last list. What the data showed was a standard serial position curve (as shown in Figure 10.15). Now the reason that this is surprising is that neither primacy nor recency effects should have occurred on

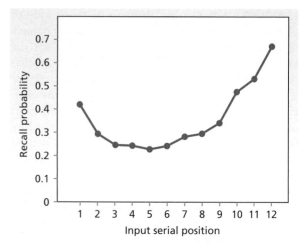

**Figure 10.15  Data from the study by Whitten and Bjork (1972)**
Although this serial position curve appears normal, neither the primacy nor recency effects are predicted from the modal model. The primacy effect was surprising on the basis of the fact that participants were instructed to rehearse only certain items. The recency effect was surprising on the basis of the fact that the end of the list was followed by a filled retention interval of 19 s.

*Source*: Bjork, R. A., & Whitten, W. B. (1974). Recency-sensitive retrieval processes in long-term memory. *Cognitive Psychology, 6,* 173–189 (fig. 1, p. 175). Reproduced with permission from Elsevier.

the basis of the predictions of the modal model. The primacy effect was not expected on the grounds that participants were explicitly instructed to rehearse only particular items during list presentation and not just the first few items. The recency effect was not expected on the grounds that there was a filled retention interval of 19 s interposed between the end of the list and the cue to recall. At the end of the list participants engaged in the number distractor task. According to the modal model, the material included in the distractor activity ought to have entered the short-term store and displaced the last few list items (the 'new stuff' pushing the 'old stuff' out of your brain). Hence by this account there ought not to have been any recency effect. In contrast, such an effect was found and it extended back to items that were presented around 2 minutes prior to the cue to recall: such an interval is well outside the traditionally assumed time limit of short-term memory.

### Long-term recency effects

So what we have here is something known as a *long-term recency effect* that bears considerable similarity to the traditional short-term recency effect. Indeed, a case is beginning to emerge that, more generally, recency

## For example . . .

Think about the last lecture you had. You probably remember more from the start and end of the lecture rather than the middle. This demonstrates your own personal primacy and recency effects for time periods much longer than short-term memory predicts.

effects reflect something other than readout from a transitory short-term store. Two other long-term recency effects are also particularly noteworthy. First there are the data reported by Baddeley and Hitch (1977). They interviewed rugby players immediately after a game and asked each participant to write down as many names of the teams that they recalled having played against during the season. They were given 2 minutes to complete this task and then the data were scored in such a way to reflect the percentage correct recall as a function of intervening games played (e.g., how many players correctly reported playing Fulcester Rovers when the actual game was four matches ago, and so on).

The finding of interest was a marked recency effect such that players' memory for matches tailed off as the number of intervening matches increased. Baddeley and Hitch were also able to eliminate the confound of elapsed time that necessarily exists here using statistics and showed that the effect of forgetting was essentially determined by the number of intervening matches (and not elapsed time). Given that such tests reflected

memory for events spanning weeks and months, the recency effect observed was clearly long term in nature and again cannot possibly be due to the read-out from some short-term store.

The second long-term recency effect is shown in Figure 10.16 as reported by Crowder (1993) and reveals American undergraduates' ability to recall the names of the US presidents. In these data there is clear evidence of both recency and primacy effects. The fact that recency effects can be observed for memory of distant events casts some considerable doubt on the simple idea that such an effect reflects the operation of a specialised short-term memory system. Some have even taken the similarities between the short-term and the long-term recency effects to reflect the operation of the very same memorial processes, and have gone so far as to question the idea for separate memory systems (Crowder, 1993; Nairne, 2002; Neath & Brown, 2006). In contrast, Baddeley and Hitch (1977) preferred to claim that 'we should retain the concept of a short-term or working memory, but that we should not use this to explain recency effects' (p. 664).

**Figure 10.16 Data taken from Crowder (1993)**

Free recall data of American undergraduates' memories for the names of American presidents. Reading from right to left: B = Bush (senior), R = Reagan, C = Carter, F = Ford, N = Nixon. . . . The notable blip in the middle of the curve is for Lincoln. Apart from that, the function clearly reveals both primacy and recency effects. More importantly, this sort of recency effect cannot reflect read-out from some form of short-term store!

*Source*: Crowder, R. G. (1993). Short-term memory: Where do we stand? *Memory & Cognition, 21,* 142–145 (fig. 1, p. 143). Copyright © 1993 by Psychonomic Society. Reproduced with permission.

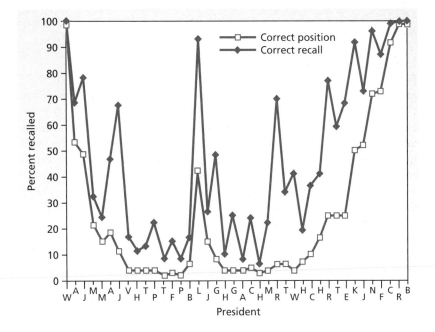

## Faithful all ye come: serial position effects in hymns

One of the problems that Maylor (2002) hinted at, in previous studies of serial position effects, is that individuals are likely to have had greater exposure to the earlier items than the later items. For example, the rugby players in Baddeley and Hitch (1977) would have had more time to discuss matches that occurred earlier on in the season. Therefore, one important control in serial position research with semantic memory is to ensure 'exposure to each item in the sequence is equivalent' (Maylor, 2002, p. 817). This led to the selection of hymn verses as the stimuli of interest, with the assumption being that once you start a hymn you finish it and so have encountered each verse an equivalent number of times.

Fifty-four participants were divided into two groups: churchgoers (27) and non-churchgoers (27), with the understanding that semantic memory for hymns would be considerably reduced in the non-churchgoers. Eighteen hymns each containing six verses were carefully selected, avoiding hymns that told a story and whose order could therefore be easily derived, and also Christmas carols which were considered far too popular, thereby rendering the title of this Research focus box incorrect. Very simply, participants were asked to put the verses for each hymn in the correct order. So top marks for those of you who notice that this is a serial order task rather than a free recall task.

Both primacy and recency effects were observed for this holy hollering, with the first verse being more consistently identified as the first verse (primacy effect) and the last verse being more consistently identified as the last verse (recency effect). Correct positioning of the intermediate verses appeared to be less accurate than the verses at either end, although in all cases churchgoers tended to be more accurate than non-churchgoers. In sum, both churchgoers and non-churchgoers showed both primacy and recency effects for hymn verse ordering, although these effects were bigger for churchgoers.

Before we start to pontificate over one outstanding observation that primacy effects were larger than recency effects, Maylor (2002) suggests that there is a rather trivial explanation for this in that 'the first verse of a hymn probably receives greater exposure than the remaining verses through its inclusion in the announcement of a hymn' (p. 819). Since church hymns are unlikely to fall within the remit of short-term memory, the data demonstrate serial position effects for longer-term semantic memory. There's no reason we can see that you couldn't apply these principles with another kind of lyrical music that takes your fancy, so we look forward to the replication using Napalm Death songs.

*Source*: Maylor, E. A. (2002). Serial position effects in semantic memory: Reconstructing the order of verses of hymns. *Psychonomic Bulletin & Review*, *9*, 816–820.

## Alternative accounts of the recency effects

How else might recency effects be explained? Well, maybe what the data are actually revealing is a fundamental principle of how remembering operates. The basic idea is that as the to-be-recalled items are presented, they are represented (by the participant) in some form of mind-blowing multidimensional psychological space in which various sorts of defining dimensions are possible. To keep it simple, one idea is that the items are represented along some form of psychological time line where the distances between items represent the time between the offset of one item and the onset of the next. Now, in the simplest case, the dimension (the scale) will be an **equal interval**

**scale** where the distance between adjacent units is the same across all points on the scale and corresponds to the same temporal interval at every place on the scale. This is just like the marks on a tape measure, in which 1 cm is the same regardless of whether you're talking about the differences between 1 cm and 2 cm or 147 cm and 148 cm. Let us assume that the current list of to-be-remembered items starts with the presentation of the first item at time 0. The items are spaced every one second so item 2 will occur at time 1, 3 at time 2, 4 at time 3 and so on. In immediate recall situations the prompt to recall the items is coincident with the offset of the last item.

What we know is that with immediate recall there is a large and robust recency effect. If, however, we introduce a filled retention interval between the end of the list and the prompt to recall, then the recency effect is typically abolished. In addition, we also know that long-term recency effects occur in which much longer intervals are at play both between the to-be-remembered items (e.g., rugby matches in a given season) and the prompt to recall. In considering all of these cases, one aim has been to try to provide a unified account that covers all of the findings. Happily, some success at providing such an account has indeed been achieved.

### The ratio rule

The central idea is that performance is critically sensitive to both the interval between items and the interval between the last item and the prompt to recall; respectively, these are known as the **inter-item interval** (or $\Delta t$) and the *retention interval* (or $T$). Indeed, as Figure 10.17 shows, what seems to capture the basic pattern of findings is the ratio of these two intervals (i.e., $\Delta t/T$). If this value is computed for each

to-be-remembered item, then the corresponding series of values correlates highly with memory for the to-be-remembered items. The function for $\Delta t/T$, as plotted by item position in the list, reveals similar sorts of recency effects as do the real memory data. Such ideas define what has come to be known as the **ratio rule** (see Baddeley, 1986, ch. 7; Ward & Tan, 2004): it is the ratio of the inter-item interval to the retention interval that reflects memory for a given item.

Such ideas as these have been discussed in less formal terms by making analogy with a set of equally spaced telephone poles (yet again we should rue the advent of mobile phones!). By this view 'The empirical rule . . . seems to be one that obeys the laws of temporal perspective – as telephone poles vanish into the distance, the relative nearness of the closest one changes less rapidly if they are widely spaced than if they are narrowly spaced' (Crowder, 1982, p. 294). As with the telephone poles, so are the memory traces of to-be-remembered items.

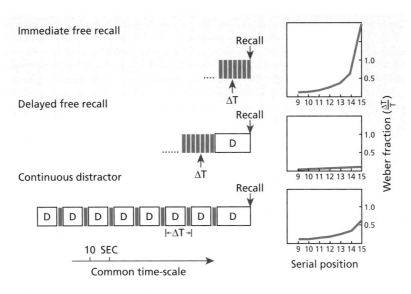

**Figure 10.17 Examples of the operation of the ratio rule**
In the top case the list of to-be-remembered items is presented at a steady pace with no intervening distractor task and is followed by immediate recall. The Weber fraction (see text for details) is computed for each item in the list, and these values are plotted, by item, in the right-hand graphs. Values are included only for the last eight items of the list. If we take the Weber values to be an indicator of how well the items will be recalled, then the graphs indicate the predictions for each case. In the delayed free recall case the items in the list are presented at a steady pace with no intervening distractor task, but now there is a delay to recall. As can be seen, under these conditions no recency effect is expected and none is found. Finally, in the continuous distractor case the items are presented at a steady pace, but now there is an intervening distractor task between every adjacent pair of items (as in the Brown–Peterson technique). With immediate recall the recency effect reappears. Clearly this simple account does a good job of explaining performance across all three conditions.
*Source*: Baddeley, A. D. (1986). *Working memory* (fig. 7.4, p. 157). Oxford, England: Oxford University Press. Reproduced with permission.

## Item distinctiveness

Although such ideas expressed in the ratio rule have been used to account for recency effects, they have been extended more recently to attempt to account for all other characteristics of forgetting. One way in which we can extend the ideas is to think in terms of the $\Delta t/T$ values and think of these as providing an index of something known as **item distinctiveness**. Murdock (1960) has provided perhaps the clearest account of what is meant by distinctiveness in this context – 'the distinctiveness of a given stimulus is the extent to which it "stands out" from other stimuli' (pp. 16–17). So as to avoid any criticism that the notion is circular, Murdock provided a useful mathematical example of how distinctiveness might be quantified (see Figure 10.18).

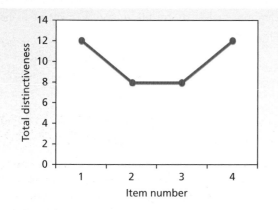

**Figure 10.18 Distinctiveness plotted as a function of item sequence number**

Consider the possibility that items in a list are scaled on some form of psychological dimension, and for ease of exposition assume the dimension is time. The first item is presented at 2 s after a start signal, item 2 is presented at 4 s, item 3 is presented at 6 s and the final item is presented at 8 s. So the list values on the dimension are 2, 4, 6 and 8. Now we can work out each item's distinctiveness value by comparing an item's value with the values for all other items and summing these difference scores.

Item 1: 4 – 2 = **2**; 6 – 2 = **4**; 8 – 2 = **6** Total distinctiveness
$\quad$ (2 + 4 + 6) = 12

Item 2: 4 – 2 = **2**; 6 – 4 = **2**; 8 – 4 = **4** Total distinctiveness
$\quad$ (2 + 2 + 4) = 8

Item 3: 6 – 2 = **4**; 6 – 4 = **2**; 8 – 6 = **2** Total distinctiveness
$\quad$ (4 + 2 + 2) = 8

Item 4: 8 – 2 = **6**; 8 – 4 = **4**; 8 – 6 = **2** Total distinctiveness
$\quad$ (6 + 4 + 2) = 12

Given these distinctiveness values we can plot a serial position curve. If we assume that distinctiveness is the main determiner of memory for a given item, then we can see that the values produce the classic U-shaped serial position curve.

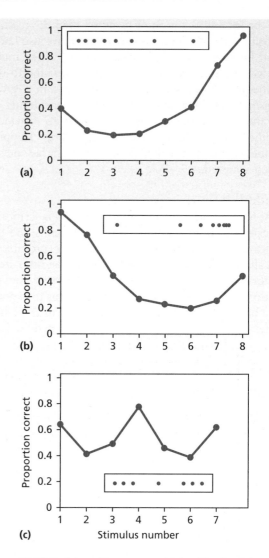

**Figure 10.19 Serial position curves obtained in absolute identification experiments**

Dots connected with solid lines illustrate various serial position curves. In each case the rectangular box contains a schematic representation of item presentation over time. The horizontal dimension of the rectangle represents time (running from left to right) and the dots within the box reflect the instant when a given item was presented. (a) Curve analogous to recency effect. (b) Curve analogous to primacy effect. (c) Isolation effect – memory for an item isolated in the list presentation sequence will be recalled particularly well.

*Source*: Brown, G. D. A., Neath, I., & Chater, N. (2007). A temporal ratio model of memory. *Psychological Review, 114*, 539–576. Reproduced with permission from APA.

More particularly, these kinds of ideas about item distinctiveness are central to several of the more recent accounts of forgetting over the short term (see Neath & Crowder, 1996; and Neath & Surprenant, 2003, ch. 6, for a review). For instance, Brown and Neath (Neath & Brown, 2006; Brown, Neath & Chater, 2006) have developed the basic ideas into a formal model of forgetting known as SIMPLE. Consistent with the name, a fundamental aim here is to try to provide the simplest possible account of memory processes. A stricture is to avoid a proliferation of different memory principles and memory systems – let's just take one idea and push it as far as we can go. According to Brown and Neath, their notions of item distinctiveness can be pushed quite a long way in explaining forgetting. Murdock's (1960) idea of distinctiveness is defined over the whole list of to-be-remembered items and hence we can refer to this as **global distinctiveness**. In contrast Brown and Neath are much more concerned with **local distinctiveness**.

In simplifying greatly, the basic idea is that memory traces are represented internally in some form of multidimensional space. Regions of this space can either be densely or sparsely populated. Take, for example, a simple 1D psychological space related to music bands in which the axis relates to the first word in a band's name. The space around 'The' would be densely populated (*The Beatles*, *The White Stripes*, *The Bonzo Dog Doo-Dah Band*, *The The* even), whereas the space around *Einstürzende* would be much less crowded (containing *Einstürzende Neubauten* only, as far as we know). As a consequence, in densely populated parts of space, it will be difficult to discriminate the individual traces from one another. Hence recall of these traces will be impaired. Alternatively, regions of the space can be sparsely populated in which case, traces will be easily discriminable from one another and they will be easily remembered. Again if we just take the simple case, and assume that the most important dimension is time, then we can use indices of time and the corresponding values on the psychological time line to define item distinctiveness within any region on this dimension. Figure 10.19 shows how such ideas can in principle account for not only the recency effect and the primacy effect but also other item spacing effects in the literature. → See 'What have we learnt?', below.

## Pinpoint question 10.8

**1938, 1940, 1942 and 1976. Which year is more distinctive and why?**

## → What have we learnt?

Currently there is a stand-off in the literature over the issue of whether the distinction between primary and secondary memory is psychologically valid. Neath and Brown (2006) make a very strong case for unifying our conceptions of memory and memory processes under a set of simple principles – this approach is almost a throw-back to behaviourist roots in which we should replace functional accounts of cognitive processes with accounts couched in terms of mathematical equations that describe principles of operation (see also Hintzman, 1993). The major thrust is to try to understand memory in terms of principles of remembering that operate over all time scales. On the understanding that the same principles underlie remembering over the short and the long-term, then maybe the short-term/long-term store distinction needs to be rethought? (Remember Occam's Razor? Right back in Chapter 1.)

Some might object that, in and of themselves, such principles provide little insight into the nature of psychological processes, but in fact Neath and Brown (2006) discussed this as being something of a virtue! Slightly more worrying, though, is that appeals are constantly being made to the notion of 'distinctiveness'. Unfortunately, how this is defined seems to shift in every next paper that is published. Initially, distinctiveness was defined in terms of the temporal proximity of the delivery of the items during exposure. This definition has been refined because other critical factors have emerged. Now *distinctiveness* is discussed in terms of some undefined, multi-dimensional space. In this respect, distinctiveness is being used in much the same way that the behaviourists argued that stimulus generalisation could be explained in terms of *similarity*. In order to explain why animals make generalisation responses to novel instances, simply appeal to some sort of similarity metric: the new instances are similar to these old familiar instances. However, history teaches us that unless such key terms are defined properly, little progress will be made (see Goldstone & Son, 2005).

In contrast to such single mechanism accounts, claims about different isolable memory systems live on in the recent work of Davelaar, Goshen-Gottstein, Ashkenazi, Haarmann and Usher (2005) and Baddeley and colleagues (see Repovš & Baddeley, 2006, for a recent review). It is usually the case that, when such

▶

opposing views confront each other, the higher ground is claimed by the side that can produce a working computer model. However, the debate about one memory system or many systems seemingly cannot be settled by computer simulations only because different working computer models reside in the competing camps. Rather than attempt to adjudicate between these alternatives here, it is perhaps best to draw the current discussion to a close: the controversy still rages and there is no consensus. Indeed it seems that even though the foundational description of the SIMPLE model has (at the time of writing) still to be published (see Brown et al., 2006), important changes to the model have already had to be introduced so as to address more challenging data (see Lewandowsky, Brown, Wright & Nimmo, 2006).

**modal model** The general view that memory comprises different short-term and long-term stores. Specifically attributed to the model of Atkinson and Shiffrin (1968).

**equal interval scale** Some scale of measurement in which the distance between any two adjacent points is the same regardless of where on the scale the two points fall.

**inter-item interval** The time between the presentation of items within a list.

**ratio rule** An attempt to account for recency effects by considering the relationship between the inter-item interval and the retention interval.

**item distinctiveness** The extent to which one particular item stands out from all the others.

**global distinctiveness** In memory experiments, distinctiveness of an item computed relative to the whole of the set of to-be-remembered items.

**local distinctiveness** In memory research, the distinctiveness of an item computed relative to its neighbouring items in a list.

## Memory as a vertical faculty

As noted at the beginning of the chapter, we can either define memory as conforming to Fodor's (1983) notion of a horizontal faculty or we can take a different view and discuss it in terms of vertical faculties. So far our discussion has focused on horizontal faculties and now we should consider vertical faculties. We have already discussed the notion of processing modularity as introduced by Crowder (1989), but he also drew a distinction between this and something he called **coding modularity**. According to coding modularity, memory is not so much some kind of depository of information – a mental warehouse – but should be understood in a completely different way. Memory ought to be understood in terms of the mental operations (the mental procedures) that were brought to bear when the to-be-remembered material was originally perceived. By this view, memory of a particular event is defined not as a passive record of the event but more in terms of the actual encoding operations that were enacted when the event occurred. Memory of a sound is quite different from memory of a sight simply because sound and vision invoke quite different coding operations. In this regard the ideas are very in tune with those about vertical faculties – different sorts of processes are operating in different domains. In his own words, 'If the memory is, in some sense, an aspect of the original event, then the memory resides in wherever in the nervous system the event did' (p. 273).

Although there is clearly something of a neurophysiological flavour to these ideas, the focus of interest is with functional consequences – what sorts of cognitive representations and processes are implicated by this form of theorising? The basic claim is that, rather than think in terms of generic stores or generic processes, a more fruitful idea is to explore special-purpose mechanisms. The most famous such account is that provided by the working memory model (Baddeley & Hitch, 1974).

## The working memory model

In stark contrast to the monolithic memory accounts in which all forms of forgetting reflect the operation of a single system and a common set of processes (e.g., Neath & Brown, 2006), there are those who take a completely contrary perspective. The contrasting argument is that the data actually point in a quite different direction, namely one in which many different components are found (Baddeley, 1986; Hitch, 1980; Monsell, 1984).

The most famous and sustained attempt at establishing evidence for this view has been carried out by Baddeley and colleagues (Repovš & Baddeley, 2006, provide a very good summary overview). The resulting framework for thinking is contained in his **working memory** account of performance. In some respects, the motivation for the working memory models can be thought of as being an exercise in thinking at the computational level (Marr, 1982; see Chapter 1). Here the aim was to stand back a little from the production line approach to data generation and ask more pressing questions about what the purpose of some form of short-term memory system might actually be. The answer, in broad stokes, is that it should provide on-line support for the current cognitive demands that are placed on the human processing system. More formally, it supports, via various different types of temporary storage mechanisms, the ability to carry out complicated cognitive tasks. For instance, in being able to understand speech, some temporary record must be maintained over the course of several seconds so that the listener can comprehend what is being said as the speech signal unfolds over time. Information from different parts of the sentences must be integrated over time such that a coherent message is recovered. Consequently, working memory mechanisms are posited for the temporary storage of the speech signal so that speech understanding can take place (see Monsell, 1984).

Another example is the case of attempting to do mental arithmetical problems. What is a quarter of 368? Well, halve it and then halve it again. In order to do this, some form of representation of the original problem must be stored together with some notion of a plan (i.e., What are the steps to take? In what order should they be taken?), and some representation of interim results (e.g., half of 368 is 174). It is these sorts of tasks and these sorts of mechanisms that are being thought about in terms of the working memory model. Underlying the working memory approach is the desire to show just what the functions of the short-term storage mechanisms really are.

More specifically, the basic assumption is that it is best to conceive of the model in terms of a set of temporary storage mechanisms (known as *slave systems*) together with a component or controller (the central executive) responsible for co-ordinating how processing takes places across the slave system. More particularly, the central executive is seen to be 'some type of supervisor or scheduler, capable of selecting strategies and integrating information from several different sources' (Baddeley, 1986, p. 225). In fact, in

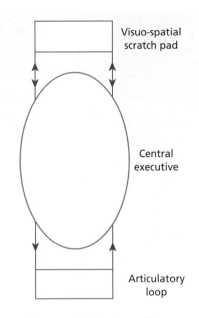

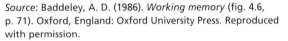

**Figure 10.20 The original tripartite working memory model as discussed by Baddeley and Hitch (1974)**

*Source*: Baddeley, A. D. (1986). *Working memory* (fig. 4.6, p. 71). Oxford, England: Oxford University Press. Reproduced with permission.

the original model proposed by Baddeley and Hitch (1974) a tripartite model was put forward comprising the **central executive** (as just defined) and two slave systems, namely a **phonological loop** and a **visuospatial scratch pad** or **sketch pad** (see Figure 10.20).

### The phonological loop

As originally conceived, the phonological loop is a speech-based system that is implicated in the on-line processing of verbal material; in particular it is implicated in the comprehension and production of speech. For instance, it is used to hold word forms that a person is preparing to speak aloud. The loop itself was further decomposed into a phonological store and articulatory rehearsal process. This store/rehearsal division echoes the similar distinction in Broadbent's (1958) model. Items may be held in the store and unless they are reactivated by the act of rehearsal they decay away and are lost (Baddeley, 2000b, p. 419). Fundamentally, therefore, the model is quite clear in accepting that short-term forgetting can be attributed to trace decay. Trace decay can be overcome by the reactivation of the traces through the use of rehearsal. The most recent and detailed account of the phonological loop is shown in Figure 10.21 as discussed by Baddeley (2003).

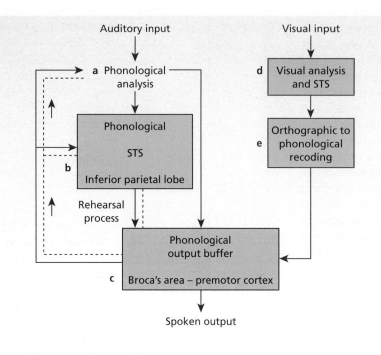

**Figure 10.21 The present-day incarnation of the phonological loop**

Other key distinctions currently being discussed in the working memory literature are also included in the figure. Central to the figure is the idea that 'Auditory information gains direct access to a phonological store, after which it passes to an output buffer for recall or recycling through rehearsal. Visual material can be recoded verbally and then gain access to the phonological store through rehearsal' (Baddeley, 2003). (a) indicates phonological analysis; (b) short-term storage; (c) programming of speech; (d) visual encoding; and (e) grapheme-to-phoneme conversion.

*Source*: Baddeley, A. D. (2003). Working memory: Looking back and looking forward. *Nature Reviews Neuroscience*, 4, 829–839 (fig. 2, p. 831). Reproduced with permission from Macmillan Publishers Ltd.

## The phonological loop: relevant data

More particularly, it has been accepted that the characteristics of the phonological loop have been revealed by various well-established effects in the literature.

1. *The phonological similarity effect* – similar sounding items are more difficult to recall over the short term than are dissimilar items. The original work was carried out with letters (*V, B, D, T* etc. vs. *X, K, H, Y* etc., Conrad, 1964), but the effect generalises when words are used (Baddeley, 1966).

2. *The irrelevant speech effect* (alternatively, the unattended speech effect) – memory for visually presented verbal items (consonants in the study by Colle & Welsh, 1976; digits in the study by Salamé & Baddeley, 1982) is impaired by the simultaneous presentation of spoken material (e.g., words, consonants, non-words, etc.) that the participant is told to ignore. Performance is gauged relative to control conditions in which no additional auditory material is presented.

3. *The word length effect* – A central reference here is to the work of Baddeley, Thomson and Buchanan (1975). They found that immediate serial recall for short monosyllable words was considerably better than that for longer five-syllable words.

4. *Articulatory suppression* – the effects of articulatory suppression are many and varied. Here it suffices to note that the idea is to have participants repeatedly articulate a word unrelated to the material presented in a concurrent memory task. For instance, have participants repeat '*the, the, the . . .*' over and over while they are also engaged in some form of immediate serial recall task.

Having very briefly summarised the foundational evidence-base, it is now important to look at how this has been used to support the working memory construct of a phonological loop.

## The phonological similarity effect

The **phonological similarity effect** has been taken to reflect the fact that some form of speech-based storage system is implicated by certain immediate memory tasks. The idea is that in certain circumstances the to-be-remembered items are temporally coded into some form of phonological code that captures information about how each item sounds. As Baddeley (2007, p. 61) has recently asserted, 'Items are stored as a series of phonological features'. If you don't know the language and are asked to repeat a Turkish sentence, then phonological information is the only thing you can use to assist in parroting the phrase back. The phonological similarity effect shows that, whatever the nature of the maintenance processes are, they are clearly compromised when attempts are made to recall similar sounding items over the short-term relative to dissimilar sounding items. According to the working memory model, if similar sounding items are held in the store then as they decay it is quite possible that they become less distinguishable from each other and hence errors in recall emerge (although in the most recent discussion of the effect, quite a variety of mechanisms are considered – Baddeley, 2007, p. 61).

## The irrelevant speech effect

Such conclusions as these are also backed up by the **irrelevant speech effect**. In a critical experiment Salamé and Baddeley (1982, Experiment 3) examined serial digit recall under various conditions. Importantly, the digits were presented visually, serially one at a time. Performance was best in a quiet control condition in which the serial recall task was tested in isolation. Performance was systematically poorer when irrelevant words were played concurrently as the digits were presented visually (this is the basic irrelevant speech effect). Such evidence fits well with the idea of a phonological loop on the understanding that the digits, though presented visually, are recoded into some form of sound-based (phonological) coding. Items are then stored in terms of how they sound. The evidence suggests that the irrelevant speech in some way interferes with the phonological coding of the visually presented digits. Problems arise in recoding the visually presented items into a phonological form because of the concurrent presentation of irrelevant speech, and the similar codes required in both cases.

In addition, performance under the same conditions was also tested when participants undertook **articulatory suppression** (repeating a single word such as 'the the the . . .' aloud over and over again). Generally, performance was much worse under conditions of suppression but more importantly the irrelevant speech effect was also abolished. Participants were generally poor in recalling items under conditions of articulatory suppression but they were no worse in the presence of irrelevant speech than they were in its absence. From the working memory point of view the results were interpreted in the following way. It was assumed that because suppression completely compromises the ability to recode the visually presented digits into some form of phonological code, there can be no additional effects attributable to irrelevant sound.

There are many vexed issues here, however, and the field has moved on considerably since the initial data were reported. For instance, more recently, Larsen and Baddeley (2003) have argued that effects of irrelevant speech are located in the phonological store, whereas the effects of articulatory suppression are twofold. First, suppression prevents visual items from being recoded into the phonological store, and second, it also prevents rehearsal (p. 1262). A thorough discussion of the specific issues, though, would take us too far into an almost impenetrable thicket of claims and counterclaims. Needless to say, little consensus has emerged, and although the data have been discussed as being perfectly consistent with the working memory model (Baddeley & Larsen, 2003), others have taken a quite different view (e.g., Neath, Farley & Surprenant, 2003). When initially reported, however, the data were pleasingly consistent with the working memory model.

## The word length effect

Much has been made of the **word length effect**. For instance, Baddeley et al. (1975) reported data that they took to be extremely revealing about the processes of sub-vocal rehearsal. One major finding was the fairly direct linear relationship between how quickly words could be articulated and how well such words could be recalled. More critically, the idea was that the capacity of the articulatory loop seemed to be best considered in terms of how many words could be articulated within a fixed interval (i.e., the temporal duration as given by the amount of mental recoding tape) that constituted the articulatory loop. Essentially, memory span seemed to reflect the number of words that could be spoken within a fixed interval: that is, more short, quickly spoken words than longer, more slowly spoken words. More formally:

Words held on loop
= temporal duration of loop × speech rate

or

Words correctly recalled
= T seconds × words articulated/second

Within the working memory model the idea is simply that 'the number of items that can be immediately recalled depends on how often each item can be rehearsed subvocally' (Neath & Surprenant, 2003, p. 72). In the working memory account the duration of the loop is assumed to be of a constant amount of time, say T = 1.5 seconds. What varies, therefore, is how long it takes to articulate the words that are to be remembered. For instance, assume four short words can be articulated in 1 s but that only two long words can be articulated in 1 s. This means that six short words can be held on the loop (i.e., 1.5 × 4) but only three long words can be (i.e., 1.5 × 2). Such an account provides a relatively straightforward explanation of why there is such a systematic (linear and direct) relation between speech rate and memory span. As noted succinctly by Neath, Brown, Poirier and Fortin (2005, p. 230), 'Short and long items both decay, but because shorter items take less time to say, more items can be refreshed.'

As with the irrelevant sound effect, however, the working memory account of the word length effect has its critics. Challenging data do exist (Tehan & Humphreys, 1988; see Brown & Kirsner, 1980, for related concerns) and alternative explanations have been put forward. For instance, one idea is that the effect can be explained without recourse to the notion of rehearsal whatsoever. The alternative idea is that longer words (by their very nature) contain more components than short words and it may be that the ability to maintain many components places more demands on storage than is the case when few components have to be stored (see Brown & Hulme, 1995; Hulme, Surprenant, Bireta, Stuart & Neath, 2004; Neath & Nairne, 1995). Yet again, though, the arguments continue to go back and forth (see Baddeley, Chinocotta, Stafford & Turk, 2002; Nairne, 2002) and the competing camps remain facing off against each other.

**What four effects support the notion of a phonological loop?**

## Visuo-spatial, short-term memory

In the same way that there is a slave system posited to subserve verbal tasks, the *visuo-spatial scratch pad* or sketch pad is posited to subserve the maintenance of visual/spatial information over the short term. One experiment nicely summaries some of the properties of such a system (Logie, Zucco & Baddeley, 1990, Experiment 2). In this experiment two sorts of memory span tests were used. In the letter span tests a sequence of visually presented letters was presented on the screen of a computer one at a time every 3 s. There then followed a gap of 2 s before a comparison sequence was then presented. In the comparison sequence, one of the original letters was replaced by a different letter, and participants were asked to indicate when such a replacement occurred in the sequence. The sequence lengths were increased until participants were unable to respond correctly over three such sequences. To be clear, the letter span tests were taken

to reflect something about the capacity of the phonological loop.

In contrast, additional visual span tests were run. Now matrix patterns were used comprising adjoining outline squares. On the first trial two squares were presented (one above the other) and one of the squares was filled. Participants viewed this pattern; there was then a 2 s blank interval (in which the matrix was removed) and a comparison matrix was presented. One square in the comparison matrix that was previously white was changed to black. The participants' task was to indicate which square had changed. In order to estimate span, the size of the matrix of squares increased by two as long as the participants were correct. When participants began to err, an estimate of span was made relative to the most complex matrix that they were able to remember correctly.

Estimates of both verbal and visual span were made in single- and dual-task conditions. Two versions of a secondary task were used (after Brooks, 1967; see Figure 10.22). In the visual version of the task, participants were asked to form a visual image of a 4 × 4 matrix and imagine the nature of the matrix when given instructions of the type 'In the starting square put a 1. The next square to the right put a 2.' The task was to imagine the sequence of instructions using visual imagery as an aid. In the verbal version of the task, participants were not asked to use any form of imagery but they were asked to remember a series of 'instructions' that were formally equivalent to the visual commands but made no sense; for example, 'In the starting square put a 1. The next square to the quick put a 2.'

The aim here was to look at the pattern of interference in the span tests as a function of the verbal/visual nature of the Brooks secondary tasks. On the assumption that there are separate, functionally independent slave systems, then there ought to be selective interference but only when the primary and secondary tasks call on the same slave system. So, if a verbal span primary task is combined with a verbal Brooks secondary task, then performance on the verbal span task should suffer. In addition, if a visual span primary task is combined with a visual Brooks secondary task, then performance on the visual span task should suffer. Less interference ought to occur if visual and verbal tasks are combined.

The results were generally clear-cut and showed that the measures of span decreased significantly when measures were taken under dual- as compared to single-task conditions. Most critically, though, performance suffered the most when both tasks called upon verbal

**Figure 10.22 Examples of the sorts of matrix memory tasks used to study visual aspects of short-term memory, devised by Brooks (1967)**

*Source*: Hitch, G. J. (1980). Developing the concept of working memory. In G. Claxton (Ed.), *Cognitive psychology: New directions* (pp. 154–196). Reproduced with permission.

| Spatial material | Nonsense material |
|---|---|
| In the starting square put a 1. | In the starting square put a 1. |
| In the next square to the *right* put a 2. | In the next square to the *quick* put a 2. |
| In the next square *up* put a 3. | In the next square to the *good* put a 3. |
| In the next square to the *right* put a 4. | In the next square to the *quick* put a 4. |
| In the next square *down* put a 5. | In the next square to the *bad* put a 5. |
| In the next square *down* put a 6. | In the next square to the *bad* put a 6. |
| In the next square to the *left* put a 7. | In the next square to the *show* put a 7. |
| In the next square *down* put an 8. | In the next square to the *bad* put an 8. |

mechanisms or both tasks called upon visual mechanisms. When the tasks called upon separate verbal and visual mechanisms then the dual-task decrement was not as pronounced. As Logie et al. (1990) argued, 'The results are certainly highly consistent with the hypothesis of a specialized short-term visual storage system, that is independent of an analogous system for short-term verbal storage' (p. 68).

Given that this experiment demonstrates how interference operates in such a selective fashion then it provides converging evidence for the separate slave systems in the working memory account. Much further work has shown how the visuo-spatial scratch pad may itself fractionate into separate systems that are selectively dedicated to the maintenance of visual and spatial information respectively. So although in its original guise the scratch pad was a catch-all memory system for all kinds of non-verbal material of a visual nature, more recently the idea has been that there may well be separate systems that code visual and spatial material separately (see Baddeley, 2000a, p. 85; Repovš & Baddeley, 2006).

Indeed, a thorough defence of this idea has been provided by Klauer and Zhao (2004). The implication is that, whereas visual characteristics of the stimuli may be captured by one system (e.g., the display contains a big red square, a small green triangle, a small blue circle), a different system is assumed to be responsible for keeping track of whereabouts in the displays the objects actually were (one object is to the upper left, another is central, the third is to the lower left). Here there is an acknowledgement that 'what' and 'where' information may be coded separately in the human visual system. Upon a moment's reflection, keeping track of this sort of information is vitally important in cases where you are frantically searching for your house keys just as the bus is coming down the road.

## The central executive

In positing a variety of temporary memory mechanisms, it was acknowledged that to avoid chaos some scheduler or controller is needed, which, in a sense, oversees the moment-by-moment operations that are taking place across the system as a whole. Given this, the *central executive* was posited as 'some type of supervisor or scheduler . . . related to the control of attention' (Baddeley, 1986, p. 225) – 'an attentional control system' (Baddeley, 2000b, p. 418). Others have been less kind, and have referred to the central executive as 'that grossly overworked functionary on whom all inconvenient failures of explanation of cognitive phenomena are loaded by our generation' (Rabbitt, 2001).

Relatively early on, the central executive was fleshed out in terms of the Norman and Shallice (1986) model of attentional control (Baddeley, 1986). In that model, two basic control processes are posited. In the first the idea is that behaviour may be controlled by common repertoires, habits or so-called *schemata*. So routine, highly familiar tasks such as driving, making tea and toast, tying shoelaces, etc. are controlled in a semi-automatic fashion by running off the typical actions as specified in the behavioural schemata. For instance, first fill the kettle, then switch it on, then select a tea bag, and so on. Within the model it was acknowledged that on a moment-to-moment basis more than one schema could be activated – the kettle is boiling but the phone has started to ring. To operate effectively, the system must be able to schedule what to do next and in this respect the current conflicts must be resolved. Such conflict resolution may be carried out in a so-called *semi-automatic fashion* (via something termed *contention scheduling*) by attending to priorities and current environmental cues. The kettle switches itself off so it is okay to answer the phone.

In addition to such semi-automatic processes, there is the notion of an overall controller known in the account as the *supervisory attentional system* (the dramatic sounding SAS) – a limited capacity attentional component. Such a system is particularly useful when the individual is confronted by a novel situation – a situation for which there are no stored schemata. For instance, think of the first time you ever played Sudoku. The rules are simple, but because you have never played before, you have no stored routines about how to go about filling in the numbers. In such a novel situation you have to be able to plan out what to do. Even though there are no schemata to call on, there may well be useful information stored in memory that you may well be able to bring to bear on the task. Such operations as these were assumed to be carried out by the SAS.

According to Baddeley (1986), the SAS is also called upon in a variety of other cases such as when the semi-automatic control processes break down, such as when the kettle does not switch itself off, smoke begins to pour out of the plug, someone knocks at the front door and the telephone is still ringing. Something has to take charge and decide what action to take next – this is where the SAS steps forward.

In 1986 Baddeley adopted the Norman and Shallice idea of the SAS as an appropriate mechanism for thinking about the central executive component in the working memory model. Later in 1996 Baddeley extended the discussion of the central executive in terms of four basic capacities: 'the ability to focus, to divide and to switch attention, and the ability to relate the content of working memory to long-term memory' (Repovš & Baddeley, 2006, p. 13). When cast in these terms it becomes immediately apparent that the operations associated with the central executive are fundamental to task switching (see Chapter 9) and the ability to co-ordinate performance in dual-task situations, such as those previously described. In this regard the study by Logie et al. (1990) is informative. Although the selective patterns of interference converge on the idea of special-purpose memory systems with their own processing resources, the overall dual-task decrement reveals how general resources may also be consumed (see Chapter 8). From a working memory perspective, such general processing resources are associated with the central executive. Figure 10.23 provides in schematic form the basic working memory model as discussed so far.

Research focus 10.3

## Standing in the way of control: restarting the central executive after brain injury

So far we have been discussing the issues associated with a normally functioning working memory, such as how the slave systems of the phonological loop and visuo-spatial scratch pad are controlled and overseen by the central executive. But what happens if something goes wrong with one of these systems? Does the whole of working memory collapse around our ears (somewhat literally) or can the system be restarted through the processes of rehabilitation? Serino, Ciaramelli, Di Santantonio, Malagu, Servadei and Làdavas (2007) were inter-

ested in exactly these kinds of questions and sought to find individuals with central executive deficits.

Serino et al. (2007) found a sample of nine individuals, all of whom had experienced traumatic brain injury and were experiencing working memory difficulties. The idea here was that, instead of retraining individuals on specific cognitive functions, if an attempt was made to improve more general central executive processes then these benefits might be passed on to other processes such as divided attention and long-term memory which rely on the

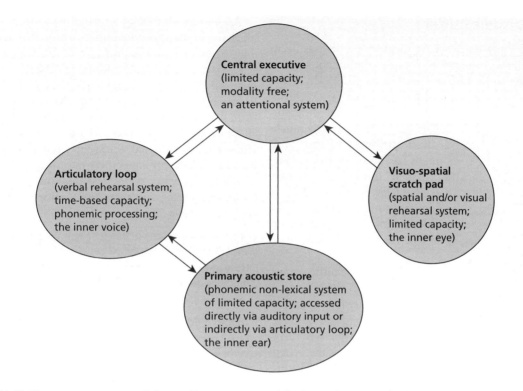

**Figure 10.23 The core components of the working memory model prior to the introduction of the episodic buffer**

*Source*: Cohen, G., Eysenck, M. W., & Le Voi, M. E. (1986). *Memory: a cognitive approach* (fig. 2.4, p. 67). Milton Keynes, England: Open University Press. Reproduced with permission of the Open University Press Publishing Company.

central executive for successful operation. Participants completed a battery of tests before undergoing working memory training, after a period of general stimulation training (labelled GST) in which central executive function was not predicted to improve, and after the experimental training (labelled WMT) which directly sought to improve working memory. Serino et al. (2007) stated that the important difference between GST and WMT was that, while both employed the same materials, 'WMT required the continuous manipulation and updating of information in WM [working memory] and therefore tapped CES [central executive system] processes, the tasks used during the GST only required basic-level attention demands . . .' (p. 15).

A significant effect of session was observed in that participants began to show improvement within test battery scores but, as predicted, this was only after training that was designed to improve working memory (WMT) and not general skills (GST). In addition, the success of the WMT was contingent upon aspects of the test battery that focused on measuring central executive processes. For example,

long-term memory and divided attention were shown to improve after working memory training, but things like processing speed and sustained attention were not shown to improve. As Serino et al. (2007) stated, improved divided attention reflects an increased ability to distribute resources among competing tasks which fits neatly with the central executive's job description.

In sum, retraining the central executive after traumatic brain injury appeared to facilitate a broad range of tasks concerned with the division of resources between slave systems, keeping track of current and future goals and the maintenance of longer-term memory traces. Importantly Serino et al. (2007) also noted that WMT also improved self-efficacy and everyday functioning, leading to a promising outlook for those individuals who found their working memory had actually stopped working.

*Source*: Serino, A., Ciaramelli, E., Di Santantonio, A., Malagu, S., Servadei, F., & Làdavas, E. (2007). A pilot study for rehabilitation of central executive deficits after traumatic brain injury. *Brain Injury*, *21*, 11–19.

## The episodic buffer

More recently the working memory model has been extended by the addition of a new component known as the **episodic buffer** (see Figure 10.24). In 1986 the claim was that one role for the central executive was 'integrating information from several different sources' (Baddeley, 1986, p. 225). More recently much more importance has been attributed to this, and therefore a new component has been posited to take responsibility for this; namely the episodic buffer (Baddeley, 2000b; Allen, Baddeley & Hitch, 2006) – 'a limited-capacity temporary storage system that is capable of integrating information from a variety of sources' (Baddeley, 2000b, p. 421) to form integrated episodes.

Part of the motivation for the episodic buffer came from certain perceived limitations of the original tripartite system. For instance, although memory span for random items is well described by the magic number 7 +/–2 (i.e., the typical memory span is between five and nine items), span increases dramatically when the to-be-remembered words can be organised into sentences – as with other cases of chunking (Miller, 1956b) – estimates of up to 16 words have been reported (Baddeley, Vallar & Wilson, 1987). These fall outside the bounds of normal estimates of the capacity of the phonological loop hence some other form of storage back-up is needed. The episodic buffer is a possible mechanism that is being tapped in such cases.

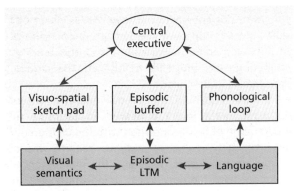

**Figure 10.24 The extended working memory model with the incorporation of the episodic buffer**
It is of current interest whether there should be direct connections between the episodic buffer and, on the one hand, the phonological loop, and on the other, the visuo-spatial sketch pad.

*Source*: Baddeley, A. D. (2000b). The episodic buffer: A new component of working memory? *Trends in Cognitive Science, 4,* 417–423 (fig. 1, p. 421). Reproduced with permission from Elsevier.

Aside from providing a further temporary storage mechanism, the episodic buffer is primarily responsible for taking information cast in different formats (e.g., visual, verbal, etc.) and integrating this in some form of multi-dimensional coding (Baddeley, 2003). It has been discussed as being the storage system from which information can be consciously retrieved (Repovš & Baddeley, 2006). The episodic buffer provides a sort of mental workspace; the storage component of the central executive into which all manner of information can be represented and stored on a temporary basis (Baddeley, 2007). → See 'What have we learnt?', page 383.

→ See 'What have we learnt?', page 383.

### Pinpoint question 10.10

How are earlier and later conceptions of the working memory model different?

**coding modularity** According to Crowder (1989), the idea that memory is a function of the processes that were brought to bear on the material when it was initially encountered.

**working memory** A framework of thinking about short-term memory, first devised by Baddeley and Hitch (1974). It is assumed that there are specific temporary storage mechanisms related to different types of information and these are controlled by a central executive.

**central executive** In the working memory model, a mechanism that oversees the operation of the slave systems in terms of scheduling and control.

**phonological loop** In the working memory model, one of the slave systems controlled by the central executive concerned with the on-line processing of verbal information.

**visuo-spatial scratch pad (sketch pad)** In the working memory model, one of the slave systems controlled by the central executive concerned with the short-term maintenance of visual and spatial information.

**phonological similarity effect** An experimental effect related to working memory in which similar-sounding items are more difficult to recall than dissimilar-sounding items.

**irrelevant speech effect** Where the presentation of irrelevant speech concurrently with to-be-remembered items impairs memory performance.

**articulatory suppression** The active repetition of spoken items in a bid to inhibit sub-vocal rehearsal. Used primarily to disrupt the phonological loop component of the working memory model.

## → What have we learnt?

It would be quite easy to write in much more length and detail about the working memory model. It is without doubt the most influential account of short-term memory to emerge over the last 30 years. It has been, and continues to be, used as a framework for thinking about short-term memory processes throughout cognitive psychology, developmental psychology and, indeed, clinical psychology. It is currently the most written-about account of the short-term memory, and therefore it should come as little surprise that it has many detractors and critics.

Some of the alternative points of view have been mentioned in passing here, but a more detailed critique would take us too far from our present concerns. The fact that the theory has such wide application can be seen as either a strength or as a fatal weakness. On the one hand, the fact that such a large body of evidence converges on the unifying framework is astonishingly impressive. Indeed, the account marries well with the modularity of mind thesis which has underpinned much of what has been written about here. In this regard, the idea of special-purpose memory systems fits well with the idea of input modules and the vertical faculties (Fodor, 1983).

On the other hand, the fact that the model appears to account for almost any aspect of remembering over the short term could be taken as a weakness. We might ask whether the theory is truly falsifiable (as discussed in Chapter 1) especially when challenging data are addressed by the generation of a new memory component such as the episodic buffer. Under what circumstances must we abandon the model and begin to think seriously in terms of alternative frameworks? If we can simply bolt on a new component or store, while leaving the original architecture intact, then we may pause to wonder whether the model can really be falsified.

---

**word length effect** The finding that recall for short words is better than recall for long words.

**episodic buffer** In the extended working memory model, a component responsible for integrating information from different sources and different modalities.

**chunking** The fact that memory over the short term is facilitated if the material can be recoded into a smaller number of meaningful packets or chunks. The sequence of letters R E M B B C C I A will be better recalled if coded into REM BBC CIA.

---

## Concluding comments

Although we have covered much ground, the landscape of memory research is vast. One notable characteristic of much of the work is that there are high aspirations to ask questions about the fundamental nature of memory. In practice, though, a downside is that much of the research is obsessively transfixed with particular laboratory-based paradigms. Indeed the obsession with immediate serial order tasks is particularly unhealthy, especially when we are making such little progress on basic issues. It is particularly alarming that we still do not understand the conditions under which forgetting is due to decay or interference (or indeed whether forgetting can ever be adequately explained in terms of decay). Maybe such questions are just too difficult to answer? Given that they are, then we might as well run another span task.

Although the working memory model was developed with aspirations to explain how such short-term storage mechanisms subserve more general cognitive tasks, much of the associated research has been constrained by laboratory-based tasks that have only tenuous relations with anything that goes on outside the laboratory. This is not the place to rehearse the arguments for and against everyday memory research (Banaji & Crowder, 1989; Conway, 1989; Morton, 1989; Roediger, 1989). All that is being suggested is that basic issues still remain over how performance in the laboratory directly informs ideas about memory outside the laboratory. We will consider some of these issues in much more detail in the next chapter.

In closing, it is perhaps best to stand back and ask some fairly basic questions. Nairne (2005) made some extremely sensible observations. According to him, 'Our capacity to access and use the past did not develop in a vacuum: instead our memory systems evolved to help us solve particular problems, adaptive problems that arose in our ancestral past . . . Nature designs, or selects, particular structural features because they aid in solving a problem faced by the species' (p. 116). What is being discussed here are concerns about computational level issues (see Marr, 1982) – questions need to be asked about the logic and purpose of the system. What is particularly interesting about Nairne's comments is the emphasis that is placed on how memory must be intimately connected with problem solving. In much the same way that the argument has been made here (see Chapter 6) that perception cannot be divorced from problem solving, Nairne also sees intimate relations between memory and problem solving. On these grounds, it seems that yet again the evidence leads us to conclude that it is the ability to solve problems that is central to being human.

## CHAPTER SUMMARY

- One view of memory is that it is a horizontal faculty because the same set of processing constraints apply across all domains. Associative theory, as discussed by Bower (1970), provides a prime example of this view of memory. Memory traces of to-be-remembered items are formed and these may be linked by an associative bond between them. Evidence against an associative account of memory was derived from paired associate learning studies, in which participants who were invited to rote learn the pairs of stimuli recalled the items less successfully than those who generated interacting memory imagery for the two items. Reasons as to why such effects arise are also discussed.

- Bower (2000) identified three main associative causes of forgetting. First, memory traces can simply decay as a function of time. Second, memory representations can change over time, reducing the amount of material available at the time of recovery. Third, individual memories can interfere with one another, of which there are two kinds: proactive interference is when old information interferes with new information while retroactive interference is when new information interferes with old information.

- In contrast to such a behaviourist account of memory, Mandler (1967) argued that the organisation of the to-be-remembered materials is just as important as the strength of associative bonds between them. He found that both the identification of consistent relations between items and the organisation of these items into hierarchies facilitated memory recall. However, it is possible to discuss this kind of organisation in terms of propositions (Bower & Bryant, 1991) and to reconcile the ideas with associative accounts of memory.

- Alternative frameworks for thinking about memory have yielded substantially more interest. In the levels of processing framework (Craik & Lockhart, 1972), memory is thought to be intimately connected with perception, in that memory traces become more durable as the depth of processing the item receives becomes deeper. For example, semantic analysis is deeper than phonological analysis, and phonological analysis is deeper than physical analysis. The framework has been criticised on the grounds that the definition of depth of processing is based on a circular argument (Eysenck, 1978). It also seems that the basic effects may be explained in terms of simple associative mechanisms (Bower & Bryant, 1991).

- Tulving (1972) provided a critical distinction in the literature between episodic (personal life experiences) and semantic (acquired world knowledge) memory. Episodic memory has an autonoetic quality in that when recalling previous personal life events, the event is in some sense re-experienced. This makes possible both backward and forward mental time travel (Tulving, 2002), in that one can think about what has happened (backward) in order to predict what will happen in the future (forward).

- Memory may be further divided in terms of shorter-term and longer-term systems. According to Broadbent (1958), external stimuli are received by an early sensory system (the S system) which has an unlimited capacity. However, items from the S system are quickly lost via a process of natural decay if they do not enter a later processing system (the P system) which has a limited capacity. Information from the P system can be fed back to the S system via maintenance rehearsal. Within these systems two mechanisms of forgetting may be identified – whereas forgetting associated with information committed to long-term memory was assumed to be at the mercy of the principles of interference, forgetting associated with information committed to the short-term store was assumed to be associated with decay.

- Issues remain over how best to describe forgetting over the short term, though, and interference accounts of short-term forgetting have been discussed in the literature. Indeed, while evidence has accrued for both decay and interference as an account of forgetting within a short-term memory system, the issue is unresolved (Baddeley, 2000a) although there is some suggestion of a greater effect for interference than decay.

- One way of collecting evidence regarding the distinction between short- and long-term memory systems is examining serial position curves. Here, participants are typically presented with lists of items and memory performance is examined as a function of whereabouts in the list the item came. Two effects are typically apparent: the primacy effect in which performance for the first few list items are improved, and the recent effect in which performance for the last few list items are improved. The guiding principle is that the recency effect should reflect read-out from the short-term memory system while the primacy effect should reflect the operation of long-term memory.

- Manipulations such as retention interval (e.g., Glanzer & Cunitz, 1966) reveal dissociations in serial position curve experiments in that longer retention intervals tend to impact more on the recency effect than the primacy effect. In contrast, other manipulations such as item spacing seem to have a much larger primacy than recency effect. The double dissociation provides evidence for discrete memory systems, each sensitive to their own constraints. However, the idea that the recency effect reflects the operation of short-term memory has come under scrutiny with the observation that recency effects can still be observed for longer retention intervals than short-term memory would allow for (Baddeley & Hitch, 1977; Crowder, 1993). Alternative explanations regarding the recency effect have arisen, which tend to focus on the distinctiveness of an item among its other members of the list (Murdock, 1960).

- All of the above may be treated as a discussion of memory as a horizontal faculty, breaching all cognitive domains and operating in the same way regardless of input or context. One famous approach that treats memory as a vertical faculty, invoking the use of special-purpose mechanisms, is the working memory model of Baddeley and Hitch (1974). In essence, the working memory model involves temporary storage mechanisms related to different types of information, the control of which are overseen by a central executive. Two of these 'slave' systems have been identified: the phonological loop and the visuo-spatial scratch pad. The phonological loop is thought to be concerned with the on-line processing of verbal information, and evidence for it may be derived from the phonological similarity effect, the irrelevant speech effect, the word length effect and articulatory suppression. In contrast, the visuo-spatial scratch pad is thought to be involved with the short-term retention of visual and spatial information, and evidence for dissociations between the phonological loop and the visuo-spatial scratch pad have been reported (Logie, Zucco & Baddeley, 1990). As an extension of the original model, in addition to the central executive, there is also an appeal to an episodic buffer (Baddeley, 2000b) which is thought to bring together discrete pieces of information.

## ANSWERS TO PINPOINT QUESTIONS

10.1  A useful way to remember the pairing of ELEPHANT–RIBBON is to generate a mental imagery of the two items interacting (e.g., an elephant tying a ribbon).

10.2  The three associative causes of forgetting are decay, modification of trace over time and (proactive or retroactive) interference.

10.3  Craik and Tulving (1975) revealed a depth of processing effect in that deeper processing led to better memory and a congruency effect in

that affirmative responding led to better memory than negative responding.

10.4  Semantic memory refers to memories of learnt rather than experienced knowledge, whereas episodic memory refers to memories of life experience (after Tulving, 2002). KC supports the distinction between the two because he presents with a single dissociation – his semantic memory is intact but his episodic memory is impaired.

10.5    Overt or covert rehearsal would help retain information in short-term memory, and you should also try to avoid hearing other people's shopping lists.

10.6    The biggest cause of forgetting appears to be interference rather than decay.

10.7    The two effects common to serial position curves are the primacy effect – words early in a list are recalled well – and the recency effect – words that appeared towards the end of a list are recalled well.

10.8    1976 is the most distinctive year because the sum of the difference between this year and all other years is the greatest (Murdock, 1960).

10.9    The phonological similarity effect, the irrelevant speech effect, the word length effect and articulatory suppression all support the phonological loop component of the working memory model.

10.10    Later versions of the working memory model incorporate an episodic buffer, to allow for the integration of information from a number of different sources.

## CHAPTER 11

# HUMAN MEMORY
## Fallibilities and failures

## LEARNING OBJECTIVES

**By the end of this chapter, you should be able to:**

- Describe the headed record model of memory (Morton, Hammersley & Bekerian, 1985).
- Discuss the data related to eyewitness testimony and the implication for memory.
- Discuss multiple accounts of the misleading information effect with respect to headed records, the destructive actualisation hypothesis (Schwarz & Stahlberg, 2003) and the encoding specificity principle (Tulving & Thomson, 1973).
- Recognise the way in which signal detection theory can be applied to explaining false memories.
- Identify how false memories apply to the real world and to aging samples.

## CHAPTER CONTENTS

# Night

MAN: I'm talking about that time by the river.

WOMAN: What time?

MAN: The first time. On the bridge. Starting at the bridge.

*Pause*

WOMAN: I can't remember.

MAN: On the bridge. We stopped and looked down at the river. It was night. There were lamps lit on the towpath. We were alone. We looked up the river. I put my hand on the small of your waist. Don't you remember? I put my hand under your coat.

*Pause*

WOMAN: Was it winter?

MAN: Of course it was winter. It was when we met. It was our first walk. You must remember that.

WOMAN: I remember walking. I remember walking with you.

MAN: The first time? Our first walk?

WOMAN: Yes, of course I remember that.

*Pause*

We walked down a road into a field, through some railings. We walked to a corner of the field and then we stood by the railings.

MAN: No. It was on the bridge that we stopped.

*Pause*

WOMAN: That was someone else.

MAN: Rubbish.

WOMAN: That was another girl.

MAN: It was years ago. You've forgotten.

*Pause*

I remember the light on the water . . .

(Pinter, 1969/1991, pp. 213–214)

## REFLECTIVE QUESTIONS

1. What happens when you can't *remember* something from your past but you *know* it took place? What implications does this have for the way in which memory is structured? Have you ever struggled to retrieve an individual's name, yet could describe exactly what they looked like, what clothes they used to wear, and the way they ate their cereal in the morning?

2. Have you ever convinced yourself you experienced something you actually didn't? Perhaps you remember an event quite differently from your friend. How did this memory feel compared to other memories that you know to be true? How easy was it to retrieve details from your apparently false memory?

## Introduction and preliminary considerations

In the last chapter we were concerned with the detailed theories that have been put forward to account for remembering over the short and very short term. Despite the more popular obsession with memory for the serial order of lists of words, other researchers have been interested in trying to make their work speak to memory as it occurs in the real world. In this chapter, therefore, we focus on ideas about how dependable memory is when confronted with events that occur naturally outside the laboratory. We have to tread a fine line here because, of course, experiments on the serial recall of lists of nonsense materials may well tell us about basic memory processes that apply generally. There is therefore little point in trying to build a case against such work on the grounds of artificiality alone. All that is being asserted is that the subject matter of the work to be covered in this chapter is much more easily related to personal impressions of the world than we have considered so far. Performance in tasks in which the participant is asked to report back in reverse order a list of rare and unrelated words, at a given tempo, is not something that will concern us now.

More generally, this chapter is concerned with the basic nature of memory as revealed by its fallibilities and failures. This is why quite a lot of the chapter is taken up with research concerning the validity of eyewitness recollection. One of the rather striking things about the research on eyewitness memory is that it points to a rather dim view of what human memory is actually like: one that underlines the unreliability of memory. So despite the fact that you are convinced that it was Tim who hid Gareth's stapler, actually it was Dawn. Why do such errors in recollection occur? Are such errors indicative of some fatal flaw in the way in which memories are maintained? Or are there more mundane reasons for such failures?

We have all had cases where our recollections of an event do not match other people's memories of the same event, such as the couple in Harold Pinter's *Night*. We are all familiar with the caricature of the absent-minded professor who is so immersed in thinking about third-order differential equations that the baby has been left in the supermarket trolley. We also take great delight in the fragile memories of the grandparents as we insist that they have failed to sugar their tea. Examples such as these typify familiar cases of memory limitations. In this chapter, we go much further than simply listing such phenomena. We address concerns about the fallibility of human memory in general – memory failures that apparently plague us all.

There will also be some close scrutiny of how sensitive our memories are to suggestion. We'll also examine how false memories come about and also how memory changes with age, particularly with respect to the ability to recollect old memories. By the end of the chapter, we'll still be none the wiser whether the old couple actually stopped on the bridge or the railings, but we should be in a better position to understand why these discrepancies occur.

We begin our discussion by focusing on one framework for thinking that helps set the scene for many of the issues we consider. This framework is provided by the headed records account of Morton, Hammersley and Bekerian (1985). There is no implication that this account provides an adequate explanation of memory processes in general or that it is correct in detail. Indeed, it is only fair to point out that the account is surrounded by controversy. All that is being accepted, though, is that the account provides a very useful vehicle by which we can introduce and discuss some basic issues about the nature of human memory.

## Headed records

Let's push things forward by returning to the computer metaphor of memory and by focusing on a human information processing account that has taken this metaphor to be a rather literal framework for thinking about human memory. The account is known as the **headed records model** (Morton et al., 1985). (There has been some controversy over whether to call this account a *framework* or *model*. Indeed, according to Morton, 1997, some critics have even stooped low enough to refer to it as 'Southern Californian soft-porn philosophy'. In the present context the terms *account*, *framework* and *model* will be used interchangeably.) In the headed records model there is a distinction between the thing being remembered and (essentially) its index or catalogue number (to revert to our library analogy). The actual distinction is discussed in terms of the **memory unit** (the information being remembered) and the **access key** (the thing that is used to retrieve the information being remembered).

The memory units are referred to as records. They are discrete (i.e., independent of one another, like items in a warehouse – see Figure 11.1), but there appears to be no commitment in the model to any particular organisational principles. There is no assumption that the records themselves are interlinked or organised, as in a network model of memory (see Chapter 12), nor are there any claims about similar items being stored in similar places. The account does not rule out such principles of organisation (see Morton, 1991), but it commits itself to none. In this regard, the furniture warehouse could be completely disorganised (there is no table section, chair section, etc.) – all the items could be stored at random. Records can be of any size and anything can be stored in a record. Again the warehouse analogy is exact because the storage units can contain items of any type (tables and chairs, not just

**Figure 11.1 Does memory operate like a warehouse?** Is the memory of your first day at college behind one of these doors?

books as in the library) and the items themselves can be of any size (a wardrobe or bar stool).

Turning to the access keys: in the headed records account these are referred to as headings. Headings act as the means by which records are retrieved. A simple way to think about this is in terms of searching for someone to fit a kitchen in the Yellow Pages. So start by looking under Kitchens, or Joiners, or Builders. It may be that the same firm is listed under all three. What this means is that the same record (the firm) can be accessed under different headings. Each entry in the phone book provides an access key to the same phone number. Take a more psychological example: to retrieve information about the Rolling Stones from the (mental) record of *The Rolling Stones*, headings could exist for *Mick, Keith, Charlie, Ronnie, Brown Sugar, hip OAPs, tax-exiled musicians*, etc.

What we have here is a notion of memory comprising two sorts of stores:

1. We have a compartment in which the headings are kept.
2. We also have a different compartment in which the records are kept.

Given this, it is important to understand how it is that the two components are supposed to interact. In the model, the basic idea is that memory retrieval follows a particular set of operations. Initially something known as a *description* is formed. This is a combination of an intentional search strategy plus current retrieval cues, and could be formulated on your own or someone else's need to know. For instance, you might be asked, 'What band does Keith Richards play in?' In this case,

the description would contain the basic information KEITH RICHARDS and the specified goal of recovering which rock band he plays for. This description is then used to try to find a match with a corresponding heading. All headings in the store are compared in parallel, and the most recently used relevant heading is then appropriated and used to recover its corresponding record. Information from that record is then interrogated and the answer to the question is provided (one hopes). Clearly, if no match is found (between a description and a heading), then the question cannot be answered because no record can be retrieved.

In summary, and as Morton et al. (1985, pp. 8–9) noted, the retrieval cycle is decomposed into four steps:

1. The formation of a description.
2. Attempting to secure a match between a description and a heading.
3. Retrieval of the associated record.
4. Evaluation of the retrieved record.

**Pinpoint question 11.1**

**If you have correctly encoded and stored a memory, how might you still not be able to find it again?**

## Headed records and various memory phenomena

It should be stressed that this is just one of many possible frameworks (models? Southern Californian soft-porn philosophies?) for thinking about memory, but what is of interest here is how it has been applied in attempting to address common memory phenomena. For instance, Morton et al. (1985) discussed the frequent occasions on which a person can be reminded of a particular incident in their past, but they are completely unable to recall anything about it. Various cues to recall can be provided such as the time and place and the protagonists in the to-be-remembered episode, but to no avail. Perhaps surprisingly, though, some other minor detail may trigger the memory. Remember that time we all went down to the beach? You know, when we buried you up to your neck in sand? It was a public holiday? You lost your sunglasses? Now you've got it! According to the theory, the minor detail that is the effective cue to recall is contained in the critical heading. In contrast, the other details that proved to be ineffective cues to recall are contained in the record. The record can only be activated by an appropriate heading.

A similar explanation is provided for the other familiar lapse of memory in which many personal details can be provided about an individual, but it is still impossible to recall their name. You know, the guy who hangs around the coffee bar, drinking Earl Grey tea, wears a beret, smokes cheroots, works in the Sociology Department . . . According to the headed records account, here is a case in which accessing the correct heading is problematic. All of the information provided as clues to the person's identity is stored in the record, yet the person's name is included in the heading, not the record. The cues to recall are included in the record but this cannot be used to retrieve the heading: it is the heading that is used to retrieve information stored in the record. Retrieval does not operate in reverse in this account. What the account allows for is the possibility that successful retrieval of a given memory may depend on something that is apparently incidental to or irrelevant to the memory. For instance, his name may leap to mind once you catch a waft of Earl Grey tea (Morton, 1991, pp. 200–1). It is the smell of Earl Grey tea that is part of the heading for the record of *Ronnie Spart*.

One aspect of the model that is reasonably provocative is the idea that each event that is stored, is stored independently of all others, and that each stored event has its own retrieval cue (heading). In addition, there is the central claim that once a record is stored it cannot be changed. Such claims as these have been used to explain certain phenomena usually discussed under the title of 'eyewitness memory'.

## Pinpoint question 11.2

**Is the retrieval of a heading or record a more efficient cue to recall?**

**headed records model** A human information processing account in which memory units are separate from access keys. Information is recovered from memory by first forming an access key and then using this to recover appropriate stored memories.

**memory unit** In the headed records model, information that is stored in long-term memory that holds the content of some to-be-remembered material.

**access key** In the headed records model, the mental cue that is used to retrieve information from long-term memory.

## Eyewitness memory

There is now an extensive literature on eyewitness memory (Loftus, 1979a), but a simple aim here is to describe the basic phenomena and show how these might be explained. (Special reference will later be made to how the headed records account fares with the data.) The classic demonstration was originally documented by Loftus and colleagues (Loftus, 1975, 1979a, 1979b; Loftus & Palmer, 1974) in a (now) standard paradigm. In an initial *exposure phase*, participants are presented with some material; following this they are provided with further related material; finally they are given an *unannounced memory test* for the material presented in the exposure phase. One particular example suffices. Loftus and Palmer (1974) showed groups of participants seven very short films, each of which showed a car accident. Following each film a short questionnaire was administered: participants were asked to give a brief account of what they had just seen and they were also quizzed with a specific question. The critical question was about the speed of the vehicles: 'About how fast were cars going when they $x$ with each other?' Across different participants the $x$ was replaced with 'smashed' (40.5), 'collided' (39.3), 'bumped' (38.1), 'hit' (34.0) and 'contacted' (31.8). Here the numbers in the brackets refer to average estimates of the cars' speed (in mph) when the different verbs were used. So as can be seen (from the numbers), the manner in which the question was framed fundamentally changed the kinds of responses that the participants provided.

Now, of course, there are (at least) two possible explanations of this effect. The first is slightly uninteresting – namely that participants were merely induced into responding in a particular way because of the language used. If asked, 'How fast were the cars travelling when they smashed into one another?' this has the implication that the cars were travelling at some considerable speed, whereas if anything the opposite is true when the term 'contacted' is used. You are hardly likely to respond that the cars were travelling at 40 mph when they *contacted* with each other! The second possibility is slightly more interesting and seems to indicate that the language used actually altered the participants' memory of the event. Participants remembered the accident to be more (or less) severe than it actually was because of the type of language used after they had witnessed the events.

To follow up on the latter so-called *memory hypothesis*, Loftus and Palmer (1974) ran a second experiment in which participants again saw a short film of a car accident and they were again quizzed about the memory of the depicted events. Now the same sorts of loaded questions were included, but importantly a further crucial question was also included. Now participants were asked, 'Did you see any broken glass?' In replicating the original result, participants again estimated that the cars were travelling faster when quizzed with 'smashed' than when quizzed with 'hit'. More importantly, though, participants quizzed with the 'smashed' question were much more likely to report the presence of broken glass than were those quizzed with the 'hit' question. This was despite the fact that there was no broken glass shown in the film of the accident. In this respect the memory hypothesis was supported: not only did participants misremember the actual speed of the cars but they also misremembered other plausible information that was not included in the original event. McCloskey and Zaragoza (1985) named this kind of result the **misleading information effect** and there are now many documented cases in which this kind of effect occurs (see Ayers & Reder, 1998, for an extensive review, and for further discussion see Wright & Loftus, 1998).

---

### Pinpoint question 11.3

'She ran across the finishing line' or 'She limped across the finishing line'. Which one would be more likely to lead to misremembering the occurrence of cramp after the race?

---

## Reconstructive and destructive processes: the misleading information effect

For Loftus and Palmer (1974) the primary claim was that the later misinformation was incorporated into the actual memory of the original event. By this view, and as Morton et al. (1985) noted, the claim is that 'memory is modified to conform to post-event information, resulting in reconstructive errors' (p. 15). Some have referred to this as the **destructive actualisation hypothesis** (see Schwarz & Stahlberg, 2003 – see Figure 11.2) on the grounds that, in actuality, the post-event information destroys stored memories. (A later, but consistent, idea – Loftus and Loftus (1980) – is that the post-event information over-writes or substitutes for the original memory of the event.) When the person is later quizzed about a given target event, the understanding is that the memory for the target event may in fact have been contaminated by later information. The later information is incorporated into the stored representation of the target event. At test the person attempts to reconstruct the original event on the basis of, not the original memory, but the altered representation of the target event.

If this sort of hypothesis is true, however, then it is quite perturbing. What it seems to suggest is the rather worrying possibility that there is no such thing as a true memory because any stored information about a given event can be changed by subsequent information. In this respect, we can never be certain that what we remember is a veridical record of what

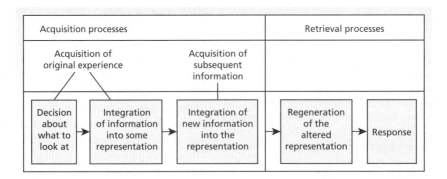

**Figure 11.2 Schematic representation of acquisition and retrieval processes that are assumed to be tapped in a typical eyewitness/misleading information experiment**
The main point of contention concerns the psychological validity of the component labelled, 'Integration of new information into the representation' (see text for further details).

*Source*: Loftus, E. F. (1975). Leading questions and eyewitness report. *Cognitive Psychology*, 7, 560–572 (fig. 1, p. 569). Reproduced with permission from Elsevier.

## But I heard them with my own ears! An exploration in earwitness testimony

Despite being much more flappy and protruding than our eyes, all too often our ears seem to get ignored in terms of cognitive psychology. So in among all this talk of eyewitness testimony, it's important to consider earwitness testimony and remember that our ears can also serve as important instruments for the amateur detective in us all. As Campos and Alonso-Quecuty (2006) pointed out, there is an unpleasant sub-set of crimes in which sound is the only reliable source of information; for instance, in cases where a conversation takes place over the telephone or when the victim is hooded. Moreover, the accurate report of verbal content is critically important in legal settings and so, in addition to visual memory, it's just as germane to consider how good our acoustic memory is under these kinds of settings.

Eighty participants were exposed to a videotape in which two shady characters were discussing a planned theft, although both the method of delivery and the retention period differed across individuals. For 40 participants, these reprobates could be both seen and heard, while for the remaining 40, only their law-breaking voices could be heard. The participant groups were further subdivided, half of which were asked to report immediately on the content of the discussion while the other half had to report back four days later.

Campos and Alonso-Quecuty (2006) sliced the data in a number of ways and were particularly interested in the distinction between verbatim recall (exact recall of an idea from the conversation) and gist recall (getting the basic message without

accurate retrieval of specific words). They found that gist recall was significantly greater than verbatim recall, with both types of recall showing greater success at immediate report relative to a four-day wait. Most importantly in terms of method of delivery, participants who experienced both audio and visual presentation of the criminal conversation recalled more gist information, with gist information significantly declining over the long retention period for the auditory-only group. In addition, participants provided more fabricated information under the auditory-only condition and with long retention interval. While this suggests that the participants themselves were criminal (fabrication of evidence, your honour!), all this means in the present context is that they recalled something that was not in the original conversation.

In terms of the consequences for earwitness testimony, the data do not bode well. There appear to be different rates of forgetting according to the way in which the initial information has been presented, with auditory-only information recalled after long delay being particularly susceptible to decay and error. Unfortunately, as the authors state, these are often the very conditions experienced for earwitnesses giving legal evidence. As Campos and Alonso-Quecuty (2006) concluded, 'accounts of "ear-witnesses" who could *only* listen to a criminal conversation should be treated with extreme caution in court' (p. 35). The eyes, it seems, have it.

*Source*: Campos, L., & Alonso-Quecuty, M. L. (2006). Remembering a criminal conversation: Beyond eyewitness testimony. *Memory*, *14*, 27–36.

actually took place. Consider the following: you go to watch a football match on Saturday afternoon and then read the match report on Sunday (after McCloskey & Zaragoza, 1985). What the destructive actualisation hypothesis suggests is that your memory for the match will incorporate (i) aspects of your experience of going to the match, together with (ii) aspects of what it is that you read in the paper. More troubling, though, is that it suggests that (to a quite significant degree) you will now be unable to discriminate your memory of the match from that of the match report. Your memory of the match is altered by what you later read about it (Loftus, 1979b). Regardless of whether or not

you are a football fan, think of the more general consequences and shudder!

## Headed records and the misleading information effect

How, therefore, might we explain the data but not accept the rather terrifying implications of the destructive actualisation hypothesis? Well, the headed records account provides one such alternative. According to the headed records account, each stored event remains immutable – it does not change over time. The record is the record is the record. Therefore, almost by fiat, the account rules out the destructive actualisation hypothesis. So if stored memories cannot change, how does the headed record account explain the misleading information effect? According to the headed records account, the first relevant event to be stored as a record is a representation of the actual film of the car accident itself. The second record to be stored concerns the post-event phase of the experiment, namely information concerning the questionnaire. These records are independent of one another and have different access keys (i.e., different headings) associated with them.

By this account, what the misinformation effect reveals is a mistake of reporting information about the post-event instead of the event itself. The error occurs because it is the most recent (relevant) record that is retrieved, and it is this that refers to the post-event information, not information about the original event. Although the headed records account of the misinformation account reported by Loftus and Palmer (1974) is a little strained, in other cases it seems more comfortable. In casting around for supporting evidence, Morton et al. (1985) referred to the work of Bekerian and Bowers (1983). In that study Bekerian and Bowers (1983) examined a slightly different task originally described by Loftus, Miller and Burns (1978).

Continuing the rather gruesome theme, the participants in the Loftus et al. (1978) experiment were initially presented with a series of slides depicting an auto–pedestrian accident. Next they were quizzed over what they had seen, and one critical question introduced potentially misleading information. For some participants, the information was consistent with what had been seen, and for others it was inconsistent with what had been seen. In a final phase, participants were shown pairs of slides and were asked to decide which of the two had originally been presented. Performance with one critical slide pair was of primary interest. One member of the slide pair was an original and the other was new, but matched with the inconsistent post-event information.

Evidence for the misleading information effect was that, of those participants who had received consistent post-event information, 75 per cent selected the slide originally seen, whereas 55 per cent of the participants who had received inconsistent information chose the slide that matched with this. However, in a later appraisal of this work, Bekerian and Bowers (1983) expressed concerns with how these data had been collected. In the original experiment the order of the slides in the final test phase were presented in a different and random order to that originally used in the exposure phase. What Bekerian and Bowers (1983)

were concerned about was that, by randomising the order of the slides at test, slide order could not now be used as an effective cue to recall.

For Bekerian and Bowers (1983), a critical point is that part of the heading for the record of the original slide sequence contains information about slide order. So the most effective means for recovering the original record would be to cue memory with the same slide order that had been used initially. As a consequence, Bekerian and Bowers (1983) compared performance across different groups of participants. For one (*random*) group the slide order was randomised and in a different (*sequential*) group the slide order was preserved. The results were apparently clear-cut. Whereas the original Loftus et al. misleading information effect was found for the random group, there was no such effect in the data for the sequential group. In actual fact, participants in the sequential group were as likely to pick the original slide as the new (inconsistent) slide. In other words, when the recognition materials closely matched the original materials, there was no evidence of a misleading information effect.

Again, taken at face value, the results of the Bekerian and Bowers (1983; see also Bowers & Bekerian, 1984) study are consistent with the headed records account of the misleading information effect, namely that the effect is not so much evidence for the alteration of extant memories, but it is more in line with the idea that post-event information can alter the ease with which particular memories can be recovered. The data ought not be taken to show how stored memories of past events can be altered by new information. Instead, the evidence reveals more about memory retrieval. The evidence suggests a default mode of operation in which retrieval is of the most recent relevant memories. This means recovering the misinformation in the post-event questionnaire and not in the original material. As a consequence, the misleading information effect does not necessitate the destructive actualisation hypothesis.

Against this, though, McCloskey and Zaragoza (1985) and Ayers and Reder (1998) have taken issue with both the evidence and the argument. Importantly, McCloskey and Zaragoza (1985) failed to replicate the pattern reported by Bekerian and Bowers (1983), and they were also concerned that the data that Bekerian and Bowers reported did not unequivocally support the headed records account. Critically, McCloskey and Zaragoza (1985) argued that the account should predict that the participants in the consistent condition ought to have performed better than participants in the inconsistent condition even if the misleading information had no effect at all. This pattern, however, was not found in the data.

How does the headed records model account for the misleading information effect?

## Alternative accounts of the misleading information effect

In this respect the evidence, so far reviewed, is, at best, neutral with regard to the headed records account, although the situation is somewhat worse for the destructive actualisation hypothesis. The data so far discussed in no way necessitate the ideas espoused in the destructive actualisation hypothesis. So how else might the misleading information effect come about? A useful example has been provided by Loftus and Hoffman (1989) and is abridged here. Harry interrupts a thief robbing a cash register in a hardware store. The thief brandishes some form of weapon, robs the till, grabs an electronic calculator (and a hammer) and throws all of this into a bag and legs it. Harry commiserates with the shop assistant, Sarah, who claims the robber escaped with an electronic calculator and a screwdriver. When the police then subsequently question Harry, 'Did you see if it was a hammer or a screwdriver?', he says, 'Screwdriver'.

In terms of the experimental paradigm, the robbery is the original event and the conversation with Sarah provides the post-event misleading information. Loftus and Hoffman (1989) provided four possible reasons for Harry's erroneous response:

1. He might never have seen the hammer and merely reported back 'Screwdriver' because he heard Sarah mention it.

2. He was unsure in his own mind whether it was a hammer or a screwdriver, but he reported 'Screwdriver' because he was convinced by Sarah.

3. He may have never seen the hammer, paid no attention to Sarah and guessed 'Screwdriver'.

4. He may have stored the original events in a veridical fashion, so that the original memory did contain a record of the hammer, but this memory became distorted, suppressed or impaired in some way.

Clearly these are not the only possibilities, but they do represent several important alternatives that have been considered in the literature. The fourth option fits most comfortably with the destructive actualisation

hypothesis – the idea that memory for the original event is impaired by acquisition of the later information. As we have seen, this hypothesis is disputed by the headed records account and it also faces some challenging data. (In fact, the headed records account is not actually covered by any of these alternatives because it allows for the fact that Harry actually saw the hammer but he retrieves information about the more recent conversation with Sarah and bases his response to the police on this.)

To examine the alternatives other than point 4, McCloskey and Zaragoza (1985) carried out a modified test procedure. The design of the experiment was as follows. In an initial exposure phase participants were presented with a slide sequence depicting a robbery in a cluttered office environment. A maintenance man enters an office, repairs a chair, finds some cash and a calculator and leaves. Certain target items were shown in the slide sequence lying around the office. Assume one critical target item is a hammer and one is a coffee jar. Next, participants were given a written narrative of what they had just seen. Finally they were given a 36-item forced choice questionnaire to complete.

For every participant, the narrative contained misleading information about two of the objects (such as the hammer) referred to as *misled items*, and neutral information about two other objects (such as the coffee jar) referred to as the *control objects*. In the final questionnaire participants were quizzed about the target items. In each case participants were forced to choose between two alternatives. Questions were either based on the original Loftus et al. (1978) procedure or were of a modified type. Take the case where a Nescafé coffee jar was a control object. Now participants with the original test procedure would be quizzed with 'Nescafé' vs. 'Folgers'. Nescafé had featured in the original slide sequence and Folgers had only occurred in the narrative in neutral terms. Given that they had not been misled about the coffee jar, then their memory for Nescafé ought to have been good. In the modified test, though, they were quizzed with 'Nescafé' vs. 'Maxwell House'. Maxwell House had not occurred in the slide sequence and it had also not occurred in the narrative. Again memory for Nescafé ought to have been good. Indeed, memory for the control items was generally very good when tested against items that had been mentioned in neutral terms in the narrative (Folgers) or completely novel items (Maxwell House).

The critical comparisons, though, were with the misled items. Now take the case where participants were misled about the hammer by having read about a screwdriver in the narrative. So when they were quizzed about the hammer with the choices 'hammer' vs. 'screwdriver' the prediction was that they would report the screwdriver – this is the misleading information effect. These alternatives conform to the original test conditions reported originally and the original misleading information effect was replicated in the data. Participants were seduced into reporting 'screwdriver'.

Modified test questions were also presented and contained 'hammer' vs. 'wrench' – the wrench is a totally new item neither seen nor mentioned before. Now it was found that memory for the misled hammer was as good as was memory for the control items. Participants chose the hammer, not the wrench. So even though misleading information about the hammer, as seen in the slide sequence, had been provided in the narrative, memory for the hammer was good when the alternative choice involved a completely new item. Problems only arose when participants were forced to choose between the (seen) hammer and the (described) screwdriver. The memory for the hammer was recoverable if the choice was between the hammer and a completely novel object.

One account of the misleading information effect – given by the destructive actualisation hypothesis – is that the memory for the hammer is over-written because of the misinformation about the screwdriver. However, this cannot be the full story: when the participants were misled by the screwdriver in the narrative, but were forced to choose between the hammer and the (novel) wrench, there was no decrement in the ability to recognise the hammer. At the very least, these data show that subtle differences in how memory is tested can lead to quite different conclusions about what the misleading information effect actually reveals. Nevertheless, as with nearly everything we have touched upon, the debate has moved forward since the original findings were reported. Further extensions and clarification of the effects reported by McCloskey and Zaragoza (1985) have been followed up by Belli (1989), Chandler (1989), Loftus and Hoffman (1989) and Tversky and Tuchin (1989) (see Payne, Toglia & Anastasi, 1994, for a useful and comprehensive review).

## Further evidence that bears on destructive processes

Something that remains of concern, though, is whether the destructive actualisation hypothesis is true – does subsequent information corrupt (even over-write) what is already stored? Evidence that stands against

the hypothesis is present in the work carried out by Lindsay and Johnson (1989), and replicated by Abeles and Morton (1999). In these cases a variant of the eye-witness paradigm was carried out, but critically, prior to seeing any movie or slide sequence, participants were presented with a narrative that might contain misleading information about the as yet-to-be seen episode. As in the original experiments (e.g., Loftus et al., 1978), and withstanding this change in the order of the narrative and slide sequence, a misinformation effect was found. As Abeles and Morton (1999) noted, the vital point here is that because the misleading information was presented first, it could not over-write information about the target episode that was presented later!

In the replication by Abeles and Morton (1999), initially all the participants were presented with a narrative description of a bedroom scene cluttered with a variety of objects. Next they were shown a photograph of a corresponding bedroom scene and were told that their memory for the objects in the scene would be tested. For the misled participants the narrative included (misleading) information about some objects that did not actually occur in the scene. For the control participants no such misleading information occurred in the narrative. Participants' recognition memory was tested with either pictures of objects that may have been present in the scenes or verbal descriptors of such objects. A principal aim was to see whether the misleading information effect would occur – despite the fact that the narrative appeared before the picture. In addition, a subsidiary aim was to see whether such an effect could be abolished if participants were cued to remember the actual pictorial scene rather than the narrative of the scene.

In discussing the headed records account, Abeles and Morton (1999) argued that a record would be laid down for the narrative and a second record would be laid down for the pictured scenes. The record of the narrative would primarily contain textual information and the record for the pictured scene would contain primarily pictorial information. However, they went further and stated that when the pictures were presented, participants actually retrieved the record for the narrative and used this to 'process the pictures' (p. 590). As a consequence, the second record would contain details of the pictures and details of the narrative. The main point was that storage of the two records was separate and that the initial record remained intact and unaltered by the second.

Abeles and Morton (1999) predicted that no misleading information effect should obtain in the data for the misled participants who were tested with pictures, but that the effect should be present in the data for the participants tested with verbal descriptors. This follows from the claim that cues at test will act as headings for retrieval of relevant records. Part of the heading will contain information about the modality within which the material is presented (either verbal or pictorial) and this can be used as effective retrieval cues for relevant records. Overall the data were in line with these predictions. There was no misinformation effect for misled participants tested with pictorial images of objects. For these participants the cues provided at test tapped into the actual memory of the pictured scenes. However, a substantial misleading information effect was revealed for participants tested with written descriptors and misled by a written narrative. Such an effect occurred even though the misleading information occurred prior to the presentation of the to-be-remembered information.

In broad strokes, the headed records account is supported by the data. In other regards, the account comes under some strain. If it is admitted that the record for the pictured scenes incorporates information about the actual scenes and from the narrative, then surely all of the misled participants should have shown the misleading information effect? In contrast, what Abeles and Morton (1999) argued was that participants who received test pictures gained only selective access to the pictorial information stored in the composite record of the pictured scenes. They did not gain access to the misleading material contained in the narrative. Clearly this is all very post hoc and much further work of both an empirical and theoretical nature is needed before the issues are finally settled. Nevertheless, the demonstration that information presented prior to a target episode can mislead, fits very uncomfortably with the destructive actualisation hypothesis.

### Pinpoint question 11.5

**How does modality influence the effect of misleading information?**

## The misleading information effect and encoding specificity

In backing up their arguments about how the format in which the information was presented may affect retrieval, Abeles and Morton (1999) were making an appeal to something known as the **encoding specificity**

**principle**. The principle is defined thus: 'specific encoding operations performed on what is perceived determine what is thought, and what is thought determines what retrieval cues are effective in providing access to what is stored' (Tulving & Thomson, 1973, p. 369). In other words, memory is best when aspects of the encoding context are replicated at test. In other words, the most effective retrieval cues are those that replicate features that were present during the encoding of the events that are committed to memory.

The now classic paper on encoding specificity is that by Tulving and Thomson (1973). In one experiment, participants were given a list of 24 pairs of words such as 'chair' paired with 'glue'. The word 'glue' was taken to be a weak associate of the target word 'chair'. Next, in phase 2, participants were given a list of words, each of which was a high associate of a corresponding and previously exposed target word (e.g., 'table'). In this phase of the experiment, participants were simply asked to provide the first four words that came to mind when they read each of these new words. They were not explicitly told of the link to the previous items.

The results of this free association test did reveal that there was a significant propensity to include the original target words in responses to these new words (on 66 per cent of cases). Next, participants were asked to look back on their four responses and circle which might have occurred originally. So if, to the word 'table', the participant had freely associated 'chair', 'lamp', 'drawer', 'mat', then the correct choice would be 'chair'. Under these conditions participants correctly recognised only 53.5 per cent of the 66 per cent of target words that had been produced in phase 2. On the assumption that some of the 53.5 per cent were lucky guesses, then the final estimate of correctly remembered items was adjusted downwards to 38 per cent (see Crowder, 1976, p. 403, for more details and some concerns about the legitimacy of this adjustment procedure).

The killer point relates to what happened in a final phase 3 of the experiment. Now participants were given the original weak associates of the target words. For each cue (such as 'glue') the participants were now asked to recall the original target word (i.e., 'chair'). The results were striking and revealed that participants were now able to recall 61 per cent of the original targets. So in phase 2 we have a demonstration of recognition failure of the target words – participants failed to recognise the targets from their own list of responses. More critically, when the original cue words were supplied at test, participants were now able to recall the original targets – we have an example of the

**recognition failure of recallable words** (see Tulving & Wiseman, 1975).

In terms of the encoding specificity principle, memory works best when the cues used at encoding are reinstated at test. To return to our discussion of the misleading information effect, it seems that what the work of Morton and associates (Abeles & Morton, 1999; Bekerian & Bowers, 1983) has done is provide other examples in which the encoding specificity principle applies. An additional proviso, though, is that they have offered a more precise theoretical account of how the principle may be operating in the production of the misleading information effect. What the data reported by Abeles and Morton (1999) (essentially) reveal is that if participants are provided with cues that tap into the misleading information contained in the record for the narrative (via the use of written narratives at test, for example), then it is most likely that participants will be misled in their reporting of the events. However, if the cues match better with the record of the critical events than with the narrative, then participants are unlikely to be misled.

## Going beyond encoding specificity

According to the encoding specificity principle, what is recovered is the memory that accords best with cues given later at test. Toth and Hunt (1999, p. 254) have even gone so far as to claim that this is 'one of the most important principles ever articulated about memory' (see Nairne, 2005, p. 120). In shorthand, Nairne (2005) used the phrase **cue–target match** to refer to the encoding specificity principle: it is the similarity between the retrieval cue and the stored memory (the target) that is critical (according to the principle) if remembering is to take place. However, as Nairne (2005) noted, the data actually reflect a more subtle point. Although high cue–target similarity may help some of the time, in other cases it may hurt.

For instance, in a study by DeLosh and Nairne (1996) participants on each trial learned to associate a single non-word with three simultaneously presented words. For instance, the non-word PAVIS would occur alongside ROUND, RED, and SOFT. Two of these words, ROUND and RED, were only paired with PAVIS; however, SOFT was also paired with a different non-word that occurred elsewhere in the learning phase. At test, participants were given a cued recall test. Three types of cued recall were tested. Participants received a unique word cue such as ROUND, or they received two unique words cues such as ROUND

and RED, or they received two word cues, one unique (ROUND) and one non-unique (SOFT). In all cases, memory for PAVIS was being tested.

The data were clear in showing that recall improved significantly when two unique word cues were used as compared with when only one unique word cue was used. This result is completely in line with the idea that the more the conditions at test replicate those that existed during encoding, then the more memory will benefit – very much in the spirit of the encoding specificity principle. However, when recall was tested with one unique and one non-unique cue word, performance actually declined. It seems, therefore, that something other than cue–target match is actually driving performance. As Nairne (2005, p. 122) noted, 'The shared cue was predictive of a number of other target responses rather than specifying only one target response', and because of this, it added to the load of trying to discriminate the correct target from other potential competitors. → See 'What have we learnt?', page 399.

→ See 'What have we learnt?', page 399.

### Pinpoint question 11.6

According to the encoding specificity principle, what is the most critical factor in determining whether a cue to recall will be effective?

**misleading information effect** The use of loaded questions which leads to the misremembering of plausible information related to the original event (McCloskey & Zaragoza, 1985).

**destructive actualisation hypothesis** After Schwarz and Stahlberg (2003), the idea that post-event information can actually destroy stored memories: stored information is over-written by new information.

**encoding specificity principle** After Tulving and Thomson (1973), the idea that memory is most successful when the conditions at encoding are replicated at retrieval.

**recognition failure of recallable words** An experimental finding in which participants are able to recall words better than they recognise them (see, for example, Tulving & Thomson, 1973).

**cue–target match** An alternative characterisation of the encoding specificity hypothesis which states that the similarity between retrieval cue and stored memory predicts remembering (Nairne, 2005).

## → What have we learnt?

What Nairne (2002, 2005) was at pains to point out is that even though cue–target match can be a persuasive factor in other memory conditions, it is not the overriding factor in the study by DeLosh and Nairne (1996) – what is apparently more important 'is the ability of a retrieval cue to help us discriminate an appropriate response from an inappropriate response that drives retention, not cue–target similarity per se' (Nairne, 2005, p. 121). Indeed this particular pattern fits well with the data reported by Abeles and Morton (1999) – participants were most likely to fall victim to the misleading information effect when the retrieval cues did not clearly distinguish between the record for the target event and the record for the narrative.

The more challenging point that Nairne is driving at is that something more profound is going on in the data. This is reflected in the claim that 'Cues in short-term memory are effective only to the extent that they are distinctive – that is, they uniquely predict target items' (Nairne, 2005, p. 73). So, although cue–target match may influence performance in some cases, the more fundamental factor is the degree to which a cue uniquely discriminates between competing stored memories. As we saw in Chapter 10, here is another example of how notions about 'distinctiveness' are beginning to play a central role in current models of memory performance.

## Research focus 11.2

## Do you remember the first time? Remembering misleading information about upcoming novel events

While we have been predominantly focusing on adult performance during misinformation paradigms, a clearly contentious issue is whether children also suffer from similar kinds of influence, and whether we can identify the conditions under which such information might be more persuasive than others. Salmon, Yao, Berntsen & Pipe (2007) set out to test this idea by preparing the child for a novel upcoming event: the treatment of a poorly bear (stuffed, not alive; toy, not real). Also of particular interest was that, similar to studies by Lindsay and Johnson (1989) and Abeles and Morton (1999), the misleading information here was presented *before* rather than after the event.

Ninety-seven 6-year-old children were used in the experiment. In the first part of the experiment, children were provided with preparatory information about the forthcoming Animal Hospital-esque event. Although many more conditions and hypotheses were tested, the crucial comparisons were between a condition in which the children received misleading information verbally and one where they received the information via the use of props. In the second part of the experiment, which took place the day after, the children actually assisted in help-

ing the sick bear according to a standard procedure which was either consistent or inconsistent with the information they received the day before. For example, while children might have been told (verbal condition) or shown (props condition) that they would be 'wiping bear's forehead with [a] cloth', during the actual event they were 'stroking bear's fur with [a] brush' (Salmon et al., 2007, p. 104). In the third part of the experiment some six to seven days later, the children were asked to recall everything they could about the time they helped a sick bear. One of the hypotheses was that the amount of correct and incorrect recall would be influenced by the way in which the misleading information was presented.

Relative to control conditions in which no misleading information was presented, Salmon et al. (2007) found that misleading information did not influence the amount of correct information that was recalled about our sickly grizzly. However, it was found that children exposed to misleading information via props did generate significantly more incorrect recall (5.19 per cent) than children exposed to misleading information via verbal presentation (1.82 per cent). Importantly, when errors in recall related to the misleading information were removed, errors did not differ between misleading prop and misleading verbal conditions. As Salmon et al. (2007) confirm, 'most of the additional errors made in the misleading condition were due to the inclusion of the pre-event misleading information' (p. 110).

In sum, the data suggest that children are more likely to recall events incorrectly when cued with misleading information in the form of props. Salmon et al. (2007) state that perhaps the reason that misleading information conveyed using props led to an increase in incorrect recall was that props are more like the eventual event than a simple verbal description. Therefore it is easier to link the preparatory information and eventual event information together

(encoding specificity, anyone?). Now obviously this similarity has a downside as children confuse what actually happened with what they were told what would happen. However, Salmon et al. (2007) also put a positive spin on this conclusion and claim that the data show that the children are actually learning to integrate information from different sources. It is hoped that you yourself are learning to integrate information from different sources (e.g., Research focus, Glossary, Pinpoint questions, For example . . . ) in this book, although we trust all of the information is of an accurate nature!

*Source*: Salmon, K., Yao, J., Berntsen, O., & Pipe, M. E. (2007). Does providing props during preparation help children to remember a novel event? *Journal of Experimental Child Psychology, 97*, 99–116.

## Even more accounts of the misleading information effect

We have spent some considerable time discussing alternative accounts of the misleading information effect in a bid to avoid the rather alarming consequences of the destructive actualisation hypothesis. A final alternative account of the misleading information effect is best described in terms of guessing (option 3 above – see page 395). By this view, participants rely less on their memory for key events; they merely guess or are biased to respond in particular ways. According to this line of argument, what the experiments are doing is tapping into some form of plausible reconstruction of events that only partially reflects anything about memory. The experiments reveal some things that are more generally referred to as **false memories**. In order to understand these sorts of ideas, though, we need to refresh our own memories of signal detection theory.

### Signal detection theory, recognition memory and explaining false memories

In a typical recognition memory experiment some material is initially presented to participants in what can be termed an exposure phase of the experiment. In an **intentional learning paradigm** participants are explicitly instructed to try to remember the material because later they will be tested on it. In an **incidental learning paradigm** the material is exposed but partici-

pants are not told about the subsequent test phase. To make the exposure phase more plausible, participants are given some form of orienting task that demands that the participants pay attention to the material. For instance, participants might be asked to rate the pleasantness of each member of a list of words. In this way the task becomes plausible even though also deceptive: the intention is to get participants to think that they are involved in anything but a memory task!

Turning to the test phase, memory can be probed under conditions either of recall or of recognition. At least two forms of recall test can be administered. In *free recall*, participants are simply asked to report any of the material that they can remember. In *cued recall*, hints (cues) are provided at the time of test. For instance, in a *paired associate learning paradigm* pairs of words are presented during the exposure phase. At recall the first word of each pair is presented in turn and the participant has to try to remember the corresponding second word, with the first word therefore acting as a cue for the second (cf. DeLosh & Nairne, 1996).

With recognition memory there is a standard procedure: participants at test are now presented with NEW material and OLD material. NEW material was not included in the exposure phase, whereas OLD material was. On each trial, in the test phase, participants typically have to make what is known as an old/new judgement. In **free recognition** the participant is typically asked, 'Was this particular material included in the exposure phase? (Yes[OLD]/No[NEW])', whereas in **forced recognition** the participant is presented with two or more alternatives and is asked to

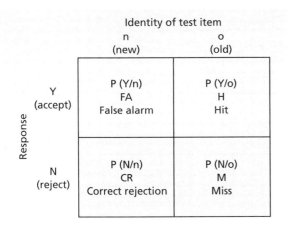

**Figure 11.3 How best to represent the data from a simple recognition memory experiment**
Following an exposure phase, in which OLD items are presented, there follows a test phase. In the test phase, the OLD items are re-presented, mixed together in a random fashion with NEW items. The participant has to decide, for each item, at test, whether it is OLD or NEW. The four possible outcomes are shown in the above matrix. The P (x) notation is that the different types of response have been converted into proportions.

*Source*: Banks, W. P. (1970). Signal detection theory and human memory. *Psychological Bulletin, 74*, 81–99 (fig. 1, p. 82). Reproduced with permission from APA.

indicate which the OLD item(s) is(are). To flesh out the terminology, a *hit* is where the participant correctly reports an OLD item as an OLD item – they are correct. They can also be correct in stating that a NEW item is a NEW item – this is a case of a *correct rejection*. A *false alarm* occurs when a NEW item is incorrectly classified as an OLD item and a *miss* occurs when an OLD item is incorrectly classified as a NEW item (for further details see Figure 11.3).

One of the main problems with all of this is that participants, in order to try to do their best, guess. To address this problem, we can ask participants to rate their confidence every time that they make a response, for example, 1 – certainly old, 4 – pure guess, 7 – certainly new (see Kintsch, 1970a, p. 231). In a recall test, every time they recall an item, we ask them to provide a confidence rating and in a recognition test we ask them to provide a rating every time they make an old/new judgement. As Figure 11.4 shows, in collecting such confidence ratings it is possible to generate something known as a **memory operating characteristic** (remember performance operating characteristics from Chapter 8). From this we can begin to infer detailed characteristics of the sorts of strategies that

participants bring to bear in the tasks (although, as recent reports have shown, this may not be as straightforward as all that – see Malmberg, 2002).

In setting up our experiments in this way we can begin to harness the power of signal detection theory, and according to Norman (1970) the first clear application of the theory to the recognition memory for words was set out by Egan (1958). Since then, the general approach was adopted in several key attempts to explain memory performance in traditional laboratory-based tasks (Banks, 1970; Kintsch, 1970b; Macmillan & Creelman, 1991; Neath & Surprenant, 2003; Snodgrass & Corwin, 1988; Wickelgren & Norman, 1966). As Swets (1996, 27) noted, the assumption is that there is an underlying continuum of memory strength upon which all potential items fall. Items that are stored in memory from the exposure phase accrue large amounts of strength and are located to the right of the continuum (see Figure 11.5) (the right-hand distribution corresponds to the OLD items) and those items that are stored in memory but were not included in the exposure phase will have less strength and be located towards the left of the distribution (the NEW distribution).

In signal detection theory it is now possible to distinguish the two parameters of $d'$ and $\beta$ where $d'$ reflects the distance between the OLD and NEW distributions and $\beta$ reflects the placement of the criterion on the continuum. The implication is that $d'$ reflects something about item familiarity (i.e., recency defined in terms of the context of the actual experimental setting) whereas $\beta$ reflects something about biases associated with the response. If the OLD and NEW distributions were completely overlapping then $d'$ (the distance between their means) would be 0 and it would be impossible to tell OLD from NEW. More typical is the case in which the participants can make these discriminations and therefore $d'$ will take on some non-zero value. The larger $d'$, the better the OLD/NEW judgements should be.

Of course, all of this is modulated by whereabouts the criterion is placed on the continuum. Values of $\beta$ reflect whereabouts the criterion is located. A value of 1 reflects no bias either way, values less than 1 reflect a bias towards responding OLD more than NEW, values greater than 1 reflect a bias towards responding NEW more than OLD. More importantly, values of $\beta$ are assumed to reflect decisional processes and not memorial processes. First you retrieve something from memory. Success at this stage will depend, in part, on the strength with which the memory trace is stored. Having retrieved the information, it is now important

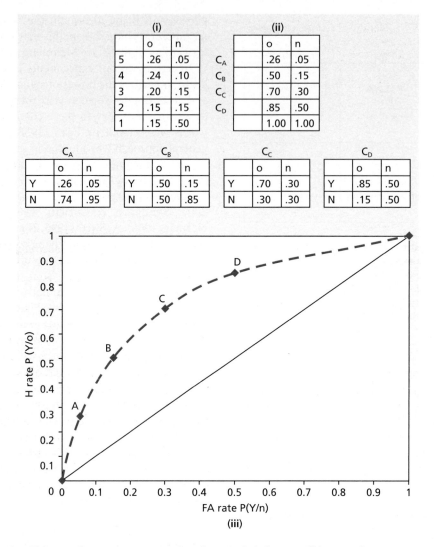

**Figure 11.4 Example of how to plot a memory operating characteristic from confidence ratings**
In this case, a 5-point scale has been used, wherein 5 indicates certainly an old item, and 1 indicates certainly a new item. In (i) the relative proportion of old (o) and new (n) responses are broken down for every point on the scale. In (ii) the data are collated in a cumulative form so that $C_B$ contains the data for $C_A$ and $C_C$ contains the data for $C_B$ and $C_A$, and so on. From these data it is possible to compute the hit rates, and false alarm rates for intervals along the scale. The four data points are indicated as A–D on the memory operating characteristic shown in (iii).

The curve traced out in the dashed line is known as the isomnemonic function (Banks, 1970). This defines cases where the strength of the evidence in favour of a set of items is the same, but that participants' confidence changes across the curve. Points towards 0,0 reflect cautiousness (few false alarms are committed); points towards 1.0,1.0 reflect liberalism (a good hit rate is associated with a high false alarm rate). The diagonal line shown reflects chance performance. Any points in the space above this diagonal reflect better than chance performance, points on the line reflect the fact that the participant is guessing, and points below the line reflect the fact that something is very much awry. The participant has perhaps misunderstood the instructions or is otherwise acting in opposition to the instructions.

*Source*: Banks, W. P. (1970). Signal detection theory and human memory. *Psychological Bulletin*, *74*, 81–99 (fig. 2, p. 83). Reproduced with permission from APA.

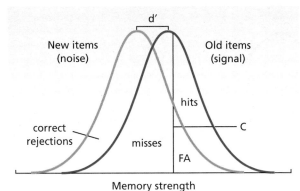

**Figure 11.5 The signal detection theory approach to memory**

In this case the continuum is defined in terms of evidence for having something stored in memory within the context of the experimental setting. Banks (1970) refers to this evidence as familiarity defined relative to 'an abstract dimension known as the likelihood axis' (p. 84). How likely is it that this item occurred within this experimental context? As before (see Chapter 4), this evidence is contaminated by noise such as similar information that is stored in memory. If evidence in favour of a given item falls above the criterion, then the participant will accept it as being an OLD item (i.e., an item remembered), otherwise it will be rejected as a NEW item (i.e., not one that has been committed to memory).

*Source*: Banks, W. P. (1970). Signal detection theory and human memory. *Psychological Bulletin*, *74*, 81–99 (fig. 3, p. 84). Reproduced with permission from APA.

to decide whether or not it is a target memory in the context of the present task.

There has been much debate about which signal detection parameters are most appropriate to use with memory data and several variants of indices akin to $d'$ and $\beta$ have been discussed (Banks, 1970; Macmillan & Creelman, 1991; Neath & Surprenant, 2003; Snodgrass & Corwin, 1988). Nonetheless, the basic idea is that when an item recurs at test, the participant (implicitly) determines its familiarity/strength and notes where this value occurs on the continuum. If that value is higher than (to the right of) the criterion, then it is recognised and is responded to as OLD, otherwise it is not recognised and is classified as NEW. In applying this logic the argument is that measures of sensitivity (e.g., $d'$) reflect memorial processes whereas measures of response bias (e.g., $\beta$) reflect things other than memorial processes such as decisional processes.

In the memory operating characteristic shown in Figure 11.4, the curved dashed line shows that performance in the task accords well with the standard

account of SDT just described. The function is consistent with the idea that participants' sensitivity does not change across the rating scale – what is changing is their response bias. More importantly, if the data systematically deviate from this particular sort of function then it is quite possible that a different model of decision is needed (see Malmberg, 2002, and Macmillan & Creelman, 1991). The basic point is that the tools that SDT provides are extremely useful if we wish to address detailed questions about how participants perform in various kinds of recall and recognition tasks (see Figure 11.6 for a further illustration of this point.)

What we have done here in adopting this signal detection theory approach is to acknowledge a difference between remembering and making a decision about whether something has been remembered or not. Any variation in $d'$ is taken to reflect something selective about the memory system; for instance, how well something is actually remembered. In contrast, any variation in $\beta$ is taken to reflect *decisions* about whether something has been remembered or not (see Erdelyi & Stein, 1981; Feenan & Snodgrass, 1990). The ultimate aim is to unconfound memory processes from decision processes (cf. Lockhart, 2000), and we need to be confident that we have independent measures of these. At the very least we want to remove effects of guessing and response bias from our estimates of memory processes. So if we get an effect on $d'$ the assumption is that this is indicative of some aspect of memory and not decision.

**Pinpoint question 11.7**

You think Jerry is an old girlfriend when in fact she is not. According to signal detection theory, what category of response have you just made?

## False memories and response bias

Having established that the really interesting effects are with measures of sensitivity rather than bias, it is now useful to consider how evidence of the fallibility of memory might actually be confounded with response bias. Here the central reference is to a study reported by Roediger and McDermott (1995).

Six lists of 12 words were constructed; each list was associated with a particular key word. For example, for the key word *chair* (known as a **critical lure**) the list contained 'table', 'sit', 'legs', 'seat', 'soft', 'desk', 'arm', 'sofa', 'wood', 'cushion', 'rest' and 'stool'. Each of these 12 words is known to be an associate of the word

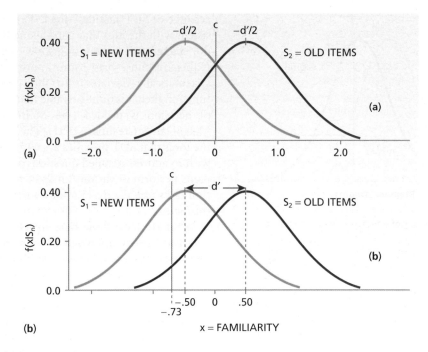

**Figure 11.6 Look into my eyes**
This example, taken from Macmillan and Creelman (1991), indicates two different scenarios in an experiment on the recognition of faces. Initially, participants were exposed to a set of faces and then were tested in a standard OLD/NEW recognition test. In (a) the data are taken to reflect control performance. In (b) the data are taken to reflect performance of hypnotised participants. From the upper panel, it can be seen that the control participants are unbiased in their reports because their criterion is located mid-way between the NEW and OLD distributions. In the lower panel, the hypnotised participants show the same level of sensitivity (the NEW and OLD distributions are the same distance apart as in the control case); however, their criterion has shifted dramatically. The hypnotised participants are much more liberal in accepting any face as having been seen before.

*Source*: Macmillan, N. A., & Creelman, C. D. (1991). *Detection theory: A user's guide* (fig. 2.2, p. 35). Cambridge, England: Cambridge University Press. Reproduced with permission of Prof. Neil Macmillan.

## For example . . .

Duvet. Cosy. Pillow. Mattress. Sheets. Blanket. Sleep. Feeling tired yet? But did anybody mention bed? Often we falsely remember the presence of certain items (known as critical lures) on the basis that they are strongly associated with all the other presented items.

'chair'. Participants were presented with a list and then were asked to try to recall all of the words in the list. After the final recall test of the sixth list, participants were given a recognition test. Participants were now presented with a new list of 42 items, 12 of which were old words. Of the 30 new words (which had not been previously presented), 6 were the critical lures (e.g., 'chair'), 12 were weakly related to the words on the original lists (e.g., 'bench') and 12 were completely unrelated to any of the words (e.g., 'weather'). For each word participants were asked to rate their confidence that it was an OLD item.

The results of the experiment were relatively clear-cut. First, the critical lures were (incorrectly) recalled with a similar frequency to other words that were present in the lists (on about 40 per cent of occasions). Other intrusions (i.e., recall of words completely unrelated to the list items) only occurred about 14 per cent of the time. The data therefore reflect that recall of the critical lures was not indicative of wild guessing. Second are the data from the recognition test. Now the critical lures were falsely recognised at about the same level as were correctly recognised OLD items. Indeed, the false alarm rate for the critical lures was considerably higher than the other control items (i.e., the unrelated and weakly related lures). Taken together, theperformance in the recall and in the recognition tasks was used as evidence for the formation of so-called false memories. Participants behaved as though the critical lures had actually been presented – they falsely remembered the critical items as having occurred.

So, on the face of it, we have another apparent demonstration of the fallibility of human memory. However, some caution is perhaps warranted, given our previous concerns about differences between measures of $d'$ and response bias. Perhaps participants are not really remembering the critical lures? Perhaps, instead, they are just acting with a very liberal criterion? Clearly the list made me think of chair-like things so presumably the word *chair* must have been present?

To test this particular alternative account of the laboratory-induced false memories, Miller and Wolford (1999) carried out a further experiment. Now they replicated the general methods used by Roediger and McDermott (1995), but in some lists they actually included the critical lures. In this way performance could be compared directly between critical lures that had been presented with those that had not been presented. Indeed, both related items and unrelated items were used, and at test, memory for presented and non-presented cases was examined. By using presented and non-presented items in this way, measures of $d'$ and response bias could be computed. The overall aim was to see if the memory for presented and non-presented cases was the same.

Particular import was attached to performance with the critical lures relative to the other cases. The data were revealing in showing that the probability of assigning an OLD response to non-presented critical lures was lower than that assigned to presented critical lures. So participants were more likely to recognise an OLD (presented) critical lure correctly (on 0.97 of occasions) than falsely recognise a NEW (non-presented) critical lure (on 0.81 of occasions). OLD and NEW critical lures were therefore being treated differently by participants – their 'memories' of the two different sorts of items was apparently not the same. Non-presented related and unrelated items were generally associated with false recognition rates (0.36 and 0.11 respectively).

Analysis of the signal detection parameters was also very revealing. Now the measures of true memory (e.g., $d'$) revealed no systematic differences across the three item types. However, there was a marked difference in response bias across the different items. Generally speaking, the data revealed that participants were simply more prone to respond Yes(OLD) to the critical lures than they were to respond Yes(OLD) to the other item types. Their criterion for responding to a critical lure was much more liberal than it was for the other items (see Figure 11.6 for an illustration of this in SDT terms). Such a conclusion is diametrically at odds with the idea that false memories are actually created for the critical lures. According to Miller and Wolford (1999), all that the experiments reveal is that participants are seduced into believing the critical lures did occur originally simply because they are highly associated with the list members.

More generally, they argued that the whole concept of false memories needs to be addressed with caution. For instance, although the notion of 'implanting' false memories has some currency in popular beliefs about how human memory is fallible, the less alarming prospect concerns a criterion shift. Accordingly, they argued that some forms of false memories result from a criterion shift, such that participants are more easily seduced into accepting that some event actually took place when in fact it did not. If there was Posh, Baby, Scary and Ginger, then there must have been Sporty there too. What they had demonstrated is that some false memories arose at a decisional stage of processing, and therefore could not be taken to reflect anything significant about memory processes.

Now, for some, this conclusion is both unpalatable and untenable (see replies by Roediger & McDermott, 1999; and Wixted & Stretch, 2000). The counterargument, regarding the effect reported by Miller and Wolford (1999), is that the three word types are each associated with a different criterion. According to Wixted and Stretch (2000), this means that participants must have had to shift the criterion on an item-by-item basis at test in an ad-hoc fashion; but this is not the only conclusion to draw. As Miller and Wolford (1999) originally suggested, participants may actually have built up some reasonable knowledge of the structure of the lists so that when a highly related item occurs at test, a liberal criterion is applied. The issues remain unsettled.

### Pinpoint question 11.8

**What is a critical lure?**

## False memories in the real world

Although we may be impressed by the methodological inventiveness of the various memory researchers, the thorny issue of real-world significance is also lurking in the undergrowth. What has all of this talk about $d'$ and response bias got to do with anything of any real-world importance? Well, in this case, the real-world significance is painfully evident given the sometimes lurid descriptions of false and recovered memories that occasionally occur in the media. Rather than attempt to try to settle the clearly emotive issues here, let us try to take a more disinterested approach and focus on exactly what has been reported in the psychological literature (see Loftus & Bernstein, 2005, for a recent and useful review).

One now classic experimental example can be referred to as the *lost-in-the-mall paradigm*. This technique was originally documented by Loftus and Pickrell (1995). Participants read short descriptions of some childhood events. The vast majority of these were true and had been corroborated by other members of the individual participant's family. One of these events was false, however. The false event described a scenario in which the participant, at around 5–6 years of age, had been lost in a shopping mall for some considerable time but was helped by an elderly person and reunited with their family. Twenty-five per cent of participants were seduced into believing this particular false scenario, and remembered some details about it.

Later research has established that in using such procedures around 20 per cent of participants can be classified as having what Loftus and Bernstein (2005)

described as *complete* or *rich false memories*: the participants genuinely report remembering the (virtual) event. Moreover, they confidently report having experienced the event, they provide details about the event, and they even express emotions about the event, even though it never happened (paraphrasing Loftus & Bernstein, 2005, p. 103).

One particularly intriguing set of experiments in this genre has examined similar effects. It is accepted that false memories can be created and implanted using misleading narratives but researchers have also been increasingly interested in whether similar effects arise through the use of doctored photographs. Here a most influential study was carried out by Wade, Garry, Read and Lindsay (2002). Here participants were interviewed about childhood events and experiences over a series of days. During the interviews they were quizzed about a sample of four photographs. Three of these were real photographs of the participant as a child, but one was doctored to show the participant as a child enjoying a hot air balloon ride (see Figure 11.7). Family members verified that the ride had never taken place. Participants were quizzed at an initial interview and a final interview about the same photographs around a week later.

Participants' recollections of the various photographed events were then scored. To classify a response as a clear false memory, participants had to report recalling the balloon event and also had to elaborate

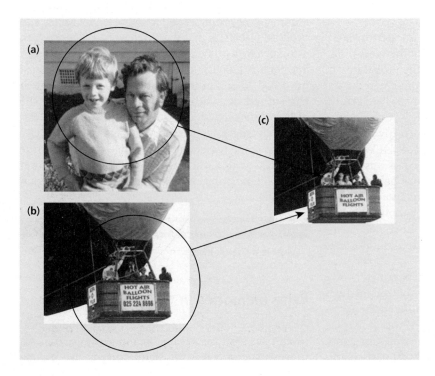

**Figure 11.7 You remember that balloon trip, don't you?**
Example of how doctored photographs can be generated in experiments on implanted memories of fictitious past lifetime events (i.e., a balloon trip, in this case).

*Source*: Garry, M., & Gerrie, M. P. (2005). When photographs create false memories. *Current Directions in Psychological Science*, *14*, 326–330 (fig. 1, p. 322). Reproduced with permission from Blackwell Publishing Ltd.

on the actual trip with information not included in the picture. To classify a response as a partial false memory, participants had to elaborate the event (say what else may have transpired, who else had been there, etc.) but failed to report actually taking the ride. Data from the initial interview revealed that 35 per cent of the participants reported either a clear or partial false memory of the event but this figure increased to 50 per cent by the final interview. Although these false memory rates are considerably higher than the 25 per cent reported by Loftus and Pickrell (1995), more tightly controlled experiments carried out by Garry and Wade (2005) revealed that the false memory rates are actually higher when narratives are used than when doctored photographs are used to mislead.

Lindsay, Hagen, Read, Wade and Garry (2004) had participants remember three school events: two of the events were real but one was false. The false one described an event putting Slime in the teacher's desk drawer. All the participants read narratives of the events and half the participants saw a photograph of their class members in addition so as to 'help them remember the events'. The results were clear in showing that, although around half of the participants given only the narrative reported false memories of the Slime episode, over 70 per cent of the participants shown the additional photograph reported similar false memories. The critical thing to note here is that the photographs were in no way deceptive, nor were they directly relevant to the supposed incident that was being remembered. So the effects have nothing to do with deception or misinformation. Even more recently, Garry and Gerrie (2005) have reported cases of false memories occurring even when actual photographs from a person's childhood are used. So, one upshot of all of this is that if you go on holiday and it's a bit rubbish, you can always generate a completely different and much more exciting story on the basis of your photos!

## Remembering the mothership: false memories and alien abductees

Most of us have been struck with the idea that we used to go to Cornwall for our summer holidays only to find it was the Cotswolds, or that our favourite security blanket as a baby was blue when it was actually pink. For other people, potential errors in memory can be much more damaging such as the claims of sexual and ritual abuse. However, one issue in testing individuals with childhood sexual abuse is that it is often very difficult to know whether the recovered memory of abuse is actually true or not. So Claney, McNally, Schacter, Lenzenweger and Pitman (2002) examined memory performance in individuals who all had a traumatic event that seemed 'unlikely to have occurred' (p. 455) – that is, all claimed to have been alien abductees.

Claney et al. (2002) actually selected three different groups for study: those who believed that they had been abducted by aliens but had no autobiographical memory of the event, those alien abductees who had recovered their memories after a period of those memories being inaccessible (among the reasons for inaccessibility were alien control of memories and the abduction happening in a different dimension), and a control group who didn't believe they'd had any extraterrestrial experience at all. Both age and educational level was controlled across groups. One hypothesis was that those individuals who had recovered (statistically unlikely to be anything other than) false memories would be more likely to show evidence of memory distortions in other domains than the control groups.

All groups were given a version of the Roediger and McDermott (1995) paradigm previously described. The idea was that the recovered memory alien abductees group would be more likely to identify 'sweet' as a critical lure they had previously seen, after being exposed to the items 'sour, sugar, tooth, honey, tart' and so on, relative to the other groups. What Claney et al. (2002) found was that, although the recovered memory alien abductees did not differ significantly from the other groups in terms of producing false recall (i.e., spontaneously putting forward 'sweet' as a word they had seen before), they were more likely to recognise falsely words that they actually hadn't seen before.

So we're left with the conclusion that the differences between alien abductees and controls are related to false recognition rather than false recall. While the interpretation of the whole data set clearly depends on whether you believe alien abduction to be a reality or not, Claney et al. (2002) did draw links between the potential error in something called source monitoring in both the case of the alleged abductees and the false recognition of critical lures. Both problems stem from judging where certain information originated from. That is, one might have had a weekend binge on *The X-Files* some years ago, whose on-screen events then become integrated into your own history because you've forgotten that the source of the abduction memory was actually external (i.e., from the TV). False recognition for the critical lures in the Roediger and McDermott paradigm are thought to work in a similar way, with subjects forgetting the

origin of the memory, leading to the retrieval of false associations (in this case, 'sweet' within the list of 'sour, sugar, tooth, honey, tart'). So, this probably means that the time you were chased by that huge boulder while retrieving some precious historical artefact, it wasn't actually you, it was Indiana Jones. Best of luck next time, Indy.

*Source*: Claney, S. A., McNally, R. J., Schacter, D. L., Lenzenweger, M. F., & Pitman, R. K. (2002). Memory distortion in people reporting abduction by aliens. *Journal of Abnormal Psychology*, *111*, 455–461.

## False memories and aging

What we have established so far is that, for whatever reasons, what we actually remember of real-life events can be sketchy at best, and completely wrong at worst! However, if you think this scenario is bleak, then brace yourself because it seems that things can only get worse (see Figure 11.8). It is simply the case that the incidence of memory failures increases with age (Jacoby & Rhodes, 2006). For instance, Karpel, Hoyer and Toglia

**Figure 11.8 Did I ever tell you about the time I was a roadie for Black Sabbath?**
Passing on information from generation to generation becomes more difficult as problems in memory become compounded by age.
*Source*: Helen King/Corbis.

(2001) reported that older people were far more prone to fall foul of the misinformation effect than younger people. Moreover, it seems that older people are far more confident of their erroneous memories than are younger people (Jacoby & Rhodes, 2006). More particular details about elderly memory were reported by Hay and Jacoby (1999).

During an initial *training phase*, and on each trial, a given stimulus word was presented on the screen of a computer and the participant had then to guess a related word. The response word that had been chosen as being correct was then displayed once the participant had made their guess. During this phase of the experiment, each stimulus word was paired with a typical response on 75 per cent of occasions (e.g., stimulus word 'organ' – response word 'music', known as *typical pairs*) and an atypical response on 25 per cent of occasions (e.g., stimulus word 'organ' – response word 'piano', known as *atypical pairs*). Sixteen stimulus words were repeatedly sampled over several blocks of trials. Using associative terminology, across the trials the S–R bond between a given typical pair was strengthened more than was the bond for a given atypical pair, simply because typical pairs occurred more frequently than atypical pairs. Hay and Jacoby (1999) referred to such S–R bonds as *habits*. The point of this training phase was to keep participants engaged with a task in which they would become sensitised to the different exposure rates of the word pairs. Incidentally, they would be picking up on the differences between typical and atypical word pairs.

Next, participants entered a *study–test phase*. Now they were presented with a list of eight word pairs. They were told to remember these particular pairs for an ensuing memory test. Following presentation of a given list of pairs, memory for that list was tested with a cued recall task. Each stimulus word of each pair was presented and the participant had to provide the associated response word as had just appeared in the study list. This study–test procedure was repeated for 16 lists of words. Most critically, all of the lists comprised pairs of words used in the training phase. Typical word pairs again occurred more often than atypical pairs.

To clarify the situation, during the initial training phase differential habits were set up between competing associates of given stimulus words – there was a typical response word and an atypical response word. During the later study–test phase, memory was being tested for which of these response words had just occurred in the immediately previous word list (e.g., was it 'music' or 'piano' that just occurred with 'organ'?). The experiment was intended to examine what influence prior exposure had on immediate memory of the word pairs. How does habit strength determine memory for recent events?

The rather convoluted procedure was deemed necessary so that estimates could be made for (i) processes of **recollection**, and, separately, (ii) processes of **habit**. The ultimate objective was to throw light on the actual reasons for poorer memory performance in the elderly. In this regard, old and young participants were tested and the data were analysed in terms of something known as the **process-dissociation procedure**.

Central here is the distinction between (i) memory based on habit (also known as automatic responding), and (ii) memory based on recollection (the consciously controlled act of remembering). Hay and Jacoby (1999) used this framework to argue that slips in remembering come about when failures in recollection occur. In such cases, performance then reflects responses based on habit. If this is accepted, then the increases in memory failure with age might be explained in terms of problems with recollection and a higher dependence on habit. Older people cannot depend on having intact memories of particular events and, as a consequence, they default to a strategy based on habit.

To examine these ideas in detail, further terminology is needed. We have already been introduced to the distinction between typical and atypical word pairs in which typicality is defined in terms of how frequently a given pairing was exposed during the training phase. We now need to consider the difference between *congruent* and *incongruent cases*. Congruence is now defined in terms of performance in the study–test phase. Let us assume that 'organ–music' is presented during the study part of the study–test phase. This is known as a congruent case because both recollection and habit are pointing in the same direction. When given the stimulus word 'organ' at test, respond 'music'.

If, however, the pair 'organ–piano' is presented during the study part of the study–test phase, then this is an incongruent case because habit and recollection are now placed in opposition. When the stimulus word 'organ' is presented at test, whereas recollection is favouring 'piano', habit is favouring 'music'. So although 'piano' is the correct response, the habitual response is 'music'.

By this account, recollective processes support correct recall for congruent and incongruent cases. However, when recollection fails, other processes are seen to operate.

### Process-dissociation logic

Essentially we can divide total recall into two components:

$$\text{Total recall} = \text{Recollection} + \text{Other processes} \tag{11.1}$$

Expressing equation (11.1) in proportions we may write:

$$1 = \text{Recollection} + \text{Other processes} \tag{11.2}$$

and rearranging this we have:

$$\text{Other processes} = 1 - \text{Recollection} \tag{11.3}$$

Other processes can now be decomposed into two further components, namely, habit and everything else. More formally:

$$\text{Other processes} = \text{Habit} + \text{Everything else} \tag{11.4}$$

expressed as proportions and rearranging we have:

$$\text{Everything else} = 1 - \text{Habit}. \tag{11.5}$$

What Figure 11.9 shows is that for congruent cases the operation of both recollection and habit accord and will conspire to generate correct recall. So even when recollection fails, the default response, as provided by habit, will produce a correct response. Both will result in the recall of the typical response word for the stimulus word. However, when both recollection and habit fail, recall fails completely.

The situation is quite different for the incongruent cases. Now when recollection fails, habit will result in an incorrect response. Habit will produce the typical response word, but this will be incorrect in

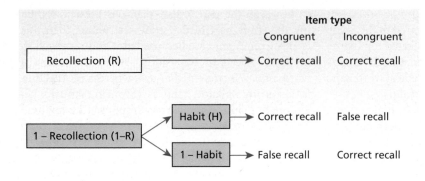

**Figure 11.9 Schematic representation of memorial processes that underlie performance in the experimental task described by Hay and Jacoby (1999)**

*Source*: Jacoby, L. L., & Rhodes, M. G. (2006). False remembering in the aged. *Current Directions in Psychological Science, 15*, 49–53 (fig. 2, p. 51). Reproduced with permission from Blackwell Publishing Ltd.

the incongruent cases. In order to be correct on incongruent trials, participants should respond with the less common associate. By extension, though, if both recollection and habit fail, the correct response is produced, essentially, by mistake.

In following the logic, we can now attempt to estimate the incidence of recollection, and separately, the incidence of habit over trials. Equation (11.6) provides an estimate of the probability of making a correct (typical) response on a congruent trial:

$$P(\text{Typical–Cong}) = R + H(1–R) \qquad (11.6)$$

Being correct on a congruent trial is the sum of cases where recollection is successful and those cases were habits are successful. The H(1−R) term reflects cases where habits are successful but only when recollection fails. You fail to recollect the word correctly but you nevertheless get it correct because you respond on the basis of habit. This is a conditional probability, H multiplied by (1−R) – the success of habit (H) given that recollection fails (i.e., the 1−R).

Equation (11.7) provides a similar estimate of the probability of making an incorrect (typical) response on an incongruent trial (this provides an estimate of making a memory slip based on habit):

$$P(\text{Typical–Incong}) = H(1–R) \qquad (11.7)$$

We can now amalgamate equations (11.6) and (11.7) and rearrange to give equation (11.8). This provides an estimate for R (i.e., recollection):

$$\begin{aligned}\text{Recollection} = &\, P(\text{Typical–Cong}) \\ &- P(\text{Typical–Incong}) \qquad (11.8)\end{aligned}$$

Our estimate of the incidence of recollection is given by the difference in correctly responding typical on congruent trials and incorrectly responding typical on

incongruent trials. This value we can easily compute directly from the data.

Moreover, by rearranging equation (11.7) and by dividing throughout by (1−R) we have:

$$\text{Habit} = \frac{P(\text{Typical–Incong})}{1–R} \qquad (11.9)$$

Again this computation is a little more involved but can be derived from the data. So having arrived at equations (11.8) and (11.9), we now have the means to estimate (i) the incidence of memories attributable to recollection (conscious memory processes), and separately, (ii) the incidence of memories attributable to habit (unconscious/automatic memory processes). Indeed this is a critical point. The process-dissociation methodology holds the promise that it provides tools with which we may be able to distinguish conscious from unconscious memory processes. Although the approach has its detractors (Graf & Komatsu, 1994; Hirshman, 1998), the method has been applied in a wide variety of settings (see, for example, Kelley & Jacoby, 2000) with some considerable success.

Indeed, when these techniques were used by Hay and Jacoby (1999), the data were particularly revealing. Young people were more accurate on both congruent trials and incongruent trials than were elderly people – as expected. However, when recollection and habit were estimated separately for the different age groups it was clearly shown that, whereas there was no difference in the age groups' reliance on habit to respond, there was a significant difference in their reliance on recollection. Elderly people were less reliant on recollection than were the young people. As Hay and Jacoby (1999) concluded, this evidence suggested that the larger prevalence of memory slips in the elderly than in the young is due to problems in being consciously able to take control of the act of remembering. → See 'What have we learnt?', page 411.

**According to Hay and Jacoby (1999), are memorial problems with aging related to recollection or habit?**

## False autobiographical memories

VLADIMIR: But we were there together, I could swear to it! Picking grapes for a man called . . . [He snaps his fingers] . . . can't think of the name, at a place called . . . [snaps his fingers] . . . can't think of the name of the place, do you not remember?

*(Beckett, 1952/1986, p. 57)*

Evidence that converges on the issue of false autobiographical memory – the misremembering of your personal history – comes from a form of memory research in a so-called **diary study** (Barclay, 1986). Conway, Collins, Gathercole and Anderson (1996) had two participants keep diary records over a period of five months (i.e., records were made on 147 days over a 21-week period). For every entry, the participants were asked to provide one true event and one true thought that had occurred. In addition, they were asked to provide either an altered event and a false thought or a false event and an altered thought. In this way the participants were providing veridical autobiographical facts alongside fabricated material that were either based on these facts or were simply made up. Various other ratings or impressions of these records were also made at the time of their production.

### → What have we learnt?

Much of the material covered so far has involved research concerned with what has come to be known as **ecological memory** (Bruce, 1985). With this approach, the focus is on how memory operates in everyday situations. Although all of the work covered here has been carried out in the laboratory, the issues addressed have concerned aspects of memory that we have all either experienced directly or come across in the media.

Fundamentally, what the work reviewed here demands is a careful appraisal of what fundamentally human memory is really like. One caricature of the constructivist account (Loftus, 1975) is that memory is apparently infinitely malleable. Any given memory of an event may be corrupted by subsequent information. The record of the event can be modified by future information; indeed it can be over-written by future information. This is a rather extreme conclusion that might be drawn on the basis of what the literature on the misinformation effect and false memories has shown. However, there are dissenting views.

For instance, from the work of McCloskey and Zaragoza (1985) it seems clear that, if the conditions are right at test, then uncorrupted material from the original event can be recovered. Consistent with this line of research is the view that we should exhaust various other possibilities before we need accept the claim that human memory is so unreliable that it is fundamentally untrustworthy. This is

a fundamental issue because, although everyone agrees that forgetting does take place, there are huge disagreements over how or why it takes place.

In the present chapter, we have concentrated on the literature concerning misinformation effects and false memories. Regarding the misinformation effect, we have concluded that this may arise for any one of several reasons – indeed, more than one factor may be operating in any one case. A rather guarded conclusion is that the effect does not necessitate the conclusion that stored memories are fundamentally changed or eradicated by subsequent incongruent information.

- Participants may not have registered critical facts but are willing to accept that the critical information was indeed presented.
- Participants also may remember both the misleading information and the critical information but are unable to recover which is associated with the actual to-be-remembered events – a possibility that has been discussed in terms of something known as *source monitoring* (see Johnson, Hashtroudi & Lindsay, 1993).
- Participants may remember both the critical and misleading information but only retrieve a record of the misleading information (Abeles & Morton, 1999; Morton et al., 1985).
- Participants may remember both the critical and misleading information but are quite happy to

▶

accept the misleading information simply because the experimenter provided it (see Abeles & Morton, 1999, p. 582).

This latter possibility is particularly pertinent when the literature on false memories is considered. Just think how you would feel if an earnest experimental psychologist took you aside and showed you a sample of pictures 'from your childhood' – some of which you clearly recognise. If you do not want to appear awkward and you are particularly obliging (think about it – there is course credit at stake here!) then why not play along in the cases that you are unsure of? Now you leave, only to return a week later when yet again you are probed about 'your childhood memories'. You have had plenty of time to think about it. These things may well have happened after all (and probably did) and if they did happen, then what else can you remember? Oh yes, the hot air balloon was coloured Norwegian blue.

Clearly there are many vexed issues here, and it seems most sensible to adopt a degree of scepticism. At the very least, what Miller and Wolford (1999) have demonstrated is that (in their experimental conditions) true and 'false' memories could be distinguished on behavioural grounds. Moreover, the incidence of false memories may indeed be tied to participants adopting a fairly liberal criterion – well, it seems plausible enough, so I guess it probably did occur. The alternative (and perhaps disturbing) view is that engendered false memories are as real as any other memory that you have.

Seven months after the final diary entry was made, recognition tests were carried out. At the time of the recognition tests, various ratings were also taken of the individual memories. First, participants were asked to say whether a particular item was true or false. If false, they were then asked to judge whether it was an altered or false record.

For the recognition test, among the records that the participants had originally generated were records contrived by the experimenter. So if recognition memory were perfect, then all of the experimenter-generated records ought to have been classified as false alongside all of the records that the participants had altered or made up originally. In scoring the data, false memories were cases where participants classified as true any altered or made-up records, regardless of whether they were self- or experimenter-generated.

So the experiment tested memory for actual events when foils (the contrived items) were either based on the same actual events or were made up entirely. Some of the foils were those made up by participants at the time of making their diary entries. In this way, participants were then forced at test to try to discriminate real from imagined events and real from contrived thoughts. In also including foils created by the experimenter, participants were also having to discriminate true records of the past from completely new fabrications.

## Memory and the remember/know distinction

For each response at test, participants were also asked to say whether they consciously remembered the record.

If they did not consciously remember the record, they were then asked whether it evoked feelings of familiarity or whether there was no distinct state of awareness. Were the participants actually recollecting the event or were they guessing? The reason for these questions stemmed from a consideration of Tulving's (1985) description of two different types of memory awareness associated with true memories. According to this view, a so-called **remember response** is 'characterized by recollective experience and features the conscious recollection of the previously studied item or experience: recall of details such as thoughts, feelings, and sensory-perceptual experiences associated with the encoding event' (Conway et al., 1996, p. 69). In contrast, there is a **know response**. Such responses do not have an associated recollective experience: they only present with a feeling of familiarity or knowing. In the above example, Vladimir seems to know that he spent time picking grapes, but the details of the recollection are missing and he looks to his friend Estragon for help. What Conway et al. were particularly interested in was whether false memories are accompanied by any form of recollective experience. In probing the participants about their impressions of their memories for their diary records, Conway et al. were attempting to garner further evidence that might distinguish true from false memories.

In brief: the results were clear in showing that the overwhelming tendencies were that true memories were accompanied by recollective experiences, whereas false memories were typically accompanied by feelings of familiarity or no distinct state of conscious awareness. However, in other respects, memory performance was different for events and thoughts. In broad strokes, memory for events was accompanied by recollective experience, memory for thoughts was accompanied by feelings of familiarity: this was irrespective of whether the events and thoughts were true or not. In addition, there were more false memories for thoughts than events. The false memories that arose for thoughts were overwhelmingly accompanied by some feeling of familiarity, and only very rarely were they accompanied by any form of recollective experience. In contrast, false memories of events were equally likely to be accompanied by recollective experience, feelings of familiarity or no distinct conscious recollections.

In answer to the question of whether false memories can be accompanied by some form of recollective experience, then the answer is 'yes but rarely'. Of the false memories documented by Conway et al., approximately one-quarter were accompanied by some form of recollective experience. So we cannot conclude that the distinction between true and false memories can be gauged categorically by whether or not remembering is accompanied by some form of recollective experience (see Heaps & Nash, 2001, for a further endorsement of this view). Although the study by Conway et al. does throw some light on an important issue, many vexed questions are left unanswered. Whether more fine-grained analyses can deliver the critical tools for discriminating the truth or falsity of any given memory remains, essentially, unresolved.

## Pinpoint question 11.10

Are false memories typically characterised by recollection or familiarity?

**false memories** Memories of states of affairs that never actually took place.

**intentional learning paradigm** Where participants are explicitly instructed to remember materials that they will be tested on later.

**incidental learning paradigm** Where participants are not explicitly instructed to remember items that they will be tested on later.

**free recognition** Participants' recognition memory is tested by having them freely decide whether an item is old or new.

**forced recognition** Participants' recognition memory is tested by having them decide as to which of one or more of the alternatives has been previously experienced.

**memory operating characteristic** A memory function plotted across a range of paired hit and false alarm rates, in a bid to understand the nature of decision-making processes.

**critical lure** From Roediger and McDermott (1995), an item that is closely associated with a list of items but is never actually presented during the initial study phase of the experiment.

**recollection** A conscious act of remembering.

**habit** Enduring memories that lead to default responding when recollection fails.

**process-dissociation procedure** After Hay and Jacoby (1999), a way of estimating the incidence of memories attributable to recollection and the incidence of memories attributable to habit.

**ecological memory** After Bruce (1985), how memory operates in everyday situations.

**diary study** A study in which participants' experiences are recorded on a regular basis over a relatively long period of time. Examination of the diary records is undertaken as the means of data analysis.

**remember response** A state of awareness associated with recollection.

**know response** A state of awareness – a feeling of familiarity – that an item was actually committed to memory.

## Concluding comments

The main thrust of the chapter has been to concentrate on certain phenomena that are assumed to reflect what might be taken to be certain key properties of memory – such as what we remember and why. In particular, the focus has been with the evidence of the degree to which we can depend on our memories – just how reliable are our memories, given that we live in such busy times and in such busy environments? One clear thread, in the literature, emphasises that we must exhibit much caution in relying too much on personal recollections. The most extreme position seems to be one in which it is assumed that our memories are infinitely malleable – no memory is insulated and free from contamination. All our memories are potentially fallible. However, much of the evidence reviewed in this chapter is difficult to square with such a negative view. A less extreme opinion is that memories can be fallible, but, given the right cues and the right testing conditions, a truthful record of past events may be recoverable. Indeed, we have also seen how it could be that people rely on habit. Maybe, given the right kind of support and time, they would be able to recollect the actual events that transpired?

Of course, there can be no doubt that people misremember past events: the critical issue is with how best to interpret such phenomena. By one view, such errors are taken as being evidence that people may indeed possess false memories – that is, they possess incorrect records of virtual past events. Such personal mental records are as true to the individual as are memories of actual past events. In accepting this, there is an emerging research trend manifest in the various attempts that have been made to try to discriminate true from false memories. The major issue is whether there are any means by which true and false memories can be discriminated. Although the behavioural evidence is equivocal on this particular issue, it may turn out that some other form of physiological or indeed neurophysiological marker may exist that can be used to distinguish between true and false memories (see Loftus & Bernstein, 2005, for a brief review).

As is probably clear, the debates are far from settled, and many profound issues about the fundamental nature of human memory remain unresolved. The field remains wide open. For some, this state of affairs may be slightly deflating – we seem to have come so far and yet we know so little. To others, though, the fact that many of the fundamental properties of human memory remain something of a mystery will stand out as being a real challenge. The importance of trying to resolve these issues cannot be underestimated. Large swathes of the judicial systems, throughout the world, rest upon beliefs in the veridical nature of human recollection. Having read about the fallibilities and failures of memory, how confident are you now that you would make a good eyewitness? Moreover, and on a more personal level, if you cannot rely on your own memories about your past self, what does this really mean about your concept of your current self?

## CHAPTER SUMMARY

- The chapter addresses fallibilities and failures of memory. The chapter begins with some remarks about general issues and features one particular framework (or model) of memory – headed records (Morton, Hammersley & Bekerian, 1985). There is no implication that this framework is particularly well specified or should be particularly favoured. In the current context, it merely provides a very useful backdrop for considering key concepts and key findings. Within the account, a distinction is made between the memory unit itself (the information being remembered) and the access key (the tag that can be used to retrieve the information). Memory retrieval is then a process of forming a description, attempting to link the description to a heading, accessing the record via the heading, and evaluating the recovered information.

- Headed records work under the assumption that, once formed, records do not change. However, there is evidence from the eyewitness testimony literature that memory is in fact much more (re)constructive than the above theory suggests. For example, Loftus and Palmer (1974) provided loaded questions related to a videotape of a car accident. Participants were sensitive to these questions such that cars that 'smashed' with one another were reported as going faster than cars that 'contacted' with one another. In addition, participants were also more likely to misremember plausible information related to the scene (such as the presence of broken glass), something known as the misleading information effect (McCloskey & Zaragoza, 1985).

- There are a number of competing accounts for the misleading information effect. The headed records account states that the record for post-event information containing the misleading information is more easily accessed than the record for the original event itself. The destructive actualisation hypothesis (Schwarz & Stahlberg, 2003) states that post-event information over-writes information related to the original event. The encoding specificity principle (Tulving & Thomson, 1973) argues that the relationship between cue and memory is critical, with retrieval more likely when cue and memory are similar to one another.

- Signal detection theory (SDT) also attempts to account for the misleading information effect by arguing that these kinds of paradigms simply induce a response bias in participants. In addition, SDT can also be applied more directly to false memories. In a classic paradigm by Roediger and McDermott (1995), participants are presented with a list of words in which a critical lure is related to the list items but never presented. The data revealed that responding to critical lures as OLD was more likely to be the result of response bias ($\beta$) rather than sensitivity ($d'$). They argued that false memories arose at a decisional stage of processing, rather than reflecting anything significant about memory itself.

- False memories have also been investigated using doctored personal materials. For example, Wade, Garry, Read and Lindsay (2002) presented participants with both real and fictional photos from their childhood, in an attempt to convince individuals that they had taken a balloon ride when they were young when in fact they had not. Approximately half of the individuals reported at least a partial false memory for the balloon incident. Moreover, Garry and Gerrie (2005) went on to show that it was not necessary to doctor photos in order to produce false memories. Misremembered events could also be generated on the basis of associating real and fictitious events with childhood photos.

- Aging appears to compound problems of false memory. Hay and Jacoby (1999) stated that memorial problems associated with the elderly are more likely to do with less reliance on recollection than younger participants. Problems arise with elderly people as they tend to respond on the basic memorial habits than recollections of actual events. Such points were made in the context of an introduction to the process dissociation paradigm and its rationale.

- There are certain characteristics that appear to distinguish between false and true memories, such as recollective experience (Conway, Collins, Gathercole & Anderson, 1996) but the predictive value of these measures is not enough to distinguish sufficiently between what is real and what is not.

## ANSWERS TO PINPOINT QUESTIONS

11.1 Remembering might also be a problem of retrieval, in that the event has been encoded and stored properly but the address of where in memory it has been stored is lost.

11.2 A heading is a more useful cue to recall than the record.

11.3 'She limped across the finishing line' is more likely to lead to misremembering the runner having cramp after the race, in the same way that 'smashed' cars lead to the misremembering of broken glass (Loftus & Palmer, 1974).

11.4 The headed records model accounts for the misleading information effect by claiming that the record for post-event information containing the misleading information is more easily accessed than is the record for the original event itself.

11.5 If participants are presented with misleading verbal descriptions and tested with verbal information, the misleading information effect should be stronger than when participants are tested with misleading visual information following exposure to verbal descriptions (Abeles & Morton, 1999).

11.6 The encoding specificity principle states that the greater the similarity between the conditions at presentation and the conditions (cue to recall) at test, the better the chance of retrieval.

11.7 Identifying Jerry as an old girlfriend when she was not can be described as a false alarm.

11.8 A critical lure is an item that is closely associated with a list of to-be-remembered items but is never actually presented as part of the list at study.

11.9 Older individuals appear to be less reliant on recollection than younger individuals (Hay & Jacoby, 1999).

11.10 False memories are typically characterised by familiarity. The feeling of recollection is rare for misremembered events.

## CHAPTER 12

# SEMANTIC MEMORY AND CONCEPTS

## LEARNING OBJECTIVES

**By the end of this chapter, you should be able to:**

- Describe the Collins and Quillian (1969) semantic network model.
- Describe the Smith, Shoben and Rips (1974) feature model of semantic memory.
- Recognise the difference between localist and distributed models.
- Describe the Rumelhart and Todd (1993) connectionist model of semantic memory.
- Discuss prototypes and mental taxonomies in relation to semantic knowledge.

## CHAPTER CONTENTS

So the summer is nearly upon us and you've decided that you're going to clear out your wardrobe once and for all, and finally get rid of all those unwanted jumpers and socks collected over many Christmases and birthdays. Once you've got over the fact that it was possible to stuff your wardrobe with what seems like a whole department store, you're left with the unenviable task of sorting your clothes. Right – maybe we could start

# Wardrobe refreshing and memories of the Pyramid stage

off with tops and bottoms? Great. Soon t-shirts and jumpers are piling up on one side of the room, and trousers, skirts and shorts are piling up on the other side. Hmm – a dress? If you're male and living on your own then you might ask how that got in there in the first place, but the problem that you're faced with now is that it's clothing that neither fits into the 'tops' category nor the 'bottoms' category. A dress is for top and bottom so it looks like it needs a new category. Curses. Maybe start again but break down these categories into smaller subdivisions. So, one pile for t-shirts, one pile for shirts, one pile for shorts and so on. Pretty soon the one big pile from your wardrobe has amassed into numerous little piles all around your bedroom. Hang on, weren't we meant to be throwing some of these clothes out? Okay, time to sub-categorise again.

Focusing on the stockpile of t-shirts for the time being, you decide that because this summer is going to be the hottest summer ever (no, really), you won't be needing any black t-shirts, so now you can sub-divide your t-shirts by colour. Two or three black tees down the line, you come across your bootleg Radiohead t-shirt from when they headlined Glastonbury in 2003 – a classic! After some deliberation, you decide this is what a t-shirt is really all about and, although it's black and you're going to be very hot this summer, it's staying in the 'keep' pile. After getting a nice big bin liner together for the charity shop, right at the bottom of your wardrobe you find what can only be described as a piece of cloth with some holes in it that could potentially be a piece of clothing. After making a mental note to buy some mothballs next time you're shopping, you set about the task of trying to figure out whether the limp piece of cloth you hold in your hand could actually pass as a pair of shorts. Okay. What does it mean for something to be some shorts? For starters, it needs three holes – one for the waist and two for the legs. Hmm. It's got four holes! Maybe it's a t-shirt then, since in terms of holes you need one hole for the head, two for the arms and one for the waist. Four holes – check! The only problem is, the holes are all at the front of the material and they go all the way through. It appears to be a dishcloth. You throw the rejected item in the bin and decide if you really need to keep that Radiohead t-shirt after all . . .

## REFLECTIVE QUESTIONS

1.  Think about all the different people that you know. What's the first way of categorising them that comes to mind? Do you find that some people actually don't fit into these schemes? Are there too many people in one category? If you have had to create lots of categories, how are these organised? Have you got bigger groups that then break down into smaller groups? How do these different categories interact with one another?

2. Rifle through your CD or download collection and figure out what your favourite music is to put on before you go out on a Saturday night. Why did you pick this as the best example of this type of music? What kind of qualities does it have? Are there other pieces of music that fit this bill, sort of, but aren't quite as good examples? How do these qualities compare with music that you listen to on Sunday morning?

## Introduction and preliminary considerations

Pause and take a deep breath: so far we have looked at very brief forms of information storage, brief forms of information storage, longer-term forms of storage and how information in the long-term store may be lost or corrupted. We have yet to consider, in any detail, what the nature of the long-term store/memory system is actually like. We still need to consider how knowledge is represented in long-term memory. As a start, we can call upon the episodic/semantic memory distinction, as applied to long-term memory, because we are primarily concerned with the nature of semantic knowledge. To reiterate, episodic memory refers to memories of personal life experiences, whereas semantic memory is more about world knowledge in general. Semantic memory concerns knowledge about the world that resides in the public domain. Paris is the capital of France. However, we will discover that there is much more to semantic memory than is conveyed by a list of facts. Indeed, we will spend some considerable amount of effort in discussing how our knowledge of the world is actually structured. How is knowledge of the world organised in the mind? What is the structure of semantic memory? Are all the (mental) books on trains and train spotting gathered together in the same place? Are the books organised alphabetically? By subject?

More particularly, and given such concerns, we will discuss how we mentally group objects into categories and how we establish what kinds of properties are associated with one category (t-shirts) and not another

(shorts). Mental categories are critically important because they allow us to manage and make sense of the wealth of sensory information around us. So much more is conveyed by stating that 'Edward is an insurance adjuster' than by saying 'Edward works in the city'. We will examine why this should be so, as we proceed. Before we get too carried away, however, it is probably best to begin by going over some key terms.

## Key terms and key concepts

One thing that is central is the notion of a **category**, that is, a collection or a set of things. To keep it simple there is a category of, for example, *Birds* and this category comprises all birds. The category *birds* can be referred to as a **superordinate category** because it can be broken down into sub-categories, or more technically, **subordinate categories**. So the superordinate category *birds* comprises sub-categories that themselves contain different kinds of birds such as *seabirds*, *birds of prey*, *domesticated birds*, and so on. Indeed, the hierarchical nature of this category scheme is made even more transparent because each of these subordinate categories can be broken down further into smaller sub-categories still: so *seabirds* contain species such as *grebes* and *fulmars*, *domesticated birds* contain the species *chickens* and *turkeys*, *birds of prey* contain the species *eagles* and *falcons* (see Figure 12.1).

So at one level of analysis, *bird* is the superordinate category that includes the subordinate *seabird*, but, as we have seen, this sub-category may also be broken down into further sub-categories. Alternatively, we may use the language of sets (where here the term

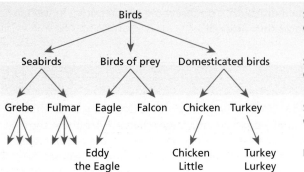

Figure 12.1 A hierarchical illustration of how a superordinate category (i.e., birds) can be subdivided into various kinds of more particular subordinate categories

**set** can be used interchangeably with 'category'). When we use this language, we can use the phrases 'superordinate sets' and 'subordinate sets', and also think in terms of 'set inclusion'. With set inclusion, a subordinate set is said to be included in a superordinate set – we have the idea of set inclusion. So a superordinate set is, by definition, larger than a set that it includes – there are more birds than there are seabirds.

Right down at the very bottom of the hierarchy is the individual or the instance, and now we can talk in terms of the instances of a category or the instances of a set. So when you look out in the garden and see a particular blackbird, then that is a particular instance of the *blackbird* category. The idea of organising category instances into hierarchical sets also allows us to draw certain inferences and conclusions about the world easily, for example, 'All seagulls are birds' and 'Not all birds are seabirds'. Stated thus, it becomes almost immediately apparent that categories and their instances are implicated when we discuss other concerns about problem solving and inference – 'Some birds are not seagulls', true?

In extending the superordinate/subordinate distinction, we need to emphasise that hierarchies can have many levels. For example, there are many different types of seabirds – gulls, terns, guillemot, etc. Then there are many different types of gulls – common gull, herring gull, etc. *Then* there are many different types of tern – common tern, arctic tern, etc. Alternatively, we could also think about *bird* being a subordinate rather than superordinate category, since birds are animals, animals are living beings, living beings are concrete entities, concrete entities are just one sort of entity, and so on.

In setting the scene in this way, the discussion has strayed onto the topic of **taxonomic systems** and the study of classification (see Sokal, 1974, for example). Such a science has its roots in that branch of biology where the aim is to generate classification schemes for any kind of living being – let's call these *biological taxonomies*. Think back to those school trips to the Natural History Museum. Remember all those glass cases filled with specimens of butterflies or insects mounted in such a way as to reveal how the different instances are related: similar kinds of instances grouped together, distant relatives being kept far apart. For a taxonomy (a classification scheme) to be at all useful, it must provide a way of organising the world in such a way that the hierarchical relations and the similarities between the instances are made apparent. So to speak of 'a taxonomy' is to discuss one way of organising instances into categories.

That there can be more than one way to organise collections is clear when CDs are considered – is it better to organise the CD collection by year, artist, album title, or even by make-up or break-up music? For now it is best to skirt around the thorny issue of whether there is *a* correct way to organise the world, and concentrate instead on the fact that psychologists have merely attempted to discover how knowledge of the world is organised mentally. As we will see, ideas about biological taxonomies have been astonishingly influential in how psychologists have thought about the organisation of human long-term memory and the nature of concepts.

In turning to the topic of human long-term memory we assume that this is the internal store of knowledge that every person carries around with them. Semantic memory is the mental store containing knowledge of basic facts about the world, for example, 'Paris is the capital of France' 'A penguin is a bird'. More generally, such knowledge is also assumed to include the meanings of words – 'Rage is an extreme form of anger' – and also concepts, for example, what a bachelor is. So part of your semantic memory might include the facts about what happened on 11 September 2001 in New York. You may also remember quite vividly where you were when you heard the news. This latter personal fact, though, would be designated as being part of episodic memory and will be different from anyone elses.

Having mentioned the term **concept** in passing above, it is important to be clear about what we actually mean by the term (the concept of concepts, if you will). This is particularly important because, sometimes, semantic memory is also referred to as the human conceptual system – the mental store of concepts. To avoid getting too embroiled in philosophical digressions, let us start with a fairly basic definition of what a concept is. According to Savin, a concept is simply a class of objects (Savin, 1973, p. 229). To take a concrete example, there is the concept of a BIKE. The concept applies to all instances of bikes. However, as cognitive psychologists, we are much more concerned with the mental than the physical, and so we are much more concerned with knowledge than with actual collections of real-world objects. In this regard Smith (1988) simply asserted that 'concepts are mental representations of classes' (p. 19).

## Extensions and intensions

A more precise definition comes about through consideration of the distinction between a concept's

**Figure 12.2 There are bikes, and there are 'bikes'**
Left: All bikes have two wheels, right? Right: Wrong!

*Sources*: (left) alveyandtowers.com; (right) Lester Lefkowitz/Corbis.

**extension** and its **intension** (Anglin, 1977; Markman & Seibert, 1976; Savin, 1973). Put simply, the extension of a concept is the set of all instances of the concept, so the extension of the BIKE concept is the set of all bikes found in the real world. The intension of a concept is the definition, defining properties, criteria or description of the members of the extension of the concept (after Markman & Seibert, 1976, p. 562). The intension of the concept BIKE underlies the decision over what is and what is not a bike. The intension specifies the criteria that you would use to classify something as a bike. Now while this all might seem pretty obvious, it actually may not be as easy as you first thought. For example, you might imagine that it's a pretty safe bet to assume that part of the intension of the concept of a bike is that it has two wheels. On the basis of Figure 12.2a we might be inclined to agree, but if you take a look at the quad bike in Figure 12.2b, you'll see that two wheels are not necessary for the concept of a BIKE to apply. The cognitive psychologist's job is to try to determine how concepts are represented in the mind, but clearly this is no minor undertaking.

For now it is useful to reiterate Smith's (1988) thoughts about concepts. In having an internal representational system based around concepts, this confers some advantages in terms of both processing efficiency and storage space. The concept name (e.g., 'bike'), in a sense, acts as a shorthand symbol that conveys a lot of information. For example, we might tell a friend that 'Monty' has four legs, barks and likes chewing bones. Basically, that's a lot of words that can be simply replaced with the concept that Monty is a DOG. On the assumption that you already had the concept DOG stored, then you'd know that, on the balance of probability, Monty has four legs, barks and indeed does like chewing bones. The sender did not have to state this explicitly because it is implicit in stating that 'Monty is a dog', and this is how concepts allow us 'to go beyond the information given' (Bruner, 1957).

Moreover, on the assumption that having the concept DOG implies having an intension, then all of the contingent knowledge about DOG (wags tail, fond of sticks) does not have to be duplicated when you hear that Barnsley is also a dog. General knowledge about dogs (regardless of whether it's Monty or Barnsley) need only be stored once. Of course, when we find out that Barnsley is a toy dog, then we need to call upon a particular subordinate category of DOG to draw the correct inferences (see Figure 12.3).

**Figure 12.3 Toy dogs share some, though not all, of the properties of real dogs**

If we assume that we do store intensions, then other benefits become apparent. We need only store the intensions once, so long as we can easily access this information. As in any dictionary, the definition of a given word is stored under the word's entry and does not have to be re-duplicated and placed in parentheses after every time ('the continuous passage of existence in which events pass from a state of potentiality in the future, through to the present, to a state of finality in the past', p. 1686) the ('used preceding a noun that has been previously specified', p. 1669) word ('one of the units of speech or writing that native speakers of a language usually regard as the smallest isolable meaningful element of the language', p. 1847) is ('a form of the present tense', p. 857) written ('the past participle of write', p. 1853; all definitions from the *Collins English Dictionary*, 2005). There is therefore economy in storage space in not having to duplicate information unnecessarily throughout the knowledge store. Indeed, as we will see, cognitive psychologists have been particularly taken with the notion of **cognitive economy** – economy in mental storage space – as discussed below.

Of additional interest is the assertion that 'concepts are the building blocks of thoughts – the building blocks of a mental life of judging, believing, wondering, and meaning' (Editorial, *Mind & Language*, 1989, 4 (1 and 2), p. 4). What this means is that concepts can be combined in giving rise to complex concepts and thoughts. So the combination of the concepts PET and FISH gives rise to the complex concept PET FISH. As Smith (1988) indicated, though, there are many vexed issues here (see, for example Connolly, Fodor, Gleitman & Gleitman, 2007) and we will return to consider some of these as the chapter draws to a close. The general point is that concepts are critically involved in thinking.

### Pinpoint question 12.1

**What is the difference between a concept's intension and its extension?**

## Propositions and propositional networks

Quite a lot of work on semantic memory in the cognitive psychological literature has addressed very particular issues concerning how the meanings of words are represented and how everyday sentences are understood. For instance, close ties have been drawn in the literature between the nature of propositions and understanding sentences. The notion of a pro-positional representational system was introduced in the chapter on mental representation (Chapter 7), and there the terms 'predicate', 'argument' and 'proposition' were used in discussing, not just natural language, but also the language of thought.

Consider the following example:

Give $(x, y, z)$

According to Norman and Rumelhart (1975), this is an example of a predicate as defined as a generic function that specifies a relation (i.e., 'Give') that holds between a number of arguments ($x$, $y$ and $z$). So we have a generic function called 'Give()' and this takes on a number of arguments – the $x$, $y$ and $z$. When we assign the $x$, $y$ and $z$ values, the generic function is now referred to as a proposition. Having introduced this way of thinking, more generally the relation specified in a proposition (Give) is referred to as being the predicate and because of this it is probably best to use the phrase **predicate expression** (Guttenplan, 1986) when discussing generic functions of the sort Give($x$, $y$, $z$). It is therefore more commonplace to discuss a proposition as being composed of a predicate together with a number of arguments.

So in the example

Give $(x, y, z)$

can be replaced by the more meaningful rendition:

Give (*agent, recipient, object*)

in which 'Give' is the predicate, and *agent, recipient* and *object* are the arguments. This, in turn, can be converted into a proposition by assigning values to the agent, recipient and object arguments:

Give (Ann, Charles, the book)

So we now have the **propositional representation** – Give (*Ann, Charles, the book*) – of the natural language sentence, '*Ann gives Charles the book*' in which *Ann* is the agent, *Charles* is the recipient and *the book* is the object.

The most straightforward application of this form of representational system is in terms of generating a code for expressing linguistic material because there is a fairly transparent correspondence between propositions and phrases used in natural language. Indeed, some of the earlier work on propositions (see, for instance, the work of Anderson, 1976; Anderson & Bower, 1973; and various examples in Norman

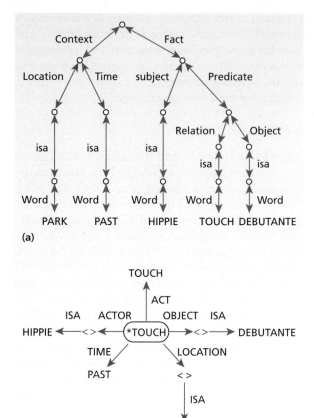

**(a)**

**(b)**

**Figure 12.4 Propositional network representational systems**
Two examples of propositional network representational systems that have been discussed in the literature on how best to think about knowledge representation. (a) is taken from Anderson and Bower (1973). (b) is taken from the work of Norman and Rumelhart (1975).

*Source*: Johnson-Laird, P. N., Herrmann, D. J., & Chaffin, R. (1984). Only connections: A critique of semantic networks. *Psychological Bulletin*, *96*, 292–315 (fig. 2, p. 297; fig. 3, p. 298). Reproduced with permission from APA.

& Rumelhart, 1975) concerned developing so-called *propositional networks* capable of capturing the meanings of sentences (Anderson, 2005). Figure 12.4 provides just two examples of this sort of enterprise, with respect to the somewhat curious sentence 'In a park a hippie touched a debutante.'

According to Anderson (2005, p. 151), with propositional networks, it is useful to think in terms of the nodes (the small unfilled circles in the figure) as standing for particular ideas and the connections (the double-headed arrows) between the nodes as standing for associations between ideas. Beneath all of this, however, is the desire to generate a form of representation

that supports the interpretation of natural language – it is a form of representation that conveys the meaning of a message. If we need to analyse the meaning of a word or concept, then we can try to generate a propositional network of that word or concept. The far-reaching claim is that such a form of representation can provide a mechanism for understanding the nature of thought!

Such issues as these will be considered in much more detail later. For now, the intention is merely to concentrate on how propositions relate to more enduring forms of memory representations known as *semantic network representations*, or more simply, **semantic networks** (Johnson-Laird, Herrmann & Chaffin, 1984). We have seen how a given proposition can help in conveying individual concepts – the proposition for 'Give' conveys something of its essence – and we have also seen how, more generally, combining different propositions in propositional networks aids in understanding sentences. Now we shall see how propositions can help us understand how the human conceptual system may be structured. A very particular kind of propositional network is known as a semantic network. Semantic networks are a kind of propositional network that specifies conceptual knowledge.

## Semantic network representations of human memory

Typically semantic network models have been attempts to specify how basic facts about the world are stored. Overwhelmingly the literature has concentrated on providing accounts of how taxonomies of various biological and other real-world instances are organised into mental categories. The general assumption has been that there is a fairly transparent mapping between the logical/biological nature of categories and their representation in the mind. According to such a view, semantic memory is organised in the same way that the butterflies are organised in the glass cabinet in our museum – close relatives are stored close together and far apart from distant relatives. More extreme still are the realist ideas that the world is actually structured in a particular way. If this is accepted, then it follows that all semantic memory does is reflect this structure in its own organisation (see later discussion of the work by Rosch and co-workers). The claim is that the world is actually composed of distinct objects that naturally group themselves in particular ways and the organisation of human semantic memory is merely a reflection of this. Real-world categories are represented as mental categories in the mind.

Before we consider such realist views in more detail, it is more important to consider how knowledge of things may be organised. What semantic memory theorists are particularly concerned with is how such conceptual knowledge is both represented and organised in the mind. The first sort of model of the human conceptual system we shall address is known as a *semantic network*. As Johnson-Laird et al. (1984) noted, 'semantic networks are designed to represent intensional relations' and as such they are not best suited to capture all attendant knowledge that an individual might possess about a class of things. We should be mindful therefore that the work on semantic networks has concentrated on how intensional knowledge of concepts may be represented. For example, knowing all of the defining characteristics of a dog is one thing, but how this knowledge is represented may tell us little about how everything else you know about dogs is represented. The implication is that semantic network formalisms may not be best suited to explain how it is that you know that your previous next-door neighbour's daughter knew someone who used to breed poodles. Thus the semantic memory literature has been primarily focused on the nature of concepts as intensions and how these might be represented in the mind. Semantic networks provide a form of representational system aimed to capture the intensions of concepts.

## Semantic networks

### Semantic networks and propositions

Here we explore the very close link between propositional representations and semantic networks. Although only very simple propositions have been discussed so far, it is quite possible to envisage more complex examples such as the following:

Shot (*Ann*, the-brother-of (*Charles*))

(the propositional representation of the sentence '*Ann shot the brother of Charles*'). As can be seen from this example, propositions can be embedded within other propositions: the argument of one proposition can be a proposition itself. Shot (*agent, recipient*) is one proposition but recipient is defined in terms of an embedded proposition, namely 'the-brother-of (*individual*)'. In this way propositions can take on an embedding or hierarchical structure. In allowing this, a highly structured representational system can be built up. It is the notion of a hierarchical organisation that provides a connection between propositional representational

systems and more specific network representational systems. Such kinds of networks are typically referred to as *semantic networks* and one of the earliest examples is shown in Figure 12.5.

The diagram is taken from a paper by Quillian (1968) in which he described a computer instantiation of how knowledge conveyed by words could be stored in a computer. It is a model of how word meanings may be represented. On the understanding that such meanings are typically unchanging, the model has been taken by some as a useful first step at attempting to characterise the nature of semantic memory.

### Semantic networks and cognitive economy

Nowadays the idea of a computer database is very commonplace, but at the time of Quillian's work, his model was one of the first to describe how knowledge might be represented and stored in a computer *in a psychologically plausible fashion*. He wanted to address the problem of how it is that knowledge could be stored in the mind. In this regard, an overarching objective of this model was to incorporate ideas about what came to be known as *cognitive economy*. This is in much the same way that, if you were moving house, you'd want to make the best use of space within the removal van as possible. For example, you'd make sure to pack all your cutlery in such a way that they take up the minimum amount of space. The basic assumption is that, as with the removal van, storage space is limited. There is only so much psychological space between your ears and so this has to be used sparingly.

Support for this assumption comes from the common-sense observation that there are only a limited number of facts that humans can learn and remember. If this is accepted, then it is argued that the human representational system must use mental space efficiently. To be able to cram as much as possible into this knowledge store, any given fact must take up a minimum amount of space. So what we are trying to do here is provide a representational system that uses space efficiently. Every time something is added to the database, we try to use as little additional space as possible. In this regard the distinction between **type nodes** and **token nodes** in Quillian's model was central.

### Type and token nodes

A type node is where all the information regarding a particular concept is stored. In the example given in Figure 12.5, PLANT 3 is a type node for the sense of the word *plant* that represents 'to plant something

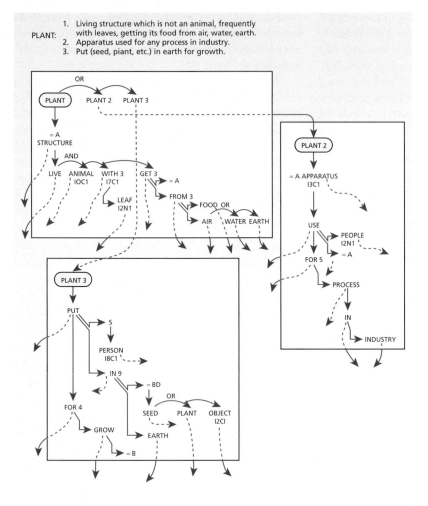

PLANT:
1. Living structure which is not an animal, frequently with leaves, getting its food from air, water, earth.
2. Apparatus used for any process in industry.
3. Put (seed, piant, etc.) in earth for growth.

**Figure 12.5 Quillian's (1968) semantic network representation of the various senses of the term 'plant'**
Type nodes are shown in the lozenge shapes, PLANT, PLANT 2 and PLANT 3. All other labelled nodes are token nodes.

*Source*: Quillian, M. R. (1968). Semantic memory. In M. L. Minsky (Ed.), *Semantic information processing* (pp. 227–259) (fig. 4.1a, p. 236). Cambridge, Massachusetts: The MIT Press. Reproduced with permission.

to grow'. In this particular database, this meaning is unique and hence needs to be stored only once in one particular place at a given type node. The intension of each concept is stored at its type node. However, this system is only feasible if this meaning can be easily accessed: there has to be some way of retrieving the information from the type PLANT 3 node and this is where token nodes come in.

In the horticultural sense of *cultivate* (let us label it CULTIVATE – see Figure 12.6), reference needs to be made to PLANT 3. So the type node for CULTIVATE is linked to a token node for PLANT 3, and this token node then links directly to the PLANT 3 type node. The meaning of PLANT 3 is stored only once in the database, but it is accessed via token nodes that are generated in places where they are needed. So there is a single link from each token node to its type node, all further necessary links emanate from the type node and the meaning of the underlying concept is given by the nature of links to and from the corresponding type

node. By making savings in not duplicating information throughout the store, the model was adhering to the notion of cognitive economy. The meaning of 'to plant', as in 'to plant seeds', is only stored once at its associated type node. Access to this meaning is via relevant token nodes.

Although the division between type and token nodes is straightforward, things were slightly more complicated. In this formalism, five different kinds of links were described (see Johnson-Laird et al., 1984, for more on this, and Figure 12.6). On these grounds, some of the links signified more than just an associative connection between two nodes. In this way, a semantic network is something more than just an **associative network**. In an associative network nodes stand for entities and links represent associative bonds between the entities. The fact that 'horse' and 'cart' are associatively related is signified by the presence of a link connecting the corresponding nodes. The link merely represents that 'horse' and 'cart' go together. With a

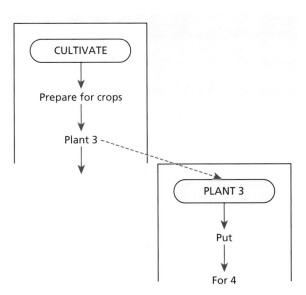

**Figure 12.6 Quillian's representational system for the word 'cultivate'**

Schematic representation of linking the representation of the meaning of the word *cultivate* with the representation of the meaning of the word *plant*. The lozenge shapes are type nodes and the other letter strings designate token nodes. As can be seen, there is a token node for PLANT 3 contained in the representation of the meaning of CULTIVATE. This token node points to the type node for PLANT 3 where the complete specification of the meaning of PLANT 3 is stored. As can be seen in Figure 12.5, the type node for PLANT 3 specifies the meaning of 'planting seeds'. Different kinds of links are posited, for instance, the link from the PLANT 3 token node to its type node is dashed and is different from the other kinds of links in the network.

semantic network, though, links can signify something other than 'goes together'. Indeed in Quillian's scheme, a given link could be assigned a tag or label that provided further information as to what the connection signified. In Figure 12.5, it can be seen that PLANT 3 needs a person as the subject of the planting. Later we will see that one specialised link used in many semantic network systems is known as an ISA link. Such a link represents a set–subset relation – 'A canary ISA bird'. We will return to this point soon. The general point, though, is that within this kind of semantic network representational system, the meaning of a concept is determined by how it is interconnected with other things in the knowledge store.

A more detailed consideration of Quillian's model is not warranted here (see Johnson-Laird et al., 1984) because it was not primarily intended as a fully fledged psychological account of how word meanings are represented in the mind. However, some of the basic characteristics of the model were incorporated into the now classic semantic network account put forward by Collins and Quillian (1969). In this model, ideas about cognitive economy were again brought to the fore. Figure 12.7 provides a schematic representation of this model. Fundamentally, this is a hierarchical model of how knowledge of natural categories (of real-world objects) is organised in memory. So whereas Quillian experimented with a particular formalism as to how word meanings may be represented, Collins and Quillian built on this work and extended the ideas in attempting to understand how conceptual knowledge may actually be organised in the mind.

**Figure 12.7 The now classic example of a semantic network representation as developed by Collins and Quillian (1969)**

*Source*: Collins, A. M., & Quillian, M. R. (1969). Retrieval time from semantic memory. *Journal of Verbal Learning and Verbal Behavior, 8*, 240–247 (fig. 1, p. 241). Reproduced with permission from Elsevier.

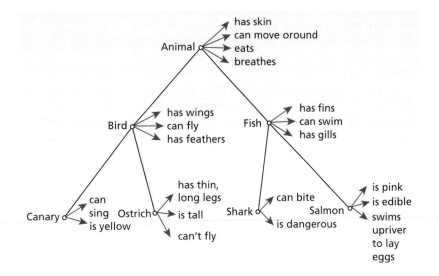

# A psychologically plausible semantic network?

Since the seminal paper of Collins and Quillian (1969), the typical example discussed is of the concept of an animal. At the highest, superordinate level is the ANIMAL (type) node and it is at this level that all the defining characteristics of animals are stored. Subordinate nodes for members of the animal category are stored at the next level, so the BIRD node is connected directly to the ANIMAL node. Now all of the defining characteristics of the category *birds* are now stored at the BIRD level. Subordinate nodes for members of the BIRD category are stored next and details of particular individual birds are now set out.

## Cognitive economy and property inheritance

However, you'll notice some interesting properties regarding this type of organisation (see Figure 12.7). For example, canaries are not listed as being able to breathe! Bad news for our feathered friend, but you'll notice that they are not listed as being feathered either! Rather than having a dead, bald canary on our hands, what we're actually seeing here are examples of cognitive economy and, more specifically, 'the principle of inheritance' (Rumelhart & Todd, 1993, p. 14). We could, of course, store the fact that canaries, bluebirds and ostriches breathe at each of the individual nodes for canaries, bluebirds and ostriches, but this would violate the principle of cognitive economy. Defining characteristics of members of a given category need only be stored once at the appropriate category node. The fact that 'canaries breathe' is implicit in the network because it is not stored at a unique place in the network – the fact must be recovered through a process of **property inheritance** (Rumelhart & Todd, 1993): 'if an *x* is a *y* and a *y* has a certain property, then generally speaking *x* can be said to have inherited that property.' (p. 14).

We will return to this notion of property inheritance in a moment, but it is worth noting that it shows how there was an attempt to marry concerns about the organisation of knowledge with concerns about problem solving. Property inheritance provided a means by which inferences about instances can be made on the basis of recovering knowledge about their categories. So good news for the canary after all. The basic point again is that problem solving is the key to what the mind has evolved to do and if we are to discuss the representation of knowledge then we should be clear about how it facilitates problem solving.

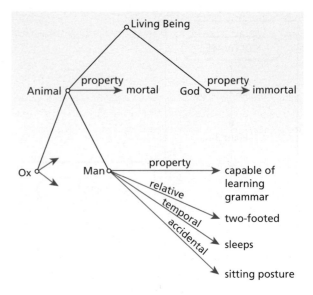

**Figure 12.8 Extending semantic network representations to capture life, the universe and everything!**
According to Kintsch (1980), this structure can be traced back to Aristotle.

*Source*: Kintsch, W. (1980). Semantic memory: A tutorial. In R. S. Nickerson (Ed.), *Attention and performance VIII* (pp. 595–620, fig. 30.4, p. 606). Reproduced with permission.

As a brief aside, for those of you who think that ideas generated in 1969 might be too far back in time to apply to contemporary cognitive psychology, some of the old ideas are often the best. Indeed Kintsch (1980) managed to trace back ideas about semantic network formalisms all the way to Aristotle (see Figure 12.8).

## Pinpoint question 12.2

**According to the Collins and Quillian (1969) model in Figure 12.7, why are sharks not listed as being able to breathe or swim?**

In terms of cognitive economy, savings in space are assumed to be good, in and of themselves. There is only a finite amount of space in the head, so use it wisely. To reinvoke an example from our previous discussion of SIT (see Chapter 6), it will take less space to store '$\alpha \times 1000000$' than it will to store one million $\alpha$s. If we recode a lot of information into a shorter form, then this is known as **data compression**. We can see data compression is at work in the semantic network formalism provided by Collins and Quillian (1969). *Breathes* is stored only once at the superordinate node – it is not duplicated throughout the store.

However, any form of data compression carries a processing cost in terms of information retrieval or data decompression. Indeed this sort of processing overhead became the main subject of empirical tests. If the human conceptual system conforms to the structures and principles of cognitive economy discussed by Collins and Quillian (1969), then certain empirical predictions can be made and tested.

### Testing the Collins and Quillian semantic network model

In order to test their model, Collins and Quillian (1969) ran a **sentence verification task**. On a given trial, the participant was presented with a visual sentence. The task was to decide whether the sentence was true or false and make an appropriate speeded response.

Two forms of sentences were generated: (i) *property sentences* such as 'A canary can sing', and (ii) *super-set sentences* such as 'A canary is a bird'. The basic idea was that any sentence targeted at a particular node should be directly verifiable, so 'A canary is a canary' should be responded to quickly because a single node in the network represents all of the information in the sentence. It was also assumed that retrieving a property from a node takes time, so 'A canary can sing' will take a little longer to verify. In addition, moving between nodes also takes time, so 'A canary is a bird' will take longer to verify than 'A canary is a canary'. Sentences of the type 'A canary can fly' will take longer still because there are time penalties associated with moving between nodes (canary → bird) and then in retrieving the property from the node (birds → fly). As Figure 12.9 shows, the data provided a very convincing support for the basic account.

In describing the model, Collins and Quillian (1969) made relatively strong claims about both how categorical knowledge may be represented and how information retrieval operates. Here the central idea is about **spreading activation** (Collins & Loftus, 1975; after Quillian, 1968). Consider the sentence 'A canary is a bird'. On recognising the word 'canary' the CANARY node would become activated. Immediately activation would emanate out along all links from this node. Now on recognising the word 'bird', the BIRD node would become activated and immediately activation would spread outwards from this node in a similar way. Critically, at the point when activation from one node spreads to an already activated node (when activation from two nodes intersects), an evaluation of the path traced by the activation is then put into place. In the simple case, activation from the CANARY node spreads

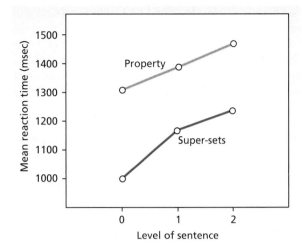

**Figure 12.9 The mean reaction time data for correct responses in the sentence verification task carried out by Collins and Quillian (1969)**
See text for further details.
*Source*: Kintsch, W. (1977). *Memory and cognition*. New York: Wiley.

towards the BIRD node and, given the task constraints, this is sufficient upon which to base a 'yes' response.

The current discussion of spreading activation, in the context of semantic networks, does little more than convey a general impression of the basic ideas. Many more assumptions were introduced and discussed later by Collins and Loftus (1975). For instance, it was assumed that activation decreased in strength as it spread away from the original node, and aligned with this is the idea that activation takes a significant amount of time to spread between nodes (see Ratcliff & McKoon, 1981). However, these amendments were added much later, and currently we are most concerned with the model in its original incarnation.

In the semantic network set out by Collins and Quillian (1969), the property links, connected to a given node, specify critical (i.e., defining) characteristics of the concept – that is, characteristics that apply to whole members of the class associated with the concept. Moreover, such general characteristics of the subordinate members of the category (e.g., BREATHES) could only be retrieved from the superordinate (ANIMAL) node via the notion of spreading activation just described. In this way the knowledge store provides constraints on the order in which different characteristics of a given instance of a category are accessed. Very particular aspects of an instance are accessed first (e.g., IS YELLOW). It is only later that more general characteristics are retrieved (e.g., CAN BREATHE).

The initial data described by Collins and Quillian provided some support for this view. The findings accord well with the intuition that it should take less time to verify 'A canary is yellow' than 'A canary has lungs' even though both are true. However, it was not long before data began to emerge that undermined such a theoretically elegant proposal.

### Pinpoint question 12.3

Which sentence should be recognised as being correct faster and why: 'Rugby balls are oval shaped' or 'Rugby balls contain air'?

## Data that challenge the Collins and Quillian account

In following up on the initial data reported by Collins and Quillian (1969), Conrad (1972) showed that sentence verification RTs (reaction times) did not necessarily reflect the sorts of taxonomic constraints discussed in their model. In her first experiment, she began by collecting some norms on how often people mentioned a given property when probed with an instance name – how often, across a bunch of people, do they report 'curly tail' for 'pig'? Next, she computed the frequency with which each property was listed for each instance. In this way the **production frequency** of a property given an instance was computed (i.e., the **property-instance production frequency**). The simple idea was that the results reported by Collins and Quillian (1969) may have been confounded by a factor other than super-set/subordinate-set relations. The contrary view is that it is the associative strength between a property and an instance that is critical. Maybe the speed of information retrieval in the Collins and Quillian task merely reflected how strongly two items of information were associated? By this alternative view, the reason that responses were quicker to 'Canaries are yellow' than 'Canaries have lungs' is that 'canaries' and 'yellow' are more highly associated than are 'canaries' and 'lungs'.

Having obtained such norms, Conrad constructed sentences in which production frequency was controlled. The central result was that production frequency was a much more potent explanatory variable than set/sub-set relations. Participants were much quicker to verify sentences in which the instance and property were highly associated ('A shark can move') than a sentence in which the instance and the property were less highly associated ('A salmon has a mouth'). Although it is possible to accommodate such data in

various modified versions of the model (cf. Collins & Loftus, 1975), such changes are post hoc. Without serious modifications to the model, the data do undermine the rather strict notions of cognitive economy set out by Collins and Quillian (1969).

The early semantic network model was further weakened by various other data sets in which contradictions to the original predictions became apparent. According to Kintsch (1977), one study by Smith, Shoben and Rips (1974), in particular, rendered the model untenable. In 1971 Loftus and Scheff had published a set of norms that tabulated the frequency with which a given superordinate had been produced in response to a particular instance – yes, another form of production frequency that came to be known as **category dominance** (Loftus, 1973). Seafood–Shrimp has a low category dominance because only 26 per cent of respondents replied 'Seafood' when asked to think of categories to which 'Shrimp' belonged.

Smith et al. (1974) used these measures as indicators of overall similarity between the instance and its superordinates and found that in several cases a given instance was more similar to its higher-order category than to its immediate superordinate category. For example, SCOTCH was found to be more similar to DRINK than to LIQUOR (*Scotch* being a type of *liquor* and *liquor* being a type of *drink*). They then generated a set of sentences to be used in a speeded sentence verification experiment and found that the similarity between category and instance labels was a potent predictor of speed of response. As Glass and Holyoak (1974/1975) noted, it was easier for participants to decide that Scotch is a drink than it was to decide that scotch is a liquor (for ease of exposition we can term this the **hierarchy violation effect**). By the strict notion of a conceptual hierarchy, as in the Collins and Quillian account (1969), this is not possible since LIQUOR is further down the hierarchy than DRINK. That is, there are many additional instances other than Scotch that make up the superordinate category of liquor, and many additional instances other than liquor that make up the (super) superordinate category of drink. → See 'What have we learnt?', page 429.

---

**category** A collection or set of things.

**superordinate category** A category that itself contains categories.

**subordinate category** A category that is contained within another (superordinate) category.

**set** Used here interchangeably with the phrase 'mental category'.

## → What have we learnt?

So despite its apparent elegance and simplicity, the basic semantic network model of Collins and Quillian (1969) has actually been tested to destruction. The model failed to stand up to empirical test, and it was also attacked at a more fundamental theoretical level. Since their introduction, semantic networks proliferated in both the psychology and artificial intelligence/computer simulation literature (see Johnson-Laird et al., 1984, for an early review). However, despite their popularity, it became very difficult to be clear about what exactly defined a semantic network. When do our doodlings on a piece of paper constitute a semantic network rather than any other formal system of knowledge representation? As has already been pointed out, there are propositional networks, and awkward questions can be asked over what it is that really sets semantic networks apart from these kinds of representational systems.

According to Woods (1975), semantic networks are an attempt 'to combine in a single mechanism the ability not only to store factual knowledge but also to model the associative connections exhibited by humans which make certain items of information accessible from certain others' (p. 44). This is relatively straightforward to grasp on the understanding that nodes stand for concepts, and links merely capture the associative relationships between concepts. However, on further analysis this is not so straightforward, and, as has been repeatedly pointed out (Woods, 1975; Johnson-Laird et al., 1984), the strict division between nodes and links is blurred when different types of nodes and different types of labelled links are posited. Even in Quillian's earliest model there were two sorts of nodes and five sorts of links.

The generic form of link shown in the Collins and Quillian (1969) network is known as an ISA link (*A canary IS A bird*), but the links from nodes to properties are many and varied (see Figure 12.7). These sorts of considerations reveal that such networks are much less constrained than might otherwise have been thought. If we take it that a representational system comprises some basic set of symbols together with rules that govern how such symbols may be combined, then we need a clear statement of what the basic constituents and rules for combining the constituents are. As Johnson-Laird et al. (1984) pointed out, there is quite a variety of different semantic network models and it is not at all clear what general principles of knowledge representation emerge from considering this variety.

Despite the very promising beginnings, network models, as models of human semantic memory, began to fall out of fashion. Collins and Loftus (1975) extended the original model, but in doing so created something that was difficult, if not impossible, to test (Kintsch, 1980). The eventual model was so encompassing that it was no longer clear which result could possibly falsify the account. In addition, the early ideas about spreading activation were of little help in explaining performance with false statements. According to Kintsch (1980), participants responded faster to statements of the kind 'A robin is a car' than to statements of the kind 'A robin is a mammal'. Just how a semantic network can explain this remains something of a mystery. So given that semantic networks are in such a poor state of health, it is important to consider what the alternatives are. One class of contenders is known as feature models and it is to these that we now turn.

**taxonomic systems** Systems for grouping instances into categories.

**concept** A mental representation that captures knowledge of what constitutes a given category of things.

**extension** The actual instances picked out by a given concept. For example, the actual objects that we call 'bikes'.

**intension** The description or defining characteristics of a concept.

**cognitive economy** The principle of minimising cognitive storage space for any item of information.

**predicate expression** A generic function which operates on one or more arguments (e.g., GO(x) is a predicate expression in which the predicate GO applies to one argument x). A corresponding proposition would be, for example, GO(home).

**propositional representation** A means of conveying information in terms of a relation that holds for one or more arguments.

**semantic networks** Systems that represent the conceptual information in terms of labelled nodes and links.

**type nodes** In semantic network models, the place in memory where the intension of a concept is stored.

**token nodes** In semantic network models, pointers to the place in memory where the intension of the associated concept is stored.

**associative network** A network model of memory in which nodes signify entities and links represent associative bonds (e.g., the nodes for A and B are connected by a link that signifies that A and B are associated).

**property inheritance** Where a subordinate category or instance adopts certain characteristics as specified at the level of the superordinate category.

**data compression** Taking any form of message and coding it in a reduced form such that any redundancies have been removed. '9xa' rather than 'aaaaaaaaa'.

**data decompression** Taking a coded message and recovering the original. For example, taking '9xa' and generating 'aaaaaaaaa'.

**sentence verification task** On each trial, a string of words is presented to a participant and the task is to decide as quickly and as accurately as possible whether the sentence makes sense or not.

**spreading activation** A metaphor for how information is communicated in a cognitive system, much like how heat emanates throughout a central heating system.

**production frequency** The number of times something is produced in response to a probe. For instance, the number of times 'horse' is produced in response to the probe 'cart'.

**property-instance production frequency** The number of times a given property is produced for a given instance. For instance, how many times 'barks' is reported for 'dog'.

**category dominance** The frequency of reporting a superordinate in response to a category instance.

**hierarchy violation effect** Cases where instances of categories show stronger links to higher-order categories relative to their immediately superordinate category. So 'Whisky' is more highly associated with 'Drink' than 'Liquor'.

## Feature models

Feature models are based on the assumption that 'a concept consists of a set of values on a large number of semantic dimensions' (Collins & Loftus, 1975, p. 410). Here we have the idea that there is a finite set of basic **semantic dimensions** upon which we all construe the

world. For example, you might describe next-door's dog on various physical dimensions such as size and weight together with other more abstract dimensions relating to temperament and intelligence. Despite the apparent simplicity of such a scheme, though, no one has provided a satisfactory list of what such dimensions actually are. Collins and Loftus (1975) mention *animateness (animacy)* and *colour*, but presumably abstract dimensions (such as temperament and intelligence) are necessary. Moreover, on the assumption that there are such dimensions, then entities are defined as comprising certain values on these dimensions, such as large, heavy, snappy and stupid. Such dimensional values are otherwise known as **semantic features**.

To take a different example, in discussing the concept FRUIT, Smith (1988) illustrates this with the following list of dimensions and values:

> Colour – red
> Shape – round
> Size – small
> Taste – sweet
> Texture – smooth
> Juiciness – juicy

It's quite possible that you may have thought 'apple' while you were reading the list of semantic features (although 'cherry' or indeed 'peach' might also have occurred to you). The basic idea, though, is that any given entity, be it a real-world object or abstract notion, can be defined by the values that it takes on the semantic dimensions. In our FRUIT example, all of the dimensions are perceptual in nature and specify physical features, but the basic understanding is that other dimensions could also be purely semantic in nature (e.g., temperament, intelligence, etc.). The dimensions need not be defined in terms of physical attributes; other more abstract characteristics are possible too. By such a view, any entity can be described by the values that it takes on the set of semantic dimensions. It is, therefore, useful to consider some preliminary evidence that provides some support for the notion of a semantic dimension.

## Psychological space and multi-dimensional scaling

Rips, Shoben and Smith (1973) provided participants with lists of instance–category pairs (e.g., robin–bird) and participants were asked to rate how related the instance and the category were – just how closely related are robin and bird? In subsequent discussion,

In furthering your research into semantic memory, it might be advisable to watch the TV show *Family Fortunes*. Here, two families compete against each other to guess typical category instances, given certain category labels. 'We asked 100 people, what are the top five things you wouldn't say to your mother-in-law?', 'Name something that you need to recharge' and 'Give me the name of a famous bear'. The family that provides answers highest in instance–category typicality win. Who thought cognitive psychology could be so much fun?

though, such ratings have been taken to be akin to ratings of typicality, so in a sense, when asked to rate relatedness, participants were in fact assessing typicality – just how typical a bird is a robin? (Smith et al., 1974, p. 217). Such ratings indicate **instance–category typicality**. The data revealed that 'robin' was rated as the most typical bird and 'goose' as the least. 'Deer' was rated as the most typical mammal and 'pig' the least. Having amassed numerical ratings of category typicality, Rips et al. analysed the data using a technique with the slightly intimidating title of **multi-dimensional scaling**. As an example, this WORD is located at a particular point in multi-dimensional space, in terms of how far up (first dimension) and how far along (second dimension) it is on the page.

Simply put, this technique takes the numerical ratings and attempts to arrange the associated items into a multi-dimensional space such that highly similar items are clustered together and highly dissimilar items are located apart. The distance between any two points in this space is taken to reflect the psychological similarity of the two instances directly. Highly similar items are close together in this abstract psychological space. The technique determines an optimum number of dimensions for capturing the data and we end up with a working definition of how knowledge is structured within psychological space.

Figure 12.10 shows the psychological space for the bird category, and, as can be seen, the space is rendered into two dimensions. However, you'll notice for feature models both 'subordinate' (e.g., robin) and 'superordinate' (e.g., bird) categories have no hierarchical relation and are instead contained within the same multi-dimensional space. In offering an interpretation of the horizontal dimension of the bird space, Rips et al. (1973) took this to reflect, essentially, physical size of the instance (wing span, perhaps) with larger sizes running to the left of space, whereas the vertical dimension was taken to reflect predacity (the degree to which *x* could be construed as a predator) with greater likelihood of predacity lower down in space.

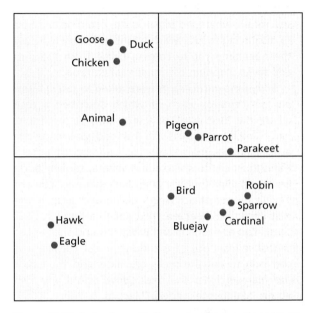

**Figure 12.10 A simple multi-dimensional semantic space as discussed by Rips et al. (1973)**
Here only two dimensions are shown. The horizontal dimension captures variation in wing span and the vertical dimension captures predacity. 'Turkey' would probably be located above and to the left of 'goose'.

*Source*: Rips, L. J., Shoben, E. J., & Smith, E. E. (1973). Semantic distance and the verification of semantic relations. *Journal of Verbal Learning and Verbal Behavior, 12*, 1–20. Reproduced with permission from Elsevier.

The basic idea therefore is that psychologically the instances of the bird category are mentally represented along these two semantic dimensions – one analogous to the physical dimension of *size* and one analogous to the abstract *predacity* dimension. It is not as though participants consciously use these dimensions in arriving at their ratings, but that their ratings implicitly reflect this kind of psychological space. Distances between points in the space reflect some notion of psychological similarity. In this case, the semantic dimensions have been revealed by a statistical technique

## 'I think I'm gonna barf': the different dimensions of disgust

While the feeling of disgust is, we hope, a long way from your thoughts as you're reading this book, there is little doubt that it serves as a powerful and pretty unpleasant emotion in everyday life. While disgust can be produced within many contexts, Martins and Pliner (2006) were particularly interested in what makes certain foods disgusting and specifically what kind of attributes could be ascribed to disgusting foods, which might be handy to know the next time you're coming home from the pub and fancy stopping off for some fast food.

Sixty-nine participants were asked to rate a number of scenarios, each of which described a case where the food itself, or a secondary element that had come into contact with the food, was made disgusting. The authors identified a number of 'potential disgust elicitors' including viscera, squishy body parts and slime (hungry yet?). For example, 'You are having dinner at a friend's house and soup is the first item that is served. You notice a bone in your soup. You ask your friend what it is and she replies that it is the neck of a turkey; in her culture it is common to eat the meat on necks and then suck the marrow from the neck. How would you feel about eating the neck?' (Martins & Pliner, 2006, p. 78). Once the disgusting nature of these scenarios was established, a second sample of 70 participants rated these foods on a number of attributes. The authors then used multi-dimensional scaling to uncover the different dimensions of disgust.

Two dimensions were essentially identified on the basis of multi-dimensional scaling. The first was labelled 'aversive textural properties' and referred to any foodstuff that was slimy, gooey, mushy or rotten. The second dimension was identified as 'reminder of livingness/animalness'. This was where individuals were reminded that the food that they were eating was once an animal, or at the very least, living. For example, a squishy tomato would score high on the first dimension and low on the second, whereas observing a cow in a field while tucking into a steak would score low on the first dimension and high on the second.

As Martins and Pliner (2006) point out, the use of multi-dimensional scaling is instructive as it shows that there are two independent dimensions to disgust. Previous work had focused on the disgust associated with animal foods and the idea that one was reminded of its living status. However, by introducing the relatively novel observation of disgust as a result of food that feels or looks unpleasant, our understanding of disgust becomes more inclusive such that vegetarian food can be as disgusting as non-vegetarian food if we really put our mind to it!

*Source*: Martins, Y., & Pliner, P. (2006). 'Urgh! That's disgusting!': Identification of the characteristics of foods underlying rejections based on disgust. *Appetite, 46*, 75–85.

that generated a spatial representation from ratings of instance–category typicality.

**How does the structure of a featural model differ from that of a semantic network?**

## The Smith et al. (1974) featural model

In fleshing out their featural model, Smith et al. (1974) discussed the distinction between **defining features** and **characteristic features**. Here the idea is that any instance of a category is represented as comprising

a list of discrete semantic features (e.g., has wings, breathes, has two legs) and that such features vary in their importance in being associated with a given category. Critically, a distinction can be drawn between defining features (e.g., has wings, lays eggs) that are necessarily associated with the category (e.g., bird), and characteristic features (e.g., being domesticated) that are not *necessarily* associated with the category but are nevertheless *variously* associated with the category (e.g., bird). Table 12.1 provides some further examples.

As with all such distinctions, attempting to defend the boundary is fraught with difficulties, and because of this Smith et al. (1974) introduced the notion of a **definingness continuum**. The argument was as follows.

**Table 12.1** Examples of how various categories may be described relative to their defining and characteristic features.

| Category | Defining features | Characteristic features |
|---|---|---|
| Bird | Has wings, lays eggs, has feathers . . . | Domesticated, lives in an aviary, eats seed . . . |
| House | Has roof, has walls, at least one door . . . | Single storey, detached, modern, freehold/leasehold . . . |
| Hammer | Blunt heavy head, has handle . . . | Wooden handle, metal head, rubber head . . . |

Features are rank ordered according to their importance and the distinction between defining features and characteristic features is simply determined by the placement of a criterion on the definingness dimension. Anything above the criterion was a defining feature and anything below was a characteristic feature. For example, 'has wings' is more highly ranked (and so is closer to a defining characteristic) than 'can fly' in the representation of the concept BIRD.

By setting up this continuum between defining and characteristic features, Smith et al. tried to sidestep the highly problematic issue of trying to provide well-defined, necessary and sufficient criteria for category membership (as pointedly discussed by Kintsch, 1980). Just how many whiskers and legs does the ship's cat have to lose before it is no longer a cat? No matter how hard you think, there is a serious problem in attempting to set out the defining characteristics for most things in the real world. Most things do not have the rigid definition of an equilateral triangle or a square. So despite the fact that the line to be drawn between defining and characteristic features is blurry, Smith et al. persevered. They argued that all members of a given category must possess the *defining* features of the category. Consequently, the differences between instances as revealed by the multi-dimensional scaling reflect the extent to which instances differ on *characteristic* features. So the large distance between pigeon and eagle reflects both a difference in size and a difference in predacity. The fact that they both have wings and feathers cannot account for these differences.

Of some further import was the finding that the typicality ratings, which defined the similarity space, correlated highly with performance in a variation of the sentence verification paradigm as used by Collins and Quillian (1969). Now Rips et al. (1973) used sentences of the type 'A robin is a bird', 'A robin is an animal', and found that the verification times were well predicted from the ratings. Low typicality ratings were associated with long verification times – 'A goose is bird' took longer to verify than 'A robin is a bird'. (Remember, a goose is an atypical bird: a robin is a typical bird.) Moreover, and as has already been

noted, the critical result was that such ratings were more potent in predicting performance than were the set/sub-set relations between the category and instance terms. It was therefore concluded that data from the sentence verification experiments reveal more about semantic relatedness/similarity/instance–category relatedness/association strength and the accessibility of certain kinds of information, given various cues, than anything directly about the cognitive economy of conceptual hierarchies.

To flesh out their featural model Smith et al. introduced the process of feature comparison to account for their sentence verification data. In schematic form the model is shown in Figure 12.11. Stage 1 recovers the feature lists for the two items and determines a rough indication of featural similarity. If the items are highly similar or highly dissimilar, a rapid response

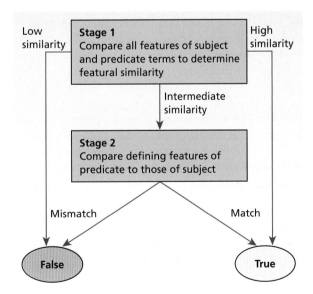

**Figure 12.11 A flow diagram of the component stages of processing that constitute the feature comparison model of sentence verification put forward by Smith et al. (1974)**

*Source*: Smith, E. E., Shoben, E. J., & Rips, L. J. (1974). Structure and process in semantic memory: A featural model for semantic decisions. *Psychological Review, 81*, 214–241 (fig. 2a, p. 219). Reproduced with permission from APA.

can be made, 'Yes, a robin is a bird', 'No, an alligator is not a bird'. If the judged similarity is neither very high nor very low, then further processing is needed and it is now that the defining characteristics of the two items are assessed in more detail – Is an orange a vegetable? As Kintsch (1977) stated, this means that 'true sentences that are not closely related semantically as well as false sentences that are related semantically are verified relatively slowly' (p. 291) and because of this the model succeeds where the original semantic network model of Collins and Quillian fails.

## Difficult findings for the featural account

It will come as no surprise by now that, as the literature unfolded, the particularities of the featural comparison model were scrutinised and criticised (see Glass & Holyoak, 1974/1975, for an in-depth review). The experiments of Smith et al. (1974) were also the focus of some controversy. In a careful reappraisal, McCloskey (1980) demonstrated that a further potent variable was **item familiarity** and that this had not been controlled for properly in the original experiments. According to McCloskey (1980), both category size and instance–category relatedness were confounded by item familiarity. He went on to argue that, in the Smith et al. (1974) work, item familiarity was, in fact, the critical variable that could most adequately explain performance in the verification tasks. Think in terms of how familiar you are with the term 'Drink' as compared with 'Liquor' (we hope it is not the other way round). When couched in these terms, the basic hierarchy violation effect does not seem so surprising after all. The higher-order category related to Scotch (i.e., drink) is simply more familiar than its immediately superordinate category (i.e., liquor), hence the faster verification response for 'Scotch is a drink' than for 'Scotch is a liquor'.

A further awkward finding, for the featural comparison account, was also uncovered when two contrasting measures of associative strength were considered. **Instance dominance** provides an index of how often an instance is produced when probed with a category label ('canary' generated on the basis of a category prompt 'bird'). In contrast, *category dominance* refers to the frequency with which the category label is given in response to the instance ('bird' generated on the basis of an instance prompt 'canary'). With the bird–canary example, both forms of dominance would be high. Insect–butterfly is a case of low instance dominance, but high category dominance. If asked to provide

instances of the category 'insect', 'butterfly' would not spring to mind immediately. However, if asked to provide a category label for 'butterfly', then 'insect' would spring to mind readily. Seafood–shrimp is a case of high instance dominance but low category dominance. Provide an example of seafood. Now provide a category for shrimp.

Loftus (1973) simply gave participants a speeded task in which on each trial they were presented with an instance name together with a category name and they had to respond as to whether or not the instance was a member of the category. The critical finding was that for instance–category pairs (e.g., robin–bird), instance dominance determined the RT, whereas for the category–instance pairs (bird–robin), category dominance determined RT. Such effects of order are particularly difficult for the featural comparison model because if semantic similarity is being assessed, why should such order effects obtain? → See 'What have we learnt?', page 435.

### Pinpoint question 12.5

Given the statements 'David Bowie' and 'Rock Gods', what would be an example of category dominance and what would be an example of instance dominance?

---

**semantic dimensions** A theoretical construct in which it is assumed that some characteristic of the world can be captured in psychological space by a point on a dimension that fixes all possible values of that characteristic.

**semantic feature** A theoretical construct by which it is assumed that some real-world characteristic can be captured, at the psychological level, by a discrete fact. For example, IS YELLOW. In cases where semantic dimensions are posited, then a semantic feature is a value on a semantic dimension.

**instance–category typicality** An index of how typical an instance is of a given category. How typical is a Shih Tzu of the category DOG?

**multi-dimensional scaling** A statistical technique whereby the similarity between entities (typically real-world category instances) is represented by distances in an abstract space defined by many dimensions.

**defining features** Attributes that are necessarily associated with a category.

**characteristic features** Attributes that are not necessarily associated with the category but that are, nevertheless, variously associated with the category.

→ What have we learnt?

## → What have we learnt?

In looking back over this early literature it becomes clear that, in a sense, the research effort on semantic memory lost its way. One of the problems seems to have been that issues about the organisation of semantic memory became muddled up with issues concerned with trying to understand speeded sentence/statement verification. Kintsch, in writing in 1980, even went so far as to claim that 'the sentence verification data of the last ten years have told us precisely nothing about the structure of semantic memory' (p. 603). Arguably, therefore, here is a rather unfortunate (and, even more unfortunately, not the only) example in cognitive psychology where the empirical tool became, in and of itself, the object of enquiry. Attention was diverted away from attempting to understand the organisation of semantic memory, to attempting to understand what is going on when sentences of the type 'Many arrows are intelligent' (Glass & Holyoak, 1974/1975, p. 317) are presented to participants.

Telling in this regard is the fact that several competing variables were uncovered that were used to explain performance in the various verification tasks. The list includes instance–category relatedness/typicality (Rips et al., 1973; Smith et al., 1974), various versions of production frequency/associative strength (Conrad, 1972; Loftus, 1973; Wilkins, 1971), category size (Smith et al., 1974) and item familiarity (McCloskey, 1980). As a consequence, some effort was directed to trying to tease these apart in attempting to discover *the* critical factor that was driving the sentence verification effects (Ashcraft, 1978; Glass & Holyoak, 1974/1975; Malt & Smith, 1982). It is therefore perhaps not so surprising that what started out as being an empirical tool to address issues in the organisation of semantic memory – speeded sentence verification – became the subject of research itself.

In other regards, there is a feeling that the baby may have been thrown out with the bathwater. True, the original Collins and Quillian model has not withstood the ensuing empirical onslaught, but it did provide interesting insights into how inferences about real-world objects may take place. As Kintsch (1977) noted, realising that *Napoleon had toes* is presumably based on inferring that Napoleon was a man and that men have toes. The fact that *Napoleon had toes* is probably not stored in memory; consequently, it must be inferred. It would be entirely sensible, therefore, that semantic memory should be organised in such a way as to facilitate inference making. Such considerations were the primary motivating factors behind the original semantic network models. Nonetheless, the basic issues remain to be properly understood.

## Research focus 12.2

### Do geese or squirrels lay eggs? Semantic memory in a schizophrenic

Individuals suffering from schizophrenia experience a number of changes to the way they think, feel and act. One of these is known as formal thought disorder (FTD). Generally associated with problems in thinking, FTD is understood to represent some sort of impairment to semantic memory. Leeson, McKenna, Murray, Kondel and Laws (2005) set up a number of tests to investigate whether FTD was the result of impaired access to the semantic store or the result of damage to the semantic store itself.

The paper presents the case study of patient TC. TC showed the first signs of schizophrenia around the age of 17, presenting with a number of symptoms including delusions related to John Lennon in addition to auditory hallucinations. TC eventually became hospitalised around the age of 30, and as a man of 46 at the time of publication has been on clozapine for the last 12 years in order to combat his symptoms. However, it was observed around three years ago that TC was spontaneously improving with respect to his disordered thought. Leeson et al. (2005), having already studied TC when his symptomatology was much worse, were interested in seeing how performance on tasks such as sentence verification differed as a result of changes in the severity of FTD.

TC performed a number of tests including sentence verification. Here, statements related to

▶

category instances and attributes were presented (e.g., 'a tiger has stripes') and TC had to indicate whether the statements were true or false. While performance has improved from the last time TC was tested, unfortunately this was not enough to be statistically significant. However, Leeson et al. (2005) investigated this further and presented a modified version of sentence verification in which two sentences were presented and TC had to say which one was true. Three different kinds of sentence pair were created: one that utilised the same category instance ('horses are mammals' vs. 'horses have shells'), one that utilised the same attribute ('geese lay eggs' vs. 'squirrels lay eggs') and a final type in which both instance and attribute were different ('cups are crockery' vs. 'geese are poisonous'). It was found that TC was much better deciding

which sentence was true when the instance was the same, relative to when both instance and attribute were different.

The authors took these (and other) findings to represent an improvement in TC's disordered thought and particularly in tasks in which true and false statements were compared (such as the modified sentence verification task). In general, the case was made for TC's remaining symptomatology as a reflection of semantic memory disorganisation and the hope that, although false beliefs related to the world had been established in the past, these could be remedied in the future.

*Source*: Leeson, V. C., McKenna, P. J., Murray, G., Kondel, T. K., & Laws, K. R. (2005). What happens to semantic memory when formal thought disorder remits? Revisiting a case study. *Cognitive Neuropsychiatry, 10*, 57–71.

---

**definingness continuum** A theoretical construct introduced by Smith et al. (1974), a psychological dimension upon which the attributes of a given entity can be rank ordered in terms of their significance for defining the entity.

**item familiarity** An index of how familiar a given entity is. How familiar are you with liquor? Drink? Malibu and Coke?

**instance dominance** The frequency of reporting a category instance in response to a superordinate.

## Semantic features, semantic primitives and cogits

So far we have considered the two generic types of models of semantic memory, namely network models and featural models. We have seen how both models have struggled to accommodate evidence that has been amassed since the original work was carried out. Although flaws have been seen in both sorts of theories, it is nevertheless true that both incorporate assumptions about how semantic properties are used to represent the meanings of words and concepts. Featural models are explicit and discuss semantic features at length; semantic networks are less specific but nonetheless these accounts assume that each concept has associated semantic properties. Given that these ideas

about semantic properties are so central to the debate, we really should consider these in more detail.

## Semantic features as defined on semantic dimensions

Central to the featural model of Smith et al. (1974) is the idea that semantic features reflect values on semantic dimensions: our apple (or tomato) is red on the colour dimension and round on the shape dimension, etc. So dimensional accounts are based on the assumption that there exist semantic dimensions upon which all entities are defined. By this view, every concept takes on particular values across the same basic set of semantic dimensions even though for most cases the values on most of the dimensions would be zero – whereas the edible dimension applies to fruits and vegetables, it does not apply to vehicles or places (Collins & Loftus, 1975).

## Semantic primitives as the atoms of meaning

An alternative approach is simply to discuss *semantic primitives* (Winograd, 1978). The analogy here is with chemistry where a basic claim is that every substance is a composite of primitive atomic elements. In terms of psychology, every concept is assumed to be a composite of primitive semantic elements. (Remember our discussion of cogits in Chapter 7? Semantic primitives

= cogits = primitive atoms of meaning.) Semantic dimensions are not fundamental; semantic primitives are. So 'has two legs' would be one semantic primitive and 'has four legs' would be another. Consequently, Monty the DOG can be thought of as being composed of the semantic primitives: barks, has fur, has four legs, buries bones, etc. There is no assumption that such primitives are defined on dimensions. All that is being asserted is that each concept can be decomposed into a set of atomic semantic primitives. Cast this way, the idea is that each concept can be decomposed into a particular set of semantic primitives that cannot themselves be analysed into smaller components. To reiterate: Hayes-Roth (1977) coined the term *cogit* in referring to 'the smallest information structure perceptually or cognitively delineated' (p. 261). So there is a division between the indefinite number of concepts of which we can conceive – such as air hockey, ice hockey, street hockey, etc. – and the finite number of primitives (cogits) from which these are composed.

It is a struggle to offer further clarification on these issues because no one has ever arrived at a generally acceptable scheme for defining what *the* actual semantic primitives are. Hinton and Shallice (1991) provided a list of 68 possible semantic features, but the arbitrariness of some of the choices is notable, as 'got from animals' and 'found near streams' are included alongside primitives for both 'pleasant' and 'unpleasant'. An alternative is simply to give up on trying to define the semantic primitives on the grounds that it is probably not the case that 'semantic knowledge is stored in the brain literally as a list of verbalizable features' (Cree & McRae, 2003). An alternative is simply to accept the view that semantic primitives exist, but to remain silent as to what exactly these are (a safe but perhaps uninspiring position). We could agree therefore that there are **semantic micro-features** (again a different way of saying cogits) but also assume that such atoms of meaning probably do not correspond to concepts that are expressible in words (Hinton, McClelland & Rumelhart, 1986).

## Semantic features and semantic feature norms

It would be wrong to state that no progress has been made, though, because people are rather good at explaining what they mean by a given concept. Indeed, a rather straightforward approach has been to gather norms of features, from having participants list the attributes of various familiar items. 'Please write down all the attributes of DOG.' Such studies are known as **feature-norming studies** and perhaps the most ambitious of these has been carried out by Cree and McRae (2003). They collected feature lists for 541 concepts referred to by concrete nouns (e.g., chisel, cheese, cello) and taken from 34 different categories (see previous discussion of *property-instance production frequency*). In this way, it was possible to arrive at lists of attributes that are associated with particular concepts. In turn, the importance of the attributes and the important correlations between attributes for a given concept can be assessed. This is because the norms contain data on the frequency with which different participants note the attribute associated with each concept. Such norms are referred to as **semantic feature production norms**.

Aside from the consistency and systematic nature of the data contained in the norms, they have been used successfully to predict performance in a variety of priming and property verification tasks (see McRae, de Sa & Seidenberg, 1997). This is further evidence that, at a psychological level, concepts may be expressed in terms of their associated features. Unfortunately, no one has yet attempted to use such semantic feature production norms to build a working computer model of some aspect of semantic memory. Even though McRae et al. (1997) initially collected such norms, they did not use these directly to inform their own model-building exercise.

## Semantic features and semantic relatedness

The interest with semantic features continues and bears on a recurring theme in the literature relating to the distinction between *semantic relatedness* and **associative relatedness** (for a much more comprehensive review of this issue see Lucas, 2000). The evidence bears on the issue of whether or not semantic memory is organised according to feature lists or conceptual categories (or indeed some amalgam of both?).

Semantic relatedness is used to refer to cases where two instances belong to the same 'restricted category' and consequently share many common features (McRae & Boisvert, 1998) – using these criteria, 'horse' and 'donkey' are highly semantically related. In contrast, it is possible also to discuss associative relatedness. Here the idea is that two instances are related but not through membership of a common category or because of shared characteristics. The instances are related merely because of frequency of co-occurrence – here, think of 'horse' and 'cart'. Although this distinction may seem rather subtle, it lies at the heart of much controversy. As we shall see, the critical cases involve instances that are semantically related but are not associatively related, for instance 'horse' and 'pony'. Now a critical issue is whether we can get effects that reveal the importance of category membership but that cannot be explained away by principles of associationism. If everything can be captured by some form of associative memory, why on earth are we bothering with all these complex ideas about the hierarchical organisation of the human conceptual system?

As McRae and Boisvert (1998) noted, there is now an immense amount of evidence to suggest that associative relations are of great psychological significance in both the organisation of knowledge and the retrieval of information from semantic memory. Indeed, as we have already seen, hierarchy violation effects clearly show that conceptual relations (Scotch–liquor) may be of little significance when associative relations are considered (Scotch–drink). Therefore, for McRae and Boisvert (1998), the more pressing issue was whether semantic relatedness is of any functional significance at all. Maybe the traditional semantic memory literature is misleading? The alternative is that semantic memory is organised in terms of simple associative relations and any conceptual hierarchies that are apparent are due to the operation of a simple associative network.

To test this, therefore, it is important to consider materials in which associative relations are controlled for but semantic relations are varied. Can we find any examples of where there are effects of semantic relatedness, when associative relations have been controlled? If there are, then this would be particularly strong evidence for a conceptual system that is based on something other than associative links.

Their first experiment is of prime interest. Central here was a set of 38 target words taken from 10 familiar categories. For each of these targets two prime words were also selected, namely a semantically similar prime and a semantically dissimilar prime, respectively. The semantically similar primes were selected from the same category as the target. Take the case where 'turkey' is the target word and the semantically similar prime was 'goose'. Goose/turkey are known as **category co-ordinates** because they both come from the same category, namely they are both *domesticated birds*. A semantically dissimilar prime (for 'turkey') was 'axe' because 'axe' and 'turkey' are taken from different categories. Importantly, though, the materials were screened so that primes and their targets were not highly associated.

A preliminary group of 20 participants were asked to associate to the primes and a different 20 participants were asked to associate to the target. Whereas no targets were produced in response to the primes, only one participant responded with the prime to the target. McRae and Boisvert (1998) concluded that the primes and target pairings were not associatively related, but did differ in terms of semantic relatedness. Primes were either from the same category as target or they were taken from a different category to that of the target.

Two speeded tasks were now developed for use with these stimuli. In the *lexical decision task* participants were asked to respond as to whether or not a visually present string of letters was a word or not. In the **semantic decision task** participants were asked to respond as to whether or not the visually presented word named a concrete object. In the lexical decision task, the words stimuli were intermixed with non-words. In the semantic decision task, only words were used. In both tasks the critical experimental materials occurred among other trials in which filler items were used.

In the simple case, only a single stimulus was presented on a trial, and participants were expected to make a speeded response to it. The critical cases were where the prime occurred on one trial (i.e., trial $n$) and the target occurred on the next (i.e., on trial $n + 1$). Primary interest was with how responses to the targets varied as a consequence of the type of prime used – whether it was preceded by a semantically similar or semantically dissimilar prime. The rationale was that if semantic relations are important then participants ought to be facilitated in responding to the target by the immediately prior presentation of the semantically similar prime (goose–turkey) than a semantically dissimilar prime (axe–turkey).

Even the most simple spreading activation account predicts that activation from the prime will spread to the target but only if the prime and target are either close in semantic space or share some common superordinate category node (cf. Collins & Loftus, 1975). If this happens then the subsequent response to the target will be facilitated relative to the case where a semantically unrelated prime is presented. When primes and targets are unrelated, activation will spread from the prime but not to the representation of the target.

The results of the experiment were clear-cut and revealed significant priming in both the lexical decision and semantic decision tasks. The central point is that priming arose in cases where there was essentially no associative relation between the primes and targets. So responses to 'turkey' were facilitated if primed by the semantically related but not associatively related 'goose'. Without further context, this result is perhaps unsurprising, but a critical point is that on the basis of prior research it had been concluded that there were no effects of semantic relatedness independent of those that could be attributed to associative relatedness

(Lupker, 1984; Moss, Ostrin, Tyler & Marslen-Wilson, 1995; Shelton & Martin, 1992). In these studies, there was no evidence of priming for category co-ordinates (goose–turkey). In contrast, priming that did occur seemed to reflect associative relatedness. Clearly there is something of a conflict here.

McRae and Boisvert (1998) had found the contrary result and argued that the contrasting pattern arose because of a difference in the materials used across the different studies. McRae and Boisvert had selected prime-target category co-ordinates (e.g., goose–turkey) that were rated as being highly similar, where for them, similarity was with respect to shared features. In their study, the highly similar instances shared many common features. By this view, it is so-called featural overlap that is the critical factor. If the instances (the category co-ordinates) share many common features

then it is highly *likely* that they will activate one another. In contrast, if the instances have few features in common (e.g., penguin–sparrow) then it is highly *unlikely* that category co-ordinates will prime one another. So common category is not the critical factor when featural similarity is taken into account (for a further detailed review, see Hutchison, 2003). In other words, it is possible to show semantic priming even for cases that are not associatively related. However, such priming is most likely to occur when the instances share many common features. → See 'What have we learnt?', below.

### Pinpoint question 12.6

**How did McRae and Boisvert (1998) control for associative links between prime and target words in their study?**

### → What have we learnt?

Evidence continues to be amassed over the psychological significance of semantic features and issues remain over how best to interpret the evidence. As we have seen, appeals to semantic features have been made in attempts to explain semantic priming effects in experiments on word recognition (see Hutchison, 2003). In this regard, semantic features do play a useful role in attempting to understand how meanings and concepts are represented in the mind. Indeed, a tentative conclusion from the priming work is that knowledge may well be structured according to mental categories but such categories are themselves structured primarily with respect to common features. Arguably, the evidence, such that it is, suggests that the human conceptual system is something more than an associative network. Relations other than simple associations are represented.

Further issues about semantic features have played a pivotal role in the computer modelling literature in which particular kinds of network models, known as **connectionist models** (see Quinlan, 1991) have been developed. We will discuss these kinds of models in more detail. As in featural models, in connectionist models it is typically assumed that there is a fixed set of semantic primitives/micro-features that collectively encode all concepts. The semantic dimension/semantic primitive distinction is blurred and reference is simply made to semantic micro-features or, alternatively, **sub-symbols** (Smolensky, 1988). A basic assumption is that each micro-feature

signals the presence/absence of an associated attribute (remember our previous discussion of the atoms of meaning – the cogits). By this view, there is a micro-featural processing unit for each form of attribute and each code for the presence/absence of a particular attribute. It is easiest to think in terms of nameable attributes such as 'has four legs', but typically the nature of the micro-features is left unspecified. Occasionally, though, there have been cases in which the problem is taken seriously, and attempts have been made to flesh out the ideas and provide easily understandable sets of features. Figure 12.12 (taken from Rogers & McClelland, 2004) provides one case in point. Nevertheless, it is generally the case that the final sets of semantic features that are posited are based upon the theorists' intuitions (cf. Hinton & Shallice, 1991) (and we really need something other than intuition on which to base our theories of meaning!).

As an alternative, there is the tradition, in the psychological literature, of having participants produce lists of features/attributes/characteristics to various instance and category labels. In this way, feature norms have been produced and so firmer evidence about what semantic features are has been forthcoming. There apparently has been little communication between the modellers and the experimentalists. Although very detailed featural connectionist models have been developed in the modelling literature (e.g., Hinton & Shallice, 1991), such models have not been based upon feature

▶

| CONTEXT | PROPERTY | PINE | OAK | ROSE | DAISY | ROBIN | CANARY | SUNFISH | SALMON |
|---|---|---|---|---|---|---|---|---|---|
| ISA . . . | Living thing | 1 | 1 | 1 | 1 | 1 | 1 | 1 | 1 |
| | Plant | 1 | 1 | 1 | 1 | 0 | 0 | 0 | 0 |
| | Animal | 0 | 0 | 0 | 0 | 1 | 1 | 1 | 1 |
| | Tree | 1 | 1 | 0 | 0 | 0 | 0 | 0 | 0 |
| | Flower | 0 | 0 | 1 | 1 | 0 | 0 | 0 | 0 |
| | Bird | 0 | 0 | 0 | 0 | 1 | 1 | 0 | 0 |
| | Fish | 0 | 0 | 0 | 0 | 0 | 0 | 1 | 1 |
| | Pine | 1 | 0 | 0 | 0 | 0 | 0 | 0 | 0 |
| | Oak | 0 | 1 | 0 | 0 | 0 | 0 | 0 | 0 |
| | Rose | 0 | 0 | 1 | 0 | 0 | 0 | 0 | 0 |
| | Daisy | 0 | 0 | 0 | 1 | 0 | 0 | 0 | 0 |
| | Robin | 0 | 0 | 0 | 0 | 1 | 0 | 0 | 0 |
| | Canary | 0 | 0 | 0 | 0 | 0 | 1 | 0 | 0 |
| | Sunfish | 0 | 0 | 0 | 0 | 0 | 0 | 1 | 0 |
| | Salmon | 0 | 0 | 0 | 0 | 0 | 0 | 0 | 1 |
| Is . . . | Pretty | 0 | 0 | 1 | 1 | 0 | 0 | 0 | 0 |
| | Big | 1 | 1 | 0 | 0 | 0 | 0 | 0 | 0 |
| | Living | 1 | 1 | 1 | 1 | 1 | 1 | 1 | 1 |
| | Green | 1 | 0 | 0 | 0 | 0 | 0 | 0 | 0 |
| | Red | 0 | 0 | 1 | 0 | 1 | 0 | 0 | 1 |
| | Yellow | 0 | 0 | 0 | 1 | 0 | 1 | 1 | 0 |
| Can . . . | Grow | 1 | 1 | 1 | 1 | 1 | 1 | 1 | 1 |
| | Move | 0 | 0 | 0 | 0 | 1 | 1 | 1 | 1 |
| | Swim | 0 | 0 | 0 | 0 | 0 | 0 | 1 | 1 |
| | Fly | 0 | 0 | 0 | 0 | 1 | 1 | 0 | 0 |
| | Sing | 0 | 0 | 0 | 0 | 0 | 1 | 0 | 0 |
| Has . . . | Skin | 0 | 0 | 0 | 0 | 1 | 1 | 1 | 1 |
| | Roots | 1 | 1 | 1 | 1 | 0 | 0 | 0 | 0 |
| | Leaves | 0 | 1 | 1 | 1 | 0 | 0 | 0 | 0 |
| | Bark | 1 | 1 | 0 | 0 | 0 | 0 | 0 | 0 |
| | Branch | 1 | 1 | 0 | 0 | 0 | 0 | 0 | 0 |
| | Petals | 0 | 0 | 1 | 1 | 0 | 0 | 0 | 0 |
| | Wings | 0 | 0 | 0 | 0 | 1 | 1 | 0 | 0 |
| | Feathers | 0 | 0 | 0 | 0 | 1 | 1 | 0 | 0 |
| | Gills | 0 | 0 | 0 | 0 | 0 | 0 | 1 | 1 |
| | Scales | 0 | 0 | 0 | 0 | 0 | 0 | 1 | 1 |

Note: Each row corresponds to a different output property. The first two columns indicate the context in which the property occurs and the name of the property, respectively. The remaining columns indicate the target patterns for the eight concepts in Rumelhart's model. To present a pattern to the network, we activate the *Item* unit corresponding to the particular concept, and one of the four *Context* units. The numbers in the table then indicate the target values for the context in question. For example, if the input is *pine has*, target values for the properties *roots*, *bark*, and *branches* are set to 1, and all other targets are set to 0.

**Figure 12.12 The most fully fleshed-out semantic feature account of how to capture the sort of conceptual hierarchy discussed by Collins and Quillian (1969) (see Figure 12.7)**
Taken from Rogers and McClelland (2004). Each column shows the distributed representation for a different category instance. Each row corresponds to a different output property.

*Source*: Rogers, T. T., & McClelland, J. L. (2004). *Semantic cognition: A parallel distributed processing approach* (Appendix B.2, p. 395). Cambridge, Massachusetts: The MIT Press. Reproduced with permission.

norms collected from human participants. Nonetheless, this is not to argue that an impasse has been reached. Indeed, to gain a better understanding of what the computer modelling work can promise, it is important to consider a quite different type of processing architecture to that proposed by Collins and Quillian (1969) and it is to this that discussion now turns.

## Localist vs. distributed models

At this stage it might be helpful to stand back from our menagerie of three-legged cats, curly-tailed pigs and balding canaries for the moment, and consider the wider picture. One way to think of the difference between the Collins and Quillian (1969) semantic network model and the featural model of Smith et al. (1974) is in terms of a card index system. Consider accessing the card headed HAMMER. By the network account, the card would contain a list of all the characteristic attributes of a hammer plus a list of other places in the indexing system to find out more information about the sort of thing a hammer is. In contrast, and by analogy, in the featural account the card would contain an ordered list of all of the attributes of HAMMER starting with the defining attributes and leading on to the characteristic attributes (see Table 12.1 on page 433).

### Localist representation

In the network model, a thing is represented as a node, with connections between nodes signifying relations between different things. Each node is unique and defined in part by where it is in the network. A simple analogy may help here – it is not perfect but it helps convey some basic ideas. Let us assume each node in the network can be thought of as a book in a library. In order to recover a book from the library, you would have to go to a particular floor in the library, to a particular section, to a particular shelf, and, finally, to a particular location on that shelf. In a similar fashion, in the actual network, each node is located in a particular place. In order to recover information associated with that node, you (metaphorically) have to go to that particular place in memory. Information associated with a given node is stored and recovered from a particular place in memory. Each node has its unique place in the network: hence we have the **place metaphor for memory**. (Remember our library/warehouse analogies of human memory used at the start of Chapter 10?) This kind of memory system is known as a **localist theory of memory**. Each concept is stored at a particular *locale* in memory. It is also the case that the featural model of Smith et al. (1974) is a localist model. Each concept is located in some place in memory. In this case, though, different places are defined in terms of the sort of multi-dimensional semantic space as shown in Figure 12.10.

### Distributed representation

These assumptions about locating concepts in some kind of space of meanings are not, however, universally accepted. More recently, radically different alternative approaches have been put forward – the library metaphor has been replaced by something much less book-like. More recent incarnations of featural models have been developed within a relatively new framework for thinking. Now the terminology is of **parallel-distributed processing** (PDP) and connectionist modelling (Quinlan, 1991). Fundamentally, the ideas are based on quite different conceptions about the nature of mental representation than those conveyed by traditional localist accounts. It is these models that adopt the micro-featural (alternatively, the sub-symbolic) approach to explaining conceptual knowledge. According to these models there is a set of micro-features upon which all entities are defined – bagels and cats and dogs can be defined relative to the same set of basic semantic features (McClelland & Rumelhart, 1986). These ideas are quite different from what has gone before and therefore it is probably best to think in terms of a simple example.

According to the PDP view, the ideas are fleshed out in terms of an interconnected collection of processing units, and again the description of the models is couched in the language of activation, partial activation, excitation, inhibition and thresholds. Given this, perhaps the simplest way to think of a processing unit is that each unit codes for a particular semantic micro-feature (Smolensky, 1988). To simplify matters further, assume each unit is like a light bulb. When the unit/light bulb is ON this signals the presence of the corresponding attribute and when the unit/light bulb is OFF this signals the absence of the attribute. For instance, a cat might be associated with the attribute of mortality such as either 'living' (light bulb ON) or 'non-living' (light bulb OFF). Such a unit is known as a **binary unit** because it can only be in one of two states (either fully ON or fully OFF) at any given time. So we can take a single unit and say that this stands for the LIVING micro-feature. Depending on the state of this unit, either living or non-living is being represented.

Now what we do is take a set of these units and use these to define the fundamental semantic attributes. To represent CAT we turn on all the units that code for the attributes associated with CAT (e.g., the 'coughs up hair balls' unit, the 'meows' unit, the 'will only be nice to you if it wants food' unit and so on) across all of the units. So collectively the states of all of the units are taken as being the internal representation of CAT. Critically, though, if we alter the states of any of the units then the represented concept changes. For example, switch off the 'hair balls' unit and the 'four paws' unit, switch on the 'barks' and 'bury bones' units, etc., and now DOG is being represented. What is central here is the current snapshot of all of the units – the so-called *current pattern of activation* across all of the units. Each different pattern of activation stands for a different concept. In this way information about any concept is distributed across the entire set of units and it is only possible to be certain about what exactly is being represented when all of the states of all of the units are taken into account. In other words, the pattern of activation across the units is the **distributed representation** of a given concept.

What is also critical here is that the place metaphor for memory no longer applies. Although all concepts are being represented via the same set of units (Hinton & Shallice, 1991; McClelland & Rumelhart, 1986), it is no longer the case that information about different categories and instances are located in different places in memory. There is only a finite set of semantic attributes given by the units and all concepts are represented via these units. If the states of the unit change, then so does what is being represented. Switch off the 'meows' unit and switch on the 'barks' unit, etc. Central is the idea that it is the current pattern of activation distributed across the semantic micro-features that defines what is being represented. What this means is that, for most concepts, the majority of the micro-feature units will remain OFF (see Fodor & McLaughlin, 1990, for this and other concerns).

**For example . . .**

What is a bicycle? A bicycle . . .

**Micro-featural description**

does not taste of raspberries
does not float
does not purr
does not tell you the time
does have a chain
does have spoked wheels
does have a saddle
does not cry
. . .

So according to the PDP approach, the list of attributes that are relevant for defining a bicycle is considerably smaller than the list of attributes that are not relevant. Indeed, in adopting this perspective, this is also true for anything else that you can think of.

## Distributed representation and mental chemistry

This is a quite different approach to that of the **mental chemistry** view of semantic primitives discussed previously in the literature (see Winograd, 1978). There the alternative view is that to define a given concept only certain primitives are considered and all others are left out. In the physical world, there are a hundred or so basic elements and each substance comprises atoms of these elements. By analogy, the mental chemistry idea is that all concepts can be derived by simply selecting the appropriate semantic primitives and leaving out all others. For example, in representing *cup* there is no assumption that a value on the (totally irrelevant) predacity dimension is incorporated at all. It is not that the value on this attribute is set to zero, but rather that this attribute is totally irrelevant to the intension of the concept CUP.

**For example . . .**

What is raw milk?

**Micro-featural description**

milk produced by the secretion of the mammary glands of one or more cows, ewes, goats or buffaloes not been heated beyond 40°C (104°F) or undergone an equivalent treatment . . .

So according to the mental chemistry approach, only the relevant attributes of any concept are represented for that concept.

*Source:* Article 2 of Directive 92/46/EEC.

So both the PDP and more traditional views of semantic representation implicate semantic primitives. The central difference is with respect to how such primitives are used. From the PDP perspective, all semantic micro-features play a role in the representation of every concept. In contrast, the more traditional mental chemistry view is that only certain micro-features (semantic primitives) are needed to define any given concept (see Figure 12.13 for illustrative examples). Central to both accounts, though, are that fundamentally semantic primitives play a crucial role. So although we may quibble about how semantic primitives are put to use, it seems that all the accounts

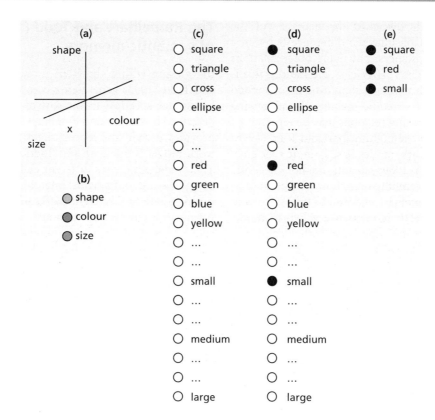

**Figure 12.13 Various representational schemes that implicate semantic features**
(a) shows the multidimensional space of semantic memory described by Rips *et al*. (1973). In this case each instance is defined relative to a unique position in this space. The space is defined via basic semantic dimensions (in this case, shape, colour and size). The *x* is supposed to signify the position in this 3D space that corresponds to a small, red square as defined by the intersection of the different values (i.e., semantic features) on the dimensions.
(b) shows a different way of conceptualising this space. Now each dimension is captured by a unique simple processing unit. There is one unit for each dimension. The states of the units are continuous and each different state of a unit signifies a different featural value.
(c) A fully distributed system in which a different binary unit is posited for every semantic feature. If the square unit is ON then a square is being represented. Similar to the scheme used by Rumelhart and Todd (1993; see Figure 12.12).
(d) shows the distributed representation for a small, red square. Depending on which units are switched ON, different concepts can be represented in exactly the same set of units. The concurrent pattern across the same set of units corresponds to the current distributed representation.
(e) The mental chemistry account of the same small, red square. Only the semantic primitives associated with a given concept are implicated in the representation of that concept.

of the human conceptual system that we have considered posit some form of primitive base by which meanings are defined.

### Semantic features and semantic relations

So far the discussion of PDP accounts of semantic representation (i.e., Hinton & Shallice, 1991; McClelland & Rumelhart, 1986; McRae et al., 1997; see also Masson, 1995) has focused on how concepts defined by features might be represented in a distributed fashion. Moreover, in most of these accounts, the distinction

between semantic dimensions and semantic features is blurred, with the preference being merely to discuss different sorts of processing units that code different aspects of meaning (i.e., semantic micro-features) such as 'is brown', 'has fur', etc. However, in defining micro-features in this way, the distinction between (i) being a property (e.g., 'brown') and (ii) being a relation (e.g., 'is alive', 'has fur') is also blurred. To some this is a very unfortunate state of affairs. A more complete account of the nature of semantic memory really does need to honour the property/relation distinction.

We have already discussed the necessity of the ISA relation in establishing the difference between a category and its instances, but many other relations have useful roles (CAN, HAVE, IS, etc.) and if this is accepted then such relations should be incorporated into our models of semantic memory. In addressing how both properties and relations may be represented in a connectionist system, Rumelhart and Todd (1993) built a PDP network model based on the original Collins and Quillian (1969) semantic memory network. We need to tread carefully here, however, because as we discuss the Rumelhart and Todd (1993) account, you will notice that it is more like a hybrid model because it incorporates aspects of both localist and distributed forms of representation.

## The Rumelhart and Todd (1993) model of semantic memory

In working within the PDP framework, Rumelhart and Todd (1993) generated a computer model of the knowledge specified in the sort of semantic network described by Collins and Quillian (1969). Figure 12.14 provides a schematic representation of the actual network model Rumelhart and Todd (1993) developed. The model comprises different collections, or banks, of processing units with interconnections or links running between different banks of units. Such is the nature of a connectionist model. Where such interconnections exist, then every unit in one bank is linked with every unit in the other bank. Again the lighting

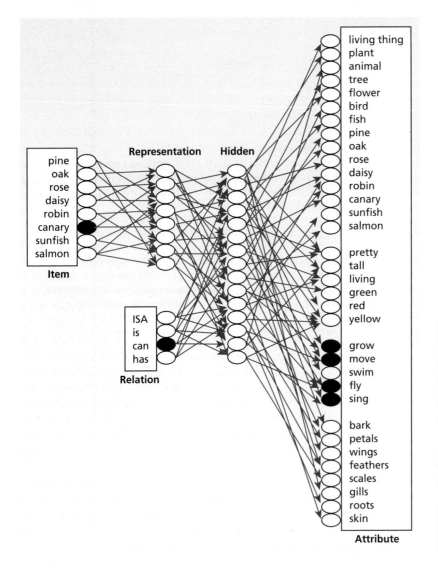

**Figure 12.14 A schematic representation of the connectionist network that Rumelhart and Todd (1993) used to simulate the semantic network described by Collins and Quillian (1969)**
In this case the input pattern (over the item and relation units) specifies 'A CANARY CAN . . .' and the output units code the things that a canary can do.

*Source*: Rogers, T. T., & McClelland, J. L. (2004). *Semantic cognition: A parallel distributed processing approach* (fig. 2.2, p. 56). Cambridge, Massachusetts: The MIT Press. Reproduced with permission.

circuit may help, by thinking in terms of light bulbs standing for units and that these light bulbs have wires (connections) running between them. Activation flows through the network via the links between units. In simple terms, if a given unit (light bulb) is switched ON then this in turn causes activation to travel down the links (wires) to all the units to which it is connected. An additional assumption is that each light bulb needs a certain amount of current before it turns on. Each unit possesses a modifiable threshold. In more formal terms, each unit has a threshold that defines its critical value – activation below this value means that unit will remain OFF; activation above this value means that unit will switch ON. This is very much like tipping some kitchen scales in that you can load up one side of the scales, but only at a certain point (or threshold) do the scales tip (or switch ON).

At the bottom of the network (left-most side of the figure) are two different collections of units, namely (i) units representing items and (ii) units representing relations. In the item bank of units, each unit stands for a particular category instance (e.g., rose, daisy, salmon). Here, you'll notice the localist aspect of the model, as there is a one-to-one mapping between an instance and a place where it is stored in the representational system. Remember, however, that each microfeature is associated with a particular processing unit located at a particular place in the knowledge store and only one instance unit can be ON at a given time (in the figure the CANARY unit is ON while all other units remain off). Similar principles of coding now arise at the bank of relations units. Here each unit stands for a different relation and again only one unit in this bank can be ON at a given time (in the figure the CAN unit is ON).

In this representational scheme the basic desire was to be able to represent concept/relation pairs, so in the example given the current state of the network represents: concept – CANARY, relation – CAN. Given this, it can be seen why the banks of units are as they are. To express such a concept/relation pair, only one concept and one relation are allowed to be active at a given time – hence the mutual exclusivity in the design of the banks of the units. Nevertheless it is the distributed pattern of activation across all of the units in the items and relations banks that is critical at any given time. It is this distributed pattern that represents a concept/relation pair.

At the top-most level (right-most level in the figure, where the mental spaghetti gets particularly messy), there is a separate bank of attribute units divided into nodes, properties, qualities and actions. As can be seen, more than one attribute unit can be ON at a given time and this is necessary for the task in hand. What Rumelhart and Todd were attempting to do was to provide an account of how concept/relation pairs become associated with certain outcomes. In completing CANARY CAN ___ the network is signalling the set of actions (i.e., GROW, MOVE, FLY and SING) that are valid of the overall assertion. In other words, the network is capturing all the actions associated with canaries.

## Connectionist models and the simulation of knowledge acquisition

So far we have seen how the connectionist network of Rumelhart and Todd (1993) represents the conceptual structures that were described by Collins and Quillian (1969). A much more important aspect of the modelling exercise, though, concerns the issue of how such knowledge may be acquired. True, the structure of the network was fixed at the outset, but Rumelhart and Todd (1993) went on to show how, given such a structure, particular aspects of conceptual knowledge may be acquired. In this regard, the idea was to show how certain inputs to the model could become systematically associated with certain outputs from the model. Basically the idea was to train the network to associate input patterns with their corresponding desired output patterns. We first assume that the network assumes almost nothing about the biological taxonomies that Collins and Quillian focused on. We go on to try to teach the network about this micro-world.

In this example, a so-called **input pattern** was a pattern of activation across item and relation units with the constraint that only one item unit and one relation unit were switched ON at a given time. The corresponding desired **output pattern** was the distributed pattern of activation across the attribute units appropriate for the current input pattern. So, in our current example, when the CANARY item unit and CAN relation unit were switched ON and presented as the input pattern, then the desired output pattern would be where the GROW, MOVE, FLY and SING units were also switched ON.

In this regard, the model goes considerably further than the work of Collins and Quillian (1969). Rumelhart and Todd (1993) not only provided a formalism for capturing semantic knowledge, but they also explored how such knowledge may be learnt.

## Basic components of connectionist networks

We have already drawn the distinction between processing units and the connections between the units. In a corresponding fashion it is possible to discuss variable thresholds on units and variable weights on connections. Both thresholds and weights can be assigned numerical values known as **coefficients**. We have already discussed the notion of a modifiable threshold when discussing word detectors (see Chapter 4). As with thresholds on line and word detectors, a low threshold means that a processing unit needs only a small amount of activation to come ON, whereas a high threshold means that the unit needs a large amount of activation to come ON. Now we have to consider the notion of a modifiable connection strength or **connection weight**.

In connectionist network models such as this, connection strengths or weights are allowed to vary in the same way that thresholds are allowed to vary. Each connection in the network has an associated number or weight.

- A positive number indicates an excitatory connection. If activation spreads down a positively weighted connection, then this will increase the possibility that the receiving unit will come ON.

- A negative number indicates an inhibitory connection. If activation spreads down a negatively weighted connection then this will decrease the possibility that the receiving unit will come ON.

- A value of zero signifies no connection. Activation cannot pass through a connection with zero weight.

Take the simple case of a representation unit, where each representation unit shares connections with all the item units. Whenever an item unit is switched ON, it sends activation to all of the representation units. Depending on whether the total activation arriving at a given representation unit is greater than its threshold, then the representation unit is switched ON; its activation value is set to 1 (ON) rather than 0 OFF. This means that the representation unit is in a state such that it can propagate activation down its interconnections.

## Training connectionist networks

Having discussed the overall structure of the network and having discussed the various representational issues, we need now to turn to issues related to training. How does the network acquire the correct mappings between the states of its input units and the states of the output units? What we are attempting to do is take a naïve network and train it such that it learns what should be produced on its output units when a given input is presented. At the beginning of training, all thresholds and weights in the network are initialised with random values. In this way, the network is initialised such that there are no systematically weighted pathways in the network. The rough analogy here is with the naïve infant's brain. In the naïve state there are no systematic pathways in the infant's brain that capture the knowledge that a canary grows, for instance. If the network is to learn which input patterns are related with which output patterns, then it must acquire sets of coefficients that capture the appropriate associative relations that exist between input and output patterns.

As a first step we take an input pattern at random and present it to the network. Let us say that the value between item unit 1 and representation unit 1 has been randomly set at 0.5. When item unit 1 is switched on, it sends a value of 1 down all of its connections to all of the representation units. As this value travels down the connections, each connection transforms this value by multiplying it by the connections weight. So when the value of 1 travels down the connection between item unit 1 and representation unit 1, it arrives as the product of 1 and 0.5, namely 0.5. What this actually means is that item unit 1 excites representation unit 1 to the value of 0.5. If the weight on this connection was 0 then clearly the eventual activation arriving at the representation unit would itself be 0 (anything multiplied by 0 is 0), hence the idea that a 0 indicates no connection.

What representation unit 1 actually does is sum up the amount of activation that it receives by adding up these so-called weighted products across all of the connections from the item units. If this total amount of activation is greater than its threshold value then it will be switched on. Let us say that a given unit has a threshold of 0.4; if the total activation arriving at the unit is greater than 0.4 then the unit is switched ON. If the total activation does not exceed the current threshold value (e.g., is less than 0.4), then the unit will remain off.

Given that units are summing activation, then it is easy to appreciate the operation of negatively weighted connections. If a connection is weighted with a negative number, then when activation is finally being summed the negative connections act against the unit coming on because the negative values are hindering the unit from reaching its threshold level of activation. An activation of 0.7 arriving from one particular connection would be cancelled out by an activation of −0.7 arriving from a second connection to the same representation unit.

When a representation unit does come ON, however, this means that it too will send activation down its connections onwards to the next bank of units – the so-called **hidden units** (see Figure 12.14). Hidden units are the intermediary units internal to the model – they neither receive input directly from the outside world nor do they produce outputs directly to the outside world. In turn, the hidden units propagate patterns of activation forward onto the final output units (i.e., the attribute units). In operation both item and relation units contribute activation to the network that converges onto the hidden units and onwards to the attribute units. As information from both the item and relation units converges on the hidden units, what the hidden units do is transform the localist representations from the input pattern into a distributed representation that is then fed forward towards the output attribute units.

Let us take a simple case and assume that we wish to train the network to associate CANARY CAN with GROW, MOVE, FLY and SING. Remember, initially all of the weights and thresholds in the network are assigned random values. When this is completed we take the first input pattern (CANARY – unit ON, CAN – unit ON) and present this to the network. This pattern of activation produces outputs from the input units and this is then fed forward through the various layers of connections and units until a distributed pattern of activation arises on the output (attribute) units. Given that the coefficients were initialised with random values, then a random set of attribute units will be switched ON. The pattern of activation over the complete set of attribute units is known as the *actual output pattern* – it is a distributed pattern of activation. Moreover, it is highly likely that this actual output pattern does not match the *desired pattern*. If the actual and desired patterns (in which the desire is that only the GROW, MOVE, FLY and SING attribute units will be switched ON) do not match, then there is a discrepancy and this discrepancy is known as **output**

error. So if, instead of the FLY unit being switched ON, the SWIM unit is switched ON, then there is a discrepancy between the actual output and the desired output.

The ultimate aim of training is to minimise this error. What we hope to achieve is a state of affairs such that whenever we present the network with an item/relation pair, then the correct attribute units switch ON. In other words, if there is output error then we will need to change the coefficients in the network (the thresholds and weights) such that the same discrepancy is minimised. The ultimate aim is to ensure that there is no discrepancy; the ideal is where every input pattern produces its correct (desired) output pattern.

Imagine you are learning to play darts. You are desperately trying to hit a treble twenty. So you know what the desired outcome is (i.e., hit the treble twenty), but when you throw a dart, it lands off to the left and misses the treble twenty. There is a discrepancy (an error) between the actual outcome and the desired outcome. You need to adjust your aim to the right. Every time you throw a dart you have a desired outcome, an actual outcome, and an index of error. You can then use this error to recalibrate your next throw – aim slightly to the right of where you aimed before. Clearly, if you hit the treble twenty then there is no error and there would be no point in altering anything. Learning in this example is using the error on each previous throw to alter what you do next time you throw. Of course, the indices of error will vary depending on which number you are trying to hit. So the changes to your throwing will depend on which numbers you are throwing for and what the previous errors were. It could be that you are particularly bad with numbers off to the right, but okay with numbers to the left. If this is the case then you really only need make adjustments for the right-hand and not the left-hand numbers.

### Back-propagation

In very broad strokes, this is exactly the same sort of learning process that occurs when connectionist networks are trained to associate sets of input patterns with corresponding output patterns. Most of the models discussed in the cognitive psychology literature implement something known as **back-propagation** (Rumelhart, Hinton & Williams, 1986). This is a so-called **supervised training** method because every time that the network produces an actual output during training, a corresponding desired output pattern is also presented for comparison purposes. This is vital because for every output unit, the discrepancy between the value it is signalling and the corresponding value in the desired pattern must be derived. Clearly, if the actual and desired values for a given output unit are the same, then the error is zero and that part of the network has the correct coefficients (weights and thresholds). You hit the treble twenty so don't change anything!

If the actual and desired outputs do not agree, then the error will be some non-zero value. The pattern of error values over all of the output units is computed and the network is, in a sense, reversed. Now the so-called **error signal** (the discrepancy between what the network responds with and what it should actually be responding with) now acts as a reverse input to the network. The error pattern acts as a signal that is sent back down the many layers of the network.

Think of it this way. You are trying to teach a young child to speak English. You present the child with a picture of a cat and they say 'dog' and you say 'cat'. In terms of the sounds of English, there is a very big difference between cat and dog. So a measure of this difference is computed and fed back down the network (i.e., through the child's brain) and subtle changes are made to the neural pathways so that it is unlikely that they will make the same mistake again. You now show the child a picture of a cat and they now say 'cog' and you say 'cat'. Again a measure of the difference between 'cog' and 'dog' is computed and fed back down the network, and so on. The discrepancy between the actual output 'cog' and 'dog' is now smaller than that previously so the error signal will be smaller as well. Nevertheless, the error signal is back-propagated and the coefficients are changed as the signal passes through the network. This iterative procedure continues until the child finally says 'cat' and you say 'cat' and there is no longer a difference between the actual output (what they say) and the desired output (what you say).

Without going into any details, when the error signal is back-propagated down the network, the coefficients that define the weights and thresholds are altered as the error signal passes by. Generally speaking, the coefficients are altered in proportion to the error signal so bigger changes are made to those pathways through the network that generated large errors at the output layer. Smaller changes are made on the pathways through the network that were responsible for small errors at the output units and no changes are made to pathways that resulted in no errors (because they are exactly how they should be). In a sense, the idea is to make bigger changes to those pathways that resulted in the biggest mistakes.

Back-propagation is also known as an iterative procedure because this process of activation feed-forward and error back-propagation is repeated time and time again for the complete set of patterns that we wish to train the network on. In fact, in the sample case, one so-called **epoch of training** is where:

1. we take each input pattern from the training set and present this once to the network;

2. carry out a forward pass of activation from the input units;

3. compute the error; and

4. carry out a backwards pass in which changes to the coefficients are made.

Typically, the patterns are chosen at random and each pattern is only presented once in every epoch. However, many hundreds of training epochs are usually needed to train a multi-layered network of the sort just described successfully. More training is needed for larger than small pattern sets, and more training is needed for more complex than simple pattern sets.

Generally speaking, the back-propagation method of training does produce gradual decrements in the overall error computed over the whole set of input–output pairings over the training epochs. Occasionally, however, the procedure fails and is unable to achieve a good fit between the actual and desired output patterns. In such cases, the network gets stuck with a set of coefficient values that cannot be changed in a way that brings about a reduction in the overall error – the technical phrase here is that the network has arrived at a **local minimum** instead of a **global minimum** in which the overall error would be minimal – near zero, if not actually zero. The ideal global minimum is where there is never any error whenever an input pattern is presented. In every case the actual and desired output patterns are the same for all inputs. In some cases, though, the network fails to achieve this ideal and it simply gets stuck with coefficients that produce notable errors – this state of affairs is termed a local minimum.

When this happens, typically training is halted, the network is re-initialised with new coefficients and the training is restarted. So although back-propagation has been proved to be a method for reducing error, there is no guarantee that it will reduce the error to an acceptable minimum – there is no guarantee that the network will achieve a global minimum (see Quinlan, 1991, ch. 2 for a more thorough exposition of back-propagation). The network may unfortunately converge on a set of coefficients that simply do not allow the network to learn appropriate mappings between the input and output patterns.

## Hidden unit representations

Perhaps the most mysterious aspect of the particular network described here relates to the hidden units – a name that doesn't really do anything to dispel the impression of some unseen magic within the connectionist network. A cash dispenser analogy may be of some help here. Your card, PIN and commands resemble the input, the desired output may be some cash or a mini-statement, and the hidden units are all those computations, clicks and whirrs that are hidden in the hole in the wall. Unless your card gets swallowed, due to some unfortunate circumstance, then the bank machine is like a connectionist network that thankfully has found its global minimum. It produces an appropriate output for a given input.

Hidden units are so-called because they are insulated from the outside world by the input and output units. Critically the hidden units in the Rumelhart and Todd model act as a means for generating, for each concept/relation pair, an internal distributed representation of the concept/relation pair (see Figure 12.14). As we have already noted, the input representations are essentially localist in nature because for each concept/relation pair only one unit could be in the ON state in the item units and only one unit could be in the ON state in the relation units. However, given the connectivity in the network, every input unit is either directly (in the case of the relation units) or indirectly (in the case of the item units) linked with every hidden unit. In this regard, the bank of hidden units will acquire a distributed pattern of activation for each pattern of activation across the input units (i.e., for a given input pattern).

Central to this work is the understanding that real-world categories are, essentially, defined such that similar characteristics are shared by all category instances. Clearly this is not absolutely true, in that sparrows fly but penguins do not, but, generally speaking, it is true that all birds have feathers, beaks, legs, wings, etc. In other words, the very different members of a category's extension must come to be associated with (or map onto) the very same category intension. In terms of the network model, this means that, at some level, the different category instances must give rise to similar internal representations. Specifically, the different category instances will map onto similar representations at the level of the hidden units. This is because similar hidden unit representations give rise to similar patterns of activation at the level of the attribute (output) units.

In essence, what we are trying to do is to take a collection of input patterns that individually code instances of particular categories and train the network to classify this sub-set of patterns as being members of category $x$ (the input patterns for Labrador, Poodle, Corgi are DOGS) and this sub-set of patterns as being members of category $y$ (the input patterns Persian, White Persian, Turkish Angora are CATS). Although each input pattern is distinctive in itself, the network must learn to overcome these subtle differences so as to assign the different instances of the same category to the same internal hidden unit representation. What the network has to learn to answer is, 'What is it about these particular patterns that makes them members of the same category?' The network has to figure out how best to configure its sets of weights and thresholds such that the different instances of the same category give rise to similar outputs on the attribute units. To achieve this it must learn to produce similar hidden unit representations for the different instances of a given category.

In effect, during training what happens is that the network configures itself, by adapting its coefficients (i.e., its weights and thresholds) such that similar hidden unit representations are derived for the different instance patterns of a given category (or, more simply, *instance patterns*) such that similar hidden unit representations then give rise to similar output patterns of activation at the attribute units. What eventually happens is that the different instance patterns give rise to hidden unit representations that are very similar to one another.

Remember, initially, the coefficients are randomised so that the different instance patterns are likely to give rise to different patterns across the attribute units. As training proceeds, however, the different instance patterns become associated with similar output patterns and during the course of training the corresponding hidden unit representations tend to reflect this. The different instance patterns give rise to similar patterns of distributed activation at the level of the hidden units.

Overall what the network is being forced to do is to recover what are known as the **statistical regularities** between the set of input patterns and the set of desired output patterns. In other words, the commonalities that bring together instances of the same category must at some level reflect statistical regularities across the instances in the real world. All birds possess beaks, wings, legs, feathers, etc.; moreover, beaks, wings, feathers and legs co-occur in those animals we refer to as birds. In this way it is not only the co-occurrence of the attribute *wings* with the category BIRD but also the co-occurrence of wings and feathers and legs and beaks with the category BIRD that the networks are adept at picking up on. What the network models are trying to achieve, therefore, are internal representations that, in some sense, reflect the real-world regularities in the co-occurrence of bundles of features and attributes of real-world category instances.

More concretely, Figure 12.14 shows the network clamped with the CANARY CAN input pattern and with the correct configuration of attribute units. Now consider what happens when the input is changed to the ROBIN CAN input pattern. In this case the CANARY unit is switched off and the ROBIN unit is switched ON. Having trained the network, what this means is that when activation spreads from the input units, eventually the same GROW, MOVE, FLY, SING attribute units will come ON at the level of the attribute units. So these different instance patterns (of the category BIRD) give rise to the identical pattern of activation at the level of the attribute units. Therefore the hidden unit representations for CANARY and BIRD are either the same or are very similar to one another.

Figure 12.15 is more expansive. What this figure shows is, essentially, hidden unit representations for various instance and category inputs that a version of the Rumelhart and Todd network acquired during training. Inputs that coded item/relation pairs such as BIRDS CAN _____, TREES CAN _____ and LIVING THINGS CAN ___ were used as well as those such as CANARY CAN ____. The network was simplified from Figure 12.14 as only eight hidden units were incorporated in the network. What the figure shows is that the different hidden units, in a sense, operated like semantic dimensions. As Rumelhart and Todd (1993) noted, what they found was 'the major conceptual dimensions of the (Collins & Quillian, 1969) semantic network are represented by particular features in the connectionist network' (p. 16; text in parentheses added). More specifically, and in terms of the figure, the first unit seems to support the plant/animal distinction. It comes ON for all plants.

Slightly more complicated is the fourth unit. This unit represents the tree/flower distinction when a plant is presented but represents bird/fish distinction when an animal is presented. So although the behaviour of the hidden units may accord well with standard notions concerning the internal representation of

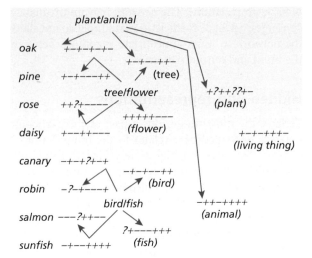

**Figure 12.15 Various hidden unit representations that a version of the Rumelhart and Todd connectionist network acquired during training**

Eight hidden units were incorporated in the network. Each is designated by a '+', '−' or '?' in the figure. These symbols signify the weights on the connections from the input units to the corresponding hidden units. The '+' signs indicate that the corresponding weighted connections are positive in nature, the '−' signs indicate that the corresponding weighted connections are negative in nature and the '?' signs indicate that the corresponding weighted connections are near zero. Roughly these signs convey the corresponding states of the hidden units. So two + marks in position 1 signify that both hidden unit representations agree on the state of activation of the first unit. Comparisons across the different hidden unit representations convey how the network is capturing both commonalities and differences across the categories fish, birds and flora. As can be seen, the plant/animal distinction is captured by hidden unit 1. In its + state the unit signifies a plant and in its '−' state it signifies an animal.

*Source*: Rumelhart, D. E., & Todd, P. M. (1993). Learning and connectionist representations. In D. E. Meyer & S. Kornblum (Eds.), *Attention and performance XIV. Synergies in experimental psychology, artificial intelligence, and cognitive neuroscience* (pp. 3–35, fig. 1.10, p. 17). Cambridge, Massachusetts: The MIT Press. Reproduced with permission.

semantic dimensions, in other regards the mapping may not be so obvious. The states of the hidden units are extremely sensitive to the states of the other units in the network. It is for this reason that there is no necessary correspondence between hidden units and the more traditional notion of semantic dimensions. Yet again, therefore, consideration of this kind of connectionist model makes us reassess traditional claims about how semantic dimensions may be realised in the mind. → See 'What have we learnt?', page 451.

## → What have we learnt?

Overall, what we have, in this sort of connectionist model is a powerful alternative account of the nature of semantic representations together with a provocative account of how such internal representations may be learnt. Fundamentally such models reveal the importance of distributed representations. For example, different input representations of members of the same semantic category come to be associated with similar hidden unit representations. Hidden unit representations are internal distributed representations that reflect higher-order contingencies between input micro-features.

Aside from these remarks about knowledge representation, connectionist models are also particularly notable for their learning capabilities. A criticism of previous work on semantic networks is that the models were hand-built and hand-tuned to reflect current interests. With those models, issues concerning knowledge acquisition were simply not addressed. How on earth did such complex conceptual structures develop? Indeed, as the field itself developed, new properties and capabilities were introduced into semantic networks, simply by adding a new node or link to capture this or that feature or relation (see Woods, 1975). In contrast, processes of knowledge acquisition are germane to connectionist networks and these have been addressed in a much more systematic fashion. It is the adaptive changes in the coefficients (the weights and thresholds) that underpin learning in connectionist parallel distributed processing (PDP) networks. When a network learns, it acquires coefficients that capture the statistical regularities that exist in the mappings between input patterns and their desired output patterns.

However, at another level, it can be seen that some of the basic characteristics of traditional semantic network models have been retained. For instance, the models honour the distinction between the representation of features and relations, they are also committed to some form of localist representation (the individual micro-features are stored somewhere), and they retain the notion of spreading activation. Stated thus, the differences between traditional semantic networks and PDP models are not as marked as might be thought.

The advent of PDP models in the 1980s brought about a re-conception of learning. The connectionist movement was driven by a desire to offer biologically plausible mechanisms for cognitive/perceptual processes. Think about it. Artificial neural networks do bear a passing resemblance to the sorts of neuronal networks that reside between your ears. Open up your head and what you will find are a bunch of 'simple' processing units (i.e., neurons/brain cells) that share many interconnections. At the time, such a view of cognitive/perceptual mechanisms was a radical departure from traditional ways of thinking. Now, though, it is generally the case that wherever there resides an arrows-and-boxes account of some aspect of cognition, there also lurks a PDP counterpart. Although PDP models are not without their critics (see, for example, Fodor & Pylyshyn, 1988; Quinlan, 1991), their influence and applicability have been immense. Connectionist thinking pervades most aspects of present-day cognitive psychology. Indeed, and as we will see, connectionism poses serious challenges to the traditional cognitivist forms of theorising. Why bother with all those arrows-and-boxes when a bunch of interconnected and simple 'light bulbs' will do?

## Pinpoint question 12.8

**How are both localist and distributed approaches to representation apparent in the Rumelhart and Todd (1993) model?**

semantic micro-features Atoms of meaning that cannot be rendered into expressible language.

feature-norming studies Identifying the most common properties associated with any one object

or category by having a large sample of people produce responses to a probe item. How often are 'hooves' produced in response to the probe 'horse'?

semantic feature production norms The frequency with which concepts are assigned to certain properties.

associative relatedness Items that are associatively related are typically bound together by what may appear to be an otherwise arbitrary state of affairs. For example, 'horse' and 'cart' belong

▶

## What should I call you? Networks, nominal competition and naming

One of the curses of being a rich and famous actor (we imagine) is that not only would you get stopped in the street, but you would get stopped in the street by people shouting your fictitious name rather than your real name: 'Joey!' rather than 'Matt!' or 'Phoebe!' rather than 'Lisa!' (not that we ever watch that particular show, you understand). This phenomenon has been labelled the *nominal competitor effect*, which, in psychology-speak, is where the retrieval of one name becomes difficult as a result of having more than one possible name available. Stevenage and Lewis (2005) wondered how this nominal competitor effect could be explained in terms of cognitive architecture and particularly connectionist models.

Forty-four participants were presented with 28 faces of famous celebrities. Half of these faces were related to individuals who were associated with both their fictitious and real names (e.g., 'Frasier' a.k.a. 'Kelsey Grammer') and half of the celebrities were associated simply with their real name (e.g., 'Nicholas Cage'). In the first experiment, participants were simply asked to name the actor as quickly and as accurately as possible. The nominal competitor effect was shown in that individuals were both slower and less accurate in naming when the celebrity face was associated with multiple names. In a second experiment, the critical manipulation was how participants judged the familiarity of actors with two names compared to those associated with a single name. Participants were faster in judging familiarity for actors with two names.

We don't need to go into details here, but Stevenage and Lewis (2005) took these data to suggest that the difference between 'Dana Scully' and 'Gillian Anderson', essentially, occurs at the level of naming (or as they put it, lexical output units – LOUs) and not in terms of different semantic information (or, as they put it, person identity nodes – PINs) being activated for each name (i.e., 'it's that FBI agent off the *X-Files*' versus 'it's that actress who was voted Sexiest Woman in the World in 1996'). Perhaps most importantly in the current context, the authors successfully modelled these data using a connectionist network. The network contained structures shown in Figure 12.16. They were able to replicate the nominal competitor effect for

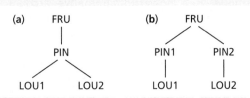

**Figure 12.16 The figure shows two different possible architectures that could account for the nominal competitor effect and the familiarity enhancement effect reported by Stevenage and Lewis (2005)**
FRU stands for face recognition unit. Such a unit codes the visual characteristics of each person's face. So there s one FRU for Kelsey Grammer and a different FRU for Gillian Anderson. PIN stands for person identity node. Each PIN captures semantic knowledge about a given individual. In (a) there is only one PIN for any one person: Kelsey Grammer has one PIN and Gillian Anderson has one PIN. In (b) the alternative is where Kelsey Grammer's FRU is connected with two PINs – one for Kelsey Grammer and one for Frasier. Finally each LOU (lexical output unit) essentially codes a person's name. For example, LOU1 represents *Kelsey Grammer*, LOU2 represents *Frasier*. The aim was to see whether the empirical findings with humans could be replicated with these sorts of networks.

two-name actors shown in experiment 1 and the familiarity enhancement effect for two-name actors shown in experiment 2. Critically, though, the effects arose in cases where two different names mapped onto the same PIN (see Figure 12.16a).

Remember, though, that this is a network that knows nothing about movies, film stars, culture or even what it might be like to have anything other than 0s and 1s flying round its head. The central point is that the competitor effects can arise merely on the basis of having had to map different names onto the same type node for a given person. This is irrespective of any other semantic knowledge that you might have about the person. So, next time you bump into Sarah-Michelle Gellar (a.k.a. Buffy the Vampire Slayer) with a sense of heightened familiarity but you're having trouble remembering her name, you could be acting because of the same sorts of architectural constraints present in the connectionist network described by Stevenage and Lewis (2005).

*Source*: Stevenage, S. V., & Lewis, H. G. (2005). By which name should I call thee? The consequences of having multiple names. *The Quarterly Journal of Experimental Psychology, 58A*, 1447–1461.

to different semantic categories but they are associatively related through the fact that they commonly co-occur.

**category co-ordinates** Short-hand for instances that belong to the same category.

**semantic decision task** Deciding whether or not a word refers to a referent of particular type (e.g., is × man-made?).

**connectionist models** Computer models in which simple processing units with modifiable thresholds are interconnected with modifiable weighted connections. Adaptive means for changing weights and thresholds results in learning mappings between inputs to and outputs from the network.

**sub-symbols** See semantic micro-features and cogit.

**place metaphor for memory** The localist assumption that individual memories are stored in unique places in memory.

**localist theory of memory** See place metaphor for memory.

**parallel-distributed processing (PDP)** An idea central to connectionist models, in which it is the entire pattern of activation across a bank of processing units that stands for the current entity that the network is representing. Such distributed patterns induce patterns of activation that spread throughout the network at the same time.

**binary unit** A processing unit in a connectionist network which can only be in one of two states at any given time (i.e., either ON or OFF).

**distributed representation** The current pattern of activation across a bank of processing units contained in a connectionist network.

**mental chemistry** The idea that concepts are composed from a finite number of semantic primitives (or mental atoms). Different concepts arise from the combination of different primitives.

**input pattern** In a connectionist model, the distributed pattern of activation across the input units.

**output pattern** In a connectionist model, the distributed pattern of activation across the output units.

**coefficients** The modifiable weights and thresholds in a connectionist model.

**connection weight** Strength of a link between nodes in a connectionist network.

**hidden units** Units in a connectionist network that are only connected to other units and do not receive activation directly from or produce activation directly to the outside world.

**output error** In a connectionist network, the difference between the actual distributed pattern of activation on the output units and desired pattern of activation on the output units.

**back-propagation** A training procedure in connectionist networks in which the aim is to minimise the discrepancy between desired and actual outputs. An iterative process in which the coefficients in the network (the weights on the connections and the thresholds on the units) are changed whenever the network makes an error in producing the wrong output for a given input.

**supervised training** A term most commonly used in the connectionist literature, regarding a training method in which, for every output of a network, a complete specification of the desired output is provided. In other words, a teaching signal is provided on an input-by-input basis.

**error signal** In a connectionist network, where the output error is used as a reverse input pattern to the network. This 'input' pattern is fed back down the network and used to change the coefficients as it passes back down the network.

**epoch of training** In the current context, this applies to the back-propagation learning algorithm. On each trial an input pattern is presented, the eventual error signal is derived at the output layer and this is fed backwards through the network as changes to the coefficients are made. One epoch is where each input pattern, used in the training regimen, is presented once to the network.

**local minimum** The state of a connectionist network in which the overall error is not close to zero but further reductions cannot be made.

**global minimum** The state of a connectionist network in which the overall error (computed over all of the input patterns) is either zero or very close to zero. If the network reaches this state then it has been successful in learning the desired mappings between input and output mappings.

**statistical regularities** In terms of connectionist models, the systematic relations that hold between the input patterns and output patterns in a given training case.

# Prototypes

Our discussion of semantic memory has so far been focused on general issues concerning various kinds of representational systems. We have contrasted network and featural models and we have explored basic issues that relate to how best to understand the notion of a semantic feature. Are there semantic primitives that act as the atoms of meaning? If so, how are they realised? Is it best to think in terms of values on abstract dimensions? Or abstract particles of meaning that are combined in different ways? Are the same semantic primitives used to code every concept? Or are the primitives used in a much more circumspect fashion, like the compounds in chemistry? To what extent is the human conceptual system based on a localist representational system? Is it more sensible to think in terms of distributed representations? To what degree should our consideration of the adult human conceptual system be governed by consideration of processes of learning and knowledge acquisition? We may not have provided very satisfactory answers to these questions but we have, at least, covered foundational assumptions that should allow you to arrive at your own conclusions.

We now need to move on and consider a different, but related, theme in the literature. This concerns yet another mental construct known as a *mental prototype* or simply a **prototype**. We will discover that there are several ways in which to define a prototype (so you will have to bear with us). However, the general ideas crop up time and again in the literature, so it is important that we do understand what is at stake.

Earlier on in the chapter a very crude distinction was drawn between network and featural models, but as we keep on concluding, such simple distinctions never are very hard and fast. The extended network model discussed by Collins and Loftus (1975) grew out of the work on the Collins and Quillian model (1969). This extended model incorporated aspects of both network and featural accounts. Indeed, Collins and Loftus accepted that concepts with many shared features have a correspondingly large number of shared connections. Indeed the distinction between network and featural models is further blurred in the PDP models in which both features and relations are captured by nodes in the network – see our discussion of the Rumelhart and Todd (1993) connectionist network. Aside from these concerns, about how best to represent category attributes and hierarchical relations, Rosch (1975) began to examine more carefully what conceptual categories might be like. This line of enquiry eventuated in the proposal of *mental prototypes of categories* or, more simply, **category prototype**s.

## Early experimental work on prototypes

In one case Rosch (1975) merely asked participants to rate instance–category typicality and found, in agreement with Smith et al. (1974), that not all instances are equally typical of a given category. Whereas *apples* are typical of the *fruit* category, *figs* and *olives* are not – at least not in Northern Europe. As we have seen, such evidence as this fits uncomfortably with the so-called classical view of concepts (Smith, 1988) in which there are 'singly necessary and jointly sufficient' properties that define each concept. By the classical view, either the instance possesses the defining properties of the category or it does not. Each instance is an equally good member of the category if it contains the defining characteristics of the category. This is not to argue that such well-defined concepts do not exist – think of the equilateral triangle, odd and even numbers, chemical elements, etc. Rather, the view is that most concepts are not like this – they have so-called **fuzzy boundaries** (see Osherson & Smith, 1981, 1982; Zadeh, 1982). Not all instances of a so-called **fuzzy concept** share the same set of properties. Think of the category of chairs. It is quite possible that your initial assumption about a chair is that it would have four legs, but there are examples of chairs that do not possess four legs (or indeed have no legs at all). If you dwell on this, then you'll start to ask questions like, 'When is a chair not a chair? When is a chair more like a stool?', begin to enter into the realm of fuzzy categories, and probably end up with a fuzzy headache.

Further experimental evidence bears on such ideas. For instance, Rosch and Mervis (1975) simply provided participants with category instances and asked them to list all of the attributes they could (e.g., *peas*, *carrots*, *string beans* were the instances from the category *vegetable*). On the understanding that there are necessary and sufficient attributes that define the associated category, then these ought to be listed by participants as common to all instances. In contrast to this, they found very few cases where this occurred. It was generally the case that several attributes were listed for some but not all instances of a given category.

Measures of so-called **family resemblance** were also computed from these ratings. Each attribute was weighted according to the number of instances in the category which were reported as possessing that attribute. Each category comprised 20 instances, so family resemblance scores ranged from 0 to 20 – a score of 20 meant that all instances possessed the attribute. Now a family resemblance score was computed for each category instance, which was simply the sum of the attribute scores just defined. Such scores in a sense indicated how typical the item was to the category. The thinking was that typical items share many attributes in common with other members of the category whereas atypical members share few attributes with other members of the category. Compare the typicality of a sparrow and an ostrich to the concept of a bird. Sparrows share many characteristics with other birds whereas ostriches do not.

To provide further support for these ideas, Rosch and Mervis (1975) correlated these family resemblance scores with previous prototypicality ratings collected by Rosch (1975). For the previous ratings Rosch (1975) had participants numerically rate 'the extent to which items fit the participants' idea or image of the meaning of the category names' (Rosch & Mervis, 1975). The critical results now showed that there were very strong correlations between the prototypicality ratings and the family resemblance scores. Simply put, the data provided good evidence that highly typical instances share many attributes in common with each other, whereas atypical category members share either very few or no attributes with other members.

## Conceptual categories and family resemblance

Such results as these were interpreted not in terms of the classical view of concepts. Instead the notion of family resemblance came to the fore. The basic ideas can be traced back to Wittgenstein (1953) and the problems he identified in trying to define the concept of a game. As Armstrong, Gleitman and Gleitman (1983) noted, he concluded that a game is 'a cluster concept, held together by a variety of gamey attributes only some of which are instantiated by any one game' (p. 269). You'll be able to unpack this quote by thinking about a variety of different games. Maybe a game is something that involves toy money? Well, that would be fine for Monopoly but what about chess? Okay, well, maybe a game is something that involves moving pieces around a board? Works for chess but not for charades, and so on.

Unsurprisingly, we can extend the idea of family resemblance to actual families themselves. Let us introduce you to the Smith clan in Figure 12.17. As Armstrong et al. (1983) pointed out, 'not all Smith Brothers have the same Smith-features, and no one criterial feature defines the family' (p. 269). Nevertheless, *Smithness* is apparent across all the siblings. The more critical point, though, is that, in terms of mental representation, concepts are not captured by some form of definition, but rather that they emerge from the family resemblance relations that exist across the members of the category. Aligned to this is the idea that each concept is associated with a category prototype – as is the case with the Smith brothers. In other cases, though, there may be more than a single prototype

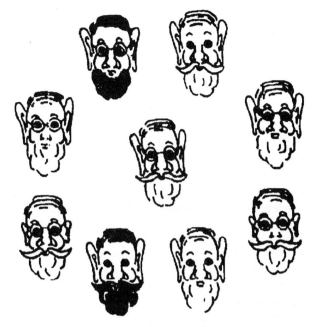

**Figure 12.17 The Smith brothers gravitate around the central prototypical Smith male sibling (taken from Armstrong et al., 1983)**

*Source*: Armstrong, S. L., Gleitman, L. R., & Gleitman, H. (1983). What some concepts might not be. *Cognition*, *13*, 263–308 (fig. 3, p. 269). Reproduced with permission from Elsevier.

and now the category prototypes are known as core members. For instance, the Smith siblings may include sisters and therefore there will be a prototypical Smith sister. The representation of the concept of the Smith siblings comprises the conceptual core (i.e., the prototypical brother and the prototypical sister) and instances of this category cluster around this core. By this view, a concept can be viewed as roughly being associated with 'bundles of statistically reliable features, hence having a concept is knowing which properties the things it applies to reliably exhibit' (Fodor, 1998, p. 92). 'Being able to fly isn't a *necessary* condition for being a bird . . . ; but it is a property that birds are quite reliably found to have.' (Fodor, 1998, p. 92).

In summary, by the prototype view, a category's prototype can be thought of as some form of summary representation that captures an example or ideal that possesses all the characteristics of the category. The prototype is useful because it provides a template against which category membership can be judged. So a novel instance will be classified on the basis of how similar it is to the category's prototype. As Armstrong et al. (1983) noted, the basic theory asserts that, at the psychological level, concepts comprise (i) a core description – a prototype, and (ii) an identification procedure that operates so as to pick out concept instances in the world (p. 295). We might imagine a nice, perfectly round, bright red, shiny, juicy apple as a prototype, but when we find a green, bruised, misshapen lump of fruit in our local supermarket, we can still recognise it for what it is.

## Prototype formation

Of some additional importance is the notion that the category's prototype may not actually correspond to any real-world entity – have you actually been on a 'romantic date' that involved red roses, candle-lit dinner with violin accompaniment, Belgian chocolates, midnight horse-drawn carriage ride, and then was all capped off by a proposal of marriage at the end of the evening (if you have, good for you!)? So the issue is, how can someone possess a category prototype if it does not correspond to a real-world entity? The simple answer is that the mental representation of a prototype emerges from experience with real-world exemplars of the category even though the eventual category prototype has never been experienced in and of itself. The basic idea is that it is quite possible to form a category prototype of the Smith brothers by merely encountering all of the peripheral Smith brothers.

Various accounts have been put forward to explain this and there is a very large experimental literature that bears on the issue of prototype formation (see Smith & Medin, 1981, 1984, for reviews). In the standard paradigm there is an *initial learning phase* followed by a *transfer test phase*. During the initial learning phase, participants are (typically) presented with instances taken from artificially constructed categories. Participants are exposed to various category instances and are trained to classify these correctly up to a certain criterion level of performance. In the test phase participants are then provided with a mixture of old and new instances and they have to classify them into the categories they learnt initially.

The most popular sorts of artificial categories used have consisted of dot patterns (Posner & Keele, 1968, 1970), schematic or identikit faces (Reed, 1972), configurations of geometrical patterns (Franks & Bransford, 1971), line drawings based on dot patterns (Homa, 1978), strings of alpha-numeric characters (Reitman & Bower, 1973), written descriptions of fictitious individuals (Reed & Friedman, 1973), and occasionally stick figures (Rosch, Simpson & Miller, 1976), multi-dimensional regular figures (Medin & Schaffer, 1978) and contrived line-drawn symbols (Caldwell & Hall, 1970).

In the majority of these experiments, each category was defined relative to a single prototype. For instance, in the dot pattern studies, category instances were physical transformations of a single prototypical dot pattern. Each instance was created by perturbing the position of each dot in the prototype. Such changes were systematically governed by a certain amount defined by a statistical rule. Figure 12.17 provides a different example of how face instances might be generated from a central prototype. Of the immense number of results, findings and effects reported, the most robust is that even though prototype instances are not presented to participants in the initial learning phase of the experiments, these prototypes are classified on both immediate and delayed testing more quickly and accurately than all other new category instances (Homa & Chambliss, 1975; Posner & Keele, 1968, 1970; Solso & McCarthy, 1981). This result has even occured when testing was delayed for a period of ten weeks (Homa & Vosburgh, 1976). Moreover, even though substantial forgetting was evident for the initially trained instances, performance with the prototypes either remained high or in some cases improved over time (Homa, Cross, Cornell, Goldman & Schwartz, 1973; Posner & Keele, 1970; Strange, Kenney, Kessel & Jenkins, 1970).

One way to think of this is that prototype formation comes about as a consequence of some form of mental averaging whereby the category's prototype represents 'the average value on each dimension' upon which the category is defined (Osherson & Smith, 1981, p. 37). By this view, the prototype is a mental representation of the characteristic attributes of the category; it represents the central tendency of the category. There is no average man on the street but we can of course conjure up what the average man might look like.

Evidence for prototype formation is so pervasive that this led Smith (1988) to state that 'Even classical concepts have prototypes' (p. 26). One of the most striking demonstrations of this was reported by Armstrong et al. (1983). In their first experiment, participants effortlessly rated the typicality of certain instances of classically defined concepts, for example, even number, odd number, plane geometric figure and female. It turns out that '3 was rated as being a better odd number than *501* and *mother* a better female than *comedienne*' (Armstrong et al., 1983, p. 277). In addition, square was rated as a better geometric figure than ellipse, and in a speeded sentence verification task, participants were quicker to respond to statements of the form '7 is an odd number' when the sentence

→ What have we learnt?

Despite basic intuitions about concepts having definitions, it seems that the actual evidence points to a much more complicated state of affairs. Whatever the nature of the actual to-be-represented category, there is an overwhelming sensitivity to favour certain characteristics and instances over others. It seems that there is an overwhelming tendency, at the psychological level, to generate some notion of prototypicality for any given concept. Even though people may be able to offer the exact definition of a concept, such as what is an even number, the behavioural evidence reflects a conceptual system that is fundamentally sensitive to instance typicality. There are inherent biases that operate so as to favour certain category instances over others. This contrast between definitions and prototypes has led to real tensions in the literature concerning the nature of the human conceptual system and we shall consider some of the issues as we draw the chapter to a close.

contained a good exemplar of the concept (e.g., *7*) than a poor exemplar of the concept (e.g., *23*). → See 'What have we learnt?', above.

Pinpoint question 12.9

**What makes a boundary 'fuzzy'?**

## The internal structure of mental taxonomies

Aside from the very influential work on category prototypes, Rosch was also responsible for introducing a different way of thinking about the internal representation of mental taxonomies. In this regard Rosch (1978) discussed the vertical dimension of a given taxonomy, that is, from instance to intermediate category to superordinate category (e.g., KITCHEN CHAIR – CHAIR – FURNITURE), which you'll recall from our earlier discussion of hierarchical network models in this chapter. Via the vertical dimension, category size decreases from the top of the hierarchy to the bottom (i.e., FURNITURE to KITCHEN CHAIR) but alternatively the level of inclusiveness increases from the bottom of the hierarchy to the top (i.e., KITCHEN CHAIR to FURNITURE).

The horizontal dimension of the taxonomy refers to cutting the hierarchy across at the same level of inclusiveness. For example, it is possible to divide the FURNITURE category into CHAIRS, TABLES, WARDROBES, etc. At a lower level, another horizontal cut gives rise to the distinction between different chairs (high chair, garden chair, electric chair), different tables and different wardrobes. For Rosch (1978), however, the most interesting questions concerned the psychological significance of these different levels of the hierarchy.

Figure 12.18 is of some help here (adapted from Fodor, 1998, p. 90) and maps out a semantic network representation of part of the knowledge associated with man-made things. The network is hierarchically organised into superordinate and subordinate cases. Two basic claims are made when the mental representation of conceptual hierarchies is being discussed:

1. There is a so-called **basic level**.
2. There will be a stereotype structure associated with each level (in other words, the different levels possess prototypes).

Much of the preceding discussion has concerned the evidence relevant to category prototypes and now it is sensible to move on to discuss the notion of a *basic level*.

## The basic level and the structure of mental categories

Central here is the idea that the world is structured in a particular way and that this structure is incorporated into the internal representational system. The structure of the represented world is mirrored in the structure of the representing world (see Chapter 7). More particularly the idea is that objects in the world naturally cluster into their categories by possessing correlated attributes. As Malt (1995) remarked, 'features in the world are not distributed randomly across entities, but instead tend to occur in clusters . . . "feathers", "wings" and "beaks" frequently occur together . . . and form our category "bird" ' (p. 88). In extending these ideas, members of a typical superordinate category share only a few common attributes (what do all household objects have in common?) whereas members of a less abstract category share many common attributes (what do all cups have in common?). Rosch

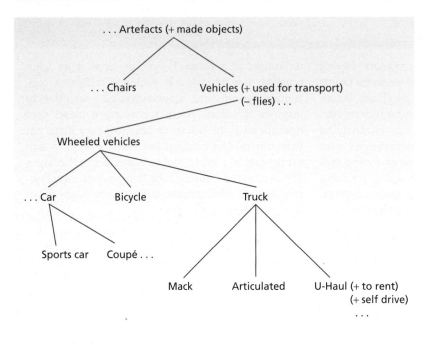

... Artefacts (+ made objects)

... Chairs      Vehicles (+ used for transport)
                 (– flies) ...

Wheeled vehicles

... Car      Bicycle                    Truck

Sports car   Coupé ...

        Mack      Articulated      U-Haul (+ to rent)
                                          (+ self drive)
                                              ...

**Figure 12.18 The conceptual hierarchy mapped out for vehicles (from Fodor, 1998)**
The basic level is located at CAR, BICYCLE, TRUCK.

*Source*: Fodor, J. A. (1998). *Concepts. Where cognitive science went wrong* (fig. 5.1, p. 90). Oxford, England: Clarendon Press. Reproduced with permission from Oxford University Press.

(1978) went further and argued that there is a basic level which is 'the most inclusive level at which there are attributes common to all or most members of the category' (p. 31) and, moreover, at this level few attributes are shared with members of other categories.

To flesh these ideas out, Rosch discussed the fact that the attributes of an instance vary in their significance for category membership and here we are discussing something known as **featural diagnosticity** (Tversky, 1977) or **cue validity** (Rosch, 1978; Rosch & Mervis, 1975; Rosch, Mervis, Gray, Johnson & Boyes-Braem, 1976). According to Rosch (1978, p. 30), 'the validity of a given cue $x$ as a predictor of a given category $y$ (the conditional probability $y/x$) increases as the frequency with which cue $x$ is associated with category $y$ increases and decreases as the frequency with which cue $x$ is associated with categories other than $y$ increases' (after Beach, 1964). Given this definition, in principle it is possible to add up the cue validities of the attributes associated with a given category to arrive at the total cue validity known as **category cue validity** (Murphy, 1982). Categories that have high category cue validity are now said to be more differentiated than those that have lower category cue validity. More critically, it is claimed that at the basic level total cue validity is maximised – so the total cue validity for, say, furniture is lower than that for chair. The total cue validity for deckchair is also lower than that for chair. Furniture is the superordinate category, chair is

located at the basic level and deckchair is at a lower subordinate level.

Evidence generally consistent with the claim came from studies in which participants were presented with various labels for things and were merely asked to write down lists of properties associated with those things (Rosch, Mervis et al., 1976). In collating the results it became clear that very few attributes were listed for superordinate categories. More attributes were listed for the basic level and only marginally but not significantly more attributes were listed for the subordinate level. To take an example from Fodor (1998), 'it's a car tells you a lot about a vehicle; but that it's a sports car doesn't add a lot to what "it's a car" already told you' (p. 91).

Unfortunately real problems have been uncovered with the particular index of category cue validity. As Murphy (1982) showed, the fundamental problem is that category cue validity actually tends to increase with class inclusiveness so it cannot be the correct measure that defines category differentiation (see also Jones, 1983). Technical fixes to this problem have more recently been proposed (see Gosselin & Schyns, 2001), and despite such detailed criticisms, the overall thrust of the theory has been extremely influential.

In summarising the supportive literature, Rosch (1978) noted the following: when asked to describe the motor movements made when using or interacting with a given object, entities at the basic level shared the most motor sequences in common. In other words, it is difficult to produce a very detailed description of how to interact with furniture and the kitchen chair, but much easier to provide such a description for chairs (Rosch, Mervis et al., 1976).

Studies were also carried out in trying to quantify the similarity of shapes of objects (Rosch, Mervis et al., 1976). Here again the data revealed converging evidence for the utility of the basic level. Whereas objects at the basic level share highly similar shapes, objects at other levels do not, the conclusion being that 'the basic level is the most inclusive level at which shapes of objects of a class are similar' (Rosch, 1978, p. 34) – a conclusion backed up by the finding that the basic level was also the most inclusive level at which a mental image of the class of objects as a whole could be formed.

From a developmental point of view, basic level effects were also observed in the classification behaviour and naming patterns of children. In one study the children were given triads of pictures and had to select the two pictures of objects that were the same kind of thing. For one group of children (the basic level group) the target pair of pictures was selected from the same basic level (e.g., two cats vs. car). In contrast, a different group of children (the superordinate group) were presented with triads in which the target pair was selected from the same superordinate level (e.g., a car and a train vs. a cat). Performance was essentially perfect for the basic level group and relatively poor for the superordinate group of children.

In analysing a corpus of early language utterances Rosch, Mervis et al. (1976) uncovered the fact that at the very early stages of language acquisition the children peppered their utterances with labels for objects at the basic level, for example, calling a dog a DOG rather than an animal or a poodle (for further converging evidence see Mervis & Pani, 1980). Indeed Fodor (1983) has even gone so far as to argue that in many cases the basic level of description is the one that is most naturally exposed in adult language use. On being asked to describe the scene of a lady walking a dog, a respondent is most likely to state seeing a lady walking a dog rather than 'A lady walking an animal' or 'A lady walking a silver-grey, miniature poodle bitch' (p. 96).

## Prototype models vs. exemplar-based models

It would be disingenuous to leave the discussion of the mental representation of concepts without a mention of **exemplar-based accounts**. Although there is a plethora of exemplar-based accounts (see Medin & Rips, 2005, for a review, and Shanks, 1997, for a discussion), all are united by the common assumption that there is no need to posit a mental representation of a category prototype. A fairly extreme exemplar view is that all of the evidence that has been amassed for the mental representations of category prototypes can be explained by accounts that merely assume that every exemplar that is encountered is stored in memory along with the appropriate category label. As Medin and Rips (2005) noted, parsimony suggests that there is no need to posit prototypes if stored instances can do the job (paraphrasing, p. 45). There are of course many vexed issues. Nonetheless, if we can do without stored representations of prototypes, and yet still account for all the data, then we should leave them out of our theories. Although a detailed discussion of the many issues would take us far from present concerns, one example is worth considering before we bring the discussion to a close. The example is taken from a recent review by Ashby and Maddox (2005).

Consider the idea that the human conceptual system is a psychological space much like the solar system. The individual planets correspond to category instances that are stored in the psychological space that makes up the human conceptual system – remember the multi-dimensional space for the bird category (as shown in Figure 12.10). By the prototype view, alongside the planets is the sun: the sun stands for our category prototype – it is the centre of our solar system. In contrast, according to the exemplar-based account, although the individual planets are represented, the sun (the category prototype) is not.

When a new planetary body is discovered, we have to decide whether it belongs to our solar system or not. According to prototype theory, to decide whether a new instance is part of our category, we have to judge whether it is closer to our category prototype than it is to any other category prototype. Exemplar-based accounts make different assumptions. For instance, category membership might be gauged by judging how close the new instance is to all instances of all categories. The new instance is then allocated to the category to whose members it is nearest overall. There are, though, many variations on this theme.

The main issue, over the years, has been how to test between these two general theories. In this regard, Ashby and Maddox (2005) noted that a recent study by Smith and Minda (2001) has provided some critical data. The issue relates to how category judgements change as new instances begin increasingly to resemble the category prototype. Again, think in terms of the solar system: now a meteor moves past Pluto, on the outer edge of the solar system, towards the sun. As the meteor steadily heads towards the sun it is getting closer to our category prototype but it is getting further and further away from the majority of other planets. From this analogy it becomes clear that the prototype and the exemplar-based accounts make different predictions about category judgements as new instances vary in their distance from the centre of the category. Without going into any further details, Smith and Minda (2001) found that the evidence from their experiments that tested these predictions favoured prototype theories over exemplar-based accounts.

Of course, this is not to argue that exemplar-based accounts are all fundamentally undermined by this result. On the contrary, it is true that, for some cases, in some situations, exemplar-based accounts fare better than prototype theories (Smith & Minda, 1998; Shanks, 1997). All that is being noted is that when certain critical predictions have been tested, the data favour prototype accounts. Much work is still needed therefore to understand what is really going on – perhaps we need to think in terms of hybrid accounts? The evidence is compelling for memory for particular instances (see Shanks, 1997, p. 117) and the evidence for mental prototypes is pretty convincing, so maybe some form of hybrid account will turn out to be the most parsimonious?

The present discussion draws to a close having just laid bare a fraction of the evidence for conceptual prototypes. It can be concluded that, even though none of the basic issues is resolved, there is an enormous amount of evidence that reveals sensitivities to category prototypes. Indeed as Rosch (1978) concluded, 'The persuasiveness of prototypes in real world categories and of prototypicality as a variable indicates that prototypes must have some place in psychological theories of representation, processing and learning' (p. 40). Indeed we will take these ideas a little further when we discuss language and its relations with the other faculties (in Chapter 14). If we posit some form of mental representation of a prototype then this will come in useful when we need to communicate thoughts about whole classes of instances.

## Pinpoint question 12.10

**What is one critical difference between exemplar-based and prototype theories?**

**prototype** An instance of a category that is most representative of the category. A mental prototype is the mental representation of a category's prototype.

**category prototype** A mental representation of the most representative member of a category.

**fuzzy boundaries** When it is impossible to draw a sharp division between where one concept begins and where another ends. When is an object a chair and when is it a stool?

**fuzzy concept** Concepts that do not have defining and necessary criteria for fixing the extension of the concept.

**family resemblance** An assessment of the extent to which all instances of a category possess certain attributes. Instances of a given category may only be so classified because they share a certain family resemblance to one another. They are similar in certain overall respects.

**basic level** According to Rosch, the primary level of entry in accessing semantic memory. 'Duck' rather than 'Bird', 'Duck' rather than 'Mallard'.

**featural diagnosticity** The degree to which a given feature is diagnostic of a given category. How diagnostic is 'beak' of the category 'birds'? (See also cue validity.)

**cue validity** The sum extent to which a given attribute (the cue) predicts membership of a given category.

**category cue validity** The degree to which a given category reflects a well-differentiated set of instances.

**exemplar-based accounts** Theories of the human conceptual system that posit that individual traces of every category instance are stored together with their category labels.

## Concluding comments

In the present chapter we have taken a glimpse into the area of research that has been focused on issues relating to that part of the human long-term memory system known as semantic memory, or alternatively, the human conceptual system. Many different perspectives on the nature of the internal representational system have been described and the discussion drew to a close with a more detailed look at Rosch's ideas about category prototypes and the putative structure of conceptual hierarchies. What the chapter has omitted to do, however, is convey the real tensions that exist in the literature between accepting that concepts are the building blocks of thought and also accepting that concepts are prototypes.

There is quite a lengthy thread in the literature that has dealt with issues in trying to marry these two competing propositions (Connolly et al., 2007; Jones, 1983; Fodor, 1994, 1998; Fodor & Lepore, 1992; Osherson & Smith, 1981, 1982; Zadeh, 1982). The fundamental problem has come to be known as the *pet fish problem* (Fodor, 1998). By the prototype account of concepts, each concept has an associated prototype together with an identification procedure that is invoked for classification processes. So think of a prototypical fish (trout, perhaps) and think of a prototypical pet (hamster, perhaps). On the assumption that complex concepts are merely the combination of their constituents, the problem is that we cannot put together trout and hamster to arrive at the concept of a PET FISH. Critical here is the idea that goldfish is neither the prototypical pet nor the prototypical fish yet it is the prototypical exemplar of the PET FISH category. Being able to predict what the prototypical PET FISH is cannot be based on some combined measure of the similarity of goldfish to the PET category and of its similarity to the FISH category – goldfish is far from being the prototypical member of either category. So grasping the concept PET FISH conflicts with the simple mental chemistry account of combining the concepts (i.e., prototypes) of PET and FISH to arrive at the complex concept PET FISH. Something else is therefore going on when we understand complex concepts and this is very different from merely combining the prototypes of the underlying constituents.

So the evidence for conceptual prototypes is compelling, and the evidence for mental problem solving is overwhelming, yet there does not appear to be any obvious way in which the two can be fitted together. Moreover, it is totally unclear how these problems will be resolved in the future. You may wish to step forward at this point . . .

## CHAPTER SUMMARY

- Certain classification systems are organised hierarchically in which smaller (subordinate) categories are combined to form larger (superordinate) categories. Such schemes have been taken to reflect how the human conceptual system is organised.

- The term 'concept' can relate to a group of objects 'out there' in the real world or to a form of mental representation. This chapter focused on how concepts are represented in the mind. A useful distinction is between a concept's extension and its intension. Concepts are understood with respect to examples of that class of item (extension) and also what the defining properties of that class of item are (intension). It is assumed that the human conceptual system is based on a representational system that captures the intensions of concepts.

- Various different forms of representational systems have been discussed in the literature and the present treatment begins with a discussion of propositions and how propositions can be organised into propositional networks. Propositional networks have been primarily concerned with representing mental structures that are invoked in the understanding of natural language. The relationship between propositional networks and semantic networks is explored. Semantic networks (Quillian, 1968; Collins & Quillian, 1969) provide one way to represent the organisation of knowledge regarding categories of real-world instances. Biological taxonomies have featured heavily in this work. With semantic networks, categories are represented hierarchically, with more general categories at the top of the hierarchy giving way to more specific categories at the bottom of the hierarchy. Categories lower down the hierarchy inherit the properties of categories higher up the hierarchy. However, empirical predictions on the basis of semantic network structure are not always borne out.

- In contrast, featural models (Smith et al., 1974) propose that items can be defined relative to specific values on a number of perceptual or semantic dimensions. Multi-dimensional scaling is used to represent the similarity between items via proximity in space. Rips et al. (1973) supported the idea that similarity in dimensional space accounted for the ability to verify sentences like 'a robin is a bird' as true or false, although potential confounds such as item familiarity have obscured any definitive evidence.

- Despite the apparent differences between network and featural models, both make appeals to semantic features/semantic primitives. These may be understood as some sort of basic building block with which all concepts can be decomposed and described. Various different perspectives on the nature of semantic features/primitives are considered. Is every instance of every concept represented by the entire set of primitives or are other possibilities more plausible? What are these semantic primitives really like? If we are to discuss the atoms of meaning then maybe we have to accept that it may not be possible to express what exactly these are in natural language. Maybe we should just accept that the atoms of meaning are semantic micro-features couched at some sub-symbolic level?

- Ideas relating to semantic relatedness, however, have persisted and evidence has been provided that supports the idea that processing facilitation can occur for a target word preceded by a prime word, when that word pair is not associatively related but is semantically related (McRae & Boisvert, 1998). Specifically, the shared number of features between items seems to be key in the organisation of semantic memory. Maybe semantic memory captures the category relations between instances as well as their featural commonalities? Semantic memory is more than a simple associative network.

- Researchers also make the distinction between localist and distributed models of semantic memory. For localist models, concepts are located in unique places in memory. For **distributed models of semantic memory**, concepts are defined relative to the total activation across the entire network at any one time.

- Connectionist (or parallel-distributed processing – PDP) accounts of semantic memory contain aspects of both localist and distributed models. PDP networks – which mimic semantic networks – consist of a layer of input units typically representing items (canary) and relations (can), a layer of hidden units, and a layer of output units representing attributes (fly). Such networks can be taught to produce correct outputs for particular inputs. The aim of a connectionist network is to reduce the discrepancy between the desired and actual output units by adjusting the thresholds of individual units and the weights between units (collectively known as coefficients).

- Category prototypes have also been introduced as a way of talking about how information related to real-world objects is organised. While certain members of a category might be more representative of that category than others, it is likely that all members of a category share family resemblance in that common attributes arise out of the consideration of a number of category examples.

- Prototypes are also integrated into a discussion of mental taxonomies (Rosch, 1978). Similar to the hierarchical network models of Collins and Quillian (1969), taxonomies have both a vertical dimension differing in terms of inclusiveness and a horizontal dimension in which categories are divided at the same level of inclusiveness. There are prototypes at each level of the taxonomy and also a basic level at which the clustering of category instances is more natural.

- The contrast between exemplar-based accounts and prototype accounts was discussed briefly and both the advantages and limitations of mental prototypes were mentioned.

---

**distributed models of semantic memory** The idea that concepts are defined relative to the current pattern of activation across an entire network of processing units at any one time.

---

## ANSWERS TO PINPOINT QUESTIONS

12.1  The intension of a concept refers, essentially, to its definition, whereas the extension of a concept refers to all possible instances to which the description applies.

12.2  Sharks are not listed as being able to breathe or swim as a result of cognitive economy. However, sharks belong to the superordinate category of 'fish' (all of whom can swim), and fish belong to the superordinate category of 'animal' (all of whom can breathe). Therefore this information can be recovered via the process of property inheritance.

12.3  'Rugby balls are oval shaped' should be responded to faster than 'Rugby balls contain air' because all of the information in the former sentence can be retrieved from a single node at the level of the rugby ball itself.

12.4 Featural models organise items according to values along several so-called semantic dimensions. Semantic networks organise items hierarchically and in terms of set/sub-set relations.

12.5 'David Bowie' in response to 'Rock Gods' would be an example of instance dominance, whereas responding 'Rock Gods' to the 'David Bowie' would be an example of category dominance.

12.6 Primes and targets were selected such that they very rarely occurred as being associates of one another in the associative norming stage of the experiment.

12.7 One concept, one relation and multiple attributes could be activated at any one time.

12.8 Localist approaches to representation are apparent in the Rumelhart & Todd (1993) model in that there is a unique unit for each particular category instance (canary), particular relation (can) and particular attribute (fly). Aligned to this are distributed patterns of activations that obtain on the hidden units. Moreover, distributed input and output patterns are being associated in the model.

12.9 A boundary becomes fuzzy when there are no clear distinctions between the instances of one category and another.

12.10 Exemplar-based theories do not assume that a mental representation of a prototype is derived and stored.

# OBJECT RECOGNITION

## CHAPTER CONTENTS

You're pretty sure it's some time in between 4 and 5 in the morning, possibly Tuesday. You've just come back from Hawaii where your best friend was getting married and are currently waiting in the passport control line at London Gatwick. You are wearing shorts and a t-shirt. It is 14 December. Although your current lobster complexion does not quite match the pasty features staring out from your passport, the officer lets you back into the country anyway.

# But mine was small, grey and shiny as well
## Disputes at baggage carousel number 6

Once you've managed to make the complex association between the combination of numbers and letters that was your flight and the baggage carousel number, you now stand – trolley in hand – waiting for your bag to be returned, the first step in a long line of events that will eventually lead back to your soft and warm bed. After an interminable wait, a number of rectangular objects start making their way round the carousel as individuals jostle for position. Suddenly you spy your case making its entry back into the country. Small? Check. Grey? Yup. A bit shiny? But of course. Making a bee-line for the edge of the carousel you see someone in front of you examining your case in a rather personal manner and start to lift it off the conveyor. Taking matters into your own hands, you tackle the individual resulting in two sun-burnt tourists wrestling on the carousel pulling for supremacy over the suitcase. 'Oi mate! This is my case! Look – it's got me initials on it.' And sure enough, you look down to see JD painted on the case, which were, as far as the customs officer was concerned, definitely not your initials. You look up to see your luggage coming round the corner with the 'Aloha from Hawaii' sticker you remember buying at the airport, thinking it would help distinguish it from every other small, grey and shiny case you saw. If you could turn any redder, you would.

## REFLECTIVE QUESTIONS

1. Think about a visual domain in which you'd consider yourself fairly knowledgeable. This could be recognising different kinds of meat after working in a butcher's, or learning about different types of knot after a sailing class. How do you find yourself categorising this information in your head? When talking to other people, are you using the same level of description you would use if you were talking to another individual with the same expertise? If not, how has this changed?

2. Take a bunch of everyday objects and lay them out on a table. Look at how you have arranged each object in turn. Is there anything special about this kind of orientation relative to your viewpoint? What information about the object is it giving you? Could you move the object to make it more or less obvious what it is? What visual information changes when this is so?

## Introduction and preliminary considerations

This chapter deals with visual object recognition. We look at the world and we recognise the things that populate it. We'll see how object recognition can take the form of classification (registering suitcase rather than pushchair) or identification (registering your particular case) and how expertise influences the way in which we interpret the world around us. How do the train spotter and the ordinary commuter differ in their train recognition abilities? We'll also get to grips with various theories about how object recognition is actually performed. One idea to come out of these theories is that objects are sometimes easier to recognise when viewed from certain angles of regard rather than others. Would you have walked off with JD's case had it been turned over, proudly displaying your 'Aloha from Hawaii' sticker on the front? Probably not. We'll also examine the role of context in object recognition and ask whether a suitcase is more easily spotted than a steering wheel on a luggage reclaim carousel. Yes, cognitive psychologists really have engaged with questions like these.

More specifically, when cognitive psychologists refer to 'object recognition', what they are typically referring to is the ability of humans to recognise familiar, concrete things, such as items of furniture, vehicles, fruits and vegetables, etc. In testing this ability in the laboratory, very particular (and perhaps very peculiar) tasks have been used. For instance, in **speeded classification tasks** a picture of a thing is shown and the participant has to decide quickly whether or not it belongs to a certain category – 'Is this is bird?' Yes/No. Alternatively, **speeded naming tasks** have been used in which the same picture is shown but participants now have to blurt its name out quickly – 'Bird!' Clearly, therefore, what is typically discussed under the title 'object recognition' is rather narrowly defined both in terms of experimental methods and the type of stimuli used.

Outside a police interrogation room, it is very difficult to think of any experimental cases where a person has been placed in a room with an actual object and is then asked to identify it ('Is this *your* pick axe, madam?'). There are some cases, in the cognitive psychology literature, where people have been tested with actual objects, but here we are talking about tests of recognition memory for bent pieces of wire and strange curved surfaces. Possibly not the most exciting of scenarios, but, nevertheless, such tasks formed the basis of the influential work of Rock and colleagues,

and we will consider this in due course. More typically, however, object recognition has been examined in terms of people's abilities to name or classify real-world objects depicted in some form of drawing.

Indeed cognitive psychologists (e.g., Snodgrass & Vanderwart, 1980) have even gone so far as to generate sets of line drawings of common objects and then collect from a large sample of participants various ratings for these particular drawings. How familiar is the depicted object? Does everyone agree about how the depicted object is named? Are they a pair of pants? Or maybe trousers? Even chinos? How many syllables has the object's name? It is because such quantitative measures of these materials have been derived that they have been used repeatedly in studies of object recognition. Using these line drawings means that it is easy to control for any unwanted variation in factors that are incidental to processes of object recognition. For instance, let's assume that you want to measure object recognition using a speeded naming task and what you discover is that, on average, people name a pen quicker than a typewriter. On the basis of this result, you may want to conclude that it is easier to recognise a pen than a typewriter, but if you think a little harder this is probably not a very safe conclusion to draw. 'Pen' is just easier to say than 'Typewriter'!

Although many benefits accrue from using well-controlled materials such as the Snodgrass and Vanderwart (1980) line drawings, the drawbacks are appreciable as well. For instance, line drawings really are very unlike the actual objects they depict, and because of this, two-dimensional (2D) line drawing recognition may provide a rather limited understanding of three-dimensional (3D) object recognition. Just how sensible is it to draw conclusions about object recognition from cases where a frail pensioner is handed a postcard with a line drawing of an accordion on it and asked, 'And what do you call this, Irene?' With the advent of more sophisticated technology, however, things are improving slightly because more realistic photographic and indeed holographic material is becoming available.

We shall examine the more typical experimental literature as the discussion proceeds. Other relevant material will also be covered, and because of this, the term 'object' will be interpreted rather liberally to include not only natural and man-made things but also computer-generated avatars (fictional characters), faces, patches of colour, gratings, etc. As will become clear, the discussion will also cover aspects of perceptual processing and aspects of mental representation that we have already touched upon in previous chapters (see Chapters 6 and 7). The fundamental questions concern how objects are coded by the perceptual system and how they are represented in long-term memory. Quite a lot of effort has been expended in trying to establish the degree to which object recognition is constrained by the manner in which information is stored in the human processing system. Yet again, therefore, we will need to confront the recurrent issue of trying to tie down the degree to which what we know about the world determines our perceptions of it. To begin, though, it is perhaps best to try to define some key terms and provide a general framework for thinking about object recognition.

> **speeded classification tasks** Reaction time paradigms in which participants are required to respond, on each trial, as to whether a stimulus belongs to a certain designated category or not (e.g. 'Is it man-made?').

> **speeded naming tasks** Reaction time paradigms in which participants are required to respond, on each trial, verbally with the name of the stimuli.

## A general framework for thinking about object recognition

Although there are many different accounts of object recognition, the majority share the following critical assumptions. Following the registration of the stimulus at the senses, some form of internal representation of the *proximal stimulus* (i.e., the stimulation of the senses)

is generated – let us call this the perceptual representation (see Chapter 6). The **distal object** (i.e., the object that is out there in the world) is then recognised when a match is secured between the perceptual representation of the proximal stimulus and some form of stored counterpart (see Figure 13.1). Although this might sound relatively uncontentious, as we shall see, not all accounts accept this idea and even fewer accept the following. In Chapter 6, evidence was set out that supports the possibility that the perceptual representation comprises a description of the proximal stimulus. The contingent idea is that long-term memory comprises, in part, a kind of mental library that contains listings of entries that are themselves descriptions of real-world objects. So 'to recognise your suitcase' means to secure a match between the derived perceptual representation and its stored description (see Edelman, 1999, p. 11).

## Sorting out 'recognition', 'identification' and 'classification'

Although the terminology is slippery, let us draw some distinctions between **recognition**, **identification** and **classification** so as to aid the exposition. Here 'identification' means to identify a given instance uniquely as a particular thing – this mug is Philip's mug. To classify something means to assign a stimulus to a particular category, for example, to conclude that this thing is a mug. Unfortunately, sometimes the term 'recognition' is used interchangeably with 'identification' and 'classification'. Part of the reason for this is that it is possible to recognise something as being a member of a particular category – this thing I'm

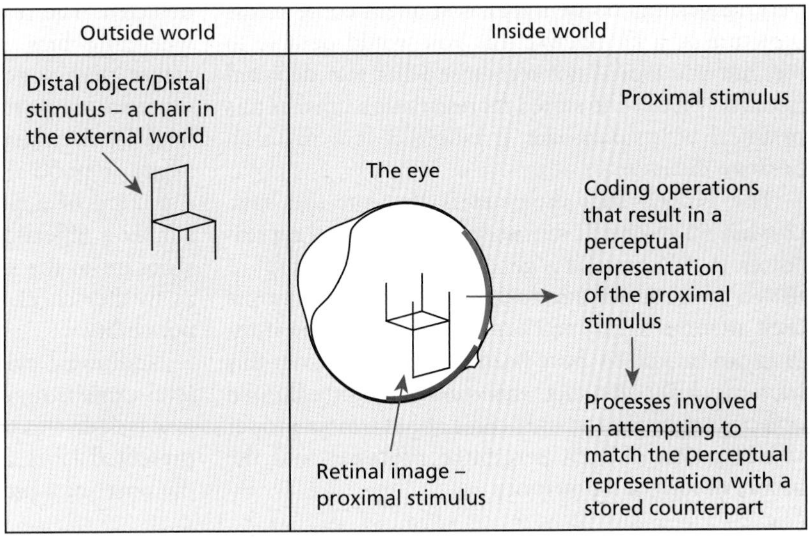

**Figure 13.1 Important distinctions in discussing object recognition** Distal objects refer to entities 'out there' in the real world. The information that we receive at our senses related to this object is known as the proximal stimulus. We then work on the proximal stimulus to form a perceptual representation. Recognition in this account is achieved when the perceptual representation of the proximal stimulus is matched with a stored counterpart.

| Outside world | Inside world |
|---|---|
| Distal object/Distal stimulus – a chair in the external world | Proximal stimulus<br><br>The eye<br><br>Coding operations that result in a perceptual representation of the proximal stimulus<br><br>Processes involved in attempting to match the perceptual representation with a stored counterpart<br><br>Retinal image – proximal stimulus |

currently holding is a mug – or as being a particular exemplar of a category – this thing I'm currently holding is Philip's mug.

In terms of theory, to recognise this stimulus you see before you as being your mug, you must secure a match between the perceptual representation of what you see with the stored description of your mug. On other occasions, though, you may only be able to recognise that this thing is a mug without being able to recognise it as being a particular mug with which you are familiar. Under these circumstances, you *categorise* the perceptual representation as being of a mug rather than any other form of crockery. The assumption in this case is that a match is being secured between the perceptual representation of the stimulus and the general category level description of MUG. (A much more detailed account of these ideas is included later.)

For completely novel objects (i.e., objects that have never before been encountered), the theory is less clear. Classifying a novel thing as belonging to a superordinate category, such as 'it is man-made' or 'it is an animal', may be quite straightforward. So if it walks, crawls, swims or flies (in a biologically plausible manner), it is most probably an animal. Some forms of interpretation are possible even though there is no stored internal description of the particular instance because it has never before been encountered. Under such circumstances, it is quite possible to be able to see something but not recognise what it is, and so the distinction between seeing and recognising is germane here (see Chapter 6). According to the theory, recognition only occurs when a match is made between the current perceptual representation and its stored counterpart. Since novel objects have no stored counterpart they cannot be identified. You might come across a picture of a *Flandrewke* that you would be able to see, but you would not recognise what was depicted because you have no stored representation of what this mythical beast looks like, if indeed it is a mythical beast at all . . .

The general idea therefore is that on the basis of what we receive at our senses, a perceptual representation of a stimulus is generated and an attempt to match this representation with a stored counterpart is then attempted. If a match is achieved, then the stimulus can be said to 'have been recognised'. Given this framework for thinking, then understanding human object recognition can only come about from a proper consideration of both perceptual processes and the nature of long-term memory.

**Pinpoint question 13.1**

**What is the difference between classification and identification?**

**distal object** An object 'out there' in the real world.

**recognition** The cognitive processes involved in classification or identification.

**identification** Recognition of a stimulus as being of a particular unique type.

**classification** The assignment of a stimulus to a mental category.

## The basic level advantage

In the previous chapter, little was given away about how the organisation of conceptual knowledge may relate to the ability to recognise objects. Clearly there is no necessary link between the two, but some early evidence provided by Rosch, Mervis et al. (1976) was interpreted as showing how object recognition may be influenced by the organisation of knowledge (i.e., the structure of human conceptual memory). Here the assumption is that conceptual knowledge is organised in an hierarchical fashion with superordinates at the top of the tree; at the next level are the basic level items and right at the bottom come the subordinates (see Figure 12.18 on page 458). In a speeded naming task, participants were presented with hard copies of pictures of real-world objects and were asked to write down, for each picture, the name of the thing depicted. The results were clear in showing an overwhelming bias to respond with basic level labels rather than superordinate or subordinate labels. In other words, participants wrote down 'dog' (the basic level label) rather than 'animal' (the superordinate label) or 'poodle' (the subordinate label) when shown a picture of a poodle. Moreover, this bias was not simply a reflection of the fact that participants were ignorant of the superordinate and subordinate labels as further checks were carried out to eliminate this possibility.

Additional evidence for the primacy of the basic level came from a separate speeded category verification task. In this case, and on a given trial, an auditory-presented label was presented immediately prior to the onset of a picture of a real-world entity. The task was to verify the correspondence between the label and the pictured referent; in other words, to respond 'Yes' if the picture of a dog followed the presentation of the label 'dog'. Now the results showed that participants were faster to respond on those trials when the picture was preceded by a basic level label (DOG) rather than by either a superordinate (ANIMAL) or a subordinate (POODLE) label.

Collectively this evidence was taken to reflect something that can be termed a **basic level advantage** (Jolicœur, Gluck & Kosslyn, 1984; Murphy & Wisniewski, 1989). The rather bold claim, attributed to Rosch, Mervis et al. (1976), is that there is a bias in the recognition system to carry out a match initially between a perceptual representation and a stored counterpart at the basic level. By this view, the basic level advantage arises because of the inherent bias of attempting to secure a match first between a given perceptual representation of a distal stimulus and the description of that stimulus couched at the basic level. As Tanaka and Taylor (1991) stated, 'people first identify objects at the basic level and then access the superordinate and subordinate categories' (p. 458; see also Jolicœur et al., 1984). In other words, first you recognise this thing as a mug and then you recognise it as your mug, and only then would it be safe to take a sip. The matching process operates initially at the level of basic level descriptions, and it is only subsequent to this that further comparisons are carried out at the subordinate level. Tanaka and Taylor (1991) called this the **basic first hypothesis** (p. 479).

Clearly there are many issues here. It is therefore perhaps best to stand back a little and try to get a better handle on what is being argued. Indeed, as Biederman, Subramaniam, Bar, Kalocsai and Fiser (1999) have pointed out, some caution is warranted over the basic effects because the data might be telling us more about the ease of naming and retrieving the names of basic level categories than about visual object recognition. The experimental effects, discussed so far, all relate to cases where verbal labels are being used but, clearly, everyday recognition occurs regardless of any verbalisation on the part of the observer. For example, it seems that you can effortlessly prepare and eat your breakfast without having constantly to name the egg, the toast, the tea, the cereal, etc. This is where a clear understanding of the experimental tasks is important in trying to appreciate exactly what has been shown. We are trying to understand object recognition, not verbal labelling, and in looking back over the literature there is a real issue about what the

experiments on 'object recognition' have really been telling us. Nevertheless, let us begin by taking the claims at face value and see where the evidence has led.

## The crude-to-fine framework reappears

The claims enshrined in the basic first hypothesis accord reasonably well with the crude-to-fine account of perception discussed in Chapter 6. There it was argued that the processes of stimulus analysis operate in a crude-to-fine manner. By that view, gross characteristics are recovered prior to the fine details. This is a claim about the nature of perceptual encoding, but the current ideas go further than this and stipulate that stimulus recognition proceeds from a crude to fine level. What is being argued is that Lucky is recognised as a dog prior to being recognised as your dog with the one eye and the three legs.

A perhaps subtle distinction is being drawn here: on the one hand, we have just discussed a claim about stimulus analysis proceeding from a crude-to-fine level. On the other hand, there is a claim about recognition proceeding from a crude to fine level. The process of securing a match between the input and its stored counterpart operates first at the basic (crude/category) level and then, possibly, further analysis is undertaken at the subordinate (fine/instance) level. Such claims are about how the categorisation of stimuli takes place, and this is what the basic first hypothesis is all about.

Although the processes of stimulus encoding and categorisation may be discussed independently from one another, these general ideas about crude-to-fine sequencing do go hand in hand. It may well be that because the initial perceptual representation only codes crude characteristics of the stimulus, such as its gross size and shape, then the categorisation process must proceed only on the basis of this information. On the basis of the currently available information the stimulus is clearly a dog but which dog, or what sort of dog it is, remains to be determined following further analysis. Couched thus, there is a certain logical consistency to the general crude-to-fine theoretical framework. Indeed, there is some intuitive appeal to these ideas especially when perception in the real world is considered. When walking across the park, it may be fairly obvious that there is a dog chasing a ball but at a distance it is not at all obvious what sort of dog it is. Similarly, in a department store you might primarily notice the jeans sections without being able to spot straight away whether the jeans you were looking at were boot-cut or loose-fit or skinny.

basic level advantage A bias in the human recognition system to match a perceptual representation to an internal representation existing at a basic level of categorisation.

basic first hypothesis The idea that perceptual representations have privileged access to basic level descriptions as a first step, after which superordinate and subordinate descriptions may be accessed.

## Further claims about the basic level advantage and perceptual processing

Despite the possibility of a very close coupling between perceptual analysis and accessing long-term memory, Fodor (1983) has made a very strong claim about the independence of the two. In Chapter 2 we saw that Fodor (1983) distinguished between *sensory transducers*, *input systems* and *central processors* (see Figure 5.1 on page 146 for a diagrammatic illustration of these differences). The sensory transducers are the sense organs, and are responsible for taking the proximal stimulus and converting this into a basic sensory code. This coding then acts as the input to the corresponding input system. The input systems operate as the interface between the sensory transducers and the central processors. They deliver to the central processors (what amounts to) the best first guess of what the distal stimulus is that gave rise to the sensory stimulation. The final decision, about what the distal stimulus may actually be, is made by the central processors.

By this view, perceptual processing (which is undertaken by the sensory transducers and input modules) operates quite independently of the knowledge that is accessed by the central processors. Perceptual processing is, essentially, stimulus driven. More particularly, in discussing the operation of input modules, Fodor (1983) argued that the perceptual representation generated from the sensory input captures a description of the proximal stimulus at the basic level. That is, the input modules deliver outputs that provide descriptions of basic level categorisations. For example, the output from the visual input module specifies 'dog' rather than 'poodle' or 'animal'. It is this form of representation that is used as a key to access information stored in long-term memory.

This view, however, is not without its critics (see Marshall, 1984, p. 224; Putnam, 1984, p. 262), and

because of this it is necessary to examine the relevant empirical evidence carefully. What we have here, though, are statements about how the perceptual representation of a stimulus is derived from the bottom up. There is stimulation at the sense organs, next there is some form of sensory encoding (carried out by the sensory transducers) and then the input modules come into play. The input modules produce a representation of the stimulus that codes its basic level status: DOG rather than ANIMAL or POODLE, SPOON rather than KITCHEN UTENSIL or SOUP LADLE, NEWSPAPER rather than PRINTED MATERIAL or YESTERDAY'S EDITION OF THE *NEW YORK TIMES*. The perceptual representation then acts as the best first-guess approximation to what is out there in the real world.

All of the foregoing provides a description of the operation of the perceptual system and a basic claim here is that perceptual processing operates quite independently of, and is not influenced in any way by, stored knowledge. So the perceptual system is able to derive a best first-guess representation of DOG without having made access with any stored knowledge about dogs. In this way the perceptual system operates in an essentially bottom-up fashion. The perceptual representation, which is produced as an output from the perceptual system, is then fed forwards to the central processors. These take the perceptual representation and make a final decision about what object is actually out there on the basis of stored knowledge.

The modularity account, as just described, accords well with the evidence cited above for the basic first hypothesis. By this view what the input modules do is produce perceptual representations that are couched at the basic level and it is these that are used to access stored knowledge. Such a view fits perfectly with the framework for thinking about object recognition described at the beginning of the chapter, namely that the derived perceptual representation must be matched against a stored counterpart in order that the distal stimulus be recognised.

More particularly, the idea is that the perceptual representation in some sense makes contact or accesses information stored in long-term memory, and when a match is secured, then the stimulus is recognised. Here the idea of the **entry point level** is important (Jolicœur et al., 1984, p. 273). What the entry point level refers to is where in the conceptual hierarchy the first point of contact is made between the perceptual representation and a relevant long-term memory representation. As we have already seen, there is evidence to suggest that, according to the basic first hypothesis, the first point of contact is at the basic level (Rosch, Mervis et al., 1976).

Although this operates as a useful working hypothesis, exceptions to this general default were discussed by Rosch, Mervis et al. (1976) and we will turn to these in a moment. Quite independently, though, other contrasting data were reported by Jolicœur et al. (1984). Here the experiments were guided by the intuition that atypical category members may be identified first at the subordinate level rather than at the basic level. For example, a picture of a penguin may actually be first classified as showing a penguin rather than a bird.

To test this idea, Jolicœur et al. (1984) ran a speeded naming task in which, on each trial, a picture of a category instance was presented and participants were merely asked to name out loud the instance shown. Two types of categories were tested. 'Basic low' categories were where the basic level was situated at the exemplar level. So the category FRUIT acts as a superordinate for various basic level sub-categories such as APPLE, PEAR and ORANGE. In contrast, 'basic high' categories were defined such that now the basic level was situated at the level of the category label itself such as BIRD, BOAT and CAR. Within both of these categories typical and atypical category instances were generated.

The results of the study were generally in line with the initial intuitions. A central result was that participants were actually quicker to provide a subordinate label for an atypical item from a 'basic high' category than they were to provide a basic level label for it. Participants were quicker to name a *penguin* as a 'penguin' than they were to name a *penguin* as a 'bird'. Jolicœur et al. (1984) therefore questioned the claim that invariably the entry point level for recognition was at the basic level. The contrary view was that different entry points exist for atypical and typical category instances. For atypical instances the entry point level is situated at the subordinate and not the basic level, since the bias is to recognise a *penguin* as a 'penguin' rather than a 'bird'. In contrast, for typical instances the basic level operates as the entry point level as a *robin* is recognised as a 'bird' first and a 'robin' second.

**entry point level** The primary point of contact between a perceptual representation and a long-term memory representation during the process of object recognition.

## The basic level advantage and expertise

Clearly the evidence from the Jolicœur et al. (1984) study fits rather uncomfortably with the general claim about the basic level always operating as the entry point level. However, in setting out the basic first hypothesis, Rosch, Mervis et al. (1976) were open to the possibility that recognition abilities may depend rather critically upon the level of expertise of the observer. Successful pig breeders are clearly able to discern which are the good sows to buy at market yet for most of us we would not know where to begin. Clearly, looking for a pink, curly-tailed thing would be a start upon arrival, but as to their breeding capacity we would be at a loss. Upon reflection, it would be odd for the recognition system to operate in such a way that prior entry always takes place at the basic level especially when an expert possesses so much more knowledge about a particular domain than the novice.

Indeed, in addressing this issue, Tanaka and Taylor (1991) had experts and novices engage in a *feature norming study* (see Chapter 12). Twelve dog and twelve bird experts were asked to provide feature lists of various category and instance labels. With cases of which the participants had no expert knowledge, the pattern of results was the same as that reported by Rosch, Mervis et al. (1976). The most features were provided for basic level cases and fewer were provided for subordinate and superordinate cases. Critically, though, a different pattern emerged when the participants were listing features for cases relevant to their expertise. So the dog experts provided more features for the subordinate dog cases (poodle, beagle) than the basic level dog case. Similarly the bird experts provided more features for the subordinate bird cases (robin, jay) than the basic level bird case.

More provocative data came from a **category verification study**. As before, a category or instance label was initially presented and immediately replaced by a picture of a category instance. Participants had to make a speeded judgement as to whether the label and picture matched. Dog and bird experts acted as the participants. Critically, when the experts were

**Pinpoint question 13.2**

According to Jolicœur et al. (1984), why would a whale be easier to identify as a whale rather than a mammal?

responding to items with which they were relatively unfamiliar, then there was a clear basic level advantage – participants were quicker to verify pictures following basic level labels than either superordinate or subordinate labels. However, when participants were responding to items in their area of expertise, the basic level advantage was abolished. Now participants were as quick to respond following a subordinate label as they were to respond after a basic level label.

Evidence such as this (see also Johnson & Mervis, 1997) can be used to argue against both the generality of basic first hypothesis and the Roschian view of conceptual structure. From Rosch's work, the understanding was that conceptual hierarchies are organised such that one level is basic and that subsidiary to this level are various superordinate and subordinate levels. Against this, however, the later data fit more comfortably with a much more malleable view of the knowledge store. In this regard, Murphy and Brownell (1985) discussed something called the **category differentiation hypothesis**. According to this, categories can change as a result of experience and expertise – they can become more distinctive, and in the limit, subordinate categories may in and of themselves come to operate as basic level categories. Whereas to the novice all pigs look the same, to the pig breeder even fine distinctions between different Gloucestershire Old Spots are quite apparent.

From this perspective it is a mistake to assume there is only one basic level in a given taxonomy. What operates as the basic level, in any particular case, may be determined by the level of expertise of the observer. Indeed, as Johnson and Mervis (1997) argued, one signature of the expert is the ability to attend to 'different and more subtle perceptual features than novices do' (p. 274). This is not to argue that the basic level loses its significance, but merely that subordinate levels can begin to behave like a basic category given the necessary experience. As Murphy and Brownell (1985) stated, 'each category may fall on a continuum of differentiation rather than on a dichotomy of basic and non-basic categories' (p. 82).

## Experts and 'experts'

The studies just cited – by Johnson and Mervis (1997) and Tanaka and Taylor (1991) – examined the performance of people who were clearly experts in their chosen field, that is, dog breeders and bird watchers. Such expertise is typically built up over many years; for instance, and as Gauthier and Tarr (1997, p. 1674) noted, it takes ten years with a particular breed to become a dog judge. Perhaps because of such constraints, other claims about the recognition abilities of 'experts' come from laboratory-based studies in which undergraduates have undergone some form of training. Performance pre- and post-training is compared and claims are then made about how such training impacts on recognition abilities. Indeed, one would hope that after being at university, undergraduates would be a little closer to being an expert in at least one particular domain relative to when they arrived!

A recent study provides a good example of this sort of experiment. Tanaka, Curran and Sheinberg (2005) trained undergraduates to become experts in recognising pictures of birds. One group of participants learnt to categorise pictures of owls at the basic level (elf owl = 'owl', saw-whet owl = 'owl') and pictures of wading birds at the subordinate level (green heron = 'green heron', purple sandpiper = 'purple sandpiper'). Learning about wading birds at the subordinate level meant that participants were having to distinguish between different kinds of wading birds. In this way, Tanaka et al. (2005) were training this group to become experts at recognising wading birds, but not experts in owls. In the interests of counterbalancing the design, a different group learnt to categorise wading birds at the basic level and owls at the subordinate level. However, all participants were exposed to ten different species of owls and ten different species of wading birds.

Training was carried out over seven consecutive days and, across the days, participants were given various speeded naming and speeded classification tasks. As expected, average response speeds decreased over the days for all tasks and, interestingly, the basic level advantage still obtained even after training. For instance, participants were faster to name the pictures as owls/wading birds than they were to provide subordinate labels (e.g., elf owl, green heron) even after the training period. In this case therefore the functional significance of the basic level was robust despite the very directed training.

More critically, though, are the particular effects of expertise training. To assess expertise, a discrimination task was used in which on each trial a pair of sequential images of individual birds was presented and the participant had to decide whether the instances were taken from the same species or not. Three conditions were administered: (i) old instances/old species, (ii) new instances/old species, and (iii) new instances/new species. Condition (i) simply tested the participants' ability to discriminate the previously exposed material. Here the data showed that participants' discrimination performance improved for both basic and subordinate training regimes but the improvement was particularly marked following subordinate training. So if you were given subordinate training on wading birds, your ability to discriminate a great blue heron from a little blue heron improved dramatically. In contrast, if you were given basic level training on wading birds, then there was only some improvement in being able to discriminate between members of the different wading bird species.

Subordinate level training also conferred a marked ability to be able to discriminate new members of the old species in condition (ii). Again, if trained on subordinate categories of wading birds, then your ability to discriminate between new members of the now familiar wading bird species was markedly better than if you had only received basic level training on the wading birds. Finally, in condition (iii), if given subordinate training on wading birds your ability to discriminate new members of unfamiliar wading bird species was also better than if given only basic level training on wading birds. These final results were taken to show the benefits of subordinate training through (a) improvements in being able to discriminate new instances of already familiar species and (b) improvements in being able to discriminate new instances of related but unfamiliar species – having been trained on green herons the participants were better able to discriminate whooping cranes and snowy egrets.

The more far-reaching claims were that subordinate training 'selectively tuned participants' perceptions of color, shape and texture cues that were specific to the species' (Tanaka et al., 2005, p. 150). Again, therefore, here is the claim that one signature of expertise relates to perceptual encoding: experts are far more adept at picking up the finer details that can be used to discriminate selectively between instances of different categories than are novices. So jean designers would be able to spot a boot-fit cut from a loose-fit cut remarkably easily.

Further supportive evidence for this general conclusion comes from another recent study by Archambault, O'Donnell and Schyns (1999). They addressed the effect that training might have on the basic level advantage. Initially participants were exposed to images of objects in isolation and were trained to classify these objects either at the basic level – 'This is a computer' – or at a subordinate level – 'This is Peter's computer'. Participants were trained so that they were completely familiarised with a set of images of computers and mugs – two sets of objects that surely make up the

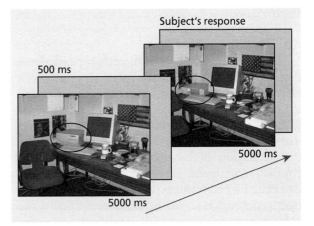

**Figure 13.2 Examples of the interchanging images used by Archambault et al. (1999) in their experiment on change-blindness**
The image sequence was iterated until participants perceived the change and reported it.
*Source*: Archambault, A., O'Donnell, C., & Schyns, P. G. (1999). Blind to object changes: When learning the same object at different levels of categorization modifies its perception. *Psychological Science, 10*, 249–255 (fig. 2, p. 251). Reproduced with permission from Blackwell Publishers Ltd.

backbone of any successful psychology laboratory. As in the Tanaka et al. (2005) study, half the participants were trained to distinguish the computers at the basic level and the mugs at the subordinate level, while the remaining participants were trained at the basic level for mugs and the subordinate level for computers. Now the same objects were used in a change blindness experiment (see Chapter 6). Figure 13.2 shows the typical office scene used in the experiments and provides an example of the alternating images used on one trial in the experiment. The pairs of images were alternated repeatedly until the participant could report what change had been introduced across the two images. The number of iterations to detect the change was the measure of interest.

Various change trials were tested:

1. a mug change – in which two different mugs were shown in the two images;
2. a computer change – in which two different computers were shown in the two images;
3. a mug disappearance – in which the mug was removed from one image;
4. a computer disappearance – in which the computer was removed from one image; and
5. another object disappearance – in which a different object was removed from one image.

Performance was gauged both as a function of the initial training regime and the type of change introduced in the images.

Regardless of training, an object disappearance was detected very quickly. However, of much more import were the findings relating to changes introduced to the mugs and the computers. Now training had a critical effect. Put simply, participants trained to make discriminations of objects at the subordinate level detected change in those objects very rapidly, be they computers or mugs. However, they were unable to detect rapidly any change relating to objects that they had learnt to classify at the basic level. Indeed such changes were only noticed after a relatively large number of image iterations.

Archambault et al. (1999) used these data to argue that 'the level of categorization at which an object is learned can affect its visual encoding and perception' (p. 254). One implication is that if a person is forced to make fine discriminations between different instances of the same category when learning about those instances, this will ensure that the next time a now familiar instance is encountered, a much more detailed representation of its features will be picked up. → See 'What have we learnt?', below.

## Pinpoint question 13.3

According to Tanaka et al. (2005), what are the advantages of learning at a subordinate level?

## → What have we learnt?

Various claims have been made about the differences between the recognition abilities of experts and novices. Despite the particularities, it is possible to distinguish general claims about perception from claims about conception. On the one hand, it is argued that the perceptual encoding of the stimuli changes as the process of becoming an expert unfolds. On the other hand, it is argued that the nature of the conceptual system changes as novices develop into experts. By the perceptual view, the signature of expertise is that a more detailed perceptual representation of the stimulus is derived or a more particular representation is derived because the expert has learnt to attend to critical features that discriminate between exemplars of different categories. By the conceptual view, claims are made about changes in the long-term representations of categories – the representation of subordinate categories become enriched and begin to take on the attributes of basic level categories. Of course, aspects of both could be true. Further discussion of these possibilities is contained in the next chapter, when inter-relations between perception, conception and language are examined. For now, it is important to continue to focus more narrowly on object recognition. Although we will consider more elaborate cases towards the end of the chapter, the discussion will adopt the standard approach and merely consider the recognition of single objects in isolation.

## Research focus 13.1

### Knowing your plonk from your plink: what makes a wine expert?

You'll notice that the prevailing wind in cognitive psychology is to focus on visual and, to a lesser extent, auditory phenomena. However, our discussion of expertise allows us to tackle olfactory (smell) sensations and perhaps more importantly the subject of booze. Now most of us like a drop of red or white now and then, but usually our interest in wine extends to detecting an empty bottle. Parr, Heatherbell and White (2002) decided to tackle the topic in a more systematic manner and look at exactly what it is that makes a wine expert.

Twenty-two adults were studied – 11 wine experts and 11 wine novices. Both groups were matched for age, gender, diet and smoking status. The wine experts were categorised as such on the basis of being either a winemaker, wine researcher, wine professional, graduate student in viticulture and oenology, or simply people with more than ten years' involvement with wine. Participants took part in a variety of cognitive tests including an old/new recognition test. Participants were exposed to 12 odours (included 'ripe or rotting fruit/apple', 'grape-like/foxy' and 'earthy/musty/mouldy') in a study phase and then asked, in a test phase, to categorise 24 odours as having been previously presented at study (i.e., old) or not (i.e., new). Identification was also tested for each odour, with participants attempting to recall the label of the odour presented at study.

Wine experts were significantly better at categorising the odours as old or new relative to wine novices; however, the groups failed to differ on the ability to identify the semantic labels for the various smells. The relationship between categorisation and identification was less clear, with certain smells such as vanilla/oak being easy to recognise but hard to identify, and other odours such as floral/rose being harder to recognise but easier to identify.

Parr et al. (2002) concluded that, since wine experts showed greater odour recognition in the absence of showing greater odour identification, then the superiority of expertise in this domain is perceptual in nature. In fact, the authors appealed to the idea of 'verbal overshadowing' in the absence of expertise (Melcher & Schooler, 1996), in that learning the verbal labels for odour might actually make you remember the name but not the smell. So in order to become a wine expert, it seems as though you really must 'follow your nose' rather than anything else.

*Source*: Parr, W. V., Heatherbell, D., & White, G. (2002). Demystifying wine expertise: Olfactory threshold, perceptual skill and semantic memory in expert and novice wine judges. *Chemical Senses, 27*, 747–755.

**category verification study** A paradigm in which participants are asked to respond whether or not a category label and category instance match.

**category differentiation hypothesis** The idea that the organisation of categories can change as a result of expertise. Categories become more distinctive from one another.

## Further issues and controversies in visual object recognition

We'll begin the next section with a nice bold statement: to recognise an object is to recognise its shape. According to Pizlo and Salach-Golyska (1995), 'Shape is defined . . . conventionally as the property of the contour of a figure or the surface of an object that does not change under translation, rotation, and size scaling' (p. 692). If something like shape constancy were not operating, then the perceptual experience of a receding object would be that it diminishes in size. Pizlo and Salach-Golyska (1995, p. 692) also explained that 'Perception of shapes of objects involves making inferences about the three-dimensional (3-D) shape of an object on the basis of its 2-D retinal image (or several images)' (see Chapter 5 for more on the notion of *perceptual inferences*). To appreciate the difficult nature of this problem, it should be remembered that the 2D image is both a function of the shape of the object and the angle of regard (i.e., the physical point of view of the observer).

Take a round coin out of your pocket and place it on the table. Under a physical description, the shape of the coin is a round disc and this does not change (unless of course you go at with a hammer) – it is constant for all views. This shape is independent of how the coin is viewed and because of this the intrinsic nature of the object's shape is known as being **viewpoint-independent**. It remains the same regardless of the position of the observer. However, the impression of the coin (the perceptual representation) will change as a consequence of how it is viewed. Given that the perceptual representation changes with each alteration in position between the observer and the object, then the perceptual representation is known as being **viewpoint-dependent**. Stand over the coin and look down on it: it will now appear circular. Crouch down with the table top at eye level. Now the coin will appear to be a small rectangular bar.

### Viewpoint-dependent vs. viewpoint-independent representations

So far we have drawn a distinction between (i) the viewpoint-independent intrinsic nature of the shape of an object – this can be said to exist out there in the real world as a property of the distal object, and (ii) the viewpoint-dependent impression of the object that changes every time there is a change in position between the observer and the object. It is hoped that all of this is relatively uncontroversial, but one of the more controversial topics in the area of visual object recognition is whether there are viewpoint-independent representations that reside in the head. Consider the following theoretical perspective.

## Object recognition and shape constancy

Pizlo and Salach-Golyska (1995) framed the problem of object recognition as being essentially akin to achieving something known as **shape constancy**: the impression that the shape of an object remains the same regardless of how it is viewed. For example, shape constancy accords well with the idea that you just know that the shape of your telephone does not change as you approach it to pick up the receiver. Figure 13.3a shows two different views of a telephone and, according to Pizlo and Salach-Golyska (1995), if you perceive these two different images as representing the same shape then you have achieved shape constancy. Well done. While you're strutting around with

shape constancy bravado, take a look at Figure 13.3b and watch your confidence in shape constancy fall around you. Here the same crumpled piece of paper looks quite different from the two different views! Clearly, therefore, there are cases where shape constancy succeeds and cases where it fails. To understand the psychology behind shape constancy, we will need to explore some reasons as to why this might be so.

For Pizlo and Salach-Golyska (1995), the recognition of objects depends on achieving shape constancy, and they attributed this view to Helmholtz. According to them, the Helmholtzian theory of shape constancy involves 'mentally constructing a 3-D Euclidian structure of the object . . . from the retinal image after taking into account the object's orientation relative to the

(a)                                                                    (b)

**Figure 13.3 Easy and difficult shape constancy**
(a) provides an illustrative example of where it is relatively easy to achieve shape constancy. (b) provides a contrary case where shape constancy is difficult to achieve. Are these two images of the same crumpled piece of paper or images of different pieces?

*Source*: Pizlo, Z., & Salach-Golyska, M. (1995). 3-D shape perception. *Perception & Psychophysics, 57,* 692–714 (fig. 1, p. 693; fig. 2, p. 693). Copyright © 1995 by Psychonomic Society Inc. Reproduced with permission of the Psychonomic Society.

observer' (p. 692). To reinvoke our coin example, in order to recognise the coin the understanding is that the perceptual system must generate an internal model of the coin. In this example the representation or internal model codes a solid disc rather than a circle; because there is a coding of the 3D shape of the object it is sometimes known as a **3D model description** (Marr, 1982, p. 307). It is an internal description that codes the so-called volumetric nature of the distal object (the object out there in the real world).

A physical example here is between a real-world aircraft and those plastic replicas they try and sell you duty-free at a cruising altitude of 39,000 feet. The plastic model conveys, in a literal way, the volumetric nature (the overall 3D shape) of the actual aircraft to which it corresponds. The correspondence between the shape of the replica and that of the real plane is the same as the correspondence between the shape information captured in the internal 3D model representation and shape of the associated real object.

With respect to object recognition, Pizlo and Salach-Golyska (1995) stated that, if the construction of the internal model description 'is always performed correctly, the perceived shape will be the same regardless of the orientation of the object relative to the observer' (p. 692). So the idea is that a precursor to recognition is the derivation of a 3D model description of the object that is viewpoint-independent. In our coin example, this kind of perceptual representation codes 'solid disc'. Shape constancy therefore works because the same 3D model (the Euclidean model quoted before) is generated for all of the different views of the coin.

To be able to recognise the coin from any view means to be able to generate the same 3D model description from any view of the object. The argument goes that the perceptual system takes a 2D representation of a stimulus derived from the retinal images and is able to generate a 3D description of a solid object from these images. Of course, this is only half the story because, as we noted above, to recognise any object you have to be able to match that perceptual representation with the stored description of the object. So a further implication here is that there is also an internal library of 3D model shape descriptions that makes up a person's knowledge about the visual nature of real-world objects. Such is the Helmholtzian view of object recognition, and quite an impressive array of processes for recognising coins, we're sure you'll agree. As we will see, many, but not all, of the key assumptions of the Helmholtzian framework are shared by present-day theories of object recognition.

## Pinpoint question 13.4

**What is the difference between viewpoint-independent and viewpoint-dependent representations?**

**viewpoint-independent** An object representation that is independent of the position of the viewer.

**viewpoint-dependent** An object representation that changes according to the position of the viewer.

**shape constancy** The tacit knowledge that the shape of an object does not change when there is a change in the relative position between the observer and the object.

**3D model description** According to Marr (1982), this is an internal representation that codes the volumetric nature of an object.

## Additional useful terminology: introduction to Marr's theory

### 2D representations

Some terminology is necessary to carry the discussion forward. One way to think of what a 2D visual representation is, is to think in terms of anything depicted on a piece of paper (a flat plane). This includes pictures, photographs and line drawings as found in the real world (and indeed in this book), but, in the abstract, it also includes mental icons and retinal images (see Chapter 3). In addition, we have also been introduced to a 3D model description of an object's shape and here the idea is that such a representation codes the volumetric nature of the object's shape. We have moved from 2D considerations into the world of three dimensions.

### $2\frac{1}{2}$D representations

In addition, Marr (1982) introduced the notion of a $2\frac{1}{2}$**D sketch**, but there is no easy analogue here. Marr assumed that in processing the information from the retinal images, the visual system recovered a representation of the viewed object that coded the object's visible shape in a very particular way. The idea was that the $2\frac{1}{2}$D sketch contains a description of the object's surfaces and edges and also provides information about the orientation and depth of the surfaces and edges relative to an observer. Figure 13.4 provides

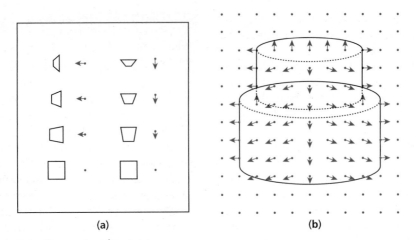

**(a)**                                                    **(b)**

**Figure 13.4 Further information on the 2½D sketch**

(a) shows the surface primitives from which the 2½D sketch is composed. The aim is to recover a description in which square patches of surfaces are labelled as specifying orientation relative to a viewer.

(b) shows the sort of surface information of a two-tier cake captured by a 2½D sketch (after Marr, 1982). The description codes the depth, surface orientation and distance from a viewer of the elements of the shape's surface.

*Source*: Marr, D. (1982). *Vision. A computational investigation into the human representation and processing of visual information* (fig. 3.12, p. 129). San Francisco: W. H. Freeman.

a schematic of the sort of information that is captured by the 2½D sketch.

What is being discussed here is a form of viewpoint-dependent representation. In this scheme it is possible to think in the following simple terms. Take an object such as a coffee cup and assume that the object's surfaces are covered with little postage stamps where each postage stamp has been pierced by a drawing pin. Take a stamp and push through a drawing pin. We now have a postage stamp with a drawing pin poking through it. Now take the stamp/pin and stick it on your coffee cup. Now repeat these operations until the whole of the surface of the cup is covered with the stamp/pins. For a less attractive idea of how this might look, revisit the movie *Hellraiser* and check out the character Pinhead. The position of each stamp/pin is defined relative to a surface point on the object and the direction in which the pin is pointing reveals the orientation of the surface point relative to the angle of regard of the observer. As you rotate the cup in your hand and fixate on one pin, then when it is perpendicular to your line of sight the length of the pin will be apparent, but when the pin is in the line of sight then it will appear like a dot.

So in this way the 2½D sketch codes the orientation of each surface point relative to the viewer, and the depth (or distance) of these points from the observer is also coded. Clearly, therefore, the 2½D sketch is a viewpoint-dependent representation because it

essentially defines the dispositions of the object's surfaces relative to the observer and these will change every time there is a change in position between the object and the observer.

Clearly the 2½D sketch is a highly abstract theoretical construct, and because of this, Marr took great pains to argue for its usefulness. Primarily the information in the 2½D sketch is critical for the purposes of interacting with an object. Although you may never have thought of this before, the information coded in the 2½D sketch (or something very much like it) must be being recovered every time you swing a bat to hit a ball, you lean in for a smooch with your partner, or you pick up a pint of beer and take a swig. In order to configure a reach and grasp and pick up your pint, the visual system must have recovered a representation of where the pint is relative to you and where its critical surfaces and edges are. So despite the very abstract nature of the 2½D sketch you should now be able to appreciate why it is nevertheless very useful: the information represented in the 2½D sketch is vital and supports successful interactions with objects within your immediate environment. You could not go down the pub without it!

## Marr's levels of representation in vision

In very simple terms Marr (1982) posited three basic forms of representation that seem to be important in terms of being able to recognise and interact with objects following on from the retinal image, namely:

1. Primal sketch.
2. $2\frac{1}{2}$D sketch.
3. 3D model description.

### The primal sketch

During early stages of visual information processing, operations on the retinal image give rise to a representation known as the **primal sketch**. In very broad strokes, this is a 2D representation that codes important information about light intensity in the image and where possible edges and contours of objects may be positioned. Such a representation is important because in specifying edges the extremities of the object can be estimated. To avoid bumping into the table you pay attention to the table's edges rather than the table's middle.

### The $2\frac{1}{2}$D sketch

From this kind of representation further processes operate to provide information about the disposition of an object's surfaces relative to the observer and this information is captured by the $2\frac{1}{2}$D sketch. If you want to place your cup of tea down on the table it is important to be able to judge where the table top is in relation to yourself. Primarily the information captured by the $2\frac{1}{2}$D sketch is useful for guiding interaction with the objects in your immediate vicinity.

### The 3D model description

Retinal image, primal sketch and $2\frac{1}{2}$D sketch are all viewpoint-dependent and because of this they are constantly being updated as the observer moves relative to the viewed object. It could therefore be argued that such representations are unstable and are therefore of little use for the purposes of recognising objects. Indeed, as Marr (1982, p. 295) noted: 'Object recognition demands a stable shape description that depends little, if at all, on the viewpoint.' In other words, viewpoint-dependent representations seem to be little use for the purposes of object recognition – how could they possibly support shape constancy, for instance? Therefore a characteristic of a representation that is suitable for the purposes of object recognition is that it must be *viewpoint-independent*, and for that Marr called upon the 3D model description as the final kind of visual representation.

So Marr's theory is, essentially, a Helmholtzian theory because it assumes that object recognition is based upon the generation of a viewpoint-independent representation that codes the volumetric nature of an object. As we have already noted, if the process of generation is working correctly then the same model description will be derived for the many different views of the same object. This in effect means that the same representation should be generated every time the object is viewed. However, as we have already appreciated, this poses immense problems for the perceptual system and for Marr the basic solution can be achieved by allowing an interaction to take place between information derived from the bottom up and information stored in our 3D library of visual representations. Remember, in order that the distal object can be recognised, the derived description must be matched with some kind of stored counterpart in long-term memory.

### Pinpoint question 13.5

**Following the retinal image, what are the three levels of Marr's model of visual representation?**

## The catalogue of 3D models

> TED: Now concentrate this time, Dougal. These [he points to some plastic cows on the table] are very small, those [pointing at some cows out of the window] are far away . . .
>
> *(Linehan & Mathews, 2000)*

Figure 13.5 provides an illustration of the sort of knowledge system that Marr took as being the store of shape descriptions – the so-called catalogue of 3D models. This catalogue was central to his ideas about how ultimately object recognition is achieved. Each entry in the catalogue comprises a 3D model description of a real-world entity and, as you can see, the catalogue is organised in an hierarchical crude-to-fine fashion. Each 3D model description contains one or more so-called **volumetric primitives**. The highest level in the hierarchy comprises a simple cylinder. This basic shape provides a very rough description of the overall size and orientation of an object – perhaps a cow seen at a distance on Craggy Island, as in the above example from *Father Ted*. The basic idea is that the cylinder provides a rough estimate of the amount of space that the cow takes up. (Not wanting to drain all the humour here, it is interesting to note that, in one sense, Dougal is quite right to point out that the retinal image of a small plastic cow close up and a

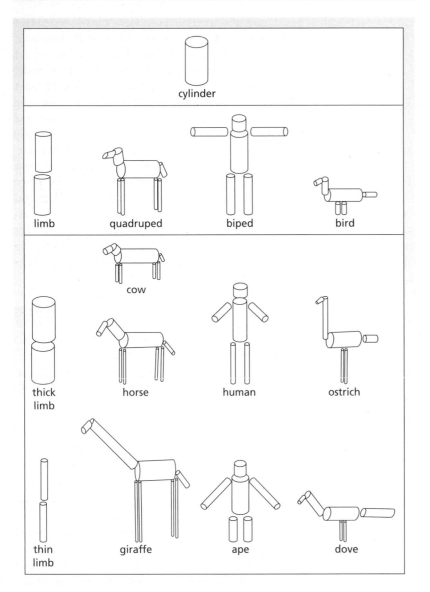

**Figure 13.5 The catalogue of 3D model descriptions described by Marr (1982)**
The catalogue is organised in a crude-to-fine hierarchical fashion. Each 3D model comprises one or more generalised cones (after Marr, 1982).

*Source*: Marr, D. (1982). *Vision. A computational investigation into the human representation and processing of visual information* (fig. 5.10, p. 319). San Francisco: W. H. Freeman.

real-life cow far away actually produce the same perceived size shape.)

Without going into too many details, it is this kind of cylindrical shape that is the basic 3D volumetric primitive that forms the building block of all shapes in the store. Each 3D model in the store comprises one or more 3D primitives. What we are discussing here is a form of representational system that comprises basic elements (the 3D primitives) together with rules of combination. As is evident in Figure 13.5, at the lower levels of the hierarchy the model descriptions become more specific (e.g., ape rather than biped) and as several primitives are combined in particular ways, the relative positions of limbs, torso, head, etc. are captured.

To be precise, the actual 3D primitive used in this scheme is known as a generalised cone and, as Figure 13.6 shows, there can be many different tokens of this type of structure. As Marr (1982) stated, 'generalized cone refers to the surface created by moving a cross section along a given smooth axis' (p. 224). The cross-section may change in size but it must maintain its shape (see Figure 13.6). In Marr's account any given 3D model comprises a set of generalised cones. Clearly this is quite an abstract notion but, as we will see, other influential theories of object recognition are also wedded to these kinds of ideas. Overall what a particular object's 3D model description provides is a fairly rich description of both the overall shape of an object,

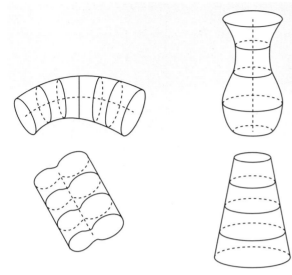

**Figure 13.6 Examples of the particular volumetric primitive known as a generalised cone**
The term 'cone' may be a little misleading. The primitive can take on a cross-section that may vary in size throughout its length (as in a cone) or it can remain the same size across its length as in a cylinder. The only constant is that the cross-section is the same shape throughout (circular, ellipse, figure-of-eight, etc.) (after Marr, 1982).

*Source*: Ullman, S. (1979). *The interpretation of visual motion* (fig. 3.11). Cambridge, Massachusetts: The MIT Press. Reproduced with permission.

the overall shapes of the parts of the object and how the parts are interconnected with one another.

## Object recognition and the process of matching

The critical step now is to examine how it is that information from the stimulus is matched with its appropriate counterpart in the store. Here Marr was particularly concerned with attempting to simplify this problem. One step he discussed was pairing the problem down to one in which surface shape and surface detail were initially eliminated from consideration. Instead the assumption is that each component of a shape is replaced by its intrinsic axis. We now try to match an axis of one of the generalised cones in the stored 3D model description with an axis derived from the input. All of this might seem a bit dense, so Figure 13.7 provides a now famous example of how this might proceed. Each panel in the figure provides a snapshot of the sort of information that has been recovered

from the input image – a line drawing of a donkey – after a given step in the process has been carried out.

In Figure 13.7, (a) shows the extraction of the actual contour of the donkey shape. (b) shows how the contour has been used to separate figure from ground. The '−' signs fall within the bounded contour and hence define the figure, the '+' signs fall outside the bounded contour and hence define the ground. (c) provides further information recovered from the contour. Now the so-called points of maximum curvature have been recovered. These are points where the direction of the contour changes dramatically. Such points are critical for the next step of carving up the overall contour into component parts as shown in (d). What you must remember here is that all of these operations are being carried out from the bottom up. There is no sense in which knowledge of particular objects is influencing these operations. The visual system does not need to know what a donkey looks like, in order to run through these early encoding operations. According to this scheme, the perceptual system is simply running through a set of procedures that aim to provide a reasonable first best guess as to what is figure, what is ground, and, importantly, what the components of the figure are.

## Object recognition and axis-based descriptions

Having made a guess as to what the parts of the figure are, the next step in (e) is to add in information about where plausible axes of these parts might be. Finally in (f) an attempt is made to connect all the axes of the component parts in a reasonable way. The basic underlying rationale for this scheme is that it shows how a description of the components of a figure can be recovered and defined in terms of component axes. The purpose of these axis-finding operations is to provide a frame of reference that specifies a co-ordinate system for defining the locations of the parts of the object (e.g., where the legs are in relation to the torso, where the head might go, and so on). The critical point is that the axis-based system is centred on the object and not the observer (as Figure 13.8 shows). This means that the eventual **axis-based description** provides a viewpoint-independent description of the object. More particularly, the reason that such axes are assumed to be so important is that the putative 3D model descriptions are defined relative to the axes of component generalised cones. So the ultimate aim is to try to secure a match between an axis-based description derived from the input image and an

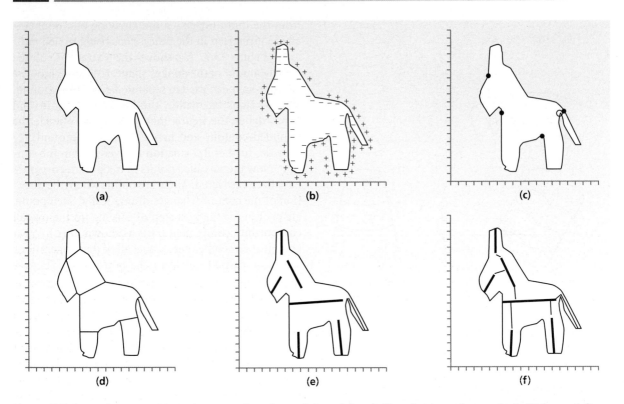

**Figure 13.7 A step-by-step guide to the generation of an axis-based description of a shape from a single 2D image (after Marr, 1982)**
See text for further details.

*Source*: Marr, D., & Nishihara, H. K. (1978). Representation and recognition of the spatial organization of three-dimensional shapes. *Proceedings of the Royal Society of London, Series B, 200*, 269–294. London: The Royal Society. Reproduced with permission.

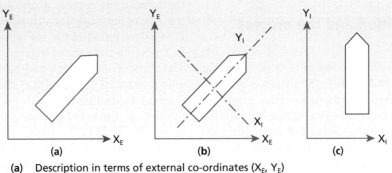

(a)   Description in terms of external co-ordinates ($X_E$, $Y_E$)
(b)   Position of the intrinsic axes $Y_I$ and $X_I$ in the external frame
(c)   Description in terms of intrinsic co-ordinates ($X_I$, $Y_I$)

**Figure 13.8 Different co-ordinate systems for describing the structure of an object**
Illustrative examples of the difference between a description of a pencil-shape input couched in terms of an external set of co-ordinates (i.e., $Y_E$ and $X_E$) shown in (a), and a description couched in terms of an internal set of co-ordinates (i.e., $Y_I$ and $X_I$) shown in (c). The co-ordinates shown in (c) reflect an intrinsic frame of reference based on the major axis of the pencil-shape, as shown in (b).

*Source*: Wiser, M. (1981). The role of intrinsic axes in shape recognition. *Proceedings of the 3rd annual meeting of the Cognitive Science Society*, Berekeley, California (fig. 3, p. 184). Hillsdale, New Jersey: Erlbaum. Reproduced with permission.

axis-based description (i.e., a 3D model description) as stored in the internal catalogue.

---

$2\frac{1}{2}$D sketch  According to Marr (1982), this is an internal description of an object containing information about the orientation and depth of surfaces and edges relative to a given angle of regard.

primal sketch  A 2D representation that codes information regarding light intensity values. Some primitive edges and lines are also coded.

volumetric primitives  Basic building blocks which are used to construct a mental representation of the volume of a 3D object.

axis-based description  According to Marr (1982), an axis-based description comprises a specification of a connected set of axes of an object composed of parts. Each axis is associated with a single generalised cone as included in the 3D model description of a familiar object.

---

## Connections with the previous material

### The basic first hypothesis revisited

At this point it is useful to take a step back and make some connections with the previous material. In describing the catalogue of 3D models as being hierarchical in nature, this should be ringing some bells because we have already discussed Rosch's (1978) ideas on the organisation of the human conceptual system. Arguably, the second tier of the 3D model catalogue (see Figure 13.6) corresponds to the superordinate level as discussed by Rosch and the lowest tier of the hierarchy corresponds to the basic level. Previously we discussed the data showing a basic level advantage such that the entry point between input and long-term memory was assumed to always be at the basic level. It's a chicken first rather than a corn-fed chicken or bird; it's a wedding ring rather than a 16-carat topaz-encrusted wedding ring or item of jewellery. However, Marr discussed several alternative ways in which the catalogue might be accessed (or indexed).

This is not to argue that evidence for the basic level entry point is flawed, but merely that it may capture only one of many ways in which contact is made with long-term memory. For instance, the catalogue might be accessed from the top down proceeding from the crude-to-fine levels. This seems a plausible account of

what might be happening when approaching an object from a distance. Initially a rough outline is apparent, but eventually it is obvious that there is a horse grazing in the field. Upon a strict reading of the basic level advantage, however, the claim is that contact is initially made at the lowest level in Figure 13.6 where (in a sense) the 3D model descriptions of the prototypical instances reside.

## Object recognition via the recognition of part of an object

In contrast, it might be that an object is recognised through recognition of one of its parts. So when wandering through some stables you will be able to recognise a horse even though only its head is protruding over the stall door. Although all of this may come across as being patently obvious, more subtle points are actually implied. For instance, the critical claim here is that it is not just that you recognise this thing as a horse because you recognised the horse's head, but that in recognising the head you will have recovered a complete specification of the other parts of the horse relative to where its head is. This might be particularly useful information if the horse bolts. In accessing the 3D model of the horse you will have recovered a representation that codes the 3D spatial disposition of the component parts of the whole animal. So the basic idea is that the entry level to the catalogue can sometimes be driven by recognition, not of the whole object, but of a single part of the animal. What the stored 3D model description is therefore providing is a means to make predictions about (i) what hidden parts there should be, and (ii) where these hidden parts are in relation to the parts that are currently visible.

## Empirical evidence that bears on Marr's theory

A useful framework for thinking about different theories of object recognition has been provided by Tarr (1995). For him Marr's theory of object recognition can be termed a **complete viewpoint-invariant theory** (p. 56). This is because the theory posits that recognition depends on the derivation of a form of representation that codes the object in terms of a viewpoint-independent co-ordinate system. For instance, it is assumed that recognition depends on the recovery of a 3D model description. The 3D model description is known as viewpoint-independent because it does not change as the position between the observer and the object changes. In Marr's theory, recognition takes place either because of (i) recovering a 3D model description through an analysis of the nature and disposition of intrinsic axes, or (ii) the recovery of some salient feature (such as the horse's head) provides access to the appropriate 3D model. Several predictions arise from this sort of theory. For example, in accessing a 3D model description, it should be possible to imagine what the object looks like from any angle of regard. Moreover, it has been suggested (Bültoff & Edelman, 1992) that the theory asserts that an object should be easy to recognise irrespective of the angle of regard. Both of these predictions have been the subject of experimental test.

## Can we imagine how objects look from other viewpoints?

Rock, Wheeler and Tudor (1989) posed the question, 'Can we imagine how objects look from other viewpoints?' and concluded with a guarded 'No'. Here participants on each trial viewed a real wire object (such as a bent and twisted paper clip – see Figure 13.9) for an unlimited amount of time. In an *imagination condition* participants were instructed to imagine how the form would look if they were to sit in a chair at 90° to the one they were currently seated in. When they were ready they then had to decide which of four alternative views matched the imagined view. In a separate *perception condition*, the participants were merely asked to decide which of four alternative views matched the actual view they had been presented with.

Performance in the perception condition was very good (levels of 97 per cent accuracy and above were found), but performance in the imagination condition was very poor. Of the four test objects used, performance ranged from 35 to 71 per cent accuracy. Data such as these fit reasonably uncomfortably with complete viewpoint-invariant accounts of recognition. In accessing a 3D model, it should be a relatively easy matter to generate an impression of how an object

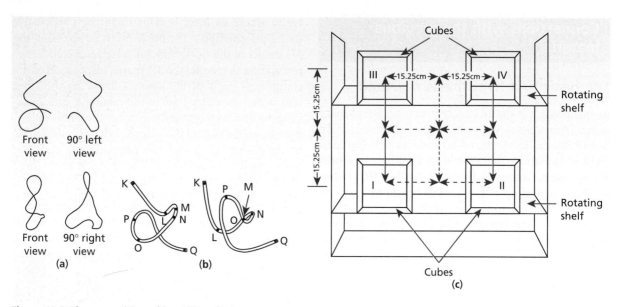

**Figure 13.9 The recognition of bent bits of wire**
On the left of (a) are examples of front views of two wire objects used by Rock et al. (1989). On the right of the figure are the corresponding side views of the objects.
(b) shows other examples of wire figures in which corresponding salient points are marked in the two views so as to convey the correspondence between the two different views.
(c) shows the actual apparatus used in the experiments reported by Rock and colleagues showing how viewing positions could change across learning and test phases.
When positions changed from exposure to test, wire objects could move from I to IV or from II to III. In cases where positions changed but the same retinal projection occurred across exposure and test, then the wire objects were rotated within the horizontal and vertical planes.

*Sources*: (a) Rock, I., Wheeler, D., & Tudor, L. (1989). Can we imagine how objects look from other viewpoints? *Cognitive Psychology*, *21*, 185–210 (fig. 1, p. 189). (b, c) Rock, I., & Di Vita, J. (1987). A case of viewer-centered object perception. *Cognitive Psychology*, *19*, 280–293 (fig. 2, p. 283; fig. 3, p. 284). Reproduced with permission with permission from Elsevier.

looks from a different position. This information is simple to recover from the putative 3D model because by mentally interrogating the 3D model it should be possible to generate an impression of any view of the object, but the data of Rock et al. (1989) stand against this suggestion.

As a brief aside, the original evidence from the mental rotation literature (see Chapter 7) also does not accord well with the idea of 3D model descriptions. If it really is the case that such representations are naturally derived for any object, then the data from the rotation studies are very puzzling. Look at view 1 and derive a 3D model. Look at view 2 and derive a 3D model. Now compare the two. There is now no obvious reason as to why the angular separation between 1 and 2 would have any influence on the time to respond, and yet it does! (For further interesting limitations on people's abilities in mental rotation tasks, see Parsons, 1995.)

## Pinpoint question 13.6

**Why does the Rock, Wheeler and Tudor (1989) study not support the notion of a complete viewpoint-invariant account?**

The second issue now concerns how a change in orientation of the object may affect its recognition. In taking a very strict reading of complete viewpoint-invariant accounts, it has been argued that all views of an object ought to be equally easy to recognise. Against this, however, further work by Rock and colleagues (Rock & Di Vita, 1987; Rock, Di Vita & Barbeito, 1981) provided evidence to the contrary. In one experiment twisted wire objects were constructed and participants were exposed to 12 of these during a learning session. A rig was constructed with four place holders (labelled I, II, III and IV in Figure 13.9c) and each object was assigned to a particular position. Each place holder was used three times across the 12 objects so participants were exposed to only one view of each object. Participants were asked to rate each object on an aesthetic scale. Exposure to the objects during this rating task constituted the learning phase of the experiment.

Following on from the learning phase there was a test phase in which a mixture of old and new objects were presented. Each test object was now presented and participants were asked to say whether or not they had seen it before. Critically, for the old objects, performance was tested as a function of the relation between the old view (as seen during the learning phase) and the new view used at test. In the *same position condition* (condition A) the old objects were pre-sented as in the learning phase with no change between the old and new views (e.g., initially exposed in I and reshown in I). In the *different position, different retinal projection condition* (condition B) the object changed not only position but also orientation between learning and test (e.g., initially exposed in I and reshown in IV). Finally, in the *different position, same retinal projection condition* (condition C) the position of the object was changed but it maintained the same orientation so as to give the same retinal projection as that seen initially in the learning phase. A wire figure could be initially exposed in I and reshown in IV but now the figures were rotated both within the horizontal and vertical planes so as to give rise to the same retinal projection in the two different positions.

The data were extraordinarily clear-cut. Whenever the view of the object was maintained as in conditions A and C, participants were over 70 per cent accurate in recognising the objects. In contrast, when the view of the object changed between learning and test as in condition B, performance dropped to around 40 per cent. Such data as these do not fit so comfortably with complete viewpoint-invariant accounts of performance. According to such accounts, if the same 3D (viewpoint-independent) description is being accessed then changes in view ought to have little effect on recognition performance. However, in following up on this study, Farah, Rochlin and Klein (1994) were able to show that changes in view were not so detrimental to recognition if the wire objects were replaced with similar bounded contours containing a curved surface (see Figure 13.10). When surface details were added, recognition performance improved. Clearly, though, view invariance is potentially very difficult to achieve. This suggests that the recognition system is particularly sensitive to viewpoint-dependent information.

More recent evidence, which converges on a similar conclusion, has been provided by Bültoff and Edelman (1992). They also used a training and test paradigm (as in the Rock and Di Vita work) and used computer-generated renditions of wire objects as the stimuli. In the training phase, each object was presented either in a so-called 0° position or at a position 75° away from this position. So every object was viewed in two positions and these positions were derived by rotating the object around its vertical axis. Pick up a bottle of wine and hold it so you can read the front label. Now rotate so that you can read the back label. What you have done is rotate it around its vertical axis. Now pick up the bottle and go to pour a glass of wine – you are now rotating it around its horizontal axis.

So with the wine bottle example the 0° position would be where the front label is face on and the 75°

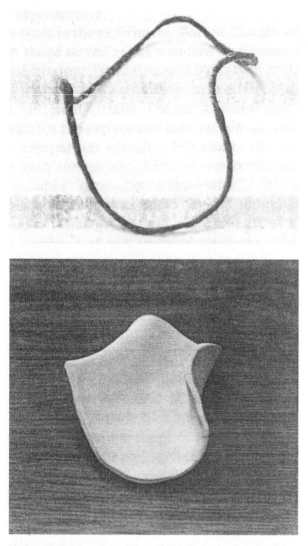

**Figure 13.10 The recognition of bits of string and plasticine shapes**
Examples of the sorts of contour and solid objects used by Farah et al. (1994).

*Source*: Farah, M. J., Rochlin, R., & Klein, K. L. (1994). Orientation invariance and geometric primitives in shape recognition. *Cognitive Science*, *18*, 325–344 (figs. 1a and 1b, p. 330). Reproduced with permission from the Cognitive Science Society.

position is where the bottle has been rotated so that you can still see most of the front label but now the back label is also partially visible. In addition, to clarify to the participants the object's 3D structure, whenever it was presented it was shown to rotate slightly back and forth. So jiggle your bottle back and forth a bit to recreate exactly what the participants were seeing (see Figure 13.11 for more details). At test both old and new objects were presented and participants were asked to respond as to whether they recognised

the object from the learning phase. Critical here was the mapping of recognition accuracy as a function of the relationship between the previously exposed orientations of the objects and the orientation of those objects at test. The data are also shown in Figure 13.11c.

Generally speaking, accuracy was very good for all orientations between 0° and 75° as defined previously. Such cases were known as INTER cases because these positions were essentially **interpolation**s between the previously exposed orientations. Interpolation essentially means figuring out what a new instance of something might be if it fits within the range of what you have been previously exposed to. Therefore, given these two extremes, you can estimate what values in between might look like. So, given that you have seen the bottle at 0° and 75°, it is easy to recognise when presented at 15°, 45°, 60° and so on.

EXTRA cases were where the object appeared as being rotated in the opposite direction to those positions shown during training. EXTRA here refers to **extrapolation**s from the orientations of the object that were originally exposed. Extrapolation basically means estimating what a new view of an object might look like when it goes beyond the range of what you've previously encountered. When we first took a look at the bottle we saw it face on and then at a position rotated to the left at 75°. To examine performance in EXTRA positions what we now do is test for positions rotated to the right that we have never seen before. The basic finding was that when EXTRA positions were tested, recognition accuracy was now significantly worse than for the INTER cases.

Now the final tested positions were cases where the objects were tested in rotations around the horizontal axis (the orthomeridian cases in Figure 13.11). We have tested the 'reading labels' cases; now we test the 'pouring wine' cases. Again in cases when the objects were rotated in this way recognition accuracy showed a marked decrement. Participants were particularly poor in recognising the objects when the objects were rotated around the horizontal axis. Essentially what the Bültoff and Edelman (1992) data show is that not all views of familiar objects are equally accessible.

However, in case you're wondering whether all of this is something purely to do with the recognition of wire frame objects as opposed to solid objects, similar patterns of performance also obtained when computer renditions of amoeba-like solid objects were used. So in this respect, providing surface information did not materially alter the viewpoint-dependent nature of the effects (cf. Farah et al., 1994). → See 'What have we learnt?', page 488.

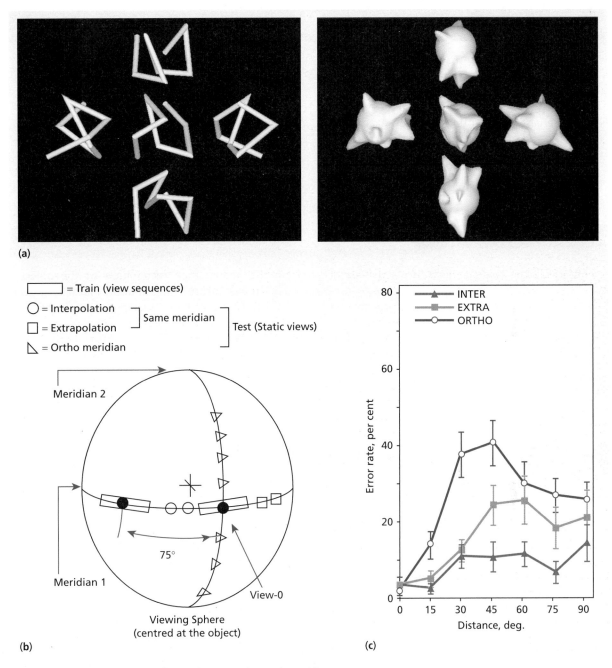

**Figure 13.11 The recognition of pipe-cleaner and amoebae objects**
(a) shows examples of the sorts of pipe-cleaner objects and amoebae objects discussed by Bültoff and Edelman (1992). The central object can be taken as the default 0° rotation view. The surrounding examples show +/– 75° views of the central object defined either in the vertical or the horizontal plane.
(b) shows in schematic form the virtual sphere about which the objects were rotated during initial exposure and subsequent test. Solid disks show the 0° and the 75° projections of the target object. Each disk is centred in a rectangle that reveals the extent to the perturbations that the participant saw during the exposure phase. Interpolated positions are shown as unfilled disks, extrapolations are shown as unfilled squares and the meridian extrapolations are shown as unfilled triangles. (c) shows the actual recognition data. Small numbers reflect good performance.

*Source*: Bültoff, H. H., & Edelman, S. (1992). Psychophysical support for a two-dimensional view interpolation theory of object recognition. *Proceedings of the National Academy of Sciences of the United States of America, 89*, 60–64 (fig. 1, p. 61; fig. 2, p. 62; fig. 3, p. 62). Washington: National Academy of Sciences. Reproduced with permission.

## For example . . .

Next time you're passing your local art gallery, you might want to have a bit of art appreciation of a different kind. Once you've got past the sheep in formaldehyde and the crumpled bed sheets, go find some Renaissance paintings and see exactly what tricks the 'old masters' used in conveying a 3D scene on a flat, two-dimensional canvas. Foreshortening is certainly one, but there are a whole bunch of others. Look at the way the lines of the buildings are structured and the relative size of objects. Remember, though, that these ideas are rampant outside the gallery too. Right now, you are receiving 2D retinal information but managing to transform it into a 3D impression of the world.

## → What have we learnt?

Collectively the evidence just discussed is particularly revealing because it shows just how sensitive people are to particular views of objects. Irrespective of the claims about view-invariant recognition, it seems that what is primarily being recovered is a representation of the object that codes viewpoint-specific characteristics. At one level this is breathtakingly obvious. Think of your television. Easy, right? But you're probably only imagining the front view. Now think of what it looks like from behind. Now imagine placing it on a glass tabletop, crawl under the table and look up. Now what does it look like? For some, this intuitive line of reasoning and the contingent empirical evidence fundamentally undermine the complete viewpoint-invariant account of recognition (see Tarr & Bültoff, 1998).

If anybody is still in doubt about difficulties in imagining how an object looks from a different view, there was a situation where one of the authors was waiting for a late experimental participant – we'll call her Michelle. Given the somewhat labyrinthine nature of the department, often participants would wait at the sign-up board in the main entrance. On arriving at the main entrance, there was a person with long blonde hair looking at the experimental sign-up board. Our brave and confident experimenter asked if they were Michelle, only for a male undergraduate to turn round with a less-than-pleased look on their face. Such anecdotal evidence fits uneasily with the idea of view-independent models. However, it is only fair to point out that Marr (1982) did discuss examples of where effects of view are most likely to obtain.

Here the basic idea was that in any case where it proved difficult to recover an object's intrinsic axes from the image, then recognition of the object would prove difficult and indeed might fail. As Figure 13.12 shows, it may well prove impossible to recognise the bucket in (c) because its principal axis is obscured in the image because of **foreshortening**, which is essentially a trick in art to make the object appear shorter by angling it towards the viewer. Remember, according to Marr's theory a critical step is to be able to recover at least one intrinsic axis of the object so that this can be used as means for accessing a 3D model description that is based upon axis-based generalised cones. Object recognition may therefore be compromised if problems arise in the recovery of a shape's intrinsic axes. Indeed, in a speeded naming task reported by Humphrey and Jolicœur (1993), participants were particularly slow and inaccurate in naming line drawings of common objects when the drawing depicted the object in a foreshortened perspective.

Despite the very best efforts of some (e.g., Quinlan, 1988) there is very little evidence that confirms the details of Marr's theory of object recognition. Although there is the evidence regarding poor performance when participants are presented foreshortened images of objects, this does not necessarily imply that the problems reflect difficulties in finding a shape's intrinsic axes. It may well be that foreshortening produces a very unfamiliar view of the object in which critical characteristics of the object's shape are either obscured or become distorted (see Lawson & Humphreys, 1998, p. 1058, for more on this). Nevertheless, the influence and importance of the theory and of Marr's legacy cannot be denied.

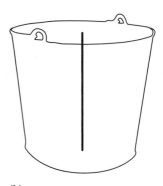

(a)

(b)

**Figure 13.12 Axis-based descriptions and problems with axis-finding processes**

An example taken from Marr (1982) of how difficult it may be to derive the same axis-based description of a rotated shape. In (a) and (c) different salient aspects of the shape are made apparent. Even though the same major axis is shown in (b) and (d), it may be difficult to derive in the latter case. Objects that are foreshortened as in (c) are likely to be difficult to recognise.

*Source*: Marr, D., & Nishihara, H. K. (1978). Representation and recognition of the spatial organization of three-dimensional shapes. *Proceedings of the Royal Society of London, Series B, 200*, 269–294. London: The Royal Sociey. Reproduced with permission.

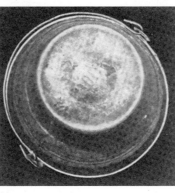

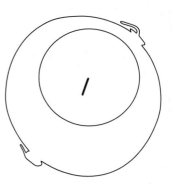

(c)

(d)

## Research focus 13.2

## 'Narrowing towards the back': foreshortening without sight

As we saw in the above discussion, foreshortening is a way of reducing the size of the object by angling it more towards or away from the viewer. Return to the wine bottle you were playing around with a couple of paragraphs ago, and pretend to drink from it. What you'll experience is a reduction in the overall size of the bottle, from the bottle being quite large in a vertical orientation to the looking-down-the-barrel-of-a-gun phenomenon when the bottle is horizontal. The general process of fore-shortening is also useful for the representation of depth on a 2D image. Think of a humble cube and you'll note that while all its faces are of equal size, actually the sides that recede into the distance are foreshortened – they are retinally smaller than the

side facing you – and the edges of the receding sides will actually meet up at a vanishing point (convergence). While this might be something we largely take for granted, Kennedy and Juricevic (2006) were interested in how the blind use these ideas of foreshortening and convergence in draw-ing images with which they have no prior visual experience.

Esref, a 47-year-old Turkish male at the time of study, was deemed totally blind from birth – he only had one eye and this was insensitive to light. Despite this, he had an interest in drawing and Kennedy and Juricevic (2006) encouraged him to draw a number of cubes. He was asked to draw both solid and wire cubes (echoing the previous

▶

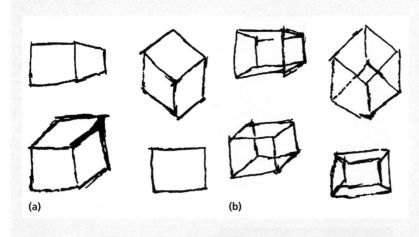

**(a)** **(b)**

**Figure 13.13 Visually impaired impressions of the world**
Examples of the drawings produced by Esref of (a) a solid cube (the four cases on the left of the figure) and (b) of a wire cube (the four cases on the right of the figure) (discussed by Kennedy & Juricevic, 2006).

*Source*: Kennedy, J. M., & Juricevic, I. (2006). Foreshortening, convergence and drawings from a blind adult. *Perception*, *35*, 847–851 (figs. 1 and 2, p. 848). Reproduced with permission from Pion Limited, London.

concern we've seen in this chapter for different kinds of representation for solid and wire objects), cubes that were directly in front of him, cubes that had a corner pointing towards him, cubes that were oriented to the left, and cubes that were oriented leftward and downward.

Figure 13.13 shows the results of these requests. Although there are slight errors in the drawing, such as the face-on solid cube actually being a horizontally elongated rectangle rather than a square (if you get your ruler out), the pictures show a remarkably accurate use of depth cues, including foreshortening and convergence. For example, both solid and wire leftward-oriented cubes (top left-hand drawings in (a) and (b)) show a right-hand trapezoid representing the side of the cube receding into the distance which is both narrower than the front side of the cube and whose sides will eventually join at a single vanishing point.

The authors pointed out Esref's remarkable ability to hide lines accurately in the solid cube condition that otherwise would be seen in the wire cube condition, in addition to representing convergence and foreshortening successfully, or to use his own words, 'narrowing towards the back'. But how does Esref know how to draw like this? Kennedy and Juricevic (2006) reported that it was probably a combination of factors including gleaning object information from haptic (i.e., touch) experience in addition simply to being provided with information about visual phenomena such that pictures of roads tend to converge. A rare case, then, but one that also should make us appreciate our own senses much more.

*Source*: Kennedy, J. M., & Juricevic, I. (2006). Foreshortening, convergence and drawings from a blind adult. *Perception*, *35*, 847–851.

**complete viewpoint-invariant theory** A theory of object recognition in which recognition depends on the coding of an object with respect to a view-independent, co-ordinate system.

**interpolation** Estimating a new value that falls between the extremes of a previously exposed range of values.

**extrapolation** Estimating a new value that falls outside the extremes of a previously exposed range of similar values.

**foreshortening** Shortening the appearance of an object by angling the object towards or away from the viewer.

## Restricted viewpoint-invariant theories

The next class of accounts that Tarr (1995) discussed he termed **restricted viewpoint-invariant theories**. The essence of these accounts is that they posit that object recognition will be achieved 'as long as the same viewpoint-configuration of features or parts is available' (p. 56). So given that the horse's head and neck are poking over the stable door, the horse will be recognised. More importantly, the assertion is that unless critical parts or features are visible, then the object will not be recognised. Perhaps the most famous such account is associated with Biederman and colleagues.

## Biederman's recognition by components account

From Paul Cézanne to Emile Bernard, 1904: 'treat nature by the cylinder, the sphere, the cone' (p. 234)

*John Rewald (1948). Paul Cézanne: Letters – London, England: Cassirer (cited in Chipp, 1968)*

In Marr's account only one sort of volumetric primitive was defined – the generalised cone. This was based on the assumption that variations of this basic primitive can be assembled in different ways so as to give rise to the different 3D models in the internal catalogue (one set of six cones gives a description of a human, another set of six cones gives a description of an ostrich – see Figure 13.5). However, other sorts of volumetric primitives have been discussed in the literature and these differ in their mathematical definitions (see Dickinson, Pentland & Rosenfeld, 1992a, 1992b; Pentland, 1986, even went so far as to discuss mathematical 'lumps of clay'). The basic idea here is that an object can be decomposed into its constituent parts and that it is recognised as a consequence of recognising these parts – hence 'recognition by components' or RBC. Figure 13.14 (taken from Pentland, 1986) conveys the basic flavour of the ideas. It may help to transport yourself back to your childhood here and consider sticklebricks and all the other different shaped toy blocks you spent happy hours with, trying to fashion cows, telephones, rockets and tractors.

One way of thinking about these kinds of accounts is that assumptions are made about the basic building blocks from which all objects can be derived and into which all objects can be decomposed. At a very primitive level, a house, for example, may be described as being composed of a cube and pyramid and most children's drawings will convey this by a triangle sitting on top of a square. Marr (1982) put forward the idea that the basic mental building block was the generalised cone, and as Figure 13.15 shows, such a simple idea lies at the heart of quite a variety of different shapes. Indeed, in extending the theory, one idea has been to try to establish a basic set of 3D primitives that can be combined in various ways to give rise to a large and indefinite number of 3D model descriptions.

This may seem like a small point, but its importance should not be overlooked. Biederman (1987), in setting out the theory, drew parallels between object recognition and language. In simple terms, words can be taken to be the building blocks of language. There are only so many words in the language, and yet there is an indefinitely large number of sentences that can be composed from combining these words in particular ways. Importantly, though, and as with any form of representational system, there is a set of primitive elements (the words) and a set of rules of combination (the grammar of the language) that defines the manner in which the words can be put together to give rise to sentences. 'The closed swan felt circular' is grammatically correct, but it makes no sense.

For Biederman (1987), the operation of the object recognition system was identical to this kind of representational system. As we will see, he posited a particular kind of volumetric primitive (which defined the basic elements of the system) that can be combined in an indefinite number of ways so as to give rise to a vast variety of object descriptions. For example, Goldstone (1998) considered a system in which each object is composed of five parts selected from a 'dictionary' of 15 possible parts. Okay, think in terms of some toy blocks system such as Lego and now consider the possibility that there is a basic set of 15 such blocks. Now take five of these at random and put them together. Now take a different set of five blocks and make another shape. Such a system is capable of generating $(15 \times 8)^5$, or in other words, 24 billion whole-object descriptions. The notion of rules of combination is perhaps a little strained, though. In terms of biological shapes there are clear constraints on how anatomical components are put together (e.g., hands and feet are typically found at the ends of limbs), but with man-made objects it seems that anything is possible.

Although Biederman accepted the usefulness of generalised cones as a basic volumetric primitive, he went further in a bid to distinguish different instantiations of generalised cones such as blocks, cylinders, spheres and wedges. Such volumetric primitives he termed **geons** – a geon is a particular sort of volumetric primitive in the same way that a generalised cone is a volumetric primitive. Over the course of the development of the theory different sets of geons have been considered with various numbers and types of geons – 36 in Biederman (1987), 24 in Biederman (1995) and eventually 8 in Hummel and Biederman (1992). The critical point, though, is that such 'components can be differentiated on the basis of perceptual properties in the two-dimensional image that are readily detectable and relatively independent of viewing position and degradation' (Biederman, 1987, p. 118). In other words, what makes the chosen 3D primitives useful is

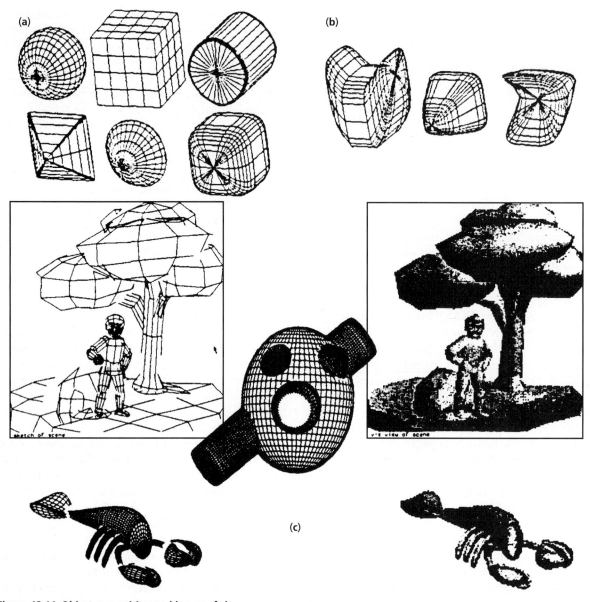

**Figure 13.14 Object recognition and lumps of clay**
Rather exotic examples of how computational lumps of clay can be deformed and conjoined to give rise to articulated descriptions of scenes, objects and animals.
(a) shows the basic forms, (b) shows deformations of these forms and (c) shows how such forms can be combined to give rise to articulated objects.
*Source*: Pentland, A. P. (1986). Perceptual organization and the representation of natural form. *Artificial Intelligence*, *28*, 293–331 (fig. 3, p. 303). Reproduced with permission from Elsevier.

that they are easily recoverable from the 2D retinal image. If you are to claim that object recognition is based on being able to recover a description that codes for the parts of the object in terms of the basic component geons, then this will be greatly facilitated if the geons are easy to recover from 2D impressions of the world. Clearly, if you posit a particular kind of geon that is very difficult to recover from a 2D snapshot of the world, then this really does compromise the usefulness of the theory because object recognition is both fast and (typically) effortless (see, for example, Thorpe Fize & Marlot, 1996).

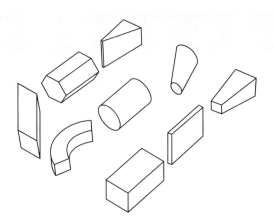

**Figure 13.15 Even more generalised cones**
The flexibility of the computational notion of a generalised cone gives rise to this variety of basic shapes. Each is a different instantiation of a generalised cone.

*Source*: Brady, M. (1982). Computational approaches to image understanding. *Computing Surveys*, *14*, 3–71 (fig. 58, p. 64). Reproduced with permission from Elsevier.

## Pinpoint question 13.7

**What is a geon?**

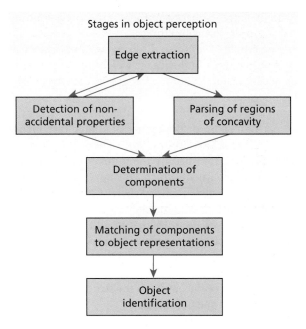

Stages in object perception

**Figure 13.16 The RBC theory of visual object recognition in schematic 'arrows-and-boxes' form (from Biederman, 1987)**
*Source*: Biederman, I. (1987). Recognition-by-components: A theory of human image understanding. *Psychological Review*, *94*, 115–147 (fig. 2, p. 118). Reproduced with permission from APA.

As Figure 13.16 shows, central to the RBC theory is the idea that objects are recognised via recognition of their components. The reason that Tarr (1995) dubbed RBC a restricted viewpoint-invariant theory is that it predicts that recognition will only be successful if there is sufficient information in the image to allow the recovery of a unique description of the object's geons (for more on this see Biederman & Gerhardstein, 1993, 1995).

In broad strokes Figure 13.16 describes the theory in terms of an arrows-and-boxes diagram. *Edge extraction* and *Parsing at regions of concavity* have already been explained in terms of Figure 13.7 and Marr's (1982) theory. In contrast, **detection of non-accidental properties** refers to the recovery of features in a 2D image that place rather tight constraints on what the 3D nature of the distal object must be. For instance, a straight line in the image is most probably associated with a straight edge in the object. Curved lines in the image are also most probably associated with curved edges on the object. Symmetry is also an important cue on the understanding that symmetries in a 2D image are very likely to have arisen because of symmetries in the distal object. Parallel curves in the image are also likely to correspond to parallel edges in the object. The point is that if certain characteristics are

present in an image of an object, then it is highly likely that these characteristics provide information about the structure of the object. So if there is a straight line in the image then your best guess is that there is a straight edge on the object. The theory works on the principle that many characteristics of the image of an object are *non-accidental*. Sketch your house and you'll find that the reason that the drawing contains

**Figure 13.17 Y-shapes are all over the place**

straight lines is because there are corresponding straight walls in the building.

Biederman (1987) also discussed the importance of cues to junctions in the image which may correspond to points of termination of edges in the object. For instance, a 'Y' in the image probably signals the termination of three surfaces in the image such as the corner of a room or the corner of a table (see Figure 13.17). Take a look around you right now and you'll probably be astonished by the number of Ys that are in your environment which you never even spotted before. They really are everywhere! Clearly such cues are not infallible guides but they are nevertheless plausible first guesses about the nature of the structure of the distal object. So if the perceptual system capitalises on such non-accidental properties then it can use these to build a perceptual representation that provides a best first guess of the nature of the structure of the distal object from the bottom up.

In combination, edge extraction, parsing at regions of concavity and the detection of such non-accidental properties provide inputs into the next stage at which the actual geons are determined. Having established the nature of the geons in the image, these can then be used to index the catalogue of 3D models stored in long-term memory and eventually the object will be recognised. We are now trying to match a geon description derived from the image to secure a match with a stored counterpart. If such a match is achieved then the object will be recognised.

More particularly for Biederman, object recognition 'is the activation in memory of a representation of a stimulus class' (1995, p. 121), but in fact this is a further endorsement of the basic first hypothesis. The implication is that the primary level of access is at the basic level. Indeed, as Kurbat (1994, p. 1341) noted, 'The class of basic-level categories RBC is intended to recognise is the broad class of concrete objects with specified boundaries which can be named by count nouns (in contrast with the things named by mass nouns like sand or water).' So count nouns refer to things that can be counted like four calling birds, three French hens and two turtle doves, while mass nouns are things you can't make a plural out of, for instance, two sands or three waters.

## Appraisal of RBC

Despite the fact that RBC features heavily in many discussions of object recognition, it is probably not a good idea to dwell too long on the account because it has so little support in the literature. The critical aspect of the theory is that geon recognition is taken to be a precursor to object recognition. By one line of reasoning, the theory predicts that if perceptual cues to the recovery of a geon description are degraded or omitted from an image, then the object will either be difficult or impossible to recognise. If you can't recover the geons, then you won't be able to recognise the object. Indeed, in garnering support for this view, Biederman reported a naming study in which participants were asked to name various line drawings of common objects. Figure 13.18 shows the sorts of line drawings used and the distinction between recoverable and so-called 'non-recoverable' items. The non-recoverable items were generated in such a way that the deleted aspects were critical for the geon recovery process. Moreover, in some cases, misleading cues to geon identity were also introduced such as a spurious cue to symmetry or parallelism. The data were clear in showing that participants were particularly impaired in being able to name the non-recoverable items.

As is the trend with these sorts of things, since the theory was put forward it has come under intense attack from a number of quarters (Bültoff & Edelman, 1992; Edelman, 1998, 1999; Kurbat, 1994; Liu, 1996; Moore & Cavanagh, 1998; Tarr & Bültoff, 1995, 1998). Kurbat (1994), for instance, has provided a particularly penetrating critique in which detailed difficulties for the component process account of recognition are laid bare. Much effort has also been directed towards attempting to justify the psychological significance of generalised cones. Very early on, however, Brady (1982) pointed out that although generalised cones are particularly well suited to describing objects with clear intrinsic axes, they tend to be ill-suited in cases in which 'objects [are] produced by molding, beating, welding or sculpture' (p. 64; see Kurbat, 1994, for more on this). So don't expect a geon analysis of Henry Moore's nudes any time soon, because although these sculptures represent the human form, the rather fluid nature of their composition seems to preclude a decomposition into clearly delineated, volumetric primitives such as geons.

More problematic, though, are the empirical data that clash with the predictions of the theory. Perhaps the most compelling examples have been provided by Moore and Cavanagh (1998). Figure 13.19a provides examples of the sorts of displays used. Here the participants' task was to indicate whether the star was located on the surface of the depicted object or not. As can be seen from the figure, two-tone images were generated of single generalised cones. Critically the images

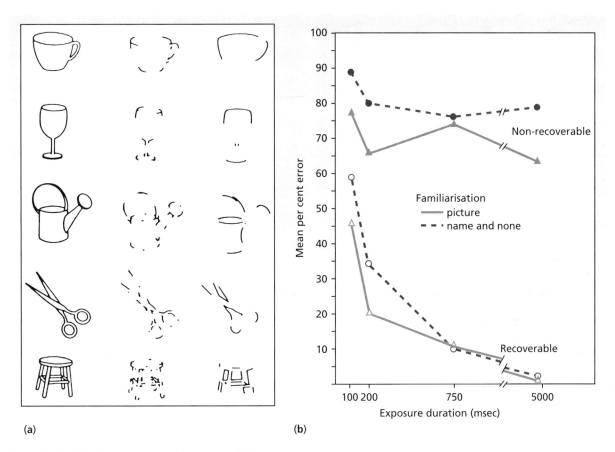

(a)                                                    (b)

**Figure 13.18 Stimuli and data used to support RBC**
(a) shows examples of the complete line figures (left-most column), recoverable examples of the figures (centre column) and non-recoverable examples of the figures (right-most column). The images of the objects were made non-recoverable by deleting aspects of the contour that are critical to the operations concerned with geon parsing and geon recovery. (b) shows data from a naming study in which naming accuracy is plotted as a function of exposure duration. Clearly participants experienced great difficulties in recognising any of the non-recoverable images even when the individual images were displayed for 5 s. Prior to the identification tasks, participants were familiarised with intact versions of the pictures (picture); they were provided with names of the objects (name); or they were given no familiarisation (none).
*Source*: Biederman, I. (1987). Recognition-by-components: A theory of human image understanding. *Psychological Review, 94*, 115–147 (fig. 16, p. 135; fig. 17, p. 136). Reproduced with permission from APA.

could be divided into regions that corresponded to the white surface of the object, the white surface (or ground plane) upon which the object was situated, the black surface of the object and a black shadow cast by the object on the plane.

The results were clear in showing that participants had great difficulty in seeing images of volumetric objects as defined as generalised cones. Instead there was a large bias to parse the image into black and white regions with some participants seeing the black regions as defining the objects and the white regions as defining the backgrounds. The situation changed dramatic-

ally, though, when two-tone images of familiar items were used and the items were composed from simple volumetric primitives. As Figure 13.19b shows, the face and the coffee pot are readily recognised, leaving a seemingly paradoxical pattern. Whereas the recovery of a 3D description of a complex object composed of volumetric primitives was possible, no such 3D impression was created by images of single primitives. Moore and Cavanagh (1998) therefore concluded that 'recognition of familiar objects in 2-tone images cannot be mediated by bottom-up recovery of generalised cones' (pp. 55–6). Further demonstrations that are awkward

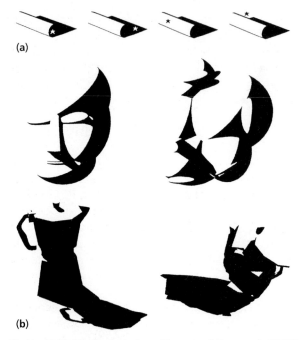

(a)

(b)

**Figure 13.19 Illustrations from Moore and Cavanagh (1998)**
(a) shows examples of the sorts of displays used in the experiments by Moore and Cavanagh (1998). The participants' task was to decide whether the star was or was not on the surface of the object.
(b) Images on the right of the figure comprise the same set of volumetric primitives as those on the left, but whereas the familiar objects are seen as taking up space in three dimensions, the images on the right appear flat or as silhouettes.

*Source*: Moore, C., & Cavanagh, P. (1998). Recovery of 3D volume from 2-tone images of novel objects. *Cognition*, *67*, 45–71 (fig. 3, p. 50; fig. 6, p. 55). Reproduced with permission from Elsevier

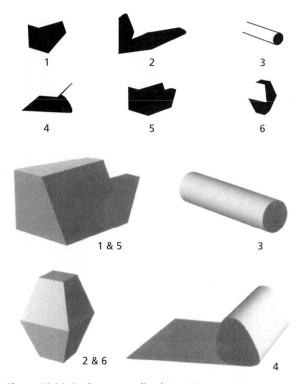

**Figure 13.20 Seeing generalised cones?**
The images in the upper panel are renditions of the generalised cones shown in the bottom panel. The numbers in the two panels show how the two sets of images are related. Again participants showed immense difficulties in recovering any sense of the shapes and their cast shadows from the images in the upper panel (from Moore & Cavanagh, 1998).

*Source*: Moore, C., & Cavanagh, P. (1998). Recovery of 3D volume from 2-tone images of novel objects. *Cognition*, *67*, 45–71 (fig. 4, p. 51; fig. 15, p. 68). Reproduced with permission from Elsevier.

for RBC are shown in Figures 13.20 and 13.21. With the cases in Figure 13.21, it is the amount of obscured contour that seems critical rather than the type of occlusion. Even in cases where junctions are obscured, the volumetric appearance of each object is apparent.

On the basis of all of this, Moore and Cavanagh (1998) went so far as to argue that, to large measure, the recognition of familiar objects in two-tone images is primarily a top-down process. For a given case, a hypothesis is generated from a stored representation of the object (see the previous discussion of analysis by synthesis, Chapter 6) that codes a viewpoint-dependent impression. This then leads the interpretation of the object or scene. Such a conclusion leads nicely on to the final class of theories of object recognition described by Tarr (1995).

## Viewpoint-dependent theories

Such accounts avoid any strict adherence to the notion of a 3D model description of an object and instead posit a catalogue of shape descriptions that code viewpoint-dependent characteristics of the objects. One possibility here is that, in a sense, the best view of each object is stored and recognition is based on notion of similarity to this best view. Remember that we agreed that we would probably all recognise a TV from the front but would be less successful if we were to view it from underneath. Ideas such as these were thoroughly explored by Palmer, Rosch and Chase (1981).

They carried out a series of tasks, the data from which all converged on the notion of a privileged or **canonical view**. For instance, goodness ratings were

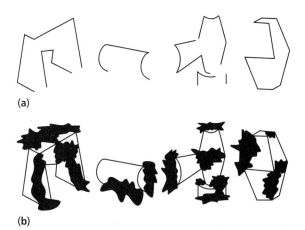

(a)

(b)

**Figure 13.21 Evidence that is difficult to square with the RBC account of object recognition**
Images in (a) show that when aspects of contour are deleted, such as deleted Y or arrow junctions, then the line drawings appear flat. This is as predicted by RBC. However, when the ink splodges are added, as in (b), the volumetric nature of the shapes becomes apparent. This latter result is not readily explained by RBC. The presence of the occluding patches allows the visual system to generate hypotheses about how the object's contours may continue behind the occluder. Such hypotheses are not generated for the cases in (a) because no impression is conveyed of objects being in any sense occluded.

*Source*: Moore, C., & Cavanagh, P. (1998). Recovery of 3D volume from 2-tone images of novel objects. *Cognition*, *67*, 45–71 (figs. 9 and 10, p. 59). Reproduced with permission from Elsevier.

taken from participants of photographs of 12 common objects. Each of these objects was photographed from 12 different perspective views. Participants were asked to rate for each of these views 'how good or typical the presented picture was of the object shown' (p. 140). Figure 13.22 shows ratings and views of a photographed horse. For all objects used there was very good agreement about the ordering of the different perspective views and in particular participants agreed about the best or privileged views. This Palmer et al. (1981) termed the *canonical perspective*. Indeed, other data indicated that the canonical perspective was the one 'spontaneously experienced in imagery' (p. 151). In other words, if asked to imagine a horse

then the image you are most likely to report is that captured by the canonical perspective.

What seems to be particularly important about the canonical view is that it maximises the amount of information that is useful for recognition. Important surfaces and components of the object are most apparent in this view. In other words, if you wanted to maximise the visual information that is critical for identifying an object, then this would be captured by the canonical view. Indeed, in a speeded naming task it was shown that naming speed varied indirectly with so-called 'canonicalness'. As the ratings in Figure 13.22 show, the different views varied in their distance from the canonical perspective. What the data showed was that such measures reflected speed of naming. The canonical perspective was named fastest and response speed slowed as the distance from the canonical view increased.

Since this initial study there have been others that underline the importance of privileged views both in inspecting views of human heads (Harries, Perrett & Lavender, 1991), novel objects (Perrett, Harries & Looker, 1992) and, indeed, potatoes (Perrett & Harries, 1988). Recently Blanz, Tarr and Bültoff (1998) provided evidence suggesting that, to large measure, it is the familiarity of the view of an object that determines its canonicalness. In this respect, the data show that not all views of an object are of the same psychological importance, either for (i) learning about the structure of an object, or indeed for (ii) the purposes of recognition.

## Pinpoint question 13.8

How does a canonical view assist in object recognition?

**restricted viewpoint-invariant theories** A theory of object recognition in which recognition depends on the recovery of the same viewpoint configuration of the object presented across time.

**geons** According to Biederman (1987), the volumetric primitives such as spheres and cylinders that make up the mental building blocks of objects.

## For example . . .

The idea of canonical views is also, of course, where we come across those favourite pastimes of droodles. This is where objects are presented to us in non-canonical views leading to 'hilarious' results such as a Mexican riding a bicycle (see Figure 13.23, and www.droodles.com for many more examples).

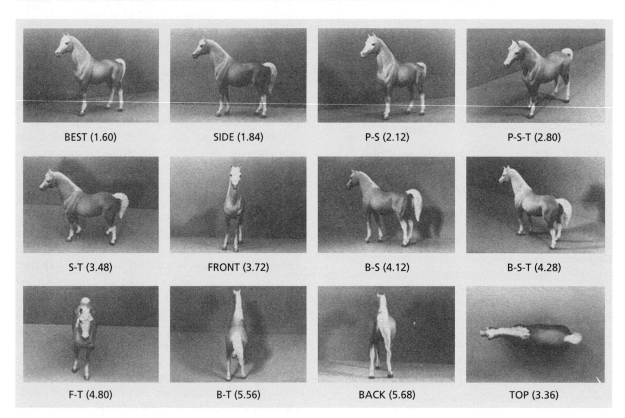

**Figure 13.22 Examples of the photographic images used by Palmer et al. (1981) in their rating study**
Numbers in brackets are the average goodness ratings with small values indicating high goodness.

*Source*: Palmer, S. E., Rosch, E., & Chase, P. (1981). Canonical perspective and the perception of objects. In J. Long & A. Baddeley (Eds.), *Attention and performance*, IX (pp. 135–151, fig. 8.2, p. 139). Hillsdale, New Jersey: Erlbaum. Reproduced with permission.

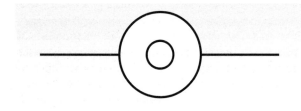

**Figure 13.23 A droodle: a non-canonical view of a Mexican riding a bicycle**

**detection of non-accidental properties** The recovery of properties contained in a 2D projection of a 3D scene that constrains the interpretation of the scene. For instance, parallel lines in the image typically arise because of parallel lines or edges in the scene. Discussed at length by Biederman in his RBC theory of object recognition.

**canonical view** After Palmer et al. (1981), a specific (typical/familiar) view of an object which is thought to best represent that object.

## Privileged view or privileged views?

In exploring alternative accounts of this kind of evidence, Tarr (1995) drew a distinction between the Palmer et al. (1981) idea of a mental catalogue comprising single canonical views of different objects and an alternative idea in which multiple views of objects are stored. The contrast is between viewpoint-dependent accounts that posit one canonical view/object and those that posit a family of privileged views/object. In this regard, the data from the previously described Bültoff and Edelman (1992) study is of some import. Here recognition performance was critically determined not so much by similarity to a canonical view but to whether or not the tested view fell within the range of views previously experienced, from which participants were able to interpolate. In this regard, theories that posit a family of privileged views for a given object seem to have the most support. For instance, the most common views of a car will be

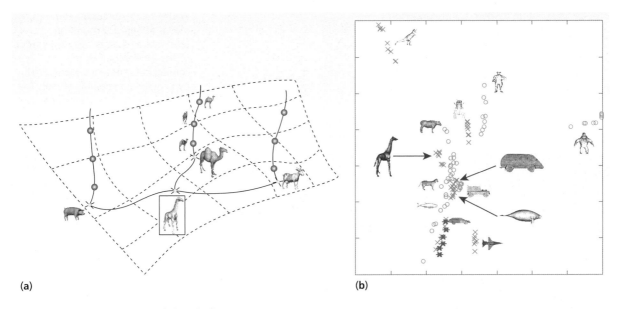

**(a)**                                                                                            **(b)**

**Figure 13.24 Edelman's view of the mind**
(a) shows a schematic of a multi-dimensional surface that captures shape descriptions of animals. Each point on the surface corresponds to an actual or possible volumetric and componential object. Distances in this space reflect shape similarity: close points in the space correspond to different but similarly shaped animals.
(b) provides a related idea in which both prototypical views and new views of objects are represented. Various prototypical views of animal types are shown.

*Sources:* (a) Edelman, S. (1999). Representation and recognition in vision (fig. 4.8, p. 94). Cambridge, Massachusetts: The MIT Press. Reproduced with permission. (b) Edelman, S. (1998). Representation is representation of similarities. *The Behavioral and Brain Sciences*, *21*, 449–498 (fig. 7, p. 463). Reproduced with permission from Cambridge University Press.

stored, such as the view from the side or the front but not the view from underneath – unless of course you are a car mechanic.

## The chorus of prototypes

In exploring these ideas Edelman (1998, 1999) has discussed the notion of a mental multi-dimensional shape space such that points in the space correspond to particular 3D shapes (see previous discussion of multi-dimensional spaces in Chapter 12). Figure 13.24a provides an illustration of the concept. Each point in the space corresponds to a particular 3D object and points close together correspond to similarly shaped objects. The basic ideas are actually fleshed out in terms of the connectionist architecture sketched in Figure 13.25.

As you'll remember from Chapter 12, a connectionist network contains a number of banks (or levels) of simple processing units. The basic idea is to try to train the network to produce correctly on its output units the desired pattern of activation for each pattern of activation across its input units. Typically the network contains weighted connections between banks of

units and modifiable thresholds on units. The weights and connections are known as coefficients. Also it is typical to start off with randomised coefficients and alter these via some form of training procedure (such as back-propagation). Whenever an input pattern is presented and the network is unable to produce the desired output pattern, then the discrepancy between the actual and desired pattern is used as an index by which the coefficients in the network can be altered.

For Edelman (1998, 1999; see also Poggio & Edelman, 1990), the input units in a sense looked down on a 2D retinal mosaic that contained a representation of a view of an object. Think of your computer screen and the fact that it is made up of pixels. Each pixel captures a point of light in which the intensity and wavelength of the light can vary. Now turn it around so that, instead of giving off light, the pixels act as light receptors. They receive light of different intensities and wavelength, code this information up and forward it on. So what we are really dealing with here is the notion of the image captured by a digital camera. This kind of image acted as the input for the input units in the network. Here it is best to think in terms of some form of feature detector such that the

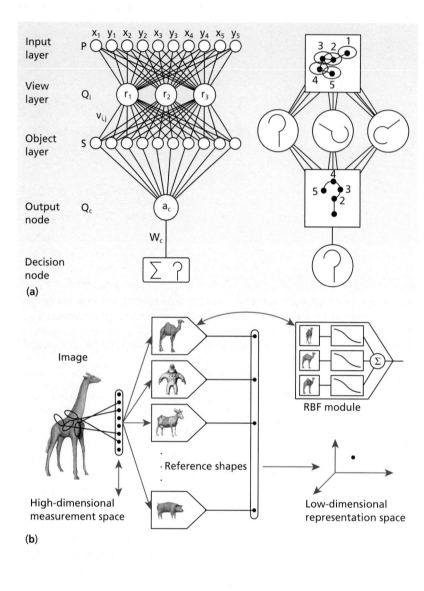

**Figure 13.25 A neural network model of object recognition**
(a) shows a schematic representation of the architecture of the connectionist network developed by Poggio and Edelman (1990). The input layer consists of units each of which captures a description of critical feature points on the input object. The view layer contains units that code a particular view of an object. Each unit in the object layer responds maximally to a particular object. In this case even though the '?' may be presented in any orientation there is a unique object unit that responds to all of these views – the object units are, in this sense, view-invariant. On the left in (a) is a schematic of the actual architecture, and on the right in (a) is a corresponding sketch of the sorts of representations that are being coded at each level of the network. (b) shows Edelman's extensions to the Poggio and Edelman model. Now individual modules are trained to recognise a given object and then these individual modules are combined into one monolithic network that deals with animal recognition in general.

*Sources*: (a) Rouder, J. N., Ratcliff, R., & McKoon, G. (2000). A neural network model of implicit memory for object recognition. *Psychological Science, 11*, 13–19 (fig. 2, p. 16). Reproduced with permission from Blackwell Publishers Ltd. (b) Edelman, S. (1999). *Representation and recognition in vision* (fig. 5.1, p. 112). Cambridge, Massachusetts: The MIT Press. Reproduced with permission.

detector has a receptive field located on some part of the retinal mosaic. In the network model, outputs from the input units feed forward to the next layer that contains view-tuned units.

This view layer is composed of units, each of which represents one particular view of a given object. So they will fire maximally if the view of the object in the image matches the unit's own view and fire less vigorously as the views depart from one another. The final object layer comprises units that code object identity independently of view, and Riesenhuber and Poggio (2000) referred to these as *view-invariant output units*. The network is therefore sensitive to both viewpoint-dependent and viewpoint-independent information.

At the level of the view-tuned units, privileged views of particular objects are coded. At the level of the view-invariant information, output units respond to a particular object regardless of view.

In some instantiations of the model (Edelman, 1998, p. 460; Edelman, 1999), separate mini-networks, so-called *reference-object modules*, were configured so that each was dedicated to recognising a particular object. Instead of configuring one mammoth network to recognise a variety of different objects, here the idea was initially to examine cases when separate networks (or modules) were each trained to recognise a given object. As Edelman (1998, p. 462) stated, 'the modules tuned to specific shapes can be considered as feature detectors, spanning a feature space in which each dimension codes similarity to a particular feature class'. Each module in a sense captures a range of prototypical views of an object. The so-called **chorus of prototypes**, though, refers to individual reference-objects that are collectively coded by the reference-object modules. So there is a module for giraffe, monkey, rhino, elephant, etc. and it is the prototypes for giraffe, monkey, rhino and elephant, etc. that collectively define the chorus of prototypes.

Once individual networks for each prototype had been configured, then these modules were gathered together into one multiple-network network. Edelman was then able to examine the resulting shape space that this huge network had acquired (see Figure 13.25b) and consider where within this space novel objects would be located. → See 'What have we learnt?', below.

## Pinpoint question 13.9

How are view-dependent and view-independent representations captured by the same connectionist model as discussed by Edelman (1999)?

## → What have we learnt?

There is much to commend the computer modelling of object recognition, and as Rouder, Ratcliff and McKoon (2000) have recently shown, the sort of connectionist architecture discussed by Edelman (see, in particular, Poggio & Edelman, 1990) can be easily extended to account for stable patterns of performance in a variety of priming experiments with humans. However, there is still much work to be done. For instance, there is a lack of clarity over what the dimensions of the shape space could actually be (Goldstone, 1998). The assumption seems to be that plums and lawnmowers are defined relative to the same set of basic shape dimensions (Edelman, 1999, p. 231), and this seems to be stretching plausibility a bit. It is also of some concern as to whether such a scheme could be scaled up to account for object recognition in the real world. Some success has been achieved with the toy worlds that the computer models inhabit but, realistically, can this sort of account be made to work in the real world? (See Goldstone, 1998.)

There is also a sense in which the representations in the chorus model that are being derived are holistic and not componential, and this may be problematic. The input images are of single shapes in isolation. Through exposure to these, the view-tuned units are trained to recognise particular views of whole objects. The representations of these objects therefore are not composed of volumetric primitives. This is apparently problematic because, as Edelman (1999) admitted, the current implementation fails to provide a principled solution to the problem of identifying an **occluded object** or an object in a cluttered scene. If you take your coin *and* your bottle of wine this time, and place the coin so that it is standing up, peeking out from behind the bottle, you will have occluded the coin by the wine bottle. Componential accounts of recognition (see the above discussion of Marr's axis-based account) are particularly suited to cope in cases where an incomplete view of an object is presented. What seems to be called for, therefore, is some form of hybrid account in which structured representations of objects are posited but that such information is conveyed in a manner commensurate with a familiar view of the object (see Moore and Cavanagh, 1998, for more on this).

Despite the progress that has been made in trying to tie down the nature of internal representations that underlie object recognition, the work is fundamentally limited by the desire to focus on the recognition of single objects in isolation. We haven't even considered how individuals might recognise objects within a busy visual scene. Unless you're sitting alone reading this book in a sensory deprivation chamber, your visual environment is filled to the brim with objects to recognise. To just consider the recognition of isolated objects is consistent with a common step in science in which the topic is simplified so that it becomes tractable. Of course, one of the problems with such an approach is that, by the time laboratory conditions are met, many of the interesting and perhaps fundamental characteristics of the initial problem no longer obtain. Indeed a fatal problem is that by paring the situation down to its bare minimum, any observations made will no longer apply in the real world. Some may wish to level this kind of criticism at the sort of work in object recognition just reviewed, and it is difficult to resist such a perspective. Rather than adopt such a negative view, though, it is perhaps more useful to consider some empirical data that reveal how object recognition can be affected by context.

## Meet the Greebles: the effects of training on an individual with visual agnosia

Most of us take object recognition for granted and it would only be when experiencing a completely novel object for the first time (such as the mysterious *Flandrewke*) that our cognitive system might fail us. Others, however, are not so lucky. Behrmann, Marotta, Gauthier, Tarr and McKeeff (2005) identified patient SM who suffered from visual agnosia – essentially the inability to recognise objects and faces. Specifically, Behrmann et al. (2005) were interested in training SM to learn a certain class of object, first to see whether this was possible at all, and second, to see if this training extended to other forms of objects.

SM was 24 at the time of study, and had developed visual agnosia as a result of a motor vehicle accident. SM was exposed to the wonderful world of the Greebles (see Figure 13.26), a set of creatures who can be categorised by gender and family, as well as identified as individuals. SM learnt to acquire information about the various visual forms of the Greebles via a number of different paradigms, including gender matching and individual

matching. At a later stage, SM was tested on pairs of Greebles that he had never seen before, to see whether he was able to recognise the new pairs as having 'same' or 'different' gender or family. In addition, SM was also presented with pairs of everyday objects and faces, and asked to make similar distinctions related to whether the objects shared the same subordinate description or whether the faces shared the same gender.

Although SM was much slower at acquiring this knowledge relative to other samples, there was substantial improvement in Greeble recognition over four months of training. More importantly, SM was able to generalise learnt Greeble attributes of gender and family to new examples of Greebles that he had never seen before. And perhaps most interestingly of all, SM's ability to recognise everyday objects was improved while his ability to recognise faces became even more impaired.

While Behrmann et al. (2005) showed substantial effects on training, not all of these were to SM's benefit as it seems what was gained in terms of

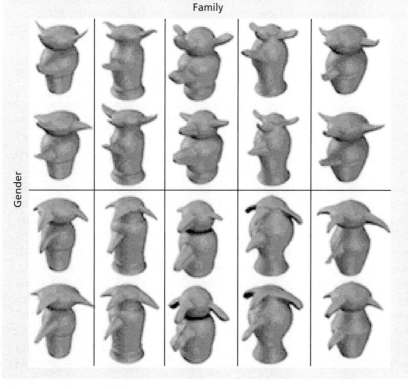

Family

Gender

**Figure 13.26 The wonderful world of Greebles**
Individual examples of Greebles as divided up according to 'gender' and 'family' (taken from Behrmann et al., 2005).

*Source*: Behrmann, M., Marotta, J., Gauthier, I., Tarr, M. J., & McKeeff, T.J. (2005). Behavioral change and its neural correlates in visual agnosia after expertise training. *Journal of Cognitive Neuroscience, 17*, 554–568 (fig. 1, p. 556). Reproduced with permission from MIT Press.

Greeble expertise was lost in terms of face expertise. Indeed, additional neuro-imaging data in the paper demonstrated that the fusiform gyrus (an area thought to be important in face recognition) showed less selectivity to faces and more selectivity to Greebles. The authors state that with intact fusiform gyri individuals can become experts in both face and

Greeble recognition. With limited resources, as in SM's case, expertise from two different domains fight for competition. In SM's case it seems the Greebles won.

*Source*: Behrmann, M., Marotta, J., Gauthier, I., Tarr, M. J., & McKeeff, T. J. (2005). Behavioral change and its neural correlates in visual agnosia after expertise training. *Journal of Cognitive Neuroscience, 17*, 554–568.

**chorus of prototypes**  A collection of prototypical representations of individual objects as defined by Edelman (1998, 1999).

**occluded object**  An object, only part of which is seen because it is obscured by something nearer to the viewer.

# Evidence regarding context and object recognition

So far we have focused on what possibly underlies the ability to recognise familiar objects in isolation. Also as we have just noted, the work on this problem has been underlined by a desire to simplify the topic so as to try to understand some basic characteristics of the human object recognition system. However, we need to be confident that what we are proposing about object recognition abilities transfer into the real world. Is what we are learning in the lab really telling us anything of more general application? Are we learning anything about the mental representations and processes that underpin object recognition in cluttered environments?

In addressing the issue of how scene information may influence object recognition, Murphy and Wisniewski (1989) adopted Rosch's hierarchical framework, posed the question 'What is a superordinate level good for?' and carried out a series of experiments to examine this question. What advantage is conferred by being able to recognise a chair as an 'item of furniture'?

In all of the experiments carried out by Murphy and Wisniewski (1989), computer-controlled displays were used in which a written label was presented prior to a target display. Figure 13.27a provides examples of the sorts of target displays used. On the left of the figure is a scene in which the target object occurs and on the right of the figure is the object depicted in isolation. On *matching trials* the label named the target

object and on *mismatching trials* there was no correspondence between the label and the target object. Critically, on half the matching trials superordinate labels were used (e.g., 'tool') and on the remaining half trials basic labels were used (e.g., 'hammer'). Participants were timed in making a yes/no response on every trial and the target displays were presented very briefly (i.e., 250 ms). In this respect, the Murphy and Wisniewski (1989) experiment is a lot like the category verification studies described earlier in the chapter.

In their first experiment, participants were quicker to respond following a basic label than a superordinate label when isolated objects were used (hammer < tool). However, when coherent scenes were used, this basic level advantage was abolished and participants took the same amount of time to respond following a basic label than when following a superordinate label (hammer = tool). Although the evidence is not very convincing, the general claim was that part of the information stored at the superordinate level specifies relations between different objects that occur in cohesive scenes. For example, when primed with the label 'crockery', relations between cups and saucers and knives and forks become readily available. Such information is not recovered when a basic level label such as 'cup' is presented because its relations with other objects do not form part of the concept CUP.

Although the experiment just cited was motivated by an attempt to understand a particular issue concerning the nature of superordinate categories, the actual experiments revealed much more about the role of context in recognising objects. In the first experiment reported by Murphy and Wisniewski (1989), context was defined in terms of whether the target object was presented in a scene or in isolation. However, in a later experiment, only scenes were used and now the target objects were embedded in either a probable or improbable setting. As Figure 13.27b shows, the target object saxophone occurred either in the probable concert setting or the improbable camping setting.

Again the same paradigm was used in which either a superordinate ('musical instrument') or basic level

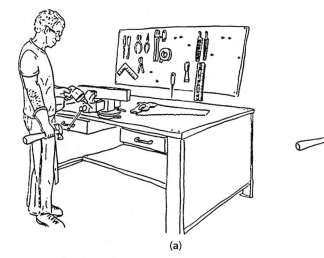

(a)

(b)

**Figure 13.27 Examples of the sorts of materials used by Murphy and Wisniewski (1989) in their experiments on object recognition**

In (a) on the left of the figure is an example of a pictured scene in which the hammer is the target and on the right is an example of a hammer in isolation. Prior to the pictured materials a written label was presented and participants were timed to respond as to whether the named item was present or not.

(b) shows an example of the manipulation of scene congruence/item probability on object recognition.

*Source*: Murphy, G. L., & Wisniewski, E. J. (1989). Categorizing objects in isolation and in scenes: What a superordinate is good for. *Journal of Experimental Psychology: Learning, Memory, and Cognition, 15*, 572–586 (fig. 1, p. 575; fig. 2, p. 582). Reproduced with permission from APA.

label ('saxophone') was presented prior to a picture and participants made speeded judgements as to whether the target was present in the scene or not. The results were relatively clear-cut: although there were no effects in the RT data, the error data revealed that overall participants were less accurate in responding to the improbable scenes than the probable scenes. Moreover, participants were particularly inaccurate in responding when an improbable scene followed a superordinate label. This Murphy and Wisniewski (1989) took as

being further evidence that superordinate conceptual information contains a specification of inter-object relations that occur in particular familiar scenes. When such information is primed, however, then it will interfere with the identification of objects that appear in unfamiliar scenes. In other words, you don't expect to see musical instruments in a camp site, so when you are primed to see musical instruments and a camp site is then presented, the recognition system is tripped up.

Again alternative accounts of these particular data have yet to be ruled out, but there are nevertheless good grounds for arguing that the recognition of particular objects is affected by the nature of the context within which such objects occur. Perhaps the best evidence for this comes from a recent study by Davenport and Potter (2004). On a trial in their experiments participants were briefly presented with a coloured photograph (see Figure 13.28 for examples). More exactly, an initial fixation point was presented for 300 ms, and

**Figure 13.28 Examples of the photographic images used by Davenport and Potter (2004) in their experiments on object recognition in consistent and inconsistent contexts**
(a) shows figures in consistent scenes, (b) shows figures in inconsistent scenes and (c) shows two control cases, background with no figure (on the left), and figure with no background (on the right).

*Source*: Davenport, J. L., & Potter, M. C. (2004). Scene consistency in object and background perception. *Psychological Science, 15*, 559–564 (fig. 1, p. 561). Reproduced with permission from Blackwell Publishers Ltd.

was followed by a blank screen for 200 ms; next a photograph was presented for 80 ms and was immediately followed by a masking screen for 200 ms. At the end of the trial participants were to respond with what they saw.

In different conditions, participants were asked to respond to the foreground object, the background scene or to both. Across different conditions, objects were presented in consistent (probable) or inconsistent (improbable) scenes. Also in control conditions either (a) only the foreground object was presented or (b) the scene without a foreground object was. As in the study by Murphy and Wisniewski (1989), accuracy served as the main measure of interest.

Overall the data showed that scene consistency was an important determining factor for accuracy; not only for the foreground objects, but also for the background scenes. Accuracy of report was higher for consistent than inconsistent cases. In addition, object report was more accurate than scene report, and objects in isolation were generally more accurately reported than when in a scene, despite scene consistency.

Taking this final result first, this can be understood on the grounds that pictures of isolated objects and objects in scenes are very different. For instance, when confronted by a scene the participant may need to search out the target and segment it from the background prior to being able to recognise it. It could be argued that neither searching nor segmenting is needed when the object is presented in isolation and on the understanding that both these processes take time, then recognition may be compromised only because the photographs were presented very briefly.

More interesting, perhaps, are the findings of scene consistency. As Davenport and Potter (2004, p. 564) concluded, 'information about the semantic relationship between objects and their background is available when a scene is presented very briefly' and this materially affects how the information in the scene is processed (see also Biederman, Mezzanotte & Rabinowitz, 1982). Object recognition appears to be facilitated if the scene is consistent and is inhabited with familiar items relative to cases where this is not the case. There are, currently, no convincing accounts as to why this is so.

## Pinpoint question 13.10

**According to Murphy and Wisniewski (1989), are you less likely to recognise a 'kitchen utensil' or an 'egg whisk' in a tanning salon?**

## Concluding comments

Much ground has been covered and many of the issues that face object recognition theorists have been laid bare. Clearly tensions remain between proponents of viewpoint-invariant representations and those who posit viewpoint-dependent representations that rely on privileged or canonical views. It might be tempting to argue that some form of hybrid model is therefore warranted, but this simple catch-all can be resisted. Something that is worth bearing in mind is the following. Even though we have the ability to attain shape constancy and to recognise an object from a variety of views and in a variety of cluttered scenes, this does not necessarily license claims about the psychological reality of internalised 3D models. There is simply no convincing evidence that such a theoretical construct has any psychological validity. Such a theoretical construct imbues us with powers of recognition that we simply cannot live up to. In contrast, on the basis of the work reviewed here, the evidence clearly shows sensitivities to particular views of objects. Any putative theory of object recognition must take this evidence into account.

We must also accept that an object may be recognised once a critical part has been identified, for example, it must be an elephant because of its trunk. Nonetheless, we must be clear about what this evidence suggests. Marr (1982) did discuss such cases but, for him, the implication was that part recognition was merely an intermediary step towards recovering a 3D model description of the whole object. An alternative is to think in terms of some form of object classifier that becomes activated once a critical amount of information from the image has been processed. There is no necessity that such a classifier must represent the kind of structural information that is captured in a 3D model.

We generally go about our business in the world without a care of how object recognition proceeds. Despite this, some of the component processes and internal representations that have been discussed must be coming into play every moment of every waking hour. It is easy to forget about these issues, primarily because in 'normal healthy adults' object recognition is so fast and so effortless. Indeed it has been estimated that within 150 ms of stimulus presentation, critical information about object identity can be recovered from a scene (Thorpe et al., 1996). This sort of timing constraint must be honoured by any theory that is put forward as an explanation of how humans recognise objects. So despite the fact that some might claim that much progress has been made, many fundamental problems have yet to be solved.

Here again, therefore, is an invitation to engage with the topic and to think about the difficult challenges that still remain.

## CHAPTER SUMMARY

- Object recognition involves either the classification or the identification of a stimulus in the external world. Any kind of recognition, however, relies on accessing stored internal descriptions of the thing that is to be recognised. When a novel object is seen for the first time, it can only be 'seen', not identified.

- Researchers have been interested in the first (or entry) point of contact between external perceptual representations and stored internal descriptions. The basic first hypothesis (Tanaka & Taylor, 1991) stated that there is a bias to access the internal store of descriptions initially via the basic level as defined by Rosch (1978). While some data are consistent with this hypothesis, other data have demonstrated that atypical members of a category can access a subordinate category prior to an assumed basic level (Jolicœur et al., 1984).

- Tanaka and Taylor (1991) showed that experts tend to provide more features when prompted with subordinate levels of description relative to basic levels of description. Therefore recognition on a subordinate level may be one of the factors leading to expertise. Both Tanaka et al. (2005) and Archambault et al. (1999) showed that novices who learn to categorise at a subordinate level went on to substantial improvement on future discrimination and also detect change quickly within their chosen field of acquired expertise.

- In terms of visual object recognition, we are typically faced with the difficult job of attempting to recognise a 3D object on the basis of 2D retinal information (Pizlo & Salach-Golyska, 1995). So that objects do not appear to change shape as we move around our environment, we require shape constancy and to do this we need to transform view-dependent representations into view-independent representations.

- Marr (1982) proposed three forms of representation that help transform the retinal image into an internal model of an object. The primal sketch is a 2D representation that codes information about light intensity in order to establish the edges and extent of the object in question. The $2^1/_2$D sketch also contains information about an object's edges and surfaces, together with the orientation and depth of these properties relative to the observer's viewpoint. The final 3D model of the object is view-independent and is typically characterised as a collection of basic building blocks of shape known as volumetric primitives.

- According to Tarr (1995), Marr's theory can be described as being a *complete viewpoint-invariant theory* in which a 3D view-independent model is accessed typically on the basis of partial information regarding the object. However, the empirical support for such theories is weak. Rock, Wheeler and Tudor (1989) found that people are generally poor at being able to imagine what abstract shapes look like from a different perspective. Rock and Di Vita (1987) demonstrated that participants were particularly sensitive to object orientation in tests of recognising previously exposed novel objects – departures from previously seen views led to poor levels of recognition. Moreover, Bültoff and Edelman (1992) showed that in a test of recognising previously exposed novel objects, while interpolated views of previous positions could be recognised with ease, extrapolated views were difficult to recognise. Object recognition seems therefore to be particularly sensitive to the similarity relations between familiar and novel views.

- Tarr (1995) drew a second set of ideas regarding object recognition under the heading of *restricted viewpoint-invariant theories*. Here the claim is that object recognition can be achieved given various constraints about what information is available in the image. One example of such a model was proposed by Biederman (1987), namely recognition by components (RBC). Here, various volumetric primitives known as geons are defined as forming the building blocks of object recognition. Specifically, an image of an object is essentially decomposed into its parts and an attempt is made to map onto these parts respective geons. Such a geon description is then used to search long-term memory (i.e., the library of 3D object models) for a matching description. If a match occurs then the object is recognised.

▶

- A final class of object recognition theory is defined by Tarr (1995) as *viewpoint-dependent*. Here, one or more canonical views of each object is stored on the understanding that such a representation codes what the object looks like from its most familiar orientation. TVs are most easily recognised and imagined in a position where the screen is visible (Palmer, Rosch & Chase, 1981). Computer instantiations of these ideas have been carried out and the most famous of these is the chorus of prototypes account put forward by Edelman (1998).

- It is also important to consider how objects are recognised in everyday scenes in which they may be occluded or surrounded by other objects. Murphy and Wisniewski (1989) suggested that the use of superordinate categories of object led individuals to consider the relationship between object and scene. Davenport and Potter (2004) also emphasised the importance of context in object recognition, even when participants were exposed to the scene for a very short period of time.

## ANSWERS TO PINPOINT QUESTIONS

13.1 Classification means that a stimulus has been assigned to a particular category (e.g., it's a mobile), whereas identification means that the stimulus has been uniquely recognised (e.g., it's Sarah's mobile).

13.2 A whale is an atypical member of the mammal category and so the subordinate level of whale would act as the entry level rather than the basic level of fruit.

13.3 Learning at a subordinate level improves the categorisation of both new and old examples in the area of expertise in question. It is also possible that perceptual encoding becomes more attuned to detecting finer detail relevant to the categorisation.

13.4 View-dependent representations change every time there is a change in the viewing angle between the observer and the object. View-independent representations remain the same regardless of the angle of regard.

13.5 The three levels of Marr's model of visual representation are the primal sketch, the $2\frac{1}{2}$D sketch and the 3D model description.

13.6 The Rock et al. (1989) study shows that we are very poor at imagining objects (or at least wire objects) from other perspectives. If we do have access to view-independent 3D models of objects, then these kinds of transformations should be easy to perform.

13.7 According to Biederman (1987), a geon is a volumetric primitive that constitutes a mental building block into which all objects are decomposed. Object recognition is achieved by securing a match between a geon description of an input stimulus with a stored counterpart in long-term memory.

13.8 A canonical view is useful for object recognition in that it maximises the amount of information that is useful for recognition. It holds a specification of an object that is most typically encountered – an impression of the front of a television is stored and not the back; a canonical view of a mug would show the position of the handle from the side, etc.

13.9 View-dependent representations are captured by the view-tuned units in the network model, while view-independent representations are captured by the view-invariant object units.

13.10 You'd be less likely to notice a kitchen utensil than an egg whisk in a tanning salon.

## CHAPTER 14

# THE NATURE OF LANGUAGE AND ITS RELATION TO THE OTHER MENTAL FACULTIES

## LEARNING OBJECTIVES

**By the end of this chapter, you should be able to:**

- Describe the difference between language performance and language competence (Chomsky, 1965).

- Distinguish between the phonological, syntactical and semantic structure of a sentence.

- Describe the language characteristics of productivity, systematicity, compositionality and recursion.

- Identify syntactic and semantic parsing mechanisms.

- Compare the establishment and connectionist approaches to explaining the acquisition of past-tense rules.

- Discuss the potential relationship between language and perception in terms of categorical perception.

## CHAPTER CONTENTS

▶

# Off the starting blocks Language on a lazy Sunday afternoon

It's a beautiful summer's day in England and for once it's not raining. You've been invited over to a friend's house and are enjoying one of those lovely Sunday afternoons in the garden, complete with nibbles, orange squash and the occasional wasp. Your friend's young child is busily playing with a newly acquired collection of coloured shapes on the lawn and also busily playing with their newly acquired language. 'I builded three spacesips!' he exclaims and drags you out of your comfortable deckchair to show you the results. 'Look, here's a blue block which is where the people go and the red pointy rocket.' Moving on to the second creation: 'And here's another yellow square with the red pointy rocket at the top – there are more astronauts in this one,' he points out by way of explanation. 'And the third one is the biggest one of all – it's lots of carriages for the people to sit in and places for their food so they don't get hungry and it's got the red pointy rocket at the top.' Looking over at the now empty bowl of nibbles on the garden table, you start to wish you were in the third rocket and slowly lean over for a closer examination. With that, the family dog goes bounding over, sending you sprawling over the child's creations. 'You breaked my rockets!' he exclaims, but after a period of quiet reflection continues, 'That's okay, I was going to make racing cars now.'

## REFLECTIVE QUESTIONS

1. What does it mean to be able to produce language? How do we know when sentences make sense and when they don't? What kind of knowledge are we applying in order to understand language? How do we anticipate language and how does this help structure our world? What makes us different from a dictionary or a talking parrot?

2. What happens when you think and what form do these thoughts take? Are they verbal or non-verbal? Do you always think in terms of language, or are there other forms of non-linguistic thought? How do language, thought and perception interact with one another?

## Introduction and preliminary considerations

Much of what has been written so far has been accepting of the general modularity of mind framework for thinking as set out by Fodor (1983). By this view, and in simple terms, there is a set of independent, purpose-specific input processing modules that operate autonomously and independently from one another in an, essentially, stimulus-driven fashion. Outputs from these distinct mental modules are fed forward towards the central systems whose purpose is to assign meaning and interpret the world. Accordingly, we could argue that there is a language module, a maths module, a music module, etc. For Fodor, though, the actual claims were more specific than this. It is assumed that, within each of these domains (i.e., language, mathematics, music) there is a variety of input modules, each of which is dedicated to carrying out a very specific task. For instance, the listening and speaking skills in language can be broken down into different components that call on quite different processing abilities. The module concerned with decoding these marks on this page is quite different from the module concerned with decoding speech.

Recently, however, issues have been raised over the degree to which the cognitive operations associated with one module are so very different from those associated with another at the most basic of levels (see Marcus, 2006, and Chapter 2 for the discussion of the difference between horizontal and vertical faculties). For instance, given that all of the modules inhabit the brain, 'they are likely to emerge from relatively similar bits of six-layered neocortex' and therefore 'the neural tissues that they rely on have at least something in common' (Marcus, 2006, p. 448). Accordingly there may well be some fairly basic functional commonalities that run across the different modules.

In taking the particular example of language, Marcus made several observations:

- Language use is heavily dependent on memory and the underlying mechanisms for the encoding, storage and retrieval of memory in language may overlap considerably with underlying mechanisms for the encoding, storage and retrieval of memory in other domains.

- Language fundamentally concerns processing sequences and here again the basic problems in producing and decoding sequences cut across many other domains. (Think of constructing a sentence, tying your shoelaces, making a cup of tea, buying a round of drinks, etc.)

- The ability to manipulate the components of language may reflect a more basic cognitive ability that underpins other faculties.

The intention here is to concentrate on this third point, and although the discussion is primarily about language, the assumption is that the basic properties of language are common to other forms of cognition and perception: for example, dealing with sequences cuts across many cognitive domains. Tying shoelaces, playing that arpeggio while practicing the harp, making sure that the tea bag is in the cup before you pour from the kettle, etc. To appreciate why sequences are so important in language use, we need to consider some of what the basic characteristics of natural language are.

## Some basic characteristics of natural language

### Performance vs. competence

The phrase **natural language** refers to any form of human language such as French, German, Cantonese, etc. We can set these apart from, say, computer programming languages. There is only so much you can say in a computer programming language, whereas with natural language the possibilities are, essentially, limitless. Moreover, in the normal course of events, natural languages are acquired naturally and effortlessly, and this cannot be said for the task of learning computer programming languages like PROLOG and LISP. In discussing natural language an important distinction can be drawn between *performance* and *competence* (Chomsky, 1965, p. 4).

#### *Performance*

Language performance (or more simply **performance**) refers to language use in all its forms: spoken, written, signed, etc. by humans. Within the context of cognitive psychology, or more exactly within the sub-discipline of psycholinguistics, the focus is on the performance characteristics of humans. Ultimately, it is these that define the language behaviours we are attempting to explain. There are many such performance limitations. Take, for example, the constraints on how quickly we can speak, or what the maximum rate of speech is that we can understand, or indeed, what is the longest sentence that we can decipher. We are not so concerned with the capabilities of the talking clock or the talking parrot, as these have very particular constraints that do not apply to humans. Indeed, even though we may well have a desire to talk to the animals, all of the evidence is that they have very little to say. As Pinker (1994) remarked, where natural language is concerned, 'they just don't get it' (p. 340). To appreciate this point, we must examine language **competence**.

### Competence

If we limited ourselves solely to the study of language performance, the claim is that we would end up with only a very narrow understanding of natural language (see Chomsky, 1965, pp. 19–20, for a very pessimistic appraisal of the usefulness of empirical methods in this regard). Most importantly, we need to be able to understand the underlying principles of how the language operates. In this respect, and in contrast to language performance, there is language competence, and here there is a very particular definition that we must consider. The phrase 'language competence' refers to a speaker's knowledge of their particular language, but now we must tread carefully. Clearly there will be individual differences across language users in what they know about their language: compare William Shakespeare with Forrest Gump. Ultimately, though, this is not what is being discussed, for what is at stake is knowledge of a natural language in some idealised form.

Traditionally it has been accepted that such knowledge is captured by a **grammar** or system of rules that specifies how sentences of a language are built up. It is assumed that all language users have such knowledge but most likely they will be unable to articulate this knowledge. Language competence is (in the main) *tacit knowledge* (Chomsky, 1980) – implicit knowledge of the grammatical rules of the language. Ordinary language users must possess such knowledge because they can be understood when they speak and write, and they understand when they listen and read. However, it is highly unlikely (unless they have studied linguistics) that they will be able to articulate what such rules actually are. Try it yourself and explain why it is quite acceptable to say, 'Who did John see Mary with?' but not 'Who did John see Mary and?' (Pinker & Bloom, 1992).

If this notion of tacit knowledge is still a mystery, then consider the following non-linguistic examples.

Most people 'know' how to ride a bike but they are unable to articulate this knowledge. They might be able to give some hints about how not to fall off but they would be unable to explain how the limbs are co-ordinated or how the body remains upright as the weight is directed first in one direction and then in the next. It is also not very likely that David Beckham really understands the kinematics behind taking a free kick but he must 'know' something, given the highly proficient manner in which he expresses this competence. This distinction between competence and performance is therefore important in domains other than language.

As we will see, therefore, psycholinguists face quite a challenge. On the one hand, there are all the issues concerning language performance, and it would be quite legitimate to focus on these. For instance, one research question, pertinent to the film industry, is, 'What is the best way to generate sub-titles when during a critical scene there are several speakers talking at once and an important message is broadcast over the PA?' On the other hand, there are issues concerning the fundamental nature of the language system. What are the fundamental constituents of the language? And what are the rules that govern how such constituents are combined? According to Chomsky (1965), the challenge is further complicated by the fact that language performance may provide only a very imperfect impression of the underlying system of rules.

What Chomsky (1965) urged us to do was to consider what the nature of language competence is, irrespective of any performance limitations. More particularly, the aim (for him) is to try to arrive at an adequate description of the constituents of the language and the rules of combination of these constituents. According to him, however, the ultimate aim is to be able to explain what it is that allows language users to decide about what is and what is not an acceptable sentence in the language. Psycholinguists should therefore strive to generate testable hypotheses about language and develop experiments that address such hypotheses. As a consequence, in this chapter we will examine some of the most important data that have been collected so far. However, irrespective of the methods used or the theoretical stance adopted, it should be accepted that a full understanding of natural language depends on understanding both the nature of observable performance and underlying competence. Put simply, there is much more to language than meets the eye or the ear!

## Pinpoint question 14.1

**Is being unable to understand someone who speaks in a heavy regional dialect a reflection of problems concerning performance or competence?**

**natural language** Human languages such as Italian or Japanese.

**performance** In Chomsky's terms, all observable human language behaviour.

**competence** In Chomsky's terms, the tacit knowledge that underlies the ability to produce and understand all and only the sentences in a natural language.

**grammar** According to Chomsky, the set of mental rules that allows a person to produce and understand the sentences in a natural language.

## The difference between the surface forms of language and the deeper forms

At this point it may be helpful to draw the distinction between the surface forms of the language and its deeper forms: the distinction between the superficial structure and the underlying structure (Chomsky, 1965; Postal, 1964). For our purposes, we can use **superficial structure** to refer to any example of observable language use – an utterance, a written sentence, a signed message, etc. **Underlying structure**, in the present context, refers to the mental representations that underpin the superficial structure. The notion of underlying language structure forms the basis of this chapter and we will discuss several examples as we proceed.

Chomsky (1965) actually discussed two related distinctions: (i) between the outer and inner form of a sentence, and (ii) between the surface and deep structure of a sentence. A detailed discussion of these would take us far from the topics of interest here (see Harley, 1995, ch. 5 for a clear and thorough treatment of the difference between deep and surface structure). Instead we will cling on to the phrase 'underlying structure' and use this with reference to putative mental representations that underpin language production and perception. In contrast, 'superficial structure' refers to language that is directly observable.

To clarify this point, consider the following two sentences:

| | |
|---|---|
| Flying planes are dangerous. | (1) |
| Flying planes is dangerous. | (2) |

A comprehensive analysis of these sentences is offered by Lyons (1968, pp. 249–51), but we need only consider them in broad strokes. Chomsky (1965) argued that, despite these two sentences appearing very similar on the surface (they only differ with respect to one word), at a deeper level they are actually very different (they mean very different things). In accounting for this difference, appeals must be made to differences in their underlying structures. The argument is that each superficial structure is generated from an underlying structure by taking the components in the underlying structure and manipulating these in particular ways. The construction of (1) starts from an abstract statement (let us call this a **base sentence** that contains a string of abstract symbols) that codes something like 'Planes are flying' where flying planes as opposed to stationary planes are dangerous. In contrast, (2) starts from a base sentence that codes something like 'Amelia flies planes' where the act of flying planes is a dangerous enterprise. In this account, the rules of grammar are then brought to bear on these base sentences (essentially the deep structures) so as to generate (1) and (2). It is only by considering the differences in the underlying structure that the real difference between (1) and (2) is made apparent.

In addition, and for Chomsky (1957), deep structure captures the intuitions we have about related sentences. Remember, every surface sentence is derived from a deeper base sentence. For example, consider the sentence:

| | |
|---|---|
| William drinks that cup of tea. | (3) |

According to Chomsky (1957), the base sentence that corresponds to (3) (the base sentence is captured by abstract symbols, not words) underlies the following set of sentences, in which the same subject (William), verb (drink) and object (tea) feature:

William drank that cup of tea.
That cup of tea was drunk by William.
William is drinking that cup of tea.
That cup of tea is being drunk by William.
Which cup of tea did William drink?

In Chomsky's early writings (1957, 1965) it was asserted that the base sentence is constructed through the application of fundamental rules of sentence

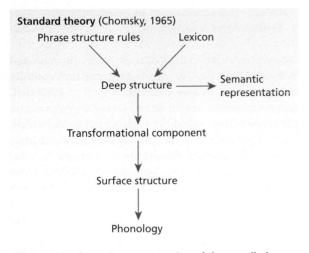

**Figure 14.1 Schematic representation of the so-called standard theory of natural language as described by Chomsky (1965)**

The basic core components of the language module are shown, together with their interrelations. In generating a base sentence, phrase structure rules are applied and information from the mental lexicon is accessed. A given base sentence constitutes what is known as deep structure. Having derived a base sentence, meanings can then be accessed. In the original transformational account, Chomsky (1965) argued that further operations were undertaken so as to generate the surface form of a sentence from its deep structure. In addition to the initial phrase structure rules, other rules of grammar known as transformational rules were posited. For instance, if roughly the base sentence codes 'John read the book', then in order to generate the question 'Which book did John read?' further transformational rules are applied. In this example, the final output is in terms of a sentence as coded in phonological terms.

*Source*: Jackendoff, R. (2003). Precis of foundations of language: Brain, meaning, grammar, evolution. *The Behavioral and Brain Sciences*, *26*, 651–707 (fig. 1, p. 655). Reproduced with permission from Cambridge University Press.

construction known as **syntactic rules** (or phrase structure rules). Next, more advanced syntactic rules known as **transformations** are brought to bear on the base sentence. Figure 14.1 (taken from Jackendoff, 2002) provides an illustration of the general ideas in schematic form. So, for Chomsky (1965), the grammar of the language comprises syntactic rules of sentence construction that specify how a base sentence is constructed and how such a base sentence is transformed in the generation of a surface form. Indeed, it is only by considering the contrast between the superficial and underlying structures that ambiguities in particular sentences can be understood. For instance, consider the following:

Visiting relatives can be difficult. (4)

Now the same surface form has more than one reading: either the relatives themselves can be difficult, or going to visit them can be. The important point is that the very same superficial structure can be derived from quite different underlying structures. The ambiguity of the sentence is only revealed once an analysis of the underlying, rather than the superficial, structures is undertaken.

Unfortunately, there are many difficult issues here. First, let us start with a fairly uncontentious claim, namely that we are right to draw the distinction between the superficial and underlying structure of language, and that, as cognitive psychologists, we are right to focus on the nature of underlying structures. Aside from this there are many unresolved issues and one is highlighted by the difference between a *linguistic analysis* and a *psycholinguistic analysis* of some aspect of language behaviour.

## Linguistics vs. psycholinguistics

One aim of a linguistic analysis is to provide an account of grammar by trying to arrive at the set of rules that defines the language in much the same way that a mathematician goes about proving a theorem. As cognitive psychologists, though, we are right to ask whether the rules and representations that are discussed in the linguistic analysis provide any insights into the cognitive processing of language. As we'll see later in the chapter on reasoning, it's all very well establishing rules related to logical reasoning, but it's not all that clear that we actually use them in any systematic way. In other words, what is the relation (if any) between our descriptions of grammar and our descriptions of mental representations and processes? (See Clark & Clark, 1977, pp. 6–7; see also Postal, 1964, p. 264.) Although some linguists would argue with Chomsky's particular linguistic analysis of sentences of the type (1) and (2), as cognitive psychologists we are much more concerned about whether such analyses tell us anything useful about the cognitive processes that underlie language comprehension and production. For instance, is it literally true that in understanding sentences, we access rules of sentence construction to help us to recover what is being conveyed? Are there really such things as base sentences? And is it really true that the rules of syntax govern sentence production and comprehension?

An issue to which we will continually return is whether any particular linguistic description of a sentence implies anything of note about mental representations and processes. Such issues as these should be at the forefront of our thoughts as we consider the complex structures that have been described in relation to the componential status of language.

### Pinpoint question 14.2

**Why is the sentence 'Students hate irritating lecturers' ambiguous?**

**superficial structure** The surface nature of language, how it looks when written, how it sounds when spoken, etc.

**underlying structure** The mental representations that underlie language production and comprehension.

**base sentence** According to Chomsky, an abstract statement containing a series of symbols from which the surface form of an actual sentence is produced.

**syntactic rules** The rules responsible for the grammatical (de)construction of a sentence.

**transformations** According to Chomsky (1965), the mechanisms in converting a base sentence into a surface sentence.

## The componential nature of language

To return to Marcus's (2006) concerns, in this chapter the aim is to reflect upon the nature of language and how it relates to other mental faculties. As we have noted, Marcus pointed out that the ability to manipulate the components of language reflect a basic cognitive ability that underpins other faculties. It is important therefore to appreciate exactly what the components of language are.

In its written form, words are composed of letters; phrases and sentences are composed of words; sentences may contain phrases; and paragraphs are composed of sentences. Other distinctions are also possible. Words may also be described in terms of morphemes – where a **morpheme** can be defined as 'the minimal unit of grammatical analysis' (Lyons, 1968, p. 181). So *walker* and *walking* share the same root morpheme (the morpheme *walk*) but they have different affixes (the morphemes *er* and *ing* respectively). So even

some single words can be decomposed into more basic constituents that convey meaning. The general idea of componential structure is perhaps best conveyed in Figure 14.2 taken from Jackendoff (2002) in which the componential nature of language is revealed in all its forms.

Three types of structure are shown and each is taken to code an aspect of language connected to the state of affairs shown at the bottom of the figure, namely a picture showing a pair of stars side by side. In this particular case, the linguistic description of this state of affairs is given by the sentence 'The little star is beside a big star.'

## The phonological structure

In this particular scheme, the **phonological structure** is centred on the *segmental level* (or tier) which contains a description of discrete speech sounds or phonemes that constitute the spoken form of the sentence. Without going into too many details, three further tiers are defined within the context of the phonological structure:

1. The *morphophonological tier* sets out how the phonemes are group(ed) together to form words and morphemes.

2. The *syllabic structure* captures how spoken words can be decomposed into syllables (sy, lla, bles).

3. The *prosodic structure* specifies how words are grouped into spoken phrases and how, within phrases, intonation and stress are assigned. Take a sentence like 'You are taking the dog for a walk.' Say it out loud as a statement, then change how you say it so that it now sounds like a question. The difference across this contrast has to do with intonation. Now take a word like *record* and say it as a verb and now say it as a noun. The difference across this contrast has to do with which syllable is carrying the stress. With the noun the stress is on the first syllable, with the verb the stress is on the second syllable.

## The syntactic structure

With **syntactic structure**, we are dealing with grammar, or alternatively, the rules that govern sentence construction. What is shown in Figure 14.2 is just one of a vast number of different ways of setting out the structural relations between words and phrases that go to make up sentences. From a traditional perspective, as taught in schools, the grammar is primarily

**Phonological structure**

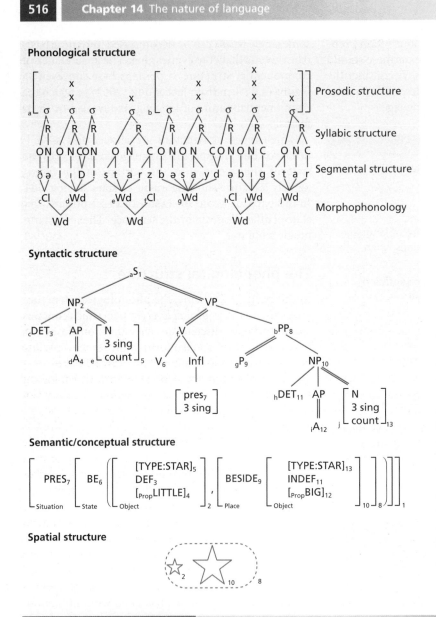

**Syntactic structure**

**Semantic/conceptual structure**

**Spatial structure**

**Figure 14.2  A componential view of language**
The main components of natural language as applied to an example of the English sentence, 'The little star is beside a big star' (from Jackendoff, 2002) – see text for further details. The segmental structure is conveyed in terms of phonetic transcription. So 'big' is /bɪg/ where now /b/ /l/ and /g/ convey the individual phonemes.

*Source*: Jackendoff, R. (2002). *Foundations of language. Brain, meaning, grammar, evolution* (fig. 1.1, p. 6). Oxford, England: Oxford University Press. Reproduced with permission.

## For example . . .

'Good day. My name is Spooner. Spoctor Dooner. I was just frassing the punt of your shop, and I thought I'd book in for a look. Look in for a book. Do excuse me, I sometimes get one word nuddled up with a mother. I'm stequently made a laughing frock.' (Barker, 2001, p. 248)

Named after English clergyman William Spooner, spoonerisms are essentially mistakes in phonologi-cal plans where phonemes are exchanged between words. There are a number of interesting character-istics associated with spoonerisms, such as that they predominantly involve the first sound of a word, and also that the exchanges often result in valid words (such as punt, mother and frock). Although hard to elicit spontaneously in the lab, they remain a fourse of sun for the pognitive csychologist.

concerned with the notion of word classes or parts of speech (such as noun, verb, adverb, etc.). More gener-ally, though, in psycholinguistics, the grammar provides a specification of the rules of sentence construction –

how word classes, and ultimately individual words, are combined to give rise to acceptable sentences. More formally, 'a grammar is a finite system of rules for characterizing . . . all and only the sentence of the language' (Wasow, 1989, pp. 163–4). Here 'all and only' means the grammar should pick out all the sentences in the language and discard everything else.

This form of representation, as shown in Figure 14.2, is known as a **tree diagram**. There is a root node (the S1 node is sometimes known as the start node) in the figure, branches (or the links between nodes), and finally the leaves or terminal nodes – the nodes at the lowest level in the tree. A useful distinction here is between the **terminal vocabulary** and the **non-terminal vocabulary**. The terminal vocabulary comprises the actual words in the language. Jackendoff (2002) omitted these from his tree diagram because he argued that the terminal vocabulary is not strictly part of the syntax of the language. By this view the syntax of the language comprises a set of abstract symbols (the non-terminal vocabulary) and the rules of how such symbols can be combined so as to generate acceptable sentences. The grammar therefore specifies the underlying structures that determine which words go where in the superficial structure.

More formally, the idea is that the rules of syntax can also be termed *rewrite rules*. There is a direct mapping between a tree diagram of syntactic representation and a set of corresponding rewrite rules. In a sense the rewrite rules determine the structure of the tree diagram. Here are the sorts of rules that underpin the generation of the sentence shown in Figure 14.2:

$$S \rightarrow NP + VP \qquad \text{(Rule 1)}$$
$$NP \rightarrow DET + AP + N \qquad \text{(Rule 2)}$$
$$VP \rightarrow V + PP \qquad \text{(Rule 3)}$$
$$PP \rightarrow P + NP \qquad \text{(Rule 4)}$$

- Rule 1: a sentence (S) can be rewritten as ($\rightarrow$ denotes 'can be rewritten as') a noun phrase (NP) plus a verb phrase (VP).
- Rule 2: a noun phrase can be rewritten as a determiner (DET, e.g., *a*, *the*) plus an adjectival phrase (AP) plus a noun (N).
- Rule 3: a verb phrase can be rewritten as a verb plus a prepositional phrase (PP).
- Rule 4: a prepositional phrase can be rewritten as a preposition (P) plus a noun phrase.

The S, NP, VP, PP, V, P, AP, DET and N make up the non-terminal vocabulary in this very simple grammar. Many other technicalities could be introduced at this juncture: for instance, the numbering in the syntactic structure tree diagram in Figure 14.2 shows how the system keeps track of the different tokens of the same type – there is a noun, $N_5$ (which might refer to Kylie)

and another noun, $N_{13}$ (which might refer to Jason). However, such technicalities would lead us far from current concerns. The primary intention is to examine the basic ideas concerning syntax and syntactic structure. Fundamentally, syntax provides a structural description of each sentence in a natural language as given by the grammatical rules of the language. A phrase that occurs frequently in this context is **syntactic parsing**. This refers to the process of dividing up linguistic input into its syntactic constituents, namely words, phrases, clauses, sentences, etc. As we will see, some cognitive psychologists have expended a tremendous amount of effort in attempting to explain language understanding in terms of the manner in which sentences are parsed into their possible constituents.

## The semantic structure

Both in Figure 14.2, and more generally, syntactic structure is distinguished from semantic structure. Whereas **syntax** refers to the form of a sentence in terms of the relations between its constituent phrases and words, **semantics** refers to its meaning. This division of syntax from semantics allows for syntactically acceptable strings of words that are, essentially, meaningless. For example, 'Colourless green ideas sleep furiously' (Chomsky, 1957, p. 15) is okay in terms of grammar, it's just that it doesn't make a blind bit of sense, whereas 'Furiously sleep ideas green colourless' is an example of a string of words that is both grammatically and semantically unacceptable. More importantly, though, cognitive psychologists have been concerned about the degree to which factors attributable to syntax and factors attributable to semantics govern sentence comprehension and production. We will consider some of this evidence shortly.

For Jackendoff (2002), regardless of how the mental representation of meaning is conceived, the semantic analysis must show how particular thoughts and ideas are expressed in words and sentences. For instance, in the notation adopted in Figure 14.2, the bracketing delimits five so-called **conceptual constituents**. Each pair of left and right brackets '[ ]' captures one conceptual constituent (an idea) and, in this scheme, each conceptual constituent may specify a situation, event, state, object or property. Collectively these specify 'that there is a Situation in the present, consisting of a State. This State is one of an Object being located in a Place' (p. 11), and also that the place is further qualified by another object. So in general terms, this kind of semantic structure conveys aspects of sentence meaning. It does this by providing a specification of the basic concepts (e.g., the STARs) and their properties (e.g., LITTLE, BIG) together with a specification of the time (the present) and place (spatial information is also conveyed, i.e., BESIDE).

Aside from these technical points, the basic ideas can be understood in terms of the so-called *propositional content* of the sentence (Clark & Clark, 1977). The **propositional content** specifies the ideas and concepts contained in a sentence. For example, with a sentence like the following:

The young troops defeated the army.                    (5)

the two important ideas (propositions) are that 'The troops were young' and 'The army was defeated' (Clark & Clark, 1977, p. 29). Clark & Clark (1977) went further and provided a useful example of how syntactic and semantic structure may relate to one another. Figure 14.3 provides a simplified tree diagram of the following sentence:

The old man lit his awful cigar.                    (6)

| Constituent | Underlying proposition |
| --- | --- |
| old man | $Man(E_{57})$, $Old(E_{57})$ |
| the old man | $Known(E_{57})$ |
| awful cigar | $Cigar(E_8)$, $Awful(E_8)$ |
| his awful cigar | $Known(E_8)$, $Belong(E_8, X)$ |
| the old man lit his awful cigar | $Light(E_{57}, E_8)$ |

As with Jackendoff's analysis, the numbering here allows the system to keep track of who is who and what is

what. The Es are in a sense much like variables in algebra. E can take on a particular value and the actual values are signified by the different numbers so $E_{57}$ signifies the particular thing that is both old and a man called Mr Smith and $E_8$ signifies the particular thing that is both awful and a cigar. As you can see, however, the X is without a value and this is because, without further information, the term 'his' is indefinite. The cigar could be Mr Smith's, but he may have been given it by Mr Jones.

According to Clark and Clark (1977) the hypothesis now is obvious – 'As listeners go along, they parse a sentence into its constituents and for each one build up the appropriate propositions' (p. 49). If this is true, though, the obvious question is, how on earth do listeners (and of course readers) do this? This is a basic question and one to which we will return shortly. As we will discover, cognitive psychologists have expended a tremendous amount of effort over how to best account for how it is that people parse sentences into meaningful constituents.

---

**Pinpoint question 14.3**

If *Monty Python's Flying Circus* was discussed with reference to 'proper noun, adjective, noun', would this be a phonological, syntactic or semantic reading?

---

**morpheme** The smallest unit of meaning in natural language.

**phonological structure** According to Jackendoff (2002), the mental representations that code how components of language sound when spoken.

**syntactic structure** Some form of representation that specifies how a sentence is decomposed into its constituent phrases and words.

**tree diagram** In terms of natural language, a schematic representation that shows the constituents of a sentence and how these are related.

**terminal vocabulary** The actual words of a language.

**non-terminal vocabulary** Abstract mental symbols that play a role in the generation and comprehension of sentences in a natural language.

**syntactic parsing** The processes involved in dividing sentences into constituent grammatical components such as verb phrases, verbs, nouns, adjectives, etc.

**syntax** The grammatical nature of natural language sentences.

**semantics** A term for meaning.

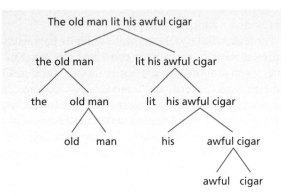

**Figure 14.3 Tree diagram that shows the structure of the sentence, 'The old man lit his awful cigar'**

*Source*: Clark, H. H., & Clark, E. V. (1977). *Psychology and Language. An introduction to psycholinguistics* (fig. 4, p. 47). New York: Harcourt Brace Jovanovitch. Reproduced with permission.

## I know it, I know it, it's on the tip of my fingers: failure of sign retrieval in the deaf

So far we have been discussing a ruthlessly efficient system in which language gets meticulously broken down into smaller and smaller components. Equally, though, we've all been in situations where language has momentarily failed us: what was the name of the film we saw last week, the boy you sat next to in English at secondary school or your fifth wife? These 'tip-of-the tongue' (TOT) phenomena are common, but are they limited to spoken language? This was the question Thompson, Emmorey and Gollan (2005) asked in investigating the possibility that similar retrieval failures might also apply to different domains, such as sign language, leading to the identification of potential 'tip-of-the-fingers' (TOF) phenomena.

Thirty-three deaf individuals were used in the study, all of whom used American sign language as their first choice of communication. Participants were presented with both pictures of famous individuals and written English words, and asked to sign their answer. TOFs in this experiment were explicitly defined as 'when you temporarily cannot retrieve a word you are sure that you know' (Thompson et al., 2005, p. 857).

The data showed that there were some interesting similarities between TOTs and TOFs. First, for the TOFs produced after exposure to the famous individuals, 56 per cent contained at least some correct phonological information. That is, participants signed the first letter of the first and/or last name of the celebrity in question. However, retrieving more phonological information did not necessarily lead to the resolution of the TOF, despite the fact that around 60 per cent of these annoying little interruptions in retrieval were solved during the experiment. Participants were also more likely to recall the initial hand shape, location and orientation of the sign rather than the movement involved in the sign.

Thompson et al. (2005) argued that TOF phenomena point very strongly to a separation between phonological and semantic retrieval. That is, the amount of semantic information that the signer could provide regarding the famous individual was simply not related to the likelihood of resolving the TOF by accessing the phonological word-form. In another example they described (p. 858), even though the sign for Switzerland mimics the actual cross on the Swiss flag, a close relation between phonological and semantic aspects did not seem to help retrieving its access during a TOF. Their data also suggest that these failures of retrieval appear to be language-universal phenomena, regardless of which body part you happen to be using at the time!

*Source*: Thompson, R., Emmorey, K., & Gollan, T. H. (2005). 'Tips of the fingers' experiences by deaf signers: Insights into the organization of a sign-based lexicon. *Psychological Science, 16*, 856–860.

---

**conceptual constituents** According to Jackendoff (2002), the units of semantic analysis related to language. Components of meaning conveyed by a sentence or phrase.

**propositional content** The ideas and concepts embodied within a sentence.

## Other basic characteristics of natural language

The fundamental idea that we have explored so far is that essentially, at the psychological level, language is a symbolic system that is composed of constituents (the basic symbols) and that these constituents are governed by rules of combination. As Figure 14.2 shows, this idea of the constitutive nature of language applies to phonology, syntax and semantics. However, to get a better understanding of the issues, it is important to consider other general characteristics that make natural language a very particular kind of symbolic system. The rules of combination that apply at the level of phrases and sentences have been discussed, by Fodor and Pylyshyn (1988), in terms of three general characteristics, namely *productivity*, *systematicity* and *compositionality*. According to them, it is only when we consider these characteristics that the true nature of natural language is revealed. A much more far-reaching claim, however, is that these three characteristics also provide fundamental insights into how the mind works in general.

## Productivity

In terms of sentences and other forms of complex expressions, Fodor and Pylyshyn (1988) have discussed the combinatorial nature of language in terms of something they labelled **productivity**. Given that sentences have constituent structure and that there is a combinatorial syntax that governs how the constituents are combined, then this provides an indication of how it is that an infinite number of sentences can be expressed and interpreted. So the basic observation is that there is an infinite number of sentences that can be expressed and interpreted, and the challenge is to provide an explanation of how this could be. Fodor and Pylyshyn (1988), in following Chomsky (1957), explained this by assuming that underlying language performance is a grammar – a generative grammar – that specifies a finite set of rules which, when applied, define all and only the sentences of the language. Such a grammar 'allows us in principle to generate(/understand) an unbounded number of sentences' (Fodor & Pylyshyn, 1988, p. 34).

## Systematicity

In addition to the productivity of language, Fodor and Pylyshyn (1988) also discussed the notion of **systematicity**. Systematicity refers to the fact that 'the ability to produce/understand some sentences is intrinsically connected to the ability to produce/understand certain others' (Fodor & Pylyshyn, 1988, p. 37). So the classic example here is that if the language user understands 'John loves Mary' then the same user will understand 'Mary loves John'. Grasping the meaning of the sentence 'John loves Mary' implies that each individual word has been assigned an interpretation. In addition, understanding the sentence implies recovering the appropriate structural description that codes the semantic relations in the sentence. In this regard, the assertion is that the sentence is coded via the sort of semantic/conceptual structure as shown in Figure 14.2 and discussed by Jackendoff (2002).

The claim is that the sentences 'John loves Mary' and 'Mary loves John' are systematically related both because they share common constituents and they also share the same structural description. Each sentence has the underlying structure $xRy$ in which two entities (the $x$ and $y$) are linked by a relation (the $R$). We have an $x$ and we have a $y$ and they share a relation $R$. For example, let $x$ be 'John', let $y$ be 'Mary' and 'loves' is the relation. In order to understand sentences of the type $xRy$ we need to be able to recover the meanings of the individual constituents. The assumption is that

this process of understanding only works because each individual word carries with it its own meaning and this remains the same regardless of the context.

So 'having a natural language', or 'being a proficient natural language user', implies being able to understand sentences – not just one sentence but lots of systematically related sentences. More particularly, understanding one sentence of a particular type (i.e., one that conforms to $xRy$) implies the ability to understand other sentences of the type $xRy$. By this view understanding sentences is based on (i) knowing the meanings of the individual words and (ii) knowing the structural (semantic) relations that hold between those words. According to Aizawa (1997), the systematicity of language is a claim that if a person understands 'John loves Mary' then the implication is that they will also understand:

*John loves John*   *Mary loves John*   *Mary loves Mary*

We can set out the complete set of sentences they will understand if they also know who *Jane* is and what *hates* and *fears* means. They are:

| | | |
|---|---|---|
| *John loves John* | *John hates John* | *John fears John* |
| *John loves Mary* | *John hates Mary* | *John fears Mary* |
| *John loves Jane* | *John hates Jane* | *John fears Jane* |
| *Mary loves John* | *Mary hates John* | *Mary fears John* |
| *Mary loves Mary* | *Mary hates Mary* | *Mary fears Mary* |
| *Mary loves Jane* | *Mary hates Jane* | *Mary fears Jane* |
| *Jane loves John* | *Jane hates John* | *Jane fears John* |
| *Jane loves Mary* | *Jane hates Mary* | *Jane fears Mary* |
| *Jane loves Jane* | *Jane hates Jane* | *Jane fears Jane* |

This discussion of systematicity is again based on a claim about the difference between superficial and underlying structures. The systematicity of language is only understood in terms of the underlying structural relations that hold between sentences. Sentences are said to be related systematically if they share the same underlying structure such as $xRy$. More importantly, though, Aizawa (1997) was at pains to point out there are no cases where a person's language comprehension skills apply on a case-by-case basis:

one does not find normal cognitive agents who think all and only the thoughts

*John loves Mary*
*Einstein studied physics*
*Bears hibernate*
*Cats chase mice and other rodents*

*(Aizawa, 1997, p. 119)*

In contrast, it is quite possible to conjure up examples where language use could be very much predicated on a case-by-case basis. Take Charlie the talking parrot, for instance. Charlie quite readily says, 'Charlie wants a chip', when he see the family gathered round for tea. He is, however, quite incapable of expressing 'Penny wants a chip', 'Charlie wants a beer' or indeed 'Penny wants a beer'. There is a very important difference therefore between 'talking' and 'having a language'.

## Compositionality

Finally, Fodor and Pylyshyn (1988) discussed the notion of **compositionality** and this is fundamentally about how grasping the meaning of a complex expression is determined by grasping the meanings of its constituents and how these are related. In simple terms, take a complex expression like *brown cow*. According to Fodor and Pylyshyn (1988), the meaning of 'brown cow' is completely determined by the meaning of 'brown', the meaning of 'cow' and the rule of combination that designates the intersections of brown things and cows. So unless you already know the meaning of *awning* you won't understand what a *purple awning* is.

According to Fodor and Pylyshyn (1988), the success of any account of natural language must be gauged against how well it accounts for productivity, systematicity and compositionality. Indeed they were also at pains to point out that these three characteristics apply more generally, and reveal basic properties of the mind. In the same way that the basic units of language are combined and different combinations of units are related to one another, so are the basic units of thought. The characteristics of natural language are shared with the language of thought (Fodor, 1975; see also Chapter 7). On the understanding that mental operations in general are akin to a language of thought, then thinking in general reflects the following:

- Productivity – an infinite number of thoughts can be entertained.

- Systematicity – various thoughts are systematically related to one another. Thinking *John loves Mary* implies the ability to think *Mary loves John*.

- Compositionality – reasoning about *brown cows* in one context implies being able to reason about such concepts in other contexts.

The main point to take home from all of this is that these three basic characteristics reveal the fundamental nature of natural language. They show how it is that this sort of symbolic system operates. Perhaps one way to appreciate this is with regard to the following

example. There are various basic components to the rules of poker – initial stakes are placed and the dealer deals the cards, there is a round of betting, some cards are revealed or cards are exchanged, and another round of betting takes place. Some variation of these steps is iterated until all players, bar one, drop out or two players end up going head-to-head.

Let us assume that understanding the rules of poker is akin to understanding sentences. 'Having the language of poker' means that a person is able to grasp all variations of the game of poker – we will have three rounds of betting instead of two, certain cards are wild, we will play no-limit Texas Hold 'Em rather than fixed-limit Texas Hold 'Em. Understanding and being able to play one game of poker implies understanding/being able to play the next.

The situation could be quite different, however. Now it could be that instead of 'having the language of poker' the person stores the rules of the different variations of the game on a case-by-case basis. This person knows the rules of Texas Hold 'Em, knows the rules of Five Card Stud but fails to grasp that the different variations of the game are still poker. In the limit the person could be in a situation where, even though they know how to play Five Card Stud, they have no idea that this is, essentially, the same game as Texas Hold 'Em. The point is that the evidence strongly suggests that language users possess a symbolic system in which being able to generate and understand one kind of sentence (one kind of poker) implies the ability to generate and understand an infinite number of other sentences (kinds of poker). The problem for cognitive psychologists is to try to explain how this comes about.

### Pinpoint question 14.4

**What are the three characteristics of language according to Fodor and Pylyshyn (1988)?**

## Recursion

In addition to the productivity, systematicity and compositionality, there is a final characteristic of natural language that is also taken to be fundamental and this is known as **recursion**. Corballis (2003) has gone so far as to claim that recursion is 'the key to the human mind'. Clearly, therefore, it would be remiss not to discuss this in a book about human cognition. Corballis (2003) defined recursion as a means 'for generating terms in a sequence, in which the rule for generating the next term in a sequence involves one or more of the preceding terms' (p. 155). A concrete example will help. Consider the simple phrase structure grammar:

Rule 1.   S → NP + VP
Rule 2.   NP → article + noun + [RC]
Rule 3.   RC → relative pronoun + VP
Rule 4.   VP → verb + [NP]

The symbols S, NP, VP are as defined previously (sentence, noun phrase and verb phrase, respectively), the RC refers to 'relative clause' and the parentheses indicate optional terms.

The recursive nature of this grammar is given by the fact that it is possible to 'cycle endlessly from Rule 2 to Rule 3 to Rule 4 and back to Rule 2' (p. 156). Indeed, in using such a system of rewrite rules it is possible to generate sentences of the sort 'The dog that chased the cat killed the rat' (see Figure 14.4 for the corresponding tree diagram).

It is because of our ability to generate and understand such so-called *embedded sentences* (the subordinate clause 'that chased the cat' is embedded in the main clause 'The dog . . . killed the rat') that claims are made about the underlying recursive nature of the rewriting rules. However, caution is warranted here. The point about recursion is that, in principle, it is possible to 'cycle endlessly', but clearly this does not happen because the 'sentence' would be essentially meaningless. There is apparently an important clash between competence and performance. The theorists claim that the underlying system of rewrite rules includes the property of recursion, but the potential of such a system is never realised in performance. People simply cannot manage with infinitely embedded sentences. Try the following:

> The malt that the rat that cat that the dog worried killed ate lay in the house that Jack built.     (7)
>
> *(Corballis, 2003, p. 157)*

However, the performance limitations do not just point to a limitation in some form of short-term memory system because troubles also occur with relatively short sentences (see Pinker, 1994, p. 205). Try the following:

> Bulldogs bulldogs bulldogs fight fight fight.     (8)

In this regard, the performance limitations reveal something both about the in-principle characteristics of the sentence parser together with how such a parser is also constrained. Some embedded sentences are more difficult to interpret than others. Indeed, it is this clash between the claimed in-principle characteristic of the sentence parser and the clear performance limitations that have led some authors (e.g., McClelland & Kawamoto, 1986) to a different conclusion. They have argued that even though some sentences can be defined in terms of recursive structures (such as those embodied in our simple phrase structure grammar considered previously – see Figure 14.4), it does not necessarily follow that 'the mechanisms for parsing them must themselves operate recursively' (p. 322).

Clearly this is an important and unresolved issue. On the one hand, Corballis (2003) is wedded to the idea that the underlying mechanisms do operate recursively. He pointed to the fact that, fundamentally, recursion underpins many other forms of cognitive activity including language, music, memory and object manipulation. For instance, 'man is the only animal that to date has been observed to use a tool to make a tool' (Corballis, 2003, p. 168, in citing Beck, 1980, p. 218). The alternative position is that, even though this sort of behaviour appears to be underpinned by a system

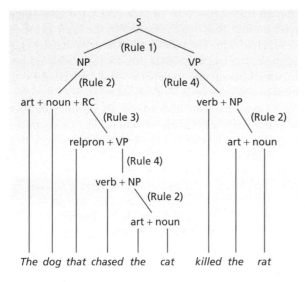

**Figure 14.4 A tree diagram illustrating syntactic recursion**
S = Sentence, NP = noun phrase, VP = verb phrase, art = article, RC = relative clause, relpron = relative pronoun. The rules are specified in the text. Recursion is shown because once Rule 4 is applied it is possible to return to the higher levels of the tree so as to apply Rule 2 and repeat the rewrite operations all over again.

*Source*: Corballis, M. (2003). Recursion as the key to the human mind. In K. Sterelny & J. Fitness (Eds.), *From mating to mentality. Evaluating evolutionary psychology* (pp. 155–171, fig. 7.1, p. 157). New York: Psychology Press. Reproduced with permission.

## For example . . .

Recursion does not just belong to the psycholinguists, however. It's very common to find versions of recursion in children's poems, such as 'The House That Jack Built' by Randolph Caldecott.

This is the Farmer who sowed the corn,
That fed the Cock that crowed in the morn,
That waked the Priest all shaven and shorn,
That married the Man all tattered and torn,
That kissed the Maiden all forlorn,

That milked the Cow with the crumpled horn,
That tossed the Dog,
That worried the Cat,
That killed the Rat,
That ate the Malt,
That lay in the House
    that Jack built.

*Source*: Caldecott, R. (2004). 'The house that Jack built'. Accessed from http://www.gutenberg.org/etext/12109 on 16 July 2007. (Original work published in 1878.)

## → What have we learnt?

By now you have been introduced to the key concepts upon which the rest of the chapter is based. The distinction between the superficial and underlying structure of language is important and may not have been at all obvious. We are primarily concerned with the cognitive nature of language, and because of this we will focus on ideas concerning (underlying) mental structures and processes. The material has also stressed the componential nature of language. Language is made up from various kinds of mental building blocks and when we describe the various facets of language – its sounds, its syntax and its semantics – various different sorts of building blocks are implicated.

There is no assumption that the framework for thinking provided by Jackendoff is correct in every detail. All that is being accepted is that it provides a very useful description that lays bare the componential nature of language. We have also considered more general characteristics of natural language. We have accepted that it is a symbolic system that has the characteristics of productivity, systematicity, compositionality and recursion. It is

asserted that, unless we have a proper account of these characteristics, then we have failed to account for natural language. There are many vexed issues, though.

As we have stressed, merely because we can provide such an elegant description of some mental faculty, this does not mean that the description is correct. Linguistic analyses may or may not prove useful in the hands of psycholinguists. It is the job of the psycholinguist to try to validate linguistic analyses in terms of establishing psychological plausibility. Do the sort of structures and processes that linguists discuss when they examine the nature of a given natural language, map onto corresponding mental structures and mental processes?

Much of the rest of the chapter concerns evidence that bears on the psychological plausibility of the sorts of language components that have so far been discussed. Additional concerns are with various mechanistic accounts of how such components are combined so as to give rise to everyday language use. We will begin by addressing evidence relating to something known as 'syntactic parsing'.

of recursive rules of operation, the actual mechanisms are much simpler than this. To appreciate the full force of this point, however, it is important to consider more carefully the nature and status of mental rules and this is something to which we will return shortly. → See 'What have we learnt', above.

**productivity** A property of natural language discussed by Fodor and Pylyshyn (1988) such that humans are capable of generating an indefinitely large number of sentences.

**systematicity** The idea put forward by Fodor and Pylyshyn (1988) that the ability to understand or produce certain sentences entails the understanding or production of other related sentences.

**compositionality** The idea put forward by Fodor and Pylyshyn (1988) that the meaning of a complex expression rests upon understanding its component constituents.

recursion A means 'for generating terms in a sequence, in which the rule for generating the next term in a sequence involves one or more of the preceding terms' (Corballis, 2003, p. 155).

## Syntactic parsing on-line

To reiterate, *syntactic parsing* refers to the process of dividing up linguistic input into its syntactic constituents, namely words, phrases, clauses, sentences, etc. Parsing, in this context, refers to the generation of a syntactic description of the linguistic input. The 'on-line' means that it is assumed that syntactic parsing takes place immediately as linguistic material unfolds over time. Perhaps the most convincing evidence that syntax is important at a cognitive level comes from the many demonstrations of the sorts of expectations that are built up as a sentence unfolds. With a sentence that starts as follows:

> Freddy knocked the nail in with a small red-handled . . .

it would be reasonable to expect 'hammer' but not 'feather'. Inclusion of 'feather' would violate the meaning of the sentence, not least because feathers do not have handles. However, it is the rules of syntax that lead to the expectation that a word of a particular type will occur next; that is, it is most likely that either another adjective (e.g., 'plastic') or a noun (e.g., 'hammer') will crop up. It is these kinds of syntactic expectations that are of initial interest here. It is these that have been most thoroughly discussed in terms of something called the *garden-path model of sentence parsing* (see Frazier, 1987).

### Syntax and the garden path

The basic idea here is that as the linguistic material (either spoken words or printed sentences) unfolds over time, each word is incorporated into a syntactic description of the sentence. This description is continually being updated in the face of more input. Figure 14.5 provides a schematic representation of an unfolding syntactic tree of the sentence 'John put the book on the table' on a word-by-word basis. (A more detailed analysis of the sentence is included later.) Now, of course, the sorts of syntactic predictions that could be made (i.e., which type of word comes next)

depend critically on the sort of grammar that is assumed and the order in which particular rules are applied. Let us sidestep these issues for a moment and simply accept the scheme as given.

Let us assume that we have a good idea about the basic rules of grammar and the order in which such rules are applied. Such assumptions are important because, according to **garden-path theory** (as defended by Frazier, 1987), it is syntactic parsing that drives the process of sentence comprehension. Primarily the parsing mechanism is governed by the recovery of the syntax of the sentence. Once this has been established, the syntactic structure constrains the analysis of the meaning of the sentence. The interpretative process can, in turn, be influenced by further syntactic information. However, problems may arise when attempting to marry early and later readings of the sentence. For example, an initial syntactic assignment may need to be reassessed in the face of later in-coming information. When this happens, a re-analysis is invoked. The derivation of a new syntactic description is required and this will take a measurable amount of time.

The 'garden path' here refers to demonstrations that the listener/reader can, in a sense, be tripped up by an unexpected type of word because the current syntactic description is predicting one type of word but another type is encountered. Some caution is warranted here, however. It turns out that there is more than one sort of garden-path model (see Clark & Clark, 1977, pp. 80–1), and the critical issue is with whether the garden path is defined by semantic or syntactic factors. For instance, Clark and Clark (1977) discussed a garden path account in which the primary factor is semantics, not syntax. That is, people adopt one interpretation of the material as it unfolds and this may result in misunderstandings. For example, consider the following (abridged from Clark & Clark, 1977, p. 81):

> I was afraid of Tyson's powerful punch, especially since it had laid out tougher men who had bragged they could handle that much alcohol.   (9)

('Punch', geddit? Well, perhaps not. Mike Tyson used to be the heavyweight champion of the world, hence the default reading of 'punch' in this context would implicate boxing.)

We can refer to these sorts of garden-path errors as *semantic garden-path errors*, but in Frazier's garden-path model it is the current *syntactic* reading of the sentence that points one way (down the garden path),

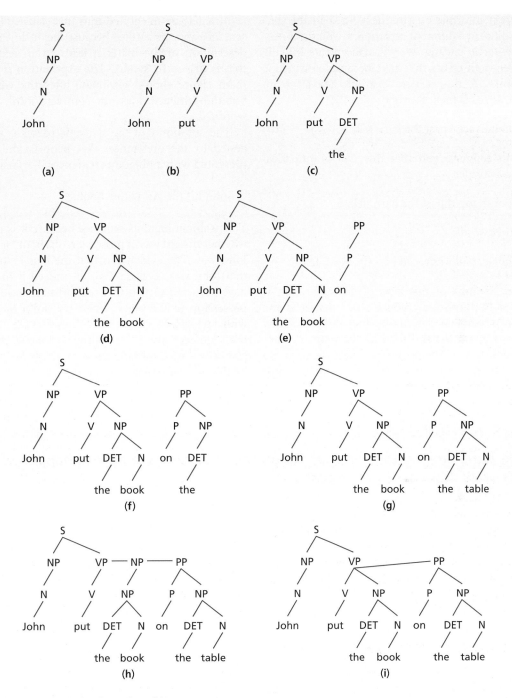

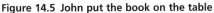

**Figure 14.5 John put the book on the table**

(a)–(g) illustrate how a syntactic tree is generated as the sentence 'John put the book on the table' unfolds over time. However, two alternative trees are shown in (h) and (i). (h) shows the reading where something like 'John put the book on the table facing towards him' is implied, whereas (i) shows the reading where something like 'John actually put the book on the table' is implied. The sequence of words 'John put the book on the table' could quite easily induce a garden-path error if included in a larger sentence.

but current information (the next word in the sentence) points in a different direction. Given this interest in syntactic parsing, we will concentrate initially on garden-path errors that arise because of syntactic constraints. A now classic example (taken from Kimball, 1973) is the following:

The horse raced past the barn fell. (10)

To try to convince you that this is a grammatical sentence, consider:

The horse, raced past the barn, fell.

or, in other words:

The horse, *that was* raced past the barn, fell.

One way to think of this kind of demonstration is that what is purportedly going on is that it is the syntactic parser that determines that the words *the, horse, raced, past, the* and *barn* are brought together into a main clause 'The horse raced past the barn'. So when *fell* occurs to finish off the sentence, it cannot

legitimately be integrated into this clause. Hence the sentence appears garbled because the on-line syntactic description of the material leads to an expectation that is driven by syntax. The expectation is that the main clause should terminate after the word *barn* but the sentence does not complete until after the word *fell*.

The autonomy of the syntactic parser is also suggested by the preferences that people exhibit when presented with ambiguous sentences. For instance:

John hit the girl with a book. (11)

This is an ambiguous sentence because it is not clear whether the girl was in possession of a book or whether John was. The evidence is that the bias is to assume that John was (Frazier, 1987) – indeed it may never have occurred to you that the girl may have been in possession of the book. Okay, try 'John hit the girl with a fringe'. This in turn indicates that the parsing of the sentences into its constituents follows particular proscribed methods and these methods are governed by the rules of syntax.

## Research focus 14.2

## While Anna dressed the baby spit up on the bed: what we believe happened as we walk down the garden path

Was Anna getting dressed? Did the baby really throw up? And who was on the bed again? While reading these intentionally tricky sentences, you're struck by the numerous interpretations that the sentence has to offer. In this respect, a garden-path sentence might act as the linguistic equivalent of an ambiguous figure (see Chapter 5), in which different versions of reality present themselves to us and we have to adjudicate between them. Ferreira, Christianson and Hollingworth (2001) were particularly concerned that there had been relatively little research on confirming these versions of reality that we assume are taking place as individuals read these sentences. For instance, in our initial parsing of the above sentence do we really think Anna is dressing the baby, and in our second parsing do we really think the baby spat?

In one part of an experiment, participants were presented with a number of garden-path sentences – stand by, here's another one: 'While Bill hunted the deer ran into the woods' – and were then asked

questions about what they had just read. Plausible garden-path statements were compared with implausible garden-path statements like 'While Bill hunted the deer paced into the zoo'. Here the implausibility comes from Bill walking round the zoo with a shotgun. A final category of sentence, 'While Bill hunted the pheasant the deer ran into the woods', was considered to be non-garden path as it was clear that Bill was after the pheasant, and it was deer that ran into the woods.

When asked, 'Did Bill hunt the deer?' participants differed in terms of their incorrect responses ('yes' being incorrect in all cases) as a function of the type of sentence used. That is, participants reported Bill hunting the deer during the plausible garden-path sentence, indicating that there was a belief based on the initially incorrect parsing of the sentence. However, as Ferreira et al. (2001) stated, it's unlikely that Bill would be hunting himself, which is why using 'reflexive absolute transitive' verbs such as 'dress' or 'bathe' are better for garden-path sentences, since such a verb could be applied to the agent or the subject, hence 'While Anna dressed the baby spit up on the bed'.

From the data, it's clear that we make mistakes with language pretty regularly, especially when given these fiendishly difficult sentences designed to send us flying down the garden path. From Ferreira et al.'s (2001) point of view, data from garden-path studies suggest that people often make do with a very rough and often incomplete interpretation of the language laid out before them, in addition to developing some false beliefs about the current situation. All of this again makes us wonder how much of what we experience is really just the faulty workings of our own minds. And give that baby some gripe water!

*Source*: Ferreira, F., Christianson, K., & Hollingworth, A. (2001). Misinterpretation of garden-path sentences: Implications for models of sentence processing and reanalysis. *Journal of Psycholinguistic Research, 30*, 3–20.

## Parsing according to minimal attachment

So what are the principles that govern sentence parsing and are thus responsible for the garden-path errors? Well, the first principle discussed by Frazier (1987) is known as the principle of **minimal attachment**. According to Frazier (1987), 'At each step . . ., the perceiver postulates the minimal number of nodes required by the grammar . . . given the structure assigned to preceding items.'

Look at Figure 14.6 and consider the following:

We painted all the walls with cracks.          (12)

Problems here arise because the prepositional phrase *with cracks* wants (in a sense) to go with (i.e., attach itself to) the initial verb phrase *We painted*, instead of the noun phrase *all the walls*.

Reconsider Figure 14.5 because this provides a more detailed example. The issue is with how the prepositional phrase 'on the table' attaches to the previous

**Figure 14.6 Is the man painting with cracks?**
*Source*: Alamy/SAS.

**For example . . .**

A quick trawl of the internet and soon 'garden-path newspaper headlines' come to the surface . . .

'French left torn in two in row over EU Constitution'
'British left waffles on Falklands'

syntactical structure for 'John put the book'. The alternatives are set out in Figure 14.5(h) and 14.5(i) and the ambiguities arise because different syntactic rules can be applied to the same structures. For instance:

VP → V + NP + PP                (Rule 5)
VP → V + NP                     (Rule 6)
NP → DET + NP                   (Rule 7)
NP → NP + PP                    (Rule 8)

As can be seen in Figure 14.5, there are alternative ways of rewriting the symbols VP and NP. In (h) Rule 6 has been used to rewrite the first VP whereas in (i) Rule 5 has. A knock-on consequence of this is that (h) has one more node than does (i) (i.e., an additional NP node). In (h) the additional NP node is used to delimit the phrase 'the-book-on-the-table' (as in 'John put the book on the table facing towards him'), whereas in (i) the prepositional phrase is attached to the verb phrase (as in 'John actually put the book on the table'). According to the principle of minimal attachment, therefore, (i) will be preferred to (h) because the tree in (i) has one less node than does the tree in (h). Minimal attachment explains why in sentence (11) 'a book' is taken to be in John's possession and in sentence (12) why the painting seems to have been undertaken with cracks (whatever that means!). Such examples as these clearly show that there is much more to language understanding than meets the eye (or indeed the ear). However, despite these simple examples, what is the actual empirical evidence for the operation of the principle of minimal attachment?

Here a seminal reference is to the work of Rayner, Carlson and Frazier (1983). Central were sentences of the type (13) and (14) shown in Figure 14.7. Whereas the structure of (13) is in keeping with the principle of minimal attachment, sentences of this sort (let's call them MA sentences) should be easy to read. In contrast, sentences of the sort shown in (14) (let's call them non-MA sentences) should be less easy to read. The rationale was that, if the principle of minimal attachment operates without regard to so-called pragmatic plausibility, then it will cause a garden-path

error in the non-MA sentences. Simply put, non-MA sentences will be more difficult to read (i.e., will be read more slowly) than will MA sentences. According to the principle of minimal attachment, the default is to assign both 'with the binoculars' and 'with a revolver', in the respective cases, as being part of a prepositional phrase of a main verb phrase relating to 'The spy'. Such an operation will result in problems in (14) but not in (13). If this syntactic assignment is made, then difficulties will arise in (14) because there will then be a problem in trying to interpret how anyone could see with a revolver!

To test this prediction, Rayner et al. (1983) generated a set of MA and non-MA sentences and measured participants' eye movements when the participants read the sentences. On a given trial, a sentence was presented on a computer screen and the participant simply had to read it. (On some occasions participants were asked, after having read the sentence, to paraphrase the material they had just read. This was to check that they were actually reading rather than merely looking at the material.) Throughout the experiment eye movements were measured using sophisticated eye-tracking equipment. Such equipment, when harnessed to a computer, can deliver a veridical record of where participants are looking when confronted with printed material. The methods are so exact that they can provide records of direction of gaze in terms of which letters within a given word are being processed on a moment-by-moment basis (see Radach & Kennedy, 2004, for a recent overview).

In undertaking careful analyses of these eye movement records, inferences can then be made about which cognitive processes are taking place during reading. For instance, one assumption is that the time it takes to scan a sentence reflects the time it takes to decipher the text. More particularly, Rayner et al. (1983) argued that the eye movement records in their experiment also reflected garden-path errors when these occurred. The argument was that if participants were misled down a garden path by the principle of minimal attachment in the non-MA sentences, then these sentences ought to take longer to process than the MA sentences. This

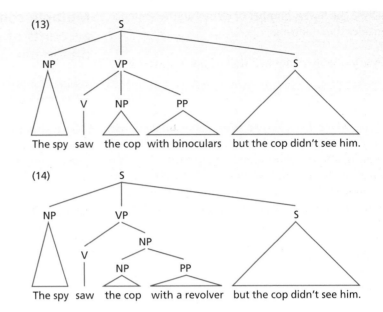

**Figure 14.7 More tree diagrams of two difference sentences**
In sentence (13) the structure is in keeping with minimal attachment, whereas with sentence (14) the structure stands in contrast to minimal attachment.

*Source*: Rayner, K., Carlson, M., & Frazier, L. (1983). The interaction of syntax and semantics during sentence processing: Eye movements in the analysis of semantically biased sentences. *Journal of Verbal Learning and Verbal Behavior, 22*, 358–374 (fig. 3, p. 368). Reproduced with permission from Elsevier.

pattern of performance was indeed what Rayner et al. (1983) reported.

Of particular note, though, were the detailed predictions about whereabouts in the sentence such slowing ought to take place. To examine this prediction they divided the eye movement records into regions of interest. So in (13) and (14) *the cop with* defined the so-called ambiguous region and everything before this defined the initial region. Finally, the biased region in (13) started with *binoculars* and in (14) with *revolver*. Evidence for a garden-path error and therefore re-analysis of the sentence was shown because participants were particularly slowed in processing the biased region in non-MA as compared with MA sentences. The data revealed that participants were slowed considerably in exactly the place in the non-MA sentences in which participants should realise that they had been led down the garden path.

Rayner et al. (1983) took such evidence to indicate the operation of an on-line syntactic parser that operated independent from any other form of sentence analysis. Their evidence was that this kind of parser was sensitive to the structural nature of the material separately from any pragmatic considerations such as what meanings were being conveyed. The garden-path errors that they examined arose because expectations of future words and phrases were built up from the syntactic assignments that had occurred earlier in the sentence. The current syntactic description of the sentence dictated that a word or phrase of a particular type would occur and if this expectation was violated,

then a processing cost was incurred. On these grounds, participants would be tripped up if the sentence did not complete in a fashion consistent with the current syntactic structure that had already been assigned. This is exactly what Rayner et al. discovered.

On the basis of this kind of evidence, they argued that, primarily, the parsing of the sentence is governed by syntactic considerations. It was asserted that syntactic analysis takes place initially and without regard to any semantic considerations. The interpretation of the material (the assignment of meaning) is something that takes place subsequently and via the operation of a so-called *thematic processor*. The thematic processor operates upon the structural description of the material generated by the syntactic parser and its role is to attempt to assign a meaning to this structure. As Rayner et al. stated, 'If the thematic selection process turns up a set of relations which is incompatible with the chosen syntactic analysis of the input string, then revision of the analysis will be attempted' (1983, p. 367).

## Parsing according to late closure

Aligned with minimal attachment is the principle of **late closure**. Now the idea is to incorporate incoming material into the syntactic constituent that is currently being processed. Both minimal attachment and late closure are driven by considerations of parsimony. Whereas minimal attachment is a principle based on the desire to minimise the number of nodes in the syntactic tree, late closure is driven by the desire to generate the fewest number of clauses in the sentence. Consider the following:

> Mary said that Tom had walked the dog yesterday. (15)

*Mary said that* . . . is known as the main clause; *Tom had walked the dog* is known as the subordinate clause. According to the principle of late closure *yesterday* will be attached to the subordinate clause rather than the main clause because the subordinate clause is the clause that is currently being processed. Another well-known example is given here (from Frazier & Rayner, 1982):

> Since Jay always jogs a mile seems like a very short distance to him. (16)

The principle of late closure states that 'jogs a mile' will be parsed as one constituent and because of this, the sentence will lead to a garden-path error. Again, the evidence from eye-movement monitoring tasks (Frazier & Rayner, 1982) was consistent with this line of reasoning.

What you may have spotted is that the two principles (minimal attachment and late closure) can make conflicting predictions as in 'John hit the girl with a book'. Given that such conflicts will arise, Frazier (1987) argued that the primary principle was minimal attachment and that late closure adjudicates in cases where different minimal attachments are possible (p. 562). Nevertheless, the overarching view, from this sort of garden-path model, is that it is syntax that is the primary factor that governs sentence parsing. Once a syntactic reading has been derived it is only then that a semantic interpretation is attempted.

Such a position accords well with Fodor's (1983) modularity of mind framework wherein the language input module delivers a structural description of the sentence which is free of semantics – remember, it is the job of the central systems to interpret the outputs from the input modules. (Indeed the ideas are very much in keeping with the theoretical account of perception discussed in Chapters 5 and 6 – the input systems put forward a first guess as to what is out there but it is the job of the central systems to try to interpret this material.)

### Pinpoint question 14.5

**How do parsing according to minimal attachment and late closure differ from one another?**

## Multiple-constraint satisfaction accounts of parsing: semantically driven parsing

Figure 14.8 provides a simple schematic that provides a framework for thinking about the many different accounts of sentence comprehension that have been discussed in the literature. Processor A is the syntactic processor and Processor B is the semantic (thematic) processor. Both alternatives (a) and (b) are syntax first accounts, in which initially some form of syntactic analysis is carried out prior to the operation of any interpretative processes. The difference between (a) and (b) is that in (b), and following some form of semantic assignment, a feedback signal is sent to the syntactic processes in such a way that semantic

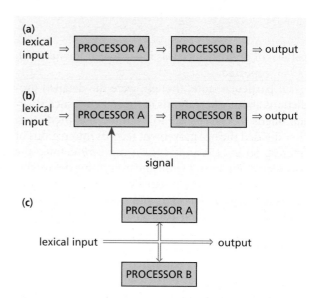

**Figure 14.8 Alternative frameworks for thinking about sentence parsing**
Processor A is taken to be the syntactic processor and Processor B is taken to be the semantic processor. (a) therefore shows in schematic form syntactic garden-path models in which syntactic analysis is a necessary precursor to semantic analysis. (b) is a slightly more sophisticated account in that semantic factors can influence the syntactic analysis through the provision of feedback. (c) conveys the idea of multiple-constraint analyses. Both syntactic and semantic factors operate concurrently (from Taraban & McClelland, 1990).

*Source*: Taraban, R., & McClelland, J. L. (1990). Parsing and comprehension: A multiple-constraint view. In K. Rayner, M. Balota, & G. B. Flores D'Arcais (Eds.), *Comprehension processes in reading* (pp. 231–263, fig. 11.2, p. 234). Hillsdale, New Jersey: Erlbaum. Reproduced with permission.

analysis can now influence any further processing. Alternative (b) is the account nearest to the kind of garden-path model favoured by Frazier (1987). Alternative (a) is a caricature of Chomsky's accounts (1957, 1965) of parsing – everything is driven by syntax! For Taraban and McClelland (1990), however, alternative (c) is perhaps more plausible. In this account both syntactic and semantic processes operate in parallel and there is no sense in which either takes precedence over the other.

Each processor has its own rules of operation and brings to bear quite different guidelines for how the sentence ought to be parsed. In other words, each processor comes with its own set of constraints and, given that there is more than one sort of processor, there is more than one set of constraints. Therefore what we now have are **multiple-constraint accounts of parsing**. Indeed, Taraban and McClelland (1990) went further and argued that the parsing of a particular sentence may be governed, more generally, by constraints provided by extra-sentential material or indeed the non-linguistic context of the language. By this view, there are many more sorts of constraints than those provided by the syntax and the semantics of the particular sentence under consideration. For simplicity, though, we will limit ourselves to just sentence syntax and sentence semantics in a bid to understand the alternatives to the 'syntax first' accounts that have just been described.

Taraban and McClelland (1990) were particularly interested in testing the empirical predictions of the multiple-constraint account. To this end they reported a sentence-reading experiment in which sentences of four different types were presented.

The dictator viewed the masses from the
***steps but he was not*** very sympathetic.  (17)
The dictator viewed the masses from the
***city but he was not*** very sympathetic.  (18)
The dictator viewed the petitions from the
***prisoners but he was not*** very sympathetic.  (19)
The dictator viewed the petitions from the
***podium but he was not*** very sympathetic.  (20)

Aside from the obvious syntactic garden-path errors, Taraban and McClelland were interested in other difficulties that might arise because of semantic expectations built up during the early part of a sentence.

According to them the preference in (17) is to expect *the masses* to be viewed from somewhere (e.g., we viewed the horserace from the grandstand, we viewed the fireworks from the hill) whereas in (19) the preference is to expect *the petitions* to be from someone (e.g., we viewed the painting from the artist, we viewed the letter from the council). So both (17) and (19) are consistent with these expectations and (18) and (20) are inconsistent with these expectations. Critically, such expectations are not defined relative to the syntactic principle of minimal attachment. They arise from a different constraint concerning the interpretation of the noun phrase in the sentence context – not a syntactic constraint at all.

The relevant data that were reported by Taraban and McClelland were the average amount of time participants spent reading words following the biasing region in the various sentences. These words are bold and in italics in (17)–(20). What the data revealed was that there was a statistically significant effect of consistency with participants being faster to read the material in the consistent sentences (i.e., 17 and 19) than they were to read the material in the inconsistent sentences (i.e., 18 and 20). This effect of consistency is simply not predicted by the sort of syntactic garden-path model discussed by Frazier (1987). So whereas the garden-path account made no prediction about the effect of consistency, the multiple-constraint account made a directional prediction as supported by the data. As Taraban and McClelland (1990) concluded, 'the main verb in a sentence (e.g., *viewed* in (17)–(20) above) is not necessarily the sole bearer of information about the likely arrangement of constituents in a sentence, but that the information may in fact be more widely distributed' (p. 250; material in parentheses added). This is not to argue that syntactic constraints do not matter, but merely that additional constraints need to be taken account of.

In demonstrating the influence of thematic roles in parsing, Taraban and McClelland set out the foundations for theories of sentence comprehension that are not primarily driven by syntactic constraints but which do posit multiple forms of constraint that mutually interact on-line. In such accounts, the overarching principle is that different sorts of constraints are brought to bear. Such constraints operate at every step in time as the linguistic material unfolds. The eventual parsing of the sentence reflects the structure that is most strongly supported by the different sources of information. The claim is not that syntactic constraints don't exist or that they are not important, but merely that these constraints are just one sort of constraint that governs parsing. Moreover, and as the data from Taraban and McClelland (1990) show, syntactic constraints may not be the most important. → See 'What have we learnt?', page 532.

## → What have we learnt?

We have only scratched the surface of the literature on sentence comprehension and on-line parsing, and it should come as no surprise to learn that the field has moved on since 1990. Evidence in favour of multiple-constraint parsers has grown considerably in the interim (e.g., McRae, Spivey-Knowlton & Tanenhaus, 1998; Spivey-Knowlton & Sedivy, 1995; Trueswell, Tanenhaus & Garnsey, 1994), but more recently, even these relatively unconstrained accounts have come under attack. The one framework for thinking that has moved into the ascendancy can be construed as being a hybrid account of the multiple-constraint and the two-stage accounts outlined in Figure 14.8. It is known as the **unrestricted race model** (Traxler, Pickering & Clifton, 1998; van Gompel, Pickering, Pearson & Liversedge, 2005; van Gompel, Pickering & Traxler, 2001). The account is a two-stage account because an initial best guess at the correct parse can be reanalysed if it turns out to be garbled. Stage 1 is where an initial parse of the sentence is offered up for further analysis which is undertaken at Stage 2. However, the initial stage allows for multiple constraints to operate: it is not just syntactic constraints that come into play initially and it is because of this that the model is known as being *unrestricted*.

More particularly, in the model it is assumed that during the initial stage, alternative parses of the sentences are pursued in parallel, but as the sentence unfolds only one of these will be favoured. In a sense, each of the different parses is entered into a race and the parse that wins the race (i.e., completes first) is then offered up for further analysis. However, even the winning parse may turn out to be garbled, and under these circumstances, the sentence must be reanalysed. Moreover, the theory allows for the fact that different sentences may result in different parses depending on which of the many possible constraints apply. So, thinking back to the data reported by Taraban and McClelland (1990), the unrestricted race model allows for the fact that some of the time minimal attachment will apply and some of the time it will be overridden by other semantic considerations. What van Gompel and colleagues have attempted to do is to set out the conditions under which the different sorts of constraints apply and why. Nevertheless, a clear picture has yet to emerge.

Yet again, therefore, there is much still to do. What the extant research has established is that there is much more to sentence parsing than deriving a syntactic description. What is still largely unknown are the conditions under which one sort of parsing constraint applies and how this may or may not be overridden when alternative sources of information are considered. Such issues as these will clearly guide the direction of future work on sentence comprehension, but at present, the final story remains to be told.

---

**garden-path theory** The idea that sentence comprehension is primarily determined by syntactic parsing.

**minimal attachment** According to Frazier (1987), the stricture that the preferred interpretation of a sentence is that which requires the fewest number of nodes in its syntactic tree structure.

**late closure** According to Frazier (1987), the rule stating that the preferred interpretation of a sentence is that which requires the fewest number of clauses.

**multiple-constraint accounts of parsing** Where sentence parsing is determined by a large variety of syntactic, semantic and pragmatic influences.

**unrestricted race model** An account of parsing in which multiple syntactic and semantic constraints operate at an early stage, leading to an initial interpretation of the language in question. A second stage allows the output to be reanalysed if the primary analysis leads to a nonsensical interpretation.

## Mental rules

So far we have been accepting of the view that knowledge of language is encapsulated in some form of grammar and that this grammar comprises rules for sentence construction. More particularly the idea is that the grammar comprises rules that are represented in the mind – so-called *mental rules*. Such a framework for thinking has been adopted because it is this that provides a very useful means to understanding the work that has been carried out on sentence parsing. However, we now need to stand back a little and begin to survey some basic assumptions. We really do need to consider this notion of mental rules in much more detail. Is it really the case that we need to posit mental rules in order to make sense of how we produce and understand sentences?

Two fundamentally opposing views on this issue may be characterised as the *establishment* and the *connectionist* positions, respectively (cf. Fodor & Pylyshyn, 1988). The **establishment position** is, essentially, based on the assumptions of the physical symbol system – the computation theory of mind – as discussed in Chapter 2. By this view, language use is predicated on the operation of an internal system of rules that specify the grammar of the language. Importantly, the key assumption is not that language use may be described by a system of rules, but that particular rules are instantiated in the brain and that these play a causal role in the production and understanding of language. The claim is, for instance, that the rules of sentence parsing are actually operating when participants attempt to make sense of the language.

As was described in Chapter 2, a typical analogy here is with a computer program where the rules of operation of the machine both determine the behaviour of the machine and are also instantiated (i.e., are represented) within the machine. The computer program is stored in the machine and it is this that determines the behaviour of the computer. The idea that language is a rule-based system is taken, in the establishment position, to apply to the mind in general – cognition may be characterised by a system of mental rules (which we have referred to as the 'language of thought'; Fodor, 1975) that describes the operations that underlie all forms of intellectual ability.

The contrasting, **connectionist position** is that, regardless of such claims about mental rules, how these are represented and how these govern mental processing, the mind is simply not like that. Although it is possible to describe the mind as if it were just like a computer with its programmed instructions, this is merely a description and bears little or no correspondence with what is actually going on. What is being observed is the operation of a highly complex neural network in which distributed patterns of activity are propagated along millions of weighted and adaptively changing interconnections.

## Rule-following vs. rule-governed devices reconsidered

The basic distinction being discussed is about the difference between *rule-following* and *rule-governed* devices. Rule-governed mechanisms may be said to act in accordance with a set of rules. By contrast, the notion of rule following applies only to cases where 'a representation of the rules they follow constitutes one of the causal determinants of their behavior' (Fodor, 1975, p. 74). From the establishment position, brains and programmable devices (computers, mobile phones, electronic calculators) are rule-following devices that have programmed instructions that determine their behaviour. Such a view forms the basis of the computational theory of mind (see Chapter 2, and Pinker, 1997, for an extended exposition and defence of this position). Connectionists do not accept the computational theory of mind and argue that the brain is a rule-governed device – it is not a rule-following device. No matter which set of rules are assumed to describe its behaviour, such rules play no causal role in its operation.

Here the classic example is that of the planets. It is quite possible to define the trajectory of the moon around the sun in terms of momentum and gravitational forces, but there is no sense in which the moon consults such rules and there certainly is no sense in which a computer analogy will help here. There is no sense in which such laws of momentum are represented inside the moon! Connectionists assert that, as with the moon, so it is with the mind.

**establishment position** Standard computational theory of mind accounts of cognition and perception (see Fodor & Pylyshyn, 1981).

**connectionist position** Accounts of the mind in which it is assumed that rule-like behaviour emerges from the complex interactions of many simple interconnected processing units.

## The past-tense debate

To put some flesh on these fairly abstract ideas, the contrasting arguments have been played out in attempting to understand the mental representations and processes that underlie the ability to generate the correct past-tense forms of verbs. So if you know the word 'talk' you should also know its past-tense form, 'talked'. This general area is centred around what has come to be known as 'the past-tense debate' (see Pinker & Ullman, 2002a). Central to this debate are certain basic facts about English morphology and the morphological relations between past- and present-tense forms of verbs. Originally it was accepted that English verbs could simply be divided into *regular* and *irregular forms*. Although this simple classification scheme has since been the focus of some debate (McClelland & Patterson, 2002a), so as to keep things simple we will concentrate on the division between regular and irregular forms. An example of a regular verb is 'talk' and its past-tense form 'talked'. An example of an irregular verb is 'go' and its past-tense form 'went'. For regular verbs, the present-tense form is converted into a past-tense form with the addition of the suffix *ed*. This is most easily conveyed by the rule:

$$V \rightarrow V + ed$$

where V is the present-tense form of the verb (sometimes known as the root morpheme), '$\rightarrow$' signifies 'is rewritten as', and the *ed* signifies the past tense or stem morpheme. Yes, here too we have a rewrite rule that applies at the level of single words – the rule explains how to generate the past-tense form of a verb from its present-tense form. For example, take the word 'talk'. Now how do you generate the past tense of this? Well, simply add 'ed' to 'talk'. This is what our rule for regular verbs (such as talk, walk, lift, laugh, etc.) stipulates. Things are much more complex for irregular verbs because this simple rule does not apply (e.g., the past tense of 'go' is not 'goed'!). If we concentrate, for now, on regular verbs by the establishment view, there is a mental counterpart to the 'ed' rule that is used when people generate the past tense of regular verbs. As we will see, not everyone subscribes to such a view and the dispute forms the basis of the past-tense debate. Primarily the dispute is between theorists who inhabit establishment and connectionist camps, respectively.

**How would you represent the rule for generating regular plural nouns?**

## The establishment account of past-tense learning

In functional terms, the establishment account, as couched in terms of the 'words-and-rules theory'

(Pinker & Ullman, 2002a), is that past-tense forms are productively generated from the present-tense via such a rule. However, the generality of such a rule is limited by the existence of irregular verbs. Now the claim is that no such formal rule applies: the mapping between the present- and past-tense forms is not as straightforward: contrast a regular verb such as *walk* ($\rightarrow$ *walked*) with an irregular verb such as *teach* ($\rightarrow$ *taught*). Given that there is no generic rule of production that applies to irregular verbs, the claim is that particular morphological relations must be specified on, essentially, an item-by-item basis. That is, you learn and store the mapping between fight and fought separately from come and came, and so on.

By this view, therefore, there is an important division between a grammatical system that specifies the rules of morphology that apply to regular verbs, and a memory system or *mental lexicon* (the mental dictionary) that specifies 'the thousands of arbitrary sound-meaning pairings that underlie morphemes and simple words of a language' (Pinker & Ullman, 2002a, p. 456). Whereas the present–past tense mappings are generated by the rule system for the regular verbs, the corresponding mappings for the irregular verbs must be recovered from the lexicon. There are so-called *type-distinct mechanisms* that govern the processing of regular and irregular verb forms, respectively. In Fodor's (1983) terms, there is a module for dealing with regular past-tense verbs and a different module for dealing with irregular past-tense verbs. In summary, the mapping between the present-tense and past-tense forms for regular verbs is carried out by application of a rule. In contrast, the mapping for irregular verbs is recovered from long-term memory. As irregular verbs are idiosyncratic the language learner must, in a sense, memorise 'go $\rightarrow$ went', 'hit $\rightarrow$ hit', 'drink $\rightarrow$ drank', 'sleep $\rightarrow$ slept', etc. on a case-by-case basis.

At the heart of the past-tense debate lies a claim about the derivation of the regular past-tense forms. According to the establishment view, fundamentally, mental operations comprise combinatorial operations defined over variables. In much the same way that algebra and programming languages contain variables, the claim is that so do mental processes (the software that defines the mind – see Chapter 2). A useful example was discussed by Marcus (1998, p. 250). The sentence 'All ducks can swim' can be coded into a conditional rule 'For all *x*, if *x* is a duck, then *x* can swim' where *x* operates as a variable that can take on particular values, such as 'Daffy'. If the condition of the rule is satisfied then the consequent holds true. If Daffy turns out to be a duck then it is concluded that Daffy can swim. Indeed, such putative mental rules form the basis of rational generalisations. For example, as soon as novel instance Howard is classified as a duck, then it automatically inherits the properties of the category duck that are specified in the rules for that category.

More particularly, it is argued in the words-and-rules theory that the mental software that governs the processing of regular verb forms comprises variables that take on values. The establishment view is that the mental processes that reflect competence with regular verb morphology critically consist of combinatorial operations involving variables. In this case, any given variable relates to a present-tense verb form – the V in the rule specified above. For instance, the value of V could be walk, talk, crawl, etc. and when combined with *ed* by application of the rewriting rule V → V + *ed*, walked, talked, crawled, etc. are generated, respectively.

The contrary view is that espoused by connectionists. They claim that, irrespective of the system of rules that may be used to describe the language, such rules are incidental to how the language is produced and understood. By this view the linguistic rules, which are encapsulated in terms of syntactic and morphological structures, merely reflect the statistical regularities that exist in the linguistic input. What the brain has done, through exposure to the language, is to recover the statistical regularities by adapting weighted connections between its myriad component processing units. So although it may be possible to describe the language in terms of its grammatical rules, such rules play no causal role in language behaviour.

## Connectionist accounts of past-tense learning

Connectionist research involves writing computing programmes that simulate cognitive processes in terms of networks of simple processing units interconnected by many links. An introduction to connectionist research is included in Chapter 12, when we discussed the Rumelhart and Todd (1993) model of semantic memory. Exactly the same general principles of distributed representation and distributed processing have been used to model the acquisition of the ability to map present-tense verbs onto their past-tense counterparts. The network architectures are very different in the two cases, but the same general principles of operation apply. In the simulations of past-tense learning the aim is to develop a computer program that provides the correct output (the past-tense verb form) for each input (the corresponding present-tense

verb form). That is, the model should produce a representation for 'walked' when presented with the input representation for 'walk' and it should be able to carry the present-to-past tense mapping for all verbs. More particularly, central is the idea that the account ought to demonstrate how such an ability is acquired. In this regard, much effort is expended in examining how it is that a network might learn the mapping between present-tense and past-tense versions of verbs.

If successful, then, a key point emerges. This is that such computer models, in solving this mapping problem, do not acquire or contain the rules of operation that are taken by the establishment theorists to be fundamental. The models do not acquire a system of morphological rules (such as V → V + *ed*). A provocative conclusion, therefore, is that if the network models do not need such a system of rules, then neither do we.

Our discussion of this topic is limited to consideration of the original work carried out by Rumelhart and McClelland (1986). Since this work was reported, there are now several other connectionist accounts showing how the mapping between present- and past-tense forms of English verb forms may be learnt (see, for example, Plunkett & Marchman, 1991, 1993; Plunkett & Juola, 1999). Despite this later work, consideration of the original model suffices for present purposes.

## Past-tense learning according to Rumelhart and McClelland (1986)

The original model, which sparked all of the controversy, is that by Rumelhart and McClelland (1986) and the architecture of this connectionist network is shown in Figure 14.9. The network comprised four layers of units. The outer-most layers (left-most and right-most) we shall call the input and output layers, respectively. In each of these layers phonemic information was coded. Phonemes are the basic units of speech. For example, the phonetic form of the letter 'T' is 'tuh'. In phonetic transcription, the sound of 'T' is rendered /t/. In terms of the simulations, the basic idea was to arrive at the following situation: present the phoneme string for /walk/ to the network on the input layer, allow information from the input units to percolate through the network to the output units, and see the appropriate output units come ON and signal the phoneme string for /walked/. More particularly, the general aim was to try to teach the network to generate the correct past-tense form of a verb (in phonemes) when the corresponding present-tense

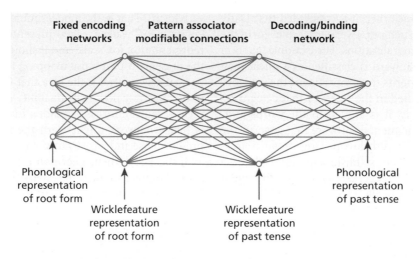

**Figure 14.9 The connectionist network used by Rumelhart and McClelland (1986) in the original past-tense learning simulations**

There are four layers of units to this network. It is best to think that the network is divided into two components, each of which includes two layers of units: an input component comprising the two sets of the representational units on the left of the figure and an output component comprising the two sets of representational units on the right of the figure. An input representation of a present-tense verb is presented to the network as a pattern of activation across the input units on the far left of the figure. Activation then propagates through the network moving from left to right. Eventually a distributed pattern of activation is produced on the output units on the far right of the figure. This pattern of activation is known as the actual output pattern and during learning this is compared with a desired pattern of activation. Any difference between these two patterns of activation is known as the error pattern and this is then used as an error signal to alter the weighted connections between the two middle layers of units in the network.

*Source*: Rumelhart, D. E., & McClelland, J. L. (1986). On learning the past tenses of English verbs. In J. L. McClelland & D. E. Rumelhart (Eds.), *Parallel distributed processing. Explorations in the microstructure of cognition. Volume 2: Psychological and biological models* (pp. 216–271, fig. 1, p. 222). Cambridge, Massachusetts: The MIT Press. Reproduced with permission.

form of the verb (in phonemes) is presented to the input units. It should be able to learn to do this for all the verbs of English.

### Phonemic representations in the model

At the heart of the network are two internal banks of units – let us call them the *present-tense layer* and the *past-tense layer*, respectively. The units in these layers were quite complex and represented phonemic information in a special way. Coding was based on something called a *Wicklephone*. Each Wicklephone represents an ordered triple of phonemes. So the phonemic representation of *bid* – /b/ /i/ /d/ – comprises three Wicklephones:

1. /#bi/
2. /bid/
3. /id#/

Here the '#' signals a word boundary. In addition, each phoneme can itself be represented by so-called phonetic features which are themselves defined on basic speech dimensions. Such dimensions coded things

about how the phonemes are articulated and what their acoustic properties are. So in the same way that a letter can be broken down into constituent features (lines and curves), so a phoneme can be broken down into constituent features (such as the place, manner and timing of the articulators, i.e., the lips, tongue and vocal chords).

Each Wicklefeature unit coded one phonetic feature for the first position in the Wicklephone (i.e., the /b/ – the preceding context), one phonetic feature of the central phoneme (i.e., the /i/ – the current phoneme) and one phonemic feature for the final position (i.e., the /d/ – the following context). Sixteen such units are shown in Table 14.1 with one unit being represented as one row in the table. The columns in the table provide the phonetic features of the corresponding phoneme given at the head of the associated column.

The upshot of all this is that each Wicklephone such as /bid/ was captured by 16 so-called Wicklefeature units (see Table 14.1) in the network. Assume /bid/ is presented to the network: this is broken down into its constituent Wicklephones (i.e., /#bi/, /bid/, /id#/) and

**Table 14.1** Example of how the Wicklephone /ᵇiᵈ/ is captured by 16 Wicklefeatures units (see text for further details).

| Wicklefeature unit | Preceding context /b/ | Central phoneme /i/ | Following context /d/ |
|---|---|---|---|
| 1 | Interrupted | Vowel | Interrupted |
| 2 | Front | Vowel | Middle |
| 3 | Stop | Vowel | Stop |
| 4 | Voiced | Vowel | Voiced |
| 5 | Interrupted | Front | Interrupted |
| 6 | Front | Front | Middle |
| 7 | Stop | Front | Stop |
| 8 | Voiced | Front | Voiced |
| 9 | Interrupted | High | Interrupted |
| 10 | Front | High | Middle |
| 11 | Stop | High | Stop |
| 12 | Voiced | High | Voiced |
| 13 | Interrupted | Short | Interrupted |
| 14 | Front | Short | Middle |
| 15 | Stop | Short | Stop |
| 16 | Voiced | Short | Voiced |

each of these activated 16 Wicklefeature units in the present-tense layer of the network.

In the network, there were 460 so-called Wicklefeature units in each of the present-tense and past-tense layers. Each node in these two layers shown in Figure 14.9 corresponds to a Wicklefeature unit and coded information as given in one of the rows of Table 14.1.

Why was such a convoluted form of representation chosen? Well, the answer to this was all to do with how the network might be able to generalise knowledge acquired from familiar verbs to verbs it had never encountered. If we take the verb 'talk', the Wicklephone coding of this is /₍#₎tₒ/, /ₜɔːₖ/, /ₒk₍#₎/. (The vowel sound in /talk/ is given by the symbol /ɔː/.) Similarly, if we take the verb 'walk', then the Wicklephone coding of this is /₍#₎tₒ/, /ₜɔːₖ/, /ₒk₍#₎/. If we train the network on /talk/ then it is, in a sense, inadvertently learning something about /walk/. This is because both /talk/ and /walk/ share some of the same set of Wicklefeature units. That is, they are both encoded via the /ₒk₍#₎/ unit. So in reinforcing certain pathways through the network when training /talk/ → /talked/, these same pathways will be activated when /walk/ is now presented to the network.

### Network operation and training

More specifically, when a phonetic representation of a present-tense root morpheme was presented to the input layer, the fixed encoding network took this representation and mapped it onto the Wicklefeature units in the present-tense layer. Critically, the crucial 16 Wicklefeature units were activated but the representation of this present-tense form was distributed across the whole 460 units. Activation across these units was then fed forward to the past-tense layer of 460 units and this gave rise to a distributed pattern across the whole layer of units. This distributed pattern was then operated upon by the decoding network so as to produce a final distributed representation across the output layer of units. This final distributed representation coded a phonemic specification of the network's best guess as to what the past-tense version of the input verb was.

A simple variant of gradient descent learning (see Chapter 12) was used to train this network. In this network only the connections between the present-tense and past-tense layers of units were modifiable through training. On each training trial, the network was provided with the present-tense root morpheme as rendered into phonemes and as captured by a distributed pattern of activation across the input layer. This information percolated through the network until a distributed pattern occurred over the Wicklefeatural units in the present-tense layer and onto the Wicklefeatural units in the past-tense layer. Now this distributed pattern of activation was compared to the correct distributed pattern for the past-tense equivalent – this was supplied as a teaching signal. Supervised learning was undertaken such that for every present-tense form presented to the input side of the network, the correct past-tense form was also made available to the past-tense layer. When /walk/ was presented at the input layer, the teaching signal (the desired pattern of activation) for /walked/ was made available for comparison at the past-tense layer. Any disparities between the actual output across the past-tense units and the desired pattern was now used to compute an error signal. This error signal was now used to alter the coefficients (the weights on the connections and the thresholds on the units) in the network in such a way that the disparity would be lessened the next time the same present-tense form was presented to the network. The learning algorithm was very similar to the back-propagation techniques described in Chapter 12.

### Results of the initial simulations

Clearly little of significance would have arisen had the network been a lamentable failure but, of course, it was not, and indeed Rumelhart and McClelland (1986) claimed a great deal of success. Such success was gauged by the manner in which the model revealed a similar developmental trajectory to that which children are supposed to follow as they master the past tense of English. Three stages of development have been discussed:

1. In stage 1 the children use only a very limited set of verbs, and if they do use the past-tense forms, they use these correctly.

2. In stage 2 they use many more verbs, most of which are regular verbs. Moreover they also tend to exhibit something called **over-generalisation**. That is, they seem to be applying the regular rule even with irregular items. So they tend to produce attempts at past-tense forms such as 'comed' or even 'camed', and as we saw in the introduction, 'builded' instead of 'built' and 'breaked' instead of 'broke'. This is even with verbs that they were using correctly in stage 1.

3. Finally stage 3 is where the child masters the past tense and uses both regular and irregular forms correctly.

A striking characteristic of this developmental trajectory is associated with the learning of the irregular forms and has come to be known as U-shaped learning. Figure 14.10 provides a graphical representation of this in which the *x* axis maps out developmental time and the *y* axis indicates some measure of performance with the irregular forms. High values of *y* indicate good performance with the irregular verbs

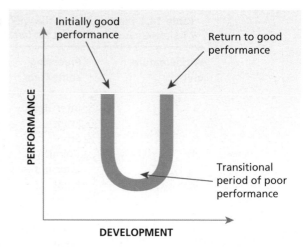

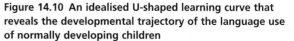

**Figure 14.10 An idealised U-shaped learning curve that reveals the developmental trajectory of the language use of normally developing children**
After some period of exposure to the language, they attain good levels with both irregular and regular verbs; there then follows a transitional period in which the children overgeneralise the '+ *ed*' rule with irregular instances. Finally, they develop into adult language users and master the past tense of all verbs.

and low values of *y* indicate poor performance with the irregular verbs. The developmental trajectory with the irregular verbs follows a U-shape function. The children start out doing very well but then they begin to make errors. Finally they recover and master the irregular forms.

### Modelling U-shaped learning

In modelling stage 1 performance Rumelhart and McClelland trained the network initially on only ten high frequency verbs (verbs that appear commonly in language such as 'walk'). This training set contained eight regular and two irregular verbs. Following training, the network was tested and it was found that it had mastered the mappings for these verbs. To model stage 2 performance, training was continued, but now an additional 410 medium frequency verbs were added to the original training set. Initially, during this extended training period, the responses of the network were taken to reflect the child at stage 2 – the network made interesting errors (see below). Following this extended training period, the network was virtually perfect in responding and had essentially mastered the past-tense forms for all 420 verb forms. Figure 14.11 shows the data collected from the network in its responses to the original test set of 10 high frequency verbs. Two things are striking:

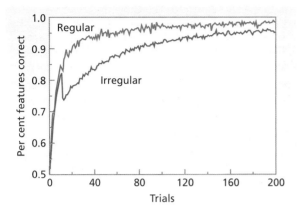

**Figure 14.11 Data taken from the actual Rumelhart and McClelland (1986) simulations of past-tense learning**
Performance with the ten initial high frequency verbs is shown. The model was continuously tested throughout the training. U-shaped learning is shown in the function for the irregular verbs. At around trial 10 or so, the performance of the model drops dramatically and it is only at about trial 40 that the model recovers and begins to perform better with the irregular verbs.

*Source*: Rumelhart, D. E., & McClelland, J. L. (1986). On learning the past tenses of English verbs. In J. L. McClelland & D. E. Rumelhart (Eds.), *Parallel distributed processing. Explorations in the microstructure of cognition. Volume 2: Psychological and biological models* (pp. 216–271, fig. 4, p. 242). Cambridge, Massachusetts: The MIT Press. Reproduced with permission.

1. The network learnt the mapping from present to past tense for both regular and irregular forms.
2. In learning the correct past-tense forms it exhibited U-shaped learning with the irregular forms. Initially the network was correct with the regular and irregular verbs to which it had been exposed; next it began to err and overgeneralise the rule of *ed* with irregular forms (e.g., it began to produce things like 'comed'); finally it reached a level of adult competence with both verb forms.

In the current discussion, the most critical finding is point 1 because what this shows is that there are not type-distinct mechanisms that govern the processing of regular and irregular forms respectively. The same network (i.e., the same set of weighted connections) captures the statistical regularities between the present- and past-tense forms for both sets of words. Moreover, there is no sense in which the network embodies the regular 'V + *ed*' rule. Such a rule plays no role in the operation of the network. Given this, the network could be said to be rule-governed (because it can handle the regular verbs), but it is definitely not rule-following.

More far-reaching, though, is the claim that such models indicate that rule-based accounts of language are not demanded by the data. The network models do not acquire a rule-based system that in some sense operationalises the rules of grammar. What they acquire is a set of weighted connections that capture the statistical regularities that exist in the mapping between the present and past tenses of the verbs.

## Pinpoint question 14.7

**In what way is a connectionist network like a child in acquiring past-tense knowledge?**

## Research focus 14.3

### Holded the front page! Sex differences in past-tense overgeneralisations

There's nothing quite like a discussion of sex differences to ensure a heated debate between psychologists. Hartshorne and Ullman (2006) have recently entered into the fray by assessing whether boys or girls tend to overgeneralise the past tense more. Ladies and gentlemen – take your corners please!

In order to do this, Hartshorne and Ullman (2006) re-examined an old data set in which overgeneralisations were observed in 10 girls and 15 boys. The children were balanced across gender in some important ways, including age (children were between the ages of 3 and 5 for the duration of the experiment), the total number of utterances recorded during the experiment, the number of irregular form past-tense words that the children knew already, and so on.

It was hypothesised that since females are purportedly better at verbal tasks than males and males are purportedly better at spatial tasks than females – yes, it's that old 'why men don't listen and women can't read maps' chestnut (Pease & Pease, 2001) – then females should show less overgeneralisation of the past-tense rule than boys. Apparently not! Girls produced an average of 5.7 per cent misapplied rules while boys only produced an average of 1.8 per cent.

Hartshorne and Ullman (2006) examined a number of reasons that girls might misapply the past-tense

▶

rule more than boys. One possible explanation related to the correlation between overgeneralisation and the number of similar-sounding regular words (folded, moulded) the girls could remember. On the basis of this, it was concluded that individuals who were more likely to remember regular past-tense words would also be more likely to generalise these to new words (holded). This was seen as distinct from the application of a rule (V → V + ed) since overgeneralisation would be more likely with increased phonological similarity between the regular word and the irregular word, whereas rule-based production would not depend on such factors. Interestingly, Hartshorne and Ullman (2006) concluded that females still had 'superior lexical abilities' (p. 21), despite the fact that in this instance it also led to the production of more errors. The battle between the sexes, it seems, continues . . .

*Source*: Hartshorne, J. K., & Ullman, M. T. (2006). Why girls say 'holded' more than boys. *Developmental Science, 9*, 21–32.

## Appraising the Rumelhart and McClelland past-tense model

From these very simple beginnings, there has followed a storm of controversy over what the simulations actually show, and what the actual human data are. Moreover, the work has been followed up with further connectionist models (Joanisse & Seidenberg, 1999; MacWhinney & Leinbach, 1991; Plunkett & Marchman, 1991, 1993; Plunkett & Juola, 1999), more traditional rule-based models (Ling & Marinov, 1993; Taatgen & Anderson, 2002), work in developmental psycholinguistics (Marcus, 1996), behavioural work with normal adults (Kim, Pinker, Prince & Prasada, 1991; Ramscar, 2002), neuropsychological studies (Joanisse & Seidenberg, 1999; Marslen-Wilson & Tyler, 1997; Miozzo, 2003; Ullman et al., 1997) and indeed further debate (Marcus, 1995; Marslen-Wilson & Tyler, 2003; McClelland & Patterson, 2002a, 2002b, 2003; Pinker & Prince, 1988; Pinker & Ullman, 2002a, 2002b, 2003; Ramscar, 2003). Despite all this effort, there remains little agreement on any of the fundamental issues.

Two points suffice. One of the major criticisms of the early connectionist work is that, in several critical ways, the behaviour of the models was, essentially, an artefact of the training regime used. In particular, the characteristic U-shaped pattern of performance primarily came about because of the radical changes introduced to the training set of verbs to which the models were exposed during the training phase of the simulations. For instance, in the Rumelhart and McClelland (1986) simulations the training set was dramatically increased from 10 verbs to 420 verbs. It was only following such a dramatic increase in the size of the training set that the model began to err on the irregular items. Similar points of criticism have been made by Marcus (1995) about the later simulations reported by Plunkett and Marchman (1993).

The simple fact is that such a dramatic increase in exposure to verbs does not occur naturally in the language environment of the developing child. All of the evidence, from real human data, is that the point at which children begin to make overgeneralisations is not linked with a similar dramatic increase in exposure to a vastly larger sample of verbs. In this sense, the language environment that the network model 'grows up in' does not accord well with that of the child.

The second point concerns the nature of the phonological coding used by the Rumelhart and McClelland (1986) model. Here again criticisms have been levelled at the Wicklephone encoding used, and clear problems and limitations have been established (Lachter & Bever, 1988) with this form of coding. Against such criticisms, though, the simulations of Plunkett and Marchman (1991) have shown that other connectionist models of past-tense learning have been developed that do not depend on such coding schemes. However, a more important point is buried away in all this.

### Generalisation in the model

One advantage of the Wicklephone coding shown in Table 14.1 is that a given unit responds to more than one word. The units that code the phonemes /Ɓk/ will become activated when words such as 'talk' and 'walk' are presented to the model. What this means is that whatever the model learns about one of these words, this knowledge will transfer to (or generalise to) the other because the same pathways within the model become activated when /ɔːk/ is presented. So, to large measure, this means that the model could be trained on 'talk' but not 'walk', yet in learning the mapping from 'talk' to 'talked' this knowledge would generalise to 'walk'. That is, when exposed to 'walk' for the first time there is a large probability that it will correctly respond on the output layer with the phonological representation for 'walked'.

The reason that this is of some considerable importance is that in the ensuing debate, arguments rage over whether the regularities that exist between the morphological structure of the past- and present-tense forms of verbs emerges because of regularities that exist at the phonological level. To reiterate: we have drawn a distinction between the root morpheme (e.g., 'talk') and the stem morpheme (e.g., 'ed'). This distinction is critical for the rule-based account because the relations that are captured by rules of the sort 'V → V + *ed*' are defined in terms of these sorts of morphemes. However, what the connectionists are keen to assert is that any such relations exist purely as a consequence of the statistical regularities that are present at the phonological level.

For instance, McClelland and Patterson (2002a) have argued that 'nearly all exceptional past-tenses in English are quasi-regular to some extent' (p. 464). What they mean by this is that there are systematic relations that exist between the present- and past-tense forms of irregular verbs that are not carried at the level of morphemes, but are carried by the fact that these words contain similar clusters of phonemes. For instance, they cited the examples such as 'bleed', 'slide' and 'fight'. The corresponding past-tense forms 'bled', 'slid', 'fought', come about through a change in the vowel and the addition of a final /d/ or /t/. Such quasi-regularities occur at the phonological, not morphemic level. Critically, the connectionist network models are exquisitely sensitive to exactly these sorts of regularities and acquire weighted coefficients that reflect these correlations across input and output patterns.

### Eliminating the morphological level?

Referring back to Figure 14.2, if such phonological quasi-regularities lie at the heart of the acquisition of verb tenses, then one possible consequence is that the morphological level identified by Jackendoff (2002) can be eliminated from our concerns. The regularities that exist between present- and past-tense verb forms are captured by relations at the phonological level, not the more abstract morphological level. The more threatening implication is that if we can eliminate these forms of mental rules and representations from our theories, then it may well turn out that we can eliminate many of the others as well. → See 'What have we learnt?', below.

### → What have we learnt?

In adopting Jackendoff's (2002) framework for thinking, it has been accepted that natural language can be analysed in several different ways. As Figure 14.2 shows, it is possible to offer a componential analysis of the sounds, syntax and semantics that collectively define a natural language. It has been accepted that natural language is highly complex in terms of its structures. A recurring theme in the discussion, though, has been with the degree to which such componential analyses inform about actual psychological mechanisms. Do the structures we draw out in our psycholinguistic tree diagrams reflect psychological structures in the mind?

As we have seen, there has been controversy over whether syntax is the primary driver of sentence parsing, especially as other pragmatic factors have also identified as being important. A challenge for the future is to determine when and how such constraints come into play when people process natural language sentences. There has also been much controversy over the notion of mental rules. This has been discussed in terms of the past-tense debate. The central issue has been with whether the acquisition of the past tense of English verbs relies on a mechanism that is sensitive to morphemes (a morphemic parser, perhaps?) or whether the mechanism is fundamentally driven by regularities that exist at the level of phonology. The debate has arisen primarily because of the growth in popularity of connectionist models and connectionist theorising (see Quinlan, 1991, for a critical review).

More generally, though, what connectionist theorists do is attempt to replace one form of mental construct with a construct of a different kind. For example, localist representations are replaced with distributed patterns of activation over a set of processing units, mental rules are replaced with sets of coefficients (weights and thresholds) that capture statistical regularities that exist in the learning environment, rule-following mechanisms are replaced with rule-governed mechanisms, and so on. The desire is either to replace traditional cognitive constructs with so-called neurally, plausible mechanisms or to discard such constructs completely. By this view everything can be explained by simple processing units interconnected with weighted

▶

connections on the understanding that the brain comprises simple processing units interlinked with weighted connections. The central issue with regard to language is whether we can replace the theoretical constructs of the sort shown in Figure 14.2 with connectionist alternatives. For example, we have seen how attempts have been made to eliminate the morphemic level of description from our understanding of the acquisition of the past tense of English verbs. Such a componential analysis has been replaced by a consideration of the so-called quasi-regularities that exist at the level of phonology between 'talk' and 'talked', 'walk' and 'walked', etc.

Nevertheless, it seems that the biggest challenge facing the connectionists is to provide a workable account of the productivity, systematicity and compositionality (Fodor & Pylyshyn, 1988) of language. For Fodor and Pylyshyn (1988), the central issues remain over understanding the basic operations of the mind, and, in the same way that natural language exhibits productivity, systematicity and compositionality, they argued that so does the language of thought. That is, natural language exhibits such properties because fundamentally these reflect the nature of thinking. In the same way that you can express an infinite number of thoughts in language, you can also entertain an infinite number of thoughts. Indeed as Goldstone and Barsalou (1998) argued, 'The operation of productivity . . . is important for abstract thought because it produces mundane creativity; a potentially infinite number of new thoughts can be generated by recombining existing thoughts in new arrangements' (p. 253). The fact that such thoughts are systematically related to other thoughts, and that understanding complex thoughts depends on understanding the constituents of those thoughts, indicates that the connectionist principles of learning by association and generalising on the basis of similarity may not prove adequate for the job at hand. In this regard Fodor and Pylyshyn (1988) strongly defended the representational theory of mind against the connectionist challenge.

Fundamentally the claim is, therefore, that language and thinking share many common characteristics. This is not an attempt to equate language with thinking, but merely to set out their common characteristics, namely productivity, systematicity, compositionality and recursion. It is also important to consider other possible synergies between language and thinking and to do this we must return to issues concerning mental categories and the nature of the human conceptual system.

---

over-generalisation With respect to past-tense learning, the cases where children misuse the '+ ed' rule, in producing utterances such as 'breaked'.

## Language, knowledge and perception

We must move on if we are to consider more generally how language relates to other mental faculties. We have been accepting of the modular view of mind, in which language is considered to be a vertical faculty (Fodor, 1983). Natural language is the primary vehicle by which we communicate about the world and so our use of language must be intimately connected with how we construe the world. Indeed it is the relation between communication and construal that underpins much of the remainder of the chapter. We begin by returning to a general framework for thinking that

has been put forward by Jackendoff, we then move on to more empirical matters before closing.

## A final general framework for thinking about the relations between language and the other related faculties

Rather surprisingly, there are precious few attempts in the literature at tying everything together within one general framework for thinking (cf. Miller & Johnson-Laird, 1976). Recently, though, a notable exception is provided in the work of Jackendoff (1987a, 1987b, 2002), for he has tried repeatedly to develop a theory in which specific claims are made about connections between linguistic and non-linguistic forms of knowledge (1987a, 1987b, 2002). Figure 14.12 provides a schematic of the most recent incarnation of these ideas. Although the account is reasonably vague, it does nevertheless make some sensible distinctions that may prove useful.

**Figure 14.12 The mind according to Jackendoff**
Situating the mind (everything within the ellipse) in the world (everything outside the ellipse) and decomposing the mind into its constituents (after Jackendoff, 2002). See text for further details.

*Source*: Jackendoff, R. (2002). *Foundations of language. Brain, meaning, grammar, evolution* (fig. 11.1, p. 348). Oxford, England: Oxford University Press. Reproduced with permission.

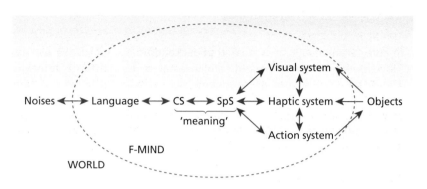

*F-MIND* stands for functional mind and is essentially an indication that the account is couched at the functional level (see Chapters 1 and 2). There is division between the external and internal worlds and within the internal world the F-MIND is divided into various forms of knowledge and various forms of processing systems. Meaning is divided into a CS component and an SpS component. The CS component is the conceptual structure that was discussed previously in relation to Figure 14.2. The SpS component stands for spatial structure. As Jackendoff (2002) noted, 'CS . . . encodes such aspects of understanding as category membership . . . , and predicate argument structure. SpS . . . is concerned with encoding the spatial understanding of the physical world – not just moment-by-moment appearance, but the integration over time of the shape, motion and layout of objects in space' (p. 346). So whereas the CS encodes *the what* and *the how*, the SpS encodes *the when* and *the where*. Critically for abstract objects of thought such as judgement and truth, the CS exists in the absence of a corresponding SpS.

In this regard, the SpS plays a crucial role in dealing with real-world concrete objects. Consequently, a core component of SpS is that it contains information captured by the sorts of 3D model representations that Marr (1982) advocated in his theory of the representation and recognition of objects from vision (we discussed in detail in Chapter 13). Again to quote Jackendoff (2002), 'SpS must encode the shape of objects in a form that is suitable for recognizing an object at different distances and from different perspectives, i.e., it must solve the classic problem of object constancy' (p. 346). In addition, the SpS encodes aspects of objects that are hidden or otherwise occluded, as well as variation in the shape and dispositions of parts of objects of similar structure (see Figure 14.13).

In his earlier writings Jackendoff (1987a, 1987b) went to some lengths to try to bolster his claims about the centrality of the 3D model description in his framework for thinking, but in his more recent writings he is more accepting of the problems that exist with this theoretical construct. As we concluded in Chapter 13, there is no convincing evidence that has established the psychological validity of 3D model descriptions. There is much more convincing evidence for representations that code information about an object's shape in terms of viewpoint-dependent

**Figure 14.13 Object recognition vs. categorisation**
Examples of (a) object categorisation and (b) object identification as conceived by Jackendoff (1987a).

*Source*: Jackendoff, R. (1987a). *Consciousness and the computational mind* (fig. 10.1, p. 199). Cambridge, Massachusetts: The MIT Press. Reproduced with permission.

**(a) Object categorisation**

| | | |
|---|---|---|
| Conceptual level: | [TOKEN]$_i$ IS-AN-INSTANCE OF | [TYPE]$_k$ |
| 3D level: | visually derived 3D model | 3D model from memory |

**(b) Object identification**

| | | |
|---|---|---|
| Conceptual level: | [TOKEN]$_i$ IS-TOKEN-IDENTICAL-TO | [TYPE]$_j$ |
| 3D level: | visually derived 3D model | 3D model from memory |

## → What have we learnt?

In sum, even though it is clear that Jackendoff is (almost) alone in writing about fundamental issues about the relation between language and perception, his general approach has associated problems. Uppermost is the fact that the theory is couched at such a level that it is very difficult to see how it can be tested. Nevertheless, what is particularly appealing is the idea that it is desirable to think in terms of some single point of contact between the words we use and the things we know about. For instance, it may well be that when we use the word 'dog' as a default, the prototypical dog comes to mind.

Clearly, much further theoretical work is needed, and other alternatives need to be developed and tested. There is a very large hole in our understanding here. Many questions remain over the relations between language and other forms of knowledge.

---

co-ordinates. It is perhaps for this reason that in his more recent writings (2002) he concedes this point by noting 'the criteria for SpS must be satisfied by some cognitive structure or combination of structures' (p. 347). If we replace the comments about 3D model descriptions with comments about some form of representation that codes a prototypical view, then maybe the account can be salvaged?

Initially the theory was motivated by a desire to integrate constructs developed in the area of perception with those developed in the area of language. Clearly this is highly desirable if we are to ever make any headway in understanding how it is that we converse about things that we experience outside the realm of language. However, aside from providing some useful distinctions – there must be some form of mental apparatus that allows us to think about those things that are perceptible and those things that are not, since we have knowledge of things that we cannot express in words (the smell of teen spirit) – the account falls somewhat short in providing little else that might form the basis of generating and testing empirical predictions. → See 'What have we learnt?', above.

## Language, mental categories and perception

Having considered lofty theoretical ideas about basic issues, it is now fitting to return to the rather mundane matters of what the relevant experimental data are. We will begin by considering some key findings, the most basic of which concerns the evidence that is taken to show that our mental categories determine what we perceive. Is it possible that the way people organise their world into categories alters the actual appearance of the world (Goldstone, 1994, p. 178)? In approaching this issue, we must tread very carefully because, from our discussion of perception (Chap-

ters 4, 5 and 6), we accepted a very general framework for thinking in which the perceptual mechanisms are insulated from any interference from higher-order central systems. We adopted the modularity of mind hypothesis that the input systems operate in a bottom-up fashion and are insulated from the human conceptual system. Now, though, we are in a position to question this basic assumption. Is it really true that the perceptual system is fixed and unalterable through experience and learning?

Having digested the relevant evidence, we then move on to an associated claim that our perceptions of the world are, to large measure, determined by the language that we use. An implication of this is that users of different natural languages – French, German, English, Hindi, etc. – perceive the world in very different ways. Such an astonishing claim does deserve to be treated with some care.

## Influences of categorisation on perceptual discrimination – Goldstone (1994)

Let us begin by considering some more basic terminology as this is central to the discussion that follows. **Stimulus generalisation** refers to an observer's ability to classify different stimuli as being the same. *The Guardian*, *The Sun* and *The Racing Post* are all newspapers. Usually the phrase is used with reference to novel instances – that is, stimulus generalisation occurs when a participant assigns a novel instance to a familiar category. If you were to go to Italy, you would recognise *Il Giorno* as a newspaper even though you may never have seen it before. In this context, a useful distinction is known as the **type–token distinction**. By way of example, the characters a, A, *a*, *A*, **a**, **A**, etc. are different tokens of the same letter type – the letter 'aie'. So 'aie' is the letter type and the six different characters in the different fonts and cases are tokens of this type. Stimulus generalisation occurs when an observer treats the different tokens of a particular stimulus type as being the same – all of the characters are taken to designate the letter 'aie'.

From a traditional cognitive psychological perspective, such stimulus generalisation abilities have been examined in terms of the operation of mental categories. Different instances (tokens) of the same category (type) have been classified with respect to some form of mental representation that captures the corresponding concept. It has been accepted that what participants are doing when making stimulus generalisations, is assigning different stimuli to the same type on the basis of the relevant mental categories. That is, they have some form of internal representation of what it is that specifies the letter 'aie' and that they consult this in order to assign the different stimulus tokens to this particular type. Stimuli that appear to fit with this mental category are treated as being the same, and stimuli that do not are treated as being different. In this respect **stimulus discrimination** (in a sense the opposite of stimulus generalisation) occurs when stimuli are assigned to different categories.

## Categorical perception

As you can possibly imagine, there is a vast literature on stimulus generalisation and discrimination in both the behavioural and cognitive literatures. Much of this work has also been carried out on artificially contrived categories (see Estes, 1994, for a review). The assumption has been that it is only by using such artificial categories that complete control can be exercised over the participant's exposure to the instances of these categories. We will consider examples of this work shortly. However, a very important effect was established using spoken syllables and it is this effect that is central to the studies that have attempted to show how it is that our mental categories may actually influence perceptual processes. The basic effect is known as *categorical perception* (Harnad, 1987). We have already discussed the effect in terms of speech perception (see Chapter 6), but, more generally, the demonstration is that 'people are better able to distinguish between physically different stimuli when the stimuli come from different categories than when they come from the same category' (Goldstone, 1994, p. 179).

Indeed, in discussing categorical perception Goldstone cited the classic study by Liberman et al. (1957) as providing supporting evidence. Some of the details of this study are worth repeating again. Liberman

et al. generated a range of sound stimuli where each sound comprised a spoken vowel–consonant syllable. The stimuli ranged in likeness from /be/ to /de/ to /ge/ so any given stimulus could be located at one of 14 possible points on this syllable continuum. On each trial a participant was presented with three sounds in an ABX paradigm. The first A sound was followed by the B sound and the participant had to respond with whether the X sound was a repetition of A or B. The central finding was that participants were more accurate in their judgements when A and B were taken from different syllable categories than when the sounds were taken from the same syllable category.

It is exactly this sort of result that indicates how it might be that our categories of the world influence our perceptions of it. In terms of the current results, the A/B pairings were configured so that the sounds were adjacent with one another on the syllable continuum and in this way each A and B pair were as physically similar to one another as any other A and B pair. Irrespective of this, however, what critically affected the participants' judgements was where the category boundaries fell on this continuum. Sounds either side of a boundary appeared to be more different from one another than did sounds adjacently placed within the boundaries of a given syllable. The ability to discriminate between two sounds (i.e., the A from the B stimuli) critically depended on whether they were taken from the same syllable category or different syllable categories. One contingent (and controversial) claim, from such a demonstration, is that our mental categories influence the manner in which we perceive the world. If you don't have the phonetic categories that distinguish between /be/ and /de/ then the world will sound very different to you!

Goldstone (1994) was particularly interested in this kind of categorical perception effect and examined it more thoroughly with the set of multi-dimensional stimuli shown in Figure 14.14. The figure shows 16 square stimuli organised into a 4 × 4 array in which the *x* dimension reflects variation in size and the *y* dimension reflects variation in brightness. Each corresponding square was an individual stimulus figure used in the experiment.

In a critical experiment (Experiment 2) three groups of experimental participants were tested in addition to a control group. The experimental groups underwent an initial training phase that involved making categorical judgements about the individual squares shown in the figure. On each trial, an individual square was presented and the participant simply had to make an unspeeded response about which category the square

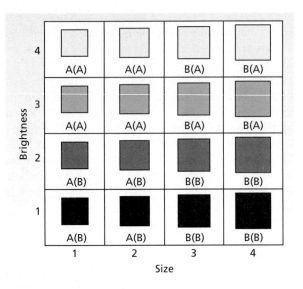

**Figure 14.14 The 2D space that defined the stimuli used by Goldstone (1994) in his experiments on categorical perception**

*Source*: Goldstone, R. L. (1994). Influences of categorization in perceptual discrimination. *Journal of Experimental Psychology: General*, *123*, 178–200 (fig. 3, p. 183). Reproduced with permission.

belonged to. For the group of *size categorisers*, squares in columns 1 and 2 were assigned to Category A (let's say *small*) and squares in columns 3 and 4 were assigned to Category B (let's say *large*). For the group of *brightness categorisers*, squares in rows 3 and 4 were assigned to Category A (let's say *bright*) and squares in rows 1 and 2 were assigned to Category B (let's say *dim*). So different participant groups were being trained to discriminate on the basis of the size or brightness of the stimulus.

In following the logic of the experiment, it should be clear that the size categorisers needed only to attend to the size dimension in order to make their category judgements, and that the brightness categorisers needed only to attend to the brightness dimension in order to make their category judgements. All experimental participants were given the same amount of training. In the judgement task, after a square had been presented and the participant had made a response, feedback was given over the correctness of the response and the correct category label was also presented. In these regards, the experimental participants were both pre-exposed to the stimuli and they were trained on a particular classificatory scheme defined in terms of the size or brightness dimension. Control participants were given no such pre-exposure or training.

In a final phase of the experiment, all participants undertook a same–different judgement task in some-

thing known as a *discrimination experiment*. On 'same' trials the same square was presented twice in succession on the screen of a computer. So square S1,B4 would have been replaced by another presentation of square S1,B4. On different trials the first square was replaced with a square that was adjacent to it in the stimulus space. For instance, square S1,B4 was replaced by square S1,B3. Participants simply had to indicate whether they thought the two squares were identical or not.

Performance in the discrimination experiment was of most interest and the critical measures were $d'$ values, the understanding being that $d'$ reflects perceptual sensitivity with larger $d'$ values signifying greater perceptual discriminability than smaller $d'$ values (see Chapter 4). Moreover, it was comparisons between the $d'$ values for each experimental group and the $d'$ values for the control group that were paramount. Any difference in the experimental $d'$ values and those of the controls could be taken as an index of the degree to which the pre-exposure/training phase had altered the perceptual sensitivity of the perceptual mechanisms, an underlying assumption being that acquiring a particular classification scheme fundamentally altered the way in which the proximal stimulus was perceived. The perceptual system had become tuned to make certain category distinctions and not others.

In this regard, Goldstone (1994) discussed the notion of **acquired distinctiveness** whereby category judgements based on a relevant dimension become particularly highly tuned. Subtle differences between adjacent categories become easily detected when the differences are on the relevant dimension. In terms of the experiment, and following training, size categorisers ought to be particularly attuned to the discriminating values on the size dimension, and brightness categorisers ought to be particular attuned to the discriminating values on the brightness dimension. So for example, and according to the principles of categorical perception, size categorisers ought to become particularly adept in discriminating between adjacent stimuli on the size dimension when the adjacent stimuli are taken from different categories. Indeed the data revealed that they were more accurate in making a different response to a stimulus pair containing a square from column 2 and a square from column 3 relative to control participants). A similar prediction concerning the brightness categorisers and stimuli that flanked the critical brightness category boundary (between rows 2 and 3) was also supported by the data. Brightness categorisers were more accurate than controls with these pairs of stimuli. Overall, therefore, predictions

Taken overall, the results were interpreted within a framework in which the acquisition of a particular perceptual classification scheme alters the perceptual encoding mechanisms in ways that, in a sense, sharpen the boundaries between the adjacent categories. It is not so much that tokens of the same type become all lumped together in a difficult-to-discriminate mass, but merely that the boundaries between the different types (the underlying categories) are forced apart. It is not that all ducks begin to look the same, but rather that it becomes easier to discriminate ducks from swans – ducks begin to look more different from swans than they did prior to acquiring the associated categories. Indeed Notman, Sowden and Özgen (2005) have recently called this a **categorical perception expansion effect** – it is as though the space between adjacent categories is expanded through training. Such evidence as this is perfectly in line with the notion of perceptual tuning – experience sharpens the perceptual boundaries between stimuli taken from different categories.

made about performance of both groups of categorisers were borne out by the results.

The data also speak to the notion of **acquired equivalence**. Simply put, there may be evidence of training giving rise to a blurring between values on the category dimensions. For instance, it may be that participants become less adept at telling stimuli apart on the dimension on which they have not been trained – that is, on the irrelevant dimension. Goldstone found no evidence of this. In addition, it may also be the case that stimuli within each category become less discriminable from one another as a result of training. That is, values on the relevant dimension that are contained within a given category become less distinct (i.e., more equivalent). Again, though, there was no strong evidence for this taking place. The results actually revealed a slight tendency for stimuli within categories to be treated as being more distinctive from one another as gauged relative to the controls – quite the opposite effect to that of acquired equivalence. Overall, therefore, there was no evidence of acquired equivalence of within-category stimuli; there was, however, evidence of acquired distinctiveness. → See 'What have we learnt?', above.

## Categorical perception and verbal labelling

The data just described were interpreted without any reference to the operation of language. However, concerns have been aired over the degree to which such categorical perception effects reveal more about verbal labelling than anything to do with perception. As Goldstone, Lippa and Shiffrin (2001) stated, 'participants adopt the strategy of labelling the object they see with their assigned categories, and respond "same" or "different" depending on whether the objects receive the same label' (p. 30). Stimuli that are adjacent across a category boundary have different labels but stimuli adjacent within a category share the same label (Pilling, Wiggett, Özgen & Davies, 2003, p. 539). It could therefore be that the effect reveals more about our descriptions of the world than our perceptions of it. To address this issue, and to try to rule out any labelling accounts of the basic effects, Goldstone et al. (2001) carried out an ingenious experiment on training participants to categorise faces. Figure 14.15 provides an illustration of the stimuli used.

Four groups of participants were trained to make A/B discriminations between faces assigned to a contrived category A and faces assigned to a contrived category B. Two faces were assigned to each category. Prior to such training, however, similarity ratings were collected for the faces – participants rated how similar each face was to every other face in their set of four. Critically, ratings were also taken for each of these faces relative to a so-called neutral face. The neutral face was not assigned to either category and was therefore not used in the subsequent training. During training, and on every trial, a single face was presented and the participant was asked to categorise it as either an A or a B. Participants were given explicit feedback on every trial and extended training was undertaken (216 categorisation trials). Finally the same similarity judgement task as carried out initially was undertaken again.

Initially the data were discussed in terms of how the similarity ratings for the trained faces altered as

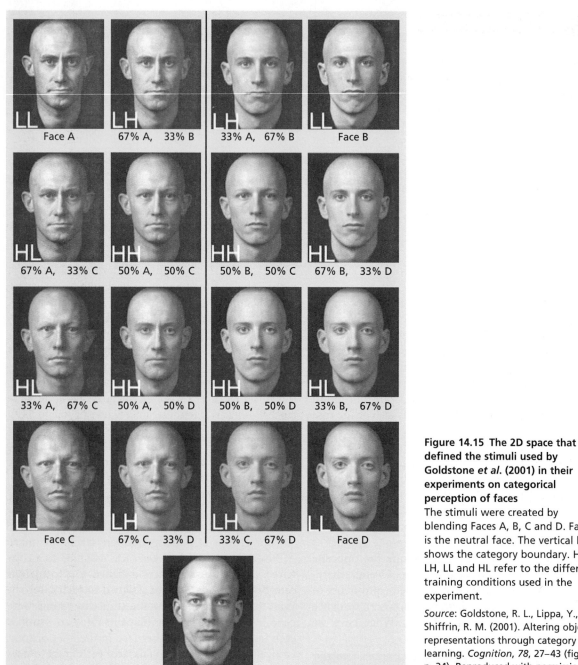

Face A | 67% A, 33% B | 33% A, 67% B | Face B

67% A, 33% C | 50% A, 50% C | 50% B, 50% C | 67% B, 33% D

33% A, 67% C | 50% A, 50% D | 50% B, 50% D | 33% B, 67% D

Face C | 67% C, 33% D | 33% C, 67% D | Face D

Face E

**Figure 14.15 The 2D space that defined the stimuli used by Goldstone *et al*. (2001) in their experiments on categorical perception of faces**
The stimuli were created by blending Faces A, B, C and D. Face E is the neutral face. The vertical line shows the category boundary. HH, LH, LL and HL refer to the different training conditions used in the experiment.

*Source*: Goldstone, R. L., Lippa, Y., & Shiffrin, R. M. (2001). Altering object representations through category learning. *Cognition*, *78*, 27–43 (fig. 1, p. 34). Reproduced with permission from Elsevier.

a consequence of the training. The data were clear in showing a categorical perception expansion effect. That is, faces that were assigned to different categories during training were rated as being less similar to one another following the category training than they were at the outset.

Of perhaps more importance, though, are the similarity ratings of the faces relative to the neutral face. The neutral face was not assigned to any category and was therefore not used during the training. What this meant was that this particular face was never associated with a category label. Hence judgements involving this face cannot be due to accessing any particular category label. The results were clear in showing that the ratings for the instances from the same category relative to the neutral faces converged after training. So whereas there was a reasonable amount of variability in how faces of one category were judged relative to the neutral face prior to training, this variability was reduced after training. In a sense, each of the faces within a given category began to appear as similar to the neutral face as every other face in that category.

In other words, there was an indirect measure of the degree to which different members of the same category became more similar to one another as a consequence of training – there was evidence of acquired equivalence. This is in contrast to acquired distinctiveness, and refers to the blurring between values on a category dimension. As Goldstone et al. (2001) concluded, 'The elements that the objects share, elements that by definition specify their category, become more important parts of the objects' descriptions' (p. 41). The claim is that category learning enhances the representation of object attributes that are critical to membership of the category. So the dog's wet nose and the cat's whiskers become important attributes that determine how best to assign a new instance to its appropriate category. Certain category attributes gain special status in how the corresponding internal category description is maintained in the mind. Category training brings about a representational change in weighting certain attributes over others. Such changes are in addition to the sorts of changes to the perceptual encoding mechanisms that have also been discussed (cf. Notman et al., 2005). Moreover, representational changes are quite independent from anything to do with the language that is used to describe the world.

### Pinpoint question 14.9

If the Seven Dwarfs look more similar to one another thanks to the presence of Snow White, is this an example of acquired distinctiveness or acquired equivalence?

## Categorical perception, colour perception and colour naming

So far we have explored the nature of categorical perception and have considered the claim that such an effect arises simply as a consequence of the language that is used to describe the associated stimulus categories. We have also seen that despite such a possibility, experience with particular category instances can bring about representational change that has nothing to do with concomitant language use. This shows that there is more to the categorical perception effect than verbal labelling: categorical perception effects arise independently from anything to do with accessing the

same category label for all items of a particular category. Therefore the data reveal that the perceptual apparatus is insulated from language. In this regard the data reveal that our perceptions of the world are determined by things other than how we label the world. However, another branch of the literature has addressed itself to the more controversial topic of how it might be that language can *determine* how we categorise the world.

## The Whorf hypothesis vs. the Roschian hypothesis

This research has examined a famous claim that is enshrined in something known as the linguistic relativity hypothesis (Roberson, Davies & Davidoff, 2000), or alternatively, the **Whorf hypothesis** (Davidoff, 2001). The associated claim (enshrined in *the Whorfian view*) is that 'We dissect nature along the lines laid down by our native language' (Whorf, 1956, cited by Davidoff, 2001, p. 383). In other words, how we construe the world is primarily determined by how we describe it. Put bluntly, the language we use determines our perceptions of it.

The counter-claim is that, essentially, our conceptual structures mirror structures in the real world. Our mental categories are therefore not determined by natural language but are given by the nature of the world. Language does not determine our perceptions of the world, it is merely the system we use to describe our perceptions of the world. As Malt (1995) stated, according to this (realist view, see Chapter 3), it is the presence of structure in the world that is taken to be the 'primary determinant' of what objects group together (p. 94). For short-hand, let us dub this the **Roschian hypothesis** – the view that the nature of the human conceptual system is, in a sense, given by the external world and it should be considered independently from language that is used to describe it (after Rosch, 1978).

Evidence against the Whorfian hypothesis comes from cases where the same sort of conceptual system appears to be at work regardless of the natural language of the culture being studied – evidence consistent with a doctrine referred to as **universalism**. Evidence in favour of the Whorfian hypothesis is where the conceptual system differs according to the language of the culture – evidence consistent with a doctrine referred to as **relativism** (see Kay & Regier, 2007). We have used the phrase 'natural language' to apply to any naturally occurring human language such as Spanish, English, French, Japanese, Cantonese, etc. So given that there are different words for the same sorts of things across these different languages, it seems sensible to ask whether the speakers of these different languages actually construe and (in the limit) perceive the world in radically different ways – ways that are determined by the language that they speak. Do speakers of different languages actually perceive the world in quite different ways? The Whorfian and the Roschian hypotheses provide starkly contrasting answers to this question.

## Colours and colour categories

In attempting to tease apart these two diametrically opposed views, the study of colour categories has come to the fore. Underpinning all of this is the fact that there are objective ways of classifying colours and these can be established independently of the language that is used to describe the colours. For instance, the wavelength of light can be quantified and this can be used to quantify differences in hue. More particularly, any colour can be fixed by specifying its **hue**, **saturation** and **brightness**. Hue is the more precise term for what is meant by 'colour' when we refer to red or green or blue, etc. Saturation refers to how vivid the colour is, for example, red is more saturated than pink. Colours that contain a lot of white are essentially *desaturated*. Brightness expresses how dark or light the colour is – the same colour can be viewed in daylight or a dimly lit room. By this view there are three dimensions that define colours and any particular colour (such as pea green) can be fixed within this 3D space.

According to Wandell (1995), a more formal system for expressing the nature of colours is provided by the 'Munsell Book of Colors'. Approximating a painting wall chart in a hardware store, the 'Munsell Book of Colors' contains colour samples that are ordered such that the perceptual distance between an adjacent pair of colour values is equal. Values of perceptual distance were gauged from ratings of similarity, hence the system provides a means for ordering colours in terms of their perceptual similarity. Moreover, the Munsell system also provides tokens of the various colours rendered onto so-called *Munsell colour chips* – much like gambling chips or checkers. The set of these colour chips spans the visible space of colours. There is a colour chip for nearly every discernible colour. In using the Munsell system it is possible to map out how a person carves up the visible spectrum into different colour categories by examining how they organise these Munsell chips.

## The early work of Heider/Rosch

Early research by Rosch (Heider, 1972; Rosch, 1973, 1975 [Heider and Rosch are one and the same person]; see also Berlin & Kay, 1969) was taken to show that a given mental colour category conforms to the notion of a cluster of instances that form around a prototype or focal category colour (see Chapter 12 for a more thorough discussion of category prototypes). In the same way, a spider is a better prototype of an insect than a dust mite. Such focal colours were shown to be better remembered and also learned earlier in developmental time than non-focal colours. By this view there is a prototypical red, green, blue, etc. and the mental representation of the colour space is divided up into distinct regions that form around the focal colours. According to universalism (i.e., the Roschian hypothesis) such a category structure reflects natural colour groupings that are non-arbitrary and reflect the nature of the colours found in the world. If this is true – blue is blue is blue – then the colour groupings should therefore be evident across all cultures regardless of the native language of the observer.

To test this idea, Rosch compared performance across two different cultures on a variety of colour judgement tasks. Participants were either American undergraduates or members of the Dugum Dani tribe, a so-called Stone Age agricultural culture (Davidoff, 2001) indigenous to Indonesian New Guinea. At the time (in the early 1970s) the claim was that the language of the Dani only contained two colour terms – light and dark. In one critical experiment (Heider, 1972) Rosch generated a stimulus set that contained eight focal colours and 16 non-focal colours. On a given trial one colour was presented for 5 s and, following a pause of 30 s, an array of 160 colours was shown. The participant had to indicate which one of the 160 colours had just occurred. The now classic result was that participants of both samples performed better on focal colour trials than on non-focal colour trials. So the claim was that even though the Dani participants possessed a very impoverished system for labelling colours (try describing a Kandinsky painting using only 'light' and 'dark'), they possessed the same underlying mental colour categories as the American undergraduates. The nature of the mental colour category system was the same across the different cultures. Such evidence has been taken to favour the idea of universal basic colour categories (Davidoff, 2001): universalism was upheld.

## More recent work by Roberson and colleagues

Since publication of these original studies the work of Rosch (just cited) has been heavily criticised to such a point that the conclusions drawn can no longer be justified on the strength of the evidence (see Davidoff, 2001; Lucy & Shweder, 1979; Ratner, 1989). Rather than dwell on these negatives, it is more appropriate to consider more recent work that is apparently much more in line with relativism. For example, an important paper was published in 2000 by Roberson, Davies and Davidoff. Here the performance of native English-speaking participants was compared with members of another New Guinea tribe (the Berinmo) whose language contains only five basic colour terms.

First a simple naming task was used. Participants were presented with Munsell chips and simply asked to name the colour of each chip. Figure 14.16 provides a schematic representation of how the array of 160 colour chips were named in the different participant groups. In the figure, the chips are arranged according to the Munsell ordering but the colour groupings convey how the chips were named by, respectively, the Berinmo and English participants.

In and of itself, this contrasting pattern of results is only to be expected; after all, there are only five colour regions identified for the Berinmo participants but eight for the English-speaking participants. The more interesting findings, though, concern the later experiments. For instance, Roberson et al. (2000) examined short-term memory for both focal (prototypical) and non-focal (non-prototypical) colours in an attempt to replicate Rosch's earlier experiment (Heider, 1972). The procedure was the same as described, but this time Berinmo and English monolinguals were compared.

Generally speaking, the data were clear in showing better recognition memory for focal than non-focal colours for both participant samples and again overall memory performance differed across the two groups. The English-speaking participants were more accurate than the Indonesian participants.

The important novel finding was that the data revealed a systematic response bias effect for the Berinmo participants. When the Berinmo participants made an error, they simply tended to choose a focal rather than a non-focal colour – they adopted the strategy that 'if in doubt, guess a focal colour that had been previously presented'. What this means is that part of the reason the Berinmo participants were accurate on focal colour trials is that they tended to guess that a focal colour occurred even though they were unsure which colour had been presented. When this response bias was taken into account, the 'memory' advantage for the focal colours shown by the Berinmo participants was abolished. It is no longer surprising that the Berinmo participants did so well on the focal colour trials because, in all probability, some of these responses were guesses. Such a finding as this has been taken to undermine the original claims for universal colour categories provided by Rosch.

More striking, perhaps, are the categorical perception effects that Roberson et al. (2000) found. Now participants were given triads of coloured chips and had to choose the two that essentially were the most similar to one another. Three sorts of triads were used: within-category triads in which all three chips were taken from the same colour category; boundary triads in which two of the chips were clear members of the same category and the third chip was positioned on the boundary of this category; finally, across-category triads were tested, where two of the chips

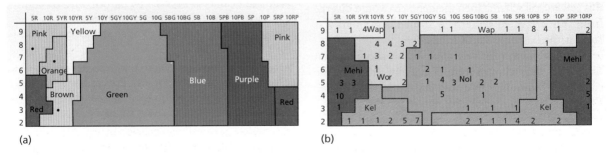

(a)  (b)

**Figure 14.16 The contrasting 2D colour spaces**
How colour labels correspond to points in Munsell colour space in Berinmo (a) and English (b).

*Source*: Davidoff, J. (2001). Language and perceptual categorisation. *Trends in Cognitive Science*, 5, 382–387 (fig. 1, p. 385). Reproduced with permission from Elsevier.

## → What have we learnt?

As Kay and Regier (2007) have recently concluded (despite Rosch's original findings), there is now ample evidence that the colour categories given by different natural languages influence (and perhaps even determine) memory for particular colours, and learning to name individual colours and to discriminate particular colours. However, we do need to be careful because, from accepting this, it does not follow that colour categories are completely determined on an arbitrary basis. So what may actually be going on? According to Roberson et al. (2000), the colour system adopted by the Berinmo speakers does have a rational basis in their culture. For example, 'it might be that tulip leaves, a favourite vegetable, are bright green when freshly picked and good to eat, but quickly yellow if kept. Agreement over the colour-term boundary coincides with agreement over when they are no longer good to eat' (p. 395). In this respect, even a subtle change from green to yellow is important to detect. What the adopted colour labelling system is doing, therefore, is highlighting what otherwise might seem a very subtle difference in hue. Language is therefore helping to emphasise a subtle difference in hue that might otherwise be missed (with fatal consequences!).

were from one category and the third was from a different category.

The clever aspect of the design was that triads were tested in which the categories were either associated with names used by English speakers (blue/green) or they were associated with names used by Berinmo speakers (noi/wor) (see Figure 14.16). Speakers from both cultures were tested with all triads and participants' choices were scored for the degree to which they conformed to the different categorical distinctions. One set of triads (let us call this the *English set*) was defined relative to the blue/green boundary. The *Berinmo set* was defined to the noi/wor boundary. So within the English set an across-category triad would consist of two green chips and one blue chip or two blue chips and one green chip. If the participants were using this category boundary they should discard the blue chip in the first instance and the green chip in the second. However, if the participants were not using this categorical scheme then their choices would diverge from this predicted pattern. A similar argument was run for the Berinmo set of triads.

The data were relatively clear-cut in showing that the participants' choices were, essentially, driven by the categorical boundary that was present in their native tongue. If the language did not mark the category boundary, then choices deviated significantly from the predicted pattern of responses. As Roberson et al. (2000) concluded, 'Speakers of both languages made judgments in line with their own colour vocabulary more consistently than judgments relating to the other language' (p. 389). The English speakers showed a categorical perception effect for the blue/green boundary and not the noi/wor boundary. The reverse categorical

perception effect was shown by the Berinmo speakers. Such evidence was taken to support the linguistic relativity hypothesis. → See 'What have we learnt?', above.

### Pinpoint question 14.10

**What do universalists claim about the relation of language to other forms of knowledge?**

**stimulus generalisation** The ability to classify different objects as being tokens of the same type.

**type–token distinction** The distinction between individual instances (tokens) and the category (type) to which they belong.

**stimulus discrimination** The ability to class different objects as being different.

**acquired distinctiveness** When participants, through experience, begin to treat different instances as being different from one another and assign them different responses.

**acquired equivalence** Where participants, through experience, treat different instances as being similar to one another and assign them the same response. Both a and A belong to the A category.

**categorical perception expansion effect** Where the perceptual space between categories appears larger as a result of training.

**Whorf hypothesis** Also known as the 'linguistic relativity hypothesis', the idea that the way we perceive the world is determined by natural language.

**Roschian hypothesis** The view that the nature of the human conceptual system is, in a sense, given by the external world and it should be considered independently from the language that is used to describe it.

**universalism** The idea that conceptual systems across individuals are basically the same and are independent of the natural language used to describe the world.

**relativism** The idea that that the human conceptual system differs according to the language of the culture.

**hue** Essentially, the category of a colour such as 'red' or 'green'.

**saturation** Essentially, the vividness of a colour.

**brightness** Essentially, how light or dark something is.

# Concluding comments

So much for the details, what of the more general issue about language determining how we perceive the world? Fundamentally, this issue relates to the more basic issue of whether the perceptual system is insulated from any interference by cognitive mechanisms. To reiterate: relativist theorists take the data from the studies with colour to support the idea that cultural experience determines our perceptions of the world. More particularly, they take the data to reflect how language use can alter the perceptual mechanisms responsible for stimulus encoding – language is the cause for a particular sort of perceptual tuning. By this view subtle distinctions between adjacent colours are enhanced by the categorical boundaries that are given by the language. The colours that straddle a category boundary appear more distinctive from one another than is the case for colours that are adjacent within a category. What the data with the Berinmo suggest is that the language provides a categorical system that sharpens up the boundary between where one category ends and another category begins. This turns out to make perfect sense from an evolutionary perspective. The colour/language categories highlight the perceptual cues that signal differences between foods that are edible and those that it is inadvisable to eat.

For universalists, however, the data can be taken to reflect a quite different conclusion. This conclusion is much more in line with the modularity of mind idea

that the input systems are insulated from the central systems. Here the understanding is that the input systems operate in an, essentially, stimulus-driven fashion: a fashion that has evolved over the history of the human species and is therefore innate. By this view, what the data actually show is that it is the interpretation of the perceptual representation that is determined by culture and it is this that changes with the language that is used.

The basic issues remain and there is still no agreement over how best to interpret the empirical data. Most problematic for the universalist camp are the data – the categorical perception effects – that have been used to support the notion of perceptual tuning (Goldstone, 1994; Goldstone et al., 2001; Notman et al., 2005; Özgen & Davies, 2002). Such effects are taken to show in a transparent way that the categories that are used to describe the world are in this sense determining how the world is perceived. However, much of this evidence depends on arguments regarding $d'$ (or similar measures of sensitivity). As we saw in Chapter 6, changes in $d'$ do not necessarily reflect operations within the perceptual system (see, for example Pylyshyn, 1999, for an extended discussion).

Perhaps one useful way forward is to think more generally in terms of how attention may be operating. As Notman et al. (2005) argued, 'Categorization acts to direct attention to stimulus features that are diagnostic of category membership thereby modulating perceptual learning about those particular features' (p. B10). By this view, what the data from the colour judgement and labelling studies may be revealing is that what the language is doing is drawing attention to a difference in hue that might otherwise go unnoticed. Indeed, Pylyshyn (1999) has gone further and argued, 'cognition only affects perception by determining where and what (and perhaps the degree to which) attention is focused' (p. 405). For him, all of the effects taken to show how language determines perception are more appropriately considered in terms of attention. Language use and other cultural experiences may simply operate so as to force an individual to attend to certain aspects of the world more than others – language aids in the direction of selective attention. So learning that face A and face B belong to the same category means learning which features the faces have in common, or which features of the two faces are most important for the category assignment.

By this view, it is not so much that the perceptual analysis of the faces has changed because of the training, but merely that participants have become more efficient at detecting what characteristics are most diagnostic of a given category. (Whether all such appeals to attention fit so comfortably with the idea that perceptual analysis remains completely insulated from any top-down control remains the topic of much controversy – see, for example, Carrasco, Ling & Read, 2004.)

For some, this may seem like a slightly depressing stalemate on which to end – we seem to have argued ourselves into an unfortunate impasse. Neither camp will give ground and the arguments continue to go to and fro. For others, though, the outlook is less gloomy. Indeed a whole new area of research is beginning to open up over the interactions between speech processing and the direction of attention in tasks in which participants listen to speech, observe some form of visual display and have their eye movements monitored. In this way detailed measures can be taken online, and these are being used to inform about the very close synergies that exist between speech comprehension and visual cognition (see Henderson & Ferreira, 2004, for a recent review).

Yet again, therefore, we have a case where, despite the work that has been done, basic questions about human cognition remain unanswered. What has been achieved is a much fuller understanding of the experimental tools that have been used to inform theoretical problems. The ingenuity of researchers is constantly being demonstrated in their developments of newer methods and techniques that overcome some of the shortcomings that have been revealed by past research.

## CHAPTER SUMMARY

- According to the principles of modularity (Fodor, 1983), there should be specific cognitive processes related to language. However, as Marcus (2006) stated, language modules are likely to be similar to other cognitive modules in virtue of their reliance on (a) memory, (b) the processing of sequences, and (c) the requirement to manipulate symbols.

- With respect to natural language, Chomsky (1965) made a distinction between performance, which refers to the constraints associated with language production and comprehension, and language competence, which refers to the speaker's knowledge regarding their particular language. Language competence is thought to be (in the main) a form of tacit knowledge, which underpins language but which itself cannot be articulated.

- A distinction was also made between the surface and deep forms of language. For Chomsky (1965), the surface or superficial structure referred to the physical appearance of language while the deep or underlying structure referred to the mental representations responsible for language production and comprehension. A base sentence containing the abstract symbols relating to subject (Rupert), verb (read) and object (paper) leads to the production of a number of surface structures such as 'Rupert read the paper', 'The paper is being read by Rupert' and 'That is the paper Rupert is reading'. Syntactic rules establish the structure of the base sentences while transformations allow the conversion of the base sentence into a surface sentence.

- One can think about a variety of different types of language structure. Phonological structure contains the morphophonological (establishing the grouping of phonemes into words), syllabic (how words can be decomposed into syllables) and prosodic (how words are grouped into phrases) structures. In contrast, syntactic structure concerns itself with the rules that govern sentence construction and semantic structure is involved with the meaning of the sentence. Meaning can be derived by considering the conceptual constituents of the sentence (Jackendoff, 2002) or more generally by the propositional content of the sentence (Clark & Clark, 1977).

- Fodor and Pylyshyn (1988) identified three further characteristics of language. Productivity refers to the ability to generate an infinite number of sentences on the basis of a finite number of rules. Systematicity refers to the ability to understand similar kinds of sentence. Being able to understand 'John loves Mary' implies the ability to understand a whole host of related sentences. Compositionality refers to the understanding of a complex expression on the basis of its constituent parts and the interactions between them. In addition, Corballis (2003) defined recursion as a means 'for generating terms in a sequence, in which the rule for generating the next term in a sequence involves one or more of the preceding terms' (p. 155).

- Syntactic parsing refers to the general principles involved in decomposing linguistic input into its constituent parts such as words, phrases and sentences. One specific way in which words group together to form sentences is provided by the garden-path theory (Frazier, 1987). Here, predictions regarding future elements of language are made according to the previous syntactic structure of the sentence. We are essentially being led down one garden path on the basis of what has gone before. Although there are cases where garden-path errors are due to semantic constraints, interest has been with similar errors caused by syntactic constraints.

- Sentence parsing can take place according to minimal attachment, in which the preferred syntactical structure of a sentence is that one that demands the fewest number of nodes within a tree diagram of the sentence. Parsing can also take place with respect to late closure, in which the preferred syntactical structure of a sentence is the one that generates the fewest number of clauses. According to Frazier (1987), minimal attachment is the dominant parsing rule whereas late closure only comes into play when minimal attachment cannot resolve the syntactical structure.

- Semantic parsing can be used in conjunction with syntactic parsing in multiple-constraint accounts of language parsing. Specifically, Taraban and McClelland (1990) revealed that participants were faster to read consistent rather than inconsistent sentences, when consistency was defined relative to the semantic interpretation of the noun phrase of the sentence. Therefore, when a sentence is ambiguous, it is likely to be resolved as a function of both syntactic and semantic parsing. This combination of syntactic and semantic processes is also reflected in the unrestricted race model (Traxler, Pickering & Clifton, 1998). Here, multiple constraints operate at an initial stage, in which multiple interpretations compete at once. A second stage allows the winning parsed sentence from the first stage to be reanalysed if the primary analysis leads to a nonsensical interpretation.

- Research has also focused on whether mental rules exist for language, such as the rule of adding 'ed' for the past tense or adding 's' for plurals. Those in support of mental rules are said to come from an establishment position; those who are not are said to come from a connectionist position. The 'words-and-rules theory' (Pinker & Ullman, 2002a) suggests that rules are employed for the application of past-tense rules on regular words, and that morphological relations for irregular words are stored on an item-by-item basis. In contrast, connectionist modelling (Rumelhart & McClelland, 1986) has been able to reproduce both past-tense performance for regular and irregular words, in addition to replicating similar errors regarding overgeneralisation (e.g., sleep – sleeped) as seen in human infants.

- Language is also thought to play an important role in the way in which we perceive the world. In previous chapters, we have seen how categorical perception plays an important role in determining our experience. However, a crucial aspect to this research is the extent to which categorical perception effects may simply be the result of verbal labelling. While the evidence for this account is limited (Goldstone, Lippa & Shiffrin, 2001), the contrast between Whorfian (Davidoff, 2001) and Roschian (Heider, 1972) hypotheses also addresses the relationship between language and perception. If different cultures with different colour category systems group colour chips in similar ways, then this is evidence for the Roschian hypothesis and universality, in which mental categorisation is independent from language. In contrast, if the colour chip grouping is different, then this is support for the Whorfian hypothesis and relativism, where language and perception are interdependent. The current state of the literature supports the Whorfian hypothesis (Kay & Regier, 2007) and more general conclusions regarding the interaction between language and perception remain open.

## ANSWERS TO PINPOINT QUESTIONS

14.1   The problems will be most likely to do with performance problems. You both speak and understand the same natural language – what varies is how the individual words are pronounced.

14.2   On one reading of the sentence it is the students who are irritating and on the other it is the lecturers.

14.3   Describing *Monty Python's Flying Circus* as 'proper noun, verb, noun' reflects the syntactic components of the sentence.

14.4   Productivity, systematicity and compositionality are the three basic characteristics of language as defined by Fodor and Pylyshyn (1988).

14.5   Parsing according to minimal attachment takes place on the basis of which sentence interpretation demands the fewest number of nodes within a tree diagram of the sentence. Late closure parsing selects the sentence that generates the fewest number of clauses.

14.6   $N \rightarrow N + s$

14.7   A connectionist network is like a normally developing child in that it is able to mimic the U-shaped learning that children reveal as they acquire the ability to master past-tense verbs.

14.8   In terms of the Goldstone (1994) experiment, it means that two physically similar stimuli that belonged to different categories could be easily told apart.

14.9   Acquired equivalence is when the Seven Dwarfs all start to look alike in the presence of Snow White.

14.10  Universalists assert that the conceptual systems across individuals are basically the same and are independent of the natural language used to describe the world. This means that we all construe the world in the same way independently of the natural language that we use.

## CHAPTER 15

# REASONING

**By the end of this chapter, you should be able to:**

- Describe both associative and rule-based components of the dual system of reasoning (Sloman, 1996).
- Identify the heuristics related to the conjunction fallacy, representativeness, availability and neglect of base rate information.
- Contrast between problems described in terms of natural frequencies and conditional probabilities.
- Describe the way in which satisficing works (Gigerenzer & Goldstein, 1996).
- Distinguish between deductive and inductive reasoning.
- Describe variants of the Wason selection task.
- Discuss the conclusions reached by syllogistic reasoning in terms of the figural effect and visual imagery.

## CHAPTER CONTENTS

# A day at the races

Since your idea of becoming a professional psychology participant hasn't really led to the wealth of riches you were expecting, you decide to go double or quits with a day at the races. The 'going' is 'soft' today, you heard on the TV before you set off, which you think is a pertinent piece of information but aren't sure. You purchase the Racing Form of a rather haggard old man outside the racecourse, who mentions that the conditions are perfect for Boy Racer in the 4.35. He confirms: 'It's soft under foot, the wind is coming from the east and he's just had his birthday. The horse is in a good mood today.' Looking at the odds, you wished that 'Boy Racer at 11:5' meant more than two numbers separated by a colon. Then you think back to all those apples-and-oranges examples you were given at school and reason that if you give the bookmaker 50p and the horse wins then you'll get £1.10p back. Plus that all-important initial stake. You spot a rather small individual in chequered pants staggering around the paddock with a half empty bottle of some dark and rather strong-smelling liquid. You decide it's probably a good idea not to bet on any nags this jockey will be riding. 'Excuse me, you're not riding on Boy Racer today, are you?' The individual swerves around to reveal a chef's hat in his other, non-bottle-clutching hand. As you make your apologies and retreat to a safe position on the grandstand, you decide to forego the canteen food today. At least that's money you'll be saving to put on Boy Racer in the 4.35.

While perhaps your first mistake was to assume you could make money at the races, there were a number of other errors made that day. It seems like you were working on the premise that all small people are jockeys, he was a small person, therefore he was a jockey. The chequered pants seemed to fit with the colourful silks that the jockeys seem to wear. But presumably this had something to do with the context on being at a racecourse too. Surely if you had been visiting a primary school, you wouldn't have thought all the tiny people were horse riders, would you?

## REFLECTIVE QUESTIONS

1. How logical do you think you are? Are all your decisions governed by valid conclusions derived from unarguable premises or are you a bit more spontaneous? What do you think these more spontaneous decisions are based on? Have you ever sat down and weighed out the pros and cons of certain options? Have you ever tried to prove someone or something wrong? How did you go about it and what techniques did you employ?

2. How many times have you been given a problem to solve, only to be completely mesmerised by its contents? How have you tried to better understand the problem? Does visualising a problem hinder or help and if so, why? Maybe $48 = 20*x + 8$ doesn't really make much sense, but if I've got 48 toffees left and I've got 20 friends but want to keep 8 toffees for myself, this might give me a better idea of how many sweeties to spread around to my mates.

## Introduction and preliminary considerations

In this chapter, we'll be examining the ways in which people reason about the world. We'll examine to what extent we reach conclusions that are logical, unbiased and rational, but also explore the idea that people use all manner of short cuts and rules of thumb in order to make decisions. We'll see how people deal with single ('the going is soft') and multiple pieces ('it's soft under foot, the wind is coming from the east and the horse has just had his birthday') of information when making decisions. We'll also see how understanding certain problems might be facilitated by using the right language, just as thinking about pounds and pence in concrete terms is easier to deal with than abstract ratios or probabilities. We'll look at how you can reach valid conclusions that do not actually follow from the use of logic and also how the context in which particular problems are framed might be useful or indeed damaging in helping us make the right decisions. As well as all this, by the end of the chapter we hope you'll have also reasoned that perhaps betting on racehorses is not the best way to make your fortune.

One theme that we can pick up from the previous chapter concerns the nature and status of mental rules. A mental rule is clearly an abstract cognitive construct but it is understandable when cast in terms of functional accounts of the mind (see Chapters 1 and 2). A mental rule has been taken to be akin to an instruction in a computer programming language. The assumptions are (i) that such rules make up mental software, and (ii) it is only by understanding the nature and operation of such rules that a proper understanding of the mind will ensue. Despite stating these assumptions, repeatedly we have been confronted with dissenting views, and real concerns rest on the distinction between rule-governed systems and rule-following systems. Do we really want to insist that the brain is a rule-following machine in which its rules of operation are stored and that mental rules determine its operation? Is the brain literally a biological computer? Alternatively, are the rules that we use to describe cognitive processes nothing more than a description, that is, a short-hand way of avoiding talk about neurally plausible mechanisms?

This chapter is about reasoning, and the overarching question concerns the extent to which our ability to reason about the world implies the operation of mental rules. Previously we have discussed attempts to eliminate discussion of particular kinds of mental constructs from our theories, such as eliminating morphemes from our accounts of acquiring the mappings between the present and past tense of English (see Chapter 14). Soon we will address similar eliminative claims that have been made about human reasoning. Initially, though, we will consider a dual systems account of reasoning that merely attempts to draw a distinction between two different types of reasoning mechanisms. Such an account allows for both associative processes and rule-based operations, which we will explain in due course. We will therefore start by considering accounts that are based on an acceptance that both associations and rules are necessary if we are to explain human reasoning.

## The dual system account of reasoning

Although there are several flavours of **dual system theory** (see Evans, 2003, for a recent discussion), we will begin by a consideration of the account put forward by Sloman (1996). He discussed at length the differences between two putative systems of reasoning, namely (i) an *associative system* and (ii) a *rule-based system*.

### The associative system

The **associative system** fits very well with the sorts of connectionist principles of operation that have been discussed previously (see Chapter 12). For example, Sloman (1996) argued that 'associative thought uses temporal and similarity relations to draw inferences and make predictions that approximate those of a sophisticated statistician. Rather than trying to reason on the basis of an underlying causal or mechanical structure, it constructs estimates based on statistical structure' (p. 4). The associative system would presumably conclude that, because all swans encountered to date have been white, then all swans are white. Inferences are drawn on the basis of co-occurrence relations that hold in the world together with estimates of how similar novel events are related to a previously experienced event. Clearly there are leanings here towards behaviourist principles (see Chapter 1).

### The rule-based system

In contrast the **rule-based system** has various defining characteristics. First, reasoning that is assumed to arise from the rule-based system exhibits productivity, systematicity and compositionality as discussed in Chapter 14. Moreover, this system is assumed to operate with variables. For instance, a generic rule of the type *If the precondition is satisfied then the action is to be taken* comprises variables for *the precondition* and *the action*. The rule is applied when a particular precondition is satisfied (i.e., the precondition variable is given a value) and a particular action is carried out (i.e., the action variable is given a value). For example, *If the water has boiled then I can make the tea* – if *precondition* (water has boiled) then *action* (make tea). We will examine much more carefully the putative nature of this rule-based system as the discussion proceeds. Fundamentally, though, the rule-based system is assumed to underpin what we normally mean when we discuss human problem solving, reasoning and considered thought, namely deliberation, explanation, ascription of purpose, and so on (see Sloman, 1996, tab. 1).

## Distinguishing between the two systems

The difference between the two systems is also drawn out with regard to the sort of relations that each handles. Within the associative system only one relation is considered and this is an association, that is, A and B are related associatively. It is perhaps best to think of an association as being nothing more than a link or a connection between two things. Nothing else should be concluded about the nature of the association nor what the association could mean other than 'goes together'. Just because Kate and Sterling share the same surname does not mean that they are members of the same family. Just because Tim and Mary were seen sitting in the back row of the cinema does not mean that they are dating. In contrast, in the context of a rule-based system, finer distinctions than mere associations are accommodated, and various forms of relations are countenanced. Several different kinds of relations have been discussed, for instance:

1. *A* and *B* are causally related, that is, *A* causes *B*. For example, I pot the black ball with the white. The white ball striking the black causes the black to be potted.

2. *A* and *B* are logically related. For example, 'if *A*, then *B*' sets up a logical relation between *A* and *B*. For instance, *If (A) there is no error message, then (B) the program compiled* (Johnson-Laird, 1983, p. 34).

3. *A* and *B* are hierarchically related. If all *A*s are *B*s and there are more *B*s than *A*s, then *A*s make up a subset of *B*s. All turkeys are birds but there are some birds that are not turkeys.

In discussing these sorts of relations the basic (and somewhat contentious) idea is that associations alone do not suffice. There has to be some kind of mental representational system that captures the sorts of semantic notions that seemingly go beyond this rather wishy-washy notion of 'goes together' as captured by mere associations.

On paper, therefore, the distinction between the rule-based and associative systems of reasoning is apparently clear-cut. Nevertheless, there is a critical difference between drawing a theoretical distinction and providing empirical support for it. So what is the supporting evidence? Well, according to Sloman (1996, p. 11), the supporting evidence for the dual system account of reasoning is in the form of something he called **Criterion S**. The claim is that people may hold a so-called **simultaneous contradictory belief** – a person can be in a particular mental state such that they are in part compelled to believe one thing that they otherwise know to be false. The main cornerstone of this argument concerns something that is known as the *Linda-the-bank-teller* problem (a teller is another name for a clerk). The main point is that such conflicted states arise because the associative system has reasoned one way, and the rule-based system has reasoned a different way. As a consequence, the two systems have arrived at different conclusions! The (mental) right hand therefore doesn't know what the (mental) left hand is doing.

## Linda-the-bank-teller problem

Consider the following:

> Linda is 31 years old, single, outspoken and very bright. She majored in Philosophy. As a student, she was deeply concerned with issues of discrimination and social justice, and also participated in anti-nuclear demonstrations.

Now consider which of the two statements about Linda is more probable:

1. Linda is a bank teller.
2. Linda is a bank teller and is active in the feminist movement.

If you are inclined towards statement 2 this is perhaps not so surprising because the description of Linda has been contrived to convey a person more representative of a feminist than a bank teller. Indeed, in the original study that examined performance with these sorts of puzzles (see Tversky & Kahneman, 1983), the results showed that, when 142 undergraduates from the University of British Columbia were probed, 85 per cent responded that statement 2 was more probable than statement 1. (Don't conclude from this that the results are anything to do with living in Canada!)

The critical fact, however, is that statement 2 cannot be more probable than statement 1. Put simply, 'A conjunction can never be more probable than one of its constituents' (Sloman, 1996, p. 12). Here the conjunction refers to statement 2 because the two constituents *bank teller* and *active in the feminist movement* are conjoined by *and*. Specifically, a conjunction statement such as *bank teller and feminist* cannot alone be more probable than either *bank teller* or *feminist* because the conjunction presupposes *bank teller* and it presupposes *feminist*. The overwhelming choice of the students revealed something that has come to be known as the **conjunction fallacy**. They reasoned incorrectly that a conjunction could be more probable than one of its constituents.

## The conjunction fallacy and representativeness

From such a demonstration Sloman (1996) argued the following. The participants were seduced in their thinking by something known as **representativeness**. The description of Linda matched that of a typical feminist. Linda's description was representative of (i.e., was very similar to) a typical feminist's. Therefore, on the balance of all probabilities, Linda must be a feminist. The influence of representativeness was so potent that the participants were seduced into drawing an incorrect conclusion. This was even though they may well have fully appreciated the logical error that they committed when they committed the conjunction fallacy. In other words, they may well have appreciated that a conjunction can never be more probable than one of its constituents, but nevertheless they still ranked statement 2 as being more probable than statement 1. This being so, the data revealed evidence of a *simultaneous contradictory belief*. According to Sloman (1996) such a simultaneous contradictory belief arose because of the conflicting operations of the two systems of reasoning. Sloman (1996) argued that responding statement 2 revealed the operation of the associative system, but on the basis of the fact that participants could also appreciate the conjunction

fallacy, this revealed the operation of the rule-based system.

Upon reflection, however, this particular line of argument is reasonably unconvincing, a point made clearly by Gigerenzer and Reiger (1996). Simply put, they explained that 'two conflicting responses need not imply two . . . systems of reasoning' (p. 24). Such contradictions may arise for one of any number of reasons, and merely demonstrating a simultaneous contradictory belief does not necessarily indicate the operation of qualitatively different systems of reasoning such as rule-based and associative systems. Indeed, the influence of representativeness in the Linda-the-bank-teller problem may reflect the operation of cognitive processes that are quite different from those that give rise to an association drawn on the basis of similarity. To appreciate these sentiments, though, it is important to unpack these ideas carefully because many issues are at stake. For the time being we can simply conclude that some of the evidence, which Sloman (1996) cited as supporting his dual system account of reasoning, is less than compelling. We should, however, consider other evidence and then see whether this converges on the dual system account. → See 'What have we learnt?', page 562.

---

### Pinpoint question 15.1

**What two forms of reasoning are considered in the dual system model (Sloman, 1996)?**

---

**dual system theory** After Sloman (1996), the idea that human reasoning can be based on the operation of either an associative system or a rule-based system.

**associative system** The idea that there is one system of reasoning that operates by making inferences purely on the basis of statistical regularities such as co-occurrences between events.

**rule-based system** In reasoning research, the idea that there is one system of reasoning that operates by making inferences on the basis of rules of logic. This system is defined in terms of the language of thought (Fodor, 1975).

**Criterion S** Sloman's assertion that a person can entertain a simultaneous contradictory belief.

**simultaneous contradictory belief** A claim by Sloman (1996) that a person can be conflicted in concurrently believing two mutually contradictory conclusions. An outcome of the dual system theory of reasoning in which the rule-based and associative outputs produce conflicting information.

▶

## → What have we learnt?

Underpinning much of the research on human reasoning is the idea that there are two independent sets of mechanisms that operate according to their own principles. These may, or may not, generate the same conclusion about a given problem. In support of such a view, Sloman (1996) has argued that it is possible that a person can be in a conflicted mental state characterised by that individual entertaining a simultaneous contradictory belief. This arises when the two putative systems produce different conclusions. For Sloman (1996) such a state of affairs is evidenced by performance on the Linda-the-bank-teller problem. The fact that participants commit a conjunction fallacy has been taken to show that the two systems of reasoning may operate in conflict with one another. Participants may well understand the logical nature of conjunctions yet still they commit the conjunction fallacy.

Some caution however, has been expressed over using this evidence to argue for two systems of reasoning. Conflicts may arise for any number of reasons. Discomfort over this particular line of argument, however, does not discount the potency of representativeness which provides something of an account as to why it is that participants are so poor at making correct probability judgements in certain cases. Judgements may be clouded by the intrusion of thoughts about what is typically the case in the real world. It is therefore important to consider more convincing evidence if we are to accept the dual system account.

---

**conjunction fallacy** The incorrect belief that the combination of two events is more likely than either event alone.

**representativeness** A heuristic that appeals to a stereotype or most likely occurrence.

---

## Reasoning by heuristics and biases

In pursuing the issues, the research into reasoning has invoked a distinction between (i) reasoning based on logic and (ii) reasoning based on what are known as **heuristics** (i.e., short cuts or rules of thumb). Perhaps this distinction will allow us to conclude in favour of some form of dual system of reasoning?

At the outset a dictionary definition is of some considerable help because in many cases in the literature the term *heuristics* is left unspecified. Accordingly a heuristic is the means by which a conclusion is drawn 'by exploration of possibilities rather than by following set rules' (*Collins English Dictionary*). So in the present context we are contrasting cold logic with, essentially, educated guess work. Maybe these different forms of reasoning reflect qualitatively different systems of reasoning?

The basic claim to be explored now is that in some important respects, aspects of human reasoning reveal the operation of cognitive heuristics. Such a claim is fundamental to what has come to be known as the **heuristics and biases approach** to human reasoning (Kahneman, Slovic & Tversky, 1982). The claim is not that humans never reason logically, but that there is compelling evidence that reveals circumstances in which they do not reason logically. A somewhat worrying implication of this claim is that human reasoning can therefore be described as being irrational. What the heuristics and biases approach to human reasoning has led to is the conclusion that human reasoning is not so much random, but that it can be wrong in consistent ways.

People tend to make the same sorts of errors when confronted with particular sorts of problems. Such systematic errors point to the operation of cognitive heuristics. The point is that whereas cognitive heuristics (or educated guesses) work most of the time, crucially they fail to deliver the correct outcome some of the time. Indeed, and in the limit, a conclusion drawn on the basis of a cognitive heuristic may lead to dire consequences: you normally do switch the iron off before you leave the house, therefore you must have switched the iron off this morning. To carry this discussion forward, we will accept that humans can and may reason logically, but what we are also going to explore is the possibility that they may in fact reason in irrational ways.

Systematic departures from rationality we will take as being symptomatic of the operation of cognitive heuristics and possible biases in reasoning. Tversky and Kahneman (1983) discussed such behaviours in terms of the operation at the cognitive level of so-called **natural assessments**. Accordingly, such natural assessments do not reflect a careful appraisal of actual probabilities, conditional probabilities and logical relations that actually hold. Rather they reflect certain rules of thumb, intuitions and biases. By this view, humans are typically not cold, calculating statistical computers but mere mortals forced to make best guesses on the basis of a ragbag of mental tricks and biases (i.e., the natural assessments).

It is relatively easy to see both the pros and cons of reasoning on the basis of heuristics. From an evolutionary perspective, and as Sutherland (1992) noted, 'Our ancestors in the animal kingdom for the most part had to solve their problems in a hurry by fighting or fleeing' (p. 137). So when confronted by a predator it is inadvisable to stand around pondering which is the best route to escape. Consequently 'it is better to be wrong than eaten' (p. 137). The assumption is that heuristics provide a good answer quickly but they are not guaranteed to provide the best answer. In this regard heuristics are useful because they work most of the time (clearly if they did not then the species could well have died out). Of course the disadvantage of using heuristics is that they do not work some of the time. What cognitive psychologists have endeavoured to explore and understand is the cases where reasoning goes wrong. Several such departures from rationality are now considered in detail.

## The representative heuristic

From our previous discussion of the Linda-the-bank-teller problem, the evidence was taken to reveal the operation of the influence of representativeness that has come to be termed the *representativeness heuristic*. This reveals a basic tendency to estimate the likelihood of something on the basis of how well it fits a proto-type of a familiar category. Participants were induced to classify Linda as a feminist. On the basis of this attribution, they then reasoned accordingly and they incorrectly committed the conjunction fallacy.

## The availability heuristic

Apart from the representativeness heuristic there is also the **availability heuristic**. In simple terms, conclusions drawn may reflect the fallacious acceptance of, essentially, the first thing that comes to mind (see Kahneman & Frederick, 2005, p. 271).

Tversky and Kahneman (1983) quoted an earlier study of theirs (Tversky & Kahneman, 1973) as an example of the operation of this heuristic. Participants were asked to complete the following word frames: (i) _ _ _ _ i n g, and (ii) _ _ _ _ _ n _. For each frame, participants were given one minute to produce words consistent with the frame. The results showed that participants produced on average 6.4 vs. 2.9 words for frame (i) and (ii), respectively. So what? Well, unless you have already caught on, all seven-lettered words ending in *ing* include all words in which *n* is the penultimate letter so there just are more words that fit frame (ii) than frame (i). Despite this (now obvious fact), participants behaved in a completely contrary manner. Tversky and Kahneman (1983) explained the results by arguing that, for whatever reason, *ing* words are far more accessible in memory than are the _n_ words. Hence the availability (recoverability from memory) of the items governed participants' responses.

---

### For example . . .

Using the availability heuristic, that is, essentially choosing the first thing that comes to mind, can have dire consequences. If you think back to that classic 1980s flick *Ghostbusters*, you'll remember towards the end of the film Gozer 'invites' them to choose the form in which the destructor of New York City will appear. Three of the Ghostbusters manage to clear their heads, but the Stay Puff Marshmallow Man is the first thing that pops into Dr Ray Stantz's mind and all hell breaks loose (see Figure 15.1).

**Figure 15.1 An example of the dire consequences of utilising the availability heuristic**
*Source*: Kobal Collection Ltd/Columbia.

(Indeed in attempting to complete word frame (ii) it was with some considerable effort to finally come up with *confine*.)

In a follow-up study Tversky and Kahneman (1983) went on to ask participants to estimate the frequency with which words consistent with the two word frames occurred in text. From what we have already considered, words consistent with frame (ii) must occur more frequently than those consistent with (i) simply because there are more of them. Yet the results showed that participants' ratings indicated the opposite. Average estimates for (i) were 13.4 and they were 4.7 for (ii). Such examples as these were taken to reflect a basic inability to reason logically about the world. Estimates of frequency of occurrence were heavily influenced by the availability of information in memory.

A more familiar case of evidence consistent with the availability heuristic are the results of those now popular TV shows that sap the whole of your evening's viewing of the 100 greatest *x* where *x* could be films, albums, rock groups, actors, etc. One of the striking things about these lists are that they typically reflect cases that exist in recent memory – so even though Girls Aloud may be ranked the greatest girl band of all time, this is clearly at odds with the fact that the truth lies with the Beverley Sisters.

## Base rate neglect

Other major fault lines in the human reasoning architecture have (allegedly) been exposed by demonstrations of an inability to reason accurately about probabilities. Although the evidence has been taken to reflect the potency of representativeness heuristics, the data actually reveal basic inabilities to reason about probabilities and likelihoods. To understand this, though, it is important to consider **Bayes' theorem**.

### An introduction to Bayes' theorem

In formal terms the theorem is given by the following formula:

$$\frac{p(H_1|D)}{p(H_0|D)} = \frac{p(D|H_1)}{p(D|H_0)} \times \frac{p(H_1)}{p(H_0)} \tag{15.1}$$

In this form the theorem provides a means to choose between two alternative hypotheses about the nature of the world (i.e., $H_1$ and $H_0$). A probability is a quantity that conveys the likelihood that something is true or is the case. In the current discussion, a value of 1 signifies a dead cert whereas 0 signifies no chance. Values in

between these two extremes are possible, for example a probability of 0.5 can be taken to reflect a 50 per cent chance that something is true or will happen.

So H stands for a hypothesis and D stands for a piece of evidence (i.e., some form of data). (The following example is unashamedly taken and abridged from Fischoff, 1982.) So $H_1$ is the hypothesis 'she loves me' ($P(H_1)$ is the actual probability that this is true), and $H_0$ is the hypothesis that 'she loves me not' ($P(H_0)$ is the actual probability that this is true). D (the evidence) is an unfinished lover letter found in a wastebasket. The ratio:

$$\frac{p(H_1)}{p(H_0)} \tag{15.2}$$

refers to the prior probabilities or the odds of $H_1$ and $H_0$ being true irrespective of finding the love letter, D. Equation (15.2) is known as the **prior odds**. Given that we are dealing in probabilities, and, in this simple case, there are only two states of the world worth considering, then $P(H_1)$ and $P(H_0)$ must add up to 1. Either she loves you or she loves you not – there is no third option. If the ratio results in a number greater than 1, then $H_1$ has more weight than $H_0$ and the odds are that she does love you independently of ever having found the letter. A value of 1 is evens, and a value less than 1 is an indication that $H_0$ is more likely than $H_1$ and that she does not love you (again irrespective of you having found the letter).

The ratio:

$$\frac{p(D|H_1)}{p(D|H_0)} \tag{15.3}$$

is known as the **likelihood ratio**. Now you are in the situation of having found the letter and you have to try to assess the impact of this piece of data for each hypothesis. p(D|H) is the probability of the data given the hypothesis. Take $p(D|H_1)$; on the assumption that $H_1$ is true (i.e., that she loves me), how probable is D (i.e., that she wrote me an unfinished love letter)? So one way to read equation (15.3) is that it reveals how probable it is that the actual love letter supports each hypothesis. Values greater than 1 are possible and are indicative that she loves you.

In words the theorem can be written as:

The posterior odds = the likelihood ratio
× prior odds (15.4)

that is, the product of likelihood ratio and the prior odds gives the **posterior odds**, or, more specifically, the relative truth of the two hypotheses given the new piece of data. The posterior odds combine initial expectations (based on prior odds) with the evidence that has been obtained (as weighted by the likelihood ratio). So by applying Bayes' theorem you should now be in a better position to judge whether or not she loves you. In other words, the posterior odds provide an index of how likely it is that one hypothesis is true relative to another. When the two hypotheses are equally likely prior to receiving D (when the prior odds equal 1, i.e., it is equally likely that she loves you as not), then the posterior odds equal the likelihood ratio. This is because you're essentially multiplying something by 1. Under these circumstances your judgement will now solely be based on D – finding the unfinished letter. When the posterior odds equal 2, then she is twice as likely to be in love with you than not.

Although the theorem will produce the most rational outcomes when all the critical probabilities are known or are recoverable, different outcomes will obtain when, for instance, the prior odds are unknown and must be estimated. What Kahneman and Tversky (1974) showed was, irrespective of the tenets of Bayes' theorem, that is, people were particularly inept in estimating outcomes given certain probabilities.

## Evidence against the use of Bayes' theorem in human reasoning

In one study participants were given hard copies of brief autobiographical (fictitious) descriptions of individuals. One group of participants were told that the descriptions were taken from 100 individuals, 70 of which were engineers and 30 of which were lawyers. A separate group of participants were given similar instructions but now the ratio of engineers to lawyers was reversed. Critically, though, both groups of participants received the same set of descriptions. The only thing that changed across the groups was the cover story. Participants were asked to work through the list of descriptions and rate the probability that each described individual was either an engineer or a lawyer. So here goes. Consider the following:

*Jack is a 45-year-old man. He is married and has four children. He is generally conservative, careful and ambitious. He has no interest in political and social issues and spends most of his free time on his many hobbies that include home carpentry, sailing and mathematical puzzles.*

Overall both groups of participants rated Jack as probably being an engineer, and participants from both groups produced similar ratings. This result, though, of course contrasts with what might otherwise have been predicted if the participants had taken the actual prior odds (see equation (15.2) above) into account. Most importantly, in the 30 per cent engineers group the prior odds indicated that it was highly likely that Jack was actually a lawyer (participants in this group were told that the underlying distribution from which the sample of descriptions had been taken was composed of 70 per cent lawyers and 30 per cent engineers). In this regard participants were shown to have neglected the base rate (the prior odds). Of some additional import was the fact that when the participants were simply asked to rate the probability of a given occupation of an anonymous individual from the same distributions as used in the study, they were highly accurate. As Tversky and Kahneman (1974) concluded, therefore, 'When no specific evidence is given, prior probabilities are properly utilized; when worthless evidence is given, prior probabilities are ignored' (p. 328; Johnson-Laird & Wason, 1977).

In a later reappraisal of the original findings, though, Kahneman and Tversky (1996) were more circumspect and conceded that the evidence revealed not so much a neglect of base rate information but a discounting or 'underweighting' (p. 584) of this information. Nonetheless, performance departed radically from a correct application of Bayes' theorem. Indeed, as Gigerenzer and Murray (1987) have pointed out, 'To explain that neglect of base rate by saying that the participant uses a representativeness heuristic is in essence saying that the participant uses the likelihood in Bayes' formula, but not the base rate (i.e., the prior odds, see equation (15.4))' (p. 162; material in parentheses added).

---

### Pinpoint question 15.2

**How are posterior odds calculated using Bayes' theorem?**

---

**heuristics** Rules of thumb or educated guesses.

**heuristics and biases approach** The understanding that some human reasoning is not logical or rational (Kahneman, Slovic & Tversky, 1982), but that it is based on educated guesswork and rules of thumb.

**natural assessments** Decisions based on heuristics and biases.

**availability heuristic** Reasoning on the basis of how easily information is recovered from memory.

## You are either with us or against us: the heuristics of terror

We seem to be in a constant state of increased vigilance and heightened awareness with respect to another terrorist attack that is always round the corner. The warning lights hover from yellow to orange to red, but it seems unlikely we will ever return to green. Mandel (2005) sought to demonstrate exactly how inconsistent risk assessments might be carried out with respect to the likelihood of terrorist attacks, leading to the somewhat worrisome conclusion that even when the future of society is potentially at stake, illogical reasoning is still at play.

Mandel's (2005) first experiment was intentionally scheduled to be carried out at the same time as the war in Iraq began (first strike 20 March 2003). Here he investigated something known as 'additivity violations due to unpacking'. For example, someone might assess the risk of 'at least one major terrorist attack' at 2 per cent. A violation of additivity due to unpacking would be then assessing the likelihood of 'at least one major terrorist attack that is plotted by al Qaeda' along with 'at least one major terrorist attack that is NOT plotted by al Qaeda' and finding that the joint likelihood is larger than 2 per cent. Clearly in both cases, the single assessment and joint assessment refer to exactly the same set of possible instances, but unpacking inflates the risk. Another violation of additivity can be caused as a result of refocusing. When two mutually exclusive outcomes are available (i.e., 'terrorist attack' versus 'no terrorist attack') then rating their collective probability should equal 1, just as in the 'she loves me, she loves me not' example. However, Mandel (2005) found that calculating the likelihood of a terrorist attack on the basis of subtracting the likelihood of 'no terrorist attack' from 1 led to a larger estimate than simply assessing the likelihood of a terrorist attack alone. So here we

have at least two cases where inflated risk assessment of terrorism is simply a result of the nature of the assessment itself.

Thankfully, Mandel (2005) also reported some good news. Violations of additivity, as a result of judging the likelihood of two potential outcomes, can be reduced by 'presenting the complementary hypotheses in close succession' (p. 283). Among a short set of distractor items, participants were asked, 'What do you think the probability is that there will be at least one major terrorist attack in the US within the next two months?' and 'What do you think the probability is that there will NOT be at least one major terrorist attack in the US within the next two months?' Using this manipulation, approximations of unity probability (that is, a probability of 1) for complementary events was improved and reported by around 50 per cent of participants.

Additional biases in assessing the risk of a terrorist attack were also reported in this series of studies, but it is perhaps best not to dwell on these too much and rather focus on how we can improve the coherence of risk assessment. Mandel suggests that individuals working in intelligence should check how stable their risk assessments are by reversing the focus of the assessment – instead of asking what is the likelihood of event $x$ occurring, ask what is the likelihood of event $x$ NOT occurring. Any violations of additivity can then be identified and addressed. Increasing the accuracy of terrorist attack risk assessment would therefore provide a more realistic picture of the current global environment. We might not be able to return to the way we were, but we can move into the future better informed.

---

*Source*: Mandel, D. R. (2005). Are risk assessments of terrorist attack coherent? *Journal of Experimental Psychology: Applied, 11*, 277–288.

---

**Bayes' theorem** A statistical method of deciding which of two hypotheses is true given the data.

**prior odds** In Bayes' theorem, the probability of each of the alternative hypotheses in advance of learning about the data.

**likelihood ratio** In Bayes' theorem, the likelihood that a piece of data supports one hypothesis rather than an alternative hypothesis.

**posterior odds** In Bayes' theorem, the estimate of how relatively likely it is that each hypothesis is true given the data.

## The medical diagnosis problem

Such examples as the Linda-the-bank-teller problem might be dismissed on the grounds that they are of no consequence: who cares about Linda? And surely these are nothing other than irritating puzzles, party games, etc. However, far more worrying cases do exist. Casscells, Schoenberger and Graboys (1978) presented the following problem (let us call it the *medical diagnosis problem*) to faculty and advanced students at Harvard Medical School. (In order for you to understand the following problem, a 'false positive' is where an individual is diagnosed with the disease but doesn't actually have it.)

*If a test to detect a disease whose prevalence is 1/1000 has a false positive rate of 5 per cent, what is the chance that a person found to have a positive result actually has the disease, assuming that you know nothing about the person's symptoms or signs?*

(We will get round to the correct answer in a minute. . . . ) In fact, only 18 per cent of the participants came close to the correct answer, but 45 per cent of the (highly educated) participants gave the (grossly incorrect) answer of 95 per cent. Simply put, such erroneous answers have been taken to reflect base rate neglect – remember, the respondents were told that the prevalence rate of the disease was only 1 per 1000 cases. To answer 95 per cent stands in stark contrast to this base rate, and could be taken as further evidence of the fallibility of human reason. Try not to think about this next time you are sitting in the doctor's waiting room! (If you really do wish to frighten yourself with further shortcomings of decision-making in the medical professions, see chs 5 and 8 in Gigerenzer, 2002.)

There are many other biases in quantitative and probabilistic reasoning that have been uncovered and several of these are summarised in Table 15.1. (The most entertaining treatment of these can be found in Sutherland, 1992, and a different and highly readable account is that of Gigerenzer, 2002: both are likely to induce panic, though.) However, rather than simply

## For example . . .

### Bayes' theorem and the medical diagnosis problem

To solve the medical diagnosis problem using Bayes' theorem, the following formula is needed:

$$P(H_1|D) = \frac{p(H_1) \times p(D|H_1)}{p(H_1) \times p(D|H_1) + p(H_0) \times p(D|H_0)} \quad (15.5)$$

Alternatively:

p(disease|test+)

$$= \frac{p(disease) \times p(test+|disease)}{p(disease) \times p(test+|disease) + p(no\ disease) \times p(test+|no\ disease)}$$

p(disease|test+) means the probability of actually having the disease given that the test produces a positive outcome.
p(disease) means the probability (or the prevalence) of the disease.
p(test+|disease) means the probability of the test producing a positive outcome given that a person has the disease.
p(no disease) means the probability of the lack of disease.

p(test+|no disease) means the probability of the test producing a positive outcome given that a person is clear of the disease.

p(disease) = 0.001
p(no disease) = 0.999
p(test+|no disease) is equal to the false positive probability, namely 0.05
p(test+|disease) is assumed to be 1. In other words, we assume that the test will always produce a positive outcome whenever a person presents with the disease.

Inserting these values into equation (15.5) gives:

$$p(disease|test+) = \frac{0.001 \times 1}{(0.001 \times 1) + (0.999 \times 0.05)}$$

p(disease|test+) = 0.0196

So the probability of a person actually having the disease given a positive test result is approximately 2 per cent.

**Table 15.1** Heuristic biases in dealing with probabilities (abridged from Poulton, 1994).

| Bias | Evidence | Heuristic/bias | Representative references |
|---|---|---|---|
| Conjunction fallacy | A conjunction is judged to be more probable than a component of that conjunction. Arises when a less likely event is paired with a more likely event. | The conjunction is taken to be more representative (hence more probable) than the less likely component. | Tversky and Kahneman (1983). |
| Base rate neglect | In judging a possible outcome, the prior possibility of a given event is either ignored or downplayed. | The prior probability is ignored or downplayed because it is taken to be less representative than the likelihood probability. | Tversky and Kahneman (1983). |
| Availability bias | Systematic mistakes are made in judging prevalence when the actual prevalence is unknown. | Estimates of prevalence are made on the basis of the ease of accessibility of relevant instances from memory. | Tversky and Kahneman (1973, 1974, 1983). |
| Anchoring and adjustment bias | Numerical estimates can be biased by a numerical context. For example, estimates of the product $8 \times 7 \times 6 \times 5 \times 4 \times 3 \times 2 \times 1$ are greater than of $1 \times 2 \times 3 \times 4 \times 5 \times 6 \times 7 \times 8$. | 'People make estimates by starting from an initial value that is adjusted [and] . . . adjustments are typically insufficient' (Kahneman & Tversky, 1974, p. 1128). In the example given, the initial value is determined by the numbers that begin the sequences. | Kahneman and Tversky (1974); Chapman and Johnson (2002). |
| Hindsight bias | Participants who are informed of outcomes judge these outcomes as more probable than participants who are not so informed. | Sutherland (1992) cites two forms of this bias – (i) 'is believing that an event that has already happened was inevitable and could have been predicted given the initial circumstances' ('I knew it all along'); and, (ii) 'is the belief that if you had taken a decision . . . made by someone else, you would have taken a better one.' (p. 236). | Fischoff (1982); Sanna and Schwarz (2006). |
| Overconfidence | Participants exhibit overconfidence in their judgements. For example, in a survey of British motorists, 95% thought that they were better than the average driver (Sutherland, 1992, p. 240). However, this overconfidence can be reversed (Sutherland, 1992, pp. 241–2): if participants are given a mixture of easy and difficult problems to solve, they may underestimate their ability to solve the difficult questions. | Generally speaking, participants are overconfident about the correctness of their judgements. | Griffin and Tversky (2002). |

| | | | |
|---|---|---|---|
| Small sample fallacy | Participants fail to appreciate sample size when judging representativeness. Aligned with this is the gamblers' fallacy: after a short run of coin tosses coming up heads, a tail is more likely. A more homely example is the familiar 'My grandfather smoked 100 cigarettes a day and never had a day off work due to ill health.' | The belief that small and large samples should be equally reliable and regular (Poulton, 1994, pp. 78–9). This is tempered by the belief that small samples ought not to be too regular. | Tversky and Kahneman (1971). |
| Regression fallacy | Participants take a person's present score which is either above or below their average to be representative of that person's performance. | This is a general failure to appreciate regression to the mean – the statistical fact that extreme outcomes are less likely to recur over time and are therefore less representative. For example, parents with very high IQs are simply less likely to have children with similarly high IQs. | Nisbett and Ross (1980); Tversky and Kahneman (1971). |
| Expected utility fallacy | People are generally very poor at working out what is a good bet. From statistical theory (known as utility theory, von Neumann & Morgenstern, 1944) the rational decision is to take the option of £2.5 million with a probability of 0.5 rather than the option of £1 million with a probability of 1. In the latter case the expected value is £1.25 million (i.e., $0.5 \times 2.5$); in the former it is £1 million (see Anderson, 2005, p. 340). | When two outcomes have similar and moderate expected gains and losses, people prefer a high probability gain but a low probability loss. With very low probabilities though this is reversed. People tend to buy lottery tickets (to attempt to achieve a low possibility gain) and they also buy house insurance (to attempt to avoid a low probable loss). | Kahneman and Tversky (1979); Poulton (1994, ch. 11). |
| Bias by frames | Depending on how two alternatives are presented (or framed) then contrasting decisions can be made. For example, consider the following: a disease has broken out and two programmes to combat the disease are mooted. Case 1. Programme A – 200 lives saved with certainty. Programme B – 600 saved with a probability of 0.33. Case 2. Programme A – 400 die with certainty. Programme B – 600 saved with a probability of 0.67. For Case 1 predominantly participants choose A. For Case 2 predominantly participants choose B. The contingencies, however, are the same for both cases. | More participants choose the risky alternative (Programme B in the example) when it is presented as avoiding losses than when it is presented as producing gains (see Sutherland, 1992, ch. 16). | Poulton (1994, ch. 12.); Tversky and Kahneman (1981). |
| Affective bias | There can be a disparity between rating the attractiveness of different bets and actual amounts placed on the different bets. For instance, although the option of 29/36 to win $2 was rated more attractive than the option 7/36 to win $9, participants then went on to wager a smaller amount on the former than the latter (Slovic, Finucane, Peters & MacGregor, 2002). | Reasoning is clouded by emotion and the affective value of possible outcomes. In the example given higher probability bets were more attractive than high payoff bets but high payoff bets are typically assigned lower amounts. It seems that 'probabilities are more readily coded as attractive or unattractive than are payoffs' (Slovic et al., 2002). The attractiveness of $9 may well depend on what else is on offer. | Slovic et al. (2002). |

*Source*: Poulton, E. C. (1994). *Behavioral decision theory: A new approach* (table 1.1, p. 7). Cambridge, England: Cambridge University Press. Reproduced with permission.

proceed down the list, it is more important to appreciate what of theoretical consequence has been concluded. What do such heuristics and biases actually tell us about human nature and human reasoning?

## Heuristics and biases and the competence/performance distinction

A useful framework for thinking about the issues has been put forward by Samuels, Stitch and Faucher (2004). They discussed the issues in terms of a competence/performance distinction (see Chapter 14) and explored whether the failures in rationality merely reflect slips in performance or whether they reflect limitations in competence and much more serious problems in the fundamental nature of the human reasoning system. The most pessimistic conclusion they discussed is the claim that such flaws in reasoning reflect fundamental limitations in humans' abilities to reason: human reasoning is basically irrational. A less severe conclusion is that the flaws merely reflect limitations in other cognitive mechanisms (relating to performance) such as failures in attention, motivation and short-term memory. Think about it – the real reason that you did badly on the test was nothing to do with your poor reasoning skills but merely because you could not be bothered to revise properly.

## The standard picture

To begin to assess these issues, Samuels et al. (2004) reasonably pointed out that we need to agree about what standards are to be used to evaluate human reasoning. This led them on to discuss the so-called **standard picture**. According to the standard picture, 'to be rational is to reason in accordance with principles of reasoning that are based on rules of logic, probability theory and so forth. . . . principles of reasoning that are based on such rules are normative principles of reasoning, namely they are the principles we ought to reason in accordance with' (Stein, 1996, cited by Samuels et al., 2004, p. 140). The standard picture therefore provides a template against which any reasoning system can be judged.

The initial step is to try to agree on a set of principles by which we can define rationality so that any examples of reasoning that depart from what is dictated by such principles can be classified as being irrational. The problem for the cognitive psychologist is to discover whether such examples of irrationality point to fundamental flaws in the mechanisms of human reasoning (limitations in competence) or whether they reflect other quite different constraints (limitations in performance). What the standard picture does is provide a checklist against which we can define rationality, and part of this checklist contains Bayesian statistics (as embodied in Bayes' theorem). What the heuristics and biases approach highlights

## For example . . .

*The Curious Incident of the Dog in the Night-Time* (Haddon, 2004) tells the story of Christopher Boone, an autistic child who sets out to solve the mystery of the titular hound. Fascinated by puzzles, he describes to the reader the famous Monty Hall problem, and also the ensuing real-life debate between Marilyn vos Savant (said to have the highest IQ in the world at the time) who answered the question in popular magazine *Parade*, and the academic community who claimed her answer was wrong. Christopher writes:

> You are on a game show on television. On this game show the idea is to win a car as a prize. The game show host shows you three doors. He says that there is a car behind one of the doors and there are goats behind the other two doors. He asks you to pick a door. You pick a door but the door is not opened. Then the game show host opens one of the doors you didn't pick to show a goat (because he knows what is behind the doors). Then he says that you have one final chance to change your mind before the doors are opened and you get a car or a goat. So he asks you if you want to change your mind and pick the other unopened door instead. What should you do? (Haddon, 2004, p. 62)

If you guessed that you have an equal chance of getting a car or a goat at this stage, you would have been on the side of the academics. And you also would have been wrong.

You might like to spend a vexed hour or two trying to prove how Marilyn was right, reflecting all the while how indeed humans might deviate from the standard picture (Samuels et al., 2004) . . .

is the significant number of cases in which human reasoning departs from, or contrasts with, what is predicted on an application of Bayes' theorem. So one question is, 'Why is it that people seem to find Bayesian reasoning so difficult?', and we must not forget that the related concerns about such examples provide cast-iron evidence for the fundamental nature of natural stupidity!

## Why people are not Bayesian reasoners

Part of the answer seems to be that people have real problems in dealing with probabilities, and especially conditional probabilities. As Sutherland (1992) discussed, people have profound problems in understanding the basic Bayesian language – so let us all agree this stuff does not come easy. In particular the evidence is that people find the difference between p(D|H) and p(H|D) to be particularly difficult to grasp – the difference between (i) the probability of the data given an hypothesis and (ii) the probability of an hypothesis given the data. Okay, take D to be a positive outcome of a test for cancer and H to be the state of the world in which the person actually has cancer. Sutherland (1992) reported that 95 per cent of doctors, in a survey undertaken in the USA, thought that because the probability of testing positive if a woman had breast cancer was 0.92 (i.e., p(D|H = 0.92) then the probability of having breast cancer if the test result was positive was also 0.92 (i.e., p(H|D) must therefore equal 0.92). This is despite the fact that this could only be the case if the test never produced a positive result for someone without the disease.

Ultimately, therefore, there is no getting away from the fact that the vast majority of people find that this sort of reasoning is hard. (Doctors are only human too, remember!) The pressing question, though, is, 'Is this clear evidence of natural stupidity, and if not, why not?' Part of the answer may have something to do with the manner in which the problems are framed. The thrust of what has just been described is that part of the difficulty in being able to solve these problems lies in difficulties in understanding the language that is used (see *The Bayesians vs. frequentists* on page 572). If this is accepted then the evidence does not necessarily point toward the conclusion of natural stupidity. Misunderstanding language is categorically not evidence for fatally flawed reasoning.

For instance, Casscells et al. (1978) offered a more common-sense alternative to the rather cumbersome mental computations that are demanded by applying Bayes' theorem to the medical diagnosis problem. Now

if the problem is approached differently the answer becomes more obvious. Consider the following:

One in every 1,000 people tested will have the disease, yet because the test is not infallible it will (wrongly) diagnose 5 per cent of the remaining 999 individuals as having the disease. Five per cent of 999 is roughly 50 individuals. So after testing 1,000 people 51 will have tested positive even though only one of these actually has the disease. Therefore only 1 in 51 positive test scores is associated with a person who has the disease – this corresponds to approximately a 2 per cent chance of finding a person with the disease given a positive test outcome.

We hope you will agree that things are a lot easier now that we have avoided engaging in Bayesian statistics. However, such appeals to intuition are not necessary because such a point has considerable empirical support. For instance, Cosmides and Tooby (1996) showed that when the medical diagnosis problem was framed in terms of frequencies (e.g., '1 out of every 1,000 Americans has disease X . . .'), 56 per cent of respondents now answered correctly. Indeed, when further orienting questions posed in similar so-called **frequentist terms** were introduced after the problem had been presented, the incidence of correct answers increased to 76 per cent.

What these sorts of demonstrations reveal is that people are much more likely to arrive at the correct answer if the problems are framed in frequentist terms. This shows that their reasoning cannot be fundamentally flawed, because if it were, then they would never be able to figure out the answers. Indeed, over many years Gigerenzer and colleagues (Gigerenzer, Todd & the ABC Research Group, 1999) have made much progress in attempting to understand the conditions under which reasoning is either difficult or easy. From this amassed evidence it seems that we need to exert much caution before leaping to any conclusions about the basic nature of human irrationality.

### Pinpoint question 15.3

**Broadly speaking, what are the two explanations for failing to follow Bayes' theorem?**

**standard picture** Reasoning based on principles of logic and probability.

**frequentist terms** Descriptions that provide information about the frequency of occurrence of certain states of affairs.

## For example . . .
### The Bayesians vs. frequentists

A problem is framed accordingly:

- *Scenario 1: Probabilities.* Consider the case where the probability of any woman having cancer is 0.8 per cent. If a woman has breast cancer, the probability is 90 per cent that she will have a positive mammogram. If a woman does not have breast cancer, the probability is 7 per cent that she will still have a positive mammogram. Imagine a woman who has a positive mammogram. What is the probability that she actually has breast cancer?

- *Scenario 2: Natural frequencies.* Eight out of every 1,000 women have breast cancer. Of these 8 women with breast cancer, 7 will have a posi-

tive mammogram. Of the remaining 992 women who do not have breast cancer, some 70 will still have a positive mammogram. Imagine a sample of women who have positive mammograms during screening. How many of these women actually have breast cancer?

Figure 15.2 clearly illustrates that the manner in which the problem is framed can place drastically different demands on the human reasoner. This is even though the structure of the basic equation is exactly the same in both cases. It is patent that the one containing natural frequencies is much simpler to work through than the one that contains conditional probabilities (for more on this, see Gigerenzer & Hoffrage, 1995).

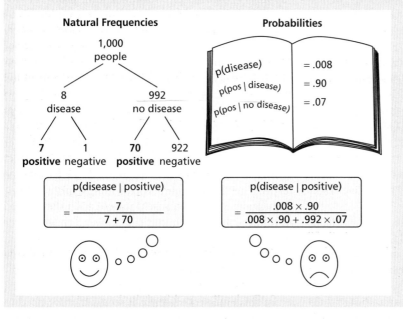

**Figure 15.2 Natural frequencies vs. probabilities**
Contrasting computations framed in terms of natural frequencies (on the left) vs. probabilities (on the right). The structure of the two equations is the same but the right-hand equation implicates conditional probabilities and (for most of us) these are hard.

*Source*: Gigerenzer, G. (2002). *Reckoning with risk. Learning to live with uncertainty* (fig. 4.2, p. 45). London: Penguin Books. Reproduced with permission.

## Natural frequencies vs. conditional probabilities

What the example above is intended to show is that people are much more comfortable when reasoning with so-called natural frequencies than conditional probabilities. Indeed, this kind of argument has been developed within an evolutionary perceptive, for both Cosmides and Tooby (1996) and Gigerenzer (1994)

have argued that human reasoning has evolved to be particularly sensitive to frequencies of events (natural frequencies) of the form *x* per *y* (e.g., 8 out of 10 cats prefer tuna) than either probabilities or conditional probabilities of the form *z* per cent (e.g., there is a 0.8 probability that my cat will prefer tuna). As a consequence, 'the minds of living systems should be understood relative to the environment in which they evolved, rather than to the tenets of classical rationality' (Gigerenzer & Goldstein, 1996, p. 651).

The principal point is that our minds evolved to be primarily sensitive to frequencies (i.e., counts) rather than conditional probabilities. The basic claim is that during the process of human evolution our ancestors developed cognitive mechanisms 'that took frequencies as input, maintained such information as frequentist representations, and used these frequentist representations as a database for effective inductive reasoning' (Cosmides & Tooby, 1996, p. 17). Information in the environment 'does not present itself in terms of single event probabilities and odds/ratios. It comes . . . in the form of frequencies of entities and events' (Cummins, 2004, p. 357).

The argument is not that probabilities are completely ignored, but merely that the probabilistic information that is available in the environment is converted into a frequentist format and that the natural way of reasoning about the world is in terms of frequencies. For instance, assume that it is true that the appearance of rain clouds is imperfectly correlated with actual rain. In other words, there is a probability of less than 1 that when the rain clouds come, so does the rain. Mentally such facts could be represented in terms of some proportion such as, for example, there is a 0.7 chance that it will rain when the rain clouds appear (a statement most probably true in York). What the frequentists argue, though, is that the mental representation of this fact is instead something like 'of the last 10 occasions that rain clouds appeared it rained on 7'. The contingent claim is that such frequentist representations confer certain advantages.

For instance, according to Cosmides and Tooby (1996), in converting counts into proportions or percentages, information is lost about the overall sample size. Fifty per cent of four observations equals 2; 50 per cent of 400 observations is 200. Moreover, when numbers are stored in terms of frequencies then such memories can be updated with ease. If the rain clouds now appear and it rains, then the contingency now becomes 'it rained on 8 out of the last 11 times the rain clouds came'. The overall claim is that frequentist representations facilitate thought because they place fewer demands on the cognitive system (see the example box above in which the mental computations demanded by the frequentist format are considerably less than those demanded by the Bayesian approach).

Aligned to these points are concerns about dealing with single-event probabilities (as evidenced by the medical diagnosis problem). Gigerenzer's (2002) point is that such statements are inherently ambiguous unless further information is provided. So to claim that 'there is a 30 per cent chance that it will rain tomorrow' is open to several interpretations – it could mean that it will rain 30 per cent of the time, that it will rain in 30 per cent of the target area, or that there is a 30 per cent chance that there will be some rain tomorrow (Gigerenzer, 2002, p. 33). On the understanding that statements about single probabilities are ambiguous in these ways, then this may reveal why people err in problems like the medical diagnosis problem (see also Kahneman & Tversky, 1996, and the reply by Gigerenzer, 1996). Different people interpret the information given in probabilities in different ways and only a few of these may interpret the information in the ways that the experimenters intended. In this way it could be that the experimenters are picking up on language problems, not thinking problems!

Indeed such issues have also been discussed in relation to the Linda-the-bank-teller problem. As Gigerenzer (1996) discussed, some 10–20 per cent of respondents interpret 'Linda is a bank teller and is active in the feminist movement' as meaning 'If Linda is a bank teller, then she is active in the feminist movement'. In addition, some 20–50 per cent of respondents apparently infer that the alternative 'Linda is a bank teller' implies that she is not active in the feminist movement. Critically, such problems in interpretation are not problems in reasoning! Therefore we may question the degree to which poor performance on such problems fundamentally reflects human irrationality.

Other experiments have examined how performance with the Linda-the-bank-teller problem can be improved by conveying the information in frequentist terms. For instance, following the description of Linda, Fiedler (1988) provided participants with the following statements:

There are 100 people who fit the description above. How many of them are:
1. Bank tellers?
2. Bank tellers and feminists?

In its standard form Fiedler (1988) found that 91 per cent of participants committed the conjunction fallacy but in the frequentist version of the problem only 22 per cent of participants committed the error. So again here is evidence that providing information in a frequentist format can aid reasoning. However, we need to tread carefully here because the actual facts are more complicated. It seems that performance is only facilitated when participants are exposed to both alternatives 'bank tellers' and 'bank tellers and feminists'. It is the contrast between these alternatives in the context of the frequentist format that facilitates

## → What have we learnt?

Despite the clear evidence of poor performance on certain problems concerning probability judgements, such evidence needs to be considered carefully before concluding proof of human irrationality. Performance can be greatly improved (i) if frequentist terms are used and/or (ii) if the problems are framed in ways that clearly reveal the set/sub-set relations that are to be considered.

Further evidence that is difficult to square with the idea that the data necessarily point towards natural stupidity, is that training with probability judgements improves performance (see Poulton, 1994, ch. 15, for a comprehensive review). For instance, in one example, in which variants of the Linda-the-bank-teller problem were used, whereas 86 per cent of statistically naïve students committed

the conjunction fallacy, only 50 per cent of statistically sophisticated psychology graduate students made the same error (Kahneman & Tversky, 1982). Indeed, it is now well established that participants' ability to solve such problems can improve through training or because of the acquisition of relevant knowledge. So even though an inability to solve such problems when first confronted with them may seem to indicate a fundamental flaw in the human reasoning system, such a conclusion needs to be treated with caution. By definition, fundamental flaws cannot be re-mediated by training. Nevertheless, what the evidence does point to is that humans do not naturally adopt Bayesian statistics when attempting to reason about probabilities.

being able to draw the correct conclusion. It is this contrast that makes the set/sub-set relations more apparent than the mere fact that the information is conveyed in frequencies (see Kahneman & Tversky, 1996). → See 'What have we learnt?', above.

### Pinpoint question 15.4

How might we improve performance on conditional probability problems?

## The two systems of reasoning revisited

Fundamental to the heuristics and biases approach is an acceptance of the dual system account of reasoning. The quick and dirty responses of the associative system are to be contrasted with the more thoughtful and considered responses of the rule-based system. The basic implication is (see Kahneman & Frederick, 2005) that 'system 1 (the associative system) quickly proposes intuitive answers to judgement problems as they arise, system 2 (the rule-based system) monitors the quality of these proposals, which it may endorse, correct, or override' (material in parentheses added; pp. 267–8). (The 'system 1/system 2' distinction arises from Stanovich and West (1999) and seems more easy to confuse than the associative/rule-based nomenclature used here: system 1 – associative, system 2 – rule-based.)

By this view such factors as accessibility and representativeness are assumed to, in part, govern the operation of the (irrational) associative system, and depending on circumstances, conclusions based on these factors can be overridden by the operation of the (rational) rule-based system. As Kahneman and Tversky (1996) noted, the associative system operates according to heuristics whereas the rule-based system operates according to rules. One claim, which we have already considered, is that what the research can highlight are cases where conflicts arise between a conclusion suggested by a given heuristic (such as representativeness) and a different conclusion suggested by a rule. So the bias in the Linda-the-bank-teller problem is to allow representativeness to govern the default response as this is determined by the operation of the associative system (system 1). However, the fact that this can be overridden if the problem is framed in frequentist terms (Kahneman & Frederick, 2005, p. 279) shows that the rule-based system (system 2) can veto the outputs of the more primitive associative system (system 1). The claim is that the rule-based system uses sets and set/sub-set relations (set inclusion) and that these are easier to invoke in frequentist formats.

Having now stated the general thrust of the heuristics and biases approach, and having considered some of the evidence that is meant to support it, what are we to actually make of it all? Two criticisms will be considered briefly. The first is that without further specification the notion of a heuristic is too vague to be useful (Gigerenzer, 1996). This is not to argue that the notion of a cognitive heuristic is completely off the mark, but merely that without further details it is very difficult to be clear about what is being discussed. What is the actual nature of the underlying mechanisms that are responsible for the effects of representativeness, availability, etc.? Little progress in understanding can be made by merely labelling these as examples of the operation of cognitive heuristics.

The second criticism is the claim that the evidence taken as support for the use of heuristics can be interpreted in other, simpler terms. The most comprehensive discussion of this alternative framework for thinking is that of Poulton (1994) who took great pains to accommodate the evidence (for some of the heuristics and biases) in terms of other well-known simple biases and errors. For instance, he described something known as the **response contraction bias**. Evidence for the response contraction bias is found when a stimulus or probability that is larger than a reference is underestimated and when a stimulus or probability that is smaller than a reference is overestimated. In this respect, responses gravitate towards the reference and so the range of responses is contracted. This response contraction bias is consistent with some of the evidence cited in support of the availability fallacy, hindsight bias, over-confidence, under-confidence and the expected utility fallacy (see Poulton, 1994, ch. 13; and Table 15.1 for further explanation of these heuristics and biases). According to Poulton (1994), the apparent flaws in reasoning that are highlighted by the heuristics and biases approach are at least equally well explained in terms of simple performance errors and constraints that occur more generally. They are merely specific instances of more basic and simpler biases. By this view, the errors in reasoning may well be explained in terms of failures of mechanisms that have application outside the realm of reasoning. Again the case for the fundamental nature of human irrationality must be reconsidered.

So although the operation of heuristics and biases in reasoning cannot be denied, there remain real issues over how best to understand these in terms of psychological processes. Everyone agrees that human reasoning departs from what might be expected on the basis of the standard picture, but the debate continues over whether such examples point to fundamental flaws in the human reasoning system. As Samuels et al. (2004) recently concluded, 'We are (still) . . . unable to determine the extent to which human beings are rational' (p. 173; material in parentheses added).

response contraction bias The underestimate of values above a reference and the overestimate of values below a reference.

## Reasoning in evolutionary terms

We have already touched upon the basic idea that to understand human reasoning fully it is important to consider the environmental niche within which our species developed (e.g., see Cosmides & Tooby, 1994). By this view, it is only proper to accept that the factors that have conveyed an adaptive advantage throughout our evolutionary history underpin the nature of the present-day reasoning system. One consequence of this is that the basic issue of whether we are rational should itself be framed in a different way. As Gigerenzer and Hug (1992) noted, 'we should think of reasoning as rational insofar as it is well designed for solving important adaptive problems' (p. 129). By this view, it should come as no surprise that human reasoning may well contrast with the strictures of the standard picture. We have evolved to survive in the world, and cold logic may not provide the most useful means to a life-saving end. However, within this so-called evolutionary approach, different theoretical claims have been made.

### Evolution and the dual systems

According to Evans (2003), underpinning the dual system account is the idea that the two systems have taken different evolutionary trajectories: system 1 (the associative system) is assumed to be the more primitive system and is common to both humans and other animals; system 2 (the rule-based system) is assumed to have evolved later. 'System 2 provides the basis for hypothetical thinking that endows modern humans with unique potential for a higher level of rationality in their reasoning and decision making' (Evans, 2003, p. 458). In this regard there is supposed to be a principled distinction between the two systems with each having a different evolutionary history and each having its own characteristics and modes of operation.

For instance, it has been argued that whereas system 1 operates in an essentially autonomous, fast and unconscious fashion, system 2 operates more slowly in a sequential fashion and the operations now are under conscious control. Indeed, it has been argued that system 2 thinking broadly corresponds with the stream

...at it is only the outputs of ...are posted into consciousness ...gh here is a golden opportunity ...nature of human consciousness, ...accept for the time being that there are ca... ...he answers just pop into our heads and cases w... ...e the answers come about through a process of deliberation. Whether such a distinction can actually be maintained, however, is something to which we will return shortly – maybe we can do away with the notion of deliberation completely?

## Evolution and reasoning the fast and frugal way

Aside from the rather crude dual system distinction, one alternative framework for thinking about human reasoning has been provided by Gigerenzer, Czerlinski and Martignon (2002). In schematic form, the framework is shown in Figure 15.3. At the top of the hierarchy is the notion of reasonableness, and what the framework sets out are different conceptions of how best to characterise human rationality (i.e., reasonableness). The first division is between bounded and unbounded rationality – a distinction that Gigerenzer et al. attributed to Simon (1982, 1992). **Unbounded rationality** captures notions of (essentially) rationality in principle. Here we may discuss models of reasoning without any regard to any form of constraint, such as how long a possible solution might be worked on, how much memory is needed or indeed what sorts of knowledge sources may be called upon.

Although discussion of such models of unbounded rationality may have utility in some disciplines, such as economics or computer science, Gigerenzer et al. (2002) expressed the preference that, as cognitive psy-

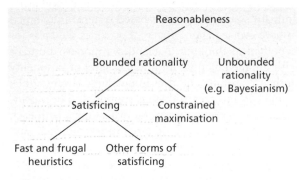

**Figure 15.3 Different conceptions of human reasonableness**

*Source*: Gigerenzer, G., Czerlinski, J., & Martignon, L. (2002). How good are fast and frugal heuristics? In T. Gilovitch, D. Griffin, & D. Kahneman (Eds.), *Heuristics and biases: The psychology of intuitive judgment* (fig. 31.1, p. 560). Cambridge, England: Cambridge University Press. Reproduced with permission.

chologists, we ought to focus on the notion of bounded rationality. If we are to develop plausible models of human reasoning then we must take account of both psychological and other real-world constraints, such as memory constraints, limited knowledge constraints, time constraints, etc. Such constraints are of no relevance when discussing models of unbounded rationality, but for humans they are paramount. For instance, do you catch this very crowded bus right now or wait for the next on the assumption that there will be a seat free? The implication, therefore, is that, since human reasoning is carried out within strict bounds and typically within strict time limits, this means that we should be exploring models of **bounded rationality**.

Given this, there is now a further distinction between **satisficing** and **constrained maximisation**. Taking the latter first, with constrained maximisation the idea is that part of the process of solving a given problem is attempting to figure out which of several possible solutions may produce the optimal trade-off between accuracy and various costs. For instance, there may be very little point in rounding costs to fractions of a penny when the overall budget must be stipulated to the nearest pound. This is not to argue that humans never or cannot engage in constrained maximisation but merely that it does not provide a very useful framework for thinking about human reasoning in general. As a consequence, Gigerenzer et al. (2002) emphasised the notion of satisficing, a word that amalgamates the meanings of *sufficing* and *satisfying* (Gigerenzer & Goldstein, 1996, p. 651).

## Human reasoning as a process of satisficing

This concept again can be traced to the work of Simon (1956, 1982) who argued that the human information processing system operates in a way so as to satisfice rather than optimise. The distinction is essentially between striving to attain a workable solution and striving for the best possible solution. The contingent claim is that the human reasoning system has evolved by adopting operations that satisfice and therefore these operations may not lead to optimal solutions. In caricature: by the time you have figured out which lifeboat looks the sturdiest, so as to ascertain the best possible (i.e., optimal) solution to your very pressing need, the ship may have sunk. The survivors, in adopting a satisficing approach, probably opted for the nearest lifeboat. By this view workable solutions need not be optimal but they do need to satisfice. Gigerenzer et al. (2002) briefly discussed one example of Simon's (1956) that illustrates one such satisficing strategy. Here the default is to 'start with an aspiration level and then choose the first object encountered that satisfies this level' (op. cit., p. 561). Difficult to accept perhaps, but such a strategy might actually help you cut down on time spent in the shops or indeed in looking for a (soul) mate.

In adopting such a bounded rationality perspective, a contingent claim is that 'our minds have evolved all sorts of nimble tricks to perform well in the quirky structures of the real world' (Gigerenzer et al., 2002, p. 561). Unsurprisingly, this leads naturally on to consider Gigerenzer's favoured perspective as given by so-called *fast and frugal heuristics*. In being sufficing strategies, such reasoning heuristics place few demands on memory and other processes, and they call upon limited knowledge. They are therefore fast and frugal. Gigerenzer and colleagues (Gigerenzer et al., 2002; Gigerenzer & Goldstein, 1996; Gigerenzer et al., 1999;

Marsh, Todd & Gigerenzer, 2004) have explored many such reasoning strategies and fast and frugal heuristics provides a detailed account of one. The approach, however, is based on the belief that the mind has evolved such that it can be construed as an **adaptive toolbox** comprising 'specific heuristics to solve particular types of problems that are commonly faced in real environments' (Marsh et al., 2004, p. 275). Such ideas as these accord well with the associated claim that the mind is composed of many different kinds of reasoning modules. → See 'What have we learnt?', page 578.

---

### Pinpoint question 15.5

On average, how many objects does a satisficer need to consider before making a decision if all those objects satisfy the desired criteria?

---

### Research focus 15.2

## When enough is enough: satisficing, maximising and the way you feel

Are you one of those people who picks up the first can of soup you see, or are you likely to comparison-shop between supermarkets at opposite ends of the town just so you can get that 6p saving on chicken nuggets? In broad strokes, we can probably all see ourselves as either a satisficer or a maximiser, and Schwartz, Ward, Lyubomirsky, Monterosso, White and Lehman (2002) set out to examine exactly how these different kinds of approaches impact on other aspects of our lives.

Schwartz et al.'s (2002) first step was to develop a questionnaire that set out to measure whether you were a satisficer or a maximiser, testing an incredible total of 1,747 subjects. Maximisers tended to agree strongly with items like 'I treat relationships like clothing: I expect to try a lot on before I get the perfect fit.' An interesting analogy, but you get the general picture. Also of interest was the observation that those who scored highly on the maximising scale also reported more regret and less life satisfaction than satisficers. Additional studies also showed that maximisers were much more concerned with social comparison, and that they were more sensitive to the opinions of others, even when they were just performing the rather mundane task of completing anagrams.

In a final study, Schwartz et al. (2002) followed up the idea of being a maximiser and experiencing regret by getting subjects to play an 'ultimatum game'. Here and at each round, subjects were allo-

cated a pot of money (e.g., $15) and were asked to offer an amount to a second (virtual) player (e.g., $7). If the virtual player accepted the amount, the subject would receive the money that was left. If the second player did not accept, neither player would receive anything. Then came the twist. A second version of the game was introduced in which the subject was told after each round what was the lowest amount the virtual player would have accepted, in order to increase regret levels if they offered too much!

The manipulation wasn't quite as successful as had been hoped, with maximisers not being particularly dissatisfied during the second condition in which the lowest bidding price of the virtual subject was revealed. However, maximisers were less satisfied than satisficers in general, and offered less money during the second version of the game (the tightwads). In sum, the studies of Schwartz et al. (2002) are fairly persuasive in taking up the satisficer route. Unless of course you enjoy being dissatisfied, more regretful, having less life satisfaction and more concern about social comparison, in which case maximising is the way for you. As they succulently put it, 'just as happiness may be a matter of choice . . . choice may also be a matter of happiness' (p. 1195).

*Source*: Schwartz, B., Ward, A., Lyubomirsky, S., Monterosso, J., White, K., & Lehman, D. R. (2002). Maximizing versus satisficing: Happiness is a matter of choice. *Journal of Personality and Social Psychology*, *83*, 1178–1197.

## → What have we learnt?

Perhaps a slightly puzzling aspect of the literature is how Gigerenzer and colleagues have criticised the heuristics and biases approach of Kahneman and Tversky but have themselves advocated reasoning by fast and frugal heuristics. Such a paradox is understandable on two counts. First, the main complaint (by Gigerenzer and colleagues) is about specificity. The claim is that, over the years, Kahneman and Tversky have conveyed very little about particular cognitive mechanisms that might be responsible for the various heuristics and biases they have documented. How exactly is it that effects of representativeness, accessibility, etc. come about? What is the nature of the underlying cognitive processes that give rise to such effects?

The subsidiary complaint is about the claim that reasoning via heuristics reveals that 'human inference is systematically biased and error prone' (Gigerenzer & Goldstein, 1996, p. 650). The alternative, more positive view is that the departures from the norms, as captured by the standard picture, should be treated not as flaws but as characteristics of a system that has evolved in the real world.

Although sometimes this system generates answers that do not accord with the tenets of the standard picture, in the main, it does a thoroughly acceptable job. Indeed, as Gigerenzer and Goldstein (1996) demonstrated, the fast and frugal heuristics can deliver about the same if not more correct inferences in less time than standard statistical models. So even though it is possible to distinguish the psychological from the rational in theoretical terms, such a distinction may not be that useful in practice.

In conclusion, the evidence for reasoning via heuristics is substantial. This does not, however, lead inevitably on to a proof of natural stupidity! Indeed, how best to interpret the evidence remains hotly contested. One particularly influential view is that the evidence for the use of reasoning heuristics can be more fully understood if an evolutionary perspective is taken. A basic claim, in this regard, is that 'human reasoning is, to some important degree, an adaptation to specific environments' (Gigerenzer & Hug, 1992, p. 169). This particular claim is explored in much more detail in the following sections.

## For example . . .
### Fast and frugal heuristics

One fast and frugal heuristic that has been documented by Gigerenzer and Goldstein (1996) is known as the take-the-best algorithm. Evidence for the operation of this heuristic comes from cases where an individual has to choose between two alternatives.

For example, you are faced with a decision about which bar to go to after work: bar *x* or bar *y*. This is how the *take-the-best algorithm* operates. If you have never heard of bar *y* then you will choose to go to bar *x*. Now assume that you are familiar with both bars, and now the choice is more involved.

For simplicity, assume that there are three characteristics that you consider important when choosing where to drink. The bar has a no smoking policy, it serves food, and it serves food at a reasonable price. Such characteristics are rank ordered from most important to least. So first consider the smok-

ing factor – do both bars prohibit smoking? If 'no', then choose the bar that prohibits smoking. If 'yes', then go on to consider the first food factor – do both bars serve food? If 'no', then choose the bar that serves food. If 'yes', go on to consider the final price factor. If one bar sells food cheaper than the other, then choose that bar. If both bars serve equally priced food, then choose one at random.

This *take-the-best algorithm* satisfices because it stops after the first discriminating factor (or cue) between the two alternatives is found. It does not exhaustively search through all possible cues in a bid to arrive at the optimal criteria upon which to base a decision. Indeed, in simulating various reasoning strategies with computer models, Gigerenzer et al. (2002) were able to demonstrate the advantages of the take-the-best algorithm over much more involved reasoning strategies.

Moreover, they also cited some counter-intuitive evidence best interpreted on the assumption that humans do actually use certain strategies utilising such fast and frugal heuristics. Here the prediction was that participants with a little knowledge of some domain might do better than participants with more knowledge of that domain – the less-is-more effect. Here German participants were tested with questions about the populations of American cities and American participants were tested with questions about the populations of German cities. Participants drew slightly more correct inferences about the other country than they did about their own. In this respect too little knowledge was a good thing.

**unbounded rationality** Accounts of reasoning in which in-principle statements are considered (e.g., how would the ideal logic machine work it out?).

**bounded rationality** The idea that human reasoning is best understood when basic performance limitations (such as memory and time constraints) are taken into consideration.

**satisficing** Adopting a solution to a problem that simply works.

**constrained maximisation** Finding a solution to a problem by figuring out which of several possible solutions produces the optimal trade-off between benefits and costs.

**adaptive toolbox** The idea that the mind comprises a whole bunch of special-purpose heuristics, each of which applies to a particular problem typically encountered in the real world.

## Evolution and the modularity of mind

In setting the scene for the current chapter, we explored the possibility that there are two fundamentally different systems of reasoning and that each has its own modes of operation and each has a different evolutionary history. A quite different view is that we have evolved many different systems of reasoning and that the dual system view grossly underestimates the vast variety of ways in which we as humans can reason. The notion of an adaptive toolbox provides one example of such a heterogeneous view of the human reasoning system.

We will return to the dual system idea shortly but more pressing is a consideration of the one system/many systems distinction – the distinction between a **non-modular view** and a so-called **massively modular view** (Samuels, 1998) of the human mind. In this respect, the overarching issue is whether it is best to discuss a central black box processor that is essentially a general-purpose problem solver or whether we need to think in terms of the mind as being composed of multiple, problem-specific, autonomous subsystems.

According to the non-modular view (Fodor, 1983, 2000), the claim is that there is just one central black box that is a domain-general (i.e., general-purpose) computational device whose operations govern all problem solving and thinking. Although this is not an acceptance of the view that the mind is literally like a digital computer, there is an acceptance that, like the computer (with its binary operations), the mind carries out just one sort of mental computation. Similar sorts of computational operations underlie all forms of thought (see Chapter 2 for a discussion of the computational theory of mind). In this regard the mind is taken to be a general-purpose computer or a general-purpose problem solver (cf. Newell et al., 1958). In contrast, the massively modular account (generally attributed to Cosmides & Tooby, 1992, 1994, 1996) is the complete antithesis of this. Now the claim is that there is an indefinite number of mental processors – each one specific to a different kind of problem that can be solved. According to this view, adaptive reasoning is served most efficiently by cognitive mechanisms that have been specifically tailored to meet the individual task demands of particular types of problem. That is, there are type-distinct ways of reasoning and that each of these has followed a different evolutionary trajectory. Cosmides (1989) referred to these as **Darwinian algorithms**, Samuels (1998) as *Darwinian modules*.

As much of what has been written in this book has adhered rather closely to the original modularity of mind theory developed by Fodor (1983), it is important to appreciate that the massively modular hypothesis (Cosmides & Tooby, 1996) is a radical departure from this. Whereas Fodor (1983) was happy to posit a multitude of different *input* modules, he also defined a non-modular view of the central processor in which the same general principles governed the operation of the higher levels of cognition. Here the higher levels of cognition refer to reasoning, problem solving and thinking. In contrast to this, Cosmides and Tooby (1996) discussed the possibility of a multitude of problem-specific processors (the Darwinian modules), each of which is dedicated to a particular type of thinking. To put further flesh on these ideas it is important to consider why it is that Cosmides and Tooby set out on such a radical departure from the original modularity theory. In order to appreciate the issues fully, though, it is important first to introduce a rather critical difference between two different forms of reasoning.

> **non-modular view** The idea that the mind contains a single general-purpose problem solver.
>
> **massively modular view** The idea that the mind comprises a variety of special-purpose mechanisms by which problems can be solved.
>
> **Darwinian algorithms** Type-distinct ways of reasoning that have developed throughout the evolution of the species.

## Deductive and inductive inference

### Deductive inference

**Deductive inference** is typically distinguished from **inductive inference**. Drawing an inference on the basis of deduction means essentially following the rules of logic. If we view logic as a game, then the rules of logic are the rules of the game. To play the game properly we must follow the rules. Similarly if we follow the rules of logic, we will be seen to reason rationally and deductively. A valid deductive inference is one that follows logically from the premises. One such valid argument is as follows:

| (1) | If $p$ then $q$ | If it is raining then I will get wet |
| (2) | $p$ | It is raining |
| --- | | |
| (3) | Therefore $q$ | Therefore I will get wet |

(1) and (2) are known as *premises* (or antecedents) and (3) is known as the *conclusion* (or consequent). In applying the rules of logic, the aim is to generate, from the premises, an appropriate conclusion. The rules of logic are akin to the rules of syntax of a language – they are also known as formal rules because the rules

are only described in terms of their form and not their content. This is one of the reasons that logical rules are typically discussed in terms of abstract symbols such as $p$ and $q$. Different symbols are distinguished only by their form, and in terms of symbolic logic there is no implication that we need to know what the symbols stand for or what they mean – the symbols are, in this sense, without content.

Indeed things can go very badly awry if, instead of using abstract symbols, we mix together the rules of logic with real words. A very basic and important distinction is between the validity of an argument and its truth. An argument can be perfectly valid but this does not mean that its conclusion will be true. How can this be? Well, as long as we adhere to the rules of logic we will generate valid arguments – we will reason deductively. If we apply the rules of logic properly then our arguments will be valid. However, this may lead us to rather unfortunate conclusions as can be seen by this rather silly example:

> If there is cloud cover then I will get sunburned
> There is cloud cover
> _____
> Therefore I will get sunburned

Here we have a perfectly valid argument but the conclusion is patently false. Johnson-Laird (2001) has provided a slightly different example of the clash between validity and sensibleness.

> Eva is in Rio or she's in Brazil
> She's not in Brazil
> _____
> Therefore she's in Rio.

The inference is perfectly valid but it makes no sense! (See Figure 15.4.)

### Inductive inference

In contrast to deductive inference, there is *inductive inference*. An inductive inference is one that goes beyond the information given in the premises. So whereas validity in terms of a deductive argument means that the conclusion necessarily follows from the premises, with an inductive argument this is not so. Here the notion of validity is strained and it is the truth of the inference that becomes critical. An inductive inference can give rise to a true conclusion but it will not necessarily follow from the premises.

other words, participants exhibited something known as a **confirmation bias** – the difficult-to-resist bias to seek confirmatory evidence of your current hypothesis. Recall from Chapter 1 our discussion of Popper (1963/2000) who noted that 'Every genuine test of a theory is any attempt to falsify it, or refute it. Testability is falsifiability . . .'. The confirmation bias operates in a completely contradictory fashion to this, hence it could be argued that the participants are behaving irrationally in exhibiting the confirmation bias.

> **deductive inference** Inferences made on the basis of logic.
>
> **inductive inference** Inferences made on the basis of information that goes beyond the premises.
>
> **confirmation bias** The inclination to seek out evidence in support of currently held hypotheses. A bias against seeking out evidence that might disconfirm such hypotheses.

**Figure 15.4 Just another late night**
Just another fashion victim wearing shades indoors or an individual trying to counteract the valid (but untrue) conclusion from the premises:
If I am on the New York subway I will get sunburned
I am on the New York subway

I will get sunburned

*Source*: Photolibrary.com/Monsoon Images.

A different experimental task devised by Wason (1960) provides a classic example of an inductive reasoning task. Here the simple problem was to give participants the number series '2 4 6' and to ask them to continue the series with a further plausible triple that continued the series. After each response the experimenter simply said whether the participant's triple conformed to the rule that generated the initial series or not. The participant's ultimate task was to uncover the original rule. (This is a particularly good case of how you may be able to infuriate friends and relatives so as to test their natural stupidity!)

As you can see, there is no rule of logic that applies here. It is knowledge of numbers that is germane, and as a consequence, the problem highlights inductive reasoning. The only way to engage with this problem is if you possess knowledge of the number system – logic is of little help. The actual rule to be discovered was 'any ascending sequence' but the participants tended to generate much more particular rules than this and, critically, there was real resistance to disconfirm any hypotheses that immediately received support. In

## The Wason selection task

Although it is an easy matter to define the difference between deductive and inductive inference, it still remains true that, as Wason and Johnson-Laird remarked (in 1968), 'As yet there is no clear psychological distinction between the two types of inference' (p. 11). Indeed this fact has been most clearly demonstrated with what is perhaps the most significant problem-solving task ever devised, namely the *Wason selection task* (see Figure 15.5). As we will see, despite the fact that the problem should be solved in a deductive fashion using rules of logic, whether this happens or not depends critically on how the problem is framed. In order to appreciate this, however, we must consider what exactly the Wason selection task is.

The Wason selection task, in its original form, is shown in Figure 15.5. In this form it is known as an *abstract deductive reasoning task*. The rule that participants are asked to consider is, 'If a card has a vowel on one side, then it has an even number on the other.' In this version, the problem is abstract because there really is no further contextual information that can be brought to bear that might facilitate solving the problem. In addition, the problem demands to be solved via processes of deductive reasoning. When presented in this form, the typical (and incorrect) choices that participants make are (i) the A card or (ii) the A and the 4 cards. The logically correct cards are the A card (because the rule would be violated if this card had an

You know that every card has a letter on one side and a number on the other. Consider the rule: 'If a card has a vowel on one side, then it has an even number on the other.'

'Your task is to say which of the cards you need to turn over in order to find out whether the rule is true or false.'

The abstract version
'If a card has a vowel on one side, then it has an even number on the other.' (if *p* then *q*)

Figure 15.5 **The original and abstract version of the Wason (1960) selection task**

odd number on the other side) and the 7 card (because if this card did have a vowel on the other side then again the rule would be violated). To be clear, to verify the rule 'If a card has a vowel on one side, then it has an even number on the other', the logically correct cards are the A card together with the 7 card.

Initially, Wason argued that the standard response (i.e., the A and 4 cards) reflected a verification or confirmation bias because participants were driven to prove rather than disprove the rule. Later work elaborated on this basic idea (Johnson-Laird & Wason, 1970). However, very soon after the original work had been published, it became apparent that performance on the task could be improved if the problem was phrased differently (or alternatively, *framed* differently) – in the same way that the conditional probability problems benefit from being transcribed in frequentist terms (see Pinpoint question 15.4), performance on the Wason selection task benefits if the problem is framed in less abstract terms.

Figure 15.6 provides an illustration of the version of the problems used by Johnson-Laird, Legrenzi and Sonio Legrenzi (1972). Now 24 participants were tested on a concrete version of the task in which a postal scenario was contrived and the rule was now 'If a letter is sealed then it has a 5p stamp on it', and an abstract version of the task (as originally formulated – see Figure 15.6a). The results showed that when presented with the concrete version, 22 of the participants responded correctly but that this number dropped to only 7 when the abstract version was tested (see Figure 15.6b). Moreover, there was almost no transfer across the problems. Participants apparently did not benefit from having been exposed to the concrete version before attempting the abstract version and only 2 participants reported seeing the logical connection between the two versions of the problem.

This sort of demonstration is (now) just one example of how performance, on what is basically a deductive reasoning task, can be moderated by **thematic content** (see Evans, Newstead & Byrne, 1993, ch. 4 for a comprehensive review). Performance may improve if the problem is cast in more concrete and less abstract terms. Evans et al. (1993) referred to this basic pattern – the improved performance with concrete versions of the problem – as 'thematic facilitation'. The existence of **thematic facilitation** reveals why, at a psychological level, the distinction between deductive and inductive thinking is blurred. Variations in performance with exactly the same deductive reasoning problem can change depending on how the problem is framed. The logic of the problem does not change; what changes is how it is worded. Moreover, the fact that performance improves with changes in framing is another example of treating with caution any assertion that human-reasoning is somehow fatally flawed. Even though an abstract version of a problem may seem impossible

Imagine you are a postal worker sorting letters. Now consider whether the following rule has been violated:

'If a letter is sealed then it has a 5p stamp on it.'

'Your task is to select only those envelopes that definitely need to be turned over to find out whether or not they violate the rule.'

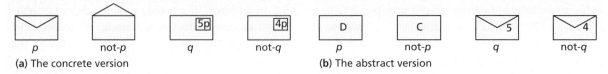

(a) The concrete version          (b) The abstract version

Figure 15.6 **A more realistic version of the Wason selection task (Johnson-Laird, Legrenzi & Sonio Legrenzi, 1972)**

to solve, a logically equivalent version can be solved because the problem is framed in realistic terms.

It would, however, be misleading to conclude that merely framing the problem in concrete terms produces thematic facilitation. Evans et al. (1993) reviewed quite a considerable body of research that showed that thematic facilitation does not occur in all cases. The relevant evidence suggests that such facilitation is most likely to occur if the material accords well with the participants' own experience. Performance improves if the problem is framed in such a way that it probes particular associations and specific information as stored in memory. In this respect, there is a link between performance on the task and the availability heuristic as discussed above. As Evans et al. (1993, p. 121) concluded, 'When the correct responses are "available" participants' logical performance will be facilitated . . . '. Cosmides (1989), however, has made a different and more particular claim. She has argued that unless the problem is framed as a **social contract** then the likelihood of obtaining thematic facilitation is small. To appreciate this point, though, it is important to examine the social contract theory of performance in the selection task.

## Social contract theory

Figure 15.7 shows a different form of the selection task and it is to this that discussion now turns. The examples shown in the figure are most closely associated with the work of Cosmides (1989) and Cosmides and Tooby (1992). As just noted, there may well be cases where a thematic facilitation effect does not occur, but Cosmides (1989) went further and examined more particularly how performance on the task varies according to how the problem is framed. Fundamental to this line of research is a theoretical approach rooted firmly within an evolutionary perspective. Central is the idea that the task may be providing evidence for something known as **cheater detection**.

In adopting an evolutionary perspective, a basic claim is that performance on the task may reflect (albeit in a fairly indirect way) how we, as a species, have internalised rules of social exchange. Here social exchange is defined as co-operation between two or more individuals for mutual benefit (Cosmides, 1989, p. 195) (e.g., you scratch my back then I will scratch yours). From an evolutionary point of view, the emergence and coherence of social groups depends upon mutual support and co-operation between individuals. Such interactions may be defined according to implicit rules of operation. Cosmides (1989, p. 196) cited one example as follows (in paraphrase):

In an exchange, an individual is usually obliged to pay a cost in order to be entitled to receive a benefit.

The associated claim is that 'the capacity to engage in social exchange could not have evolved unless, on average, both participants realized a net benefit by engaging in exchange'. To be successful is to avoid exchanges in which the cost exceeds the benefit. Moreover, it is argued that 'the capacity to engage in social exchange *cannot evolve* in a species unless the members of the social group are able to detect individuals who cheat (fail to reciprocate) on social contracts'. An inability to detect cheaters would therefore have associated dire consequences for the protagonist. The strictly Darwinian claim is that to be constantly cheated upon would not accord well with the survival of the fittest. The lineage of the cheated upon would soon come to a rather unfortunate end!

So it appears there are good grounds for arguing that the ability to detect cheaters confers a real adaptive advantage. Given this, two further contingent claims are as follows:

1. The human mind must contain algorithms that produce and operate on cost–benefit representations of exchange interactions.

(a) Rule 1 – Standard social contract (STD–SC): 'If you take the benefit, then you pay the cost.'
   (If $p$ then $q$)

(b) Rule 2 – Switched social contract (SWC–SC): 'If you pay the cost, then you take the benefit.'
   (If $p$ then $q$)

| | benefit accepted | benefit not accepted | cost paid | cost not paid |
|---|---|---|---|---|
| STD–SC | $p$ | not-$p$ | $q$ | not-$q$ |
| SWC–SC | $q$ | not-$q$ | $p$ | not-$p$ |

**Figure 15.7 Social contract versions of the Wason selection task (Cosmides & Tooby, 1992)**

2. The human mind must include inferential procedures that make humans very good at detecting cheating on social contracts.

So what is the empirical evidence upon which such claims have been based? Figure 15.7 shows an example of the actual task used that illustrates the *standard version of the social contract*. According to Cosmides (1989), when the problem is so framed – 'If you take the benefit, then you pay the cost' – this accords well with the notion of a basic social contract. Furthermore, if this also induces the participants to treat the problem as being akin to brokering a social contract then the predominant responses should be to choose both the 'cost not paid' (the not-$q$) card and the 'benefit accepted' (the $p$) card because these will reveal potential cheaters. In addition they should also ignore the 'cost paid' (the $q$) card and the 'benefit not accepted' (the not-$p$) card because these will represent individuals who could not possibly have cheated. That is, predominantly participants ought to be able to solve this form of the selection task. The results reported by Cosmides (1989) confirmed this prediction: over 70 per cent of the participants answered the problem correctly even when the problems were framed in the context of hypothetical and therefore unfamiliar scenarios. In this regard, the evidence was taken to be a powerful demonstration of thematic facilitation that could not have been due merely to availability/accessibility of information stored in long-term memory.

More provocative, though, was performance with a second form of the task known as the *switched social contract*. Now the rule was framed in these terms: 'If you pay the cost, then you take the benefit.' As can be seen in Figure 15.7, the logical assignment of the cards to the various categories has now changed. Now under this reassignment, logic and social contract theory provide different predictions. According to the social contract theory, the default position, that underpins cheater detection, is always to choose the 'cost not paid' and 'benefit accepted' cards regardless of what logical category these cards fall into. So whereas social contract theory predicts that the choices will be the 'cost not paid' (not-$p$) and the 'benefit accepted' (the $q$) card, logic still dictates that the response should be the 'cost paid' (the $p$) card and the 'benefit not accepted' (the not-$q$) card. The data were clear, however, in revealing that the majority of participants (over 66 per cent) responded according to the predictions of social contract theory.

So here again is a very clear case where there is a contrast between (i) the tenets of the standard picture where rationality is defined by the rules of logic, and (ii) actual human reasoning. Responses on the switched social contract version of the problem contrast with the predictions of the standard picture. The claim is, though, that human reasoning is both understandable and sensible given that there is an overwhelming evolutionary prerogative to detect cheaters. The more far-reaching claim was that the thematic facilitation shown when the selection task was framed as a rule involving a social contract was taken as evidence that 'people have reasoning procedures that are specifically designed for detecting cheaters in situations of social exchange' (Cosmides & Tooby, 1992, p. 181). In other words, the evidence was taken to support a Darwinian algorithm that had evolved specifically for the purpose of cheater detection. → See 'What have we learnt?', below.

### Pinpoint question 15.6

**What two characteristics might lead to thematic facilitation in the Wason selection task?**

### → What have we learnt?

As you can probably imagine, the original studies provoked a flurry of activity and many follow-up experiments and papers have been published since the work first appeared. Different theoretical perspectives have also been offered. Emphasis for thematic effects has been attributed to the influence of pragmatic reasoning schemata (see the work of Cheng and colleagues: Cheng & Holyoak, 1985, 1989; Cheng, Holyoak, Nisbett & Oliver, 1986), deontic reasoning modules (Cummins, 1996) and relevance theory (Sperber, Cara & Girotto, 1995; Sperber & Girotto, 2003). Each is, essentially, based on revealing cases not originally covered by social contract theory. Rather than cover the fine details of all of these alternatives, just one example of relevant work will allow us to convey something of the flavour of how the debate has advanced.

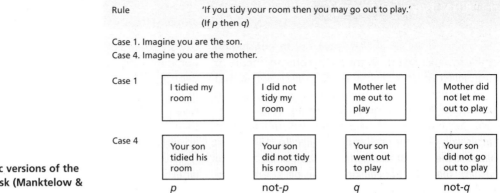

| Rule | 'If you tidy your room then you may go out to play.' (If *p* then *q*) |

Case 1. Imagine you are the son.
Case 4. Imagine you are the mother.

**Figure 15.8 Deontic versions of the Wason selection task (Manktelow & Over, 1991)**

## Feeling obliged? Deontic and indicative conditionals

Manktelow and Over (1991) examined performance with what are known as **deontic conditional**s such as 'if you do *p* then you *must* do *q*' and in this form the conditional relates to some form of obligation. The more typical case of the selection task involves **indicative conditional**s such as 'if there is a *p* then there is a *q*'. So the keen-eyed among you will have already noticed that a critical difference between the social contract examples of the task and the original versions of the task maps onto the difference between deontic and indicative conditionals, respectively. Whereas indicative conditionals assert truths, deontic conditionals impose obligations (see Fodor, 2000, p. 102). As Manktelow and Over (1991, p. 88) noted, 'Deontic thinking takes place when we consider what we may (or are allowed to) do, or what we ought to (must or should) do, rather than what was, is, or will actually be the case. So basic forms of deontic thought are those concerned with permissions and obligations.' They went on to test examples of the selection task in which deontic inference was being tapped. For instance, they discussed their earlier work in which they examined the following rule:

If you clear up spilt blood, you must wear rubber gloves

Participants did particularly well when faced with this rule in the selection task, and yet, there is no sense in which the rule implies any form of social contract. It seems, therefore, that something more general than an appreciation of social contracts is being tapped. More importantly, the social contract theory, as originally described, failed to take account of the difference between law makers and law breakers. For example,

Manktelow and Over (1991) examined performance with the following rule:

If you tidy your room then you may go out to play

Now different groups of participants were tested with this rule couched in terms of the selection task (see Figure 15.8). For one group the participants were to consider the rule from the point of view of being a teenage son when faced with an ultimatum given by his mother (i.e., case 1); for another group the participants were to consider the rule when wearing the shoes of the mother of a teenage son (case 4). So in case 1 participants were asked to adopt the perspective of trying to ascertain whether the mother was breaking the rule, whereas in case 4 they were asked to ascertain whether the son was breaking the rule. In other words, in case 1 (as the child) participants should choose the *p* and not-*q* cards ('I tidied my room' and 'Mother did not let me out to play') whereas in case 4 (as the mother) the preferences ought to be the not-*p* and the *q* cards ('Your son did not tidy his room' and 'Your son went out to play'). Although the data for case 1 were not so clear-cut, the data for case 4 were particularly compelling and in line with the predictions. Moreover, in probing a slightly modified case 1 rule in a further experiment, the data were now as predicted. → See 'What have we learnt?', page 586.

## The selection task and attempts to eliminate system 2

A final theoretical thread in this discussion of the selection task concerns the work of Oaksford and Chater (1994, 2001, 2003) and their repeated attempts to avoid discussion of system 2 (the rule-based system) in accounting for performance in the task. Put simply: they have argued from an eliminative perspective in

## → What have we learnt?

So where does all of this leave us? In concluding their review of work on the social contract theory of the selection task, Evans et al. (1993) noted that none of various researchers, 'appear to be equating rationality with logical reasoning, but rather assume that selections are rational in the sense of achieving goals or maximising utility' (p. 134). So in the mother/son scenario, responses can be seen to reflect the fact that reasoning can be altered radically depending on which utilities are being maximised – is it okay to go out to play? vs. is it okay to let him go out to play?

In addition, we must accept that the thematic effects that have been identified in the Wason selection task are many and varied, and as Leighton (2004) has recently stated, given that participants' responses on the task vary as a consequence of 'contextual changes to the thematic rule, then it supports the notion that the thematic tasks are not necessarily eliciting formal logical reasoning' (pp. 305–6). This, however, is a long way from concluding that responses are irrational or merely arbitrary. Some responses may well be quite odd, especially when the abstract version of the task is used (see the very entertaining account by Wason, 1960). However, what the empirical research has shown is that performance does tend to vary systematically and that some of the conditions for this systemati-

city are reasonably well understood. For instance, as Cummins (2004) has argued, performance on the deontic versions of the task (rules containing 'must' or implying obligation in some other way) may well reveal basic understanding of social norms rather than social contracts that bring with them the notion of reciprocation for mutual benefit.

There remains something of an issue over whether the evidence with the selection task points to the operation of the sort of type-distinct reasoning mechanisms – the Darwinian modules – postulated by Cosmides (1989). Many have argued that it does not (Cummins, 2004; Fodor, 2000; Johnson-Laird & Byrne, 2002; Sperber & Girotto, 2003). Of the many concerns that have been raised, one that has recurred is that much of the evidence reflects differences between reasoning with deontic conditionals and reasoning with indicative conditionals (Fodor, 2000, p. 104; Johnson-Laird & Byrne, 2002). Although performance with these two different sorts of conditionals does show marked differences, it is perhaps a step too far to then argue that each implicates a different sort of reasoning module for the various cases. The alternative is to argue that the same reasoning apparatus is responsible throughout, but that different sorts of inferences are being drawn in the two cases.

which performance in the task can be explained without any acknowledgement of the sort of rule-based cerebral thinking that is typically associated with system 2.

According to them, performance in the task can be adequately explained in terms of (as yet to be specified) neural mechanisms that slavishly obey the tenets of Bayesian reasoning. Now the contrast is between logical reasoning and reasoning according to the generation and testing of hypotheses according to Bayesian formulations. In pursuing the latter alternative, Oaksford and Chater developed a so-called **information gain model** of performance as a mechanistic account of system 1.

They frame the problem accordingly: in the Wason task what participants are attempting to find out is which of two hypotheses best describes the actual disposition of the letters and the numbers on the cards.

The two hypotheses are either (i) for each vowel there is an even number on the other side of the card, in which case there is a dependency between the presence of even numbers and vowels, or (ii) there is no such dependency between the presence of vowels and even numbers. In trying to decide between these two hypotheses, participants are seen to behave so as to reduce uncertainty over which could possibly be true. Remember, participants are not actually allowed to turn the cards over – they simply have to say which cards they would turn over in order to see if the rule were true.

What the information gain model does is provide a detailed mathematical account of the typical choices people make in the task on the understanding that reasoning reduces to computing concurrent levels of uncertainties in addition to projected levels of uncertainties given that certain cards could be turned over. In this framework the mind is essentially reduced to a sophisticated statistical (Bayesian) machine that can, to varying degrees of competence, figure out which card selections will provide optimal information about how the world is configured. The theoretical enterprise therefore is to provide an adequate account of the behaviour of this sort of abstract statistical machine.

According to the information gain model, the participants' task is to select those cards that will provide the most information about discriminating between these two hypotheses. As Oaksford and Chater (2003) stated, 'The most informative data (i.e., the choices about the cards) are those that produce the greatest reduction in the uncertainty about which hypothesis is true' (material in parentheses added; p. 291). So, very briefly, the expected information gain depends on the nature of the assumptions that the participants make about the proportions of $p$ to not-$p$ cases and the proportions of $q$ to not-$q$ cases. The underlying assumption here is that, generally speaking, the negation of any given state of the world is more prevalent than that state of the world. Clearly there is only one 10 o'clock on 13 November 2006 and an infinite number of other states of the world that are not 10 o'clock on 13 November 2006. There are more things that are not dogs than are dogs (Anderson, 2005) and so on. On this basis alone, therefore, $p$ and $q$ are taken to be less frequent than not-$p$ and not-$q$. Therefore $p$ and $q$ ought to provide the greatest expected information gain and indeed these are the most frequent choices.

Think of it this way. Let us cast the problem thus: 'If drug A is given then a rash will appear'. The four cards are 'drug A', 'no drug', 'rash' and 'no rash'. Now reflect on which of these four cards are going to be most informative – 'the drug A' (the $p$) and the 'rash' (the $q$) cards, right? Most of the time most people are not on prescription medication and most of the time most people do not suffer from rashes. In developing the mathematical argument the model correctly predicts the rank ordering of choices in the Wason selection task (i.e., $p > q >$ not-$q >$ not-$p$; here the notation $p > q$ means that the $p$ card is chosen more often than the $q$ card). By this account, the not-$p$ card is hardly ever chosen because it is simply not informative. An overarching point is that by assuming that uncertainty reduction underpins performance in the task, then there is clearly a rational basis to participants' performance. Therefore the $q$ choice that is typically made is another example that should not be taken as being indicative of natural stupidity (Oaksford & Chater, 2001). Such a choice follows on the understanding that rare cases can prove to be most informative.

## Appraising the information gain account

Oaksford and Chater have amassed a great deal of evidence that is consistent with their information gain model, and in a sense they have rested their case on the assertion that 'no account of the selection task is sufficiently general if it cannot take account of the set size of $p$ and the set size of $q$ or the probability judgements which reflect these' (Green & Over, 2000). However, some problems are evident with the model when such concerns are taken into consideration. For instance, as Anderson (2005) has remarked, in the standard Wason selection task, 'it does not seem in this situation that there are many more even numbers than odd numbers' (p. 320). More particularly, there are now data that contrast with the idea that choices in the task should vary as a function of the frequency with which the corresponding concepts occur.

Oberauer, Weidenfeld and Hörnig (2004) put this idea to the test in the following way. Initially participants underwent a training phase in which they had to learn to classify schematic objects according to features on three binary dimensions. One class of object was playing cards and each card could have round or sharp edges (dimension 1), a number (i.e., 1 or 2) on one face of the card (dimension 2) and finally a letter (i.e., A or B) on the other face of the card (dimension 3). So on a given learning trial a card would appear on a computer screen and participants were probed to respond with, for instance, the featural value on the other side of the card. Participants were trying to figure out the rule connecting the one set of feature values on one side of the card and the set of feature values on the other side of the card.

Critically for each binary dimension one frequent value occurred on 0.9 (or 9 out of 10 times if you're a frequentist) of the occasions and the rare value occurred on the remaining 0.1 (or 1 every 10 times) occasions. For example, 9 times out of 10 the card had round rather than sharp edges. In this way the base rates for the different values were configured within the experiment. The frequency of $p$ (an odd or even number) and the frequency of $q$ (a vowel or a consonant) were being set up during the course of the experiment. Participants were not explicitly told of this manipulation, however. All that happened was that a stimulus and probe question were presented, the participant made a response and feedback was then given as to whether the response was correct or not.

The experiment was set up in this way so as to test the basic assumption of the information gain model that it is the featural base rates that, in part, determine selections in the Wason task. To test this assumption, Oberauer et al. (2004) went on to require that participants undertake various selection problems defined in terms of the actual learning materials used in the experiment. A rather strict prediction from the information gain theory is that choices in the task should now be tied to how often the participants had been exposed to the criterial values during training.

The data were relatively clear-cut in this regard. Remember, participants were not told which featural value was the most frequent during training. However, the data revealed that participants were sensitive to the contingencies and their choices in the selection tasks began to reflect the 9 to 1 bias in favour of the frequent value. More interesting, though, was that the data in the selection task problems did not accord well with the particular predictions derived from application of the information gain model. There was no evidence that participants' responses varied as a function of the base rate of the values probed in the problems in the manner predicted by the theory. As Oberauer et al. (2004) concluded, even though these data do not refute the theory, the evidence does 'undermine the key assumption . . . used for linking the theory to empirical test' (p. 527). → See 'What have we learnt?', below.

### Pinpoint question 15.7

Does the information gain theory put more value on rare or common events?

**thematic content** Refers to the meanings conveyed by the terms in a problem. What the problem is about.

**thematic facilitation** A common finding that solving the Wason selection task is facilitated if the problem is cast in a plausible and familiar scenario.

**social contract** Implicit agreements regarding social exchanges and cultural norms.

**cheater detection** From an evolutionary perspective, the need to be able to discover those individuals who renege on social contracts.

**deontic conditional** A conditional statement relating to obligation.

**indicative conditional** A conditional statement relating to the assertion of truths.

**information gain model** A model developed by Oaksford and Chater (1994), in which problem solving amounts to the desire to acquire the maximum amount of information that can be used to adjudicate between various hypotheses.

### → What have we learnt?

There is no doubt that the information gain theory provides an interesting and rather radical account of how people reason in ways that depart from the standard picture. For instance, we can account for task performance without an appeal to mental logic, or indeed mental cogitation of any kind – input the values into the (neural) statistical machine and stand back until the cogs finish whirring and the answer is spat out. As the work of Oberauer et al. (2004) shows, however, the theory is perhaps not as watertight as Oaksford and Chater have suggested (2001, 2003). Indeed, even more recently, the fault lines in theory have widened because it performed poorly in accounting for other data collected by Oberauer (2006). It seems therefore to be an open question as to whether the account can be salvaged by further embellishments.

Moreover, whereas Oaksford and Chater in 2001 were happy to acknowledge the system 1/system 2 framework for thinking, it seems that their attitudes have hardened more recently (2003). It seems that they now feel system 2 may be eliminated from consideration altogether (see 2003, p. 312). By this view all the interesting questions about reasoning can be answered by considering how system 1 operates. By this view, the unconscious neural networks propagate activity across the myriad connections between the millions of simple processing units and then merely catapult a conclusion into the theatre of consciousness. It seems as though they want to rid any discussion of *thinking* from our explanations of human problem solving.

## For example . . .

## The rights and wrongs of conditional inference

Conditional premise:      If *p* then *q*
Categorical premises:      *p*
     *q*
     not *p*
     not *q*

To appreciate the logical force of this material really it is best to try to think in terms of *p*s and *q*s. However, as cognitive psychologists we know that people tend to think best in concrete terms (see Simon, 1972), hence concrete examples have been provided to the right of the page. We begin by considering two locally valid forms of argument known as modus ponens and modus tollens.

*Reasoning by modus ponens (affirming the antecedent)*

(In these cases, *p* is known as the antecedent and *q* is known as the consequent.)

| If *p* then *q* | If I am thirsty then I drink |
| *p* | I am thirsty |
| --------------- | ----------------------------------- |
| ∴ *q* | ∴ I drink |

The symbol ∴ stands for 'therefore'.

*Reasoning by modus tollens (denying the consequent)*

| If *p* then *q* | If I am thirsty then I drink |
| not *q* | I do not drink |
| --------------- | ----------------------------------- |
| ∴ not *p* | ∴ I am not thirsty |

Now consider two logically invalid forms of argument, (i) *to affirm the consequent*, and (ii) *to deny the antecedent*.

*Affirm the consequent – illogical, invalid argument*

| If *p* then *q* | If I am thirsty then I drink |
| *q* | I drink |
| --------------- | ----------------------------------- |
| *p* | ∴ I am thirsty |

*Deny the antecedent – illogical, invalid argument*

| If *p* then *q* | If I am thirsty then I drink |
| not *p* | I am not thirsty |
| --------------- | ----------------------------------- |
| not *q* | ∴ I do not drink |

Again the evidence is that people do not appear to behave rationally. According to Oaksford and Chater (2001), participants endorse arguments of the modus ponens form more often than they do arguments of the modus tollens form. Remember, both forms of argument are equally valid! In addition, they endorse arguments of the 'affirm the consequent' form and 'deny the antecedent' form at levels significantly above zero. Now we have people agreeing with invalid conclusions!

Try out a different concrete example and set the antecedent to 'If I sing well' and the consequent to 'I will win *The X Factor*'. The rather perplexing result is that, regardless of what you conclude, there is bound to be a conflict between validity and truth.

## Deductive reasoning and syllogisms

Aside from the experiments on the Wason selection task and variants thereof, an alternative thread in the literature has examined deductive reasoning using problems known as **syllogism**s. It is only fair to point out that this is a particularly challenging topic and for this reason quite a bit of the following dwells on simple examples and descriptions of key concepts. Without considering the basics, it would be impossible to be able to appreciate what has been found out and what is now known about this form of deductive reasoning. Furthermore, the terminology should come in useful if you do feel inclined to engage further with the topic.

## Some definitions and useful terminology

The basic unit of meaning here is known as a **categorical term** which designates a class of things – so it is typically expressed as a common noun or noun phrase:

chairs, tables, dance moves, things found in the bottom of the laundry basket, etc. Importantly, use of such a categorical term implies a well-defined distinction between things, to which the class refers, and things outside the class (the so-called complementary class). There is a categorical distinction being drawn.

A **categorical proposition**, therefore, is a statement that declares a relation between the classes designated by two categorical terms. Traditionally the first term in such a statement is known as the *subject* and the second is known as a *predicate*. So in *Some of Andrew's clothes are embarrassing, Andrew's clothes* is the subject and *embarrassing* is the predicate.

It is also possible to speak of the quality of a categorical proposition – it can either be an **inclusive** or **positive assertion** about members of the participant class being included in the predicate class as in *Some of Andrew's clothes are embarrassing.* Alternatively it can be an **exclusive** or **negative assertion** about members of the participant class being excluded from the predicate class as in *Some of Andrew's clothes are not embarrassing.*

Finally there is the quantity of a categorical proposition which refers to the degree to which the relation holds between the members of the two classes. We can distinguish:

(i)    a universal affirmative proposition (known in shorthand form as **A**)

> All S are P
> *All of Andrew's clothes are embarrassing*

(ii)    a universal negative proposition (**E**)

> No S are P
> *None of Andrew's clothes are embarrassing*

(iii)    a particular affirmative proposition (**I**)

> Some S are P
> *Some of Andrew's clothes are embarrassing*

(iv)    a particular negative proposition (**O**)

> Some S are not P
> *Some of Andrew's clothes are not embarrassing*

The terms *All, Some, No, None* are known as *quantifiers* (words that modify a noun and indicate how many or how much).

### Pinpoint question 15.8

Identify the subject term, predicate, quality and quantity of the following categorical proposition: *Some of Edward's examples are tough.*

By definition, a syllogism comprises three propositions, respectively, two premises and a conclusion. The first premise is known as the **major premise** and the second premise is known as the **minor premise**.

For instance:

| | |
|---|---|
| Major premise | All men are mortal |
| Minor premise | All fathers are men |
| ------------------------------ | |
| Conclusion | All fathers are mortal |

The mood of a syllogism is given by the collective description of the type of statements included. So classify each of the statements as **A, E, I** or **O** and you will get the mood – in this case **AAA** (since all of the propositions are universally affirmative).

Also, as can be seen from this example, only three categorical terms are included. The three categorical terms are known respectively as:

1. The *middle term* (or **M**) is common to both premises but is missing from the conclusion (*men*).
2. The *minor term* (or **S**) which is the participant of the conclusion and is present in one of the premises (*fathers*).
3. The *major term* (or **P**) which is the predicate of the conclusion and is present in the other premise (*mortal*).

By arranging these terms in different ways, we arrive at what are known as the four figures of the syllogism. These are summarised below:

| Figure | 1st | 2nd | 3rd | 4th |
|---|---|---|---|---|
| Major premise | M–P | P–M | M–P | P–M |
| Minor premise | S–M | S–M | M–S | M–S |
| Conclusion | S–P | S–P | S–P | S–P |

In this traditional scheme, the participant of the conclusion is always contained in the second (minor) premise. More particularly, this way of discussing the figures of syllogisms fails to acknowledge that more possibilities exist because the logical nature of the problems can be preserved even when the major and minor premises are swapped around. An appreciation of this point has allowed Johnson-Laird, on a number of occasions (1980; Johnson-Laird & Byrne, 1991; Johnson-Laird & Steedman, 1978), to remark that there are double the number of syllogisms than was previously thought.

## For example . . .

### Just how many possible kinds of syllogism are there?

There are 64 possible combinations of moods of the syllogism:

| Major premise | × | Minor premise | × | Conclusion |
|---|---|---|---|---|
| (A, E, I, O) | | (A, E, I, O) | | (A, E, I, O) |

that is, three combinations of four choices. In other words:

$$4 \quad \times 4 \quad \times 4 = 64$$

In accounting for the different figures of the syllogism, we must now multiply the 64 by 4 to arrive at a total of 256. However, as Johnson-Laird has pointed out, if we now swap the major and minor premises we arrive at a total of 512.

---

**syllogism**  An argument structure that comprises two premises and a conclusion.

**categorical term**  The basic unit of meaning in a syllogism.

**categorical proposition**  A statement that declares a relation between the classes designated by two categorical terms.

**inclusive (or positive) assertion**  In a categorical proposition where members of a subject class are included in the predicate class. For example, 'Some of Amy's nights out are memorable'.

**exclusive (or negative) assertion**  In a categorical proposition where members of a subject class are excluded in the predicate class. For example, 'Some of Amy's tattoos are not lady-like'.

**major premise**  The first premise in a syllogism.

**minor premise**  The second premise in a syllogism.

## Psychological aspects of syllogistic reasoning

Now the basic terms and concepts are in place, we can (thankfully) return to cognitive psychology. What we have just concluded is that even though, on first blush, a syllogism is quite straightforward to define, on further inspection, this simplicity is misleading. For instance, given the large array of syllogistic forms, it is now possible to ask whether they are all equally easy (okay, difficult) to solve. The unsurprising finding (of course) is that performance is not the same across all syllogisms. Indeed, a now classic effect is known as the **figural effect**, and this was first examined, in detail, by Johnson-Laird and Steedman (1978).

In their first experiment, Johnson-Laird and Steedman (1978) generated pairs of premises with a conclusion missing. For example:

Some of the musicians are inventors
All of the inventors are professors

-------------------------------------

???

On each trial a participant was given such a pair and simply asked to generate what they thought a logical conclusion was. Twenty participants were tested. The most interesting finding was that participants consistently gave particular conclusions depending on the figure of the syllogism. In summary, a central pattern of performance was as follows (the text in parentheses provides the number of participants who generated the respective conclusion):

**Example 1**

Some A are B
All B are C

---------------

| | | |
|---|---|---|
| Conclusion 1 | Some A are C | (15 participants) |
| Conclusion 2 | Some C are A | (2 participants) |

**Example 2**

All B are A
Some C are B

---------------

| | | |
|---|---|---|
| Conclusion 1 | Some A are C | (16 participants) |
| Conclusion 2 | Some C are A | (1 participant) |

In both examples both conclusions are equally valid, but there is an overall bias to generate a conclusion that preserves the order of mention of the terms in the problem – this is the figural effect.

## The figural effect and mental models

As you read more and more about deductive reasoning you will soon realise that there is a variety of different accounts of the underlying putative processes. One particularly influential account was put forward by Johnson-Laird and Steedman (1978). They began by discussing something called *analogy theory* but this was eventually superseded by the **mental models account** (Johnson-Laird, 1980, 1983, 2001).

One particularly attractive aspect of the mental models account of reasoning is that it acknowledges close synergies between perception, imagination and thinking. Such an acknowledgement has been repeatedly emphasised at various points throughout this book. The central idea is that in thinking about the world, a person, in a sense, constructs an inner model of it and then operates on this model to derive predictions and conclusions about states of the world. (Remember the flat pack furniture from Chapter 7.) In an alternative form of words, the notion of operating on a mental model is known as **mental simulation**. (Again, remember our discussion of mental rotation – there mental simulation of a physical act was cast in terms of mental rotation.) These basic ideas are usually attributed to Craik (1943).

One important claim is that the mental model is an analogical representation (see Chapter 7) that captures parts and relations that exist in the represented world with analogical parts and relations. So for instance, to represent:

The cat is above the ape.
The dog is below the ape.

a model would be constructed in which tokens for cat, dog and ape would be arrayed accordingly:

Cat
Ape
Dog

In this representing world, the vertical dimension in the model stands for the vertical dimension in the represented world. Hence the representation is analogical in nature. In building a mental model, the basic idea is that mental tokens for particular individuals are generated and are represented within a kind of mental workspace. Although the account seems best placed to examine reasoning about the dispositions of objects in the real world (see Johnson-Laird & Byrne, 1991, ch. 5), the basic formalism has been discussed in terms of more general reasoning capacities. For instance, the basic mental models account can explain how participants deal with syllogisms. Examples are provided in our 'For example . . .' boxes below.

In brief, according to the theory, when participants are confronted with attempting to reason syllogistically, they incrementally construct mental models that abide by the constraints contained in the problems. So the ease or difficulty associated with the different sorts of syllogisms is indicative of the number and complexity of the models that are generated. As Rips (1986) stated, 'the larger the number of models that you must consider, the greater the demand on memory'. Given that working memory is limited in capacity and that in certain cases several models must be kept in mind, then it is most likely that you will overlook one or more of these models which produces an inappropriate conclusion (paraphrasing p. 277, op. cit.). The evidence is such that it provides some support for these ideas (see Johnson-Laird & Byrne, 2002, for a recent review). → See 'What have we learnt?', page 593.

### Pinpoint question 15.9

**According to Johnson-Laird and Steedman (1978), which conclusion is most likely from the premises:** *Some academics are failed musicians, All failed musicians are failed writers.* **Is it 'Some academics are failed writers' or 'Some failed writers are academics'?**

## → What have we learnt?

Recently Johnson-Laird (2004) has provided a useful checklist of the principles that underlie the mental models framework for thinking. Some of these principles are repeated here (paraphrasing Johnson-Laird, 2004, p. 200):

1. Each mental model represents a possibility. 'A conclusion is necessary if it holds in all of the models of the premises, probable if it holds in most of the equi-possible models, and possible if it holds in at least one model.'

2. Mental models represent what is true and not what is false. The claim here is that, in operating in this way, few demands are placed on working memory. A downside is that this may lead to systematic errors in reasoning.

3. Reasoners develop different strategies using inferential tactics based on mental models. These strategies may well depart from the tenets of the standard picture.

4. Individuals check the consistency of a set of assertions by searching for a single model in which all the assertions are true. If the initial model turns out not to be working – is inconsistent with an assumption – then further mental work is needed and a new model needs to be considered.

5. A mismatch principle can be seen to be at work when an inconsistency occurs between clear evidence and a set of propositions. Under such circumstances they tend to reject the proposition represented by mental models that conflict with the evidence.

## For example . . .

## The mental models account of reasoning syllogistically

Consider these premises (taken from Johnson-Laird, 1980):

| Major premise | All of the singers are professors |
| Minor premise | All of the poets are professors |

On reading the first premise the claim is that the following mental model is created in the human representational system. A sample of mental tokens is set up for the two categorical terms. One sample of tokens for *singers* and a different sample of mental tokens for *professors* are set up. These tokens are arranged accordingly:

```
singer = professor
singer = professor
singer = professor
        (professor)
        (professor)
        (professor)
```

What is assumed is that there is some kind of mental workspace (a blackboard?) within which an

internal model of the world is constructed. As with any representational system there are both primitives (the tokens and other symbols, e.g., the equals sign and the parentheses) and rules of combination of these primitives. Here the equals sign signifies identity and the parentheses indicate individuals that may or may not exist. In the current example the mental model allows for the fact that there may well be professors who are not singers.

Having constructed a model for the major premise, we now need to work on this model so as to incorporate the new information provided by the minor premise. Alternatively the idea is to generate a number of different models, each of which is consistent with the premises. For instance:

```
Minor premise    All of the poets are professors

singer = professor   = poet
singer = professor   = poet
singer = professor   = poet
        (professor)
        (professor)
        (professor)
```

In generating a model in this way, although the information is consistent with the premises, it may lead to mistakes in reasoning. For instance, a participant might conclude incorrectly that *All the singers are poets* or that *All the poets are singers*. To avoid such mistakes, a different model may be constructed. For instance:

singer = professor   = poet
singer = professor   = poet
singer = professor
        (professor) = poet
        (professor)
        (professor)

This model, however, may also lead to the invalid conclusions, *Some of the singers are poets*, or its converse, *Some of the poets are singers*. A final alternative may therefore be considered:

singer = professor
singer = professor
singer = professor
        (professor) = poet
        (professor) = poet
        (professor) = poet

All three of these models are consistent with the premises. Importantly, though, because the models give contradictory hints about the relations between singers and poets, participants ought to conclude that no valid conclusions can be drawn. The fact that different models can be constructed that fit with the premises provides some insights into why participants draw the types of erroneous conclusions that they do (see Johnson-Laird, 1980, and Johnson-Laird & Steedman, 1978, for more on this). In this regard, the mental models account is important, not least because it provides some insights into why people do not reason like logic machines.

## For example . . .
## Mental models and the figural effect

According to the mental models account of reasoning, as people process the information in the premises, they construct models that represent this information. Consider the following two premises:

Major premise    Some of the A are B
Minor premise    All of the B are C

-----------------------------

### Model 1: This model represents the information in the major premise

A  = B
A  = B
(A)   (B)

Again the (A) and (B) provide for cases in which other As and Bs exist but as yet we are uncertain as to how or if at all they are related.

### Model 2: This model represents the information in the major premise

A  = C
A  = C
(A)   (C)

What has happened here is, because the quantifier *All* occurs in *All of the B are C*, all of the tokens for B can be replaced with tokens for C. In this way the most natural conclusion, consistent with the model, is *Some of the A are C*. Hence the figural effect is explained.

A similar argument can be made for the bias to conclude *Some of the C are A* when presented with the following:

Major premise    Some of the B are A
Minor premise    All of the B are C

-----------------------------

## Looking at the evidence: eye movements and syllogistic reasoning

As we mentioned in the conclusion of the previous chapter, an interesting development is the use of new technology such as eye tracking to address old questions regarding language comprehension or, indeed, syllogistic reasoning. Espino, Santamaria, Meseguer and Carreiras (2005) recorded eye movements in an attempt to distinguish exactly why some syllogisms are harder to understand than others and, in doing so, provide support for one kind of model over another. In the case of syllogism difficulty, both Johnson-Laird (1980) and Oaksford and Chater (1994) posit differences between simple and complex problems but for different reasons. In the case of the mental models theory (Johnson-Laird, 1980) the harder syllogisms will be those that produce the greater number of mental models. Comparing a figure 1 with a figure 4 syllogism, the composite model should be easier to build for a figure 4 syllogism since the predicate of the first premise and the subject of the second premise are identical. This is in contrast to the information gain model (Oaksford & Chater, 1994; see also Chater & Oaksford, 1999) that predicts that the hard syllogisms will be those with the uninformative conclusions. In this respect, the influence of figure should have a late effect on processing since difficulty is defined relative to the conclusion and not the premises. This is in contrast to the mental models theory which predicts an earlier effect of figure.

Thirty-two participants completed the investigation in which all individuals were exposed to both simple and complex syllogistic problems, in the form of both a first or fourth figure. This led to the following premises:

|  | Figure 1 | Figure 4 |
| --- | --- | --- |
| Simple problem | All Italians are politicians All geographers are Italians | All politicians are Italian All Italians are geographers |
| Complex problem | All Italians are politicians No geographer is Italian | No geographer is Italian All Italians are politicians |

Participants were told to 'draw a conclusion that had to be true given that the premises were true' (Espino et al., 2005, p. B5) and while doing so, their eye movements over the syllogisms were recorded. The time of a first-pass reading (considered to reflect 'early effects'), total reading time (considered to reflect 'late effects') and percentage of correct conclusions were all noted for each of the four different categories of syllogism.

In terms of early effects, differences in first-pass reading were only observed for the second premise, in that participants were faster to read the second line of a figure 4 than a figure 1 structured syllogism. Focusing on total reading time for later effects, participants were significantly slower in reading the first premise and second premise of complex problems relative to simple problems, and they also took longer to read the second premise when it was embedded in a figure 1 problem relative to a figure 4 problem. As one would expect, more correct conclusions were generated for simple than complex problems and also for figure 4 problems than figure 1 problems.

Espino et al. (2005) conclude that, while all models predict that easier problems will be read quicker than harder problems, the data are most interesting in terms of revealing differences between the presentation of the syllogism and the use of various figures. As we 'saw' ourselves from the data, the effect of figure in the absence of an effect of complexity at first-pass reading suggests that syllogism difficulty is established on the basis of the nature of the premises rather than the conclusions, thereby supporting the mental models theory (Johnson-Laird, 1980). Therefore, simply looking at where we look can help to delineate between theories of reasoning in ways that behavioural data never could.

Source: Espino, O., Santamaria, C., Meseguer, E., & Carreiras, M. (2005). Early and late processes in syllogistic reasoning: Evidence from eye-movements. Cognition, 98, B1–B9.

## → What have we learnt?

There is much to like about the mental models approach despite the fact that it has been heavily attacked over the years (Broadbent, 1984; and see the particularly incisive review by Rips, 1986). The critical point is that in avoiding any discussion of the mental rules of logic, Johnson-Laird has put forward a whole different set of rules concerning the construction of mental models and the operations that are carried out on such models. More perplexing is that some of these rules may in fact be equivalent to standard rules of logic (see Rips, 1986). A different concern now is that, whereas the rules of logic are generally well understood, the rules of mental models are not (and they have changed somewhat over the years).

Nevertheless one of its strengths is that the theory does take very seriously the evidence (see Chapter 7) that mental problem solving is intimately connected with perception. The account deals with the idea that in some sense the mental representations that underpin reasoning reflect perceptual properties of possible states of the world. For example, in being told that *All the beekeepers are artists*, the claim is that a first step is to imagine, or more generally, simply construct a mental scenario that represents a corresponding state of the world. For instance, a number of individuals are imagined in such a way that each is identified as being both a beekeeper and an artist. Alternatively, imagine a room full of people and ask all beekeepers to raise their left hand and all the artists to raise their right hand. Consequently the imagined scene will contain a room in which there are some (perhaps all) of the people with both hands raised. It is these sorts of mental operations (of constructing an internal and analogical model of some state of the world) that are implicated by mental modellers.

A slight hesitancy here, though, is whether participants are conscious of particular visual images when they carry out such operations. There is no necessary implication of visual imagery here because all that is being argued is that the mind operates on an analogical model of some state of the world. Mental models are said to be *iconic* in that 'parts of the mental model correspond to the parts of what it represents, and so its structure corresponds to the structure of what it represents' (Johnson-Laird, 2004, p. 171). This particular conclusion has most strikingly been demonstrated recently by Knauff and Johnson-Laird (2002).

## Mental models and mental imagery

We bring the chapter to a close by considering one final experimental study by Knauff and Johnson-Laird (2002). The paper examined possible interplays between visual imagery and reasoning. Participants were initially asked to rate individual propositions of the following kind:

1. Visual:        The dog is cleaner than the cat
2. Control:       The dog is smarter than the cat
3. Visuo-spatial: The dog is in front of the cat

Participants were asked to judge each of the propositions on how easy it was to form a visual image of the content, and separately, how easy it was to form a spatial image of the content. While proposition (1) is visual in nature, it does not immediately suggest any spatial relationships between *dog* and *cat* whereas proposition (3) does. Perhaps not surprisingly, the visual propositions scored high for visual judgements and low on the spatial judgements. The control proposi-

tions scored low on both judgements, and the visuo-spatial propositions scored high on both judgements.

The litmus test now was to see how participants fared with such statements when embedded in problems of the following sort:

The dog is cleaner than the cat
The ape is dirtier than the cat
Does it follow:
The dog is cleaner than the ape?

Over several experiments it was shown that participants performed relatively badly with such inference problems when the problems comprised visual as opposed to visuo-spatial or control propositions. Participants were slower and less accurate in cases where visual propositions were used. There were also some indications that participants did best with problems framed with visuo-spatial propositions.

Overall these data were taken to support something dubbed the visual-imagery impedance hypothesis. This is the claim that 'Relations that elicit visual images containing details that are irrelevant to an inference should impede the process of reasoning' (Knauff & Johnson-Laird, 2002, p. 364). A corollary of this is that if the content contains information relevant to the inference then this may facilitate performance.

Rather unsurprisingly, Knauff and Johnson-Laird (2002) took the data to be perfectly consistent with a mental models account, although they failed to provide a very detailed explanation of the overall patterns of performance. Several other points are worthy of note before concluding. Primary among these is the claim that the data sit very uncomfortably with the idea that the reasoning in these cases reflects the operation of some form of mental logic (see Rips, 1994). As Knauff and Johnson-Laird (2002) noted, according to mental logic accounts all reasoning is carried out via abstract symbols and rules (sentences or their logical forms). Such constructs as these are stripped of any content or so-called 'extra baggage' (Shepard & Feng, 1972). If every proposition were couched in such abstractions then the account fails to explain the basic effects.

Moreover, the data sit poorly with the idea that reasoning is based upon visual imagery. People can reason about relations that they cannot visualise, hence something else must be implicated by the tasks. What the data show instead is that, when people reason they cannot help but operate with mechanisms that are primarily adapted to deal with concrete things. This conclusion accords very well with a number of demonstrations of the same point (see Simon, 1972; Shepard & Cooper, 1982). One example will suffice here (abridged from Simon, 1972, p. 195):

A 3 cm cube is painted blue on one side. Sides adjacent to the blue side but opposite from one another are painted red. The cube is now divided into smaller 1 cm cubes. How many 1 cm cubes have exactly one blue side and one red side?

Although this problem could be conceived in terms of a calculation problem, participants typically report that they solve this problem through a process of mental simulation. They mentally simulate the aspects of the physical processes involved in painting and cutting the cube. In addition, if now asked 'Which side did you paint blue?' the participant can immediately reply. The important point is that this information is completely irrelevant to solving the problem. It is as if participants cannot help but cast problems in concrete terms. A consequence of this is that reasoning may be

far from optimal, as Knauff and Johnson-Laird (2002) have more recently demonstrated.

**Pinpoint question 15.10**

**When do mental images help and when do they hinder reasoning performance?**

---

**figural effect** The bias in syllogistic reasoning that the information in the conclusion is likely to preserve the order of that information in the premises.

**mental models account** After Johnson-Laird (1980), the idea that an inner model is constructed and operated upon so as to draw conclusions about the state of the world.

**mental simulation** Operating upon a mental model so as to reason about the represented world.

## Concluding comments

As is probably very clear, there are many different schools of thought about thinking and reasoning. The present discussion has examined several of these in terms of various issues that recur in the literature. Primary among these are concerns about the system 1 (associative) vs. system 2 (rule-based) distinction and the associated dual process accounts, and concerns about the degree to which human reasoning is rational. What has emerged from the discussion is that it is probably best to frame arguments in terms of adaptive usefulness. Why might it be that certain mechanisms have developed? If human reasoning is seen to depart from the standard picture, what are the possible adaptive reasons as to why this is so? Consideration of these types of questions leads to an appreciation as to why theories of competence must be informed by considerations of actual performance. Humans have developed natural ways of thinking, and as we have seen, these do not always accord with ideas of mental logic and the standard picture of what is rational.

In reflecting on the material, a very important conclusion does emerge, and this is that humans are not logic machines. In fact, it seems that considered logical analyses do not come naturally to most of us. On the contrary, we reason best in concrete terms. A very clear example of this is provided by Feynman (1965/1992) in his discussion of the quantum theory of light. He explains the basic principles in terms of firing a machine gun at a metal plate with two holes in for the bullets to pass through! Aligned to this point is that we have concluded that our perceptions of the world fundamentally affect our ability to reason about the world. This is not to argue that we cannot be taught to use logic, nor that, for some, the *p*s and *q*s come very easy, but for most of us, this kind of abstract thinking is hard.

Nothing so far has been concluded about the validity of the dual system framework for thinking. The fact that your thinking is accompanied by your inner voice, and that you are typically capable of explaining to someone else why it is that you reasoned the way you did, provide a strong justification for a conscious component to problem solving. Indeed, see Ericsson and Simon (1984; after Newell & Simon, 1972) for a thorough examination of *protocol analysis* or how

the study of a person's verbal reports of engaging in a problem-solving task may be used as indicators of their reasoning processes. However, this cannot be the whole story. A moment's reflection reveals that much of what goes on when you try to figure things out is not available to conscious introspection. In this regard, the distinction between tacit and explicit knowledge is important. Many cognitive processes that support reasoning remain well hidden within the central black box.

The most fitting, and yet unforgiving, conclusion has been provided by Johnson-Laird (2004, p. 199): 'Reasoning matters. People who are good reasoners are likely to make progress in life. Those who are bad reasoners are likely to make a hash of things.' Cast in these terms, understanding reasoning may allow you to do a whole host of other things aside from being able to pass the exam at the end of the course!

## CHAPTER SUMMARY

- An initial distinction between associative and rule-based systems can be made when discussing human reasoning (Evans, 2003). Here, reasoning may be based on the product of inferences (as generated by an associative system) or logic (as generated by a rule-based system). One potential outcome of this dual process system is that individuals can hold a simultaneous contradictory belief (Sloman, 1996) and this is seen to be due to each system producing a different conclusion.

- Tversky and Kahneman (1983) identified a number of heuristics (or rules of thumb) used in reasoning. These are reflected in the conjunction fallacy, representativeness, availability and base rate neglect. The advantage of using heuristics is that they are quick and are generally reliable; however, the disadvantage is that they do not lead to the correct conclusion all of the time. Both novices and experts in particular domains employ heuristics, as demonstrated by the medical diagnosis problem (Casscells, Schoenberger & Graboys, 1978). The use of heuristics stands in contrast to the standard picture (Samuels, Stitch & Faucher, 2004), which assumes that human reasoning is determined by rational decision-making.

- One issue surrounding failures of logical reasoning and why people do not appear to be rational relates to the way in which the problem is framed. Cosmides and Tooby (1996) noted that individuals are more accurate in their estimates when the issue is presented in terms of natural frequencies (i.e., 8 out of 10 cats) rather than in probabilities or proportions (e.g., 0.8 of all cats).

- Bounded rationality refers to reasoning processes that take into account the limits of human performance. With this in mind, Gigerenzer, Czerlinski and Martignon (2002) identified a style of reasoning captured by so-called fast and frugal heuristics.

- Another important distinction in the reasoning literature is between deductive and inductive reasoning. Deductive reasoning refers to conclusions drawn from premises based on the rules of logic. Inductive reasoning refers to conclusions drawn by going beyond the information currently available. Attempts to distinguish between deductive and inductive reasoning have been made by Wason (1960) in the famous selection task. The task is based around conditional inference and the selection of valid and invalid arguments. Valid reasoning given an initial statement (if *p* then *q*) follows from affirming the antecedent (*p* therefore *q*; modus ponens) and denying the consequent (not-*q* therefore not-*p*; modus tollens). Invalid reasoning stems from affirming the consequent (*q* therefore *p*) or denying the antecedent (not-*p* therefore not-*q*).

- A critical manipulation is the nature of thematic content within the task (Evans, Newstead & Byrne, 1993). If the task is framed in a concrete rather than abstract way, then subjects are much better in identifying which cards need to be turned over in order to assess whether the stipulated rule is correct. A specific form of thematic content is known as a social contract (Cosmides, 1989) in which rules of social exchange are explored. Other variants of the task have been developed in which deontic (i.e., if $p$ then you must do $q$; an assertion of obligation) conditionals have been compared with indicative conditionals (i.e., if $p$ then $q$; an assertion of truth) (Manktelow & Over, 1991). A final aspect of the card-sorting literature is the proposal of the information gain model (Oaksford & Chater, 2003) in which performance in the task is accounted for by participants selecting those options that lead to the greatest amount of information gain in an attempt to reduce uncertainty.

- The extent to which humans can carry out deductive reasoning has also been explored with the use of syllogisms, in which a single conclusion is drawn from two premises. Johnson-Laird (1980) identified a total of 512 syllogisms available. One psychological phenomenon related to the use of syllogisms is known as the figural effect. This shows that individuals tend to reach different conclusions depending on the structure of the syllogism. Related to this, it has also been proposed that we build a mental model of the premises to assist in this process. However, Knauff and Johnson-Laird (2002) noted that mental imagery can both help and hinder the processing of syllogisms, depending on whether the visualised information is relevant to the task.

## ANSWERS TO PINPOINT QUESTIONS

15.1 Both rule-based and associative reasoning comprise the dual system theory.

15.2 Posterior odds are calculated as the prior odds multiplied by the likelihood ratio.

15.3 Failure to follow Bayes' theorem might be the result of not understanding the theorem itself, or not understanding the language in which such problems are couched.

15.4 Performance on conditional probability problems might be improved by describing them in terms of frequencies, thereby making the set/sub-set relations more apparent.

15.5 One object that fulfils the desired criteria is all the satisfiser needs.

15.6 Both framing the problem in familiar, concrete terms and describing the task in terms of a social contract can improve performance in the Wason selection task.

15.7 The information gain theory puts more value on rare events because they are typically more informative than are common events.

15.8 Subject term (Edward's examples), predicate (tough), quality (inclusive or positive) and quantity (particular affirmative).

15.9 'Some academics are failed writers' is the most likely conclusion as this is in accordance with the figural effect.

15.10 Visual imagery can help reasoning when the problem depends on thinking about problems that contain visual and spatial aspects. Visual imagery can also hinder reasoning when the visuo-spatial aspects of the problem are irrelevant to the solution.

## CHAPTER 16

# COGNITION AND EMOTION

## CHAPTER CONTENTS

# Master of your mood?

So, it's the final chapter and the end of the book and emotions are perhaps running a little high. Perhaps you're reading the last topic with some fear and loathing as this is the one you chose for your essay and there are only three weeks until the deadline and this is the first time you've even thought about emotion. Perhaps you're reading this with great joy, as your love for cognitive psychology has been exponentially increased as a result of this book, and you're sitting on a beach after finishing term and have decided to take us with you as your holiday reading. The normally distributed fact of the matter is that it's more likely you'll be somewhere among these extremes.

We hope that by the end of the chapter you'll also be 'master of your mood' in an alternative sense in that you'll be much more aware of the issues involved in recognising emotion in yourself and others as well as how mood might seep in-between the gaps in our little black boxes and influence our cognition in quite fundamental ways.

## REFLECTIVE QUESTIONS

1. Do you sometimes wake up in a bad mood? How do you think this influences how you behave throughout your day? Do you think you make better or worse decisions when you're feeling sad? How could you induce positive moods in individuals?

2. How can you tell what other people are feeling? Would a person who had just got a pay rise look the same as a person who had just got fired? If not, what kinds of difference exist between these two people? What kind of information do you look for? Which parts of the body do you consider the most expressive? Is this information always reliable?

## Introduction and preliminary considerations

Since the 1980s there has been gathering interest in the area of cognition and emotion. This is not to imply that there was no relevant research carried out prior to that time, but merely that there has been a noticeable growth in interest over the recent past. It is difficult to be clear as to why this has happened, but it must be partially due to the advances in computer technology.

It simply is the case that computer graphics have developed to a point where things that previously only existed in fertile imaginations are now commonplace in the world of personal computing. For instance, it is now possible to generate a sequence of photographic images of your favourite historical figure metamorphosing into their pet dog. You might well ask why anyone would want to do that sort of thing, but aside from such flights of fancy, this technique of **morphing** has featured in recent research into the recognition of facial expressions of emotional states (see, for instance,

Hsu & Young, 2004). (Figure 16.1 provides a slightly more 'old school' approach to morphing in terms of representing changes in facial expression of emotion.) Put simply, some topics within the area of cognition and emotion could not take place (or perhaps, more exactly, would be exceedingly difficult to carry out) if it were not for the advances that have been made in computer technology. Examples that clarify this point will be considered shortly.

Another mundane reason as to why the topic of emotion has featured little in cognitive psychology is probably to do with the sorts of participants that typically feature in experimental studies. You will be hard-pressed to find an experiment in cognitive

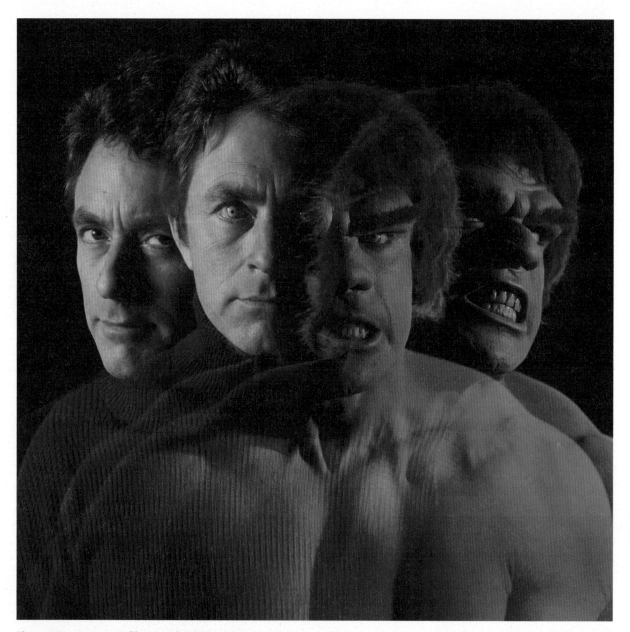

**Figure 16.1 You won't like me when I'm angry**
Although quite recent in terms of cognitive psychology, Bruce Banner (a.k.a. The Incredible Hulk) demonstrates that the idea of morphing emotional facial expressions has been around for some time.
*Source*: Kobal Collection Ltd/Universal TV.

psychology on 'normal, healthy' adults that is not based on research carried out on undergraduate students. Of course, children and the elderly feature in work in developmental psychology, and interesting case studies are prevalent in cognitive neuropsychology, but work in cognitive psychology is primarily based on experiments with undergraduate students. In contrast, traditionally the topic of emotion has been carried out with clinical populations or, indeed, in clinical settings with clinical populations. In this regard, our current understanding of human emotion has grown against a backdrop of work of cases where emotions do not seem to be working properly. For instance, much of the early work in psychoanalysis was concerned with extreme forms of anxiety and neurotic behaviour (Freud, 1964/1973).

There are several basic issues here and we will focus on some of these before continuing. Part of the justification for some work on emotion is that if you really want to understand, say, anxiety, then why not study anxious people; if you want to study depression, then study depressives. The thing about undergraduate students, though, is that on the whole they are a pretty normal bunch of individuals. Much like any other normal (Gaussian) distribution that describes a sample of participants, the majority of individuals are of a normal disposition (they fall within the normal range), and although some of these individuals will be inordinately happy or inordinately sad, the majority of individuals won't be. So if you want access to consistently sad individuals, as a means to understand sadness, then chances are that these will be difficult to find within undergraduate samples. Such individuals will be there, but they will be relatively few in number. Cognitive psychologists, though, have attempted to work round such problems, and as we will see later, they have developed means to try to examine how mood states may affect cognitive processes in so-called 'normal, healthy' adults.

There is also a further detectible reluctance of traditional cognitive psychologists to engage with the topic of emotion. Why should this be? Well, part of the answer takes us right back to Chapters 1 and 2 in which we discussed the roots of the discipline and, in particular, the computational metaphor of mind. What traditional cognitive psychologists are most happiest with are causal accounts in which an explanation is couched in terms of some sort of mechanism or continuation of mechanisms. An over-simplified view of the mind is that, in the same way that there is a causal connection between the keys you press on the keyboard and the characters that appear on the screen,

there is a causal connection between the marks you see on the page and the sounds that you utter when you begin to read out loud. Within the confines of such a mechanistic account of the mind there appears to be no room for emotion to play a role. How could it be that the computer breaks the causal chain by presenting different characters on the screen simply because it is feeling happy or sad? To put this another way, a central problem is whereabouts in our arrows-and-boxes diagrams of the mind we should put the box called emotion.

In reply, one answer is that this is simply the wrong approach – it is simply inappropriate to think that there is such a thing as an 'emotional box'. A more promising approach is to think in terms of emotional states (or, as they are sometimes called, *affective states*), on the understanding that these somehow influence the operations that are carried out by the various boxes that form our cognitive model. It may be that we can make some headway by assuming that emotional states alter or influence the operations that take place when we process the information that the world provides. How might this be? Well, perhaps the clearest statement of such sentiments has been provided by Oatley and Johnson-Laird (1987) and it is to this theory of emotions that we now turn.

> **morphing** A computer technique which enables the production of a sequence of images across which small changes are introduced. The impression is created of the start image and the end image being joined by an apparently seamless set of indiscernible transformations.

## Towards a cognitive theory of emotions

The Oatley and Johnson-Laird (1987) theory is, essentially, based on the modularity of mind hypothesis. Although there probably are some basic disagreements with the strict Fodorian account (see Chapter 1), they adopted the view that the mind is composed of a set of modules or autonomous processors, each of which is self-contained and has an associated information processing goal (such as to generate a name code of a visually presented letter – see Chapter 3 and the discussion of the dual code account of iconic memory). They also assumed that such modules are organised hierarchically, but that there is some overarching controller, or operating system (much like the central executive as discussed in the working memory model – see Chapter 10). The controller co-ordinates the operations of the processing modules in such a way that sensible sequences of behaviour are generated. Just think of preparing a meal for a bunch of friends and the operations concerning shopping for the ingredients and preparing the meal. Reflect on how important it is to get the sequencing of these operations correct. Now think of the sort of scheduling that the mental controller must be continuously undertaking as it goes about its business of co-ordinating the mental modules!

In describing the nature of these control processes, Oatley and Johnson-Laird (1987) introduced the notion of **signal propagation** throughout the modular system. The controller sends out emotional signals that convey information about the emotional state of the person. Such signals act to 'set the whole system suddenly into a particular mode [known as an emotional mode] and to maintain it tonically in that mode' (p. 32). In effect, the signals selectively switch the processing modules on and off according to the emotional state of the person. For instance, given the imminent presence of a bear in the campsite, switch on the flight modules and switch off the fight modules.

## The 'five' basic emotions

In fleshing these ideas out, Oatley and Johnson-Laird discussed the view that there exist a small number of basic human emotions that constitute a universal set of emotions. The word 'universal' implies that they occur for everyone regardless of upbringing and culture. Following the work of Ekman, Friesen and Ellsworth (1982), Oatley and Johnson-Laird set out the assumption that there are five basic emotion modes, namely 'happiness, sadness, anxiety (or fear), anger, and disgust' (p. 33). You may well ask what happened to love and jealousy/envy (cf. Sabini & Silver, 2005) and Oatley and Johnson-Laird (1987) also considered the case for surprise/interest. In this regard, they argued that (at the time they were writing) the actual number of basic emotions was unresolved but, nevertheless, they concentrated on the five that are listed because the evidence for the universality of these was strongest.

In later work by Ekman (1999), the five basic emotions became 15, although, again, *interest* was left out because Ekman stated that it ought to be treated as a cognitive state rather than an emotion. To try to help adjudicate on these issues, Ekman (1999) provided a list of criteria (see Table 16.1) to help us try to decide

**Table 16.1 Basic emotions.** The table sets out those characteristics that distinguish basic emotions from one another and from other affective phenomena (from Ekman, 1999).

1. Distinctive universal signals
2. Distinctive physiology
3. Automatic appraisal, tuned to:
4. Distinctive universals in antecedent events
5. Distinctive appearance developmentally
6. Presence in other primates
7. Quick onset
8. Brief duration
9. Unbidden occurrence
10. Distinctive thoughts, memories, images
11. Distinctive subjective experience

*Source*: Ekman, P. (1999). Basic emotions. In T. Dalgleish & M. J. Powers (Eds.), *Handbook of cognition and emotion* (pp. 45–60, table 3.1). Chichester, England: Wiley. Reproduced with permission from John Wily & Sons Limited.

what is and what is not a basic emotion. For instance, one idea is that each basic emotion has a distinctive signal and here a prime example is that of facial expression. The claim is that a person's emotional state can be conveyed, and can be recognised, via their facial expression. Think about it – you would have a fair idea whether your friend had either just won the lottery or bitten into a rancid apple merely on the basis of observing their facial expression. Ekman went further and stated that each basic emotion has an associated and distinctive facial expression alongside other distinctive physiological markers: fear can induce freezing, for example (see Research focus 16.3 on page 631). Although the actual details are still to be worked out, the idea is that each basic emotion has its own distinctive and associated physiological state. We will address some of the other criteria as we proceed, but for now it is more important to continue with the theoretical consequences of these ideas as discussed by Oatley and Johnson-Laird (1987). Indeed, it is only fair to point out that Ekman's views about how best to define basic emotions have been critically appraised by Sabini and Silver (2005) and they did show that alternative schemata are possible.

## Emotional vs. non-emotional modes of the cognitive system

Having accepted the idea of a basic set of emotions, Oatley and Johnson-Laird (1987) distinguished emotional modes from non-emotional modes of the

## Research focus 16.1

### If you're happy and you know it, press a key: cultural differences in recognising basic emotions

Earlier, we hinted at the idea that basic emotions are universal, essentially independent of culture and upbringing. This being cognitive psychology, clearly a bold conjecture like that is not going to stay unchallenged for long. In particular, the concern of Shioiri, Someya, Helmeste and Tang (1999) was that if identifying problems in emotional recognition were to be used in helping investigate psychiatric patients, then a facial expression test set up as part of a test battery over in America should work as well on Japanese as on American participants.

One hundred and twenty-three Japanese and 271 American individuals were shown the Japanese and Caucasian facial expressions of emotion (JACFEE) set which was made up of 56 images, 8 containing expressions of anger, contempt, disgust, fear, happiness, sadness and surprise. Also of interest was the fact that for each of these collection of 8 images, 4 were Japanese faces and 4 were Caucasian faces. Participants were required to rate both the emotion displayed and the intensity of the emotion for each picture, in a bid to see whether Japanese and Americans differed in their assessment of basic facial emotions.

Shioiri et al. (1999) found that Japanese individuals were particularly poor at judging negative facial emotions such as anger, contempt and fear. Moreover, this inability to recognise emotions did not seem to be related to rating the intensity of the image as being weak. For example, if an individual is only weakly exhibiting a barely audible murmur, we might not know whether they are laughing or crying. More intense versions of sadness and happiness, such as bawling one's eyes out and wide-mouthed cackling, respectively, are much less ambiguous. However, this did not seem to be an adequate account of performance for the Japanese participants since they performed as well as Americans in judging positive emotions such as happiness.

So how might we account for these differences in recognising negative emotions? Shioiri et al. (1999) discuss cultural differences between the US and Japan as one possible explanation. In (very) broad strokes, it is said that Japan is a culture that discourages the outward expression of emotion, particularly emotion that is negative. In contrast, the US is well known for supporting the externalisation of feeling, to which anyone who has ever seen the Jerry Springer show will attest. Therefore, it is possible that reduced exposure to negative emotions limits the ability to spot them. It is even possible that there is 'an unconscious denial when a Japanese person is confronted with a face that is expressing negative emotion' (p. 630) such that they will fail to recognise it. We wonder: where do you think your country fits on this scale?

*Source*: Shioiri, T., Someya, T., Helmeste, D., & Tang, S. W. (1999). Cultural differences in recognition of facial emotional expression: Contrast between Japanese and American raters. *Psychiatry and Clinical Neuroscience, 53*, 629–33.

cognitive system. One such non-emotional mode is the conscious construction of a plan; another is free association or day-dreaming. However, it is difficult to get a firm grip on this distinction because it is easy to think of plans that clearly do invoke emotions (such as revenge) and day-dreams that are highly emotional (think about that first date). Nevertheless the distinction between emotional and non-emotional modes of the cognitive system is otherwise useful because clearly there are cases where we do things in a non-emotional way (such as painting a window frame) and there are other cases where we are consumed by our emotions (such as phoning the ex despite the fact that everyone else thinks that you should just let it go). In the theory, however, plans are typically constructed consciously in a non-emotional mode, and emotions are seen to operate as the plan unfolds.

For Oatley and Johnson-Laird (1987), the basic idea is that the system can only be in one emotional mode at once and aligned to this is the idea that the different emotional modes mutually inhibit one another. If you are happy, you cannot be concurrently sad, and vice versa. You cannot be happy and sad at the same time, but the theory allows for those occasions where you oscillate between being happy and sad. Sometimes the reminiscences during a funeral may bring about a happy frame of mind. However, most particularly, Oatley and Johnson-Laird (1987) asserted that emotions have 'evolved as a primitive means of co-ordinating a modular nervous system' (p. 35). So when the controller sends out an emotional signal, this acts to interrupt the concurrently ongoing plan of action.

Indeed, in attributing functions to emotions, the basic idea is that plans of action can be broken down into various sub-plans with their various sub-goals. Transitions between these sub-plans are referred to as *junctures* and it is at these junctures that emotions come into play. The basic idea is that the 'cognitive system adopts an emotion mode at a significant juncture in a plan' (p. 35). Essentially, in moving through a set of planned stages, emotions operate at the transitions between the stages such that the current plan is appraised and can be changed according to a person's emotional frame of mind.

Let's assume that you are cooking a meal for a bunch of friends (again) – the recipe you are following sets out the sequence of stages that you need to go through to prepare the food – (i) first peel the potatoes, then (ii) slice them into smaller pieces, then (iii) place them in a pan of water, then (iv) bring them to the boil. This caricature of the plan of cooking potatoes has been broken down into four sub-plans. Moving between the sub-plans lays bare the junctures in the plan. Let us now assume that when you switch on the cooker the lights in the kitchen fuse, and smoke and then flames begin to emerge out of the ceiling rose. It is highly likely that this could arouse feelings of anxiety. According to the theory, when you see the smoke and flames, the controller will issue an emotional signal that acts to interrupt the cooking-the-potatoes plan and induce an anxiety mode in which you reach for the phone and ring for the fire service. The general idea is that a consequence of adopting a particular emotional state results in the disruption of ongoing cognitive processes 'in order to promote basic biosocial goals' (Öhman, 1999, p. 345). Okay, you were making a meal but now you are looking for the nearest exit.

In elaborating these ideas Oatley and Johnson-Laird (1987) gave some specific examples:

1. A happy frame of mind is consistent with the state of affairs where all current sub-goals are being achieved so, as a consequence, continue.

2. A sad frame of mind is consistent with the state of affairs where the current plan has failed to achieve its sub-goal so, as a consequence, do nothing or devise a new plan.

3. An anxious frame of mind is consistent with the state of affairs where self-preservation is threatened so, as a consequence, stop, concentrate and/or attempt to escape.

4. An angry frame of mind is consistent with the state of affairs where the current plan is frustrated so, as a consequence, try harder or aggress.

5. A disgusted frame of mind is consistent with the state of affairs where a gustatory goal is violated so as a consequence, reject substance and/or withdraw (paraphrasing tab. 1, Oatley & Johnson-Laird, 1987).

Aligned to this is the idea that emotions relate to our basic biosocial needs. They operate so as to control the operations of an internal modular processing system by forcing these into one of a small number of characteristic modes of processing. For example, the controller issues the following emotional signal to the processing modules: 'Okay everybody, we are now in a happy frame of mind so act accordingly'. In addition, it is asserted that emotions are fundamental to our social interactions with others. Our emotional state is intimately defined in terms of our relations with others. As anyone with good friends and family will attest, happiness can be brought about through successful interactions with others. In this regard, a person's emotional states are, in part, assessed in terms of the success or failure of the social plans that are entertained between that person and others. ➔ See 'What have we learnt?', page 607.

## Pinpoint question 16.1

**According to Oatley and Johnson-Laird (1987), when are emotional modes thought to come more into play: during the construction of a plan or when it is being carried out?**

→ **What have we learnt?**

It would be disingenuous to state that the Oatley and Johnson-Laird (1987) model is the only model that has attempted to integrate ideas about emotions with ideas about human information processing (see Buck, 1986a, for a review of alternative accounts). However, it demonstrates very nicely how emotional states may affect cognitive processes – ultimately the idea is that our emotions play a critical role in controlling the execution of planned behaviours. It is not so much that our emotions critically alter how a particular cognitive operation is carried out, rather the claim is that emotional states determine which cognitive operations will take place when. The basic ideas have been fleshed out in terms of how it is that our emotions influence the scheduling of planned behaviour. In this regard, there is no sense in which our functional accounts of the mind need incorporate an 'emotional box' in an arrows-and-boxes account; the alternative is that there is some executive controller that propagates emotional signals throughout such a system and these determine which operations are carried out and in what order.

Being slightly more negative, it is perhaps also worth asking, what is the utility of the Oatley and Johnson-Laird model? In reviewing the work it has proved difficult to find any reference to any empirical work that has been based on the model. This must be because it fails to provide any unique predictions. The model is very much a descriptive piece of work, and although it all seems very sensible, it provides no critical empirical predictions. Here again, therefore, we have an opportunity to return to some of the earliest material contained in the book, when we discussed the nature of scientific theories (see Chapter 1). Unless the theory provides a testable set of predictions that allows for the theory to be falsified, then it has little utility. This is perhaps the main reason that Oatley and Johnson-Laird (1987) framed their ideas as constituting a model rather than a theory. The ideas provide a rather general framework for thinking about how it is that emotions may affect cognitive processes, and as we have noted, it provides a useful example of how it is that emotional states may, in some sense, guide the execution of planned behaviours. What is currently lacking, though, are any testable empirical predictions.

**signal propagation** According to Oatley and Johnson-Laird (1987), the transmission of information across the whole of the cognitive system.

## Conscious versus unconscious processing

In a later consideration of the theory, Öhman (1999) stated that, according to Oatley and Johnson-Laird (1987), emotions 'are related to basic biosocial needs and they do not depend on conscious appraisal for their elicitation . . . they are sometime elicited after merely an automatic, unconscious analysis of the situation' (p. 346). From Table 16.2, as provided by Öhman (1999), it can be seen that 'automatic appraisal' is listed as one of Ekman's characteristics that define basic emotions. However, there are many vexed issues here. Primarily there is the claim that, fundamentally, our emotions are beyond our control – they come upon us irrespective of how else it is that we are

currently disposed. It seems that the argument is that, whenever an individual is confronted by a particular emotional scenario, then that individual will experience the relevant emotion, despite their best intentions otherwise. Buck (1986b) has even gone so far as to state that 'we feel *before* we know, and in an important sense, feeling *determines what we know*' (p. 363).

There is a more useful way to think about what Öhman (1999) was intimating, and this has been discussed by Öhman and Mineka (2001). For them, the paradigm case is of experiencing fear. When confronted by a fearful scenario, 'behavior is likely to be elicited whether we want it or not and whether the stimulus has been represented in consciousness. Evolutionary fear-relevant stimuli therefore show characteristics of preconscious automaticity (i.e., they may trigger responses in the absence of any conscious awareness of the stimulus event . . . )' (p. 485). As Öhman has stated (1999, p. 334), 'a particular feeling could result from the unconscious appraisal of a stimulus as emotionally significant . . .'. So the claim is that our emotional states may be elicited after some form of unconscious appraisal of the current

**Table 16.2** Characteristics of automatic and controlled processing (from Öhman, 1999).

| Characteristic | Automatic processing | Controlled processing |
| --- | --- | --- |
| Cognitive resources | Independent | Heavily dependent |
| Intentional control | Incomplete | Complete |
| Attention | Not required, may be called | Required |
| Effort | Little, if any | Much |
| Serial-parallel dependence | Parallel | Serial |
| Awareness | Little, if any | High |
| Indivisibility | Wholistic | Fragmentised |
| Performance level | High | Low, except for simple tasks |
| Practice | Gradual improvement | Little effect |
| Modification | Difficult | Easy |

*Source*: Öhman, A. (1999). Distinguishing unconscious from conscious emotional processes: Methodological considerations and theoretical implication. In T. Dalgleish & M. J. Powers (Eds.), *Handbook of cognition and emotion* (p. 326, table 17.1). Chichester, England: Wiley. Reproduced with permission from John Wily & Sons Limited.

environment. So we may feel fear without any clear understanding of why.

Such ideas do, however, stand in contrast to the sorts of claims that have been made about how the unconscious may be operating in those instances of perceptual defence (see Chapter 4). In the perceptual defence literature, the basic idea was that the unconscious operates so as to protect the conscious processor from panicking in the face of imminent threat. Here, though, the idea is that the unconscious actually operates so as to generate early warning signals of possible threats so that the conscious processor can begin to deal with these quickly and effectively. We will consider such ideas in more detail as we proceed.

## Automatic vs. controlled processes

Central to such sentiments is a distinction between so-called **automatic** and **controlled processes**. Such a distinction has a very long history in attentional research (see Styles, 2006, ch. 7), but it is unfortunately the case that there is no generally accepted view as to how best to define this distinction. From our previous discussion of attention, an important contrast was drawn between *early processes* that operate in a parallel fashion without any mutual interference (see Chapters 8 and 9) and *central processes* that are capacity limited and can, essentially, only deal with one thing at once. For some theorists (e.g., Treisman & Gelade, 1980), the early vs. central distinction mirrors the automatic vs. controlled distinction.

However, we can go further because Table 16.2 captures several key factors that have been used to flesh out the distinction. Even though such a list provides a

useful crib sheet, the devil is in the detail. Reynolds and Besner (2006) have recently pointed out that, if we assume that there are 11 such factors that can be attributed to mental processes, then there are 2,047 possible definitions of the term 'automatic'! It is because of this vast space of possibilities that there remains debate over how best to define the difference between automatic and controlled processes. Nevertheless, without discussing all of the listed factors in any depth, it is generally accepted that whereas automatic processes operate at an unconscious level, controlled processes operate at the conscious level. In the current context, the key assumption is that the basic emotions may be elicited automatically, prior to a conscious appraisal of a given scene. Such sentiments have been most clearly articulated with respect to the elicitation of fear (Öhman & Mineka, 2001).

### The automatic detection of threat

A central point is that, fundamentally, a person must be able to recognise threatening situations quickly. Threatening situations are likely to invoke fear, and for Öhman and Mineka (2001) a consequence of our evolutionary history is that a **fear system** or 'an evolved module for the elicitation of fear and fear learning' (p. 483) has developed. It is this fear system that incorporates defence mechanisms (and emotional reactions) for dealing with threatening situations. As Öhman has bluntly stated (1999, p. 338), 'Predators strike hard and fast, and therefore time has always been a primary consideration of the fear system. The faster it can be activated the better the odds of escaping the predator.' In line with this view is that such activation of the fear system should happen quickly and automatically.

The underlying assumption here is that threat must be detected quickly, hence the putative threat detection system must operate quickly and automatically – it simply cannot wait around until everything in the current environmental snapshot has been exhaustively identified. As we noted before, if you're about to be hit by a speeding car then you need to know about it pretty quickly so you could actually do something about it. There has to be some kind of unconscious processing of the scene that rapidly (automatically) detects threat (cf. Ekman, 1977). This unconscious system operates as an early warning system which alerts the conscious processes so that these can be brought to bear on the threat-provoking entity. The person must now concentrate all their resources on dealing with the threat. A simple prediction of this sort of claim is that threatening objects should be detected rapidly in cluttered visual scenes. It is this kind of prediction that has been examined in a variety of visual search experiments.

## Searching for emotionally charged stimuli

There are many variants on the basic visual search paradigm (see Wolfe, 1994, for a comprehensive review). A classic example is where, on a given trial, a participant is told to look for a target stimulus of a particular type in a **search display** containing one possible target or several possible targets. Participants have to respond by pressing one key if they find the item (i.e., they make a 'present' response) and a different key if they are unable to find the item (i.e., they make an 'absent' response). The typical measures of interest are response time (RT) and/or response accuracy. If the experiment is an RT experiment then participants are asked to respond as quickly and as accurately as they can, and both measures are used to inform about contingent cognitive processes. However, if accuracy is the main measure of interest, then RTs are typically not of interest. Participants are merely told to respond as accurately as they can without regard to speed.

Although the possible manipulations are many and varied, it is typically the case that performance is assessed as the number of to-be-searched items (or more typically, *search elements*) contained in the search displays is varied across trials. Across trials the search displays contain different numbers of search elements. In the typical experiment displays of four different sizes are used. On some trials only one element is present whereas on others 5, 15 or 30 elements

are present (see, for example, Treisman & Gelade, 1980). This factor of display set size is usually referred to, in short-hand, as **display size**. In addition to display size, the factors of interest are with the type of target element, the kind of non-target elements, and the relations that exist between the target and non-target elements (see Duncan & Humphreys, 1989). Typically, the research has involved search for neutral things like coloured letters, but an interesting version of the traditional visual search task was carried out by Hansen and Hansen (1988) in which the search elements were images of faces.

## The face-in-the-crowd effect

In their search tasks the to-be-searched elements were black and white photographs of faces and each search display comprised a $3 \times 3$ matrix of faces of nine different individuals. (Here is a good example of where advances in computer technology have expedited research into emotion and cognition.) The basic task was a slightly different variant to the present/absent search task just described because, in this case, participants were instructed to press one key if all the faces wore the same expression (on a 'same' trial) and they were to press a different key if one of the faces (the discrepant face) wore a distinctive expression (on a 'different' trial). Search performance was examined as a function of the type of expression of the discrepant face and the type of expression of the rest of the crowd.

On 'same' trials the crowd wore an angry expression, a happy expression or a neutral expression. Discrepant faces, on 'different' trials, were themselves angry, happy or neutral. An angry target face could occur in a neutral or happy crowd; a happy target face could occur in an angry or neutral crowd and neutral target face could occur in a happy or angry crowd. The results of their first experiment were mixed. The data showed that angry faces were detected relatively quickly and accurately when presented in a neutral or happy crowd. Detection of a neutral face in an angry crowd was less efficient, as was detection of a happy face in an angry crowd. Happy faces were generally hard to find in both neutral and angry crowds. Surveying this pattern of results provides some evidence in favour of a particular face-in-the-crowd effect known as the **anger superiority effect**. The effect is consistent with the claim that it should be relatively easy to detect a discrepant angry face in an otherwise neutral or happy crowd on the grounds that we are particularly adept at detecting negatively emotionally charged facial expressions. The basic idea here is that it is important to be able to detect such so-called 'threatening facial expressions' efficiently because these act as a warning that 'aversive consequences are likely' (Öhman, Lundqvist & Esteves, 2001, p. 381). If any angry face is looking directly at you then it is possible that you could, imminently, become the victim of some form of attack.

However, further consideration of the results reported by Hansen and Hansen (1988) reveals that the data were perhaps not as clear-cut as they might have been. For instance, the results also showed that it was relatively easy to find a discrepant *neutral* face in a happy crowd. There was no obvious reason for this finding, and in a bid to examine some possibilities, Hansen and Hansen ran a second experiment (Experiment 2). Now instead of using crowds composed of pictures of different individuals, they used displays in which every picture was of the same individual. Now the 'crowd' wore the same expression and the discrepant photograph depicted a different individual. → See 'What have we learnt?', below.

## → What have we learnt?

Again, although it is possible to express concerns about how contrived and artificial much of experimental cognitive psychology is, there is a sense in which such complaints apply with some force to this particular line of research. It seems that the work on the detection of particular facial expressions has taken a rather dramatic change in direction from the outset – the work has become more divorced from the real world as time has progressed. In many other areas of cognitive psychology, experimenters have tried at the outset to simplify a given task in a bid to understand its fundamentals before they have attempted to examine full-blown real-world performance. For instance, if we only understood how it is that single letter features are picked up in visually presented words then we might be able to understand reading for pleasure (cf. Henderson, 1982). However, with the problem of facial expression detection, the research has gone in a quite different direction. Hansen and Hansen (1988) started, in their first experiment, with displays that bear some analogy with the situation of looking for someone distinctive in a crowd. The crowd comprises many different individuals but you are looking for a unique individual. By their second experiment, though, any such real-world analogy had been abandoned because now the displays were changed in a critical way.

Outside the cinematically contrived cases such as with *Being John Malkovich* (see Figure 16.2), there is no scenario in which the same individual's face is duplicated throughout the visual field. Despite this, Hansen and Hansen (1988) went on and used displays in which images of the same person recurred. Indeed, this sort of design step underlines a slightly disappointing aspect of this area of research. As time has progressed, the stimuli and tasks have continued to move further from reality. As we will see, photographic images have more or less been abandoned in favour of using schematic (cartoon) faces (though see Juth, Lundqvist, Karlsson & Öhman, 2005, for a recent return to the use of photographic images).

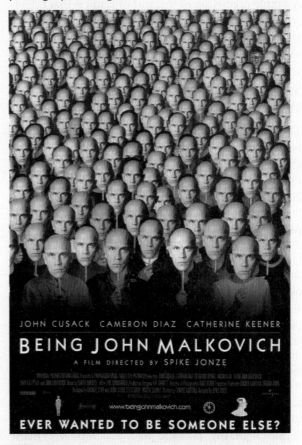

**Figure 16.2 Being a participant in a face-in-the-crowd experiment**
Outside cinematic flights of fancy, you are unlikely to ever have to search through a crowd of faces in which there is only one individual's face duplicated throughout the crowd.

*Source*: Alamy Images/Universal/Gramercy.

Hansen and Hansen (1988) now changed the task so that the constraints of the visual search task were altered from the same/different judgement used previously. Now each display (i.e., the crowd display) contained a discrepant face – either an angry face in a happy crowd or a happy face in an angry crowd – and the participant had to indicate *whereabouts* the discrepant face was in the display. On each trial a central fixation was replaced by four face stimuli, each of which was located in a different quadrant in the periphery. The crowd display was presented very briefly and was followed by a masking display (a standard backward masking procedure was used – see Chapter 3). Scrambled letters were presented at each face location after the offset of the crowd display. Over trials the duration of the crowd display was altered so that the same level of performance was attained across the different conditions. What the results showed was that overall participants needed less time to detect an angry face in a happy crowd than they did to detect a happy face in an angry crowd. In this respect the data are in line with the original idea that a discrepant angry face grabs attention.

## Pinpoint question 16.2

**What is the anger superiority effect?**

### Search as a function of display size

In a final experiment, the same/different procedure was revisited and the same sort of crowd displays as in Experiment 2 were used again. Now, however, display size was varied. Displays contained either four or nine to-be-searched elements. This manipulation in display size is central to theories of visual search that make predictions about the differences between automatic/parallel search processes and serial/controlled search processes (Wolfe, 1998). If the time to search for a target is unaffected by the number of to-be-searched elements in a display, then performance is taken to reflect a parallel search process. It is as if every display location is processed at once without interference. If it takes the same time to respond to the target present regardless of the number of display elements, then this is sometimes referred to as **target pop-out** (Treisman & Gormican, 1998). More particularly, target pop-out occurs when responses are generally quick (less than half a second) and RTs do not increase as display size increases (or rather, RTs do increase but only very slightly as display size increases). Target pop-out is

therefore taken to be a signature of automatic **parallel search**.

In contrast, it is also found that when target detection is more difficult, RTs do increase linearly as a function of display size such that a unit amount of time is added to the RT every time the display increases by one element. Such a pattern of performance is taken to reflect search operations in which each display element is scrutinised in turn. This kind of one-at-a-time process is known as **serial search** and is assumed to reflect controlled processes. Indeed, when a target element is hard to detect, performance reflects something known as **serial self-terminating search**. Scrutinise each element in turn and if the current element is a target, press the 'present' key. Continue searching and if all elements have been exhausted and a target has not been found, then press the 'absent' key.

The main measure that is taken to reflect the difference between parallel and serial search is the slope of the best-fitting straight line to the mean RTs plotted for each display set size. If the function resembles a flat line, then search is taken to be parallel. This corresponds to the case where responses are unaffected by the number of to-be-searched elements in the display. However, given that some increases in RT may occur, then slope values of less than 10 ms/element are accepted as being in line with parallel search processes and the notion of target pop-out (see Wolfe, 1998). In contrast, if the function relating RT to display set size is linear and the slope is noticeably greater than 10 ms/element then search is taken to be serial – the target does not pop out and search is taken to reflect some form of controlled process (see Figure 16.3 for illustrative examples). In this context, a value such as 10 ms/element indicates that it takes on average 10 ms to process each search element. Values of less than 10 ms indicate that the search process is astonishingly rapid and suggests that more than a single search element is being processed at once.

So, on the assumption that the detection of a threatening face reflects automatic processing, then, strictly speaking, RT ought not to depend on the size of the crowd. Angry faces should be detected fast and efficiently regardless of whether there are four or nine faces to search through. This is exactly what Hansen and Hansen (1988) found. In contrast, when participants were confronted with an angry crowd and the target was a happy face, the time to respond increased in line with display size. The more search elements there were, the longer it took to detect a happy face.
→ See 'What have we learnt?', page 613.

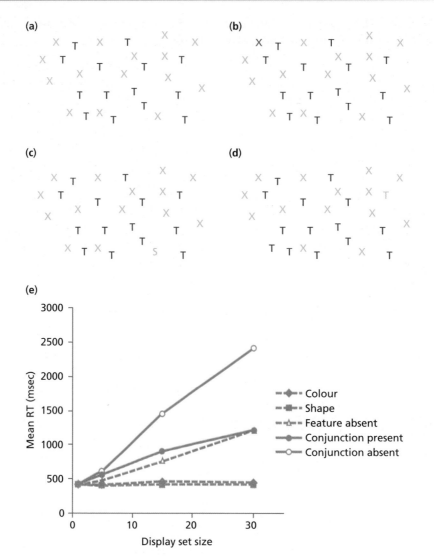

**Figure 16.3 A contrived visual search task and made-up data**
(a) shows a typical sort of visual search display in which the to-be-searched elements are coloured letters. In this case the display contains the non-target letters, green Xs and red Ts.
(b) and (c) show corresponding 'target present' cases. Here the task that participants are faced with is known as *feature search* and they have to respond 'present' if they register a distinctive colour (i.e., blue letter), as in (b), or a distinctive shape (i.e., an S), as in (c).
(d) shows a corresponding 'target present' case when participants undertake something known as conjunction search. In this cases participants must respond 'present' if they register a distinctive combination of the colour green and the shape T (i.e., a green T).
(e) shows illustrative data. Here mean RTs are plotted both as a function of display set size and of condition. As can be seen, with the 'feature present' responses (indicated as colour and shape, respectively) there is, essentially, no effect of display size on speed of response. Participants are equally as fast to respond when the display contains a single search element as when the display contains 30 search elements. For completeness, the data for 'feature absent' responses are also shown. In this case RTs do tend to increase as the display size increases.
Effects of display size are most apparent in the data from the conjunction search condition. For both present and absent responses RTs increase linearly as display size increases. There is a constant increment in RT as the display size increases by each new element. Moreover, for these cases when the slopes of the corresponding best-fitting straight lines are computed, the slope value for the absent responses is twice that of the slope for present responses. This pattern fits comfortably with the idea of a serial self-terminating search. Search each element in turn until you find a target. As soon as you find a target, respond 'present'; otherwise keep searching and when you have considered all elements and have not found a target, respond 'absent'.

### → What have we learnt?

Overall, therefore, the data across the three experiments reported by Hansen and Hansen (1988) provided mixed and thus slightly provocative support for the idea that threatening facial expressions automatically grab attention. Indeed, one concern about the final set of data they reported relates to the fact that different non-target faces were used across the two search conditions. Remember, the task was to press one key when the display contained a discrepant facial expression and a different key when all faces wore the same expression. However, the target displays contained either an angry face in a crowd of happy faces or a happy face in a crowd of angry faces. In the absence of further data we cannot ascertain the exact reasons for the advantage for detecting the angry face (i.e., the so-called **angry face advantage**). It could be because a discrepant angry face automatically grabs attention or it could be because happy faces are simply easier to search through. Alternatively, the relatively poor performance in detecting a discrepant happy face could be due to the fact that such faces fail to grab attention or it could be due to the fact that angry faces are much more difficult to search through.

### Pinpoint question 16.3

How is it possible in visual search experiments to evaluate whether participants are conducting serial or parallel search?

## Further work on the face-in-the-crowd effect

In a bid to try to untangle all of these factors, further studies have been carried out (see, for instance, Fox, Lester, Russo, Bowles, Pichler & Dutton, 2000; Öhman, Lundqvist & Esteves, 2001; Eastwood, Smilek & Merikle, 2001). However, in reviewing these studies a rather murky picture emerges. Purcell, Stewart and Skov (1996) were unable to replicate the basic angry face advantage in their search tasks. Moreover, they found that the original efficient detection of the angry faces reported by Hansen and Hansen (1988) may have been due to the presence of irrelevant but confounded visual features. Inadvertently there were 'extraneous dark areas' (dark patches) on the angry faces. Given such problems in trying to control for such incidental visual features, Fox et al. (2000) chose to run their experiments with the sorts of schematic face displays shown in Figure 16.4.

In their experiments a search display comprised four randomly positioned schematic faces and the participant's task was to make a same/different (or odd-one-out) response on every trial. The discrepant face target was either an angry or happy face. An angry face target occurred in a crowd of happy or neutral faces. A happy target occurred in a crowd of angry or neutral

**Figure 16.4 An example of the sort of display used by Fox et al. (2000, Experiment 1) in their experiments on facial expression detection**

*Source*: Fox, E., Lester, V., Russo, R., Bowles, R. J., Pichler, A., & Dutton, K. (2000). Facial expressions of emotion: Are angry faces detected more efficiently? *Cognition and Emotion, 14*, 61–92 (fig. 1, p. 66). Reproduced with permission from Taylor & Francis, Ltd.

faces. Such conditions replicated the original Hansen and Hansen (1988) experiment.

One very clear result was that the time to search through an angry crowd was slow relative to the time to search through happy or neutral crowds when the search display was presented very briefly (for 300 ms). However, when the display duration was increased (to 800 ms) then search through crowds expressing any emotion was slow relative to searching through a neutral crowd. An implication here is that it is relatively difficult to search through a set of angry faces even when these are displayed briefly. In this regard, there is something about angry expressions that disrupt the search process – Fox et al. (2000) stated that 'anger tends to hold visual attention' (p. 87). However, given the other effect of display duration, Fox et al. (2000) went on to argue that, more generally, it takes time to recover emotionally laden expressions. So although threat may be processed very quickly, the recovery of other emotional expressions takes further processing time.

In contrast, when performance on target present trials was examined, it was found that an angry face was detected rapidly among neutral faces regardless of the display duration. So here we have further support for the anger superiority effect. Angry faces were easily detectible when embedded in a crowd of non-emotional faces, and they were more noticeable than corresponding discrepant happy faces.

The evidence of whether angry faces pop out, however, is slightly mixed. When Fox et al. varied display set size and plotted RT as a function of display size (see Figure 16.3 for an explanation), they found an average slope value for present responses of 16 ms/search element when an angry/sad face was the target. They reported a value of 29 ms/search element when a happy face was the target. In these cases neutral faces defined the crowd. In very similar conditions Eastwood et al. (2001) reported values of 13 ms/search element and 20 ms/search element for the search functions for angry and happy targets, respectively. In this case, the crowd was defined by randomly positioned neutral faces and displays varied from 7 to 19 search elements. In all cases the slope values are greater than the critical 10 ms/search element rule of thumb for parallel search, and even though angry faces are easy to detect against a neutral crowd, this negative expression does not strictly pop out from the crowd. → See 'What have we learnt?', below.

## Expression detection or the pop-out of distinctive visual features?

A frown is a smile upside down.

*(Fats Waller)*

As a brief aside, it is also useful to comment on the various control search tasks that have been run alongside the facial expression search tasks (just as Purcell et al., 1996, wanted to check that dark patches on the angry faces were not the cause of the anger superiority effect). In fact, quite a lot of effort has been expended to try to see what exactly is *the* critical factor. For instance, a useful control has been where the face images have been inverted (see, for example, Eastwood et al., 2001). Here the aim has been to see whether the same pattern of differences that were originally attributed to the emotional valence of the faces occurred when the stimuli were inverted. The general point here is that when faces are inverted it is as if, at a psychological level, they are no longer treated in the same way as upright faces (see, for example, Yin, 1969). So if a face-in-the-crowd effect occurs when the stimuli are inverted it casts a shadow over the idea that emotionality must be driving the original effect. The reasoning goes along the following lines.

If inverted faces are really not treated as faces then the emotional valence of the facial expression cannot be recovered. So if the face-in-the-crowd effect still occurs with inverted faces this must be due to at least one distinctive visual feature that the discrepant face contains. For instance, an angry face contains a downward-curving mouth whereas a happy face contains an upward-curving mouth. An important result therefore in this regard is that Eastwood et al. (2001) *only* found the classic angry face superiority effect when the target faces were upright. This suggests that there is something more to the effect than merely distinguishing one sort of curve from another.

## → What have we learnt?

The evidence (such that it is) provides some support for the anger superiority effect, in that the detection of a threatening facial expression among a crowd can be accomplished rapidly. However, there are important caveats because the effect is apparently limited to cases where schematic faces are used and when the crowd wears a neutral expression (Eastwood et al., 2001; Fox et al., 2000; Öhman, Lundqvist & Esteves, 2001, Experiment 1). In this regard the empirical evidence provides very little in favour of the idea that threatening facial expressions capture attention automatically. There is an emerging consensus that although the detection of a threatening expression can be fast, there is insufficient evidence to conclude that such facial expressions pop out (Öhman, Lundqvist & Esteves, 2001).

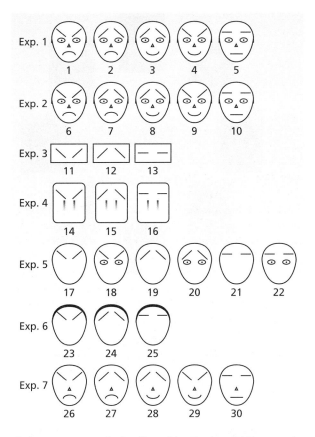

**Figure 16.5 Sorts of stimuli used by Tipples, Atkinson and Young (2002) in their series of experiments on what visual characteristics underlie the angry face advantage**

*Source*: Tipples, J., Atkinson, A. P., & Young, A. W. (2002). The eyebrow frown: A salient social signal. *Emotion*, *2*, 288–296 (fig. 1, p. 290). Reproduced with permission from APA.

A different thread in the literature involves studies that have focused on detection of the particular facial features themselves. The primary aim has been to try to ascertain which of these, or indeed which combination of these (Fox et al., 2000; Öhman, Lundqvist & Esteves, 2001; Schubö, Gendolla, Meinecke & Abele, 2006; Tipples, Atkinson & Young, 2002), are critical to the various face-in-the-crowd effects. Figure 16.5 taken from Tipples, Atkinson and Young (2002) provides just one sample of stimuli that have been used to address

this issue. Rather than attempt to discuss this literature in detail – the eyebrow configuration seems to be particularly important with a downward-pointing 'V' shape being particularly easy to detect (under certain situations; see Tipples, Atkinson and Young 2002) – it is perhaps more useful to make some general points.

One thing that is particularly notable is that this line of research is in danger of moving too far away from the original issues regarding threat detection. Remember, a basic question is: do threatening stimuli automatically grab attention? Instead, what we are beginning to learn about are the factors that make the detection of schematic images of faces and parts of faces either easy or difficult. It seems that basic issues concerning the detection of threat are in danger of getting lost in a morass of details regarding the conditions under which an upward- or downward-pointing 'V' is easy or difficult to find. Again, similar charges might be made against many others areas of cognitive psychology in which the research has become paradigm-driven rather than issue-driven. The danger is that performance in the experimental task becomes the object of interest and the basic theoretical issues are forgotten about. It would be a pity if this relatively new and important area of research degenerates in a similar fashion.

### A happiness superiority effect?

To return to the more interesting issues, the picture has recently been complicated by the data recently reported by Juth et al. (2005). They have documented what might otherwise be called a **happiness superiority effect**. Put simply, they have found that, despite all other evidence to the contrary, it is happy facial expressions that are easy to detect. Figure 16.6 provides examples of the search displays they used. Now what we have are displays containing eight colour photographic images of faces of different individuals. In this regard, there is something of a return to ecological validity. Moreover, the orientation of the head to the viewer is varied across the facial images. Critically each face can either be looking directly at the viewer or be looking away from the viewer.

## For example . . .

In a famous scene in the film *Taxi Driver*, Travis Bickle squares off with a source of potential threat by asking, 'Are you looking at me? Are you looking at ME?' Although clearly Travis was aware that threatening faces require particular attention when the individual is directing their threat at you, the problem was that he was looking at *himself* in a mirror when he said it.

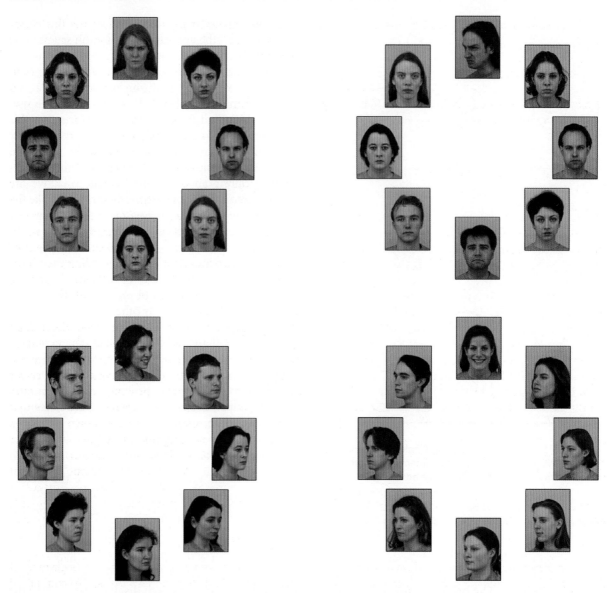

**Figure 16.6 Examples of the displays used by Juth et al. (2005) in their experiments on facial expression detection**

*Source*: Juth, P., Lundqvist, D., Karlsson, A., & Öhman, A. (2005). Looking for foes and friends: Perceptual and emotional factors when finding a face in the crowd. *Emotion*, *4*, 379–395 (fig. 1, p. 381). Reproduced with permission from APA.

Clearly this is an important factor because if a face in the crowd belongs to someone who is concentrating on you, then their face should be looking directly at you. Such a social cue is particularly important if the face in the crowd intends to do you imminent harm. In any case, the predictions in the Juth et al. (2005) study were relatively clear-cut because, if the anger superiority is robust, then it ought to be particularly evident when the angry face was looking directly at the participant. However, quite contrary to

this prediction Juth et al. (2005) found that it was the happy faces that stood out. Moreover, there was no evidence to support their prediction regarding threat enhancement when an angry face looked directly at the participant.

Given this contrasting pattern of effects – happiness superiority with real images of faces but anger superiority with schematic faces – it is probably best to simply concur with Juth et al. (2005) and agree that at present 'there are several aspects of visual search for emotional faces that are poorly understood' (p. 393).

**Pinpoint question 16.4**

Under what conditions in the Juth et al. (2005) study did the happiness superiority effect arise?

## Appraisal of the work on facial expression detection

In several places a rather critical stance has been taken over the work on facial expression detection. Part of the reason for this is that there is some evidence that the work is beginning to become fixated on particular experimental paradigms. The danger is that we are more likely to learn about performance in a particular laboratory task than we are to learn about how particular facial expressions may be detected and recognised. This is not to argue that no progress has been made, but merely that if the research continues in this vein then we may soon lose sight of the basic issues.

A related concern is with the rather contrived stimulus displays that have been used so far. A moment's reflection will reveal that a critical component of facial expression concerns change. Faces are dynamic entities and expressions are constantly changing. Indeed, it may be that what is critical to the detection of emotions is how the face changes. In really frightening scenarios it is the sudden change of expression that grabs attention, not the fact that one individual wears one distinctive and static expression among a crowd that wear a different but homogenous expression, like so many showroom dummies. Although this may be dismissed as being too negative a view, there is some empirical evidence that underlines the importance of the dynamic nature of faces and how critical this is to face recognition.

For example, Lander and Chuang (2005) have shown how it is that facial images may only become recognisable once the face is viewed in motion. For one experiment, videos were made of an individual facing a camera such that only the head was in view. The head was initially fully facing the lens and then the individual was instructed to (i) move their head slowly up and down – in the rigid case, (ii) continue to face the camera, hold a neutral expression and then smile – the smiling case, or (iii) start reciting the letters of the alphabet – in the talking case. In a final static case a still image of the individual's face with a neutral expression was selected. The images were then taken and filtered such that much of the fine detail was removed – they were blurry and all colour was removed.

The experiment was simplicity itself because each participant was tested individually and on each trial one static image or video clip was presented. The task was simply for the participant to provide any information about the viewed individual that they could. Critically the images were of members of staff within a university psychology department and the participants in the study were undergraduates of the same department. The point is that the individuals in the videos were assumed to be familiar to the participants (because, of course, all the participants turned up to all the lectures). However, as a check, at the end of testing, clear colour photographs of each filmed individual was shown to the participants and they were asked to rate how familiar they were with the photographed individual.

In analysing the data, the scores were divided up according to whether the filmed individuals were highly familiar to the participants or whether they were not so familiar, but the pattern of results was the same across this distinction. Generally speaking, recognition rates were low when either static images were shown or when the rigid motion videos were shown. However, recognition rates were significantly higher when either the smiling or talking videos were shown.

Although this work does not cement the point about the importance of using dynamic images in research on facial expression detection, it does provide a very strong hint that future work should seriously consider such options. Some fairly obvious experiments suggest themselves, and, given the advances in computer technology alluded to at the beginning of the chapter, such experiments could be configured and carried out.

## Other attentional tasks and facial expression processing

Aside from visual search, yet another classic task which has a long history in attentional research has come to be known as the **flanker task** (Eriksen & Eriksen, 1974). The task is simple enough. Participants merely have to make a speeded choice reaction time (CRT) response to a display containing three visually presented items (typically, letters) – a central target and two flanking items (or flankers). In the Eriksen & Eriksen (1974) experiments a central target letter was flanked on each side by three letters but a simpler variation on this kind of display is being considered here. Consider the

## Going for gold? What your face looks like when you come second

As we have already seen, one potentially big problem for the facial expression literature is that the data will tell us less and less about facial expression and more and more about the often bizarre practices of cognitive psychologists. Happily, in addition to data generated in the lab, data also continue to come in from 'the field'. In particular, Matsumoto and Willingham (2006) examined that most emotional of sporting events – the Olympics – and the spontaneous facial expressions of judo competitors as they won or lost a medal match.

In a sample that you don't see everyday, 84 judo competitors (representing 35 countries from six continents) had their photo taken at various points during the competition. This included the very second they knew that they had won a medal match to approximately 10–15 seconds after the final move in which the referee called the decision, during the receipt of their medal and during the delightfully titled 'podium posing'. Facial expressions were then coded according to a particular system known as the facial affect coding system (FACS; Ekman & Friesen, 1978), which served as a detailed account of exactly what emotions the competitors were displaying at these critical times in an athlete's career.

Matsumoto and Willingham (2006) reported a preponderance of *Duchenne* (or genuine) smiles in gold and bronze medallists. Here, a Duchenne smile stands in contrast to something that has historically been known (rather unkindly) as a *Pan American* smile, in which the former involves an upward movement of the lip corners and muscles around

the eyes and is thought to represent genuine happiness while the latter is thought to represent the kind of professional smile you get from air stewards and stewardesses (hence the term 'Pan American'). Interestingly, none of the silver medallists smiled and most expressed sadness. However, this seems preferable to the 14 per cent of silver medallists who displayed contempt! As the authors confirmed, 'the silver medallists indeed did not display flat, enjoyable emotions as much as either the gold or the bronze medallists' (p. 575). However, things changed slightly at the podium. Silver medallists started smiling, but these expressions were characterised as largely non-genuine smiles. Furthermore, the silver medallists stopped smiling as the national anthem of the gold medal winner was played.

While we have largely been focusing on negative facial emotion, it is also interesting to think about what evolutionary purpose the transmission of positive emotions serve (the happiness superiority effect, anyone?), which Matsumoto and Willingham (2006) saw as a potential avenue for future research. As a final thought, who would've guessed becoming an Olympic silver medallist would elicit so much negative emotion? From an emotional point of view then, it almost seems better to come third than second.

*Source*: Matsumoto, D., & Willingham, B. (2006). The thrill of victory and the agony of defeat: Spontaneous expressions of medal winners of the 2004 Athens Olympic Games. *Journal of Personality and Social Psychology, 91*, 568–581.

following contrived example. In running such an experiment two target letters (e.g., *A* and *B*) are assigned to one key press response and two other letters (e.g., *X* and *Y*) are assigned to the other key press response. Same displays all contain the same letter (e.g., *A A A*). With same displays all the letters point to or, alternatively, prime the same response. This is also true of *consistent displays* such as *B A B*. With consistent displays the target and flankers are different letters, but again they all prime the same response (both *A* and *B* are assigned to the same response key). In contrast, in *inconsistent displays* (such as *X A X*) the target and flankers are different and whereas the target *A* primes

one response, the flankers prime the alternative response.

Performances in such flanker tasks have been used to address several issues in attentional research, and it should come as no surprise that the central result is that responses on inconsistent trials are typically slower and less accurate than they are on consistent trials. This is the typical **flanker interference effect** and the poor performance on inconsistent trials has traditionally been interpreted as showing something known as *response competition*. The basic idea is that even though participants are told to focus on the target and (essentially) to ignore the flankers, the flankers do influence performance. This is the equivalent of somebody starting to vacuum while you're trying to watch a TV show with the words 'Just ignore me, pretend I'm not here'. We cannot help listen to the drone of the cleaner just as we cannot help process flanker information. It is as if information from both the target and the flankers reaches the stage of processing in which responses are selected for execution. In all cases – except on inconsistent trials – all three letters activate the same response. In contrast, on inconsistent trials, whereas the target letter activates one response, the flankers activate the alternative response. Given this, a state of response competition ensues because the system must now decide which of the two competing responses to emit. For an interesting discussion of the relevant psychological issues relevant to the flanker task, see the recent review by Latcher, Forster and Ruthruff (2004).

Although the inconsistency effect (i.e., poor performance on inconsistent trials) is assumed to arise at a response organisation stage of processing, it is assumed to be due to an inability to filter out information from the flankers – it is, essentially, an effect that reveals a failure of selective attention. Participants are unable selectively to process the central target and ignore the flankers. The most convincing evidence in favour of this particular view is that if the flankers are moved further away from the central target and into the periphery, the size of the inconsistency effect diminishes accordingly (Miller, 1991).

**Pinpoint question 16.5**

**'EDE' and 'FDF' might be consistent and inconsistent trials in a flanker task, respectively. How would we know?**

## The flanker task and emotional faces

Given the basic line of reasoning behind the flanker task, it is now possible to garner further converging evidence for the cognitive operations that are implicated in the detection of facial expressions. A good example here is the recent work by Fenske and Eastwood (2003). Illustrations of the sorts of displays used in their experiments are shown in Figure 16.7. The task was, on each trial, simply to classify the central target face as expressing either a negative or positive emotion.

The results were different according to whether the target expression was positive or negative. For negative responses there was no differential effect of flanker compatibility. That is, responses were as fast regardless

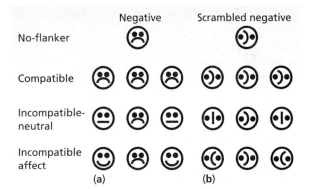

**Figure 16.7 Examples of the sorts of displays used by Fenske and Eastwood (2003) in their examination of the flanker effect driven by conflicting facial expressions**
(a) Shows examples of the schematic face displays and (b) shows examples of the corresponding non-face stimuli

*Source*: Fenske, M. J., & Eastwood, J. D. (2003). Modulation of focused attention by faces expressing emotion: Evidence from flanker tasks. *Emotion*, 3, 327–343 (fig. 1, p. 331). Reproduced with permission from APA.

of what expression was shown by the flanking faces when participants classified the target face as showing a negative emotion. In contrast, for positive responses there was an effect of flanker consistency. Responses were faster when the flankers wore a happy expression – that is, they were consistent with the target in contrast to when the flanking faces were either negative or neutral. Hostmann, Borgstedt and Heumann (2006) have more recently referred to this overall pattern as a **flanker asymmetry effect** – namely responses to a positive expression flanked by negative expressions suffer from more interference than do responses to a negative expression flanked by positive expressions.

Fenske and Eastwood (2003) took the lack of any consistency effects with the negative targets as evidence that a consequence of attending directly to a negative expression 'constricts' attention. Attentional resources are devoted to the negative expression and, as a consequence, the flanking faces are simply not processed – the central negative expression holds attention that might otherwise be diverted by the flanking faces. Here again, though, is a problem: whereas Fenske and Eastwood (2003) attributed their findings to the processes associated with the central target, an alternative view is that results reflect more to do with the processing of the flankers. Indeed Hostmann et al. (2006) replicated the basic effects reported by Fenske and Eastwood (2003) with more complex schematic faces but discussed the findings in terms of angry flanking faces attracting attention away from the happy central target face. Given that happy faces are assumed not to attract attention (though see Juth et al., 2005), then flanking happy faces will not interfere with processing the central angry face.

However, upon further examination (see Hostmann et al., 2006) it seems that the basic effects reflect more about the perceptual characteristics of the stimuli than they do about facial emotional valence. For instance, the basic flanker asymmetry effect even occurred with stimuli that were unlike faces, such as those shown in Figure 16.7. Overall data such as these should make us extremely cautious about the sorts of claims that have been made about the attention-getting attributes of stimuli that have otherwise been taken to depict facial expressions. The basic effects may reflect more about low-level perceptual processes that take place regardless of the supposed emotional content of the stimuli.

In closing this discussion about processing facial expressions, it is useful to return to an issue that was aired earlier, namely that it is possible to, in some sense, register the emotional valence of an expression independently of awareness. This particular issue has recently been re-examined by Pessoa, Japee and Ungerleider (2005) in a visual masking experiment designed to examine the recognition of fearful facial expressions. In this experiment a single photographic image of a target face was briefly presented, and this was followed immediately by a masking face. The target face wore a fearful, happy or neutral expression and the masking image was always of a neutral expression. The participant's task was to classify the target as 'fear or no fear' (p. 244). In addition, participants on every trial gave a confidence rating associated with their initial response so that a value of 1 signified that they were essentially guessing and 6 signified that they were highly confident in their response. Across trials the target display was presented for either 17, 33 or 83 ms.

The data were analysed using signal detection theory techniques (see Chapter 4). Without going into too many details, the data were clear in showing high participant variability in the ability to detect fear across the various display durations. Indeed, of the participants that were tested, two were performing above chance at the shortest display duration and two showed a trend to above-chance performance. This pattern provides something of a cautionary note for research undertaken to look at the claimed unconscious/automatic effects of emotion detection (cf. Esteves & Öhman, 1993). The data reported by Pessoa et al. (2005) show conclusively that some participants were consistently aware of masked faces even at the shortest target durations. Furthermore, the evidence also indicated that other participants did, on some trials, have

a clear impression of what had been presented. Such data as these again reveal limitations of backward masking (see previous discussion of Smithson & Mollon, 2006, in Chapter 4, p. 138) and show that there are no guarantees that the technique will make a stimulus inadmissible to consciousness.

Indeed such concerns have recently been echoed by Wiens (2006). Moreover, Wiens also pointed out that rapidly switching between different facial images could produce an illusion of facial motion which could act as a confound in the experiment. The message therefore is very clear: we need to be especially cautious about claims regarding unconscious processing of facial expressions when the evidence is taken from masking experiments.

---

### Pinpoint question 16.6

**How does the flanker asymmetry effect manifest itself?**

---

**automatic processes** Operations at an unconscious level, thought to be capacity unlimited and outside the control of the person.

**controlled processes** Operations at a conscious level, thought to be capacity limited.

**fear system** A cognitive module that has evolved to automatically service fearful and threatening stimuli.

**search display** In visual search paradigms, the stimulus as defined by a collection of to-be-searched elements.

**display size** In visual search paradigms, the number of to-be-searched elements presented in any given search display.

**anger superiority effect** The ease of detecting a discrepant angry face within a crowd, gauged relative to the difficulty of detecting a discrepant neutral or happy face.

**target pop-out** When it takes the same amount of time to detect the presence of a target, regardless of the number of search elements.

**parallel search** Assumed to reflect automatic processes in visual search, the concurrent analysis of a number of display elements.

**serial search** Assumed to reflect controlled processes, the sequential analysis of each search element in turn.

**serial self-terminating search** A serial search process in which each search element is considered in turn. If and when a target is encountered, respond 'present'; otherwise respond 'absent' when the last element turns out not to be a target.

**angry face advantage** The apparent ease of detecting an angry facial expression in a crowd of faces.

**happiness superiority effect** The relative ease at detecting a discrepant happy face within a crowd, relative to a discrepant neutral or angry face.

**flanker task** An experimental paradigm (Eriksen & Eriksen, 1974) in which participants are presented with visual displays, each containing a row of display elements. The central element is the designated target that must be responded to; the surrounding (flanking) elements must be ignored.

**flanker interference effect** In the flanker task, where flankers that are inconsistent with the target produce less accurate and/or slower responses than flankers that are consistent with the target.

**flanker asymmetry effect** After Hostmann et al. (2006), where responses to a positive expression flanked by negative expressions suffer from more interference than do responses to a negative expression flanked by positive expressions.

## Eye gaze, facial expression and the direction of attention

Trent and Sue are trying to look like they're not paying attention to the group of ladies they saw across the room

TRENT: Is she looking at me, baby?

SUE: No.

TRENT: Now?

SUE: No.

TRENT: Is she looking now?

SUE: No! She's not looking at you. She hasn't looked at you once. Will you stop asking if . . . Wait, she just looked.

TRENT: See, baby?

Mike and Rob walk up to Trent and Sue

MIKE: How you guys doing?

TRENT: It's on.

MIKE: Which one?

TRENT: (indicates the group of girls with a subtle head move) Groucho.

Mike and Rob STARE DIRECTLY at the girls like a deer in the headlights . . . a big no-no.

MIKE: The one with the cigar? She's cute.

Trent and Sue react with frustrated disappointment.

TRENT: What are you doing?

MIKE: What?

TRENT: You looked right at her, baby.

MIKE: She didn't notice.

SUE: Yes she did.

TRENT: Damn. Now I gotta go in early.

MIKE: I'm sorry.

TRENT: Don't sweat it, baby. This ones a layup.

Trent crosses away.

*(Favreau, 2000, pp. 66–8)*

For the time being we will stick with research concerned with information conveyed by facial characteristics. Now, though, the issue is not so much to do with attention-getting capabilities of a facial image, but with how information conveyed by facial characteristics may direct your attention. Obviously if you want to get your friend to attend to something, then say 'Look over there' – you could also point when saying this. In the present context, though, the research has not considered the use of language but the more constrained case in which only visual stimuli are used. We all have the experience of following someone else's gaze. The question is, can we get design experiments to examine this? For instance, we may ask, is gaze following an automatic process? The subjective impression is that gaze following is a pretty natural thing to do, but the empirical issue concerns whether in fact we cannot help but do it. It may be that when you see a directed gaze in someone else, you cannot help but follow it. Yes, it could be that we are all inherently curious (well, nosey). To appreciate this research, however, it is important to go back to some basics and consider the original laboratory-based work.

### The basic spatial cueing task

*Central cueing*

The basic paradigm to this particular line of research has a relatively long history in experimental cognitive psychology. Here we will concentrate on the work of Posner, Nissen and Ogden (1978; but see Sanders, 1972, for a review of previous relevant work). The paradigm involved something that has come to be known as **spatial cueing**. In the original task participants were asked to fixate a central location marked as a vertical line bisecting an outline square box. The task was simplicity itself as participants had merely to press a left response key if a target X was subsequently presented to the left of the centre, and a right response key if the target was presented to the right. This is known as a **choice reaction time (CRT) task**. However, on some trials prior to the target (also known as the **imperative signal** – this is the signal that demands a response) a cue (or warning signal) was presented.

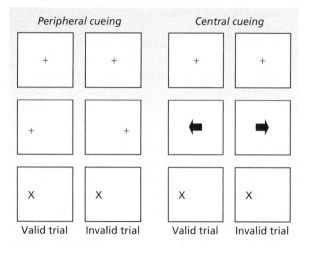

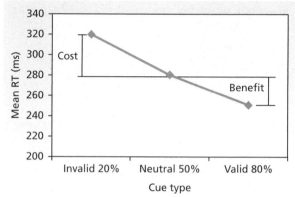

**Figure 16.8 Four cases of spatial cueing**
Participants are asked to fixate at a central location and then respond to onset of the target X. The target X can be preceded by a cue that either correctly predicts (*valid*) or incorrectly predicts (*invalid*) the location of the target. Moreover, the nature of the cue can either be *peripheral* by appearing at one of the actual target locations, or *central* by providing information regarding the possible location of the target without appearing in any of the possible positions. Neutral peripheral trials where both pre-cue '+'s are presented simultaneously to both fields. Neutral central trials are where the central fixation '+' is presented as a pre-cue.

**Figure 16.9 Idealised data from a made-up spatial cueing experiment**
On 50 per cent of the trials a neutral cue is presented and on the other 50 per cent of trials a directional cue is presented. Critically, though, the experiment examines performance with informative cues. Of the 50 per cent of trials on which a directional cue was presented, 80 per cent of the trials included a valid cue and 20 per cent of the trials included an invalid cue. Valid cues are where the cue correctly indicates the target's location. Invalid cues are where the cue misleads and indicates a location other than where the target will occur.

In this example the participant merely responds as soon as the target is registered. Hence mean RT in ms is plotted as a function of type of cueing trial. An RT cost is shown as being the difference between mean RTs on invalid and neutral trials. An RT benefit is shown as being the difference between the mean RTs on valid and neutral trials.

The warning signal was either a '+' or a leftward- or rightward-pointing arrow displayed at a central fixation location – a so-called **central cue**. Later experiments utilised peripheral cues, and we will discuss these shortly. A **peripheral cue** is a stimulus that is presented at one of the possible target locations prior to the target. Figure 16.8 provides schematic examples of central and peripheral cues in a made-up visual cueing experiment.

One obvious thing we could do is to examine performance in cases where the cue correctly indicates the location of the subsequent target and compare this with performance where the cue indicates a different location to that of the target. This is exactly what Posner et al. (1978) did: on **valid trials** the arrow correctly indicated the subsequent location of the target, and on **invalid trials** the arrow pointed to the contra-lateral position. The '+' warning signal provided the so-called **neutral trials** because such a symbol provides no directional information. Half the time the cue was a + and on the remaining half trials the cue was an arrow. On those trials when an arrow cue was presented it was valid on 80 per cent of the trials; so if you follow the cue, then eight out of ten times you would be correct. In other words, when the cue

was presented it was highly informative as to the location of the target. In short-hand, it is possible to refer to the arrow cues as central **informative cues** – they were presented at central fixation and provided information about the highly probable location of the impending target. Figure 16.9 provides an illustration of idealised data that obtain when this sort of experiment is carried out.

Posner et al. (1978) went further though and varied the SOA between the cue and the target across separate blocks of trials. No cue trials were referred to as 0 SOA trials. When a cue was presented, SOAs of 50, 150, 300, 500 and 1000 ms were tested. The response time (RT) and accuracy data were now mapped out as a function of cue and SOA. The RT data revealed how both performance benefits and costs emerged relative to the neutral baseline. Here a benefit is defined when performance was better on a cued trial than a neutral trial and a cost is when performance is worse on a cued trial than a neutral trial. It is typically the case that benefits accrue on a valid trial and costs accrue on invalid trials (see Figure 16.9 for further information).

The basic point here is that such experiments provide information about attentional control in the visual modality. By examining how the costs and benefits change as a consequence of cueing and the temporal relation between the cue and target, then the understanding is that this will reveal how attention is moved about the visual field.

Figure 16.10 provides a graphical illustration of the actual data reported by Posner et al. (1978). Strikingly, both the size of the benefits and the costs in the RT data increased dramatically as the delay between the onset of the cue and the target (the SOA) increased. No such effects arose when the cue and target were presented simultaneously, but as soon as there was a 50 ms delay both effects were observed. Both effects peaked at around 150 ms and then slowly diminished. However, these effects were accompanied by a striking pattern in the accuracy data. Participants showed

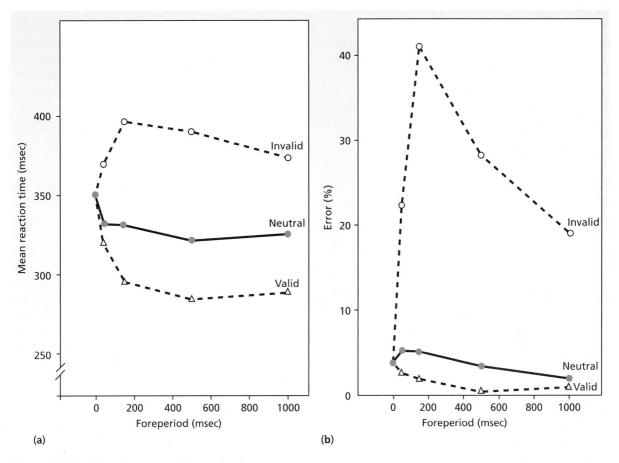

(a)

(b)

**Figure 16.10 Real data from a spatial cueing experiment**
(a) shows the actual mean RTs plotted as function of both cue type (invalid, neutral, valid) and the interval between the onset of the cue and the onset of the target from Posner et al. (1978). There is no difference in performance when the cue and target were presented at the same instance (i.e., the 0 ms case). However, both costs and benefits begin to emerge as soon as a delay is introduced between the cue and the target. All of the ensuing valid data points are below the neutral data points. The pair-wise differences reveal RT benefits because responses on valid trials are quicker than those on neutral trials. All of the ensuing invalid data points are above the neutral data points. Now the pair-wise differences reveal RT costs because responses on invalid trials are slower than those on neutral trials.

(b) shows the corresponding accuracy data. Now error rates are plotted as a function of both cue type (invalid, neutral, valid) and the interval between the onset of the cue and the onset of the target. With these data is the striking tendency for participants to make errors on invalid trials. What this shows is that there was a real tendency to respond to the direction of the pointing of the cue and not to the location of the target.

*Source*: Posner, M. I., Nissen, M. J., & Ogden, W. C. (1978). Attended and unattended processing modes: The role of set for spatial location. In H. L. Pick & E. Saltzman (Eds.), *Modes of perceiving and processing information* (pp. 137–157, fig. 1, p. 141; fig. 2, p. 142). Hillsdale, New Jersey: Erlbaum. Reproduced with permission.

marked inaccuracies at the shortened SOAs on invalid trials – at the shortest SOA participants had an overwhelming tendency to respond to the direction of the cue and not the position of the target. This **speed/error trade-off**, however, also dissipated as the SOA increased.

## Explaining spatial cueing

Posner (1978) discussed this overall pattern of performance as being indicative of the development of a so-called *mental set*. For Posner (1978), 'set is an active process that arises from participants' knowledge about the nature of the input they will receive', and it 'is produced only through the deliberate turning of attention toward some expected event' (p. 186). So what we have are statements about how the data reflect some form of attentional mechanism, particularly those concerning the control and direction of spatial attention.

In terms of the spatial cueing data, four alternative accounts of these set effects were considered (and, as will become clear, the favoured interpretation was option 2):

1. They might be due to the programming of a preparatory eye movement to the cued location of the target.

2. They might be due to the movement of some form of **attentional spotlight** to the cued location of the target in the absence of any eye movement.

3. They might arise as a consequence of 'a shift of attention to a position in the brain that would be contacted by the external event' (Posner et al., 1978, p. 143).

4. Finally the effects might simply reflect some form of response priming; for example, a leftward-pointing arrow primes a left key response. In other words, the effects have nothing to do with attentional mechanisms, instead they simply tell us about how responses are linked to environmental signals. If left arrow, press left key; if right arrow, press right key.

### Peripheral cueing

Evidence that rules out a response priming account (option 4) and also casts some doubt on the idea that the effects are solely concerned with eye movements (option 1) was presented in a **simple reaction time (SRT) task** (see Posner et al., 1978, Experiment 3). In a critical condition, the warning signal was presented

for 1 s and the target – now a small filled-in square ('a square of light', p. 144) – was presented at the offset of the cue, left or right of fixation. Now instead of using the 'central' arrow cues, a 'peripheral' cue was used. The flash of light occurred at one of the two possible target locations out in the visual periphery. The task was to make a single key press when the target appeared. Importantly, eye position was monitored and of most importance are the data from trials in which participants were able to retain central fixation. Under these conditions both costs and benefits arose. Moreover, the size of these effects were both of the order of 30 ms. These findings clearly show that costs and benefits arise even when the eyes remain stationary and they cannot be attributed to any form of differential response priming because there is only one key to press!

## Covert vs. overt shifts of attention

The favoured explanation was all to do with what is known as **covert shifts of attention**. We will define these in a moment. Such covert shifts in attention are typically distinguished from **overt shifts of attention** as these are associated with shifts in eye position. If you want to *attend* to what is going on outside your window, then *look* outside your window. In this regard, changing where you look is a case of an overt shift of visual attention. You decided to look out of the window and you moved your eyes in order to do this. Your focus of attention is locked to where your eyes are pointing. In the experiments under discussion, though, we can rule out overt shifts of attention because we still get costs and benefits when participants maintained a central fixation. On these grounds, we must turn to the notion of covert shifts of attention in a bid to explain the data. Covert shifts of attention are where the focus of attention changes but, in this case, the eyes remain stationary. To get an intuitive feel of what is being discussed, look at this **WORD** but try to focus your attention on something off to the right of the book.

### Endogenous vs. exogenous control

To get a feeling for what spatial attention is all about, perhaps the simplest analogy is with the notion of shining a torch in a pitch-black room. In order to see what is in the room, you must direct the beam of the torch to various points in the room. Using such an analogy, it is possible to discuss the notion of a *mental spotlight of attention* such that the current focus of attention is where the mental spotlight points. The argument is that the current focus of attention is given by everything that falls within the beam of the mental spotlight. Moreover, this mental spotlight is moveable, if you decide to attend to the television then let your eyes do the work and direct your attention by looking at it. This intentional control is also known as *endogenous control*. Alternatively the spotlight can be summoned by external events – if someone decides to take a flash photograph in an otherwise darkened theatre you will be hard pressed not to look at the position of the flash. Your attentional spotlight is summoned to the location of the flash. This stimulus or external control of your mental spotlight is known as *exogenous control*. Moving the attentional spotlight is known as the **spatial orienting** of attention.

Traditionally in discussing the sorts of cueing experiments so far considered, various arguments and explanations have been put forward. A basic idea is that a peripheral cue automatically summons your attention to its location. You simply cannot help but ignore the onset of a peripheral cue; alternatively, the peripheral cue is said to exert exogenous control over your mental spotlight. Your mental spotlight is automatically summoned to the position of the cue. On a valid trial, because the cue summons your spotlight to its location, you are then speeded in making a response. This is because the subsequent target falls at the location of your mental spotlight and within your current focus of attention. As a consequence, a performance benefit is found on valid trials. Remember, costs and benefits are gauged relative to performance on neutral trials. On neutral trials because the cue does not provide any useful directional information there is no sense in which the mental spotlight can be directed in any systematic fashion. Perhaps the mental spotlight simply loiters at the location of the central fixation?

In contrast to performance on valid trials, a cost will arise on an invalid trial because the position of the subsequent target is contra-lateral (on the other side of the screen) to cue. The cue summons your spotlight to its location, but the target appears elsewhere. As a consequence, you have to re-orient your attention to the location of the target. Although the details of this kind of re-orientation have become quite involved over the years – first disengage from the cue, then move the spotlight, then engage with the target (see, for instance, Fan, McCandliss, Fossella, Flombaum & Posner, 2005) – the basic idea is that such additional processes produce performance decrements that are revealed as RT costs. In simple terms, in having the

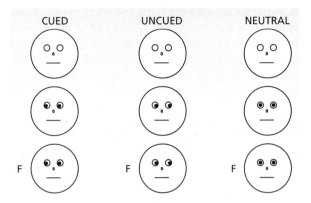

**Figure 16.11 Examples of displays used by Friesen and Kingstone (1998)**
The three columns show different cueing conditions. Here the terminology is such that 'cued' means 'valid', and 'uncued' means 'invalid'. The sequence of events on each trial type unfolds from top to bottom (see text for further details).
*Source*: Friesen, C. K., & Kingstone, A. (1998). The eyes have it! Reflexive orienting is triggered by nonpredictive gaze. *Psychonomic Bulletin & Review*, 5, 490–495 (fig. 1, p. 491). Copyright © 1998 by Psychonomic Society. Reproduced with permission of Psychonomic Society, Inc.

target appear at a different location to that signalled by cue, this produces a performance cost.

Similar sorts of arguments have also been put forward in terms of how endogenous control operations underlie cueing when central cues (e.g., arrows) are used. However, it should come as no surprise that accounts of spatial orienting have been hotly debated over the years, a huge literature has been spawned, and there remain many vexed questions. A whole host of issues exist over how sensible the notion of a mental spotlight is; concerns remain over how best to distinguish endogenous vs. exogenous forms of cueing; and the difference between controlled and automatic processes remains in dispute. Rather than attempt to grapple with such controversial topics here, we need to return to our present concerns. We need to consider the cueing experiments that have examined the degree to which an individual's attention can be controlled by some external agent's eye gaze.

## Experimental work on following eye gaze

A useful starting place here is with a clear demonstration described by Friesen and Kingstone (1998). Figure 16.11 provides examples of the sorts of displays that they used. Each trial began with the presentation of a schematic face with blank eyes (i.e., eyes with no pupils showing) for 680 ms. Next a pair of pupils were presented – on neutral trials the pupils were facing the viewer and on cued trials the pupils were either directed to the right or the left. Following the onset of the pupils a target letter (an F or a T) was presented in the periphery to the right or left of the head. Three conditions were tested. In the *detection condition* participants were under **go/no go task** instructions. This meant that participants had to press the space bar if a target letter occurred after the cue, but if no target was presented, then participants were therefore instructed not to make a response. (In other cases, go/no go conditions exist in which participants only respond to stimuli of a particular type – press the key if you see an X but not if you see a Y.) In the *localisation condition* participants were instructed to press a right key if the target letter appeared on the right of fixation and a left key if the target appeared on the left of fixation. Finally in the identification condition participants were instructed to press one key if the letter was an F and a different key if it was a T. On cued (i.e., valid) trials the pupils looked in the direction of the target letter and on uncued (i.e., invalid) trials the pupils looked in the contra-lateral direction.

As in the previous Posner et al. study (1978), the delay between the cue (the pupils) and the target (letter) was varied – delays of 105, 300, 600 and 1005 ms were used. Despite the fact that the data were being mapped out according to cue validity, SOA and condition, a very clear pattern emerged. Summarising greatly, the data revealed significant benefits for all tasks in that responses were facilitated on valid trials and these effects were most pronounced at the shortest SOA. There was no strong evidence of associated costs because performance on neutral and invalid trials was equivalent. → See 'What have we learnt?', below.

## Further experiments on the potency of eye gaze

Many demonstrations, such as those reported by Friesen and Kingstone (1998), have now appeared in the literature (for another interesting example, see Gibson & Kingstone, 2006), and all point towards the special status of so-called **social attention**. Cognitive psychologists are only now beginning to explore socially relevant factors that govern the direction of visual attention. What is clearly beginning to emerge is that socially significant cues are extremely powerful determinants of a person's attentional focus.

Figure 16.12 shows the sorts of displays used recently by Ristic and Kingstone (2005). The face displays were used in conditions very similar to those reported by Friesen and Kingstone (1998). The target was a peripherally positioned asterisk and an SRT go/

---

### → What have we learnt?

One reason that the effects are of interest are that the experiments were run with **uninformative cues** in that the direction of eye gaze was uncorrelated with the position of the target. The pupils in the schematic faces provided no useful information as to where the target would occur, and participants were explicitly instructed that this was so. This is in stark contrast to the previous work of Posner et al. (1978) in which an informative cue was used – their informative cue was a valid predictor of the target's location 80 per cent of the time. Friesen and Kingstone (1998) found that with uninformative cues there were still facilitative effects on valid cue trials. Furthermore, these effects also occurred at relatively short SOAs.

Overall, therefore, this pattern suggests the potency of the effects of eye gaze on directing attention. Put simply, it seems that it is impossible not to avert your attention and follow the direction of another's eye gaze. As Friesen and Kingstone (1998) would have it, 'a nonpredictive shift in gaze can trigger reflexive orienting' (p. 494). In other words, even though the pupils did not predict where the target would appear, participants could do nothing other than follow this cue. If such orienting were under strategic control (i.e., under endogenous control) then participants should have been able essentially to ignore the cue because it was irrelevant to the task. The fact that they were not able to ignore the direction of gaze underlines just how powerful an attentional cue another's eye position is. This suggests that the emotional state of someone as conveyed by their gaze can determine where you next attend. Just think, if someone else has found something interesting to look at, you may be missing out if you don't look too.

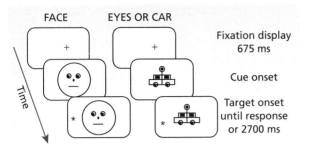

FACE        EYES OR CAR

Fixation display
675 ms

Cue onset

Target onset
until response
or 2700 ms

Time

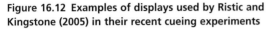

**Figure 16.12 Examples of displays used by Ristic and Kingstone (2005) in their recent cueing experiments**

*Source*: Ristic, J., & Kingstone, A. (2005). Taking control of reflexive social attention. *Cognition*, *94*, B55–B56 (fig. 1, p. B57). Reproduced with permission from Elsevier.

no go task was configured – make a response as soon as you see the target, otherwise do not respond. The data from the face condition were generally as reported by Friesen and Kingstone (1998). Here, though, strong validity effects were found at slightly longer SOAs (i.e., 300 ms and 600 ms) and the effects dissipated at the longest (1000 ms) SOA.

Of more interest are the data that obtained when the so-called EYES or CAR display was used. Now in the EYES condition participants were actually informed, prior to testing, that the displays contained a schematic representation of a hat pulled down to the eyes of a face. In contrast, in the CAR condition, they were told that the schematic was that of a car. The findings were clear: when participants were informed that eyes were represented, then the cueing effect found for the schematic faces was replicated. However, when the participants were informed that the diagram was of a car, no such cueing effects obtained.

These data are interesting for a number of reasons. It could be argued that the EYES provide some form of exogenous cue that operates automatically to direct attention to one side of the display or the other. This may well be part of the story, but it cannot be the whole of the story. The reason is that when exactly the same stimulus is used, the cueing effects depended on whether participants, in some sense, formed the impression of eyes. It was only when participants treated the displays as containing eyes did the cueing effects occur. If the participants did not interpret the cues as eyes, then there was no such attentional orienting. In other words, it is only when participants interpret the cues in socially significant terms that attentional orienting is affected. The eye cueing effect therefore clearly contains an important endogenous component.

One final case of socially significant visual orienting is worth discussing before moving on. This is a recent study reported by Tipples (2006). This is another examination of the social orienting of attention, but added to the mix is a manipulation of facial expression. Does the emotional expression on the face interact in any way with the social orienting of attention? The question was whether the orienting mechanism is particularly sensitive to fearful expressions. In particular, are the orienting effects more potent when a fearful rather than a happy expression is viewed?

Figure 16.13 provides examples of the sorts of displays Tipples (2006) used in his experiment. He used a variant of the identification condition described by Friesen and Kingstone (1998) and examined performance at two SOAs (300 ms and 700 ms). In addition to the happy and fearful expressions shown in the figure, Tipples also included trials in which the face wore a neutral expression. As before, the actual eye gaze was completely uninformative about the location of the target letter. So 50 per cent of the time the eyes pointed in the (valid) direction of the target and on the remaining 50 per cent of trials the eye direction was invalid. In this regard, the eye gaze provided no useful information as to the target's eventual position. The pattern of results was as follows. Overall the cueing effects did not vary as a consequence of SOA; however, there was some slight evidence that the size of the cueing effects did vary as a function of the type of expression of the face. Broadly speaking, the evidence (such as it is) shows that the cueing effects were largest when a fearful face was used, next largest when a happy face was used and smallest when a neutral face was used. Even though the effects are not as clear-cut as they might have been, this general trend is in line with the idea that fearful faces provide particularly potent forms of cues for orienting attention. Just think about it: if you do detect that someone is expressing fear and is staring off to the left, maybe you too need to determine quickly what it is that they are fearful of!

**Pinpoint question 16.7**

**What role does facial expression play in spatial cueing experiments using eye gaze?**

**spatial cueing** An experimental paradigm (e.g., Posner, Nissen & Ogden, 1978) in which a cue either correctly or incorrectly predicts the location of a subsequent target.

Trial with fearful expression    Trial with happy expression

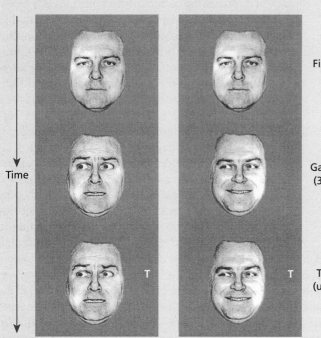

Time

Fixation display
(750 ms)

Gaze cue display
(300 or 700 ms)

Target display
(until response)

**Figure 16.13 Examples of displays used by Tipples (2006)**

*Source*: Tipples, J. (2006). Fear and fearfulness potentiate automatic orienting to eye gaze. *Cognition and Emotion*, *20*, 309–320 (fig. 1, p. 313). Reproduced with permission from Taylor & Francis Ltd.

**choice reaction time (CRT) task** In a CRT task, participants are asked to decide about the nature of an imperative signal and make one of a number of alternative possible responses under speeded constraints.

**imperative signal** A stimulus that demands a response.

**central cue** A cue in a spatial cueing paradigm which provides information regarding the possible location of the target but the cue itself is not presented at a possible target location.

**peripheral cue** A cue in a spatial cueing paradigm which provides information regarding the location of the target by appearing at one of the possible target locations.

**valid trials** In a spatial cueing experiment, when a cue correctly indicates the location of the target.

**invalid trials** In spatial cueing experiments, when a cue incorrectly indicates the location of the ensuing target.

**neutral trials** In a spatial cueing experiment, when the cue provides no useful information about the location of the target.

**informative cues** In a spatial cueing experiment, where the cues are highly predictive of the location (or nature) of the ensuing target.

**speed/error trade-off** This particular pattern of performance relates to reaction time tasks in which, in order to speed up, participants make many errors.

**attentional spotlight** A metaphor used for the current focus of visual attention. Like the spotlight of a torch, attributes of the visual world are clearer within the focus of the beam than they are outside the focus of the beam.

**simple reaction time (SRT) task** In SRT tasks the participant is typically asked to respond to the onset of a pre-defined imperative signal.

**covert shifts of attention** Movements of visual attention that are not locked to changes in eye position.

**overt shifts of attention** Movements of visual attention that are locked to changes in eye position.

**spatial orienting** Moving the focus of attention around in space.

**go/no go task** A speeded response task in which participants are required to respond only when a target is presented. They must withhold responses when no target appears.

**uninformative cues** Cues that are uncorrelated with what response the target requires. In spatial cueing experiments, uninformative cues provide no useful information as to where the target will be presented.

**social attention** The effect of social factors on attention.

## Detecting threatening objects

Aside from the emerging thread in the literature regarding the 'automatic' detection of emotionally charged facial expressions, recent work has also been undertaken on the automatic detection of other forms of threat as characterised by various sorts of threatening objects. Again the work of Öhman and colleagues provides a useful starting place for discussion. For example, Öhman, Flykt and Esteves (2001) reported a series of visual search experiments in which the detection of images of threatening targets was examined. In their first experiment, they used a variant of the same/different search task, described above (e.g., see the discussion of Hansen & Hansen, 1988). Participants were now instructed to press one key if all the images in a stimulus display depicted exemplars taken from the same category (i.e., they had to make a same response) and another key if there was a discrepant target image of an instance taken from another category (i.e., they had to make a different response). The categories of interest were snakes, spiders, flowers and mushrooms. The snakes and spiders were taken to be the threatening instances, whereas flowers and mushrooms were taken to be neutral. Would participants be particularly adept at detecting a discrepant threatening category instance among members of non-threatening category members?

The reasoning was the same as before. It was hypothesised that because snakes and spiders, when confronted in the wild, may be life-threatening, there are good grounds for assuming that these will be detected automatically. Over the course of human evolution, the putative fear system (Öhman & Mineka, 2001) has adapted so as to provide an early warning signal when confronted by a scene that contains any form of threatening item. In this particular experimental context the prediction was as follows. Target detection responses to snakes and spiders, when such items occurred in a background of flowers or mushrooms, should be faster than similar responses to flowers and mushrooms when these occurred against a background of snakes or spiders.

Search displays were therefore constructed accordingly, and each display contained a $3 \times 3$ matrix of nine colour photographic images. The data were clear in showing that, as predicted, the so-called fear-relevant targets accrued shorter response times than did the neutral targets. Importantly, the time to respond 'same' (i.e., target absent) was unaffected by whether participants were confronted with a display containing only fear-relevant images or neutral images. On these grounds, the effects on 'different' trials (i.e., target present) could not be attributed to the ease of searching through a background of neutral vs. fear-relevant non-targets. Times to search through displays containing just neutral or just fear-relevant non-targets were equivalent. In this regard, target detection did seem to be influenced by the emotional valence of the target.

These findings were supported further when display set size was manipulated in a second experiment. In replicating the procedure of the first experiment, the task constraints were persevered, but displays contained either four or nine images. Here the idea was to examine whether the time to detect a fear-relevant target would scale with the number of to-be-searched images. What the data showed, though, was that target responses to fear-relevant items were hardly affected when display size increased. In contrast, similar responses to neutral items increased noticeably when the display size increased. Öhman, Flykt and Esteves (2001) concluded that the RT increase for the target responses to fear-relevant items was so small that there was evidence on these trials of target pop-out. Their data suggested that detection of a threatening object operated in an automatic fashion.

In following up on this particular line of research, Tipples, Young, Quinlan, Broks and Ellis (2002) reported a rather disappointing series of experiments that failed to endorse the findings reported by Öhman, Flykt and Esteves (2001). The results of their first experiment, though, were somewhat encouraging. This experiment was a replication of the second experiment reported by Öhman, Flykt and Esteves (2001), and again there was an RT advantage found for fear-relevant targets. Each fear-relevant picture contained a coloured photographic image of a snake, bear or wild dog poised to attack. Neutral stimuli were photographic images of plants and leaves (see Figure 16.14a for an example of the sort of display used). Target detection RTs were shorter on fear-relevant trials than neutral trials and there was a smaller effect of an increase of display set size on RTs to fear-relevant targets than neutral targets. (Again displays containing four or nine images were used.) In addition, performance on 'target absent' trials revealed that displays containing only fear-relevant images were responded to quicker than were displays containing only neutral stimuli.

Tipples, Young et al. (2002) were concerned that the basic threat advantage might be attributable more to the perceptual characteristics of the stimuli than to their threatening nature. For instance, all of the threat

**Figure 16.14 Examples of the sorts of displays used by Tipples, Young et al. (2002) in their 'threat detection' experiments**

In both (a) and (b) displays of set size four are shown. (a) shows an example of where a discrepant image of a threatening animal is present among non-threatening images of plants. (b) shows an example of where a discrepant image of a non-threatening animal is present among non-threatening images of plants.

stimuli were depictions of animals with bared fangs or teeth. Perhaps the efficient detection of these arresting visual features was at the heart of the 'threat' advantage. This is in much the same way as the V-shaped eyebrows might have been a dead giveaway of an angry demeanour. In a bid to test this idea, Tipples, Young et al. changed the stimulus sets so that now detection of pleasant animals vs. plants was tested (see Figure 16.14b for an example of the sort of display used). What the data now showed was that there was an animal advantage that bore all of the hallmarks of the original threat advantage found in their first experiment. RTs to animal targets were shorter than RTs to plant targets, and moreover the RT increase due to the increase in display set size was considerably less for the animal than plant targets.

This particular pattern of results cast something of a cloud over the original threat advantage. It seems that the efficient detection of the threatening animals was apparently more to do with the fact that they were animals rather than that they were threatening. Indeed, when performance for pleasant and threatening animals was tested in the same search task with the same participants in the context of plants, a **general animal advantage** was found. Responses were generally quicker to target animals as compared with target plants and there was no difference in responses as a function of the threatening nature of the animals. So, in a sense, it doesn't matter whether the target is grizzly bear or Yogi Bear. All that matters is that it is a bear among other non-animals.

## Further evidence for the animal advantage

This general animal advantage has since been replicated by Lipp, Derakshan, Waters and Logies (2004), but even more recently Lipp and Waters (2007) have examined this finding in much finer detail. They described a variant on the basic visual search task in which target detection was examined as a consequence of the other non-targets included in the display. Each display contained nine colour photographic images of animals. Two main conditions were examined: in the *bird condition* birds were the designated targets, and in the *fish condition* fish were the designated targets. Participants were instructed to press one key if an image of a designated target was present in the display, and another key if no target was present. The critical manipulation was whether or not a fear-inducing target was present in the display. In the bird condition the fear-inducing foil image was of a spider and the control neutral image was of a cockroach. In the fish condition the fear-inducing foil image was of a snake and the control neutral image was of a lizard. The intention was to see what would happen when a critical foil image was present among the other non-targets.

So here primarily was a desire to see whether or not target detection would be affected by the presence of an otherwise irrelevant foil image among the other non-target images. Particular interest was with whether target responses would be slowed when a fear-inducing image was also present in the display. The data were clear: in this regard, participants were slowed in making 'target present' responses when the display contained a fear-inducing image. Most critical perhaps were the results from a second experiment. Now Lipp and Waters (2007) pre-screened participants according to whether they were particularly fearful of spiders or particularly fearful of snakes. Now the data were broken down according to the presence of an image of a most fearful foil image or the presence of a least fearful foil image. In general the data showed that although participants were slowed whenever an irrelevant fearful foil image was present, they were particularly slowed in the presence of the foil that they feared the most. For later reference, we will refer to

this evidence as support for the **inertia hypothesis** – the claim that it is difficult to move on mentally from having detected an emotionally provoking stimulus. → See 'What have we learnt?', page 632.

→ See 'What have we learnt?', page 632.

### Pinpoint question 16.8

Why did the data from Tipples, Young, Quinlan, Broks and Ellis (2002) cast doubt on the finding that there is a processing advantage for threatening animals?

### Research focus 16.3

## Freeze! Coming face to face with threat

So far we have looked at the claim that threatening stimuli have a processing advantage over non-threatening stimuli, and have been weaving our way around the data that both support and refute this idea. However, the evidence for the privileged processing of things that go bump in the night has been largely derived from reaction times and error rates, and we hope you'd agree that there is much more to being human than looking at these two measures of performance! Azevedo, Volchan, Imbiriba, Rodrigues, Oliveira, Oliveira, Lutterbach, and Vargas (2005) were particularly interested in changes in posture as a result of being presented with threatening pictures.

Forty-eight male participants were asked to stand on a triangular aluminium plate which helped record changes in posture, while being shown pictures from the international affective picture system (IAPS; Lang, Bradley & Cuthbert, 2005). Now some of the pictures in here are likely to be among the most disturbing things you have seen outside an Ali Roth film (dead children, car crash victims, etc.). Bizarrely, there's also a picture of a very young Sir Ian McKellen in among these rancid images, which does not appear to belong to this negative affect category unless you find English thespians particularly threatening. In any case, participants were shown images of mutilation, along with positively rated sports scenes and neutrally rated pictures of everyday objects for comparison. The idea here was that mutilation would be perceived as threatening,

since death and dismemberment are rather un-attractive prospects from a survival point of view. In addition to seeing how much participants wobbled, their heart rate was also recorded as a further index of threat.

Very simply, the authors found that participants swayed much less when confronted with threatening images, in addition to observing significantly reduced heart rate, with beats per minute averaging about 86 for the pleasant and 87 for the neutral images, but only 83 during the presentation of the unpleasant images. So what do reduced body sway and reduced heart rate ('bradycardia', for those of you who wanted to be doctors) afford the organism faced with threat?

At a first pass, it would seem counter-intuitive that the cognitive benefit for processing threatening stimuli would be so that we can stand still quicker and slow our heart rate down a bit. However, as Azevedo et al. (2005) point out, heart rate decreases suggest the activation of a defensive system, and when the organism is still, they can more accurately monitor danger and get 'ready for fight or flight in an instant' (p. 255). Therefore 'freezing' might actually be your best option before either facing your fear or simply running for the hills.

*Source:* Azevedo, T. M., Volchan, E., Imbiriba, L. A., Rodrigues, E. C., Oliveira, J. M., Oliveira, L. F., Lutterbach, L. G., & Vargas, C. D. (2005). A freezing-like posture to pictures of mutilation. *Psychophysiology, 42,* 255–260.

## → What have we learnt?

In discussing their findings, Tipples, Young, Quinlan, Broks and Ellis (2002) outlined three possible ways in which fearful stimuli may influence the allocation of attention in visual search tasks:

1. Threatening stimuli may automatically grab attention to themselves such that it is these stimuli that are automatically processed first.
2. Threatening stimuli are consciously recognised more quickly than are non-threatening stimuli.
3. Once a threatening stimulus has been identified then it is harder to shift or relocate attention from it.

Tipples, Young et al. (2002) concluded that it is the final possibility that garnered the most support from the then extant data. Interestingly, it is this conclusion that, at this time, provides the most sensible account of the data reported by Lipp and Waters (2007). In their tasks participants were instructed to try to detect an animal of a particular class (i.e., a fish or a bird) but it was interference from an otherwise irrelevant fearful image that was apparent. What this seems to indicate is that if participants do register the presence of a threatening item, then this will interfere with (slow them down or otherwise impede) their ability to process the other items in the display (see Brosch & Sharma, 2005, and Fox, Russo & Dutton, 2002, for further support for this view). There is growing evidence for the inertia hypothesis. In common-sense terms, if there is an imminent possibility that something is about to do you harm, then it probably is a good idea to keep an eye on it!

---

**general animal advantage** Relatively good performance in quickly detecting a discrepant animal among other non-animal search items.

**inertia hypothesis** The hypothesis that it is the difficulty in disengaging attention away from an emotionally provoking stimulus that is special about them.

---

## Other indications of the influence of emotion on cognition

As is probably clear by now, one of the most prominent avenues of research on emotion and cognition is how attention and attentional control may be influenced by emotionally inducing stimuli. There are, of course, many other areas of human cognition that show effects of the emotional state of the participants and we shall look at some of these before bringing the chapter to a close. However, it is, yet again, useful to consider some rather basic practical and theoretical issues before continuing.

### Mood induction in 'normal, healthy adults'

Outside clinical settings in which pathological emotional states are examined, alternative techniques for studying emotions and emotional effects on cognitive processing in 'normal, healthy adults' have been developed. For example, some experiments have employed a technique known as **mood induction** and have used this with undergraduate students as participants. Here the idea is to try to induce a particular emotion for the duration of the experiment (just think of the ethical issues that begin to emerge!), and then go on to study what effects such a mood state gives rise to. A concrete example can be found in the work of Bradley, Mogg and Lee (1997). They selected students who scored low on a standardised test of depression (i.e., Beck's Depression Inventory) on the grounds that these particular participants were not depressive nor were they inclined to depression. These individuals were then randomly allocated to one of two different mood induction procedures. For one case participants were induced to feel depressed, while for the other case the participants were induced to feel in a neutral frame of mind.

Although the exact hypotheses under test will be addressed later, the basic idea here was to try to examine the effects of particular emotional states on cognitive processes. Bradley et al. (1997) even went so far as to suggest that the particular emotional states of depression and anxiety 'influence all aspects of information processing, including perception, attention, memory and reasoning' (p. 911). So by inducing a particular mood, it is hoped that we can see how this affects perception, attention, memory and reasoning.

However, given the basic modularity of mind hypothesis that we have adopted throughout this book, such a claim is clearly contentious. As we covered in Chapter 4, it is of some considerable concern, for instance, as to whether emotional states can influence or interfere with the operation of the input (perceptual) modules. Put simply, it is pretty important that you rapidly recognise the fast approaching bus when you are crossing the road irrespective of whether you are blissfully happy or worrying about what fresh hell awaits when you get into college. Clearly such general theoretical concerns are important and it is useful to bear these in mind as we proceed. However, for now it is more helpful to avoid getting too distracted by such controversies, and concentrate on more concrete factors such as the methodology of mood induction.

To reiterate: Bradley et al. (1997) attempted to induce particular mood states in their participants. When participants had had such a mood state induced, they were then tested in a particular cognitive task. To induce a depressive frame of mind, participants were asked to recall unhappy memories while they listened to sad music – 'Prokofiev's Russia under Mongolian Yoke, played at half speed' (Bradley et al., 1997, p. 914) for seven minutes. In contrast, participants in the neutral mood induction procedure were asked to recall routine journeys that they had taken in the past while they listened to Kraftwerk's 'Pocket Computer' for seven minutes. Such mood induction procedures were justified on the grounds that they had been shown to be effective in previous studies.

More critically, participants were given other questionnaires regarding their mood at the very start of the experiment and again at the very end. Comparing across these two test phases, it was found that participants who had undergone depressive mood induction were, according to the self-report measures, 'feeling more depressed and sad' after mood induction than were the participants who had undergone neutral mood induction.

## Mood induction and ethical considerations

We will consider what the actual theoretical issues Bradley et al. (1997) were interested in shortly, but for now mention of this work has allowed us to discuss the technique of mood induction in otherwise normal, healthy adults. The understanding is that such techniques provide the means by which we can examine emotional effects on cognitive processes in otherwise

normal, healthy adults. Of course, detractors could argue that such techniques are limited in their application. We have already hinted at ethical issues, but to be less obtuse, we should be rightly concerned when considering whether mood induction techniques are to be condoned. Bradley et al. (1997) pre-screened their participants so that no so-called **dysphoric individuals** (depressives or individuals prone to depression) underwent depressive mood induction. That is, individuals who scored highly on the depression inventory were weeded out from the sample of possible participants and were not included in the remaining phases of the experiment.

However, given that such experiments are being carried out in a bid to induce something other than boredom (pressing keys for over 40 minutes!) or fatigue (pressing keys for over 40 minutes!), caution is clearly warranted. Indeed, to quote from the current British Psychological Society's (2004) 'Ethical Principles for Conducting Research with Human Participants', 'The essential principle is that the investigation should be considered from the standpoint of all participants; foreseeable threats to their psychological well-being, health, values or dignity should be eliminated' (British Psychological Society, 2004, *Code of Conduct: Ethical Principles and Guidelines*. Retrieved 9 January 2006 from http://www.bps.org.uk, p. 8). So, although we might get away with temporarily inducing a sad frame of mind in otherwise 'normal, healthy adults', would we really want to be involved in an experiment that induced fear, anxiety or disgust? Or indeed making depressive people feel even more depressed than they already are? So unlike other, more traditional areas of cognitive psychology, the area of cognition and emotion forces us to consider some very particular and important ethical questions.

### Pinpoint question 16.9

What was used as a mood inducer in the Bradley et al. (1997) study and what precautions were taken when inducing mood?

## 'Mood' induction and 'mood'

Apart from such delicate ethical issues, we might also express some other concerns. It seems appropriate to ask about the degree to which the sorts of emotions that are conjured up in the laboratory are the very same emotions as those that naturally occur outside the laboratory. As we have seen, there is a growing area of research on how threatening or fear-provoking stimuli are processed relative to non-threatening or neutral stimuli. However, this research is typically carried out with pictures of threatening objects (such as guns, knives, snakes and spiders) and not with the objects themselves. Just ask yourself which is the more threatening to you: a rattlesnake poised to strike on the desk in front of you or a picture of a rattlesnake poised to strike on the desk in front of you? On these grounds, how confident should we be that experiments on processing fear-provoking objects tell us anything about fear?

Of course, similar arguments can be made about almost every topic that we have covered in the book. For example, to what extent can learning the serial order of words in a list tell us anything about memory in the real world? What kind of insights does the examination of 'sentences' like 'The horse raced past the barn fell' give us into the cognitive psychology of everyday language? All that is being intimated here, though, is that, when confronted by any sort of grandiose claims about emotional effects on cognitive processes, some caution is perhaps warranted. Put bluntly, pictures of poisonous snakes simply are not threatening. Of course, this is not to argue that such stimuli cannot induce a possibly extreme emotional reaction in some individuals, such as will probably occur with snake phobics, in this case. We should not, however, take such pathological cases as evidence that, more generally, pictures of threatening or fear-provoking objects induce the same sorts of emotional states to those that are conjured up when the corresponding objects are confronted. Issues such as these should be addressed when we attempt to appraise exactly what it is that the work on the 'emotional effects on cognitive processes' is actually telling us.

## More evidence for the inertia hypothesis?

Bearing all of this in mind, we should, nevertheless, return to what the experimental work is perhaps telling us. To this end, Bradley et al. (1997) employed their mood induction technique in a bid to examine a version of the inertia hypothesis as applied to the processing of single words. In the context of their work the basic effect is known as an attentional bias. The particular hypothesis under test was that emotionally charged words capture attention and, as a consequence, accrue preferential processing. On each trial in their experiment the sequence of events was as follows. Initially a central fixation cross was presented for 500 ms and this was immediately replaced by a display

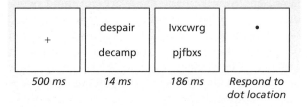

**Figure 16.15 A schematic representation of the events as they unfolded in the dot probe task examined by Bradley et al. (1997)**
Time from the start of a trial moves from left to right across the page.

containing two vertically aligned words, one above and one below the fixation point. In one condition, the words were briefly presented for 14 ms and were then immediately pattern masked by random letter strings that occurred at the same positions as the words. The masks were presented for 186 ms and then a dot appeared at one of the word locations. The participants' task was to respond to the location of the dot as quickly and as accurately as they could (see Figure 16.15).

On some of the trials one of the presented words was negatively emotionally charged, such as 'hopeless' and 'despair'. Of prime import was what would happen to responses to the following dot probe as a function of the emotional valence of the preceding word. A simple prediction was that if attention was preferentially allocated to the emotionally charged word, then the response to the dot that subsequently appeared at the location of this word should be emitted faster than would be the case if the probe were placed at the position of a neutral word. Responses to a dot at the position of 'despair' would be faster than would be responses to a dot at the position of 'decamp'.

Despite the simplicity of this prediction, though, a rather complex pattern of performance emerged. Very briefly, support for the prediction was that participants who had been induced to feel depressed showed the basic effect. That is, when the words were presented for relatively long durations (over 500 ms) and were not masked, then the depressed participants were faster to respond to the dot probe when it fell at the position of a negative word than when it fell at the position of a control word. Such an attentional bias, if anything, was reversed in a group of participants who had not been mood induced prior to the dot probe task. No such attentional biases were found when the words were briefly presented and were backward masked.

This latter finding poses something of a problem for the idea that there is an unconscious bias towards emotionally charged words that are presented below the conscious threshold (also see Chapter 4 and the discussion of perceptual defence). Some evidence for such a possibility, however, was reported in a second experiment. In this case, highly anxious individuals revealed an attentional bias towards anxiety-provoking words (e.g., 'disgrace', 'incurable', 'attacked') even when the words were briefly presented and backward masked.

Overall, such an unexpected and complex pattern of results is difficult to square with any simple hypotheses about how emotional mood states may affect the cognitive processes concerning word processing. The research questions have yet to be answered satisfactorily and the topic remains wide open.

---

**mood induction** An attempt to create a particular mood state in a person prior to testing them in some experimental setting.

**dysphoric individuals** Individuals who are either depressed or prone to depression.

---

## Mood and judgement

In closing this chapter, it is important to consider alternative means by which emotional states may influence cognitive processes outside effects concerning attention and attentional allocation. We have already expressed some concerns over the rather grandiose claim made by Bradley et al. (1997) that the particular emotional states of depression and anxiety 'influence all aspects of information processing, including perception, attention, memory and reasoning' (p. 911) and now it is time to appraise this view more carefully. We begin by focusing on something that has come to be known as **depressive realism**.

### Depressive realism

A seminal reference to depressive realism is that by Alloy and Abramson (1979). The basic task was concerned with the perception of, or more appropriately, the judgements made about response–outcome contingencies. So fundamentally the topic concerns how mood influences reasoning (see Chapter 15). The tasks used were designed to tap into an individual's estimates of how much control they thought they had over their environment. Take riding a bike, for example; there is typically a causal link between pushing down on the pedal and moving forwards. The link is

such that the cyclist rightly judges that there is a causal contingency between making a particular response (i.e., pushing down on the pedal) and a particular outcome (i.e., moving forwards). As ubiquitous as such things are in everyday life, sometimes the relation between responses and outcomes is not so clear-cut. For instance, sometimes you will put the required amount of money in the coffee machine but, for whatever reason, it does not provide the expected drink. The machine spits out the coins, it takes your money and nothing happens, it delivers the wrong drink, etc. Take another example: no matter how hard and how often you go fishing there is only an imperfect correlation between casting in the baited line and catching a fish.

In summary, what Alloy and Abramson (1979) did was to test participants in their ability to judge a very particular response–outcome contingency, namely that between making a key press response and the onset of light flash. Using computer control it was possible to vary the degree of correlation between such a response and such an outcome. Statistically a **correlation coefficient** provides a numerical index of the degree to which two types of events (say A and B) co-occur. Correlation coefficients can vary from $-1$ to $+1$: $+1$ signifies that A and B always co-occur, a value of 0 signifies that A and B vary independently of one another and a value of $-1$ signifies that A and B never co-occur. The most important thing to note about correlation is that it is different from causality. However, despite this basic fact, it is nevertheless sometimes easy to be seduced into believing that because A and B always co-occur, they are causally related. Just think: if B always follows A, then it could be a reasonable bet that B is caused by A.

Unless the plug has fused there is normally a $+1$ correlation between (A) switching the kettle on and (B) the water boiling. Such a case also provides an example of a causal chain because the boiling of the water is causally related to switching the kettle on. The fact that such high correlations reflect causal relations in some cases may also lie at the heart of the development of superstitious behaviour. Sometimes you do your rain dance just before it rains; therefore, clearly, your dance causes it to rain.

To reiterate: what Alloy and Abramson (1979) were interested in was how well participants were able to estimate the contingency between a certain response (i.e., pressing a response key) and a certain outcome (i.e., a light flash). On each trial, participants were given the opportunity to make a key press response and, following this window of opportunity, either a light flashed or it did not. At the end of a block of trials the participants were asked to rate their control over the outcome. What Alloy and Abramson reported was that, generally speaking, when participants were tested under varying levels of response–outcome correlation, their estimates of these correlations were usually fairly accurate. A critical finding, though, was that such judgements varied as a function of the mood of the participant.

Alloy and Abramson (1979) ran different participants in two conditions. The participants were classified as being depressed or non-depressed and, across the two conditions, the frequency with which an outcome followed a response was varied. In one condition, namely the *25–25 condition*, the flash of light occurred on 25 per cent of trials following a key press and on 25 per cent of the trials when no key press was made. The incidence of the flash of light was therefore low. In contrast, in the *75–75 condition*, the flash of light occurred on 75 per cent of trials following a key press and on 75 per cent of the trials when no key press was made. The incidence of the flash of light was therefore reasonably high. However, in both conditions, outcomes were not contingent upon responding – making a response and experiencing a particular outcome were uncorrelated. Across trials, therefore, if participants were operating optimally, then they ought to have learnt this, namely that the responses and outcomes were uncorrelated or independent of each other. However, what Alloy and Abramson found was that non-depressed participants judged that they had more control over the outcomes when these occurred frequently than when they occurred less often. This finding has been referred to as the *outcome-density effect*. Non-depressed participants exhibited what has come to be known as *an illusion of control*. The outcome density effect is that this illusion of control will be greater when the incidence of the to-be-judged outcome is high rather than low. In contrast, the depressed participants judged that they had no control over the outcome in both conditions. Hence the label *depressive realism* – the judgements of the depressed participants were more realistic because they did not make inflated judgements about their control of the environment, unlike the non-depressed individuals. The conclusion is that depressed individuals are 'sadder but wiser'.

## Further work on depressive realism

Since this original finding has been reported, both replications and failures to replicate have been reported in the literature. However, recently a careful review of this area of research has been completed by Allan, Siegel and Hannah (2007). They discussed three possible reasons for the basic effect. These can be referred to as follows:

- a motivational hypothesis
- an ITI hypothesis
- a response-criterion hypothesis.

### The motivational hypothesis

Allan et al. (2007) attributed this to Alloy and Abramson (1979) who stated that the difference between depressed and non-depressed individuals reflects differences in their self-esteem. Non-depressed individuals have higher self-esteem than depressives and, as a consequence, distort reality in an optimistic fashion. Not only do they always look on the bright side of life but they fail to see the darker side. Depressives, in contrast, have little desire to protect their feeling of self-worth and therefore do not distort the evidence accordingly.

### The ITI hypothesis

This hypothesis relates to the finding that ITI (or the inter-trial interval – the time between trials) affects the participants' judgements. Here the focus is with a finding reported by Msetfi, Murphy, Simpson and Kornbrot (2005; see also Msetfi, Murphy & Simpson, 2007), namely when the ITI was short there was no outcome density effect but when the ITI was long there was such an effect but only for non-depressed individuals. Depressives still exhibited depressive realism. Without going into too many details, the basic idea is that whatever mechanisms are being tapped by the task, the effect of ITI reflects that in non-depressed participants the rate of presentation of trials is taken into account when estimates of response–outcome contingency are made, but this factor is essentially ignored by depressed individuals. Msetfi et al. (2005) did acknowledge, however, that the hypothesis is incomplete and Allan et al. (2007) did reference cases when the outcome density effect is present at short ITIs.

### The response-criterion hypothesis

In simple terms, we can think of this hypothesis in terms of the depressive attitude of 'just say no'. As soon as the notion of response criterion is mentioned then this takes us right into the realm of signal detection theory (see Chapter 4). On a given trial, a participant may approach the task from either of two different

## → What have we learnt?

The work of Allan et al. (2007) forces us to be cautious in accepting the claim that the particular emotional state of depression can influence 'all aspects of information processing, including perception, attention, memory and reasoning' (Bradley et al., 1997, p. 911). What has been concluded stands in contrast to this. For instance, the data provide no support for the claim that the mechanisms responsible for judging response–outcome contingencies operate any differently in depressed and non-depressed individuals. On the contrary, what the data show is that depressives fail to show a shift in a response bias that non-depressed individuals do exhibit under certain circumstances.

perspectives – judgements can reflect either a disposition based on 'What do I perceive the likelihood of the outcome to be on this trial?' or 'Given that likelihood, how should I respond?' The basic idea here is that behaviour in the experiment could reflect something about the processes concerning estimating response–outcome contingencies or it could reflect something quite different about how best to respond given that a certain estimate has been made. In other words, the behaviour could reflect (i) something about the mechanism responsible for estimating correlations in the environment, or (ii) something about mechanisms that are responsible for actions that are carried out once such estimates have been made.

Basically, if the response-criterion hypothesis is true, then we should conclude that the experiments on depressive realism reveal much about how depressives act and rather less about how they actually construe the world. Depressives, unlike non-depressed individuals, are simply less likely to say 'yes, the outcome will occur'. According to Allan et al. (2007), the basic outcome density effect reflects, in non-depressives, a greater response bias to say 'yes, an outcome will occur if the frequency of the outcome increases' – depressives, on the other hand, simply do not exhibit such an eagerness to say 'yes'. Allan et al. (2007) concluded that 'Depressives may be sadder but they are not wiser, rather so-called "depressive realism" results from the bias of depressives to say "no"'. → See 'What have we learnt?', above.

### Pinpoint question 16.10

**What are the three alternate explanations for depressive realism?**

**depressive realism** The idea that depressed individuals make more accurate judgements regarding response–outcome contingencies than do non-depressed individuals.

**correlation coefficient** A numerical index of the degree to which two things or states of affairs co-occur.

## Concluding comments

Clearly the area of cognition and emotion is growing in popularity. The first issue of the first volume of *Emotion*, an American Psychological Association journal, was only published in March 2001. Coincidentally the first issue of the first volume of *Cognitive Affective & Behavioral Neuroscience* (a Psychonomic Society journal) was also published at exactly the same time. The field holds much promise, and it will be interesting to see how the research develops over the coming years. Indeed, on reflection, it may turn out that this area of research produces a spur to cognitive psychologists for them to reconsider what laboratory research really contributes to our understanding of what it is to be a sentient being.

One example suffices before closing. Over the past 30 or so years much has been discovered about how people search for simple things like a red letter, a T and (easy now) even a red T in displays containing other coloured letters. Much has been learnt and several integrative reviews have been written (see Wolfe, 1994, 1998; and indeed Quinlan, 2003). Some of this work informed a now extremely influential model of visual search put forward by Itti and Koch (see, for example, Itti & Koch, 2000). Without going into any details, the model works primarily from the bottom up. A so-called *saliency map* is built up from input that codes the current visual scene. Information in this 2D spatial array of the scene codes 'the saliency or conspicuity of objects in the visual environment' (p. 1489). So, in caricature, shiny, bright objects grab attention because such salient attributes are coded as being important in the saliency map. The model accounts for a fair amount of the data, and it is being taken very seriously by a lot of serious people.

A fly in the ointment, though, is that the model does a very poor job of accounting for what a person does when confronted by more socially relevant search tasks with real-world scenes. For instance, Henderson, Brockmole, Castelhano and Mack (2007) have recently reported experiments in which people were given a task in which, on a given trial, they were expected to count the number of people contained in a photograph of a real-world scene. While participants viewed the photographs, their eye movements were monitored. So for every participant, and for every picture, records of eye scan paths across the images were derived. For comparison purposes, the same photographic images were presented to the Itti and Koch computer model and, essentially, saliency maps for the images were derived. Such maps provided regions of interest in the images and such regions of interest will be 'looked' at by the model. In other words, it was possible to derive patterns of eye movements for the model and compare these with patterns of eye movements made by actual people. In brief, and to be blunt, the model failed to provide an adequate fit with the human data. There were many glaring cases where humans simply failed to look at the regions of interest as defined by the model.

Now, of course, it may well be that the model can be extended to account for these data, by providing it with top-down mechanisms that will allow it to carry out the 'people search' task, but this is beside the point. The basic point is that models of the sort put forward by Itti and Koch may, in fact, be rather misleading. This is not to say that stimulus factors are not important – what else do you have to go on in contrived or novel environments? On the contrary, the claim is that a quite different view of visual search emerges if the task is situated in more realistic sorts of situations. You may never have had to count the number of people in a visual scene but you probably will have been placed in the situation of waiting for a friend or relative coming off a plane at an airport, a train at a railway station or a bus at a bus station. Does knowing about searching for red Ts really help here?

Maybe if we begin to take the real world a little more seriously in our research, then we will really begin to make significant progress in understanding the mind. So the question is, how do you feel about that?

## CHAPTER SUMMARY

- Interest in the relationship between emotion and cognition is growing as a result of the advances in computer technology (e.g., morphing), but has been historically slow, possibly as a result of assuming that only clinical populations would be able to tell us anything meaningful about the mechanisms underlying emotion. Another central issue, when discussing emotion in relation to cognition, is how it fits in the grand scheme of things. Rather than argue that emotion has its own set of autonomous processors in keeping with the modularity of mind hypothesis, other researchers such as Oatley and Johnson-Laird (1987) have argued that emotion propagates the entire cognitive system.

- Five basic emotions have been identified as happiness, sadness, anxiety/fear, anger and disgust (Ekman, Friesen & Ellsworth, 1982). According to Ekman (1999), basic emotions are thought to have a number of properties, including distinctive signals and physiological markers. With the notion of basic emotions, it is possible to distinguish between emotional and non-emotional modes of the cognitive system (Oatley & Johnson-Laird, 1987). By this view, emotion makes itself known during the execution of planned behaviour and, more specifically, in the transitions between sub-plans (also known as junctures). In this way, emotions change the ongoing cognitive processes in order to ensure the maintenance of basic biosocial needs (Öhman, 1999).

- Öhman (1999) went further to suggest that as a result of the basic nature of emotions, they do not always need conscious evaluation. For example, fear responses can often operate after an unconscious, automatic appraisal of the environment (Öhman & Mineka, 2001). Unfortunately, the distinction between automatic (unconscious) and controlled (conscious) processes is problematic, with little consensus regarding the properties of these two classes of operations.

- Certain types of emotion have been associated with automatic processing. For example, the processing of fear-relevant or threatening stimuli is thought to occur much faster than any other type of emotional stimulus. In order to test these ideas, visual search paradigms (e.g., Treisman & Gelade, 1980) have been established in which individuals are required to look out for a target stimulus of a particular type in a display containing a varying number of to-be-searched elements (display size). Hansen and Hansen (1988) have examined how certain target emotional facial expressions were detected within visual search experiments, by instructing participants to judge the visual arrays as either containing all the same facial expressions or whether one of the faces had a different expression. An anger superiority effect was found in that angry faces were easier to detect in a sea of happy faces, relative to the detection of a happy face in an angry crowd. However, this finding was compromised by the observation that participants also found it relatively easy to find a neutral face in a happy crowd.

- A further advantage of the visual search paradigm is that the idea of automatic processing can be experimentally assessed. Essentially, automatic (or parallel) search is when the display size increases but the speed of target detection remains marginally unaffected – the target is said to 'pop out'. This is in contrast to serial searches in which the reaction time for target detection is slowed by an increase in display size (typically more than 10 ms per display element; Wolfe, 1998). Hansen and Hansen (1988) also provided data to suggest that the increase in reaction time for detecting a happy face in an angry crowd as a result of increased display size was larger than the increase for detecting an angry face in a happy crowd. However, the reaction time increase was not small enough to claim that the detection of angry faces is an automatic process (Eastwood et al., 2001), although it is certainly fast. Arguments for an anger superiority effect have been compromised by critiques of the stimuli used (Purcell et al., 1996) and also by the occurrence of a happiness superiority effect (Juth et al., 2005). One important factor appears to be the use of real or schematic faces, with a happiness superiority effect more likely with real faces and an anger superiority effect more likely with schematic faces.

- In addition to the visual search paradigm, other experimental protocols have been employed to examine the detection of emotion. In the flanker task (Eriksen & Eriksen, 1974), participants are typically required to respond to a centrally presented item while being flanked by additional items either side. In terms of response, the flanker items are either consistent or inconsistent with the target item. Therefore participants often experience response competition on inconsistent trials in which the centrally presented item is suggesting one response while the flanker items are suggesting another response, resulting in slower reaction times than consistent trials. Using emotional faces as target and flankers, Fenske and Eastwood (2003) found that negative emotion target faces did not suffer from flanker interference, but positive emotion target faces did suffer from being surrounded by negative emotion flanker faces. This has been labelled as a flanker asymmetry effect (Hostmann et al., 2006). Although in one sense this supports the idea that negative facial expressions capture attention, it is not clear whether the effect is due to target processing or flanker processing.

- Spatial cueing (Posner et al., 1978) is a third cognitive psychology paradigm that speaks to the mechanisms underlying the processing of emotion. Typically, participants are required to respond to the spatial location of a target item. Prior to the presentation of a target, however, a cue is presented which provides information regarding the possible location of the subsequent target. On valid trials, the cue correctly predicts the location of the target. On invalid trials, the cue incorrectly predicts the location of the target. In addition to manipulating the validity of the cue–target relation, the time between the onset of cue and target (stimulus onset asynchrony – SOA) is also varied. A typical finding is that at very short SOAs (e.g., 50 ms) participants have a tendency to respond to the cued location rather than the actual location of the target. Distinctions have been made in the spatial cueing paradigm between covert and overt shifts of attention, in which covert shifts of attention do not involve eye movements. Further delineations have been made between attention being under exogenous and endogenous control. The exogenous control of attention is essentially driven by stimulus factors, whereas the endogenous control of attention is essentially driven by the intention of the individual.

- Ideas of social attention have come to fruition on the basis of applying the spatial cueing paradigm to faces. For example, Friesen and Kingstone (1998) used eye gaze as the cue to the position of a letter which participants then had to decide whether it was a pre-defined target or not. Individuals were greatly speeded on valid trials in which the cue face was looking in the direction of where the eventual letter would appear. Therefore it seems very difficult not to be able to follow the gaze of another person. Moreover, when presented with schematic cues, participants had to believe that the cue represented eyes in order for the effect to occur (Ristic & Kingstone, 2005), thereby demonstrating an endogenous component to the effect. Tipples

▶

(2006) combined eye gaze with facial expression, and found that valid cues produced greater speeding when the face wore a fearful expression than a happy expression.

● However, it is not just faces that can be perceived as threatening or fearful. Öhman, Flykt and Esteves (2001) showed that snakes and spiders were responded to much faster than flowers and mushrooms in visual search tasks. Moreover, a manipulation of display size in the same experiment suggested that threatening stimuli did indeed pop out, given that there was little effect on increasing the display size on reaction time. Attempts to replicate this finding have met with mixed results (Tipples, Young, Quinlan, Broks & Ellis, 2002), with the growing idea that it might be that animals per se give rise to the advantage rather than threatening animals (see also Lipp et al., 2004). However, there is some indication that individually fear-inducing images may influence cognition more than individually fear-irrelevant images (Lipp & Waters, 2007).

● A final interaction between emotion and cognition is the consideration of mood and judgement. Depressive realism (Alloy & Abramson, 1979) is the phenomenon by which depressive individuals are thought to have more realistic assessments of situations than normal, healthy individuals. For example, depressive individuals were more likely to learn that responses and outcomes were uncorrelated in an experiment than non-depressed individuals. Allan et al. (2007) suggest three possible reasons for the depressive realism effect. First, a motivational account suggests that depressed individuals do not see any reason to protect their feeling of self-worth so do not adjust evidence in the world accordingly. Second, an inter-trial interval (ITI) account suggests that the ability of normal, healthy individuals to perceive an illusion of control critically depends on a large ITI. Third, the response-criterion hypothesis suggests that the effect arises from a bias of depressive individuals simply to say 'no'.

## ANSWERS TO PINPOINT QUESTIONS

16.1 Emotional modes are thought to come more into play when a plan is being carried out.

16.2 The anger superiority effect is the relative ease at detecting a discrepant angry face within a crowd, relative to detecting a discrepant neutral or happy face.

16.3 Serial and parallel searches are evaluated on the basis of the slope of the linear function between increases in display size and increases in RT. Traditionally, if the slope is less than 10 ms per item, the search is said to be parallel, and if the slope is clearly above 10 ms per item, the search is said to be serial.

16.4 The happiness superiority effect came about in the Juth et al. (2005) study by using colour photographic images of faces of different individuals which were either looking towards or away from the viewer.

16.5 We would know 'EDE' was consistent if both E and D were assigned to the same response and we would know 'FDF' was inconsistent if both F and D were assigned to different responses.

16.6 The flanker asymmetry effect (Hostmann et al., 2006) manifests itself in the fact that responses

to a positive expression flanked by negative expressions suffer from more interference than do responses to a negative expression flanked by positive expressions.

16.7 According to the evidence provided by Tipples (2006), participants experienced greater spatial cueing effects for eye gaze when the facial expression was one of fear.

16.8 It appeared that in the context of being tested alongside plants, the detection of a discrepant image of a pleasant animal was essentially the same as the detection of a discrepant image of a threatening animal.

16.9 Music was used as a mood inducer in the Bradley et al. (1997) study and care was taken to ensure that no depressives or individuals prone to depression took part in the study.

16.10 Depressive realism may be accounted for by differences in motivation between depressed and non-depressed individuals, the fact that depressed individuals might ignore the length of time in between trials, or the increased likelihood of depressed individuals to just say no.

# Bibliography

Abeles, P., & Morton, J. (1999). Avoiding misinformation: Reinstating target modality. *The Quarterly Journal of Experimental Psychology, 52A*, 581–592.

Achtman, R. L., Hess, R. F., & Wang, Y.-Z. (2003). Sensitivity for global shape detection. *Journal of Vision, 3*, 616–624.

Adams, D. (1979). *The Hitchhiker's Guide to the Galaxy.* London: Pan Books.

Adelson, E. H. (1983). What is iconic storage good for? *The Behavioral and Brain Sciences, 6*, 11–12.

Aizawa, K. (1997). Explaining systematicity. *Mind & Language, 12*, 115–136.

Allan, L. G., Siegel, S., & Hannah, S. (2007). The sad truth about depressive realism. *The Quarterly Journal of Experimental Psychology, 60*, 482–495.

Allen, R. J., Baddeley, A. D., & Hitch, G. J. (2006). Is the binding of visual features in working memory resource-demanding? *Journal of Experimental Psychology: General, 135*, 298–313.

Alloy, L. B., & Abramson, L. Y. (1979). Judgement of contingency in depressed and non-depressed students: Sadder but wiser? *Journal of Experimental Psychology: General, 108*, 441–485.

Allport, D. A. (1968). Phenomenal simultaneity and the perceptual moment hypothesis. *British Journal of Psychology, 59*, 395–406.

Allport, D. A. (1977). On knowing the meaning of words we are unable to report: The effects of visual masking. In S. Dornic (Ed.), *Attention and performance, VI* (pp. 505–533). Hillsdale, New Jersey: Erlbaum.

Allport, D. A. (1989). Visual attention. In M. I. Posner (Ed.), *Foundations of cognitive science* (pp. 631–682). Cambridge, Massachusetts: The MIT Press.

Allport, D. A., Antonis, B., & Reynolds, P. (1972). On the division of attention: A disproof of the single-channel hypothesis.

*The Quarterly Journal of Experimental Psychology, 24*, 225–235.

Allport, D. A., Styles, E. A., & Hsieh, S. (1994). Shifting intentional set: Exploring the dynamic control of tasks. In C. Umilta & M. Moscovitch (Eds.), *Attention and performance XV: Conscious and nonconscious information processing* (pp. 421–452). Cambridge, Massachusetts: The MIT Press.

Allport, D. A., Tipper, S. P., & Chmiel, N. R. J. (1985). Perceptual integration and post-categorical filtering. In M. I. Posner & O. S. M. Marin (Eds.), *Attention and performance, XI* (pp. 107–132). Hillsdale, New Jersey: Erlbaum.

Allport, D. A., & Wylie, G. (1999). Task-switching: Positive and negative priming of task-set. In G. W. Humphreys, J. Duncan & A. Treisman (Eds.), *Attention space and action. Studies in cognitive neuroscience* (pp. 273–296). Oxford, England: Oxford University Press.

Allport, D. A., & Wylie, G. (2000). Task switching, stimulus–response bindings and negative priming. In S. Monsell and J. Driver (Eds.), *Attention and performance XVIII: Control of Cognitive processes* (pp. 35–70). Cambridge, Massachusetts: The MIT Press.

Amirkhiabani, G., & Lovegrove, W. J. (1996). Role of eccentricity and size in the global precedence effect. *Journal of Experimental Psychology: Human Perception and Performance, 22*, 1434–1447.

Anderson, J. R. (1976). *Language, memory and thought.* Hillsdale, New Jersey: Erlbaum.

Anderson, J. R. (1978). Arguments concerning representations for mental imagery. *Psychological Review, 85*, 249–277.

Anderson, J. R. (1979). Further arguments concerning representations for mental imagery: A response to Hayes-Roth and

Pylyshyn. *Psychological Review, 86*, 395–406.

Anderson, J. R. (2005). *Cognitive psychology and its implications* (6th ed.). New York: Worth.

Anderson, J. R., & Bower, G. H. (1973). *Human associative memory.* Washington: Winston.

Anderson, J. R., & Bower, G. H. (1974). A propositional theory of recognition memory. *Memory & Cognition, 2*, 406–412.

Anderson, L. (1995). *Word of mouth: On the ugly one with the jewels.* New York: Warner Bros.

Anglin, J. M. (Ed.). (1974). *J. S. Bruner: Beyond the information given. Studies in the Psychology of Knowing.* London: George Allen & Unwin Ltd.

Anglin, J. M. (1977). *Word, object, and conceptual development.* London: Academic Press.

Archambault, A., O'Donnell, C., & Schyns, P. G. (1999). Blind to object changes: When learning the same object at different levels of categorization modifies its perception. *Psychological Science, 10*, 249–255.

Armstrong, S. L., Gleitman, L. R., & Gleitman, H. (1983). What some concepts might not be. *Cognition, 13*, 263–308.

Ashby, F. G., & Maddox, W. T. (2005). Human category learning. *Annual Review of Psychology, 56*, 149–178.

Ashcraft, M. H. (1978). Property dominance and typicality effects in property statement verification. *Journal of Verbal Learning and Verbal Behavior, 17*, 155–164.

Atkinson, R. C., & Shiffrin, R. M. (1968). Human memory: A proposed system and its control processes. In K. W. Spence & J. T. Spence (Eds.), *The psychology of learning and motivation*, Vol. 2 (pp. 89–195). New York: Academic.

Atkinson, R. C., & Shiffrin, R. M. (1976). The control of short-term memory. *Scientific American, 225,* 82–90.

Averbach, E., & Coriell, A. S. (1961). Short term memory in vision. *Bell Systems Technical Journal, 40,* 309–328.

Ayers, M. S., & Reder, L. M. (1998). A theoretical review of the misinformation effect: Predictions from an activation-based memory model. *Psychonomic Bulletin & Review, 5,* 1–21.

Azevedo, T. M., Volchan, E., Imbiriba, L. A., Rodrigues, E. C., Oliveira, J. M., Oliveira, L. F., Lutterbach, L. G., & Vargas, C. D. (2005). A freezing-like posture to pictures of mutilation. *Psychophysiology, 42,* 255–260.

Baddeley, A. D. (1966). Short-term memory for word sequences as a function of acoustic, semantic and formal similarity. *The Quarterly Journal of Experimental Psychology, 18,* 362–365.

Baddeley, A. D. (1986). *Working memory.* Oxford, England: Oxford University Press.

Baddeley, A. D. (1990). *Human memory: Theory and practice.* Hove, England: Erlbaum.

Baddeley, A. D. (2000a). Short-term and working memory. In E. Tulving & F. I. M. Craik (Eds.), *The Oxford handbook of memory* (pp. 77–92). Oxford, England: Oxford University Press.

Baddeley, A. D. (2000b). The episodic buffer: A new component of working memory? *Trends in Cognitive Science, 4,* 417–423.

Baddeley, A. D. (2003). Working memory: Looking back and looking forward. *Nature Reviews Neuroscience, 4,* 829–839.

Baddeley, A. D. (2007). *Working memory, thought, and action.* Oxford, England: Oxford University Press.

Baddeley, A. D., Chinocotta, D., Stafford, L., & Turk, D. (2002). Is the word length effect in STM entirely attributable to output delay? Evidence from serial recognition. *The Quarterly Journal of Experimental Psychology, 55A,* 353–369.

Baddeley, A. D., & Hitch, G. J. (1974). Working memory. In G. H. Bower (Ed.), *Recent advances in learning and motivation*, Vol. VIII (pp. 47–90). New York: Academic.

Baddeley, A. D., & Hitch, G. J. (1977). Recency re-examined. In S. Dornic (Ed.), *Attention and performance, VI* (pp. 647–667). Hillsdale, New Jersey: Erlbaum.

Baddeley, A. D., & Larsen, J. D. (2003). The disruption of STM: A response to our commentators. *The Quarterly Journal of Experimental Psychology, 56A,* 1301–1306.

Baddeley, A. D., & Scott, D. (1971). Short term forgetting in the absence of proactive interference. *The Quarterly Journal of Experimental Psychology, 23,* 275–283.

Baddeley, A. D., Thomson, N., & Buchanan, M. (1975). Word length and the structure of working memory. *Journal of Verbal Learning and Verbal Behavior, 14,* 575–589.

Baddeley, A. D., Vallar, G., & Wilson, B. A. (1987). Sentence comprehension and phonological memory: Some neuropsychological evidence. In M. Coltheart (Ed.), *Attention and performance, XII: The psychology of reading* (pp. 509–529). Hove, England: Erlbaum.

Banaji, M. R., & Crowder, R. G. (1989). The bankruptcy of everyday memory. *American Psychologist, 44,* 1185–1193.

Banks, W. P. (1970). Signal detection theory and human memory. *Psychological Bulletin, 74,* 81–99.

Banks, W. P., & Barber, G. (1977). Color information in iconic memory. *Psychological Review, 84,* 536–546.

Barber, P. J., & de la Mahotiere, C. (1982). Perceptual defence: An attempted replication using the dark adaptation paradigm. *Canadian Journal of Psychology, 36,* 94–104.

Barclay, C. R. (1986). Schematization of autobiographical memory. In D. C. Rubin (Ed.), *Autobiographical memory* (pp. 82–99). Cambridge, England: Cambridge University Press.

Barker, R. (2001). *All I ever wrote: The complete works.* London: Sidgwick & Jackson.

Barlow, H. B. (2001). Redundancy reduction revisited. *Network: Computation in Neural Systems, 12,* 241–253.

Bartlett, F. C. (1932). *Remembering: A study in experimental and social psychology.* Cambridge, England: Cambridge University Press.

Beach, L. R. (1964). Recognition, assimilation and identification of objects. *Psychological Monographs, 78* (Whole No. 582a).

Beck, B. B. (1980). *Animal tool behavior: The use and manufacture of tools by animals.* New York: Garland STPM Press.

Becker, M. W., Pashler, H., & Anstis, S. M. (2000). The role of iconic memory in change-detection tasks. *Perception, 29,* 273–286.

Beckett, S. (1952/1986). *The complete dramatic works.* London: Faber.

Behrmann, M., Marotta, J., Gauthier, I., Tarr, M. J., & McKeeff, T. J. (2005). Behavioral change and its neural correlates in visual agnosia after expertise training. *Journal of Cognitive Neuroscience, 17,* 554–568.

Bekerian, D. A., & Bowers, J. M. (1983). Eyewitness testimony. Were we misled? *Journal of Experimental Psychology: Learning, Memory and Cognition, 9,* 139–145.

Belli, R. F. (1989). Influences of misleading postevent information: Misinformation interference and acceptance. *Journal of Experimental Psychology: General, 118,* 72–85.

Benton, S., & Moscovitch, M. (1988). The time course of repetition effects for words and unfamiliar faces. *Journal of Experimental Psychology: General, 117,* 148–160.

Berlin, B., & Kay, P. (1969). *Basic color terms: Their universality and evolution.* Berkeley and Los Angeles, California: University of California Press.

Bernbach, H. A. (1967). Decision processes in memory. *Psychological Review, 74,* 462–480.

Bernbach, H. A. (1969). Replication processes in human memory and learning. In G. H. Bower & J. T. Spence (Eds.), *The psychology of learning and motivation*, Vol. 3 (pp. 201–240). New York: Academic.

Biederman, I. (1987). Recognition-by-components: A theory of human image understanding. *Psychological Review, 94,* 115–147.

Biederman, I. (1995). Visual object recognition. In S. M. Kosslyn & D. N. Osherson (Eds.), *An invitation to cognitive science* (2nd ed., pp. 121–165). Cambridge, Massachusetts: The MIT Press.

Biederman, I., & Gerhardstein, P. C. (1993). Recognizing depth-rotated objects: Evidence and conditions for three-dimensional viewpoint invariance. *Journal of Experimental Psychology: Human Perception and Performance, 19,* 1162–1182.

Biederman, I., & Gerhardstein, P. C. (1995). Viewpoint-dependent mechanisms in visual object recognition: Reply to Tarr and Bültoff (1995). *Journal of Experimental Psychology: Human Perception and Performance, 21,* 1506–1514.

Biederman, I., Mezzanotte, R. J., & Rabinowitz, J. C. (1982). Scene perception: Detecting and judging objects undergoing relational violations. *Cognitive Psychology, 14,* 143–177.

Biederman, I., Subramaniam, S., Bar, M., Kalocsai, P., & Fiser, J. (1999). Subordinate-level object classification reexamined. *Psychological Research, 62*, 131–153.

Bjork, R. A., & Whitten, W. B. (1974). Recency-sensitive retrieval processes in long-term memory. *Cognitive Psychology, 6*, 173–189.

Blakemore, C., & Cooper, G. F. (1970). Development of the brain depends on the visual environment. *Nature, 228*, 477–478.

Blanz, V., Tarr, M. J., & Bültoff, H. H. (1998). What object attributes determine canonical views? *Perception, 28*, 575–599.

Blumberg, M. S., & Wasserman, E. A. (1995). Animal mind and the argument from design. *American Psychologist, 50*, 133–144.

Boles, D. B. (1984). Global versus local processing: Is there a hemispheric dichotomy? *Neuropsychologia, 22*, 445–455.

Boring, E. G. (1930). A new ambiguous figure. *The American Journal of Psychology, 42*, 444–445.

Boselie, F., & Leeuwenberg, E. L. J. (1986). A test of the minimum principle requires a perceptual coding system. *Perception, 15*, 331–354.

Bower, G. H. (1970). Imagery as a relational organizer in associative learning. *Journal of Verbal Learning and Verbal Behavior, 9*, 529–533.

Bower, G. H. (2000). A brief history of memory research. In E. Tulving & F. I. M. Craik (Eds.), *The Oxford handbook of memory* (pp. 3–32). Oxford, England: Oxford University Press.

Bower, G. H., & Bryant, D. J. (1991). On relating the organizational theory of memory to levels of processing. In W. Kessen, A. Ortony & F. I. M. Craik (Eds.), *Memories, thoughts, and emotions: Essays in honor of George Mandler* (pp. 149–168). Hillsdale, New Jersey: Erlbaum.

Bower, G. H., Clark, M. C., Lesgold, A. M., & Winzenz, D. (1969). Hierarchical retrieval schemes in recall of categorized word lists. *Journal of Verbal Learning and Verbal Behavior, 8*, 323–343.

Bowers, J. M., & Bekerian, D. A. (1984). When will postevent information distort eyewitness testimony? *Journal of Applied Psychology, 69*, 466–472.

Bowman, R., & Sutherland, N. S. (1969). Discrimination of 'W' and 'V' shapes by goldfish. *The Quarterly Journal of Experimental Psychology, 21*, 69–76.

Bradley, B. P., Mogg, K., & Lee, S. C. (1997). Attentional biases for negative information in induced and naturally occurring dysphoria. *Behaviour Research and Therapy, 35*, 911–927.

Brady, M. (1982). Computational approaches to image understanding. *Computing Surveys, 14*, 3–71.

Brandimonte, M. A., & Gerbino, W. (1993). Mental image reversal and verbal recoding: When ducks become rabbits. *Memory & Cognition, 21*, 23–33.

Broadbent, D. E. (1954). The role of auditory localization in attention and memory span. *Journal of Experimental Psychology, 47*, 191–196.

Broadbent, D. E. (1956). Successive responses to simultaneous stimuli. *The Quarterly Journal of Experimental Psychology, 8*, 145–152.

Broadbent, D. E. (1958). *Perception and communication*. Oxford, England: Pergamon Press.

Broadbent, D. E. (1970). Stimulus set and response set: Two kinds of selective attention. In D. I. Mostofsky (Ed.), *Attention: Contemporary theory and analysis* (pp. 51–60). New York: Appleton-Century-Crofts.

Broadbent, D. E. (1971). *Decision and stress*. London: Academic Press.

Broadbent, D. E. (1977). The hidden preattentive processes. *American Psychologist, 32*, 109–118.

Broadbent, D. E. (1982). Task combination and selective intake of information. *Acta Psychologica, 50*, 253–290.

Broadbent, D. E. (1984). Mental models: A critical notice of Johnson-Laird, P.N. Mental Models. *The Quarterly Journal of Experimental Psychology, 36A*, 673–681.

Broadbent, D. E., & Gregory, M. H. P. (1967a). Perception of emotionally toned words. *Nature, 215*, 581–584.

Broadbent, D. E., & Gregory, M. H. P. (1967b). Psychological refractory period and the length of time required to make a decision. *Proceedings of the Royal Society of London, Series B, 168*, 181–193.

Broadbent, D. E., & Gregory, M. H. P. (1971). Effects on tachistoscopic perception from independent variation of word probability and of letter probability. *Acta Psychologica, 35*, 1–14.

Brooks, L. R. (1967). The suppression of visualization by reading. *The Quarterly Journal of Experimental Psychology, 19*, 289–299.

Brosch, T., & Sharma, D. (2005). The role of fear-relevant stimuli in visual search: A comparison of phylogenetic and ontogenetic stimuli. *Emotion, 5*, 360–364.

Brown, G. D. A., & Hulme, C. (1995). Modeling item length effects in memory span: No rehearsal needed? *Journal of Memory and Language, 34*, 594–621.

Brown, G. D. A., Neath, I., & Chater, N. (2006). A temporal ratio model of memory. *Psychological Review, 114*, 539–576.

Brown, H., & Kirsner, K. (1980). A within-subjects analysis of the relationship between memory span and processing rate in short-term memory. *Cognitive Psychology, 12*, 177–187.

Brown, J. (1958). Some tests of the decay theory of immediate memory. *The Quarterly Journal of Experimental Psychology, 10*, 12–21.

Brown, R., & McNeill, D. (1966). The tip-of-the-tongue phenomenon. *Journal of Verbal Learning and Verbal Behavior, 5*, 325–337.

Bruce, D. (1985). The how and why of ecological memory. *Journal of Experimental Psychology: General, 114*, 78–90.

Bruner, J. S. (1957). On perceptual readiness. *Psychological Review, 64*, 123–152.

Bruner, J. S., & Goodman, G. C. (1947). Value and need as organizing factors in perception. *Journal of Abnormal and Social Psychology, 42*, 33–44.

Bruner, J. S., & Postman, L. (1949). On the perception of incongruity: A paradigm. *Journal of Personality, 18*, 206–223.

Brysbaert, M. (1995). Arabic number reading: On the nature of the numerical scale and the origin of phonological recoding. *Journal of Experimental Psychology: General, 124*, 434–452.

Buck, R. (1986a). The psychology of emotion. In J. E. LeDoux & W. Hirst (Eds.), *Mind and brain. Dialogues in cognitive neuroscience* (pp. 275–300). Cambridge, England: Cambridge University Press.

Buck, R. (1986b). A psychologist's reply. In J. E. LeDoux & W. Hirst (Eds.), *Mind and brain. Dialogues in cognitive neuroscience* (pp. 359–366). Cambridge, England: Cambridge University Press.

Buffart, H., Leeuwenberg, E. L. J., & Restle, F. (1983). Analysis of ambiguity in visual pattern completion. *Journal of Experimental Psychology: Human Perception and Performance, 9*, 980–1000.

Bültoff, H. H., & Edelman, S. (1992). Psychophysical support for a two-dimensional view interpolation theory of object recognition. *Proceedings of the National Academy of Sciences of the United States of America, 89*, 60–64.

Bundesen, C. (1990). A theory of visual attention. *Psychological Review, 97*, 523–547.

Bundesen, C., Pedersen, L. F., & Larsen, A. (1984). Measuring efficiency of selection from briefly exposed visual displays: A model of partial report. *Journal of Experimental Psychology: Human Perception and Performance, 10,* 329–339.

Burgess, A. (1962). *A clockwork orange.* London: Penguin Books.

Burgess, N., & Hitch, G. J. (1999). Memory for serial order: A network model of the phonological loop and its timing. *Psychological Review, 106,* 551–581.

Burmann, B., Dehnhardt, G., & Mauck, B. (2005). Visual information processing in the lion-tailed macaque (macaca silenus): Mental rotation or rotational invariance? *Brain, Behavior & Evolution, 65,* 168–176.

Caldwell, E. C., & Hall, V. C. (1970). Distinctive-features versus prototype learning reexamined. *Journal of Experimental Psychology, 83,* 7–12.

Campos, L., & Alonso-Quecuty, M. L. (2006). Remembering a criminal conversation: Beyond eyewitness testimony. *Memory, 14,* 27–36.

Carrasco, M., Ling, S., & Read, S. (2004). Attention alters appearance. *Nature Neuroscience, 7,* 308–313.

Casscells, W., Schoenberger, A., & Graboys, T. B. (1978). Interpretation by physicians of clinical laboratory results. *The New England Journal of Medicine, 299,* 999–1001.

Cattell, J. M. (1886). The time taken up by cerebral operations. *Mind, 11,* 220–242.

Chambers, D., & Reisberg, D. (1985). Can mental images be ambiguous? *Journal of Experimental Psychology: Human Perception and Performance, 11,* 317–328.

Chambers, D., & Reisberg, D. (1992). What an image depicts depends on what an image means. *Cognitive Psychology, 24,* 145–174.

Chandler, C. C. (1989). Specific retroactive interference in modified recognition tests: Evidence for an unknown cause of interference. *Journal of Experimental Psychology: Learning, Memory and Cognition, 15,* 256–265.

Chapman, G. B., & Johnson, E. J. (2002). Incorporating the irrelevant: Anchors in judgments of belief and value. In T. Gilovich, D. Griffin & D. Kahneman (Eds.), *Heuristics and biases. The psychology of intuitive judgment* (pp. 120–138). Cambridge, England: Cambridge University Press.

Chater, N. (1996). Reconciling simplicity and likelihood principles in perceptual organization. *Psychological Review, 103,* 566–581.

Chater, N., & Oaksford, M. (1999). The probability heuristics model of syllogistic reasoning. *Cognitive Science, 22,* 25–51.

Cheesman, J., & Merikle, P. M. (1984). Priming with and without awareness. *Perception & Psychophysics, 36,* 387–395.

Cheesman, J., & Merikle, P. M. (1985). Word recognition and consciousness. In D. Besner, T. G. Waller & G. E. MacKinnon (Eds.), *Reading Research: Advances in theory and practice* (Vol. 5, pp. 311–352). New York: Academic Press.

Cheesman, J., & Merikle, P. M. (1986). Distinguishing conscious from unconscious perceptual processes. *Canadian Journal of Psychology, 40,* 343–367.

Cheng, P. W., & Holyoak, K. J. (1985). Pragmatic reasoning schemas. *Cognitive Psychology, 17,* 391–416.

Cheng, P. W., & Holyoak, K. J. (1989). On the natural selection of reasoning theories. *Cognition, 33,* 285–313.

Cheng, P. W., Holyoak, K. J., Nisbett, R. E., & Oliver, L. M. (1986). Pragmatic versus syntactic approaches to training deductive reasoning. *Cognitive Psychology, 18,* 293–328.

Cherry, C. (1978). *On human communication. A review, a survey and a criticism* (3rd ed.). Cambridge, Massachusetts: The MIT Press.

Cherry, E. C. (1953). Some experiments on the recognition of speech, with one and two ears. *Journal of the Acoustical Society of America, 26,* 554–559.

Chipp, H. B. (1968). *Theories of modern art: A source book by artists and critics.* Berkeley, California: University of California Press.

Chomsky, N. (1957). *Syntactic structures.* The Hague, Holland: Mouton.

Chomsky, N. (1965). *Aspects of the theory of syntax.* Cambridge, Massachusetts: The MIT Press.

Chomsky, N. (1980). Rules and representation. *The Behavioral and Brain Sciences, 3,* 1–61.

Churchland, P. M. (1984). *Matter and consciousness.* Cambridge, Massachusetts: The MIT Press.

Claney, S. A., McNally, R. J., Schacter, D. L., Lenzenweger, M. F., & Pitman, R. K. (2002). Memory distortion in people reporting abduction by aliens. *Journal of Abnormal Psychology, 111,* 455–461.

Clark, H. H., & Clark, E. V. (1977). *Psychology and Language: An introduction to psycholinguistics.* New York: Harcourt Brace Jovanovich.

Clark, S. E. (1969). Retrieval of color information from the preperceptual

storage system. *Journal of Experimental Psychology, 82,* 263–266.

Colle, H. A., & Welsh, A. (1976). Acoustic masking in primary memory. *Journal of Verbal Learning and Verbal Behavior, 15,* 17–32.

Collins, A. M., & Loftus, E. F. (1975). A spreading-activation theory of semantic processing. *Psychological Review, 82,* 407–428.

Collins, A. M., & Quillian, M. R. (1969). Retrieval time from semantic memory. *Journal of Verbal Learning and Verbal Behavior, 8,* 240–247.

Collins, A. M., & Quillian, M. R. (1970). Facilitating retrieval from semantic memory: The effect of repeating part of an inference. *Acta Psychologica, 33,* 304–314.

Coltheart, M. (1972). Visual information processing. In P. C. Dodwell (Ed.), *New horizons in psychology 2* (pp. 62–85). Harmondsworth, England: Penguin Books.

Coltheart, M. (1980a). Iconic memory and visible persistence. *Perception & Psychophysics, 27,* 183–228.

Coltheart, M. (1980b). The persistences of vision. *Philosophical Transactions of the Royal Society of London, (Series B), 290,* 57–69.

Coltheart, M. (1983a). Ecological necessity of iconic memory. *The Behavioral and Brain Sciences, 6,* 17–18.

Coltheart, M. (1983b). Iconic memory. *Philosophical Transactions of the Royal Society of London, (Series B), 302,* 282–294.

Coltheart, M. (1984). Sensory memory. In H. Bouma & D. G. Bouwhis (Eds.), *Attention and performance X: Control of language processes. Proceedings of the tenth international symposium on attention and performance* (pp. 259–285). Hillsdale, New Jersey: Erlbaum.

Coltheart, M. (1999). Modularity and cognition. *Trends in Cognitive Science, 3,* 115–120.

Coltheart, M. (2001). Assumptions and methods in cognitive neuropsychology. In R. Rapp (Ed.), *The handbook of cognitive neuropsychology* (pp. 3–21). Hove, England: Psychology Press.

Coltheart, M., & Davies, M. (2003). Inference and explanation in cognitive neuropsychology. *Cortex, 39,* 188–191.

Coltheart, M., Lea, C. D., & Thompson, K. (1974). In defence of iconic memory. *The Quarterly Journal of Experimental Psychology, 26,* 633–641.

Connolly, A. C., Fodor, J. A., Gleitman, L. R., & Gleitman, H. (2007). Why stereotypes don't even make good defaults. *Cognition*, *103*, 1–22.

Connolly, G. N., Wayne, G. D., Lymperis, D., & Doherty, M. C. (2000). How cigarette additives are used to mask environmental tobacco smoke. *Tobacco Control*, *9*, 283–291.

Conrad, C. (1972). Cognitive economy in semantic memory. *Journal of Experimental Psychology*, *92*, 149–154.

Conrad, R. (1964). Acoustic confusion in immediate memory. *British Journal of Psychology*, *55*, 49–54.

Conway, A. R. A., Cowan, N., & Bunting, M. F. (2001). The cocktail party phenomenon revisited: The importance of working memory capacity. *Psychonomic Bulletin & Review*, *8*, 331–335.

Conway, M. A. (1989). In defense of everyday memory. *American Psychologist*, *46*, 19–26.

Conway, M. A. (1990). Autobiographical memory and conceptual representation. *Journal of Experimental Psychology: Learning, Memory and Cognition*, *16*, 799–812.

Conway, M. A. (2005). Memory and the self. *Journal of Memory and Language*, *53*, 594–628.

Conway, M. A., Collins, A., Gathercole, S. E., & Anderson, S. J. (1996). Recollections of true and false autobiographical memories. *Journal of Experimental Psychology: General*, *125*, 69–95.

Corballis, M. (2003). Recursion as the key to the human mind. In K. Sterelny & J. Fitness (Eds.), *From mating to mentality. Evaluating evolutionary psychology* (pp. 155–171). New York: Psychology Press.

Cosmides, L. (1989). The logic of social exchange: has natural selection shaped how humans reason? Studies with the Wason selection task. *Cognition*, *31*, 187–276.

Cosmides, L., & Tooby, J. (1992). Cognitive adaptations for social exchange. In J. Barkow, L. Cosmides & J. Tooby (Eds.), *The adapted mind: Evolutionary psychology and the generation of culture* (pp. 163–228). New York: Oxford University Press.

Cosmides, L., & Tooby, J. (1994). Origins of domain specificity: The evolution of functional organization. In L. Hirschfield & S. Gelman (Eds.), *Mapping the mind: Domain specificity in cognition and culture* (pp. 85–116). New York: Cambridge University Press.

Cosmides, L., & Tooby, J. (1996). Are humans good intuitive statisticians after all? Rethinking some conclusions from the literature on judgment under uncertainty. *Cognition*, *58*, 1–73.

Cowan, N. (1988). Evolving conceptions of memory storage, selective attention, and theory mutual constraints within the human information-processing system. *Psychological Bulletin*, *104*, 163–191.

Cowan, N. (1995). *Attention and memory: An integrated framework*. Oxford, England: Oxford University Press.

Craik, F. I. M. (2002). Levels of processing: Past, present, and future? *Memory*, *10*, 305–318.

Craik, F. I. M., & Birtwistle, J. (1971). Proactive inhibition in free recall. *Journal of Experimental Psychology*, *91*, 120–123.

Craik, F. I. M., & Lockhart, R. S. (1972). Levels of processing: A framework for memory research. *Journal of Verbal Learning and Verbal Behavior*, *11*, 671–684.

Craik, F. I. M., & Tulving, E. (1975). Depth of processing and the retention of words in episodic memory. *Journal of Experimental Psychology: General*, *104*, 268–294.

Craik, K. (1943). *The nature of explanation*. Cambridge, England: Cambridge University Press.

Cree, G. S., & McRae, K. (2003). Analyzing the factors underlying the structure and computation of the meaning of Chipmunk, Cherry, Chisel, Cheese and Cello (and many other such concrete nouns). *Journal of Experimental Psychology: General*, *132*, 163–201.

Crossley, M., Hiscock, M., & Foreman, J. B. (2004). Dual task performance in early stage dementia: Differential effects for automatized and effortful processing. *Journal of Clinical and Experimental Neuropsychology*, *26*, 332–346.

Crowder, R. G. (1976). *Principles of learning and memory*. Hillsdale, New Jersey: Erlbaum.

Crowder, R. G. (1982). The demise of short-term memory. *Acta Psychologica*, *50*, 291–323.

Crowder, R. G. (1989). Modularity and dissociations in memory systems. In H. L. Roediger III & F. I. M. Craik (Eds.), *Varieties of memory and consciousness. Essays in honor of Endel Tulving* (pp. 271–294). Hillsdale, New Jersey: Erlbaum.

Crowder, R. G. (1993). Short-term memory: Where do we stand? *Memory & Cognition*, *21*, 142–145.

Cummins, D. D. (1996). Evidence for innateness of deontic reasoning. *Mind and Language*, *11*, 160–190.

Cummins, D. D. (2004). The evolution of reasoning. In J. P. Leighton & R. J. Sternberg (Eds.), *The nature of reasoning* (pp. 339–374). Cambridge, England: Cambridge University Press.

Daniels, G. (1994). Secrets of a successful marriage. In M. Groening, *The Simpsons*. USA: Fox.

Davelaar, E. J., Goshen-Gottstein, Y., Ashkenazi, A., Haarmann, H. J., & Usher, M. (2005). The demise of short term memory revisited: Empirical and computational investigations of recency effects. *Psychological Review*, *112*, 3–42.

Davenport, J. L., & Potter, M. C. (2004). Scene consistency in object and background perception. *Psychological Science*, *15*, 559–564.

Davidoff, J. (2001). Language and perceptual categorisation. *Trends in Cognitive Science*, *5*, 382–387.

Davidson, M. L., Fox, M.-J., & Dick, A. O. (1973). Effect of eye movements on backward masking and perceived location. *Perception & Psychophysics*, *14*, 110–116.

de Fockert, J. W., Rees, G., Frith, C. D., & Lavie, N. (2001). The role of working memory in visual selective attention. *Science*, *291*, 1803–1806.

DeLosh, E. L., & Nairne, J. S. (1996). Similarity or discriminability? An evaluation of the fundamental assumption of the encoding specificity principle. Paper presented at the 68th Annual Meeting of the Midwestern Psychological Association, Chicago, Illinois.

Dennett, D. C. (1981). The nature of images and the introspective trap. In N. Block (Ed.), *Readings in Philosophy of Psychology* (Vol. 2, pp. 128–134). Cambridge, Massachusetts: Harvard University Press.

Deutsch, J. A., & Deutsch, D. (1963). Attention: Some theoretical considerations. *Psychological Review*, *70*, 80–90.

Deutsch, J. A., & Deutsch, D. (1967). Comments on 'Selective attention: Perception or response?' *The Quarterly Journal of Experimental Psychology*, *19*, 362–363.

Di Lollo, V., Enns, J. T., & Rensink, R. A. (2000). Competition for consciousness among visual events: The psychophysics of reentrant visual processes. *Journal of Experimental Psychology: General*, *129*, 481–507.

Dickinson, S. J., Pentland, A. P., & Rosenfeld, A. (1992a). 3-D shape recovery using distributed aspect matching. *IEEE Transactions on Pattern Analysis and Machine Intelligence*, *14*, 174–198.

Dickinson, S. J., Pentland, A. P., & Rosenfeld, A. (1992b). From volumes to views: An approach to 3-D object recognition. *CVGIP: Image Understanding*, *55*, 130–154.

Dijksterhuis, A., & Aarts, H. (2003). On wildebeests and humans: The preferential detection of negative stimuli. *Psychological Science*, *14*, 14–18.

Dijksterhuis, A., Corneille, O., Aarts, H., Vermeulen, N., & Luminet, O. (2004). Yes, there is a preferential detection of negative stimuli: A response to Labiouse. *Psychological Science*, *15*, 571–572.

Dixon, N. F. (1971). *Subliminal Perception. The Nature of a Controversy*. London: McGraw-Hill.

Dolan, T. G., & Rainey, J. E. (2005). Audibility of train horns in passenger vehicles. *Human Factors*, *47*, 613–629.

Doyle, J. R., & Leach, C. (1988). Word superiority in signal detection: Barely a glimpse, yet reading nonetheless. *Cognitive Psychology*, *20*, 283–318.

Draine, S. C., & Greenwald, A. G. (1998). Replicable unconscious semantic priming. *Journal of Experimental Psychology: General*, *127*, 286–303.

Duncan, J. (1980). The locus of interference in the perception of simultaneous stimuli. *Psychological Review*, *87*, 272–300.

Duncan, J., & Humphreys, G. W. (1989). Visual search and stimulus similarity. *Psychological Review*, *96*, 43–458.

Dunn, J. C., & Kirsner, K. (1988). Discovering functionally independent mental processes: The principle of reversed association. *Psychological Review*, *95*, 91–101.

Durgin, F. (2000). The reverse Stroop effect. *Psychonomic Bulletin & Review*, *7*, 121–125.

Eastwood, J. D., Smilek, D., & Merikle, P. M. (2001). Differential attentional guidance by unattended faces expressing positive and negative emotion. *Perception & Psychophysics*, *63*, 1004–1013.

Edelman, S. (1998). Representation is representation of similarities. *The Behavioral and Brain Sciences*, *21*, 449–498.

Edelman, S. (1999). *Representation and recognition in vision*. Cambridge, Massachusetts: The MIT Press.

Efron, R. (1970). The relationship between the duration of a stimulus and the duration of a perception. *Neuropsychologia*, *8*, 37–55.

Egan, J. P. (1958). Recognition memory and the operating characteristic (Technical Note AFCRC-TN-58-51): Indiana University, Hearing and Communication Laboratory.

Ekman, P. (1977). Biological and cultural contributions to body and facial movement. In J. Blacking (Ed.), *Anthropology of the body* (pp. 34–84). London: Academic.

Ekman, P. (1999). Basic emotions. In T. Dalgleish & M. J. Powers (Eds.), *Handbook of cognition and emotion* (pp. 45–60). Chichester, England: Wiley.

Ekman, P., & Friesen, W. V. (1978). *The Facial Action Coding System (FACS): A technique for the measurement of facial action*. Palo Alto, California: Consulting Psychologists Press.

Ekman, P., Friesen, W. V., & Ellsworth, P. (1982). What emotion categories or dimensions can observers judge from facial behavior? In P. Ekman (Ed.), *Emotion in the human face* (pp. 39–55). Cambridge, England: Cambridge University Press.

Ellis, A. W., & Marshall, J. C. (1978). Semantic errors or statistical flukes? A note on Allport's 'On knowing the meaning of words we are unable to report'. *The Quarterly Journal of Experimental Psychology*, *30*, 569–575.

Enns, J. T., & Di Lollo, V. (2000). What's new in visual masking? *Trends in Cognitive Science*, *4*, 345–352.

Epstein, W., & Rock, I. (1960). Perceptual set as an artefact of recency. *The American Journal of Psychology*, *73*, 214–228.

Erdelyi, M. H. (1974). A new look at the New Look: Perceptual defense and vigilance. *Psychological Review*, *81*, 1–25.

Erdelyi, M. H., & Stein, J. B. (1981). Recognition hypermnesia: The growth of recognition memory (d') over time with repeated testing. *Cognition*, *9*, 23–33.

Ericsson, K., & Simon, H. A. (1984). *Protocol analysis*. Cambridge, Massachusetts: The MIT Press.

Eriksen, B. A., & Eriksen, C. W. (1974). Effects of noise letters upon the identification of a target letter in a nonsearch task. *Perception & Psychophysics*, *16*, 143–149.

Espino, O., Santamaria, C., Meseguer, E., & Carreiras, M. (2005). Early and late processes in syllogistic reasoning: Evidence from eye-movements. *Coginition*, *98*, B1–B9.

Estes, W. K. (1994). *Classification and cognition*. New York: Oxford University Press.

Esteves, F., & Öhman, A. (1993). Masking the face: Recognition of emotional facial expressions as a function of the parameters of backward masking.

*Scandinavian Journal of Psychology*, *34*, 1–18.

Evans, J. S. B. T. (2003). In two minds: dual-process accounts of reasoning. *Trends in Cognitive Science*, *7*, 454–459.

Evans, J. S. B. T., Newstead, S. E., & Byrne, R. M. (1993). *Human reasoning: The psychology of deduction*. Mahwah, New Jersey: Erlbaum.

Eysenck, M. W. (1978). Levels of processing: A critique. *British Journal of Psychology*, *69*, 157–169.

Fagot, C. (1994). Chronometric investigations of task switching. Unpublished PhD Thesis, University of California, San Diego.

Fan, J., McCandliss, B. D., Fossella, J., Flombaum, J. I., & Posner, M. I. (2005). The activation of attentional networks. *Neuroimage*, *26*, 471–479.

Fant, G. (1967). Auditory patterns of speech. In W. Wathen-Dunn (Ed.), *Models for perception of speech and visual form. Proceedings of a Symposium sponsored by the Data Sciences Laboratory Air Force Cambridge Research Laboratories Boston, Massachusetts, November 11–14, 1964* (pp. 111–125). Cambridge, Massachusetts: The MIT Press.

Fantz, R. L. (1964). Visual experience in infants: Decreased attention to familiar patterns relative to novel ones. *Science*, *30* (October), 668–670.

Farah, M. J., Rochlin, R., & Klein, K. L. (1994). Orientation invariance and geometric primitives in shape recognition. *Cognitive Science*, *18*, 325–344.

Favreau, J. (2000). *Swingers*. London: Faber and Faber.

Feenan, K., & Snodgrass, J. G. (1990). The effect of context on discrimination and bias in recognition memory for pictures and words. *Memory & Cognition*, *18*, 517–527.

Felician, O., Ceccaldi, M., Didic, M., Thinus-Blanc, C., & Poncet, M. (2003). Pointing to body parts: A double dissociation study. *Neuropsychologia*, *41*, 1307–1316.

Fendrich, R., Rieger, J. W., & Heinze, H. J. (2005). The effect of retinal stabilization on anorthoscopic percepts under free-viewing conditions. *Vision Research*, *45*, 567–582.

Fenske, M. J., & Eastwood, J. D. (2003). Modulation of focused attention by faces expressing emotion: Evidence from flanker tasks. *Emotion*, *3*, 327–343.

Ferreira, F., Christianson, K., & Hollingworth, A. (2001). Misinterpretation of garden-path sentences: Implications for models of sentence processing and reanalysis. *Journal of Psycholinguistic Research, 30,* 3–20.

Feynman, R. P. (1965/1992). *The character of physical law.* Harmondsworth, England: Penguin.

Fiedler, K. (1988). The dependence of the conjunction fallacy on subtle linguistic factors. *Psychological Research, 50,* 123–129.

Finke, R. A., & Pinker, S. (1982). Spontaneous imagery scanning in mental extrapolation. *Journal of Experimental Psychology: Learning, Memory and Cognition, 8,* 142–147.

Fischoff, B. (1982). Debiasing. In D. Kahneman, P. Slovic & A. Tversky (Eds.), *Judgment under uncertainty: Heuristics and biases* (pp. 422–444). Cambridge, England: Cambridge University Press.

Flanagan, O. (1984). *The science of the mind.* Cambridge, Massachusetts: The MIT Press.

Flew, A. (1979). *A dictionary of philosophy.* London: Pan Books.

Fodor, J. A. (1975). *The language of thought.* Cambridge, Massachusetts: Harvard University Press.

Fodor, J. A. (1980). Methodological solipsism considered as a research strategy in cognitive psychology. *The Behavioral and Brain Sciences, 3,* 63–109.

Fodor, J. A. (1981a). The mind-body problem. *Scientific American, 244,* 124–132.

Fodor, J. A. (1981b). *Representations.* Cambridge, Massachusetts: The MIT Press.

Fodor, J. A. (1983). *The modularity of mind: An essay on faculty psychology.* Cambridge, Massachusetts: The MIT Press.

Fodor, J. A. (1984). Observation reconsidered. *Philosophy of Science, 51,* 23–43.

Fodor, J. A. (1985). Precis of *The Modularity of Mind. The Behavioral and Brain Sciences, 8,* 1–42.

Fodor, J. A. (1994). Concepts: a potboiler. *Cognition, 50,* 95–113.

Fodor, J. A. (1998). *Concepts: Where cognitive science went wrong.* Oxford, England: Clarendon Press.

Fodor, J. A. (1999). *Let your brain alone.* London Review of Books, 21, 19.

Fodor, J. A. (2000). *The mind doesn't work that way. The scope and limits of computational psychology.* Cambridge, Massachusetts: The MIT Press.

Fodor, J. A., & Lepore, E. (1992). *Holism. A shopper's guide.* Cambridge, Massachusetts: Blackwell.

Fodor, J. A., & McLaughlin, B. P. (1990). Connectionism and the problem of systematicity: Why Smolensky's solution doesn't work. *Cognition, 35,* 183–204.

Fodor, J. A., & Pylyshyn, Z. W. (1981). How direct is visual perception? Some reflections on Gibson's 'Ecological Approach'. *Cognition, 9,* 139–196.

Fodor, J. A., & Pylyshyn, Z. W. (1988). Connectionism and cognitive architecture: A critical analysis. *Cognition, 28,* 3–71.

Fodor, J. D., Fodor, J. A., & Garrett, M. F. (1975). The psychological unreality of semantic representations. *Linguistic Inquiry, 6,* 515–531.

Fox, E. (1995). Negative priming from ignored distractors in visual selection: A review. *Psychonomic Bulletin & Review, 2,* 145–173.

Fox, E., Lester, V., Russo, R., Bowles, R. J., Pichler, A., & Dutton, K. (2000). Facial expressions of emotion: Are angry faces detected more efficiently? *Cognition and Emotion, 14,* 61–92.

Fox, E., Russo, R., & Dutton, K. (2002). Attentional bias for threat: Evidence for delayed disengagement from emotional faces. *Cognition and Emotion, 16,* 355–379.

Franks, J. J., & Bransford, J. D. (1971). Abstraction of visual patterns. *Journal of Experimental Psychology, 90,* 65–74.

Franz, E. A., Zelaznik, H. N., Swinnen, S., & Walter, C. (2001). Spatial conceptual influences on the coordination of bimanual actions: When a dual task becomes a single task. *Journal of Motor Behavior, 33,* 103–112.

Frazier, L. (1987). Sentence processing: A tutorial review. In M. Coltheart (Ed.), *Attention & performance, XII. The psychology of reading* (pp. 559–586). Hove, England: Erlbaum.

Frazier, L., & Rayner, K. (1982). Making and correcting errors during sentence comprehension: Eye movements in the analysis of structurally ambiguous sentences. *Cognitive Psychology, 14,* 178–210.

French, R. M. (2000). The Turing test: The first 50 years. *Trends in Cognitive Science, 4,* 115–122.

Freud, S. (1950). A note upon the 'mystic writing pad'. In J. Strachey (Ed.), *Collected papers of Sigmund Freud.* London: Hogarth.

Freud, S. (1942/1952). *A general introduction to psychoanalysis.* New York: Washington Square Press.

Freud, S. (1964/1973). *2. New introductory lectures on psychoanalysis.* London: Penguin Books.

Friesen, C. K., & Kingstone, A. (1998). The eyes have it! Reflexive orienting is triggered by nonpredictive gaze. *Psychonomic Bulletin & Review, 5,* 490–495.

Funnell, E. (1983). Phonological processes in reading: new evidence from acquired dyslexia. *British Journal of Psychology, 74,* 159–180.

Gallace, A., Tan, H. Z., & Spence, C. (2006). The failure to detect tactile change: A tactile analogue of visual change blindness. *Psychonomic Bulletin & Review, 13,* 300–303.

Gallistel, C. R. (1990). Representations in animal cognition: An introduction. *Cognition, 37,* 1–22.

Garrett, B. E., & Griffiths, R. R. (1997). The role of DA in the behavioral effects of caffeine in animals and humans. *Pharmacology, Biochemistry & Behavior, 57,* 533–541.

Garry, M., & Gerrie, M. P. (2005). When photographs create false memories. *Current Directions in Psychological Science, 14,* 326–330.

Garry, M., & Wade, K. A. (2005). Actually, a picture is worth less than 45 words: narratives produce more false memories than photographs. *Psychonomic Bulletin & Review, 12,* 359–366.

Gauthier, I., & Tarr, M. J. (1997). Becoming a 'Greeble' expert: Exploring the face recognition mechanism. *Vision Research, 37,* 1673–1682.

Gegenfurtner, K. R., & Sperling, G. (1993). Information transfer in iconic memory experiments. *Journal of Experimental Psychology: Human Perception and Performance, 19,* 845–866.

Gibson, B. S., & Kingstone, A. (2006). Visual attention and the semantics of space. *Psychological Science, 17,* 622–627.

Gibson, J. J. (1986). *The ecological approach to visual perception.* Hillsdale, New Jersey: Erlbaum.

Gigerenzer, G. (1994). Why the distinction between single-event probabilities and frequencies is relevant for psychology and vice versa. In G. Wright & P. Ayton (Eds.), *Subjective probability* (pp. 129–162). New York: Wiley.

Gigerenzer, G. (1996). On narrow norms and vague heuristics: A reply to Kahneman and Tversky (1996). *Psychological Review, 103,* 592–596.

Gigerenzer, G. (2002). *Reckoning with risk. Learning to live with uncertainty.* London: Penguin Books.

Gigerenzer, G., Czerlinski, J., & Martignon, L. (2002). How good are fast and frugal heuristics? In T. Gilovich, D. Griffin & D. Kahneman (Eds.), *Heuristics and biases: The psychology of intuitive judgment* (pp. 559–581). Cambridge, England: Cambridge University Press.

Gigerenzer, G., & Goldstein, D. G. (1996). Reasoning the fast and frugal way: Models of bounded rationality. *Psychological Review, 103,* 650–699.

Gigerenzer, G., & Hoffrage, U. (1995). How to improve Bayesian reasoning without instruction: Frequency formats. *Psychological Review, 102,* 684–704.

Gigerenzer, G., & Hug, K. (1992). Domain-specific reasoning: Social contracts, cheating, and perspective change. *Cognition, 43,* 127–171.

Gigerenzer, G., & Murray, D. J. (1987). *Cognition as intuitive statistics.* Hillsdale, New Jersey: Erlbaum.

Gigerenzer, G., & Reiger, T. (1996). How do we tell an association from a rule? A response to Sloman (1996). *Psychological Bulletin, 119,* 23–26.

Gigerenzer, G., Todd, P. M., & the ABC Research Group. (1999). *Simple heuristics that make us smart.* New York: Oxford University Press.

Gilbert, S., J, & Shallice, T. (2002). Task switching: A PDP model. *Cognitive Psychology, 44,* 297–337.

Girgus, J. J., Rock, I., & Egatz, R. (1977). The effect of knowledge of reversibility on the reversibility of ambiguous figures. *Perception & Psychophysics, 22,* 550–556.

Glanzer, M., & Cunitz, A. R. (1966). Two storage mechanisms in free recall. *Journal of Verbal Learning and Verbal Behavior, 5,* 351–360.

Glass, A. L., & Holyoak, K. J. (1974/1975). Alternative conceptions of semantic memory. *Cognition, 3,* 313–339.

Goldstone, R. L. (1994). Influences of categorization in perceptual discrimination. *Journal of Experimental Psychology: General, 123,* 178–200.

Goldstone, R. L. (1998). Objects, please remain composed. *The Behavioral and Brain Sciences, 21,* 472–473.

Goldstone, R. L., & Barsalou, L. W. (1998). Reuniting perception and conception. *Cognition, 65,* 231–262.

Goldstone, R. L., Lippa, Y., & Shiffrin, R. M. (2001). Altering object representations through category learning. *Cognition, 78,* 27–43.

Goldstone, R. L., & Son, J. Y. (2005). Similarity. In K. J. Holyoak & R. G. Morrison (Eds.), *The Cambridge handbook of thinking and reasoning* (pp. 13–36). Cambridge, England: Cambridge University Press.

Gopher, D., & Navon, D. (1980). How is performance limited: Testing the notion of central capacity. *Acta Psychologica, 46,* 161–180.

Gordon, I. E. (1989). *Theories of visual perception* (1st ed.). Chichester, England: John Wiley & Sons.

Goschke, T. (2000). Intentional reconfiguration and involuntary persistence in task set switching. In S. Monsell & J. Driver (Eds.), *Attention and performance XVIII: Control of cognitive processes* (pp. 331–355). Cambridge, Massachursetts: The MIT Press.

Gosselin, F., & Schyns, P. G. (2001). Why do we SLIP to the basic level? Computational constraints and their implementation. *Psychological Review, 64,* 735–758.

Graf, P., & Komatsu, S. (1994). Process-dissociation procedure: Handle with caution! *European Journal of Cognitive Psychology, 6,* 113–129.

Green, D. W., & Over, D. E. (2000). Decision theoretical effects in testing a causal connection. *Current Psychology of Cognition, 19,* 51–68.

Greenwald, A. G. (1992). New look 3: Unconscious cognition reclaimed. *American Psychologist, 47,* 766–779.

Gregg, V. (1975). *Human memory.* London: Methuen.

Gregory, R. L. (1961). The brain as an engineering problem. In W. H. Thorpe & O. L. Zangwill (Eds.), *Current problems in animal behaviour* (pp. 307–330). Cambridge, England: Cambridge University Press.

Gregory, R. L. (1970). *The intelligent eye.* New York: McGraw-Hill.

Gregory, R. L. (1980). Perceptions as hypotheses. *Philosophical Transactions of the Royal Society of London, Series B, 290,* 181–197.

Gregory, R. L. (1998). Brainy minds. *British Medical Journal, 317,* 1693–1695.

Grice, G. R., Canham, L., & Burroughs, J. M. (1983). Forest before trees? It depends where you look. *Perception & Psychophysics, 33,* 121–128.

Griffin, D., & Tversky, A. (2002). The weighing of evidence and the determinants of confidence. In T. Gilovich, D. Griffin & D. Kahneman (Eds.), *Heuristics and biases. The psychology of intuitive judgment* (pp. 230–249). Cambridge, England: Cambridge University Press.

Gunderson, K. (1964). The imitation game. *Mind, 73,* 595–597.

Guttenplan, S. (1986). *The languages of logic* (1st ed.). Oxford, England: Blackwell.

Haber, R. N. (1974). Information Processing. In E. C. Carterette & M. P. Friedman (Eds.), *Handbook of perception, Volume 1. Historical and philosophical roots of perception* (pp. 313–333). London: Academic.

Haber, R. N. (1983). The impending demise of the icon: A critique of the concept of iconic storage in visual information processing. *The Behavioral and Brain Sciences, 6,* 1–54.

Haber, R. N., & Hershenson, M. (1979). *The psychology of visual perception.* London: Holt, Rinehart and Winston.

Haber, R. N., & Nathanson, L. S. (1968). Post-retinal storage? Some further observations on Park's camel as seen through the eye of a needle. *Perception & Psychophysics, 3,* 349–355.

Haddon, M. (2004). *The Curious Incident of the Dog in the Night-Time.* New York: Vintage.

Hansen, C. H., & Hansen, R. D. (1988). Finding the face in the crowd: An anger superiority effect. *Journal of Personality and Social Psychology, 54,* 917–924.

Harley, T. A. (1995). *The psychology of language: From data to theory.* Hove, England: Psychology Press.

Harman, G. (1989). Some philosophical issues in cognitive science: Qualia, intentionality, and the mind-body problem. In M. I. Posner (Ed.), *Foundations of cognitive science* (pp. 831–848). Cambridge, Massachusetts: The MIT Press.

Harnad, S. R. (1987). *Categorical perception: the groundwork of cognition.* Cambridge, England: Cambridge University Press.

Harries, M. H., Perrett, D. I., & Lavender, A. (1991). Preferential inspection of views of 3-D model heads. *Perception, 20,* 669–680.

Hartshorne, J. K., & Ullman, M. T. (2006). Why girls say 'holded' more than boys. *Developmental Science, 9,* 21–32.

Hay, J. F., & Jacoby, L. L. (1999). Separating habit and recollection in young and older adults: Effects of elaborative processing and distinctiveness. *Psychology and Aging, 14,* 122–134.

Hayes-Roth, B. (1977). Evolution of cognitive structures and processes. *Psychological Review, 84,* 260–278.

Hayes-Roth, F. (1979). Distinguishing theories of representation: A critique of Anderson's 'Arguments concerning mental imagery'. *Psychological Review, 86,* 376–382.

Hayhoe, M., Lachter, J., & Feldman, J. (1991). Integration of form across saccadic eye movements. *Perception, 20,* 393–402.

Heaps, C. M., & Nash, M. (2001). Comparing recollective experience in true and false autobiographical memories. *Journal of Experimental Psychology: Learning, Memory and Cognition, 4,* 920–930.

Heider, E. R. (1972). Universals in color naming. *Journal of Experimental Psychology, 93,* 10–20.

Helmholtz, H. v. (1867/1962). *Treatise on physiological optics (Vol. 3).* New York: Dover.

Henderson, J., Brockmole, J. R., Castelhano, M. S., & Mack, M. (2007). Visual saliency does not account for eye movements during visual search in real-world scenes. In R. van Gompel, M. Fischer, W. Murray & R. Hill (Eds.), *Eye movements: A window on mind and brain* (pp. 537–562). Oxford, England: Elsevier.

Henderson, J. M., & Ferreira, F. (2004). *The interface of language, vision, and action.* New York: Psychology Press.

Henderson, L. (1982). *Orthography and word recognition in reading.* London: Academic.

Hinton, G. E. (1979). Some demonstrations of the effects of structural descriptions in mental imagery. *Cognitive Science, 3,* 231–250.

Hinton, G. E., McClelland, J. L., & Rumelhart, D. E. (1986). Distributed representations. In J. L. McClelland & D. E. Rumelhart (Eds.), *Parallel distributed processing. Explorations in the microstructure of cognition. Volume 1: Foundations* (pp. 77–109). Cambridge, Massachusetts: The MIT Press.

Hinton, G. E., & Parsons, L. M. (1981). Frames of reference and mental imagery. In J. Long & A. D. Baddeley (Eds.), *Attention and performance, IX* (pp. 261–277). Hillsdale, New Jersey: Erlbaum.

Hinton, G. E., & Parsons, L. M. (1988). Scene-based and viewer-centered representations for combining shapes. *Cognition, 30,* 1–35.

Hinton, G. E., & Shallice, T. (1991). Lesioning an attractor network: Investigations of acquired dyslexia. *Psychological Review, 98,* 74–95.

Hintzman, D. L. (1974). Psychology and the cow's belly. *The Worm Runner's Digest, 16,* 84–85.

Hintzman, D. L. (1993). Twenty-five years of learning and memory: Was the cognitive revolution a mistake? In D. E. Meyer & S. Kornblum (Eds.), *Attention and performance XIV. Synergies in experimental psychology, artificial intelligence, and cognitive neuroscience* (pp. 359–391). Cambridge, Massachusetts: The MIT Press.

Hirshman, E. (1998). On the logic of testing the independence assumption in the process-dissociation procedure. *Memory & Cognition, 26,* 857–859.

Hirshman, E., & Durante, R. (1992). Prime identification and semantic priming. *Journal of Experimental Psychology: Learning, Memory and Cognition, 18,* 255–265.

Hirst, W. (1986). The psychology of attention. In J. E. LeDoux & W. Hirst (Eds.), *Mind and Brain. Dialogues in cognitive neuroscience* (pp. 105–141). Cambridge, England: Cambridge University Press.

Hirst, W., Spelke, E., Reaves, C., Chaharack, G., & Neisser, U. (1980). Dividing attention without alternation or automaticity. *Journal of Experimental Psychology: General, 109,* 98–117.

Hitch, G. J. (1980). Developing the concept of working memory. In G. Claxton (Ed.), *Cognitive psychology: New directions* (pp. 154–196). London: Routledge & Kegan Paul.

Hochberg, J. E. (1968). In the mind's eye. In R. N. Haber (Ed.), *Contemporary theory and research in visual perception* (pp. 309–331). New York: Holt, Rinehart & Winston.

Hochberg, J. E. (1970). Attention, organization, and consciousness. In D. I. Mostofsky (Ed.), *Attention: Contemporary theory and analysis* (pp. 99–124). New York: Appleton-Century-Crofts.

Hochberg, J. E. (1978). *Perception* (2nd ed.). Englewood Cliffs, New Jersey: Prentice-Hall.

Hochberg, J. E. (1981). Levels of perceptual organization. In M. Kubovy & J. R. Pomerantz (Eds.), *Perceptual organization* (pp. 255–278). Hillsdale, New Jersey: Erlbaum.

Hochberg, J. E. (2003). Acts of perceptual inquiry: problems for any stimulus-based simplicity theory. *Acta Psychologica, 114,* 215–228.

Hochberg, J. E., & McAllister, E. (1953). A quantitative approach to figural 'goodness'. *Journal of Experimental Psychology, 46,* 361–364.

Hodges, A. (1983). *Alan Turing: The enigma.* London: Burnett Books.

Hoffman, J. E. (1980). Interaction between global and local levels of form. *Journal of Experimental Psychology: Human Perception and Performance, 6,* 22–234.

Holender, D. (1986). Semantic activation without conscious identification in dichotic listening, parafoveal vision, and visual masking: A survey and appraisal. *The Behavioural and Brain Sciences, 9,* 1–66.

Homa, D. (1978). Abstraction of ill-defined forms. *Journal of Experimental Psychology: Learning, Memory and Cognition, 4,* 407–416.

Homa, D., & Chambliss, D. (1975). The relative contributions of common and distinctive information from the abstraction of ill-defined categories. *Journal of Experimental Psychology: Human Learning and Memory, 104,* 351–359.

Homa, D., Cross, J., Cornell, D., Goldman, D., & Shwartz, S. (1973). Prototype abstraction and classification of new instances as a function of number of instances defining the prototype. *Journal of Experimental Psychology, 101,* 116–122.

Homa, D., & Vosburgh, R. (1976). Category breadth and the abstraction of prototype information. *Journal of Experimental Psychology: Human Learning and Memory, 2,* 322–330.

Horlitz, K. L., & O'Leary, A. (1993). Satiation or availability? Effects of attention, memory, and imagery on the perception of ambiguous figures. *Perception & Psychophysics, 53,* 668–681.

Hostmann, G., Borgstedt, K., & Heumann, M. (2006). Flanker effects with faces may depend on perceptual as well as emotional differences. *Emotion, 6,* 28–39.

Hsu, S.-M., & Young, A. W. (2004). Adaptation effects in facial expression recognition. *Visual Cognition, 11,* 871–899.

Huang, L., & Pashler, H. (2005). Expectation and repetition effects in searching for featural singletons in very brief displays. *Perception & Psychophysics, 67,* 150–157.

Hubel, D. H. (1963/1972). The visual cortex of the brain. In R. Held & W. Richards (Eds.), *Perception: Mechanisms and models. Readings from Scientific American* (pp. 148–156). San Francisco: Freeman.

Hubel, D. H., & Wiesel, T. N. (1977). Functional architecture of macaque visual cortex. *Proceedings of the Royal Society of London, Series B, 198,* 1–59.

Hughes, H. C., Layton, W. M., Baird, J. C., & Lester, L. S. (1984). Global precedence in visual pattern recognition. *Perception & Psychophysics, 35,* 361–371.

Hulme, C., Roodenrys, S., Schweickert, R., Brown, G. D. A., Martin, S., & Stuart, G. (1997). Word-frequency effects in short-term memory tasks: Evidence from a redintegration process in immediate serial recall. *Journal of Experimental Psychology: Human Perception and Performance, 23,* 1217–1232.

Hulme, C., Surprenant, A. M., Bireta, T. J., Stuart, G., & Neath, I. (2004). Abolishing the word length effect. *Journal of Experimental Psychology: Learning, Memory and Cognition, 30,* 98–106.

Hummel, J. E., & Biederman, I. (1992). Dynamic binding in a neural network for shape recognition. *Psychological Review, 99,* 480–517.

Humphrey, G. K., & Jolicœur, P. (1993). Visual object identification: Some effects of image foreshortening, monocular depth cues, and visual field on object identification. *The Quarterly Journal of Experimental Psychology, 46A,* 137–159.

Humphreys, G. W., Besner, D., & Quinlan, P. T. (1998) Event perception and the word repetition effect. *Journal of Experimental Psychology: General, 117,* 51–67.

Hutchison, K. A. (2003). Is semantic priming due to association strength or feature overlap? A microanalytic review. *Psychonomic Bulletin & Review, 4,* 785–813.

Irwin, D. E., Brown, J. S., & Sun, J.-S. (1988). Visual masking and visual integration across saccadic eye movements. *Journal of Experimental Psychology: General, 117,* 276–287.

Itti, L., & Koch, C. (2000). A saliency-based search mechanism for overt and covert shifts of visual attention. *Vision Research, 40,* 489–1506.

Jackendoff, R. (1977). Towards a cognitively viable semantics. In C. Rameh (Ed.), *Georgetown University Round Table on Languages and Linguistics* (pp. 59–80). Washington: Georgetown University Press.

Jackendoff, R. (1987a). *Consciousness and the computational mind.* Cambridge, Massachusetts: The MIT Press.

Jackendoff, R. (1987b). On beyond zebra: The relation of linguistic and visual information. *Cognition, 26,* 89–114.

Jackendoff, R. (2002). *Foundations of language. Brain, meaning, grammar, evolution.* Oxford, England: Oxford University Press.

Jacoby, L. L., & Rhodes, M. G. (2006). False remembering in the aged. *Current Directions in Psychological Science, 15,* 49–53.

James, W. (1890). *Principles of psychology.* New York: Holt.

Jersild, A. T. (1927). Mental set and shift. *Archives of Psychology,* whole no. 89.

Joanisse, M. F., & Seidenberg, M. S. (1999). Impairments in verb morphology after brain injury: a connectionist model. *Proceedings of the National Academy of Sciences of the United States of America, 96,* 7592–7597.

John, E. R. (1972). Switchboard versus statistical theories of learning and memory. *Science, 177,* 849–864.

Johnson, K. E., & Mervis, C. B. (1997). Effects of varying levels of expertise on the basic level of categorization. *Journal of Experimental Psychology: General, 126,* 248–277.

Johnson, M. K., Hashtroudi, S., & Lindsay, D. S. (1993). Source monitoring. *Psychological Bulletin, 114,* 3–28.

Johnson-Laird, P. N. (1980). Mental models in cognitive science. *Cognitive Science, 4,* 71–115.

Johnson-Laird, P. N. (1983). *Mental models.* Cambridge, England: Cambridge University Press.

Johnson-Laird, P. N. (1989). *The computer and the mind: An introduction to cognitive science.* Cambridge, Massachusetts: Harvard University Press.

Johnson-Laird, P. N. (2001). Mental models and deduction. *Trends in Cognitive Science, 5,* 434–442.

Johnson-Laird, P. N. (2004). Mental models and reasoning. In J. P. Leighton & R. J. Sternberg (Eds.), *The nature of reasoning* (pp. 169–204). Cambridge, England: Cambridge University Press.

Johnson-Laird, P. N., & Byrne, R. M. (1991). *Deduction.* Hove, England: Erlbaum.

Johnson-Laird, P. N., & Byrne, R. M. (2002). Conditionals: A theory of meaning, pragmatics, and inference. *Psychological Review, 109,* 646–678.

Johnson-Laird, P. N., Herrmann, D. J., & Chaffin, R. (1984). Only connections: A critique of semantic networks. *Psychological Bulletin, 96,* 292–315.

Johnson-Laird, P. N., Legrenzi, P., & Sonio Legrenzi, M. (1972). Reasoning and a sense of reality. *British Journal of Psychology, 63,* 395–400.

Johnson-Laird, P. N., & Steedman, M. J. (1978). The psychology of syllogisms. *Cognitive Psychology, 10,* 64–99.

Johnson-Laird, P. N., & Wason, P. C. (1970). Insight into a logical relation. *The Quarterly Journal of Experimental Psychology, 22,* 49–61.

Johnson-Laird, P. N., & Wason, P. C. (1977). *Thinking: Readings in Cognitive Science.* Cambridge, England: Cambridge University Press.

Jolicœur, P., Gluck, M., & Kosslyn, S. M. (1984). Pictures and names: Making the connection. *Cognitive Psychology, 16,* 243–275.

Jones, G. V. (1983). Identifying basic categories. *Psychological Bulletin, 94,* 423–428.

Jonides, J., & Mack, R. (1984). On the cost and benefit of cost and benefit. *Psychological Bulletin, 96,* 29–44.

Jusczyk, P. W., & Earhard, B. (1980). The lingua mentis and its role in thought. In P. W. Jusczyk & R. M. Klein (Eds.), *The nature of thought: Essays in honour of D. O. Hebb* (pp. 155–188). Hillsdale, New Jersey: Erlbaum.

Juth, P., Lundqvist, D., Karlsson, A., & Öhman, A. (2005). Looking for foes and friends: Perceptual and emotional factors when finding a face in the crowd. *Emotion, 4,* 379–395.

Kadden, R. M., Litt, M. D., Kabela-Cormier, E., & Petry, N. M. (2007). Abstinence rates following behavioral treatments for marijuana dependence. *Addictive Behaviors, 32,* 1220–1236.

Kahneman, D. (1968). Methods, findings and theory in visual masking. *Psychological Bulletin, 70,* 404–426.

Kahneman, D. (1973). *Attention and effort.* Englewood Cliffs, New Jersey: Prentice Hall.

Kahneman, D., & Frederick, S. (2005). A model of heuristic judgment. In K. J. Holyoak & R. G. Morrison (Eds.), *The Cambridge Handbook of Thinking and Reasoning* (pp. 267–293). Cambridge, England: Cambridge University Press.

Kahneman, D., Slovic, P., & Tversky, A. (1982). *Judgment under uncertainty: Heuristics and biases.* Cambridge, England: Cambridge University Press.

Kahneman, D., & Tversky, A. (1974). Judgment under uncertainty: Heuristics and biases. *Science, 27,* 1124–1131.

Kahneman, D., & Tversky, A. (1979). Prospect theory: An analysis of decision under risk. *Econometrica, 47,* 263–291.

Kahneman, D., & Tversky, A. (1982). On the study of statistical intuitions. *Cognition, 11,* 123–141.

Kahneman, D., & Tversky, A. (1996). On the reality of cognitive illusions. *Psychological Review, 103,* 582–591.

Kanizsa, G. (1969). Perception, past experience and the 'impossible experiment'. *Acta Psychologica, 31,* 66–96.

Kanizsa, G. (1985). Seeing and thinking. *Acta Psychologica, 59,* 23–33.

Karpel, M. E., Hoyer, W. J., & Toglia, M. P. (2001). Accuracy and qualities of real and suggested memories: Nonspecific age differences. *The Journals of Gerontology Series B: Psychological Sciences and Social Sciences, 56,* P103–P110.

Katz, J. J., & Fodor, J. A. (1963). The structure of semantic theory. *Language, 39*, 170–210.

Kay, P., & Regier, T. (2007). Color naming universals: The case of Berinmo. *Cognition, 102*, 289–298.

Kelley, C. M., & Jacoby, L. L. (2000). Recollection and familiarity: Process-dissociation. In E. Tulving & F. I. M. Craik (Eds.), *The Oxford handbook of memory* (pp. 215–228). Oxford, England: Oxford University Press.

Kennedy, J. M., & Juricevic, I. (2006). Foreshortening, convergence and drawings from a blind adult. *Perception, 35*, 847–851.

Keppel, G., & Underwood, B. J. (1962). Proactive inhibition in short-term retention of single items. *Journal of Verbal Learning and Verbal Behavior, 1*, 153–161.

Kim, J. J., Pinker, S., Prince, A., & Prasada, S. (1991). Why no mere mortal has ever flown out to center field. *Cognitive Science, 15*, 173–218.

Kimball, J. (1973). Seven principles of surface structure parsing in natural language. *Cognition, 2*, 15–47.

Kimchi, R. (1992). Primacy of wholistic processing and global/local paradigm: A critical review. *Psychological Bulletin, 112*, 24–38.

Kinchla, R. A., & Wolfe, J. M. (1979). The order of visual processing 'top-down', 'bottom-up' or 'middle-out'. *Perception & Psychophysics, 25*, 225–231.

Kintsch, W. (1970a). *Learning memory and conceptual processes.* New York: Wiley.

Kintsch, W. (1970b). Models of free recall and recognition. In D. A. Norman (Ed.), *Models of human memory* (pp. 331–373). New York: Academic.

Kintsch, W. (1974). *The representation of meaning in memory.* Hillsdale, New Jersey: Erlbaum.

Kintsch, W. (1977). *Memory and cognition.* New York: Wiley.

Kintsch, W. (1980). Semantic memory: A tutorial. In R. S. Nickerson (Ed.), *Attention and performance VIII* (pp. 595–620). Hillsdale, New Jersey: Erlbaum.

Kirby, K. N., & Kosslyn, S. M. (1990). Thinking visually. *Mind & Language, 5*, 324–341.

Klatzky, R. L. (1975). *Human memory: Structure and process.* San Francisco: W. H. Freeman.

Klauer, K. C., & Zhao, Z. (2004). Double dissociations in visual and spatial short-term memory. *Journal of Experimental Psychology: General, 133*, 355–381.

Klein, S. B., Cosmides, L., Tooby, J., & Chance, S. (2002). Decisions and the evolution of memory: Multiple systems, multiple functions. *Psychological Review, 109*, 306–329.

Knauff, M., & Johnson-Laird, P. N. (2002). Visual imagery can impede reasoning. *Memory & Cognition, 30*, 363–371.

Koffka, K. (1935/1963). *Principles of Gestalt psychology.* New York: Harcourt, Brace & World.

Kohler, W. (1930/1971). Human perception. In M. Henle (Ed.), *The selected papers of Wolfgang Kohler* (pp. 142–167). New York: Liveright.

Kolers, P. A., & Palef, S. R. (1976). Knowing not. *Memory & Cognition, 4*, 553–558.

Kosslyn, S. M. (1976). Can imagery be distinguished from other forms of internal representation? Evidence from studies of information retrieval time. *Memory & Cognition, 4*, 291–297.

Kosslyn, S. M. (1980). *Image and mind.* Cambridge, Massachusetts: Harvard University Press.

Kosslyn, S. M. (1994). *Image and brain: The resolution of the imagery debate.* Cambridge, Massachusetts: The MIT Press.

Kosslyn, S. M., Ball, T. M., & Reiser, B. J. (1978). Visual images preserve metric spatial information: Evidence from studies of image scanning. *Journal of Experimental Psychology: Human Perception and Performance, 4*, 56–60.

Kosslyn, S. M., Ganis, G., & Thompson, W. L. (2003). Mental imagery: against the nihilistic hypothesis. *Trends in Cognitive Science, 7*, 109–111.

Kosslyn, S. M., Pinker, S., Smith, G., & Shwartz, S. P. A. (1979). On the demystification of mental imagery. *The Behavioral and Brain Sciences, 2*, 535–548.

Kosslyn, S. M., & Pomerantz, J. R. (1977). Imagery, propositions, and the form of internal representations. *Cognitive Psychology, 9*, 52–76.

Kosslyn, S. M., & Shwartz, S. P. A. (1977). A data-driven simulation of visual imagery. *Cognitive Science, 1*, 265–296.

Kouider, S., & Dupoux, E. (2005). Subliminal speech priming. *Psychological Science, 16*, 617–625.

Kubovy, M. (1983). Mental imagery majestically transforming cognitive psychology. Review of Mental images and their transformations. *Contemporary Psychology, 28*, 661–663.

Kučera, H., & Francis, W. N. (1967). *Computational analysis of present-day American English.* Providence, Rhode Island: Brown University Press.

Kurbat, M. A. (1994). Structural description theories: Is RBC/JIM a general-purpose theory of human entry-level object recognition? *Perception, 23*, 1339–1368.

Labiouse, C. L. (2004). Is there a real preferential detection of negative stimuli? A comment on Dijksterhuis and Aarts (2003). *Psychological Science, 15*, 364–365.

Lachter, J., & Bever, T. (1988). The relation between linguistic structure and associative theories of language learning: A constructive critique of some connectionist learning models. *Cognition, 28*, 195–247.

Lamb, M. R., & Robertson, L. C. (1988). The processing of hierarchical stimuli: Effects of retinal locus, locational uncertainty, and stimulus identity. *Perception & Psychophysics, 44*, 172–181.

Landauer, T. K. (1975). Memory without organization: Properties of a model with random storage and undirected retrieval. *Cognitive Psychology, 7*, 495–531.

Lander, K., & Chuang, L. (2005). Why are moving faces easier to recognize? *Visual Cognition, 12*, 429–442.

Lang, P. J. Bradley, M. M., & Cuthbert, B. N. (2005). International affective picture system (IAPS): Affective ratings of pictures and instruction manual. *Technical Report A-6.* Gainesville, Florida: University of Florida.

Larsen, J. D., & Baddeley, A. D. (2003). Disruption of verbal STM by irrelevant speech, articulatory suppression, and manual tapping: Do they have a common source? *The Quarterly Journal of Experimental Psychology, 56A*, 1249–1268.

Latcher, J., Forster, K. I., & Ruthruff, E. (2004). Forty-five years after Broadbent (1958): Still no identification without attention. *Psychological Review, 111*, 880–913.

Lavie, N. (1995). Perceptual load as a necessary condition for selective attention. *Journal of Experimental Psychology: Human Perception and Performance, 21*, 451–468.

Lavie, N. (2000). Selective attention and cognitive control: Dissociating attentional functions through different types of load. In S. Monsell & J. Driver (Eds.), *Attention and performance, XVIII* (pp. 175–194). Cambridge, Massachusetts: The MIT Press.

Lawson, R., & Humphreys, G. W. (1998). View-specific effects of depth rotation and foreshortening on the initial recognition priming of familiar objects. *Perception & Psychophysics, 60*, 1052–1066.

Leeper, R. (1935). A study of a neglected portion of the field of learning: The development of sensory organization. *Journal of Genetic Psychology, 46,* 41–75.

Leeson, V. C., McKenna, P. J., Murray, G., Kondel, T. K., & Laws, K. R. (2005). What happens to semantic memory when formal thought disorder remits? Revisiting a case study. *Cognitive Neuropsychiatry, 10,* 57–71.

Leeuwenberg, E. L. J. (1969). Quantitative specification of information in sequential patterns. *Psychological Review, 76,* 216–220.

Leeuwenberg, E. L. J., & Boselie, F. (1988). Against the likelihood principle in visual form perception. *Psychological Review, 95,* 485–491.

Leeuwenberg, E. L. J., & van der Helm, P. A. (1991). Unity and variety in visual form. *Perception, 20,* 595–622.

Leighton, J. P. (2004). The assessment of logical reasoning. In J. P. Leighton & R. J. Sternberg (Eds.), *The nature of reasoning* (pp. 291–312). Cambridge, England: Cambridge University Press.

Levine, M., Jankovic, I., & Palij, M. (1982). Principles of spatial problem solving. *Journal of Experimental Psychology: General, 111,* 157–175.

Levy, J., Pashler, H., & Boer, E. (2006). Central interference in driving. Is there any stopping the psychological refractory period? *Psychological Science, 17,* 228–235.

Lewandowsky, S., Brown, G. D. A., Wright, T., & Nimmo, L. M. (2006). Timeless memory: Evidence against temporal distinctiveness models of short-term memory for serial order. *Journal of Memory and Language, 54,* 20–38.

Liberman, A. M., Harris, K. S., Hoffman, H. S., & Griffith, B. C. (1957). The discrimination of speech sounds within and across phoneme boundaries. *Journal of Experimental Psychology, 54,* 358–368.

Liberman, A. M., & Mattingly, I. G. (1985). The motor theory of speech production revised. *Cognition, 21,* 1–36.

Lindsay, D. S., Hagen, L., Read, J. D., Wade, K. A., & Garry, M. (2004). True photographs and false memories. *Psychological Science, 15,* 149–154.

Lindsay, D. S., & Johnson, M. K. (1989). The eyewitness suggestibility effect and memory for source. *Memory & Cognition, 17,* 349–358.

Lindsay, P. H. (1967). Comments on 'Selective attention: Perception or response?' *The Quarterly Journal of Experimental Psychology, 19,* 363–364.

Lindsay, P. H., & Norman, D. A. (1972). *Human information processing. An introduction to psychology.* New York: Academic.

Linehan, G., & Mathews, A. (2000). *Father Ted: the complete scripts.* London: Boxtree.

Ling, C. X., & Marinov, M. (1993). Answering the connectionist challenge: a symbolic model of learning the past tenses of English verbs. *Cognition, 49,* 235–290.

Lipp, O. V., Derakshan, N., Waters, A. M., & Logies, S. (2004). Snakes and cats in the flower bed: Fast detection is not specific to pictures of fear-relevant animals. *Emotion, 4,* 233–250.

Lipp, O. V., & Waters, A. M. (2007). When danger lurks in the background: Attentional capture by animal fear-relevant distractors is specific and selectively enhanced by animal fear. *Emotion, 7,* 192–200.

Liu, Z. (1996). Viewpoint dependency in object representation and recognition. *Spatial Vision, 9,* 491–521.

Lockhart, R. S. (2000). Methods of memory research. In E. Tulving & F. I. M. Craik (Eds.), *The Oxford handbook of memory* (pp. 45–58). Oxford, England: Oxford University Press.

Lockhart, R. S., Craik, F. I. M., & Jacoby, L. L. (1976). Depth of processing, recognition and recall. Some aspects of a general memory system. In J. Brown (Ed.), *Recall and recognition* (pp. 75–102). New York: Wiley.

Loftus, E. F. (1973). Category dominance, instance dominance, and categorization time. *Journal of Experimental Psychology, 97,* 70–74.

Loftus, E. F. (1975). Leading questions and eyewitness report. *Cognitive Psychology, 7,* 560–572.

Loftus, E. F. (1977). How to catch a zebra in semantic memory. In R. Shaw & J. Bransford (Eds.), *Perceiving, acting and knowing. Toward an ecological psychology* (pp. 393–411). Hillsdale, New Jersey: Erlbaum.

Loftus, E. F. (1979a). *Eyewitness testimony.* Cambridge, Massachusetts: Harvard University Press.

Loftus, E. F. (1979b). The malleability of memory. *American Scientist, 67,* 312–320.

Loftus, E. F., & Bernstein, D. M. (2005). Rich false memories: The royal road to success. In A. F. Healy & R. W. Proctor (Eds.), *Experimental cognitive psychology and its applications: Festschrift in honor of Lyle Bourne, Walter Kintsch, and Thomas Landauer* (pp. 101–113). Washington: APA.

Loftus, E. F., & Hoffman, H. G. (1989). Misinformation and memory: The creation of new memories. *Journal of Experimental Psychology: General, 118,* 100–104.

Loftus, E. F., & Klinger, M. R. (1992). Is the unconscious smart or dumb? *American Psychologist, 47,* 761–765.

Loftus, E. F., & Loftus, G. R. (1980). On the permanence of stored information in the human brain. *American Psychologist, 35,* 409–420.

Loftus, E. F., Miller, D., & Burns, H. (1978). Semantic integration of verbal information into a visual memory. *Journal of Experimental Psychology: Learning, Memory and Cognition, 4,* 19–31.

Loftus, E. F., & Palmer, J. C. (1974). Reconstruction of automobile destruction: An example of the interaction between language and memory. *Journal of Verbal Learning and Verbal Behavior, 13,* 585–589.

Loftus, E. F., & Pickrell, J. E. (1995). The formation of false memories. *Psychiatric Annals, 25,* 720–725.

Loftus, E. F., & Scheff, R. W. (1971). Categorization norms for 50 representative instances. *Journal of Experimental Psychology, 91,* 355–364.

Loftus, G. R. (1983). The continuing persistence of the icon. *The Behavioral and Brain Sciences, 6,* 28.

Loftus, G. R., & Irwin, D. E. (1998). On the relations among different measures of visible and informational persistence. *Cognitive Psychology, 35,* 135–199.

Logie, R. H., Zucco, G. M., & Baddeley, A. D. (1990). Interference with visual short-term memory. *Acta Psychologica, 75,* 55–74.

Long, G. M., & Beaton, R. J. (1982). The case for peripheral persistence: Effects of target and background luminance on a partial-report task. *Journal of Experimental Psychology: Human Perception and Performance, 8,* 383–391.

Long, G. M., & McCarthy, P. R. (1982). Target energy effects on Type 1 and Type 2 visual persistence. *Bulletin of the Psychonomic Society, 19,* 219–221.

Lovie, A. D. (1983). Attention and behaviourism: Fact and fiction. *British Journal of Psychology, 74,* 301–310.

Lu, Z., Neuse, J., Madigan, S., & Dosher, B. A. (2005). Fast decay of iconic memory in observers with mild cognitive impairments. *Proceedings of the National Academy of Sciences of the USA, 102,* 1797–1802.

Lucas, M. (2000). Semantic priming without association: A meta-analytic review. *Psychonomic Bulletin & Review, 7,* 618–630.

Lucy, J., & Shweder, R. (1979). Whorf and his critics: Linguistic and nonlinguistic influences on color memory. *American Anthropologist, 81,* 581–615.

Lupker, S. J. (1984). Semantic priming without association: A second look. *Journal of Verbal Learning and Verbal Behavior, 23,* 709–733.

Lyons, J. (1968). *Introduction of theoretical linguistics.* Cambridge, England: Cambridge University Press.

MacKay, D. M. (1961). Operational aspects of some fundamental concepts of human communication. *Journal of Communication, 11,* 183–189.

MacLeod, C. M. (1991). Half a century of research on the Stroop effect: An integrative review. *Psychological Bulletin, 109,* 163–203.

Macmillan, N. A. (1986). The psychophysics of subliminal perception. *Behavioral and Brain Sciences, 9,* 38–9

Macmillan, N. A., & Creelman, C. D. (1991). *Detection theory: A user's guide.* Cambridge, England: Cambridge University Press.

Macphail, E. M. (1998). *The evolution of consciousness.* Oxford, England: Oxford University Press.

MacWhinney, B., & Leinbach, J. (1991). Implementations are not conceptualizations: Revising the verb learning model. *Cognition, 40,* 121–157.

Magnuson, J. S., McMurray, B., Tanenhaus, M. K., & Aslin, R. N. (2003). Lexical effects on compensation for coarticulation: the ghost of Christmas past. *Cognition, 27,* 285–298.

Maguire, E. A., Nannery, R., & Spiers, H. J. (2006). Navigation around London by a taxi driver with bilateral hippocampal lesions. *Brain, 129,* 2894–2907.

Malmberg, K. J. (2002). On the form of ROCs constructed from confidence ratings. *Journal of Experimental Psychology: Learning, Memory and Cognition,* 380–387.

Malt, B. C. (1995). Category coherence in cross-cultural perspective. *Cognitive Psychology, 29,* 85–148.

Malt, B. C., & Smith, E. E. (1982). The role of familiarity in determining typicality. *Memory & Cognition, 10,* 69–75.

Mandel, D. R. (2005). Are risk assessments of terrorist attack coherent? *Journal of Experimental Psychology: Applied, 11,* 277–288.

Mandler, G. (1967). Organization and memory. In K. W. Spence & J. T. Spence (Eds.), *The psychology of learning and motivation: Advances in research and theory* (pp. 328–372). New York: Academic.

Mandler, G. (2002). Organisation: What levels of processing are levels of. *Memory, 10,* 333–338.

Mandler, G., & Pearlstone, Z. (1966). Free and constrained concept learning and subsequent recall. *Journal of Verbal Learning and Verbal Behavior, 5,* 126–131.

Manktelow, K. I., & Over, D. E. (1991). Social roles and uilities in reasoning with deontic conditionals. *Cognition, 39,* 85–105.

Maquestiaux, F., Hartley, A. A., & Bertsch, J. (2004). Can practice overcome age-related differences in the psychological refractory period? *Psychology and Aging, 19,* 649–667.

Marcel, A. J. (1983a). Conscious and unconscious perception: Experiments on visual masking and word recognition. *Cognitive Psychology, 15,* 197–237.

Marcel, A. J. (1983b). Conscious and unconscious perception: An approach to the relations between phenomenal experience and perceptual processes. *Cognitive Psychology, 15,* 238–300.

Marcus, G. F. (1995). The acquisition of the English past tense in children and multilayered connectionist networks. *Cognition, 56,* 271–279.

Marcus, G. F. (1996). Why do children say 'Breaked'? *Current Directions in Psychological Science, 5,* 81–85.

Marcus, G. F. (1998). Rethinking eliminative connectionism. *Cognitive Psychology, 37,* 243–282.

Marcus, G. F. (2006). Cognitive architecture and decent with modification. Cognition, 101, 443–465.

Markman, E. M., & Seibert, J. (1976). Classes and collections: Internal organization and resulting holistic properties. *Cognitive Psychology, 8,* 561–577.

Marr, D. (1982). *Vision. A computational investigation into the human representation and processing of visual information.* San Francisco: W. H. Freeman.

Marr, D., & Nishihara, H. K. (1978). Representation and recognition of the spatial organization of three-dimensional shapes. *Proceedings of the Royal Society of London, Series B, 269–294.* London: The Royal Society.

Marsh, B., Todd, P. M., & Gigerenzer, G. (2004). Cognitive heuristics. Reasoning the fast and frugal way. In J. P. Leighton & R. J. Sternberg (Eds.), *The nature of reasoning* (pp. 273–287). Cambridge, England: Cambridge University Press.

Marshall, J. C. (1984). Multiple perspectives on modularity. *Cognition, 17,* 209–242.

Marslen-Wilson, W. D., & Tyler, L. K. (1997). Dissociating types of mental computation. *Nature, 387,* 592–594.

Marslen-Wilson, W. D., & Tyler, L. K. (2003). Capturing underlying differentiation in the human language system. *Trends in Cognitive Science, 7,* 62–63.

Martin, M. (1979). Local and global processing: The role of sparsity. *Memory & Cognition, 7,* 476–484.

Martins, Y., & Pliner, P. (2006). 'Urgh! That's disgusting!': Identification of the characteristics of foods underlying rejections based on disgust. *Appetite, 46,* 75–85.

Masson, M. E. J. (1995). A distributed memory model of semantic priming. *Journal of Experimental Psychology: Learning, Memory and Cognition, 21,* 3–23.

Masson, M. E. J., & Borowsky, R. (1998). More than meets the eye: Context effects in word identification. *Memory & Cognition, 26,* 1245–1269.

Mast, F. W., & Kosslyn, S. M. (2002). Visual mental images can be ambiguous: insights from individual differences in spatial transform abilities. *Cognition, 86,* 57–70.

Matsumoto, D., & Willingham, B. (2006). The thrill of victory and the agony of defeat: Spontaneous expressions of medal winners of the 2004 Athens Olympic Games. *Journal of Personality and Social Psychology, 91,* 568–581.

Maylor, E. A. (2002). Serial position effects in semantic memory: Reconstructing the order of verses of hymns. *Psychonomic Bulletin & Review, 9,* 816–820.

McCann, R. S., & Johnston, J. C. (1992). Locus of the single-channel bottleneck in dual-task interference. *Journal of Experimental Psychology: Human Perception and Performance, 18,* 471–484.

McCarthy, J. (1979). Ascribing mental qualities to machines. In M. Ringle (Ed.), *Philosophical perspectives in Artificial Intelligence* (pp. 161–195). Atlantic Highlands, New Jersey: Humanities Press.

McClelland, J. L., & Kawamoto, A. H. (1986). Mechanisms of sentence processing: Assigning roles to constituents of sentences. In J. L. McClelland & D. E. Rumelhart (Eds.), *Parallel distributed processing: Explorations in the microstructure of cognition. Volume 2: Psychological and biological models* (pp. 272–325). Cambridge, Massachusetts: The MIT Press.

McClelland, J. L., Mirman, D., & Holt, L. L. (2006). Are there interactive processes in speech perception? *Trends in Cognitive Science, 10,* 363–369.

McClelland, J. L., & Patterson, K. (2002a). 'Words or Rules' cannot exploit the regularity of exceptions. *Trends in Cognitive Science, 6,* 464–465.

McClelland, J. L., & Patterson, K. (2002b). Rules or connections in past-tense inflections: what does the evidence rule out? *Trends in Cognitive Science, 6,* 465–472.

McClelland, J. L., & Patterson, K. (2003). Differentiation and integration in human language. *Trends in Cognitive Science, 7,* 63–64.

McClelland, J. L., & Rumelhart, D. E. (1981). An interactive activation model of context effects in letter perception. *Psychological Review, 88,* 375–407.

McClelland, J. L., & Rumelhart, D. E. (1986). A distributed model of human learning and memory. In J. L. McClelland & D. E. Rumelhart (Eds.), *Parallel distributed processing: Explorations in the microstructure of cognition. Volume 2: Psychological and biological models* (pp. 170–215). Cambridge, Massachusetts: The MIT Press.

McCloskey, M. (1980). The stimulus familiarity problem in semantic memory research. *Journal of Verbal Learning and Verbal Behavior, 19,* 485–502.

McCloskey, M., & Zaragoza, M. (1985). Misleading postevent information and memory for events: Arguments and evidence against memory impairment hypothesis. *Journal of Experimental Psychology: General, 114,* 1–16.

McGinn, C. (1994). Can we solve the mind-body problem? In R. Warner & T. Szubka (Eds.), *The mind-body problem* (pp. 99–120). Oxford, England: Blackwell.

McGurk, H., & MacDonald, J. (1976). Hearing lips and seeing voices. *Nature, 264,* 746–748.

McRae, K., & Boisvert, S. (1998). Automatic semantic priming. *Journal of Experimental Psychology: Learning, Memory and Cognition, 24,* 558–572.

McRae, K., de Sa, V., & Seidenberg, M. S. (1997). On the nature and scope of featural representations of word meanings. *Journal of Experimental Psychology: General, 126,* 99–130.

McRae, K., Spivey-Knowlton, M. J., & Tanenhaus, M. K. (1998). Modelling the influence of thematic fit (and other constraints) in on-line sentence comprehension. *Journal of Memory and Language, 38,* 283–312.

Medin, D. L., & Rips, L. J. (2005). Concepts and categories. In K. J. Holyoak & R. G. Morrison (Eds.), *The Cambridge handbook of thinking and reasoning.* (pp. 37–72). Cambridge, England: Cambridge University Press.

Medin, D. L., & Schaffer, M. M. (1978). Context theory of classification learning. *Psychological Review, 85,* 207–238.

Melcher, J. M., & Schooler, J. W. (1996). The misremembrance of wines past: Verbal and perceptual expertise differentially mediate verbal overshadowing of taste memory. *Journal of Memory and Language, 35,* 231–245.

Melton, A. W. (1963). Implications of short-term memory for a general theory of memory. *Journal of Verbal Learning and Verbal Behavior, 2,* 1–12.

Merikle, P. M. (1980). Selection from visual persistence by perceptual groups and category membership. *Journal of Experimental Psychology: General, 109,* 279–295.

Merikle, P. M. (1992). Perception without awareness: Critical issues. *American Psychologist, 47,* 792–795.

Merikle, P. M., & Reingold, E. M. (1990). Recognition and lexical decision without detection: Unconscious perception? *Journal of Experimental Psychology: Human Perception and Performance, 16,* 574–583.

Mervis, C. B., & Pani, J. R. (1980). Acquisition of basic concepts. *Cognitive Psychology, 12,* 496–522.

Meyer, D. E., Yantis, S., Osman, A. M., & Smith, J. E. K. (1985). Temporal properties of human information processing: Tests of discrete versus continuous models. *Cognitive Psychology, 17,* 445–518.

Michaels, C. F., & Carello, C. (1981). *Direct perception.* Englewood Cliffs, New Jersey: Prentice-Hall.

Michaels, C. F., & Turvey, M. T. (1979). Central sources of visual masking: Indexing structures supporting seeing at a single, brief glance. *Psychological Research, 41,* 1–61.

Miller, G. A. (1956a). Human memory and the storage of information. *IRE Transactions on Information Theory, IT–2,* 129–137.

Miller, G. A. (1956b). The magical number seven, plus or minus two: Some limits on our capacity for processing information. *Psychological Review, 63,* 81–97.

Miller, G. A. (1962). *Psychology. The science of mental life.* Harmondsworth, England: Hutchinson.

Miller, G. A., Galanter, E., & Pribram, K. H. (1960). *Plans and the structure of behavior.* New York: Holt.

Miller, G. A., & Johnson-Laird, P. N. (1976). *Language and perception.* Cambridge, England: Cambridge University Press.

Miller, J. (1982). Discrete versus continuous stage models of human information processing: In search of partial output. *Journal of Experimental Psychology: Human Perception and Performance, 8,* 273–296.

Miller, J. (1983). Can response preparation begin before stimulus recognition finishes? *Journal of Experimental Psychology: Human Perception and Performance, 9,* 161–182.

Miller, J. (1988). Discrete and continuous models of human information processing: Theoretical distinctions and empirical results. *Acta Psychologica, 67,* 191–257.

Miller, J. (1991). The flanker compatibility effect as a function of visual angle, attentional focus, visual transients, and perceptual load: A search for boundary conditions. *Perception & Psychophysics, 49,* 270–288.

Miller, M. B., & Wolford, G. L. (1999). Theoretical commentary: The role of criterion shift in false memory. *Psychological Review, 106,* 398–405.

Minsky, M. (1975). A framework for representing knowledge. In P. H. Winston (Ed.), *The psychology of computer vision* (pp. 211–277). New York: McGraw-Hill.

Miozzo, M. (2003). On the processing of regular and irregular forms of verbs and nouns: Evidence from neuropsychology. *Cognition, 87,* 101–127.

Mitroff, S. R., Sobel, D. M., & Gopnik, A. (2006). Reversing how to think about ambiguous figure reversals: Spontaneous alternating by uninformed observers. *Perception, 35,* 709–715.

Monsell, S. (1984). Components of working memory underlying verbal skills: A 'Distributed Capacities' view. A tutorial review. In M. I. Posner, Y. Cohen, H. Bouma & D. G. Bouwhis (Eds.), *Attention and performance, X* (pp. 327–350). Hillsdale, New Jersey: Erlbaum.

Monsell, S. (1996). Control of mental processes. In V. Bruce (Ed.), *Unsolved mysteries of the mind: Tutorial essays in cognition* (pp. 93–148). Hove, England: Erlbaum and Taylor and Francis.

Monsell, S. (2003). Task switching. *Trends in Cognitive Science, 7,* 134–140.

Moore, C., & Cavanagh, P. (1998). Recovery of 3D volume from 2-tone images of novel objects. *Cognition, 67,* 45–71.

Moray, N. (1959). Attention in dichotic listening: Affective cues and the influence of instruction. *The Quarterly Journal of Experimental Psychology, 11,* 56–60.

Moray, N. (1969). *Listening and attention.* Harmondsworth, England: Penguin Books.

Morgan, M. J., Findlay, J. M., & Watt, R. J. (1982). Aperture viewing: A review and a synthesis. *The Quarterly Journal of Experimental Psychology, 34A,* 211–233.

Morris, P. E., & Hampson, P. J. (1983). *Imagery and consciousness.* London: Academic Press.

Morton, J. (1989). The bankruptcy of everyday thinking. *American Psychologist, 46,* 32–33.

Morton, J. (1991). Cognitive pathologies of memory: A headed records analysis. In W. Kessen, A. Ortony & F. I. M. Craik (Eds.), *Memories, thought and emotions: Essays in honour of George Mandler* (pp. 199–210). Hillsdale, New Jersey: Erlbaum.

Morton, J. (1997). Free associations with EPS and memory. *The Quarterly Journal of Experimental Psychology, 50A,* 924–941.

Morton, J., & Broadbent, D. E. (1967). Passive versus active recognition models or is your homunculus really necessary? In W. Wathen-Dunn (Ed.), *Models for the perception of speech and visual form. Proceedings of a Symposium sponsored by the Data Sciences Laboratory Air Force Cambridge Research Laboratories Boston, Massachusetts, November 11–14, 1964* (pp. 103–110). Cambridge, Massachusetts: The MIT Press.

Morton, J., Hammersley, R. H., & Bekerian, D. A. (1985). Headed records: A model for memory and its failures. *Cognition, 20,* 1–23.

Moss, H. E., Ostrin, R. K., Tyler, L. K., & Marslen-Wilson, W. D. (1995). Accessing different types of lexical semantic information: Evidence from priming. *Journal of Experimental Psychology: Learning, Memory, Cognition, 21,* 863–883.

Msetfi, R. M., Murphy, R. A., & Simpson, J. (2007). Depressive realism and the effect of intertrial interval on judgements of zero, positive and negative contingencies. *The Quarterly Journal of Experimental Psychology, 60,* 461–481.

Msetfi, R. M., Murphy, R. A., Simpson, J., & Kornbrot, D. E. (2005). Depressive realism and outcome density bias in contingency judgements: The effect of context and the inter-trial interval. *Journal of Experimental Psychology: General, 134,* 10–22.

Mueller, S. T., Seymour, T. L., Kieras, D. E., & Meyer, D. E. (2003). Theoretical implications of articulatory duration, phonological similarity, and phonological complexity in verbal working memory. *Journal of Experimental Psychology: Learning, Memory and Cognition, 29,* 1353–1380.

Murdock, B. B. (1960). The distinctiveness of stimuli. *Psychological Review, 67,* 16–31.

Murdock, B. B. (1961). The retention of individual items. *Journal of Experimental Psychology, 62,* 618–625.

Murdock, B. B. (1962). The serial position effect in free recall. *Journal of Experimental Psychology, 64,* 482–488.

Murdock, B. B. (1974). *Human memory: Theory and data.* Hillsdale, New Jersey: Erlbaum.

Murphy, G. L. (1982). Cue validity and levels of categorization. *Psychological Bulletin, 91,* 174–177.

Murphy, G. L., & Brownell, H. H. (1985). Category differentiation in object recognition: Typicality constraints on the basic category advantage. *Journal of Experimental Psychology: Learning, Memory, and Cognition, 11,* 70–84.

Murphy, G. L., & Wisniewski, E. J. (1989). Categorizing objects in isolation and in scenes: What a superordinate is good for. *Journal of Experimental Psychology: Learning, Memory, and Cognition, 15,* 572–586.

Myers, B., & McCleary, R. (1964). Interocular transfer of a pattern discrimination in pattern-deprived cats. *Journal of Comparative and Physiological Psychology, 57,* 16–21.

Nairne, J. S. (2002). Remembering over the short-term: The case against the standard model. *Annual Review of Psychology, 53,* 53–81.

Nairne, J. S. (2005). The functionalist agenda in memory research. In A. F. Healy & R. W. Proctor (Eds.), *Experimental cognitive psychology and its applications: Festschrift in honor of Lyle Bourne, Walter Kintsch, and Thomas Landauer* (pp. 115–126). Washington: APA.

Navon, D. (1977). Forest before trees: The precedence of global features in visual perception. *Cognitive Psychology, 9,* 353–385.

Navon, D. (1981). The forest revisited: More on global processing. *Psychological Research, 43,* 1–32.

Navon, D. (1983a). The demise of the icon or of the icon-as-a-picture metaphor? *The Behavioral and Brain Sciences, 6,* 34–35.

Navon, D. (1983b). How many trees does it take to make a forest? *Perception, 12,* 239–254.

Navon, D. (1984). Resources: A theoretical soup stone. *Psychological Review, 91,* 216–234.

Navon, D. (1985). Attention division or attention sharing? In M. I. Posner & O. S. M. Marin (Eds.), *Attention and performance, XI* (pp. 133–146). Hillsdale, New Jersey: Erlbaum.

Navon, D. (1989a). The importance of being visible: On the role of attention in a mind viewed as an anarchic intelligence system. I. Basic tenets. *European Journal of Cognitive Psychology, 1,* 191–213.

Navon, D. (1989b). The importance of being visible: On the role of attention in a mind viewed as an anarchic intelligence system. II. Application to the field of intelligence. *European Journal of Cognitive Psychology, 1,* 215–238.

Navon, D. (1990). Do people allocate limited processing resources among concurrent activities? In L. Green & J. H. Kagel (Eds.), *Advances in behavioral economics, Volume 2* (pp. 209–225). Norwood, New Jersey: Ablex.

Navon, D. (2003). What does a compound letter tell the psychologist's mind? *Acta Psychologica, 114,* 273–309.

Navon, D., & Gopher, D. (1979). On the economy of the human-processing system. *Psychological Review, 86,* 214–255.

Navon, D., & Gopher, D. (1980). Task difficulty, resources, and dual-task performance. In R. S. Nickerson (Ed.), *Attention and performance, VIII* (pp. 297–315). Hillsdale, New Jersey: Erlbaum.

Navon, D., & Miller, J. (1987). Role of outcome conflict in dual-task interference. *Journal of Experimental Psychology: Human Perception and Performance, 13,* 435–448.

Navon, D., & Miller, J. (2002). Queing or sharing? A critical evaluation of the single-bottleneck notion. *Cognitive Psychology, 44,* 193–251.

Navon, D., & Norman, J. (1983). Does global precedence really depend on visual angle? *Journal of Experimental Psychology: Human Perception and Performance, 9,* 955–965.

Neath, I., & Brown, G. D. A. (2006). SIMPLE: Further applications of a local distinctiveness model of memory. In B. H. Ross (Ed.), *The psychology of learning and motivation* (pp. 201–206). San Diego, California: Academic.

Neath, I., Brown, G. D. A., Poirier, M., & Fortin, C. (2005). Short-term and working memory: Past, progress and prospects. *Memory, 13,* 225–235.

Neath, I., & Crowder, R. G. (1996). Distinctiveness and very short-term serial position effects. *Memory, 4,* 225–242.

Neath, I., Farley, L. A., & Surprenant, A. M. (2003). Directly assessing the relationship between irrelevant speech and articulatory suppression. *The Quarterly Journal of Experimental Psychology, 56A,* 1269–1278.

Neath, I., & Nairne, J. S. (1995). Word-length effects in immediate memory: Overwriting trace-decay theory. *Psychonomic Bulletin & Review, 2,* 429–441.

Neath, I., & Surprenant, A. M. (2003). *Human memory* (2nd ed.). Belmont, California: Wadsworth/Thomson.

Neisser, U. (1967). *Cognitive Psychology.* New York: Appleton-Century-Crofts.

Neisser, U. (1976). *Cognition and reality: Principles and implications of cognitive psychology.* San Francisco: W. H. Freeman.

Newell, A. (1973). You can't play 20 questions with nature and win: Projective comments on the papers of this symposium. In W. G. Chase (Ed.), *Visual information processing* (pp. 283–308). New York: Academic.

Newell, A. (1980). Physical Symbol Systems. *Cognitive Science, 4,* 135–183.

Newell, A., Shaw, J. C., & Simon, H. A. (1958). Elements of a theory of human problem solving. *Psychological Review, 65,* 151–166.

Newell, A., & Simon, H. A. (1972). *Human Problem Solving.* Englewood Cliffs, New Jersey: Prentice Hall.

Nielsen, J. M. (1958). *Memory and amnesia.* Los Angeles: San Lucas.

Nieuwenhuis, S., & Monsell, S. (2002). Residual costs in task switching: Testing the failure-to-engage hypothesis. *Psychonomic Bulletin & Review, 9,* 86–92.

Nisbett, R. E., & Ross, L. (1980). *Human inference: Strategies and shortcomings of social judgment.* Englewood Cliffs, New Jersey: Prentice-Hall.

Norman, D. A. (1969). Towards a theory of memory and attention. *Psychological Review, 75,* 522–536.

Norman, D. A. (1970). Introduction: Models of human memory. In D. A. Norman (Ed.), *Models of human memory* (pp. 1–15). New York: Academic.

Norman, D. A., & Bobrow, D. G. (1975). On data-limited and resource-limited processes. *Cognitive Psychology, 7,* 44–64.

Norman, D. A., & Bobrow, D. G. (1976). On the analysis of performance operating characteristics. *Psychological Review, 83,* 508–510.

Norman, D. A., & Rumelhart, D. E. (1975). Memory and knowledge. In D. A. Norman & D. E. Rumelhart (Eds.), *Explorations in cognition* (pp. 3–32). San Francisco: W. H. Freeman.

Norman, D. A., & Shallice, T. (1986). Attention to action: Willed and automatic control of behaviour. In R. J. Davidson, G. E. Schwartz & D. Shapiro (Eds.), *Consciousness and self-regulation, Vol. 4* (pp. 1–18). New York: Plenum.

Norman, J. (2002). Two visual systems and two theories of perception: An attempt to reconcile the constructivist and ecological approaches. *The Behavioral and Brain Sciences, 25,* 73–144.

Norris, D. (1986). Word recognition: Context effects without priming. *Cognition, 22,* 93–196.

Norris, D. (1995). Signal detection theory and modularity: On being sensitive to the power of bias models of semantic priming. *Journal of Experimental Psychology: Human Perception and Performance, 21,* 935–939.

Norris, D., McQueen, J. M., & Cutler, A. (2002). Merging information in speech recognition: Feedback is never necessary. *The Behavioral and Brain Sciences, 23,* 299–370.

Notman, L. A., Sowden, P. T., & Özgen, E. (2005). The nature of learned categorical perception effects: A psychophysical approach. *Cognition, 95,* B1–B14.

Oaksford, M., & Chater, N. (1994). A rational analysis of the selection task as optimal data selection. *Psychological Review, 101,* 608–631.

Oaksford, M., & Chater, N. (2001). The probabilistic approach to human reasoning. *Trends in Cognitive Science, 5,* 349–357.

Oaksford, M., & Chater, N. (2003). Optimal data selection: Revision, review, and reevaluation. *Psychonomic Bulletin & Review, 10,* 289–318.

Oatley, K., & Johnson-Laird, P. N. (1987). Towards a cognitive theory of emotions. *Cognition and Emotion, 1,* 29–50.

Oberauer, K. (2006). Reasoning with conditionals: A test of formal models of four theories. *Cognitive Psychology, 53,* 238–283.

Oberauer, K., Weidenfeld, A., & Hörnig, R. (2004). Logical reasoning and probabilities: A comprehensive test of Oaksford and Chater (2001). *Psychonomic Bulletin & Review, 11,* 521–527.

Öhman, A. (1999). Distinguishing unconscious from conscious emotional processes: Methodological considerations and theoretical implications. In T. Dalgleish & M. J. Powers (Eds.), *Handbook of cognition and emotion* (pp. 321–352). Chichester, England: Wiley.

Öhman, A., Flykt, A., & Esteves, F. (2001). Emotion drives attention: Detecting the snake in the grass. *Journal of Experimental Psychology: General, 130,* 466–478.

Öhman, A., Lundqvist, D., & Esteves, F. (2001). The face in the crowd revisited: A threat advantage with schematic stimuli. *Journal of Personality and Social Psychology, 80,* 381–396.

Öhman, A., & Mineka, S. (2001). Fears, phobias, and preparedness: Toward an evolved module of fear and fear learning. *Psychological Review, 108,* 483–522.

Olivers, C. N., Chater, N., & Watson, D. G. (2004). Holography does not account for goodness: A critique of van der Helm and Leeuwenberg (1996). *Psychological Review, 111,* 242–260.

Olsson, A., Ebert, J. P., Banaji, M. R., & Phelps, E. A. (2005). The role of social groups in the persistence of learned fear. *Science, 309,* 785–787.

O'Regan, J. K. (1994). The world as an outside memory: No strong internal metric means no problem of visual acuity. *The Behavioral and Brain Sciences, 17,* 270–271.

Osherson, D. N., & Smith, E. E. (1981). On the adequacy of prototype theory as a theory of concepts. *Cognition, 9,* 35–58.

Osherson, D. N., & Smith, E. E. (1982). Gradeness and conceptual combination. *Cognition, 12,* 299–318.

Özgen, E., & Davies, I. R. L. (2002). Acquisition of categorical color perception: A perceptual learning approach to the linguistic relativity hypothesis. *Journal of Experimental Psychology: General, 131,* 477–493.

Page, M. P. A., & Norris, D. (1998). The primacy model: A new model of immediate serial recall. *Psychological Review, 105,* 761–781.

Paivio, A. (1990). *Mental Representations: A dual coding approach.* New York: Oxford University Press.

Paivio, A. (1991). Dual coding theory: Retrospect and current status. *Canadian Journal of Psychology, 45,* 255–287.

Palmer, S. E. (1975). Visual perception and world knowledge: Notes on a model of sensory-cognitive interaction. In

D. A. Norman & D. E. Rumelhart (Eds.), *Explorations in cognition* (pp. 279–307). San Francisco: W. H. Freeman.

Palmer, S. E. (1977). Hierarchical structure in perceptual organisation. *Cognitive Psychology, 9*, 441–474.

Palmer, S. E. (1978). Fundamental aspects of cognitive representation. In E. Rosch & B. B. Lloyd (Eds.), *Cognition and categorization* (pp. 259–303). Hillsdale, New Jersey: Erlbaum.

Palmer, S. E. (1992). Common region: A new principle of perceptual grouping. *Cognitive Psychology, 24*, 436–447.

Palmer, S. E., & Kimchi, R. (1986). The information processing approach to cognition. In T. J. Knapp & L. C. Robertson (Eds.), *Approaches to cognition: Contrasts and controversies* (pp. 37–77). Hillsdale, New Jersey: Erlbaum.

Palmer, S. E., Rosch, E., & Chase, P. (1981). Canonical perspective and the perception of objects. In J. Long & A. Baddeley (Eds.), *Attention and performance, IX* (pp. 135–151). Hillsdale, New Jersey: Erlbaum.

Paquet, L., & Merikle, P. M. (1984). Global precedence: The effect of exposure duration. *Canadian Journal of Psychology, 38*, 45–53.

Parks, T. E. (1965). Post-retinal visual storage. *American Journal of Psychology, 78*, 145–147.

Parr, W. V., Heatherbell, D., & White, G. (2002). Demystifying wine expertise: Olfactory threshold, perceptual skill and semantic memory in expert and novice wine judges. *Chemical Senses, 27*, 747–755.

Parsons, L. M. (1995). Inability to reason about an object's orientation using an axis and angle of rotation. *Journal of Experimental Psychology: Human Perception and Performance, 21*, 1259–1277.

Pashler, H. E. (1994). Dual-task interference in simple tasks: Data and theory. *Psychological Bulletin, 116*, 220–244.

Pashler, H. E. (1998). *The psychology of attention.* Cambridge, Massachusetts: The MIT Press.

Pashler, H. E. (2000). Task switching and multitask performance. In S. Monsell & J. Driver (Eds.), *Attention and performance XVIII: Control of cognitive processes* (pp. 277–307). Cambridge, Massachusetts: The MIT Press.

Pashler, H. E., & Johnston, J. C. (1989). Chronometric evidence for central postponement in temporally overlapping tasks. *The Quarterly Journal of Experimental Psychology, 41A*, 19–45.

Pashler, H. E., Johnston, J. C., & Ruthruff, E. (2001). Attention and performance. *Annual Review of Psychology, 52*, 629–651.

Pastore, R. E., Crawley, E., Berens, M. S., & Skelly, M. A. (2003). 'Nonparametric A' and other modern misconceptions about signal detection theory. *Psychonomic Bulletin & Review, 10*, 556–569.

Pastore, R. E., Crawley, E., Skelly, M. A., & Berens, M. S. (2003). Signal detection theory analyses of semantic priming in word recognition. *Journal of Experimental Psychology: Human Perception and Performance, 29*, 1251–1266.

Payne, D. G., Toglia, M. P., & Anastasi, J. S. (1994). Recognition performance level and the magnitude of the misinformation effect in eyewitness memory. *Psychonomic Bulletin & Review, 1*, 376–382.

Pear, T. H. (1922). *Remembering and forgetting.* London: Methuen.

Pease, A., & Pease, B. (2001). *Why men don't listen and women can't read maps: How we're different and what to do about it.* London: Orion.

Penrose, R. (1989). *The Emperor's new mind: Concerning computers, minds, and the laws of Physics.* Oxford, England: Oxford University Press.

Pentland, A. P. (1986). Perceptual organization and the representation of natural form. *Artificial Intelligence, 28*, 293–331.

Perrett, D. I., & Harries, M. H. (1988). Characteristic views and the visual inspection of simple faceted and smooth objects: 'tetrahedra and potatoes'. *Perception, 17*, 703–720.

Perrett, D. I., Harries, M. H., & Looker, S. (1992). Use of preferential inspection to define the viewing sphere and characteristic views of an arbitrary machined tool part. *Perception, 21*, 497–515.

Persaud, N., McLeod, P., & Cowey, A. (2007). Post-decision wagering objectively measures awareness. *Nature Neuroscience, 10*, 257–261.

Pessoa, L., Japee, S., & Ungerleider, L. G. (2005). Visual awareness and the detection of fearful faces. *Emotion, 5*, 243–247.

Peterson, L. R., & Peterson, M. J. (1959). Short-term retention of individual verbal items. *Journal of Experimental Psychology, 58*, 193–198.

Peterson, M. A., & Hochberg, J. (1983). Opposed-set measurement procedure: A quantitative analysis of the role of local cues and intention in form perception. *Journal of Experimental Psychology: Human Perception and Performance, 9*, 183–193.

Peterson, M. A., Kihlstrom, J. F., Rose, P. M., & Glisky, M. L. (1992). Mental images can be ambiguous: Reconstruals and reference-frame reversals. *Memory & Cognition, 20*, 107–123.

Piccirilli, M., Sciarma, T., & Luzzi, S. (2000). Modularity of music: Evidence from a case of pure amusia. *Journal of Neurology, Neurosurgery and Psychiatry, 69*, 541–545.

Pilling, M., Wiggett, A., Özgen, E., & Davies, I. R. L. (2003). Is color 'categorical perception' really perceptual? *Memory & Cognition, 31*, 538–551.

Pinker, S. (1994). *The language instinct. The new science of language and mind.* London: Penguin Books.

Pinker, S. (1997). *How the mind works.* London: Penguin Books.

Pinker, S., & Bloom, P. (1992). Natural language and natural selection. In J. H. Barkow, L. Cosmides & J. Tooby (Eds.), *The adapted mind: Evolutionary psychology and the generation of culture* (pp. 451–493). Oxford, England: Oxford University Press.

Pinker, S., & Prince, A. (1988). On language and connectionism: Analysis of a parallel distributed model of language acquisition. *Cognition, 28*, 73–193.

Pinker, S., & Ullman, M. T. (2002a). The past and future of the past tense. *Trends in Cognitive Science, 6*, 456–463.

Pinker, S., & Ullman, M. T. (2002b). Combination and structure, not gradedness, is the issue. Reply to McClelland and Patterson. *Trends in Cognitive Science, 6*, 472–474.

Pinker, S., & Ullman, M. T. (2003). Beyond one model per phenomenon. *Trends in Cognitive Science, 7*, 108–109.

Pinter, H. (1969/1991). *Plays 3.* London: Faber and Faber.

Piolat, A., Olive, T., & Kellogg, R. T. (2005). Cognitive effort during note taking. *Applied Cognitive Psychology, 19*, 291–312.

Pizlo, Z., & Salach-Golyska, M. (1995). 3-D shape perception. *Perception & Psychophysics, 57*, 692–714.

Plaut, D. (2003). Interpreting double dissociations in connectionist networks. *Cortex, 39*, 138–141.

Plunkett, K., & Juola, P. (1999). A connectionist model of English past tense and plural morphology. *Cognitive Science, 23*, 463–490.

Plunkett, K., & Marchman, V. (1991). U-shaped learning and frequency effects in a multi-layered perception: Implications for child language acquisition. *Cognition, 38*, 43–102.

Plunkett, K., & Marchman, V. (1993). From rote learning to system building: Acquiring verb morphology in children and connectionist nets. *Cognition, 48*, 21–69.

Poggio, T., & Edelman, S. (1990). A network that learns to recognize three-dimensional objects. *Nature, 343*, 263–266.

Pollatsek, A., Well, A. D., & Schindler, R. M. (1975). Familiarity affects visual processing of words. *Journal of Experimental Psychology: Human Perception and Performance, 1*, 328–338.

Pomerantz, J. R. (1983). Global and local precedence: Selective attention in form and motion processing. *Journal of Experimental Psychology: General, 112*, 516–540.

Pomerantz, J. R., & Kubovy, M. (1986). Theoretical approaches to perceptual organization. In K. R. Boff, J. P. Kaufman & J. P. Thomas (Eds.), *Handbook of perception and human performance* (pp. 36-31–36-45). New York: Wiley.

Popper, K. (1963/2000). Conjectures and refutations. In T. Schick (Ed.), *Readings in the Philosophy of Science* (pp. 9–13). Mountain View, California: Mayfield.

Posner, M. I. (1978). *Chronometric explorations of mind. The third Paul M. Fitts lectures.* Oxford, England: Oxford University Press.

Posner, M. I., & Keele, S. W. (1968). On the genesis of abstract ideas. *Journal of Experimental Psychology, 77*, 353–363.

Posner, M. I., & Keele, S. W. (1970). Retention of abstract ideas. *Journal of Experimental Psychology, 83*, 304–308.

Posner, M. I., & Konick, A. F. (1966). On the role of interference in short term retention. *Journal of Experimental Psychology, 72*, 221–231.

Posner, M. I., Nissen, M. J., & Ogden, W. C. (1978). Attended and unattended processing modes: The role of set for spatial location. In H. L. Pick & E. Saltzman (Eds.), *Modes of perceiving and processing information* (pp. 137–157). Hillsdale, New Jersey: Erlbaum.

Posner, M. I., & Rogers, M. G. K. (1978). Chronometric analysis of abstraction and recognition. In W. K. Estes (Ed.), *Handbook of learning and cognitive processes. Vol. 5. Human information processing* (pp. 143–188, Fig. 2, p. 149) Hillsdale, New Jersey: Erlbaum.

Posner, M. I., & Warren, R. E. (1972). Traces, concepts, and conscious constructions. In A. W. Melton & E. Martin (Eds.), *Coding processes in human memory* (pp. 25–43). Washington: Winston.

Postal, P. M. (1964). Underlying and superficial linguistic structure. *Harvard Educational Review, 34*, 246–266.

Postman, L., Bronson, W. C., & Gropper, G. L. (1953). Is there a mechanism of perceptual defense? *The Journal of Abnormal and Social Psychology, 48*, 215–224.

Postman, L., & Keppel, G. (1969). Short-term memory. In L. Postman & G. Keppel (Eds.), *Verbal learning and memory. Selected readings* (pp. 345–351). Harmondsworth, England: Penguin Books.

Pothos, E. M., & Ward, R. (2000). Symmetry, repetition and figural goodness: an investigation of the Weight of Evidence theory. *Cognition, 75*, B65–B78.

Poulton, E. C. (1994). *Behavioral decision theory: A new approach.* Cambridge, England: Cambridge University Press.

Power, R. P. (1978). Hypotheses in perception: their development about unambiguous stimuli in the environment. *Perception, 7*, 105–111.

Pribram, K. H. (1971). *Languages of the brain: Experimental paradoxes and principles in neuropsychology.* Englewood Cliffs, New Jersey: Prentice-Hall.

Purcell, D. G., Stewart, A. L., & Skov, R. B. (1996). It takes a confounded face to pop out of a crowd. *Perception, 25*, 1091–1108.

Purves, D., & Lotto, R. B. (2003). *Why we see what we do: An empirical theory of vision.* Sunderland, Massachusetts: Sinauer Associates.

Putnam, H. (1984). Models and modules. *Cognition, 17*, 253–264.

Pylyshyn, Z. W. (1973). What the mind's eye tells the mind's brain: A critique of mental imagery. *Psychological Bulletin, 80*, 1–24.

Pylyshyn, Z. W. (1978). What has language to with perception? Some speculations on the Lingua Mentis. In D. L. Waltz (Ed.), *Theoretical Issues in Natural Language Processing, Vol. 2* (pp. 172–179). Urbana, Illinois: University of Illinois at Urbana-Champaign.

Pylyshyn, Z. W. (1979). Validating computational models: A critique of Anderson's indeterminacy of representation claim. *Psychological Review, 86*, 383–394.

Pylyshyn, Z. W. (1981). The imagery debate: Analogue media versus tacit knowledge. *Psychological Review, 88*, 16–45.

Pylyshyn, Z. W. (1999). Is vision continuous with cognition? The case for cognitive impenetrability of visual perception. *The Behavioral and Brain Sciences, 22*, 341–423.

Pylyshyn, Z. W. (2002). Mental imagery: In search of a theory. *The Behavioral and Brain Science, 25*, 157–238.

Pylyshyn, Z. W. (2003). Return of the mental image: are there really pictures in the brain? *Trends in Cognitive Science, 7*, 113–118.

Quillian, M. R. (1968). Semantic memory. In M. L. Minsky (Ed.), *Semantic information processing* (pp. 227–259). Cambridge, Massachusetts: The MIT Press.

Quinlan, P. T. (1988). *Evidence for the use of perceptual reference frames in two-dimensional shape recognition.* Birkbeck College, University of London. Unpublished doctoral dissertation.

Quinlan, P. T. (1991). *Connectionism and psychology: A psychological perspective on new connectionist research.* Hemel Hempstead, England: Harvester Wheatsheaf.

Quinlan, P. T. (2003). Visual feature integration theory: Past, present and future. *Psychological Bulletin, 129*, 643–673.

Quinn, P. C., & Bhatt, R. S. (2006). Are some Gestalt principles deployed more readily than others during early development? The case of lightness versus form similarity. *Journal of Experimental Psychology: Human Perception and Performance, 32*, 1221–1230.

Rabbitt, P. (2001). Review essay: 'How strange are the tricks of memory'. *The Quarterly Journal of Experimental Psychology, 54A*, 1261–1264.

Rabbitt, P. M. A. (1964). Ignoring irrelevant information. *British Journal of Psychology, 55*, 404–414.

Rabbitt, P. M. A. (1967). Learning to ignore irrelevant information. *American Journal of Psychology, 80*, 1–13.

Radach, R., & Kennedy, A. (2004). Theoretical perspectives on eye movements in reading: Past controversies, current issues, and an agenda for future research. *European Journal of Cognitive Psychology, 16*, 3–26.

Ramscar, M. J. A. (2002). When the fly flied and when the fly flew: The effects of semantics on the comprehension of past tense inflections. Paper presented at the Proceedings of the Annual Conference of the Cognitive Science Society, Fairfax, Virginia.

Ramscar, M. J. A. (2003). The past-tense debate: exocentric form versus the evidence. *Trends in Cognitive Science, 7*, 107–108.

Rapp, R. (Ed.) (2001). *The handbook of cognitive neuropsychology*. Hove, England: Psychology Press.

Ratcliff, R., & McKoon, G. (1981). Does activation really spread? *Psychological Review, 88*, 454–462.

Ratner, C. (1989). A sociohistorical critique of naturalistic theories of color perception. *Journal of Mind and Behavior, 10*, 361–372.

Rayner, K., Carlson, M., & Frazier, L. (1983). The interaction of syntax and semantics during sentence processing: Eye movements in the analysis of semantically biased sentences. *Journal of Verbal Learning and Verbal Behavior, 22*, 358–374.

Reed, S. K. (1972). Pattern recognition and categorization. *Cognitive Psychology, 3*, 382–407.

Reed, S. K. (1974). Structural descriptions and the limitations of visual images. *Memory & Cognition, 2*, 329–336.

Reed, S. K., & Friedman, M. P. (1973). Perceptual and conceptual categorization. *Memory & Cognition, 1*, 157–163.

Reed, S. K., & Johnsen, J. A. (1975). Detection of parts in patterns and images. *Memory & Cognition, 3*, 569–575.

Reisberg, D., & Chambers, D. (1991). Neither pictures nor propositions: What can we learn from a mental image? *Canadian Journal of Psychology, 45*, 336–352.

Reitman, J. S., & Bower, G. H. (1973). Storage and later recognition of exemplars of concepts. *Cognitive Psychology, 4*, 194–206.

Rensink, R. A. (2002). Change detection. *Annual Review of Psychology, 53*, 245–277.

Rensink, R. A., O'Regan, J. K., & Clark, J. J. (1997). To see or not to see: The need for attention to perceive changes in scenes. *Psychological Science, 8*, 368–373.

Repovš, G., & Baddeley, A. D. (2006). The multi-component model of working memory: Explorations in experimental cognitive psychology. *Neuroscience, 139*, 5–21.

Reynolds, M., & Besner, D. (2006). Reading aloud is not automatic: Processing capacity is required to generate a phonological code from print. *Journal of Experimental Psychology: Human Perception and Performance, 32*, 1303–1323.

Reynvoet, B., & Brysbaert, M. (1999). Single-digit and two-digit Arabic numerals address the same semantic number line. *Cognition, 72*, 191–201.

Rhodes, G., & Kalish, M. L. (1999). Cognitive penetration: Would we know it if we saw it? *Behavioral and Brain Sciences, 22*, 390–391.

Riesenhuber, M., & Poggio, T. (2000). Models of object recognition. *Nature Neuroscience Supplement, 3*, 1199–1203.

Rips, L. J. (1986). Mental muddles. In M. Brand & R. M. Harnish (Eds.), *The representation of knowledge and belief* (pp. 258–286). Tucson, Arizona: The University of Arizona Press.

Rips, L. J. (1994). *The psychology of proof: Deductive reasoning in human thinking*. Cambridge, Massachusetts: The MIT Press.

Rips, L. J., Shoben, E. J., & Smith, E. E. (1973). Semantic distance and the verification of semantic relations. *Journal of Verbal Learning and Verbal Behavior, 12*, 1–20.

Ristic, J., & Kingstone, A. (2005). Taking control of reflexive social attention. *Cognition, 94*, B55–B56.

Roberson, D., Davies, I., & Davidoff, J. (2000). Color categories are not universal: Replications and new evidence from a Stone-Age culture. *Journal of Experimental Psychology: General, 129*, 369–398.

Robertson, L. C. (1986). From Gestalt to neo-Gestalt. In T. J. Knapp & L. C. Robertson (Eds.), *Approaches to cognition: Contrasts and controversies* (pp. 159–188). Hillsdale, New Jersey: Erlbaum.

Robinson, J. O. (1972). *The psychology of visual illusion*. London: Hutchinson.

Rock, I. (1983). *The logic of perception*. Cambridge, Massachusetts: The MIT Press.

Rock, I. (1986). Cognitive intervention in perceptual processing. In T. J. Knapp & L. C. Robertson (Eds.), *Approaches to cognition: Contrasts and controversies* (pp. 189–221). Hillsdale, New Jersey: Erlbaum.

Rock, I., & Di Vita, J. (1987). A case of viewer-centered object perception. *Cognitive Psychology, 19*, 280–293.

Rock, I., Di Vita, J., & Barbeito, R. (1981). The effect of form perception of change of orientation in the third dimension. *Journal of Experimental Psychology: Human Perception and Performance, 7*, 719–732.

Rock, I., Hall, S., & Davis, J. (1994). Why do ambiguous figures reverse? *Acta Psychologica, 87*, 33–59.

Rock, I., & Mitchener, K. (1992). Further evidence of failure of reversal of ambiguous figures by uninformed subjects. *Perception, 21*, 39–45.

Rock, I., Wheeler, D., & Tudor, L. (1989). Can we imagine how objects look from other viewpoints? *Cognitive Psychology, 21*, 185–210.

Roediger III, H. L. (1980). Memory metaphors in cognitive psychology. *Memory & Cognition, 8*, 231–246.

Roediger III, H. L. (1991). They read an article? A commentary on the everyday memory controversy. *American Psychologist, 46*, 37–30.

Roediger III, H. L., & McDermott, K. B. (1995). Creating false memories: Remembering words not presented in lists. *Journal of Experimental Psychology: Learning, Memory and Cognition, 21*, 803–814.

Roediger III, H. L., & McDermott, K. B. (1999). False alarms about false memories. *Psychological Review, 106*, 406–410.

Rogers, R. D., & Monsell, S. (1995). Costs of a predictable switch between simple cognitive tasks. *Journal of Experimental Psychology: General, 124*, 207–301.

Rogers, T. T., & McClelland, J. L. (2004). *Semantic cognition: A parallel distributed processing approach*. Cambridge, Massachusetts: The MIT Press.

Roodenrys, S., & Quinlan, P. T. (2000). The effects of stimulus set size and word frequency on verbal serial recall. *Memory, 8*, 71–78.

Rosch, E. (1973). On the internal structure of perceptual and semantic categories. In T. E. Moore (Ed.), *Cognitive development and the acquisition of language* (pp. 111–144). New York: Academic.

Rosch, E. (1975). Cognitive representations of semantic categories. *Journal of Experimental Psychology: General, 104*, 192–233.

Rosch, E. (1978). Principles of categorization. In E. Rosch & B. B. Lloyd (Eds.), *Cognition and categorization* (pp. 27–48). Hillsdale, New Jersey: Erlbaum.

Rosch, E., & Mervis, C. B. (1975). Family resemblance: Studies in the internal structure of categories. *Cognitive Psychology, 7*, 573–605.

Rosch, E., Mervis, C. B., Gray, W. D., Johnson, D. M., & Boyes-Braem, P. (1976). Basic objects in natural categories. *Cognitive Psychology, 8*, 382–439.

Rosch, E., Simpson, C., & Miller, R. S. (1976). Structural basis of typicality effects. *Journal of Experimental Psychology: Human Perception and Performance, 2*, 491–502.

Rouder, J. N., Ratcliff, R., & McKoon, G. (2000). A neural network model of implicit memory for object recognition. *Psychological Science, 11*, 13–19.

Rumelhart, D. E. (1977). Towards an interactive model of reading. In S. Dornic (Ed.), *Attention and performance, VI* (pp. 265–303). Hillsdale, New Jersey: Erlbaum.

Rumelhart, D. E., Hinton, G. E., & Williams, R. J. (1986). Learning internal representations by error propagation. In J. L. McClelland & D. E. Rumelhart (Eds.), *Parallel distributed processing: Explorations in the microstructure of cognition. Volume 2: Psychological and biological models* (pp. 318–362). Cambridge, Massachusetts: The MIT Press.

Rumelhart, D. E., & McClelland, J. L. (1986). On learning the past tenses of English verbs. In J. L. McClelland & D. E. Rumelhart (Eds.), *Parallel distributed processing: Explorations in the microstructure of cognition. Volume 2: Psychological and biological models* (pp. 216–271). Cambridge, Massachusetts: The MIT Press.

Rumelhart, D. E., & Norman, D. A. (1985). Representation of knowledge. In A. M. Aitkenhead & J. M. Slack (Eds.), *Issues in cognitive modelling* (pp. 15–62). Hillsdale, New Jersey: Erlbaum.

Rumelhart, D. E., & Todd, P. M. (1993). Learning and connectionist representations. In D. E. Meyer & S. Kornblum (Eds.), *Attention and performance XIV. Synergies in experimental psychology, artificial intelligence, and cognitive neuroscience* (pp. 3–35). Cambridge, Massachusetts: The MIT Press.

Ruthruff, E., Johnston, J. C., & van Selst, M. (2001). Why practice reduces dual-task interference. *Journal of Experimental Psychology: Human Perception and Performance, 27,* 3–21.

Ruthruff, E., Johnston, J. C., van Selst, M., Whitsell, S., & Remington, R. (2003). Vanishing dual-task interference after practice: Has the bottleneck been eliminated or is it merely latent? *Journal of Experimental Psychology: Human Perception and Performance, 29,* 280–289.

Sabini, J., & Silver, M. (2005). Ekman's basic emotions: Why not love and jealousy? *Cognition and Emotion, 19,* 693–712.

Sackitt, B. (1976). Iconic memory. *Psychological Review, 83,* 237–276.

Salamé, P., & Baddeley, A. D. (1982). Disruption of short-term memory by irrelevant speech: Implications for the structure of working memory. *Journal of Verbal Learning and Verbal Behavior, 21,* 150–164.

Salmon, K., Yao, J., Berntsen, O., & Pipe, M. E. (2007). Does providing props during preparation help children to remember a novel event? *Journal of Experimental Child Psychology, 97,* 99–116.

Samuel, A. (1981a). The role of bottom-up confirmation in the phonemic restoration illusion. *Journal of Experimental Psychology: Human Perception and Performance, 7,* 1124–1131.

Samuel, A. (1981b). Phonemic restoration: Insights from a new methodology. *Journal of Experimental Psychology: General, 110,* 474–494.

Samuel, A. (1996a). Phoneme restoration. *Language and Cognitive Processes, 11,* 647–653.

Samuel, A. (1996b). Does lexical information influence the perceptual restoration of phonemes? *Journal of Experimental Psychology: General, 125,* 28–51.

Samuel, A. G. (2001). Knowing a word affects the fundamental perception of the sounds within it. *Psychological Science, 12,* 348–351.

Samuels, R. (1998). Evolutionary psychology and the massive modularity hypothesis. *The British Journal of the Philosophy of Science, 49,* 575–602.

Samuels, R., Stitch, S., & Faucher, L. (2004). Reason and rationality. In I. Niiniluoto, M. Sintonen & J. Wolenski (Eds.), *Handbook of epistemology* (pp. 131–179). Dordrecht, Holland: Kluwer.

Sanders, A. F. (1972). Foreperiod duration and the time course of preparation. *Acta Psychologica, 36,* 60–71.

Sanna, L. J., & Schwarz, N. (2006). Metacognitive experiences and human judgment: The case of hindsight bias and its debiasing. *Current Directions in Psychological Science, 15,* 172–176.

Savin, H. B. (1973). Meaning and concepts: A review of Jerrold J. Katz's semantic theory. *Cognition, 2,* 213–238.

Scharf, B., & Lefton, L. A. (1970). Backward and forward masking as a function of stimulus and task parameters. *Journal of Experimental Psychology, 84,* 331–338.

Schmidt, H. G., Peeck, V. H., Paas, F., & van Breukelen, G. J. P. (2000). Remembering the street names of one's childhood neighbourhood: A study of very long-term retention. *Memory, 8,* 37–49.

Schubö, A., Gendolla, G. H. E., Meinecke, C., & Abele, A. E. (2006). Detecting emotional faces and features in a visual search paradigm: Are faces special? *Emotion, 6,* 26–256.

Schumacher, E. H., Seymour, T. L., Glass, J. M., Fencsik, D. E., Lauber, E. J.,

Kieras, D. E., et al. (2001). Virtually perfect time sharing in dual-task performance: Uncorking the central cognitive bottleneck. *Psychological Science, 12,* 101–108.

Schwartz, B., Ward, A., Lyubomirsky, S., Monterosso, J., White, K., & Lehman, D. R. (2002). Maximizing versus satisficing: Happiness is a matter of choice. *Journal of Personality and Social Psychology, 83,* 1178–1197.

Schwarz, S., & Stahlberg, D. (2003). Strength of hindsight bias as a consequence of meta-cognitions. *Memory, 11,* 395–410.

Seamon, J. J., & Virostek, S. (1978). Memory performance and subject-defined depth of processing. *Memory & Cognition, 6,* 283–287.

Searle, J. (1980). Minds, brains and programs. *Behavioural and Brain Sciences, 3,* 417–424.

Searle, J. R. (1994). *The rediscovery of mind.* Cambridge, Massachusetts: The MIT Press.

Searle, J. R. (2001). *Rationality in action.* Cambridge, Massachusetts: The MIT Press.

Seinfeld, J., & David, L. J. (1998). *The Seinfeld Scripts.* New York: Harper Paperbacks.

Seki, K., Ishiai, S., Koyama, Y., Sato, S., Hirabayashi, H., & Inaki, K. (2000). Why are some patients with severe neglect able to copy a cube? The significance of verbal intelligence. *Neuropsychologia, 38,* 1466–1472.

Selnes, O. A. (2001). A historical overview of contributions from the study of deficits. In R. Rapp (Ed.), *The handbook of cognitive neuropsychology* (pp. 23–41). Hove, England: Psychology Press.

Serino, A., Ciaramelli, E., Di Santantonio, A., Malagu, S., Servadei, F., & Làdavas, E. (2007). A pilot study for rehabilitation of central executive deficits after traumatic brain injury. *Brain Injury, 21,* 11–19.

Shaffer, L. H. (1975). Multiple attention in continuous verbal tasks. In P. M. A. Rabbitt & S. Dornic (Eds.), *Attention and performance V* (pp. 157–167). New York: Academic.

Shallice, T. (1984). More functionally isolable subsystems but fewer 'modules'? *Cognition, 17,* 243–252.

Shallice, T. (1988). *From neuropsychology to mental structure.* Cambridge, England: Cambridge University Press.

Shanks, D. R. (1997). Representation of categories and concepts in memory. In M. A. Conway (Ed.), *Cognitive models of memory* (pp. 111–146). Hove, England: Psychology Press.

Shannon, C. E., & Weaver, W. (1949). *The mathematical theory of communication.* Urbana, Illinois: Illinois Press.

Shelton, J. R., & Martin, R. C. (1992). How semantic is automatic semantic priming? *Journal of Experimental Psychology: Learning, Memory and Cognition, 18*, 1191–1210.

Shepard, R. N. (1990). On understanding mental images. In H. Barlow, C. Blakemore & M. Weston-Smith (Eds.), *Images and understanding* (pp. 365–370). Cambridge, England: Cambridge University Press.

Shepard, R. N., & Cooper, L. A. (1982). *Mental images and their transformations.* Cambridge, Massachusetts: The MIT Press.

Shepard, R. N., & Feng, C. (1972). A chronometric study of mental paper folding. *Cognitive Psychology, 3*, 228–243.

Shepard, R. N., & Metzler, J. (1971). Mental rotation of three-dimensional objects. *Science, 171*, 701–703.

Shioiri, T., Someya, T., Helmeste, D., & Tang, S. W. (1999). Cultural differences in recognition of facial emotional expression: Contrast between Japanese and American raters. *Psychiatry and Clinical Neuroscience, 53*, 629–633.

Simon, H. A. (1956). Rational choice and the structure of the environment. *Psychological Review, 63*, 129–138.

Simon, H. A. (1972). What is visual imagery? An information processing interpretation. In L. W. Gregg (Ed.), *Cognition in learning and memory* (pp. 183–204). New York: Wiley.

Simon, H. A. (1982). *Models of bounded rationality.* Cambridge, Massachusetts: The MIT Press.

Simon, H. A. (1992). *Economics, bounded rationality, and the cognitive revolution.* Aldershot, England: Elgar.

Simon, H. A., & Feigenbaum, E. A. (1964). An information processing theory of some effects of similarity, familiarization, and meaningfulness in verbal learning. *Journal of Verbal Learning and Verbal Behavior, 3*, 385–396.

Simons, D. J., & Ambinder, M. S. (2005). Change blindness: Theory and consequences. *Current Directions in Psychological Science, 14*, 44–48.

Simons, D. J., & Levin, D. (1998). Failure to detect changes to people during a real-world interaction. *Psychonomic Bulletin & Review, 5*, 644–649.

Sivonen, P., Maess, B., & Friederici, A. (2006). Semantic retrieval of spoken words with an obliterated initial phoneme in a sentence context. *Neuroscience Letters, 408*, 220–225.

Skinner, B. F. (1948/1976). *Walden Two.* Englewood Cliffs, New Jersey: Prentice Hall.

Skinner, B. F. (1985). Cognitive science and behaviourism. *British Journal of Psychology, 76*, 291–301.

Sloman, A. (1978). *The computer revolution in philosophy: Philosophy, science, and, models of mind.* Hassocks, England: Harvester Press.

Sloman, S. A. (1996). The empirical case for two systems of reasoning. *Psychological Bulletin, 119*, 3–22.

Slovic, P., Finucane, M., Peters, E., & MacGregor, D. G. (2002). The affect heuristic. In T. Gilovich, D. Griffin & D. Kahneman (Eds.), *Heuristics and biases. The psychology of intuitive judgments* (pp. 397–420). Cambridge, England: Cambridge University Press.

Smith, E. E. (1988). Concepts and thought. In R. J. Sternberg & E. E. Smith (Eds.), *The psychology of human thought,* (pp. 19–49). Cambridge, England: Cambridge University Press.

Smith, E. E., & Medin, D. L. (1981). *Categories and concepts.* Cambridge, Massachusetts: Harvard University Press.

Smith, E. E., & Medin, D. L. (1984). Concepts and concept formation. *Annual Review of Psychology, 35*, 113–138.

Smith, E. E., Shoben, E. J., & Rips, L. J. (1974). Structure and process in semantic memory: A featural model for semantic decisions. *Psychological Review, 81*, 214–241.

Smith, J. D., & Minda, J. P. (1998). Prototypes in the mist: The early epochs of category learning. *Journal of Experimental Psychology: Learning, Memory and Cognition, 24*, 1411–1436.

Smith, J. D., & Minda, J. P. (2001). Distinguishing prototype-based and exemplar-based processes in category learning. *Journal of Experimental Psychology: Learning, Memory and Cognition, 28*, 800–811.

Smith, M. C., & Fabri, P. (1975). Post-cueing after erasure of the icon: Is there a set effect? *The Quarterly Journal of Experimental Psychology, 27*, 63–72.

Smithson, H., & Mollon, J. (2006). Do masks terminate the icon? *The Quarterly Journal of Experimental Psychology, 59*, 150–160.

Smolensky, P. (1988). On the proper treatment of connectionism. *Behavioral and Brain Sciences, 11*, 1–74.

Snodgrass, J. G., & Corwin, J. (1988). Pragmatics of measuring recognition memory: Applications to dementia and amnesia. *Journal of Experimental Psychology: General, 117*, 34–50.

Snodgrass, J. G., & Vanderwart, M. A. (1980). Standardized set of 260 pictures: Norms of name agreement, usage agreement, familiarity, and visual complexity. *Journal of Experimental Psychology: Learning, Memory, and Cognition, 6*, 174–215.

Sokal, R. R. (1974). Classification: Purposes, principles, processes, prospects. *Science, 185*, 1115–1123.

Solso, R. L., & McCarthy, J. E. (1981). Prototype formation: Central tendency model vs. attribute frequency model. *Bulletin of the Psychonomic Society, 17*, 10–11.

Spector, A., & Biederman, I. (1976). Mental set and mental shift revisited. *American Journal of Psychology, 89*, 669–679.

Sperber, D., Cara, F., & Girotto, V. (1995). Relevance theory explains the selection task. *Cognition, 52*, 3–39.

Sperber, D., & Girotto, V. (2003). Does the selection task detect cheater-detection? In K. Sterelny & J. Fitness (Eds.), *From mating to mentality: Evaluating evolutionary psychology* (pp. 197–226). London: Psychology Press.

Sperling, G. (1960). The information available in brief visual presentations. *Psychological Monographs, 74*, 1–29.

Sperling, G. (1963). A model for visual memory tasks. *Human Factors, 5*, 19–31.

Spivey-Knowlton, M. J., & Sedivy, J. (1995). Resolving attachment ambiguities with multiple constraints. *Cognition, 55*, 227–267.

Stanovich, K. E., & West, R. F. (1999). *Who is rational? Studies of individual differences in reasoning.* Mahwah, New Jersey: Erlbaum.

Stein, E. (1996). *Without good reason.* Oxford, England: Clarendon Press.

Steinfeld, G. J. (1967). Concepts of set and availability and their relation to the reorganization of ambiguous pictorial stimuli. *Psychological Review, 74*, 505–522.

Sternberg, S. (1967). Two operations in character recognition: Some evidence from reaction-time measurements. In W. Wathen-Dunn (Ed.), *Models for the perception of speech and visual form. Proceedings of a symposium sponsored by the Data Sciences Laboratory Air Force Cambridge Research Laboratories, Boston, Massachusetts, November 11–14, 1964* (pp. 187–201). Cambridge, Massachusetts: The MIT Press.

Stevenage, S. V., & Lewis, H. G. (2005). By which name should I call thee? The consequences of having multiple names. *The Quarterly Journal of Experimental Psychology, 58A*, 1447–1461.

Stevens, K. N., & Halle, M. (1967). Remarks on analysis by synthesis and distinctive features. In W. Wathen-Dunn (Ed.), *Models for the perception of speech and visual form. Proceedings of a Symposium sponsored by the Data Sciences Laboratory Air Force Cambridge Research Laboratories, Boston, Massachusetts, November 11–14, 1964* (pp. 88–102). Cambridge, Massachusetts: The MIT Press.

Stork, E. C., & Widdowson, J. D. A. (1974). Learning about linguistics. *An introductory workbook*. London: Hutchinson.

Strange, W., Kenney, T., Kessel, F., & Jenkins, J. (1970). Abstraction over time of prototypes from distortions of random dot patterns. *Journal of Experimental Psychology, 83,* 508–510.

Strayer, D. L., Drews, F. A., & Johnston, W. A. (2003). Cell phone-induced failures of visual attention during simulated driving. *Journal of Experimental Psychology: Applied, 9,* 23–32.

Stroop, J. R. (1935). Studies of interference in serial verbal reactions. *Journal of Experimental Psychology, 18,* 643–661.

Styles, E. A. (2006). *The psychology of attention* (2nd ed.). Hove, England: Psychology Press.

Suddendorf, T., & Corballis, M. (in press). The evolution of foresight: What is mental time travel and is it unique to humans? *Behavioral and Brain Sciences.*

Sutherland, N. S. (1967). Comments on the session. In W. Wathen-Dunn (Ed.), *Models for the perception of speech and visual form. Proceedings of a symposium sponsored by the Data Sciences Laboratory Air Force Cambridge Research Laboratories, Boston, Massachusetts, November 11–14, 1964* (pp. 239–243). Cambridge, Massachusetts: The MIT Press.

Sutherland, N. S. (1968). Outlines of a theory of visual pattern recognition in animals and man. P*roceedings of the Royal Society of London, Series B, 171,* 297–317.

Sutherland, N. S. (1974). Object recognition. In E. C. Carterette & M. P. Friedman (Eds.), *Handbook of perception III* (pp. 157–185). London: Academic.

Sutherland, N. S. (1988). Simplicity is not enough. In B. A. G. Elsendoorn & H. Bouma (Eds.), *Working models of human perception* (pp. 381–390). London: Academic.

Sutherland, N. S. (1992). Irrationality: The enemy within. London: Penguin Books.

Sutherland, N. S., & Williams, C. (1969). Discrimination of checkerboard patterns by rats. *The Quarterly Journal of Experimental Psychology, 21,* 77–84.

Swets, J. A. (1973). The Relative Operating Characteristic in psychology. *Science, 182,* 990–1000.

Swets, J. A. (1996). *Signal detection theory and ROC analysis in psychology and diagnostics.* Malwah, New Jersey: Erlbaum.

Taatgen, N. A., & Anderson, J. R. (2002). Why do children learn to say 'broke'? A model of learning the past tense without feedback. *Cognition, 86,* 123–155.

Tanaka, J., Curran, T., & Sheinberg, D. (2005). The training and transfer of real-world perceptual expertise. *Psychological Science, 16,* 145–151.

Tanaka, J. W., & Taylor, M. (1991). Object categories and expertise: Is the basic level in the eye of beholder? *Cognitive Psychology, 23,* 457–482.

Taraban, R., & McClelland, J. L. (1990). Parsing and comprehension: A multiple-constraint view. In K. Rayner, M. Balota & G. B. Flores D'Arcais (Eds.), *Comprehension processes in reading* (pp. 231–263). Hillsdale, New Jersey: Erlbaum.

Tarr, M. J. (1995). Rotating objects to recognise them: A case study of the role of viewpoint dependency in the recognition of three-dimensional objects. *Psychonomic Bulletin & Review, 2,* 55–82.

Tarr, M. J., & Bültoff, H. H. (1995). Is human object recognition better described by geon structural descriptions or by multiple views? Comment on Biederman and Gerhardstein (1993). *Journal of Experimental Psychology: Human Perception and Performance, 21,* 1494–1505.

Tarr, M. J., & Bültoff, H. H. (1998). Image-based object recognition in man, monkey and machine. *Cognition, 67,* 1–20.

Tatler, B. W. (2001). Characterising the visual buffer: Real world evidence for overwriting early in each fixation. *Perception, 30,* 993–1006.

Tehan, G., & Humphreys, M. S. (1988). Articulatory loop explanations of memory span and pronunciation rate correspondences: A cautionary note. *Bulletin of the Psychonomic Society, 26,* 293–296.

Telford, C. W. (1931). The refractory phase of voluntary and associative responses. *Journal of Experimental Psychology, 61,* 1–35.

Thomas, L. E., & Irwin, D. E. (2006). Voluntary eyeblinks disrupt iconic memory. *Perception & Psychophysics, 68,* 475–488.

Thompson, R., Emmorey, K., & Gollan, T. H. (2005). 'Tips of the fingers' experiences by deaf signers: Insights into the organization of a sign-based lexicon. *Psychological Science, 16,* 856–860.

Thorpe, S., Fize, D., & Marlot, C. (1996). Speed of processing in the human visual system. *Nature, 381,* 520–522.

Tieges, Z., Snel, J., Kok, A., Wijnen, J. G., Lorist, M. M., & Ridderinkhof, R. (2006). Caffeine improves anticipatory processes in task switching. *Biological Psychology, 73,* 101–116.

Tipples, J. (2006). Fear and fearfulness potentiate automatic orienting to eye gaze. *Cognition and Emotion, 20,* 309–320.

Tipples, J., Atkinson, A. P., & Young, A. W. (2002). The eyebrow frown: A salient social signal. *Emotion, 2,* 288–296.

Tipples, J., Young, A. W., Quinlan, P. T., Broks, P., & Ellis, A. W. (2002). Searching for threat. *The Quarterly Journal of Experimental Psychology, 55A,* 1007–1026.

Tolman, E. C. (1948). Cognitive maps in rats and men. *Psychological Review, 55,* 189–208.

Tolman, E. C. (1932/1967). *Purposive behavior in animals and man.* New York: Appleton-Century-Croft.

Tombu, M., & Jolicœur, P. (2003). A central capacity sharing model of dual-task performance. *Journal of Experimental Psychology: Human Perception and Performance, 29,* 3–18.

Tombu, M., & Jolicœur, P. (2004). Virtually no evidence for virtually perfect time-sharing. *Journal of Experimental Psychology: Human Perception and Performance, 30,* 795–810.

Tombu, M., & Jolicœur, P. (2005). Testing the predictions of the central capacity sharing model. *Journal of Experimental Psychology: Human Perception and Performance, 31,* 790–802.

Toth, J. P., & Hunt, R. R. (1999). Not one versus many, but zero versus any: Structure and function in the context of the multiple memory systems debate. In J. K. Foster & M. Jelicic (Eds.), *Memory: Systems, process, or function? Debates in psychology* (pp. 232–272). New York: Oxford University Press.

Traxler, M. J., Pickering, M. J., & Clifton, C. (1998). Adjunct attachment is not a form of lexical ambiguity resolution. *Journal of Memory and Language, 33,* 285–318.

Treisman, A. M. (1964). Contextual cues in selective listening. *The Quarterly Journal of Experimental Psychology, 12,* 242–248.

Treisman, A. M. (1967). Reply. *The Quarterly Journal of Experimental Psychology, 19,* 364–367.

Treisman, A. M. (1969). Strategies and models of selective attention. *Psychological Review, 76,* 282–299.

Treisman, A. M., & Davies, A. (1973). Dividing attention to ear and eye. In S. Kornblum (Ed.), *Attention and performance, IV* (pp. 101–117). New York: Academic.

Treisman, A. M., & Geffen, G. (1967). Selective attention: Perception or response? *The Quarterly Journal of Experimental Psychology, 19*, 1–17.

Treisman, A. M., & Gelade, G. (1980). A feature-integration theory of attention. *Cognitive Psychology, 12*, 97–136.

Treisman, A. M., & Gormican, S. (1998). Feature analysis in early vision: Evidence from search asymmetries. *Psychological Review, 95*, 15–48.

Trueswell, J. C., Tanenhaus, M. K., & Garnsey, S. M. (1994). Semantic influences on parsing: Use of thematic role information in syntactic ambiguity resolution. *Journal of Memory and Language, 33*, 285–318.

Tulving, E. (1962). Subjective organization in the free recall of 'unrelated' words. *Psychological Review, 69*, 344–354.

Tulving, E. (1972). Episodic and semantic memory. In E. Tulving & W. Donaldson (Eds.), *Organization of memory* (pp. 232–272). New York: Academic.

Tulving, E. (1983). *Elements of episodic memory*. Oxford, England: Clarendon.

Tulving, E. (1985). Memory and consciousness. *Canadian Psychologist, 26*, 1–12.

Tulving, E. (1993). Varieties of consciousness and levels of awareness in memory. In A. D. Baddeley & L. Weiskrantz (Eds.), *Attention: Selection, awareness, and control. A tribute to Donald Broadbent* (pp. 283–299). Oxford, England: Oxford University Press.

Tulving, E. (2002). Episodic memory: From mind to brain. *Annual Review of Psychology, 53*, 1–25.

Tulving, E., & Colotla, V. A. (1970). Free recall of trilingual lists. *Cognitive Psychology, 1*, 86–98.

Tulving, E., & Thomson, D. M. (1973). Encoding specificity and retrieval processes in episodic memory. *Psychological Review, 80*, 352–373.

Tulving, E., & Wiseman, S. (1975). Relation between recognition and recognition failure of recallable words. *Bulletin of the Psychonomic Society, 6*, 79–82.

Turvey, M. T. (1973). On peripheral and central processes in vision: Inferences from an information-processing analysis of masking with patterned stimuli. *Psychological Review, 80*, 1–52.

Turvey, M. T. (1977). Contrasting orientations to the theory of visual information processing. *Psychological Review, 84*, 67–88.

Turvey, M. T. (1978). Visual processing and short-term memory. In W. K. Estes (Ed.), *Handbook of learning and cognitive processes, Volume 5: Human information processing* (pp. 91–142). Hillsdale, New Jersey: Erlbaum.

Turvey, M. T., & Kravetz, S. (1970). Retrieval from iconic memory with shape as the selection criterion. *Perception & Psychophysics, 8*, 171–172.

Turvey, M. T., Shaw, R. E., Reed, E. S., & Mace, W. M. (1981). Ecological laws of perceiving and acting: In reply to Fodor and Pylyshyn (1981). *Cognition, 9*, 237–304.

Tversky, A. (1977). Features of similarity. *Psychological Review, 84*, 327–352.

Tversky, A., & Kahneman, D. (1971). The belief in the 'law of small numbers'. *Psychological Bulletin, 76*, 105–110.

Tversky, A., & Kahneman, D. (1973). Availability: A heuristic for judging frequency and probability. *Cognitive Psychology, 5*, 207–232.

Tversky, A., & Kahneman, D. (1974). Judgment under uncertainty: Heuristics and Biases. *Science, 185*, 1124–1131.

Tversky, A., & Kahneman, D. (1981). The framing of decisions and the psychology of choice. *Science, 211*, 453–458.

Tversky, A., & Kahneman, D. (1983). Extensional versus intensional reasoning: The conjunction fallacy in probability judgment. *Psychological Review, 90*, 293–315.

Tversky, B., & Tuchin, M. (1989). A reconciliation of the evidence on eyewitness testimony: Comments on McCloskey and Zaragoza. *Journal of Experimental Psychology: General, 118*, 86–91.

Ullman, M. T., Corkin, S., Coppola, M., Hickok, G., Growdon, J. H., & Koroshetz, W. J. (1997). A neural dissociation within language: Evidence that the mental dictionary is part of declarative memory, and that grammatical rules are processed by the procedural system. *Journal of Cognitive Neuroscience, 9*, 266–276.

Ullman, S. (1979). The interpretation of visual motion (fig. 3.11). Cambridge, Massachusetts: The MIT Press.

Underwood, G. (1976). *Attention and memory*. Oxford, England: Pergamon Press.

van der Heijden, A. H. C. (2003). *Attention in vision: Perception, communication and action*. London: Wise.

van der Helm, P. A. (2000). Simplicity versus likelihood in visual perception: From surprisals to precisals. *Psychological Bulletin, 126*, 770–800.

van der Helm, P. A., & Leeuwenberg, E. L. J. (1996). Goodness of visual regularities: A nontransformational approach. *Psychological Review, 103*, 429–456.

van Gompel, R. P. G., Pickering, M. J., Pearson, J., & Liversedge, S. P. (2005). Evidence against competition during syntactic ambiguity resolution. *Journal of Memory and Language, 52*, 284–307.

van Gompel, R. P. G., Pickering, M. J., & Traxler, M. J. (2001). Reanalysis in sentence processing: Evidence against current constraint-based and two-stage models. *Journal of Memory and Language, 45*, 225–258.

van Selst, M., Ruthruff, E., & Johnston, J. C. (1999). Can practice eliminate the Psychological Refractory Period. *Journal of Experimental Psychology: Human Perception and Performance, 25*, 1268–1283.

van Taylor, D. (1992). *Dream deceivers: The story behind James Vance vs. Judas Priest* [Motion Picture]. New York: First Run Features.

van Wassenhove, V., Grant, K. W., & Poeppel, D. (2006). Temporal window of integration in auditory–visual speech perception. *Neuropsychologia, 45*, 588–607.

VanRullen, R., & Koch, C. (2003). Is perception discrete or continuous? *Trends in Cognitive Science, 7*, 207–213.

Vitello, P., Hammer, K., & Schweber, N. (2006, June 12). A ring tone meant to fall on deaf ears. *The New York Times*.

von Neumann, J., & Morgenstern, O. (1944). *The theory of games and economic behavior*. Princeton, New Jersey: Princeton University Press.

von Wright, J. M. (1968). Selection in immediate memory. *The Quarterly Journal of Experimental Psychology, 20*, 62–68.

von Wright, J. M. (1970). On selection in visual immediate memory. *Acta Psychologica, 33*, 280–292.

Wade, K. A., Garry, M., Read, J. D., & Lindsay, D. S. (2002). A picture is worth a thousand lies: Using false photographs to create false childhood memories. *Psychonomic Bulletin & Review, 9*, 597–603.

Wade, N. J. (1982). *The art and science of visual illusions*. London: Routledge & Kegan Paul.

Wade, N. J., & Swanston, M. (1991). *Visual perception: An introduction*. London: Routledge.

Wagar, B. M., & Thagard, P. (2004). Spiking Phineas Gage: A neurocomputational theory of cognitive-affective integration in decision making. *Psychological Review, 111,* 67–79.

Wagemans, J. (1999). Toward a better approach to goodness: Comments on Van der Helm and Leeuwenberg (1996). *Psychological Review, 106,* 610–621.

Wandell, B. A. (1995). *Foundations of vision.* Sunderland, Massachusetts: Sinauer.

Ward, G., & Tan, L. (2004). The effect of the length of to-be-remembered lists and intervening lists on free recall: A re-examination using overt rehearsal. *Journal of Experimental Psychology: Learning, Memory and Cognition, 30,* 186–210.

Warren, R. M. (1970). Perceptual restoration of missing speech sounds. *Science, 167,* 392–393.

Warren, R. M. (1999). *Auditory Perception. A new analysis and synthesis.* Cambridge, England: Cambridge University Press.

Wason, P. C. (1960). On the failure to eliminate hypotheses in a conceptual task. *The Quarterly Journal of Experimental Psychology, 12,* 129–140.

Wason, P. C., & Johnson-Laird, P. N. (1968). *Thinking and reasoning.* Harmondsworth, England: Penguin Books.

Wasow, T. (1989). Grammatical theory. In M. I. Posner (Ed.), *Foundations of cognitive science* (pp. 162–205). Cambridge, Massachusetts: The MIT Press.

Waszak, F., Hommel, B., & Allport, A. (2003). Task-switching and long-term priming: Role of episodic stimulus-task bindings in task-shift costs. *Cognitive Psychology, 46,* 361–413.

Watkins, M. J. (1989). Wilful and nonwilful determinants of memory. In H. L. Roediger III & F. I. M. Craik (Eds.), *Varieties of memory and consciousness. Essays in honor of Endel Tulving* (pp. 59–71). Hillsdale, New Jersey: Erlbaum.

Watt, R. J. (1988). *Visual processing: Computational, psychophysical, and cognitive research.* Hove, England: Erlbaum.

Waugh, N. C., & Norman, D. A. (1965). Primary memory. *Psychological Review, 72,* 89–104.

Welford, A. T. (1952). The 'psychological refractory period' and the timing of high-speed performance: A review and a theory. *British Journal of Psychology, 43,* 2–19.

Wertheimer, M. (1925/1967). Gestalt theory. In W. D. Ellis (Ed.), *A source book of Gestalt psychology* (pp. 1–11). New York: Humanities Press.

Weschler, D. B. (1963). Engrams, memory storage and mnemonic coding. *American Psychologist, 18,* 149–153.

Whitten, W. B., & Bjork, R. A. (1972). Test events as learning triads: The importance of being imperfect. Paper persented at the meeting of the Midwestern Mathematical Psychology Association, Bloomington, Indiana.

Whorf, B. L. (1956). The relation of habitual thought and behavior to language. In J. B. Carroll (Ed.), *Language, thought and reality: Essays by B. L. Whorf* (pp. 35–270). Cambridge, Massachusetts: The MIT Press.

Wickelgren, W. A., & Norman, D. A. (1966). Strength models and serial position in short-term recognition memory. *Journal of Mathematical Psychology, 3,* 316–347.

Wickens, C. D. (1984). *Engineering psychology and human performance.* Columbus, Ohio: Charles E. Merrill.

Wickens, D. D., Born, D. G., & Allen, C. K. (1963). Proactive inhibition and item similarity in short-term memory. *Journal of Verbal Learning and Verbal Behavior, 2,* 440–445.

Wickens, T. D. (2002). *Elementary signal detection theory.* Oxford, England: Oxford University Press.

Wiens, S. (2006). Current concerns in visual masking. *Emotion, 6,* 675–680.

Wilkins, A. J. (1971). Conjoint frequency, category size, and categorization time. *Journal of Verbal Learning and Verbal Behavior,* 382–385.

Williams, P. C., & Parkin, A. J. (1980). On knowing the meaning of words we are able to report: Confirmation of a guessing explanation. *The Quarterly Journal of Experimental Psychology, 32,* 101–107.

Wilton, R. N. (1978). Explaining imaginal inference by operations in a propositional format. *Perception, 7,* 563–574.

Wilton, R. N. (1985). The recency effect in the perception of ambiguous figures. *Perception, 14,* 53–61.

Wilton, R. N. (1990). The mediation of paired associate recall by representations of properties ascribed to objects in perception and imagination. *The Quarterly Journal of Experimental Psychology, 42A,* 611–634.

Wilton, R. N. (1992). The representation of objects and their attributes in memory: Evidence concerning memory for location. *The Quarterly Journal of Experimental Psychology, 45A,* 421–450.

Wilton, R. N. (2000). *Consciousness, free will, and the explanation of human behaviour.* Lampeter, Wales: Edwin Mellen Press.

Wilton, R. N., & Mathieson, P. (1996). The supposed effect of interactive imagery in paired associate learning. *The Quarterly Journal of Experimental Psychology, 49A,* 888–900.

Winograd, T. (1978). On primitives, prototypes, and other semantic anomalies. In D. L. Waltz (Ed.), *Theoretical issues in natural language processing, Vol. 2* (pp. 25–32). Urbana-Champaign, Illinois: University of Illinois at Urbana-Champaign.

Wittgenstein, L. (1953). *Philosophical investigations.* New York: MacMillan.

Wixted, J. T., & Stretch, V. (2000). The case against a criterion-shift account of false memory. *Psychological Review, 107,* 368–376.

Wolfe, J. M. (1994). Guided search 2.0: A revised model of visual search. *Psychonomic Bulletin & Review, 1,* 202–238.

Wolfe, J. M. (1998). What can 1 million trials tell us about visual search? *Psychological Science, 9,* 33–39.

Wood, N. L., & Cowan, N. (1995a). The cocktail party phenomenon revisited: Attention and memory in the classic selective listening procedure of Cherry (1953). *Journal of Experimental Psychology: General, 124,* 243–262.

Wood, N. L., & Cowan, N. (1995b). The cocktail party phenomenon revisited: How frequent are attention shifts to one's name in an irrelevant auditory channel? *Journal of Experimental Psychology: Learning, Memory and Cognition, 21,* 255–260.

Woods, W. A. (1975). What's in a link: Foundations for semantic networks. In D. G. Bobrow & A. M. Collins (Eds.), *Representation and understanding: Studies in cognitive science* (pp. 35–82). New York: Academic.

Woodworth, R. S. (1929). *Psychology.* New York: Holt.

Worthington, A. G. (1964). Differential rates of dark adaptation to 'taboo' with 'neutral' stimuli. *Canadian Journal of Psychology, 18,* 257–265.

Wright, D. B., & Loftus, E. F. (1998). How misinformation alters memories. *Journal of Experimental Child Psychology, 71,* 155–164.

Yin, R. (1969). Looking at upside-down faces. *Journal of Experimental Psychology, 81,* 141–145.

Zadeh, L. A. (1982). A note on prototype theory and fuzzy sets. *Cognition, 12,* 291–297.

# Glossary

$2\frac{1}{2}$D sketch According to Marr (1982), this is an internal description of an object containing information about the orientation and depth of surfaces and edges relative to a given angle of regard.

3D model description According to Marr (1982), this is an internal representation that codes the volumetric nature of an object.

abstract A term that is used to refer to anything that is defined without reference to the material world.

access key In the headed records model, the mental cue that is used to retrieve information from long-term memory.

acquired disorders Neurological problems that arise during the normal course of development through injury or illness.

acquired distinctiveness When participants, through experience, begin to treat different instances as being different from one another and assign them different responses.

acquired equivalence Where participants, through experience, treat different instances as being similar to one another and assign them the same response. Both a and A belong to the A category.

active theories A phrase used to refer to theories of perception in which the person can exert some control over how they perceive the world.

adaptive toolbox The idea that the mind comprises a whole bunch of special-purpose heuristics, each of which applies to a particular problem typically encountered in the real world.

added stimuli In the phonemic restoration paradigm, where noise is added to the critical phoneme.

additive pattern In the context of the PRP, the case where the same effect of task 2 difficulty is constant for all SOAs tested.

algorithm A well-specified procedure (such as a computer program) that ensures the correct outcome when correctly applied.

all-or-nothing system A thresholded system that is either in an ON state or an OFF state. There is no state in-between ON and OFF.

alternating blocks A sequence of trials in which, respectively, odd and even trials are predictably related to two different tasks.

alternation cost Impaired performance observed during alternating blocks relative to pure blocks.

ambiguous figures A stimulus that has more than one interpretation and there is no obvious reason as to which is the 'correct' one.

ambiguous figure reversal The point at which an ambiguous figure switches between two different interpretations.

analogical representation A form of representation in which there is a correspondence between parts and relations in the representing world and parts and relations in the represented world.

analysis by synthesis Perception viewed as a process of integration of sensory information and shared knowledge on the basis of generating and testing hypotheses about the input.

anger superiority effect The ease of detecting a discrepant angry face within a crowd, gauged relative to the difficulty of detecting a discrepant neutral or happy face.

angry face advantage The apparent ease of detecting an angry facial expression in a crowd of faces.

anorthoscopic perception Perception of a world through a slit or aperture.

anterograde amnesia Inability to retrieve memories after a certain time point.

aperture viewing Viewing a stimulus through a slit.

architectural characteristics When used in the context of the mind, this phrase refers to how the mind may be composed and organised into its constituent components.

arguments One or more variables that apply to a predicate. A predicate structure is of the sort – Predicate [Argument1, Argument2, . . . Argument$n$].

arrows-and-boxes diagram Similar to a schematic blueprint; a visual representation specifying the components of a system and how the components are interconnected.

articulatory suppression The active repetition of spoken items in a bid to inhibit sub-vocal rehearsal. Used primarily to disrupt the phonological loop component of the working memory model.

artificial intelligence (AI) approach Attempts to mimic intelligent behaviour via computer simulation.

association deficit A neuropsychological case in which an individual with brain damage presents with deficits in two different domains such as an inability to understand (i) written and (ii) spoken forms of language.

association formation The laying down of associative bonds between two otherwise separate entities. Responses can be associated with stimuli, hence an associative bond is formed between the stimulus and response.

associative memory Information storage that keeps track of the associative relations between two events. Typically the strength of an associative link is indexed by the co-occurrence between the two associates.

associative network A network model of memory in which nodes signify entities and links represent associative bonds (e.g., the nodes for A and B are connected by a link that signifies that A and B are associated).

**associative processes** Psychological processes by which two entities are related. The registration of the co-occurrence of two entities.

**associative relatedness** Items that are associatively related are typically bound together by what may appear to be an otherwise arbitrary state of affairs. For example, 'horse' and 'cart' belong to different semantic categories but they are associatively related through the fact that they commonly co-occur.

**associative system** The idea that there is one system of reasoning that operates by making inferences purely on the basis of statistical regularities such as co-occurrences between events.

**attended channel** An input channel that participants concentrate on.

**attentional resources** The equivalent of mental electricity. A finite amount of mental energy that must be distributed among competing stimuli and tasks.

**attentional spotlight** A metaphor used for the current focus of visual attention. Like the spotlight of a torch, attributes of the visual world are clearer within the focus of the beam than they are outside the focus of the beam.

**attenuated filter account** Treisman's (1964) revision of Broadbent's (1958) filter theory in which relevant portions of an unattended signal may be semantically processed. In this account filtering is partial and not all-or-nothing as in Broadbent's earlier theory.

**automatic processes** Operations at an unconscious level, thought to be capacity unlimited and outside the control of the person.

**autonoetic aspect of memory** According to Tulving (1985), a phenomenological aspect of remembering in which previous events are re-experienced.

**availability heuristic** Reasoning on the basis of how easily information is recovered from memory.

**axis-based description** According to Marr (1982), an axis-based description comprises a specification of a connected set of axes of an object composed of parts. Each axis of component is associated with a single generalised cone as included in the 3D model description of a familiar object.

**back-propagation** A training procedure in connectionist networks in which the aim

is to minimise the discrepancy between desired and actual outputs. An iterative process in which the coefficients in the network (the weights on the connections and the thresholds on the units) are changed whenever the network makes an error in producing the wrong output for a given input.

**backward masking** A situation under which one visual event is obscured by an immediately following event (known as the mask).

**base sentence** According to Chomsky, an abstract statement containing a series of symbols from which the surface form of an actual sentence is produced.

**basic first hypothesis** The idea that perceptual representations have privileged access to basic level descriptions as a first step, after which superordinate and subordinate descriptions may be accessed.

**basic level** According to Rosch, the primary level of entry in accessing semantic memory. 'Duck' rather than 'Bird', 'Duck' rather than 'Mallard'.

**basic level advantage** A bias in the human recognition system to match a perceptual representation to an internal representation existing at a basic level of categorisation.

**battery of tests** A series of psychological tests carried out in order to assess an individual's ability across a number of domains.

**Bayes' theorem** A statistical method of deciding which of two hypotheses is true given the evidence.

**behavioural dispositions** Statements about common ways of behaving.

**behaviourism** A research programme that attempts to describe human nature but only in terms of observable events and entities.

**beta** In signal detection theory, the symbol for the location of the criterion. Changes in beta are typically taken to reflect changes in response bias.

**binary coding** Representations that can contain only 0s and 1s.

**binary unit** A processing unit in a connectionist network which can only be in one of two states at any given time (i.e., either ON or OFF).

**binocular retinocentric representation** A representation of the visual world derived from both eyes but which preserves locational information in terms of retinal co-ordinates.

**bivalent lists** Experimental stimuli in which each stimulus is associated with two tasks. In the absence of other

information, such as a cue or its order in the list, the response is ambiguous.

**bottom-up processing** Processes driven by the stimulus in a feed-forward fashion.

**bounded rationality** The idea that human reasoning is best understood when basic performance limitations (such as memory and time constraints) are taken into consideration.

**brightness** Essentially, how light or dark something is.

**brightness constancy (invariance)** The ability to discount absolute brightness in identifying shape.

**canonical view** After Palmer et al. (1981), a specific (typical/familiar) view of an object which is thought to best represent that object.

**capacity sharing** The idea that multiple tasks may be able to share central processes at the same time.

**categorical identity** A specification of the category to which a stimulus belongs.

**categorical perception** Where the detection of the difference between an A and a B stimulus is better if A and B are taken from different psychological categories than when A and B are taken from the same psychological category.

**categorical perception expansion effect** Where the perceptual space between categories appears larger as a result of training.

**categorical proposition** A statement that declares a relation between the classes designated by two categorical terms.

**categorical term** The basic unit of meaning in a syllogism.

**category** A collection or set of things.

**category co-ordinates** Short-hand for instances that belong to the same category.

**category cue validity** The degree to which a given category reflects a well-differentiated set of instances.

**category differentiation hypothesis** The idea that the organisation of categories can change as a result of expertise. Categories become more distinctive from one another.

**category dominance** The frequency of reporting a superordinate in response to a category instance.

**category prototype** A mental representation of the most representative member of a category.

**category verification study** A paradigm in which participants are asked to respond whether or not a category label and category instance match.

**cathode-ray tube metaphor** The proposal that the internal medium of representation used in various mental imagery tasks corresponds to a 2D array of light intensity values.

**central cue** A cue in a spatial cueing paradigm which provides information regarding the possible location of the target but the cue itself is not presented at a possible target location.

**central executive** In the working memory model, a mechanism that oversees the operation of the slave systems in terms of scheduling and control.

**central masking** Masking occurring at the level of central decision mechanisms. Introduced in terms of the concurrent and contingent model of Turvey (1973).

**central processes** Internal operations that eventuate in the assignment of a stimulus representation to a mental category. Processes that are concerned with stimulus identification; interpretative mechanisms.

**central state identity theory** The idea that to understand the mind we must understand the brain. Mental states and processes are identical with neurological states and processes.

**change blindness** The inability to detect a critical change in alternating images of the same scene.

**characteristic features** Attributes that are not necessarily associated with the category but that are, nevertheless, variously associated with the category.

**cheater detection** From an evolutionary perspective, the need to be able to discover those individuals who renege on social contracts.

**choice reaction time (CRT) task** In a CRT task, participants are asked to decide about the nature of an imperative signal and make one of a number of alternative possible responses under speeded constraints.

**chorus of prototypes** A collection of prototypical representations of individual objects as defined by Edelman (1998, 1999).

**chunking** The fact that memory over the short term is facilitated if the material can be recoded into a smaller number of meaningful packets or chunks. The sequence of letters R E M B B C C I A will be better recalled if coded into REM BBC CIA.

**classification** The assignment of a stimulus to a mental category.

**coding modularity** According to Crowder (1989), the idea that memory is a function of the processes that were brought to bear on the material when it was initially encountered.

**coding transformation** Used in reference to stimulus processing – taking one internal code and translating this into another. For instance, the earliest representation of the stimulus is converted into a code that specifies its name, its physical appearance, its identity, etc.

**coefficients** The modifiable weights and thresholds in a connectionist model.

**cogit** The smallest unit of information within mental language. Cogits are the atoms of thought.

**cognition** Operations associated with the central processes.

**cognitive economy** The principle of minimising cognitive storage space for any item of information.

**cognitive map** An internal representation of an external environment that captures salient landmarks and salient spatial relations between those landmarks.

**cognitive neuropsychology** A cognitive approach that concentrates on comparisons between performance of individuals suffering from some form of brain damage with individuals with intact brains.

**cognitive system** Interpretative mechanisms.

**combinatorial syntax** A system of rules for the combining units of some form of language or form of representational system.

**compatible S–R relations** Cases where the meaning or physical position of a stimulus maps directly onto the physical position of a response. A stimulus on the left of the display is assigned to the compatible left response.

**competence** In Chomsky's terms, the tacit knowledge that underlies the ability to produce and understand all and only the sentences in a natural language.

**complementarity** The reciprocal interaction between the resource demands of two tasks. If the demands on one task increase, performance on a competing task suffers.

**complete viewpoint-invariant theory** A theory of object recognition in which recognition depends on the coding of an object with respect to a view-independent, co-ordinate system.

**compositionality** The idea put forward by Fodor and Pylyshyn (1988) that the meaning of a complex expression rests upon understanding its component constituents.

**compound letter** A stimulus in which a larger letter is composed of smaller letters (after Navon, 1977).

**computational metaphor** The position that the mind/brain relation is the same as the computer software/hardware relation. Mental processes are computational processes.

**computational processes** Individual operators that can be specified in terms of a physical symbol system.

**computational theory level** Marr's (1982) first level of description is concerned with what the device does and why it does it.

**computer metaphor of memory** A view of the mind in which each memory trace or mental record is stored at its own place (address) in the mental store.

**concept** A mental representation that captures knowledge of what constitutes a given category of things.

**conceptual constituents** According to Jackendoff (2002), the units of semantic analysis related to language. Components of meaning conveyed by a sentence or phrase.

**condition/action pair** Conditional statement specifying that if a condition is met then the action will be taken. Discussed here in terms of the computational processes of control.

**confirmation bias** The inclination to seek out evidence in support of currently held hypotheses. A bias against seeking out evidence that might disconfirm such hypotheses.

**confirmed identity** Final judgement of an object's identity based on available perceptual evidence.

**congruity effect** Responding with affirmation leads to better memory than does responding with negation.

**conjunction fallacy** The incorrect belief that the combination of two events is more likely than either event alone.

**connection weight** Strength of a link between nodes in a connectionist network.

**connectionism** A discipline that attempts to generate computer models of the mind based on brain-like architectures – simple processing units (based on brain cells) are interconnected with adaptable connections or links. Very much a telephone exchange approach to modelling the mind.

**connectionist models** Computer models in which simple processing units with modifiable thresholds are interconnected with modifiable weighted connections. Adaptive means for changing weights and thresholds results in learning mappings between inputs to and outputs from the network.

**connectionist position** Accounts of the mind in which it is assumed that rule-like behaviour emerges from the complex interactions of many simple interconnected processing units.

**constrained maximisation** Finding a solution to a problem by figuring out which of several possible solutions produces the optimal trade-off benefits and costs.

**constructive process** Perception construed as a process in which the percept is built up from sensory information and stored knowledge.

**constructivist theory** A theory of perception that assumes constructive processes; that is, the percept is built up from the evidence at the senses together with knowledge about the world.

**contralateral** Opposite side to the side being considered.

**control participants** A group of individuals with intact brains who provide a profile of normal performance on some test or battery of tests in a cognitive neuropsychological study.

**controlled parallel processing** The general view, espoused by Pashler (1998), that parallel processing of stimuli is possible but this is not without restraint and is under executive control.

**controlled processes** Operations at a conscious level, thought to be capacity limited.

**converging evidence** A variety of different forms of evidence that all lead to the same sort of conclusion. The evidence converges on the one conclusion.

**correct rejections** Cases where a signal is not present and a correct absent response is made.

**correlation coefficient** A numerical index of the degree to which two things or states of affairs co-occur.

**covert shifts of attention** Movements of visual attention that are not locked to changes in eye position.

**criterion** In signal detection theory, a movable threshold that determines the decision as to whether or not the signal or target stimulus was present on a given trial.

**Criterion S** Sloman's assertion that a person can entertain a simultaneous contradictory belief.

**critical lure** From Roediger and McDermott (1995), an item that is closely associated with a list of items but is never actually presented during the initial study phase of the experiment.

**cue–target match** An alternative characterisation of the encoding specificity hypothesis which states that the similarity between retrieval cue and stored memory predicts remembering (Nairne, 2005).

**cue validity** The sum extent to which a given attribute (the cue) predicts membership of a given category.

**cued recall test** Where participants are asked, in a memory experiment, to reinstate a previously experienced item with the aid of a cue or cues.

**curtailment** A form of masking by interruption where the processing of one stimulus stops when a second stimulus is presented.

**cyclopean retinocentric frame of reference** Spatial co-ordinates derived from combined information from both eyes.

**d prime ($d'$)** In signal detection theory, perceptual sensitivity or the distance between the noise and the signal + noise distributions. According to Estes (1994, p. 232), a $d'$ of 0 indicates a complete inability to distinguish a signal from noise (the distributions overlap completely); a $d'$ of 2 or 3 reflects a high degree of discrimination between signal + noise and noise (the distributions are spaced far apart).

**Darwinian algorithms** Type-distinct ways of reasoning that have developed throughout the evolution of the species.

**data compression** Taking any form of message and coding it in a reduced form such that any redundancies have been removed. '9xa' rather than 'aaaaaaaaa'.

**data decompression** Taking a coded message and recovering the original. For example, taking '9xa' and generating 'aaaaaaaaa'.

**decay** Forgetting that occurs naturally as a function of time. Memory traces are said to fade away over time.

**deductive inference** Inferences made on the basis of logic.

**defining features** Attributes that are necessarily associated with a category.

**definingness continuum** A theoretical construct introduced by Smith et al. (1974), a psychological dimension upon which the attributes of a given entity can be rank ordered in terms of their significance for defining the entity.

**demonstration proof** Taking any hypothesis and demonstrating that it can work in practice. Demonstrating that something works.

**deontic conditional** A conditional statement relating to obligation.

**depictive representation** A form of representation that denotes by resemblance.

**depressive realism** The idea that depressed individuals make more accurate judgements regarding response–outcome contingencies than do non-depressed individuals.

**depth of processing effect** Deeper (e.g., semantic) processing leads to better memory than does less deep processing. It is easier to remember material when semantic judgements are made than when judgements are made about the surface characteristics of the material. Is it the antonym of 'ambitious'? Does it rhyme with 'capricious'?

**descriptive representation** A form of representation that denotes by description.

**destructive actualisation hypothesis** After Schwarz and Stahlberg (2003), the idea that post-event information can actually destroy stored memories: stored information is over-written by new information.

**detection of non-accidental properties** The recovery of properties contained in a 2D projection of a 3D scene that constrains the interpretation of the scene. For instance, parallel lines in the image typically arise because of parallel lines or edges in the scene. Discussed at length by Biederman in his RBC theory of object recognition.

**detection task** An experimental task in which the participant simply has to respond on every trial as to whether a stimulus is present or not.

**deterministic system** Consequents are causally determined by their antecedents. For instance, each response is causally linked to a stimulus.

**developmental disorders** Neurological problems that develop as a person ages. Typically such problems are noted in childhood and may arise as a result of genetic factors, during pregnancy or birth.

**diary study** A study in which participants' experiences are recorded on a regular basis over a relatively long period of time. Examination of the diary records is undertaken as the means of data analysis.

**dichoptic** Cases where one stimulus is delivered to one eye and a different stimulus is delivered to the other eye.

**dichotic listening** Situations that involve different acoustic material being presented to left and right ears at the same time.

**different brains problem** An issue for type identity theory in that no two brains are the same, hence the same mental event cannot be associated with a particular neurological event because different neurological events take place in different brains.

**discrete moment hypothesis** Where visual perception over time is derived from individual non-overlapping snapshots of the world.

**display elements** Individual components of a stimulus display. For instance, the individual letters in a matrix of letters.

**display set size** The number of individual display elements in a stimulus display.

**display size** In visual search paradigms, the number of to-be-searched elements presented in any given search display.

**dissociation deficit** A neuropsychological case in which an individual with brain damage presents with a marked deficit in one domain but has preserved, or relatively preserved, function in a related domain. For instance, a person is able to read words but not non-words.

**distal object** An object 'out there' in the real world.

**distal stimulus** The external entity in the outside world from which stimulation of the sense organs arises.

**distributed models of semantic memory** The idea that concepts are defined relative to the current pattern of activation across an entire network of processing units at any one time.

**distributed representation** The current pattern of activation across a bank of processing units contained in a connectionist network.

**domain-specific** The notion that individual processing modules are responsible for a discrete aspect of processing. For example, there is a particular module responsible for colour perception and a different module for pitch perception, etc.

**double dissociation** Where individual 1 performs well on task A but poorly on task B, but individual 2 performs poorly on task A but well on task B.

**dual system theory** After Sloman (1996), the idea that human reasoning can be based on the operation of either an associative system or a rule-based system.

**dualism** The philosophical position that the mind is a mental entity distinct from the physical world.

**dual-task decrement** A reduction in performance when performing two tasks together, relative to performing the same two tasks separately.

**dynamic mask** A mask that changes over time.

**dysphoric individuals** Individuals who are either depressed or prone to depression.

**ecological memory** After Bruce (1985), how memory operates in everyday situations.

**egocentric frame of reference** A head-based frame of reference used by the visual system to specify object positions relative to the viewer's head.

**eliminative materialism** The viewpoint that once we understand the precise electro-chemical workings of the brain, we will understand the mind. When we reach this point, we can eliminate any talk of the cognitive level.

**empirical** A scientific experiment or observation involving measurement.

**encoding specificity principle** After Tulving and Thomson (1973), the idea that memory is most successful when the conditions at encoding are replicated at retrieval.

**end-code** According to SIT, the end-code is the ultimate version of an internal description of a shape when all of the redundancy reducing operations have been carried out.

**endogenous control** The ability to change cognitive processing at will. In spatial cueing experiments, the idea that the movement of attention is under the control of the participant.

**entry point level** The primary point of contact between a perceptual representation and a long-term memory representation during the process of object recognition.

**episodic buffer** In the extended working memory model, a component responsible for integrating information from different sources and different modalities.

**episodic memory** Memories of life experiences (after Tulving, 2002).

**epoch of training** In the current context, this applies to the back-propagation learning algorithm. On each trial an input pattern is presented, the eventual error signal is derived at the output layer and this is fed backwards through the network as changes to the coefficients are made. One epoch is where each input pattern, used in the training regimen, is presented once to the network.

**equal interval scale** Some scale of measurement in which the distance between any two adjacent points is the same regardless of where on the scale the two points fall.

**erasure** A form of interruption masking in which the current stimulus is completely over-written by the delivery of the mask.

**error signal** In a connectionist network, where the output error is used as a reverse input pattern to the network. This 'input' pattern is fed back down the network and used to change the coefficients as it passes back down the network.

**establishment position** Standard computational theory of mind accounts of cognition and perception (see Fodor & Pylyshyn, 1981).

**exclusive (or negative) assertion** In a categorical proposition where members of a subject class are excluded in the predicate class. For example, 'Some of Amy's tattoos are not lady-like'.

**exemplar-based accounts** Theories of the human conceptual system that posit that individual traces of every category instance are stored together with their category labels.

**exogenous control** Cognitive processes that are driven by events external to the person. A bright flash will grab your visual attention and there is nothing that you can do to avoid this from happening. In spatial cueing experiments, the idea that the movement of attention is governed by salient stimulus characteristics such as a sudden onset of a visual event.

**expectancy (set) effects** Empirical findings that reveal how expectancy can influence our perceptions of the world.

**extension** The actual instances picked out by a given concept. For example, the actual objects that we call 'bikes'.

**extrapolation** Estimating a new value that falls outside the extremes of a previously exposed range of similar values.

**facilitation** When performance is faster (and/or more accurate) on a given type of trial relative to performance on some form of comparison, baseline, control or neutral trial.

**false alarms** Cases where a signal is not present and an incorrect present response is made.

**false memories** Memories of states of affairs that never actually took place.

**familiarity effects** Empirical findings that reveal how familiarity influences our perceptions of the world.

**family resemblance** An assessment of the extent to which all instances of a category possess certain attributes. Instances of a given category may only be so classified because they share a certain family resemblance to one another. They are similar in certain overall respects.

**fear system** A cognitive module that has evolved to service automatically fearful and threatening stimuli.

**featural diagnosticity** The degree to which a given feature is diagnostic of a given category. How diagnostic is 'beak' of the category 'birds'? (See also *cue validity*.)

**feature detectors** A putative neural mechanism such as a brain cell that is dedicated to collect evidence in favour of one particular kind of perceptual feature such as line orientation, size, position, colour, etc. A feature detector is switched ON (alternatively, it fires) when evidence consistent with the target feature is present in the input.

**feature-norming studies** Identifying the most common properties associated with any one object or category by having a large sample of people produce responses to a probe item. How often are 'hooves' produced in response to the probe 'horse'?

**feedback** Where later processes provide information to (or influence, in some other way) earlier processes.

**feedforward** Where earlier processes provide information to (or influence, in some other way) later processes.

**feedforward system** Information processing system in which only feedforward operations are carried out.

**field theory** Tolman's account of the learning behaviour of rats in mazes explained in terms of means–end expectation.

**figural effect** The bias in syllogistic reasoning that the information in the conclusion is likely to preserve the order of that information in the premises.

**first-level representation** A representation of the stimulus that contains a record of its identity. However, further operations are needed before a response can be generated (see discussion of the three component account of iconic memory in Chapter 3).

**flanker asymmetry effect** After Hostmann et al. (2006), where responses to a positive expression flanked by negative expressions suffer from more interference than do responses to a negative expression flanked by positive expressions.

**flanker interference effect** In the flanker task, where flankers that are inconsistent with the target produce less accurate and/or slower responses than flankers that are consistent with the target.

**flanker task** An experimental paradigm (Eriksen & Eriksen, 1974) in which participants are presented with visual displays, each containing a row of display elements. The central element is the designated target that must be responded to; the surrounding (flanking) elements must be ignored.

**forced recognition** Participants' recognition memory is tested by having them decide as to which or one or more of the alternatives has been previously experienced.

**foreshortening** Shortening the appearance of an object by angling the object towards or away from the viewer.

**formal system** A notational system governed by the form of symbols (their structure) with no reference to what those symbols represent or mean.

**forward masking** A situation under which one visual event is obscured by an immediately preceding event (known as the mask).

**frame** After Minsky (1975), a mental representation of a stereotyped or typical real-world event or object. Slots in the frame are associated with attributes and the slots are filled with default or prototypical values.

**free recall test** Where participants are asked to reinstate previously exposed items in any order without the aid of cues.

**free recognition** Participants' recognition memory is tested by having them freely decide whether an item is old or new.

**free will** The idea that an entity is free to choose how to behave and is capable of deciding how to behave. Linked to the idea that although I did do *x* I could have done *y* if I had so wished.

**frequentist terms** Descriptions that provide information about frequency of occurrence of states of affairs.

**full-report condition** In the Sperling (1960) paradigm, reporting all the display items from some form of briefly presented and masked display.

**function** A term used to refer to what a thing does.

**functional account** A description of a system primarily in terms of what purpose(s) it serves.

**functional architecture** A specification of the components of an information processing system, how they are interconnected and what functions the components serve.

**functional description** A description of some form of device that sets out what function each component has.

**functional role** A phrase used to refer to what the purpose of a component of an information processing system is.

**functional space** The idea that there is some form of psychological workspace that allows a person to reason about spatial relations in the real world.

**functionalism** The endeavour to attempt to define the properties of any device in terms of the functions that it and its components serve.

**fuzzy boundaries** When it is impossible to draw a sharp division between where one concept begins and where another ends. When is an object a chair? And when is it a stool?

**fuzzy concept** Concepts that do not have defining and necessary criteria for fixing the extension of the concept.

**garden-path theory** The idea that sentence comprehension is primarily determined by syntactic parsing.

**general animal advantage** Relatively good performance in quickly detecting a discrepant animal among other non-animal search items.

**geocentric frame of reference** A scene-based frame of reference in vision which takes into account both body-centred and scene-based attributes.

**geometric relations** Spatial relationships as defined within a geometric system.

**geons** According to Biederman (1987), the volumetric primitives such as spheres and cylinders that make up the mental building blocks of objects.

**Gestalt laws** A set of statements backed up by demonstrations of how it is that the perceptual system groups elements (the parts) into coherent wholes. Collectively the laws specify principles of perceptual organisation.

**global addressability** The assumption that any input segment corresponds to a global constituent of some object and not to some local constituent.

**global advantage** When responses to the general nature of a stimulus are better than responses to its local aspects.

**global distinctiveness** In memory experiments, distinctiveness of an item computed relative to the whole of the set of to-be-remembered items.

**global minimum** The state of a connectionist network in which the overall error (computed over all of the input patterns) is either zero or very close to zero. If the network reaches this state then it has been successful in learning the desired mappings between input and output mappings.

**global precedence** The idea that the global aspects of a shape are recovered prior to its local aspects.

**global-to-local interference** Cases where responses to local aspects of a stimulus are impeded by conflicting global information.

**global-to-local processing** The idea that the general nature of a stimulus is derived prior to its local aspects.

**go/no go task** A speeded response task in which participants are required to respond only when a target is presented. They must withhold responses when no target appears.

**grammar** According to Chomsky, the set of mental rules that allows a person to produce and understand the sentences in a natural language.

**habit** Enduring memories that lead to default responding when recollection fails.

**happiness superiority effect** The relative ease at detecting a discrepant happy face within a crowd, relative to a discrepant neutral or angry face.

**hardware implementation level** Marr's (1982) third level of description concerned with the physical nature of an information processing device.

**headed records model** A human information processing account in which memory units are separate from access keys. Information is recovered from memory by first forming an access key and then using this to recover appropriate stored memories.

**hemi-retina** Either the left half or the right half of the retina.

**heuristics** Rules of thumb or educated guesses.

**heuristics and biases approach** The understanding that some human reasoning is not logical or rational (Kahneman, Slovic & Tversky, 1982), but that it is based on educated guesswork and rules of thumb.

**hidden units** Units in a connectionist network that are only connected to other units and do not receive activation directly from or produce activation directly to the outside world.

**hierarchy violation effect** Cases where instances of categories show stronger links to higher-order categories relative to their immediately superordinate category. So 'Whisky' is more highly associated with 'Drink' than 'Liquor'.

**hits** Cases where a signal is present and a correct present response is made.

**horizontal faculties** General competencies such as memory or attention that cut across all cognitive domains.

**hue** Essentially, the category of a colour such as 'red' or 'green'.

**hypothesis-and-test cycle** First a hypothesis is generated and then analyses are carried out to test the validity of the hypothesis. If the test fails, the cycle begins again with another hypothesis, and so on.

**iconic memory** Traditionally, taken to be a very short-term visual memory system which briefly preserves the physical characteristics of the stimulus.

**identification** Recognition of a stimulus as being of a particular unique type.

**immediate memory span** The length of sequence of items for which an individual can recall all the items in their correct order.

**imperative signal** A stimulus that demands a response.

**incidental learning** A situation in which participants are oriented to materials without being aware that they will have to remember them and be tested on them later.

**incidental learning paradigm** Where participants are not explicitly instructed to remember items that they will be tested on later.

**inclusive (or positive) assertion** In a categorical proposition where members of a subject class are included in the predicate class. For example, 'Some of Amy's nights out are memorable'.

**incompatible S–R relations** Cases where the meaning or physical position of a stimulus does not directly map onto the physical position of a response. For example, stimuli on the right of a display are mapped to a left response key.

**indicative conditional** A conditional statement relating to the assertion of truths.

**inductive inference** Inferences made on the basis of information that goes beyond the premises.

**inertia hypothesis** The hypothesis that it is the difficulty in disengaging attention away from an emotionally provoking stimulus that is special about them.

**information gain model** A model developed by Oaksford and Chater (1994), in which problem solving amounts to the desire to acquire the maximum amount of information that can be used to adjudicate between various hypotheses.

**information processing system** A descriptive phrase that is used to refer to any kind of device whose operations are causally defined in terms of the information presented to it.

**information theory** A mathematical account of how a communication system works (Shannon & Weaver, 1949).

**informational persistence** The retention of information following the offset of a stimulus, as revealed by the partial-report advantage. A technical phrase for iconic memory in its traditional guise.

**informationally encapsulated** A property of a processing module (Fodor, 1983) in which its operations are determined locally by information contained within the module.

**informative cues** In a spatial cueing experiment, where the cues are highly predictive of the location (or nature) of the ensuing target.

**inhibition** When responding is slower (and/or less accurate) on a given type of trial relative to performance on some form of comparison, baseline, control or neutral trial.

**input channels** The idea that the sensory apparatus can be divided into independent streams of processing. Descriptions of an input channel can include whole senses (e.g., touch) or specific sensory transducers (e.g., the left ear).

**input pattern** In a connectionist model, the distributed pattern of activation across the input units.

**input processes** Early stage of processing associated with the initial physical registration and encoding of the stimulus. It is also referred to as early or peripheral processes or pre-bottleneck processes.

**instance–category typicality** An index of how typical an instance is of a given category. How typical is a Shih Tzu of the category DOG?

**instance dominance** The frequency of reporting a category instance in response to a superordinate.

**instructional set** An expectation towards a certain kind of stimulus, usually as a result of explicit guidance by the experimenter.

**integration hypothesis** According to Kahneman (1968), cases where two visual events are coded as one.

**Integration masking** When mask and stimulus are combined (psychologically) into a single montage.

**intension** The description or defining characteristics of a concept.

**intentional learning paradigm** Where participants are explicitly instructed to remember materials that they will be tested on later.

**intentionality** When thoughts and feelings refer to particular things in the world.

**interactive activation models** Processing systems in which information can both feed forward information from lower levels to higher levels and be fed back from higher levels to lower levels.

**inter-item interval** The time between the presentation of items within a list.

**internal representation** Some property of the inner workings of a device that stands for some property of the outside world. For instance, in a computer 01 represents '1'.

**interpolation** Estimating a new value that falls between the extremes of a previously exposed range of values.

**interruption masking** When processing of a stimulus is stopped by the presentation of an ensuing stimulus or masker.

**inter-stimulus interval (ISI)** The time between the offset of one stimulus and the onset of a subsequent stimulus.

**invalid trials** In spatial cueing experiments, when a cue incorrectly indicates the location (or nature) of the ensuing target.

**ipsi-lateral** Same side to that being discussed.

**irrelevant speech effect** Where the presentation of irrelevant speech concurrently with to-be-remembered items impairs memory performance.

**item distinctiveness** The extent to which one particular item stands out from all the others.

**item familiarity** An index of how familiar a given entity is. How familiar are you with liquor? Drink? Malibu and Coke?

**know response** A state of awareness – a feeling of familiarity – that an item was actually committed to memory.

**knowledge driven** A claim about perception being governed by stored knowledge.

**language of thought** A phrase used to refer to the internal system of representation and the operations that take place within this system in order to explain thought and thinking (after Fodor, 1975).

**late closure** According to Frazier (1987), the rule stating that the preferred interpretation of a sentence is that which requires the fewest number of clauses.

**late processes** Processes associated with decision/response stages of processing.

**latent learning** The acquisition of knowledge in the absence of reward or feedback.

**law of effect** A behaviourist law proposing that responses are strengthened when

associated with positive outcomes and weakened when associated with negative outcomes.

**law of exercise** A behaviourist law proposing that associative bonds are strengthened the more often a particular stimulus is followed by a particular response.

**laws of behaviour** Statements that specify the conditions under which certain types of behaviour will come about.

**lenient analogical representation** Such representations merely preserve spatial information in some way or other.

**levels of processing** A theory of memory in which the strength of trace is related to the level of analysis, with shallower processing associated with the retrieval of physical characteristics and deeper processing associated with retrieval of semantic information. Deeper levels of processing produce better memory performance than does shallower processing.

**lexical decision task** An experimental paradigm in which participants must judge whether, on a given trial, a letter string is a word or a non-word. Typically performance is carried out under reaction time conditions.

**likelihood principle** The idea that 'sensory elements will be organized into the most probable object or event (distal stimulus) in the environment consistent with the sensory data (the proximal stimulus)' (Pomerantz & Kubovy, 1986, pp. 36–9).

**likelihood ratio** In Bayes' theorem, the likelihood that a piece of data supports one hypothesis rather than an alternative hypothesis.

**limited capacity channel** A notion that is based on the view that information must be transmitted in human information processing between different processing modules – for instance, between the peripheral and the central mechanisms. The understanding is that processing modules are connected by processing channels, any one of which can only cope with a certain amount of information at any given time.

**line detector** An abstract feature detector that is dedicated to registering information in the proximal stimulus that corresponds to a line of a particular length, orientation, position, etc. in the external world.

**lingua mentis** A phrase synonymous with the language of thought.

**list length effect** Memory performance for short lists is typically better than for longer lists.

**literal picture** A representation of an object or scene that strictly resembles the subject of the picture, in the same way that an undoctored photograph depicts a scene.

**local distinctiveness** In memory research, the distinctiveness of an item computed relative to its neighbouring items in a list.

**local minimum** The state of a connectionist network in which the overall error is not close to zero but further reductions cannot be made.

**localist theory of memory** See *place metaphor for memory*.

**local-to-global interference** Cases where responses to global aspects of a stimulus are impeded by conflicting local information.

**logical behaviourism** The doctrine that all talk about mental states and processes can be replaced by talk of behavioural dispositions. For example, to say that Andrew is clever is to say nothing other than that Andrew behaves in an intelligent way.

**major premise** The first premise in a syllogism.

**many-to-one mapping** When a single proximal stimulus may have been produced by several distal causes. The many distal causes map onto the one proximal stimulus.

**masking by object substitution** Specifically, this occurs when the target display and masker are initially presented simultaneously, then the target display is removed (but the masker remains present), and finally the masker is removed. The effect can even occur when the masker has no contours (e.g., it is composed of a small number of dots).

**massively modular view** The idea that the mind comprises a variety of special-purpose mechanisms by which problems can be solved.

**materialism** The philosophical position that mental events equate with/reduce to physical events.

**means–end expectations** Knowledge that carrying out a certain set of behaviours will result in a specific goal.

**mechanistic account** One that details operations that could be undertaken by some form of machine or device.

**memory operating characteristic** A memory function plotted across a range of paired hit and false alarm rates, in a bid to understand the nature of decision-making processes.

**memory set** List of to-be-remembered items.

**memory unit** In the headed records model, information that is stored in long-term memory that holds the content of some to-be-remembered material.

**mental category** Stored knowledge regarding the nature of a class of objects or entities.

**mental chemistry** The idea that concepts are composed from a finite number of semantic primitives (or mental atoms). Different concepts arise from the combination of different primitives.

**mental images** A mental image is taken to be a visual recreation in the mind of some concrete object or event. A picture in the mind.

**mental lexicon** The 'mental'dictionary in which knowledge about words in a given natural language is represented.

**mental model** Generally associated with Johnson-Laird. The idea that in solving problems a person will construct an internal model of the current state of affairs so as to reason about that state of affairs. Mental models support predictions about possible future states of affairs.

**mental models account** After Johnson-Laird (1980), the idea that an inner model is constructed and operated upon so as to draw conclusions about the state of the world.

**mental representation** Stored knowledge as captured by internal forms of presentation in the mind.

**mental resources** The mental equivalent of energy or power that supports cognitive performance in some task. Difficult tasks are assumed to demand more mental resources than simple tasks.

**mental set** A person's frame of mind or expectancies about an up-and-coming stimulus.

**mental simulation** Operating upon a mental model so as to reason about the represented world.

**mentalese** A term to describe mental language as discussed by Fodor (1975), for instance.

**methodological behaviourism** A kind of behaviourism which aims to detail the correlations between stimuli and responses.

**minimal attachment** According to Frazier (1987), the stricture that the preferred interpretation of a sentence is that which requires the fewest number of nodes in its syntactic tree structure.

**minimum principle** The idea that of all possible perceptual organisations, the one that will be selected will be the simplest.

**minor premise** The second premise in a syllogism.

**misleading information effect** The use of loaded questions which leads to the misremembering of plausible information related to the original event (McCloskey & Zaragoza, 1985).

**misses** Cases where a signal is present and an incorrect absent response is made.

**mnemonic strategy** An aid to memory.

**modal model** The general view that memory comprises different short-term and long-term stores. Specifically attributed to the model of Atkinson and Shiffrin (1968).

**modular decomposition** Specifying the intervening component processes involved in some functional account of the mind.

**modularity hypothesis** The idea that the mind may be decomposed into smaller and discrete sub-processes (or modules) (after Fodor, 1983).

**molar descriptions of behaviour** Behaviour described in terms of the ultimate goals that the organism is attempting to achieve.

**molecular descriptions of behaviour** Behaviour described in terms of atomic units. For example, behaviour broken down into sequences of S–R bonds.

**monocular retinocentric frame of reference** Spatial co-ordinates derived within an eye and defined in terms of some form of retinal co-ordinate system.

**monoptic** Cases where the stimulus is delivered to only one eye.

**mood induction** An attempt to create a particular mood state in a person prior to testing them in some experimental setting.

**morpheme** The smallest unit of meaning in natural language.

**morphing** A computer technique which enables the production of a sequence of images across which small changes are introduced. The impression is created of the start image and the end image being joined by an apparently seamless set of indiscernible transformations.

**multi-dimensional scaling** A statistical technique whereby the similarity between entities (typically real-world category instances) is represented by distances in an abstract space defined by many dimensions.

**multiple-constraint accounts of parsing** Where sentence parsing is determined by a large variety of syntactic, semantic and pragmatic influences.

**multi-tasking** Being able to do more than one thing, at a cognitive level, at the same time.

**naïve realism** The idea that the perception directly and passively mirrors the stimulus as it is presented at the senses.

**name code** A mental encoding that captures information about the name of a stimulus.

**nasal hemi-retina** The half of the retina closest to the nose.

**natural assessments** Decisions based on heuristics and biases.

**natural language** Human languages such as Italian or Japanese.

**negative priming** Typically discussed in terms of performance on trial $n + 1$ of an adjacent pair of trials (trial $n$ and trial $n + 1$). Negative priming is characterised by poor performance on trial $n + 1$ when an ignored stimulus characteristic on trial $n$ becomes the imperative signal on trial $n + 1$.

**network diagram** See *tree structure*.

**neutral trials** In a spatial cueing experiment, when the cue provides no useful information about the location of the target.

**New Look** The idea that our perceptions of the world are influenced by our knowledge, expectations, beliefs, needs and desires about the world.

**non-modular view** The idea that the mind contains a single general-purpose problem solver.

**non-switch trial** A trial that implicates the same task as the immediately preceding trial.

**non-terminal vocabulary** Abstract mental symbols that play a role in the generation and comprehension of sentences in a natural language.

**object schema** Similar to Minsky's (1975) frame, a memory representation that codes the perceptual nature of a familiar object.

**objective threshold** The point at which perceptual discrimination is at chance.

**Occam's Razor** The principle that, given two competing theories that make the same predictions, the preferred theory is the one that is simpler.

**occluded object** An object, only part of which is seen because it is obscured by something nearer to the viewer.

**Old Look** A passive view of perception in which encoding principles are applied to any stimulus independently of its nature and irrespective of the mental state of the participant.

**orthographic description** A mental coding that specifies a sequence of letters. It is assumed that something like an orthographic description must be stored internally for us to read and spell words.

**outcome conflict** Conflicts that arise in cases where competing stimuli are present in a display and it is difficult to resolve which to respond to.

**output error** In a connectionist network, the difference between the actual distributed pattern of activation on the output units and desired pattern of activation on the output units.

**output pattern** In a connectionist model, the distributed pattern of activation across the output units.

**output processes** Processes associated with physically making a response.

**over-generalisation** With respect to past-tense learning, the cases where children misuse the '+ ed' rule, in producing utterances such as 'breaked'.

**overt shifts of attention** Movements of visual attention that are locked to changes in eye position.

**P system** Strictly, the perceptual system in Broadbent's (1958) filter theory of attention. In this scheme the P system assigns meanings to signals propagated down the limited-capacity channel.

**paired associate learning** An experimental paradigm in which participants are presented with pairs of items during a study phase, which must be committed to memory. In some cases, during a later test phase, participants are presented with one member of each pair (stimulus item) and are asked to produce the other member (i.e., the response item).

**paralexic errors** A fancy phrase for semantic errors.

**parallel-distributed processing (PDP)** An idea central to connectionist models, in which it is the entire pattern of activation across a bank of processing units that stands for the current entity that the network is representing. Such distributed patterns induce patterns of activation that spread throughout the network at the same time.

**parallel processing** Within some form of information processing system, allowing the system to process more than one stimulus at once.

**parallel processor** A mechanism that can operate on more than one thing at once.

**parallel search** Assumed to reflect automatic processes in visual search, the concurrent analysis of a number of display elements.

**partial-report condition** In the Sperling (1960) paradigm, reporting only the cued items from a briefly presented and masked display.

**partial-report superiority** The finding that estimates of iconic memory derived from partial report are larger than those derived from full report.

**passive theories** A phrase used to refer to theories of perception in which the person has no control over their perceptions of the world.

**perception** According to Fodor (1983), operations associated with the input modules.

**perceptual cue** An aspect of the proximal stimulus that is used to infer what the distal stimulus is.

**perceptual defence** A form of semantic activation without conscious identification in which taboo words are harder to detect than neutral words.

**perceptual inference** Certain plausible hypotheses are made about the possible link between the proximal and distal stimuli and these are then tested out against the available sensory evidence.

**perceptual load** The amount of perceptual analysis demanded by a given task.

**perceptual representation** Stimulus representation derived through the operation of the perceptual mechanisms.

**perceptual system** Mechanisms responsible for the generation of an initial internal representation of a stimulus.

**perceptual threshold** The point at which a stimulus of a certain kind is said to be perceptible. Usually defined in terms of some stimulus factor such as stimulus intensity that can be varied experimentally.

**perceptual vigilance** A form of semantic activation without conscious identification in which emotional words are easier to detect than neutral words.

**performance** In Chomsky's terms, all observable human language behaviour.

**performance operating characteristic (POC)** A function relating performance on two tasks when the two tasks are combined. The POC functions can be traced out as the difficulty of the tasks is varied or as participants vary their commitment to either or both tasks.

**peripheral coding mechanisms** Internal operations that are responsible for generating sensory codes for a given stimulus.

**peripheral cue** A cue in a spatial cueing paradigm which provides information regarding the location of the target by appearing at one of the possible target locations.

**peripheral masking** According to Turvey (1973), masking occurring at the level of peripheral encoding mechanisms.

**pertinence** According to Norman (1969), the level of activation of any given stored stimulus representation calculated as a combination of sensory analysis and top-down influence.

**phoneme** The minimum unit of speech in a natural language.

**phonemic restoration** The perception of an intact phoneme when it is in fact not present in a spoken utterance.

**phonological description** The internal specification of how a word is pronounced. A pronounceable non-word also has a phonological description.

**phonological loop** In the working memory model, one of the slave systems controlled by the central executive concerned with the on-line processing of verbal information.

**phonological rules** The specification of the rules of pronunciation.

**phonological similarity effect** An experimental effect related to working memory in which similar-sounding items are more difficult to recall than dissimilar-sounding items.

**phonological structure** According to Jackendoff (2002), the mental representations that code how components of language sound when spoken.

**photoreceptor cells** Cells that make up the retina and that are sensitive to light.

**phrenology** After Francis Joseph Gall (1758–1828), the idea that vertical faculties could be measured relative to the sizes of bumps on the head. Each bump was related to an underlying brain region.

**physical symbol system** A kind of symbol system, defined by Newell (1980), as comprising mental representations and mental processes as defined in computational terms.

**place metaphor for memory** The localist assumption that individual memories are stored in unique places in memory.

**post-categorical information** A specification of the categorical nature of a stimulus.

**post-categorical selection** Selection on the basis of semantic information.

**posterior odds** In Bayes' theorem, the estimate of how relatively likely it is that each hypothesis is true given the data.

**post-field** Some form of visual event immediately after the stimulus field has been presented on a given trial.

**poverty of the stimulus** The assumption that the proximal stimulus is a very poor under-specification of what the distal stimulus is.

**pre-categorical** When a representation of a stimulus does not contain the category identity of the stimulus.

**pre-categorical level** A stage in processing at which the categorical identity of the stimulus is not known. For example, it's red and it's small but what is it?

**predicate** Within propositional representation, a generic function which applies to one or more arguments.

**predicate expression** A generic function which operates on one or more arguments (e.g., GO(x) is a predicate expression in which the predicate GO applies to one argument x). A corresponding proposition would be, for example, GO(home).

**predictive veridicality** Going beyond the information provided by the current stimulus representation so as to predict future events.

**pre-field** Some form of visual event immediately before the stimulus field on a given trial.

**presbycusis** Loss of high frequency sensitivity in hearing traditionally associated with aging. An inability to hear high frequencies.

**primacy effect** In a serial position curve, memory is good for the first few items in a list.

**primal sketch** A 2D representation that codes information regarding light intensity values. Some primitive edges and lines are also coded.

**prime** In a priming experiment, a stimulus that occurs before a target stimulus.

**priming effects** Changes in behaviour that are due to relations that hold between a prime stimulus and target stimulus. Priming effects are observed on responses to targets.

**primitive code** According to the structural information theory (Boselie & Leeuwenberg, 1986), a collection of primitive symbols that are used in generating the internal code for a shape.

**primitive symbol** The atomic symbolic unit contained in a primitive code.

**principle of Prägnanz** As pointed out by Gestaltists, perceptual elements tend to cohere into 'good' groupings.

**principles of associationism** Statements that collectively specify how association formation takes place.

**prior odds** In Bayes' theorem, the probability of each of the alternative hypotheses in advance of learning about the data.

**proactive interference/inhibition** The negative influence of present events on future performance. Interference of new material by old material.

**probabilistic syllogism** A collection of statements in which the major premise and minor premise lead to a likely conclusion.

**probe item** In the Sternberg memory scanning task, an item to be compared with a memory set.

**process-dissociation procedure** After Hay and Jacoby (1999), a way of estimating the incidence of memories attributable to recollection and the incidence of memories attributable to habit.

**processing constraint** A non-architectural limitation within a system that places an upper bound on the amount of information that can be processed at any one time.

**processing modularity** Crowder's (1989) view the same memory processes apply throughout cognition. For example, remembering and forgetting are the same regardless of which cognitive domain is being discussed.

**production frequency** The number of times something is produced in response to a probe. For instance, the number of times 'horse' is produced in response to the probe 'cart'.

**productivity** A property of natural language discussed by Fodor and Pylyshyn (1988) such that humans are capable of generating an indefinitely large number of sentences.

**profile of test scores** The complete set of individual test scores across a *battery of tests*.

**property inheritance** Where a subordinate category or instance adopts certain characteristics as specified at the level of the superordinate category.

**property-instance production frequency** The number of times a given property is produced for a given instance. For instance, how many times 'barks' is reported for 'dog'.

**propositional content** The ideas and concepts embodied within a sentence.

**propositional network** A representational system in which propositions are coded in terms of nodes and links.

**propositional representation** A means of conveying information in terms of a relation that holds for one or more arguments.

**propositional system** A formal system of representation based upon propositions.

**prototype** An instance of a category that is most representative of the category. A mental prototype is the mental representation of a category's prototype.

**proximal stimulus** Stimulation of the sense organs that is caused by a particular distal stimulus.

**proximity** As pointed out by Gestaltists, elements that are close together tend to group together.

**psychological refractory period (PRP)** The amount of temporal lock-out that occurs while one stimulus engages central (so-called bottleneck) processes.

**psychophysical function** A graphical/mathematical means for relating a participant's responses to some variation in a stimulus factor.

**pure blocks** A set of trials in which only one task is demanded throughout.

**ratio rule** An attempt to account for recency effects by considering the relationship between the inter-item interval and the retention interval.

**rational decision-making** The selection of appropriate means to produce the desired result.

**recency effect (in serial memory)** In a serial position curve, where memory is good for the last few items in a list.

**recency effects** In perception research, experimental findings that reveal how the recency with which a stimulus has been encountered influences the perception of the stimulus. In memory research, how items towards the end of a list of to-be-remembered items are well recalled.

**recognition** The cognitive processes involved in classification or identification.

**recognition failure of recallable words** An experimental finding in which participants are able to recall words better than they recognise them (see, for example, Tulving & Thomson, 1973).

**recognition test** Where previously seen items are mixed with previously unseen items, and participants are required to categorise each item as either being old or new.

**recollection** A conscious act of remembering.

**recursion** A means 'for generating terms in a sequence, in which the rule for generating the next term in a sequence involves one or more of the preceding terms' (Corballis, 2003, p. 155).

**reductionism** The notion that we can reduce ideas relating to mental events to a basic physical level. At a fundamental level, mental events can be understood in terms of the operations of physical mechanisms.

**redundancy** The extent to which a message can be predicted or recovered from other parts of the message.

**re-entrant processing** Operations that feed back information from higher stages of processing to lower levels. A particular form of feedback in which previously derived stimulus representations are over-written by higher levels (see Enns & Di Lollo, 2000).

**rehearsal** Allowing information to be recirculated in a processing system. In Broadbent's (1958) account, information from the P system is returned to the S system.

**relativism** The idea that the human conceptual system differs according to the language of the culture.

**release from proactive inhibition** Where memory performance improves as a result of switching the category of to-be-remembered items in a run of trials.

**remember response** A state of awareness associated with recollection.

**repetition priming** When a stimulus is repeated, responses to the second presentation are changed relative to when the stimulus is not repeated. A priming effect is typically revealed as facilitation whereby responses are quicker and/or more accurate on a repeated presentation than on a non-repeated presentation.

**replaced stimuli** In the phonemic restoration paradigm, where the critical phoneme is replaced by noise.

**replacement** A form of masking by interruption where the processing of one stimulus is over-written when a second stimulus is presented.

**representation and the algorithm level** Marr's (1982) second level of description concerned with how a device represents information and how such representations are operated upon.

**representational system** A set of symbols and their rules of combination that form the basis of capturing information about a particular set of entities in some represented world.

**representativeness** A heuristic that appeals to a stereotype or most likely occurrence.

**represented world** The set of things being represented in a representing world (e.g., the London Underground system in a map of the Underground).

**representing world** A means by which information in a represented world is captured. For instance, a map of the London Underground system is a representing world of the actual represented Underground system.

**residual switch cost** In the task-switching literature, a performance decrement associated with changing tasks even in the presence of a substantial interval between the two tasks.

**resistance to damage** The way in which a larger system can still retain its functions even though some components of the system fail. The lights on the car have gone out but the engine keeps on turning.

**resource artefacts** This refers to accounting for a single dissociation by claiming that task difficulty is not equated across the various tasks that show the dissociation.

**response competition** Conflict that occurs when more than one response is invoked by a stimulus.

**response contraction bias** The underestimate of values above a reference and the overestimate of values below a reference.

**response item** In paired associate learning, the item in the pair that must be reinstated during the test phase.

**response organisation** Stages of processing that concern the planning of the appropriate actions for a response.

**response set** Stimuli defined as targets because they share the same mental category. No one physical characteristic defines the targets.

**response-to-stimulus interval (RSI)** The time between the response made on the current trial and the presentation of the next stimulus.

**restricted viewpoint-invariant theories** A theory of object recognition in which recognition depends on the recovery of the same viewpoint configuration of the object presented across time.

**retention interval** The length of time that individuals are required to hold items in memory before memory is tested.

**retinal co-ordinate system** Defining retinal positions in terms of a 2D co-ordinate system. For example, using $x$ (left/right) and $y$ (up/down) values with the origin fixed at the fovea. Such codings are preserved at some of the higher levels of the visual system. It is possible to find retinotopic maps in the cortex.

**retinal painting** According to Morgan, Findlay and Watt (1982), the piecemeal exposure of a stimulus over adjacent parts of the retina as is assumed to take place in studies of aperture viewing.

**retinal position constancy (invariance)** The ability to discount retinal position in identifying shape.

**retinal receptive field** The region of the retina that can be linked directly to feature detectors of a particular sort – such as a line detector.

**retinotopic map** See *retinal co-ordinate system.*

**retroactive inhibition** Interference of old material by new material.

**retrograde amnesia** Inability to retrieve memories before a certain time point.

**reverse engineering** Attempting to understand how a pre-existing device works on the basis of how it behaves.

**Roschian hypothesis** The view that the nature of the human conceptual system is, in a sense, given by the external world and it should be considered independently from language that is used to describe it.

**rule-based system** In reasoning research, the idea that there is one system of reasoning that operates by making inferences on the basis of rules of logic. This system is defined in terms of the language of thought (Fodor, 1975).

**rule-following device** A device acting according to a set of rules which are represented within the device itself (i.e., minds and computers).

**rule-governed device** A device acting according to a set of rules which are not represented within the device itself.

**rules of operation** Statements specifying condition/action pairs that determine and control computational processes.

**S system** The early sensory storage and coding mechanisms in Broadbent's 1958 model of human information processing.

**saccades** Generally used as short-hand of eye movements, but a saccade is the jump between one fixation and the next.

**same/different judgement task** Experimental paradigm where, on each trial, participants are required to compare two stimuli and respond as to whether they are the same or whether they differ from one another.

**satisficing** Adopting a solution to a problem that simply works.

**saturation** Essentially, the vividness of a colour.

**schematic diagram** A visual representation specifying each component of a system and how the components link together.

**search display** In visual search paradigms, the stimulus as defined by a collection of to-be-searched elements.

**second-level representation** A representation of the stimulus that contains a record of its identity. Sufficient information is coded such that a response can be organised (see discussion of the three-component account of iconic memory in Chapter 3).

**selection by categorisation** The ability to select items for further processing on the basis of the category membership.

**selection by filtering** A specific kind of selection taken from Broadbent's (1958) filter theory in which information is chosen from sensory memory on the basis of physical characteristics of the input.

**selection by pigeonholing** The ability to select items because of lowering of a category threshold – if it looks like a duck and walks like a duck, it must be a duck.

**semantic activation without conscious identification** The claim that the meaning of a stimulus can be accessed even though the person has no conscious awareness that any stimulus has been presented.

**semantic decision task** Deciding whether or not a word refers to a referent of particular type (e.g., is *x* man-made?).

**semantic dimensions** A theoretical construct in which it is assumed that some characteristic of the world can be captured in psychological space by a point on a dimension that fixes all possible values of that characteristic.

**semantic errors** Errors in report that are semantically related to the desired target response.

**semantic feature** A theoretical construct by which it is assumed that some real-world characteristic can be captured, at the psychological level, by a discrete fact. For example, IS YELLOW. In cases where semantic dimensions are posited, then a semantic feature is a value on a semantic dimension.

**semantic feature production norms** The frequency with which concepts are assigned to certain properties.

**semantic memory** Memories of learnt rather than experienced knowledge (after Tulving, 2002).

**semantic micro-features** Atoms of meaning that cannot be rendered into expressible language.

**semantic networks** Systems that represent the conceptual information in terms of labelled nodes and links.

**semantic priming** Where responses to a target stimulus are influenced by the semantic nature of the prime.

**semantic primitives** Atomic units of meaning within mental language.

**semantic relatedness** Typically, the degree to which items are related by virtue of the fact that they share the same category.

**semantically related** Items that share commonalities in meaning (e.g., doctor–nurse).

**semantics** A term for meaning.

**sensitivity** In signal detection theory, the distance between the noise and the signal + noise distributions. An index of the efficacy of perceptual encodings mechanisms (i.e., $d'$).

**sensory encoding** The manner in which stimulus information that impinges on the senses is transformed into some form of internal code.

**sensory experience** The subjective sensations associated with stimulation of the senses.

**sensory transduction** Transforming stimulation of the sense organs into some form of internal signal.

**sentence verification task** On each trial, a string of words is presented to a participant and the task is to decide as quickly and as accurately as possible whether the sentence makes sense or not.

**sequential stage model of processing** A view of stimulus processing in which intervening stages of processing are ordered. In strictly serial accounts each stage must run to completion before the next stage can begin.

**serial exhaustive processing** The sequential examination of a list of items, with testing continuing until all items have been considered.

**serial order task** Where participants are asked to reinstate previously exposed items in the order in which they were presented.

**serial position curves** The pattern of memory performance plotted as a function of whereabouts each item was presented within a list.

**serial processor** A mechanism that can only operate on one thing at once.

**serial search** Assumed to reflect controlled processes, the sequential analysis of each search element in turn.

**serial self-terminating processing** The sequential examination of a list of items, with examination stopping after the item of interest has been found.

**serial self-terminating search** A serial search process in which each search element is considered in turn. If and when a target is encountered, respond 'present'; otherwise respond 'absent' when the last element turns out not to be a target.

**set** Used here interchangeably with the phrase 'mental category'.

**shadow** To report back verbally the contents of an attended channel in real time.

**shape constancy** The tacit knowledge that the shape of an object does not change when there is a change in the relative position between the observer and the object.

**signal detection theory** A theoretical framework that provides a rationale for separating the effects of perceptual sensitivity from those of response bias.

**signal propagation** According to Oatley and Johnson-Laird (1987), the transmission of information across the whole of the cognitive system.

**similarity** As pointed out by Gestaltists, elements that are similar tend to group together.

**simple horse-race account** Where the processes associated with different aspects of a stimulus race to completion.

**simple reaction time (SRT) task** In SRT tasks the participant is typically asked to respond to the onset of a pre-defined imperative signal.

**simultaneous contradictory belief** A claim by Sloman (1996) that a person can be conflicted in concurrently believing two mutually contradictory conclusions. An outcome of the dual-system theory of reasoning in which the rule-based and associative outputs produce conflicting information.

**single-case study** Research that involves the examination of only a single participant's performance. Most typically used in cognitive neuropsychological research.

**single dissociation** See *dissociation deficit*.

**size constancy/invariance** The perceptual inference that an object retains its size regardless of the size of its image on the retina. The ability to discount absolute size in identifying shape.

**slack time** In PRP studies, the time the second task has to wait before the first task has cleared the central bottleneck.

**slot-and-filler** In thinking about a stereotypical object or event, there are a number of characteristics (or slots) that the entity has (e.g., legs) and these must be assigned (or filled) with a certain value (e.g., four).

**social attention** The effect of social factors on attention.

**social contract** Implicit agreements regarding social exchanges and cultural norms.

**spatial cueing** An experimental paradigm (e.g., Posner, Nissen & Ogden, 1978) in which a cue either correctly or incorrectly predicts the location of a subsequent target.

**spatial orienting** Moving the focus of attention around in space.

**speech spectrograph**  A visual representation of sound energy in speech.

**speed/error trade-off**  This particular pattern of performance relates to reaction time tasks in which, in order to speed up, participants make many errors.

**speeded classification tasks**  Reaction time paradigms in which participants are required to respond, on each trial, as to whether a stimulus belongs to a certain designated category or not (e.g., 'Is it man-made?').

**speeded naming tasks**  Reaction time paradigms in which participants are required to respond, on each trial, verbally with the name of the stimuli.

**spreading activation**  A metaphor for how information is communicated in a cognitive system, much like how heat emanates throughout a central heating system.

**staircase method**  A psychological procedure whereby the limits of performance are assessed by an experimenter systematically increasing or decreasing a parameter over trials.

**standard picture**  Reasoning based on principles of logic and probability.

**statistical regularities**  In terms of connectionist models, the systematic relations that hold between the input patterns and output patterns in a given training case.

**Sternberg memory scanning task**  A task in which participants are initially given a set of possible target items to hold in mind; they are then presented with a single item and are asked to decide if it is a target.

**stimulus discrimination**  The ability to class different objects as being different.

**stimulus display**  The presentation of visual information that the participant must operate upon so as to respond accordingly.

**stimulus-driven**  Operations that are invoked by the stimulus – see *bottom-up processing*.

**stimulus duration**  The length of time that a stimulus is presented.

**stimulus factors**  Dimensions upon which a stimulus may vary.

**stimulus generalisation**  The ability to classify different objects as being tokens of the same type.

**stimulus item**  In paired associate learning, the item in the pair that is presented during the test phase.

**stimulus onset asynchrony (SOA)**  The time between the onset of one stimulus and the onset of a subsequent stimulus.

**stimulus representation**  The phrase used to refer to how a stimulus is encoded following the operation of the perceptual mechanisms.

**stimulus set**  The common physical characteristics shared by items that are designated targets.

**stimulus-driven processing**  See *bottom-up processing*.

**strict analogical representation**  According to Palmer (1978), in this form of representation 'Spatial information is not only preserved but it is preserved in (1) a spatial medium and (2) in such a way that the image resembles that which it represents' (p. 295).

**strong AI**  One version of artificial intelligence in which an appropriately programmed computer is assumed to have the same sorts of mental states as humans.

**structural bottleneck**  A claim that not all information arriving at a particular stage of processing can be dealt with concurrently; only information associated with one task can pass through to the next stage at once.

**structural constraint**  A limitation within the architecture of the system that limits the amount of information that can pass through at any one time. Also known as a structural bottleneck.

**structural description**  A form of internal representation that codes key parts of a shape and some of the salient relations between those parts.

**structural information load**  The number of primitive symbols contained within an end-code.

**structural information theory**  A model originated by Boselie and Leeuwenberg (1986) which attempts to operationalise how the minimum principle might work in vision.

**subjective factors**  Factors that are inherent to participants – indicative of individual differences.

**subjective threshold**  The point at which a person feels as though they are performing at chance even though, in actual fact, they are performing better than chance.

**subliminal perception**  Perception thought to occur below the threshold of consciousness.

**subordinate category**  A category that is contained within another (superordinate) category.

**sub-routines**  Smaller sections of a larger program which can run independently of one another.

**sub-symbols**  See *semantic micro-features* and *cogit*.

**sub-threshold**  Below threshold – subliminal.

**suggested identity**  First guess of an object's identity.

**superficial structure**  The surface nature of language, how it looks when written, how it sounds when spoken, etc.

**superordinate category**  A category that itself contains categories.

**supervised training**  A term most commonly used in the connectionist literature, regarding a training method in which, for every output of a network, a complete specification of the desired output is provided. In other words, a teaching signal is provided on an input-by-input basis.

**supra-threshold**  Above threshold.

**switch trial**  A trial that implicates a task different from the immediately preceding trial.

**switching the filter**  In Broadbent's (1958) account, whereby the focus of attention is changed from one input channel to another.

**syllogism**  An argument structure that comprises two premises and a conclusion.

**symbol processing**  Acts of symbol manipulation including the retrieval of a symbol from memory, the transformation of one symbol into another, and the storage of the new symbol back into memory.

**symbol system**  A representational system comprising a set of well-defined symbols, each of which stands for a particular entity, and a set of rules by which such symbols can be manipulated.

**symbolic pictures**  A symbolic picture is a representation of an object or scene that does not necessarily resemble the subject of the picture.

**symbolic representation**  Some form of notational system used to denote, depict or represent an entity or set of entities.

**syntactic parsing**  The processes involved in dividing sentences into constituent grammatical components such as verb phrases, verbs, nouns, adjectives, etc.

**syntactic rules**  The rules responsible for the grammatical (de)construction of a sentence.

**syntactic structure**  Some form of representation that specifies how a sentence is decomposed into its constituent phrases and words.

**syntax**  The grammatical nature of natural language sentences.

**systematicity**  The idea put forward by Fodor and Pylyshyn (1988) that the ability to understand or produce certain sentences entails the understanding or production of other related sentences.

**tacit knowledge** The knowledge that a person has but which they are unable to express in language.

**target** A generic term for a stimulus that demands some form of response. Within a priming experiment it is preceded by a prime stimulus.

**target display** Alternative phrase for the imperative stimulus (i.e., the stimulus that the participant must act upon). See *stimulus display*.

**target pop-out** When it takes the same amount of time to detect the presence of a target, regardless of the number of search elements.

**task carryover account** Task switching explained according to the presence or absence of priming from the previous trial.

**task set** The collection of processes associated with the completion of a particular task.

**task set inertia** The claim that the processing system has a default of maintaining operations with an immediately preceding task even if the task demands change.

**task set reconfiguration** The need to discard one set of processes and engage another set of processes when faced with a change in task.

**task-switching** Changing from doing one task to doing another.

**task-switching cost** The impairment in performance associated with changing between one set of operations and another. There are many reasons as to why such costs may occur.

**taxonomic systems** Systems for grouping instances into categories.

**template** According to Gestalt theories, an exact perceptual copy of an input stimulus.

**template matching** Taking a representation of an input stimulus and attempting to match this against stored templates of known stimuli.

**temporal hemi-retina** The retinal half furthest from the nose.

**terminal vocabulary** The actual words of a language.

**thematic content** Refers to the meanings conveyed by the terms in a problem. What the problem is about.

**thematic facilitation** A common finding that solving the Wason selection task is facilitated if the problem is cast in a plausible and familiar scenario.

**thresholded system** A system whose outputs are not a continuous function of their inputs.

**time-sharing** Where one stage of processing is dealing with more than one stimulus at the same time.

**token identity theory** A version of central state identity theory which argues that any one of several different sorts of neurological events gives rise to a particular sort of mental event.

**token nodes** In semantic network models, pointers to the place in memory where the intension of the associated concept is stored.

**transformations** According to Chomsky (1965), the mechanisms in converting a base sentence into a surface sentence.

**travelling moment hypothesis** Where perception is built up from an overlapping sequence of snapshots.

**tree diagram** In terms of natural language, a schematic representation that shows the constituents of a sentence and how these are related.

**tree structure** A form of representation which is composed of nodes and connections between nodes. From a topmost node the structure branches out until at the very bottom are the leaves.

**trigram** A collection of three letters.

**two-alternative forced choice** Paradigm in which participants are required to choose between one of two possible alternatives on every trial.

**type identity theory** A version of central state identity theory which asserts that there is a one-to-one mapping between each mental event and its corresponding neurological event.

**type nodes** In semantic network models, the place in memory where the intension of a concept is stored.

**type–token distinction** The distinction between individual instances (tokens) and the category (type) to which they belong.

**unattended channel** An input channel that participants are asked to ignore.

**unbounded rationality** Accounts of reasoning in which in-principle statements are considered (e.g., how would the ideal logic machine work it out?).

**unconscious inference** A perceptual inference that operates unconsciously.

**uncontrolled serial model** A framework of processing in which all items must be processed but in a sequential fashion.

**under-additive pattern** In the context of the PRP, the case where the effect of task 2 difficulty increases as SOA increases.

**underlying structure** The mental representations that underlie language production and comprehension.

**uninformative cues** Cues that are uncorrelated with what response the target requires. In spatial cueing experiments, uninformative cues provide no useful information as to where the target will be presented.

**univalent lists** Experimental stimuli in which each stimulus is only associated with its own particular task. For instance, a vowel/consonant judgement can only be made of a letter, whereas an odd/even judgement can only be made of a number.

**univariate lists** Experimental stimuli in which each stimulus is unambiguously associated with only one task and hence only one set of operations.

**universalism** The idea that conceptual systems across individuals are basically the same and are independent of the natural language used to describe the world.

**unrestricted race model** An account of parsing in which multiple syntactic and semantic constraints operate at an early stage, leading to an initial interpretation of the language in question. A second stage allows the output to be reanalysed if the primary analysis leads to a nonsensical interpretation.

**valid trials** In a spatial cueing experiment, when a cue correctly indicates the location of the target.

**veridical representation** An internal record of an external stimulus that is a truthful specification of it.

**vertical faculties** Specific competencies that reflect independent intellectual capacities, such as being a competent musician, language user, mathematician, etc. Such capacities are assumed to have domain-specific characteristics.

**viewpoint-dependent** An object representation that changes according to the position of the viewer.

**viewpoint-independent** An object representation that is independent of the position of the viewer.

**visible persistence** Neural activity following the offset of a visually presented stimulus. Think of the impression created when you look at the camera and the flash accompanies the photograph.

**visual code** Encoding that captures the visual characteristics of a stimulus.

**visual frames of reference** After Wade and Swanston (1991), a collection of coding schemes that exist at different levels of the visual system. Each codes the spatial disposition of the parts of a stimulus in its own co-ordinates such as positions relative to the fovea – as in a retinal frame of reference.

**visual masking** A situation under which one visual event is obscured either by an immediately preceding event or an immediately following event.

**visual noise mask** A display field containing densely scattered letter fragments or randomly positioned black and white squares. A mask that contains no pattern information.

**visual sensory memory** An assumed temporary memory system that fleetingly records the physical characteristics of sensory stimulation.

**visuo-spatial scratch pad (sketch pad)** In the working memory model, one of the slave systems controlled by the central executive concerned with the short-term maintenance of visual and spatial information.

**volumetric primitives** Basic building blocks which are used to construct a mental representation of the volume of a 3D object.

**weak AI** One version of artificial intelligence in which computer modelling is taken to be a methodological tool that aids our understanding of human cognition.

**Whorf hypothesis** Also known as the 'linguistic relativity hypothesis', the idea that the way we perceive the world is determined by natural language.

**word frequency effect** Differences observed in word processing as a result of the frequency of occurrence in natural language. Common words are typically dealt with more effectively than rare words.

**word length effect** The finding that recall for short words is better than recall for long words.

**word recognition advantage** For example, the finding that words are more accurately recognised from a briefly presented display than strings of random letters. More generally, where performance with words is better than with any other form of strings of letters.

**word superiority effect** Generally speaking, when performance with words is superior relative to performance with non-words.

**working memory** A framework of thinking about short-term memory, first devised by Baddeley and Hitch (1974). It is assumed that there are specific temporary storage mechanisms related to different types of information and these are controlled by a central executive.

# Name index

# Subject index

# Publisher's acknowledgements

We are grateful to the following for permission to reproduce copyright material:

## Figures and illustrations

Figure 2.2: Haber, R. N. (1974). Information processing. In Carterette, E. C., & Friedman, M. P. (1974). *Handbook of perception* (Vol. 1, fig. 1, p. 315). London: Academic Press. Reproduced with permission from Elsevier; Figure 2.5: Newell, A. (1980). Physical symbol systems. *Cognitive Science*, 4, 135–183 (fig. 2, p. 145). Reproduced with permission from the Carnegie Mellon University Pittsburgh, Pennsylvania; Figure 2.9: From Damasio, H., Grabowski, T., Frank, R., Galaburda, A. M., & Damasio, A. R. (1994). The return of Phineas Gage: Clues about the brain from the skull of a famous patient, *Science, 264(5162)*, pp. 1102–1105. Reproduced with permission from AAAS; Figure 3.1: Coltheart, M. (1972). Visual information processing. In P. C. Dodwell (Ed.), *New horizons in psychology 2* (fig. 1, p. 64). Harmondsworth, England: Penguin Books. Reproduced by permission of Penguin Books Ltd; Figure 3.3: Sperling, G. (1963). A model for visual memory tasks. *Human Factors*, 5, 19–31 (fig. 3, p. 24). Reproduced with permission from Human Factors. Copyright © 1963 by The Human Factors and Ergonomics Society. All rights reserved; Figure 3.4: Coltheart, M. (1972). Visual information processing. In P. C. Dodwell (Ed.), *New horizons in psychology 2* (fig. 2, p. 67). Harmondsworth, England: Penguin Books. Reproduced by permission of Penguin Books Ltd; Figure 3.5: Smithson, H., & Mollon, J. (2006). Do masks terminate the icon? *The Quarterly Journal of Experimental Psychology*, 59, 150–160 (fig. 1, p. 152). Reproduced by permission of Taylor & Francis Ltd; Figure 3.6: Coltheart, M. (1972). Visual information processing. In P. C. Dodwell (Ed.), *New horizons in psychology 2* (fig. 7, p. 75). Harmondsworth, England: Penguin Books. Reproduced by permission of Penguin Books Ltd; Figure 3.7: Turvey, M. T. (1973). On peripheral and central processes in vision: Inferences from an information-processing analysis of masking with patterned stimuli. *Psychological Review*, 80, 1–52 (fig. 1, p. 2). Reprinted with permission from APA; Figure 3.8: Averbach, E., & Coriell, A. S. (1961). Short term memory in vision. *Bell Systems Technical Journal*, 40, 309–328 (fig. 2, p. 313). Reproduced by permission of John Wiley & Sons Limited; Figure 3.12: Turvey, M. T. (1977). Contrasting orientations to the theory of visual information processing. *Psychological Review*, 84, 67–88 (fig. 2, p. 79). Reprinted with permission from APA; Figures 3.13 and 3.14: Tatler, B. W. (2001). Characterising the visual buffer: real world evidence for overwriting early in each fixation. *Perception*, 30, 993–1006 (fig. 1(a), p. 994; fig. 7, p. 1004). Reproduced with permission from Pion Limited, London; Figure 3.16: Wade, N. J. (1996). Frames of reference in vision. Minimally Invasive *Therapy and Allied Technologies*, 5, 435–439 (fig. 1, p. 436). Reproduced with permission from Taylor & Francis Ltd; Figure 3.19: Turvey, M. T. (1973). On peripheral and central processes in vision: Inferences from an information-processing analysis of masking with patterned stimuli. *Psychological Review*, 80, 1–52 (fig. 2, p. 4). Reprinted with permission from APA; Figure 3.23a: Snodgrass, J. G., & Vanderwart, M. A. (1980). Standardized set of 260 pictures: Norms of name agreement, usage agreement, familiarity, and visual complexity. *Journal of Experimental Psychology: Learning, Memory, and Cognition*, 6, 174–215 (43, p. 198). Reprinted with permission from APA; Figure 3.24: Morgan, M. J., Findlay, J. M., & Watt, R. J. (1982). Aperture viewing: A review and a synthesis. *The Quarterly Journal of Experimental Psychology*, 34A, 211–233. Reprinted by permission of Taylor & Francis Ltd (www.informaworld.com); Figures 4.2 and 4.3:

Enns, J. T., & Di Lollo, V. (2000). What's new in visual masking? *Trends in Cognitive Science, 4*, 345–352 (figs. 4 & 5, p. 348). Reproduced with permission from Elsevier; Figure 4.6: Haber, R. N., & Hershenson, M. (1979). *The psychology of visual perception* (fig. 5.1, p. 89). London: Holt, Rinehart and Winston. Reproduced with permission from Ralph Haber; Figure 4.7: Greenwald, A. G. (1992). New Look 3: Unconscious cognition reclaimed. *American Psychologist, 47*, 766–779 (fig. 1, p. 767). Reprinted with permission from APA; Figure 4.8: Willingham, D. (2004). *Cognition: the thinking animal* (2nd ed., p. 511) Upper Saddle River, NJ: Prentice Hall. Reproduced with permission of Pearson Education, Inc.; Figure 4.13: Smithson, H., & Mollon, J. (2006). Do masks terminate the icon? *The Quarterly Journal of Experimental Psychology, 59*, 150–160 (fig. 2, p. 153). Reproduced with permission from Taylor & Francis Ltd; Figure 5.2: Kanizsa, G. (1985). Seeing and thinking. *Acta Psychologica, 59*, 23–33 (fig. 1, p. 24). Reproduced with permission from Elsevier; Figure 5.5: Pollatsek, A., Well, A. D., & Schindler, R. M. (1975). Familiarity affects visual processing of words. *Journal of Experimental Psychology: Human Perception and Performance, 1*, 328–338 (fig. 1, p. 337). Reproduced with permission from APA; Figure 5.6: Doyle, J. R., & Leach, C. (1988). Word superiority in signal detection: Barely a glimpse, yet reading nonetheless. *Cognitive Psychology, 20*, 283–318 (fig. 1, p. 301). Reproduced with permission from Elsevier; Figure 5.7a: Fisher, G. H. (1966). Materials for experimental studies of ambiguous and embedded figures. *Research Bulletin, No. 4*. Department of Psychology, University of Newcastle upon Tyne, reproduced with permission; Figure 5.8: Mitroff, S. R., Sobel, D. M., & Gopnik, A. (2006). Reversing how to think about ambiguous figure reversals: Spontaneous alternating by uninformed observers. *Perception, 35*, 709–715 (fig. 1, p. 711). Reproduced with permission from Pion Limited, London; Figure 5.10: Cherry, C. (1978). *On human communication* (fig. 7.8, p. 278). Cambridge, MA: The MIT Press. Copyright © 1978 Massachusetts Institute of Technology. Reproduced with permission from The MIT Press; Figure 5.12: Leeper, R. (1935). A study of a neglected portion of the field of learning – The development of sensory organization. *Journal of Genetic Psychology, 46*, 41–75 (fig. 1, p. 49). Reprinted with permission of the Helen Dwight Reid Educational Foundation. Published by Heldref Publications, 1319 Eighteenth St., NW, Washington DC 20036-1802. Copyright © 1935; Figure 5.13: Haber, R. N., & Hershenson, M. (1979). *The psychology of visual perception* (fig. 8.10, p. 191). London: Holt, Rinehart and Winston. Reproduced with permission from Ralph Haber; Figure 5.16: Palmer, S. E. (1992). Common region: A new principle of perceptual grouping. *Cognitive Psychology, 24*, 436–447 (fig. 2, p. 439). Reproduced with permission from Elsevier; Figure 5.17: Quinn, P. C., & Bhatt, R. S. (2006). Are some Gestalt principles deployed more readily than others during early development? The case of lightness versus form similarity. *Journal of Experimental Psychology: Human Perception and Performance, 32*, 1221–1230 (fig. 1, p. 1223, fig. 2, p. 1225, fig. 3, p. 1226). Reprinted with permission from APA; Figure 5.19: Seki, K., Ishiai, S., Koyama, Y., Sato, S., Hirabayashi, H., & Inaki, K. (2000). Why are some patients with severe neglect able to copy a cube? The significance of verbal intelligence. *Neuropsychologia, 38*, 1466–1472 (fig. 5, p. 1470). Reproduced with permission from Elsevier; Figure 5.20a: Robinson, J. O. (1972). *The psychology of visual illusion* (fig. 2.1, p. 21, fig. 3.3, p. 67, fig. 3.19, p. 73 and fig. 3.33, p. 7). London: Hutchinson. Reproduced with permission; Figure 5.20b,c,d: Palmer, S. E. (1992). Common region: A new principle of perceptual grouping. *Cognitive Psychology, 24*, 436–447 (fig. 7, p. 445). Reproduced with permission from Elsevier; Figure 5.22: Kanizsa, G. (1969). Perception, past experience and the 'impossible experiment'. *Acta Psychologica, 31*, 66–96 (fig. 18, p. 85). Reproduced with permission from Elsevier; Figure 5.23: Achtman, R. L., Hess, R. F., & Wang, Y.-Z. (2003). Sensitivity for global shape detection. *Journal of Vision, 3*, 616–624 (fig. 2j, p. 619). Copyright © AVRO. Reproduced with permission from The Association for Research in Vision and Ophthalmology; Figure 5.24: Leeper, R. (1935). A study of a neglected portion of the field of learning – The development of sensory organization. *Journal of Genetic Psychology, 46*, 41–75 (fig. 1, p. 49). Reprinted with permission of the Helen Dwight Reid Educational Foundation. Published by Heldref Publications, 1319 Eighteenth St., NW, Washington DC 20036-1802. Copyright © 1935; Figure 5.25: Gregory, R. L. (1998). Brainy minds. *British Medical Journal, 317*, 1693–1695 (fig. 3, p. 1694). Reproduced with permission from the BMJ Publishing Group; Figure 6.1: Pomerantz, J. R., & Kubovy, M. (1986). Theoretical approaches to perceptual organization. In K. R. Boff, J. P. Kaufman, & J. P. Thomas (Eds.), *Handbook of perception and human performance* (fig. 36.43, pp. 36–42). New York: Wiley. Reproduced with permission from John Wiley & Sons; Figure 6.3: Kanizsa, G. (1985). Seeing and thinking. *Acta Psychologica, 59*,

23–33 (fig. 3, p. 30). Reproduced with permission from Elsevier; Figure 6.4: Peterson, M. A., & Hochberg, J. (1983). Opposed-set measurement procedure: A quantitative analysis of the role of local cues and intention in form perception. *Journal of Experimental Psychology: Human Perception and Performance, 9,* 183–193 (fig. 1, p. 184). Reprinted with permission from APA; Figure 6.6: Kanizsa, G. (1985). Seeing and thinking. *Acta Psychologica, 59,* 23–33 (fig. 8, p. 32). Reproduced with permission from Elsevier; Figure 6.10: Navon, D. (1981). The forest revisited: More on global processing. *Psychological Research, 43,* 1–32 (fig. 3a,b, p. 6). Reproduced with kind permission from Springer Science and Business Media; Figure 6.11: Navon, D. (2003). What does a compound letter tell the psychologist's mind? *Acta Psychologica, 114,* 273–309 (fig. 2, p. 283). Reproduced with permission from Elsevier; Figure 6.13: Watt, R. J. (1988). *Visual processing: Computational, psychophysical, and cognitive research* (fig. 5.9, p. 134). Hove, England: Erlbaum. Reproduced with permission; Figures 6.16 & 6.17: Simons, D. J., & Ambinder, M. S. (2005). Change blindness: Theory and consequences. *Current Directions in Psychological Science, 14,* 44–48 (fig. 1, p. 45, fig. 2, p. 46). Reproduced with permission from Blackwell Publishers, Ltd; Figure 6.18: Leeuwenberg, E. L. J., & van der Helm, P. A. (1991). Unity and variety in visual form. *Perception, 20,* 595–622 (fig. 19, p. 617). Reproduced with permission from Pion Limited, London; Figure 6.19: Stevens, K. N., & Halle, M. (1967). Remarks on analysis by synthesis and distinctive features. In W. Wathen-Dunn (Ed.), Models for perception of speech and visual form. Proceedings of a Symposium sponsored by the Data Sciences Laboratory Air Force Cambridge Research Laboratories Boston, Massachusetts November 11–14, 1964 (pp. 88–102). Fig. 3. Cambridge, MA: The MIT Press. Copyright © 1967 Massachusetts Institute of Technology. Reproduced with permission from The MIT Press; Figure 6.20: Warren, R. M. (1999). *Auditory Perception. A new analysis and synthesis* (fig. 7.5, p. 165). Cambridge, UK: Cambridge University Press. Reproduced with permission; Figure 6.21: Fry, D. B. (Ed.) (1976). *Acoustic phonetics* (fig. 1, p. 335, fig. 2, p. 338). Cambridge, MA: Cambridge University Press. Reproduced with permission; Figure 6.22: Minksy, M. (1974). A framework for representing knowledge. MIT-AI Laboratory Memo 306, June, 1974 (fig. 1.5). Reproduced with permission of Prof. Marvin Minsky; Figure 6.26: Leeper, R. (1935). A study of a neglected portion of the field of learning – The development of sensory organization. *Journal of Genetic Psychology,*

46, 41–75 (fig. 1, p. 49). Reproduced with permission of the Helen Dwight Reid Educational Foundation. Published by Heldref Publications, 1319 Eighteenth St., NW, Washington, DC 20036-1802. Copyright © 1935; Figure 7.7: Tolman, E. C. (1958). *Behavior and psychological man* (fig. 2, p. 74). Berkeley, CA: University of California Press; Figures 7.11 & 7.12: Kosslyn, S. M. (1980). *Image and mind* (fig. 3.6, p. 43, fig. 3.7, p. 44). Cambridge, Massachusetts: Harvard University Press. Reprinted by permission of the Harvard University Press, Copyright © 1980 by the President and Fellows of Harvard College; Figure 7.13: Pylyshyn, Z. W. (1981). The imagery debate: Analogue media versus tacit knowledge. *Psychological Review, 88,* 16–45 (fig. 1, p. 24). Reprinted with permission from APA; Figures 7.14 & 7.15: Palmer, S. E. (1977). Hierarchical structure in perceptual organisation. *Cognitive Psychology, 9,* 441–474 (fig. 7, p. 463; fig. 8, p. 465). Reproduced with permission from Elsevier; Figure 7.16: Reed, S. K. (1974). Structural descriptions and the limitations of visual images. *Memory & Cognition, 2,* 329–336 (fig. 2, p. 330). Copyright © 1974 by Psychonomic Society Inc. Reproduced with permission of Psychonomic Society Inc. in the format Textbook via Copyright Clearance Center; Figure 7.17: Chambers, D., & Reisberg, D. (1985). Can mental images be ambiguous? *Journal of Experimental Psychology: Human Perception and Performance, 11,* 317–328 (fig. 1, p. 320). Reprinted with permission from APA; Figure 7.18: Pylyshyn, Z. W. (2002). Mental imagery: In search of a theory. *The Behavioral and Brain Sciences, 25,* 157–238 (fig. 6, p. 173). Cambridge, England: Cambridge University Press. Reproduced with permission; Figure 7.19: Mast, F. W., & Kosslyn, S. M. (2002). Visual mental images can be ambiguous: insights from individual differences in spatial transform abilities. *Cognition, 86,* 57–70 (fig. 2, p. 61). Reproduced with permission from Elsevier; Figure 7.20: Shepard, R. N., & Cooper, L. A. (1982). Mental images and their transformations (fig. 3.1, p. 35, fig. 3.2, p. 36). Cambridge, MA: The MIT Press. Copyright © 1982 Massachusetts Institute of Technology. Reproduced with permission of The MIT Press; Figure 7.21: Bowman, R., & Sutherland, N. S. (1969). Discrimination of 'W' and 'V' shapes by goldfish. *The Quarterly Journal of Experimental Psychology, 21,* 69–76 (fig. 1, p. 72). Reproduced with permission from Taylor & Francis Ltd; Figure 7.23: Sutherland, N. S. (1974). Object recognition. In E. C. Carterette & M. P. Friedman (Eds.), *Handbook of perception III* (pp. 157–185; fig. 3, p. 165). Reproduced with permission from Elsevier; Figure 7.24: Sutherland, N. S.

(1968). Outlines of a theory of visual pattern recognition in animals and man. *Proceedings of the Royal Society of London, Series B, 171*, 297–317 (fig. 16, p. 306). London: The Royal Society. Reproduced with permission; Figure 7.25: Henderson, L. (1982). *Orthography and word recognition in reading* (fig. 11, p. 228). London: Academic Press. Reproduced with permission from Elsevier; Figure 7.27: Hinton, G. E., & Parsons, L. M. (1981). Frames of reference and mental imagery. In J. Long & A. D. Baddeley (Eds.), *Attention and performance, IX* (pp. 261–277; fig. 15.1, p. 262, fig. 15.2, p. 263). Hillsdale, NJ: Erlbaum. Reproduced with permission; Figure 8.6: Kahneman, D. (1973). *Attention and effort* (fig. 1.1b, p. 6). Englewood Cliffs, New Jersey: Prentice Hall. Reproduced with permission; Figure 8.8: Norman, D. A. (1969). Towards a theory of memory and attention. *Psychological Review, 75*, 522–536 (fig. 1, p. 526). Reprinted with permission from APA; Figure 8.10: Kahneman, D. (1973). *Attention and effort* (fig. 1.2, p. 10). Englewood Cliffs, New Jersey: Prentice Hall. Reproduced with permission; Figure 8.12: Navon, D., & Gopher, D. (1980). Task difficulty, resources, and dual-task performance. In R. S. Nickerson (Ed.), *Attention and performance VIII* (pp. 297–315; fig. 15.3a & b, p. 309). Hillsdale, NJ: Erlbaum. Reproduced with permission; Figure 8.13: Navon, D. (1990). Do people allocate limited processing resources among concurrent activities? In L. Green & J. H. Kagel (Eds.), *Advances in behavioral economics.* Volume 2 (pp. 209–225). Fig. 3, p. 219. Norwood, NJ: Ablex. Copyright © 1990 by Ablex Publishing Corp. Reproduced with permission of Greenwood Publishing Group, Inc., Westport, Connecticut; Figure 8.16: Pashler, H. E. (1998). *The psychology of attention.* Fig. 1.6, p. 22. Cambridge, MA: The MIT Press. Copyright © 1998 Massachusetts Institute of Technology. Reproduced by permission of The MIT Press; Figure 8.17: Sternberg, S. (1975). Memory scanning: New findings and current controversies. *The Quarterly Journal of Experimental Psychology, 27*, 1–32 (fig. 2, p. 5, fig. 4, p. 6). Reproduced with permission from Taylor & Francis Ltd; Figure 8.18: Pashler, H. E. (1998). *The psychology of attention.* Fig. 5.1, p. 227. Cambridge, MA: The MIT Press. Copyright © 1998 Massachusetts Institute of Technology. Reproduced by permission of The MIT Press; Figure 8.19: Lavie, N. (1995). Perceptual load as a necessary condition for selective attention. *Journal of Experimental Psychology: Human Perception and Performance, 21*, 451–468 (fig. 1, p. 455). Reprinted with permission from APA; Figure 8.21: de Fockert, J. W., Rees, G., Frith, C. D., & Lavie, N. (2001). The role of working memory in visual selective attention. *Science, 291*, 1803–1806 (fig. 1, p. 1804). Reproduced with permission from the American Association for the Advancement of Science (AAAS); Figures 9.4 and 9.5: Broadbent, D. E., & Gregory, M. H. P. (1967b). Psychological refractory period and the length of time required to make a decision. *Proceedings of the Royal Society of London, Series B, 168*, 181–193 (fig. 3, p. 189; fig. 4, p. 190). London: The Royal Society. Reproduced with permission; Figure 9.8: Pashler, H. E., & Johnston, J. C. (1989). Chronometric evidence for central postponement in temporally overlapping tasks. *The Quarterly Journal of Experimental Psychology, 41A*, 19–45 (fig. 3, p. 31). Reproduced with permission of Taylor & Francis Ltd; Figure 9.9: Pashler, H. E. (1998). *The psychology of attention* (fig. 6.7, p. 285). Cambridge, Massachusetts: The MIT Press. Reproduced with permission; Figure 9.11: Monsell, S. (2003). Task switching. *Trends in Cognitive Science, 7*, 134–140 (fig. 2, p. 136). Reproduced with permission from Elsevier; Figure 10.1: Bower, G. H., Clark, M. C., Lesgold, A. M., & Winzenz, D. (1969). Hierarchical retrieval schemes in recall of categorized word lists. *Journal of Verbal Learning and Verbal Behavior, 8*, 323–343 (fig. 1, p. 324). Reproduced with permission from Elsevier; Figure 10.2: Gregg, V. (1975). *Human memory* (fig. 5.1, p. 60). London: Methuen. Reproduced with permission from Thomson; Figures 10.4 & 10.7: Kintsch, W. (1970a). *Learning memory and conceptual processes* (fig. 4.5, p. 143; fig. 4.7, p. 148). New York: Wiley. Reproduced with permission from John Wiley & Sons; Figures 10.8 & 10.9: Postman, L. J. & Keppel, G. (Eds.), (1969). *Verbal learning and memory. Selected readings* (fig. 1, p. 355; fig. 2, p. 387). Harmondsworth, England: Penguin Books. Reproduced with permission; Figure 10.11: Waugh, N. C., & Norman, D. A. (1965). Primary memory. *Psychological Review, 72*, 89–104 (fig. 3, p. 95). Reproduced with permission; Figures 10.12 & 13a: Kintsch, W. (1970a). *Learning memory and conceptual processes* (fig. 4.13, p. 161; fig. 4.10, p. 156). New York: Wiley. Reproduced with permission from John Wiley & Sons; Figure 10.13b: Gregg, V. H. (1986). *Introduction to human memory* (fig. 4.3, p. 98). London: Routledge + Kegan Paul. Reproduced with permission from Taylor & Francis Ltd; Figure 10.14: Atkinson, R. C., & Shiffrin, R. M. (1976). The control of short-term memory. *Scientific American, 225*, 82–90. Copyright © 1976 Scientific American, Inc. Reproduced with permission; Figure 10.15: Bjork, R. A., & Whitten, W. B. (1974). Recency-sensitive retrieval processes in long-term memory. *Cognitive*

*Psychology*, 6, 173–189 (fig. 1, p. 175). Reproduced with permission from Elsevier; Figure 10.16: Crowder, R. G. (1993). Short-term memory: Where do we stand? *Memory & Cognition*, 21, 142–145 (fig. 1, p. 143). Copyright © 1993 by Psychonomic Society Inc. Reproduced with permission of Psychonomic Society Inc. via Copyright Clearance Center; Figures 10.17 & 10.20: Baddeley, A. D. (1986). *Working memory* (fig. 7.4, p. 157; fig. 4.6, p. 71). Oxford, England: Oxford University Press. Reproduced with permission; Figure 10.21: Baddeley, A. D. (2003). Working memory: Looking back and looking forward. *Nature Reviews Neuroscience*, 4, 829–839 (fig. 2, p. 831). Reproduced with permission from Macmillan Publishers Ltd; Figure 10.22: Hitch, G. J. (1980). Developing the concept of working memory. In G. Claxton (Ed.), *Cognitive psychology: New directions* (pp. 154–196). Reproduced with permission; Figure 10.23: Cohen, G., Eysenck, M. W., & Le Voi, M. E. (1986). *Memory: A cognitive approach* (fig. 2.4, p. 67). Milton Keynes, England: Open University Press. Reproduced with the kind permission of the Open University Press Publishing Company; Figure 10.24: Baddeley, A. D. (2000b). The episodic buffer: A new component of working memory? *Trends in Cognitive Science*, 4, 417–423 (fig. 1, p. 421). Reproduced with permission from Elsevier; Figure 11.2: Loftus, E. F. (1975). Leading questions and eyewitness report. *Cognitive Psychology*, 7, 560–572 (fig. 1, p. 569). Reproduced with permission from Elsevier; Figures 11.3, 11.4 & 11.5: Banks, W. P. (1970). Signal detection theory and human memory. *Psychological Bulletin*, 74, 81–99 (fig. 1, p. 82; fig. 2, p. 83; fig. 3, p. 84). Reproduced with permission; Figure 11.6: Macmillan, N. A., & Creelman, C. D. (1991). *Detection theory: A user's guide* (fig. 2.2, p. 35). Cambridge, England: Cambridge University Press. Reproduced with permission from Prof. Neil Macmillan; Figure 11.7: Garry, M., & Gerrie, M. P. (2005). When photographs create false memories. *Current Directions in Psychological Science*, 14, 326–330 (fig. 1, p. 322). Reproduced with permission from Blackwell Publishing Ltd; Figure 11.9: Jacoby, L. L., & Rhodes, M. G. (2006). False remembering in the aged. *Current Directions in Psychological Science*, 15, 49–53 (fig. 2, p. 51). Reproduced with permission from Blackwell Publishing Ltd; Figure 12.4a,b: Johnson-Laird, P. N., Herrmann, D. J., & Chaffin, R. (1984). Only connections: A critique of semantic networks. *Psychological Bulletin*, 96, 292–315 (fig. 2, p. 297; fig. 3, p. 298). Reproduced with permission; Figure 12.5: Quillian, M. R. (1968). Semantic memory. In M. L. Minsky (Ed.), *Semantic information processing* (pp. 227–259, fig. 4-1a, p. 236). Cambridge, Massachsuetts: The MIT Press. Reproduced with permission; Figure 12.7: Collins, A. M., & Quillian, M. R. (1969). Retrieval time from semantic memory. *Journal of Verbal Learning and Verbal Behavior*, 8, 240–247 (fig. 1, p. 241). Reproduced with permission; Figure 12.8: Kintsch, W. (1980). Semantic memory: A tutorial. In R. S. Nickerson (Ed.), *Attention and performance VIII* (pp. 595–620, fig. 30.4, p. 606). Reproduced with permission; Figure 12.10: Rips, L. J., Shoben, E. J., & Smith, E. E. (1973). Semantic distance and the verification of semantic relations. *Journal of Verbal Learning and Verbal Behavior*, 12, 1–20. Reproduced with permission from Elsevier; Figure 12.11: Smith, E. E., Shoben, E. J., & Rips, L. J. (1974). Structure and process in semantic memory: A featural model for semantic decisions. *Psychological Review*, 81, 214–241 (fig. 2a, p. 219). Reproduced with permission from APA; Figure 12.12: Rogers, T. T. & McClelland, J. L. (2004). *Semantic Cognition: A Parallel Distributed Processing Approach* (Appendix B.2, p. 395). Cambridge, Massachusetts: The MIT Press. Reproduced with permission; Figure 12.14: Rogers, T. T. & McClelland, J. L. (2004). *Semantic Cognition: A Parallel Distributed Processing Approach* (fig. 2.2, p. 56). Cambridge, Massachusetts: The MIT Press. Reproduced with permission; Figure 12.15: Rumelhart, D. E., & Todd, P. M. (1993). Learning and connectionist representations. In D. E. Meyer, & S. Kornblum (Eds.), *Attention and performance XIV. Synergies in experimental psychology, artificial intelligence, and cognitive neuroscience* (pp. 3–35, fig. 1.10, p. 17). Cambridge, MA: The MIT Press. Reproduced with permission; Figure 12.17: Armstrong, S. L., Gleitman, L. R., & Gleitman, H. (1983). What some concepts might not be. *Cognition*, 13, 263–308 (fig. 3, p. 269). Reproduced with permissionm from Elsevier; Figure 12.18: Fodor, J. A. (1998). Concepts. Where cognitive science went wrong (fig. 5.1, p. 90). Oxford, England: Clarendon Press. Reproduced with permission; Figure 13.2: Archambault, A., O'Donnell, C., & Schyns, P. G. (1999). Blind to object changes: When learning the same object at different levels of categorization modifies its perception. *Psychological Science*, 10, 249–255 (fig. 2, p. 251). Reproduced with permission from Blackwell Publishers Ltd; Figure 13.3a,b: Pizlo, Z., & Salach-Golyska, M. (1995). 3-D shape perception. *Perception & Psychophysics*, 57, 692–714 (fig. 1, p. 693; fig. 2, p. 693). Copyright © 1995 by Psychonomic Society Inc. Reproduced with permission of Psychonomic Society Inc. via Copyright Clearance Center; Figure 13.6: Ullman, S. (1979). *The interpretation of visual motion* (fig. 3.11). Cambridge, Massachusetts: The MIT Press. Reproduced with permission; Figure 13.7: Marr, D., & Nishihara, H. K. (1978). Representation and recognition of the spatial organization of three-dimensional shapes. *Proceedings of the Royal Society of London, Series B, 200,* 269–294. London: The Royal Society. Reproduced with permission; Figure 13.8: Wiser, M. (1981). The role of intrinsic axes in shape recognition. *Proceedings of the 3rd annual meeting of the Cognitive Science society, Berkeley, California* (fig. 3, p. 184). Hillsdale, New Jersey: Erlbaum. Reproduced with permission; Figure 13.9a: Rock, I., Wheeler, D., & Tudor, L. (1989). Can we imagine how objects look from other viewpoints? *Cognitive Psychology, 21,* 185–210 (fig. 1, p. 189). Reproduced with permission from Elsevier; Figures 13.9b,c: Rock, I., & Di Vita, J. (1987). A case of viewer-centered object perception. *Cognitive Psychology, 19,* 280–293 (fig. 2, p. 283; fig. 3, p. 284). Reproduced with permission from Elsevier; Figure 13.10: Farah, M. J., Rochlin, R., & Klein, K. L. (1994). Orientation invariance and geometric primitives in shape recognition. *Cognitive Science, 18,* 325–344 (figs. 1a, 1b, p. 330). Reproduced with permission from the Cognitive Science Society; Figures 13.11a,b,c: Bültoff, H. H., & Edelman, S. (1992). Psychophysical support for a two-dimensional view interpolation theory of object recognition. *Proceedings of the National Academy of Sciences of the United States of America, 89,* 60–64 (fig. 1, p. 61; fig. 2, p. 62; fig. 3, p. 62). Washington, DC: National Academy of Sciences. Reproduced with permission; Figure 13.12: Marr, D. & Nishihara, H. K. (1978). Representation and recognition of the spatial organization of three-dimensional shapes. *Proceedings of the Royal Society of London, Series B, 200,* 269–294. London: The Royal Society. Reproduced with permission; Figure 13.13: Kennedy, J. M., & Juricevic, I. (2006). Foreshortening, convergence and drawings from a blind adult. *Perception, 35,* 847–851 (figs. 1 & 2, p. 848). Reproduced with permission from Pion Limited, London; Figure 13.14: Pentland, A. P. (1986). Perceptual organization and the representation of natural form. *Artificial Intelligence, 28,* 293–331 (fig. 3, p. 303). Reproduced with permission from Elsevier; Figure 13.15: Brooks, R. A. (1981). Symbolic reasoning among 3-D models and 2-D images, *Artificial Intelligence, 17,* 64. Reproduced with permission from Elsevier; Figures 13.16 & 13.18a,b: Biederman, I. (1987). Recognition-by-components: A theory of human image understanding. *Psychological Review, 94,* 115–147 (fig. 2, p. 118; fig. 16, p. 135; fig. 17, p. 136). Reproduced with permission from APA;

Figures 13.19a,b, 13.20a,b & 13.21: Moore, C., & Cavanagh, P. (1998). Recovery of 3D volume from 2-tone images of novel objects. *Cognition, 67,* 45–71 (fig. 3, p. 50, fig. 6, p. 55; fig. 4, p. 51, fig. 15, p. 68; fig. 9, fig. 10). Reproduced with permission from Elsevier; Figure 13.22: Palmer, S. E., Rosch, E., & Chase, P. (1981). Canonical perspective and the perception of objects. In J. Long & A. Baddeley (Eds.), *Attention and performance, IX* (pp. 135–151, fig. 8.2, p. 139). Hillsdale, New Jersey: Erlbaum. Reproduced with permission; Figure 13.24a: Edelman, S. (1999). *Representation and recognition in vision* (fig. 4.8, p. 94). Cambridge, Massachusetts: The MIT Press. Reproduced with permission; Figure 13.24b: Edelman, S. (1998). Representation is representation of similarities. *The Behavioral and Brain Sciences, 21,* 449–498 (fig. 7, p. 463). Reproduced with permission from Cambridge University Press; Figure 13.25a: Rouder, J. N., Ratcliff, R., & McKoon, G. (2000). A neural network model of implicit memory for object recognition. *Psychological Science, 11,* 13–19 (fig. 2, p. 16). Reproduced with permission from Blackwell Publishers Ltd; Figure 13.25b: Edelman, S. (1999). *Representation and recognition in vision* (fig. 5.1, p. 112). Cambridge, Massachusetts: The MIT Press. Reproduced with permission; Figure 13.26: Behrmann, M., Marotta, J., Gauthier, I., Tarr, M. J., & McKeeff, T. J. (2005). Behavioral change and its neural correlates in visual agnosia after expertise training. *Journal of Cognitive Neuroscience, 17,* 554–568 (fig. 1, p. 556). Reproduced with permission from The MIT Press; Figure 13.27a,b: Murphy, G. L., & Wisniewski, E. J. (1989). Categorizing objects in isolation and in scenes: What a superordinate is good for. *Journal of Experimental Psychology: Learning, Memory, and Cognition, 15,* 572–586 (fig. 1, p. 575; fig. 2, p. 582). Reproduced with permission from APA; Figure 13.28: Davenport, J. L., & Potter, M. C. (2004). Scene consistency in object and background perception. *Psychological Science, 15,* 559–564 (fig. 1, p. 561). Reproduced with permission from Blackwell Publishers Ltd; Figure 14.1: Jackendoff, R. (2003). Precis of foundations of language: Brain, meaning, grammar, evolution. *The Behavioral and Brain Sciences, 26,* 651–707 (fig. 1, p. 655). Reproduced with permission from Cambridge University Press; Figure 14.2: Jackendoff, R. (2002). *Foundations of language. Brain, meaning, grammar, evolution* (fig. 1.1, p. 6). Oxford, England: Oxford University Press. Reproduced by permission; Figure 14.3: Clark, H. H., & Clark, E. V. (1977). *Psychology and language. An introduction to psycholinguistics* (fig. 4, p. 47). New York: Harcourt Brace Jovanovitch, Inc. Reproduced with permission; Figure 14.4: Corballis, M. (2003). Recursion as the key to the human mind. In K. Sterelny & J. Fitness (Eds.), *From mating to mentality. Evaluating evolutionary psychology* (pp. 155–171, fig. 7.1, p. 157). New York: Psychology Press. Reproduced with permission; Figure 14.7: Rayner, K., Carlson, M., & Frazier, L. (1983). The interaction of syntax and semantics during sentence processing: Eye movements in the analysis of semantically biased sentences. *Journal of Verbal Learning and Verbal Behavior*, *22*, 358–374 (Fig. 3, p. 368). Reproduced with permission from Elsevier; Figure 14.8: Taraban, R., & McClelland, J. L. (1990). Parsing and comprehension: A multiple-constraint view. In K. Rayner, M. Balota & G. B. Flores D'Arcais (Eds.), *Comprehension processes in reading* (pp. 231–263, fig. 11.2, p. 234). Hillsdale, NJ: Erlbaum. Reproduced with permission; Figures 14.9 & 14.11: Rumelhart, D. E., & McClelland, J. L. (1986). On learning the past tenses of English verbs. In J. L. McClelland & D. E. Rumelhart (Eds.), *Parallel distributed processing. Explorations in the microstructure of cognition. Volume 2: Psychological and biological models* (pp. 216–271, fig. 1, p. 222; fig. 4, p. 242). Cambridge, Massachusetts: The MIT Press. Reproduced with permission; Figure 14.12: Jackendoff, R. (2002). *Foundations of language. Brain, meaning, grammar, evolution* (fig. 11.1, p. 348). Oxford, England: Oxford University Press. Reproduced with permission; Figure 14.13: Jackendoff, R. (1987). *Consciousness and the computational mind* (fig. 10.1, p. 199). Cambridge, Massachusetts: The MIT Press. Reproduced with permission; Figure 14.14: Goldstone, R. L. (1994). Influences of categorization in perceptual discrimination. *Journal of Experimental Psychology: General*, *123*, 178–200 (fig. 3, p. 183). Reproduced with permission; Figure 14.15: Goldstone, R. L., Lippa, Y., & Shiffrin, R. M. (2001). Altering object representations through category learning. *Cognition*, *78*, 27–43 (fig. 1, p. 34). Reproduced with permission from Elsevier; Figure 14.16: Davidoff, J. (2001). Language and perceptual categorisation. *Trends in Cognitive Science*, *5*, 382–387 (fig. 1, p. 385). Reproduced with permission from Elsevier; Figures 15.2 and 15.3: Gigerenzer, G. (2002). *Reckoning with risk. Learning to live with uncertainty* (fig. 4.2, p. 45). London: Penguin Books. Reproduced with permission; Figure 16.4: Fox, E., Lester, V., Russo, R., Bowles, R. J., Pichler, A., & Dutton, K. (2000). Facial expressions of emotion: Are angry faces detected more efficiently? *Cognition and Emotion*, *14*, 61–92 (fig. 1, p. 66). Reproduced with permission from Taylor & Francis Ltd; Figure 16.5: Tipples, J., Atkinson, A. P., & Young, A. W. (2002). The eyebrow frown: A salient social signal. *Emotion*, *2*, 288–296 (fig. 1, p. 290). Reproduced with permission from APA; Figure 16.6: Juth, P., Lundqvist, D., Karlsson, A., & Öhman, A. (2005). Looking for foes and friends: Perceptual and emotional factors when finding a face in the crowd. *Emotion*, *4*, 379–395 (fig. 1, p. 381). Reproduced with permission from APA; Figure 16.7: Fenske, M. J., & Eastwood, J. D. (2003). Modulation of focused attention by faces expressing emotion: Evidence from flanker tasks. *Emotion*, *3*, 327–343 (fig. 1, p. 331). Reproduced with permission from APA; Figure 16.10a,b: Posner, M. I., Nissen, M. J., & Ogden, W. C. (1978). Attended and unattended processing modes: The role of set for spatial location. In H. L. Pick & E. Saltzman (Eds.), *Modes of perceiving an processing information* (pp. 137–157; fig. 1, p. 141, fig. 2, p. 142). Hillsdale, NJ: Erlbaum. Reproduced with permission; Figure 16.11: Friesen, C. K., & Kingstone, A. (1998). The eyes have it! Reflexive orienting is triggered by nonpredictive gaze. *Psychonomic Bulletin & Review*, *5*, 490–495 (fig. 1, p. 491). Copyright © 1998 by Psychonomic Society Inc. Reproduced with permission of Psychonomic Society Inc. via Copyright Clearance Center; Figure 16.12: Ristic, J., & Kingstone, A. (2005). Taking control of reflexive social attention. *Cognition*, *94*, B55–B56 (fig. 1, p. B57). Reproduced with permission from Elsevier; Figure 16.13: Tipples, J. (2006). Fear and fearfulness potentiate automatic orienting to eye gaze. *Cognition and Emotion*, *20*, 309–320 (fig. 1, p. 313). Reproduced with permission from Taylor & Francis Ltd.

## Tables

Table 2.1: Felician, O., Ceccaldi, M., Didic, M., Thinus-Blanc, C., & Poncet, M. (2003). Pointing to body parts: A double dissociation study. *Neuropsychologia*, *41*, 1307–1316. Reproduced with permission from Elsevier; Table 5.1: Bentin, S., & Moscovitch, M. (1988). The time course of repetition effects for words and unfamiliar faces. *Journal of Experimental Psychology: General*, *117*, 148–160. Reproduced with permission; Table 10.1: Roediger III, H. L. (1980). Memory metaphors in cognitive psychology. *Memory & Cognition*, *8*, 231–246. Copyright © 1980 by Psychonomic Society Inc. Reproduced with permission of Psychonomic Society Inc. via Copyright Clearance Center; Table 15.1: Poulton, E. C. (1994). *Behavioral decision theory: A new approach* (table 1.1, p. 7). Cambridge, England: Cambridge University Press. Reproduced with permission; Table 16.1: Ekman, P.

(1999). Basic emotions. In T. Dalgleish & M. J. Powers (Eds.), *Handbook of cognition and emotion* (pp. 45–60, table 3.1). Chichester, England: Wiley. Reproduced with permission from John Wiley & Sons Limited; Table 16.2: Öhman, A. (1999). Distinguishing unconscious from conscious emotional processes: Methodological considerations and theoretical implications. In T. Dalgleish & M. J. Powers (Eds.), *Handbook of cognition and emotion* (table 17.1, p. 326). Chichester, England: Wiley. Reproduced with permission from John Wiley & Sons Limited.

*Photos*

Figure 1.2(a): Alamy Images / Janine Wiedel Photolibrary; Figure 1.2(b): Kobal Collection Ltd / Warner Bros.; Figure 1.4: Courtesy of the authors; Figure 2.4: Kobal Collection Ltd / Warner Bros.; Figure 2.6: John Alex Maguire / Rex Features; Figure 2.7: Wolfgang Flamisch / Zefa / Corbis; Figure 3.2: Bettmann / Corbis; Figure 3.10: courtesy of the authors; Figure 3.11: courtesy of the authors; Figure 3.15: Rex Features / 20th Century Fox / Everett; Figures 3.17 and 3.18 (image): Photodisc; Figure 3.23(b): J. Marshall / Tribal Eye / Alamy Images; Figure 3.25: courtesy of the authors; Figure 4.1: Photolibrary.com / Blend Images LLC; Figure 4.4 (image): Courtesy of the authors; Figure 5.9: Courtesy of the authors; Figure 5.14: Courtesy of the authors; Figure 5.21: Alamy Images / Peter Jordan; Figure 6.2: Rex Features / Buenavista / Everett; Figures 6.7 and 6.9: courtesy of the authors; Figure 6.12: Giuseppe Arcimboldo. *Vertumnus*. 1590–1591. Oil on wood.

Skoklosters Castle, Balsta, Sweden / Samuel Uhrdin; Figure 6.14: Rex Features / Hanna-Barbera / Everett; Figure 6.23: Photolibrary.com; Figure 6.24 (image): 215: Kobal Collection Ltd / Warner Bros / DC Comics; Figure 7.1a: Skyscan; Figure 7.1b: Ordnance Survey; Figure 7.2: Courtesy of the National Aeronautics and Space Administration (NASA) (www.nasa.gov); Figures 7.9 and 7.10: courtesy of the authors; Figure 7.22: Olivier Douliery / ABACA / PA Photos; Figure 8.1: Katy Beswetherick / Rex Features; Figure 8.20 (top row images): Getty Images; Figure 8.20 (bottom row images): Hulton-Deutsch Collection / Corbis; Figure 8.21 (top image): Getty Images; Figure 8.21 (bottom image): Corbis; Figure 9.1 (image): courtesy of author; Figure 9.10 (images): courtesy of authors; Figure 10.3: Rex Features; Figure 10.5: Rex Features / Newmarket / Everett; Figures 10.6 and 11.1: courtesy of authors; Figure 11.8: Helen King / Corbis; Figure 12.2 (left): alveyandtowers.com; Figure 12.2 (right): Lester Lefkowitz / Corbis; Figure 12.3: courtesy of the authors; Figure 13.17: courtesy of the authors; Figure 13.26 (image): courtesy of Micael J Tarr (www.tarrlab.org); Figure 14.6: Alamy Images / SAS; Figure 15.1: Kobal Collection Ltd / Columbia; Figure 15.4: Photolibrary.com / Monsoon Images; Figure 16.1: Kobal Collection Ltd / Universal TV; Figure 16.2: Alamy Images / Universal / Gramercy; Figure 16.14: courtesy of the authors.

In some instances we have been unable to trace the owners of copyright material, and we would appreciate any information that would enable us to do so.

call me !